VISIONS *of* AMERICA

A HISTORY OF THE UNITED STATES

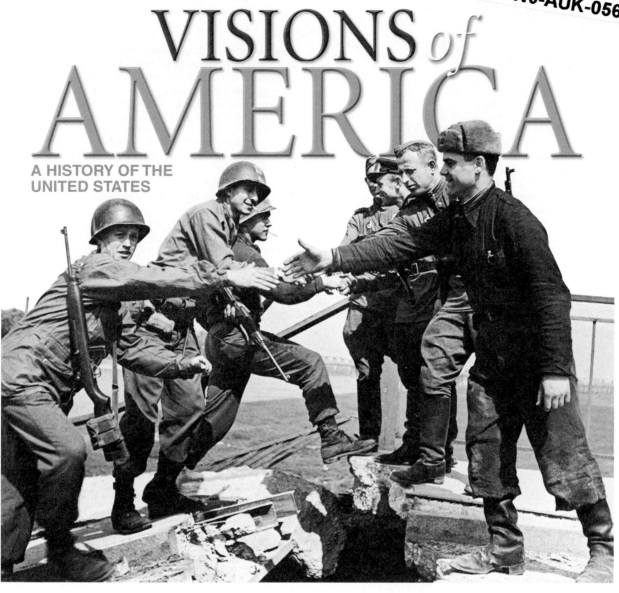

Jennifer D. Keene
Chapman University

Saul Cornell
Fordham University

Edward T. O'Donnell
College of the Holy Cross

Prentice Hall

Boston Columbus Indianapolis New York San Francisco
Upper Saddle River Amsterdam Cape Town Dubai London Madrid
Milan Munich Paris Montreal Toronto Delhi Mexico City
Sao Paulo Sydney Hong Kong Seoul Singapore Taipei Tokyo

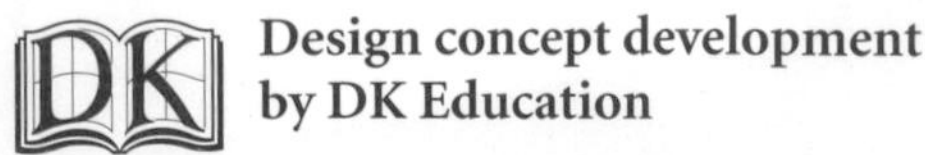

Design concept development by DK Education

Editorial Director: Leah Jewell
Publisher: Priscilla McGeehon
Senior Development Editor: Roberta Meyer
Development Editor: Philip Herbst
Editorial Assistant: Amanda Dykstra
Director of Marketing: Brandy Dawson
Senior Managing Editor: Ann Marie McCarthy
Project Manager: Debra Wechsler
Senior Operations Supervisor: Mary Ann Gloriande
Operations Specialist: Maura Zaldivar
Map Editor: Jeannine Ciliotta
Manager of Design Development: John Christiana
Art Director: Laura Gardner
AV Project Manager: Mirella Signoretto
Manager, Visual Research: Beth Brenzel
Photo Researchers: Barbara S. Salz; Jody Potter
Manager, Rights and Permissions: Zina Arabia
Image Permission Coordinator: Debbie Latronica
Manager, Cover Visual Research & Permissions: Karen Sanatar
Cover Art: Soldiers: © Bettmann/CORBIS All Rights Reserved; Family painting: Lilly Martin Spencer, "Domestic Happiness". 1849. Oil on canvas, Spencer, Lilly Martin (1827-1902) / The Detroit Institute of Arts, USA / Gift of Dr. and Mrs. James Cleland Jr. / The Bridgeman Art Library; Effects of the Fugitive Slave Law: The Granger Collection, New York; Immigrant family: Courtesy of the Library of Congress; Obama family: © Ralf-Finn Hestoft/Ralf-Finn Hestoft/Corbis
Cover Designer: Laura Gardner
Media Director: Brian Hyland
Lead Media Project Manager: Sarah Kinney
Supplements Editor: Emsal Hasan
Full-Service Project Management: Pre-Press PMG
Composition: Pre-Press PMG
Printer/Binder: Webcrafters, Inc.
Cover Printer: Lehigh-Phoenix Color/Hagerstown

Dedication

To our parents, who imbued us with a love of history; our spouses, who have learned to share this passion; and our children, present and future students of American history.

This book was set in 10.5/12.5 Minion.

Credits and acknowledgments borrowed from other sources and reproduced, with permission, in this textbook appear on appropriate page within text (or beginning on page C-1).

Library of Congress Cataloging-in-Publication Data

Keene, Jennifer D.
Visions of America / Jennifer D. Keene, Saul Cornell, Edward T. O'Donnell, — 1st ed.
p. cm.
Includes bibliographical references and index.
ISBN-13: 978-0-321-06687-9
ISBN-10: 0-321-06687-1
1. United States—History—Textbooks. I. Cornell, Saul. II. O'Donnell, Edward T. III. Title.
E178.1.K24 2009
973—dc22 2009017107

10 9 8 7 6 5 4 3 2 1

Prentice Hall is an imprint of

www.pearsonhighered.com

Student ISBN 13: 978-0-321-06687-9
ISBN 10: 0-321-06687-1
Exam ISBN 13: 978-0-205-62006-7
ISBN 10: 0-205-62006-X

Brief Contents

CHAPTER

Contents

CHAPTER 3 Growth, Slavery, and Conflict: Colonial America, 1710–1763 64

CHAPTER 4 Revolutionary America: Change and Transformation, 1764–1783 96

CHAPTER 5 A Virtuous Republic: Creating a Workable Government, 1783–1789 128

CHAPTER 6 The New Republic: An Age of Political Passion, 1789–1800 158

CHAPTER 11 "To Overspread the Continent:" Westward Expansion and Political Conflict, 1840–1848 316

CHAPTER 12 Slavery and Sectionalism: The Political Crisis of 1848–1861 342

CHAPTER 13 A Nation Torn Apart: The Civil War, 1861–1865 374

CHAPTER 28 Righting a Nation Adrift: America in the 1970s and 1980s 842

CHAPTER 29 Building a New World Order: The United States, 1989–2009 874

Maps

Charts, Graphs, and Tables

Images as History

CHAPTER

Competing Visions

CHAPTER

Choices and Consequences

CHAPTER

Preface

Jennifer D. Keene, Saul Cornell, and Edward T. O'Donnell discuss their goals in writing *Visions of America.*

Why did you write this book? What separates it from the many fine survey texts that are available?

We conceived of *Visions of America* while teaching in the kinds of classrooms familiar to most of the instructors and students who will use this book. Many of our students are the first in their family to attend college, some are international students, most are required to take the U.S. History survey, and some are passionate students of history.

Despite their differences most share the same vision of history, but it is a distorted vision. Students often see history as a series of events that unfolded as if preordained. The colonists defeated the British, the Civil War held the Union together and abolished slavery, America defeated Nazi Germany and then prevailed in the Cold War. Yet as historians we know that history is never inevitable, that vehement disagreements have shaped the past and continue to influence the present, that events are driven by choices, and that outcomes are unknowable to those who make those choices. We wrote *Visions of America* to make those perceptions just as obvious to our readers.

How did you do that? How does Visions *change students' perceptions about history?*

The title captures our unique approach. *Visions of America* explores the competing political, social, and cultural visions *for* America that have generated conflicts in virtually every period of U.S. history. We focused on competing visions so that students can learn to appreciate the dynamic debates that shaped our nation. Every element of the text reinforces the competing visions theme, from the narrative and images to the highlighted quotes and features. The Competing Visions feature presents excerpts from key primary source documents to exemplify conflicting visions for America.

- In **Chapter 5** (page 143) students will read the opposing positions Washington and Jefferson held toward Shays's Rebellion in their own words. Excerpts from their writings convey how these two patriots interpreted the meaning of the rebellion in radically different ways.
- In **Chapter 16** (page 487) Competing Visions examines two clashing views on the legitimacy of labor unions, one a searing 1877 anti-union editorial from *Scribner's Monthly* and the other a stout defense of unions found in an 1884 labor newspaper.
- In **Chapter 19** (page 576) Competing Visions pairs Rudyard Kipling's poem, "The White Man's Burden," with a poetic parody by an anti-imperialist activist, "The Real 'White Man's Burden,'" to present the internal debate over whether the United States should create a formal colonial empire.

How did you convey that history is the product of individual choices?

Choices confronting political leaders and ordinary people are a consistent theme of the narrative, but they are graphically depicted in Choices and Consequences. In each chapter, this innovative feature diagrams the choices leaders and ordinary people grappled with at key moments in America's history. By helping students to visualize complex and sometimes agonizing choices, Choices and Consequences underscores the point that historical events are the products of human agency.

- In **Chapter 10** (page 300) students consider the choices faced by Mary Cragin, a woman who joined the Oneida perfectionist community. Did free love in nineteenth-century America represent a step toward female emancipation or was it merely another way for men to dominate woman?
- In **Chapter 14** (page 434) students see the choices that the U.S. Supreme Court confronted in *Plessy v. Ferguson.* We examine the majority decision and its consequences for establishing the policy of "separate but equal" in public facilities and schools across the South. Finally we consider the continuing controversies surrounding the strategies African Americans adopted while living under Jim Crow segregation.
- In **Chapter 25** (page 769) we examine the choices Rosa Parks faced in 1955 when asked to vacate her bus seat for a white man, her decision to stay put, the consequences of that decision, and the continuing controversies surrounding how Americans mythologized this critical moment in our history.

How does Visions of America *use images differently from other textbooks?*

Images have powerfully influenced the national debate, but history textbooks typically use them as mere illustrations. Our approach is different. We selected the nearly seven hundred paintings, photographs, line drawings, woodcuts, advertisements, engravings, film stills, political cartoons, and other images in the text. Each one is discussed and treated as historical evidence. The innovative design by DK Publishing integrates images across the pages in a way that shows detail and invites scrutiny.

- In **Chapter 4** we discuss the impact of republicanism on the family in the Revolutionary era. Accompanying the narrative on page 124, contrasting portraits of families, painted before and after the Revolution, reveal the growing ideal of companionate marriage. In the bottom portrait the husband, wife, and child are not only physically closer, but their expressions suggest greater emotional connection and intimacy, a change facilitated by republican ideology. The visuals reinforce the text, allowing students to see history as well as read about it.

- In **Chapter 17** political cartoons highlight the growing concern over the rise of political machines. On page 504 we discuss Thomas Nast's cartoon, "In Counting There Is Strength." Students discover that Nast created the image to depict William "Boss" Tweed, head of New York's Tammany Hall machine, as both corrupt and arrogant. The reference to counting suggests that Tweed's power derived from his ability to conduct fraudulent vote counts on election day.

"THAT'S WHAT'S THE MATTER."
Boss Tweed. "As long as I count the Votes, what are you going to do about it? say?"

- By reading the story behind the iconic photographic of a Vietnamese Buddhist monk setting himself on fire in **Chapter 26** (page 785), students learn to see the Vietnam War as both a civil war and part of the global Cold War. The intentional ways that activists used the Western media to publicize their cause, and the ways that one photograph can alter history, also become apparent.

How does Visions *encourage students to analyze historical images effectively?*

Beyond the analysis of images in the narrative, in each chapter, Images as History focuses on one or two images in depth. This feature encourages students to "read" images as texts with multiple meanings that speak to both the past and the present. These features include:

- A PORTRAIT OF COLONIAL ASPIRATIONS (Chapter 3, page 69). The portrait of Henry Darnall III reveals the aspirations of the colonial elite and their role in the growing Anglicization of colonial life. In the painting, next to Darnall is one of the earliest depictions of an African slave in American art, a sign of the growing importance of slavery to colonial society.

- SEEING THE POOR (Chapter 17, page 509). We dissect Jacob Riis's photograph of a poor Italian immigrant mother and child, encouraging students to appreciate how Riis's image both reflected and shaped contemporary views of immigrants in the late nineteenth century.
- ADVERTISING THE NEW WOMAN (Chapter 21, page 645). The ways that advertising both shaped and reflected public perceptions of the ideal woman become apparent when analysing the image of the "Fisher Girl" in a 1920s automobile advertisement.

The slim Fisher girl appeared liberated from the confines of the home and the physical incapacity caused by too much weight. She seemed to be a modern woman on the move.

This female silhouette more closely resembled the body of an adolescent girl than a mature woman, encouraging a female preoccupation with dieting and self-denial that continues today.

Most ads of the time displayed men with both feet firmly on the ground. This woman's off-balance pose with one knee bent suggested tentativeness and instability, putting limits on her inde-pendence and strength.

THE SATURDAY EVENING POST

Of all those who express motor car body preference . . 95% Prefer "Body by Fisher".

These tall, elongated figurines depicted an ideal female body that was slim and youthful with legs that formed a straight line from toe to thigh, pointed toes, and a giraffe-like neck. These proportions suggested the women were nearly 9 feet tall!

The presence of the maid behind the Fisher girl indicates that she is rich as well as thin—an enviable combination to many women.

Her sleek body, like that of the car being advertised, served mostly as a commodity or decorative object suitable for a modern man.

"Body by Fisher"

Many students feel overwhelmed by the amount of information in history textbooks. How does Visions *help students focus on what is most important?*

Visions of America promotes active learning on every page. Each chapter opens with a large, striking image and an **enlarged quotation** designed to encapsulate the major issues of the period and spark curiosity. Throughout, lively **display quotes** from leaders and ordinary people draw students into the text. Questions running along the bottom of each page serve as **learning objectives**, prompting students to review and reflect on what they have just read. Each chapter ends with a **conclusion**, followed by a colorful **visual chronology** linking images and key events. **Review questions** help students synthesize the material in the chapter, and a list of **key terms** serves as a quick review of essential concepts.

Associating an image with a term, name, or concept can help to cement it in students' memory. *Visions of America* encourages this by providing images in abundance alongside the text to serve as mnemonic cues. For example the controversy over Andrew Jackson's Bank War produced a number of evocative cartoons. Typically most textbooks reproduce a single pro-Jackson or one anti-Jackson cartoon. *Visions of America* presents both views of the Bank War side by side so students can compare and contrast them.

Why will students read this book?

History professors and textbooks need to be good storytellers. *Visions of America's* lively writing style—active, engaging, and full of anecdotes—brings history to life. We live in an intensely visual culture, and students are always fascinated to discover the "truth" about the images they have long associated with key periods in American history, or to learn about new ones. Students will enjoy reading a text that shows them history is a living narrative open to interpretation and the product of decisions people made in the past.

Five or ten years from now, what will students remember from reading Visions of America*? How will they apply the skills they have gained?*

Students may not recall the exact terms of the Versailles Treaty or the Reconstruction Acts, but they will remember that people making individual choices are the driving force of history. When participating in the political or cultural debates of their own era, they will recall that competing visions have been a staple of the nation's historical development. The critical-thinking skills they honed while reading this book will serve them well throughout their lives. Years from now, they will know how to analyze and consume images intelligently. Most important, students will remember the moment when they realized that history was not just an endless list of names and dates but the fascinating tale of human experience.

About the Authors

Jennifer D. Keene

Jennifer D. Keene is a Professor of History and chair of the History Department at Chapman University in Orange, California. Dr. Keene has published three books on the American involvement in the First World War: *Doughboys, the Great War and the Remaking of America* (2001); *The United States and the First World War* (2000); and *World War I* (2006). She has received numerous fellowships for her research, including a Mellon Fellowship, a National Research Council Postdoctoral Award, and Fulbright Senior Scholar Awards to Australia and France. Her articles have appeared in the *Annales de Démographie Historique, Peace & Change, Intelligence and National Security,* and *Military Psychology*. Dr. Keene served as an associate editor for the *Encyclopedia of War and American Society* (2005) which won the Society of Military History's prize for best reference book. She works closely with the Gilder-Lehrman Institute, offering Teaching American History workshops for secondary school teachers throughout the country.

Saul Cornell

Saul Cornell is the Paul and Diane Guenther Chair in American History at Fordham University in New York. Professor Cornell has also taught at the Ohio State University, the College of William and Mary, and Leiden University in the Netherlands. He is the author of *A Well Regulated Militia: The Founding Fathers and the Origins of Gun Control* (Langum Prize in Legal History) and *The Other Founders: Anti-Federalism and the Dissenting Tradition in America, 1788–1828* (Society of the Cincinnati Book Prize), both of which were nominated for the Pulitzer Prize. His articles have appeared in the *Journal of American History*, the *William and Mary Quarterly, American Studies, Law and History Review*, and dozens of leading law reviews. He is also a frequent participant in Teaching American History workshops and has lectured widely on digital history both domestically and abroad.

Edward T. O'Donnell

Edward T. O'Donnell is an Associate Professor of History at the College of the Holy Cross in Worcester, Massachusetts. He taught previously at Hunter College, City University of New York. He is the author of many scholarly articles for journals such as *The Journal of Urban History, The Journal of the Gilded Age and Progressive Era*, and *The Public Historian*, as well as several books, including *Ship Ablaze: The Tragedy of the Steamboat General Slocum* (Random House, 2003) and the forthcoming *Talisman of a Lost Hope: Henry George and Gilded Age America* (Columbia University Press). Professor O'Donnell is also very active in the field of public history, curating several exhibits and consulting for others at institutions such as the Lower East Side Tenement Museum. Since 2002, he has worked with more than twenty Teaching American History grant programs across the country, offering lectures and workshops for middle and high school teachers.

Features

Dynamic **chapter openings** combine a vivid image with a narrative introduction, highlighting the major themes of the chapter. A pithy **quote** sounds a voice from the past, and a **visual outline** previews the chapter's major topics.

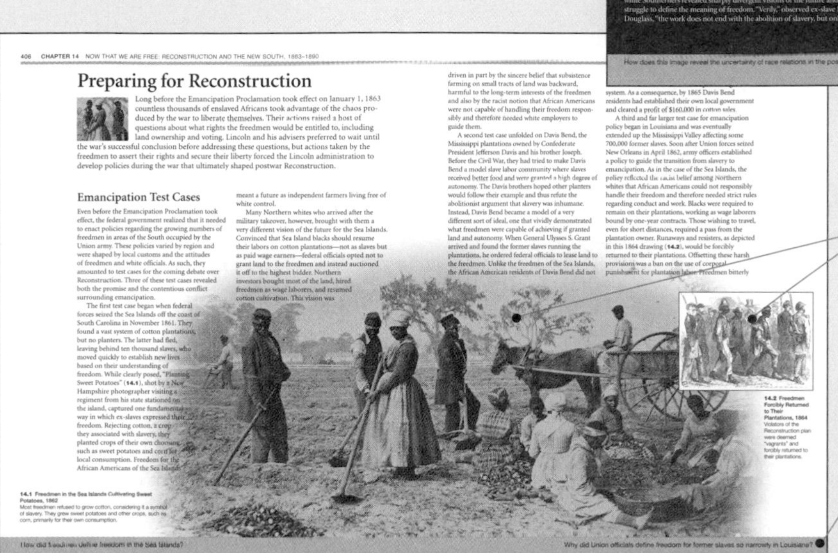

Historical **images** are imaginatively displayed. Authors explore each image as it documents events or expresses and shapes public opinion.

At the bottom of every page, a **learning objective** in the form of a question focuses students on the key message of the page.

In each chapter, excerpts from personal letters, diary entries, speeches, editorials, and other written documents highlight the **Competing Visions** that have shaped every period of American history.

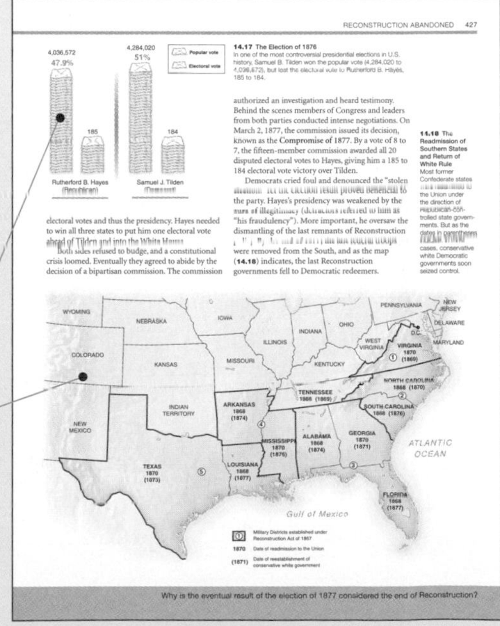

Visually engaging **maps** and **graphics** make data accessible and provide geographical context. Specially designed charts clarify the results of presidential elections.

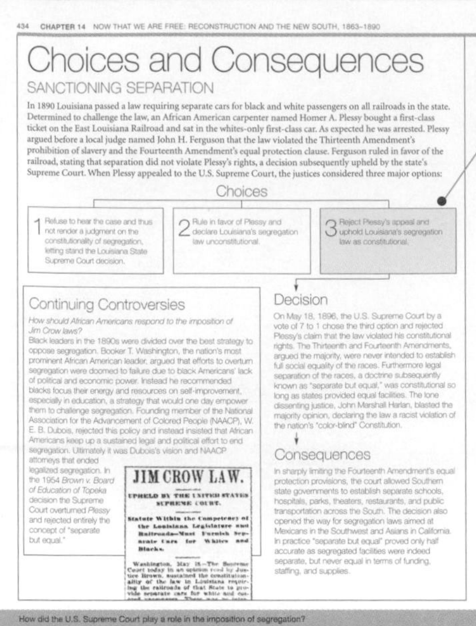
434 CHAPTER 14 NOW THAT WE ARE FREE: RECONSTRUCTION AND THE NEW SOUTH, 1863–1890

Choices and Consequences

SANCTIONING SEPARATION

In 1890 Louisiana passed a law requiring separate cars for black and white passengers on all railroads in the state. Determined to challenge the law, an African American carpenter named Homer A. Plessy bought a first-class ticket on the East Louisiana Railroad and sat in the whites-only first-class car. As expected he was arrested. Plessy argued before a local judge named John H. Ferguson that the law violated the Thirteenth Amendment's prohibition of slavery and the Fourteenth Amendment's equal protection clause. Ferguson ruled in favor of the railroad, stating that separation did not violate Plessy's rights, a decision subsequently upheld by the state's Supreme Court. When Plessy appealed to the U.S. Supreme Court, the justices considered three major options:

Choices

1 Refuse to hear the case and thus not render a judgment on the constitutionality of segregation, letting stand the Louisiana State Supreme Court decision.

2 Rule in favor of Plessy and declare Louisiana's segregation law unconstitutional.

3 Reject Plessy's appeal and uphold Louisiana's segregation law as constitutional.

Decision

On May 18, 1896, the U.S. Supreme Court by a vote of 7 to 1 chose the third option and rejected Plessy's claim that the law violated his constitutional rights. The Thirteenth and Fourteenth Amendments, argued the majority, were never intended to establish full social equality of the races. Furthermore legal separation of the races, a doctrine subsequently known as "separate but equal," was constitutional so long as states provided equal facilities. The lone dissenting justice, John Marshall Harlan, blasted the majority opinion, declaring the law a racist violation of the nation's "color-blind" Constitution.

Consequences

In sharply limiting the Fourteenth Amendment's equal protection provisions, the court allowed Southern state governments to establish separate schools, hospitals, parks, theaters, restaurants, and public transportation across the South. The decision also opened the way for segregation laws aimed at Mexicans in the Southwest and Asians in California. In practice "separate but equal" proved only half accurate as segregated facilities were indeed separate, but never equal in terms of funding, staffing, and supplies.

Continuing Controversies

How should African Americans respond to the imposition of Jim Crow laws?

Black leaders in the 1890s were divided over the best strategy to oppose segregation. Booker T. Washington, the nation's most prominent African American leader, argued that efforts to overturn segregation were doomed to failure due to black Americans' lack of political and economic power. Instead he recommended blacks focus their energy and resources on self-improvement, especially in education, a strategy that would one day empower them to challenge segregation. Founding member of the National Association for the Advancement of Colored People (NAACP), W. E. B. Dubois, rejected this policy and instead insisted that African Americans keep up a sustained legal and political effort to end segregation. Ultimately it was Dubois's vision and NAACP attorneys that ended legalized segregation. In the 1954 *Brown v. Board of Education of Topeka* decision the Supreme Court overturned *Plessy* and rejected entirely the concept of "separate but equal."

JIM CROW LAW.

UPHELD BY THE UNITED STATES SUPREME COURT.

Statute Within the Competency of the Louisiana Legislature and Railroads—Must Furnish Separate Cars for Whites and Blacks.

Washington, May 18.—The Supreme Court today in an opinion read by Justice Brown, sustained the constitutionality of the law in Louisiana requiring the railroads of that State to provide separate cars for white and colored passengers.

How did the U.S. Supreme Court play a role in the imposition of segregation?

Choices and Consequences drives home the point that history is shaped by the choices we make as a nation. Each one focuses on a significant choice that confronted ordinary citizens, political leaders, or judges. The major choices are followed by the decision, an analysis of its consequences, and the controversies that often continued for years.

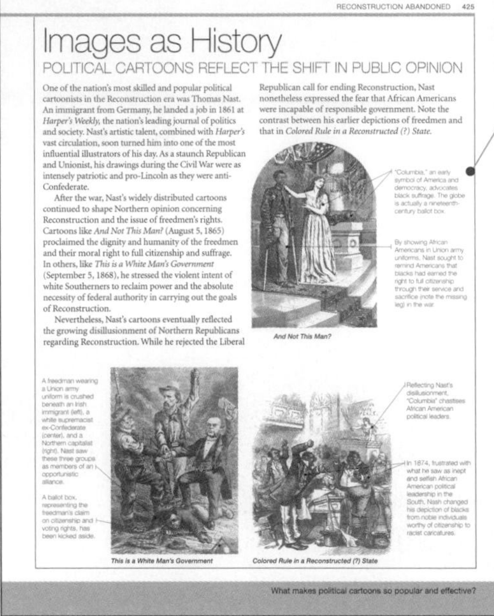
RECONSTRUCTION ABANDONED 425

Images as History

POLITICAL CARTOONS REFLECT THE SHIFT IN PUBLIC OPINION

One of the nation's most skilled and popular political cartoonists in the Reconstruction era was Thomas Nast. An immigrant from Germany, he landed a job in 1861 at *Harper's Weekly*, the nation's leading journal of politics and society. Nast's artistic talent, combined with *Harper's* vast circulation, soon turned him into one of the most influential illustrators of his day. As a staunch Republican and Unionist, his drawings during the Civil War were as intensely patriotic and pro-Lincoln as they were anti-Confederate.

After the war, Nast's widely distributed cartoons continued to shape Northern opinion concerning Reconstruction and the issue of freedmen's rights. Cartoons like *And Not This Man?* (August 5, 1865) proclaimed the dignity and humanity of the freedmen and their moral right to full citizenship and suffrage. In others, like *This is a White Man's Government* (September 5, 1868), he stressed the violent intent of white Southerners to reclaim power and the absolute necessity of federal authority in carrying out the goals of Reconstruction.

Nevertheless, Nast's cartoons eventually reflected the growing disillusionment of Northern Republicans regarding Reconstruction. While he rejected the Liberal Republican call for ending Reconstruction, Nast nonetheless expressed the fear that African Americans were incapable of responsible government. Note the contrast between his earlier depictions of freedmen and that in *Colored Rule in a Reconstructed (?) State.*

"Columbia," an early symbol of America and democracy, advocates black suffrage. The globe is actually a nineteenth-century ballot box.

By showing African Americans in Union army uniforms, Nast sought to remind Americans that blacks had earned the right to full citizenship through their service and sacrifice (note the missing leg) in the war.

And Not This Man?

A freedman wearing a Union army uniform is crushed beneath an Irish immigrant (left), a white supremacist ex-Confederate (center), and a Northern capitalist (right). Nast saw these three groups as members of an opportunistic alliance.

A ballot box, representing the freedman's claim on citizenship and voting rights, has been kicked aside.

This is a White Man's Government

Reflecting Nast's disillusionment, "Columbia" chastises African American political leaders.

In 1874, frustrated with what he saw as inept and selfish African American political leadership in the South, Nash changed his depiction of blacks from noble individuals worthy of citizenship to racist caricatures.

Colored Rule in a Reconstructed (?) State

What makes political cartoons so popular and effective?

Images as History unpacks the meaning and purpose of images—including cartoons, posters, magazine illustrations, posters, fine art, and photographs. Tightly connected to the narrative, each IAH feature analyzes the way images are used to express opinions, shape perceptions, and influence policy.

RECONSTRUCTION ABANDONED 423

Reconstruction Abandoned

By the end of Grant's first term in office, supporters of Reconstruction and freedmen's rights could look with some satisfaction at the many extraordinary changes that had taken place in the South. Yet ominous signs soon appeared that suggested Reconstruction was in trouble. Despite the crackdown on the Klan, white Southerners increasingly demonstrated their commitment to seizing power and imposing a new form of servitude on African Americans. Northerners, by contrast, seemed less and less willing to support a vigorous Reconstruction policy. Slowly, between 1872 and 1877, the extraordinary experiment in multiracial democracy and progressive government in the South was dismantled in favor of oligarchy and white supremacy.

Corruption and Scandal

A major factor in the pullback from Reconstruction was a series of corruption scandals that plagued the Grant administration. Grant himself was honest, but also politically naive and given to a hands-off style of leadership that gave officials in his administration an unusual degree of independence. Many of them took advantage of Grant's implicit trust to enrich themselves in a variety of illegal schemes.

For example, in 1869 Jay Gould and Jim Fisk, two Wall Street titans, conspired with Grant's brother-in-law in a scheme to corner the gold market. The plan eventually collapsed on September 24, 1869, a day dubbed "Black Friday, but not before hundreds of innocent investors were ruined and countless workers thrown out of work in the ensuing national economic turmoil. Fisk and Gould were pilloried in the press, but emerged unscathed. When the Credit Mobilier scandal became public, it was revealed that Grant's vice president and several high-ranking members of Congress had taken large bribes from the company involved in the completion of the government-subsidized Union Pacific Railroad. Other scandals found that three of Grant's cabinet members used their office for illegal financial gain. In the so-called "Whiskey Ring" scandal, for example, Treasury secretary Orville E. Babcock made a small fortune by illegally allowing whiskey distillers to avoid paying excise taxes. Secretary of War William W. Belknap likewise accepted bribes from companies engaged in corrupt activities on Indian reservations.

The North Retreats

Corruption scandals undermined the authority of Grant's administration. Grant soon found that to secure reelection and keep the Republican Party in power he would have to minimize political controversies. With so much negative publicity stirred up by corruption scandals, Grant's administration took steps to minimize political controversies. To secure his reelection and keep the Republican Party in power, Grant adopted a more conservative approach to Reconstruction, by now a frequent source of rancor in Washington.

In the summer of 1872, for example, Grant lobbied Congress for and then signed into law the Amnesty Act, granting a general pardon to all but a few hundred former Confederate leaders. Now eligible to vote and hold office, these planters, ex-army officers, and ex-Confederate officials wasted little time in reasserting their authority.

> "It seems to me that we are drifting, drifting back under the leadership of the slaveholders. Our former masters are fast taking the reins of government."
>
> GEORGE M. ARNOLD, African American Republican

The retreat from Reconstruction in the 1870s was also hastened by growing dissention within the Republican Party. Many Republicans, including former Radicals, began to question the wisdom of maintaining a strong federal role in the affairs of Southern states. Some Republicans now believed the fundamental goals of Reconstruction—citizenship, civil rights, and suffrage for the freedmen—had been accomplished. There was, they believed, a constitutional and moral limit to what the federal government could do on behalf of the freedmen. Now was the time, they argued, for the freedmen to elevate themselves economically, socially, and politically using their new rights.

What impact did the scandals of the Grant administration have on Reconstruction?

Spread throughout each chapter, **contemporary voices** comment on the major issues of the day.

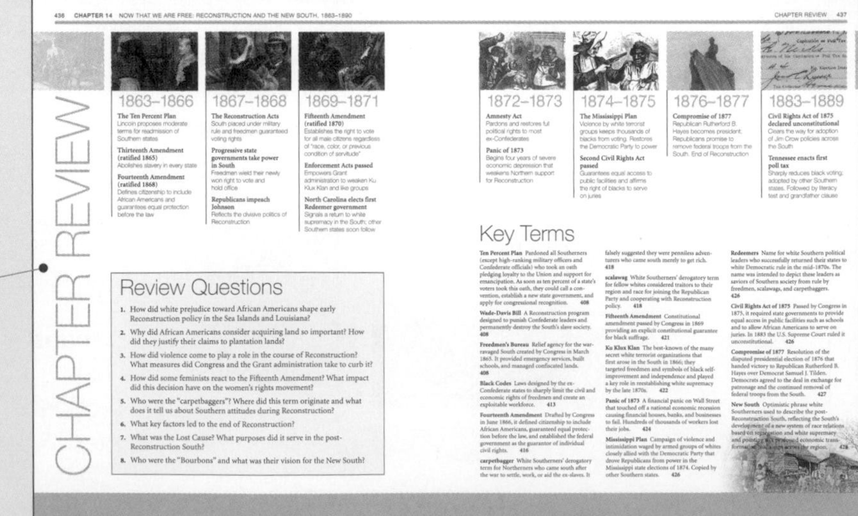
436 CHAPTER 14 NOW THAT WE ARE FREE: RECONSTRUCTION AND THE NEW SOUTH, 1863–1890   CHAPTER REVIEW 437

CHAPTER REVIEW

1863–1866

The Ten Percent Plan — Lincoln proposes moderate terms for readmission of Southern states

Thirteenth Amendment (ratified 1865) — Abolishes slavery in every state

Fourteenth Amendment (ratified 1868) — Defines citizenship to include African Americans and guarantees equal protection before the law

1867–1868

The Reconstruction Acts — South placed under military rule and freedmen guaranteed voting rights

Progressive state governments take power in South — Freedmen wield their newly won right to vote and hold office

Republicans impeach Johnson — Reflects the divisive politics of Reconstruction

1869–1871

Fifteenth Amendment (ratified 1870) — Establishes the right to vote for all male citizens regardless of "race, color, or previous condition of servitude"

Enforcement Acts passed — Empowers Grant administration to weaken Ku Klux Klan and like groups

North Carolina elects first Redeemer government — Signals a return to white supremacy in the South; other Southern states soon follow

1872–1873

Amnesty Act — Pardons and restores full political rights to most ex-Confederates

Panic of 1873 — Begins four years of severe economic depression that weakens Northern support for Reconstruction

1874–1875

The Mississippi Plan — Violence by white terrorist groups keeps thousands of blacks from voting. Restores the Democratic Party to power

Second Civil Rights Act passed — Guarantees equal access to public facilities and affirms the right of blacks to serve on juries

1876–1877

Compromise of 1877 — Republican Rutherford B. Hayes becomes president; Republicans promise to remove federal troops from the South. End of Reconstruction

1883–1889

Civil Rights Act of 1875 declared unconstitutional — Clears the way for adoption of Jim Crow policies across the South

Tennessee enacts first poll tax — Sharply reduces black voting; adopted by other Southern states. Followed by literacy test and grandfather clause

Review Questions

1. How did white prejudice toward African Americans shape early Reconstruction policy in the Sea Islands and Louisiana?
2. Why did African Americans consider acquiring land so important? How did they justify their claims to plantation lands?
3. How did violence come to play a role in the course of Reconstruction? What measures did Congress and the Grant administration take to curb it?
4. How did some feminists react to the Fifteenth Amendment? What impact did this decision have on the women's rights movement?
5. Who were the "carpetbaggers"? Where did this term originate and what does it tell us about Southern attitudes during Reconstruction?
6. What key factors led to the end of Reconstruction?
7. What was the Lost Cause? What purposes did it serve in the post-Reconstruction South?
8. Who were the "Bourbons" and what was their vision for the New South?

Key Terms

Ten Percent Plan Pardoned all Southerners (except high-ranking military officers and Confederate officials) who took an oath pledging loyalty to the Union and support for emancipation. As soon as ten percent of a state's voters took this oath, they could call a convention, establish a new state government, and apply for congressional recognition. 408

Wade-Davis Bill A Reconstruction program designed to punish Confederate leaders and permanently destroy the South's slave society. 408

Freedmen's Bureau Relief agency for the war-ravaged South created by Congress in March 1865. It provided emergency services, built schools, and managed confiscated lands. 408

Black Codes Laws designed by the ex-Confederate states to sharply limit the civil and economic rights of freedmen and create an exploitable workforce. 413

Fourteenth Amendment Drafted by Congress in June 1866, it defined citizenship to include African Americans, guaranteed equal protection before the law, and established the federal government as the guarantor of individual civil rights. 416

carpetbagger White Southerners' derogatory term for Northerners who came south after the war to settle, work, or aid the ex-slaves. It falsely suggested they were penniless adventurers who came south merely to get rich. 418

scalawag White Southerners' derogatory term for fellow whites considered traitors to their region and race for joining the Republican Party and cooperating with Reconstruction policy. 418

Fifteenth Amendment Constitutional amendment passed by Congress in 1869 providing an explicit constitutional guarantee for black suffrage. 421

Ku Klux Klan The best-known of the many secret white terrorist organizations that first arose in the South in 1866; they targeted freedmen and symbols of black self-improvement and independence and played a key role in reestablishing white supremacy by the late 1870s. 422

Panic of 1873 A financial panic on Wall Street that touched off a national economic recession causing financial houses, banks, and businesses to fail. Hundreds of thousands of workers lost their jobs. 424

Mississippi Plan Campaign of violence and intimidation waged by armed groups of whites closely allied with the Democratic Party that drove Republicans from power in the Mississippi state elections of 1874. Copied by other Southern states. 426

Redeemers Name for white Southern political leaders who successfully returned their states to white Democratic rule in the mid-1870s. The name was intended to depict these leaders as saviors of Southern society from rule by freedmen, scalawags, and carpetbaggers. 426

Civil Rights Act of 1875 Passed by Congress in 1875, it required state governments to provide equal access in public facilities such as schools and to allow African Americans to serve on juries. In 1883 the U.S. Supreme Court ruled it unconstitutional. 426

Compromise of 1877 Resolution of the disputed presidential election of 1876 that handed victory to Republican Rutherford B. Hayes over Democrat Samuel J. Tilden. Democrats agreed to the deal in exchange for patronage and the continued removal of federal troops from the South. 427

New South Optimistic phrase white Southerners used to describe the post-Reconstruction South, reflecting the South's development of a new system of race relations based on segregation and white supremacy and pointing [illegible] economic transformation [illegible] the region. [illegible]

A **Chapter Review** provides a **visual summary** of key events, thought-provoking **review questions**, and **key terms** with definitions and page references.

Supplements for Instructors and Students

FOR QUALIFIED COLLEGE ADOPTERS

Name of Supplement	Print or Online?	Instructor or Student Supplement?	Description
Instructor's Manual 0-205-72875-8	Both	Instructor	Chapter overview, lecture supplements, discussion questions, suggested assignments, and research resources for each chapter, including both general and text-specific content.
American Stories: Biographies in United States History, Third Edition Volume 1: 0-13-182654-9 Volume 2: 0-13-182653-0	Both	Student	This two-volume collection of sixty-two biographies provides insight into the lives and contributions to American history of key figures as well as ordinary citizens. Introductions, pre-reading questions, and suggested resources help students connect the relevance of these individuals to historical events.
MyHistoryLab 0-205-75326-4	Online	Both	Along with a complete e-book version of *Visions of America,* MyHistoryLab provides several hundred primary source documents, study support, test review materials, maps and activities, many of which are assignable and feed into a gradebook. The History Bookshelf includes nearly 100 of the most commonly assigned book-length sources. A Closer Look guides users through the process of analyzing visual images. The History Toolkit offers guided tutorials and helpful links. Icons in the e-book link directly to relevant materials. Visit www.myhistorylab.com.
CourseSmart 0-205-72698-4	Online	Both	CourseSmart Textbooks Online give students an inexpensive alternative to purchasing the print textbook by subscribing to the same content online and saving up to 50% off the suggested list price of the print text. Features include search, online note-taking, a print option, and bookmarking. Visit www.coursesmart.com
Instructor's Resource Center	Online	Instructor	A password-protected Web site where instructors can download Pearson supplements. Please contact your local Pearson representative for an access code or visit www.pearsonhighered.com/educator.
MyTest 0-205-75334-5	Online	Instructor	The MyTest test bank contains over 1,700 multiple-choice, short answer, and essay questions to test both general knowledge and features and content specific to *Visions of America*. Questions can be edited, and tests can be printed in several different formats. Visit www.pearsonmytest.com.
PowerPoint Presentation 0-205-74815-5	Online	Instructor	The PowerPoint slides to accompany *Visions of America* include an outline of each chapter and full-color images, maps, and figures from the text.
Comprehensive American History Transparency Set 0-673-97211-9	Online	Instructor	A vast collection of American history transparency masters. Available exclusively on the Instructor's Resource Center.
Discovering American History Through Maps and Views by Gerald Danzer 0-673-53766-8	Online	Instructor	A set of 140 full-color digital transparency masters includes cartographic and pictorial maps, views, photos; urban plans and building diagrams; and works of art. Available exclusively on the Instructor's Resource Center.
Digital Transparancy Masters	Online	Instructor	Text-specific transparency masters include all the maps that appear in *Visions of America.*

Name of Supplement	Print or Online?	Instructor or Student Supplement?	Description
Longman American History Atlas 0-321-00486-8	Print	Both	A full-color historical atlas includes approximately 100 maps covering the scope of American history from pre-Columbian Native Americans to the 1990s. Produced by a renowned cartographic firm and a team of respected historians.
Study Card for American History 0-321-29232-4	Print	Student	This timeline of major events in American social, political, and cultural history distills course information to the basics, helping students quickly master the fundamentals and prepare for exams.
Mapping America: A Guide to Historical Geography by Ken Weatherbie Volume 1: 0-321-47559-3 Volume 2: 0-321-47560-7	Print	Student	This two-volume workbook presents the basic geography of the United States, its lands and river systems, and helps students place the history of the United States into spatial perspective. The goal of this workbook is to reinforce, through practice, how to read visual materials as historical documents.
America Through the Eyes of Its People, Third Edition Volume 1: 0-321-39575-1 Volume 2: 0-321-39576-X	Print	Student	This two-volume comprehensive anthology of primary sources expertly balances social and political history and includes up-to-date narrative material.
A Short Guide to Writing About History, Seventh Edition by Richard Marius and Melvin E. Page 0-205-67370-8	Print	Student	Teaches students how to think and write like historians, to incorporate their own ideas into their papers and to tell a story about history. Covering brief essays and the documented resource paper, the text outlines the writing and researching processes, explores modes of historical writing (including argument), and offers guidelines for improving style and documenting sources.
Penguin Valuepacks	Print	Student	A variety of Penguin-Putnam texts are available at discounted prices when bundled with *Visions of America.* Complete list of available titles at http://www.pearsonhighered.com/penguin/
Library of American Biography Series	Print	Student	Pearson's renowned series of biographies spotlights figures who had a significant impact on American history. View the complete list at http://www.pearsonhighered.com/historyvaluepacks/biographies_history.html
Retrieving the American Past	Print	Student	This on-demand database offers eighty-six modules on topics such as "Women on the Frontier," "The Salem Witchcraft Scare," "The Age of Industrial Violence," and "Native American Societies, 1870–1995." Approximately thirty-five pages in length, each module includes an introduction, several primary documents and secondary sources, follow-up questions, and recommendations for further reading. Instructor-originated material can be incorporated. Contact your local Pearson representative for more information or visit http://www.pearsoncustom.com/

Acknowledgments

DEVELOPMENT STORY

More than three hundred and fifty reviewers, focus group participants, and class-testers participated in developing *Visions of America.* Each of them evaluated both the extensive visual program and the narrative text. They commented on the selection of images and on their integration into the narrative. They suggested refinements to the page design to maximize visual appeal and pedagogical effectiveness. And, through many drafts, they appraised our success in executing our twofold goal—to approach American history as the product of competing visions and to enhance that approach through an analysis of our nation's visual legacy. Always too, they focused on the value of our approach in the classroom. This book would not have been possible without their efforts, nor those of the many students who participated in focus groups and class tests.

Manuscript Reviewers

Alabama

Carl Boening, Shelton State Community College
Antoinnette Hudson, Jacksonville State University
Lawrence Kohl, University of Alabama
Lisa Lindquist Dorr, University of Alabama
Andre Millard, University of Alabama - Birmingham
Rebecca Reeves, Wallace State Community College
England Robert, Northwest-Shoals Community College
George Terrell Jr., Gadsden State Community College
John Turner, University of South Alabama
Deryl Umphrey, Calhoun Community College

Arkansas

Ken Bridges, South Arkansas Community College
James Moses, Arkansas Technical University
Charlotte Power, Black River Technical College
Carey Roberts, Arkansas Technical University
Amy Rumsey, Arkansas State University

Arizona

James Austin, Chandler-Gilbert Community College
Azusa Ono, Arizona State University
Debbie Roberts, Yavapai College
David Rudakewich, Coconino Community College

California

Guy Aronoff, California State University—Channel Islands
Josh Ashenmiller, Fullerton College
Don Bandy, Taft College
Rosemary Bell, Skyline College
Dominic Cerri, Sacramento City College
Daniel Christensen, Biola University
Tracy Davis, Victor Valley College
Philip DiMare, California State University, Sacramento
Michael Flores, Cypress College
Keith R. V. Heningburg, Sacramento City College
Jennifer Hernandez, Cuyamaca Collage
Jay Hester, Sierra College
George Jarrett, Cerritos College
Daehwan Lee, Pasadena City College
Daniel Lewis, California State Polytechnic University-Pomona
Peter Mancall, University of Southern California
Louis McDermott, Solano Community College
Aime McNamara, Cabrillo College
Jonathan Nielson, Cosumnes River College
Emily Rader, El Camino College
John Sbardellati, University of California—Santa Barbara
Bryan Seiling, Cypress College

Colorado

John Baranski, Fort Lewis College
Joanne Maypole, Metropolitan State College of Denver
Cheryl Waite, Community College of Aurora

Connecticut

Edward Donato, Sacred Heart University

Delaware

Bradley Skelcher, Delaware State University

Florida

Anthony Atwood, Florida International University
Will Benedicks, Tallahassee Community College
Tomas Bennett, Florida Hospital College of Health Sciences
Daniel Finn, Seminole Community College
David Gregory, Tallahassee Community College
Brian Harding, Lake-Sumter Community College
Kelly Minor, University of Florida
John Shaffett, The Baptist College of Florida
E. Timothy Smith, Barry University

Georgia

Don Butts, Gordon State College
Michael Hall, Armstrong Atlantic State University
Shane Hamilton, University of Georgia
Heather Lucas, Georgia Perimeter College-Dunwoody Campus
Elsa Nystrom, Kennesaw State University
George S. Pabis, Georgia Perimeter College
Jim Piecuch, Kennesaw State University
Colleen Vasconcellos, University of West Georgia

Hawaii

Allison Gough, Hawaii Pacific University

Idaho

Christian Esh, Northwest Nazarene University

Illinois

Steven DePasquale, Kankakee Community College
Melissa Dierkes, Moraine Valley Community College
Richard Filipink, Western Illinois University
Kent Gatyas, Morton College
George Gerdow, Northeastern Illinois University
Jennifer Guiliano, University of Illinois at Urbana-Champaign
Robert Harmon, Elgin Community College
Virginia Jelatis, Western Illinois University
Mark Leff, University of Illinois
Stephen Lowe, Olivet Nazarene University
Jim McIntyre, Moraine Valley Community College
Jay Nelson, DePaul University
Jay Pearce, Blackhawk Community College
Wendy Sarti, Oakton Community College
Anne Valk, Southern Illinois University—Edwardsville
Ben Whisenhunt, College of DuPage

Indiana

Eric Hall, Purdue University
Anne Kearney, Jefferson Community and Technical College
Jason Lantzer, Indiana University—Bloomington
Jonathan Nashel, Indiana University—South Bend
Dave O'Grady, University of Southern Indiana
David Vanderstel, Indiana University—Purdue University Indianapolis

Iowa

Dick Broadie, University of Northern Iowa
Kevin Gannon, Grand View University
Johanna Schoen, University of Iowa

Acknowledgments *(continued from pp. xxix)*

Kansas

Andrew Lindsay, Pittsburg State University
James B. M. Schick, Pittsburg State University

Kentucky

John Bowes, Eastern Kentucky University
John Burch, Campbellsville University
Jeff Dennis, Morehead State University
Jennifer Geouge, Somerset Community College—Laurel Campus
Carol Siler, Eastern Kentucky University
Patia Tabar, Northern Kentucky University
Fiona Halloran, Eastern Kentucky University

Maine

Patricia Bixel, Maine Maritime Academy
Karen Kimball, University of Maine—Machias
David Raymond, Northern Maine Community College

Maryland

Wayne Ackerson, Salisbury University
Angela Leonard, Loyola College
David Peavler, Towson University
Alonzo Smith, Montgomery College

Massachusetts

Vincent Cannato, University of Massachusetts Boston
Gary Donato, Massachusetts Bay Community College
Charlotte Haller, Worcester State College
Kevin Kenny, Boston College
Betty Mitchell, University of Massachusetts—Dartmouth
Gail Mohanty, University of Massachusetts—Dartmouth
Elaine Pascale, Suffolk University
Cynthia Lyerly, Boston College

Michigan

Gordon Andrews, Lake Michigan College
Kevin Brown, Lansing Community College
Kimn Carlton-Smith, Ferris State University
Todd Estes, Oakland University
Roy Finkenbine, University of Detroit Mercy
Amy French, Delta Community College
Steven Garvey, Muskegon Community College
Jeff Janowick, Lansing Community College
Malcolm Magee, Michigan State University
Ed Martini, Western Michigan University
Joshua Schier, Western Michigan University
Harold Siegel, Hillsdale College
Dave Stewart, Hillsdale College
Catherine Tobin, Central Michigan University

Minnesota

Kevin Byrne, Gustavus Adolphus College
Kathleen Gorman, Minnesota State University—Mankato
Paul Harris, Minnesota State University, Moorhead
John Hendrickson, Minnesota State University, Mankato
Linda Janke, Anoka Ramsey Community College
Judy Kutulas, St. Olaf College
Scott Laderman, University of Minnesota—Duluth
David Rayson, Normandale Community College
Gregory Schmidt, Winona State University
Terry Shoptaugh, Minnesota State University, Moorhead

Mississippi

John Arnold, Itawamba Community College
Eric Bobo, Hinds Community College
Michael Namorato, University of Mississippi

Missouri

Diana Ahmad, University of Missouri—Rolla
Kay Blalock, St. Louis Community College—Meramec
Brad Lookingbill, Columbia College
John McManus, University of Missouri—Rolla
Kay Murnan, Ozarks Technical Community College
Kim Schreck, University of Missouri—St. Louis
K. Dirk Voss, Saint Louis Community College
James Whitt, Ozarks Technical Community College
Tim Wood, Southwest Baptist University

Montana

David Bibb, University of Great Falls
Debora Bibb, University of Great Falls

North Carolina

Monika Fleming, Edgecombe Community College
Michael Kennedy, High Point University

North Dakota

Jon Brudvig, University of Mary
Joseph Jastrzembski, Minot State University
Jim Norris, North Dakota State University

Nebraska

Amy Forss, Metropolitan Community College
Heather Fryer, Creighton University

Nevada

Susan Imswiler, Truckee Meadows Community College
Cyd McMullen, Great Basin College
Jerry Parker, Truckee Meadows Community College
John Reid, Truckee Meadows Community College

New Hampshire

Andrew Moore, Saint Anselm College

New Jersey

Barbara Calluori, Montclair State University
Bill Carr, Kean University
Walter Dabrowski, Mercer County Community College
Janet Golden, Rutgers University—Camden
David Wolcott, Educational Testing Service

New Mexico

Nancy Shockley, New Mexico State University

New York

Heather Barry, St. Joseph's College
Thomas Beal, State University of New York—Oneonta
Will Corprew, Broome Community College
Andrea DeKoter, State University of New York at Cortland
Tom Dublin, The State University of New York at Binghamton
Megan Elias, City University of New York—Queensborough Community College
Andrew Feffer, Union College
David Gerber, State University of New York at Buffalo
Gary Ostrower, Alfred University
William Price, North Country Community College
Daniel Prosterman, Syracuse University
Margaret Wingate, Broome Community College
Jason Young, The State University of New York at Buffalo

Ohio

Rebecca Barrett, The Ohio State University
Diane Britton, University of Toledo
Daniel Cobb, Miami University
William Coil, The Ohio State University
Hasan Jeffries, The Ohio State University
Gregory Kupsky, The Ohio State University
Mark Mengerink, Bowling Green State University
Caryn Neumann, Miami University Middletown
Paul O'Hara, Xavier University
Judith Spraul-Schmidt, University of Cincinnati Raymond Walters College
Jim Streckfuss, Miami University
Shirley Wajda, Kent State University
Jonathan Winkler, Wright State University

Oklahoma

Jeff Carlisle, Oklahoma City Community College
Frank Gilbert, Southeastern Oklahoma State University
Paul B. Hatley, Rogers State University
Stacy Reaves, Tulsa Community College
Paddy Swiney, Tulsa Community College

Oregon

Cathy Croghan Alzner, Portland Community College
John Shaw, Portland Community College—Sylvania

Pennsylvania

Jacqueline Akins, Community College of Philadelphia
Allan Austin, College Misericordia
Andy Bacha, Harrisburg Area Community College
Brian Black, Pennsylvania State University—Altoona
Michael P. Gabriel, Kutztown University
Jolyon Girard, Cabrini College
John Hepp, Wilkes University

VISIONS *of* AMERICA

CHAPTER 1

People in Motion

The Atlantic World to 1590

The First Americans p. 4

"Your Magnificence must know that herein they are so inhuman that they outdo every custom (even) of beasts; for they eat all their enemies whom they kill or capture ... and are libidinous beyond measure."

PIERO SODERINI,
attributed to Amerigo Vespucci, 1497

To the people who had lived in the Americas for millennia, the idea that theirs was a "New World" would have seemed strange. Scientists continue to debate when the first people arrived in the Americas from Asia, but estimates range from between forty thousand and fourteen thousand years ago. In the millennia that followed, the peoples of the Americas fanned out and established a range of societies.

Yet to the Europeans who arrived in the Americas toward the end of the fifteenth century, America was indeed a "brave new world," as William Shakespeare wrote, inhabited by exotic plants, animals, and peoples. In images and words Europeans portrayed this extraordinary land in the most fantastic terms. Some accounts spoke of America as an Eden-like earthly paradise inhabited by good-natured, but primitive, peoples. Others emphasized themes like those featured in this engraving, *Amerigo Vespucci Awakens a Sleeping America.* Vespucci, an Italian-Spanish navigator from whose first name the New World came to be called the Americas, gazes upon a naked native woman rising from her hammock. Her nudity symbolizes the wild sexuality Europeans believed characterized the native inhabitants of the Americas. The cannibals behind her, devouring human flesh, represent savagery, a second prominent element of the European vision of the New World. Neither vision of the Americas was accurate, but both would greatly complicate Europeans' understanding of the American civilizations they encountered, leading to a legacy of violence, exploitation, and conquest.

The European arrival in the Americas was part of a process of exploration and colonization pursued primarily by Portugal, Spain, France, and England. This impulse was driven both by a hunger for riches as well as by profound changes in European society, religion, economics, and politics brought on by the Renaissance and Reformation. Africa was eventually drawn into this vast trading network encompassing the entire Atlantic world. Colonization almost always involved the severe exploitation of native peoples, including dispossession of land and coerced labor. Eventually Europeans turned to the international slave trade and the labor of enslaved Africans to draw the wealth from the mines and fields of the New World.

How did Europeans envision America?

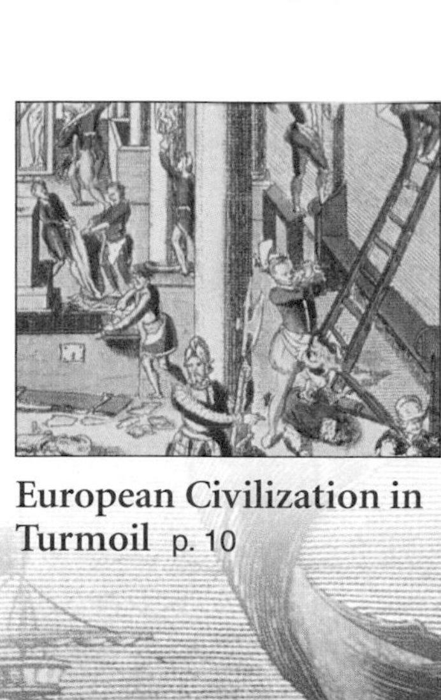

The First Americans

In one sense America *was* the New World—or at least a newer one in terms of human habitation. The oldest traces of human life have been found in Africa, where the earliest human fossil remains date to more than 100,000 years ago. In contrast the oldest human fossils found in North America are roughly 14,000 years old, far more recent than those found in Europe, Asia, or Australia. The ancient inhabitants of America, **Paleo-Indians**, were an Ice Age people who survived largely by hunting big game and to a lesser extent by collecting edible plants and fishing. Within a few thousand years of their arrival in America from Asia, they had fanned out across the Americas.

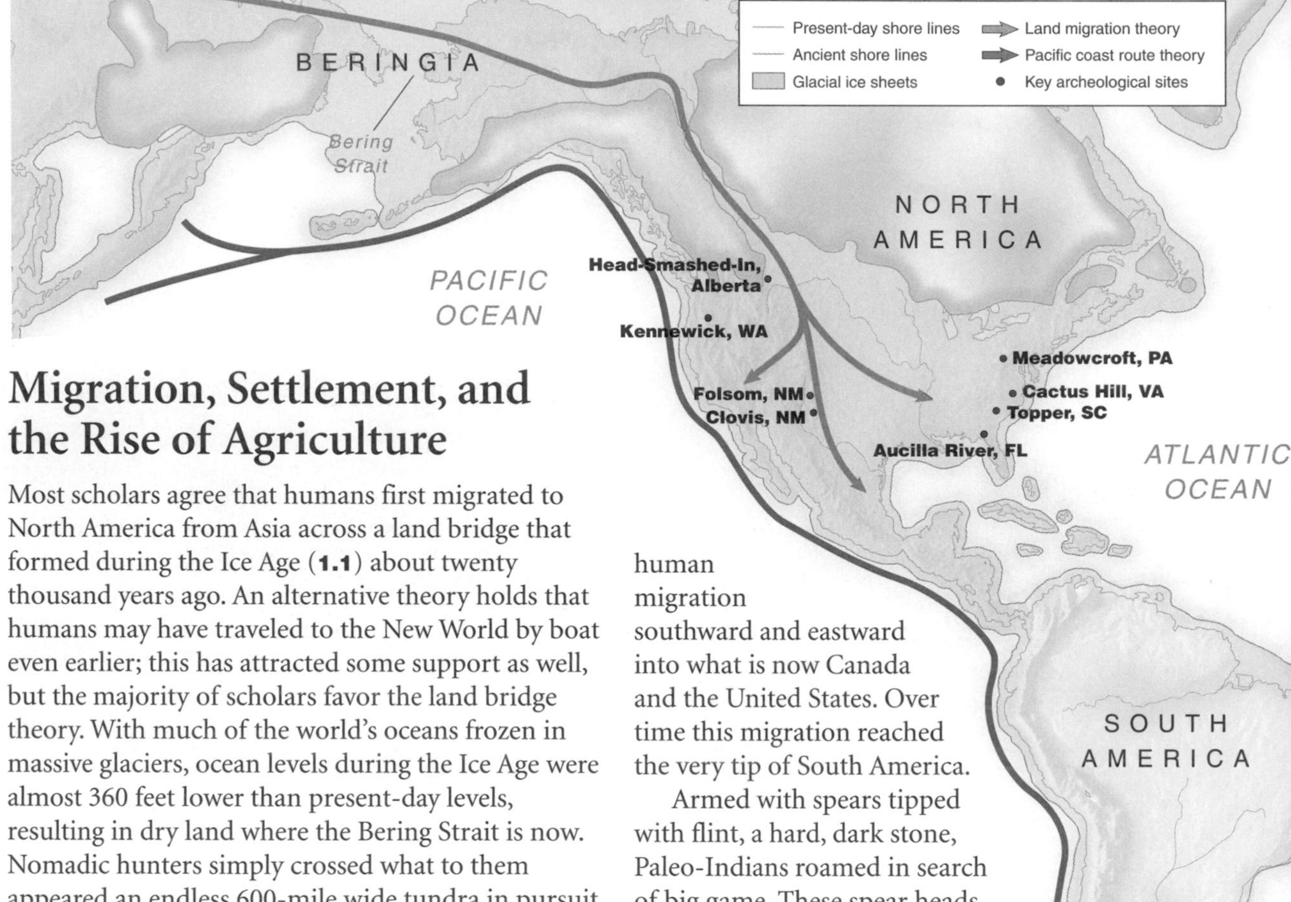

1.1 Migration from Asia to America Most scholars believe the first inhabitants of America migrated from Asia across the Bering Strait by way of the land bridge that once connected Asia and North America.

Migration, Settlement, and the Rise of Agriculture

Most scholars agree that humans first migrated to North America from Asia across a land bridge that formed during the Ice Age (**1.1**) about twenty thousand years ago. An alternative theory holds that humans may have traveled to the New World by boat even earlier; this has attracted some support as well, but the majority of scholars favor the land bridge theory. With much of the world's oceans frozen in massive glaciers, ocean levels during the Ice Age were almost 360 feet lower than present-day levels, resulting in dry land where the Bering Strait is now. Nomadic hunters simply crossed what to them appeared an endless 600-mile wide tundra in pursuit of migratory big game animals like the woolly mammoths—huge, long-tusked members of the elephant family that provided furs for warm clothing and ample stocks of meat.

Temperatures slowly warmed as the Ice Age passed, causing the great glaciers to melt and sea levels to rise. Sometime between 11,000 and 12,000 BCE, the rising waters covered the Bering Strait land bridge, cutting off migration from Asia. But the recession of the glaciers also opened the way for human migration southward and eastward into what is now Canada and the United States. Over time this migration reached the very tip of South America.

Armed with spears tipped with flint, a hard, dark stone, Paleo-Indians roamed in search of big game. These spear heads, called Clovis points, named after the New Mexico town in which scientists first discovered them, were one of the Stone Age tools used by the ancient inhabitants of America. Clovis point arrowheads like those shown in (**1.2**) were lashed to poles to make simple spears. Paleo-Indians also used other simple stone tools such as stone axes and scrapers for hunting and preparing meat, a variety of bone tools such as antler harpoons for fishing, and bone needles for sewing hides. These

What theories account for the mass extinction of large mammals in the Americas?

ancient peoples generally hunted in small bands of perhaps twenty to thirty people in cooperative kin groups. Hunting parties pursued a wide range of prey, including the woolly mammoth. They also hunted the oversized ancestors of many modern species, such as beaver, bison, caribou, and forerunners of the camel. Hunting, gathering, and other activities among Stone Age peoples were probably divided along gender lines. Men hunted and fished, while women reared children, gathered nuts and berries, and made clothing.

Many of the mammals that Paleo-Indians hunted, including mammoths, forerunners of camels, and primitive horses, eventually became extinct (the Spanish reintroduced modern horses from Europe into the Americas thousands of years later). Three competing scientific theories exist to account for the mass extinctions of large mammals in the Americas. Some scientists believe overhunting led to the demise of the large mammals. Others argue that dramatic climate change—the rising temperatures that accompanied the passing of the Ice Age—killed off certain animals that were unable to adapt to the new warmer environments. The most recent explanation for the mass extinctions focuses on diseases that may have been brought to the New World by humans and the animals that accompanied them, most notably dogs and possibly rats. Whatever the cause of the mass extinctions, the decline in large game eventually led Paleo-Indians to search for new food sources and develop new modes of providing food and other necessities.

Approximately nine thousand years ago, a period known as the **Archaic Era** began. Lasting approximately six thousand years, it ushered in significant social changes that began with increased efforts by native peoples to shape the environment to enhance food production. At first these efforts were quite primitive. Archaic Era Indians, for example, used fire to burn away forest underbrush to provide better habitats for smaller mammals such as deer, which they hunted. They also relied increasingly on gathering nuts and berries and, in some cases, harvesting shellfish from lakes, streams, or coastal waters. The gendered division of labor found in Stone Age societies persisted into the Archaic Era: women cared for children and did much of the gathering and preparing of food while men hunted and fished.

Some Archaic Era Indians even took the first steps toward agriculture. At first they encouraged the growth of edible plants, such as sunflowers and wild onions, by simply weeding out inedible plants around them. Over time Archaic Era Indians learned how to collect and plant seeds and developed basic ideas about irrigation. These primitive cultivation techniques led to increased food supplies and diminished reliance on hunting.

1.2 Clovis Point The range of tools available to Paleo-Indians was limited, but included stone tools, such as arrowheads, axes, scrapers, and bone needles and harpoons. Clovis point arrowheads were attached to spears for hunting.

By about 5,000 BCE fixed agricultural settlements appeared in what is now Mexico. There native people learned how to grow maize (corn), squash, and beans, leading to the development of food surpluses and consequently large increases in population. Planting, tending, and defending crops necessitated the creation of larger permanent settlements, leading to urbanization, the creation of towns and cities. Increased food surpluses allowed the ancient peoples of the Americas to devote more resources to a variety of cultural, artistic, and engineering projects. The combination of agriculture, urbanism, and increasing social complexity set the foundation for the emergence of the first great civilizations of the southern region of North America, an area stretching from modern Mexico to Nicaragua known as Mesoamerica.

The most advanced societies in Mesoamerica included the Olmecs (1500 BCE to about 400 BCE), Maya (peaked in 300 BCE–900 CE), and Toltecs (800 CE–1200 CE). These complex societies developed written languages, systems of mathematics, sophisticated irrigation techniques, and monumental architecture. They also experienced increased social stratification, the division of a society into classes of people ranked from low to high according

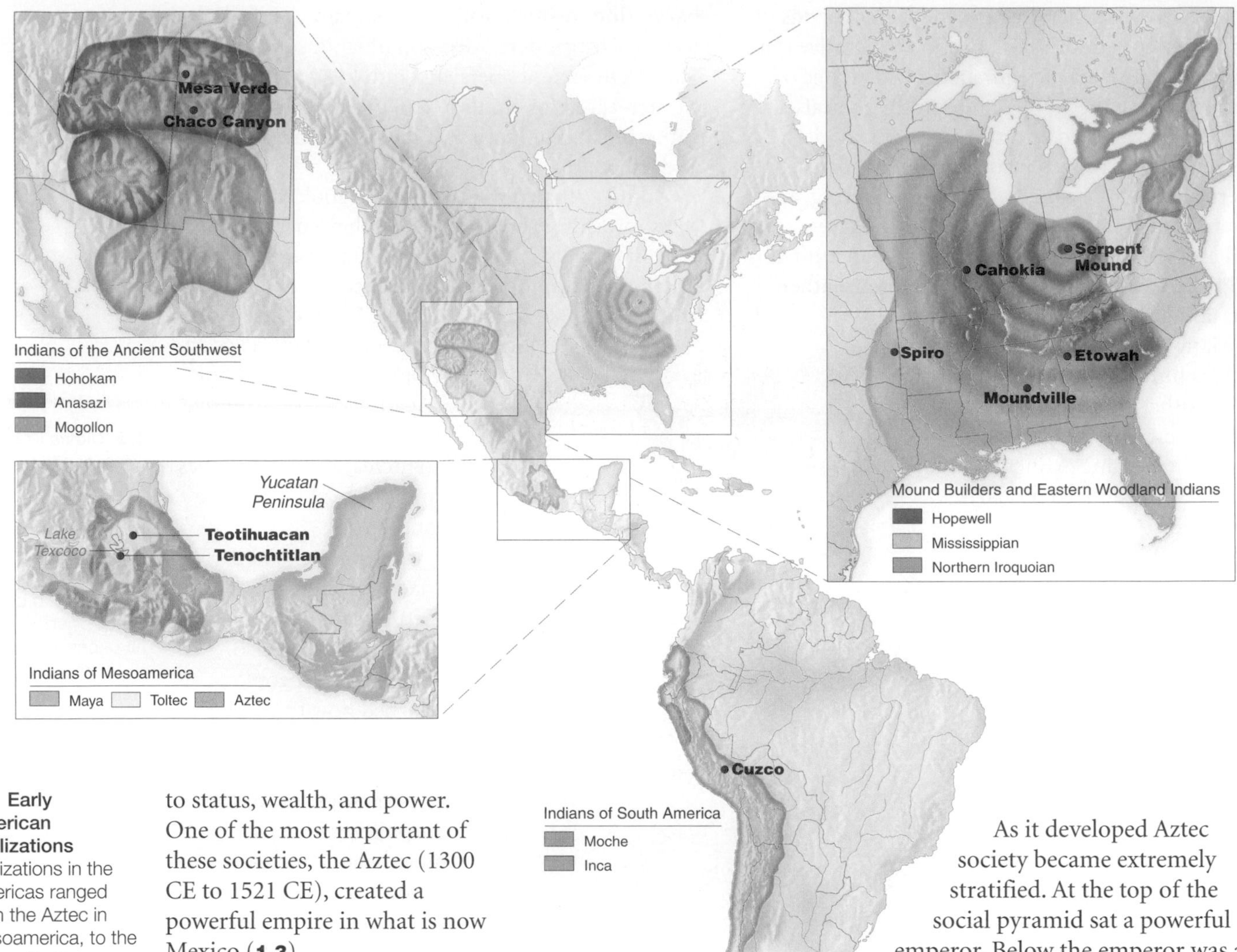

1.3 Early American Civilizations Civilizations in the Americas ranged from the Aztec in Mesoamerica, to the Anasazi in the Southwest, and the Mound builders of the Midwest.

to status, wealth, and power. One of the most important of these societies, the Aztec (1300 CE to 1521 CE), created a powerful empire in what is now Mexico (**1.3**).

The Aztec

The rise of the immensely powerful Aztec Confederacy transformed Mesoamerica. By the time the Spanish arrived in the early sixteenth century, the Aztecs controlled a vast empire of between ten and twenty million people. The **Aztec** Empire's capital, the great city of Tenochtitlán, was built on an island in Lake Texcoco in 1325 on the site of today's Mexico City. Causeways connected the city to the mainland and an elaborate system of dams controlled the water level of the lake, while aqueducts carried fresh water to the city. A sophisticated system of floating gardens produced food to feed the large urban population, which swelled to almost three hundred thousand over the next two centuries. The central plaza of the Aztec capitol was dominated by pyramid-like temples that towered over the landscape, reaching a height of close to 200 feet.

As it developed Aztec society became extremely stratified. At the top of the social pyramid sat a powerful emperor. Below the emperor was a class of nobles, a priestly class, a warrior class, and an administrative class who collected taxes and tributes. The foundation of this vast pyramid was comprised of merchants, artisans, and farmers. At the very bottom were slaves. Some were Aztec-born and became slaves temporarily as punishment for crime. Prisoners of war also added to the slave population, and human chattel was provided as part of tax debts owed to the Aztec Empire by its many conquered peoples.

Gender roles were sharply defined among the Aztec. Women helped men tend the fields but were primarily responsible for child rearing, cooking, weaving cloth, and shopping in the markets. Although the priests were invariably men, Aztec religion accorded women an important role in the family, including making religious offerings to the gods.

Trade and commerce were crucial to the Aztec economy. In the smaller towns daily markets provided a wide array of goods, but these markets

What role did commerce play in Aztec culture?

were miniscule compared to the great open-air market in Tenochtitlán. Countless foods, textiles, ceramics, and other goods were available for trade, illustrating the richness and complexity of the Aztec economy.

The Aztecs were a war-like society. Conquered peoples were forced to pay tribute in the form of textiles, agricultural products, precious stones, and ceramics, and even provide slaves for human sacrifices. Some estimates put the number of sacrificial victims at ten thousand per year. For the Aztecs human sacrifice was a central religious ritual necessary to appease the gods, especially the gods of rain and war.

> "Begin with the dealers in gold, silver, precious stones, feathers, mantles, and embroidered goods.... But why waste so many words in recounting what they sell in their great market? If I describe everything in detail I shall never be finished."
>
> Spaniard BERNAL DIAZ DEL CASTILLO, Spanish historian of the conquest of Mexico, 1568

Mound Builders and Pueblo Dwellers

Urban settlements also appeared in several other regions of North America (1.3). One group, the mound-building societies, created monumental earthen burial mounds as part of their religious practices. Some two thousand years ago, the Adena of what is now southern Ohio built The Great Serpent Mound. Still visible, it resembles a giant snake. Excavations of this and other mound-building society sites have unearthed a host of artifacts used for religious purposes and personal adornment. We can also conclude that these inland people acquired the conch shells and shark teeth found at their sites from other cultures, as part of a trade network that extended all the way to the Atlantic coast.

The most complex mound-building society, the Mississippian, developed in the Mississippi Valley (1.3). The central city of this civilization, Cahokia, arose in what is now southern Illinois near St. Louis. Cahokia developed a stratified society with a chief at the top, followed by an elite class and a lower class who provided labor for agriculture and building projects. At its height about a thousand years ago, Cahokia's population ranged somewhere between twenty thousand and forty thousand. The city was protected by a huge wooden palisade and featured at its center a massive terraced earthwork mound that covered 16 acres and rose over 100 feet above the ground. Capping this mound was a wooden temple that would have been among the tallest human-made structures in the Americas, exceeded only by the pyramids of Mesoamerica. Several other Mississippian communities developed in present-day Alabama, Georgia, and Oklahoma.

In the American Southwest, the Anasazi peoples created another complex civilization marked by a sophisticated urban culture that included a series of towns interconnected by roads (1.3). To survive in the arid climate of the Southwest, the Anasazi developed impressive engineering skills that they used to build their cities and construct complex irrigation systems to supply water for drinking and agriculture. Using adobe (clay) bricks, they built large dwellings later known by their Spanish name, *pueblos*. At the city of Chaco Canyon in what is now northwestern New Mexico, the Anasazi built Pueblo Bonito. This dwelling contained as many as 650 rooms, including forty kivas, or circular rooms intended for religious ceremonies. Until the development of modern apartment buildings in the late nineteenth century, this was the largest human dwelling in world history.

In addition to their architectural and engineering expertise, the Anasazi also developed skills in making pottery and textiles, some of which they used in a vast trade network that stretched hundreds of miles to the south. The most valuable commodity they traded was turquoise, a bright blue-green stone used to make jewelry. In exchange for it the Anasazi acquired prized luxuries such as sea shells from as far away as the Gulf of California to the west and carved images and feathers from Mesoamerica.

1.4 John White's Painting of Secoton
John White's painting of the Eastern Woodlands Indian village of Secoton includes images of wigwams, the Algonquian word for "dwelling place." (Europeans sometimes described these dwellings as longhouses.)

Eastern Woodlands Indian Societies

A very different type of society developed in a region encompassing what is now the Eastern United States and Canada. In contrast to the native societies of the Southwest and Mesoamerica, Eastern Woodlands societies were neither highly urban nor stratified. Organized into individual tribes, these Eastern Woodlands Indian peoples lived as hunters and gatherers as well as agriculturalists. Most spoke a dialect of one of two major Indian languages, Iroquois and Algonquian.

Instead of living in urban settlements, Eastern Woodland Indians moved with the seasons to take advantage of different food sources, tracking animals in forest regions or fishing in lakes, streams, and rivers. Consequently as this painting, one of the earliest European views of an actual Indian village (**1.4**), shows, their villages were composed of wood and bark structures that were easily disassembled and reassembled to make seasonal movement possible. Dwelling in small villages rather than settled urban areas, Eastern Woodlands Indians avoided many of the sanitation problems and disease outbreaks that periodically afflicted urbanized societies such as Tenochtitlán and Cahokia.

The complex religious life of Eastern Woodlands Indians embraced the concept of a supreme being, the great Manitou, but also included animism, or the belief that everything in nature possessed a spirit that had to acknowledged and respected. Rather than seeking to own land and subdue the world around them in the manner of European societies, Eastern Woodlands Indians sought to inhabit the land and to live in dynamic harmony with it. These beliefs, however, did not keep them from actively altering or managing their environments to their advantage. Indians adopted a number of strategies such as controlled burning of brush, a technique that encouraged the growth of habitats for the deer they hunted. This type of strategy contrasted with the approach of European agriculture, which used clear cutting to make land available for farming.

Compared with the more urban societies of the Southwest and Mesoamerica, the tribal societies of the Eastern seaboard had a relatively egalitarian political and social structure. Apart from the chief and a religious figure known as a shaman, most members of a tribe enjoyed a rough equality. While many indigenous societies in the Americas, particularly the more hierarchical ones of

Mesoamerica, were patrilineal, with inheritance and decision making residing in the male line, some Eastern Woodlands societies were matrilineal, tracing descent and determining inheritance from ancestors on the female side. In some tribes women enjoyed significant roles in tribal governance. When captives were taken in war, for example, the decision to either adopt or execute them was often made by women. Nonetheless Woodland Indians divided labor along gender lines, with women consigned to the fields, planting beans, corn, and squash, while men tracked and hunted animals for food, hides, and pelts.

Eastern Woodland Indians were more communal than individualistic in outlook. Although trade was important and individuals might own some goods, accumulating material wealth was not an important goal, as it was in the more stratified Mesoamerican societies. Individual tribes controlled territory, but the notion of owning land as private property was alien to most of these tribal societies.

> "They are not delighted in baubles, but in useful things.... I have observed that they will not be troubled with superfluous commodities."
>
> THOMAS MORTON, English lawyer, 1637

Warfare among many Eastern Woodlands tribes was intermittent but common. They often fought over control of tribal territory or hunting rights. Warfare typically consisted of skirmishes between rival war parties, a style of combat that usually kept causalities low. Causalities suffered in war, however, might trigger further military actions, or "mourning wars," intended to replenish the population reduced by fighting. In such a war some prisoners taken captive might be tortured and killed, while others deemed suitable were adopted by the tribe.

The persistent warfare among tribes led to the creation of the powerful Iroquois League of Five Nations, an organization that sought to reduce conflict among its members: the Seneca, Mohawk, Onondaga, Cayuga, and Oneida nations. Women played a significant role in the governance of the league. Female elders from each of the individual nations selected the men who formed the league's Great Council, a body that met to discuss matters of common concern, especially war and peace.

American Societies on the Eve of European Contact

American Indian societies were socially and culturally diverse, ranging from the highly stratified and urban Aztec in Mesoamerica to the relatively egalitarian hunter-farmer Iroquois in the Northeast. The peoples of the Americas spoke a host of different languages, developed a spectrum of distinctive religious traditions, and created different political models to govern themselves.

These societies shared many characteristics among themselves and with peoples in other parts of the world. Like their Asian and European contemporaries, the societies of the Americas were premodern, with limited scientific knowledge and widespread belief in magic. Most people worked the land, struggling to provide the basics needed to support life. Except for the privileged few, life was hard, sometimes brutal, and short.

In the Andes Mountains of South America, alpaca and llamas were domesticated, providing wool or food and, in the case of the llama, serving as a pack animal. But in contrast to Africa, Asia, or Europe, in North America and Mesoamerica there were no large domesticated animals, such as horses (extinct after the Paleo-Indian period), cattle, or camels. Without such animals the people of these regions lacked the kind of mobility and power that horses afforded Europeans and Asians and that camels provided for Africans.

American societies on the eve of contact with Europeans were distinctive in another way. While African and Asian societies had developed considerable trade with Europe, the peoples of the Americas had remained largely cut off from contact with other parts of the world for thousands of years. This isolation had prevented their exposure to a host of diseases. By the time of the first contact between Europe and America in the late 1400s, the inhabitants of Asia, Africa, and Europe, long exposed to a common pool of diseases because of their extensive trade contacts, had developed immunity to many virulent pathogens. In their relative isolation, however, the indigenous societies of the Americas were highly susceptible to the microbial invaders introduced by Europeans.

What were some of the distinctive characteristics shared by all of the societies of the Americas?

European Civilization in Turmoil

As the Aztec Empire was reaching the height of its power at the close of the fifteenth century, European society was in the midst of a profound transformation. This period of cultural, intellectual, scientific, and commercial flourishing is known as the Renaissance. The revival of interest in classical languages, including Greek and Latin, not only led to renewed interest in the civilizations of Greece and Rome but also Renaissance thinkers re-examined the early history of the church and its teachings. Reformers drawing on these traditions and reacting to the corruption of the Roman Catholic Church challenged the authority of the church. The rise of a new strain of Christian thought, Protestantism, led to creation of a host of new Protestant religious sects. Amidst this tumult powerful monarchs across Europe forged new nation-states out of the relatively weak decentralized governments of Europe. Modern nations such as England, France, and Spain were born in this era. State building required money, and these monarchs were eager to increase the wealth and power of their nations, a desire that ultimately led to the movement for colonization and exploration of Africa and the Americas.

The Allure of the East and the Challenge of Islam

The leading European powers' decision to explore, conquer, and exploit lands in the Atlantic world was facilitated by a host of economic, technological, and cultural changes. Contact with Asia led to major changes in taste and patterns of consumption during the early modern period, the time spanning the fifteenth through the seventeenth centuries. Europeans looked beyond their borders, particularly to China and the Far East, for sugar and spices to enrich their bland foods and for luxury goods, especially exotic textiles such as silk, to enliven their fashions. These commodities, not native to Europe, had to be obtained from Asia.

All of the overland trade routes to the East plied by Western traders were in territory controlled by Muslims, adherents of **Islam**, a monotheistic faith shaped by the teachings of the prophet Muhammad. Since its emergence in the seventh century Middle East, Muslim influence spread, stretching from Europe to Africa and parts of Asia. Europeans came to resent the economic power of Muslim nations who controlled the lucrative trade routes to the East.

European antagonism toward the Muslim world also sprang from an intense religious animosity. For almost three hundred years, Christian Europe had waged a holy war against Islam, launching Crusades to regain control of Jerusalem, the holy city of Jews, Christians, and Muslims. Closer to Europe, Islam's influence in Europe was most pronounced in the Ottoman Empire, whose power eventually spread throughout the Eastern Mediterranean and Baltic Regions.

Trade, Commerce, and Urbanization

Among the important changes in Europe during this period were the dramatic growth of the economy and its expansion. The Black Death (1347–1352 CE), an epidemic plague, wiped out about half of Europe's population. In the centuries following the Black Death, Europe's population began to expand slowly, eventually recouping and surpassing the size it had attained before the epidemic. The economies of Europe likewise recovered after the Black Death. At the dawn of the fifteenth century, the Italian city-states, most especially Venice, dominated trade and finance, particularly trade with the East. In part, Venice's dominance resulted from its proximity to the lucrative eastern trade routes. Italy also dominated textile production as Florence emerged as Europe's leading producer of woolen cloth. Slowly the economic center of Europe shifted eastward. By about 1500 Antwerp had become the leading commercial center of Europe but was soon surpassed by Amsterdam.

As trade and commerce expanded, Europeans developed new financial practices and services that facilitated continued economic growth. New

What trade goods from Asia were most sought after by Europeans?

accounting methods helped merchants keep track of inventories and profits and losses, and marine insurance reduced the risks of maritime trade. At the same time a more elaborate banking system helped finance trade. The growth of deposit banking, a system in which merchants could deposit funds with bankers and then draw on written checks instead of presenting cash for payment of goods, greatly bolstered trade and commerce. All these developments made economic ventures more secure and encouraged investment, some of which was directed toward overseas trade and exploration. Together the new commercial and financial practices were key elements in the growth of capitalism. Simply put, **capitalism** is an economic system in which a market economy, geared toward the maximization of profit, determines the prices of goods and services. This new, profit-driven capitalist ethos slowly transformed European life beginning in the fifteenth century.

Capitalism transformed rural Europe as well. European culture had always viewed nature as something to be tamed and exploited (see *Competing Visions: European and Huron Views of Nature*, page 12.) Rather than simply produce food for themselves, the new capitalist ethos led some farmers to seek the maximum yield from their land and plant crops that would fetch a higher price at market. In other cases landowners simply evicted farmers from their lands so that they could graze sheep on the land and produce wool that would be turned into cloth. This latter change in agriculture effectively forced many to leave the countryside and seek new employment in towns and cities.

The combination of migration from the countryside and commercial development led to greater urbanization in Europe. In the two centuries after the Black Death, the population of London increased from 50,000 to more than 200,000. Outside of London, England's changes were less dramatic, but no less significant. Populations in port cities such as Bristol, regional market towns such as Cambridge, and the new manufacturing centers in the cloth trade such as Manchester mushroomed.

Economic growth was also spurred by technological improvements and new inventions. The printing press transformed the way knowledge was produced and disseminated. While a scribe hand-copying a book onto parchment might turn out two or three books a year, the typical print run of a book produced on paper by a printing press was between a hundred and a thousand. Printed books not only made it easier to preserve knowledge already acquired but also facilitated advances in science and geographic exploration by making it easier to collect, organize, and analyze information. Printed texts and engraved images also whet the appetites of Europeans for exploration by making accounts of exotic places such as India and China more accessible. Marco Polo's (1254?–1324) influential text, *The Travels of Marco Polo*, circulated widely in manuscript form for more than a century before a printed edition appeared in 1477.

Printing created an entire new industry for the production, dissemination, and sale of books. The new technology also transformed visual culture, making it possible to create cheap images. The new technique of engraving, shown here (**1.5**), was a multistep process. On the right a skilled craftsman gouges out an image on a copper plate. In the center the plates are inked and then wiped clean. On the left the final stages in the engraving process are demonstrated, including the giant press used to create the final image.

1.5 Copper Engraving This detailed engraving shows the many steps used to make an engraving, from the artist's hand to the final drying of the printed page. [*Source:* Hans Collaert, "Sculptura in Aes". The workshop of an engraver (Sculptura in Aes), plate 19 from "Nova Reperta", Netherlandish. c. 1600. Engraving. After Stradanus (Jan van der Straet), 10 5/8" × 7 7/8". The Metropolitan Museum of Art, New York, NY, U.S.A. Image copyright © The Metropolitan Museum of Art]

What impact did printing have on European society?

Competing Visions

EUROPEAN AND HURON VIEWS OF NATURE

European capitalism was built on several deeply rooted beliefs in Western culture, including the notion of private property and the belief that nature existed as a resource for man to tame and exploit. The differences between European and Eastern Woodlands Indian culture are clearly visible in the starkly different attitudes of each culture toward the natural world. Following a mandate laid down in the biblical Book of Genesis, Europeans believed that they had a god-given right to rule over nature. The Huron, an Eastern Woodlands Indian tribe from Canada, approached nature in a radically different way that reflected their animist belief that all living things had spiritual power. What ecological consequences flowed from the Huron view of nature? How might this view have shaped the European impression of Indians? What ecological consequences follow from the Western view?

In Genesis God gave man complete control over nature. According to this view humanity was not simply enjoined to "subdue nature" but to make sure that the "fear of you and the dread of you shall be upon every beast of the earth."

And God blessed them, and God said unto them, Be fruitful, and multiply, and replenish the earth, and subdue it: and have dominion over the fish of the sea, and over the fowl of the air, and over every living thing that moveth upon the earth.

King James Bible, Genesis 1:28 (1611)

Lucas Cranach, *Adam and Eve*

One of the best sources for understanding Indian views of nature can be found in the writings of Jesuit missionaries, a Catholic order active in the French colonization of Canada. In this selection a Jesuit recounts his exchange with a Huron Indian about the proper treatment of animal bones, which had to be treated with respect to avoid angering the animal spirits that might take offense and make hunting more difficult for the Huron.

As to the Beaver which has been taken in a trap, it is best to throw its bones into a river. It is remarkable how they gather and collect these bones, and preserve them with so much care, that you would say their game would be lost if they violated their superstitions. As I was laughing at them, and telling them that Beavers do not know what is done with their bones, they answered me, "Thou dost not know how to take Beavers, and thou wishest to talk about it." Before the Beaver was entirely dead, they told me, its soul comes to make the round of the Cabin of him who has killed it, and looks very carefully to see what is done with its bones; if they are given to the dogs, the other Beavers would be apprised of it and therefore they would make themselves hard to capture. (*Paul le Jeune*, 1633)

The Jesuit Relations and Allied Documents: Travels and Explorations of the Jesuit Missionaries in New France 1610–1791 (1896–1901) 6: 211.

John White, *Indians Fishing*

How does this painting of Adam and Eve reflect European views of nature?

Renaissance and Reformation

A revival of interest in the culture of Greek and Roman antiquity, focused first in Italy, spread across Europe at the end of the fifteenth century. This rebirth of classical learning, the Renaissance, transformed the way Europeans thought about art, architecture, science, and political philosophy. The most significant change was the shift from theology, the primary subject of scholarly concern throughout the preceding centuries of the Middle Ages, to the classical subjects of the liberal arts, including poetry, history, and philosophy. Much like the ancient Greeks, Renaissance scholars emphasized the human capacity for self-improvement and exalted the beauty of the human body in painting and sculpture. For these scholars, known as **humanists**, humans were the masters of their world and obligated to study it. These Renaissance values, in particular the spirit of exploration, would soon inspire explorers to seek out new lands and trade routes.

In contrast to medieval Europe, with its cloistered monasteries where monks prayed and copied texts for their own libraries, the Renaissance placed a high value on public art, architecture, and philosophical thought aimed at civilizing humanity. Civic humanism, the new philosophy of the Renaissance, encouraged artists and philosophers to participate in public life, especially in cities, which replaced monasteries as the ideal place to encourage learning and glorify God.

Renaissance ideas inspired several religious figures to call for reforms in the Roman Catholic Church. The most intense criticism was aimed at the sale of indulgences. In essence money donated to the Church could buy forgiveness for sin. In 1517 a young German monk named Martin Luther attacked the sale of indulgences and other key elements of Catholic doctrine and practice. Luther eventually developed a new theological alternative to Catholicism. Rejecting the Catholic Church's focus on good works as the key to achieving salvation, Luther argued that only faith could bring salvation. Luther also argued that ordinary people did not need to depend on the clergy to gain access to God's word; they could and should read the Bible themselves. Luther translated the Bible to German, and the newly invented printing press made it widely accessible. Anyone who could read could now receive the word of God in his or her own home. Luther championed the idea of the priesthood of all true believers—the notion that everyone could experience salvation directly. Priests would continue to preach the word of God, but Luther would dispense with the Catholic rituals of confession, penance, and absolution. Luther also felt there was no need for monasticism. The place for the committed Christian was in this world, not cloistered away in a monastery.

In addition to his critique of church doctrine, Luther urged Christian monarchs to take up the cause of religious reform and reject the authority of the Pope. His attack on the worldly power of the Roman Catholic Church appealed to some European rulers eager to strengthen their power and weaken the Pope's. Luther was summarily excommunicated from the Church, but his calls for reform had wide appeal. His supporters, known as Protestants, began a movement for religious reform that would be known as the **Reformation**.

Protestantism spread across Europe and found an especially receptive home in Switzerland. In Geneva, a French-speaking city in Switzerland, the French Protestant reformer John Calvin (1509–1564) articulated a new variant of Protestantism with a different theological emphasis from Luther's version. Calvin's theology stressed the doctrine of predestination, the notion that God had destined some people to salvation and some to damnation prior to their birth. Another important innovation in his thinking was his belief that the true church was not embodied in any official church organization, including the Roman Catholic Church, but rather in a group of the "elect," or those chosen by God for salvation. According to this ideal the elect could continue to act as a reformed church even if they had no physical place of worship or formal ministry to serve their spiritual needs. With the Bible and personal faith, argued Calvin, Protestants could constitute a true church wherever they lived, including, eventually, a wilderness like America.

Calvinists in Switzerland took their critique of Catholic worship a step further than Lutherans, literally becoming iconoclasts, or image breakers. They took the biblical injunction to avoid "graven," or carved images literally and set about to purify churches from such unholy Catholic trappings. Decrying them as sacrilegious and a form of idolatry, Calvinists smashed the stained glass windows and religious carvings that adorned many churches. One Catholic nun, described a Protestant rampage in Geneva in these terms: "Like enraged wolves, they destroyed those fine images with great axes, and hammers, especially going after the blessed crucifix, and the image of Our Lady [Mary]." This contemporary image of one such rampage shows

What were the essential teachings of Calvinism?

1.6 Protestants Stripping a Church of Images
This image literally depicts Calvinist iconoclasm, the destruction of "graven" images such as religious statues and stained glass windows.

Protestants pulling down sculptures and smashing stained glass windows (**1.6**). Once purged of all such Catholic images, religious worship, Calvinists believed, could focus on the words of the Bible alone.

New Monarchs and the Rise of the Nation-State

By the end of the fifteenth century, the kingdoms of France, England, and Spain had evolved into sovereign nation-states. Powerful monarchs consolidated their power, eliminated rivals to their thrones, created administrative bureaucracies to rule, and built larger, more effective armies. Paying for these required huge sums of money, and if they could not raise what they needed at home, some monarchs began to look abroad. Territorial expansion and exploration of new regions, they reasoned, would increase both trade and revenues.

In England Henry VII established the House of Tudor as the ruling family of England. His son, Henry VIII, solidified and expanded the power of the monarchy, incorporating Wales in 1536 and soon after proclaiming himself king of Ireland and Scotland. Henry's VIII most important accomplishment as King of England was his break with Rome when the Pope refused to dissolve his marriage to Catherine of Aragon. After failing to obtain a divorce, Henry declared himself head of his own independent English church. He rejected the authority of the Roman Catholic Church, confiscated all the church's lands and properties in his realm, and then sold them for a handsome profit. The intensity of Henry's anti-Catholic feeling (and his particular hostility to the Pope) is evident in this portrait painted by an unknown artist in 1570 (**1.7**). Henry VIII lies in bed, pointing to his future successor Edward VI. The Pope collapses in the foreground and two monks flee the scene, while a monastery is sacked in the background.

Perhaps the most ambitious of the new monarchies was Spain's, created by the marriage

Why did Calvinists wish to remove all icons from their churches?

of Ferdinand of Aragon and Isabella of Castile. Ferdinand and Isabella followed a strategy common to all the new monarchs: They reduced the power of the nobility and strengthened their own control over the military. They also boosted crown revenue by raising taxes and making tax collection more efficient.

As part of their effort to transform Spain into a world power, Ferdinand and Isabella sought to strengthen the power of the Roman Catholic Church and ally its interests with the state. In 1481 the Spanish monarchy sought the Pope's approval for an office of **Spanish Inquisition**, a religious tribunal charged with finding and punishing heresy, or unorthodox beliefs among Christians, and for eliminating non-Christians, most notably Muslims and Jews, from Spain. Thousands of suspected heretics were arrested, tortured, and imprisoned. Hundreds were executed. Eventually in 1492 the government ordered all Jews, except those who converted to Christianity, expelled from Spain. That same year Ferdinand and Isabella achieved another goal in their effort to strengthen Church and state by conquering Granada in what is now southern Spain, the last remaining stronghold of Islamic culture within Spain.

The expulsion of the Moors, the Muslim people of Granada, in 1492 was the final phase of this *reconquista* ("re-conquest"). Spain's holy war united state and Church in a single purpose. This partnership between a militant clergy and an equally aggressive military would serve Spain well when its attention moved beyond its European borders to the wider Atlantic world.

1.7 ***Henry VIII and Edward the VI against the Pope***
In this unfinished painting England's Henry VIII passes on his authority to Edward VI, including his role as head of the new Church of England. In the upper right English Protestant iconoclasts attack a monastery. At the bottom of the image the Pope collapses and monks flee from the "worde of the Lorde."

How was the English Reformation different than the Continental Reformation?

Columbus and the Columbian Exchange

Buoyed by the conquest of Granada in 1492, Queen Isabella agreed to outfit a small expedition to find a quicker route to Asia. The expedition's leader, Italian sailor Christopher Columbus, was an experienced mariner who had worked in the Portuguese seagoing trade to Africa and the Atlantic islands. Familiar with Marco Polo's written accounts of China, Columbus believed he could find a faster and more direct route to Asia than traveling around the tip of Africa by simply crossing the Atlantic. He first asked the King of Portugal to fund the voyage, but the king's advisors warned Columbus that he had greatly underestimated the circumference of the Earth and would certainly perish long before he reached Asia. Undeterred Columbus turned to Queen Isabella, who consented.

Columbus Encounters the "Indians"

After sailing for thirty-three days, Columbus reached the Caribbean islands, most likely the Bahamas. Mistakenly convinced that he had arrived in India, he called the native peoples "Indians." Columbus claimed all the lands he visited for Spain. Concluding that the native people were savages, he believed that they were "fit to be ordered about, and made to work, plant, and do everything else that may be needed, and build towns and be taught our customs." Returning to Spain with captive Indians, exotic plants, and some gold, Columbus was greeted as a hero and secured funding for additional voyages of exploration.

> "As soon as I arrived in the Indies, in the first island which I found, I took by force some of them, in order that they might learn and give me information."
>
> CHRISTOPHER COLUMBUS, 1493

Columbus was not the first European to cross the Atlantic, nor was he the first to create a small European outpost in America. The Vikings had sailed from Iceland almost four hundred years earlier, establishing small fishing outposts in what is now Newfoundland, Canada. Nevertheless Columbus's voyage to the Americas brought the two worlds together in ways that earlier Viking ventures had not. Europe's printing presses would make accounts of his voyage widely available, providing a model for later explorers, conquerors, and settlers. Columbus's voyage also began one of the most complex ecological changes in modern history. The worlds on both sides of the Atlantic were suddenly reconnected, a development that would have far-reaching biological consequences for Europe, Africa, and America.

Modern scholars have described the biological encounter between the two sides of the Atlantic as the **Columbian Exchange**, a name that acknowledges the crucial role that Columbus played in instigating this transformation. This exchange involved a range of foods, animals, and diseases (**1.8**). Moving from the Americas to Europe by way of Columbus and the Europeans who followed him were a host of foods now closely identified with European cuisine. Before Columbus Italian cuisine had no tomatoes, Irish food no potatoes, and Switzerland no chocolate. Moving

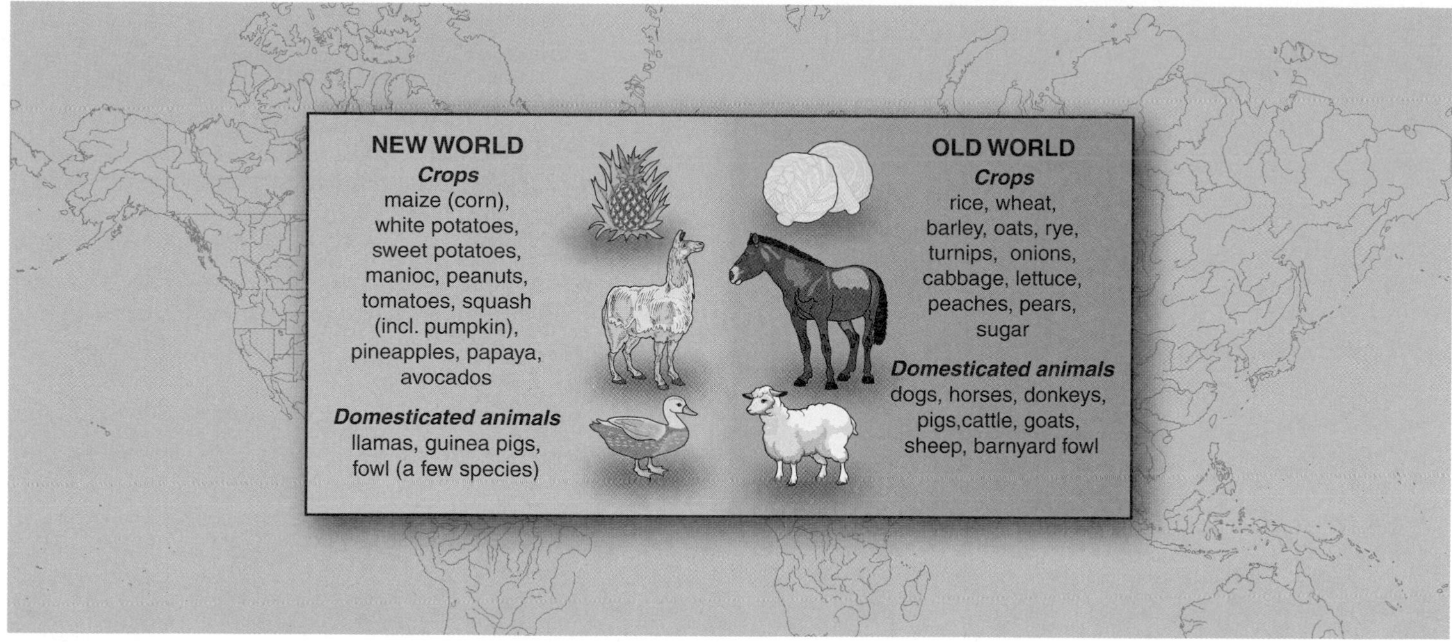

1.8 Columbian Exchange
This chart shows the most important crops and animals involved in the Columbian exchange. A host of pathogens, mostly of Old World origin, were also part of the Columbian Exchange.

in the other direction were animals, including the horse, long extinct in the Americas but reintroduced by the Spanish.

Diseases crossed the Atlantic as well. Europeans brought back a plague in the form of the sexually transmitted disease syphilis, which sailors probably first picked up in the Caribbean islands. Far more devastating were the diseases like smallpox brought to the New World. These diseases wreaked havoc on Indian societies, killing huge numbers of men, women, and children.

European Technology in the Era of the Columbian Exchange

Columbus and the Europeans who led the exploration of the Atlantic world benefited from a number of technological changes developed in Europe in the fifteenth century. Improvements in map making and the introduction of navigational devices that allowed mariners to calculate latitude more accurately aided exploration, for example. Europeans borrowed technology from the Islamic world and Asia to improve their ships. The Portuguese also made important strides in shipbuilding with the caravel, a vessel whose lateen (triangular) sails were better suited to catching wind than were those of traditional European ships.

Europeans enjoyed a clear technological and military advantage over the peoples of America, a disparity that would profoundly affect European interactions with the Aztec, and later with Eastern Woodlands Indian peoples. Foremost were the metallurgical techniques that allowed Europeans to forge iron weapons that were stronger than those of the Aztec. The domestication and breeding of horses allowed Europeans to support their armies by swift-moving cavalry. Through trade with China, Europeans had learned about gunpowder and developed powerful cannons and firearms such as the arquebus, a forerunner of the musket and rifle. Among the inventions depicted in this engraving, "Nova Reperta," ("New Discoveries") (1584), by artist Johannes Stradanus, are the compass, the mechanical clock, cannons and gun powder, and saddle with stirrups (**1.9**).

The Conquest of the Aztec and Inca Empires

Columbus's successful voyage in 1492 was followed by waves of Spanish explorers and conquerors (*conquistadores* in Spanish), who soon seized control of the islands of the Caribbean. Following a pattern first established by the Portuguese on their Atlantic islands, the Spanish took the land from the Indian inhabitants, the Taino, Caribs, and Arawaks, and established colonies. Like the Portuguese they subjugated the Indians, forcing them to pan for gold or perform agricultural work such as planting, harvesting, and processing sugar. The harsh labor regime and the deadly diseases the Spanish brought nearly wiped out these indigenous populations. On the island of Hispaniola (present-day Haiti and the Dominican Republic), 95 percent of the native peoples died within twenty-five years. Faced with the loss of this indigenous labor force, the Spanish again followed the Portuguese example and turned to the African slave trade to supply the labor they demanded for the production of lucrative cash crops such as sugar.

Spanish *conquistadores*, lured by rumors of a fabulous empire possessing great wealth, eventually turned their attention to the mainland of what is now Mexico. In 1519, eager to acquire this wealth for himself and Spain, Hernán Cortés, a brash and ambitious protégé of the Spanish governor of

1.9 ***Nova Reperta***
In this drawing of "new discoveries," the artist links the new scientific and technological discoveries with the exploration of the "New World." A printing press stands between a map of the Americas and a compass. The image is anchored by a cannon and casks of gunpowder, symbolic of European military technology.

What technological advances facilitated European expansionism?

Hispaniola, embarked on an expedition to find the famed capital of the Aztec Empire and conquer it. Landing on Mexico's southeast coast with over five hundred men and sixteen horses, he burned his ships, depriving his men of any opportunity to retreat. He forced his men to push forward to conquest or die in the attempt.

Although vastly outnumbered by the Aztecs, Cortés and his men held a number of military advantages. First they possessed horses, firearms, and steel weapons. Second they quickly gained allies among the peoples conquered by the Aztecs. After years of subjugation in which they were forced to provide the Aztecs with victims for human sacrifice, these exploited peoples now willingly sided with the Spanish (see *Images as History: Blood of the Gods: Aztec Human Sacrifice,* page 20). Finally the Spanish unknowingly carried with them a host of diseases, in particular the deadly smallpox virus, which infected and killed vast numbers of Aztecs. By 1521, just two years after his arrival, Cortés had subdued the once mighty Aztec Empire. A decade later a force of Spanish conquistadors led by Francisco Pizarro toppled a similarly powerful Inca empire in present-day Peru.

To many people of the Americas, who had never seen anything like firearms before, the Spanish *did* seem to have god-like power. The power of European firearms left an indelible impression on South American cultures. Created centuries after European contact, this Peruvian painting (**1.10**) shows an angel carrying an arquebus, the type of firearm used by the Spanish during their conquest of Central and South America.

1.10 Heavenly Militia
This South American painting done hundreds of years after the conquest shows an angel with an arquebus, a precursor of the modern rifle. The image shows the awesome power that Spanish weaponry had on the consciousness of the conquered peoples of Central and South America.

> "[A]n epidemic broke out, a sickness of pustules. ... The disease brought great desolation; a great many died of it. ... The Mexica warriors were greatly weakened by it."
>
> BERNRDINO DE SAHAGÚN 1519
> (Account of the defeat of the Aztecs published 1545)

What role did disease play in the Spanish conquest of the Aztec?

Images as History

BLOOD OF THE GODS: AZTEC HUMAN SACRIFICE

Aztec human sacrifice was a gruesome but highly public spectacle. Indeed the monumental pyramids that dominated the central Temple plaza of Tenochtitlán and other Aztec cities were designed to showcase this grisly ritual. The image here of the twin temples from the city of Texcoco, very similar in style to the main temples in Tenochtitlán, was drawn after the Spanish conquest of Mexico. Aztec artists' drawings such as this one provide important sources for understanding Aztec architecture and culture. The twin temples atop the pyramid were devoted to the rain god Tlaloc and the war god Huitzilopochtli. In front of the two temples at the top of the pyramid are the stone platforms used for human sacrifice. In the most elaborate version of this ghastly ritual, the sacrificial victim was held down by four priests while another priest plunged a ceremonial dagger into his chest and extracted a beating heart, which was offered up to the gods.

Lurid images of human sacrifice have become inextricably linked with Aztec civilization. Their legacy as a brutal people was cultivated, in fact, by their Spanish conquerors who used Aztec human sacrifice as a justification for conquering and converting the Aztec to Christianity. Theodore de Bry's engraving of Aztec human sacrifice pictured here was widely reprinted in Europe and helped spread the image of Aztec barbarism. The artist's imaginary version of a ritual sacrifice atop a pyramid bears only slight resemblance to the reality. The pyramid in de Bry's picture looks more like a European tower than a Mesoamerican structure. The two temples of the rain god and war god are entirely fanciful. Nevertheless the image effectively conveyed the Spanish colonizers' view of Aztec culture as barbaric.

Stone platforms were used during the rituals of human sacrifice.

The roof of the rain god's temple on the left was painted with four bands, symbols of rain, while the war god's shrine on the right is composed of a skull rack featuring 240 carved skull images.

Aztec Pyramid and Skull Rack

The skull rack was specifically associated with the temple of the war god, not the rain god.

Aztec sacrifice did include children and infants, but this horrifying practice was separate from the central scene depicted in which an adult was sacrificed to the god of war. By graphically mingling the two scenes together, de Bry visually heightened the barbarism of Aztec culture.

de Bry Engraving of Aztec Sacrifice

Why did the Spanish stress the cruelty and barbarism of Aztec culture?

West African Worlds

Africa, the world's second largest continent in terms of land mass, is home to some of the most ancient civilizations in the world. The range of societies in Africa in the sixteenth century rivaled those of the Americas in social complexity and cultural and religious diversity. Africa featured class-stratified urban civilizations alongside more simple egalitarian societies. Monotheistic faiths, including Christianity and Islam, flourished in parts of Africa, as did religions closer in principle to the animist beliefs of Eastern Woodlands Indians.

The North African states bordering on the Mediterranean had been trading with Europe since the days of the founding of the great ancient port city of Carthage (814 BCE). Africans possessed many commodities sought by Europeans, including salt, gold, ivory, and exotic woods. But the development of a direct sea route from Europe to West Africa in the fifteenth century greatly increased trade and contact between Europeans and Africans. The most profound consequence of the sea routes to West Africa was the development of the international slave trade, a process that changed virtually every society in the Atlantic world.

West African Societies, Islam, and Trade

The civilizations of Africa south of the Saharan Desert, including those with Atlantic ports, were socially and culturally diverse. The powerful Songhai Empire (1370–1591) extended from the Atlantic inward to the Sudan. Primarily agricultural the empire included several urban centers and a highly organized military and administrative state bureaucracy. In the great Songhai city of Timbuktu, an Islamic university rivaled many European centers of learning.

Other peoples, such as the Igbos of West Africa, lived in smaller, highly autonomous villages. These simpler, more egalitarian societies were organized mainly around kinship, more like America's Eastern Woodlands Indians than the empires of Mesoamerica or the rising nation-states of Europe. Local rulers consulted with a council of elders before making decisions affecting the community. Societies such as the Igbos were matrilineal, while other African societies traced descent and organized inheritance through the paternal line.

Before the seventh century most societies of West Africa practiced animist religions. These polytheistic faiths considered certain aspects of nature, such as the sun, wind, and animals, to be gods and spirits. Ancestor worship also played a prominent role in many West African religious traditions. But beginning in the mid-seventh century, the faith of Islam, first established in Arabia by Muhammad in 610 CE, began spreading via trade routes through northern, western, and eastern Africa. Over the centuries Islam became the dominant religion in these areas, especially in trading centers.

Trade played a key role in the economic life of both North and West Africa. Goods traded along these routes including salt, ivory, and precious metals. While salt was an essential ingredient for cooking and preserving food, the other items were sought after by artists and artisans who fashioned them into luxury goods such as jewelry. Before the end of the fifteenth century, these goods moved along an extensive network of caravan routes linking West Africa to the North African port cities of Tangier, Tunis, Tripoli, and Alexandria. But Portuguese exploration of the African coast in the late 1400s soon led to the development of direct trade between Europeans and Africans (**1.11**).

The Portuguese-African Connection

Portugal took the lead in exploring the possibility of an Atlantic route to Asia, which provided Europe with spices and exotic fabrics such as silk. Prince Henry the Navigator (1394–1460), a member of the Portuguese royal family, used his wealth and power to encourage exploration of the West African coast. Even after his death Portugal continued to explore the West African coast, leading to Portuguese navigator Vasco da Gama's successful voyage (1497–1499) around the Horn of Africa and

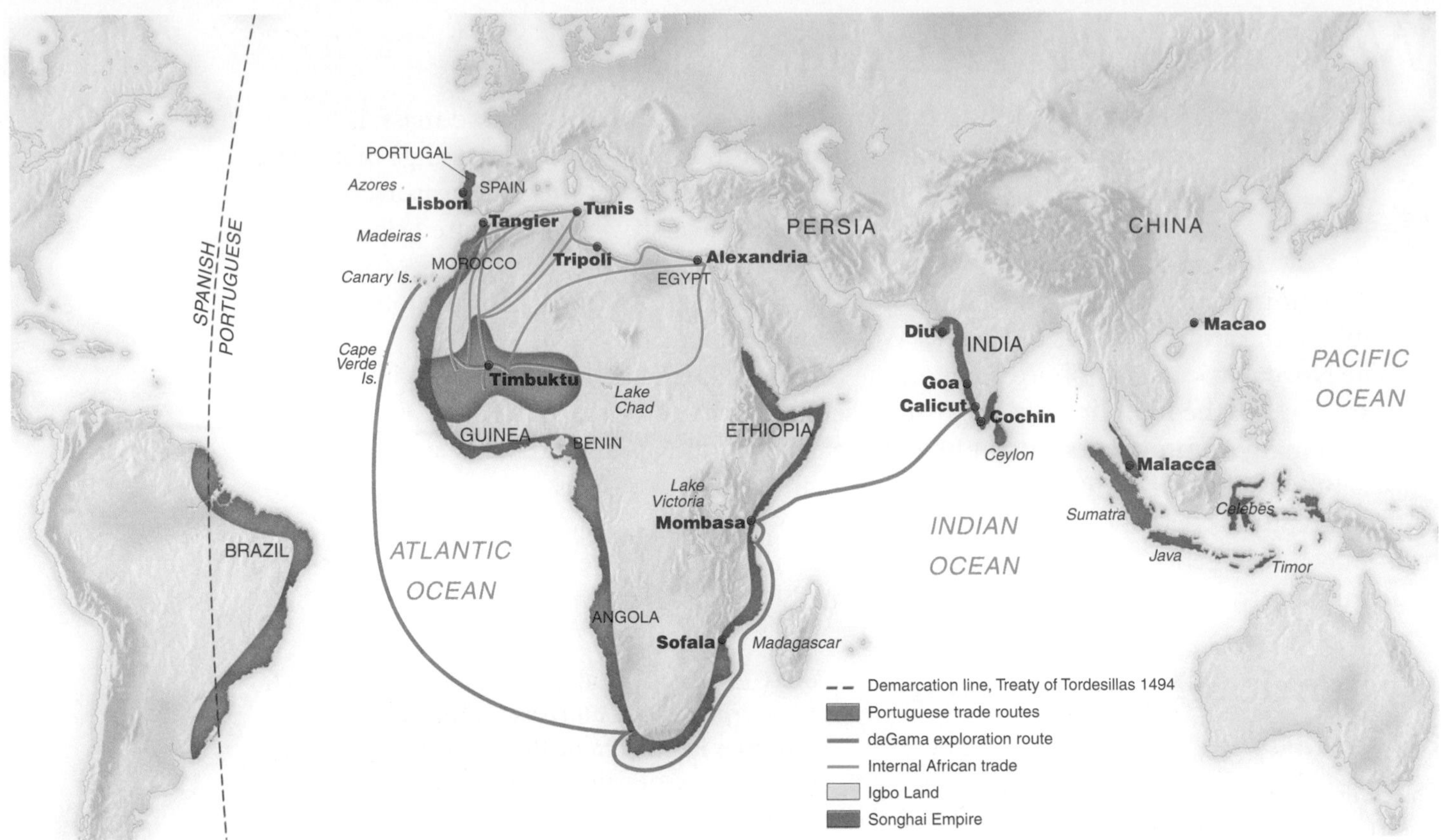

1.11 Internal African Trade Routes and Portuguese Trade with Africa West African kingdoms were linked by several different inland trade routes to North Africa and the Mediterranean. The Portuguese traded with the Atlantic islands and the west coast of Africa.

subsequent arrival at the southwest coast of India (1.11). Portuguese traders established a lucrative trade with India and began to explore trading possibilities with Africa, seeking such prized goods as ivory and gold. After 1470 Portuguese trade with West Africa increased, and within a decade the Portuguese had established forts along the African coasts to facilitate further trading opportunities.

At approximately the same time that the Portuguese were exploring the African coast, they were embarking on an ambitious but ruthless plan of conquest and colonization in the Atlantic island groups of the Madeiras, Azores, Cape Verde, and the Canaries (1.11). By the 1450s these Atlantic outposts had been converted into sugar-producing plantation economies. The Portuguese conquered and enslaved the indigenous populations of the Canary Islands, the Guanche—a North African people who had settled the islands thousands of years earlier. The semitropical climate of the Canaries was ideal for sugar cultivation, and the Portuguese forced the Guanche to labor for them on large sugar plantations. The king of Portugal assured the Pope that enslavement was entirely justified because the Guanche were, in his words, "infidels and savages." The Portuguese experience on the Canaries foreshadowed European interactions with the peoples of the Americas.

The Portuguese soon encountered an unexpected problem in conquering and enslaving the indigenous population of the Canaries. With no previous exposure to the diseases carried by the Portuguese, thousands of Guanche people became ill and died. Unable to rely on an indigenous source of labor, the Portuguese turned to Africa for slaves to provide the back-breaking labor they demanded for cultivating, harvesting, and processing sugar.

African Slavery

Slavery was widely practiced in Africa long before the arrival of the Portuguese. Rival tribes usually took slaves as spoils of war; but some prisoners attained privileged positions as petty officials, military leaders, and, in rare cases, political advisors to rulers. In Africa slavery was not always a permanent or hereditary condition, and slaves were sometimes absorbed into the societies that held them.

How did the Portuguese justify the enslavement of the Guanche?

> "[T]hey kidnap even noblemen, and the sons of noblemen, and our relatives, and take them to be sold to the white men who are in our Kingdoms ... and as soon as they are taken ... they are immediately ironed and branded with fire."
>
> NZINGA MBEMBA (King Alfonso of the Kongo, Central Africa), 1526

Initially controlled by Islamic traders, the slave trade after 1600 came increasingly under European domination. The ever-rising demand for labor in the Americas, fueled by extraordinary profits from slave-based sugar plantations, prompted rival European powers to compete with one another for a share of this lucrative trade. As the value of slaves increased, Africans began organizing raiding parties into neighboring territories with the express purpose of obtaining slaves.

European involvement in the African slave trade transformed this centuries-old institution into one of the most exploitative labor systems in world history. Europeans developed a racist conception of slavery that declared people of dark skin to be inferior beings for whom slavery was a natural and proper condition. As a consequence Europeans treated slaves as property with few legal rights or protections. Masters were free to extract the maximum amount of labor from them with minimal regard for their humanity. Slaves taken by Europeans to the Americas were often worked literally to death in the sugar fields. Those who survived found that slavery in the New World was a permanent and hereditary condition. They and their descendants faced a lifetime of slavery with no hope of ever obtaining freedom.

Some African nations managed to fend off the ravages of the slave trade. Benin, a well-organized nation-state ruled by a powerful monarch, traded slaves captured during war to the Portuguese in the fifteenth century but gradually withdrew from the slave trade (see *Choices and Consequences: Benin, Portugal, and the International Slave Trade,* page 24). Benin continued to trade with the Portuguese on its own terms. Among the goods sought by the Portuguese were pepper and ivory; the Benin sought bronze. Among the most visually impressive uses of this bronze were the finely crafted panels created for the walls of the royal palace. In the panel pictured here (**1.12**), a Portuguese soldier with a pike is surrounded by five "manilas," the bronze bars that were among the most important trade goods brought by the Portuguese.

1.12 Benin Bronze Panel The artists of Benin were widely admired for their finely crafted bronze plaques and sculptures which decorated the walls of the royal palace. The panel depicts a Portuguese soldier and the bronze bars used as a common trade item. [*Source:* Kunsthistorisches Museum, Vienna, Austria]

Choices and Consequences

BENIN, PORTUGAL, AND THE INTERNATIONAL SLAVE TRADE

By the end of the fifteenth century the Portuguese were transporting about 2,000 slaves a year from West Africa. The Portuguese took advantage of ethnic and tribal rivalries and the traditional African practice of taking captured opponents as slaves. Africans were eager to trade with the Portuguese who offered highly prized goods such as bronze, cloth, horses, and in limited cases, firearms. The Kingdom of Benin, one of the more powerful West-African kingdoms initially participated in this trade, but by 1516 the Oba (King) faced a momentous decision about continuing to participate in the slave trade.

Choices

1. Continue to trade with the Portuguese, but refuse to have any dealings with the slave trade
2. Continue to trade with the Portuguese and participate fully in the expanding international slave trade
3. Continue to trade with the Portuguese, but severely restrict Benin's participation in the international slave trade

Decision

Benin's king continued to trade with the Portuguese but restricted the trade in male slaves, the most sought after slaves for heavy agricultural labor. Benin allowed women to be traded (eventually prohibiting this trade as well) and continued to tolerate slavery within its own kingdom.

Consequences

In contrast to many other African kingdoms, Benin's decision allowed it to prosper and preserve its political autonomy far longer than many neighboring states. Benin obtained the benefits of trade by selling cloth instead of slaves. By refusing to become a major supplier of slaves Benin avoided the costly and potentially destabilizing warfare needed to obtain large numbers of slaves.

Continuing Controversies

What does the kingdom of Benin's experiences with the slave trade reveal about the nature of African slavery?

Few scholars believe Benin's actions were motivated by humanitarian concerns about the evils of slavery, which the African kingdom continued to tolerate. Scholars disagree over Benin's motivation for ending its involvement in the slave trade. Some argue that Benin's economy required a large supply of labor, which meant it could ill afford to export slaves. Others argue that Benin's rulers wisely calculated that continued expansion and warfare would only weaken their power and lead to political instability.

City of Benin

What theories account for Benin's ability to resist involvement in the international slave trade?

European Colonization of the Atlantic World

By the end of the sixteenth century, Portugal, Spain, and France had established permanent outposts in the Atlantic world, with England soon to follow. Each of these nations concentrated on a particular region of the Atlantic world (**1.13**). Portugal focused primarily on West Africa and Brazil, where trade in slaves and production of sugar generated enormous profits. Spain's massive empire in the Atlantic extended from the tip of South America to the western regions of North America. The Spanish Empire's chief export was silver. Meanwhile France directed its attention northward toward Canada, where the fur trade produced a lucrative commodity for export. Finally England, a relative latecomer to colonization, established its first outposts on the east coast of North America, in present-day North Carolina and Virginia.

The Black Legend and the Creation of New Spain

The Spanish had used images of Aztec human sacrifice to justify their conquest (see *Images as History: Blood of the Gods: Aztec Human Sacrifice*, page 20). Images and tales of Spanish brutality during the conquest of the Americas gave rise to the "Black Legend." This indictment of Spanish cruelty toward the native peoples of the Americas first appeared in the writings of the Spanish priest, Bartolomé de Las Casas. The new medium of print allowed copies of his scathing critique of Spanish colonialism to be distributed throughout Europe; his indictment of the Spanish was soon translated into French, Dutch, and English. In some cases these books contained gruesome wood-cut images such as those that appeared in the English edition, *The Tears of the Indians* (1656). The four scenes depicted on the front cover of the book, the "massacre and slaughter" of the Indian inhabitants of the Americas, are

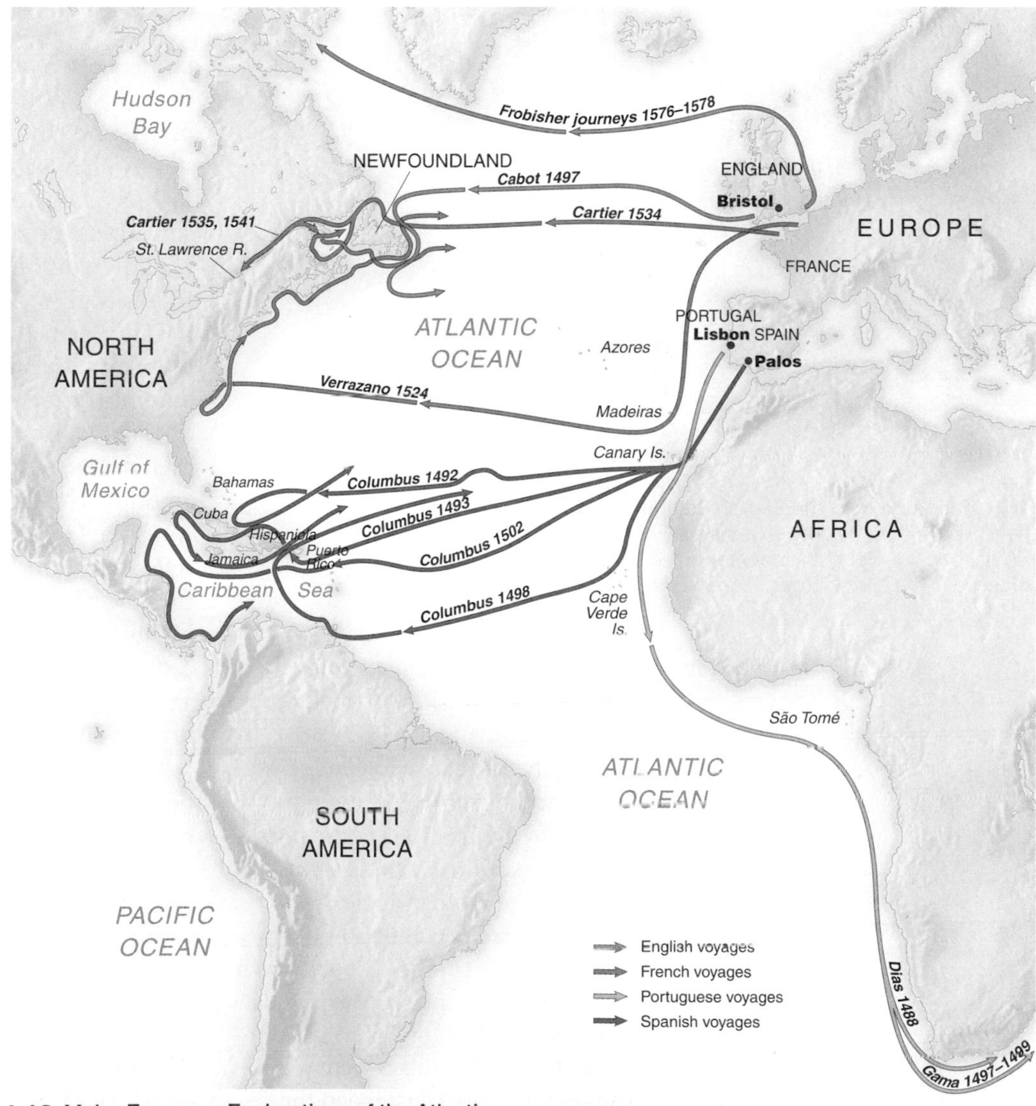

1.13 Major European Explorations of the Atlantic
The European nations that explored the Atlantic took different arcs. The Portuguese turned toward Africa, the Spanish explored Central and South America, and the English and French focused on the North Atlantic.

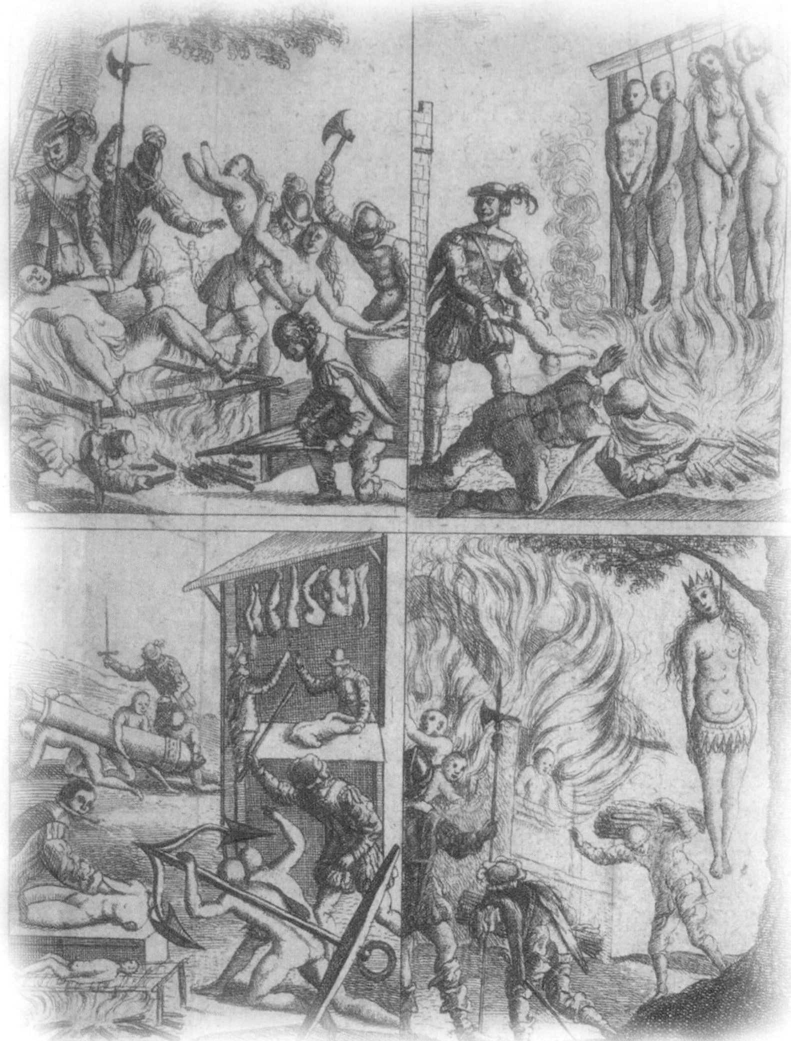

1.14 Title Page from the English Edition of Las Casas
The title page from the English translation of Las Casas's work, *The Tears of the Indians,* portrays Spanish cruelty toward Indians. The spread of these images gave credence to the "Black Legend" of Spanish conquest and violence.

described in Las Casas's narrative. The title page shows scenes of torture and punishment, including being hacked to death and burnt alive (**1.14**).

Within two decades the Spanish had conquered much of Central and South America. Inspired by tales of fabulously wealthy civilizations to the north, they launched several expeditions to explore the vast continent of North America. Hernando de Soto's expedition to Florida explored much of the southeastern United States in 1539. Another expedition in 1540, under the command of Francisco Vasquez de Coronado, traversed a huge swath of America from what is now Kansas to Colorado. Subsequent settlements in these regions greatly extended the Spanish Empire. Within a mere sixty years of conquering the Aztecs and Incas, Spain's North American colonial empire extended from Santa Fe (present-day New Mexico) in the west, to San Augustine (present-day Florida) in the east, and then all the way south to the tip of South America—an area larger than ancient Rome's vast empire. The Spanish crown had taken an active role in colonizing these regions, and the government it created to rule its American empire reflected the investment of time, money, and resources. The empire was divided into a series of administrative units and was staffed by a large number of bureaucrats and administrative officials. Of crucial importance was Spain's board of trade, headquartered in the Spanish port city of Seville. It granted licenses for trade with Spain's colonies, enforced commercial laws, and collected customs and any revenues due the crown.

Along with the colonial government, the Roman Catholic Church exercised enormous power and influence in Spanish America. Spain granted the Church sizeable amounts of land and money, and priests and church officials enjoyed a privileged status. They also bore certain responsibilities such as establishing churches, schools, and hospitals, converting native people to the faith, and enforcing religious conformity by using the powers of the Inquisition.

The Spanish established a network of interconnected urban centers to aid them in the administration of the peoples and territories they conquered. In part this policy reflected the relatively high degree of urbanization the Spanish found among the civilizations of Mesoamerica and South America. However this model of organization also reflected Spanish values and interests, allowing them to project the power of the church and state in highly visible ways. By the close of the sixteenth century, there were 225 towns in Spanish America, all laid out according to Renaissance models of urban planning in a grid-like pattern. The grand central plazas in the larger towns and cities afforded both a place for commerce and a symbolic space for monumental civic and church architecture. This painting of the central plaza in Mexico City (**1.15**) captures the use of urban planning and monumental architecture to reinforce the power of the state and the church. The cathedral and the vice regent's (local governor) and archbishop's palaces tower over the central square, vivid reminders of the dominance of church and state.

Much of the economy of New Spain was based on a highly exploitive system of labor. Ensuring an adequate labor supply for the arduous task of

What does the architecture of the central Plaza of Mexico City tell us about Spain's approach to colonization?

mining and agricultural work became a top economic priority of Spanish colonial officials. Rather than enslave the inhabitants of Central and South America as they had done to the native peoples in the Caribbean islands, the Spanish developed a system of forced labor, the *encomienda*, that was only marginally less exploitive than slavery itself. The crown declared Indians "vassals" who owed their labor to noblemen who in turn were required to provide for the Indians' spiritual welfare. The system provided labor and in theory demonstrated the Spanish commitment to saving the souls of the Indians by converting them. In reality the system led to the brutal exploitation of Indians. Criticism of the system by religious reformers such as Las Casas, combined with high levels of mortality among the indigenous population, which easily succumbed to diseases brought by the Spanish, eventually led to the use of other types of labor, including conscript (enrolled by compulsion) labor, wage labor, and slavery.

Fishing and Furs: France's North Atlantic Empire

In 1493 the Pope had settled a colonial dispute between Spain and Portugal by dividing the Atlantic world between them, a decision later ratified by a treaty signed by both countries. France rejected the authority of the treaty and sent fleets to take advantage of the abundant cod fisheries in the waters off what is now Newfoundland. In 1524 France dispatched Giovanni da Verrazano, an Italian mariner working for the king of France, to find the so-called northwest passage that would allow travel

1.15 ***Central Square of Mexico City*** Spanish urban planners sought to project imperial power onto the colonial landscape. In this painting of the town square in Mexico City, the buildings most closely identified with church and state tower over the central plaza. [*Source:* Cristobal de Villalpando (1639-1714), "Central Square of Mexico City." 1695 (oil on canvas). Corsham Court, Wiltshire. The Bridgeman Art Library, NY]

What types of labor systems were employed in the Spanish colonies?

1.16 ***France Bringing the Faith to the Indians of New France***
In this allegory France, personified as a woman, presents a willing Indian convert with a religious painting while pointing toward the heavens where Jesus, also depicted in the painting, hovers over the scene.

through the Americas to Asia. Although he failed to find such a route, his mapping of the North American coast aroused the interest of the French monarch, who decided to commit additional resources for further exploration of North America. In the 1530s French explorer Jacques Cartier made a more extensive and detailed investigation of the North Atlantic, eventually traveling up the St. Lawrence River, where he encountered a group of Micmac Indians (an Algonquian-speaking Eastern Woodlands Indian nation). Their offer of furs in exchange for European goods such as knives, kettles, and beads led the French to recognize the potential of furs as an ideal commodity. Furs could be sold to Europeans who valued their warmth and treated them as a high-status luxury commodity.

In 1604 the French established Port Royal in Nova Scotia and four years later founded the city of Quebec, now the capital of the province of Quebec, on the banks of the St. Lawrence River. Located at a strategic bend in the river, Quebec was well placed to allow the French to trade with the local Indians, who were skilled fur trappers. The beaver pelts traded to the French fetched a good price in the European markets.

The French encounter with Native Americans differed from that of the Spanish and Portuguese in three significant ways. First the relatively small size of the settlement in New France and the dependence of the French on Indians to provide furs necessitated maintaining good relations with local tribes. Second, the predominantly French male population intermarried with local Indians. Eventually the French government even encouraged intermarriage, believing it would lead to the gradual assimilation of the Indian population into the French culture of New France.

The French encounter with North American Indians differed in still a third way. The French were committed to converting the Indians to their Catholic faith, but rather than follow the Spanish example and transplant the hierarchical structures of the Church, including the Inquisition, French Jesuits adopted a different strategy. They sent out missionaries to live among Indian populations and learn their languages and customs. The French Jesuits were just as eager as the Spanish to convert the Indians, but they recognized the need to understand the culture of those they wished to convert. The French also took advantage of religious art and images to help convert the Indians. The importance of images to this process is mirrored in this allegorical painting, *France Bringing the Faith to the Indians of New France* (**1.16**). France, represented as a woman, presents a painting to an

Indian who receives it gratefully. The Indian wears a cloak with a Fleur de Lys, the symbol of the French monarchy.

English Expansion: Ireland and Virginia

Although England took advantage of the rich opportunities for fishing provided by the Atlantic Ocean, its exploration of the Americas was a relatively low priority for most of the sixteenth century. Three factors explain this lack of interest. First England faced less economic pressure to find export markets because its primary export—wool—was in high demand on the European continent. Second England faced a crisis of leadership after the death of Henry VIII in 1547. He was succeeded by his sickly ten-year-old son, Edward VI, who died only five years into his reign. Next came Henry's daughter Mary, who tried to reestablish Catholicism, a campaign that included the intense persecution of Protestants. Her reign was also short, since she died only five years after assuming the throne. Finally England was bogged down in a colonial venture closer to home, the subjugation of Ireland. While Spain easily conquered the Moors in Spain before moving on to Atlantic exploration, Irish resistance to English colonization tied up English resources for decades.

Yet even as England struggled to colonize Ireland, their experiences there provided them with a distinctive model for future colonial policy in the New World. While the Spanish set out to conquer and convert the inhabitants of the Americas, absorbing them into Spanish society as a subordinate class at the bottom of the social order, the English took a different approach. Rather than attempt to incorporate the Irish, the English expelled them from their land. They then repopulated the land with colonists from England and Scotland, creating **plantations**, or fortified outposts dedicated to producing agricultural products for export. Originally the term plantation simply meant any English settlement in a foreign land, but it later became synonymous with a distinctive slave-based labor system used in much of the Atlantic world.

One source of this policy can be traced to the deeply felt religious animosity between Protestants and Catholics. The English not only had little regard for the Catholic faith of the Irish but also they feared the Irish would support efforts to reimpose Catholicism on England and would assist Catholic nations like France and Spain if they went to war against England. Expelling the Irish and transplanting loyal Protestant farmers from England and Scotland, therefore, promised to boost the English economy and secure control of a potentially troublesome neighboring island. This colonial model developed in Ireland—expulsion and plantation—would shape subsequent English experiments in colonization.

Economic pressures eventually impelled England to follow its European rivals and engage in the exploration and colonization of the Atlantic. Its profitable wool trade with the continent began to decline in the 1550s, prompting English merchants to seek new sources of trade and commercial opportunities. These merchants founded scores of new companies devoted to overseas trade with parts of Europe, Africa, and the Mediterranean.

England's entry into exploration and colonization was also helped when the crisis of the monarchy ended with the rise to the throne of another of Henry's daughters, Elizabeth. She succeeded "Bloody Queen Mary," as Protestants called her, in 1558 and quickly established herself as a strong leader determined to project English power overseas. She eagerly pursued an aggressive policy of expansion, challenging Spain's dominance in the Atlantic. A committed Protestant Elizabeth viewed Spanish power as a serious threat to her realm. Her religious convictions and foreign policy objectives eventually brought England into direct conflict with Spain.

England's support for Spain's enemies on the continent, including the Protestant Dutch, the continuing actions of English pirates, and English anti-Catholicism, finally drove King Philip of Spain to take decisive action. In 1588 Spain launched a mighty Armada, or fleet of warships, to invade England and destroy Europe's most powerful Protestant monarchy. The Spanish considered their ships invincible, but after storms greatly reduced their numbers they were routed by the smaller, faster ships of the English navy. The defeat of the Armada shifted the balance of power in the Atlantic dramatically, as England emerged as the major force in the Atlantic world. To commemorate the stunning defeat of Spain's Armada, Queen Elizabeth commissioned a portrait that symbolized England's rise to a position of power in the Atlantic world. In the painting Elizabeth's hand rests prominently on a globe, her fingers reaching out to cover the Atlantic

What lessons did the English learn from their experiences in Ireland?

1.17 Elizabeth's Armada Portrait In this portrait commemorating England's victory over the Spanish Armada, Queen Elizabeth's hand rests on the globe, reaching out to cover much of what is now North America. In the upper left the Spanish fleet sets out toward England, while in the upper right the defeated Spanish Armada flounders. [*Source:* George Gower (1540-96), "Elizabeth I, Armada Portrait", c. 1588 (oil on panel), Gower, George (1540-96) (attr. to) / Woburn Abbey, Bedfordshire, UK / The Bridgeman Art Library]

world and North America (**1.17**). In the background the artist includes two scenes depicting the defeat of the Armada, a further reminder of England's power and supremacy of the navy.

Among the most ardent supporters of expanding England's role in the Atlantic world were former **privateers**. These were Englishmen who engaged in state-sanctioned piracy in the Atlantic against Spanish treasure fleets returning from South America. A number of them had grown rich and influential as a result of their successes. John Hawkins, for example, earned himself a fortune and an English knighthood for his daring seizures of Spanish ships. One of the most dashing of these buccaneers, Sir Walter Raleigh, had participated in the English conquest of Ireland and became a favorite of Queen Elizabeth. Raleigh sought support for a more ambitious plan of colonization in the lands north of Spanish America and south of French Canada. Queen Elizabeth bestowed her blessing on the enterprise, but not money. As a result Raleigh and the colonial ventures that followed had to turn to private capital to finance his plan.

In contrast to France and Spain's state-financed model of exploration of colonization, England adopted a more capitalist model, with private investors forming companies and issuing stock to finance exploration and settlement. Having raised the funds to outfit a small expedition of two ships, Raleigh's expedition arrived in the outer banks regions of what is now North Carolina in July 1585. Naming the new settlement Virginia, in honor of Elizabeth, known widely as the "Virgin Queen," England had finally established its first colony in the New World. Unfortunately for Raleigh and the original colonists, the first colony at Roanoke (an Algonquian Indian name for shell money) ended in disaster. To begin with, although the location near the treacherous region of Cape Hatteras protected the settlement from possible Spanish raids, it also deterred passing ships from stopping, which made re-provisioning the colony difficult. Then conflict with local Indians erupted when the colonists accused the Indians of stealing a silver cup. All the while relief for the colonists was delayed by the outbreak of war with Spain. The English navy required every available ship to repulse the Spanish Armada. When a ship finally arrived three years later, the new settlers found the colony deserted. All the residents had disappeared, leaving behind only one clue: the word "CROATOAN" carved into a door-post. The fate of the lost colony of Roanoke still remains a mystery, but scholars suspect that the term *croatan* was a vague reference to a Croatan Indian village some 50 miles south of the settlement which may have been the colonists' destination before they disappeared.

Although the first English attempt to create a fixed settlement was a dismal failure, the information gained by the colonists about the Algonquian tribes who inhabited North Carolina proved invaluable. The governor of the colony, John White, was an accomplished artist who captured scenes from Indian life in a vivid series of paintings (**1.18**).

Many of his images were popularized by the Flemish engraver Theodore de Bry, but often with notable alterations (**1.19**). Note how de Bry, in

What is the symbolic importance of the position of Queen Elizabeth's hand in the Armada portrait?

1.18 and **1.19** **John White Painting and Theodore de Bry's Engraving**
John White's painting of an Algonquian Indian man and woman eating is one of the earliest efforts to realistically represent Indians. In his popular engraving of this image, Theodore de Bry changed the Indians' features and shifted their pose to reflect postures more familiar to Europeans.

addition to altering the poses of the Indians, gave the woman features considered more beautiful by Europeans and painted her looking seductively at the viewer. Such changes in the representation of indigenous women fit the prevailing European notion that the New World was characterized by lust and promiscuity.

Conclusion

The onset of European exploration and colonization of the Atlantic world in the fifteenth and sixteenth centuries touched off a collision between the civilizations of the Americas, Africa, and Europe. The Americas had been inhabited for thousands of years before Columbus disembarked in the Caribbean in 1492 and claimed the territory for Spain. In the thousands of years before that encounter, a variety of civilizations had evolved in the Americas. Some rivaled the richest nations of Europe, while others more closely resembled the stateless societies of Africa. The mighty pyramids of the Aztec Empire would inspire awe in the first Europeans to gaze upon them, as would the remains of earlier civilizations such as the Mound Builders and Anasazi.

Columbus's voyages unleashed a process of political, economic, and biological encounter that radically transformed the lives of the peoples who inhabited Europe, Africa, and the Americas. The exchange of foods, animals, plants, and diseases altered the lives of kings and simple farmers on both sides of the Atlantic. The European desire for riches led to the oppression, and in some cases enslavement, of indigenous peoples to work in mines and sugar fields. The decline in native populations that resulted from diseases and exploitation led European colonizers to turn to African slaves as a labor source.

Portugal and Spain took the lead in overseas expansion in the fifteenth and sixteenth centuries. Indeed by the end of the sixteenth century, the Spanish Empire in the Americas had surpassed the ancient Roman Empire in size. Spain's unrivaled dominance in the Atlantic was dealt a serious setback when England destroyed the its mighty Armada in 1588. England, a relative latecomer in the race to control the Atlantic and its riches, soon turned its attention to exploration and colonization. Within a century England would surpass Spain as the preeminent power in the Atlantic world.

How did de Bry change the Indians in John White's painting?

1325

Founding of Tenochtitlán
Aztec Empire becomes dominant power in Mesoamerica

1440

Gutenberg invents printing press
Print revolution transforms the way knowledge is organized and spread

1519–1521

Hernán Cortés conquers Aztecs
Founding of Spanish empire in what is now Mexico

Review Questions

1. Why did Paleo-Indians migrate to the Americas?
2. What were the chief advantages of fixed agriculture, and how did fixed agriculture contribute to the rise of more complex civilizations?
3. What were the chief similarities between the civilizations of Africa and the Americas? What were the differences?
4. What impact did new technology have on the course of European overseas expansion in the fifteenth and sixteenth centuries?
5. What were the most important ideas associated with the Renaissance?
6. What was the Columbian Exchange?
7. How did Spanish city planning and architecture help reinforce the power of the state and the church in the Americas?
8. Why did England enter the race for colonies in the Atlantic world so late?
9. Compare the impact of Spanish, French, and English approaches to colonization on the indigenous populations of the Americas.

1534

Henry VIII breaks with Rome
Henry strengthens the forces of the Protestant Reformation and greatly weakens the English Catholic church

1585–1588

English establish colony of Roanoke on North Carolina's outer banks
England's first permanent settlement in America fails and no trace is found of the settlers when new supplies are brought to the colony

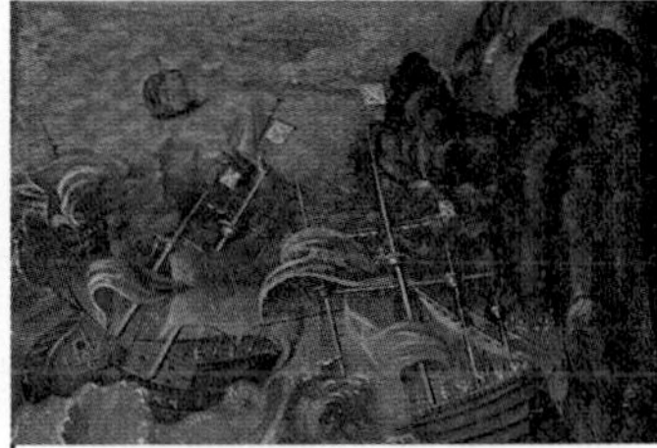

1588

English defeat Spanish Armada
Spanish dominance of the Atlantic world challenged

1608

Quebec founded
France's major settlement in North America established

Key Terms

Paleo-Indians The name given by scientists to the first inhabitants of the Americas, an Ice Age people who survived largely by hunting big game, and to a lesser extent by collecting edible plants and fishing. **4**

Archaic Era Period beginning approximately nine thousand years ago lasting an estimated six thousand years. This period was marked by more intensive efforts on the part of ancient societies to shape the environment to enhance food production. **5**

Aztec Led by the Mexica tribe, the Aztec created a powerful empire whose capital, the great city of Tenochtitlán, was created on an island in Lake Texcoco in 1325 CE. **6**

Islam Monotheistic faith whose teachings followed the word of the prophet Muhammad, and whose followers controlled most of the overland trade routes to the Far East. **10**

capitalism An economic system in which the market economy determined the prices of goods and services. **11**

humanists Individuals who advocated a revival of ancient learning, particularly ancient Greek thought, and encouraged greater attention to secular topics including a new emphasis on the study of humanity. **13**

Reformation The movement for religious reform started by Martin Luther. **13**

Spanish Inquisition A Spanish tribunal devoted to finding and punishing heresy and rooting out Spain's Jews and Muslims. **15**

Columbian Exchange The term used by modern scholars to describe the biological encounter between the two sides of the Atlantic, including the movement of plants, animals, and diseases. **16**

plantation An English settlement or fortified outpost in a foreign land dedicated to producing agricultural products for export. (Later the term would become synonymous with a distinctive slave-based labor system used in much of the Atlantic world.) **29**

privateer A form of state-sponsored piracy, usually directed against Spanish treasure fleets returning from the Americas. **30**

CHAPTER

2

Models of Settlement

English Colonial Societies, 1590–1710

The Chesapeake Colonies p. 36

New England p. 42

> **"Our First work is expulsion of the savages to gain the free range of the country ... for it is infinitely better to have no heathen among us, who at best are but thorns in our side, than to be at peace and league with them."**
>
> Virginia Governor FRANCIS WYATT, 1623–1624

Theodore de Bry's 1619 engraving, *The Chickahominy Become 'New Englishmen,'* from the book *America*, portrays treaty negotiations between Virginia Indians and the English. Captain Samuel Argall, the Englishman negotiating the treaty, sits on a mat with a tribal elder. Another tribal leader addresses his people, informing them about the terms of the treaty, which was meant to promote trade and peace between the English and the Virginia Indians. As the engraving title, which refers to the Chickahominy as "New Englishmen," suggests, the English insisted that Indian tribes submit to English rule and accept the English king as their lord. By contrast the Indians believed that negotiating a treaty with the English meant that they had entered into a diplomatic relationship as equals. These differing visions frequently led to conflict between Native Americans and English settlers throughout the seventeenth century.

At the dawn of the 1600s, England trailed far behind Spain and France in the race to exploit the wealth of the Americas. By the end of the century, however, England had become a formidable colonial power in both North America and the Caribbean. In contrast to Spain and France, whose colonization efforts relied on active support from the monarchy and church, England's first efforts to colonize America relied on joint stock companies, which were privately financed commercial ventures. The two great early English experiments in colonization, in Virginia and New England, faced many challenges in their early years, including how to deal with local Indian populations. The solution for the English was not simply rendering the Indians politically subservient to the king but also segregating themselves from the Indians whenever possible.

Relations between settlers and Indians complicated colonial politics for most of the seventeenth century. Bacon's Rebellion (1676), a popular uprising in Virginia triggered by colonists' conflict over Indian policy, shook the foundations of the colony. In New England persistent conflict between Indians and settlers exacerbated existing social and economic tensions, leading to the worst outbreak of witchcraft accusations in colonial America, the Salem witchcraft hysteria (1692). The reassertion of political control by England, whose Glorious Revolution (1688) contributed to the emergence of a new, more stable colonial world, helped facilitate the resolution of the witchcraft crisis. On many occasions in the years to come, colonists would invoke the political and constitutional ideas of the Glorious Revolution to defend their liberties.

What was the English attitude toward Indians?

The Chesapeake Colonies

The failure of the Roanoke colony in Virginia (see Chapter 1) at the end of the sixteenth century (1585–1590) was only a temporary setback for English colonial projects in America. Less than two decades later, a new group of English settlers established a colony, Jamestown, in the Chesapeake Bay area of what is now Virginia. Although the early history of Jamestown was fraught with problems, the colony eventually began to prosper. Tobacco agriculture provided a strong financial incentive to expand into the wider Chesapeake region. By the 1630s Lord Baltimore had developed an ambitious plan to found another colony in the region, Maryland.

The Founding of Jamestown

Joint stock companies charted by King James I funded the English colonial enterprises. Investors bought shares in the company, and at the end of a specified period received their investment back plus a percentage of the profits of the company. In April of 1606 the king issued a charter to the Virginia Company of London to create a colony in America. In late December 1606 three ships set sail for the Chesapeake, arriving off the coast of Virginia in May of 1607. The first settlers were a motley assortment of men; no women traveled on this first voyage. The settlers named the new settlement Jamestown, in honor of England's King James I.

> "Our men were destroyed with cruel diseases, as swellings, Fluxes, Burning fevers and by wars, and some departed suddenly, but for the most part they died of mere famine."
>
> GEORGE PERCY, Colonist, 1607

The colonists scouted a location secure from possible Spanish attack, but still accessible to the sea. They built a fortified palisade to protect them from possible attacks by hostile Indians and by Spanish ships. Unfortunately the site they chose turned out to be a public health disaster. On the edge of a swamp, Jamestown was a fertile breeding ground for mosquitoes and the pathogens they carried, including malaria. Salt water from the nearby river contaminated the wells the colonists dug to supply fresh drinking water. In addition poor drainage meant the colonists' own waste occasionally contaminated the water supply. Many settlers died within a year of disembarking from their ship.

The Virginia Company's promotional pamphlets (**2.1**) deceptively cast Virginia as an "earthly paradise" that would offer opportunities for the settlers to become rich. Almost one-third of the early settlers were gentlemen who were unprepared for the arduous life in Virginia and who viewed manual labor as undignified. Believing that vast troves of mineral wealth existed in the region, settlers wasted time searching for gold and silver instead of planting crops or repairing fortifications. Dissension and a lack of firm political leadership also nearly undermined the colony.

Relations between the settlers and the powerful Powhatan Indian confederacy had begun amicably at Jamestown. Chief Powhatan, the ruler of the confederacy, was eager to trade with the English and acquire manufactured goods, especially firearms and metal tomahawks (a type of hatchet). Powhatan had also hoped to use the English as allies against rival Indian tribes. However once the Indians realized that the English were not temporary visitors merely interested in trade, but were intending to settle permanently in the region, relations between the two peoples deteriorated.

In dealing with the Indians, Virginians applied the same principles that the English had developed in the conquest of Ireland: expelling the local population and limiting contact with them as much as possible. The English failed to grasp basic rituals of hospitality and gift giving, essential to establishing cordial relations with Indian peoples. While the French and Spanish had encouraged marriage between settlers and Indians, the English discouraged such unions. This marriage taboo not only deprived the colony of a means of establishing friendly relations between

Why did Jamestown turn out to be such a poor choice for a permanent settlement?

the two peoples but also deprived the colonists of cultural go-betweens who could have smoothed out conflicts and misunderstandings.

Among the most enduring myths associated with Jamestown and the English settlers' relations with the Indians is the tale of Pocahontas. Settler-soldier John Smith's tale of how a beautiful Indian girl saved his life is a foundational myth in American history, one that later writers often cast in romantic terms: an American Romeo-and-Juliet story of love at first sight between a beautiful Indian "princess" (a term straight from English aristocratic culture) and a dashing English officer. Smith's published account of his time in Virginia helped create this mythology. Smith took considerable liberties with the truth, highlighting his role as a romantic hero who saved Jamestown from disaster.

The events Smith described in his account almost certainly did not take place as he described them. However Smith was likely captured and eventually adopted into the tribe, and Pocahontas, then a young girl, may indeed have taken part in the adoption ritual. Among some Eastern Woodland Indian tribes, capture and ritual torture, followed by adoption into the tribe, was an essential means of conducting diplomacy. Once adopted into the tribe, prisoners became political intermediaries.

Although prone to inflate his achievements, Smith, an experienced soldier who had fought with the Dutch against Spain in the 1590s, played a decisive role in helping the colony avert disaster. In 1608 Smith negotiated an exchange of goods for food with Indians that helped stave off starvation. Smith's reforms may have staved off immediate catastrophe, but they did not prevent enormous suffering and high mortality during the difficult winter of 1609–1610, known as the "starving time." The colonists were so pressed for food that some even resorted to cannibalism to survive the winter. In his history of Virginia, Smith wrote about the starving time. Smith reported, with a somewhat macabre sense of humor, that one man "did kill his wife, powdered her, and had eaten part of her before it was knowne, for which hee was executed, as hee well deserved; now whether shee was better roasted, boyled or carbonado'd [stewed in beer], I know not, but of such a dish as powdered wife I never heard of."

Smith's role as intermediary with the Indians, a position that his alleged encounter with Pocahontas had helped solidify, did not prevent a further deterioration in relations with neighboring Indians. In 1609 Smith left Jamestown and returned to

NOVA BRITANNIA.

OFFERING MOST

Excellent fruites by Planting in

VIRGINIA.

Exciting all ſuch as be well affected to further the ſame.

LONDON

Printed for SAMVEL MACHAM, and are to be ſold at his Shop in Pauls Church-yard, at the Signe of the Bul-head.

1609.

2.1 Virginia Promotional Literature The Virginia Company produced pamphlets that promoted the riches to be had by planting in Virginia.

England. After his departure the growing hostility between the English and the Indians intensified. In 1613 Captain Samuel Argall led a party of Virginians on a mission to capture Pocahontas, whom Indians and Englishmen now knew by her adult name of Matoaka. The English hoped that by holding her hostage they could force her people to sign a peace treaty. For more on this episode, see *Choices and Consequences: The Ordeal of Pocahontas,* page 38.

Tobacco Agriculture and Political Reorganization

Jamestown had barely survived the "starving time" of 1609 to 1610, when the population dropped from between five and six hundred to sixty. Although the colony held on, it had not yet found a profitable commodity that could make it economically viable. John Rolfe solved this problem by introducing tobacco into the Virginia colony. Experimenting with various strains of tobacco, Rolfe finally settled on a variety that had been successfully cultivated in the

What was the "starving time"?

Choices and Consequences

THE ORDEAL OF POCAHONTAS

Desperate to force the local Powhatan Indians to negotiate a peace treaty, English settlers embarked on an audacious plan. They abducted a local Powhatan Indian woman named Pocahontas, now known by her adult Indian name Matoaka, hoping to force her people to accept a peace treaty. Her kidnappers took her to Henrico, a heavily fortified settlement upriver from Jamestown. The plan was to isolate her from her people. The English placed Matoaka in the household of a minister, who instructed her in the English language and customs and began indoctrinating her in Christianity. At the weekly prayer meetings hosted by the minister, she met John Rolfe, an influential Englishman recently widowed. Within a year of her abduction, Matoaka was baptized a Christian and had adopted a new English name, Rebecca. John Rolfe proposed marriage to the newly Christianized woman. Matoaka now faced a few possible options.

Choices

1 Reject the offer of marriage and remain a captive among the English until her people rescued her.

2 Attempt to escape.

3 Marry Rolfe, and through that marriage help her people forge an alliance with the Virginians.

Decision

Matoaka, now known by her English name Rebecca, chose the third option; after converting to Christianity, she married John Rolfe. Two years after their marriage, the couple journeyed to England, where she became something of a celebrity and was even introduced at court.

Consequences

Marrying Rolfe gained Matoaka (Rebecca) her freedom. In her new role as the wife of a high-status Englishman, she became a mediator between her people and the English. Indeed had she not become ill and died within a year after arriving in England, she might have been able to expand this important role.

MATOAKA ALS REBECKA FILIA POTENTISS PRINC POWHATANI IMP VIRGINIÆ
Ætatis suæ 21 A°. 1616.
Matoaks als Rebecka daughter to the mighty Prince Powhatan Emperour of Attanoughkomouck als Virginia converted and baptized in the Christian faith and Wife to the Wor.ll Mr Tho. Rolff.

Continuing Controversies

How do Indian conceptions of gender role help explain Pocahontas' decision to marry?

Scholars and analysts have suggested different explanations for her decision. Some have seen her decision as an expression of romantic love; others, as sheer expedience. The most recent and perhaps most persuasive explanation of her conversion and marriage to John Rolfe acknowledges the key role of women as cultural intermediaries in Indian diplomacy. By creating ties of kin to bind potentially warring nations in a blood bond, marriage served an important diplomatic function. This explanation, rather than viewing her decision as a slight to her Indian heritage, sees her decision as likely having increased her status with her tribe by allowing her to assume an important diplomatic role.

What role did women play in Indian diplomacy?

Caribbean. Tobacco was all the rage in Europe, a fact reflected in this humorous painting showing a group of monkeys in a tavern eagerly consuming tobacco (**2.2**). Playing on the popular notion that monkeys have a great capacity for imitation, the artist thereby ridicules the consumption of tobacco as a bad habit all to easily emulated. Smoking tobacco for pleasure became popular among all classes in European society. Tobacco was also believed to have many medicinal uses; it was recommended as a cure for colds and an aid to digestion.

Rolfe sent his first consignment of tobacco, 2,600 pounds, to England in 1614. Tobacco proved to be the colony's economic salvation: Profits from its sale created a boom in the colony, which then led inhabitants to devote nearly every acre of land to the "sot weed." Exports increased dramatically in the decades following the introduction of the crop. Yet while tobacco agriculture made some Virginians wealthy, the pursuit of profits diverted time and other resources from basic tasks, such as planting crops and repairing buildings. As a result of this neglect, settlers in boom-time Virginia continued to die at an alarming rate.

Establishing political order in Virginia proved far more difficult than the founders of the colony had expected. In 1618 Sir Edwin Sandys became the Virginia Company of London's treasurer and instituted a series of reforms to make the government of the colony more effective. A key reform was the creation of a representative body to make laws. The privilege of voting for representatives was extended to free men of property, who were to elect representatives who would then enact laws for the colony. Virginia's new legislative body, the House of Burgesses (representatives), first convened in July of 1619. Rather than take orders from company officials, the colonists gained some control over their own political affairs, a milestone in the evolution of representative government in America.

Because laborers continued to be scarce in Virginia, Sandys also introduced a new system to provide incentives to attract settlers. The **headright** system encouraged additional immigrants by giving 50 acres to anyone who would pay his own fare to

2.2 Apes Smoking
Artist Abraham Teniers mocked the popularity of smoking, substituting monkeys for humans.

What were some of the most important reforms implemented in 1618 by Edwin Sandys?

Virginia and 50 additional acres for each person he brought with him. The year 1619 also marked the arrival of the first Africans in Virginia. An English pirate vessel flying under a Dutch flag sold the Africans, captured from a Portuguese slaving ship in the Caribbean, to the Virginia colonists.

Immigrants continued to arrive in Virginia despite the continuing high mortality rates. Approximately two-thirds of the settlers died in the next three years. Deteriorating relations with local Indian communities reached a crisis point in 1622, when Powhatan's successor launched an assault on the colony that killed 347 colonists. The sensational attack inspired this engraving (**2.3**), which appeared in England six years later. To create a contrast between the imagined civility of the colonists and the alleged barbarism of the Indians, the engraver included inaccurate details, including tablecloths and a European-style walled city in the distance.

Two years after the attack, King James revoked the colony's charter. Now the king, not the Virginia Company of London, would appoint the governor. Eventually the king recognized the House of Burgesses, giving his royal sanction to the colonists' efforts at self-rule. Virginia had become England's first royal colony.

2.3 Theodore de Bry Engraving of the "Massacre" of 1622
This engraving of the 1622 Indian attack on Virginia residents contains a number of inaccuracies. To exaggerate the difference between Indian savagery and English "civilization," the artist included a European-style city in the background.

Lord Baltimore's Refuge: Maryland

James I died in 1625, and his heir, Charles I, came to the throne. Having married the French Catholic princess Henrietta Marie, Charles I resolved to make good on his marriage promise to ease the plight of England's Catholics. The vast majority of England's aristocracy was Protestant, but a small number were Catholic. One Catholic nobleman, George Calvert, Lord Baltimore, realized that he might be able to help his fellow Catholics and increase his own wealth by obtaining a royal charter for land in Virginia, making it a haven for English Catholics. After Calvert's death his son Cecil, the second Lord Baltimore, obtained a charter for a colony from King Charles in 1632. In this elegant portrait (**2.4**) painted by Gerard Soest, a court painter to King Charles, Cecil Calvert, Lord Baltimore, stands holding a copy of the map of Maryland. He hands the map to his grandson, the son of the then current governor of Maryland, Charles Calvert. Grandfather and grandson are dressed in the finest fabrics, as is the slave who stands off to the side.

Maryland began as a proprietary colony under the legal authority of Lord Baltimore. The legal title of **proprietor** gave its possessor almost king-like authority over his domains. Lord Baltimore learned an important lesson from Jamestown: The lure of profits from tobacco agriculture could drive colonists to starve themselves to death in order to get rich quick. To avoid this danger Calvert had ordered that settlers first obtain a "sufficient quantity of corn and other provisions of victual" before producing tobacco or any other commodities for export. Although he envisioned his colony as a haven for Catholics, Calvert knew that the economic success of the colony depended on attracting laborers, so the colony would need to be equally hospitable to Protestants. Maryland therefore afforded religious freedom to all Christians.

From the start the proprietor and the freemen battled over control of the

What was a proprietor?

colony. Colonists challenged Lord Baltimore. The Maryland assembly routinely voted down bills he introduced; Baltimore responded by blocking acts passed by the assembly. Exacerbating the discord was the continuing religious tension between the Catholic proprietor and the overwhelmingly Protestant assembly. Eventually the two sides accommodated each other, and within a decade Maryland had a functional legislature.

Life in the Chesapeake: Tobacco and Society

The demands of an expanding tobacco economy in the Chesapeake, an area that included parts of Virginia and Maryland bordering Chesapeake Bay, produced a society that was driven by the profit motive. Tobacco production rose dramatically in the middle of the seventeenth century, with exports from Virginia to England growing from over 200,000 pounds in the early 1620s to over 3,000,000 pounds by the end of the 1630s. By the 1670s tobacco exports to England had increased to about 20,000,000 pounds. Attracting laborers to work in the tobacco fields proved difficult. Indentured servants, individuals who contracted to be servants for a specified number of years, usually four to seven years, provided an important source of labor. Employers paid for the passage of their indentured servants to the colonies and clothed and fed them while they remained bound to their employer. At the end of the term of service, employers usually gave their indentured servants some clothes and tools and allowed them to set out on their own. African slaves provided another source of labor, but slavery was not yet the dominant labor system in the region, and slavery had not yet hardened into a fixed status. A small number of slaves did eventually obtain their freedom.

2.4 Lord Baltimore
The sumptuous clothes worn by Lord Baltimore, his grandson, and the black slave testify to the wealth and power of a proprietor. [Courtesy of Enoch Pratt Free Library, Central Library/State Library Resource Center, Baltimore, MD]

Most planters preferred men for the arduous work of growing tobacco, so immigrants to the Chesapeake society were overwhelmingly male. Scholars estimate that before 1640, men outnumbered women by as much as 6 to 1. The lopsided sex ratio meant that the small number of women who migrated to the region and managed to survive the high mortality rates enjoyed considerable control over their decision to marry. Since women often outlived their husbands, a fortunate woman could make several favorable matches over the course of her life and create a sizeable estate. By the end of the century, as food supplies, sanitation, and shelter all improved, and more children were born in the region and more women migrated there, sex ratios became somewhat less lopsided.

Tobacco agriculture shaped the distinctive pattern of settlement in the Chesapeake. Rather than organize themselves into towns, colonists spread out in search of arable land to plant. They prized locations close to navigable rivers that fed into one of the major waterways in the area, as a location close to the river made shipping tobacco easier and cheaper. A small number of wealthy planters monopolized these choice locations. The demands of tobacco agriculture led to an almost insatiable need for additional land, which exacerbated the tensions with local Indians eager to prevent further encroachments on their territories.

How did the unbalanced sex ratio of the Chesapeake impact gender roles in this colonial region?

New England

The same year that the Virginia Company of London obtained a charter to settle what is now Virginia, another group of investors organized a rival company, the Virginia Company of Plymouth, intending to settle north of Virginia. The charter they obtained included lands as far north as modern Bangor, Maine. In 1607 the company established a small plantation at the Sagadahoc (known now as the Kennebec) River. The ferocity of the Maine winter, however, proved too much for the colonists, who abandoned the settlement and returned to England.

Although the region's severe winters seemed to have doomed the prospects of settling this region, a group of Protestant religious dissenters known as Puritans expressed interest in migrating to New England. The ascension of Queen Elizabeth I (1558–1603), who had embraced the Protestant faith and supported the ideals of the Reformation, helped further the progress of the English Reformation.

The queen's support for Protestantism stopped well short of what the most zealous reformers had sought. Elizabeth opted to chart a middle path between traditional Catholicism and the most radical wing of the Protestant Reformation. Those who urged further reform earned themselves the name Puritans because of their desire to purify the Church of England of all vestiges of Catholic belief and practice.

> "The name Puritan is very aptly given to these men ... because they think themselves ... more pure than others ... and separate themselves from all other churches and congregations as spotted and defiled."
>
> JOHN WHITGIFT,
> Elizabethan clergyman, 1573

Elizabeth never married and produced no heir, so the royal line passed to James I of Scotland. Although eager to assert his own power, James was not particularly interested in pursuing the ideals of the Protestant Reformation. When his son Charles I ascended the throne in 1625 and took a French Catholic woman for his wife, proponents of reform feared the worst—a revival of Catholicism. In response to religious developments in England two factions emerged within the reformation movement. Puritans continued to believe that reform was possible within the Church of England. Another strain of English Protestantism bent on further reformation, **Separatism**, argued for complete separation from the established church.

Plymouth Plantation

In 1608 a large group of Separatists fled to Holland, renowned for its support of religious toleration and a haven for Protestant dissenters, including other Calvinists from France and England. Life there proved difficult for the English Separatists. The problem was not persecution, but rather the corrupting influences of the affluent urban culture of the Dutch Republic. Describing the Separatists' experience in the Dutch university town of Leiden, William Bradford recalled "the manifold temptations of the place" and expressed particular concern that the Separatists' children would be "drawn away by evil examples into extravagant and dangerous courses." The artist Jan Steen, a Dutch painter who explored the theme of corruption in many of his paintings, captured these fears in portrayals of Dutch urban life in his work. *Images as History: Corruption versus Piety* examines one of Steen's moralizing paintings about the temptations of Dutch life.

Why were English reformers called Puritans?

Images as History

CORRUPTION VERSUS PIETY

In his painting *The Topsy-Turvy World,* Jan Steen conjures up a chaotic household that seems to be the exact opposite of the ideals of domestic tranquility, godliness, and order. The painting depicts a multitude of sins. The seated couple in the middle represents unbridled sensuality. The duck on the shoulder of the piously dressed man mocks the couple's commitment to religion. The man and woman seem completely unaware of the lewd behavior around them. What moral lessons does this painting teach and how does the artist visually represent the vices of city life in Holland?

A small child, unattended, smokes a pipe, while another unsupervised youth steals a coin from a purse in the cupboard against the wall.

The duck on the shoulder of the man mocks his false piety. The man hides his face in his book rather than restore order to the chaotic scene around him.

The immodestly dressed woman in the center of the painting looks at viewers. She rests a wine glass suggestively in the lap of the drunken man seated next to her.

Jan Steen, *The Topsy-Turvy World*

The animals represent vice and disorder. Instead of sitting obediently in the background, the dog scavenges for food on the table, while a pig roots around on the floor for a meal.

What does Jan Steen's painting tell us about the world English Separatists encountered in Holland?

English Separatists living in Leiden decided that life in the tolerant, worldly environment of Holland posed too many temptations for the faithful. A group of the Leiden Separatists, resolving to leave the sinful world of Holland, returned to England briefly before setting out for what they believed to be the unspoiled New World. Later called Pilgrims, a term traditionally used to describe Christians on a spiritual quest for salvation, they set sail for Virginia. After a harrowing two-month journey aboard their ship the *Mayflower*, the Pilgrims found themselves not off the Virginia coast, but rather off the coast of Cape Cod, in what is now Massachusetts, in late fall of 1620. William Bradford, their leader, described the experience of arriving safely in America in emotional terms. "Being thus arrived at safe harbor, and brought safe to land" the Pilgrims then "fell upon their knees and blessed the God of Heaven who had brought them over the vast and furious ocean."

Realizing that their company charter was not legally binding on a settlement outside of Virginia, they drew up a new political document, the *Mayflower Compact* (1620), that stated the principles that would govern their community. The document asserted that its signers did "solemnly and mutually, in the Presence of God and one another, covenant and combine ourselves together into a civil Body Politick, for our better Ordering and Preservation, and Furtherance of the Ends aforesaid." The agreement also bound those non-Pilgrims traveling to America, including many servants, who promised to abide by the decisions of the community. The Pilgrims named their colony Plymouth after the port city they departed from in England. Their goal was not religious toleration, but rather Protestant purity. The Pilgrims fled England to create a community purged of all taints of unreformed Catholic practice. Tolerance for what they considered religions' error was inconsistent with the goal of creating a pure form of Christian worship.

> "For we must consider that we shall be as a city upon a hill. The eyes of all people are upon us. So that if wee shall deal falsely with our God in this work wee have undertaken, and so cause him to withdraw his present help from us, wee shall be made a story and a by-word through the world."
>
> JOHN WINTHROP, Puritan leader, 1630

The world the Pilgrims encountered in Massachusetts had been inhabited by Indians for millennia. Earlier European contact had already irrevocably altered this world. The Indian population of the area had been largely wiped out by the end of the sixteenth century. Sporadic contact with European traders and fishing fleets had exposed the Indians of this region to smallpox and other devastating pathogens.

Life in America was brutal for the Pilgrims. Half of their complement of just over one hundred men and women died within the first year. The Pilgrims would have all perished had not Squanto, a local Indian from the Patuxet, a tribe decimated by European diseases, befriended them. English traders had kidnapped Squanto some years before and taken him to England, where he lived as a slave. Through a harrowing series of events involving two further kidnappings, Squanto eventually returned to his home in New England. His skills as an interpreter and knowledge of Indian agricultural practices proved to be indispensible to the Pilgrims.

A Godly Commonwealth

In 1629 Charles I dissolved Parliament and continued his plans to restore some elements of Catholic ritual to the English church, a move that alarmed the Puritans. His assault on Parliament, which included many Puritan leaders, and his elevation of anti-Puritan bishops to powerful positions in the Church of England struck many reformers as ominous developments. The same year that Charles I dismissed Parliament, John Winthrop, a member of the Puritan gentry, wrote to his wife that "I am verily persuaded God will bring some heavy affliction upon this land." A year later Winthrop led a group of Puritans to New England where they hoped to create a church and community freed from the corruption Winthrop saw everywhere in England. By the early 1630s another twenty thousand Puritans would leave England for America. By the end of the next decade, the growing population of the Massachusetts Bay Colony had spread out into the Connecticut Valley.

John Winthrop, who became the first governor of the Massachusetts Bay Colony, captured the Puritan vision of the world when he reminded immigrants to America that they must become "a city upon a hill," an example of true reformation that would guide others toward this holy ideal. Winthrop contrasted the holy purpose of New England's Puritans with earlier colonial efforts in Virginia,

Why did John Winthrop describe New England as "a city upon a hill?"

which had been driven more by a lust for gold than by love of God. The hardships and failures of Virginia were, according to Winthrop, a direct result of their goals, which were "Carnal and not Religious." Rather than transport "a multitude of rude and misgoverned persons," the Puritans in New England would ensure their success by establishing "a right form of government" that would promote their religious mission.

The settlement of Puritan New England differed in significant ways from that of the Chesapeake. For one, in contrast to the settlers of Virginia, a large percentage of immigrants to Puritan New England were married. For another, unlike the first Virginians, who were largely drawn from the ranks of gentlemen, the Puritans came largely from the middling ranks of society, including many farmers. In some cases whole Puritan congregations followed their ministers to America during the Great Migration (1630–1642). When these settlers arrived they did not scatter in search of better lands or access to navigable waters, as did the colonists in the Chesapeake, but remained clustered in towns.

Putting a premium on building stable communities, Puritans settled in towns and villages so that communities would remain cohesive. Typically a Puritan village included a central meetinghouse and a town green. The map (**2.5**) illustrates the difference between Puritan patterns of settlement and those of the Chesapeake. In New England homes clustered close to the center of town, and fields were arranged at the outskirts of these town centers. The meetinghouse, literally the nucleus of the community, served both a religious and a civic function. A 1635 law required that new houses be built within half a mile of the meetinghouse.

Rather than expand the size of towns and allow settlers to spread out and weaken the bond of community, Puritans created new towns and villages. New England's town structure served two critical functions: It enhanced the colonists' ability to defend themselves against Indian attack, and it facilitated the enforcement of communal norms and beliefs. Deviance and misbehavior were easier to control in the small tight-knit towns of New England than was such behavior in the Chesapeake. In 1630 New England boasted eleven towns. By 1647 the number had tripled to thirty-three and would rise to more than one hundred by the start of the next century.

The family was another building block of Puritan society. Puritans migrated to New England as families, and their conception of the family was designed to further their religious ideals. John Winthrop expressed this view when he noted that "A family is a little common wealth, and a common wealth is a greate family." The foundation for this set of beliefs was the Fifth Commandment, which enjoined believers to honor one's father and mother. Puritans saw this commandment extending well beyond the requirement of honoring one's parents. Minister John Cotton reminded his parishioners that the Fifth Commandment injunction to honor parents applied to "all our Superiors, whether in Family, School, Church, and Commonwealth." In

2.5 Two Models of Settlement: A Puritan Town and a Chesapeake Community Puritan villages were clustered around a central town common and meetinghouse. Settlement in the Chesapeake followed a different model, with individuals scattering across the landscape in search of the best land and access to navigable rivers.

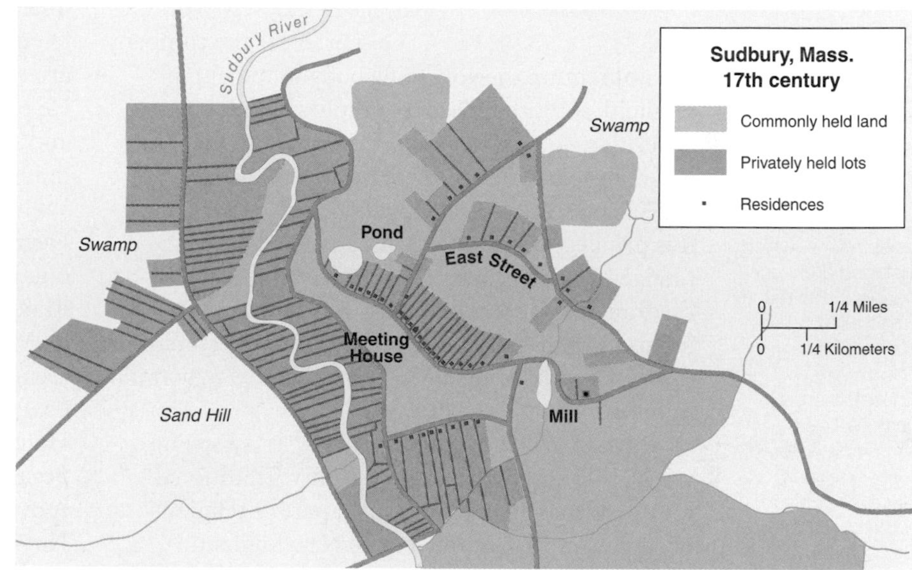

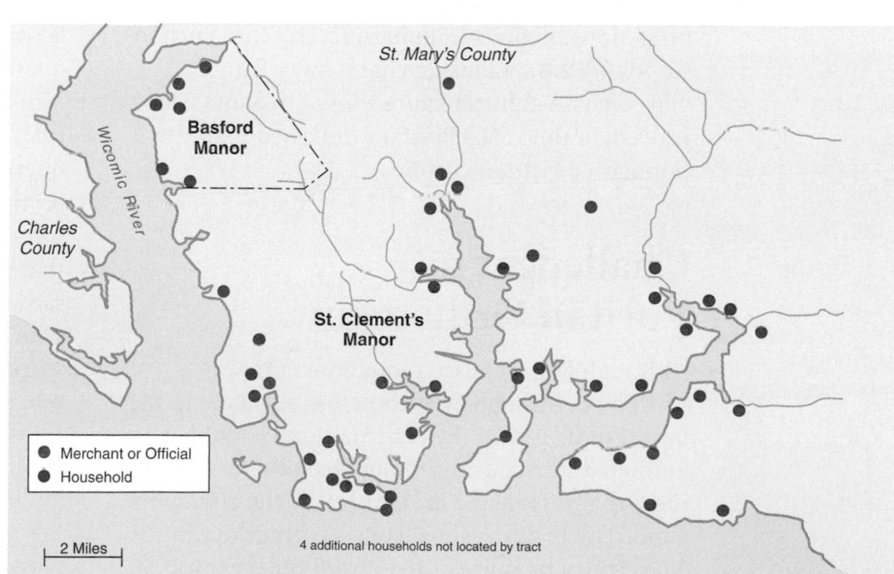

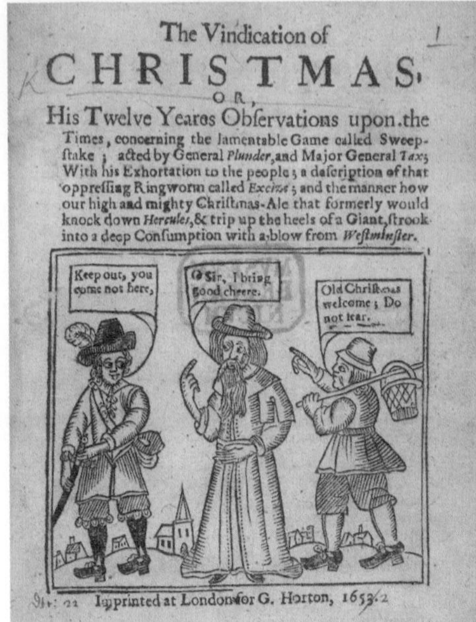

2.6 Puritans Chase Away Father Christmas
This anti-Puritan woodcut pokes fun at the Puritans' opposition to traditional Christmas celebrations, which included drunkenness and too much "mad mirth." [*Source:* The Vindication of Christmas or, His Twelve Yeares Observations upon the Times, concerning the lamentable game called Sweepstake, 1653 (woodcut), English School, (17th century)/British Library, London, UK/© British Library Board. All Rights Reserved/The Bridgeman Art Library]

Cotton's view honor meant more than reverence; it also mandated obedience. Taking these words to heart, in 1648 the Massachusetts colonists made disobedience to parents a crime punishable by death. Although this penalty was never applied, it signaled the seriousness with which the Puritans took the idea of patriarchal authority.

The government of the Massachusetts colony evolved out of the joint-stock company used to raise money to fund the Puritans' voyage to the New World. The charter for the company did not require the governing body to remain in England, so Puritan leaders simply set up their own governing body in America. In contrast to England, where property determined the right to vote, Massachusetts allowed all male church members this privilege. Since a fairly high percentage of the first generation of settlers were church members, the franchise in Massachusetts was much more inclusive than that in England. Historians estimate that 40 percent of men may have qualified to vote in the 1630s.

Puritan law encouraged sobriety and a strong work ethic and discouraged frivolity. Traditional folk customs that had long been part of religious observances were banned from New England worship. Christmas too was targeted for purging of all non-religious trappings. In this anti-Puritan woodcut (**2.6**), a Puritan chases away Father Christmas, a cultural figure similar to Santa Claus. Indeed, in the 1650s Puritans outlawed many popular Christmas customs.

Challenges to Puritan Orthodoxy

Although Massachusetts sought to enforce orthodoxy through everything from its laws to the layout of its towns, the Reformation vision that animated Puritanism contained a number of radical ideas that threatened the survival of the city upon a hill. The first great challenge to orthodoxy in Massachusetts came in 1635 from the devout Separatist minister Roger Williams. He attacked the government of Massachusetts Bay for using the power of the state to enforce religious orthodoxy. For Williams the goal of creating a purified church led to the conclusion that government ought not to meddle in religious affairs. Williams advocated the complete separation of church and state. While many modern supporters of the separation of church and state seek to prevent government from being influenced by religion, Williams sought the opposite—to protect religion from possible corruption by government. Williams also attacked the colonists for unjustly seizing Indian lands, a position that proved almost as unpopular as his novel religious views.

Although Governor John Winthrop of Massachusetts greatly respected Williams for his intellect and piety, Massachusetts Bay could not tolerate his direct challenge to the state's authority to enforce religious orthodoxy. Before he could be arrested, Williams fled the colony and headed south. He purchased land from the Narragansett Indians and settled in what is now Rhode Island. Thankful that God had rescued him from his enemies, Williams named his new settlement "Providence." Eventually he returned to England and in 1644 obtained a parliamentary charter for a new colony, Rhode Island.

While the Massachusetts Bay Colony was still reeling from the Williams controversy, a new challenge to orthodoxy emerged. In 1634 Anne Hutchinson, the wife of a prominent merchant, began holding religious meetings in her home. A dynamic speaker and forceful personality, Hutchinson was also a gifted thinker who did not accept the inferior status that Puritan theology accorded women. Although she did not directly question the role prescribed for women, her actions implicitly challenged accepted ideas about gender roles in Puritan society. Hutchinson also openly questioned the theological purity of the colony's leading ministers. In her view, only one minister, John Cotton, was preaching the true Calvinist idea that only God's grace alone could bring about salvation. Hutchinson charged the other ministers with sliding backward toward the notion that good works could contribute to salvation. Attacking the religious views of the ministry was bad enough, but for a woman to do so, especially one who attracted a following among both sexes, was too much.

The colony's leaders feared that Hutchinson and her followers had succumbed to the Antinomian heresy. Antinomians took the logic of Calvinism to its extreme: The elect, if possessed of true saving grace, need not follow any earthly laws. If good works really had no connection to salvation then why follow earthly laws? Most Puritans feared that the Antinomian heresy would lead to moral anarchy. The Puritans also charged Hutchinson with violating the Fifth Commandment by refusing to honor and obey the ministers who were the colony's patriarchs.

Hutchinson was hauled before a special court and subjected to a grueling examination. During this ordeal she brilliantly parried virtually all of the questions posed. At the end of her examination, however, she made a serious mistake. When asked how she could be so sure of her actions, she claimed that God spoke directly to her by an immediate revelation. Puritans believed that God spoke to his chosen people only by his revealed word—the Bible—not by direct revelations. For Winthrop and others the claim that God spoke directly to Hutchinson exposed the dangerous Antinomian strain in her thinking. If this was true anyone, including those who acted immorally, could simply claim to be acting according to a prophetic voice from God. Hutchinson was convicted and banished from Massachusetts Bay Colony. She headed south to Rhode Island, where she and several of her followers sought refuge before eventually settling on what is now Long Island, near the Dutch town of New Amsterdam in the colony of New Netherlands.

While Puritans in New England continued striving to build their city upon a hill and protect it from the danger of heresy, Puritans on the other side of the Atlantic had been locked in a protracted struggle with King Charles I. The political struggle between Parliament and the king eventually led to civil war. Emerging victorious, Parliament tried the king for crimes against his people and executed him. The commander of parliamentary forces, Oliver Cromwell, became England's new leader, assuming the title of Lord Protector of England. Cromwell ruled with nearly monarchical powers.

In the process of raising an army to fight against the king, Parliament had decided to lift censorship and allow freedom of the press for the first time in English history. To gain popular support and recruit soldiers for their army, Parliament also inaugurated a new policy of religious toleration for all Protestants. With censorship lifted a host of sectarian religious groups emerged in the Civil War years. One of these sects, the Society of Friends, or **Quakers**, believed each individual possessed a divine spark of grace, an inner light that could lead them to salvation. The origin of the word *Quaker* is complex. The leader of the Quakers, George Fox, had earned this name when he reminded a magistrate that the righteous ought to "tremble at the word of the Lord." The name stuck because of the nature of Quaker worship. As one contemporary noted men, women, and children would "fall into quaking fits" in response to the workings of grace within themselves. Quakers rejected the need for any ministry at all. At their meetings anyone who felt the spirit move within them was entitled to preach.

Expansion and Conflict

In contrast to the disease-ridden environment of the Chesapeake, New England's environment was reasonably healthy, and the population expanded owing to natural increase. Infant mortality in New England was somewhat lower than that in England. Although exact figures are difficult to obtain, historians estimate that just over 10 percent of the children born in colonial New England died before their first birthday. The comparable figure in England was about 15 percent. While few people in England lived past middle age, about 50 percent of New Englanders who survived to age twenty would have lived until their late sixties.

New England's growing population combined with the relative longevity of its inhabitants created enormous pressure to acquire additional land so that children might be able to start their own families. Religious leaders played a prominent role in New England's early expansion. The Puritan minister Thomas Hooker led a group of Massachusetts settlers in 1636 and founded the town of Hartford, Connecticut; the Reverend John Davenport left Massachusetts and established the town of New Haven, Connecticut, a year later. In 1638 representatives from several of these towns drafted a frame of government, the Fundamental Orders of Connecticut.

Expansion into the Connecticut Valley brought New Englanders into direct conflict with the local Pequot Indians, who refused to submit to English authority. In the resulting fierce war against the Pequots, New Englanders exploited intertribal rivalries to gain an advantage over the Pequot. New Englanders aligned with the Pequot's enemies, tribes that sought to take advantage of the colonists' firearms to destroy a rival tribe. The ferocity of English warfare horrified the Narragansett and Mohegan Indians, traditional enemies of the Pequot, who joined forces with the English in the war against the Pequots.

Why was Ann Hutchinson such a threat to the Puritan elite?

The Caribbean Colonies

From England's point of view, the real economic jewel in the Atlantic world was not the American mainland, but the Caribbean "sugar islands." Not long after Columbus landed in the Bahamas in the late fifteenth century, the Spanish established a firm colonial presence in the region. By the early sixteenth century, not just Spain but also France, England, and Holland had each established colonies in the area. The enormous wealth of the "sugar islands" encouraged intermittent warfare among these rival colonial powers that resulted in a continuous redrawing of the map of this region, as islands traded hands between different colonial powers (**2.7**). During Cromwell's rule Admiral Sir William Penn seized Jamaica from Spain in 1655, and France took part of Hispaniola (Haiti) in 1664. France and England traded islands such as St. Kitts back and forth for much of the century. Spain conquered the English colony of Providence Island in 1641. The most profitable English sugar colonies were St. Christopher (1624), Barbados (1627), Nevis (1628), Montserrat (1632), Providence Island (1630), Antigua (1632) and eventually Jamaica.

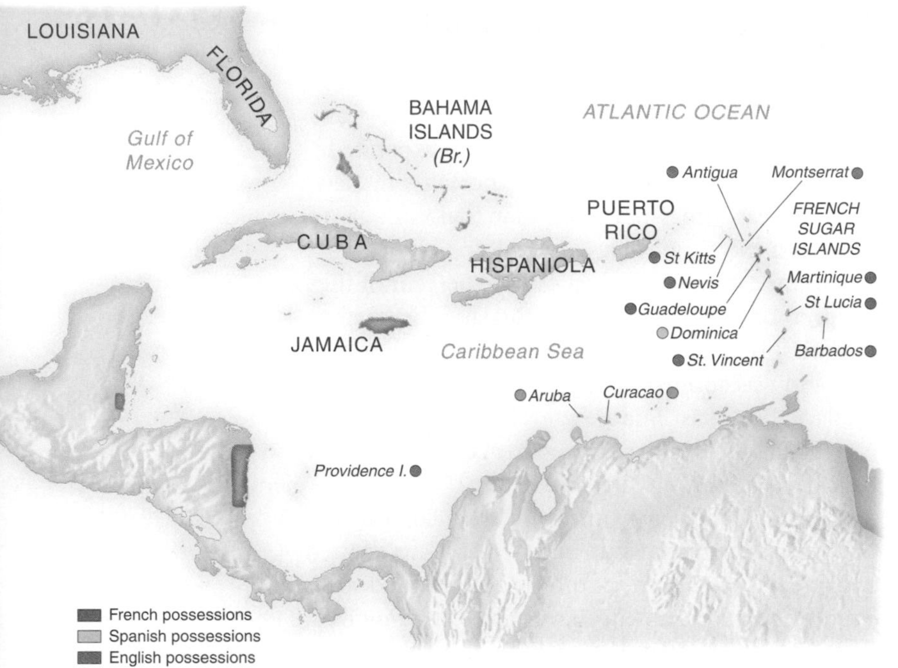

2.7 Caribbean Colonies
The sugar islands of the Caribbean became the most profitable region of the Atlantic economy. Barbados became a major producer of sugar and an example for how slavery could be accommodated to English law.

Power Is Sweet

Although the amount of acreage that the English cultivated in the Caribbean was small, the region became the richest in the English Atlantic empire. Sugar generated enormous profits for Caribbean planters, exceeding the value of all exports from the mainland colonies. Because of the enormous wealth of the West Indies, roughly two-thirds of all English migrants headed for the Caribbean. By the middle of the seventeenth century, the population of this region had reached approximately 44,000, while the population of the Chesapeake was about 12,000 and New England around 23,000.

The wealth produced by sugar could be substantial. Seventeenth-century Europe developed an appetite for sugar that seemed nearly limitless. Besides its use in desserts, sugar was sprinkled on cooked food as a condiment and used medicinally in an effort to treat a variety of afflictions. The use of sugar could also broadcast wealth, social status, or power. Wealthy Europeans displayed lavish sugar sculptures with intricately carved figurines and scenes on banquet tables for guests to admire.

Producing sugar and preparing it for export required a labor force capable of surviving the brutal heat of the Caribbean islands. Sugar production also entailed backbreaking agricultural labor. The multistage process that followed the cutting of the cane required additional labor at every phase. This French engraving (**2.8**) shows the multiple stages of sugar production, including milling and boiling.

Barbados: The Emergence of a Slave Society

The key island economically in the English Caribbean was Barbados. Far from the sea routes plied by Spanish fleets, Barbados avoided the

What was the main source of wealth in the Caribbean islands?

> "I consider the laws concerning Negroes to be reasonable, for by reason of their numbers they become dangerous, being a brutish sort of people and reckoned as goods and chattels [property] in the Island."
>
> Colonial English official, 1680

European rivalry and warfare that embroiled other parts of the Caribbean. Visitors to the island often found it "more healthful than any of her neighbors." By 1660, 26,000 English immigrants had settled there, drawn by the promise of wealth through the sugar trade.

Because of the harsh conditions for laborers on Barbados and the high mortality rates of workers in the sugar fields, maintaining an adequate labor force was a serious problem. During the first decade of colonization, planters in Barbados emulated their countrymen in Virginia, relying heavily on indentured servants as a labor source. Some unfortunate individuals were actually "barbadosed," to use the seventeenth-century turn of phrase that became a synonym for "kidnapped" but originally meant being abducted to work in the sugar fields. Desperate for workers planters even tried convict labor for a brief period. The need for agricultural labor eventually led English planters to emulate the Portuguese and Spanish and turn to slave labor. Within the first decade of turning to sugar production, Barbadian planters bought twenty thousand African slaves. Within the colonies of the English Atlantic world, Barbados became the primary destination for African slaves, who outnumbered whites by 1660.

Spanish and Portuguese law had easily accommodated the institution of slavery. But English law had no precedent upon which to draw in framing a law for slavery. The first efforts to deal with slavery occurred in a piecemeal fashion. Early laws dealt with slave theft and with other practical problems, such as slaves wandering off their plantations. By 1661 Barbados had enacted a comprehensive set of laws to govern relations between masters and slaves. Framed in 1661 the Barbadian slave code created a system of legalized segregation in which race defined servitude. Barbadians instituted harsh penalties to prevent slaves from challenging the authority of their masters. At the same time the legal code minimized penalties for masters' mistreatment of slaves. Murdering a slave incurred a modest fine, while accidentally killing a slave during punishment carried no legal penalty at all. The Barbadian slave code would provide a model for other areas of the English Atlantic, including Virginia, where slavery took hold.

2.8 Sugar Production This engraving of the various steps in the production of West Indian sugar shows the centrality of black slave labor to sugar agriculture. [*Source:* University of Virginia Library, Special Collections Department]

Why did Barbados turn to slavery as its primary source of labor?

The Restoration Era and the Proprietary Colonies

In 1660 Charles II became king of England, reestablishing the English monarchy. The **Restoration**, as this period was known, inaugurated a new phase in the evolution of English colonial America. The driving force behind colonization now came from a small group of courtiers, aristocrats close to the king who used their influence to secure colonial charters. In America, building on the model pioneered by Lord Baltimore, these new Restoration-era proprietors sought to increase their wealth while advancing their own particular political and religious ideals. The new colonies also experienced the same type of conflicts that had plagued Maryland. Proprietors struggled to impose their vision of government on settlers who demanded representation. Nevertheless by the end of the seventeenth century, England had cemented its control of the eastern seaboard of America from the Carolinas to northern New England (**2.9**).

2.9 Seventeenth-Century English Mainland Colonies This map shows the Restoration colonies of Carolina, New York, New Jersey, and Pennsylvania. By the end of the seventeenth century, England had established its dominance on the eastern seaboard of North America. English control extended from northern New England to the Carolinas.

Early 17th century colonies (founded 1607–1640)
Restoration Era colonies (founded 1660–1685)

The English Conquest of the Dutch Colony of New Netherland

Along with England the other great Protestant nation in Europe was Holland (the Netherlands), which also actively engaged in trans-Atlantic trade, including sugar, slaves, and other commodities. Although Dutch merchants traveled the entire Atlantic world, the Dutch had established only a modest presence in North America. The Dutch exploration of the Hudson River laid the foundation for the colony of New Netherland (1609). The Dutch East India Company had established fur-trading outposts in present-day Philadelphia and Albany (New York) in 1612. About a decade later the Dutch established a settlement at the tip of Manhattan Island that they called New Amsterdam in honor of Holland's most important city. The Dutch welcomed traders from various parts of Europe and embraced the ideals of religious toleration. The small but thriving city of New Amsterdam included Dutch, English, Scandinavians, Germans, and Portuguese. By the middle of the century, a small number of Sephardic Jews (Portuguese Jews), who had fled the persecution of the Inquisition in Brazil, had also joined the community.

The centrality of the fur trade to the economy of New Amsterdam emerges in this early image of the city. Although the image (**2.10**) does not accurately depict the two Indians, it does show that the wealth

What was the Restoration?

of the city depended on the cooperation of Indian trappers. The Hudson River made it easy to ship beaver pelts downriver from the area around Albany to New Amsterdam. Merchants shipped these pelts to England and Europe, where their fur was prized for hats. This image also features the city's active port, a key to its economic vitality.

Unhappy that Dutch merchants in New Netherland were getting rich in the fur trade, English merchants urged the crown to attack the Dutch stronghold in America. The thriving, long-lived communities of New England had faced the prospect of running out of land, and splinter communities had sprung up in parts of Connecticut and as far south as Long Island, just southeast of New Amsterdam. The expansion of English settlers into the region claimed by the Dutch increased friction between England and Holland.

The prospect of eliminating the Dutch corridor between English settlement in the Chesapeake and New England also appealed to Charles II, and particularly to the king's brother, James, Duke of York. Charles II gave his brother a charter for the area and dispatched a fleet to seize New Netherland in 1664. Although Peter Stuyvesant, the Dutch governor, tried to rally opposition to the English invasion, Dutch merchants in the city decided that it was better to secure favorable terms from the superior English forces than fight. After their conquest of the Dutch, the English divided the region into two new colonies, New York and New Jersey.

James II, the Duke of York, intended to take firm control of his new holdings in New York. He believed that his role as proprietor gave him almost absolute power over his dominions. Protesting their lack of adequate representation, New Yorkers refused to pay taxes. Eventually James II relented, and the first New York assembly convened in 1683.

A Peaceable Kingdom: Quakers in New Jersey and Pennsylvania

James II granted land that would become New Jersey to two courtiers who attracted settlers by promising representation and religious toleration for all Protestants. One of these men, the Quaker William Penn, saw an unprecedented opportunity for creating a religious refuge for members of his faith and others persecuted for their religious beliefs. Penn's father, Admiral Sir William Penn, had helped wrest Jamaica from the Spanish. The king also owed him a large debt. The king paid this debt with a grant for a large tract of land near New Jersey that became known as Pennsylvania (Penn's woods). As a result of this enormous gift of land, Penn's ambitious plans for Pennsylvania, a colony inspired by his Quaker vision of religious toleration, soon overshadowed his involvement in New Jersey.

One of the few radical sects to survive the tumultuous era of the English Civil War, Quakers had been persecuted for their beliefs in the Restoration era. Quakers rejected the notion of priesthood, believing that individual congregations could conduct their own worship without priests. The group also refused to abide by social customs that demanded individuals show deference to those who stood above them in society. Thus Quakers refused to doff their hat and refrained from using any form of honorific address, such as sir, lord, or lady. Quakers simply addressed each other as thee and thou, terms that sound odd to the modern ear but that signified their belief that everyone was equal before God.

Penn intended Pennsylvania to be a "holy experiment" in which Quakers would live in harmony with those of other faiths. Penn expanded his vision of religious toleration well beyond that of Lord Baltimore. To understand the differences between their views, see *Competing Visions: Lord Baltimore and William Penn: Two Visions of Religious Toleration*, page 52.

2.10 New Amsterdam
In the image, a highly Europeanized-looking Indian man hands a small furry animal to similarly unrealistic Indian woman. The fur trade was vital to the economy of this region.

Competing Visions

LORD BALTIMORE AND WILLIAM PENN: TWO VISIONS OF RELIGIOUS TOLERATION

Lord Baltimore envisioned Maryland as a means of both enriching himself and providing a refuge for English Catholics, who were persecuted by the Protestant majority in England. William Penn's plan for religious toleration went well beyond Baltimore's narrower vision. In Pennsylvania Penn sought to welcome anyone who believed in God. What aspects of Quaker belief contributed to Penn's more expansive vision of religious freedom?

Maryland passed its Toleration Act 1649 in the midst of the English Civil War, when Puritans, who were intensely anti-Catholic, were in charge of Parliament. A number of Puritans had migrated to the Chesapeake region. Catholics in the region feared that the English Parliament, dominated by Puritans, might persecute Catholics. Lord Baltimore's vision of toleration reflected his position as a Catholic in a largely Protestant society.

No person or persons whatsoever within this Province, or the islands, ports, harbors, creeks, or havens thereunto belonging professing to believe in Jesus Christ, shall from henceforth be any ways troubled, molested or discountenanced for or in respect of his or her religion nor in the free exercise thereof within this Province or the islands thereunto belonging nor any way compelled to the belief or exercise of any other religion against his or her consent, so as they be not unfaithful to the Lord Proprietary, or molest or conspire against the civil government established or to be established in this Province under him or his heirs.

Maryland Toleration Act (1649)

Lord Baltimore

Penn's Charter of Liberties extended the ideas of religious toleration beyond Christians, to include Jews, Muslims, and other monotheists—believers in one God—a definition that Penn believed included Indians as well. Penn's policy of toleration made Pennsylvania a haven for a variety of different religious groups.

That all persons living in this province, who confess and acknowledge the one Almighty and eternal God, to be the Creator, Upholder and Ruler of the world; and that hold themselves obliged in conscience to live peaceably and justly in civil society, shall, in no ways, be molested or prejudiced for their religious persuasion, or practice, in matters of faith and worship, nor shall they be compelled, at any time, to frequent or maintain any religious worship, place or ministry whatever.

Pennsylvania Charter of Liberty (1682)

William Penn

What were the most important differences between Maryland's and Pennsylvania's policy of toleration?

In formulating a government for his colony, Penn drew on a number of new ideas in English politics, including the writings of the English political philosopher James Harrington, who believed that a stable society depended on a relatively broad distribution of property. In Harrington's view owning property gave individuals a permanent stake in society and also allowed men to be independent, voting for representatives without being manipulated or intimidated.

Penn also hoped to make his colony a "peaceable kingdom" in which different religions lived in harmony. This vision was not restricted to Europeans, but embraced Indians as well. True to his Quaker principles, Penn resolved to negotiate for Indian lands and submit disputes to arbitration by a committee composed of Indians and Quakers.

Penn desired to live beside the Indians as "Neighbors and Friends." He paid generously for Indian lands and ensured that Indians could continue to live on land purchased by whites. Penn praised the local Leni-Lenape people for their eloquence and honor and tried to learn something of their language and customs. During the first generation of settlement, when land was plentiful and the immigrant population still small, Pennsylvania upheld Penn's promise to treat the Indians with respect.

> "Our worthy Proprietor treated the Indians with extraordinary humanity; they became very civil and loving to us, and brought in an abundance of venison."
>
> RICHARD TOWNSEND, Quaker, 1682

The Carolinas

A group of influential English courtiers, the Lords Proprietors, founded Carolina as a joint effort, hoping to make money and create a buffer zone between Spanish Florida and other English settlements on the eastern seaboard. Although the Lords Proprietors sought to shape their dominion according to their own vision, the settlers who migrated there had other ideas. From the outset Carolina's fortunes were closely tied to those of the West Indies, Barbados in particular. Many of the colony's first settlers emigrated from the West Indies. Rather than produce goods for export to England, Carolina began as a colony of a colony, providing naval stores such as pine tar resins to waterproof ships and food such as cattle for the West Indian islands.

The Lords Proprietors had studied the settlement of New England and Virginia and had come to the conclusion that New England–style towns were superior to the "inconvenience and Barbarisme of scattered Dwellings" that characterized settlement in the Chesapeake. The visions of Lords Proprietors and the interests and aspirations of the colonists clashed. Rather than settle in the New England–style nucleated villages as the proprietors had hoped, settlers followed the Chesapeake model, scattering to find the most productive land available and, when available, access to navigable waterways. In 1712 the proprietors divided their holdings into two colonies, North Carolina and South Carolina. The crown took over South Carolina in 1719 and North Carolina a decade later.

The close economic ties between Carolina and Barbados meant that its early settlers were well acquainted with slavery. But the settlers who tried to impose the West Indies' slave system on the frontier environment of Carolina discovered problems they had not anticipated. The rude conditions of early Carolina history, its small population and simple economy, made it harder to maintain social distance between slaves and their masters. The Carolinas were at the edge of English America. Their proximity to Spanish-controlled Florida and hostile Indian tribes meant that slaves and masters had to work closely together, including defending settlements against attack. The location of the Carolinas also encouraged a less exploitive form of slavery, as slaves in the Carolinas had more opportunities to run away and might find refuge with local Indian tribes. By contrast apart from a few mountainous regions in areas such as Jamaica, the islands of the West Indies afforded few sanctuaries for runaway slaves.

Relations with local Indian tribes were complex. Conflicts among Indian tribes provided early Carolina colonists with an unexpected economic boon: the sale of Indian slaves became a lucrative enterprise. Indians sold prisoners they had taken during intertribal warfare to the English, who then exported them to other regions of the British colonies. Indeed Indian slaves provided the most important export from the colony until about 1715, when rice surpassed it. Carolinians also engaged in an active trade with local Indian tribes for deer hides, which were then exported to England. Carolina began as a colony of a colony but soon became an integral part of the Atlantic economy, exporting slaves, deer hides, and eventually rice.

In what ways was Carolina a colony of a colony?

The Crises of the Late Seventeenth Century

The last quarter of the seventeenth century was a period of profound unrest in colonial North America. Religious and ethnic tensions sometimes produced political volatility. In Spanish New Mexico, New England, and Virginia, Europeans were pitted against indigenous populations. In Maryland religious animosities between the Catholic proprietor and a largely Protestant population caused friction. In New York the longstanding divisions between the Dutch and the English kept old wounds open. In New York and Maryland, the tensions triggered a crisis that led to government reorganization. Other forces were at work as well. Relations between the English and the Indians had settled into a pattern of mutual suspicion and antagonism. Colonial governors became entangled in mediating disputes between land-hungry settlers and tribes eager to fend them off. Seeing the brutality of Anglo-Indian warfare, many victims of witchcraft during the Salem witchcraft trials envisioned the devil as a tawny-skinned tormentor whose tortures resembled those used by Indians on their enemies. Finally at the end of the seventeenth century, the political realignment associated with the Glorious Revolution in England helped usher in a new era of political stability in the colonies.

War and Rebellion

In New England relations with the Wampanoag Indians, who had helped the Pilgrims, had deteriorated in the decades since both groups sat down for their harvest feast in 1621. The Wampanoag leader, Metacom, whom the colonists sometimes called King Philip, grew frustrated with English expansion and eventually led the Wampanoags in King Philip's War against New Englanders. The fierce fighting between New Englanders and Indians spread across New England, with hardly a town escaping the conflict. In a contemporary map of New England (**2.11**), the mapmaker provided a numbered key listing the sites of battles, including the more than a dozen settler towns that were utterly destroyed. Nearly three thousand Indians died in the conflict and almost a thousand colonists.

Puritans interpreted the ferocity of the war as a sign of God's displeasure with them. Increase Mather, a leading Puritan minister, reported that after the war ended, the government of Massachusetts appointed a committee to promote "a Reformation of those Evils which hath provoked the Lord to bring the sword upon us." Among the causes of God's displeasure, Mather listed drunkenness; the presence of what Puritans saw as "heretical" sects, such as the Quakers; an obsession with material profit; and a loss of modesty demonstrated by attention to fashion, especially "excesses in Apparel and hair."

In the Chesapeake tensions between colonists and Indians also led to violence. In Virginia, **Bacon's Rebellion**, a popular uprising named after its leader, Nathaniel Bacon, erupted in 1676. The royal governor, William Berkeley, had long played favorites, dealing out lucrative patronage positions and generous land grants to his cronies. The governor had also made a handsome profit off the fur trade with the region's Indians. Frustrated by Berkeley's policies Bacon, a relative newcomer to the colony and a distant relative of the governor, decided to challenge Berkeley's corruption and favoritism. Finding a common enemy, the area's Indians, Bacon attracted a broad range of Virginians to his cause. He drew support from planters frustrated with Berkeley's favoritism and landowners frustrated by the governor's refusal to adopt a more aggressive expansion policy and acquire additional Indian land for settlement. He drew the bulk of his supporters, however, from the bottom ranks of Virginia society, including indentured servants and slaves. Promising to exterminate Indians and distribute land to all, Bacon effectively exploited the deep class resentments that had smoldered for a long time in the Chesapeake region. The governor of the colony had to flee temporally to the eastern shore of the Chesapeake. Buoyed up by popular support for his

What were the main causes of Bacon's Rebellion?

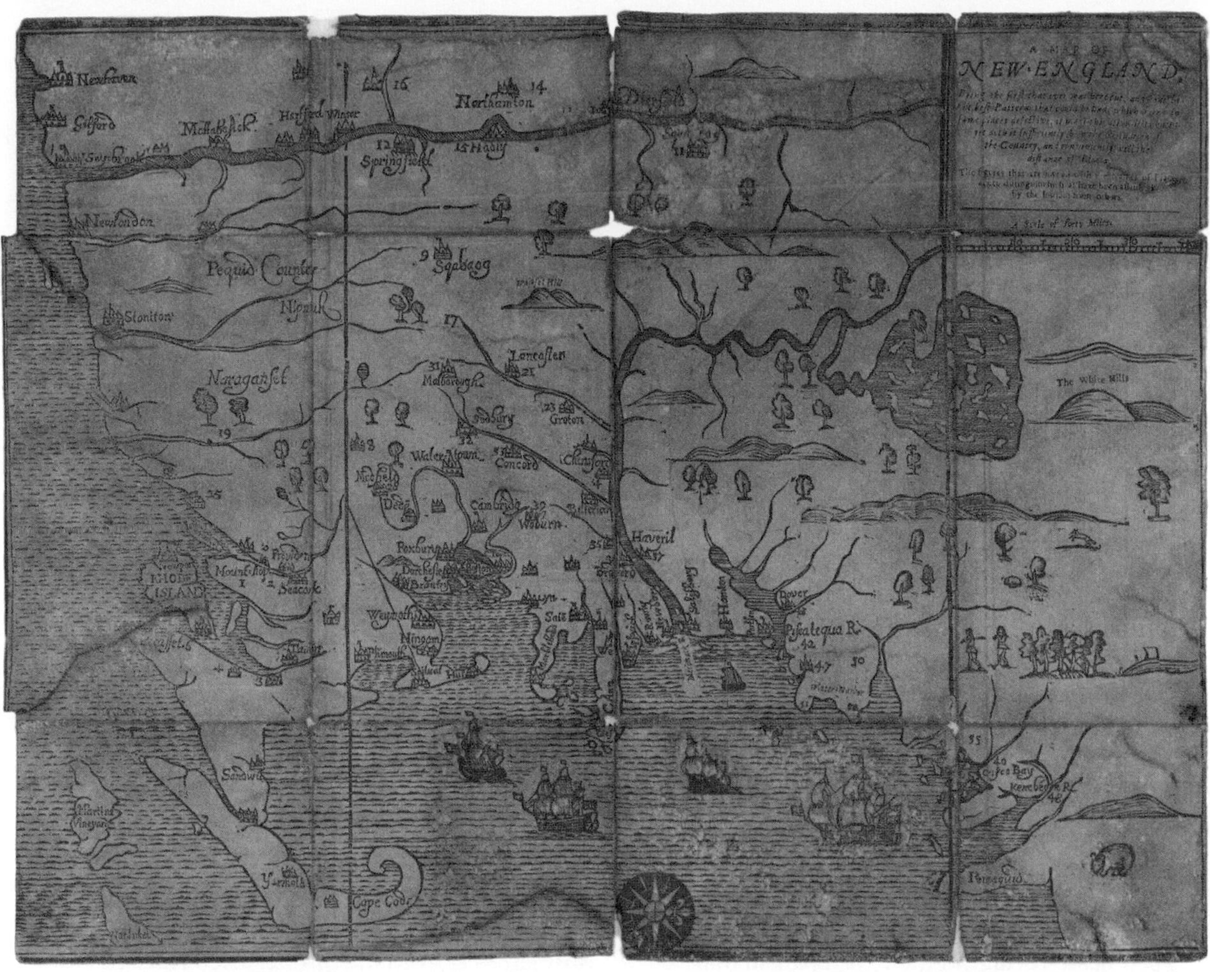

2.11 King Philip's War
This contemporary map suggests the scale of the conflict between Indians and Puritans during King Philip's War.

cause, Bacon torched the colony's capital, Jamestown. Bacon's rising star faded almost as quickly as it rose when he contracted a fever and died, leaving the rebellion leaderless. The royal governor, returning with reinforcements, easily defeated the remnants of Bacon's followers.

A commission formed to investigate the causes of the uprising concluded that the "giddy headed multitude" attracted to Bacon's Rebellion was largely composed of men "lately crept out of the condition of servants." An especially troubling aspect of the rebellion was the interracial solidarity among servants, including whites serving temporary indentures and African slaves who were permanently enslaved. Indeed one of the groups of rebels to surrender was composed of eighty blacks and twenty whites.

Slavery in Virginia began as a legally amorphous category. Earlier in the century some slaves had managed to acquire their freedom, either through grants from their master or through their own resourcefulness. One slave who had taken advantage of the earlier laxity in the law was Anthony Johnson, who became a planter himself. By the eve of Bacon's Rebellion, Virginia's laws regarding slavery had hardened into an almost impenetrable barrier preventing slaves from achieving what Anthony Johnson had achieved—freedom. Bacon's Rebellion accelerated these changes, driving Virginia to invest more heavily in slaves. The danger posed by a "giddy multitude" of landless laborers, whose frustration so-called rabble-rousers such as Nathaniel Bacon could exploit, hastened the shift away from use of indentured servants to use of African slaves, a group that would remain a permanent underclass.

A variety of economic and demographic forces also converged to push Virginia toward a slave-based economy. Among these the number of immigrants into the Chesapeake declined during the late seventeenth century, reducing the available workforce. As the price of slaves decreased and the high levels of mortality in the region, including slaves, dropped, purchasing slaves became more economical. Previously there had been little incentive to purchase a slave for twice the price of an indentured servant if the slave was unlikely to live long enough to make the difference in price economically

What economic and demographic forces contributed to the emergence of slavery in the Chesapeake region?

advantageous. At mid-seventeenth century a mere three hundred slaves resided in the Chesapeake. By the end of the century, the number had climbed to thirteen thousand.

England's colonies were not the only ones rocked by unrest at the end of the seventeenth century. Other parts of the Atlantic colonial world experience similar unrest. In Spanish New Mexico disputes culminated in the Pueblo Revolt (1680). In New Spain Indians were pitted against the Roman Catholic Church. Dispirited by severe droughts and periodic attacks by neighboring Apache and Navajo war parties, the Pueblo people sought solace in their traditional religious practices and turned away from the Catholic religion of their Spanish conquerors. Fearing a challenge to their authority, the Spanish Catholic missionaries in New Mexico brought the full force of church and state power against these "heretics." Rather than accept the new wave of repression, Indians rose up against Spanish authority, killing most of the colony's missionaries and more than four hundred settlers. The rebellion drove the Spanish from New Mexico for more than a decade. However divisions within the Pueblo community and continuing drought hampered the ability of the Pueblo people to resist Spanish power indefinitely. When the Spanish returned thirteen years later, they easily reconquered New Mexico.

The Pueblo revolt did force the Spanish to be more tolerant, at least to Indians who accepted Christianity. They could retain elements of their traditional religious practice and culture, including the use of Shamans, or religious healers. The Spanish also reformed the system of using forced labor, which improved the Indians' economic situation somewhat.

The Dominion of New England and the Glorious Revolution

Although the Pueblo Revolt demonstrated that even Spain's hierarchical colonial empire was not immune from strife, many close to England's king, including his brother James II, envied the Spanish model of empire. In 1685 James II became England's first Catholic monarch in almost 130 years. James had been closely involved in colonial affairs in New York. Believing that Spain's empire was a better administrative model, James hoped to consolidate the English colonies into larger administrative units with powerful governors similar to those in New Spain. Setting his plan in motion, King James II revoked the colonial charters of New York and New Jersey, folding them into New England as a single new administrative and political entity, the Dominion of New England. A powerful English governor and a council appointed by the king would rule the new Spanish-style dominion. Representative assemblies were abolished, and a reorganized legal system made it more difficult for colonists to have access to the courts. To extract additional wealth from the colonists, the colonial government raised taxes dramatically and revoked land deeds. To regain title to their own land, colonists would have to obtain new deeds and pay new taxes on land.

James II had a bold agenda at home as well. A Catholic, James sought to ally England with Catholic France and against Protestant Holland. He also asserted his right to tax his subjects without Parliament's consent. When Parliament refused to accept his agenda, James dissolved Parliament. In the autumn of 1688, English opponents of the king allied with the Protestant Dutch prince William of Orange and launched a successful invasion of England to oust James II from the throne. The Prince of Orange, whose English wife, Mary, was the daughter of James II, succeeded in reestablishing a Protestant monarchy. The relatively bloodless revolution that led to the ascension of William and Mary was proclaimed a **Glorious Revolution** and a vindication for English liberty. Indeed the association between the Glorious Revolution and English liberty was literally cast in metal. The commemorative medallion (**2.12**) produced for the occasion depicts William of Orange with Britannia, symbol of England. She sits under an orange tree, which was the symbol of the prince of Orange. Britannia grasps a liberty pole and has

2.12 Glorious Revolution Commemorative Medal
In this medal commissioned to commemorate the ascension of William and Mary to England's throne and the Glorious Revolution, Britannia, symbol of England, sits under an orange tree, which was the symbol of William of Orange.

her hand on the Bible. The Latin inscription announces that "the Prince of Orange restores the law to us."

An important consequence of the Glorious Revolution was the decision of William and Mary to accept Parliament's "Act Declaring the Rights and Liberties of the Subject and Settling the Succession of the Crown English," an act more generally known as the English Bill of Rights. This act excluded Catholics from the monarchy, affirmed the supremacy of Parliament, and protected certain basic procedural rights of individuals, such as the right to petition, and criminal procedural rights, such as trial by jury, bans on excessive bail, and bans on cruel and unusual punishments. In some cases the Bill of Rights both affirmed individual rights and simultaneously asserted parliamentary authority. Thus the English Bill of Rights asserted that "the subjects which are Protestants may have arms for their defense suitable to their condition and as allowed by law." Restricted to Protestants this particular right was further limited by social class and ultimately subject to Parliament's right to regulate arms.

While official word of the Glorious Revolution took time to reach the colonies, rumors about the ascension of William and Mary started to arrive in the spring of 1689. In April of 1689 two thousand militiamen, mostly from country towns, marched on Boston, arrested the governor, and restored their old colonial charter. In late May New York's militia took control of that colony. In Maryland John Coode marched with seven hundred militiamen to "vindicate and assert the Sovereign Dominion and right of King William and Mary." In the case of Maryland, Protestant resentment against the power of the Catholic proprietary government also fueled Coode's rebellion. The Glorious Revolution in America was a victory for the ideal of representative government and the notion that a well-regulated militia under local control was the best protection for liberty.

The Salem Witchcraft Hysteria

Within a decade of the close of King Philip's War (1675), New Englanders were once again at war with their Indian neighbors, this time in Maine along the northern border of Massachusetts. Fighting was fierce, and Maine's proximity to French Quebec led some English colonists to see their latest troubles as part of a French Catholic plot to rally the Indians against Protestant New England. Some colonists in Massachusetts even accused the Indians of using witchcraft against them. Complicating matters, the recent upheavals of the Glorious Revolution had not yet produced a new stable government, and a new royal governor had yet to be appointed in Massachusetts.

2.13 Signing Satan's Book In this rough woodcut image, Satan presents his book to a witch. Puritans believed that the devil required individuals to renounce their covenant with God and sign a new contract with Satan.

In the midst of this heightened anxiety came the most serious outbreak of witchcraft accusations in colonial America. The center of the witchcraft hysteria was Salem, Massachusetts, but the accusations soon spread throughout Essex County, the coastal county closest to Maine. Before the witchcraft prosecutions ended, nineteen innocent men and women would be executed and one man who refused to plead either innocent or guilty had stones piled on his chest as a means of forcing him to plead. Rather than enter a plea he was crushed to death.

The Puritans who inhabited this region thought themselves an especially attractive target for Satan, who would, they believed, have been eager to upset their effort to build a city upon a hill. New England's covenant with God was mirrored in Satan's own demonic contracts with witches. To seal these contracts, New Englanders believed, Satan made his disciples sign his book, a belief reflected in this seventeenth-century woodcut, which shows the devil and his book (**2.13**).

The witchcraft hysteria began in Salem Village, the outlying part of the coastal port of Salem town. The first purported occurrence of witchcraft occurred in the home of Minister Samuel Parris, whose daughter and her cousin, Abigail Williams, began acting

Why did New Englanders believe that the Devil made his minions sign a book or contract?

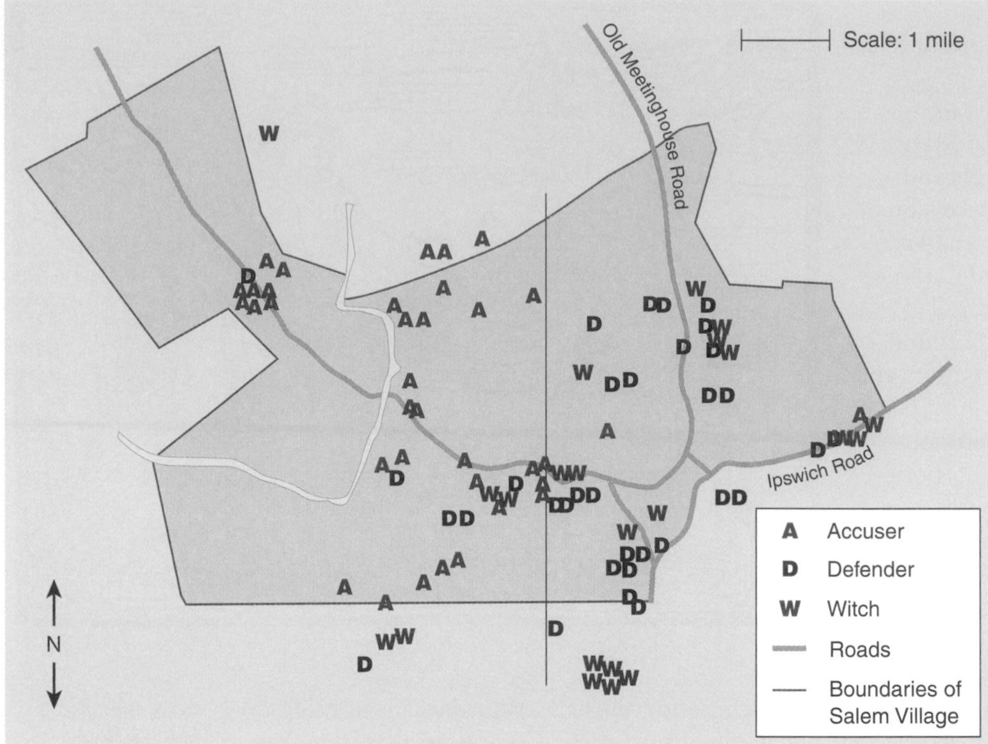

2.14 Pattern of Salem Witchcraft Accusations
This modern map shows the pattern of accusation in Salem. The town was physically divided: Accusers lived in Salem Village, the less commercial part of the town. Accused witches were more likely to have lived in the more commercial area of Salem town.

strangely. After consulting with a physician, who could find no explanation for his daughter's illness, Parris concluded that the girls were victims of witchcraft. When questioned the girls accused two Salem women and Tituba, a Caribbean Indian slave whom Parris owned, of practicing witchcraft. Parris forced a confession from Tituba. Soon the pattern of accusation grew wider and eventually engulfed the whole community. The scope of the witch hunt changed dramatically when the accusations spread to another local minister, the Reverend George Burroughs, who had left Salem to settle in Maine and had recently returned. Much of the testimony from that point forward talked about the Devil taking the shape of an American Indian, creating yet another theme in the witchcraft hysteria. The Puritans even compared the suffering they believed that Satan inflicted on them with tortures Indians used against settlers in the brutal frontier war in Maine.

Historians have identified several patterns in the web of accusations. Witches in New England were more likely to be women, particularly older women who did not live in male-headed households. Women who failed to fit the model of the pious, submissive female, ruled by a benevolent patriarch, an ideal that Puritans especially esteemed, were particularly at risk. The line between accusers and accused almost perfectly divided the Salem community in half (**2.14**). Many of the accusers lived in the more rural Salem Village while those accused were generally from the richer, more commercially oriented part of the community, Salem town. The two parts of Salem had been involved in conflicts for some time. Arguments over the choice of minister and over the efforts of Salem Village to break away from Salem town also played themselves out in charges of witchcraft.

Pressure to stop the trials mounted, particularly as accusations began to be leveled at more prominent individuals from outside Salem. At the start of the trials, ministers had approved of the use of spectral evidence—testimony that witches were using magic to torture victims. But as one of the accused, Rebecca Nurse, argued during her trial, verifying such evidence was impossible. How, she asked the court, could one know if spectral evidence were genuine? Could not Satan appear at a trial to confound the court and trick them into accusing the wrong person? Doubts began to trouble leading ministers in the colony, including Increase Mather, who had been an early supporter of the witchcraft prosecutions. Mather delivered a sermon stating a principle that became a bedrock principle of Anglo-American law: "It were better that ten suspected witches should escape, than that one innocent person should be condemned." Meanwhile the accusations had started to reach the highest levels of Massachusetts society, including the wife of the newly appointed royal governor, William Phips. Rather than allow the trials to continue, Phips dissolved the court that had handled the witchcraft trials and replaced it with a new court whose guidelines followed English law and disallowed convictions based on spectral evidence.

What does the map of the Salem witchcraft accusations tell us about this event?

The Whig Ideal and the Emergence of Political Stability

The Massachusetts legal system that produced the Salem witchcraft trials was out of step with legal developments in England, and even more so in light of the events of the Glorious Revolution (1688). The English Bill of Rights adopted by Parliament (1689) not only weakened royal power but also provided stronger protections for individual liberty, including explicit prohibitions on cruel and unusual punishments and robust affirmation of the right to a jury trial.

In the long struggle between Parliament and the monarchy, Parliament had finally emerged as preeminent in the English political and constitutional system. The group who supported Parliamentary power after the Glorious Revolution became known as **Whigs**. Their opponents, the Tories, were proponents of monarchical authority. The period after the Glorious Revolution ushered in relative political stability in Anglo-American politics. This new era of stability did not end all political debate, but it did mark clear boundaries for future discussions.

The Whig Vision of Politics

Whig theory, put into place after the Glorious Revolution, put a premium on the ideal of civic virtue, placing the public good above personal interest. To promote such virtue one needed the right type of society, a society in which property ownership was widespread. An agricultural nation, where farming was thought to encourage honesty, frugality, and independence, was less likely to become corrupt than a society dependent on commerce and manufacturing. In an agrarian society politics would be less fractious because everyone's interest would be similar. In such a society representatives would be equally affected by whatever laws they passed. This would prevent representatives from tyrannizing over the people by passing oppressive laws.

The Whig view of politics was not democratic. It assumed that only men who owned property had a sufficient permanent stake in society to be trusted with the vote. (The small number of women who owned property, mostly widows, were not allowed to vote.) According to Whig thought, only the best—most virtuous—men would serve as representatives and only those with land were entitled to vote. The notion of frequent elections became a cornerstone of Whig politics. The great danger, however, lay in the potential for electoral corruption, a fact reflected in this early political cartoon (**2.15**), which shows voters being bribed in a local tavern. The fear of corruption became an important feature of Whig political culture, underscoring the need for a virtuous elite and an electorate who could not be manipulated by unscrupulous politicians.

2.15 English Whig Cartoon on Electoral Corruption In this early political satire of an English election, the electorate mill about waiting to be bribed by a political candidate. The text below the scene warned of the dangers of "flattery and gold" which causes men to be corrupted and "liberty sold."

The Glorious Revolution also impacted English law. England had no written constitution, but the common law, the unwritten rules of law worked out over a millennium by English courts, embodied many of the essential liberties esteemed by Englishmen. To these protections Parliament had added the Bill of Rights of 1689, which codified several constitutional principles that would strongly influence the worldview of colonists in America. By asserting the ideal of the rule of law, the Glorious Revolution established the principle that no man, even the king, was above the law. The revolution also lodged the right to tax firmly in the representative branch of government, Parliament, and it rejected the practice of raising a standing army without the consent of the legislature, a practice considered a serious threat to liberty. Among the other provisions protected by the Bill of Rights were the right to petition government for redress of grievances, the right to trial by jury, bail, and a prohibition on cruel and unusual punishments. More than a century later, the U.S. Constitution's Bill of Rights codified and expanded these ideals.

Mercantilism, Federalism, and the Structure of Empire

In 1651 the English Parliament passed the first navigation act designed to limit Dutch trade with the America colonies. The act required that all goods entering or leaving colonial ports be carried on English or colonial ships. It also required that non-English goods be carried on English ships or ships of the country from which the goods originated. One motivation for the act was to eliminate Dutch traders, who had made a handsome profit, particularly as middlemen between the colonies and other parts of Europe. Later the Restoration Parliament passed another series of more restrictive navigation acts in 1660, 1663, 1673, and 1696. These acts required that all goods be transported on American or English carriers, which meant goods from other parts of Europe had to transit through English ports before arriving in the colonies. In 1696 Parliament created the Board of Trade to help coordinate policy toward the colonies. Three years later Parliament passed the Woolens Act, designed to protect the English woolen industry from competition from Ireland and the colonies. The act did not prohibit Americans from making and selling woolens within the colonies, but it did prohibit them from exporting them to England.

The great eighteenth-century Scottish economist Adam Smith called this economic system **mercantilism**. According to this theory the wealth of the "mother" country England would be increased by heavy governmental regulation of imports and exports to the colonies. Colonies existed to generate wealth for their mother country by supplying it with raw materials and purchasing consumer goods from it. To enforce its mercantile policies, Parliament used legislation such as the navigation acts to control colonial behavior. It also created admiralty courts, which were special courts to try violations of the laws governing commerce.

In 1707 the Act of Union brought together the kingdoms of Scotland and England, creating the United Kingdom of Great Britain. The act divided power in the new British Empire between local and national authority. Colonial assemblies continued to legislate on local matters, and Parliament exercised powers over the whole empire. In essence British government had created a federal system that divided power between a distant central authority and local governments. This system of divided authority paved the way for the modern U.S. division between national authority (seated in Washington, D.C.) and the individual state governments.

> "The encouragement of exportation and the discouragement of importation [of manufactured goods] are the two great engines by which the mercantile system proposes to enrich every country."
>
> ADAM SMITH, *The Wealth of Nations*, 1776

What was the theory of mercantilism?

Conclusion

Although initially beset by problems, Virginia's Jamestown, founded in 1607, became the first successful English colony in America. A few colonists earned great wealth through tobacco production, but many suffered misery and death in the new colony. England's experiences in Jamestown provided them with many useful lessons about how to structure colonial enterprises politically and make them profitable. Lord Baltimore, the proprietor of Virginia's Chesapeake neighbor, Maryland, took these lessons to heart, which helped his colony avoid many of the problems that befell early Virginia.

Settlers of the Chesapeake were driven primarily by profits, but New Englanders added a new religious set of motivations that shaped their colonial experience. Convinced that the Church of England was failing in its pursuit of true reformation, the Pilgrims and Puritans voyaged to America with the hope that they might create purified churches and communities organized around religious values. The Puritan goal of becoming "a city upon a hill" faced many challenges from without and within.

The mainland English colonies enjoyed less material prosperity than did the English sugar islands. Caribbean islands such as Barbados produced enormous wealth, and their transition to slave-based economies paved the way for the development of slavery on the mainland. The Barbadian slave code of 1661 became the foundation for an American law of slavery. Provisioning the Caribbean islands with food and the necessary naval stores provided an economic rationale for Carolina, a proprietary colony established after the Restoration of the English monarchy. Taking their cues from Lord Baltimore's colonial venture in Maryland, proprietors created colonies in Carolina, New York, New Jersey, and Pennsylvania. Pennsylvania, founded by the Quaker William Penn, sought to apply Quaker principles and establish friendly relations with the Leni-Lenape Indians. Apart from Penn and Roger Williams, few other colonists were interested in developing peaceful relations with their Indian neighbors. For most of the seventeenth century, colonist-Indian relations remained tense and often turned violent.

American society in the latter decades of the seventeenth century experienced a number of conflicts. Intermittent warfare with Native Americans, the political crisis triggered by the Glorious Revolution, and the Salem witchcraft outbreak bore witness to the underlying strains in American colonial life. By the end of the century, however, the colonies were entering a new phase of stability and growth. In the next half-century, the population of the English colonies would increase dramatically, and the simple provincial world would be replaced by a more refined society.

1607

Founding of Jamestown
First successful English colony in America

1614–1620

John Rolfe exports first tobacco crop from Virginia
The struggling Jamestown colony finally finds a cash crop for export

***Mayflower Compact* signed**
Pilgrims arrive in Massachusetts without a legal title to the land and frame their own government

1634

Colony of Maryland established
First proprietary colony

Roger Williams founds Providence
First colony founded on religious toleration established in colonial America

Anne Hutchinson banished to Rhode Island
Antinomian controversy ends

Review Questions

1. How do you account for the early failures of Jamestown and its eventual successes?
2. What explains the dramatically different pattern of settlement in the Chesapeake and New England? What forces and ideas shaped the spatial organization of each region?
3. Why was the term *Puritan* an apt characterization of the Calvinists within the English church seeking further reformation?
4. What drove the Pilgrims to leave Holland, a country noted for both its prosperity and its tolerance?
5. What differences can you assign to the visions of liberty espoused by orthodox Puritans such as John Winthrop and dissenters such as Roger Williams?
6. Why did the English sugar islands turn to slavery as their primary labor source? How did early Carolina function as a colony of a colony?
7. What role did conflicts with Native Americans play in the crisis of the latter part of the seventeenth century?
8. How did William Penn's Quaker faith shape his vision of Pennsylvania?
9. What role did spectral evidence play in the Salem witchcraft trials? What role did gender play in the dynamics of the Salem witch trials?
10. What ideas and values were most closely associated with Whig politics?

1642

English Civil War
English Puritans under Oliver Cromwell take up arms against Charles I

1664–1681

England captures New Netherland, which is renamed New York
James, Duke of York, gains control of New York and New Jersey

William Penn obtains Royal Charter for Pennsylvania
Quaker William Penn founds Pennsylvania

1688

Glorious Revolution in England
William and Mary ascend to the throne, and Whig political ideals triumph

1692

Salem Witchcraft Trials
A witchcraft hysteria engulfs Salem Village and Salem town

Key Terms

headright An incentive system to encourage additional immigrants by giving 50 acres to any man who would pay their own fare to Virginia and 50 additional acres for each person brought with him. **39**

proprietor This English legal title carried with it enormous political power, giving its possessor almost king-like authority over his domains. Colonial proprietors carried similar powers. **40**

Separatism This strain of English Protestantism argued for a total separation from the established Church of England. **42**

Quakers The Society of Friends, who believed each individual possessed a divine spark of grace, an inner light that could lead them to salvation. **47**

Restoration In 1660 Charles II became king of England, restoring the monarchy to power after the Civil War and Cromwellian rule. **50**

Bacon's Rebellion A popular uprising in Virginia in 1676 named after its leader, Nathaniel Bacon. **54**

Glorious Revolution The relatively bloodless revolution that led to the ascension of William and Mary, which was widely seen as a vindication for English liberty. **56**

Whigs (English, 17th Century) The group that supported parliamentary power after the Glorious Revolution. **59**

mercantilism Theory of empire that advocated strict regulation of trade between colonies and the mother country to benefit the latter. **60**

CHAPTER 3

Growth, Slavery, and Conflict

Colonial America, 1710–1763

Culture and Society in the Eighteenth Century p. 66

> "In 1740, I don't remember [seeing] such a thing as a [Turkish] carpet in the country… . Now nothing are so common as [Turkish] or [English] Carpets, the whole furniture of the Roomes Elegant & every appearance of opulence."
>
> JOHN WAYLES, future father-in-law of Thomas Jefferson, 1766

Life in the seventeenth-century American colonies, even for the wealthiest, was crude and primitive. Beginning in the eighteenth century, a more cosmopolitan and refined culture began to emerge. Prosperous colonists sought out the latest British and European consumer goods, such as finely woven Turkish or English carpets, tea sets, and imported pattern books with English architectural and furniture styles.

Captain Archibald Macpheadris, a fur trader living in Portsmouth, New Hampshire, built an elegant new home in 1716, complete with a series of beautifully executed wall murals, signifying his wealth and refinement. One of the most striking murals depicted two Mohawk Indian chiefs. The unknown muralist copied these images from an engraving of a group of Indians who traveled to London to meet with Queen Anne. The engraver and the muralist included the tomahawk and war club wielded by the two leaders, yet the image of the Indians also reflected the conventions of European painting: The position of the "Indian King's" hands resembled a common aristocratic pose found in English portraits from this period. The engraving of the "Indian Kings" that inspired Macpheadris's murals was part of the wide array of goods that traveled across the Atlantic.

Books, newspapers, and letters all were part of this commerce, and they facilitated a lively exchange of ideas on a wide array of subjects, including architecture, fashion, politics, religion, science, and philosophy. One highly influential set of ideas was associated with the Enlightenment and its ideals of reason and social progress. These ideas fostered new social experiments, such as the founding of the colony of Georgia.

The English evangelical minister George Whitefield traveled to the colonies, crisscrossing them from New Hampshire to Georgia. His tour helped spread the ideas of the religious revival movement known as the Great Awakening. Enlightenment ideals of liberty, human dignity, and progress and new religious ideas even led some Americans to begin questioning the institution of slavery, which had become vital to the prosperity of the colonial economy. The stark contrast between the wealthy planters and wretchedly housed slaves was not the only divide in American life. As the overall wealth of the colonies increased, so did the disparity between the wealthy and the poor.

Land itself became scarce by the mid-eighteenth century. Expansion westward was hampered by the Appalachian Mountains, and the rich lands of what is now America's Midwest were controlled by the French and a host of different Indian tribes. Ultimately the balance of power in North America was decided by the French and Indian War (1755–1763).

What do the Macphaedris House murals tell us about colonial culture?

Culture and Society in the Eighteenth Century

As trade expanded between the colonies and Britain, colonists strove to emulate the culture and sophistication of the mother country. New and grander homes, filled with the latest European-style furnishings, testified to the growing sophistication of the colonies. Yet while the colonies were striving to become more British, they were also developing their own distinctly American political culture and institutions. A native-born elite emerged, an American gentry class whose wealth, confidence, and education inspired them to become leaders in the various colonial assemblies. A distinctive American style of politics had begun to take shape.

The Refinement of America

At the end of the seventeenth century, even the homes of the most prosperous families in colonial America had few imported luxury goods. The sparse furnishing of the Hart Room (**3.1**), now in the Metropolitan Museum of Art in New York City, capture the primitive nature of late seventeenth-century American homes. Thomas Hart, a landowner in Ipswich, Massachusetts, built his house in 1639 and furnished it in the ensuing decades. This parlor room, the best room in the house, usually served as both a bedroom and a communal living space. Information obtained from probates, a list of goods assembled as part of a will, suggests that homeowners furnished even the best parlor rooms sparsely, with simple tables and cupboards. The furniture's simplicity and boxy look reflected prevailing styles and the scarcity of skilled craftsmen in the colonies at the time. The walls were generally whitewashed, with no ornamentation; the post and beams used to support the walls and the roof were clearly visible.

Colonial culture began to change with the expansion of commerce at the start of the eighteenth century. America became more fully integrated into the Atlantic economy, a huge triangle that stretched from Scotland to Africa to the interior of the British mainland colonies (**3.2**). Trade in the Atlantic world involved a staggering array of goods. Scottish merchants purchased Virginia tobacco, which was sold throughout Europe. Another side of the triangle tied New England merchants to West Indian sugar planters. West Indian sugar was distilled into rum by New Englanders. Some of this alcohol was traded to Indians in the lucrative beaver trade in upstate New York. These beaver furs were often used in hats and sometimes ended up in London or on the European continent.

By the early decades of the eighteenth century, expanding trade with the British Empire increased

3.1 The Hart Room, Metropolitan Museum of Art
The simple whitewashed walls and exposed beams in this prosperous seventeenth-century room and the simple boxy style of its furniture were typical of the lack of ornamentation in this era. [*Source:* Room from the Hart House, Ipswich, Massachusetts, American, 17th Century. Oak beams, pine panels and white plaster walls. The Metropolitan Museum of Art, Munsey Fund, 1936 (36.127). Photograph ©1995 The Metropolitan Museum of Art.]

Define Anglicization and give an example of an aspect of colonial life transformed by this process?

the number of wealthy colonists and brought a flood of new luxury goods into affluent American homes. Acquiring such goods allowed individuals and families to demonstrate that they were not simple provincials; they were part of a wider cosmopolitan world. Rather than eat with simple earthenware ceramics, as their forebears had, the wealthiest Americans now aspired to dine on fine porcelain imported from England or Holland. Refined taste was proof of gentility, a term that became synonymous with the attributes associated with wealth and sophistication. American society underwent a process of **Anglicization** as colonists emulated English society, including its tastes in furniture, foods, clothing, and customs.

Nothing better captured the rise of gentility and the increasing Anglicization of colonial America than the rage for imported tea. As the consumption of tea increased dramatically between the end of the seventeenth century and the dawn of the eighteenth, the rituals of serving tea became more refined and complicated. Serving tea to one's guests became an essential ritual. Although tea drinking started as a custom among the wealthy, it gradually spread to all levels of American society. By the middle of the eighteenth century, tea drinking had evolved from a luxury to a necessity, so much so that inmates in the Philadelphia poorhouse demanded that their meager rations include tea.

The Verplank Room (**3.3**) in the Metropolitan Museum of Art contains furniture from the New York City townhouse of Samuel Verplank and the country house of Cadwallader Colden Jr. in Orange, New York. In contrast to the simple whitewashed walls of the seventeenth-century Hart Room, the Verplank Room has painted wood paneling. The elegant card table in the Verplank Room is one of many specialized pieces of furniture likely to have adorned a prosperous home in the middle of the eighteenth century. The Verplanks, Coldens, and other genteel families would each have owned an imported china set and tea table as well.

Changes in furnishing provide insights into deeper changes in colonial society. The rising popularity of writing desks and drop-leaf bookcases with writing surfaces (see detail in 3.3) reflected the expansion of trade networks in the British Empire. Merchants needed to keep better track of a variety of written documents as they broadened the range of

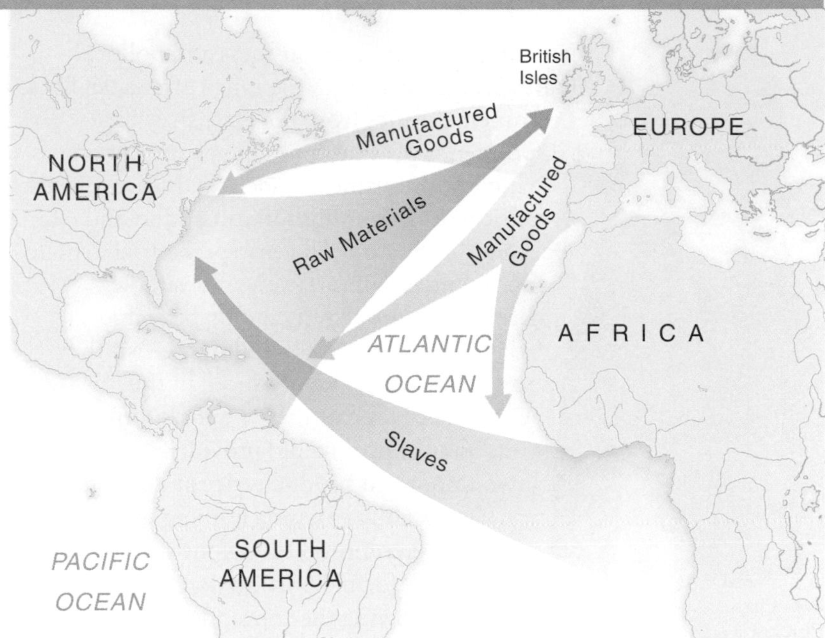

3.2 The Triangle Trade
The Atlantic economy can be visualized as a triangle. Goods from Europe were sold or traded in America or Africa. Raw materials from the Americas were sold in Europe. European goods were sold or traded for African slaves who were then shipped to the Americas.

3.3 The Verplank Room, Metropolitan Museum of Art
The highly specialized furniture reflected the growing wealth of many colonists and the Anglicization of colonial culture. In the inset image of a secretary bookcase, notice the drop-leaf writing surface and cubbyholes that made this piece of furniture well adapted to the needs of merchants.
[*Sources:* Woodwork of a Room from the Colden House, Coldenham, New York, American, ca. 1767, Pine, 252" × 213" × 113" (640.1 × 541 × 287 cm). The Metropolitan Museum of Art, Purchase, The Sylmaris Collection, Gift of George Coe Graves, by exchange, 1940 (40.127). Photograph ©1995 The Metropolitan Museum of Art. (Detail) Detail, Desk and Bookcase, English, 1700–1720; Oak, pine, 81 1/8 × 43 7/8 × 23 1/2 in. The Metropolitan Museum of Art, Gift of James DeLancey Verplanck and John Bayard Rodgers Verplanck, 1929 [39.184.1a,b]. Image copyright © The Metropolitan Museum of Art]

Why did new pieces of furniture like drop-leaf bookcases become popular in the eighteenth century?

their correspondence on business and political matters. An insight into the range of this far-flung commerce comes from the extensive correspondence of Charleston merchant Robert Pringle with business associates throughout the Atlantic world, from Lisbon to London and Barbados to Boston. The entrepreneurial Pringle experimented with a variety of desirable agricultural imports, including pistachios, Seville oranges, and olives, hoping that they might eventually be produced in the Carolinas. None of these imports took hold, but South Carolina did provide Europe with two important products, rice and indigo.

For wealthy colonists nothing was more effective at communicating one's riches and gentility than a formal portrait done in the latest English style. Following the conventions of European portraits, men and women struck standard aristocratic poses; elegant ladies dressed in flowing gowns, mimicking the style of their monarch, Queen Anne. Men and even young boys were painted wearing elegant outfits that reflected their wealth, status, and power. The portrait of the young Henry Darnall III, one of the earliest done in the American South, testifies to the growing wealth and refinement of the colonial elite (see *Images as History: A Portrait of Colonial Aspirations*).

Eliza Lucas Pinckney, an affluent South Carolina woman, exemplified the new ideal of refined female gentility. Born into a prosperous family of rice planters, Eliza introduced the profitable dye, indigo, into South Carolina (1738–1744), which became the colonies' second most important export crop in the eighteenth century. She eagerly consumed British fashions and ideas, and aspired to create a persona and a lifestyle that a visitor from London would have easily recognized. She studied French, was conversant in the ideas of the English philosopher John Locke, and actively participated in the management of her family's plantation. Her social life was equally busy. She regularly attended teas, dances, and concerts. Eliza's beautiful gold silk dress (**3.4**) was woven from silk produced on her own plantation. After the silk was harvested, she sent it to England to be dyed and woven into a fabric suitable for a gown that might be worn to the most elegant party in either London or Charleston.

For women the new customs of gentility were a mixed blessing. A wealthy woman might have servants or slaves to help her entertain in a suitable style, but it took additional time and effort to supervise these activities. Most women did not enjoy the luxury of additional help and had to handle these new responsibilities themselves.

3.4 Eliza Pinckney's Dress Silk produced on Pinckney's plantation was sent to England so that it could be spun into fine fabric, dyed, and sewn into a dress that reflected the latest London fashions.

More English, Yet More American

The exteriors of American homes also underwent a process of Anglicization. English-style manor houses such as William Byrd's home, Westover (1730–1734) (**3.5**), borrowed ideas from English pattern books (architectural guidebooks of the latest styles) (**3.6**). The main entrance of this elegant red brick mansion took guests through an impressive doorway that Byrd imported from England. The model for the door and its frame came from a London design. The classical columns and the swan-shaped broken pediment at the top of the doorframe includes a carved pineapple. If one thing best represented the ideal of refinement in the eighteenth century, it was the rage for pineapples. The exotic West Indian fruit created a sensation

3.5 Westover Plantation The doorway of Byrd's mansion was crafted in England and included the latest architectural details. Notice the carved pineapple above the door.

3.6 English Pattern Book Byrd used this picture from an influential London design book when selecting a style for his doorway. [*Source:* Courtesy, The Winterthur Library: Printed Book and Periodical Collection]

How does Westover Plantation illustrate the growing wealth of the colonies?

Images as History

A PORTRAIT OF COLONIAL ASPIRATIONS

Justus Engelhardt Kühn's portrait of the young Henry Darnall III (1710) reveals how the aspirations of colonists continued to exceed the bounds of the possible. Although the Darnalls lived a life of luxury compared with most colonists, surrounding themselves with goods that earlier generations of colonists would have envied, they did not quite live up to the standards of the typical British aristocrat.

The scene behind Darnall is pure fantasy. An elegant stone balustrade overlooking an elaborate formal garden projects an image of wealth, refinement, and power. Yet neither the fancy garden nor the stone balcony would have existed anywhere in the colonies in the first decade of the eighteenth century. Kühn's decision to include these imaginary elements in the background reflected the aspirations rather than the realities of life in the colonies. The picture symbolized the wealth, power, and gentility that the Darnalls sought to achieve, not their actual condition.

The work is also the first known painting of an African American in the colonies. Darnall's slave wears a silver collar around his neck, a symbol of his inferior status. Although much younger, Darnall towers over his slave.

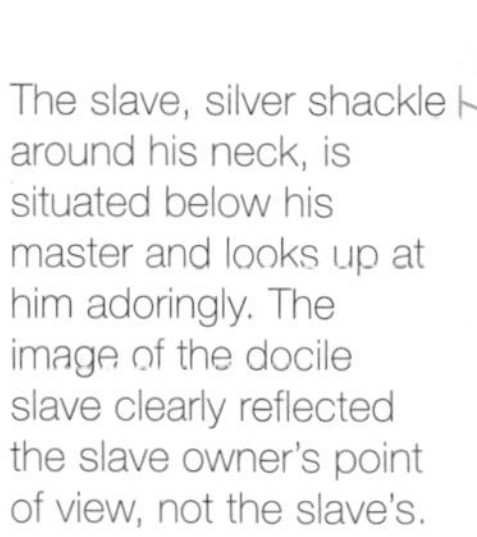

The imaginary garden in the background represents the Darnalls' desires, but this level of grandeur was not yet attainable in the colonies.
The slave, silver shackle around his neck, is situated below his master and looks up at him adoringly. The image of the docile slave clearly reflected the slave owner's point of view, not the slave's.
Darnall's elegant suit testifies to his family's wealth and cosmopolitan taste.

Henry Darnall III as a Child **by Justus Engelhardt Kühn**

How is slavery represented in this portrait?

among the wealthy on both sides of the Atlantic, as both a culinary delicacy and as a symbol of affluent hospitality. The pineapple soon became a common architectural motif in the mansions of wealthy Americans.

Anglicization transformed churches and public architecture as well. Some of the grandest buildings erected in the colonies during the first half of the eighteenth century were public structures such as the Pennsylvania State House in Philadelphia, where Pennsylvania's assembly met. Constructed between 1732 and 1756, the State House's two-and-half-story red brick structure dominated the Philadelphia skyline. Built in the Palladian style (also known as Georgian, in honor of the British monarch, King George I), the Pennsylvania State House captured two seemingly opposing trends in the evolution of American society in the eighteenth century. On the outside its architecture testified to the powerful influence of Anglicization on American society. With its beautiful windows and impressive red brick exterior, the State House visibly symbolized the colonists' esteem for and knowledge of the latest English architectural styles (**3.7**). Inside the State House, however, the debates and votes of the Pennsylvania assembly were emblematic of the growing power and assertiveness of an American-born colonial elite. Philadelphians later renamed their state house Independence Hall, reflecting its close association with two important moments in American history: the signing of the Declaration of Independence and the drafting of the U.S. Constitution.

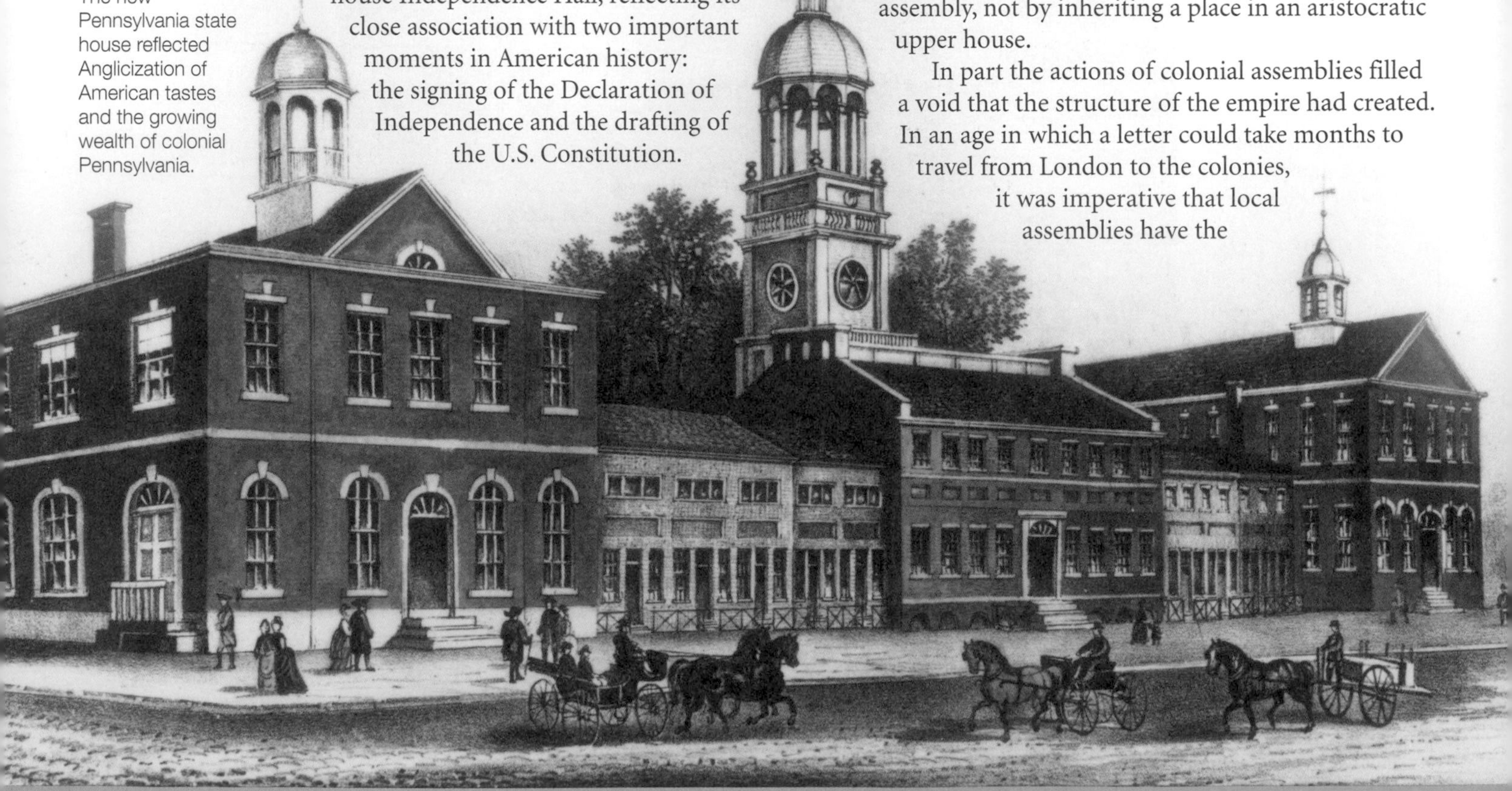

3.7 Pennsylvania State House The new Pennsylvania state house reflected Anglicization of American tastes and the growing wealth of colonial Pennsylvania.

How did the Pennsylvania State House reflect the Anglicization of the colonies?

Strong Assemblies and Weak Governors

The impressive Pennsylvania State House was a potent visual reminder of the power of the colonial assembly. The assemblies had become the preeminent political institutions in the colonies. American ideas about legislative power drew support from seventeenth-century English Whig ideas that triumphed during England's Glorious Revolution (1688) (see Chapter 2).

Several developments in American colonial history helped reinforce the growth of legislative power. Although voting in America remained restricted to adult white male land holders, the percentage of such individuals in the colonies was larger than it was in Britain. The larger size of the voting population meant that a higher percentage of Americans were politically active than Britons. Additionally none of the colonies had anything like an upper house comparable to Parliament's House of Lords. The governors' councils, the closest thing to an upper house, had little power. America's native-born elites were not a titled British aristocracy, with a distinct legislative body, the House of Lords, to guard their privileges and powers. Ambitious young Americans from good families, like the young Thomas Jefferson, expected to enter politics by election to the lower house of the colonial assembly, not by inheriting a place in an aristocratic upper house.

In part the actions of colonial assemblies filled a void that the structure of the empire had created. In an age in which a letter could take months to travel from London to the colonies, it was imperative that local assemblies have the authority to deal with a host of governmental responsibilities, from organizing the militia to providing for the poor. Although colonists had gained the right to legislate on local matters, they were also part of the larger British Empire. Most colonies had agents who represented their interests in London and lobbied Parliament. Apart from these agents the colonies had no actual representation in Parliament: No member of Parliament was elected from the colonies or watched over their interests. In this regard the American colonies were no worse off than were other British colonies, including Barbados and Jamaica. Even within Britain newer cities such as Manchester and Birmingham had no representation in Parliament, and at least one town, Dunwich, continued to send two members to Parliament even though the town had literally crumbled into the North Sea. To cast their votes "legal residents" of Dunwich had to row out to the location of the former town hall, which was submerged.

The underlying theory of representation that justified this situation was **virtual representation.** According to traditional Whig political theory, members of Parliament were expected to represent the whole nation, not any particular locality. Rather than speak for any local interest, representatives were supposed to act in the larger public good. All Britons, then, including the colonists, had virtual representation in Parliament, even if they had no actual representatives to guard their interests. As long as Parliament did not meddle much in colonial affairs, engaging in a policy of "salutary neglect," this theory of virtual representation caused few problems. When Parliament began to take a more active role in managing the empire and collecting greater revenues in the 1760s, the colonial theory of *actual* representation and the traditional British theory of *virtual* representation would come into direct conflict.

Royal governors repeatedly complained that the colonial assemblies had exercised authority that did not belong to them and frustrated their plans at every turn. The royal governors' dependence on the assembly for their salaries weakened their position with regard to the legislature. By controlling the power of the purse, colonial assemblies were able to frustrate the plans of the most ambitious royal governors: If they wished to collect their salaries, the governors dared not anger the assemblies. Colonial assemblies came to act like and think of themselves as mini-parliaments, with full legislative power over local matters.

Colonial politics could be quite nasty, and most royal governors lacked the power to tame their legislatures. No governor was more ineffective and despised than Lord Cornbury, Royal Governor of New York and New Jersey (the two colonies shared the same royal governor until 1738). Enemies of Cornbury accused him of parading around the ramparts of New York's forts in women's clothing. Cornbury's opponents used these rumors to undermine his authority, a strategy that was extremely effective. Sir Danvers Osborne, another New York governor, was so despondent over dealings with the colonial assembly that he hanged himself. To avoid the fate of Cornbury or Osborne, savvy royal governors understood the necessity of making strategic alliances with members of the assembly. The give-and-take between the governors and the assembly defined colonial politics for much of the eighteenth century.

"My Lord Cornbury has and dos still make use of an unfortunate Custom of dressing himself in Womens Cloaths and of exposing himself in that Garb upon the Ramparts to the view of the public; in that dress he draws a World of Spectators about him and consequently as many Censures."

Letter spreading rumors of Lord Cornbury's cross-dressing, 1709

Why were colonial governors so weak?

Enlightenment and Awakenings

In 1733–1734 the great English poet and essayist Alexander Pope wrote his "Essay on Man." Pope advised his readers, "know then thyself, presume not God to scan.'; The proper study of Mankind is Man." The suggestion that man, not God, was the proper focus for human inquiry was the essence of the **Enlightenment.** This broad philosophical movement extolled the virtues of reason and the methods of science and applied these insights to politics and social reform. Rejecting traditional Christian teaching that man was tainted by Adam's "original sin," Enlightenment thinkers favored the English philosopher John Locke's theory that humans were born with a *tabula rasa*, a blank slate upon which society could inscribe its moral lessons. If humans began life as virtual blank slates, they could be molded by education and environment. Crime itself could be eliminated if one understood human nature and created a proper environment to rehabilitate criminals. Not surprisingly a variety of social experiments, including prison reform, attracted considerable interest among supporters of the Enlightenment.

While some Americans were embracing the Enlightenment's commitment to science and reason, others were swept up in the evangelical fervor of the **Great Awakening.** This religious revival movement attacked traditional styles of worship and replaced them with a more emotional style of religious devotion. Communities across America were divided into those in favor of the new style of religion and those opposed to it.

3.8 ***The Goals Committee of the House of Commons*** In William Hogarth's painting, members of Parliament involved in prison reform, including James Oglethorpe (second from the left), examine a prisoner. His tattered clothes and shackles reveal the inhumanity of Britain's prison system.

How did Georgia reflect Enlightenment ideals?

Georgia's Utopian Experiment

One of the most ambitious Enlightenment endeavors was the colony of Georgia, founded as an experiment to reform criminals and the poor by transplanting them from England to a more wholesome environment in America. James Oglethorpe, a spokesman in Parliament for humanitarian causes, secured parliamentary support for his plan to use colonization as an alternative to imprisonment. The new colony of Georgia, named for King George, was strategically located between the Carolinas and Spanish Florida, where it could provide a buffer against the Spanish.

Life in British prisons in the eighteenth century was harsh. At least half of those languishing in prison were debtors, whose crime was failing to pay their bills. Oglethorpe became a leading champion for prison reform and was appointed to a committee charged with investigating the nation's jails. The committee's work attracted the interest of artist and social critic William Hogarth. In this painting of Oglethorpe's committee, Hogarth presents a stark contrast between the elegantly dressed members of Parliament and a prisoner in rags who was "clamped in irons," a painful form of physical restraint commonly used in British prisons (**3.8**).

For Oglethorpe, removing prisoners from debtors' prison and sending them to a colony in America meshed perfectly with his vision for dealing with crime and poverty in Britain. In America the poor would have a fresh opportunity to earn a living and avoid the impoverishment they faced in England. Oglethorpe's vision for Georgia reflected the views of Enlightenment thinkers such as John Locke, who rejected the notion that humans were born depraved and could not be rehabilitated if placed in a healthier environment.

The 1732 charter granted Oglethorpe and the trustees of the colony of Georgia enormous power. To prevent the colony from becoming just another slave society in which a few enjoyed great wealth and the majority were poor, the trustees banned slavery. To promote sobriety the trustees also prohibited the importation of rum. Oglethorpe and the trustees soon confronted the same types of problems that earlier proprietary colonies had experienced (see Chapter 2). Settlers demanded a greater say in their affairs, including the right to import slaves (see *Competing Visions: Slavery and Georgia*). By 1738 the colony had abandoned much of its original vision, including its ban on importing both slaves and rum. Having begun as something of a utopian experiment, Georgia became another slave society in the lower South.

Although Enlightenment ideals helped shape the early history of Georgia, defense was never far from Oglethorpe's mind. His plan for the city of Savannah drew on the ideals of Renaissance city planning that had inspired the design of many other towns in the Americas (see Chapter 1), which Oglethorpe adapted to the colony's site on the frontier of Spanish America. His rectilinear plan drew on a tradition of designing military encampments stretching back to ancient Rome (**3.9**). Oglethorpe had dreamed of using Georgia as the launching point for the conquest of Spanish America, but his attack on the Spanish town of St. Augustine in Florida in 1740 failed. Two years later when the Spanish retaliated, Oglethorpe successfully repelled them. Georgia did not become a staging ground to root out the Spanish, but it was an effective barrier, protecting the colonies from Spanish attack.

American Champions of the Enlightenment

The Enlightenment championed the work of Sir Isaac Newton, the great English scientist and mathematician who invented calculus and explored the laws of motion, optics, and gravity. The Newtonian universe was radically different than the world that had produced the Salem Witchcraft accusations (see Chapter 2). Rather than look

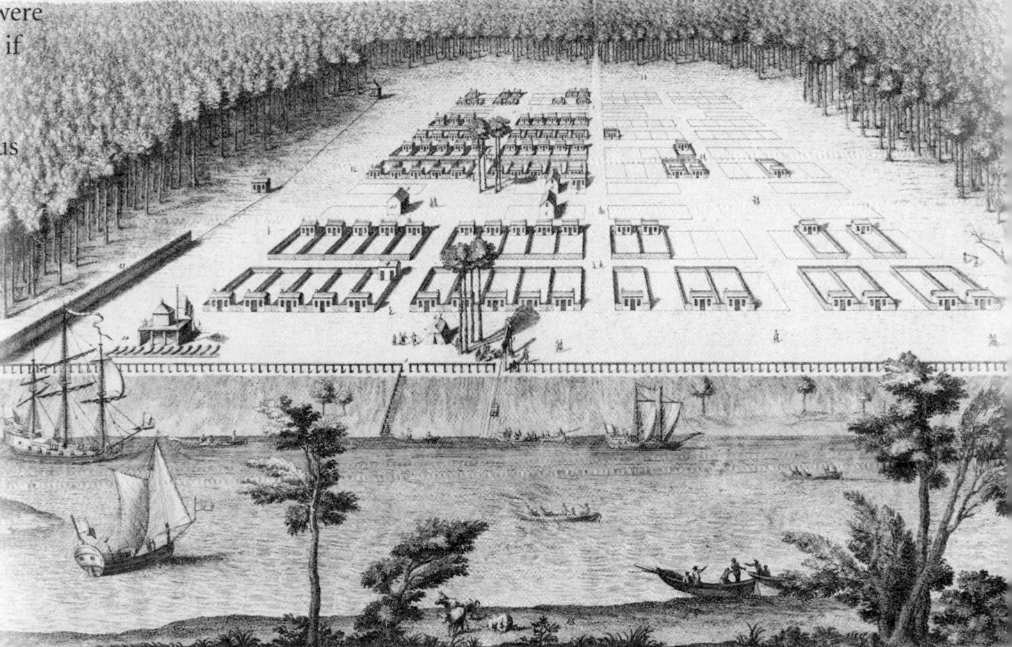

3.9 Savannah, Georgia
The layout of Savannah resembled a Roman military garrison, reflecting its strategic importance as a frontier outpost protecting the American colonies from Spanish America. [*Source:* Courtesy of the Georgia Historical Society]

What military function did Georgia serve?

Competing Visions

SLAVERY AND GEORGIA

James Oglethorpe viewed Georgia as an Enlightenment experiment that would demonstrate that the poor and debt-ridden could be rehabilitated if provided with the right environment. The desire of some colonists to import slaves threatened this vision. If Georgia turned to slave labor, it would become more like Carolina and Virginia. The profit motive would lead to the creation of the same types of inequalities that had led to the impoverishment of the debtors who had been the colony's first settlers. Why were some Georgians so eager to import slaves? What advantages did slave labor have over free labor in their view?

The Earl of Egmont, one of the leading trustees of the colony, made the following observations in his diary about the debate over introducing slavery into Georgia. In this first selection Egmont recounts the desires of colonists to import slaves into the colony.

Diary of the Earl of Egmont, 1735

Wednesday, 3 [September 1735]. The Scots settled at Joseph's Town having applied for the liberty of making use of negro slaves, we acquainted one of their number, who came over to solicit this and other requests made by them to us, that it could not be allowed, the King having passed an Act against it, of which we read part to him....

Monday, 17 [November 1735]. A letter was read from Mr. Samuel Eveleigh that he had quitted his purpose of settling in Georgia, and was returned to Carolina, because we allow not the use of negro slaves, without which he pretends our Colony will never prove considerable by reason the heat of the climate will not permit white men to labour as the negroes do, especially in raising rice, nor can they endure the wet season when rice is to be gathered in....

In this second extract from Egmont's diary, he details Oglethorpe's response to the demand that slavery be introduced into the colony.

Diary of the Earl of Egmont, 1739

Col. Oglethorpe wrote again to the Trustees, to show further inconveniences arising from the allowing the use of Negroes, viz. 1. That it is against the principles by which the Trustees associated together, which was to relieve the distressed, whereas we should occasion the misery of thousands in Africa, by setting Men upon using arts to buy and bring into perpetual slavery the poor people, who now live free there. 2. Instead of strengthening, we should weaken the Frontiers of America. 3. Give away to the Owners of slaves that land which was design'd as a Refuge to persecuted Protestants. 4. Prevent all improvements of silk and wine. 5. And glut the Markets with more of the American Commodities, which do already but too much interfere with the English produce.

TO BE SOLD on board the Ship *Bance-Yland*, on tuesday the 6th of *May* next, at *Ashley-Ferry*; a choice cargo of about 250 fine healthy

NEGROES,

just arrived from the Windward & Rice Coast. —The utmost care has already been taken, and

Slave Auction notice

Why did Georgia's trustees wish to retain a ban on slavery?

primarily to the invisible world of the supernatural, Newtonianism focused on the visible world of nature, which functioned according to the rules discerned by observation and interpreted by reason. Newtonianism was not antithetical to religion, but the god of the Newtonian universe was somewhat different from the traditional Christian notion of God as a patriarch or king. In the Newtonian vision God was the great clockmaker who fashioned the universe to run according to predictable natural laws.

In contrast to Newton's grand theorizing, the Enlightenment in America took a distinctly practical approach. No figure in America more closely approximated this ideal than Benjamin Franklin. Printer, scientist, reformer, and statesman, Franklin became a symbol of the American Enlightenment on both sides of the Atlantic. His international fame derived from his scientific experiments with lightning and electricity, which he published in 1751. Franklin coined the terms positive and negative to describe the nature of electrical current and theorized the possibility of creating a battery to store an electrical charge. Franklin also demonstrated that lightning was a form of electrical discharge. This insight led the practical-minded Franklin to develop the lightning rod. The device was designed to attract lightning and then conduct the current safely away from a building. American homes were generally built of wood, a plentiful material in most parts of the colonies that was extremely susceptible to damage by lightning. In a tribute to Franklin, John Adams wrote, "Nothing, perhaps, that ever occurred upon this earth was so well calculated to give any man an extensive and universal celebrity as the discovery of ... lightning rods." Franklin's close association with electricity in general and the lightning rod in particular was captured in this 1763 painting (**3.10**), which depicts Franklin at his desk with a lightning storm raging in the background and a lightning rod prominently positioned on a building visible through a window.

Franklin helped found the American Philosophical Society (1743), a learned society committed to the advancement of knowledge; the College of Philadelphia (1751) (later the University of Pennsylvania); and the Library Company, a private lending library. In addition to these institutions that reflected the Enlightenment's emphasis on education and the spread of knowledge, Franklin helped found a number of organizations dedicated to improving the lives of Philadelphians, including a fire company and the first public hospital in the colonies. Although Franklin owned slaves, as did many in Philadelphia, he eventually came to regard slavery as a great evil and vigorously opposed it later in his life.

3.10 Benjamin Franklin and Electricity
This contemporary painting of Franklin links him with his work on electricity. In the background, lightning destroys one building while another, to which Franklin's lightning rod is attached, survives a strike.
[*Source:* Mason Chamberlain (1727–1787), "Portrait of Benjamin Franklin". 1762. Oil on canvas, 50 3/8 × 40 3/4 inches (128 × 103.5 cm). Gift of Mr. and Mrs. Wharton Sinkler, 1956. Location: Philadelphia Museum of Art, Philadelphia, Pennsylvania, U.S.A./Art Resource, NY]

How does this portrait of Franklin reflect his reputation as a champion of the Enlightenment?

Awakening, Revivalism, and American Society

In the period between 1730 and 1770, the colonies experienced a series of religious revivals that historians group together as The Great Awakening. The resulting religious conflict divided families, split churches, and fragmented communities, forever altering the religious landscape of colonial America.

One of the early leaders of the revival movement, Gilbert Tennent, a New Jersey minister, attacked ministers for preaching an empty, "dead form of religion." Only by accepting the reality of sin and opening one's heart to grace could one hope to achieve salvation. Tennent also took aim at America's expanding consumer society and the "covetousness" that society had encouraged.

The leading intellectual champion of the Awakening was New England minister Jonathan Edwards, who captured the spirit of this movement when he wrote that "Our people do not so much need to have their heads" filled, as much as "have their hearts touched." Edwards's fiery sermon, "Sinners in the Hands of an Angry God" (1741), offered his parishioners a vision of the eternal fires of hell that awaited the unconverted. To shake his parishioners out of their complacency and remind them of the necessity of grace for salvation, Edwards compared their fate to that of a spider dangling above the pit of eternal damnation, with only God's mercy preventing them from falling in.

In 1757 Edwards became the president of the College of New Jersey (which became Princeton University), one of several new colleges founded by supporters of the Awakening to train a new generation of ministers. Princeton, allied to the Presbyterian Church, also had close ties to Scottish universities that were leading centers of Enlightenment thought. Rhode Island College (Brown University) was founded by the Baptists in 1764; Queens College (later Rutgers), by the Dutch Reformed Church in 1766. Dartmouth College was founded by the Congregationalist Eleazar Wheelock in 1769, originally as an Indian mission school.

"The God that holds you over the pit of hell, much as one holds a spider, or some loathsome insect, over the fire, abhors you, and is dreadfully provoked; his wrath towards you burns like fire; he looks upon you as worthy of nothing else, but to be cast into the fire."

JONATHAN EDWARDS, 1741

Edwards's account of his own Massachusetts revival inspired the English Anglican minister George Whitefield to take his evangelical crusade to the colonies. Whitefield's 1739–1740 tour was America's first genuinely inter-colonial event. The energetic English preacher traversed most of the eastern seaboard from New Hampshire to Georgia. His tour took advantage of improved roads and the expansion of inter-colonial shipping routes. He traveled the same routes as the merchants who hawked the latest English wares, and his gift for selling the gospel prompted one critic to describe him and other evangelical ministers as "Peddlers in Divinity." Whitefield attracted such large crowds that much of his preaching was done outdoors because few churches were big enough to hold his audience.

The Great Awakening changed American society. The evangelical methods employed by gifted preachers implicitly challenged the hierarchical assumptions of colonial society about gender, race, and social status. Individuals exercised greater choice, many chose to leave their own congregations and find one that better suited their spiritual needs. For some the Awakening provided opportunities to step forward as lay preachers. For the first time in American religious history, significant numbers of ordinary people were given a public voice. For those whose voices were seldom heard in public—women, blacks, artisans, or poor folk—the opportunity to testify, often to mixed crowds that included people like themselves or even their social betters, challenged traditional ideas about hierarchy. Mary Cooper, a resident of Long Island, noted in her diary that she heard an astonishing assortment of individuals preach, including a Quaker woman, a "Black man," and even two Indian preachers. By giving a voice to many groups previously excluded from traditional preaching, the Great Awakening contributed to the growth of a more democratic culture.

In a few cases women touched by the spirit began preaching, a decision that prompted their own ministers to denounce them for flouting the accepted roles assigned to women in colonial society. Testifying to one's religious experiences was one thing, but assuming the role of preacher, a role traditionally reserved for men, was simply too radical. After Bathsheba Kingsley stole a horse and rode from community to community preaching the gospel, Jonathan Edwards denounced her for perverting the spirit of revival. Edwards, wed to traditional ideas about women's roles, was horrified that Kingsley interpreted the Awakening's message as an invitation to become a gospel preacher.

Not all ministers approved of the ideas and methods of the revivalist preachers. Opponents of the revival, dubbed **Old Lights**, attacked the revivalists, or **New Lights**, for their excessive emotionalism. Old Light ministers ridiculed the revivalists for telling their congregants that "they were damned! damned! damned!" Rather than adopt the new, more emotional

What aspects of the Great Awakening encouraged democratization?

style, Old Lights continued to favor sermons based on learned explications of biblical texts. In response to this backlash against the Awakening, revivalist Reverend Gilbert Tennent accused his opponents of lacking "the Courage, or Honesty, to thrust the Nail of Terror into sleeping Souls." One New Light preacher, James Davenport, took the emphasis on emotionalism to an extreme, urging that books and sermons written by Old Light ministers be burned. As congregations divided between New Lights and Old Lights, many communities were pulled apart.

3.11
***Lamentation,* Moravian Painting of Christ**
This painting features the "blood of the savior." Jesus's physical pain and stoic endurance appealed strongly to American Indian men.

Indian Revivals

The Great Awakening also spilled over into Indian country. Indians won over by evangelical efforts often served as cultural mediators between their communities and the colonists. The Moravians, a German-speaking group of evangelical Protestants, were particularly effective at evangelizing among Indian tribes. In 1740 a large group of German Moravians migrated to Pennsylvania, where they settled in a town they named Bethlehem. Moravians also established communities in the Carolinas and Georgia.

Unlike the Calvinist faith of many English colonists, which shunned the use of images in their churches, the Moravians' Lutheran faith eagerly embraced the use of art as a means of promoting the gospels (see Chapters 1 and 2). In particular Moravians focused on the redemptive power of Christ's suffering as the foundation for religious salvation. Their most renowned artist in America, John Valentine Haidt, was well schooled in European styles of religious painting and used these techniques to translate the Moravians' Christian vision into visually rich images (**3.11**). The idea of Christ's suffering resonated with Indian converts, and the Moravians displayed images of the crucifixion to bring the gospel to the Indians. After viewing such pictures in the home of a Moravian missionary, two visiting Indians commented on "how many wounds he has, how much blood flows forth!" For American Indians Moravian religious imagery of Jesus suggested a brave spiritual warrior, an ideal that resonated in the minds of young male Indians, whose conception of masculinity was based on a martial ideal of physical strength, bravery, and the endurance of pain and suffering.

The Great Awakening touched a small but influential group of Indians; a different type of native religious renewal movement had an even larger impact on American Indians. As early as 1737 reports began filtering back from Indian country, the broad swath of territory from western Pennsylvania to French-controlled land in Illinois, that Indian religious leaders were preaching the need for a return to traditional ways and a complete separation from colonists. The alcohol that Europeans traded with Indians had contributed to rising levels of alcoholism among Indians. In the 1760s the Delaware Indian prophet Neolin championed the revival of traditional beliefs and the rejection of European influences. He urged his people to "learn to live without any Trade or Connections with White people." In place of dependency and trade, he counseled "Clothing and Supporting themselves as their forefathers did." Neolin and other prophets of Indian revitalization traveled as itinerants through Indian territory preaching their message. Indian revivalists attacked Indian involvement with and dependence on the world of trade and commerce with Europeans.

Why was Moravian art so helpful to missionaries interested in converting American Indians?

African Americans in the Colonial Era

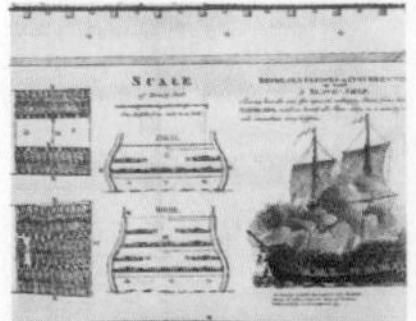

By the dawn of the eighteenth century, racial slavery had become a central feature of the Atlantic world, with firm roots in parts of British North America. The greatest demand for slaves came from the sugar-producing regions of Brazil and the Caribbean. An additional 300,000 slaves arrived in the British mainland colonies, with the greatest demand for their labor in the plantation economies of the upper and lower South. The highest proportion of slaves lived in the lower South, where Africans actually outnumbered Europeans. Slavery in British North America was not an exclusively southern phenomenon. Slaves were an important part of urban life in New York, Philadelphia, and Boston. Slavery also played a significant part in the economies of the mid-Atlantic and New England.

Slavery was a brutal and exploitative labor system, but the experience of individual slaves varied greatly from region to region. Regardless of where they were and under what circumstances they lived, slaves found a variety of ways to resist their masters' domination. Occasionally they turned to violent forms of resistance, but more often they used various kinds of economic sabotage—pretending sickness, destroying tools, or even running away—to undermine the profitability of slavery. Perhaps even more significant were the slaves' attempts to assert their humanity and create lives beyond the reach of the master's dominion. Establishing families in spite of the ever-present threat of being torn from one's loved ones and sold, building a viable community, and practicing their own religion gave slaves the cultural resources to survive and denied their masters complete control over important parts of their lives.

The Atlantic Slave Trade

Slaves had been traded internally within Africa for centuries; indeed, it took several hundred years for the Atlantic slave trade to surpass the internal African slave trade. The demand for agricultural labor in the Atlantic world created a strong market for African slaves and led to a dramatic increase in the trans-Atlantic slave trade at the end of the seventeenth century. The leading participants in the international slave trade in the seventeenth century had been Spain, Portugal, and Holland, but by the eighteenth century, Britain had become the preeminent slave-trading nation in the Atlantic world.

> "The stench of the hold ... became pestilential. The closeness of the place, and the heat of the climate, added to the number in the ship, which was so crowded that each had scarcely room to turn himself, almost suffocated us."
>
> OLAUDAH EQUIANO, *The Life of Olaudah Equiano* (London, 1789)

As the map (**3.12**) shows, the vast majority of slaves in the Atlantic trade ended up in one of the sugar colonies. Portuguese sugar production was centered in Brazil, while Dutch, French, and British sugar production was centered in the Caribbean. Only about 4 percent of the slaves imported from Africa were transported to the American colonies, but the significance of slavery to the British mainland American colonies was enormous.

Travel across the Atlantic was harrowing under the best of circumstances; in the case of the slave trade, the ordeal was horrendous. The brutality of slavery began far from the Atlantic coast of Africa in the inland regions, where slave catchers acquired most slaves. The captive slaves were then bound by ropes or wooden yokes and forcibly marched to the coast, where they were housed in pens. To prevent communication among captives and reduce the

Which regions of the Atlantic world imported the most slaves?

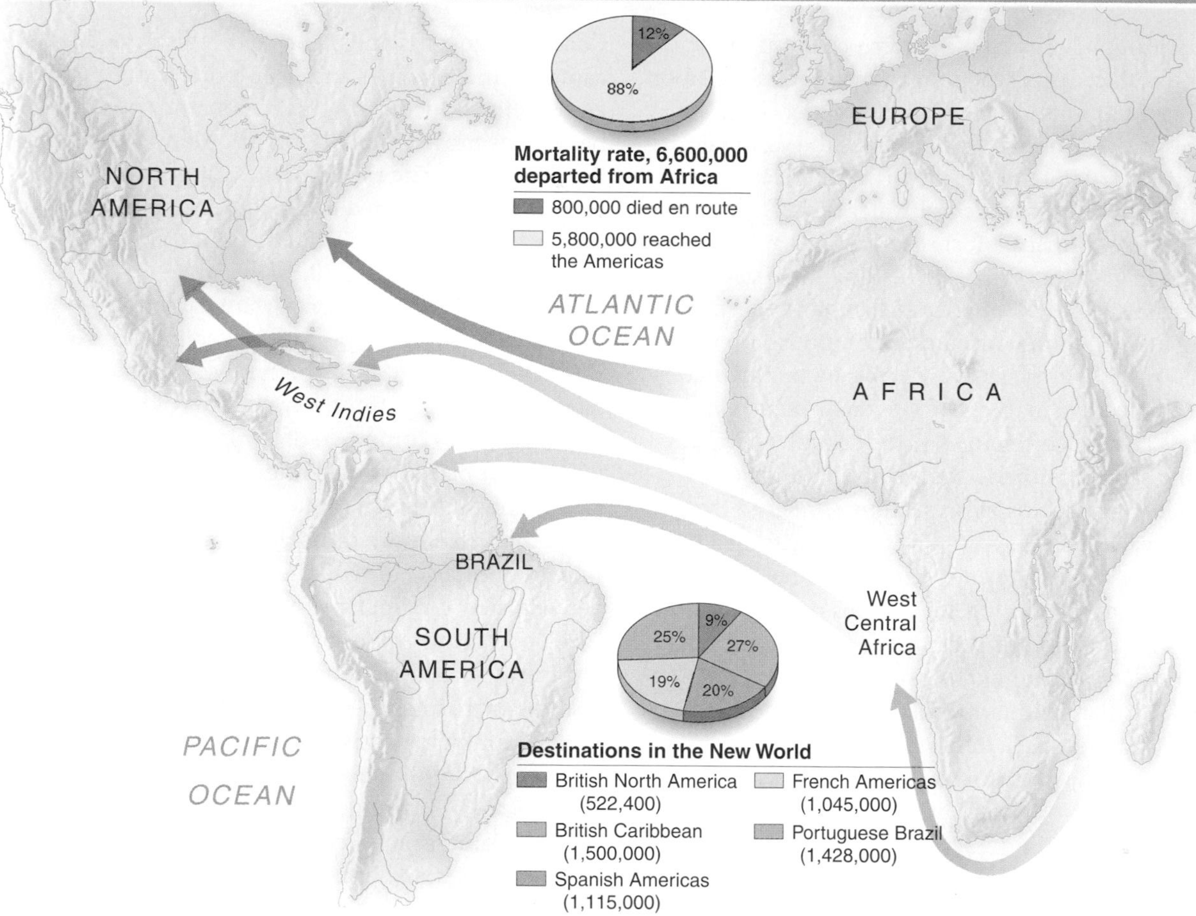

3.12 The Atlantic Slave Trade This map and the corresponding pie charts show the involvement of various nations in the slave trade in the eighteenth century. British slave traders transported the largest share of slaves, selling most to the sugar plantation owners on the islands of the British Caribbean and Brazil. Slave imports to the British American mainland were about a third of the number destined for the sugar islands of the Caribbean.

chances of slaves organizing themselves to escape or challenge their captors, the slave catchers often separated individuals from the same ethnic or language groups. They also routinely separated family members from one another. Slaves might remain housed in these deplorable and inhumane conditions for months before being boarded on slave ships bound for the Americas.

The voyage across the Atlantic from Africa to the Americas, known as the **middle passage**, was horrific. The cramped conditions on these voyages depicted in this antislavery petition barely convey the ordeal of this journey (**3.13**). Typically their captors forced the slaves to remain in shackles during the voyage. Slaves endured meager rations and unsanitary conditions, a situation that led some who preferred "death to such a life of misery" to drown themselves. Of those transported, a little over 10 percent died en route to the British colonies.

In the seventeenth century most slaves bound for the British mainland colonies in America came first to the Caribbean, where they were "seasoned," a process of physical and psychological adjustment to the rigors of plantation slavery. Afterward they would make the final leg of the voyage to the

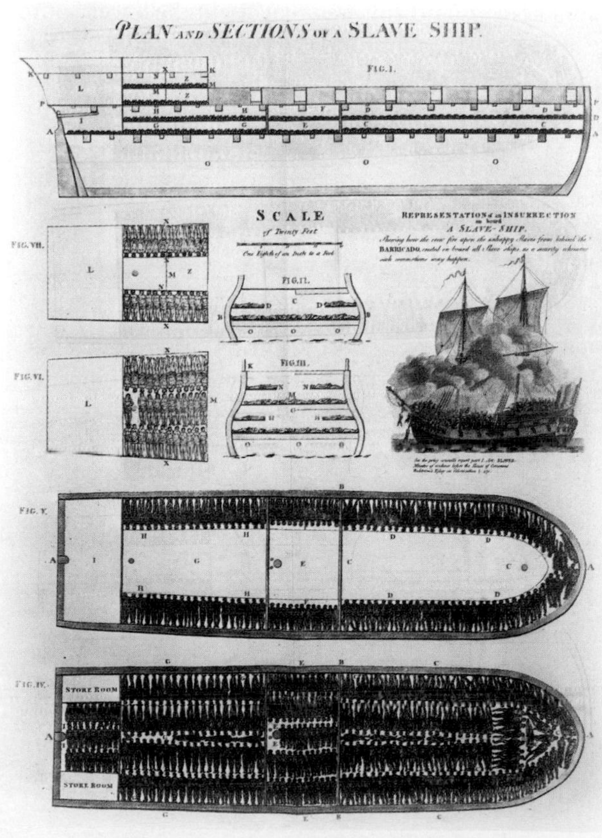

3.13 Tight Packing This abolitionist depiction of tight packing shows the cramped conditions on slave ships, which maximized the number of bodies carried with no concern for the health of the slaves transported. [*Source:* The Art Archive/Picture Desk, Inc./Kobal Collection]

American mainland. This pattern changed in the eighteenth century when the demand for slave labor increased dramatically, and many traders chose to bypass the seasoning process. Thus the vast majority of slaves arriving in British North America in the eighteenth century were "saltwater slaves," coming directly from Africa. Most slaves arrived at Sullivan's Island in Charleston harbor, leading some scholars to describe it as Black America's Ellis Island (page 506).

After being unloaded and quarantined on Sullivan's Island, slaves were typically transported for sale in the slave markets of the major port towns and cities. This was often the last time family members would see each other. After being subjected to a humiliating process of inspection, similar to that used by livestock buyers, slaves were auctioned off to their new masters. Even if family members had managed to remain together to this point, they now faced the prospect of permanent separation from their loved ones. Thus the experience of the auction block further traumatized slaves who had already suffered a multitude of horrors on their perilous journey from Africa to America.

Southern Slavery

The two regional subcultures in the colonial South—the lower and the upper South—had distinctive slave labor systems and cultures. Slavery in the lower South (parts of the Carolina and Georgia low country) had evolved as the region moved from a frontier settlement to an integrated part of the Atlantic slave economy. In the upper South slavery had gradually replaced indentured servitude (p. 83) as the main source of labor by the end of the seventeenth century.

The lower South began as a colony of a colony. Carolina was first conceived as a base for supplying food to the Caribbean sugar islands. The colony also traded captured Indian slaves and deer hides. In the 1690s rice was introduced into this region and soon became its most profitable export. Many slaves had learned to cultivate rice in Africa, and their knowledge contributed to the increase in rice production from a mere 12,000 pounds in 1698 to 18 million pounds in 1730.

In the 1740s another important cash crop—indigo, a bluish dye—was introduced into the region. By the 1730s, when the Carolinas were divided into North and South Carolina, two-thirds of the region's population was composed of African slaves. The vast majority of blacks worked under a task system that gave them considerable autonomy over their work. Once their tasks were completed, slaves might use the time to hunt, fish, or tend their own gardens, which allowed them to supplement their meager diets.

The swampy regions of the Carolina low country were fertile breeding grounds for a variety of tropical diseases, including malaria. Africans had developed partial immunity to this disease, but whites of European descent were extremely susceptible. Given the unhealthy environment of the coastal lowlands, wealthy planters preferred to spend much of the year at their Charleston homes. The large number of white absentees and the continuous influx of slaves from Africa helped blacks living in this region to preserve aspects of their African heritage despite the deprivations of slave life. The conical-shaped, thatched-roofed huts in the slave quarters on Mulberry plantation (**3.14**), South Carolina, reflect the influence of African architectural styles on this region.

Slavery in the upper South, the Chesapeake region, differed markedly from its practice in the low country Carolinas. While the task system worked for rice cultivation, growing tobacco, the dominant crop in the Chesapeake region, demanded much more oversight. The plants were easily damaged if not properly tended, so planters preferred to organize their slaves into gangs that worked together under the watchful eye of a white overseer or a black slave driver chosen by the master.

Slaves in the Chesapeake were a minority, and they lived on plantations typically smaller than those found in the lower South. Although slaves in this region preserved some elements

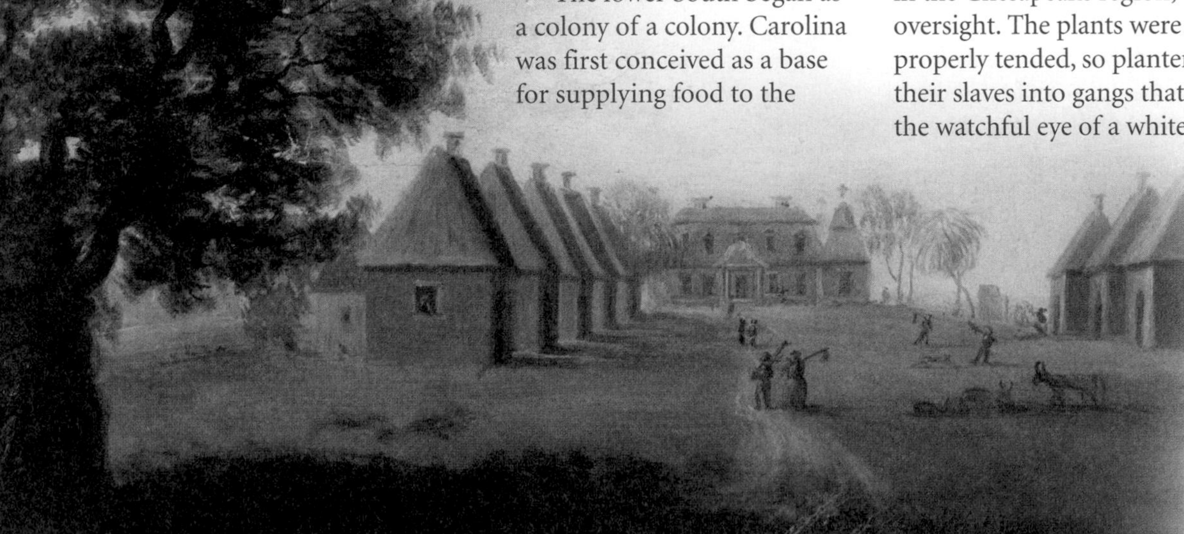

3.14 Slave Quarters, Mulberry Plantation, South Carolina The conical design of these slave cabins, including their thatched roofs, drew on West African architectural influences.

What were the main differences between the task system and the gang system of labor?

of traditional African culture, their smaller numbers and wider distribution made their African cultural heritage more difficult to preserve.

Northern Slavery and Free Blacks

Although slavery was less vital to the colonial economy outside of the South, it did play an important role in some areas and regions. For example, in parts of New York and New Jersey, the slave population might be 15 percent in some places and as high as 30 percent in others. Typically slaves in the rural North worked as field hands on small family farms. Northern slavery also included a sizeable urban population, where slaves generally worked as domestics in wealthier homes. In seaport towns and cities, slaves worked in a variety of maritime occupations. In Pennsylvania slaves were so essential to iron manufacturing that their masters petitioned the assembly to lower tariffs on slave imports so that they could continue to produce iron.

A small community of free blacks emerged and settled in northern cities such as Philadelphia, New York, and Boston. Slaves gained their freedom by several means. Some were freed by masters who recognized the evil of slavery. One of the earliest groups to condemn slavery was the Quakers. Other slaves, particularly those who had learned a skill such as carpentry, might be able to strike a bargain with their owners and gain the right to work for themselves part time, eventually saving enough money to buy their own freedom. While a small percentage of freed slaves became farmers, many ended up in one of the thriving seaport towns and cities where economic opportunities were greater.

Urban settings also provided African Americans in the North with more cultural opportunities. In both New York City and Albany, the African American communities adapted the Dutch religious holiday of "Pentecost" and turned it into a carnival-like festival they named "Pinkster." The holiday was presided over by an African American figure, "King Charles," who acted as the political leader of his community during the holiday. During Pinkster African Americans participated in music, dancing, and festive meals; they also paraded as part of their African "different nations," an explicit demonstration of their African roots.

The Great Awakening helped spread Christianity to slaves across America and also made inroads among free blacks in the North. The German evangelical sect, the Moravians, was particularly aggressive in preaching the gospel to slaves in North Carolina. Jonathan Edwards, himself a slave owner, reported that several slaves in his own community had embraced the revival. Some evangelical groups such as the Methodists encouraged free blacks to attend their revival meetings. The new more emotional style favored by so many Awakening preachers appealed to African Americans because it more closely resembled traditional African styles of religious practice.

Slave Resistance and Rebellion

The growth of slavery at the end of the seventeenth century led colonial governments to take legal steps to ensure that African slaves remained subservient to their white masters (see Chapters 2). The slave codes adopted at the end of the seventeenth century gave masters almost unlimited authority over their slaves. The codes also legally defined as slaves children born to slave mothers, even when fathered by free whites.

Although deprived of any legal means to protect themselves, slaves developed a range of strategies for coping with the horrors of slavery and escaping the domination of their masters. Stealing, shirking responsibility, feigning illness, or breaking tools: all of these actions deliberately slowed the pace of their work and provided some temporary relief. Some slaves chose to run away. Sometimes runaways simply hid in the woods or sought refuge with a family on nearby plantations, hiding out in slave quarters. Avoiding the white slave patrols that were always on the lookout for runaways made this a risky option. In those parts of the South closer to Indian country or Spanish territory, including parts of the Carolinas and Georgia, slaves might try to find refuge in territory beyond the control of the English colonists.

Slaves who took part in South Carolina's Stono Rebellion of 1739 took advantage of the colonies' close proximity to Spanish Florida. The rebels broke into a storehouse and seized arms, murdered whites, and torched the homes of slave owners. The rebels hoped that other slaves would rally to their standard, and some slaves from the surrounding countryside did join the rebellion, whose numbers rose to around 150. The slave rebels hoped to find refuge in Spanish Florida. The Carolina militia intercepted the rebels before they could reach Spanish Florida, and the better-organized and armed militia routed the Stono rebels, slaughtering them by the dozens and subsequently executing those who survived. In response to the Stono Rebellion, South Carolina passed harsher slave codes and temporarily blocked importation of slaves into the

How did slaves resist the authority of their masters?

> "Many of the white people in these provinces take little or no care of Negro marriages ... they often part men from their wives by selling them far asunder."
>
> JOHN WOOLMAN, Journal, 1774

region, a ban that was soon lifted because of the economic importance of slave labor. The Stono Rebellion was the largest African American uprising in the colonial era, but it would not be the last in the history of American slavery.

An African American Culture Emerges under Slavery

Most slaves did not adopt rebellion as their primary strategy for challenging the authority of their masters. Simply establishing families, building an African American community, and practicing their own religion were more realistic goals for most slaves—but all were extremely difficult to achieve given the constraints imposed by slavery. Forming a family under slavery was not easily accomplished. For one thing, the sex ratio among slaves during much of the colonial period was sharply skewed, with many more males than females. During the early years of the slave trade, slave owners preferred males for the backbreaking work required in the tobacco or sugarcane fields, so most slaves imported into the Americas were male; the odds of a male slave finding a wife were slim. During the eighteenth century, as more slaves were born in America, the sex ratio became more balanced because roughly comparable numbers of boys and girls were born. But even if the chances of a man finding a mate increased, slavery made family formation difficult at best. Slave marriages had no legal standing, so slaves faced the constant threat of separation from their spouses. The decision to break up slave families rested entirely with the master, and many children were sold off from the rest of their family. On relatively small plantations slaves usually sought a spouse on a neighboring plantation, which left couples at the mercy of masters who could easily withhold visiting privileges and prevent husbands and wives from seeing one another. Nevertheless many slaves did manage to find partners and create stable families.

One of the many aspects of traditional African culture preserved by slaves was naming practices. As was customary in many parts of West Africa, slave parents might name their children after the day of the week on which they were born. Plantation records commonly show West African names like Cudjo (Monday) for boys or Cuba (Wednesday) for girls, evidence that slaves continued to honor their ancestral practices.

Slaves also drew on African traditions in shaping distinctive music and dance forms, which provided an outlet for cultural expression. Using African techniques they constructed musical instruments, including a variety of drums and stringed instruments. Masters typically found African styles of dancing and singing exotic and alien to their European sensibilities. One British visitor to Maryland noted that on Sundays, the one day that masters generally allowed slaves to rest, blacks met "to amuse themselves with Dancing," which was a "most violent exercise." This rare colonial-era painting of slaves dancing not only illustrates the intensity of African-inspired dance but also shows the importance of an African-style instrument that would become a fixture in American music—the banjo (**3.15**). Music could serve ulterior purposes as well. Shortly after the Stono Rebellion, South Carolina banned drumming, fearing that slaves could drum and communicate secret messages from one plantation to another.

3.15 Slaves Dancing and Playing Banjo This image of slaves dancing in the slave quarters prominently features a banjo. The instrument was modeled on an instrument that was well-known in Africa.

What evidence exists for the persistence of African cultural traits among American slaves?

Immigration, Regional Economies, and Inequality

Although distinctions of wealth emerged almost immediately in American society, especially in the cities, the relative abundance of land in the seventeenth century allowed many rural colonists to own their own land, a goal almost unattainable in Europe, where most land was owned by the aristocracy. Even in cities those without a farmstead generally earned higher wages than they would have in Europe because labor commanded a higher price in the colonies, where skilled craftsmen were rarer. Although all of these facts contributed to the prosperity of the colonists, population growth (natural increase and immigration) and the dwindling availability of land became serious problems by the middle of the eighteenth century. In the colonies' expanding cities, the gulf between the rich and poor widened, and in rural areas young people faced the prospect that they might not be able to obtain land for their own farms.

Immigration to the Colonies

The population of British North America expanded rapidly in the eighteenth century. Between 1700 and 1750 the white population of the colonies rose from around 250,000 to more than a million. In contrast to America's first predominantly English colonists who arrived at the start of the seventeenth century, eighteenth-century immigrants varied in national origin and ethnic identity. As chart **3.16** illustrates, the colonies attracted settlers from elsewhere in Britain, including Scotland, Ireland, and Wales. Immigration from the European continent also included large numbers of Dutch and Germans.

The decision to immigrate to America was a momentous one. The financial and personal costs of immigration could demand heavy sacrifices. The trans-Atlantic crossing, which could take as long as four months, meant enduring cramped conditions on a ship with few amenities. Additionally, the cost of the trans-Atlantic passage was well beyond the yearly wages of the average Englishman and even more expensive for those traveling from the European continent. To finance their passage many immigrants, men and women alike, contracted to work as **indentured servants**. In exchange for having their passage paid, indentured servants agreed to work for a specified period of years, usually seven. In some cases the indenture system separated family members, with husband and wife indenturing themselves to different families.

Regional Economies

By the middle of the eighteenth century, the British had settled the eastern seaboard, from the southern colony of Georgia to the northern New England colony of New Hampshire. Although each of the thirteen colonies functioned as its own separate political unit, historians have grouped the colonies into five regions—New England, the mid-Atlantic, the upper South, the lower South, and the back country—reflecting their unique histories,

3.16 Eighteenth-Century Immigration to the Colonies
During the eighteenth century, the number of non-English immigrants increased. Immigrants from other parts of the British Empire, including Scotland and Ireland, rose as well. Another major source of immigration was continental Europe, especially Germany and Holland. One-fifth of this population of immigrants were enslaved Africans.

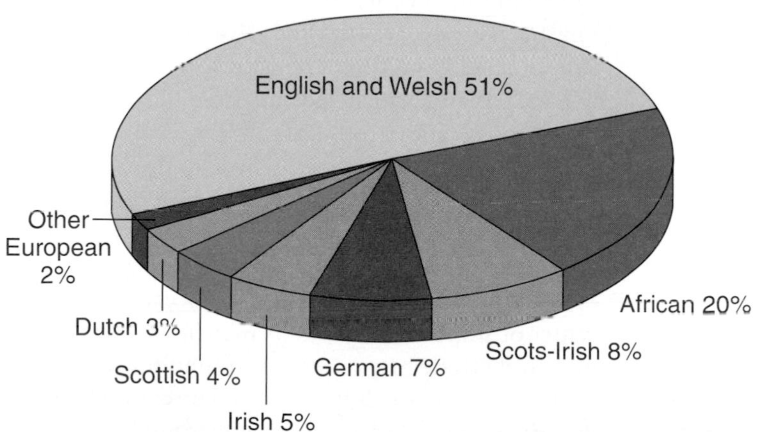

3.17 Map of Colonial Regions
By the middle of the eighteenth century, colonial America had evolved into a number of distinctive regions: New England, mid-Atlantic, upper South, lower South, back country.

distinctive patterns of settlement, and diverse economies (**3.17**). Race, ethnicity, and religious composition also lent a distinctive quality to each of the major regions of colonial America.

New England

New England (Connecticut, Massachusetts, New Hampshire, and Rhode Island) was the most ethnically homogenous region in colonial British America (see 3.17). Overwhelmingly white and English, the Congregational Church, the heir of the Puritan tradition, was the dominant religion in New England. In addition New England included several other Protestant churches—Anglicans (Church of England), Presbyterians, Quakers, and Baptists. This lent some religious diversity to the region, particularly in Rhode Island, which had embraced the principle of religious toleration from its founding.

The sea had always been central to the New England economy, but in the eighteenth century the region's maritime economy expanded dramatically. New England continued to supply fish to a variety of domestic and foreign markets, it became a major center of shipbuilding, and its merchants carried on a lively trade in a variety of commodities. Yankee trade in spirits—including the amber-colored dessert wine of Madeira, an island group in the eastern Atlantic, and rum, distilled from molasses procured in the Caribbean—was vital to New England's commercial economy.

The ministerial elite continued to play an active role in shaping the affairs of the region, but the rising merchant class became increasingly powerful over the course of the eighteenth century. Many of the region's leaders were educated at Harvard (1636), the oldest college in the colonies, or Yale (1701).

The Mid-Atlantic

The mid-Atlantic (New York, Pennsylvania, New Jersey, and Delaware) was the most ethnically diverse region in the colonies, and its hubs, New York and Philadelphia, were home to a wide range of ethnic and religious groups (see 3.17). Indeed as this engraving (**3.18**) of the eighteenth-century New York skyline illustrates, the spires and bell towers of the city's churches and lone synagogue proclaimed its religious diversity for miles around.

Philadelphia and New York became centers of commerce and finance. Each city boasted a thriving port, facilitating trade with Europe and coastal trade with other ports in the Atlantic world. Agricultural products from rural Pennsylvania and Delaware were sold in the markets of Philadelphia. New York's Hudson River carried agricultural products from upriver farms and furs from northern New York. The mid-Atlantic region had a variety of small manufacturing enterprises as well, including flour milling, lumbering, mining, and metal foundries. The region depended on indentured servants for much of its labor. In the period between 1700 and 1775, about 100,000 servants came from the British Isles and another 35,000 from German-speaking regions on the European continent.

Although Quakers were a powerful force in Pennsylvania politics, the region's merchant class was even more influential. The mid-Atlantic region was somewhat slower to create colleges than either Massachusetts or Virginia, but by the middle of the eighteenth century, Pennsylvania was home to the College of Philadelphia, 1755 (University of Pennsylvania), George III had chartered Kings College, 1754 (Columbia), in New York, and the College of New Jersey, 1746 (Princeton), and Queens College, 1766 (Rutgers), had been established in New Jersey.

Which region of colonial America was the most culturally diverse?

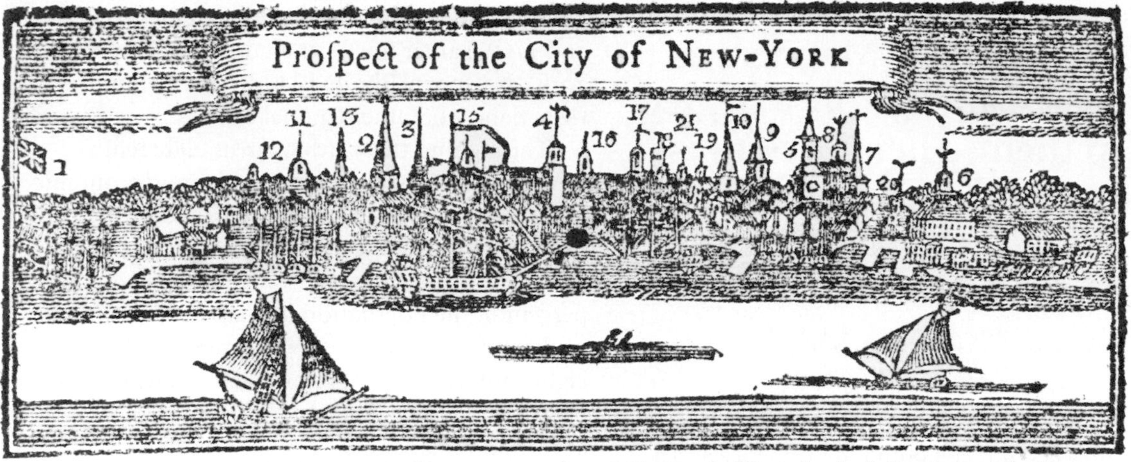

1 Fort George	6 The Priſon.	11 Old Dutch Church	16 Quaker's Meeting
2 Trinity Church	7 New Brick Meeting	12 Jew's Synagogue	17 Calviniſt Church
3 Presbyter. Meeting	8 King's College	13 Lutherian Church	18 Anabaptiſt Meeting
4 North D. Church	9 St. Paul's Church	14 The French Church	19 Moravian Meeting
5 St. George's Chapel	10 N. Dutch Cal. Church	15 New Scot's Meeting	20 N. Lutheran Church
			21 Methodiſt Meeting

3.18 Engraving of New York Skyline
This engraving of New York's skyline lists a score of churches and synagogues whose spires dominated the skyline of the colonial town.

The Upper and Lower South

The South was most closely tied to slave labor. Actually it was two distinct regions: the upper South, or Chesapeake Region, and the lower South, including parts of South Carolina and the Georgia lowcountry (see 3.17). Each produced different cash crops and employed slave labor in slightly different ways. Immigration into the two regions and the ethnic composition of the upper and lower South was also different.

Although somewhat more ethnically diverse than New England, the upper South, those areas of Virginia and Maryland tied to the Chesapeake, drew immigrants largely from England and Scotland. The powerful planter elite who dominated this region built great fortunes from tobacco grown on plantations with slave labor. Many of the area's wealthiest citizens were educated at the College of William and Mary (1693), the nation's second-oldest college.

The lower South was settled later than the Chesapeake, and so the region benefited from the growth of immigration to America. As a result of its later settlement, the region was also more religiously diverse than the upper South. In addition to Anglicans the region included Presbyterians, German Moravians, Baptists, and Quakers.

The damp, hot climate of the lowcountry regions bred diseases such as malaria. To avoid these conditions the wealthiest planters spent only part of the year on their plantations in the unhealthy lowcountry. Many preferred their second homes in Charleston, which became a major cultural and economic center of the region. Nevertheless Charleston lacked an educational institution comparable to William and Mary, so the wealthiest Carolinians typically headed to England for their education.

The Back Country

In the early days of settlement during the seventeenth century, colonists had hugged the coastline. By the eighteenth century they began pushing westward to areas such as the interior of the Carolinas, western Pennsylvania, and Virginia (see 3.17). Many new immigrants headed directly for the back country. The Scots-Irish were particularly attracted to the back country of Pennsylvania and the Carolinas, where they settled in large numbers.

The back country region lacked many of the refinements that the older, more settled regions of the colonies possessed, leading travelers to compare back country colonists with Indians. In the comparison both were described as savages.

Whatever their similarities to Indians might have been, relations between them were generally strained. Rather than seek to trade with Indians and learn their ways, the Scots-Irish wanted to create farmsteads, which required displacing Indians. The simmering tensions between residents of the back country region and the local Indians would occasionally erupt into violence throughout the eighteenth century.

Back country settlers farmed, hunted, and raised livestock for their own consumption and for local trade and were less well connected to the burgeoning Atlantic economy. The economic realities of life in the

What were the main cash crops produced by slave labor in the South?

> "They were as rude in their Manners as the Common Savages, and hardly a degree removed from them. Their Dresses almost as loose and Naked as the Indians, and differing in Nothing save Complexion."
>
> Minister CHARLES WOODMASON, observations on the back country, 1766

back country encouraged both independence and a strongly egalitarian culture. Courts were rare and so were tax officials or other representatives of either the colonial or the British government. A visitor to this region would also have noticed a lack of churches, primary schools, and institutions of higher education.

Cities: Growth and Inequality

Although the vast majority of Americans lived in the countryside during the eighteenth century, cities were growing. Philadelphia boasted 23,000 residents by 1760, making it the largest city in the colonies. Still America was far less urban than either Europe or even the Spanish colonies to the south. Compared to London, with more than 700,000 people, Philadelphia was tiny. Britain's mainland American colonies were also far less urbanized than Spain's empire in the Americas. There were a half dozen cities in Spanish America larger than Philadelphia. Mexico City, for example, had more than 100,000 inhabitants by the middle of the eighteenth century.

Although small in size, the growth rates of the cities of colonial British America were impressive. Boston, for example, doubled in size between 1700 and 1760. Larger towns, including Albany (New York), Newport (Rhode Island), and Baltimore (Maryland), became regional centers.

Throughout these urban areas eighteenth-century society became polarized along economic lines. The percentage of wealth owned by the richest Americans increased, and the number of poor people rose as well. In Boston and Philadelphia 5 percent of the population had amassed almost half of their city's wealth by the last quarter of the eighteenth century. At the same time the number of the urban poor rose dramatically in Boston, New York, and Philadelphia. The graph (**3.19**) illustrates the dramatic climb in the amount of money Boston devoted to poor relief from the middle of the century onward. During this same period many trades and crafts established their own mutual benefit societies to help the poor. The stark inequality between the lives of the destitute and those of Boston's wealthiest merchants, who lived in fine new mansions and traveled around the city in elegant coaches, grew more pronounced, especially by the last quarter of the eighteenth century.

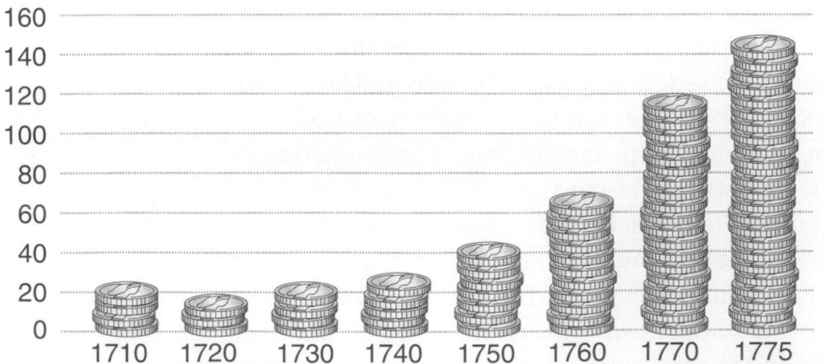

3.19 Poor Relief, Boston
Poverty increased in colonial Boston in the late eighteenth century, as did the poor relief needed to deal with this problem.

Rural America: Land Becomes Scarce

By the middle of the eighteenth century, many Americans living in the countryside or in small towns in most of the settled regions of the colonies confronted a growing scarcity of land. The problem Connecticut's colonists faced illustrates the interconnected issues of population growth and land scarcity. Between 1720 and 1760 Connecticut's population more than doubled, from 59,000 to 142,000. Beginning in the 1740s children faced the prospect that their parents would not have enough land to help them establish their own farm when they became adults.

Many sons and daughters delayed marriage until they could acquire a farmstead and establish their own independent household. Others moved to nearby towns. Many of Connecticut's young adults went as far as northern New Hampshire, and others left New England altogether, heading to the most western parts of New York, Pennsylvania, Virginia, or the Carolinas. Finally, some families simply postponed their dreams of independence, working as tenants on another farmer's land as they struggled to save enough money to purchase their own farm.

Why was American society becoming more unequal toward the end of the eighteenth century?

War and the Contest Over Empire

By the middle of the century, nearly 1.2 million people lived in the British mainland colonies, making it a far more densely populated region than New France, which numbered well under 100,000. Britain and France had been almost constantly at war since the late seventeenth century. Although these wars were generally fought over conflicts that originated in Europe, control of North America became increasingly important to both nations. The British were keen to eliminate French influence in Canada and the Great Lakes region. Eliminating France also appealed to American colonists, who viewed the rich agricultural lands controlled by France as a means of alleviating the land shortage they faced. The struggle between the British and the French for control of North America would dramatically alter the map of North America.

The relatively small population of New France was spread across a vast territory, from Quebec in the north to New Orleans in the south, and as far west as Illinois (see map 3.20). In the Great Lakes region, French traders lived and worked among the Indians, often marrying Indian women. Unlike the British, who sought to displace the tribes and resettle the land with small farmers, the French developed a complex multiracial society that included Indians.

The Rise and Fall of the Middle Ground

When the seventeenth century began, more than two million Indians lived in communities east of the Mississippi River. Lacking immunity to diseases brought by the Europeans, Indian populations who came into contact with Europeans were extremely vulnerable to infection. Tribes east of the Mississippi were repeatedly devastated by epidemics that reduced their numbers to less than a quarter million by the end of the eighteenth century. One response to this dramatic decrease in population was the rise of "mourning wars," in which rival tribes raided each other's villages and took prisoners to bolster their own populations. In these wars men were often tortured and executed, but women and children were typically adopted into the conquering tribes.

Indians were also increasingly drawn into the trans-Atlantic economy, exchanging furs for a variety of European goods, including beads, fabric, alcohol, metal tools, and even firearms. The growing European demand for furs, and increased Indian desires for European goods, led to conflict among different tribes for access to prime hunting and trapping grounds. The nature of intertribal warfare changed as limited mourning wars evolved into "beaver wars," in which Indian tribes fought one another for control of territory.

Further west in the Great Lakes region, France, not Britain, was the dominant power. In this region the French and Indians created a **middle ground**, a cultural and geographical region in which Indians and the French negotiated with each other for goods and neither side could impose its will on the other side by force. Indians traded furs for guns, metal tools, and cloth.

While the French colonial government had hoped to regulate and tax this lucrative trade by establishing a series of forts, or outposts, a group of young, fiercely independent French traders, known as *coureurs des bois* ("runners of the woods"), established their own trading networks beyond the direct control of the French government. Many married Indian women, producing children who became a distinctive group called *métis*, or people of mixed French and Indian descent. Familiar with both Indian and French customs, and fluent in both Indian languages and French, the *métis* became critical intermediaries between Indian and French cultures, even when the gulf was sometimes difficult to bridge. Like other European societies, French culture was patriarchal: Inheritance passed from father to son, a practice that gave fathers enormous power over their sons. Thus it was quite natural for the French to cast themselves as fathers to their Indian children in the Great Lakes region. Indians accepted the notion of the French as fathers, but they

What made the middle ground a distinctive region of colonial America?

understood the concept of fatherhood in radically different terms than Europeans did. In the Indian cultures of the middle ground region, fathers were not powerful patriarchs. Indeed one chief tried in vain to explain to one French colonial official the different views of paternal authority in their respective cultures: "When you command, all the French obey and go to war. But I shall not be heeded and obeyed by my nation in such a manner." Although a significant gulf continued to exist between the two cultures, intermarriage between French traders and Indian women nevertheless promoted cultural exchange and mutual understanding.

"Go and see the forts our [French] Father has created, and you will see that the land beneath their walls is still hunting ground ... whilst the English, on the contrary, no sooner get possession of a country than the game is forced to leave; the trees fall down before them, the earth becomes bare."

Contemporary Indian account of the French and English settlement, late eighteenth century

The expansion of British settlement beyond the Appalachian Mountains threatened the middle ground created in the Great Lakes region. Rather than seek to preserve a middle ground, the British hoped to incorporate this region into their colonial empire. As had been true for so much British colonization, the idea was to eliminate indigenous populations, transplant British agricultural practices, and establish permanent settlements.

The Struggle for North America

The great military powers of Europe—Britain, France, and Spain—remained locked in a struggle for political supremacy in Europe. In 1739 European conflicts once more spilled over into North America when Britain again went to war, this time with Spain. British ships smuggled goods into Spanish America depriving Spain of valuable trade and tax revenues. Spain responded by capturing British ships, seizing their crews and cargos. British outrage over Spanish policy reached a critical moment when Captain Robert Jenkins testified before Parliament that after capturing his ship, the Spanish placed him in custody and cut off his ear as punishment for his alleged smuggling. Jenkins presented his ear in a pickle jar to an outraged Parliament. The resulting conflict between Britain and Spain was dubbed the War of Jenkins' Ear (1739–1748).

Although war with Spain dragged on until 1748, King George's War (1744–1748), a conflict in which France joined with Spain against Britain and the American colonies, soon overshadowed the War of Jenkins' Ear. The most important military victory from the colonists' point of view occurred at Louisbourg. New England's militias achieved a stunning triumph over the French and seized the mighty fortress of Louisbourg, which guarded Atlantic access to the Gulf of St. Lawrence and French Canada. Although the fortress was returned to the French by the British as part of the peace treaty ending the conflict, the victory, which relied heavily on New England's militia, became a source of colonial pride.

The conflict between France and Britain occurred during a period when colonists were particularly eager to settle in the Ohio Valley, a region controlled by the French. The formation of the Ohio Company of Virginia in 1747 greatly facilitated the exploration and settlement of this region, a development that prompted the French to solidify their hold on the region by establishing a string of forts (**3.20**). The most important of these was Fort Duquesne, erected at a fork in the Ohio River in what is now Pittsburgh. Eager to dislodge the French from Duquesne, in 1755 the royal governor of Virginia dispatched a force of militiamen under the command of an ambitious young officer, George Washington, to seize the strategic fort. Overwhelmed by a force of French and Indian warriors, Washington was forced to surrender.

Washington's defeat proved to be only the first skirmish in a protracted battle to control the Ohio territory. The British dispatched General Edward Braddock with a larger force, comprising British regular troops and colonial volunteers, to take Fort Duquesne. The French and their Indian allies routed Braddock's forces. Washington had escaped, but Braddock was killed in battle and his troops suffered

Why did British expansion threaten the middle ground?

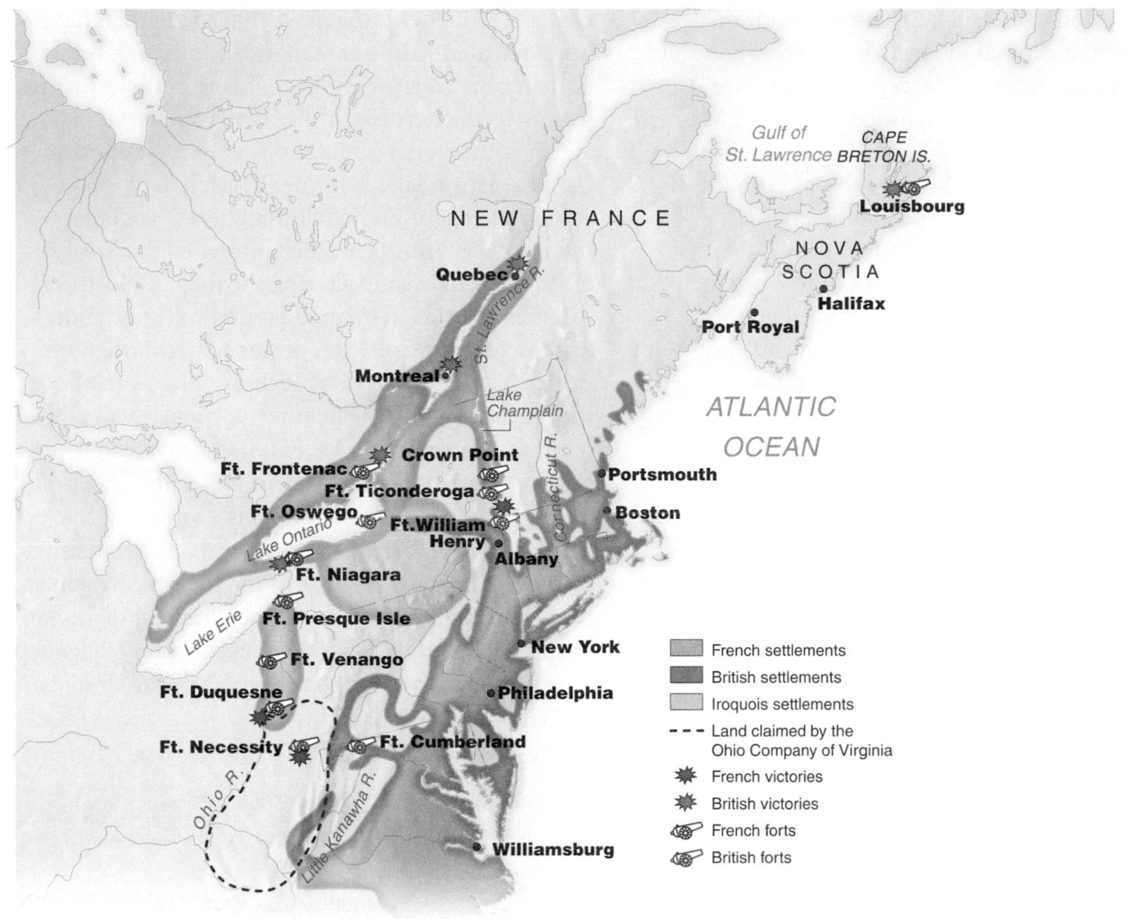

3.20 British Conquest of New France
The British and French battled one another across a huge arc of territory, fighting pivotal battles at Louisbourg, Quebec, and Montreal.

a staggering 70 percent casualty rate. It was a shocking and ignominious defeat for the British and their colonial allies.

It would be two years before the British developed an effective military strategy in response to Braddock's humiliating defeat. Meanwhile, relations between American colonists and the Indian peoples along the frontier continued to deteriorate. Many tribes were emboldened by the French victory to settle old scores with American colonists. In particular, angry Delaware and Shawnee tribes, who resented western expansion into their hunting grounds, confronted Scots-Irish settlers on the frontier of Pennsylvania. Armed conflict along the frontier disrupted the lives of colonists and Indians, resulting in death and injury for both communities.

In England William Pitt, the ambitious prime minister appointed by George II, believed that the future balance of power in Europe hinged on control of America. In 1757 the British embarked on a bold new policy: to root out the French and make a direct assault on the French strongholds of Quebec City and Montreal. Pitt promoted a number of young, talented officers including Jeffery Amherst and James Wolfe to lead the campaign against Canada. An army of ten thousand regulars and a sizeable fleet was dispatched to Canada. Defeating the French meant taking on their Indian allies as well, and so the conflict was known as the French and Indian War.

The British suffered an early setback when the French general Montcalm seized the British Fort William Henry on Lake George in northern New York.

What was William Pitt's new policy for North America?

Although Montcalm had negotiated a traditional surrender that allowed the British to retreat honorably, his Indian allies refused to accept these terms and sought scalps and other trophies of war. "The Massacre of Fort William Henry" alienated Montcalm from his Indian allies and stiffened the resolve of both the British and the colonists to defeat the French.

British fortunes began to turn when a force under Jeffery Amherst captured Louisbourg fortress in 1758. A year later British forces assailed the city of Quebec and captured it. General Wolfe, the commander of British forces, searched for a weakness in the city's formidable defenses and finally settled on a daring assault strategy. Wolfe and his men approached the city from its poorly guarded rear flank. Rather than risk a frontal assault on the heavily fortified city, Wolfe's men scaled the heights behind the city and overpowered the small detachment of troops guarding the cliffs. In the battle that followed, Wolfe and his French counterpart General Montcalm were both killed.

Pennsylvania painter Benjamin West commemorated the assault on Quebec in his painting, *The Death of General Wolfe* (1771) (**3.21**). West shows the dying general cradled in the arms of one of his officers. Contemporary viewers would have recognized this arrangement from European painting and sculpture: the position of Jesus sprawled across the Virgin Mary's lap after the crucifixion. To heighten the sense of drama in West's painting, a British soldier runs toward the dying General Wolfe with the news that the French have been defeated, while an American Indian, a symbol of the noble warrior, looks on respectfully, a further tribute to the heroism of the British general.

The other great population center in French Canada, Montreal, fell to the British in late 1760, ending the era of French domination in Canada. In early 1763 France and Britain signed the Treaty of Paris, permanently altering the map of North America. Quebec remained French culturally, but Britain now controlled all of Canada. Although the British had defeated the French in Canada, relations with Indians along the frontier, particularly in Ohio, remained tense. In 1762 the Indian revivalist prophet Neolin's pan-Indian movement rallied the tribes of the Midwest against further British colonial expansion. A year later the Ottawa Indian chief, Pontiac, led a pan-Indian force against the British garrison at Fort Detroit. Inspired by Pontiac's leadership, Indian peoples across the Midwest attacked weakly defended frontier garrisons in what is now Michigan, Indiana, and Ohio and even launched attacks against settler communities in western Pennsylvania, in what the

3.21 ***The Death of General Wolfe*** West cast the dying Wolfe in the same pose artists used to depict Jesus after the crucifixion. The messenger arriving with the news of victory enters the scene from the light-filled area of the painting, symbolizing the bright future of North America after the British victory. [*Source:* Benjamin West (1738–1820), "The Death of General Wolfe," 1770. Oil on canvas, 152.6 × 214.5 cm. Transfer from the Canadian War Memorials, 1921 (Gift of the 2nd Duke of Westminster, England, 1918). Photo © National Gallery of Canada, Ottawa, Ontario.]

What role does the Indian figure play in West's painting?

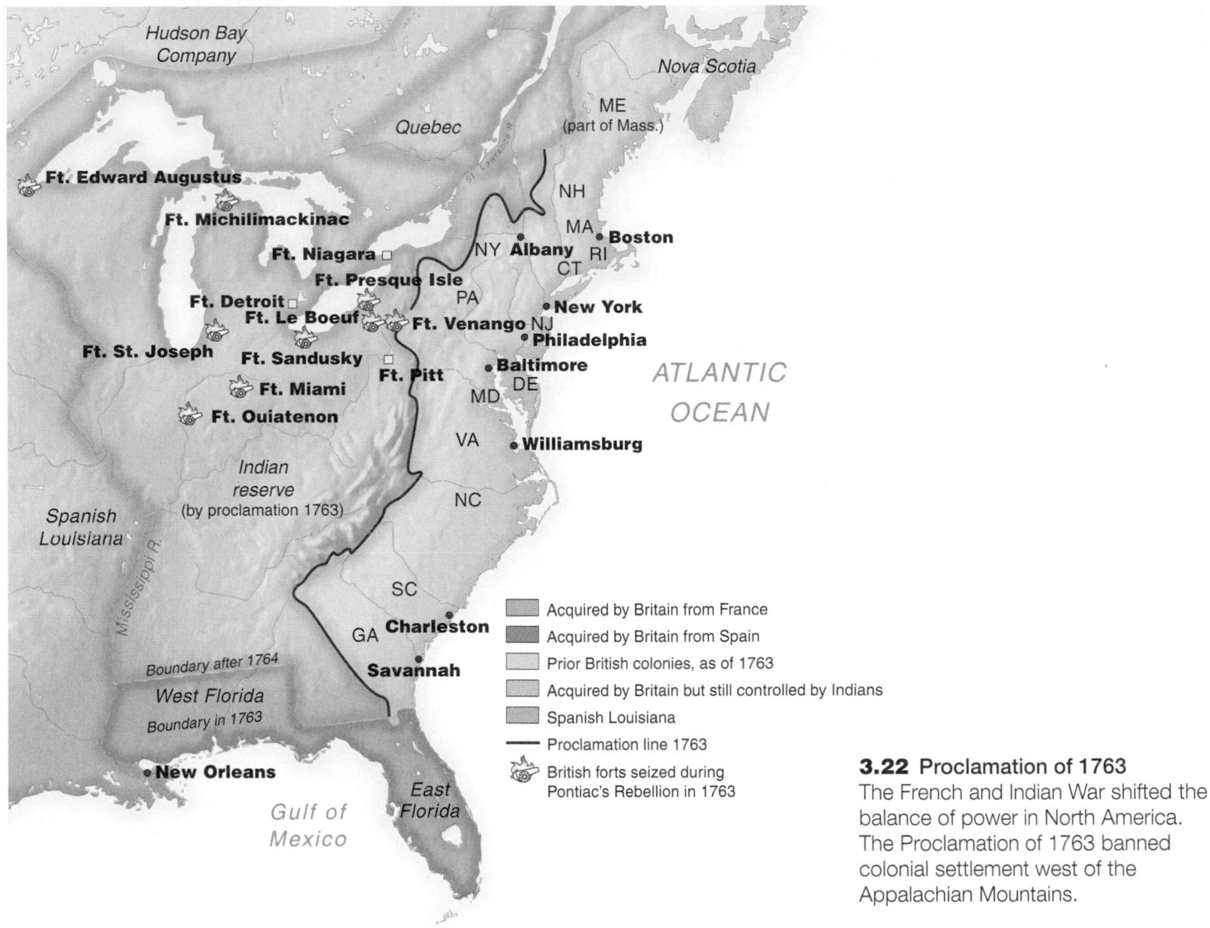

3.22 Proclamation of 1763
The French and Indian War shifted the balance of power in North America. The Proclamation of 1763 banned colonial settlement west of the Appalachian Mountains.

colonists called Pontiac's Rebellion. Anger over the failure of the colonial governments to protect frontier settlers led to protests by western residents. The most dramatic protest occurred in Pennsylvania, where settlers from the frontier settlement of Paxton sought revenge by attacking friendly Indians and marching against the city of Philadelphia demanding the creation of a militia to fight Indians. The march of the "Paxton Boys" might have plunged Pennsylvania into widespread bloodshed, but violence was averted after a group of leading Philadelphia citizens met with the protestors and agreed to present their list of grievances to the colonial assembly. (See *Choices and Consequences: Quakers, Pacifism, and the Paxton Uprising*, page 92.)

Before the defeat of the French in Canada, western Indians could count on a reliable supply of arms and ammunition from Britain's traditional rival, France. Without this vital support the pan-Indian alliance eventually collapsed. Still Pontiac's Rebellion persuaded the British to be conciliatory toward the more powerful tribes along the frontier. The peace treaty that was signed to end hostilities with Indians not only included favorable terms for trade but also placed severe restrictions on westward expansion by colonists. The Proclamation of 1763 (**3.22**) established a fixed line beyond which colonial expansion westward was prohibited, effectively restricting colonists to territory east of the Appalachian Mountains.

Choices and Consequences

QUAKERS, PACIFISM, AND THE PAXTON UPRISING

Relations between Pennsylvanians and Indians had steadily deteriorated over the course of the eighteenth century as the population grew. Newcomers, such as the Scots-Irish who dominated the backcountry, began to challenge the Quakers' political power. The violence associated with Pontiac's Rebellion only exacerbated these simmering tensions. Western settlers, including the Paxton Boys, petitioned the Quaker-dominated colonial assembly to pass a mandatory militia law and provide arms for western settlers. Quakers, however, were pacifists who continued to believe that it was possible to maintain peaceful relations with their Indian neighbors. Quakers in the assembly faced a difficult decision.

Choices

1 Support a mandatory militia law and create a well-regulated militia, properly trained and armed.

2 Continue to oppose the creation of a well-regulated militia and continue to seek peaceful non-violent solutions to Indian–settler conflicts.

3 Resign from elected office so that their pacifism would not prevent the assembly from voting to create a militia.

Decision

The legislature chose to continue its pacifist policies.

Consequences

Pennsylvania was the only colony without a militia law. This issue continued to spark controversy until the American Revolution. The 1776 Pennsylvania Constitution and Declaration of Rights not only created a militia but also it became the first state to expressly protect a right to bear arms.

Continuing Controversies

Why were Quakers so obstinately against creating a well regulated militia?

Scholars sympathetic to the plight of the Paxton supporters view their challenge to the Quaker government as an expression of the rising tide of democratic sentiment that helped bring about the American Revolution. For those more sympathetic to the Indians, the Quaker government's policies were as exceptional as they were praiseworthy.

Paxton Uprising cartoon

Why did Paxtonians demand that the Quakers create a militia?

Conclusion

The transformation of the American colonies from a crude provincial backwater to a more refined, prosperous hub of the British Empire occurred slowly over the course of the eighteenth century. A British traveler to Philadelphia, then the largest city in America, would have been impressed by the fine houses, elegant coaches, and other signs of America's refinement and gentility. The visitor would also have been struck by the signs of Enlightenment in the city: a fine lending library, the American Philosophical Society, and a new university. The city hosted scientists of international renown, such as Benjamin Franklin, the man who had tamed lightning. A visitor to the colonies might also have encountered the great evangelist George Whitefield, on one of his tours. Even if one missed hearing the "peddler in divinity," one could read about his exploits in the expanding press.

Not everyone shared equally in the growing prosperity and refinement of America. African slaves toiled under harsh conditions in rice fields or tended tobacco in the South, while slavery solidified in urban areas and seaport towns in the mid-Atlantic and New England. Many ordinary laborers in towns and cities and the farmers in the countryside faced fewer opportunities to improve their economic conditions as the century progressed. The enormous growth in the population of the British colonies meant that land was becoming scarce. Colonists looked at the fertile lands of the Ohio country as a possible source to alleviate this problem. The French and their Indian allies, however, were eager to prevent further expansion by English colonists. The French and Indian War settled the future of this important region. The decisive defeat of the French removed the main threat to American colonists and a major competitor for the potential wealth of Indian country, including trade opportunities and land.

Although colonists may have viewed the defeat of the French as opening up vast new territory for settlement, the British government in London wanted to maintain peaceful relations with the powerful Indian nations that inhabited these regions. The need to pay off the war debt and the conflict over the future of western lands would put colonists and their rulers in London on a collision course.

1728

Massachusetts House battles Crown over permanent salary for the royal governor

Massachusetts House and the royal governor disagree over salary, an important indicator of the growing power of colonial legislatures

1728

New York's Jewish community builds the first synagogue in British North America

New York's pluralistic society expands to include Jews as well as Christians

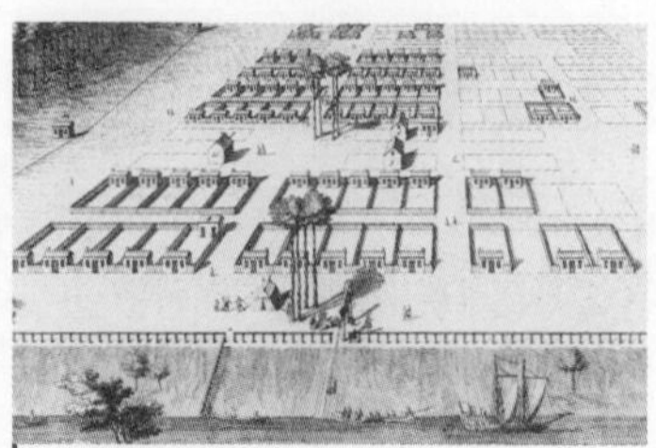

1732

James Oglethorpe founds Georgia to rehabilitate the poor

A utopian experiment and a buffer between Carolina and Spanish Florida, Georgia eventually accepted slavery and became a plantation society

Benjamin Franklin founds Library Company

America's first circulating library

Review Questions

1. How did changes in architecture and home furnishing reflect Anglicization and the rise of gentility in colonial America?
2. What accounts for the growth and power of the lower house of the assembly as one of the most powerful institutions in colonial America?
3. What were the leading Enlightenment ideals, and what was the significance of America's role in that movement? In what ways did the colony of Georgia strive to embody Enlightenment ideals?
4. Who were the "Old Lights," and how did their religious beliefs and practices differ from the "New Lights"?
5. Why were Moravian missionaries so successful at converting Indians?
6. How did the experience of slavery differ between the upper South and the lower South?
7. Where did slavery have the greatest impact in the mid-Atlantic and New England?
8. How did the scarcity of land affect Americans before the French and Indian War?
9. How did the French and Indian War affect colonial–Indian relations? What new problems did the British victory create for the empire?

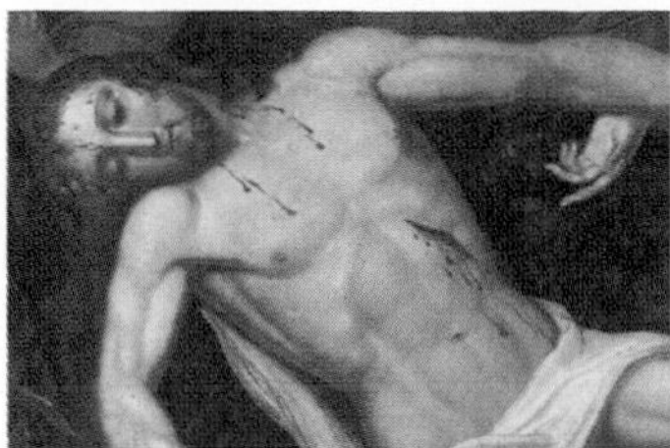

1735–1739

First Moravian community established in America in Savannah, Georgia
Moravians, an evangelical Protestant sect from Germany, bring their message to America

English preacher George Whitefield arrives in America and embarks on a tour that generates new enthusiasm for religious revival
The great evangelical preacher creates an inter-colonial sensation and extends the reach of the Great Awakening

War of Jenkins' Ear
British fight Spain, and later France

1741–1751

Academy of Philadelphia founded (later renamed the University of Pennsylvania)
Franklin helps found the University of Pennsylvania

Benjamin Franklin publishes his experiments on electricity
Earns Franklin fame and symbolizes America's contribution to the Enlightenment

Eliza Pinckney introduces indigo to South Carolina
The sought-after dye produced by indigo became Carolina's second most important export

1759

Quebec falls to British troops under General Wolfe
The decisive battle in the French and Indian War signals the defeat of the French in Canada

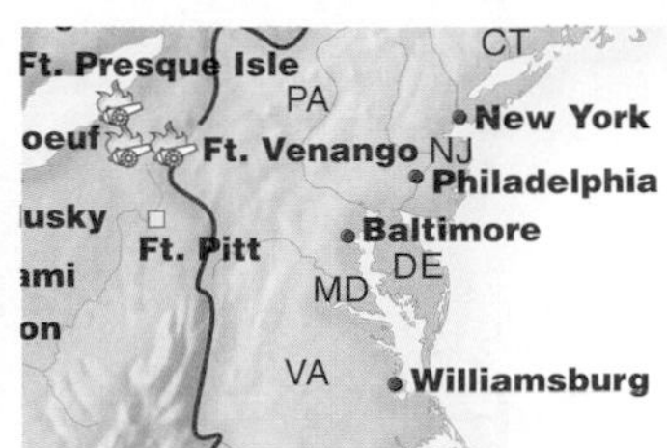

1763

Proclamation of 1763 closes land west of the Appalachians to colonial settlement
To prevent further encroachment on Indian lands and avoid future conflicts, Britain forbids colonial settlement beyond the Appalachian Mountains

Treaty of Paris between Britain and France ends French and Indian War
The formal end of hostilities legally acknowledges British domination in North America

Key Terms

Anglicization The colonial American desire to emulate English society, including English taste in foods, customs, and architecture. **67**

virtual representation A theory of representation in which legislators do not serve their localities but rather the whole nation. **71**

Enlightenment An international philosophical movement that extolled the virtues of reason and science and applied these new insights to politics and social reform. **72**

Great Awakening A religious revival movement that emphasized a more emotional style of religious practice. **72**

Old Lights Opponents of the Great Awakening who favored traditional forms of religious worship. **76**

New Lights Supporters of the Great Awakening and its more emotional style of worship. **76**

middle passage The harrowing voyage across the Atlantic from Africa to the Americas during which slaves endured meager rations and horrendously unsanitary conditions. **79**

indentured servants A form of bound labor in which servants had their passage to America paid in return for a specified number of years of service. **83**

middle ground A cultural and geographical region of the Great Lakes in which Indians and the French negotiated with each other for goods and neither side could impose its will on the other. **87**

CHAPTER 4

Revolutionary America

Change and Transformation, 1764–1783

> "Yesterday the greatest question was decided … and a greater question perhaps never was nor will be decided among men. A resolution was passed without one dissenting colony, that these United Colonies are, and of right ought to be, free and independent states."
>
> JOHN ADAMS, 1776

Britain's decisive victory in the French and Indian War in 1763 removed the French threat to its American empire. But the war had been expensive to wage, and the ongoing costs of administering and protecting North America nearly drained the British economy. To pay these costs Britain adopted a new set of policies for America, including new taxes, more aggressive ways of collecting them, and more severe methods of enforcing these measures. The colonists viewed these policies as an ominous first step in a plot to deprive them of their liberty.

When King George III assumed the British throne in 1760, monarchism was deeply rooted in American culture, and Americans were proud of their British heritage. Opposition to British policy began with respectful pleas to the king for relief from unjust policies. Gradually, over the course of the next decade, Americans became convinced that it was no longer possible to remain within the British Empire and protect their rights. Resistance to British policies stiffened, and the colonists eventually decided to declare independence from Britain.

Tensions between Britain and the American colonies reached a boiling point with the Tea Act, the theme of this cartoon, *The Tea-Tax-Tempest.* In the image "Father Time" displays the events of the American Revolution to four figures who symbolize the four continents. The "magic lantern" shows a tea pot boiling over, symbolizing revolution, while British and American military forces stand ready to face one another.

The notions of liberty and equality that Americans invoked in their struggle against British tyranny changed American society. The idea that "all men are created equal" and that every person enjoyed certain "inalienable rights," as America's Declaration of Independence asserted, were radical ideas for those who had grown up in a society that was ruled by a king and that enthusiastically embraced the idea of aristocracy.

The Revolution did bring about some radical changes in American society. New England effectively eliminated slavery after the Revolution. The new states of the mid-Atlantic adopted a more gradual approach to abolishing slavery. In the South, however, where slavery was deeply entrenched and men made huge fortunes from crops produced with slave labor, only modest gains were made in promoting the abolition of slavery. Although not yet full political participants, revolutionary notions of equality led women to demand that husbands treat them as partners in their marriage. A new idea of companionate marriage blossomed.

How did the Revolution's idea of liberty transform American society?

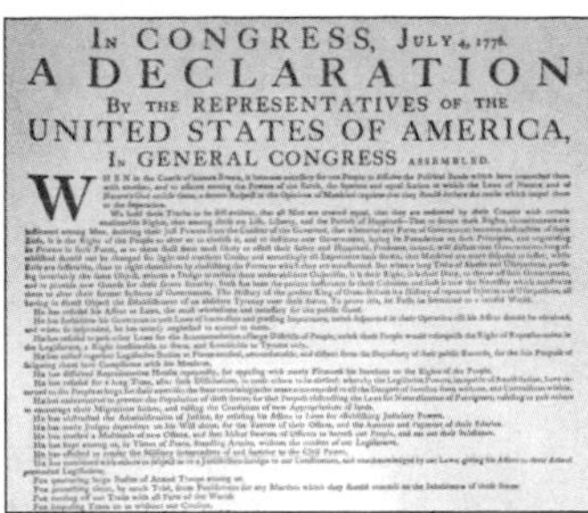

In CONGRESS, July 4, 1776.
A DECLARATION
By the REPRESENTATIVES of the
UNITED STATES OF AMERICA,
In GENERAL CONGRESS assembled.

Tightening the Reins of Empire

The British victory in the French and Indian War in 1763 secured North America against French attack. It also forced the British government to chart a new direction for dealing with America. A cornerstone of the new policy was the Proclamation of 1763, which prohibited settlement in lands west of the Appalachian Mountains (Chapter 3). Having just fought an expensive war against the French, the British were keen to prevent colonists and Indians from starting a new war. Britain also felt a renewed urgency to raise funds to pay off the war debt and cover the costs of administering the colonies.

Taxation without Representation

In 1763 George Grenville, the new prime minister, ordered a detailed investigation of colonial revenues and was unhappy to discover that American customs' duties produced less than £2,000 sterling a year. The lucrative trade in molasses between British North America and the Caribbean islands alone should have yielded something like £200,000 a year, apart from all of the other goods traded between North America and Britain, which should also have generated customs duties. To make the colonies pay their share of taxes, Grenville was determined to enforce existing laws and enact new taxes to bring in additional revenue.

The first step in Grenville's new program was the Revenue Act (1764), popularly known as the **Sugar Act**. It lowered the duties colonists had to pay on molasses, but taxed sugar and other goods imported to the colonies and increased penalties for smuggling. It also created new ways for enforcing compliance with these laws. Violators could be prosecuted in British vice-admiralty courts, which operated without jury trials. For some Americans the Sugar Act violated two long-held beliefs: the idea that colonists could not be taxed without their consent and the equally sacred notion that Englishmen were entitled to the right of trial by jury of their peers.

An outspoken critic of the new British policy was the Massachusetts lawyer James Otis, who attacked the Sugar Act as a violation of the rights of Englishmen. Otis had already achieved notoriety for his earlier opposition to the use of writs of assistance by customs officials. Otis insisted that under British law, one could only issue a search warrant for a specific premises where there was probable cause to suspect illegal activity. Rather than require that officials designate where they intended to search, the new general writs allowed customs officials to search any private property without first demonstrating probable cause or seeking the approval of a magistrate. In his pamphlet attacking the Sugar Act, *The Rights of the British Colonies Asserted and Proved*, Otis denied that the British had the authority to tax the colonists without their consent. Otis stopped short of recommending active resistance to the Sugar Act. Rather he counseled patience, reminding his readers that we "must and ought to yield obedience to an act of Parliament, though erroneous, till repealed."

While Americans viewed the new tax on sugar and other imports as a burden and a violation of their rights, for the British, the taxes were a modest imposition necessary

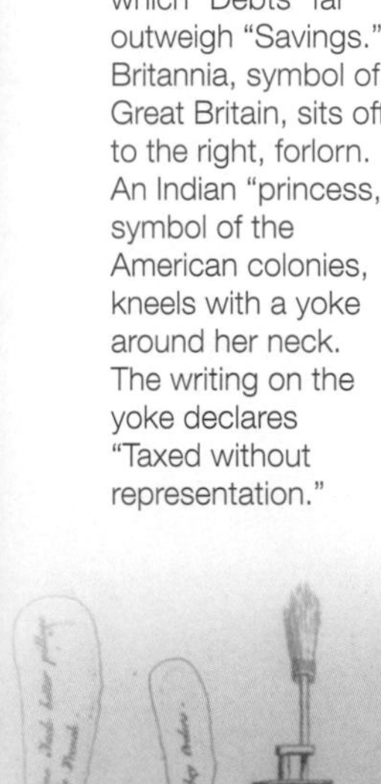

4.1 *The Great Financier* Prime Minister George Grenville holds a balance in which "Debts" far outweigh "Savings." Britannia, symbol of Great Britain, sits off to the right, forlorn. An Indian "princess," symbol of the American colonies, kneels with a yoke around her neck. The writing on the yoke declares "Taxed without representation."

Why is the scale in the cartoon, *The Great Financier,* out of balance?

> "The very act of taxing exercised over those who are not represented appears to me to be depriving them of one of their most essential rights as freemen."
>
> JAMES OTIS, *The Rights of the British Colonies Asserted and Proved* (1764)

to pay for the cost of eliminating the French from North America and administering the colonies. This political cartoon (**4.1**), which shows Grenville holding a balance in which "debts" clearly outweigh "savings," shows Britain's financial predicament. The British cartoonist who drew this obviously sympathized with Americans. He shows a Native American "princess," the most common symbol of the colonies in British cartoons, carrying a sack of money and bearing a heavy yoke around her neck. Inscribed on the yoke is the colonists' rallying cry: "No taxation without representation."

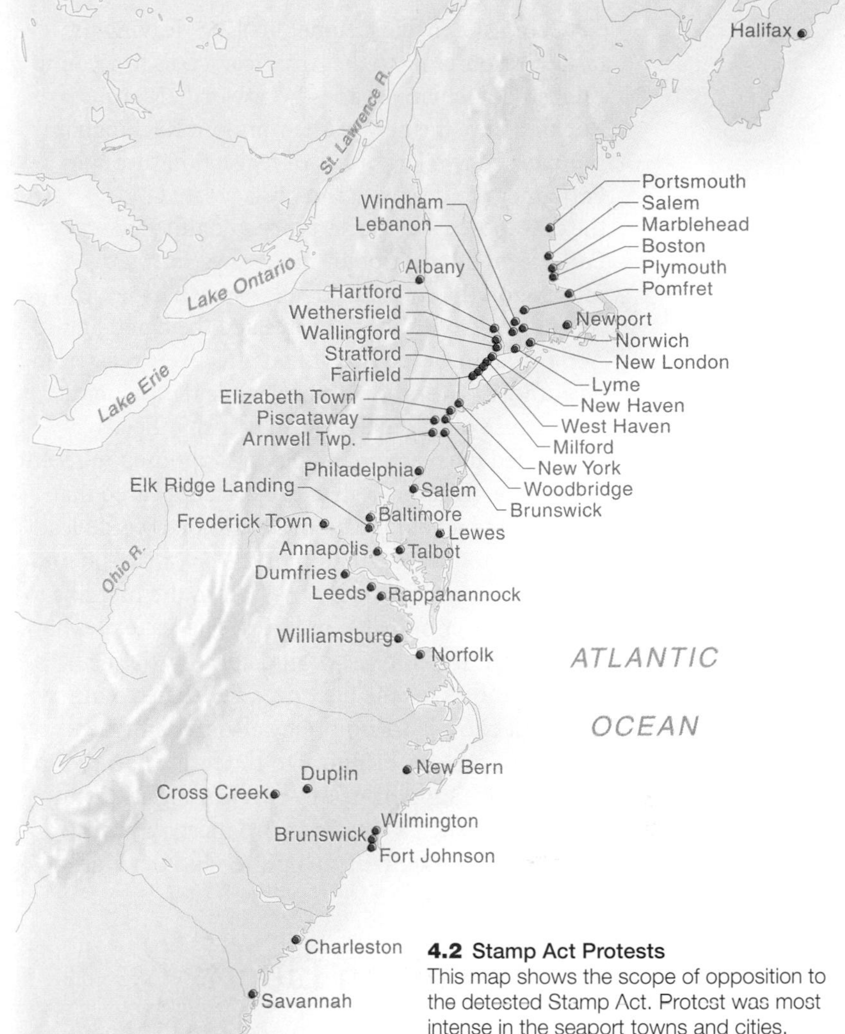

4.2 Stamp Act Protests
This map shows the scope of opposition to the detested Stamp Act. Protest was most intense in the seaport towns and cities.

The Stamp Act Crisis

Britain reacted to the colonists' resistance to the Sugar Act by imposing yet another, much harsher tax. Grenville and Parliament enacted the **Stamp Act**, which required colonists to purchase special stamps and place them on all legal documents. Stamped paper was required for everything from newspapers to playing cards. A similar tax existed in Britain, and Parliament believed that requiring colonists to pay such a tax at a lower rate than their brethren in Britain was entirely reasonable. A growing number of colonists rejected this notion. For those opposed to the Stamp Act, taxation without consent was illegal.

Opposition was most intense in the seaport towns and cities; the map (**4.2**) shows how widespread anger against this latest tax was in the colonies. Stamps had to be affixed to virtually all legal transactions and most printed documents, so the new tax act alienated a much larger group of Americans than had any previous parliamentary tax. The British could hardly have picked a worse target for their new scheme of taxation. Among the colonists most burdened by the tax were lawyers and printers, two of the most vocal and influential groups in the colonies. Protests against the Stamp Act filled the pages of colonial newspapers and produced a spate of pamphlets defending colonial rights. The Massachusetts House of Representatives called on other colonial assemblies to send delegates to New York to frame a response to the Stamp Act crisis. Nine of the thirteen colonies sent a representative to the Stamp Act congress, and although framed in respectful terms, the "Declaration of the Rights and Grievances of the Colonies" was an important step toward articulating a common response to British policy, forcing representatives from different colonies to work together for a common goal.

Protest against this latest attack on American liberty was not limited to newspapers or legislative chambers. Opposition to the Stamp Act spilled out of doors into the streets of American cities and towns. Crowds of angry colonists attacked tax collectors and government officials. In a few cases crowds attacked the homes of British officials, including the home of the lieutenant governor of Massachusetts, Thomas Hutchinson.

George Grenville resigned in 1765, leaving the task of responding to the American crisis to a young English nobleman, Charles Wentworth, Marquess of Rockingham, the new prime minister. Rockingham shepherded two key pieces of legislation through Parliament to deal with the crisis created by the Stamp Act. The Declaratory Act affirmed Parliament's authority to "make laws and statutes" binding on the colonies "in all cases whatsoever." The second piece of legislation repealed the hated Stamp Act. Britain believed that it had effectively reasserted its authority over the colonies, while removing the main cause of colonial protest. British officials misjudged the reaction of colonists opposed to recent policy. For critics of British policy, it appeared that Parliament had embarked on a path that would lead inevitably to the destruction of the colonists' liberty.

Colonial politics had moved from the margins to the very center of British politics. The issue of what to do about the colonies would come to define British politics for the next decade. In the colonies the conflict over British policy also transformed American politics, bringing to the fore a new group of aggressive supporters of American rights, including groups such as the Sons of Liberty, a group devoted to opposing British policy and defending American rights.

An Assault on Liberty

The resolution of the Stamp Act crisis did not eliminate Britain's pressing financial need for colonial revenue nor did it reduce colonial determination to resist further efforts to tax Americans. What little good will Britain's repeal of the Stamp Act generated, Britain quickly squandered as it renewed its efforts to impose a new set of taxes on the colonies. The Townshend Duties (1767), named for Charles Townshend, an ambitious government minister, levied new taxes on glass, paint, paper, and tea imported into the colonies. Townshend misinterpreted the Stamp Act protests. He believed that colonists opposed internal tax laws targeted at commerce within the colonies, but that Americans would accept external taxes such as customs duties that affected trade between the colonies and other parts of the British Empire. Again many Americans saw things differently.

The Townshend Duties prompted Americans to clarify their views on the issue of taxation. An important statement of American views came in Pennsylvania lawyer John Dickinson's pamphlet *Letters from a Farmer in Pennsylvania* (1767–1768). Dickinson disputed Parliament's right to tax the colonists at all. Parliament could regulate trade among different parts of the empire, he acknowledged, but only the people's representatives could enact taxes designed primarily to raise revenues. Since Americans had no representation in Parliament, that institution could not tax them.

In response to the Townshend Duties, Americans began a **nonimportation movement**, an organized boycott against the purchase of any imported British goods. Women took an active role in the boycott movement, urging that instead of imported fabrics, women wear only clothes made from domestic homespun fabrics. The nonimportation movement offered American women a chance to contribute actively to the defense of American rights. It also raised women's political consciousness. As thirteen-year-old Anna Green Winslow wrote in her journal regarding the decision to abandon imported fabrics, "I am (as we say) a daughter of liberty, I chuse to wear as much of our manufactory as possible."

Another import, tea, had become the basis of an important social ritual in colonial society. In the context of the growing frustration with British policy, tea drinking took on new political significance. In 1774 Penelope Barker and a group of women in Edenton, North Carolina, organized a tea boycott. Word of the Edenton protest eventually reached England, where a British cartoonist lampooned its support for the American cause (**4.3**). This satire casts the Edenton women as a motley assortment of hags and harlots, whose unfeminine actions and neglect of their proper duties as women furnish evidence of their lack of virtue. The tea boycott even inspired nine-year-old Susan Boudinot, the daughter of a wealthy Philadelphia family, who demonstrated her solidarity with the colonial cause in her own way. When invited to tea at the home of the royal governor of New Jersey, Susan curtsied respectfully, raised her teacup to her lips, and then tossed the contents out of a nearby window.

The new duties imposed by the British were only one part of a new, more aggressive policy toward the colonies. Between 1765 and 1768 the British transferred the bulk of their military forces in America from the frontier and stationed them in the major seaport cities, sites of the most violent opposition to the Stamp Act. This decision increased the already tense situation in these localities. In 1768 the simmering tensions between colonists and the British government came to a head when British customs officials in Boston seized merchant John Hancock's ship *Liberty*. Customs officials

How did nonimportation transform women's political role in the colonies?

4.3 **Patriotic Ladies of Edenton**
This sarcastic British cartoon lampoons the efforts of American women to participate in the movement to boycott British imports. The artist's caricature shows the women as unfeminine and neglectful of their proper subordinate roles as wives and mothers. [*Source:* 'A Society of Patriotic Ladies at Edenton in North Carolina', Metropolitan Museum of Art. Bequest of Charles Allen Munn]

had long suspected Hancock of smuggling and thought that seizing the *Liberty* would give them the proof they needed to prosecute him. The decision proved to be a serious blunder. The symbolic significance of the British assault on a ship named *Liberty* was not lost on Bostonians, who saw this as an assault on the idea of liberty itself. In response to the seizure of the *Liberty*, Bostonians rioted, driving customs officials from the town. To quell unrest in Boston, the British dispatched additional troops and warships to the area. By 1769 the British had stationed almost four thousand armed troops, dubbed redcoats because of their red uniforms, in a city with a population of roughly fifteen thousand.

Relations between residents of Boston and the occupying forces were tense. On March 5, 1770, a group of citizens taunted a group of soldiers and pelted them with snowballs. In the melee that followed, some of the soldiers opened fire on the crowd, killing five civilians. The Boston silversmith and engraver Paul Revere published a popular engraving of the **Boston Massacre**, as the confrontation came to be called, in which he portrayed the British as having deliberately fired on the unarmed crowd (**4.4**). Revere aligns the soldiers in a formal military pose, and portrays the commanders as giving an official order to fire. When the soldiers responsible for the shootings were indicted for murder, Boston's John Adams, a vocal critic of British policy, volunteered to defend the accused soldiers. Adams sought to demonstrate to the British that the Americans were not a lawless mob, but a law-abiding people. A gifted lawyer, Adams secured acquittals for all those accused except for two soldiers, who were convicted of the lesser crime of manslaughter. The evidence presented at the trial revealed that Revere's version of the event, while excellent propaganda, was not an accurate rendering of the circumstances.

The new taxes and pressure for compliance had stiffened the colonists' resistance. So although the British repealed most of the Townshend Duties in 1770, relations between the colonies and Britain remained strained. Colonists

4.4 **Boston Massacre**
Paul Revere's influential engraving of the Boston Massacre takes liberties with the facts to portray British actions in the worst possible light. The orderly arrangement of the troops and the stance of the officer at their side suggests that they acted under orders. Behind the troops, Revere has renamed the shop "Butcher's Hall."

How does Revere stage the events of the Boston Massacre to evoke sympathy for the colonists' cause?

continued to demand the traditional rights of Englishmen, such as trial by jury, but American protests had moved in a new direction, including the view that taxation without representation was a violation of fundamental rights. Resistance to British policy was also becoming more organized. The Sons of Liberty, created during the Stamp Act crisis, continued their criticism, but now they were joined by local committees that had formed during the protests against the Townshend Duties to coordinate and enforce boycotts.

After the repeal of the Townshend Duties, Americans enjoyed a brief respite from Parliament's attentions, as Britain turned its focus elsewhere in its far-flung empire, especially India. The temporary distraction of the British did not last long, however, and colonists soon faced another effort to tax them.

The Intolerable Acts and the First Continental Congress

In 1773 Parliament decided to help the fledgling East India Company increase its tea sales to the colonies. Many members of Parliament had sizable investments in the company. Parliament's new law lowered the price of tea to Americans, but gave the East India Company a monopoly on trade with the colonies. Once again British authorities miscalculated American reactions to their policies. Colonists resented the new policy, even though it made tea cheaper, and merchants resented the monopoly it gave to the East India Company. Others saw the act as a subtle way of reasserting Britain's right to tax the colonies.

One group of angry colonists in Philadelphia, calling themselves The Tar and Feathering Committee, issued a warning that they would tar and feather any ship's captain who landed with British tea.

The British found the colonists' actions thuggish. In this hostile British cartoon, *Bostonians Pay the Excise-Man* (**4.5**), a cruel-looking bunch of colonists force a British customs official, covered in tar and feathers, to drink British tea until he became sick. A painful form of public humiliation, tarring and feathering involved pouring hot tar onto the victim's skin and then attaching a coat of bird feathers to the molten tar.

The most dramatic response to the tea act occurred in December of 1773, when a group of Bostonians, dressed as Indians, boarded an English ship and tossed 90,000 pounds of tea into the harbor. To punish the colonists responsible for the Boston Tea Party, as the event was called, the British Parliament passed the Coercive Acts, known to colonists as **the Intolerable Acts.** This legislation closed the Port of Boston, annulled the Massachusetts colonial charter, dissolved or severely

4.5 ***Bostonians Paying the Excise-Man***
In this pro-British cartoon, Bostonians appear as cruel thugs who have tarred and feathered the custom's official and are forcing tea down his throat.

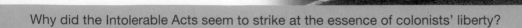

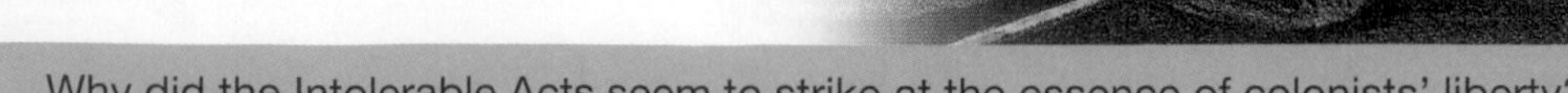
Why did the Intolerable Acts seem to strike at the essence of colonists' liberty?

4.6 ***The Able Doctor, or America Swallowing the Bitter Draught*** Paul Revere's engraving presents America as a partially clad Indian princess. Chief Judge Mansfield, a symbol of British law, holds America down. The Prime Minister, Lord North, shown with a copy of the Boston Port Bill, one of the Intolerable Acts, protruding from his pocket, forces tea down her throat.

restricted that colony's political institutions, and allowed the British to quarter (house) troops in private homes. (A generation later Americans adopted the Third Amendment to the Bill of Rights, which forbade quartering troops in civilian homes, a direct response to this detested British practice.) The acts also allowed British officials charged with capital crimes to be tried outside the colonies. Some colonists called the last provision the "Murder Act," since they feared it would allow soldiers charged with murder to avoid prosecution.

Americans were divided over how to respond to the Intolerable Acts. Some saw the Bostonians who dumped tea into the harbor as radicals whose actions besmirched Americans' reputation as law-abiding subjects of the king. Others expressed outrage at the British policy that had forced Bostonians to resort to such a dramatic protest. This cartoon, *The Able Doctor, Or America Swallowing the Bitter Draught* (**4.6**), casts Bostonians differently from the lawless ruffians depicted in *Bostonians Paying the Excise-Man* (4.5). Here the British prime minister brutally accosts America, a half-clad Indian princess, forcing tea down her throat, while Chief Justice Lord Mansfield, the symbol of British law, pins her arms down.

The most important consequence of the Intolerable Acts was the decision by the colonies to convene a Continental Congress in Philadelphia during the fall of 1774. All the colonies except Georgia sent representatives. Among the colonial leaders who attended were Patrick Henry, John Adams, and George Washington. Congress endorsed the Resolves of Suffolk County, Massachusetts, which denounced the Intolerable Acts and asserted the intention of colonists to nullify such a manifest violation of their "rights and liberties." The Congress also adopted a resolution that recommended that every town, county, and city create a committee to enforce the boycott of British goods. The informal network of committees that had previously opposed British policy now acquired a quasi-legal status from Congress.

Although many Americans hoped that a peaceful solution to the deepening crisis was possible, in March of 1774, the brilliant Virginia orator Patrick Henry addressed his fellow delegates in the Virginia Assembly and urged them to prepare for the inevitable conflict that loomed between the colonies and Britain. Although no contemporaneous copy of this dramatic speech exists, Henry's words were recounted many years later, assuming almost legendary status in American culture. In response to British assaults on America liberty, Henry boldly declared, "Give Me Liberty—or give me death!"

What is the symbolic significance of Judge Mansfield's actions in this political cartoon?

> "If we view the whole of the conduct of the [British] ministry and parliament, I do not see how any one can doubt but that there is a settled fix'd plan for enslaving the colonies, or bringing them under arbitrary government."
>
> Connecticut Minister, the Reverend EBENEZER BALDWIN, 1774

In the period between the passage of the Stamp Act in 1764 and the meeting of the First Continental Congress in 1774, relations between Britain and America had steadily deteriorated. As the chart (**4.7**) shows, Britain had tried a variety of types of revenue measures designed to raise funds from the colonies. Americans, however, remained resolutely opposed to taxation without representation. Rather than subdue the colonies, British policy only served to strengthen the resolve of Americans to defend their rights.

Lexington, Concord, and Lord Dunmore's Proclamation

Living on the edge of the British Empire, colonists had come to depend on their own **militias** as their primary means of public defense. The laws of the individual colonies regulated these organizations of citizen soldiers. During the colonial period the militia was more than just a force available to protect the colonists from hostile Indians or protect them from possible attacks from French or Spanish forces. In an era before police forces, the militia also helped enforce public order, serving to put down riots, rebellions, and other civil disturbances. In January of 1775 Virginia's George Mason foresaw the importance of the militia to the colonists' struggle with Britain and called on the colonists to put their militia in good order. Mason declared that "a well regulated Militia, composed of gentlemen freeholders, and other free-man, is the natural strength and only stable security of a free Government."

The British, too, understood the importance of the militia to colonial resistance. Not only did they pose a military threat, but they were also indispensable to helping mobilize Americans and organizing their opposition to British policy. Disarming the militias became a high priority for the British. Their first target was Massachusetts, which had become a hotbed of resistance; the British dispatched troops to Concord in April of 1775 to seize gunpowder and other military supplies. Paul Revere, an outspoken member of the Sons of Liberty, was charged with riding from Boston to Lexington and Concord to warn citizens that British troops were on the march. Revere got as far as Lexington before a British patrol captured him. Fortunately for Revere he had already encountered another member of the Sons of Liberty that night, Dr. Samuel Prescott, who was returning from the home of his fiancée. Prescott agreed to carry word that British troops were on the march from Boston. The alarm spread throughout the countryside. When the seven hundred British regulars finally arrived at Lexington's town green, they faced a determined force of sixty to seventy colonial militiamen. Although the militia agreed to disperse, someone, it is not clear who, fired a shot, and the two sides exchanged fire. The Battle of Lexington marked the first military conflict between Britain and America, and the colonists had demonstrated their mettle.

The British then marched on to Concord, where they confronted a larger and better organized detachment of colonial militia at the North Bridge in Concord. The militia stood their ground and exchanged fire with the British regulars, who were forced to retreat. While the British retreated back to Boston, colonial reinforcements poured into Concord and the surrounding countryside. The organized column of British troops marching back to Boston was an easy target for colonial militiamen, who took up positions along the roadside and in the adjacent woods. Before the end of the day, 273 British redcoats were dead and 95 members of the Massachusetts militia had been killed. A Rhode Island newspaper captured the views of those won over to the Patriot cause when it commented that British aggression marked the start of a "War which shall hereafter fill an important page in history."

Although the British had mounted a direct assault on the Massachusetts militia, they opted for a stealthier plan for disarming the Virginia militia. Under cover of darkness a detachment of Royal

What was the impact of Lord Dunmore's Proclamation on southern colonists?

Marines entered Virginia's capital of Williamsburg, seized the gun powder, and destroyed the firing mechanisms on the muskets stored in the militia's magazine. When citizens of Williamsburg learned of the assault, they marched on the governor's mansion to protest. As word of the British raid spread throughout the colony, a group of militia led by Patrick Henry planned to march on Williamsburg. Lord Dunmore, the royal governor, warned that if the militia entered Williamsburg he would "declare freedom to slaves and reduce the city of Williamsburg to ashes." At the last moment a compromise was worked out, and the governor made restitution for the stolen powder and damaged guns. Still Dunmore's threat to free Virginia's slaves had sent a shockwave through the colony.

Two weeks later colonists learned of Lord **Dunmore's Proclamation.** Dunmore offered freedom to any slave who joined the British forces in putting down the American rebellion. Within a month three hundred slaves had joined "Dunmore's Ethiopian Regiment," whose ranks would swell to some eight hundred or more. The uniforms of this unit included a sash emblazoned with the motto "Liberty To Slaves." Virginians complained that the British were "using every Art to seduce the Negroes, " while others viewed Dunmore's decision as "diabolical." Many Virginians who were wavering on the issue of American independence now concluded that a break with Britain was inevitable, even desirable. Some Virginians recognized that Virginia's slaves were seeking the very same liberty that colonists claimed. For example Lund Washington, who managed his cousin George's Mount Vernon estate, including his slaves, observed that "there is not a man of them but would leave us, if they could make their escape."

Date	Act	Policy	Consequences
1763	**Proclamation of 1763**	Prohibits colonists from moving westward	Intensifies problem of land scarcity in colonies
1764	**Sugar Act**	Reduces duty on molasses, but provides for more vigorous methods of enforcement	Colonials articulate theory that taxation without representation is a violation of "their most essential rights as freemen."
1765	**Stamp Act**	Documents and printed materials, including legal documents, newspapers, and playing cards must use special stamped paper	Riots in major urban areas, harassment of revenue officers, colonial representatives meet for Stamp Act Congress
1765	**Quartering Act**	Colonists must supply British troops with housing and firewood	Colonial Assemblies protest, New York punished for failure to comply with law
1766	**Declaratory Act/Repeal of Stamp Act**	Britain asserts its right to legislate for colonies in all cases/ Stamp Act repealed	Britain reasserts its authority, while removing the obnoxious provisions of the Stamp Act
1767	**Townshend Acts**	New duties placed on glass, lead, paper, paint	Non-importation movement gains ground
1773	**Tea Act**	Parliament gives East India Company monopoly, but duties on tea are reduced	90,000 pounds of tea tossed into Boston harbor
1774	**Coercive Acts (Intolerable Acts)**	Port of Boston closed, town meetings restricted	First Continental Congress meets and other colonies express support for Bostonians
1775	**Prohibitory Act**	Britain declares intention to coerce Americans into submission	Continental Congress adopts a Declaration of Rights asserting American rights

4.7 British Policies and Colonial Response

Why did British regulars choose Concord as their military objective?

Patriots versus Loyalists

IN CONGRESS, JULY 4, 1776.
A DECLARATIO
BY THE REPRESENTATIVES OF THE
UNITED STATES OF AMERIC
IN GENERAL CONGRESS ASSEMBLED.

By 1775 the rift between Britain and the colonies had grown precipitously large. Indeed it was not just colonists who believed that if Britain continued on its present course it would end in disaster. A satirical British cartoon, *The Political Cartoon for the Year 1775* (**4.8**), published in London, vividly captured this view. It depicts King George III riding in a coach heading straight over a cliff. Chief Justice Lord Mansfield, a symbol of British law, holds the reins of the carriage of state, which rides roughshod over the Magna Carta—a text closely linked with the Rights of Englishmen—and the British Constitution, another symbol of liberty. The cartoonist's symbolism suggested a view that was becoming increasingly popular in the colonies: Americans could no longer expect the political and legal system of Britain to protect their liberty. Although some Americans were persuaded that England was intent on trampling on Americans' liberty, other colonists remained loyal to the crown. For Patriots it was becoming increasingly clear that they could no longer count on the legal protections that had safeguarded their liberty for generations. Loyalists, by contrast, disputed this claim. For those loyal to George III, liberty could only be maintained by upholding English law. Loyalists viewed Patriots' actions as examples of lawlessness, not affirmations of liberty.

The Battle of Bunker Hill

Two months after Lexington and Concord, the two sides clashed again in Charlestown, across the Charles River from Boston. American forces had dug in at Bunker Hill and nearby Breeds Hill, prepared to hold off the British forces in Boston. The main fighting actually took place at Breeds Hill, which was closer to the harbor. The British underestimated the colonists' resolve to hold their ground. Although the British took Bunker Hill, they had purchased their casualties: 226 dead and more than 800 wounded. Americans suffered 140 dead and 271 wounded. Even more important, Americans had shown the British that they were not the "untrained rabble" the British had portrayed them as and that they could become a formidable fighting force. The painter John Trumbull immortalized the battle in his painting *The Death of General Warren at the Battle of Bunker Hill*. For a discussion of this painting and how it reflected the realities of a battle in which neither side won a clear victory, see *Images as*

4.8 *The Political Cartoon for the Year 1775*
George III rides next to Chief Judge Lord Mansfield in a carriage heading toward the edge of a cliff. The carriage crushes the Magna Carta and the British Constitution, symbols of the rule of law, while flames engulf Boston in the background.

What does *The Political Cartoon for the Year 1775* reveal about the nature of relations between the colonies and Britain?

Despite the armed confrontations at Lexington, Concord, and then Bunker Hill, the Continental Congress had not abandoned hope of reconciliation with King George III. In July of 1775 Congress drafted the "Olive Branch" petition, asking George III to intervene on their behalf. The king rejected the American appeal. With that rejection the time for reconciliation had now passed, and the supporters of American independence in the Continental Congress gained momentum. The push for independence in turn opened up a division within colonial society between colonists who supported independence and those who remained loyal to the British.

Common Sense and the Declaration of Independence

In January of 1776 a recent immigrant to America from England wrote a pamphlet that argued forcefully for American independence. In ***Common Sense***, Thomas Paine not only attacked recent British policy, he framed a stinging indictment of monarchy, and defended a democratic theory of representative government. After stating the "simple facts, plain arguments, and common sense" of the matter, Paine concluded that separation from Britain was the only course of action that made any sense for America. Paine's work was printed in a cheap format that allowed artisans, farmers, and others with little money to purchase a copy. He wrote in plain, forceful prose, avoiding literary and classical allusions that would have required knowledge of Latin. The book was a phenomenal publishing success. Paine boasted that as many as 150,000 copies of *Common Sense* were printed, but recent scholarship puts the figure closer to half that number. Still, given that few books sold more than 50,000, Paine's pamphlet popularity was impressive.

Common Sense did more than simply fuel Americans' desire for independence; it helped change the framework in which Americans thought about politics itself. Before Paine's pamphlet most Americans, even those who believed that reconciliation with Britain was impossible, still maintained a respectful attitude toward George III. Most Americans had grown up in a culture that venerated constitutional monarchy, but Paine's savage critique of this institution had a liberating impact. Paine ridiculed monarchy as "ridiculous." After demonstrating that history proved that monarchy was incompatible with liberty, Paine turned to the current British monarch George III, whom he equated with savagery itself. He denounced the king for his repeated assaults on American liberty, noting that "even brutes do not devour their young." Those who supported reconciliation with Britain found Paine's scathing attacks on George III simply appalling. Paine also gave a voice to many who wished to radically transform American political life. He was unabashedly democratic at a time when many, including those most eager to separate from Britain, viewed simple democracy as a danger to be avoided at all cost. *Common Sense* became a blueprint for those who wished to experiment with democratic forms of government, although not everyone who ardently supported American independence appreciated Paine's democratic ideas.

> "There is something absurd in supposing a Continent to be perpetually governed by an island."
>
> THOMAS PAINE, *Common Sense* 1776

In July of 1775, a month after Congress drafted the "Olive Branch Petition," pleading with George III to abandon the "cruel" policies of his ministers and "such statutes" as "immediately distress" the colonists, the king declared that the American colonists were "in open and avowed rebellion." The Prohibitory Act, which the British Parliament enacted into law at the very end of December 1775, imposed a complete ban on all trade with the thirteen colonies. Word of the ban, Parliament's most recent effort to subdue the colonists, arrived in America in February 1776. Coming on the heels of Paine's indictment of British tyranny, the policy further inflamed American resentments against Britain.

In the months after the adoption of the Prohibitory Act, support for independence gained ground. In May Congress instructed the individual colonies "to adopt such Government as shall, in the Opinion of the Representatives of the People, best conduce to the Happiness and Safety of their Constituents." Congress added a preamble five days later that affirmed "the exercise of every kind of authority under the said crown should be totally suppressed." Although Congress had not formally

Images as History

TRUMBULL'S *THE DEATH OF GENERAL WARREN AT THE BATTLE OF BUNKER HILL*

American John Trumbull's painting *The Death of General Warren at the Battle of Bunker Hill* (1786), painted eleven years after the battle, captured an important moment in the American war for independence. Like Benjamin West's *The Death of General Wolfe* (see page 90), Trumbull's painting depicts the heroic death of a military figure, but the two paintings differ in a number of fascinating ways. While *The Death of General Wolfe* portrayed a clear victory for the British, *The Death of General Warren* showed a more complex event in which neither side was completely victorious. While the Americans lost the battle, they proved themselves an effective fighting force and exacted a high price from the British for their victory. How did Trumbull's composition reflect the realities of this battle, a struggle in which neither side won a clear victory?

Trumbull's painting *The Death of General Warren* was part of a series of paintings he began to commemorate the "great events of our country's revolution." The artist intended to use his painting as the basis for a set of engravings that he could sell as cheap prints to a popular market on both sides of the Atlantic. With this in mind Trumbull captured the chaotic horror of a battle scene in which both armies displayed heroism and nobility. The American General Warren lies mortally wounded, cradled in the arms of one of his troops, in the same pose in which Benjamin West portrayed British General Wolfe.

One element of the painting meant to appeal to British viewers is the depiction of British Major John Small in the center of the composition near Warren. Small stays the hand of one of his infantryman poised to bayonet the dying Warren. By placing these two noble gestures—Warren's sacrifice and Small's humanitarian intervention—at the center of the painting, Trumbull shifts attention away from the actual outcome of the battle to the idea that virtuous men on both sides performed noble deeds. This decision enhanced the moral complexity of the events while also making it and later engravings based on it attractive to British and American customers—effectively doubling the size of his potential market.

Trumbull's canvas also advanced the democratization of art begun by Benjamin West. In this painting virtue resides neither in one nation nor in any particular class of men. Trumbull portrays a broad range of soldiers heroically—from a gentlemanly British officer to a barefoot colonial soldier. Indeed Abigail Adams, an outspoken supporter of American independence and the wife of the prominent politician John Adams, noted that Trumbull "teaches mankind that it is not rank nor titles, but character alone, which interests posterity."

Trumbull all but ignored African Americans, consigning the two he did include to minor roles in the painting. Trumbull described the African American standing in the lower right corner behind an injured colonial officer as a "faithful negro." At least fourteen African Americans were among the troops defending Breeds Hill and Bunker Hill. The African American Peter Salem played an important

The Death of General Warren at the Battle of Bunker Hill

How did Trumbull craft his painting so it would appeal to both an American and British audience?

role in the actual battle, perhaps firing the shot that killed Major Pitcairn, the British figure collapsing near the center of the painting. The painting's slighting of that role probably reflected Trumbull's own racial ideas and those of his audience, who were not used to seeing African Americans depicted in anything but a subservient role. For the moment the democratization of art was restricted to those of European descent. African Americans' treatment in American art mirrored their marginalization in the larger society.

Rather than portray an African American as heroic, Warren marginalizes this figure, literally placing him in the shadow of a white officer at the end of the canvas.
Trumbull highlights the idea of virtue and honor as universal values by showing a British officer preventing a soldier from bayoneting the dying Warren.
General Warren's pose evokes the image of Jesus being cradled in the arms of Mary.
Major Pitcairn, who led the British assault on Concord, is mortally wounded in this battle.

What does Trumbull's portrayal of African Americans tell us about his views and those of his likely audiences?

declared independence from Britain, it had effectively asserted that the colonies had become independent states no longer under the authority of Parliament or the king.

On the very same day, Richard Henry Lee of Virginia introduced his resolution that "these United Colonies are, and of right ought to be, free and independent states." Congress then debated the Lee resolution and on June 11, 1776, appointed a committee to draft a formal declaration of independence. With John Adams (Massachusetts) as its chair, the committee included Robert Livingston (New York), Thomas Jefferson (Virginia), Roger Sherman (Connecticut), and Benjamin Franklin (Pennsylvania). Adams designated Jefferson to take the lead in drafting the formal resolution. On June 28 the committee presented the congressional delegates with the draft. Congress cut about a quarter of the text and made some minor revisions to the document. On July 4, 1776, Congress approved the final text of the **Declaration of Independence**, a public defense of America's decision to declare independence from Britain that was to be printed and sent to the individual states. Congress ordered copies of the declaration, which were then widely distributed.

Thomas Jefferson, the primary architect of the declaration, admitted that his text reflected the "sentiments of the day, whether expressed in conversation or letters, printed essays." The introductory paragraph explained the reasons for separating from Britain. The second paragraph provided a powerful defense of the ideas of liberty and equality and affirmed that "all men are created Equal." The Declaration asserted that all men were therefore entitled to "life, liberty, and the pursuit of happiness." A long list of grievances against King George III took up the bulk of the text. Printed as a single broadside, the indented list of charges against George III was immediately recognizable (**4.9**).

The drafters of the Declaration of Independence aimed it at both a domestic and a foreign audience. It made the case for independence to the American people and announced to the British government the reasons for taking up arms against it. The declaration also sought to help the cause of American diplomacy. If America were to fight a war against the most powerful nation on earth, it would need help from other European powers, such as Holland and Britain's long-time rival, France. Because a powerful monarch then ruled France, the language of the declaration refrained from using the inflammatory antimonarchical rhetoric favored by Thomas Paine in *Common Sense*. George III's misdeeds, not monarchy itself, were to blame for America's demand for independence.

IN CONGRESS, JULY 4, 1776.

A DECLARATION

BY THE REPRESENTATIVES OF THE

UNITED STATES OF AMERICA,

IN GENERAL CONGRESS ASSEMBLED.

WHEN in the Course of human Events, it becomes necessary for one People to dissolve the Political Bands which have connected them with another, …

Signed by ORDER and in BEHALF of the CONGRESS,

JOHN HANCOCK, PRESIDENT.

ATTEST.

CHARLES THOMSON, SECRETARY.

4.9 The Declaration of Independence The Declaration of Independence was printed as a broadside. This single-sheet format made it easy to post in public places. The layout of the Declaration—the typography and paragraphing—guides the reader through the main parts of its argument.

The Plight of the Loyalists

The division between **Patriots**, colonists who supported American independence, and **Loyalists**, those wishing to remain loyal to the king, drove a deep wedge in colonial society. John Adams speculated that

What audiences did the Declaration of Independence address?

> "We hold these truths to be self-evident, that all men are created equal, that they are endowed by their Creator with certain unalienable Rights, that among these are Life, Liberty, and the pursuit of Happiness."
>
> Declaration of Independence, 1776

Americans were evenly divided among Patriots, Loyalists, and those striving to remain neutral. Although it is difficult to establish hard figures for how colonists divided on the issue of independence, historians estimate that Patriots constituted about 40 percent of the population, neutrals another 40 percent, and Loyalists probably about 20 percent.

Many prominent Loyalists had openly opposed British policy toward the colony, but refused to accept the decision for independence. Minister Samuel Seabury captured the view of many Loyalists when he wrote: "To talk of a colony independent of the mother-country, is no better sense than to talk of a limb independent of the body to which it belongs." The image of the dismemberment of the empire was a powerful one in the minds of colonials and Britons alike. At the start of the 1760s, supporters of American rights had used such images to try to persuade Britain to change its policy toward the colonies. At the time Benjamin Franklin was working as a colonial lobbyist in England, working for repeal of British taxes. He designed an engraving, *The Colonies Reduced*, to appeal to Parliament, evoking the horror of a possible separation between the colonists and the mother country (**4.10**). Seabury's reassertion of the horrors that would follow from the dismemberment of the empire tapped into a powerful set of fears and anxieties among Americans unsure about the question of independence.

Loyalists suffered many hardships during the struggle for independence. In some places where Patriot feelings were strongest, individuals could be ostracized for refusing to support the Patriot cause. They were excluded from juries and were disarmed. Many states passed laws seizing Loyalist property. A complicated issue arising from these laws was how to deal with women married to Loyalist husbands. Some women brought property from their own family into their marriage. Was this property also liable to confiscation? The story of Grace Gowden Galloway illustrates the rapid reversal of fortune that could befall anyone who opposed the Patriots' side in the American Revolution. For the story of her struggle, see *Choices and Consequences: A Loyalist Wife's Dilemma* (page 112).

The Loyalist cause appealed to many Americans, not just wealthy men and women like Grace and Joseph Galloway. New York boasted a sizeable Loyalist population, as did parts of the southern backcountry in the Carolinas. A number of religious sects, particularly groups such as the Quakers who were pacifists, opposed the violence of war. Beginning with Lord Dunmore's Proclamation, many slaves had sensed that a British victory, not independence, offered them the best chance for freedom. Historians estimate that as many as 100,000 slaves freed themselves by running away during the dislocation created by the war with Britain.

4.10 ***The Colonies Reduced***
This image created by Benjamin Franklin plays on the idea of the dismemberment of the empire as a development fatal to both the colonies and the mother country. Franklin used this image early in America's opposition to British policy. Loyalists later used the dismemberment metaphor to persuade Americans to oppose independence.

How did the metaphor of dismemberment influence Loyalist thought?

Choices and Consequences

A LOYALIST WIFE'S DILEMMA

Before the struggle for independence, Grace Gowden Galloway stood at the apex of Philadelphia society. Her husband, Joseph Galloway, was both wealthy and influential in Pennsylvania politics. Throughout the escalating conflict with Britain, Joseph Galloway supported reconciliation, and when war broke out, he became a Loyalist. Realizing that he could no longer count on the goodwill of his former friends and neighbors to protect him, Galloway and his daughter fled Philadelphia—perhaps the most ardent Patriot city outside of New England—for the safety of British-controlled New York in 1776. The government of Pennsylvania confiscated Galloway's estates and property, but Grace Galloway was determined to protect the property she had inherited from her own family and had brought into her marriage. She faced a difficult set of choices about what to do about her property:

Choices

1 Follow her husband and daughter into exile, accepting that neither she nor her husband would probably ever recover their property.

2 Follow her husband and daughter into exile and use every legal means available to prevent the confiscation of her property and fight an uphill battle to protect her property from afar.

3 Stay in Philadelphia and use every legal option to protect the properties that she had brought into her marriage before marrying Joseph Galloway.

Decision

Grace chose to stay and fight. She hoped that by remaining in her home she could avoid eviction. She also concluded that the chances of defending her own property against confiscation would be easier if she stayed in Philadelphia.

Consequences

Grace courageously endured great hardship while defending her rights but was ultimately evicted. Snubbed and shunned by many of her former friends and acquaintances, and driven from her home, she lived in a modest set of rented rooms. In her diary Grace recounts her struggles and the indignities she suffered, including the time she "saw My own Chariot standing at my door for the Use of others while I am forced to Walk." She never rejoined her family and died alone in 1781. Although evicted from her home, she was more successful at protecting the property she had brought into the marriage, which eventually passed on to her descendents.

Eighteenth-century coach

Continuing Controversies

What does Grace Gowden Galloway's plight reveal about the situation of Loyalists during the American Revolution?

The legal status of the property of a woman married to a Loyalist was complicated. This issue came before American courts in *Martin v. Commonwealth* (1805). Building on a new conception of women as independent political actors, the state of Massachusetts claimed that a woman's choice to stay or flee was hers alone. The Massachusetts high court, however, disagreed with this new view of women's legal autonomy. The court held that the woman's decision to leave the state had been her husband's, not her own, and therefore the state did not have the right to seize her land. Although a defeat for women's rights, the outcome of the case would have certainly pleased Grace Gowden Galloway.

What does *Martin v. Commonwealth* reveal about women's roles in Revolutionary era America?

America at War

Britain had good reason to be confident at the start of the war in the summer of 1776. Britain's navy was the most powerful in the world and its army formidable. The population of the British Isles was more than four times greater than that of the colonies. America began the war effort with only a citizen's militia. Fighting against the most powerful army in the world meant that America would have to create a professional fighting force. Congress appointed George Washington the commander of the newly formed Continental Army.

Although Britain's population was much larger than that of the colonies, the relative size of the two armies in the field was not that lopsided. Over the course of the war, around 250,000 Americans served at one time or another, but the size of the American armed forces on the ground, including regulars and militia, never exceeded roughly ninety thousand troops. British forces, which included thirty thousand German Hessian mercenaries, never topped sixty thousand. Even if the British were able to defeat the American armed forces in the field and gain control of all of America's urban centers, conquering and pacifying the entire American continent would be a virtually impossible task. The British also never grasped that they were fighting a new type of war: not a struggle against another European power, but a battle against a decentralized independence movement.

The War in the North

Stiff colonial resistance at Breeds Hill and Bunker Hill had convinced the British military that the colonial militias were not an undisciplined rabble that would retreat if confronted by a well-trained professional army. The creation of a Continental Army under the leadership of George Washington underscored this fact and led the British to change their tactics. Rather than employing the army to subdue a rebel population, the British prepared for a sustained military conflict. Realizing that Patriot sympathies in New England were strongest, the British retreated to New York, a colony with a large Loyalist population. New York not only provided a safer base of operations, but the British also believed that if they could hold New York they would effectively cut New England off from the rest of America.

Although determined to defend New York against British attack, Washington suffered a decisive defeat at Brooklyn Heights in August of 1776. Washington retreated to Manhattan, but British Major General Sir William Howe soon drove his forces from New York. Retreating south through New Jersey, Washington eventually crossed the Delaware River and set up a winter base at Valley Forge, Pennsylvania. During the winter, however, Washington's ranks, which had swelled with militiamen, dwindled as many militiamen simply returned home. These citizen soldiers had repulsed the immediate threat. They would also effectively protect the American countryside and prevent Loyalist pockets from forming outside of British-controlled territory, but they were ill suited to sustained battle. Washington lamented their unpredictable coming and going: "come in, you cannot tell how" and "go, you cannot tell when, and act you cannot tell where." The militia's lack of discipline and of long-term commitment to fight was a constant source of frustration to Washington and other American military leaders. Still the militia remained vital, contributing both to the military and to the political success of the war effort.

Washington's retreat dealt a devastating blow to American morale. Indeed the winter encampment at Valley Forge marked the low point of American confidence in the war. Writing in his essay *The American Crisis*, Thomas Paine desperately tried to inspire Americans to continue the war effort, reminding them that "These are the times that try men's souls." Believing that he had decisively defeated Washington, an overconfident General Howe established his base camp in New York City and planned to enjoy the winter holiday festivities.

Realizing that America desperately needed a victory, Washington took a bold gamble and launched a surprise attack on Christmas night 1776. Leading his soldiers across the partially frozen Delaware River under cover of darkness, he attacked a British outpost manned by German mercenaries stationed at Trenton. Winning a victory at Trenton, Washington struck out a week later

Why did Thomas Paine describe Valley Forge as one of the times that "try men's souls?"

> "The summer soldier and the sunshine patriot, will in this crisis, shrink from the service of his country; but he that stands it NOW deserves the love and thanks of men and women."
>
> THOMAS PAINE, *The American Crisis* (1780)

with another daring attack and victory at Princeton. General Howe had squandered his early advantage and allowed Washington time to regroup and score two important victories. Washington shrewdly abandoned his early strategy of fighting a conventional war against the British. He now realized that his primary goal was to wear down his opponents and avoid a decisive loss in the field. Such a strategy played to America's natural advantages and would eventually force the British to accept that they could not conquer America. To commemorate Washington's victory at Princeton, the trustees of Princeton College commissioned the eminent American painter Charles Wilson Peale to paint Washington at the Battle of Princeton (**4.11**). The portrait replaced a painting of George III, damaged during the battle when a cannonball removed the king's head.

4.11 ***Washington at the Battle of Princeton***
In this painting the officer behind Washington is posed in the same position as General Wolfe and General Warren. Washington, by contrast, stands firm, a symbol of the virtuous new republic that rises from the noble sacrifice depicted in the background. [Reproduced with permission of the Minor White Archive, Princeton University Art Museum. Copyright © The Trustees of Princeton University]

The next major turning point in the Northern field came at Saratoga in the fall of 1777. A British army under the command of General John Burgoyne marched south from Canada. Burgoyne hoped to join forces with British forces under the leadership of General Major John Howe from New York. Their goal was to divide New England from the rest of the colonies. But an American force under the leadership of General Horatio Gates defeated Burgoyne at Saratoga, in upstate New York (**4.12**). In addition to providing Americans with an important victory and morale boast, the British defeat at Saratoga persuaded the French to commit troops and naval forces to aid the colonists.

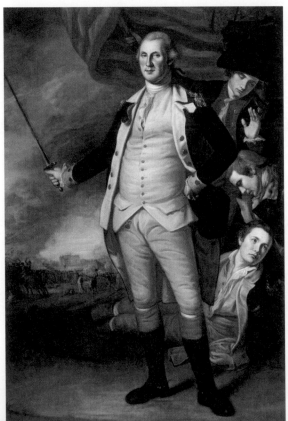

The active entry of France in the war changed the dynamics of the conflict. Rather than simply providing some resources, France was now fully committed to helping America win independence. In 1778 France and America signed a treaty promising to fight until American independence was secured. Spain soon joined France as an opponent of Britain. Within two years Britain declared war on Holland, which had become an important source of arms and other supplies for the American war effort. The great European powers were now at war. What had begun as a colonial war for independence fought exclusively in North America had mushroomed into a global conflict involving the Mediterranean, Africa, India, and the Caribbean. The wealthy sugar islands of the Caribbean were at risk from French attack. Britain had to divert important resources from the war effort in North America to protect these possessions. Fighting a war on multiple fronts drained British resources.

The Southern Campaigns and Final Victory at Yorktown

The British believed that Loyalist sympathies were greatest in the colonial South. They also saw the South, with its cash crops of tobacco, indigo, and rice, as more valuable economically than the North. Initially the British strategy seemed to pay off. British troops scored impressive victories at Savannah (Georgia), Charleston (South Carolina), and Camden (South Carolina). But still they failed to consolidate their power in the region. The colonial militias played a pivotal role, harassing Loyalists and promoting the Patriot cause. The British were especially vulnerable to hit-and-run operations by commanders such as South Carolina's Francis Marion. Nicknamed the "swamp fox" by his frustrated opponents, Marion would appear out of nowhere, attack and retreat, and then disappear into the swamps before the British could retaliate.

The course of the war in the South changed dramatically in 1781 when General Nathaniel Greene and General Daniel Morgan scored a major defeat against the British forces under Lord Cornwallis at Cowpens (South Carolina). American

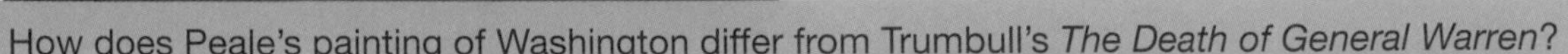

How does Peale's painting of Washington differ from Trumbull's *The Death of General Warren*?

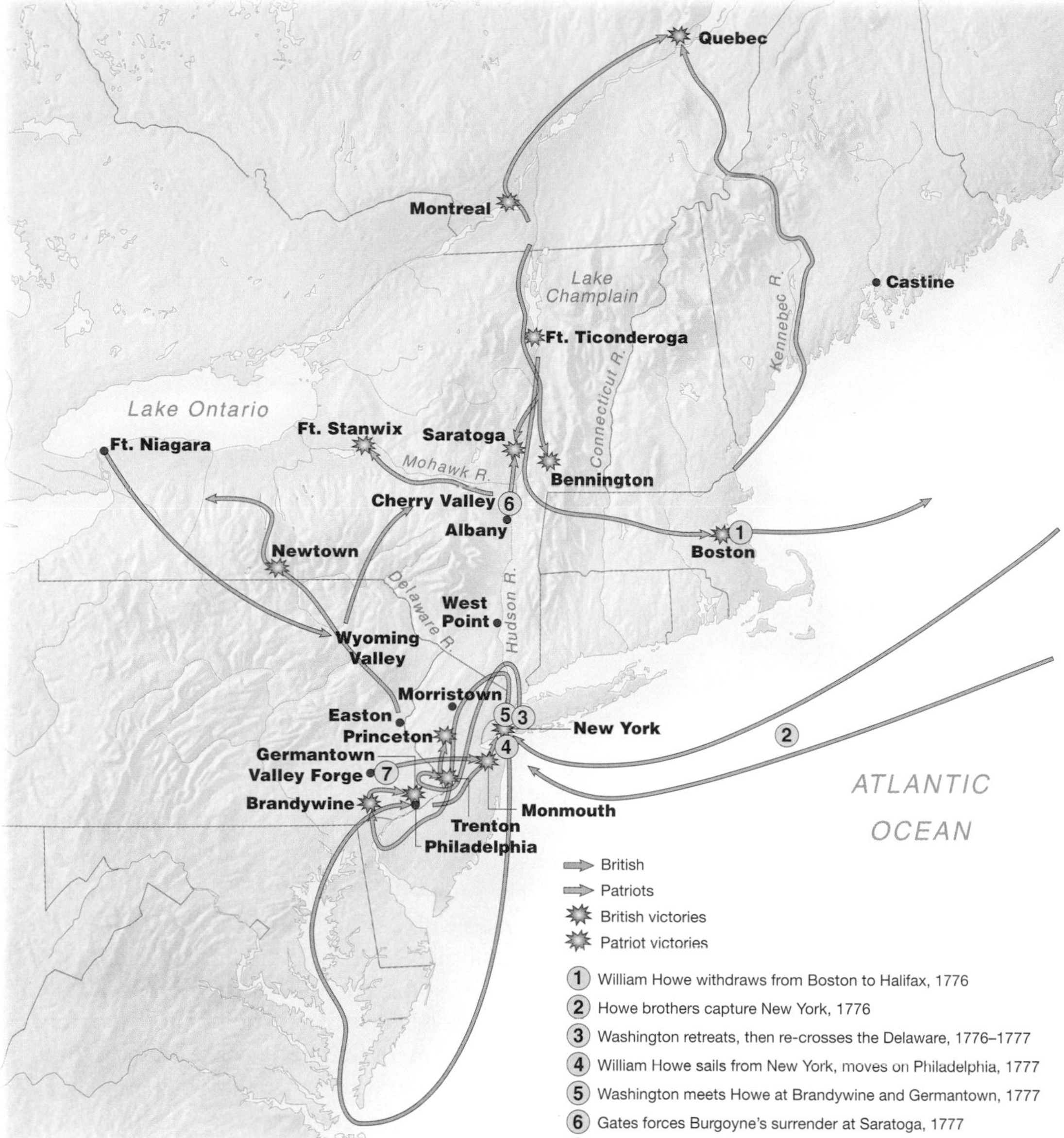

4.12 Northern Campaigns
Although the British won important victories around New York City, Washington's triumphs at Trenton and Princeton helped restore American morale. The turning point in the war in the North, however, was the defeat of the British at Saratoga, which helped persuade the French to increase their support for the American cause.

forces also inflicted heavy losses at Guilford Court House (North Carolina) in 1781. Cornwallis retreated to Virginia and established a well-fortified base at Yorktown in the winter of 1781 (**4.13**).

Cornwallis's retreat to Yorktown proved to be a strategic blunder for the British that Washington quickly turned to America's advantage. Before Saratoga the French had not committed major naval resources to the American cause, and America's own small navy was no match for the superior British fleet. With their naval superiority the British were confident that the retreat to Yorktown made strategic sense. With the guns of the British navy at their disposal, and new supplies, Yorktown seemed like a good strategic location to regroup.

But things went awry for the British when, early in the fall of 1781, the French dispatched a formidable fleet under the command of Admiral Paul de Grasse from the Caribbean to help the American cause. With the French navy supporting the Americans, the balance of power at sea shifted, giving the Americans a naval advantage. Washington seized the opportunity, ordering French forces under the Marquis de Lafayette and the Comte de Rochambeau to join American troops in an assault on Yorktown. With support from de Grasse's navy, the Americans and French trapped Cornwallis in Yorktown. Although French support was indispensable, this fanciful French image of the victory at Yorktown, drawn by a French artist, portrays this

What role did the French navy play in the victory at Yorktown?

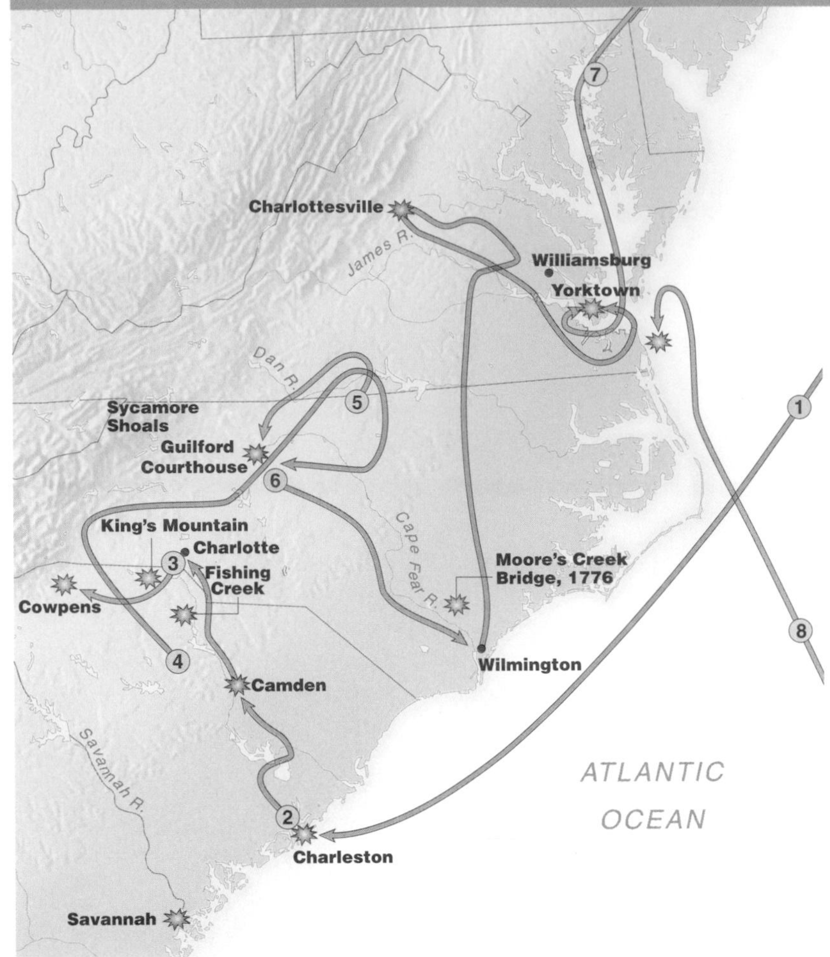

4.13 Southern Campaigns
Although the British scored impressive victories early in the South, especially at Charleston, American forces recovered and forced Cornwallis to retreat to Virginia. Cornwallis's move proved to be a strategic error, since it allowed the French fleet to cut off Cornwallis and enabled Washington to trap the British at Yorktown.

British
Patriots
British victories
Patriot victories

1. Clinton and Cornwallis force surrender of Charleston, May 1780
2. Cornwallis bests Gates at Camden and moves north, August 1780
3. Morgan meets British at Cowpens, defeats Tarleton, January 1781
4. Cornwallis pursues Greene's army across the Dan River, February 1781
5. Greene confronts Cornwallis at Guilford Courthouse, March 1781
6. After a retreat to Wilmington, Cornwallis moves to Virginia, April 1781
7. Washington moves south, pins Cornwallis at Yorktown, August 1781
8. French Admiral De Grasse from West Indies, defeats the British fleet, September 1781

historic moment as though the Americans hardly figured in it at all (**4.14**).

Outnumbered and with his land and sea escapes cut off, Cornwallis decided that he had no alternative but to surrender to Washington in October of 1781. Washington then appointed General Benjamin Lincoln to receive the British surrender, offered by a subordinate of Cornwallis. During the negotiation of the surrender, British musicians played an old popular tune called "The World Turned Upside Down." America had turned the world upside down: It had defeated the most powerful nation on earth.

The British defeat at Yorktown provided American diplomats with a strong bargaining position in negotiating a peace treaty with Britain. The **Treaty of Paris** (1783) officially ended the war between the newly created United States and Britain. The treaty recognized American independence, acknowledged America's border with Canada, and recognized American fishing rights in the area off Newfoundland.

4.14 Defeat of Cornwallis at Yorktown
A French artist's fanciful depiction of the American and French victory at Yorktown focused entirely on the French navy and army. A medieval-looking walled city in the background also signifies his lack of familiarity with the events.

Why was the song "The World Turned Upside Down" so appropriate for the surrender of Cornwallis at Yorktown?

The Radicalism of the American Revolution

The American Revolution encompassed two interrelated struggles. The Revolution was both a colonial war for independence and a revolutionary struggle to change American government and society. Thus the war was both a struggle for home rule—the right of Americans to govern themselves—and a war for who should rule at home, a contest to determine the nature of American government and the structure of society. The American Revolution set in motion a social and political transformation that affected nearly every aspect of American society. The Declaration of Independence had articulated the twin ideals of equality and liberty. Some Americans took the declaration's bold affirmation of liberty and equality to be an endorsement of more than colonial independence. For them these words were revolutionary. The message of the Declaration inspired them to undertake a radical transformation of American politics and society.

The first constitutions drafted by the states in 1776 included language that echoed the Declaration's affirmation of the ideals of liberty and equality. Few Americans doubted the importance of this affirmation; deciding how far to take it, however, proved controversial. The Pennsylvania Constitution went further than any other state constitution in embracing a democratic conception of equality—at least for white men.

Not every group in America benefited equally from the promise of the Revolution. African slaves, Indians, and women were not included fully in the Revolution's promise of equality and liberty. Although the promise of the Revolution remained unfilled for many in America, oppressed groups throughout American history would use this promise to seek to obtain the full rights of citizenship.

Popular Politics in the Revolutionary Era

British taxation was not the only set of policies that produced violent resistance during the Revolutionary era. Colonists also opposed unfair taxes imposed by their own colonial governments. The established colonial elites who dominated government also came under attack. In the Carolinas, a Regulator movement emerged that sought reform of colonial government. The Regulators, as their name implied, sought to regulate society by eliminating corruption and bringing the rule of law to places that lacked it. The Regulators resented eastern interests who were eager to tax western farmers, but not interested in sharing political power with them. Thus in backcountry North Carolina, Regulators opposed oppressive tax policies, including taxes enacted to pay for a lavish new palace for the royal governor. Some Regulators, such as Herman Husband, wove together religious themes with democratic ideas and formulated a forceful critique of corruption and inequality in North Carolina. Husband fused his religious rhetoric with a class-conscious critique of the eastern elites who dominated state politics. Husband noted that "obedience to just laws, and subjection to slavery" were not the same. Resistance to unjust authority was legitimate because "God gave all men a knowledge of their privileges, and a true zeal to maintain them." In contrast with Husband's views, the royal governor and his supporters among the clergy asserted that "subjection to lawful authority," not resistance, was the "plain and principal doctrine of Christianity."

In 1770 one thousand Regulators marched on the Orange County courthouse in Hillsborough. The protesters not only shut down the court but also publicly whipped a court official who was notorious for charging excessively high fees to process basic legal documents. The angry crowd also meted out punishments to several lawyers whose high fees were a source of irritation to backcountry residents. Such fees fell heavily on poor folk and blocked their access to the courts. The protests of the Regulators prompted the royal governor to dispatch the militia, which defeated the Regulators and restored order.

Who were the Regulators?

Although the Regulators were not victorious, their class-conscious rhetoric and critique of power and corruption struck a resonant note in many parts of the Carolina backcountry.

Constitutional Experiments: Testing the Limits of Democracy

When the Continental Congress directed the states to draft new constitutions, the new states became political laboratories for constitutional experimentation. Different visions of constitutional government were set against one another in this vibrant public debate. Virginia broke new ground by framing a detailed declaration of rights that would serve as a model for other states. By contrast virtually every other state apart from Vermont rejected Pennsylvania's radical democratic experiment. Massachusetts, like Virginia, became a model for other states, pioneering a number of constitutional developments that would become essential features of American constitutionalism, particularly in areas such as the separation of powers and checks and balances between these different branches.

4.15 Timothy Matlack
To symbolize Matlack's role in drafting the Pennsylvania Constitution of 1776, the painter included several items in the background, including law books, the great seal of Pennsylvania, the text of the Pennsylvania Constitution, and a powder horn and musket. [*Source:* Charles Willson Peale's, "Timothy Matlack," c. 1790, oil on canvas. Access. # 1998.218/ Photograph © 2010 Museum of Fine Arts, Boston.]

In June of 1776 the new state of Virginia drafted a Declaration of Rights and a Constitution. The chief architect of the Declaration of Rights was George Mason, an influential Patriot leader in Virginia. The document asserted that life, liberty, and property were fundamental rights and that "all men are by nature equally free and independent." Some Virginians worried that this language might undermine the institution of slavery, encouraging slaves to revolt. Another delegate calmed these fears by pointing out that an armed population organized as a well-regulated militia would be more than adequate to protect Virginians from its slave population. Indeed the Virginia Declaration of Rights also affirmed "That a well regulated militia, composed of the body of the people, trained to arms, is the proper, natural, and safe defense of a free state; that standing armies, in time of peace, should be avoided as dangerous to liberty; and that, in all cases, the military should be under strict subordination to, and be governed by, the civil power." The Declaration of Rights also protected other basic liberties: trial by jury, freedom of the press, and freedom of religion.

Pennsylvania drafted its constitution not long after Virginia's. While members of a slave-owning planter elite drafted Virginia's Declaration of Rights and Constitution, a more democratic coalition that included urban artisans influenced by the ideas of Thomas Paine and backcountry farmers resentful of the old eastern colonial elites, and similar to the Regulators, drafted Pennsylvania's constitution. Echoing Paine's ideas in *Common Sense*, the Pennsylvania Constitution created a form of representative government with a single legislature, a system known as **unicameralism**.

Responding to the frustration of frontier settlers, who had sought the creation of a state militia to protect them from Indian attack, and the necessities of fighting against Britain, the Pennsylvania Constitution also created a citizens' militia and became the first state constitution to expressly protect the right of citizens to bear arms "in defense of themselves and the state." In keeping with Paine's

What made Pennsylvania's Constitution so radical for its day?

democratic ideas, the constitution rejected property requirements for voting. Any male taxpayer who resided in the state for a year could vote. Timothy Matlack, who had helped write this radical constitution, commissioned a portrait that reflected its diverse influences (**4.15**). A powder horn and musket appear in the background, the text of the Pennsylvania Constitution before him on the table, and volumes of important British legal texts rest on the table behind him.

The Revolution prompted a lively public debate over how far to take the idea of democracy. Although Pennsylvania may have gone further than most in implementing these ideas, similar debates occurred in the press in other states. The traditional Whig theory of representation assumed that only property owners could exercise the independent judgment necessary to vote. Individuals without property would be at the mercy of the rich and powerful who could influence their votes on election day. Whig theory also viewed the possession of property as an essential way of demonstrating that one had a permanent stake in society. According to the Whigs only men with such an interest would be able to act in the long-term interests of society. The Revolution nurtured a competing vision of government, far more democratic in spirit. The anonymous author of the pamphlet *The People the Best Governors* championed this alternative vision of politics, asserting that "the people know best their own wants and necessities, and therefore are best able to rule themselves." According to this view, a propertied elite was not needed to act as a check on the people.

Those who rejected the radical notion of equality implicit in democracy ridiculed the new, more democratic theories being advanced. The Reverend Charles Bullman of South Carolina, for example, suggested that if these ideas were not checked, "Every silly clown and illiterate mechanic will take upon him to censure the conduct of his Prince or Governor." Among the Patriot elite no figure expressed greater reservations about the dangers of too much democracy, and of unicameralism, than John Adams. Fearful of Paine's influenced, Adams reluctantly conceded that Paine's work had helped rally Americans to the idea of independence, but Adams feared that Paine's work had "a better hand at pulling down than building" up governments. Indeed Adams worried that Paine's "feeble" ideas about government would mislead Americans when the time came to draft new state constitutions. Adams incorporated his own views on the matter into his short, but influential, essay, "Thoughts on Government," which he wrote in response to a request from North Carolina's Provincial Congress, the body responsible for framing its new constitution.

Most states were unwilling to follow Pennsylvania's radical model, opting to retain some type of property requirement for voting and office holding. In general, however, the new property requirements the states adopted were somewhat lower than they had been during the colonial period, so on balance, the pool of eligible voters increased. Although not a resounding victory for those who shared the democratic views of Thomas Paine and the author of "The People the Best Governors," the Revolution clearly led to a greater democratization of politics.

Although not the most democratic experiment in government, the Massachusetts Constitution produced interesting innovations. John Adams played a leading role in helping to draft it. Adopted in 1780 it remains the oldest continuously functioning written constitution in the world. Setting the terms for nearly all subsequent constitution-making in America, Massachusetts had taken revolutionary-era constitutional ideas in several new directions. Massachusetts saw a constitution as the supreme law that had to rest on the express consent of the government. Legislative bodies had drafted earlier state constitutions, but a special convention drafted the Massachusetts constitution, which it then submitted directly to the people for ratification. The idea of securing express consent for the constitution led Massachusetts to take the

> "Shall We Say, that every Individual of the Community, old and young, male and female, as well as rich and poor, must consent, expressly to every Act of Legislation?"
>
> JOHN ADAMS to James Sullivan, May 1776

Why did the traditional Whig view of representation oppose democracy?

unprecedented step of eliminating property requirements for this special ratification process. Thus even those white men who would not meet the property requirements for voting for the legislature under the proposed constitution were able to vote on the Constitution. The notion that a constitution had to be submitted to the people directly for ratification was a radical innovation that quickly became an accepted feature of American constitutional life.

The Massachusetts Constitution also became the first to successfully implement an effective system of checks and balances. While all of the early state governments supported the principle of separation of powers, making the powers of the legislative, executive, and judicial functions of government distinct, these early constitutions had not built in the checks and balances that would make this ideal a practical reality. To make separation of powers effective, the different branches of government had to have the ability to check one another's power. Massachusetts went further than any other state in devising a system that achieved this goal. The Massachusetts office of governor had considerable power, including the right to veto acts of the legislature. This gave the executive the ability to check the legislature. The legislature was given a check on the governor through its ability to override a gubernatorial veto by a two-thirds vote. Finally, to compensate and balance this additional power, Massachusetts made the governor an office directly elected by the people, not appointed by the legislature as many other states had opted to do.

Another important experiment in constitutional government was the Articles of Confederation, the constitution that Congress framed for the new United States of America. Although Congress drafted the articles in 1777, the states did not ratify them for another four years. The government created by the articles was not a national government, but rather "a firm league of friendship" among the sovereign states. Thus Article II of the articles affirmed that "Each state retains its sovereignty, freedom, and independence, and every power, jurisdiction, and right, which is not by this Confederation expressly delegated to the United States, in Congress assembled." Because fighting the British was then Congress's top priority, Congress cobbled together the Articles of Confederation without providing many features that the individual states had included in their constitutions. Frustration and fear of British-style government also shaped the minds of Congress. Having just cast off a powerful central government with a powerful king, the articles abandoned the idea of a single unified executive to enforce the law. Nor did the articles have the power to tax, another governmental power that the British had abused. The articles created a weak government whose ability to tax, engage in military actions, and conduct diplomacy depended entirely on the goodwill of the states.

African Americans Struggle for Freedom

The great English literary figure Dr. Samuel Johnson pointed out the hypocrisy of Americans claiming to be champions of liberty while enslaving Africans. In some cases slaves invoked the ideas of the Revolution explicitly, while in others they voted with their feet, seizing opportunities to free themselves. The dislocations associated with America's war for independence provided opportunities for African Americans seeking to escape the bondage of slavery. For some, fleeing to the British side provided the best chance for freedom. Other slaves seized on the ideas nurtured by the broader revolutionary changes that accompanied the war for independence. The ideas of liberty and equality intensified the burgeoning movement for the abolition of slavery more generally. Although the Revolution did not eradicate slavery, it did put it on the road to extinction in New England and the mid-Atlantic regions.

> "How is it that we hear the loudest yelps for liberty among the drivers of Negro slaves?"
>
> Dr. SAMUEL JOHNSON, 1775

Slaves, eager to cast off their own shackles, appropriated the Revolution's language of liberty. During the Stamp Act protests in South Carolina (1765), slaves staged their own parade chanting "liberty." Alarmed South Carolinians viewed such activities as evidence of a plan for rebellion. To thwart the imagined threat, they mobilized the militia, which also served as slave patrols. Blacks in New England fared better when they invoked the Revolution's ideals than did blacks in the South. In

What was the impact of the American Revolution on the institution of slavery?

1774 a group of slaves petitioned the governor, council, and House of Representatives of the Province of Massachusetts for their freedom. In their petition the slaves used the language of the Declaration of Independence, including the idea of natural rights and the notion that government rested on the consent of the governed. They asserted: "We have in common with all other men a naturel right to our freedoms without Being depriv'd of them by our fellow men."

Less than a decade later, another slave, Mum Bett, successfully sued for her freedom. A local jury in western Massachusetts heard the case and based their verdict on the language of the state's declaration of rights, which stated clearly that "All men are born free and equal, and have certain natural, essential, and unalienable rights; among which may be reckoned the right of enjoying and defending their lives and liberties." Mum Bett changed her name to Elizabeth Freeman, obtained employment as a housekeeper in the home of the lawyer who defended her, and eventually became a respected midwife and nurse in her community. Citing this precedent the state's highest court eventually upheld the decision and officially abolished slavery in Massachusetts.

New England went further than any other region in its support for the abolition of slavery. Vermont's 1777 Constitution expressly prohibited slavery, the first constitution in the nation to take such a bold step. In the mid-Atlantic Pennsylvania and New York adopted gradual schemes of emancipation.

The American Revolution in Indian Country

The struggle between Britain and the American colonies had enormous consequences for American Indians. Although neutrality appealed to many Indians, avoiding entanglement in the conflict between Britain and America became impossible. Faced with the need to make a choice, many Indian nations chose to side with Britain, whose colonial policies, including the Proclamation of 1763, had blocked American expansion into indigenous peoples' lands. An American victory would inevitably mean more settlers streaming into American Indian country and greater destruction of the habitats that Indians depended on for their survival.

The language of the Declaration of Independence had underscored America's deep-seated fear and hostility toward American Indians. Among the many complaints Jefferson leveled against the king was: "He has excited domestic insurrections amongst us, and has endeavoured to bring on the inhabitants of our frontiers, the merciless Indian Savages, whose known rule of warfare, is an undistinguished destruction of all ages, sexes and conditions." Jefferson's view of American Indians as "savages" engaged in acts of barbarism rallied Americans against the British.

One event that whipped up anti-Indian feelings among Americans was the murder of Jane McCrea in upstate New York at the hands of Mohawk Indians. Jane was traveling to meet her fiancé, a British soldier, when pro-British Mohawk Indians attacked her. McCrea's political sympathies did not prevent her from becoming a martyr for the Patriot cause. Colonial newspapers lamented her sad fate, which was also memorialized in poetry. In 1780 a novel about her demise appeared, and the painter John Trumbull made several sketches of McCrea's murder for a possible painting before deciding to abandon the subject and move on to other projects, including his painting of the death of General Warren. The story of McCrea continued to attract artists decades later. Writer Joel Barlow, a close friend of Jefferson and important literary figure in early America, memorialized the event in one of his poems, and artist John Vanderlyn used the event as the basis for this dramatic painting (**4.16**), which was displayed in 1804. Vanderlyn's representation of the light-skinned McCrea and the dark-skinned American Indians underscores the role of the painting as a morality tale between

4.16 Death of Jane McCrea John Vanderlyn painted this scene several decades after the event occurred. He took several liberties with history. McCrea's fiancé, the military figure rushing to rescue her (circled in red), wears the blue uniform of a Continental soldier. In reality McCrea was a Loyalist and her fiancé a British regular. [*Source:* John Vanderlyn, "The Murder of Jane McCrea". 1804. Oil on canvas, 32 1/2 × 26 1/2 in. Wadsworth Atheneum Museum of Art, Hartford, CT. Purchased by Subscription. Acc# 1855.4]

Why did so many Indians side with the British during the American Revolution?

good and evil. The American Indians are depicted as cruel savages about to murder McCrea.

Pro-British tribes siding with the British, whose policies they saw as limiting colonial expansion westward, scored notable victories on the western frontier during 1782. After these successes, many Indians were stunned to learn that the British had surrendered at Yorktown. Indians were excluded from the negotiations that ended the war. Many viewed the Treaty of Paris (1783), which ceded much of American Indian country to America, as a betrayal.

Liberty's Daughters: Women and the Revolutionary Movement

Women took an active role in the revolutionary cause. One of the most outspoken female Patriots was Mercy Otis Warren, wife of patriot leader James Warren and sister of James Otis. Warren's gifts as a poet, playwright, and eventually historian allowed her to champion the American cause in a variety of literary endeavors. Her satirical plays mocked British policy and took aim at leading British politicians and military figures. The fictional names of the characters in her plays communicated Warren's disdain for the British. Warren's scathing satire mocked the actions of Brigadier General Hateall, Secretary of State Dupe, and Governor Rapatio. These sinister plotters against American liberty were matched by equally talented and virtuous American Patriot leaders, whose names, Brutus or Honestus, signified their commitment to Roman republican virtue.

Women also served in various roles in the war effort. When mustered into service the militia often depended on support from women. An eyewitness to such a mobilization in Cambridge, Massachusetts, in 1774 noted that local women "surpassed the Men for Eagerness & Spirit in the Defense of Liberty by Arms." Women not only provided moral support, "animating their Husbands & Sons to fight for their liberties," but also helped "making Cartridges." Some women actively supported the efforts of troops, becoming "Molly Pitchers," women who hauled water and carried supplies to soldiers. Deborah Sampson took this commitment a step further, disguising herself as a man and serving the Continental Army under the name Robert Shirtliffe. A camp physician discovered Sampson while attending to her during a bout of fever. The Continental Army also had camp followers—women, including the wives of soldiers, who washed, cooked, nursed, and tended to other needs of soldiers during the Revolution.

The Revolution's emphasis on liberty and equality boosted notions of gender equality. Abigail Adams, wife of John Adams, wrote to her husband who was serving in the Continental Congress and working on his own ideas about politics in his essay "Thoughts on Government." Abigail demanded that her husband "remember the ladies" and work toward greater legal equality for women (see *Competing Visions: Remember the Ladies*). A few women went further than Abigail, demanding not only legal equality but also some measure of political equality, at least for women who owned property.

One supporter of this idea was Hannah Corbin, sister of Patriot leader Richard Henry Lee. While Abigail Adams's life was a model of female propriety, Corbin led an unconventional lifestyle that made her acutely aware of the inferior legal status of women. After her husband died an untimely death at the age of thirty-five, Corbin managed the affairs of her husband's plantation. Her husband's will stipulated that if she ever remarried, Hannah would lose control of her family's estate. The spirited Corbin was unwilling to accept the choice of remaining a widow or losing control of her property. Rejecting contemporary moral codes Hannah Corbin began a common-law relationship with another man (living together as husband and wife without being legally married). Although the two lived together as husband and wife, the fact that they were not legally married allowed her to preserve control of her estate. The defiant and independent Corbin later wrote to her brother inquiring why women who owned property were prohibited from voting. Lee could provide no reasonable explanation to his sister's inquiry. Lee even conceded that in theory, a policy allowing such women to vote was plausible, but fell back on custom, noting that "it has never been the practice either here or in England" and speculating that "Perhaps 'twas thought rather out of character for women to press into those tumultuous assemblages of men."

Every state, apart from New Jersey, limited suffrage to men. It is not clear if New Jersey's omission was deliberate or accidental. Still New Jersey women who fulfilled the state's property requirements took full advantage of this omission and voted in elections for more than three decades before state legislature revoked this right.

Although the Revolution did not usher in the legal or political changes sought by Adams and Corbin, the ideas of equality espoused by the

Was Hannah Corbin's argument for women's suffrage consistent with Whig theory?

Competing Visions

REMEMBER THE LADIES

A strong supporter of independence, and an articulate and forceful personality, Abigail Adams believed that the American Revolution provided an opportunity for women to gain much-needed legal reform. This was particularly needed in areas such as property law, where women were considered legally dead once they married.

In this spirited letter written shortly before Congress declared independence from Britain, Abigail made her displeasure with the inferior legal status of women quite clear to her husband.

Abigail Adams to John Adams, 31 Mar. 1776

I desire you would Remember the Ladies, and be more generous and favourable to them than your ancestors. Do not put such unlimited power into the hands of the Husbands. Remember all Men would be tyrants if they could. If particular care and attention is not paid to the Ladies we are determined to foment a Rebellion, and will not hold ourselves bound by any Laws in which we have no voice, or Representation.

Abigail Adams

In a somewhat dismissive reply, Adams nevertheless revealed how the Revolution's ideas about equality permeated American society.

John Adams to Abigail Adams, 14 Apr. 1776

As to your extraordinary Code of Laws, I cannot but laugh. We have been told that our Struggle has loosened the bands of Government every where. That Children and Apprentices were disobedient—that schools and Colleges were grown turbulent—that Indians slighted their Guardians and Negroes grew insolent to their Masters. But your Letter was the first Intimation that another Tribe more numerous and powerful than all the rest were grown discontented. —This is rather too coarse a Compliment but you are so saucy, I wont blot it out. Depend upon it, We know better than to repeal our Masculine systems.

John Adams

Was Abigail Adams's demand for women's rights consistent with the Revolution's ideals?

Revolution did influence ideas about marriage and family life. Lucy Knox, wife of General Henry Knox, wrote to her husband a year after the Declaration of Independence to remind him to "not consider yourself as commander in chief of your own house," but recognize that "there is such a thing as equal command." Lucy Knox viewed marriage as an egalitarian relationship between husband and wife, one in which the two lived together as companions. Scholars describe this new conception of husband and wife as **companionate marriage.** The Revolution not only altered ideas about marriage but also changed attitudes about patriarchal authority, a fact reflected in the portraiture of the day. In his painting of the Cadwalader family, Charles Wilson Peale gives a model of a companionate marriage (**4.17**). Peale's painting contrasts with a style of family portraiture seen in a painting of the Isaac Royall family done thirty years earlier. A comparison of the portraits shows how ideas of family relations, including the relationship between husband and wife, and parents and children, had changed in the intervening years (**4.18**). In Peale's painting John and Elizabeth Cadwalader look directly at one another. His hand

4.17 Cadwalader Family
Charles Wilson Peale's portrait of the Cadwalader family evokes the ideal of companionate marriage, in which husbands and wives enjoyed an intimate and egalitarian relationship within marriage. [*Source:* Charles Willson Peale, "Portrait of John and Elizabeth Lloyd Cadwalader and Their Daughter Anne". 1772. Oil on canvas, 50 1/2" × 41 1/4" (128.3 × 104.8 cm). Photo: Graydon Wood. Philadelphia Museum of Art: Purchased for the Cadwalader collection with funds contributed by the Mabel Pew Myrin Trust and the gift of an anonymous donor, 1983. Acc: 1983-90-3.]

How do these two paintings demonstrate the changing views of the family in the era of the American Revolution?

rests on hers, and their young child reaches for the peach held by his father. The intimacy of the family is evidenced in the physical closeness of its members. By contrast the portrait of the Royall family reveals little of this physical closeness. The husband has no physical contact with his wife or his children.

4.18 ***Isaac Royall and Family*****, by Robert Feke, 1741**
This portrait of the Royall family, done almost three decades before the Cadwalader portrait, captures the more patriarchal view of the family. The father stands somewhat aloof from the family.

Conclusion

American resistance to British policy impelled the thirteen colonies to declare their independence from Britain and wage war against the most powerful nation on earth. Americans had started this process convinced that they were simply defending the cherished rights of Englishmen. By the time Americans published the Declaration of Independence in 1776, their ideas had evolved and their claims asserted the fundamental rights of all men. What began as a colonial war for independence had become a genuine revolution.

The ideas of equality and liberty that inspired the American Revolution transformed American society. White men were the greatest beneficiaries of the Revolution. The ideas of liberty and equality articulated in the Declaration of Independence infused the first constitutions drafted by the individual states. These new governments experimented with how to apply these abstract principles. No state went further than Pennsylvania in implementing the ideas of democracy. Yet within a generation Pennsylvania's radical experiment in unicameralism would be cast aside in favor of the more typical bicameral model favored by most states. Only New Jersey followed the logic of equality to allow women to vote. Still the Revolution's ideas transformed ideas about women's roles and helped slaves in New England and the mid-Atlantic states to push for the abolition of slavery. One group largely excluded from the benefits of the Revolution was American Indians, many of whom had backed the British.

As the young republic confronted new problems, including how to pay for its recent war for independence, Americans began to re-examine their political institutions. Americans also grappled with how to deal with the democratic ideals unleashed by the Revolution. Even more significant, Americans would jettison the Articles of Confederation in favor of a new more powerful central government. America's experiment in constitutional government was only just beginning.

1764

Sugar Act
British tax molasses and colonies protest being taxed without their consent

1765

Stamp Act
Colonial protest intensifies against Britain's new policies

1770

Boston Massacre
British troops fire on crowd in Boston

Review Questions

1. What were the main goals of Britain's new policies toward the colonies after the conclusion of the French and Indian War?
2. In what ways did American protest against the Stamp Act inaugurate a new phase in American resistance to British policy?
3. How did Paul Revere's representation of the events of the Boston Massacre in his famous engraving stir up resentment against the British? How did Revere manipulate the events to present them in the worst possible light?
4. How did Jefferson's argument for independence in the Declaration differ from Paine's argument in *Common Sense*?
5. What advantages did the Americans possess in the war for independence? What were the important advantages of the British?
6. How did the Massachusetts Constitution depart from the earlier models of Virginia and Pennsylvania?
7. Did the Revolution's ideals of liberty and equality have any significant impact on the lives of blacks, women, and American Indians?

1773–1775

Boston Tea Party
Sons of Liberty toss tea into Boston Harbor

Intolerable Acts
Port of Boston Closed

Lexington, Concord, Bunker Hill
These early battles demonstrated the colonists' capacity to use military force to protect their rights.

Olive Branch Petition
Congress makes final attempt to persuade the king to address American grievances

IN CONGRESS, JULY 4, 1776.
A DECLARATION
BY THE REPRESENTATIVES OF THE
UNITED STATES OF AMERICA,
IN GENERAL CONGRESS ASSEMBLED.

1776

Thomas Paine publishes *Common Sense*
Paine states the case for American independence in a pamphlet that becomes an instant best seller

Declaration of Independence
American colonies declare independence

Pennsylvania Declaration of Rights and Constitution
Pennsylvania Constitution adopts simple democratic scheme of government

Washington's Victory at Princeton
Washington's victories at Trenton and Princeton boost Americans' morale

1777

Jane McCrea murdered by Mohawk Indians
The murder becomes a rallying cry for Americans against British treachery

1781

Defeat of Cornwallis at Yorktown
American and French forces defeat British army at Yorktown, ending the Revolutionary War

Key Terms

Sugar Act British tax aimed at imported sugar, molasses, and other goods imported into the colonies; it also created a new mechanism for enforcing compliance with custom's duties. **98**

Stamp Act Legislation that required colonists to purchase special stamps and place them on all legal documents. Newspapers and playing cards had to be printed on special stamped paper. **99**

nonimportation movement A boycott against the purchase of any imported British goods. **100**

Boston Massacre A confrontation between a group of Bostonians and British troops on March 5, 1770, during which the troops opened fire on the citizens, killing five of them. **101**

Intolerable Acts Legislation passed by Parliament to punish Bostonians for the Boston Tea Party. It closed the Port of Boston; annulled the Massachusetts colonial charter and dissolved or severely restricted that colony's political institutions; and allowed British officials charged with capital crimes to be tried outside the colonies. **102**

militia An organization of citizen soldiers regulated by the laws of the individual colonies that provided the primary means of public defense in the colonial period. **104**

Lord Dunmore's Proclamation Official announcement issued by Lord Dunmore, royal governor of Virginia. It offered freedom to any slave who joined the British forces in putting down the American rebellion. **105**

Common Sense Thomas Paine's influential pamphlet that forcefully argued for American independence, attacked the institution of monarchy, and defended a democratic theory of representative government. **107**

Declaration of Independence On July 4, 1776, Congress approved the final text of the Declaration of Independence, a public defense of America's decision to declare independence from Britain that was to be printed and sent to the individual states. **110**

Patriots Colonists who supported American independence. **110**

Loyalists Colonists who remained loyal to the king and Britain. **110**

Treaty of Paris (1783) Treaty between the newly created United States of America and Britain that officially ended the war between the two and formally recognized American independence. **116**

unicameralism A form of representative government with only one legislature. Pennsylvania's 1776 constitution created a unicameral system. **118**

companionate marriage A term used by scholars to describe a more egalitarian relationship between husband and wife in which the two act as companions to each other. **124**

CHAPTER 5

A Virtuous Republic

Creating a Workable Government, 1783–1789

> "We may look up to Armies for our Defense, but Virtue is our best Security. It is not possible that any State should long remain free, where Virtue is not supremely honored."
>
> SAMUEL ADAMS 1775

In 1776 patriot leader John Adams wrote that "public virtue is the only foundation of Republics. There must be a positive passion for the public good, the public interest." Adams echoed many Americans' views when he wrote that republican government depended on the concept of public virtue, which meant pursuing the public good and placing it ahead of personal interest or local attachments. Men were expected to serve in the militia, sit on juries, and, if they were truly virtuous and wise, take on the burden of public service as elected representatives. Women, too, were expected to play a major role in the political life of the new republic, assuming the role of republican mothers and wives who would instill patriotism and virtue in their children and spouses.

Americans of the revolutionary generation took their cues from the lessons of history, particularly the example of the Roman Republic and its ideal of public virtue. When Dr. Joseph Warren, physician and Patriot leader, addressed Bostonians on the fifth anniversary of the Boston Massacre in 1775, he literally donned a Roman toga, the long flowing gown that symbolized freedom and citizenship. Warren's dramatic gesture, linking himself with Roman republicanism, was mirrored in the pages of nearly every American newspaper of the day, where letters and essays on political matters were signed with pen names drawn from Roman history, such as the politicians Brutus and Cato, and the great Roman general Cincinnatus.

To mold a new generation of virtuous citizens, Americans looked to education, religion, and even architecture. No American was more enthusiastic about architecture's capacity to instruct than Thomas Jefferson. Public buildings, Jefferson wrote, "should be more than things of beauty and convenience, above all they should state a creed." Rather than emulate contemporary Georgian-style buildings such as the Pennsylvania State House (see Chapter 3), the building in which the Declaration of Independence was drafted, Jefferson argued for a return to the purity of Roman architecture. In his design for the Virginia State Capitol (pictured here), Jefferson succeeded in re-creating the simple beauty of Roman architecture. He believed that the Virginia State Capitol would inspire citizens to emulate the ideals of the ancient Roman Republic, which included an emphasis on civic participation and public virtue.

In the decade following independence, Americans' faith in their ability to create a virtuous republic was severely challenged. An aborted coup led by disgruntled Continental Army officers, conflicts between debtors and creditors, and an uprising in western Massachusetts drove the nation to a political crisis. The events of the postwar period tested America's faith in republicanism and led some leaders to abandon traditional republican theory, with its emphasis on virtue, and to embrace a new approach to constitutional government that relied on a balance of conflicting interests and a system of checks and balances. The culmination of this struggle between the two competing visions of constitutional government was the U.S. Constitution and the Bill of Rights.

What did virtue mean to the Founders of the American Republic?

ONE DOLLAR.

Republicanism and the Politics of Virtue

The American Revolution marked a decisive break from many ideas and values that had defined British culture for centuries. Monarchy and aristocracy were swept away by the Revolution. America was now a republic. Republicanism placed a premium on the ideal of virtue. As the poet, playwright, and historian Mercy Otis Warren observed, Americans needed "to cherish true, genuine republican virtue." The events of the postwar period would test this commitment in a host of ways.

George Washington: The American Cincinnatus

No individual in America was more closely identified with the ideal of virtue than George Washington. A symbol of the virtuous citizen–soldier, responding to the summons of his nation and retiring to private life once his service was no longer needed—Washington was a model of civic virtue. Washington's reputation for public virtue and his ability to command the respect of his troops had helped the beleaguered Continental Army during some of its more dire campaigns. In 1783 Washington faced a different sort of challenge. This time it was not the threat of enemy troops he faced, but the rumors of a military coup by the Continental Army's officers' corps. Washington wielded his personal authority to win over disgruntled members of the corps and made an impassioned appeal to "reason and virtue," thus crushing the revolt without firing a shot.

Washington had learned of rumors that the army's leadership would no longer tolerate Congress's failure to deal with complaints about their pay and the issue of their pensions. An anonymous essay had circulated among officers suggesting that the time might soon come when it would be necessary to turn their arms against Congress itself. The officers' anger had been simmering for some time. Frustration with the Confederation Congress was widespread among officers; Washington was well aware of the officers' grievances. He had complained about the inefficiency and ineffectiveness of Congress on many occasions. With no power to tax, Congress had to depend on voluntary contributions from the states. Without a reliable source of revenue, it was difficult to wage war or conduct the routine business of governing. Faced with the possibility of a rebellion by his own officers, Washington resolved to address his men in person and persuade them of the folly of their plan.

On a dark wintry day in March 1783, Washington traveled to Newburgh, New York, to address the officers' corps. The assembled officers met in a makeshift building that some of them had dubbed the "Temple of Virtue." Washington prepared to read a letter that he hoped would persuade the officers that their demands would be met. Fumbling to find a pair of glasses he had recently acquired, he paused, and then addressed the hushed crowd: "Gentlemen, you must pardon me. I have grown grey in your service, and now find myself growing blind." The impact on his audience was dramatic. "There was something so natural, so unaffected in his appeal," Major Samuel Shaw later wrote, "as rendered it superior to the most studied oratory, and you might see sensibility moisten every eye." Washington's own wartime sacrifices had already provided a powerful role model for the officers' corps. Now the figure of their beloved commander growing gray and blind in the service of his country struck a resonant chord. He exhorted his men to give posterity "proof of unexampled patriotism and patient virtue." Civic virtue had triumphed over corruption, and the Newburgh conspiracy was effectively crushed without a single shot being fired.

Another important event that helped spread Washington's reputation as the embodiment of republican virtue was the highly public ceremonial occasion of turning over his military commission to Congress after the war. In Annapolis, Maryland, where Congress was convened, Washington addressed a room crowded with congressional delegates and a gallery packed with well-wishers. "Having now finished the work assigned me," he

Why did Americans believe Washington was the modern Cincinnatus?

informed his audience, many of whom were brought to tears, "I here offer my commission, and take my leave" of "the employments of public life." By abandoning public life and returning to his plow, Washington was seen as placing the good of the nation ahead of personal glory. In the public's view, Washington had transformed himself into the modern Cincinnatus, an allusion to the ancient world's great symbol of public virtue, the Roman general Cincinnatus. After serving the Roman Republic as a soldier, Cincinnatus returned to life as a farmer.

After resigning, Washington went on a triumphal tour of the nation. As he entered Philadelphia, he was saluted by cannons and a chorus of bells from the city's steeples. He sat for portraits by America's leading painters and enjoyed listening to commemorative verses that compared him to Cincinnatus. Well schooled in the history of the ancient Roman Republic, Americans understood that a popular military leader's decision to emulate Rome's dictatorial general Julius Caesar rather than Cincinnatus would lead to despotism. Several years later the Virginia legislature commissioned the eminent French sculptor Jean-Antoine Houdon to create a life-sized statue of Washington as the modern Cincinnatus (**5.1**). Washington stands before a plow, the symbol of the virtuous farmer, the ideal embodied by Cincinnatus.

> "No free Government, or the blessing of liberty, can be preserved to any people but by a firm adherence to justice, moderation, temperance, frugality, and virtue . . .
>
> Virginia Declaration of Rights, 1776

5.1 George Washington as the Modern Cincinnatus George Washington is literally cast as the modern Cincinnatus in this sculpture. He stands in front of the plow and beside the Roman "fasces," a bundle of rods that symbolized the rule of law.

The Politics of Virtue: Views from the States

The republican emphasis on virtue suffused American culture. The first state constitutions drafted after independence used their declarations of rights to outline the basic rights of citizens and also instructed citizens in the basic premises of republican government. In these declarations of rights, the ideal of virtue was literally written into American law. The Virginia Declaration of Rights (1776) asserted that free government could not survive without a virtuous citizenry, a point echoed by the Massachusetts Constitution drafted four years later. Educating citizens in the importance of republican ideals became a high priority for the new nation.

Art, architecture, and even fashion were pressed into service to mold the character of a new generation of citizens. Jefferson's design for the new Virginia Capitol was the most ambitious visible symbol of the way one might instill republican values by reforming architecture. (See the chapter opening image, p. 129). The impact of the Revolution was even seen in home furnishings. Before the Revolution, decorative elements on American furniture copied British fashions, including fanciful designs such as the scrolled

5.2 Chippendale High Chest
This pre-revolutionary chest reflected British styles, including the floral decorative patterns in the fancy broken pediment on top of the chest. [Courtesy, Winterthur Museum]

pediment with rosettes on this chest of drawers (**5.2**). After the Revolution some of these purely decorative elements were replaced with symbols that represented the republican values of the new nation. A beautifully crafted example of this adorns a chest of drawers made in Salem, Massachusetts (**5.3**). The broken pediment is a simple classical design. Gone is the fancy carving in the pediment of the late colonial chest (5.2). In its place is the goddess of liberty herself. To reinforce the ideal of Roman republicanism, the chest has two classical columns, another symbol of this ideal. These flank another set of carvings that illustrate the prosperity that republicanism will bring to the new nation.

Education was another important means for inculcating virtue. The Massachusetts Constitution expressly linked republicanism, virtue, and education. The state achieved this by providing public primary education for boys and girls. Several of the larger towns also provided secondary education for boys. Thomas Jefferson framed the most ambitious proposal to create a public system of education in 1778. In "A Bill for the more General Diffusion of Knowledge," Jefferson proposed that Virginia adopt a publicly funded system of education. White children, including boys and girls, would be educated at public expense for three years. The best male students would then be selected for secondary education, and a small select group from among this cohort would later attend the College of William and Mary. Jefferson introduced his bill in the state legislature several times, although it never passed.

Jefferson's faith in education reflected his debt to the ideals of the Enlightenment, the international philosophical movement based on the notion that reason and science provided the means to improve humanity. (See discussion in Chapter 3) Following the lead of the English philosopher John Locke, Enlightenment thinkers believed that people were born a blank slate upon which society could write its own moral code. Many American Founders, including Jefferson, were also strongly influenced by other ideas drawn from the Enlightenment. Philosophers of the Enlightenment believed that humans had an innate moral sense, akin to the other five senses. In the same way that people see different shades of the color spectrum, so the moral sense helped people see the difference between right and wrong. One need only cultivate this inborn sense to produce an enlightened body of citizens. Taken together, Lockean psychology and Enlightenment moral theory led many Americans to put enormous faith in education's ability to shape morality and mold character.

Inspired by Enlightenment ideals about education and the American Revolution's faith in representative government, Americans founded new educational institutions to help create an enlightened citizenry. Ezra Stiles, the president of Yale University at the time, wrote in 1786 that "the spirit for Academy making is vigorous." The charter for one of these new academies in North Carolina declared that "the good education of youth has the most direct tendency to promote the virtue, increase the wealth and extend the fame of any people." North Carolina was one of the states that founded a university. Georgia and Vermont also founded public institutions of higher education. Among the private colleges established were Williams (Massachusetts), Transylvania (Kentucky), College of Charleston (South Carolina), and Bowdoin (Maine).

Educators also published new republican materials to instruct children in reading, writing, and arithmetic. Spellers and readers included patriotic lessons with illustrations that reinforced

5.3 Samuel McIntire Carving
This piece of furniture, produced after the Revolution, uses simple classical lines. Symbols of republicanism, such as the goddess of liberty, were carved at the center of the broken pediment. [*Source:* Samuel McIntire, "Chest-on-chest (detail)"; Mahogany, mahogany veneer, ebony and satin-wood inlay, pine; Eighteenth-century American Arts No. 4; the M. and M. Karolik Collection of Eighteenth-Century American Arts, 41.580. Museum of Fine Arts, Boston (41.58). Photograph © 2010 Museum of Fine Arts, Boston]

How did changes in furniture design reflect the influence of republican ideas?

their republican message. In a book of alphabet rhymes, for example, the bald eagle from the Great Seal of America, the new nation's official symbol, represented the letter "E" (**5.4**). The design of the great seal had gone through many versions before Congress finally approved one that included an American eagle clutching an olive branch and thirteen arrows, symbolizing the new government's power to make war and to negotiate peace. The thirteen states are represented by the same number of stars, stripes, and arrows. Charles Thomson, the secretary of Congress, observed that the eagle bore a shield to symbolize that "the United States ought to rely on their own Virtue."

The expansion of education opened up new possibilities for white women. While Jefferson's plan for educational reform called for basic education for women, other reformers recommended more ambitious plans to educate the nation's female population. Jefferson's friend, the eminent Philadelphia physician Benjamin Rush, offered a robust statement of the importance of education in a republic in general, but also framed a bold call to educate women for their role as republican citizens. Women needed to be familiar with the political ideas of republicanism. As the mothers of future citizens of the republic, women had a special role to play. Rush was not alone in championing female education. The Philadelphia Young Ladies Academy (1787) was typical of these new institutions. In addition to teaching music, dance, and needlework, these new schools taught girls a variety of subjects, such as rhetoric, oratory, and history, once exclusively taught to boys. Martha Ryan, a student at one of the new schools in North Carolina, inscribed the phrase "Liberty or Death" in her cipher book (**5.5**). Although clearly influenced by republican ideas, her book also revealed the continuing importance of traditional ideas about women's roles. Bound into the book was a series of penmanship exercises that intoned such traditional moral injunctions as "Honour Father and Mother." *Images as History: Women's Roles: Tradition and Change* explores women's roles and the effects of republican ideas on those roles (page 134).

Supporters of Enlightenment ideas such as Benjamin Rush and Thomas Jefferson believed that education would help nurture the virtue necessary for the survival of republicanism. Other Americans, however, looked to religion to foster virtue. One minister reminded his parishioners that while the "civil authority have no right to establish religion," it was still true that "religion is connected with the

5.4 Book of Children's Verses
This book of children's verse uses America's new national symbol, the bald eagle, taken from the Great Seal of the United States. Educational materials such as this one included republican and patriotic themes.

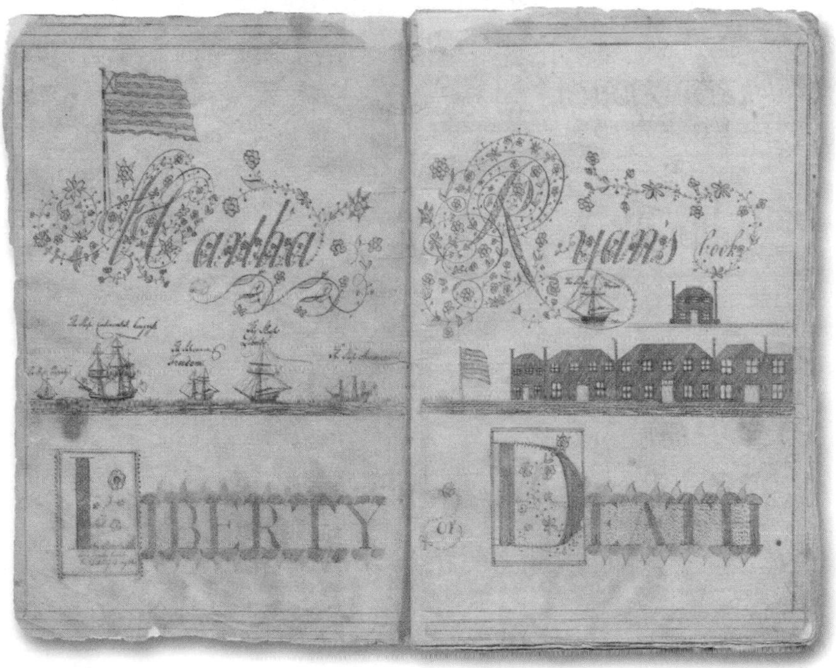

5.5 Martha Ryan's Cipher Book
The cover of Martha Ryan's cipher book proclaims liberty. Yet, the book included penmanship exercises with such traditional precepts as "Honour Father and Mother ... A good girl will mind."

Images as History

WOMEN'S ROLES: TRADITION AND CHANGE

Although republicanism did allow some women to transform the roles assigned to them, it retained the traditional view that a woman's primary duties were to her family. In the engraving *Keep Within the Compass,* the woman who stays within the compass enjoys a life of harmony and prosperity. Stepping outside of the compass carried grave consequences.

Republican ideals of womanhood were stitched into a needlework sampler prepared by a school girl, Nabby Martin of Providence, Rhode Island. Samplers were a traditional form of needlework, a standard part of a young woman's education. Nabby included images of young couples, flowers, and domestic animals, common to pre-Revolution samplers, but republican themes show through. The home, the symbol of domesticity, traditionally the heart and center image of a young girl's sampler, has been replaced by the Rhode Island state house. Politics, not home, is the center of this piece. Nabby also showed her respect for the republican emphasis on education by including the College of Rhode Island.

As a female, Nabby Martin was barred from the world of the state house and the College of Rhode Island, but the inclusion of their images in her sampler is significant. Although working with an art form closely tied to women's roles, Martin turned her gaze to the wider world both buildings represented. The republican message of the sampler is clear: Let Virtue be a Guide to Thee. How is virtue represented visually in Martin's needlework?

The text that accompanied this image advised: "Keep within the Compass and You shall be sure to avoid many troubles which others endure."

Keep Within the Compass, 1784
[Courtesy, Winterthur Museum]

When a woman steps outside the compass, she faces arrest and imprisonment.

The building pictured is The College of Rhode Island, the forerunner of Brown University.

The message of the sampler is announced in the central text: Let Virtue be a Guide to Thee

Instead of a home, the Rhode Island state house is the central image.

Nabby Martin, Sampler, 1786

How did republican ideas change notions about women's roles?

morals of the people." Another minister noted that by "instilling good sentiments into the tender minds of children and youth, you will teach them to stand fast in their liberty." Post-revolutionary America remained a predominantly Protestant culture in which religious dissent was tolerated only within limits. Some states continued to bar Catholics and Jews from holding public office. The assumption behind such laws was that only Protestants could be counted on to have the necessary virtue to seek the public good.

Although excluded from the full benefits of citizenship, religious dissenters were still allowed to worship according to the dictates of conscience. Most state bills of rights and constitutions guaranteed the free exercise of religion. Revolutionary ideas of liberty and equality slowly led states to abandon the notion that only Protestants could be trusted to hold public office. Religious tests requiring potential office holders to swear a belief in the divinity of Jesus as a requirement for public office holding were abolished in Virginia (1785), Georgia (1789), Pennsylvania (1790), South Carolina (1790), Delaware (1792), and Vermont (1793).

Before the Revolution, many colonies provided direct government support to religion or followed the English practice of having an official state church. But the Revolution gave impetus to the notion of separation of church and state. The post-revolutionary era witnessed a widespread move to disestablish the Anglican Church in those places where it enjoyed public funding. Two different justifications for the separation of church and state emerged in post-revolutionary America. For champions of the Enlightenment, such as Jefferson, separation of church and state was inspired by the fear that religion might use the power of government to oppress citizens of different religious views. Enlightenment champions of religious freedom also feared that religion might corrupt government. Dissenting Protestant sects, notably the Baptists and Methodists, opposed state support for religion for a different reason. These groups had long felt oppressed by the state-supported Anglican Church, particularly by taxation to support that church. For Virginia's Baptist community, the ideal of separation of church and state was as much a means to protect the purity of religion from corruption by government as it was a means to protect government from religious tyranny.

Evangelicals and supporters of the Enlightenment came together in Virginia in 1785 when the state legislature considered a bill for nonpreferential aid for ministers of the Christian religion. Since the scheme was nonpreferential, it would not establish an official state church but rather provide funds to all Protestant churches in a nondiscriminatory fashion. Patrick Henry and Richard Henry Lee, two of the state's leading politicians, campaigned in favor of the bill. Leading the opposition was an equally impressive duo, James Madison and Thomas Jefferson, champions of Enlightenment values.

Madison and Jefferson outlined their case against state support for religion in "The Memorial and Remonstrance Against Religious Assessments" (1785). This essay not only was instrumental in defeating the bill but also became a landmark in the history of American church–state relations.

Democracy Triumphant?

According to traditional republican theory, citizens were expected to defer to their betters, who were assumed to be the most virtuous members of society. Before the American Revolution, the state legislatures were dominated by men of wealth. As one legislator noted, "it is right that men of birth and fortune, in every government that is free, should be invested with power, and enjoy higher honours than the people." Virtue, according to this view, required one to have the wealth supposedly necessary to cultivate wisdom and knowledge. One newspaper writer captured this traditional conception of virtue when he wrote that representatives "should be ABLE in ESTATE, ABLE in KNOWLEDGE AND LEARNING."

The Revolution, however, challenged this ideal, substituting a more democratic theory of virtue. A writer calling himself "Democritus" captured the essence of this new theory when he urged that citizens only vote for "a man of middling circumstances" and "common understanding," not members of a wealthy or educated elite. In nearly every state a new type of politician emerged who embodied the more democratic version of republicanism: men such as New York's Abraham Yates, a shoemaker from Albany, and Pennsylvania's William Findley, a weaver from western Pennsylvania.

Supporters of the traditional elitist republican view of politics mocked the humble origins of the new politicians and questioned their ability to function as effective legislators. One contemporary political satirist took aim at Findley, whose humble origins as a weaver prompted this sarcastic comment: "It will be more honourable for such men to stay at their looms and knot threads, than to come forward in a legislative capacity."

The post-revolutionary debate over the meaning of virtue and democracy shaped the tone of political debate. When William Smith, a prosperous Baltimore flour merchant, ran for office in 1789 his enemies attacked him by claiming that "Mr. Smith has distilled RICHES from the tears of the POOR; and grown FAT upon their curses." Smith's supporters viewed his independence as one of his main qualifications for office. In their view Smith was "a Man of great commercial Knowledge, of known integrity, and possessed of a Character and independent Fortune which place him above Temptation." Smith's support for this traditional idea of virtue was reflected in this portrait (**5.6**) painted by artist Charles Wilson Peale. Rather than include symbols that reflected Smith's life as a prosperous city merchant, Peale depicted Smith as a simply dressed country gentlemen. The books that the artist included, poetical works on rural life, reinforce the notion that Smith was a virtuous country gentleman. Peale also placed Smith in front of a Roman column, another visual cue designed to symbolize his virtue.

5.6 William Smith and his Grandson
In this portrait of William Smith, the artist conjures up an image of a country gentleman who devoted himself to thought and contemplation. All references to Smith's life as a prosperous Baltimore merchant are deliberately excluded from the painting. [*Source:* Charles Wilson Peale (American 1741–1827), "William Smith and his Grandson". 1788. Oil on Canvas, 51 1/4" × 40 3/8" (130.2 × 102.5 cm). Signed and dated lower right C W Peale painted 1788. Virginia Museum of Fine Arts, Richmond. Museum Purchase with Funds provided by The Robert G. Cabell III and Maude Morgan Cabell Foundation, and The Arthur and Margaret Glasgow Fund. Photo: Katherine Wetzel G Virginia Museum of Fine Arts]

The debate over what qualities made a good representative in part reflected a larger process of democratization in American culture. The Revolution greatly expanded the number of white male voters eligible to participate in the political process. Most states lowered property requirements for voting, and Pennsylvania abandoned such requirements entirely. Taken together, the expansion of democratic ideas and changes in suffrage requirements changed the character of politics in America. As this graph (**5.7**) reveals, the impact on the composition of state legislatures was profound. After the American Revolution the percentage of wealthy citizens elected to the legislature dropped significantly, and the numbers of elected citizens drawn from the ranks of the "middling sort," or middling classes, increased dramatically. One Boston newspaper writer complained that "since the war, blustering ignorant men" had unfortunately pushed "themselves into office." Not everyone saw the rise of these

Why did William Smith's portrait cast him as a country gentleman rather than an urban merchant?

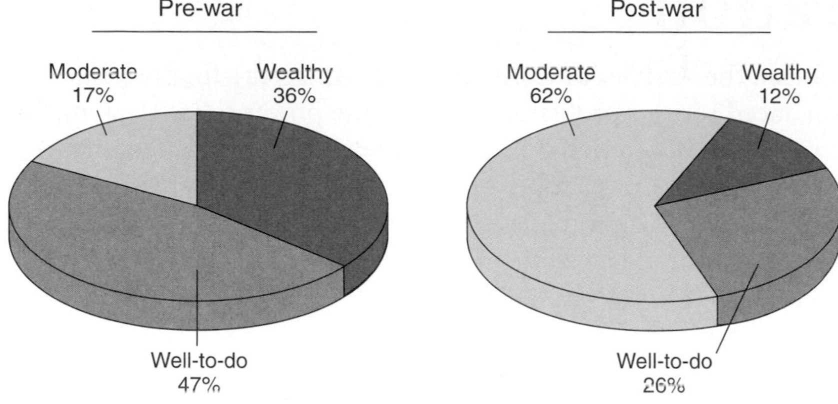

5.7 The Democratization of the State Legislatures The number of wealthy legislators decreased and the number of men of moderate wealth increased. These changes were pronounced in parts of the mid-Atlantic and New England, and are reflected in the data regarding property holdings of legislators elected in New York, New Jersey, and New Hampshire.

new politicians in negative terms. For those who believed in democracy, these trends were a positive development. Now government included "a class of citizens who hither to have thought it more for their interest to be contented with a humbler walk in life."

The new democratic politicians favored policies designed to make it easier for ordinary citizens to participate in government. They introduced, for example, higher salaries for elected representatives, encouraging ordinary people to serve in government. They also made efforts to relocate state capitals inland so that travel to them would be easier for backcountry farmers.

Debtors versus Creditors

Economic issues proved particularly contentious in post-revolutionary America. On economic matters, spokesmen for these new politicians favored policies designed to ease the burdens of farmers and artisans. Some legislatures passed "stay laws," which created generous grace periods for the recovery of debts and protected farmers from having their farms seized for nonpayment of debts. States also enacted "tender laws," which allowed farmers to pay debts with goods rather than hard currency. Merchants generally opposed these policies.

The lack of specie, currency backed by silver and gold, hindered economic exchange. Spokesmen for debtors argued that government had an obligation to use paper money to ease the shortage of currency. By expanding the money supply, printing more paper currency, government adopted a policy that encouraged inflation. Increasing the amount of money in circulation facilitated commerce. When done cautiously, this type of inflationary economic policy provided a means of pumping up the economy. As long as the government did not flood the market with paper, driving down its price, debtors and creditors could each adjust their behavior to take into account the effects of modest inflation in prices for various commodities. By encouraging economic activity, paper money could provide an important tool for economic growth. Farmers were especially fond of this system because they could repay their debts with depreciated currency—money that was worth less than the amount of the original debt. This system, however, could function only if merchants did not dramatically raise prices to compensate for the declining value of paper money. A rapid rise in prices could lead inflation to spiral out of control. Most merchants, however, viewed paper money as a bad policy that hurt their economic interests.

No state was more aggressive in using paper money to solve its financial problems than Rhode Island. Unfortunately, however, the decision to print large amounts of paper money never won the support of that state's merchants in Providence and Newport. When presented with paper money, merchants responded by dramatically increasing prices and eventually refused to accept any depreciated paper currency. Angered by the actions of merchants, the debtor interest in the state legislature responded with laws that imposed a steep fine on any merchant who refused to accept paper currency. One writer lampooned the situation of "Rogue Island" in verse: "*Hail! realm of rogues, renow'd for fraud and guile All hail, ye knav'ries of yon little isle.*"

Life under the Articles of Confederation

From the outset, the **Articles of Confederation**, America's first federal constitution, faced serious problems. Without the power to tax, lacking the power to coerce states even to follow the treaties it had negotiated, the Confederation Congress was simply unable to deal with the pressing economic problems and diplomatic issues the nation confronted. Some leaders also worried that the Confederation lacked the military power to deal effectively with internal rebellions or external foes.

No Taxation with Representation

Americans deeply resented British efforts to tax them prior to the Revolution. Given their fears of strong government and hostility to taxation, the Articles of Confederation, the constitution created by the Confederation Congress, did not empower the new central government to tax Americans. Rather than provide such a power, the Articles of Confederation relied on requisitions made to the states to fund the war effort and other government business. Few states bothered to comply with these requisitions in a timely manner, and the new government of the United States was plagued by shortages of funds.

Although it lacked the power to tax, Congress had to fund the war. To help pay for the war effort, Congress printed almost $250 million in paper currency. This paper money was not backed by gold or silver. Congress's use of paper money led to staggering inflation. By 1781 the value of this money had plunged: In that year it took more than 150 continental dollars to purchase what had taken one dollar to buy in 1777. This dramatic drop in the value of continental currency led some to the phrase "As worthless as a Continental" to describe something with no value. As **5.8** illustrates, it would literally take a pile of continentals to purchase what a single dollar might have paid for less than five years before.

5.8 Continental Paper Currency The value of Continental paper currency dropped precipitously as Congress printed more money, and faith in the value of the currency dwindled.

The **Treaty of Paris** (1783) formally ended hostilities between Britain and the new United States of America. Peace did not, however, solve the economic problems that the new nation faced. Indeed, the end of the war ushered in new economic problems. Patriot boycotts of British goods and the disruption of normal trade patterns during wartime meant that consumers had been denied access to luxury items, including china, textiles, and a host of other goods. Demand for British goods increased dramatically after the war, and soon the new nation was flooded with imports. British merchants encouraged Americans to buy goods on credit. Few American goods went to Britain to offset the huge increase in imports. America's trade deficit with Britain caused a serious drain on what little gold and silver reserves were available to the new nation. With little hard currency, American banks had to curtail loans. When merchants were forced to call in debts to satisfy their British suppliers, they in turn called in the debts owed them by individuals. Taken together this constriction of credit sent the American economy into a depression. Prices for agricultural products plummeted, and wages fell abruptly. The result: the nation's first economic depression.

Diplomacy: Frustration and Stalemate

The new nation was faced with a host of military challenges. British troops remained garrisoned in parts of the Ohio Valley. Relations with many of the Indian tribes along the frontier also remained tense. Farther from the nation's borders, Americans faced a different set of problems. Without a powerful navy to protect American commerce on the high seas, American ships were easy prey for pirates. Piracy was a particularly serious problem for merchants who wished to trade in the Mediterranean. State-sanctioned piracy was rampant among the North

Why did the Articles of Confederation lack the power to tax?

African states of Morocco, Algiers, Tunis, and Tripoli, known as the Barbary States. The Barbary pirates extorted money from merchant vessels in exchange for safe passage in the Mediterranean. Failure to pay resulted in the seizure of ships and imprisonment of sailors. American sailors taken as captives by Barbary pirates languished in North African prisons or were sold into slavery in North Africa. In July 1785, when pirates captured two American ships, Algiers demanded nearly $60,000 in ransom to release the vessels and their crews. The American navy was too weak to challenge these pirate fleets. While the loss of trade burdened the nation's fledgling economy, the sad fate of American captives became a source of national humiliation.

Frustration with the inability to defend America's interests on the high seas grew, but America faced even more serious problems closer to its borders. Defending the nation's interests in the Mediterranean would have to wait while America dealt with the threats posed by Indians and by the continuing presence of the British and Spanish in North America. The map (**5.9**) shows the continuing British and Spanish presence along America's borders, a fact that increased American anxiety.

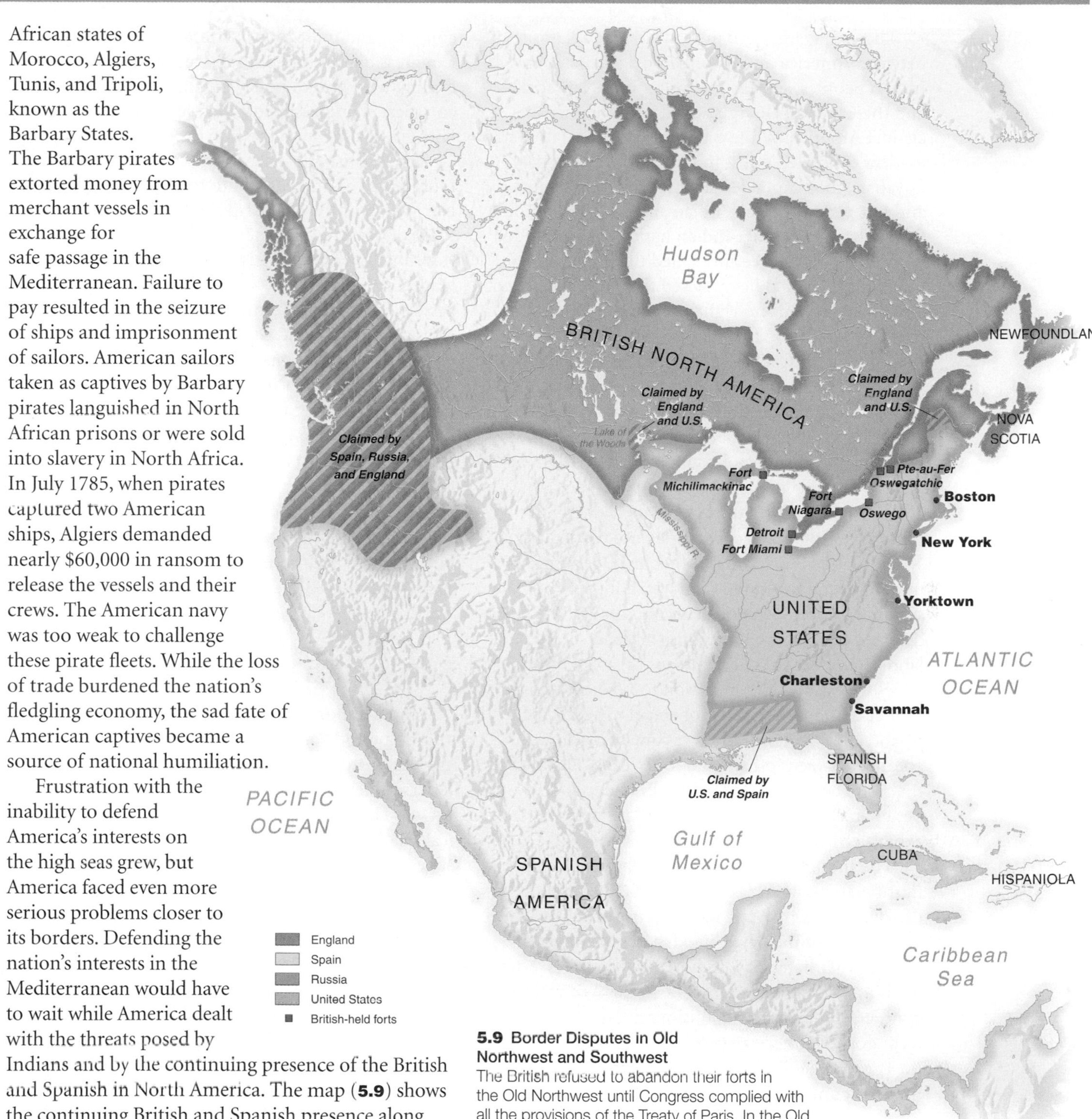

5.9 Border Disputes in Old Northwest and Southwest
The British refused to abandon their forts in the Old Northwest until Congress complied with all the provisions of the Treaty of Paris. In the Old Southwest, Spain frustrated America's efforts to secure the rights to navigate the Mississippi River.

Congress had little power to compel the states to live up to its treaty obligations, including provisions requiring Americans to pay prewar debts and compensate Loyalists for property confiscated during the war. Britain used America's failure to comply with these provisions as a pretext for retaining control of their forts in the Ohio Territory of the **Old Northwest,** the region of the new nation bordering on the Great Lakes (**5.9**). These outposts allowed the British to continue their lucrative fur trade with the Indians.

The war against Britain had strained relations between America and its Indian neighbors. Many Indian peoples, such as the Iroquois in New York and the Creek in Georgia, sided with the British against America. While British peace negotiators had made a concerted effort to protect the interests of Loyalists, they expended no effort to secure a just and fair peace for their Indian allies. The leader of the Mohawks, another Indian nation that had sided with the British, forcefully stated the point of view of his people when he observed that the government of George III had "no right whatever to grant away to the States of America their rights or properties without a manifest breach of all justice and equity."

Given the absence of Indian representation in the treaty that ended hostilities between the United States and Great Britain, it is hardly surprising that the interests of Indian peoples were not reflected in the final terms agreed upon. The Treaty of Paris ceded the entire Old Northwest territory to the United States. American diplomatic envoys were not particularly sympathetic to the claims of Indians. Operating under a theory of conquest in which Indians were "a subdued people," American negotiators assumed that defeated tribes had to relinquish all claims to Western lands. Rejecting this view, Indians organized themselves to resist further incursions onto their lands. Rather than mark the start of an era of peace, the period after the Revolution was one of continued conflict between Indians and Americans. Those tribes that were best organized politically and militarily were better able to defend their interests against American expansionism.

The Indian population east of the Mississippi numbered between 150,000 and 200,000 and was divided into eighty-five different nations. The white population of the new United States of America was approximately 2.4 million. Growing pressure to open up Indian lands for white settlement created conflict. Indians had no illusions about the long-term goal of American policy. The insatiable desire for Indian land led the Creek Indians to bestow the name "Ecunnaunuxulgee" on Georgians. Translated into English, the name meant "people greedily grasping after the lands of red people."

When confronted with the continuing determination of Indians to defend their lands with their lives, Americans were forced to abandon their conquest theory and negotiate more fairly with Indians. American leaders soon realized that missionary work and trade with the Indians were more likely to secure harmonious relations than conquest and military confrontation would. By 1787 Congress had shifted both its tone and strategy for dealing with Indian policy. In place of their theory of conquest, Congress recommended "the utmost good faith" in dealing with the Indians.

The Spanish presence in the Old Southwest represented another threat to the new United States. Navigation of the Mississippi River was crucial to the economic development of this region. Goods traveling down the Mississippi needed to be unloaded at New Orleans and placed on ocean-bound vessels. Spain denied Americans free access to the Mississippi River and the Port of New Orleans. Eager to solve their problems in the Southwest, Congress authorized Secretary of Foreign Affairs John Jay to negotiate with the Spanish. Spain proposed opening up trade with their empire if the United States renounced its rights to navigate the Mississippi. The terms set by the Spanish would have been a boon to New England merchants, who would have benefited from new trade opportunities with Spanish America, but alienated Southerners, particularly those in the West, who viewed the Mississippi as their pipeline to world markets.

Settling the Old Northwest

The most important achievement of the Confederation period was the plan Congress devised for Western settlement. A committee chaired by Thomas Jefferson devised the initial plan for settling the West (**5.10**). This proposal imagined a rational mathematical scheme for carving out as many as sixteen new states from the Northwest Territory. In fashioning his plan, Jefferson combined republican theories of self-government with Enlightenment ideas about geography. Boundaries would be drawn along an orderly grid after being carefully surveyed. Reflecting his debt to classical republicanism, Jefferson's chose names for the new territories such as Polypatamia, "land of many rivers." Republicanism guided Jefferson's plan in other ways. In his Ordinance of 1784, Jefferson proposed that new territories be incorporated into the union as states on equal footing to the original thirteen. Jefferson sought local self-government for settlers almost immediately. When the population reached twenty thousand free inhabitants, a constitutional convention would set up a permanent state government. The plan banned hereditary titles and slavery after the year 1800. Jefferson's 1784 plan recommended that land be made available in parcels small enough

What was the conquest theory and how did it influence diplomatic relations with Indian peoples?

for average Americans to purchase. He envisioned the Northwest Territory as an area populated by white yeoman farmers and their families.

The Land Ordinance of 1785 adopted by Congress departed from Jefferson's original proposal in a number of crucial areas. The 1785 plan called for the creation of townships containing 36 square miles. Land was to be sold for a sum of no less than a dollar an acre, payment to be made in hard currency. Ordinary citizens would have had trouble raising this amount of cash and therefore had little chance to purchase land directly from the government. Jefferson's hope that the Western land could be sold directly to citizens and promote his vision of a republic of small independent farmers was jettisoned in favor of a plan that favored speculators.

In 1787 Congress passed another piece of legislation dealing with Western lands, the **Northwest Ordinance of 1787**. The final plan for the governance of the new territories the act created was considerably less democratic than Jefferson's original proposal, but maintained his orderly model for dividing up the territory. According to Congress's plan, the Northwest Territories would be ruled by powerful governors appointed by Congress. When the population reached five thousand adult male inhabitants, settlers would be allowed to elect their own territorial legislatures. When the population reached sixty thousand free inhabitants, a figure that included women as well as men, the territories could seek admission to the Confederation. The language of the Northwest Ordinance echoed the republican ideals of the Revolution. Congress proclaimed that "fundamental principles of civil and religious liberty" were the foundation for the new states to be created from the territories. In keeping with the republican ideas about virtue and the need for public education, the Northwest Ordinance made provision for government funding of elementary education through the sale of land. Most important for the future of the territories, the ordinance rejected slavery in the new states to be carved out of the Northwest Territories.

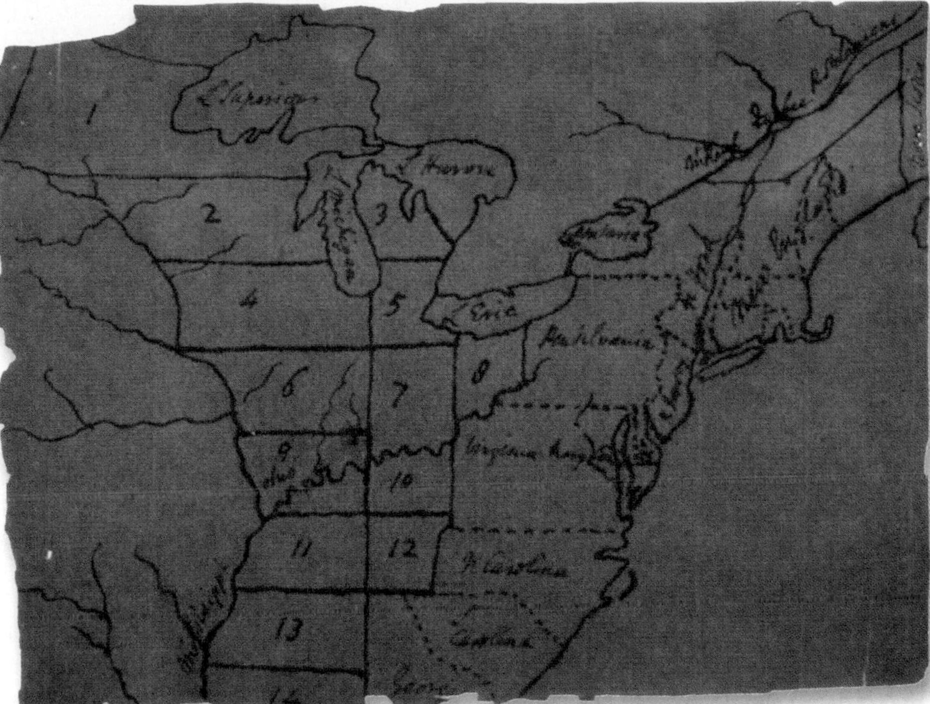

5.10 Jefferson's Plan for the West Jefferson's gridlike map of his plan for the settlement of the West was influenced by the ideas of Enlightenment thinkers. The names that Jefferson proposed for these territories were inspired by the language of classical antiquity. Thus, one potential state was named Sylvania, for "a forested region."

Shays's Rebellion

The postwar economic downturn hit farmers in Massachusetts particularly hard. As the number of farm foreclosures rose, and family after family saw their farms seized by their creditors, popular frustration mounted. Events took a dramatic turn when a contingent of ex-Revolutionary War veterans marched on the town of Northampton to shut down the local courts and prevent further foreclosures. The armed crowd prevented the judges of the court, dressed in formal judicial attire, long black robes and

"Religion, morality, and knowledge, being necessary to good government and the happiness of mankind, schools and the means of education shall forever be encouraged."

Northwest Ordinance of 1787

What republican features distinguish the Northwest Ordinance?

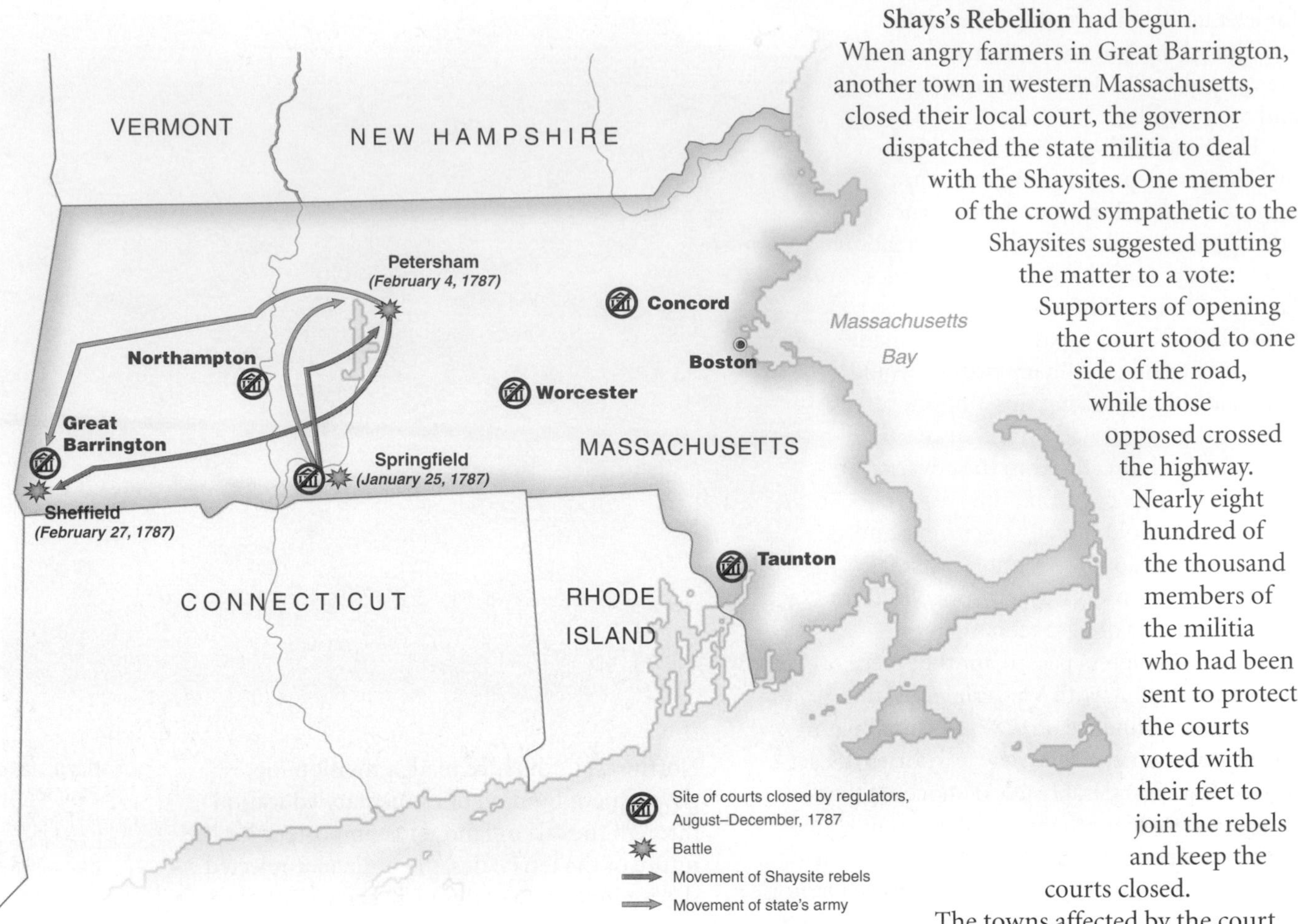

5.11 Court Closings and Major Battles in Shays's Rebellion
Shays and his supporters closed courts in several major towns in central and western Massachusetts. Shaysites and forces loyal to the state of Massachusetts fought a decisive battle at the Springfield state armory, where the Shaysites were routed.

gray wigs, from entering the courthouse. The protestors, dubbed Shaysites, after the leader, Daniel Shays, believed that they were protecting the "good of the commonwealth" and opposing the "tyrannical government in the Massachusetts State." Governor James Bowdoin condemned the court closings as "fraught with the most fatal and pernicious consequences" that "must tend to subvert all law and government."

Shays's Rebellion had begun.

When angry farmers in Great Barrington, another town in western Massachusetts, closed their local court, the governor dispatched the state militia to deal with the Shaysites. One member of the crowd sympathetic to the Shaysites suggested putting the matter to a vote: Supporters of opening the court stood to one side of the road, while those opposed crossed the highway. Nearly eight hundred of the thousand members of the militia who had been sent to protect the courts voted with their feet to join the rebels and keep the courts closed.

The towns affected by the court closing are shown in the map (**5.11**), which also shows the location of the armed confrontations between the Shaysites and government forces. Shays and his followers were defeated in a battle near the state arsenal in Springfield. The failure of Shays's Rebellion, the most serious challenge to government authority in the new nation, gave additional impetus to those eager to reform the structure of the Articles of Confederation and create a more powerful central government. The one figure among the nation's Patriot elite who seemed relatively unfazed by the rebellion in western Massachusetts was Thomas Jefferson. The reactions of Washington and Jefferson reflected their different visions of the Revolution and American politics (see *Competing Visions: Reactions to Shays's Rebellion*).

Competing Visions

REACTIONS TO SHAYS'S REBELLION

Shays's Rebellion forced Americans to ponder the meaning of the Revolution. Those who opposed the rebellion saw in it the danger of placing too much faith in virtue as a foundation for republican government. But for the farmers who took up arms against government, the rebellion demonstrated the continuing validity of the right of revolution. Shays and his supporters also couched their appeals in terms of republican ideas about the common good. Consider the different reactions of George Washington and Thomas Jefferson to the rebellion. Why do you think Washington was so shaken by the rebellion? How do you account for Jefferson's greater sympathy for the rebels?

In this letter to General Henry Knox dated December 26, 1786, Washington expressed his alarm over the uprising in western Massachusetts, lamenting that America's belief that virtue could provide a solid foundation for government may have been excessively naive.

I feel, my dear Genl. Knox, infinitely more than I can express to you, for the disorders which have arisen in these States. Good God! who besides a tory could have foreseen, or a Briton predicted them! were these people wiser than others, or did they judge of us from the corruption, and depravity of their own hearts? The latter I am persuaded was the case, and that notwithstanding the boasted virtue of America, we are far gone in every thing ignoble and bad.

I do assure you, that even at this moment, when I reflect on the present posture of our affairs, it seems to me to be like the vision of a dream. My mind does not know how to realize it, as a thing in actual existence, so strange, so wonderful does it appear to me! In this, as in most other matter, we are too slow. When this spirit first dawned, probably it might easily have been checked; but it is scarcely within the reach of human ken, at this moment, to say when, where, or how it will end. There are combustibles in every State, which a spark might set fire to.

George Washington

From Paris, where he was serving as America's minister, Thomas Jefferson wrote to James Madison on January 30th, 1787, inquiring about his views of Shays's Rebellion. Jefferson offered his own preliminary assessment in which he expressed guarded support for the rebels.

I am impatient to learn your sentiments on the late troubles in the Eastern states. So far as I have yet seen, they do not appear to threaten serious consequences. . . . I hold it that a little rebellion now and then is a good thing, and as necessary in the political world as storms in the physical. Unsuccessful rebellions, indeed, generally establish the encroachments on the rights of the people which have produced them. An observation of this truth should render honest republican governors so mild in their punishment of rebellions as not to discourage them too much. It is a medicine necessary for the sound health of government.

Thomas Jefferson

Whose view of Shays's Rebellion was more realistic, Washington's or Jefferson's?

The Movement for Constitutional Reform

The economic, political, and diplomatic problems faced by the Confederation government, including Shays's Rebellion, inspired a small but extremely talented group of politicians to promote their plans for reform of the Articles of Confederation. As nationalists—men who believed in the need for a stronger national government—they regarded constitutional reform as imperative. Rather than continue to put their faith in virtue as a foundation for republican government, nationalists sought to create a powerful central government to protect American interests abroad and deal with internal threats, such as Shays's Rebellion. For the nationalists the postwar era was a time of national crisis that demanded decisive action if America was to survive. Nationalists proposed a new model of government to protect individual liberty and promote the common good. The new Federal Constitution created by this group relied on a system of checks and balances, not virtue, to protect liberty.

The Road to Philadelphia

Delegates from Maryland and Virginia gathered at George Washington's home in Mount Vernon (1785) to discuss economic matters. A year later in Annapolis, Maryland (1786) delegates from five states gathered to discuss the problems of the Confederation. Finally, in 1787 delegates from twelve of the thirteen states gathered in Philadelphia to take up reform of the Articles of Confederation. The fifty-five delegates who gathered in Philadelphia included an impressive cast of characters. Virginia sent James Madison and George Mason, two of the state's most esteemed political figures. Pennsylvania's representatives included the oldest delegate in attendance, Benjamin Franklin, then aged 81, and James Wilson, the nation's premier legal mind. New York's delegation boasted the brilliant, but brash, Alexander Hamilton. The delegates chose George Washington to preside over the meeting. The convention was dominated by lawyers, and nearly all the delegates were wealthy men.

> "We have probably had too good an opinion of human nature in forming our confederation."
>
> GEORGE WASHINGTON, 1786

A strict rule of secrecy was imposed on the convention's proceedings, a decision that facilitated a more frank debate among the delegates, but only intensified rumors about the activities of the delegates. The rule of secrecy was stringently enforced: The windows of the Pennsylvania State House were nailed shut and a guard posted at the door.

Writing from France, where he was serving as American ambassador, Thomas Jefferson admiringly described the assembly as a meeting of "demigods" —men of such impressive accomplishments that they seemed like the mythical heroes of antiquity, part human and part divine. Some contemporaries, however, were suspicious of the convention's secrecy. One Pennsylvania newspaper warned of the "monster" being fashioned behind a "thick veil of secrecy." Later generations of Americans have tended to echo Jefferson's observations: that the convention was composed of extraordinarily talented politicians, a view beautifully illustrated by this mid-nineteenth-century painting by Thomas Rossiter (**5.12**). In the Rossiter painting the Founders are portrayed bathed in light, not shrouded in secrecy.

Large States versus Small States

Instead of arguing over reforming the Articles of Confederation, as originally intended, the Philadelphia Convention took up a bold proposal

What were the main features of the Virginia Plan?

5.12 Constitutional Convention
Jefferson's observation that the Framers of the Constitution were an "assembly of demigods" is captured in Thomas Rossiter's nineteenth-century painting of the Philadelphia Convention. Rather than appear as a dark conclave, the members of the convention are bathed in light.

offered by the Virginia delegation. The **Virginia Plan,** drafted largely by James Madison, abandoned the federal system created by the Articles of Confederation, substituting in its place an entirely new model of government that had some federal features and some national features. The states would retain considerable power, but in those areas in which the new national government was given authority, its power would be supreme.

The new government created by the **Virginia Plan** would be composed of a single executive (the branch of government charged with, among other things, the execution of laws), a two-house legislature (Congress, the lawmaking body), and a separate judiciary (courts). The lower house of Congress would be directly elected by the people, and the upper house would be elected by the lower house from a list provided by the state legislatures. Under the Articles of Confederation, small states such as Maryland had the same vote as large states such as Virginia. Rather than this one-state one-vote principle, population size would now determine representation in this new Congress.

The Virginia Plan gave considerable power to the new Congress, which had the power "to legislate in all cases to which the separate States are incompetent" or "in which the harmony of the United States may be interrupted by the exercise of individual [state] legislation." Although this grant of authority did not explicitly address nettlesome issues such as the power to tax, such powers were clearly within the purview of this broad grant of authority. The authors of the Virginia Plan, especially James Madison, thought that a more general grant of authority, rather than a long list of enumerated powers, would be more politically acceptable to the delegates.

Representatives from the small states opposed the Virginia Plan. Two weeks after the Virginia Plan was introduced, William Patterson of New Jersey made a counterproposal. This alternative plan, often dubbed the **New Jersey Plan,** called for a modified federal system based on the existing Articles of Confederation. It proposed a single legislature in which each state would have one vote, which would maintain the parity between small states and large states. In contrast to the Articles of Confederation, the new national legislature would be the supreme law of the land and would be binding on the states. The national legislature created by this plan would have the power to tax and to regulate interstate commerce. Although the New Jersey Plan was defeated, it had revealed the difficulty of reaching a consensus without accommodating the concerns of the small states, which feared that the new system would give larger states inordinate influence over the new government.

The following figure (**5.13**) shows the differences between the Virginia and New Jersey plans and how each differed from the Articles of Confederation. While both of these plans would have given the new central government broad new powers, particularly over economic matters, representatives from the large and small states continued to be divided over how the legislature would be structured. On June 29, 1788, Oliver Ellsworth of Connecticut reintroduced an earlier compromise that he and Roger Sherman (also of Connecticut) had devised. The plan provided for equal representation for large and small states in the upper house as well as a lower house in which representation would be apportioned on the basis of population. On July 16, 1787, the convention adopted the **Great Compromise** (sometimes known as the Connecticut Compromise because of Ellsworth and Sherman's role in framing it). The Great Compromise solved one of the most difficult issues facing the convention: the struggle over representation based on population versus equal representation among the states.

Conflict over Slavery

While the Connecticut Compromise solved one of the most difficult problems faced by the convention, it also focused attention on another equally contentious issue: whether to count slaves in the apportionment of the new lower house. Representatives from the Southern states, seeking sufficient representation in the new legislature to protect the interests of slavery, were determined that their slaves be counted. Opponents of slavery, by contrast, wished to see slaves taxed as a form of property but did not wish to count them when calculating the population used to determine representation in the new lower house. The convention settled on a solution in which slaves were counted as three-fifths of a person for purposes of taxation and legislative apportionment. (The three-fifths ratio had been worked out by the Confederation Congress several years earlier, when it faced another issue pertaining to slavery.)

Conflict over slavery flared up again over the issue of the slave trade. One of the most intense attacks on the slave trade was voiced by Virginian George Mason, the largest slave owner in the convention, who warned his fellow delegates of the threat to the republic of the institution of slavery. "Every master of slaves is born a petty tyrant" and

	Articles of Confederation	Virginia Plan	New Jersey Plan
Structure of the Legislature	Single house, one state one vote	Two houses, both determined by population	Single house, one state one vote
Taxation	No power to tax	Power to tax	Power to tax
Judicial Power	No judicial power apart from courts to hear admiralty cases	Federal judiciary	Federal judiciary
Executive Power	Plural executive	Single executive chosen by national legislature	Single or plural executive elected by Congress

5.13 Comparison of the Articles of Confederation, Virginia, and New Jersey Plans
Although the Virginia and New Jersey plans differed on the issue of representation, each would have given the new government the vital power of taxation.

How did the conflict over slavery shape the debates of the Constitutional Convention?

> "The states were divided into different interests not by their difference of size but by other circumstances; the most material of which resulted partly from climate, but principally from their having or not having slaves."
>
> JAMES MADISON, 1787

the institution of "slavery discourages arts & manufactures." Mason recommended ending the slave trade as a first step toward eliminating slavery. Several delegates viewed Mason's actions cynically. Virginia had an excess of slaves and would profit enormously from an internal trade among slaves if the external trade with Africa were abolished. South Carolinian Charles Pinckney defended slavery, noting that all the great republics of the ancient world had accepted the necessity of this institution. Pinckney's cousin, General Charles Cotesworth Pinckney, another delegate from South Carolina, was even blunter, reminding delegates that his state would never accept the Constitution if a ban on the slave trade was enacted. Once again compromise held the convention together. The new Congress was denied the authority to ban the slave trade until the year 1808.

Although the word slavery never appears in the Constitution, several clauses in the document protected slavery. Article IV, Section 2, prevented fugitive slaves, defined as any "person held to service or labour in one state," from fleeing to another state to seek asylum and freedom. In addition, Article I, Section 8, prohibited the national government from taxing the exports of any state, a provision that prevented the products of slave labor, such as rice, indigo, tobacco, or sugar, from being singled out for economic sanctions by those hostile to slavery. In James Madison's view, the greatest division in the convention turned out to be not the conflict between large states and small states, but slavery.

Filling out the Constitutional Design

After sorting out the structure of the legislative branch of government, the convention struggled over the executive branch. George Mason argued for a three-man executive. A plural executive, he argued, could better represent the different regional interests of the nation. Rejecting this proposal, the convention settled on a unitary executive. There was also disagreement over how to choose the executive. James Wilson wanted to see the executive elected by the people, while Mason argued that the people lacked the wisdom to make such an important decision. Roger Sherman's plan to have the national legislature pick the executive was challenged as a threat to the ideal of the separation of powers.

Eventually the convention settled on the idea of having an "electoral college" composed of men chosen by each state in a manner to be determined by the individual state legislatures. By giving the states some control over selection of the president, this system provided another way of strengthening the power of the states within the new federal system created by the Constitution. The electoral college also reflected the ideals of republicanism held by the delegates. By creating a filtering mechanism for the selection of the president, the electoral college was designed to help ensure that the men chosen were drawn from the ranks of the nation's leading citizens.

Delegates also clashed over the term of office that the executive would serve. Alexander Hamilton proposed that the executive have a life term, but this idea was rejected as leaning too close to monarchy. Some delegates favored a single term of as much as seven years, while others argued that a shorter term with the possibility of reelection would provide a greater check on the president. The convention ultimately settled on a four-year term with no limits on the number of terms a president might serve. The final structure of the executive branch was detailed in what became Article II of the Constitution.

Through August the convention continued to sketch the barest outline for the third branch of government, the federal judiciary. A new Supreme Court was created, and Congress was authorized to create such inferior courts as it deemed necessary. The Supreme Court's authority extended "in all Cases, in Law and Equity, arising under the Constitution, the Laws of the United States, and Treaties made under their authority." While a

How did the electoral college strengthen the powers of the states and further the ideals of republicanism?

number of delegates to the convention assumed that the courts would exercise the power of judicial review, the power to declare acts of Congress unconstitutional, the Constitution failed to make such power explicit.

Two delegates from New York, Robert Yates and John Lansing, left before the document was completed and therefore did not sign it. Three other delegates—Edmund Randolph, George Mason, and Elbridge Gerry—refused to sign the Constitution because of their reservations about its final draft. Despite the protests of a few delegates, Benjamin Franklin captured the feelings of many delegates when he wrote that despite its faults, it was doubtful "whether any other convention we can obtain may be able to make a better Constitution." Franklin went on to remark that "it therefore astonishes me, Sir, to find this system approaching as near to perfection as it does." After the convention concluded its work and the text of the Constitution were made public, Franklin was approached by a woman who asked the aging patriot, "'Well Doctor what have we got a republic or a monarchy?' 'A republic,' replied the Doctor, 'if you can keep it.'"

The Constitution reflected the give and take among the delegates and the spirit of compromise that prevailed at the Convention. The new Constitution was a radical departure from the Articles of Confederation (**5.14**).

The powerful national legislature created by the Constitution was given authority to enact all laws "necessary and proper" to carrying out responsibilities delegated by the Constitution. The new national legislature had an upper and a lower house. States were equally represented in the upper house, the Senate. Representation in the lower house, the House of Representatives, was based on population, with slaves counting as three-fifths of a person. Amendments to the Constitution would require the approval of three-quarters of the states, not the unanimous consent required under the Articles. While the executive under the Articles of Confederation had been very weak, the new office of president was powerful. The president could veto legislation, negotiate treaties, and issue pardons. The ill-defined powers of the new Supreme Court left many wondering if the judiciary would be the weakest of the three branches, not co-equal with the legislature and the executive.

The new federal Constitution also broke with several well-established precedents that had shaped the various state constitutions drafted in the years immediately following the Revolution. Unlike the typical state constitution, the federal Constitution did not include a declaration of rights stating the basic rights and liberties retained by the people, nor did it reassert the basic republican principles upon which government rested. Compared with many state constitutions, which directly elected their governors, the indirect method of choosing a national leader through the electoral college might have seemed less democratic.

	Articles of Confederation	Constitution
Structure of the Legislature	Single house, one state one vote	Two houses, one determined by population, upper house equal state representation
Taxation	No power to tax	Power to tax
Judicial Power	No judicial power apart from courts to hear admiralty cases	Federal judiciary
Executive Power	Plural executive	Executive chosen by electors chosen by state legislators

5.14 Comparison of the Articles of Confederation and the Constitution
As this chart shows, the new federal government created by the Constitution was far more powerful than the old government under the Articles of Confederation.

Identify the most important differences between the federal Constitution and the typical state constitutions of this period.

The Great Debate

The publication of the Constitution inaugurated one of the most vigorous political campaigns in American history. In taverns and town squares, Americans argued over the meaning of the new Constitution. As one contemporary commentator remarked, "the plan of a Government proposed to us by the convention—affords matter for conversation to every rank of beings from the Governor to the door keeper." Soon two sides emerged in the debate over ratification.

Federalists versus Anti-Federalists

In the debate the supporters of the Constitution described themselves as **Federalists,** thus saddling their opponents, who opposed it, with the name **Anti-Federalists.** Never entirely happy with their name, opponents of the Constitution complained that they were the true supporters of federalism and attacked pro-Constitutional forces as "consolidationists" who wished to consolidate the union into a single national government and rob the states of their power. Looking back on the bitter struggle over ratification, one Anti-Federalist quipped that because the issue before the nation was ratification of the Constitution, the two sides were more aptly described as "rats and anti-rats."

Citizens paraded, raised their glasses to toast, or attacked the new government, in a few instances even rioting to express their sentiments. Anti-Federalists in Carlisle, Pennsylvania, burned an effigy of Federalist James Wilson to express their disapproval of the new Constitution. Wilson, a renowned lawyer and a recent immigrant from Scotland, was one of the most important supporters of the Constitution in Pennsylvania. He was also an easy target for ridicule, since he spoke with a thick Scottish accent that his enemies mocked and lampooned. The supporters of the Constitution also took to the streets to defend the Constitution and occasionally to intimidate their opponents. In one instance a Federalist crowd wrecked the printing presses of Anti-Federalist publishers in New York City. Although these disturbances attracted considerable attention, they were the exception, however, not the rule.

The debate could be heated, but Americans typically confined their passions to the printed page. Hundreds of columns of newspaper text were devoted to the debate over the merits of the Constitution, and dozens of pamphlets were written for and against the new plan of government. *The Federalist,* for example, John Jay, Alexander Hamilton, and James Madison's sophisticated defense of the Constitution, was first published as a series of newspaper essays in New York. It is now regarded by many scholars as the most important contribution America has made to Western political philosophy. Writing under the pen name Publius, a hero of the Roman Republic, the authors hoped to cloak themselves in the toga of Roman virtue. This strategy was designed to focus the public's attention on the ideas behind, not the men responsible for, the essays. *The Federalist* not only responded to Anti-Federalist criticism but it also provided a sophisticated analysis of republican government and a point-by-point discussion of the merits of the various provisions of the Constitution. Although its influence on the outcome of ratification was modest, *The Federalist* soon became the favorite text of judges, legislators, and others interested in interpreting the meaning of the Constitution. It continues to be the text most often cited by the Supreme Court when trying to identify the original understanding of various provisions of the Constitution.

Anti-Federalists produced no single text comparable to *The Federalist.* However, the writings of Elbridge Gerry and George Mason, prominent Anti-Federalists who had participated in the Philadelphia Convention but had refused to sign the Constitution, were widely reprinted. Sophisticated critiques of the Constitution were framed by authors who adopted the pen names Brutus and Federal Farmer. Brutus invoked the same ideal of Roman virtue that Publius had appropriated for the supporters of the Constitution. The name Federal Farmer traded on the association of republican ideals of simplicity associated with the ideal of the yeoman farmer. Both texts developed an alternative vision of republican government. Rather than accept

Why did Federalist and Anti-Federalist authors adopt names such as Publius and Brutus?

5.15 ***The Looking Glass for 1787***
This Federalist political cartoon from Connecticut portrays the state as a cart stuck in the mud and weighed down by paper money and debt. While Federalists proclaim "Comply with Congress" and pull the state toward a bright sun, the Anti-Federalists exclaim "Success to Shays" and drag the cart toward a shadowy future symbolized by the dark clouds.

the need for a powerful central government, Anti-Federalists clung to the idea of a system in which the bulk of governmental functions would continue to reside in the states.

Although the struggle over ratification produced some of the most intellectually sophisticated writings in American history, in other respects it was a textbook example of negative campaigning. If Publius and Brutus provided an example of dispassionate reason, metaphorically invoking Roman ideals of virtue by their pen names, other authors, on both sides, were not above slinging mud when it served their interests. Federalists, for example, denounced their opponents as Shaysites, a charge repeated in the satirical print, *The Looking Glass for 1787* (**5.15**). In this cartoon, the state of Connecticut appears stuck in the mud, dragged in opposite directions by Federalists and Anti-Federalists. The artist who created this pro-Federalist political cartoon stooped lower than most: One Anti-Federalist character is portrayed with his trousers pulled down around his ankles and his bottom exposed to his Federalist opponents. Anti-Federalists attacked the Federalists, charging that they were part of an aristocratic elite who wished to dominate common folk. Amos Singletary, an Anti-Federalist from Massachusetts, warned his fellow citizens that the lawyers and rich merchants who backed the Constitution favored the interests of the aristocratic few over those of the democratic many. In Singletary's view, the new Constitution would undue the democratic reforms of the revolution, returning power to powerful economic groups, such as lawyers and merchants.

Although Anti-Federalism attracted supporters of democracy such as Singletary, it also appealed to wealthy planters such as Virginia's George Mason, who was less concerned about the Constitution's anti-democratic features and more worried about the centralization of power. Although Anti-Federalists did not agree about everything, there were some important points of commonality among them. The essential points of the Anti-Federalist critique of the constitution emerged early in the public debate. At the top of this list was the fear of consolidation, the concern that the federal government would absorb all power into its orbit. Anti-Federalists believed that the number of representatives was too small to represent the diverse interest of the American people adequately. Representatives would also be far removed from their constituents and lose touch with the feelings and concerns of those they served. The extensive powers of the president and the potentially vast jurisdiction enjoyed by the new Supreme Court also worried Anti-Federalists, who feared that the federal government would become tyrannical.

The absence of a bill of rights proved to be one of the Anti-Federalists' most effective criticisms. In their view history demonstrated that once in power even the most virtuous rulers were tempted to increase their powers at the expense of popular liberty. A written declaration of rights stating clearly the rights and powers retained by the people was therefore an essential safeguard for liberty. Rather than accept that the omission of a bill of rights was a

> "These lawyers, and men of learning, and moneyed men, that talk so finely, and gloss over matters so smoothly, to make us poor illiterate people swallow down the pill, expect to get into Congress themselves ... and then they will swallow up all us little folks, like the great Leviathan."
>
> AMOS SINGLETARY, 1788

How does *The Looking Glass for 1787* portray the Anti-Federalists?

serious flaw in the Constitution, Federalists argued that a bill of rights was unnecessary. Pennsylvania's James Wilson defended the absence of a bill of rights by noting that the new government was one of delegated power only, and hence all powers not ceded to the new government were retained by the people and the states. "It would have been superfluous and absurd," Wilson observed, to stipulate "that we should enjoy those privileges, of which we are not divested either by the intention or the act that brought that body into existence." In *The Federalist,* Publius adopted a different line of attack. He argued that the inclusion of a bill of rights would be dangerous. By listing exactly which rights were protected, the new government would by implication exclude a host of other important rights that it did not explicitly include among those reserved to the people. Since it would be impossible to create a list of all the rights enjoyed by the people, it was better not to list any. For an overview of the main points of disagreement between Federalists and Anti-Federalists see **5.16**.

James Madison Federalists	**George Mason** Anti-Federalists
Support strong central government	Oppose strong central government
Oppose bill of rights as unnecessary and perhaps even harmful to liberty	Favor inclusion of a bill of rights as necessary to protect liberty
Doubt effectiveness of militia and favor federal standing army	Favor militia and oppose federal standing army
Republicanism can survive only in a large and diverse republic	Republicanism can survive only in a small republic
Virtue is a weak foundation for republicanism; a system of checks and balances is better suited to preserving a republican government against corruption	Republicanism depends on a virtuous population to prevent corruption

5.16 Anti-Federalist versus Federalist Ideas Anti-Federalists and Federalists each believed in republican government, but they disagreed over how to structure such a government.

The Theory of the Large Republic: The Genius of James Madison

Anti-Federalists charged that the Constitution was a novel form of government. Federalists did not dispute this point. Political philosophers from antiquity up through the great eighteenth-century French philosopher Baron de Montesquieu agreed on one point: Republican governments only thrived in a small territory with a fairly homogeneous population. When republics grew large or their economies became complicated, conflicts intensified and political life became turbulent. These internal divisions would eventually destabilize government. It was only a matter of time before a republic would collapse into anarchy. This social chaos eventually made republics vulnerable to external conquest or internal subversion by unscrupulous leaders who invariably became despots. Although America had been fortunate that men like Washington took their cues from virtuous leaders such as Cincinnatus, others in the future might emulate the despot Caesar. Many Anti-Federalists accepted this theory, arguing that virtue could thrive only in a small republic.

Madison, however, rejected this theory. He argued that only a large and diverse republic could ward off the inevitable corruption and conflicts that destroyed previous republics. Rather than depend on virtue, Madison placed his faith in the system of checks and balances created by the Constitution, in which the interests of the different branches of government would balance one another. "Enlightened statesmen will not always be at the helm," wrote Madison, so he sought to create a constitutional system that did not depend on virtuous leaders. According to Madisonian theory the different branches of the new government would be set against one another, producing a system of checks and balances.

Before coming to the Philadelphia Convention, Madison had drafted a short document that analyzed "The Vices of the Political System of the United States." Madison had taken his raw notes on republics and shaped them into a memorandum to be used when he took up his role as a delegate to the convention. "The inconveniences of popular States, contrary to the prevailing Theory, are in proportion not to the extent, but to the narrowness of their limits," he wrote. In other words, small republics, not

Why did traditional republican theorists believe that republics needed to be small to survive?

large republics, were more prone to factionalism and political unrest.

During ratification, Madison took these theoretical musings and polished them into a formal statement of beliefs. The new theory of the extended republic was most fully elaborated in *The Federalist*. Madison proclaimed that the new Constitution provided "a republican remedy for the diseases most incident to republican government." Rather than depend on virtue, Madison's theory assumed that individuals would pursue their interests. In an expanded republic, the ongoing give and take among a multiplicity of interests would prevent any one interest from becoming oppressive. The best example of this theory was religion in America. Given the multiplicity of different sects, it was impossible for any one group to dominate and impose its will on the others. The other advantage of a large republic was the increased size of electoral districts, which would provide a bigger pool of talent for elections. The dynamics of election in such districts would also likely filter out candidates for office who lacked the requisite wisdom and knowledge for public service.

"If men were angels, no government would be necessary. If angels were to govern men, neither external nor internal controls on government would be necessary. In framing a government which is to be administered by men over men, the great difficulty lies in this: you must first enable the government to control the governed; and in the next place oblige it to control itself."

JAMES MADISON, *The Federalist* 1788

Ratification

Early and decisive Federalist successes in states such as Delaware, New Jersey, Georgia, and Connecticut helped establish a powerful momentum that Federalists capitalized on to advance their goal of unconditional ratification. If states with powerful, well-organized Anti-Federalist coalitions, such as Virginia, had held ratification conventions earlier, the Constitution might have been defeated. Federalists' willingness to compromise also won over many moderates who might otherwise have opposed the Constitution in important battleground states such as Massachusetts. Had the Federalists maintained a hard-line stance, sticking to the argument advanced by James Wilson that a bill of rights was unnecessary, the Constitution might never have been ratified. New Hampshire's positive vote on the Constitution in late June of 1788 gave Federalists the nine states needed to ratify the Constitution. Although the Constitution was now the new law of the land, Federalists recognized that it was vital to persuade Anti-Federalists in Virginia and New York to accept the Constitution.

To help persuade their state's Anti-Federalists, New York Federalists staged a "grand federal procession" in New York City to show that the Constitution enjoyed broad popular support, particularly among the city's artisans, who saw a strong government as a way of protecting their economic interests from foreign competition. The festive parade drew members from virtually all of the city's many craft trades, who turned out in style to rally behind the Constitution. The parade included dozens of different floats. Printers, for example, marched alongside a printing press mounted on a horse-drawn cart. Printers even churned out an ode written for the occasion that praised the Constitution. A banner with the name Publius, the author of *The Federalist*, flew proudly above the press, and the printers sported caps with the words "Liberty of Press" written in large letters. Marching behind them, another group of artisans carried this banner, which celebrated their work with pewter, a metal alloy of tin and lead that was widely used to make tableware such as mugs and plates (**5.17**). Their banner carried the following verses:

> The Federal Plan Most Solid And Secure
> Americans Their Freedom Will Ensure
> All Arts Shall Flourish In Columbia's Land
> And all Her Sons Join as One Social Band

New York Anti-Federalists had a dilemma: Should they continue their opposition to the Constitution or work within the new system of government? To understand how they made their decision, see *Choices and Consequences: To Ratify or Not.*

How did the argument of *The Federalist* No. 10 change republican theory?

Choices and Consequences:

TO RATIFY OR NOT

By the time New York's ratification convention met in Poughkeepsie, nine states had already ratified the Constitution, making it the new law of the land. Could Anti-Federalists continue to oppose the Constitution and thereby place New York outside of the new nation? For many Anti-Federalists such a prospect was not realistic, so they turned their attentions to the question of amendments to the Constitution. The outcome of the convention depended on the decisions of a block of moderate Anti-Federalists, led by the merchant Melancton Smith. New York Anti-Federalists faced a momentous decision: to continue their opposition to the Constitution or to work within the new system of government.

Choices

1 Agree to support the Constitution with the promise that the First Congress would take up the issue of amendments.

2 Agree to support the Constitution provisionally until amendments were made, but to consider seceding from the Union if amendments were not made.

3 Block ratification in New York and continue to oppose the Constitution.

Decision

Smith opted for the first possibility, making New York the eleventh state to ratify the Constitution. Smith delivered a powerful speech in the New York convention in which he reiterated his hope for future amendments but recognized the need to work through the "mode prescribed by the Constitution."

Consequences

If Smith and other swing Anti-Federalist votes in the Convention had opposed ratification, New York would have remained outside the new Union, and the new nation might have split into separate confederacies. If Smith and other moderates had insisted on prior amendments, Federalists would likely have stood their ground and the convention would possibly have failed to ratify the Constitution. As it was, Smith's decision put more pressure on Rhode Island and North Carolina to accept the new Constitution. The decision also gave additional impetus to the move to amend the Constitution after ratification. Federalist newspapers seized on the idea of adding a new pillar for each state that voted in favor of the Constitution. The pillars and temple metaphor, like Jefferson's model for the Virginia state capitol, evoked Roman ideals of virtue and liberty.

Continuing Controversies

What forces impelled New York Anti-Federalists to accept the Constitution and wait for subsequent amendments?

Although the Anti-Federalists were defeated in 1788, many of their fears and ideals about government still resonate in American politics. Were the Anti-Federalists backward-looking politicians who failed to grasp the genius of the new Constitution, or visionaries who predicted the growth and centralization of American politics? Americans continue to argue over the legacy of Anti-Federalism.

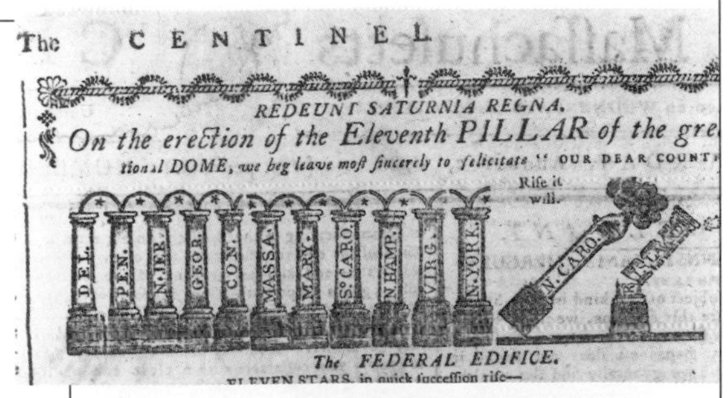

Massachusetts newspaper celebrates New York as "the eleventh pillar."

5.17 Pewterers' Banner
In a New York City parade, Federalist artisans carried a banner that included the U.S. flag and depicted artisans crafting objects of pewter. The verse at the top proclaims the bright future for America under the new Constitution. [*Source:* Collection of The New-York Historical Society, [1903.12]]

New York's ratification dashed the last hopes of the more resolute opponents of the Constitution. Federalists had waged an effective campaign to secure ratification. The majority of Americans were probably opposed to the Constitution when it was first proposed, and the final vote on ratification was close in many states. Several factors helped account for the Federalists' stunning victory. Supporters of the Constitution benefited from being able to organize themselves around a well-defined goal: ratification. By contrast, Anti-Federalists were unable to provide a clear alternative. Some opponents favored another convention to draft an entirely new Constitution, others simply favored amending the Constitution, and a few Anti-Federalists still clung to the idea of revising the Articles of Confederation. Finally, Federalists were far more effective at getting their message into print. Many newspaper editors simply refused to print Anti-Federalist materials.

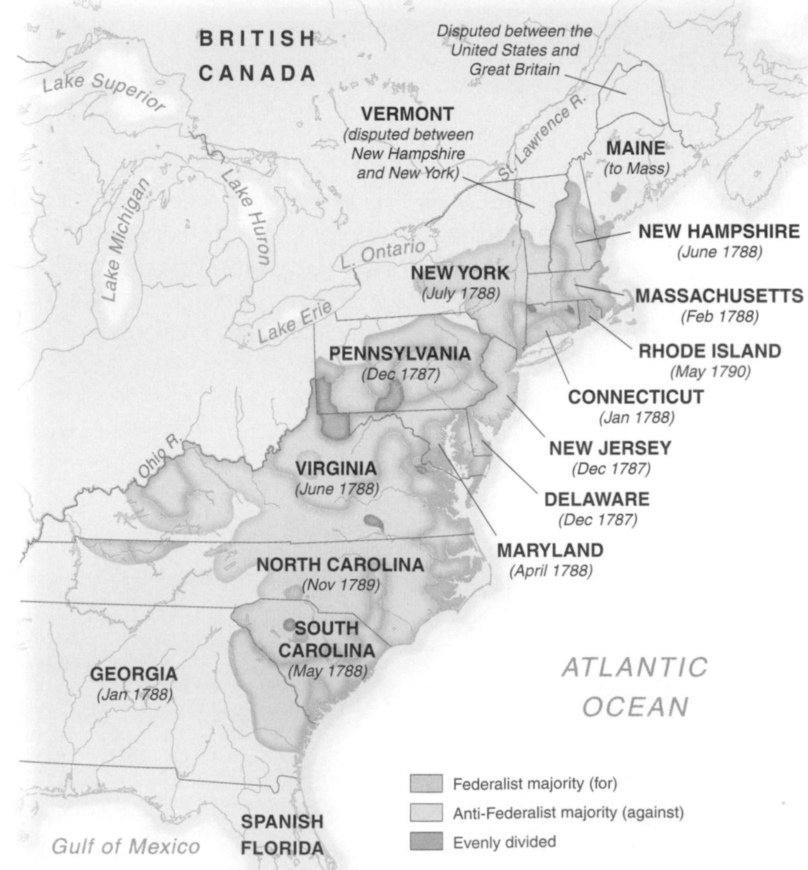

5.18 Geographical Distribution of the Vote on Ratification
Support for the Constitution was strongest along coastal regions and frontiers exposed to threats from external enemies and among small states such as Delaware, Maryland, and New Jersey. Anti-Federalism was strongest in the backcountry regions of New England, the mid-Atlantic, and the South.

The political dynamics of ratification were complex. No single theory accounts for why some individuals and regions supported the Constitution, but there were certain patterns in voting, shown in the map (**5.18**). Geography, economics, and the personal experiences of individuals all shaped the vote on the Constitution.

Merchants and artisans living in regions tied to commerce, such as coastal regions and inland areas close to navigable rivers, looked to a stronger union to protect their economic interests and became Federalists. Inhabitants of frontier regions that faced continuing Indian threats also supported the movement for a stronger central government because of these security concerns. With the exception of Rhode Island, small states supported the Constitution. Officers of the Continental Army who had experienced the difficulty of dealing with a weak Congress under the Articles also supported the Constitution.

On the other side, Anti-Federalists drew together an equally diverse coalition of groups that opposed any effort to centralize authority and lessen the power of the states. Backcountry farmers across the nation, particularly those less closely connected to major commercial market centers, opposed the Constitution. State politicians, especially the newly empowered men of moderate wealth and more humble origins who dominated politics in states such as Pennsylvania and New York, were strongly Anti-Federalist. Finally, wealthy planters in parts of the South who feared that a distant and powerful government would not faithfully represent their interests became Anti-Federalists.

The Creation of a Loyal Opposition

Despite the intensity of the struggle over ratification, Anti-Federalists did not continue their opposition to the Constitution once the nine states needed to ratify the new Constitution adopted it. Indeed, rather than choose to become an anti-Constitutional party, Anti-Federalists now accepted having to work within the framework provided by the Constitution. Continued opposition to the Constitution would only have led to anarchy, which most Anti-Federalists wished to avoid as much as did their Federalist opponents. Anti-Federalists turned their attentions to campaigning for election to the First Congress and to the project of securing amendments to the Constitution.

Conclusion

The first American constitutions drafted after Independence had literally written virtue into their texts. There was widespread agreement that republicanism could only survive where virtue was encouraged. American art and architecture reinforced these values. Preachers made appeals to virtue from the pulpit, and the idea of virtue filled the pages of newspapers. Every citizen was expected to cultivate virtue; no aspect of American life was exempt from the republican emphasis on the need for a virtuous citizenry.

The creation of a virtuous republic proved far more difficult than many had imagined. America faced many challenges under the Articles of Confederation, America's first national constitution. Without the power to tax, the government of the Articles was at the mercy of the states. The individual states seemed incapable of putting the interests of the nation ahead of local interests. Other events demonstrated the fragility of America's fledgling experiment in republican government. Shays's Rebellion, an uprising of farmers in western Massachusetts, alarmed many notable politicians, who feared that America was succumbing to anarchy. For nationalists, America's salvation lay in a stronger central government. These supporters of constitutional reform successfully agitated for a convention to reform the structure of the Articles of Confederation.

The new Constitution that Americans adopted created a much more powerful central government. The Constitution was a bold new experiment in republican government. It abandoned the traditional republican emphasis on virtue and substituted in its place a system of checks and balances designed to prevent any branch of government from becoming a threat to liberty. The Constitution did not eliminate the serious divisions within American society, nor did its adoption lay to rest all the Anti-Federalists' fears. The Constitution did, however, set the terms under which subsequent generations would debate important political questions. Although Americans are apt to be forward-looking in many areas, after more than two centuries, most Americans continue to venerate the achievements of the Framers of the Constitution.

Why was there no anti-Constitution movement after ratification?

1783

Newburgh Conspiracy
Washington prevents coup by Continental army officers

Treaty of Paris
Hostilities between United States and Britain conclude and Britain recognizes American Independence

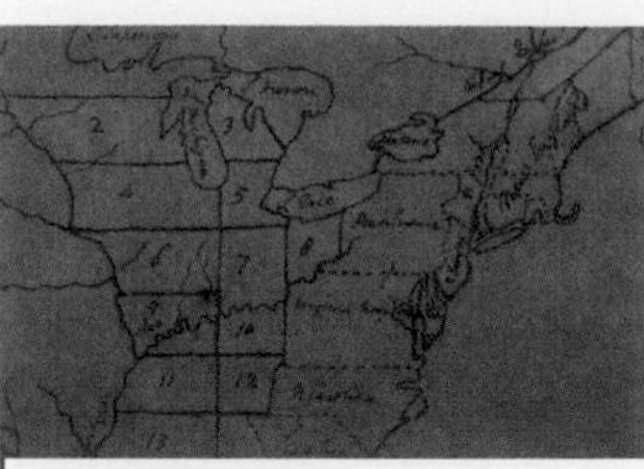

1784

Land Ordinance of 1784
Thomas Jefferson proposes a model for settling the Old Northwest Territory

1785

Thomas Jefferson Appointed Ambassador to France
Jefferson appointment as French ambassador insulates him from the hysteria surrounding Shays's Rebellion

Review Questions

1. Americans in the post-revolutionary era looked to Rome for inspiration in building a virtuous republic. How were these ideas reflected in American art and architecture in this period?
2. Discuss the most notable policy achievements and failures of the Confederation government.
3. Describe the most divisive issues faced by the Constitutional Convention and the main compromises worked out by the delegates to solve these problems.
4. Which groups in society tended to support the Constitution? Which groups opposed ratification?
5. Anti-Federalists were alarmed by the power of the federal government. Do you think the Anti-Federalist objections to the Constitution have any validity today?

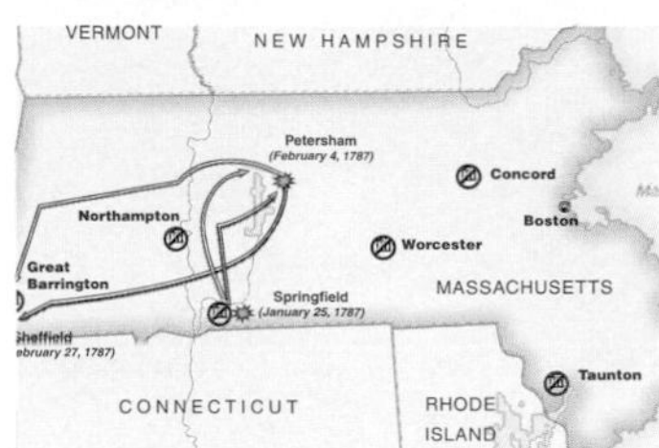

1786

Virginia Statute for Religious Freedom
Madison and Jefferson win approval of bill promoting religious freedom

Shays's Rebellion begins
Farmers in western Massachusetts close courts

1787

Philadelphia Convention Drafts Constitution
Delegates assemble in Philadelphia to revise Articles of Confederation

Hamilton, Madison, and Jay publish the first installment of *The Federalist*
The most sophisticated defense of the Constitution appears in the New York press

1788

New Hampshire becomes ninth state to ratify Constitution
Constitution becomes new law of the land

1789

University of North Carolina chartered
Although the University of Georgia was the first public university chartered in the United States (1785), the University of North Carolina (1789) was the first public institution of higher education to admit students and offer classes

Key Terms

Articles of Confederation America's first constitutional government in effect from 1781–1788. The articles created a weak decentralized form of government that lacked the power to tax and compel state obedience to treaties it negotiated. **138**

Treaty of Paris (1783) Treaty between the newly created United States of America and Britain that officially ended the war between the two and formally recognized American independence. **138**

Old Northwest The region of the new nation bordering on the Great Lakes. **139**

Northwest Ordinance of 1787 One of several laws adopted by the Confederation Congress designed to provide a plan for the orderly settlement of the Northwest Territory (the area north of the Ohio River and west of Pennsylvania). In addition to providing for a plan for self-governance, the Ordinance also prohibited slavery from the Northwest Territory. **141**

Shays's Rebellion Uprising in western Massachusetts in which farmers organized themselves as local militia units and closed down courts to prevent their farms from being seized by creditors. **142**

Virginia Plan A plan framed by James Madison and introduced in the Constitution Convention by Edmund Randolph that called on delegations to abandon the government of the Articles and create a new, strong national government. **145**

New Jersey Plan Proposal made by William Patterson of New Jersey as an alternative to the more nationalistic Virginia Plan that would have retained the principle of state equality in the legislature embodied in the Articles of Confederation. **146**

Great Compromise Compromise plan proposed by Roger Sherman and Oliver Ellsworth of Connecticut that called for equal representation of each state in the upper house and a lower house based on population. **146**

Federalists The name adopted by the supporters of the Constitution who favored a stronger centralized government. **149**

Anti-Federalists The name reluctantly adopted by opponents of the Constitution who insisted that they, not their opponents, were the true supporters of the ideal of federalism. Anti-Federalists opposed weakening the power of the states and feared that the Constitution yielded too much power to the new central government. **149**

CHAPTER 6

The New Republic

An Age of Political Passion, 1789–1800

Launching the New Government p. 160

Hamilton's Ambitious Program p. 162

> "Party spirit is the fashion of the Times ... Party spirit makes the worst of everything that opposes her folly."
>
> *Newark Centinel of Freedom*, 1799

The adoption of the Constitution did little to lessen the divisions in America that had arisen during ratification. The Federalist supporters of the Constitution splintered into two opposing groups. One side rallied around Alexander Hamilton, who became the chief theorist and driving force for an ambitious Federalist agenda. For Hamilton and his allies, the adoption of the Constitution was simply the first step in creating a powerful central government. These new Federalists envisioned a future America as a great commercial empire that would, inspired by Britain's lead, develop a strong military and pursue economic development aggressively.

Opposing this bold agenda was a group that coalesced around Thomas Jefferson, who, with his friend James Madison, a former ally of Hamilton, helped define the core of the Republican opposition. This movement, while lacking the coherence and formal organization of a modern political party, battled its Federalist opponents on a wide range of political, economic, and constitutional issues. Republicans sought to limit the powers of the new federal government, opposed to the creation of a powerful financial and military state.

The radicalism of the French Revolution further polarized American political life, and political passions intensified during the turbulent 1790s. Federalists denounced the excesses of revolutionary France even as Republicans continued to affirm their support for France.

The Cannibals are landing

By the end of the 1790s, the partisan animosities had grown intense, as reflected in this pro-Federalist political cartoon, *The Times, A Political Portrait*. George Washington, who sits in a carriage behind a group of volunteer militiamen, rides out to meet the French enemy threat. As they march forward, the militia tramples a Republican printer, while a dog urinates on a copy of his newspaper. The artist shows Republican James Madison attempting to block Washington's progress with a giant pen, while Republicans Albert Gallatin and Thomas Jefferson restrain his progress from behind. The text at the bottom announces the triumph of American government and warns traitors that they will receive their just punishments.

After a decade of Federalist domination, Americans in 1800 turned to Thomas Jefferson, head of the Republican opposition, as their leader. In a close election contest, power was peacefully transferred from the Federalists to their opponents, and Jefferson became the nation's third president.

Why was the period after the adoption of the Constitution so politically contentious?

thy master.

Volunteers
Stop de wheel

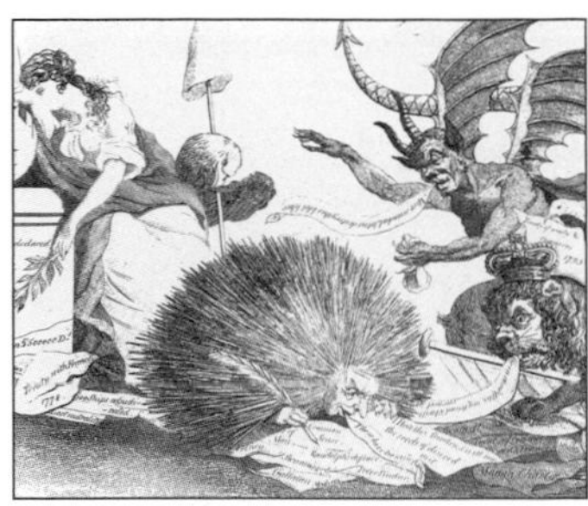

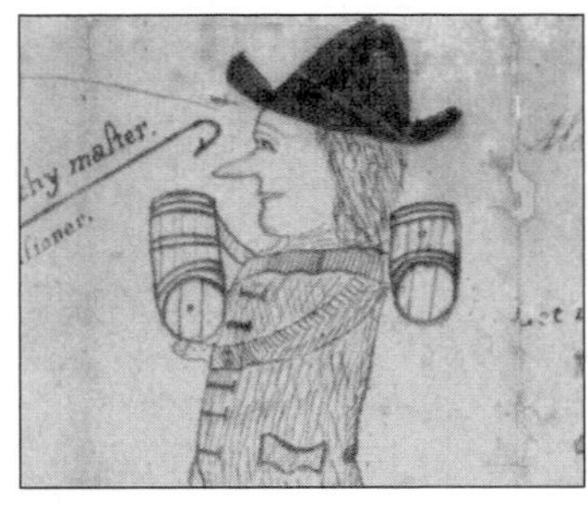

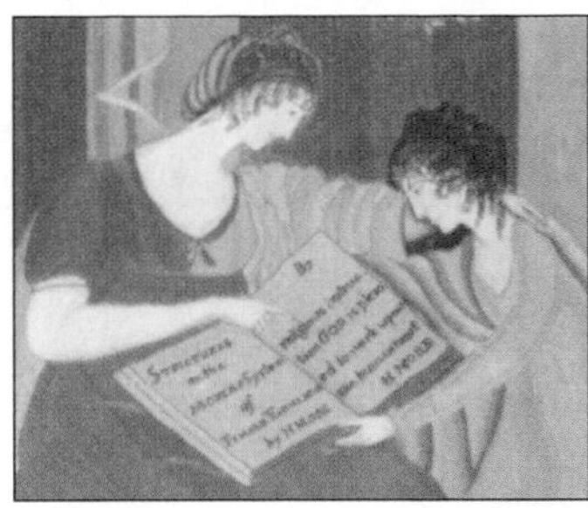

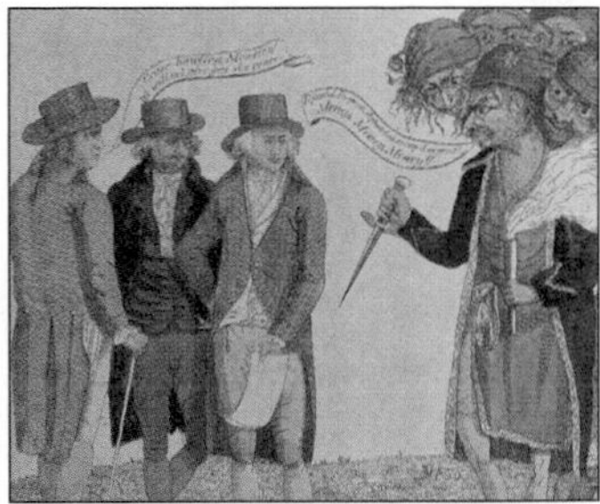

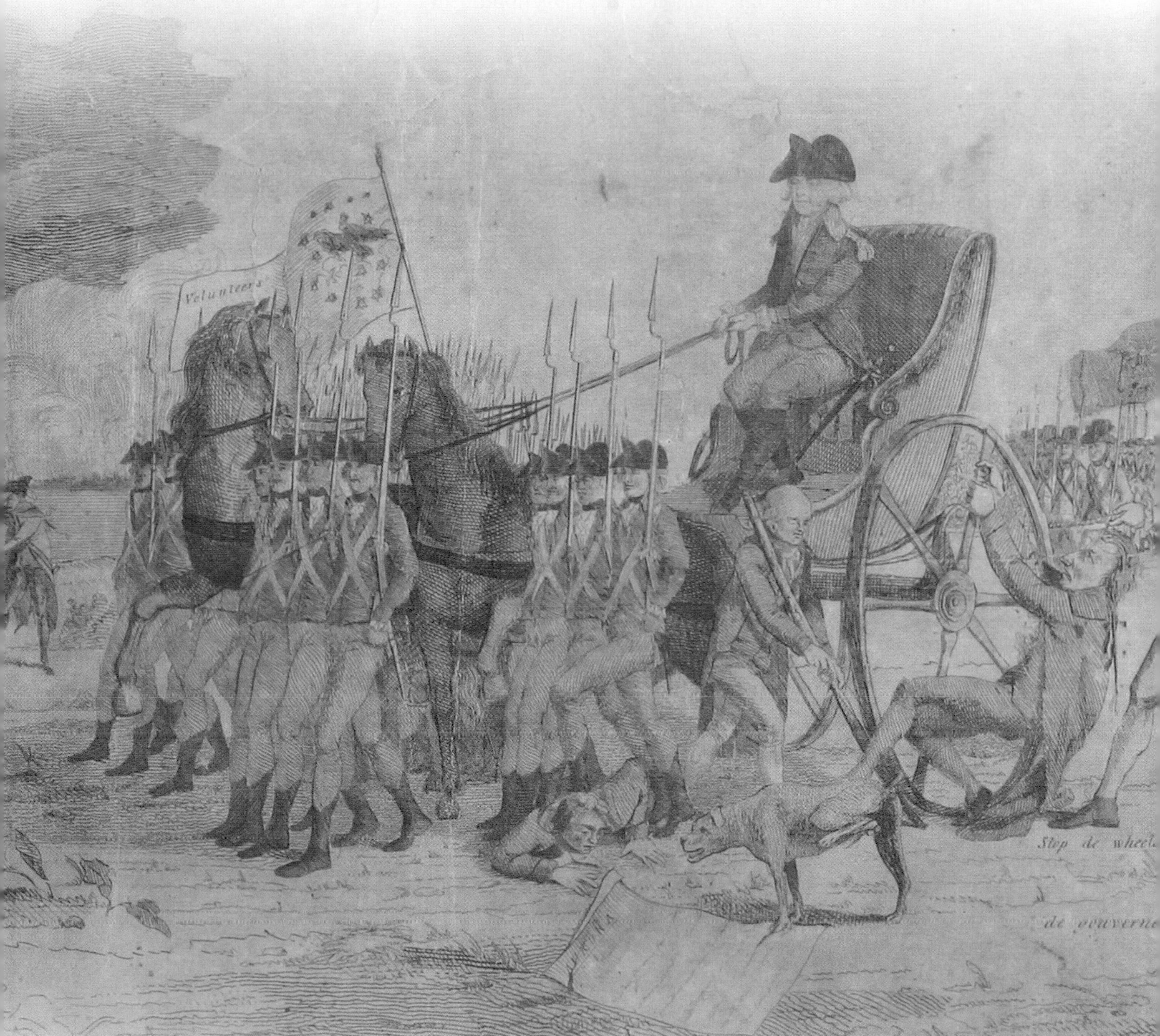

Launching the New Government

Although intense partisanship had characterized American politics during the colonial and revolutionary eras, the republican ideas championed during the Revolution stressed the need for a virtuous citizenry. The Constitution created a system designed to check the dangers of factionalism. Still, leaders were expected to put the good of the nation above any factional interest. Fortunately for America, the nation's first president, George Washington, was such a figure, a leader who tried to remain above partisanship. Appointing Alexander Hamilton and Thomas Jefferson to his cabinet demonstrated his commitment to this ideal. These were men whose views on government were almost at opposite extremes, and from them, Washington sought policy alternatives to deal with the pressing issues facing the new nation.

Choosing the First President

The Constitution had created an **electoral college**, a group of electors appointed by the states who had the responsibility of picking the president. On February 4, 1789, electors from all the states that had ratified the Constitution met in their respective state capitals and unanimously selected George Washington to be the nation's first president. John Adams, another prominent revolutionary leader, received half the number of votes that Washington did, becoming the first vice president. The remaining votes were split among ten other candidates.

The nation celebrated Washington's election in a grand style. He traveled from his home at Mount Vernon in Virginia to the site of his inaugural in New York, feted along the way. Many towns erected triumphal arches, such as this one near Trenton (**6.1**). Although typically leading men in the community would come out to greet Washington, giving him a military salute, in Trenton he met the local women who had erected the arch and who serenaded him. A large placard on the arch proudly proclaimed that "The Defender of the Mothers will also Defend the Daughters."

The First Federal Elections: Completing the Constitution

While there had been little doubt that George Washington would be America's first president, the divisions between Federalists and Anti-Federalists influenced the first congressional elections. The issue that dominated the first federal elections was that of constitutional amendments.

Federalists were eager to have James Madison run for office for Congress. Madison agreed to run, but he balked at the idea of actively campaigning for a seat in Congress, believing that such campaigning was inconsistent with republican ideals. Fortunately, Madison's supporters persuaded him that if he did not take his case directly to the people, Virginia would send an Anti-Federalist–dominated delegation to Congress. Madison faced Anti-Federalist James Monroe, and he eventually relented and won election to Congress. One group critical to Madison's success was the Baptist community, which was eager to obtain explicit protection for freedom of religion in the Constitution. The task of shaping a set of amendments fell to Federalist James Madison.

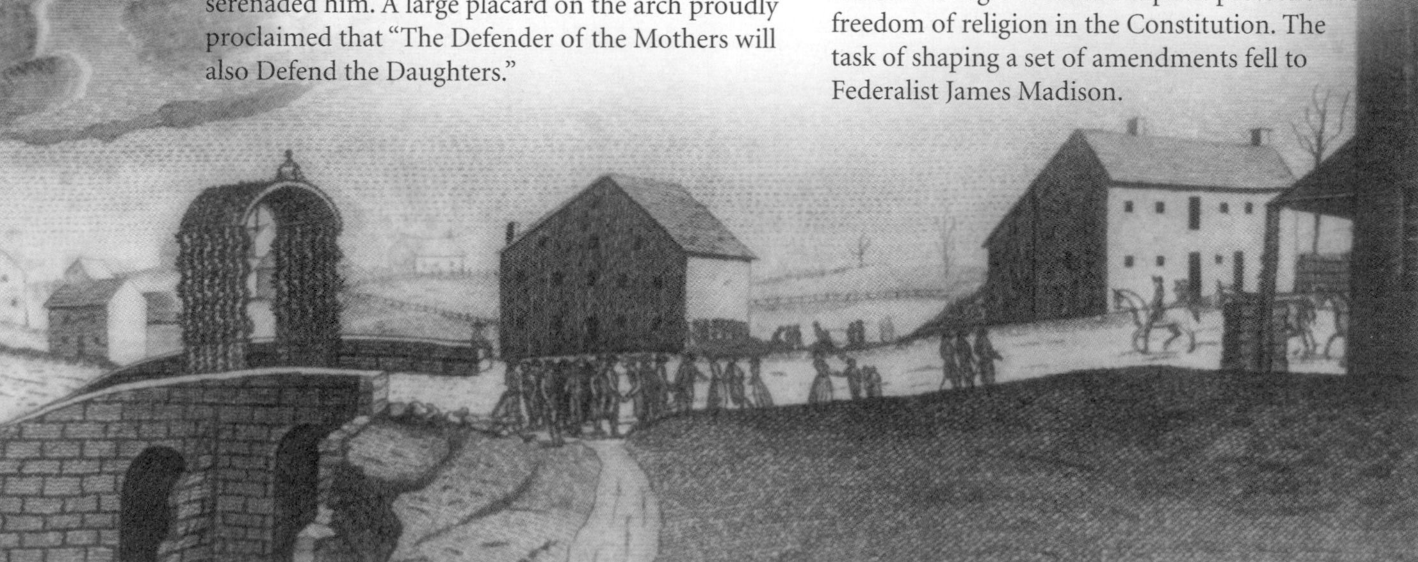

6.1 **Triumphal Arch Near Trenton** At Trenton a group of women erected a twenty-foot arch made of evergreens and laurels. On the right, Washington rides toward the arch.

Why did Madison shift his views on the need for a Bill of Rights?

Madison recognized that if properly framed, amendments might go a long way to eliminating lingering Anti-Federalist suspicions of the new federal government. Thus, although he had originally opposed Anti-Federalist calls for amendments during the struggle over ratification, Madison now recognized the political necessity of amendments. He accepted the unenviable task that he described as "the nauseous project of amendments," knowing that the process would be deeply politicized and that the few ardent Anti-Federalists in Congress would agitate for weakening the federal government. Still, Madison pared down the dozens of amendments proposed by the various state ratification conventions to a list of seventeen amendments. The Senate then whittled these down to twelve provisions and sent them to the states to ratify. The states did not adopt the first two proposed amendments, which dealt with legislative apportionment and congressional salaries. (More than two hundred years later, Congress adopted the Twenty-Seventh Amendment, which prohibited Congress from raising its own salary.)

The final form of the **Bill of Rights**, the first ten of the original twelve amendments to the Constitution, included protections for basic individual liberties and protections for the states. The First Amendment protected freedom of the press and religion. The Second Amendment guaranteed that the people would continue to have a right to keep and bear arms in a well-regulated militia. (This right has since been expanded to include private arms used for individual self defense within the home as well.) The Third Amendment forbade the government to quarter troops in the homes of private citizens. Several amendments protected the procedural rights associated with jury trial. Assuring those concerned that a bill of rights might inadvertently exclude some rights, the Ninth Amendment declared that enumeration of some rights did not mean the denial of others retained by the people. Finally, the fear that the new government would expand its powers by exploiting the vague clauses of the Constitution prompted inclusion of the Tenth Amendment, which stated that those powers not delegated to new government were reserved to the states and people.

The Bill of Rights assuaged the concerns of most moderate Anti-Federalists even if it did not satisfy the most ardent opponents of federal power. The adoption of the Bill of Rights resolved the most important issue remaining from the struggle between Federalists and Anti-Federalists, clearing the way for a new set of issues to come to the fore.

Filling Out the Branches of Government

The Constitution created a blueprint for the new federal government, but Congress and the new president still had to work out important details, including the structure of the executive and the judiciary departments. Congress filled out the structure of the executive branch, creating new cabinet positions for a secretary of state to advise the president on foreign affairs, a secretary of the treasury to oversee economic policy and a new office of attorney general to be the chief legal advisor to government. The position of secretary of war was a carryover from the government that had existed under the Articles of Confederation.

For his cabinet Washington assembled an impressive group of leaders who had distinguished themselves in American public life during the Revolutionary War. Henry Knox, the secretary of war, was a leading Revolutionary War general; Edmund Randolph, the new attorney general, had introduced the Virginia plan in the constitutional convention; Thomas Jefferson, the secretary of state, had been the primary author of the Declaration of Independence; and the first secretary of the treasury, Alexander Hamilton, had been one of the co-authors of *The Federalist* along with John Jay, who became the first chief justice of the Supreme Court. Although none of his appointments had been Anti-Federalists, Washington's choices cut across a wide section of the political spectrum, with Hamilton representing the extreme nationalist position and Jefferson taking a stance far more sympathetic to state power.

During ratification some Anti-Federalists had expressed fear that the Constitution would create a large, expensive government with a vast bureaucracy. In reality the federal government was far less imposing. Scattered among several buildings near New York's Wall Street, the temporary home of the new government, the offices of the new government bore slight resemblance to the nightmare that some Anti-Federalists had predicted. The scale of the new government was modest, and the size of the new federal bureaucracy small. As a whole, the new government included about 350 officers. Jefferson's State Department employed two clerks, two assistants, and a part-time translator. (The modern State Department employs eight thousand people in Washington, D.C., and another eleven thousand overseas.)

Why were some ardent Anti-Federalists not satisfied with the Bill of Rights?

Hamilton's Ambitious Program

In 1789 Congress requested that Secretary of the Treasury Alexander Hamilton issue a report on the state of the new nation's economy. Between 1790 and 1791, Hamilton responded with a series of reports to Congress, each report corresponding to a major part of his overall plan to bolster America's economy. These included reports on public credit, a national bank, the establishment of a mint to make money, and manufactures. Hamilton saw a strong national government as a necessity to promote American prosperity and protect the young nation's economic interests against foreign threats. In Hamilton's view the Constitution had created a central government with considerable power over the economy. In his reports he urged Congress and the president to use this authority to encourage economic growth. To accomplish this, Hamilton looked to Britain as a model for America's future. With a robust manufacturing and financial section, and the powerful Bank of England to energize its economy, Britain had the most diverse and sophisticated economy in all of Europe.

Hamilton's Vision for the New Republic

Alexander Hamilton envisioned America as a powerful nation with a strong government and a vigorous commercial economy. Before he could implement his ambitious program to realize this vision, however, Hamilton would have to overcome formidable opponents at nearly every turn. Hamilton's bold program not only frightened many former Anti-Federalists but also alarmed some strong supporters of the Constitution, notably James Madison, who did not wish to see the new government become a powerful state modeled after the government of Britain.

> "In place of that noble love of liberty and republican government which carried us triumphantly through the war, [a pro-British] monarchical aristocratical party has sprung up, whose avowed object is to draw over us the substance, as they have already done the forms, of the British government."
>
> THOMAS JEFFERSON, 1796

Another outspoken opponent of Hamilton's program was Madison's close friend Thomas Jefferson. Hamilton's economic vision clashed with Jefferson's vision of a nation composed of small farmers. The new opposition to Federalist efforts to create a powerful centralized government, who called themselves **Republicans**, united former Anti-Federalists and those Federalists who shared the concerns of Madison and Jefferson. Republicans believed that liberty could flourish only if the individual states remained powerful enough to protect their citizens from the power of the new federal government.

The leader who conceived this audacious Federalist agenda, a vision that would transform America, was a self-made man who lacked the aristocratic upbringing of his chief opponents, Virginians Jefferson and Madison. Hamilton came from an exceedingly modest background. Born in the West Indies, the illegitimate son of a Scottish merchant and a planter's daughter, Hamilton was orphaned at an early age but obtained a job as an apprentice clerk in a merchant firm. At the age of fourteen, he wrote "my Ambition is so prevalent that" he loathed the "Grov'ling condition of a Clerk or the like, to which my Fortune etc. condemns me, and would willingly risk my life, tho not my Character, to exalt my station." Hamilton was talented, ambitious, and hard working, and the proprietor of the merchant firm recognized his talent and helped him finance his education. Hamilton attended Kings College (now Columbia University) in New York City. He took advantage of the opportunities provided by the American Revolution, rising rapidly through the

What were the main features of Hamilton's economic program?

> "In almost all the questions, great and small, which have arisen since the first session of Congress, Mr. Jefferson and Mr. Madison have been found among those who are disposed to narrow the federal authority[and sound] the alarm, with great affected solemnity, at encroachments, meditated on the rights of the States."
>
> ALEXANDER HAMILTON, 1792

ranks of the Continental Army to become Washington's personal aid. Marrying into a prominent New York family, he became an important political figure in that state and developed close ties to the city's financial community.

A successful lawyer with many friends and allies within New York's merchant community, Hamilton became one of the most influential political figures in the state. The New York merchant community commissioned this portrait (**6.2**) of Alexander Hamilton to honor him for his contribution to their economic prosperity. It provides one measure of his power and influence, particularly within the new nation's financial world. Yet the painting is as notable for what the artist omitted as for what he included. Hamilton insisted that no references to his important political accomplishments be included in the painting, something that commissioners of the portrait had requested. Realizing that much about his political life was controversial, Hamilton directed the artist to avoid any such references. Rather than depicting the complex, often contentious quality of his life, the painting presents the image of a disinterested republican statesman and writer.

Hamilton was an unabashed American nationalist and an elitist who viewed democracy with suspicion. He believed that there would always be class divisions in society. To survive and prosper, the new nation had to win the allegiance of the rich and powerful, binding their interests to those of the new federal government.

6.2 Alexander Hamilton
New York City's merchant community commissioned a portrait of Hamilton in 1792. Hamilton decided against having the painting represent his political career, which was steeped in controversy; he chose instead to have himself painted in a plain brown suit standing beside a table with an inkwell and quill.

The Assumption of State Debts

Hamilton's "Report on Public Credit" addressed the war debt of the states and the federal government. The new nation and the individual states had incurred considerable debt financing the American Revolution. This debt consisted of a multitude of different types of paper currency and securities that the Confederation government and the individual states had issued. The federal and state governments now owed about $11 million of the debt to foreign bankers and governments. The remainder, around $42 million in federal debt and $21 million in state debt, was owed to American citizens who had supplied food, arms, and other materials for the Revolutionary War effort.

How does Hamilton's own life story help explain his particular vision for America's future?

Hamilton proposed consolidating the debt of the individual states and the federal government. Hamilton's scheme called for the **assumption of the state debts**, by which the federal government would take over any outstanding debts that the states owed. Creditors who held state paper would exchange their notes for a new type of paper that promised to pay the bearer interest until the bearer redeemed the original value of the note. Hamilton's "Second Report on Public Credit" focused on financing this scheme and included a plan for taxing whiskey. Hamilton envisioned a permanently funded national debt in which income from taxes would service the interest, allowing the federal government to pay its other expenses.

The most controversial feature of Hamilton's plan dealt with the problem posed by speculation in these paper notes. The value of state- and Confederation-issued paper had declined steadily as the hard-pressed states and the fledgling national government simply printed more paper to pay their debts. By the 1790s inflation had eroded the value of this paper. After the adoption of the Constitution, a small group of financial speculators had purchased large amounts of this devalued paper, hoping that the new government would finally redeem the paper at face value and net them a huge profit. Believing it was vital for the new nation to maintain excellent credit with investors, Hamilton insisted that government had an obligation to honor the debt at full face value.

Republicans feared that Hamilton's funding scheme would give a windfall to speculators. Besides being unjust, Republicans argued, such a plan would help create a powerful financial interest that would become a potential source of corruption. Rather than pay full value to speculators, Republicans favored a policy that would pay the full value of the debt to the original holders but not to the speculators. The Republican policy would have given speculators a reasonable return on their investment, but not a huge profit. Hamilton argued that this policy would violate the sanctity of contracts and undermine the credit of the new government. Eventually Hamilton defeated his opponents, and state debt certificates would be exchanged for federal ones at full face value.

Madison's Opposition

Hamilton was shocked to find his former ally James Madison leading the opposition to his policies. During ratification Madison had sided with Hamilton and together with John Jay wrote *The Federalist*, the powerful defense of the Constitution. Madison had also supported Hamilton's early efforts to create an effective Treasury Department under the Articles of Confederation. What led Madison to change his position so dramatically and mount a vigorous opposition to Hamilton in 1789?

Madison's growing opposition to Hamilton's economic program was motivated by his desire to preserve the constitutional system he had labored so hard to create. The speculative frenzy caused by Hamilton's policy of assumption shocked Madison, who came to believe that Hamilton's program would undermine the republican values that the Constitution was designed to protect. While

> "In an agricultural country like this, therefore, to erect and concentrate and perpetuate a large moneyed interest ... must ... produce one or other of two evils: the prostration of agriculture at the feet of commerce, or a change in the present form of Federal Government fatal to the existence of American liberty."
>
> Virginia's remonstrance against the assumption of state debts, 16 December 1790

Why did Virginians, including Madison and Jefferson, oppose Hamilton's economic program?

Hamilton dreamed of a powerful state that might rival Britain, Madison was more interested in preserving his constitutional vision. In Madison's view, Hamilton's system would create vast inequalities of wealth, encourage corruption, and ultimately undermine America's republican form of government. Hamilton believed that Madison had been unduly influenced by Jefferson; indeed, Madison had always shared with his fellow Virginian a similar republican vision of an agrarian republic. Hamilton, by contrast, the product of New York's commercial ethos, believed that America's future depended on creating a powerful fiscal military state.

The split between Hamilton and Madison reflected a profound shift in the dynamics of American political life. A scant few years before, Madison had decried faction in *Federalist No. 10.* Now faced with the rise of Hamilton's Federalist agenda, Madison revised his thinking about factions and politics. In an essay published in the *National Gazette,* "A Candid State of Parties," he now conceded that America had become divided into a Republican party and an anti-Republican party (the Federalists).

Opposition to his plan of assumption took a great personal toll on Hamilton. Indeed, Jefferson described the secretary of the treasury as "somb[er], haggard, and dejected beyond comparison." Jefferson invited Hamilton to dinner with Madison, where the three worked out the final details of a deal to break the impasse over assumption. In exchange for gaining support for his economic program, Hamilton agreed to the proposal to move the new capital of the United States from New York City to a site on the Potomac River. Southerners such as Jefferson and Madison feared that keeping the nation's capital in its temporary home of New York City invited domination by commercial and financial interests. Although Hamilton might gain in the short run, Madison and Jefferson believed that the bargain they struck would lessen the influence of financial interests over the government. In the meanwhile, the government temporarily relocated to Philadelphia. This cartoon (**6.3**), which shows Congress embarked on the ship *Constitution* as it sails to its eventual home on the Potomac, captures the Republicans' association of urban commercial centers such as Philadelphia with

6.3 Congress Embarked on the Ship *Constitution*
Jefferson and Madison hoped that by relocating the capital to a new home on the Potomac, they would reduce the dangers of federal government corruption. In this cartoon the devil lures Congress to its temporary home in Philadelphia.

What did Madison and Jefferson gain by moving the location of the new capital to what is now Washington, D.C.?

corruption. The devil lures the ship to its clear doom on the rocky falls leading to Philadelphia.

The Bank, the Mint, and the Report on Manufactures

In his "Report on a National Bank," Hamilton recommended that the federal government charter a national bank. The new **Bank of the United States** would serve as a depository for government funds, help bolster confidence in government securities, make loans, and provide the nation with a stable national currency. The government would own part of the stock in the new Bank of the United States, but would allow private investors to buy the majority of stock. At the time of his proposal, America's financial sector was rudimentary: there were only three private banks in the United States. A national bank would help stabilize the economy of the new nation and provide a means of linking the interests of the wealthy to the prosperity of the new nation.

Once again Madison opposed Hamilton's plan. Much of the debate on this proposal focused on the constitutionality of Hamilton's plan. Madison wanted to see the Constitution interpreted according to the original understanding of the states that ratified it in 1788. Arguing for the narrow interpretation of congressional power, Madison denied that the Constitution authorized Congress to charter a national bank. Ultimately, however, Hamilton's ideas prevailed, and the Federalist controlled Congress chartered the Bank of the United States. Having lost in Congress, Republicans held out hope for a presidential veto. Washington sought advice from the members of his cabinet about the constitutionality of the bank. Attorney General Edmund Randolph and Thomas Jefferson both agreed with Madison.

Jefferson took advantage of the occasion to articulate his own views on how to interpret the new Constitution. He acknowledged that the Constitution empowered Congress to enact laws "necessary and proper." However, while the creation of a bank was convenient and useful, it was not in his view necessary for Congress to fulfill its obligations to raise revenues. This theory of strict construction approached the text of the Constitution in an almost literal manner. If the Constitution did not grant a power, then, according to the theory of strict construction, the Tenth Amendment reserved that power to the states and the people. Madison and Jefferson designed their slightly different theories of constitutional interpretation to protect the rights of the people and the powers of the states against encroachment by the federal government.

By contrast, Hamilton's theory of loose construction interpreted the language of the Constitution broadly. Hamilton believed the federal government enjoyed enormous latitude in determining the appropriate means for accomplishing any legitimate constitutional end. Even if a specific power was not listed, such as the power to charter a bank, Hamilton believed the Constitution implied such a power. In the case of the bank, Hamilton argued that Jefferson's reasoning would effectively rewrite the constitution to restrict the powers of Congress to enact only those laws that were absolutely "necessary and proper." In response to Madison and Jefferson's suggestion of consulting the original intent of the state ratification conventions, Hamilton argued that "the intention is to be sought in the instrument itself." Interpreters of the Constitution should follow well established legal rules for understanding statutes and apply them to the words of the Constitution. In other words, the actual text of the Constitution, not the arguments of Federalists, Anti-Federalists, or state ratification conventions, ought to shape subsequent interpretation. The struggle over the proper way of interpreting the Constitution had emerged as a major political battlefield in the new republic. Indeed, the proper interpretation of the Constitution remains a controversial issue in modern America.

As would happen throughout his first term in office, Washington sided with Hamilton against Madison and Jefferson. The successful chartering of the Bank of the United States was Hamilton's second major victory in the struggle to define the character of the new republic.

Hamilton's report on the necessity of a federal mint was the one part of his program that Jefferson enthusiastically endorsed. Hamilton proposed a currency that would include a variety of coins in different denominations emblazoned with different patriotic symbols. Jefferson not only recognized the need for a federal currency but as a part-time inventor he was also fascinated by the mechanics of minting money.

Hamilton's "Report on Manufactures" detailed the remaining part of his plan to reshape the American economy. He called for a comprehensive

How did Hamilton and Jefferson differ in their interpretations of the phrase "necessary and proper?"

program to encourage domestic industry by providing incentives for industrial development and tariffs to help American industry compete against imported foreign goods, which were cheaper. Congress refused to follow Hamilton's recommendation to raise these tariffs sharply. Hamilton's more grandiose scheme to encourage industrial development generated little interest in Congress. However, Hamilton did manage to persuade Congress to enact a new series of taxes, including a duty on whiskey. In the struggle to shape the contours of the new nation's economy, Hamilton's Federalists had soundly defeated Jefferson, Madison, and the Republican opposition at nearly every turn. Hamilton was largely successful at implementing his visionary economic program.

Hamilton	Jefferson
Commercial Republic	Agrarian Republic
Broad Construction	Strict Construction
Standing Army	Militia
Pro-British	Pro-French

6.4 Political Views: Hamilton versus Jefferson

Jefferson and Hamilton: Contrasting Visions of the Republic

Jefferson and Hamilton were a study in contrasts. Their backgrounds varied greatly: Jefferson was a southern slave owner; Hamilton, a northerner with strong abolitionist sympathies. Jefferson grew up a Virginia aristocrat, with every conceivable advantage; Hamilton was a self-made man who confessed that he was determined to escape his humble origins at almost any cost.

Regarding several of the most important issues facing the new American nation, the two men found themselves in distinctly separate camps, as summarized in the table (**6.4**). In general, Hamilton sought to endow the national government with additional powers; Jefferson sought to limit the powers of the federal government and protect state authority from further incursions.

The two men also approached the economy from radically different philosophies. Hamilton's idea of a thriving commercial republic was diametrically opposed to Jefferson's vision of a nation of independent yeoman farmers tilling the land. "While we have land to labour," Jefferson wrote, "let us never wish to see our citizens occupied at a work bench." Hamilton believed that America needed to emulate the powerful and diversified economy of Great Britain and foster commerce and manufacture.

A gulf separated the two men on questions of constitutional law as well. Hamilton believed in a broad, or loose, construction of the Constitution. He believed the federal government had to have wide latitude to choose whatever means was best suited to accomplish its legitimate objects. Jefferson, by contrast, believed in a strict construction of the Constitution so that the powers of the new government would be limited to those clearly established by the Constitution.

In foreign affairs the two men opposed one another as well. Hamilton was an Anglophile who not only championed Britain but also believed that Britain's path to economic power ought to guide America. Jefferson savored all things French, from wine to pastry. He thought America's interests were better served by supporting France.

What were the most important points of disagreement between Hamilton and Jefferson?

Partisanship without Parties

The idea of political parties was inimical to the republican values of the post-Revolutionary era. In the struggle over ratification in 1788, Madison had written in *Federalist No. 10* that "the public good is disregarded in the conflicts of rival parties." The partisan struggles that dominated American politics in the years after ratification forced Madison to rethink his view of parties. In 1792 Madison conceded that in "every political society, parties are unavoidable." Although Americans increasingly used terms like *party* to describe the bitter conflicts of the 1790s, the partisan alignments they described had not yet achieved the highly organized structure of modern political parties. Political conflict in the 1790s was a transitional phase in the evolution of a modern two-party system. Some historians describe this period as that of the first party system, but many prefer to characterize it as a proto-party system that set the stage for the later developments of highly organized modern style parties. Indeed, although Americans were deeply divided politically, neither Federalists nor Republicans functioned as disciplined modern political parties. Neither group organized loyal supporters around a set of well-defined messages at a national level. Nor did either side successfully create permanent political structures that brought local and state politics under the umbrella of a coherent national organization. The partisan conflicts of this era produced two proto-parties, the Federalists and the Republicans.

A New Type of Politician

Although the aristocratic Thomas Jefferson and James Madison dominated the Republican movement, its success owed much to a new type of politician whose expertise lay in mobilizing voters and creating effective political organizations. The most influential of these new politicians was Virginia's John Beckley. In contrast to Jefferson and Madison, who were connected to the gentry elite that dominated political life in Virginia, Beckley rose from the status of an indentured servant to a lowly clerk, and eventually became the clerk of the U.S. House of Representatives. He became an indispensable player in advancing the Republican cause. Indeed, while aristocratic politicians such as Jefferson and Madison continued to view themselves as members of a virtuous elite who were not motivated by party spite, Beckley and other members of this new class of professional politicians immersed themselves in the sometimes sordid task of coordinating campaign and attacking their opponents.

Beckley and other Republicans figures who did much of the grassroots organizing were more at home in the world of taverns and coffee houses than they were in the world of elegant dinner parties that Jefferson and Madison inhabited. Beckley felt a kindred spirit with the artisans and merchants of New York City and Philadelphia, having worked as a clerk. He felt a particular kinship with other self-made men, many of whom joined the Republican movement. In many respects Beckley's life more closely resembled Hamilton's than Jefferson's. Despite this fact, Beckley threw himself into the task of promoting Jefferson's fortunes and attacking Hamilton. Gossip became one highly effective means of political warfare that Beckley developed to a fine art. Beckley leaked information about an adulterous affair Hamilton was having with the wife of a shady financier. When the press reported rumors that Hamilton had provided sensitive financial information to his lover's husband, Republican politicians pounced on Hamilton, who was forced to admit the affair but denied any financial improprieties. Beckley's efforts weakened Hamilton's political standing but did not destroy the New Yorker's influence among Federalists.

The Growth of the Partisan Press

The expansion of the press facilitated the rise of partisan politics. In the years immediately following ratification of the Constitution, there was a dramatic, nearly threefold increase in the number

What role did the partisan press play in the politics of the 1790s?

of newspapers, from a mere 92 in 1790 to nearly 235 in 1800. While eastern port towns and cities still supported the greatest number of papers, many interior market towns also boasted papers by the last decade of the eighteenth century. Many of these papers aligned themselves with one or the other main political movements in the country. John Fenno's *Gazette of the United States*, which he established "to endear the General Government to the people," articulated the Federalist point of view. To combat Fenno's influence, Jefferson and Madison persuaded the poet Philip Freneau to found the *National Gazette*, which rallied opposition to Hamilton and the Federalists. The resulting battle of words in the press between the two publications intensified the already highly charged political atmosphere. Federalists and Republicans each recognized that political success meant managing public opinion. "All power," James Madison noted, "has been traced to public opinion." A free government, therefore, calls for "a circulation of newspapers through the entire body of the people."

The level of partisan rancor in the press grew steadily over the course of the 1790s. No person was sharper in his attacks than Federalist William Cobbett, who often wrote under the pen name Peter Porcupine, a choice that reflected his prickly literary personality and barbed writing. Jefferson complained that the Federalist press was filled with "porcupines" and lamented that "a single sentence got hold of by the 'Porcupines,' will suffice to abuse and persecute me in their papers for months." Cobbett lambasted the Republicans as atheists and radical democrats who sought to destroy all government. He compared the leading Republican newspaper, the *Aurora*, to "a lewd and common strumpet" whose illegitimate offspring were falsehood and slander. The Republicans replied with their own stinging attacks. This Republican political cartoon (**6.5**) casts Cobbett as a tool of the devil and his Federalist lackeys in America.

The Democratic-Republican Societies

The emergence of a new type of political organization helped transform the political life of the new nation. Between 1793 and 1794, thirty-five **Democratic-Republican Societies** sprouted up across America. Although not official organs of the Republican movement, most of the societies had close ties to local Republican organizations. The goal of these societies was to influence public opinion. The New York Democratic-Republican Society asserted that public opinion "is the foundation of all our liberties, and constitutes the only solid groundwork for all our Rights." In addition to publishing their sentiments on the political issues of the day, the societies staged Fourth of July celebrations, gave festive dinners, and sponsored public orations.

Republicans viewed the societies as a way to improve public understanding of political issues and refine public opinion. Federalists saw them in a different light. They denounced these "self-created societies" for sowing the "seeds of jealousy and distrust of the government." For Federalists, the Democratic-Republican Societies not only sapped the people's confidence in their government but also fomented radical ideas. Federalists viewed the role of elected representatives differently than did Republicans. Federalists supported a more traditional republican ideal of virtue in which citizens deferred to the wisdom of their leaders once they had been placed in office. Republicans embraced a more democratic ideal in which the voice of the people could be brought to bear on public questions through organizations such as the Democratic-Republican Societies.

6.5 Peter Porcupine Liberty sits forlorn, while Federalist William Cobbett, "Peter Porcupine," scribbles attacks and insults. The devil and the British Lion urge on the Porcupine. A Jay bird, symbolic of Jay's Treaty, perches on the British Lion.

Conflicts at Home and Abroad

The French Revolution, the bloody toppling of the monarchy followed by the rise of a radical democratic government, sent shock waves across Europe and profoundly affected American politics. Republicans supported the revolution, and Federalist denounced its excesses. Europe was once again embroiled in conflict as France and Britain went to war with one another. Although Washington continued to have the support of Republicans and Federalists, the contest over the vice presidency in 1792 demonstrated how deeply divided America had become. Federalist John Adams defeated his Republican rival, the former Anti-Federalist George Clinton, but the Republicans carried the entire South.

Closer to home America still needed to secure its borders. The British continued to occupy forts in the Old Northwest (the modern Midwestern states of Ohio, Indiana, and Michigan) and engaged in a lively trade with Indians, including the sale of firearms. The Spanish presence in Florida and Louisiana gave them control of the Mississippi, a vital artery for Western trade. American shipping no longer enjoyed the protection of the British Navy. In the Mediterranean pirates based in North Africa harassed American shipping and captured American sailors and cargoes.

Resistance to Hamilton's economic program erupted into violence in western Pennsylvania and Kentucky. Angry over the tax on whiskey, farmers protested and eventually turned to violence to vent their anger and frustration. Washington felt compelled to call out the militia to quell the rebellion. The new federal government had survived its most serious test, but the repression of the rebellion did little to heal the divisions in American political life.

The French Revolution in America

In 1789 a financial crisis in France precipitated a revolution that transformed a powerful European monarchy into a republic. At the beginning, American support for the French Revolution cut across partisan allegiances. Even the arch-Federalist newspaper, *Gazette of the United States,* greeted the news of the revolution with excitement, describing it as "one of the most glorious objects that can arrest the attention of mankind." Republican James Madison added that events in France were "glorious to mankind and so glorious to this country, because it has grown as it were out of the American Revolution."

When the tide of the French Revolution turned more radical and violent, however, many Americans began to re-examine their support for the French cause. The execution of France's King Louis XVI and his queen Marie Antoinette in 1793 outraged Federalists, who now strongly denounced the revolution. This cartoon (**6.6**) captures the Federalist belief that the French Revolution had perverted American ideas of liberty. The French goddess of "liberty" sits next to the guillotine, a new device for execution developed in revolutionary France that used a heavy blade to decapitate its victims. Republicans remained steadfast in their support for the ideals of the French Revolution while attempting to distance themselves from its worst excesses.

The French Revolution became a symbol for both Republicans and Federalists. The former group championed the democratic ideals of the revolution, and the latter opposed its violence and radicalism. Ardently pro-French Republicans began addressing each other as "citizen," a custom borrowed from revolutionary France. Many Republican women

"The French Revolution is a political convulsion that in a great or less degree shakes the whole civilized world and it is of real consequence to the principles and of course to the happiness of a Nation to estimate it rightly."

ALEXANDER HAMILTON, 1794

Why did Federalists become such ardent critics of the French Revolution?

followed suit, some using the term *citizen* and others *citizeness* or *citess* among themselves. France's new minister Edmund Genêt arrived in America two days after word of the execution of King Louis XVI arrived in the spring of 1793. Philadelphia's Republican women turned out in red, white, and blue to welcome the new representative of revolutionary France. While Republican men worn the tricolor cockade on their hats, women attached tricolor pins to their chests to affirm support for France. One sarcastic Federalist commentator, denouncing the rage, described "these fiery frenchified dames" as "monsters in human shape."

When revolutionary France declared war on Britain in 1793, Americans found themselves reluctantly drawn into European affairs. Attitudes toward France became a political lightening rod, concentrating and focusing political feelings for both Republicans and Federalists. The French Revolution came to symbolize many of the hopes and fears of Americans struggling to come to terms with their own revolutionary heritage. Republicans defined the revolution by its ideals of liberty, equality, and fraternity; Federalists focused on the bloody excesses of the revolution's policies and saw it as a confirmation of the danger of taking ideas of liberty and equality too far.

6.6 Liberty and the Guillotine This Federalist cartoon shows the French Revolution debasing Liberty, who appears in tattered clothes but sports the tricolor cockade, symbol of the revolution, in her hair. Liberty sits in front of the bodies of victims decapitated by the guillotine, a bloody symbol of what Federalists regarded as the French Revolution's perverse theories of justice.

Adams versus Clinton: A Contest for Vice President

By 1792 Washington feared that the level of partisan conflict in the nation might tear apart the political fabric of the nation. Although Hamilton and Jefferson's mutual antagonism had hardened, both men agreed that Washington was the one figure who could rise above partisan squabbles and unite the nation. Hamilton implored Washington "to make a further sacrifice of your tranquility and happiness to the public good."

Although Republicans did not wish to challenge Washington directly, they decided to run the popular former Anti-Federalist Governor of New York George Clinton against John Adams for the office of vice president. Republican newspapers praised Washington but took aim at Adams, charging that he was an avowed supporter of monarchy and aristocracy. Invoking recent events in France, one radical newspaper editor even suggested that the time had arrived in America to "lop off every unfruitful branch, and root out of the soil of freedom all of the noxious weeds of aristocracy."

Adams weathered this challenge and handily defeated Clinton by a margin of 77 to 50 (with five additional votes scattered among other Republican candidates). The sectional character of politics was evident in the electoral college. Clinton carried the entire South, the most solidly Republican region.

Diplomatic Controversies and Triumphs

The new American nation had many diplomatic challenges, some arising from the French Revolution, but others stemming from unresolved issues with Britain. American ships traveled the oceans in search of trade opportunities, but no longer enjoyed the protection of the powerful British navy. Closer to home, the British retained control of their forts in the Northwest, defying the Treaty of Paris (1783) which required the British to relinquish them. Spain's control of the Mississippi River and the port of New Orleans, both of which were vital to the economic prosperity of the old Southwest (modern

6.7 Map of Spanish Interests in America
Spanish control of the Mississippi River and Port of New Orleans was a source of great concern to Americans. The Mississippi River was a vital conduit for goods, which were then shipped to the Port of New Orleans.

Kentucky, Tennessee and Mississippi), was another source of concern (**6.7**).

War between France and Britain in 1793 opened up economic opportunities for American merchants, who traded with both sides in the conflict. While Britain remained America's chief trading partner, trade with France was becoming increasingly important to the nation's prosperity.

Britain hoped to use its naval advantage to cut off trade between France and other nations, including America. American merchants who violated the British embargo against France had their ships and cargoes impounded. The British navy seized more than 250 American ships and confiscated many cargoes. Angry over British policy, Republicans proposed an embargo against the British. Federalists opposed this proposal, however, arguing that American economic well-being depended on good relations with Britain, not with France. President Washington appointed the respected Federalist from New York and chief justice of the Supreme Court, John Jay, as a special envoy to travel to London to negotiate a settlement with the British. Jay had helped negotiate the Treaty of Paris, ending conflict between America and Britain. In 1795 Jay successfully negotiated a treaty (thereafter called **Jay's Treaty**) with Britain, which agreed to compensate America for cargoes seized in 1793–1794 and to vacate forts in the Northwest Territory. However, America failed to win from Britain acceptance of the right of neutral nations to trade with belligerents without harassment.

When the details of Jay's Treaty were leaked to the press, Republicans responded with outrage, finding the treaty overly generous to the British. Angry protesters burned effigies of Jay and copies of the treaty in cities and towns across the mid-Atlantic and South, the regions of the country in which Republican sympathies were strongest. Jay's Treaty not only inflamed popular passions but also provoked a fierce debate in Congress over the role of the House of Representatives in foreign affairs. Republicans in the House believed that Jay had made too many concessions. The House demanded to see Jay's negotiating instructions, believing that Federalists had never intended to exact major concessions from the British. The House even threatened to withhold funding to implement the treaty until the instructions were made public. Federalists denounced the House's actions as an unconstitutional intrusion on the treaty-making powers of the president and the Senate.

Jay had negotiated with Britain from a position of weakness, but the American envoy charged with obtaining concessions from Spain was in a far stronger position. The U.S. minister to Britain, Federalist Thomas Pinckney, traveled to Spain to begin negotiations about American access to the Mississippi and New Orleans. Pinckney's Treaty (1795) secured America's right to navigate the

Why did Republicans oppose Jay's Treaty?

Mississippi River and use the Port of New Orleans. It also settled a boundary dispute between America and Spanish Florida. Spain had feared that America might try to acquire Spanish Florida and Louisiana by force, so it was more than willing to seek favorable terms over the trade and negotiate the boundary dispute between the two nations.

Violence along the Frontier

Securing America's Western frontier—an area that included the Northwest Territory, the Tennessee frontier, and the Mississippi Territory— was important for the new nation. It meant not only negotiating with Britain and Spain but also dealing with the Indian nations that occupied much of this land. In addition, the government faced strong resentments that arose among farmers over federal taxation of locally distilled whiskey.

Settlers streamed into Western territories, invariably resulting in conflicts with the indigenous populations. In the Old Northwest, the Shawnee, Delaware, and Miami confederated to defend their lands against settlers' incursions. In 1790 Little Turtle, a war chief of the Miami, led a pan-Indian war force comprising twelve different tribes that defeated an American army led by General Josiah Harmar in Ohio. A year later Indians in Ohio dealt an even more crushing blow to an army led by General Arthur St. Clair. More than nine hundred American soldiers were killed or wounded, and St. Clair barely escaped with his life.

These two demoralizing defeats prompted a major reorganization of the War Department. In the summer of 1794, a new, more professional army under the leadership of General Anthony Wayne decisively defeated Ohio's Indian tribes at the Battle of Fallen Timbers. In 1795 the defeated Indians signed the Treaty of Greenville, which stipulated that the twelve Ohio tribes relinquish their claims on most of Ohio. In Indian cultures the signing of treaties was a ceremonial occasion in which certain rituals were observed, including the exchange of gifts. Indians gave this wampum belt (**6.8**), an important ceremonial item, to American negotiators at the Treaty of Greenville ceremony. Chippewa Chief Mash-i-pi-nash-i-wish explained the meaning of this gift in these terms: "When I show you this belt, I point out to you your children at one end of it, and mine at the other.... Remember, we have taken the Great Spirit to witness our present actions; we will make a new world, and leave nothing on it to incommode our children." Wayne and the other American negotiators also believed that the indigenous peoples of Ohio had entered into a new relationship with Americans that fit a familial ideal. Americans, however, did not understand the gift of wampum in the same way as the Chippewa did. For Americans, Indians had joined the American family as dependents, not equals.

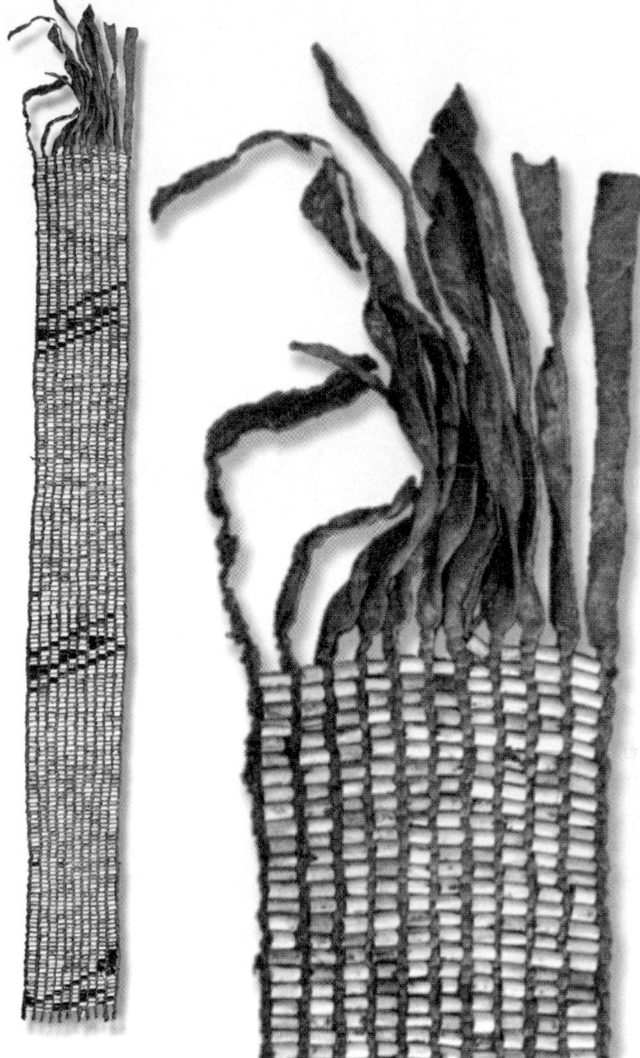

6.8 Wampum Belt
Beads, usually made from seashells, were strung together in a wampum belt. This particular belt, given during the Treaty of Greenville ceremony, symbolized the Indian belief that they would now join with the United States into one great family. The American negotiators interpreted the gift as a sign of Indian submission to America.

The most serious test of the new Republic's ability to govern came in 1794, when anger over Hamilton's economic policies turned violent. Resentment against the hated whiskey tax had festered since its enactment in 1791. The **Whiskey Rebellion** erupted when farmers from Pennsylvania and Kentucky took up arms to protest the whiskey excise tax.

Distilling had long been important economically in parts of western Pennsylvania and Kentucky, where farmers turned grain into whiskey. Once they had distilled it into alcohol, farmers could transport

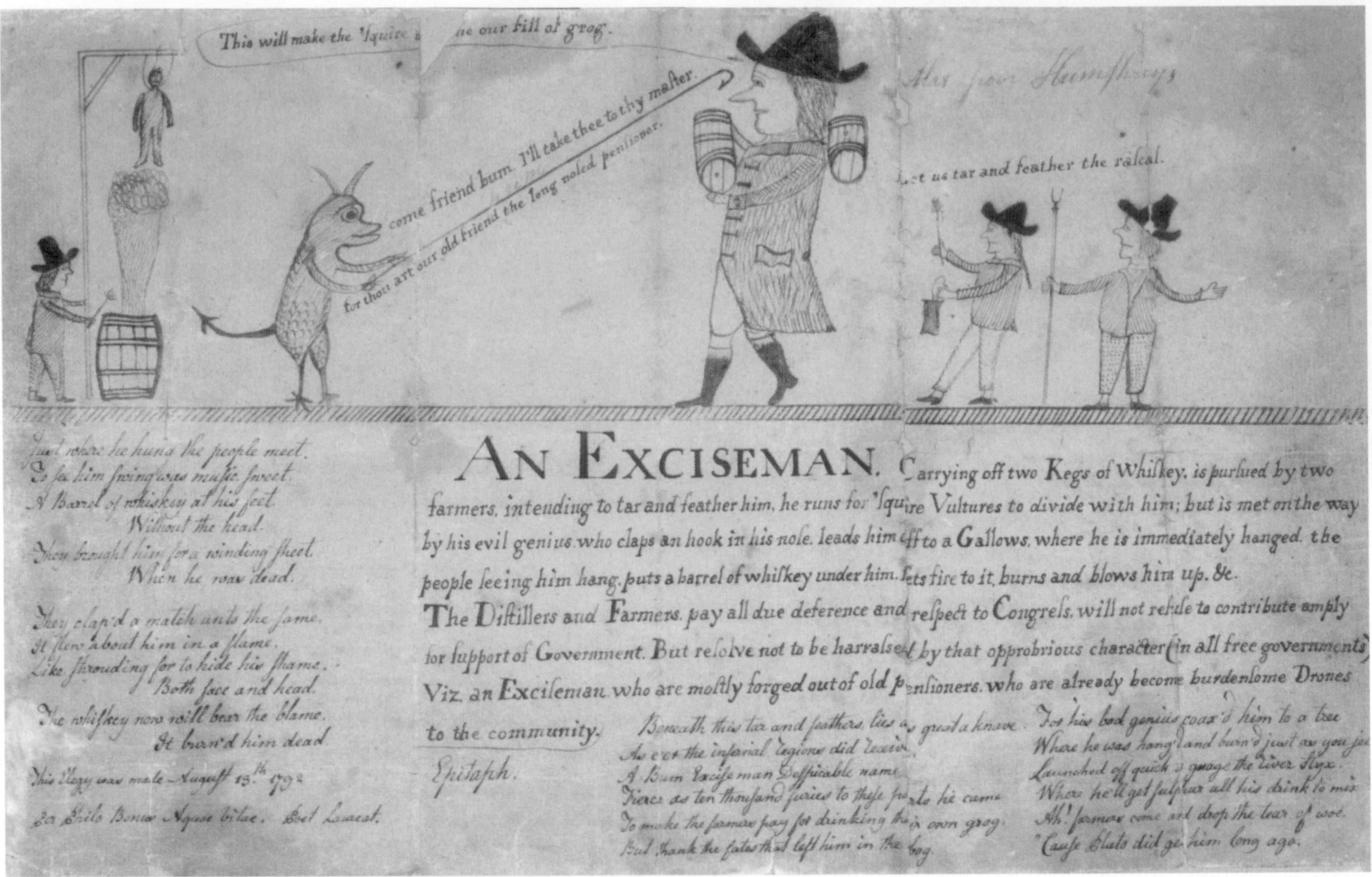

6.9 **Political Cartoon, Whiskey Rebellion**
In this cartoon, which denounces the hated whiskey tax, two distillers chase an excise man (tax collector), threatening to tar and feather him. Meanwhile, a demon hooks the tax collector by the nose and leads him to the gallows to be executed.

it more cheaply than the bulkier and heavy grains from which it was produced. Whiskey also sold at a higher price than grain, so Western farmers could earn a higher profit on their crops.

Protest against the whiskey tax began peacefully. Opponents of Federalist policy sought repeal of the law, and attacked the law in the local press. As anger intensified, angry farmers drew on the rich traditions of popular protest that Americans had used during the Revolution, such as the one depicted in this contemporary cartoon (**6.9**). The scene shows an angry crowd of tax protesters who have executed and burned in effigy a local tax collector. By July of 1794, frustration over the government's policy turned violent. A crowd of five hundred western Pennsylvania farmers, many armed with muskets, marched on the home of a government tax collector, John Neville, seeking to intimidate him. Two protestors were killed in the attack and Neville's home was burned to the ground. Two weeks later six thousand armed men gathered and threatened to attack the nearby town of Pittsburgh if the government did not meet their demand for repealing the tax. Washington's advisors were divided over the best response. Federalists and Republicans differed over the causes of the rebellion and how to respond to it. Federalist blamed the Democratic-Republican Societies for fomenting discord and favored a swift and decisive military response. Republicans faulted Hamilton's economic program and counseled moderation and patience. For an analysis of Washington's decision in dealing with this rebellion, see *Choices and Consequences: Washington's Decision to Crush the Whiskey Rebellion.*

After negotiations failed, Washington dispatched the militia and resistance to government authority quickly crumbled. One hundred and fifty individuals were arrested, and two obscure figures were convicted of treason. Rather than see the two become martyrs, however, Washington pardoned them.

Why did the Whiskey Rebellion present such a problem for Republicans?

Choices and Consequences

WASHINGTON'S DECISION TO CRUSH THE WHISKEY REBELLION

The armed resistance of Western farmers to the detested Whiskey tax posed a serious dilemma for Washington. Should the president negotiate with the rebels or use military force to put down the rebellion? Washington's cabinet differed over the best course of action. The Whiskey Rebellion tested the new government created by the Constitution. The situation was further complicated by the uncertainty over the militia. Even if Washington wished to use the militia, it was not clear if the militia would respond. During Shays's Rebellion (Chapter 5) the militia had refused to fire on other citizens and sided with the rebels. Washington had to consider this issue as well as the larger question about how the new government ought to respond to a direct challenge to its authority. Washington had three choices:

Choices

1 Call up the militia and immediately dispatch them to western Pennsylvania to subdue the rebels by force.

2 Adopt a conciliatory posture and make any necessary concessions to the rebels, including repealing the tax, and thereby avoid an armed response.

3 Offer the rebels a chance to end their protest; mobilize the militia and have it ready to march if the offer was rejected.

Decision

Republican leaders outside of the administration had hoped Washington would adopt a conciliatory posture and recognize that since an unjust tax was the root of the problem, it would make sense to accede to the rebels' demands. Hamilton and other Federalists counseled a decisive show of force. Washington opted instead for the third choice. After efforts to peacefully persuade the rebels to stand down failed, he acted quickly and decisively to put down the rebellion. Concerns that the militias of neighboring states might side with the rebels proved unfounded. The rebels were no match for the militia, and the rebellion fizzled once troops had marched westward.

Consequences

Washington's decision to put down the rebellion ended it in western Pennsylvania. In other parts of the nation, however, such as Kentucky, where support for tax resistance was more pervasive, nonviolent methods of resistance proved effective. In Kentucky few citizens were willing to act as tax collectors and juries were unlikely to convict individuals who refused to pay the taxes. One unexpected consequence of the rebellion was the undermining of the authority of the Democratic-Republican Societies, who were blamed for stirring up opposition to the government and fanning the resentments of the Whiskey Rebels.

Continuing Controversies

Why were some Federalists reluctant to use force to put down the Whiskey Rebellion? Washington's decision to use force has prompted some controversy. Supporters of Washington's actions argue that Washington wisely sought to demonstrate that armed resistance to government authority was not an affirmation of liberty, but threatened to undermine liberty and the rule of law. Detractors of Washington's actions argue that Pennsylvania's own government felt that it was unnecessary to mobilize the militia and that a peaceful resolution to the crisis was possible.

Why did Federalist policy not work in Kentucky?

Cultural Politics in a Passionate Age

Politics seeped into every aspect of popular culture in the years after the adoption of the Constitution. Even fashion became a political battleground, so much so that sporting the wrong color badge could lead to violence. The bitter political disputes of the day were also woven into the fabric of a new literary art form, the novel. Novels proved to be particularly important to women, who were not only among the main readers of novels but also became authors as well. The way the nation confronted issues of race and slavery also reflected the larger political divisions of the day. The slave uprising in the French Caribbean colony of Saint-Domingue became a flash point, focusing renewed attention on the issue of abolitionism and slavery.

Political Fashions and Fashionable Politics

Nearly every aspect of American political culture was swept up in the political passions of the age. In the politically charged environment of the 1790s, political debates spilled over into the new nation's streets and town squares. Ordinary citizens read newspapers or attended political meetings to keep abreast of the latest political developments. They also used taverns to host political meetings where Federalists and their Republican opponents offered up a range of toasts on everything from the militia to the French Revolution. Even the simple act of hoisting a glass of ale could become a political gesture, particularly when the press reported the accompanying toasts. Citizens marched in parades and occasionally even rioted to express their frustrations with political developments.

Even fashion was swept up into the political conflicts. Americans signaled their political allegiances and foreign policy preferences by adopting the latest Paris or London styles. Republican supporters of the French Revolution adorned their hats with a red, white, and blue (the colors of the French flag) tricolor cockade, a small rosette-like decoration attached to one's cap. Federalists, by contrast, favored a black cockade, a decoration that some soldiers had used during the American Revolution. By the end of the decade, sporting the "wrong" type of ornament in the streets of Philadelphia could easily trigger a small riot.

Literature, Education, and Gender

The 1790s was a period in which a huge increase in the amount of printed matter was available to Americans. In addition to the expansion of newspapers, there was a huge outpouring of books, magazines, broadsides, and pamphlets. The market for books increased dramatically in the thirty years between the American Revolution and 1800. The number of booksellers in Boston, New York, Philadelphia, and Charleston almost quadrupled in that time. In the last decade of the eighteenth century, 266 new lending libraries opened across America. The new libraries were not restricted to prosperous coastal cities, but as one contemporary noted, "in our inland towns of consequence, social libraries have been instituted composed of books designed to amuse rather than to instruct." While the cost of books may have been beyond men and women of modest means, a subscription to one of these libraries was often not.

Americans could also turn to magazines for education and amusement. The titles of several new magazines suggested a calculated effort to appeal to both men and women. For example, *The Gentlemen and Ladies Town and Country Magazine* began publishing in 1789. In a few cases magazines aimed to court the growing number of female readers directly. Thus, *The Lady's Magazine and Repository of Entertaining Knowledge,* founded in 1791 in Philadelphia, targeted a female audience.

The rise of a new literary form, the novel, in eighteenth-century England helped to spur the enormous expansion in America's publishing industry. Americans eagerly consumed imported novels, and new works written by American authors appeared as well. Women became an important audience for the novel; women also wrote many of the most successful early novels. Susanna Rowson's *Charlotte Temple,* first published in England (1791), was reprinted in America three years later, where the first edition quickly sold out. Although written in England, the story's American setting made it

How did fashion become politicized in the 1790s?

particularly popular in the new republic. The moral of the novel was unmistakable. The heroine, Charlotte Temple, foolishly leaves England for America, where she elopes with a knave who reneges on his promise to marry her. Charlotte is eventually abandoned, suffers physical and mental depredations, and dies soon after giving birth to a child out of wedlock.

Immigrating to America in 1793, Rowson fared much better than her character Charlotte. After a brief career as an actress, Rowson established the Young Ladies' Academy, in Boston (1797). Her curriculum included reading, writing, arithmetic, and needlework.

Another important female author was Judith Sargent Murray, who became an outspoken advocate of equality and education for women. Her essay "On the Equality of the Sexes," published in the *Massachusetts Magazine* in 1790 under the pen name "Constantia," argued that women's intellectual abilities were equal to those of men and that if provided with a proper education women could equal men in accomplishment. Murray not only wrote articles for literary magazines but also used the novel to spread her ideals about the equality of the sexes. Her novel, *The Story of Margaretta* (1798), used the conventions of sentimental novels such as *Charlotte Temple*, but recast them in terms that reflected her views of female education. Rather than fall prey to seduction, suffering abandonment and ruin, a fate typical for many other female characters in popular novels, Margaretta uses her intelligence and superior education to avoid these perils.

Murray helped found the Dorchester Ladies Academy in Massachusetts. A fifteen-year-old student at the academy, Maria Crowninshield, produced this remarkable allegory of female education (**6.10**). Although at one level this fine example of needlework conformed to the traditional ideas of female education, which focused on sewing skills, the subject matter chosen by the artist signaled her commitment to a modern expansive conception of female education. The young girl depicted is reading a copy of English author Hannah Moore's *Strictures on the Modern System of Female Education* (1799). Moore's volume, which advocated an expansion of educational opportunities for women, was one of a number of tracts defending the idea of women's education. The most radical voice demanding changes in women's roles was Mary Wollstonecraft, an English writer whose *A Vindication of the Rights of Women* (1792) sparked a lively debate on both sides of the Atlantic in the 1790s about the need for equality of education for men and women.

Federalists, Republicans, and the Politics of Race

Fashion and reading material were not the only aspects of American culture to be swept up in the political passions and divisions of the age. These passions also extended to the politics of race. This issue became a major concern as a result of events in the Caribbean, where slaves in Saint-Domingue rose up against their French masters and seized control of the island in 1791. Federalists and Republicans were divided over how to respond to events in Saint-Domingue (present-day Haiti).

Toussaint L'Ouverture, a talented former slave, forged an effective all-black fighting force that routed the planters. Should America embrace the most recent revolutionary struggle for liberty? At first the Washington administration supported the ruling white elite, but as L'Ouverture's forces

6.10 Allegory of Female Education In this needlework composition, young Maria Crowninshield, a student at the Ladies Academy in Dorchester, Massachusetts, depicts a young student receiving instruction from a female teacher. [*Source:* Photograph Courtesy Peabody Essex Museum]

How is virtue represented in Maria Crowninshield's allegory of female education?

solidified their hold on the island, the American government accepted the need to establish stable relations with the new government there. Indeed, as relations with France worsened, many Federalists began to urge Washington to strengthen relations with Saint-Domingue, hoping to renew the lucrative trade with the former French colony. However, while Federalists supported recognition of the former French colony, Republicans in Congress opposed such a move. Republicans' attitudes toward Saint-Domingue were motivated in part by their loyalty to France, which was eager to recapture the island; but their attitudes also reflected the party's commitment to protecting the institution of slavery. Republicans feared that America slaves might emulate their oppressed brethren in the Caribbean. Saint-Domingue conjured up a nightmare for most slave owners, such as the graphic depiction of bloodletting during the revolution produced by a German engraver (**6.11**). Although concern over slave insurrection was most keen in the South, Republicans outside of this region also voiced concerns. Republican Congressman Albert Gallatin of Pennsylvania warned Congress of the danger that supporters of L'Ouverture's ideas might "spread their views among the Negro people there [in America] and excite dangerous insurrections among them."

Even among those most opposed to slavery, few were willing to speak up in support of the ideal of racial equality. Racist attitudes can be found among ardent supporters of abolitionism. Thus, one can see evidence of condescension in the pro-abolitionist painting, *Liberty Displaying the Arts and Sciences*, commissioned by an organization founded by Benjamin Franklin, The Library Company. *Images as History:* Liberty Displaying the Arts and Sciences explores the tensions within early abolitionist thought.

6.11 Saint-Domingue Revolution For Republicans, particularly in the Southern states, images such as this one conjured up their worst nightmare—a bloody slave insurrection.

Why did Republicans oppose normalizing relations with St. Domingue?

Images as History

LIBERTY DISPLAYING THE ARTS AND SCIENCES

In the 1790s, the Library Company of Philadelphia, a premier cultural institution founded in 1731 by Benjamin Franklin, commissioned Samuel Jennings's painting *Liberty Displaying the Arts and Sciences.* The painting was to represent the ideals of the new American nation. What symbols does the artist include to show the cultural achievements of the new nation? How does the artist portray African Americans?

The Library Company directors asked Jennings to include the goddess of liberty along with "Symbols of Painting, Architecture, Mechanics, Astronomy," including a broken chain at the feet of the goddess of liberty, a symbol of the painting's abolitionist sentiments. Although Jennings added some of his own ideas to the composition, he largely followed the directors' suggestions.

The painting reflected the influence of the classical world, including copies of the writings of Homer and Virgil, two of its greatest authors, but Jennings did not slight the intellectual and cultural achievements of the modern world. He used volumes of authors Milton and Shakespeare to represent modern literary achievements, at least of the English-speaking world. A telescope, symbol of the advancement of science, appears in the lower right-hand corner. Finally, as instructed by his patrons, Jennings included the Goddess of Liberty with a liberty pole and cap, two symbols closely linked with the American Revolution.

Jennings's included a "Group of Negroes, who are paying Homage to Liberty, for the boundless Blessings they receive through her." The African Americans bow before Liberty. Cast in this subservient pose, they do not appear as masters of their own destinies. Nor does Jennings's treatment suggest that African Americans created any of the cultural achievements of the new nation. Although clearly abolitionist in sympathy, the painting does not endorse the notion of racial equality. African Americans are rendered as subservient, not as actors in charge of their own destiny.

The Goddess of Liberty sits with a liberty pole topped by a liberty cap.
A group of African Americans bows before Liberty.
The broken chains symbolize the abolition of slavery.
The telescope symbolizes the advancements made by modern science.

Liberty Displaying the Arts and Sciences [*Source:* The Library Company of Philadelphia]

What symbols does the artist use to represent the achievements of the arts and science in the new American nation?

The Stormy Presidency of John Adams

George Washington did not seek a third term of office, a decision that set a precedent for subsequent presidents. (The unofficial two-term limit that Washington established bound presidents until the middle of the twentieth century, when Franklin Delano Roosevelt won a third term.) In the election of 1796, the Federalist congressional caucus selected John Adams and Thomas Pinckney as candidates, while Republicans put forward Thomas Jefferson and Aaron Burr. Party discipline, however, was lax. When it came time for the electoral college to meet and vote for president and vice president, 52 of the 136 electors cast votes for individuals not selected by either the Federalist or Republican congressional caucuses. Adams won the most votes and became President, and Jefferson polled the next most votes and became Vice President. Although Adams defeated Jefferson, the bitter electoral contest intensified the partisan divisions within America. Conflict in Europe only exacerbated these tensions. Events in Europe threatened to drag America into war. Fearful that America was threatened from abroad and concerned that domestic radicals were working to undermine American interests, Federalists passed repressive measures that prompted Republicans to intensify their opposition to Federalist power and rally around their leader, Thomas Jefferson.

In 1800 Jefferson once again faced Adams in a presidential election. This time Jefferson defeated Adams, but the election resulted in a tie between Jefferson and his vice-presidential running mate, Aaron Burr. The Constitution provided that under these circumstances, the House of Representative would determine the election's outcome. After a flurry of politicking, Federalists agreed to select Jefferson, who became president.

In Richmond, Virginia, the debate over liberty inspired a slave named Gabriel to lead a rebellion aimed at liberating Virginia's slave population. Although the rebellion failed, it highlighted the inescapable conflict between American ideals of liberty and the realities of racial slavery.

Washington's Farewell Address

Washington never wavered in his belief that he acted above party, but by the middle of his second term in office he had adopted most of Hamilton's Federalist agenda, which in turn prompted the most outspoken Republican editors to attack Washington. Rather than respond to these attacks directly, Washington used his Farewell Address, a written statement widely printed in newspapers across the nation in September 1796, as an occasion to reiterate his basic political ideals.

In his Farewell Address Washington attacked the growing factionalism, partisanship, and growing regional tensions in American politics. He sounded an alarm, cautioning the nation "in the most solemn manner against the baneful effects of the Spirit of Party, generally." Recognizing that foreign policy disputes had been particularly divisive, he advised that in matters of diplomacy America "steer clear of permanent alliances, with any portion of the foreign world." Washington was not counseling strict isolation, but rather suggesting that America enter only into temporary alliances that served its interests. Above all, Washington wished to see America pursue a policy free of irrational hatreds or allegiances to foreign nations. The address sought to fuse idealism and realism into a workable approach to foreign policy.

In this famous portrait of Washington done at the end of his presidency (1796), the artist, Gilbert Stuart, created a painting filled with symbolism that captured the central role of Washington's presidency in launching the new nation (**6.12**). When the painting was first displayed publicly, the announcement noted that Washington was "surrounded with allegorical emblems of his public life in the service of his country, which are highly illustrative of the great and tremendous storms which have frequently prevailed." The public notice went on to assure viewers that "these storms have abated, and the appearance of the rainbow is

What advice did Washington offer the new nation in his Farewell Address?

> "Thomas Jefferson is a firm Republican, —John Adams is an avowed Monarchist.... Will you, by your votes, contribute to make the avowed friend of monarchy President?"
>
> Election statement in favor of Jefferson (1796)

introduced in the background as a sign" of America's bright future.

Although Gilbert Stuart's portrait of Washington suggested that the nation had weathered its worst storms, the period after Washington's retirement from politics proved to be even more contentious. The election of 1796 was closely fought and bitterly divisive. John Adams defeated his rival Thomas Jefferson by a narrow margin of three electoral votes. Intrigue had marred the election. Alexander Hamilton sought to undermine Adams's candidacy by backing Thomas Pinckney, who was running with Adams. When Adams learned of Hamilton's plan, he arranged to have some of his supporters in New England divert votes from Pinckney. The Constitution did not anticipate the rise of parties, nor did it envision the idea of presidential tickets with a designated candidate for president and vice president running together. The Founders' system was simpler: the president was the candidate with the most votes, and the vice president was the runner up. When Federalist plots resulted in votes being diverted from Pinckney, Thomas Jefferson became the candidate with the second most votes and hence became the new vice president. The most

6.12 Portrait of President George Washington
Gilbert Stuart's painting included several allegorical elements. The passing storm and the rainbow symbolized the new nation's stormy beginnings and bright future.

What visual elements does the artist use to represent the future of America in this painting of George Washington?

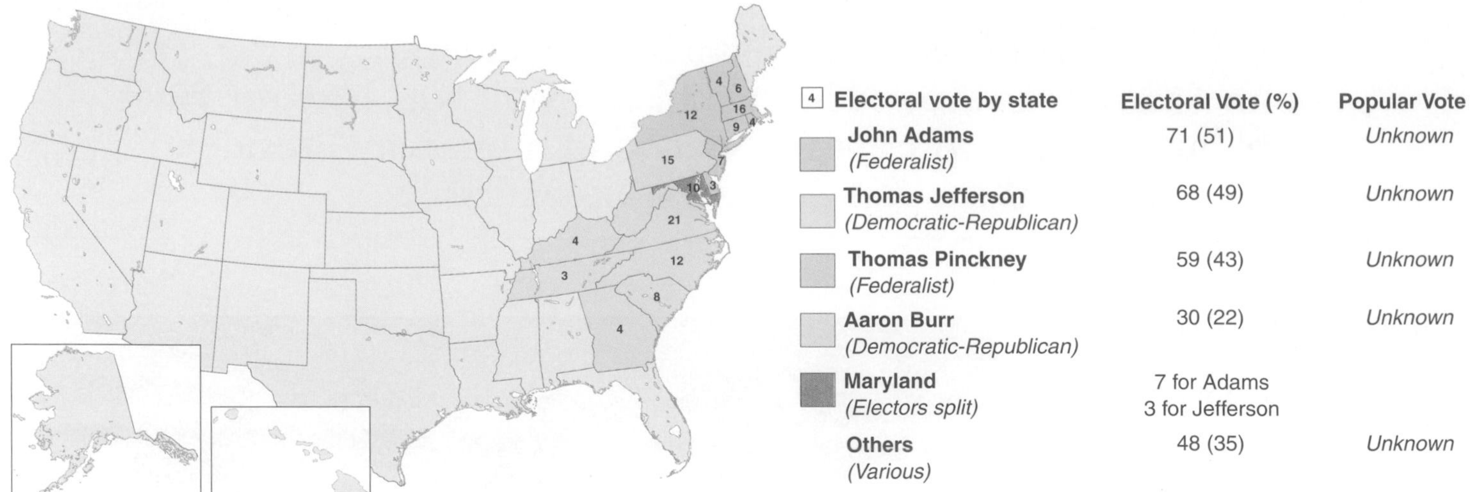

4 Electoral vote by state	Electoral Vote (%)	Popular Vote
John Adams *(Federalist)*	71 (51)	*Unknown*
Thomas Jefferson *(Democratic-Republican)*	68 (49)	*Unknown*
Thomas Pinckney *(Federalist)*	59 (43)	*Unknown*
Aaron Burr *(Democratic-Republican)*	30 (22)	*Unknown*
Maryland *(Electors split)*	7 for Adams 3 for Jefferson	
Others *(Various)*	48 (35)	*Unknown*

6.13 Electoral Map 1796
This map of the electoral votes in the presidential election of 1796 shows the regional basis of American politics at that time. The strength of Thomas Jefferson, the Republican candidate, was concentrated in the South and Pennsylvania. John Adams, the Federalist candidate, was strongest in New England, New York, New Jersey, and Delaware.

obvious pattern in the election was regional. John Adams carried New England and most of the mid-Atlantic apart from Pennsylvania. Jefferson took the entire South and Pennsylvania (**6.13**).

The XYZ Affair and Quasi-War with France

Adams, pictured in **6.14**, assumed the presidency just as a crisis with France was coming to a head. In 1796 the French government, still angry over what it viewed as a pro-British tilt in American foreign policy, had recalled its diplomatic envoy. France began seizing American ships trading with Britain. Hoping to avert a war, Adams sent three American ministers to France to negotiate a settlement. The delegates included Charles Cotesworth Pinckney of South Carolina, John Marshall of Virginia, and Elbridge Gerry of Massachusetts. At first, the French Directory, the revolutionary committee that had replaced the king after the French Revolution and ruled France from 1795 to 1799, snubbed the American delegation. When three French officials, identified simply as "X," "Y," and "Z," demanded a bribe from America's diplomats as the price of beginning negotiations, public furor erupted over what was dubbed the **XYZ Affair**. These officials sought a bribe of $250, 000 for themselves, a generous loan of $12 million to France, and an official apology from President Adams for unflattering remarks he had made about the French government. In a contemporary political cartoon (**6.15**) the five-headed "monster" of the French Directory (the revolutionary committee had five members) demands payment of a bribe from America's ambassadors.

The XYZ Affair galvanized Americans, who united behind Adams's decision to prepare for war by increasing allocations for the military. "Millions for defense, but not one cent for tribute," became the rallying cry. While Hamilton's allies among the Federalists sought an explicit declaration of war

6.14 John Adams
John Adams was elected president in 1796 in the first truly partisan presidential campaign in the new nation's brief history.

What impact did the XYZ Affair have on American politics?

against France, Adams resisted pressure to declare full-fledged war. The undeclared naval war between France and America, or Quasi-War, lasted almost two years between 1798 and 1800. In addition to creating a new Department of the Navy to coordinate America's naval war, Congress tripled the size of the regular army and created a special provisional army numbering some fifty thousand. Washington reluctantly agreed to head the provisional army if Hamilton were appointed his second in command, a request that would have given Hamilton authority over many military leaders more experienced than he. Hamilton's bold effort to elevate himself above so many other qualified officers angered many Federalists who aligned themselves with Adams. Federalists were now divided into Adams and Hamilton factions.

6.15 ***The Paris Monster*** This colorful cartoon ridicules French corruption and depravity in the XYZ Affair. The "Many Headed Monster," the symbol of French government, wields a dagger while he solicits a bribe from the American delegation. The American ministers respond, "We will not give you six pence."

The Alien and Sedition Acts

Federalists enacted a broad program designed to deal with the threats posed by the Quasi-War. To pay for the enormous expansion in the size of the military, the Federalist-controlled Congress passed a new property tax that fell on land, slaves, and buildings. Federalists in Congress then proposed a series of laws, the **Alien and Sedition Acts**, designed to protect America from the danger of foreign and domestic subversion.

The Alien Acts, which included three separate laws, made it more difficult to become a citizen and gave the government far-reaching powers to deport dangerous resident aliens. The Sedition Act made it a crime to "combine or conspire together with the intent to oppose any measure or measures of the government of the United States." The act criminalized any attempt to "write, print, utter, or publish" statements "false, scandalous, or malicious" against "the government of the United States, or either house of Congress of the United States, or the President." Conspicuously absent from the act were criminal penalties for attacking Republican Vice President Thomas Jefferson. The Federalist press was free to hurl whatever invectives it chose at Jefferson with impunity. Federalists and Republicans debated the constitutionality of the Sedition Act. *Competing Visions: Congressional Debate over the Sedition Act* discusses the congressional arguments over the constitutionality of the Sedition Act (see p. 184).

Federalists used the authority of the Sedition Act to prosecute twenty-five individuals, all Republican sympathizers. The list of targets included printers, outspoken politicians, and other prominent public figures. Federalists even prosecuted one drunken Republican for his declaration that he did not care if a cannon salute to President Adams "fired thro' his a—." The harshest sentence, a $400 fine and an eighteen-month prison sentence, went to David Brown, an itinerant preacher and political agitator who had raised a liberty pole in Dedham, Massachusetts, with a placard that read "No Stamp Act, No Sedition, no Alien Bills, no Land Tax: downfall to the Tyrants of America, peace and retirement to the President, long live the Vice-President."

Republicans had tried to use every constitutional means at their disposal to protest the Sedition Act. They first sought to petition Congress to repeal the law and then tried to use the court system to challenge its constitutionality. When both of these means failed, leading Republicans cast about for a new strategy to challenge it. Madison and Jefferson articulated such a strategy in two separate documents, the Virginia Resolution (1798) and the Kentucky Resolution (1798). Madison authored the former; Jefferson, the latter. Both documents defended the rights of the states to judge the constitutionality of federal laws and if necessary to protect their citizens against actions of

Why did the Federalists believe that it was necessary to pass the Alien and Sedition Acts?

Competing Visions

CONGRESSIONAL DEBATE OVER THE SEDITION ACT

In response to the increasing rancor of the partisan press and the belief that supporters of French Revolutionary ideas were actively working to subvert American government, Federalists passed a federal sedition law (1798). Federalists defended the constitutionality of the act, noting that individual states had enacted similar laws and further arguing that such a power was essential to the survival of any government. Republicans attacked the act as an unconstitutional violation of the First Amendment's protections for freedom of speech and the press and a violation of the Tenth Amendment's guarantee of federalism, which limited the powers of the new government to those delegated by the Constitution. Republican Matthew Lyon and Federalist Roger Griswold traded insults, then blows, as partisan tensions reached a peak in Congress. In considering the Republican and Federalist arguments presented here, which interpretation of the Bill of Rights seems more persuasive? Why?

John Nicholas, a Virginia Republican, captured the essence of the constitutional arguments against the Sedition Act in an impassioned speech in the House of Representatives. Nicholas employed the Republican theory of strict construction, arguing that the Sedition Act violated the express language of the Bill of Rights.

I have looked in vain among the enumerated powers given to Congress in the Constitution, for the authority to pass a bill like the present (one); but I found instead express prohibition against passing it.... One of the first acts of this Government was to propose certain Amendments to the Constitution ... "that the powers not delegated to the United States by the Constitution, nor prohibited by it to the States, are reserved to the States respectively, or to the people" [Tenth Amendment]; and also, "that Congress shall make no law abridging the freedom of speech, or of the press" [First Amendment].

Harrison Gray Otis, a Federalist from Massachusetts, rejected the Republican argument on constitutional grounds, arguing that government had an inherent right to protect itself against sedition. Neither the First Amendment nor the Tenth Amendment required the government to ignore sedition. Otis argued that the constitution was not a suicide pact that prevented government from taking actions to defend itself against subversion.

The present bill is perfectly harmless and contains no provision which is not practiced ... under the laws ... of the several states.... Every independent government has a right to preserve and defend itself against injuries and outrages which endanger its existence; for unless it has this power, it is unworthy of the name of a free Government.

Congressional Pugilists, Republican Matthew Lyon and Federalist Roger Griswold

What constitutional ideas were used to challenge the Sedition Act?

the federal government. Republicans based this idea on the notion that the Constitution was a compact among the people of the states who not only retained all powers not delegated to the new government but also retained a right to judge when acts of the federal government were a violation of the Constitution. Neither Madison nor Jefferson took the next logical step and asserted a right of the states to actively nullify an unconstitutional act of the federal government. Both men hoped that persuasion, not force, would be the mechanism used by the states to challenge an unconstitutional exercise of federal power. In keeping with this notion, Virginia and Kentucky distributed their resolutions to the other state legislatures hoping that other states would follow their example and rally against the Sedition Act. However, legislatures in the Federalist-dominated New England states attacked the Virginia and Kentucky resolutions as dangerous and unconstitutional assertions of state power against the power of the federal government. Federalists argued that final arbiter of the constitutionality of acts of Congress ought to be the federal courts, not the state legislatures.

Angered by the northern Federalist legislatures' reactions, Jefferson authored a second set of Kentucky Resolutions (1799). In these, he introduced the constitutional doctrine of nullification, which asserted that states could nullify unconstitutional laws. Jefferson did not answer how a state would accomplish the goal of constitutional nullification. The Virginia and Kentucky resolutions became the foundation for subsequent arguments about **states' rights**, the theory that the Constitution was a compact among the states and that the individual states retained the right to judge when the federal government's actions were unconstitutional.

The other significant outgrowth of the Alien and Sedition crisis was the development of a new theory of freedom of the press. This new theory, the basis for modern theories of freedom of the press, argued that political opinions were not subject to any government control. Rather than try to limit dissenting ideas, the new view embraced the idea of a market place of ideas. More speech, not less, was the antidote to the threat posed by dangerous ideas.

The Disputed Election of 1800

The Quasi-War with France, which was winding down by 1800, had split Federalists into two factions. Although Adams supported a military build up, he never abandoned hope of a negotiated settlement. Hamilton, by contrast, believed that the war with France provided an opportunity to crush domestic opposition and forge an alliance with Britain. Adams had little interest in such grandiose schemes, which may have included vague plans for a joint Anglo-American conquest of Spanish America. The president also resented Hamilton's meddling in the affairs of his administration.

Adams persisted in trying to negotiate a settlement with France, and changes in the French government now made a peaceful solution likely. The radical phase of the French Revolution ended when Napoleon Bonaparte, an ambitious general of the French Army, seized control of France's government in 1799. Eager to gain U.S. support for his military campaign against Spain and England, Napoleon negotiated a treaty with Adams that ended the naval conflict between the two nations. However, Adams's statesmanlike effort to seek peace angered Hamiltonians. Exacerbating the tensions between the two men, Adams privately attacked Hamilton's "British faction." In turn, believing that Adams lacked the resolve to deal with France or the Republicans, Hamilton published a pamphlet denouncing the president. The split within the ranks of Federalists could hardly have come at a worse time: the election of 1800 loomed on the horizon.

The election of 1800 presented the nation with a clear choice between Federalist Adams and Republican Jefferson. Each party indulged in campaigning that was more rancorous than anything either side had experienced in previous elections. Federalists attacked Jefferson as an atheist and radical supporter of the French Revolution, themes captured in this political cartoon (**6.16**), which shows Jefferson in league with the devil. One Connecticut minister confidently declared, "I do not believe that the Most High will permit a howling atheist to sit at the head of this nation." Republicans, in turn, prayed for deliverance from "Tories; from Aristocrats."

Despite dire predictions about the dangers of electing Jefferson—some New Englanders hid their family Bibles, fearing that President Jefferson might confiscate them—Republicans garnered enough votes to win. Still, the election was

6.16 Anti-Jefferson Political Cartoon
Jefferson's opponents portrayed him as an atheist who drew radical ideas from the French Revolution. In this image the American eagle tries to prevent Jefferson from throwing the Constitution into the flames emanating from the altar of Gallic (French) despotism.

Why did the Federalist political cartoon show Jefferson about to burn the Constitution?

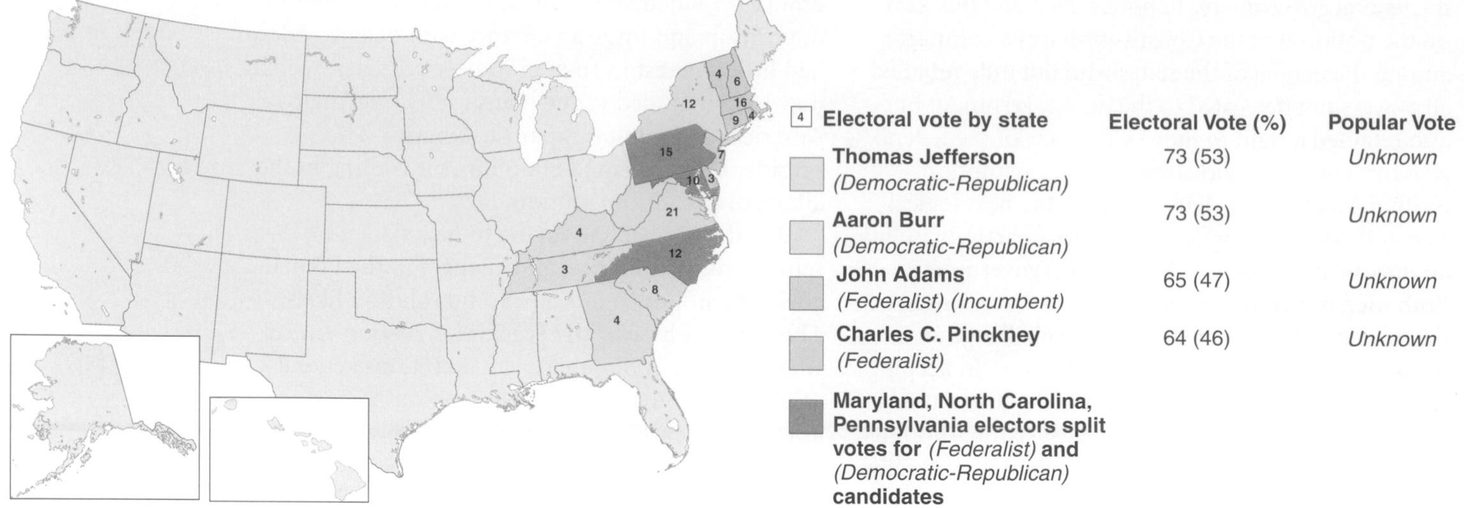

6.17 Electoral Map of 1800 Adams's support in the election of 1800 was concentrated chiefly in New England. Jefferson drew support from the South and the mid-Atlantic.

extremely close. As the map (**6.17**) shows, support for Adams was strongest in New England, while Jefferson carried the South and parts of the mid-Atlantic. A mere eight votes marked the margin of victory between the two sides.

The Republican victory triggered a constitutional crisis that few would have predicted. The actual vote in the electoral college had produced a tie between Jefferson and the Republican candidate for vice president, Aaron Burr. This was possible because the Constitution did not direct electors to cast separate ballots for president and vice president. A tie meant that the sitting House of Representatives, dominated by Federalists, would decide the election. The new Republican-dominated House would not take its seats until March of 1801. The political situation was tense. Rumors about political deals and conspiracies circulated widely. As a precautionary measure, Pennsylvania and Virginia both mobilized their militias, a decision that sent a clear message that these two states would not sit by while scheming politicians in Congress cast aside the will of the people. The politicians indeed schemed and negotiated, thus making resolution of the deadlock time consuming.

Many Federalists believed that Jefferson was a fanatic, viewing Burr as a safer alternative. This was not the case for Alexander Hamilton, however, who had been Burr's rival in New York politics for more than a decade. Rather than see Burr emerge victorious, Hamilton persuaded Federalists that Jefferson was the lesser of the two evils. Jefferson had also worked hard to assure a number of Federalists, including Hamilton, that he was not intent on a radical course that would undermine all hard-won Federalist policies of the previous decade. With Hamilton's support and some assurances from Jefferson, a deal was finally struck. It took five days and thirty-five ballots before the House finally voted to elect Jefferson.

Jefferson's victory narrowly averted another constitutional crisis. Despite the threat that Virginia and Pennsylvania had mobilized their militias while the House was casting its ballots, the election of 1800 peacefully transferred political power from Federalists to Republicans, a notable achievement given the tense political atmosphere of the 1790s. To avert any future deadlock in subsequent presidential elections, the Twelfth Amendment to the Constitution, adopted in 1804, required that electors cast separate ballots for president and vice president.

Gabriel's Rebellion

The French Revolution and the struggles between Federalists and Republicans leading up to the election of 1800 helped spread ideas about liberty throughout American society. These notions percolated down into every community of America, including slave communities in the South. The most dramatic illustration of this came in Virginia in 1800. **Gabriel's Rebellion**, a slave insurrection in Richmond, drew together free blacks and slaves in a plot to liberate the Richmond's slaves.

Gabriel, the slave leader of the rebellion, was trained as a blacksmith and enjoyed considerable mobility. His master allowed Gabriel to hire himself out to others and to keep a portion of his earnings for himself. Gabriel used his mobility to make contact with other slaves and free blacks and together with them formulated a bold plan to seize the state arsenal and distribute arms to Virginia's slaves. Gabriel was not only aware of the slave uprising in

Which events of the 1790s helped inspire Gabriel's Rebellion?

Saint-Domingue and the French Revolution but also showed himself to be keenly aware of the ideas of the American Revolution. He planned to march his troops under a banner emblazoned with the words "death or liberty." Gabriel had taken Patrick Henry's famous words, reversed them, and transformed them into the rallying cry for a slave rebellion. Governor James Monroe mobilized the state militia which easily crushed the rebellion. To deal with the rebels, the state convened a special court that tried slaves without the benefit of a jury. Twenty-six of those put on trial were convicted and sentenced to death. Although the state of Virginia showed little concern for the rights of the accused slaves, the state was obligated to pay out close to $9,000 to the slave owners, who were legally entitled to be compensated for the loss of their property.

"Mr. Jefferson, though too revolutionary in his notions, is yet a lover of liberty and will be desirous of something like orderly Government.—Mr. Burr loves nothing but himself ... and will be content with nothing short of permanent power in his own hands."

ALEXANDER HAMILTON, 1800

Conclusion

The 1790s was a time of extended crises at home and abroad, and events in Europe heightened domestic political tensions. The French Revolution contributed to this polarization of American political life. Federalists viewed that revolution as proof that an excessive devotion to liberty and equality threatened peace and stability. Republicans, by contrast, embraced the French Revolution enthusiastically; only slowly, over the course of the decade, did they withdraw their support.

The leading architect of Federalist policy for most of the 1790s was Alexander Hamilton, who supported a pro-British foreign policy, a strong federal government, and an economic policy favoring the development of a complex commercial economy. Republicans, led by Madison and Jefferson, supported France and favored an economy in which small producers, farmers, and artisans dominated economic life. For Republicans, if government were to have any role in fostering economic development, it would be the individual state governments, not the federal government.

Most political conflicts in the years following ratification of the Constitution quickly escalated into constitutional controversies as each side accused the other of advocating policies that the other believed unconstitutional. Federalists defended a policy of broad, or loose, construction, believing that in its sphere of authority the new government had wide latitude to adopt whatever policies seemed expedient to accomplish its aims. Republicans championed a policy of strict construction, construing the Constitution in an almost literal fashion.

Conflict over the economy, foreign policy, and the meaning of key provisions of the Constitution produced an age of intense political passion. Yet, despite the intense partisanship of this decade, Americans had not yet reconciled themselves to the existence of political parties as a permanent feature of public life. The peaceful transition of power from Federalists to Republicans in 1800 was a tribute to the structure of government created by the Constitution and to Americans' commitment to the principles of constitutionalism. The shift from being an opposition movement to controlling the national government posed unexpected challenges for Jefferson, Madison, and other Republicans.

What were the chief political differences dividing Federalists from Republicans in 1800?

1789

Washington inaugurated
Washington becomes America's first president

1790–1791

Hamilton's Report on Public Credit
Federalist economic program implemented

Bill of Rights ratified
Constitution amended to protect individual liberty and include additional structural supports for federalism

Bank of the United States established
Congress approves a key element of the Hamiltonian program

1793–1794

Whiskey Rebellion
Farmers in western Pennsylvania protest the whiskey excise tax

Review Questions

1. What were the main features of Hamilton's economic plan? How did each of these components contribute to the growth of the American economy?
2. Why did Jefferson and Madison wish to relocate the nation's capital away from New York City?
3. What was Hamilton's theory of constitutional interpretation, and how did it differ from Jefferson's theory?
4. How did the French Revolution affect domestic American politics?
5. How did the novel reflect and influence ideas about women's roles in the new republic?
6. What were the differences between the views of Republicans and Federalists toward the revolution in Saint-Domingue (modern-day Haiti)? What political factors might account for these differences?
7. What was the constitutional basis for the Republicans' challenge to the constitutionality of the Sedition Act? Explain.
8. What symbols does the cartoonist who created the anti-Jefferson political cartoon, "Providential Detection," use to signal his opposition to Jeffersonian political views?

1795

Jay's Treaty
Senate ratifies Jay's Treaty with Great Britain. Republicans oppose treaty

1796

John Adams elected president
Washington declines to serve a third term and is succeeded by Federalist John Adams

1798

XYZ Affair
American negotiators reject French demands for a bribe as a condition for peace treaty

Alien and Sedition Acts
Congress enacts a series of new acts to control aliens and punish attacks on the government

Virginia and Kentucky Resolutions
Madison and Jefferson draft resolutions protesting the Sedition Act and asserting the right of the states to check unconstitutional acts of the federal government

1800

Jefferson elected president
Peaceful transfer of power from Federalists to Republicans

Key Terms

electoral college A group of electors appointed by each state who had the responsibility of picking the president. **160**

Bill of Rights The first ten of the original twelve amendments to the Constitution, which included protections for basic individual liberties and protections for the states. **161**

Republicans An opposition movement led by Jefferson and Madison that opposed Federalists' efforts to create a more powerful centralized government. **162**

assumption of the state debts Hamilton's scheme for the federal government to take over any outstanding state debts. **164**

Bank of the United States A bank chartered by the federal government. The Bank served as a depository for government funds, helped bolster confidence in government securities, made loans, and provided the nation with a stable national currency. **166**

Democratic-Republican Societies A new type of political organization informally allied with the Republicans whose function was to help collect, channel, and influence public opinion. **169**

Jay's Treaty Diplomatic treaty negotiated by Federalist John Jay in 1794. According to the terms of the treaty, Britain agreed to compensate America for cargoes seized in 1793–1794 and promised to vacate forts in the Northwest Territory. However, America failed to win acceptance of the right of neutral nations to trade with belligerents without harassment. **172**

Whiskey Rebellion The armed uprising of western Pennsylvania farmers protesting the Whiskey excise in 1794 was the most serious test of the new federal government's authority since ratification of the Constitution. **173**

XYZ Affair The furor created when Americans learned that three French officials, identified in diplomatic correspondence as "X," "Y," and "Z," demanded a bribe from America's diplomats as the price of beginning negotiations. **182**

Alien and Sedition Acts Four laws designed to protect America from the danger of foreign and domestic subversion. The first three, the Alien laws, dealt with immigration and naturalization. The Sedition Act criminalized criticism of the federal government. **183**

states' rights The theory that the Constitution was a compact among the states and that the individual states retained the right to judge when the federal government's actions were unconstitutional. **185**

Gabriel's Rebellion A slave insurrection in Richmond, Virginia, that drew together free blacks and slaves in a plot to seize the Richmond arsenal and foment a slave rebellion. **186**

CHAPTER 7

Jeffersonian America

An Expanding Empire of Liberty, 1800–1824

Politics in Jeffersonian America p. 192

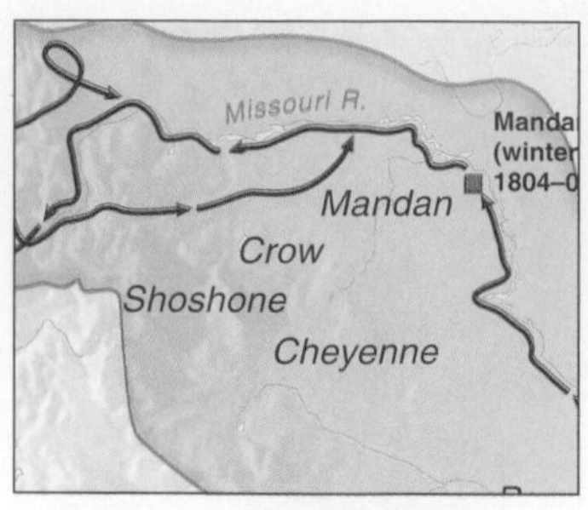

An Expanding Empire of Liberty p. 196

> "The revolution of 1800 was as real a revolution in the principles of our government as that of 1776 was in its form; not effected, indeed, by the sword, as that, but by the rational and peaceable instrument of reform, the suffrage of the people."
>
> THOMAS JEFFERSON to Judge Spenser Roane, 1819

In 1800 Republican Thomas Jefferson won the presidential election against his Federalist opponent John Adams. After nearly a decade in opposition, Republicans celebrated their presidential triumph with toasts and songs about "Jefferson and Liberty." Federalists, however, feared that the new president—whom they had denounced as an atheist, a tool of the French, and a supporter of Thomas Paine's radical democratic ideas—would undo all their work of the previous decade. In this Federalist political cartoon from 1800, *Mad Tom in a Rage,* Jefferson's ally Thomas Paine and the Devil tear down the federal edifice created by Washington and Adams.

Nevertheless, the Federalist fears captured in the cartoon proved unfounded. President Jefferson turned out to be a rather different person from Vice President Jefferson, the leader of the Republican opposition during the Adams administration. Rather than mount a full-scale attack on Federalist policy, Jefferson adopted a less confrontational approach. In his presidential inaugural, he struck a conciliatory tone and reminded Americans: "We are all republicans—we are all federalists."

In his inaugural Jefferson also promised the nation "a wise and frugal government." Implementing this vision of government, however, proved difficult as he took over the reigns of power in his first term of office. The opportunity to purchase the Louisiana Territory, thus doubling the size of the new nation, led him to cast aside the idea of strict construction, which restricted the powers of the federal government to those explicitly delegated by the Constitution. By the end of Jefferson's second term, some Americans came to believe that the Jeffersonian Republicans had become indistinguishable from their Federalist opponents. Jefferson's anointed successor, James Madison, made compromises that some of his supporters believed amounted to a betrayal of the ideas he had championed as a member of the Republican opposition in the 1790s.

Foreign affairs proved especially vexing for both Jefferson and Madison. Each had tried to prevent American entanglement in the war raging between Britain and France. Despite their efforts, however, America was dragged into the European conflict, eventually going to war against Britain in 1812. Although the war had been fought against the British, the conspicuous losers in the conflict were the Indian tribes in the Northwest and Southwest, who lost a valuable ally in Britain and suffered military defeats by American troops. The demands of fighting the war also forced Republicans to reconsider the necessity of many aspects of Hamiltonian economic policy. By the end of the presidency of James Monroe, who became the fourth Virginian to become president, the old political labels of Republican and Federalist had become nearly meaningless, soon to be supplanted by two new political parties.

What does the image of *Mad Tom in a Rage* tell us about the meaning of the Election of 1800?

Politics in Jeffersonian America

Jefferson's presidential triumph in 1800 ushered in a new era in American political life. After a decade of Federalist rule, and despite the courts remaining bastions of Federalist power, Republicans now controlled the presidency and the Congress. Despite Jefferson's efforts to avoid the bitter partisanship that had characterized politics during the previous decade, American politics remained deeply divisive. In an age when gentlemen lived by a code of honor, political sleights could easily turn into personal insult, and might result in tragic results. Before the end of his presidency, Jefferson's vice president, Aaron Burr, would slay Jefferson's longtime opponent, Alexander Hamilton, in a duel, and Burr would become a fugitive from justice. Former president John Adams sarcastically observed that his fellow citizens had made great strides in the "arts of lying and libeling and the other arts which grow out of them, such as wielding the cudgel and pistol."

Jefferson's Visions of Government

Jefferson set out his views of government in his inaugural address on March 4, 1801. While invoking a shared set of values, including faith in representative government and the rule of law, Jefferson also made clear how his idea of government differed from that of his opponents. Throughout the 1790s Federalists had worked to endow the new government of the United States with sufficient power to become a great nation, modeled on Britain's commercial and military might. Following Hamilton's lead, Federalists had successfully increased the size of the central government and military. Federalists had not only increased the size of government but they had also used their expansive view of federal power to crush political opposition. Rather than embrace the Federalists' strong centralized government, Jefferson hoped to reduce the size of the federal government.

Jefferson invoked the ideal of liberty, not power. He described the state governments as the proper defenders of liberty. In contrast to Federalists, who supported a national bank and enacted a host of taxes, including the unpopular whiskey tax, Jefferson sought to reduce the burdens government placed on the people. Rather than favor commerce he emphasized the "encouragement of agriculture" with "commerce as its handmaid." To achieve his goal of "economy in public expense," he would scale back the size of government. An alert citizenry, a vigorous militia, and strong state governments were the foundation upon which to build America's future. Finally, opposing laws such as the Sedition Act, Jefferson praised freedom of the press, reminding Americans that political conflict was a testimony to the vitality of American life, not a sign of the nation's weakness.

The Jeffersonian Style

Jefferson's inaugural not only set out his philosophical differences with Federalists but also gave him the occasion to dramatize them. Jefferson's vision had always melded democratic ideals to aristocratic tastes. He labored to create a different presidential style from those who came before him. Jefferson loathed the pomp and ceremony that his predecessors, including both Washington and Adams, had used to exalt the office of the presidency. Rather than ride to his inaugural in an elegant coach, Jefferson walked behind a small band of Maryland militia. Instead of delivering his annual address to Congress from a monarch-like throne as his predecessors in office had done, he chose to have a clerk read his addresses to Congress. Jefferson rejected the elegant balls that Federalists had staged during the Washington and Adams presidencies as smacking too much of European-style monarchy.

Yet although he sought to replace the aristocratic style of his predecessors with something more democratic, Jefferson remained a rich Virginian slaveholder whose tastes were anything but common. Although Jefferson dispensed with pomp and formality, his presidency still reflected his aristocratic tastes. Dinner with Jefferson involved an unusual mix of informality and aristocratic style. He entertained his guests in informal attire, wearing a pair of worn leather slippers, an informality that shocked some of

What was the essence of Jefferson's vision of government?

his guests. Yet guests invited to Monticello, the home he designed himself, in the mountains of western Virginia (**7.1**), found themselves in an architectural masterpiece that confidently proclaimed Jefferson's wealth and exquisite taste. The food and wine served at these dinners were equally impressive. Jefferson regaled his dinner guests with the sensual delights of his table and the dazzling brilliance of his dinner conversation, which ranged over everything from philosophy to agriculture. A connoisseur of fine wines, Jefferson's annual wine bill for his first term in office came to $2,400 dollars, almost ten times the yearly income of a typical artisan of his days.

7.1 Jefferson's Monticello
Jefferson's design for Monticello borrowed elements from English architecture, including the classical columns, and the latest Parisian styles, such as the domed roof that caps the building.

Political Slurs and the Politics of Honor

Literate and urbane, Thomas Jefferson was deeply influenced by the ideas of the Enlightenment, particularly its emphasis on reason and science. One of Jefferson's many interests was fossils. Jefferson wrote about mammoths in his book *Notes on Virginia*. Four months after his inauguration, Jefferson's friend, the artist Charles Wilson Peale, set out on an expedition to exhume the remains of a mammoth discovered in upstate New York. President Jefferson, enthusiastically supporting Peale's outing, even authorized the use of U.S. military equipment to aid in the dig. The expedition proved to be a monumental undertaking, as reflected in Peale's painting of the event (**7.2**). The disinterment of the giant fossil testified to American ingenuity. To Jefferson, the expedition was a fitting symbol of the new nation's commitment to the values of the Enlightenment.

His interest in fossils and mammoth bones, however, provided an easy target for his enemies, who mocked him as "the mammoth philosopher" or the "mammoth of democracy." In response, a group of his supporters attempted to turn Jefferson's passionate

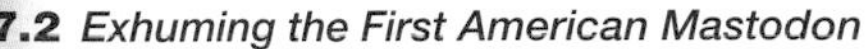

7.2 *Exhuming the First American Mastodon*
Charles Wilson Peale's painting of the exhumation of the mammoth is a tribute to American ingenuity and the Enlightenment values esteemed by Jefferson. The centerpiece of the portrait is not the fossils, but a machine designed to remove water from the dig.

What does Monticello reveal about Thomas Jefferson's ideas and values?

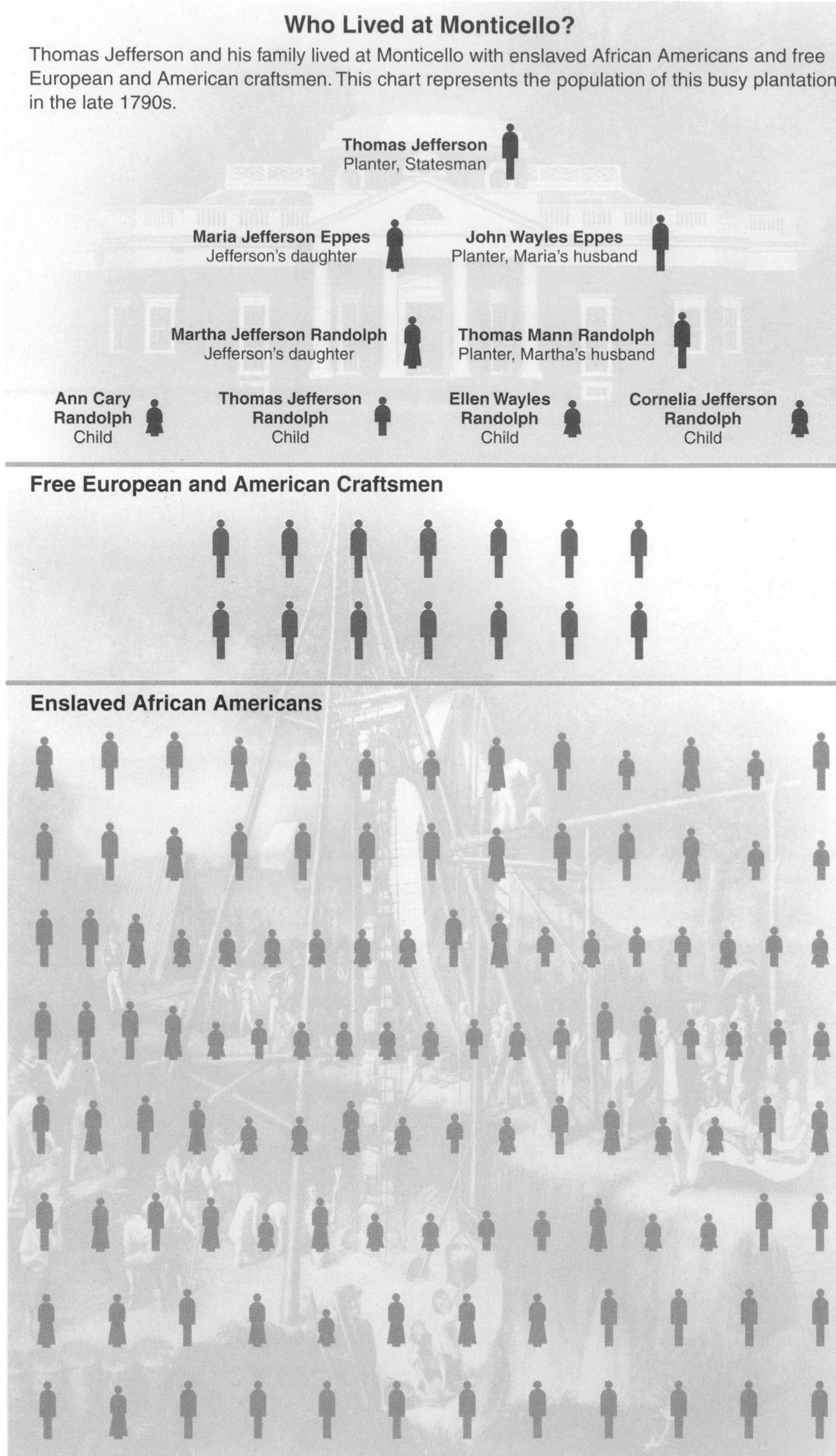

7.3 Residents of Monticello
The vast majority of those living on Jefferson's land were African American slaves.

interest in mammoths to his advantage. The president was presented with a "mammoth cheese" weighing more than 1,200 lbs. The delivery of the "mammoth cheese" to the president became a news sensation and filled newspaper columns for months. Mammoth jokes, however, were among the milder partisan attacks leveled at Jefferson. The president's lavish home at Monticello also prompted sarcastic comments. Federalists pointed out the obvious contradiction between the president's support for democracy and his own aristocratic tastes in architecture, food, and wine. His enemies also highlighted the contradiction between Jefferson's impassioned defense of liberty and his life as a slaveholder. Monticello was a large working plantation and was therefore home to a sizable African American slave community. Indeed, as the chart (**7.3**) illustrates, slaves vastly outnumbered Monticello's free white population, which included Jefferson's family and a variety of white laborers living on the mountaintop.

Attacks on the president became intensely personal. One of Jefferson's former supporters, the disgruntled newspaper editor James Callender, accused Jefferson of taking Sally Hemings, a Monticello slave, "as his concubine." This political cartoon (**7.4**) portrays Jefferson as a cock courting the hen Sally Hemings. The press repeated the charge that the president had a slave mistress, and tales of Jefferson's "Monticellan Sally" appeared in newspapers.

Although Jefferson chose to ignore these accusations, the Sally Hemings scandal persisted long after he left the presidency. Among the descendents of Monticello's slaves, the notion that Jefferson had fathered children with Sally Hemings became part of a family oral tradition that persisted for more than two centuries. Many descendents of Jefferson and modern scholars doubted the truth of these rumors until modern forensic DNA testing provided strong evidence that a male in Jefferson's blood line was the likely father of at least one child by Sally Hemings. Although not

Is it possible to reconcile Jefferson's support for slavery with his political values?

everyone has been persuaded, many scholars now believe that Jefferson did have some type of sexual relationship with Hemings.

Federalist attacks on Jefferson went well beyond attacks on his personal character. The most vocal critics of the president charged that had white Southerners not been entitled to count three-fifths of their slaves in the apportioning electoral votes in 1800, then Jefferson would have lost to Adams. However, the charge that Jefferson was a "Negro President" was not entirely true, since Jefferson won clear majorities in the North and mid-Atlantic and his margin in the Electoral College would have been even greater if presidential electors from states in those regions had more accurately reflected the popular vote in those states that supported Jefferson.

Jefferson was not the only politician whose reputation was dragged through the mud. Attacks on character were frequent, and in a culture in which honor played a central role, they were a serious matter that demanded an appropriate response. If an apology or retraction was not forthcoming, a man might demand satisfaction on the field of honor, resulting in a duel. A number of leading politicians participated in duels, and gentlemen typically owned a pair of dueling pistols. Often, friends intervened and prevented the duel. In the most famous duel of the era, no one stopped the face-off between Vice President Aaron Burr and his longtime rival in New York politics, Alexander Hamilton. Burr's candidacy for governor of New York in 1804 was undermined by Hamilton's attacks. A newspaper reported that Hamilton had described the ex-vice president as "a dangerous man and one who ought not be trusted with the reins of government." Hamilton also insulted Burr's personal integrity and honor.

These attacks on his character led Burr to demand an apology. When Hamilton refused to apologize, Burr challenged Hamilton to a duel. On July 11, 1804, the two men met across the river from New York City in Weehawken, New Jersey, where Burr fatally shot Hamilton. Authorities in both New York and New Jersey immediately charged Burr with murder, and Burr fled to Philadelphia, where he remained a fugitive.

News of the duel spread throughout the country. In Baltimore, angry citizens burned the former vice president in effigy. Eventually, the charges against Burr were dropped; although dueling was still illegal in most states, duelers were rarely prosecuted.

> "Of all the Damsels on the green
> on mountain or in valley
> A lass so luscious ne'er was seen
> As Monticellan Sally"
>
> *Boston Gazette*, 1802

7.4 Jefferson and Sally Hemings Jefferson's enemies spread rumors about his illicit sexual relationship with his slave Sally Hemings. This caricature of Jefferson as a cock and Sally Hemings as a hen presents the scandal in comic visual terms.

What role did honor play in the political culture of Jeffersonian America?

An Expanding Empire of Liberty

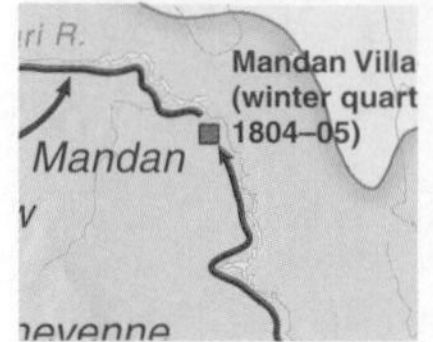

Many of Jefferson's supporters hoped that the new president would radically restructure the balance of power between the states and the federal government. They would be disappointed. Rather than a wholesale assault on the Hamiltonian system, Jefferson opted for a more modest, less confrontational approach. The exception was the judiciary. The Federalists had expanded and seeded it with opponents of Jefferson, presenting him with a major challenge.

Another challenge was posed by the unexpected opportunity to purchase the entire Louisiana Territory from the French emperor Napoleon. To justify this purchase, which required an enormous exercise of federal power, Jefferson would need to accept a Hamiltonian view of the Constitution. Jefferson's vision of an expanding "empire of liberty" peopled by independent yeoman farmers came into conflict with his vision of limited government.

Dismantling the Federalist Program

Jefferson's approach to change in government was moderate and conciliatory. Instead of purging government of all Federalists, he dismissed only those who were corrupt or inept or who posed serious obstacles to his agenda. Similarly, although Jefferson had contemplated declaring the Sedition Act unconstitutional, he simply refused to bring forward any new indictments, pardoning individuals prosecuted by Federalists and allowing the law to expire.

Jefferson remained committed to the ideal of a republican system in which the states, not the federal government, retained the bulk of authority. The powers of the federal government pertained to "the external and mutual relations only of these states." The states were responsible for the "principal care of our persons, our property." With states' rights in mind, Jefferson reduced the size of the federal government. He directed Albert Gallatin, his new secretary of the Treasury, to eradicate the national debt created by previous Federalist administrations. Gallatin severed the connection between the Bank of the United States and the federal government, using the sale of the government's interest in the bank to lower the national debt. To make up for the loss of income from the repeal of unpopular taxes, Jefferson relied on the sale of Western lands and income from tariffs on imports. Convinced that the militia was sufficient to protect America's peacetime interests, he slashed the budget of both the navy and the army, sharply reducing the size of both. It was a decision that would create serious problems for Jefferson in his second term. Without a powerful navy to protect American merchant ships, the new nation's commerce could be threatened by the navies of France and Britain.

The Courts: The Last Bastion of Federalist Power

Early in his first term, Jefferson confided to a supporter that the Federalists "have retired into the judiciary as a stronghold." One of the last acts of John Adams's Federalist administration had been the passage of the Judiciary Act of 1801, which created a host of new circuit and district court judges and a variety of other legal offices, such as clerks, federal marshals, justices of the peace, and district attorneys. With new Federalist appointments in place, Adams had hoped to solidify the Federalists' control of the judiciary. The Judiciary Act also reduced the number of Supreme Court justices from six to five. (The reduction would take effect upon the death or retirement of one of the sitting justices.) By reducing the number of judges on the Supreme Court, Federalists hoped to minimize the likelihood that Jefferson would appoint a Supreme Court justice during his tenure. Jefferson instructed his secretary of state, James Madison, to withhold any of the new commissions that arrived after he was to be sworn in as president. One of the disappointed judiciary office seekers, William Marbury, sued Madison, seeking a court order to compel Jefferson to turn over his commission. In what would become a landmark in American constitutional law, *Marbury v. Madison* finally decided the case on February 23, 1803, helping to strengthen the powers of the federal judiciary. See *Choices and Consequences: John Marshall's Dilemma.*

Did Jefferson's actions as president justify his view that his election was a genuine revolution?

Choices and Consequences

JOHN MARSHALL'S DILEMMA

The case of *Marbury v. Madison* pitted President Jefferson against the new Federalist Chief Justice of the Supreme Court, John Marshall. Jefferson, a champion of states' rights, resented the Federalist-controlled judiciary and, in particular, Marshall, an ardent nationalist who supported a strong central government and a powerful judiciary. *Marbury v. Madison* presented Marshall with a tremendous opportunity to enhance the power of the court, but it also set up the possibility of a serious conflict between the court and the executive branch. Could Marshall compel Jefferson to deliver the commission against his will? What if Jefferson refused the court order? Although Marshall sought to strengthen the power of the court, a direct confrontation with Jefferson might have the opposite effect if Marshall ruled against the president and Jefferson ignored the court's ruling. Marshall had three possible options before him.

Choices

1 Give Marbury his commission.

2 Deny Marbury the commission.

3 Acknowledge the legitimacy of Marbury's claim, while somehow avoiding a showdown between the court and the executive branch.

Decision

Marshall stated emphatically that Marbury was entitled to the commission. But he asserted just as strongly that he could not order Madison to deliver the commission because the Supreme Court lacked jurisdiction to hear the case. Thus, Marshall used a technical legal issue to avoid a showdown between the executive and the judiciary. To arrive at this result, Marshall declared part of an earlier law, the Judiciary Act of 1789, unconstitutional.

John Marshall

Consequences

Legal scholars usually regard *Marbury v. Madison* as one of the most important and brilliant opinions in Supreme Court history. Marshall gave all the parties in the case a partial victory. By affirming that Marbury was entitled to the commission, Marshall gave Marbury a moral victory, at the same time that he handed Jefferson a practical political victory. His ruling affirmed the concept of judicial review, the notion that courts might overturn acts of the legislature, thus giving the biggest victory to the Supreme Court, whose power was enhanced by his decision.

Continuing Controversies

What role should judicial review play in a democracy?

The power of unelected judges to overturn acts of the legislature struck many Americans in Jefferson's day as undemocratic and inconsistent with the notion of representative government. Modern critics still argue that judicial review is undemocratic. Supporters of judicial review argue that the courts serve a necessary *counter-majoritarian* role. By protecting minorities against overbearing majorities, a strong judiciary with the power of judicial review safeguards individual liberty. The controversy that began with *Marbury v. Madison* continues to this day.

How did John Marshall avoid a showdown with Jefferson in *Marbury v. Madison*?

The Louisiana Purchase

In his first Inaugural Address, Jefferson described America as a "chosen country, with room enough for our descendants to the thousandth and thousandth generation." For America to remain a republic of virtuous yeoman farmers and keep alive the ideal of an "empire of liberty," the nation, he argued, would have to expand westward. Jefferson's vision of an expanding empire of liberty, however, had little room for African Americans or Indians. The first test of the limits of this vision, especially of his concept of liberty, became apparent in Jefferson's response to news of Gabriel's Rebellion, the slave uprising in Richmond, Virginia, in 1800 (see Chapter 6). The uprising prompted much soul-searching on the part of white Virginians, including a proposal to emancipate slaves and settle them on Western lands. Virginia's Governor James Monroe took this proposal seriously and sought the president's advice about the prospects of implementing such a bold solution to the problem of slavery. Jefferson opposed the plan, however, because he viewed such lands as vital to America's future. He did not wish to see land that could go to whites and help preserve his vision of a yeoman republic set aside for the use of blacks.

The West was absolutely essential to Jefferson's future vision of the nation. By the time he took office, more than half a million Americans lived west of the Appalachian Mountains; access to the Mississippi River had become crucial to their economic prosperity. Agricultural produce destined for the port of New Orleans traveled on large flat boats down the Mississippi. Pinckney's Treaty (1795) with Spain provided navigation rights to this vital economic corridor. When the Spanish ceded Louisiana to France, they also turned over control of the Mississippi River to Napoleon Bonaparte, the country's ambitious military ruler. Napoleon's decision to close the port of New Orleans to American shipping alarmed many in Congress. Some Americans even advocated seizing the city. Preferring a negotiated settlement, Jefferson sent a delegation to France to purchase the port from Napoleon. When they arrived in Paris, America's diplomatic envoys were astounded to learn that Napoleon was willing to sell the entire territory of Louisiana to the United States.

This offer presented Jefferson with an opportunity to double the size of the United States. The only problem was that the Constitution did not authorize the president to purchase new territory. To fulfill his dream of securing enough land for the nation to remain a yeoman republic, Jefferson had to abandon his constitutional philosophy of strict construction, which limited the powers of the federal government to those expressly delegated by the Constitution. Although Jefferson contemplated amending the Constitution to enable such a purchase, he feared that Napoleon might withdraw his offer before such an amendment could be ratified. To help realize his vision of a yeoman nation, Jefferson abandoned his constitutional ideals. With the **Louisiana Purchase**, the United States acquired the Louisiana Territory from France in 1803, thereby securing control of the Mississippi River and virtually doubling the size of the new nation (**7.5**).

> "There is on the globe one single spot, the possessor of which is our natural and habitual enemy. It is New Orleans, through which the produce of three-eighths of our territory must pass to market, and from its fertility it will ere long yield more than half of our whole produce and contain more than half our inhabitants."
>
> THOMAS JEFFERSON, 1802

Lewis and Clark

In January 1803, six month before news of the purchase of Louisiana, Jefferson had requested funds from Congress for an expedition to explore and map the Western parts of the continent. Meriwether Lewis, Jefferson's private secretary, headed the expedition. Lewis invited Captain William Clark, an experienced army officer with extensive experience in mapmaking, to join him in commanding a "Corps of volunteers for North

Was the Louisiana Purchase consistent with Jefferson's ideals?

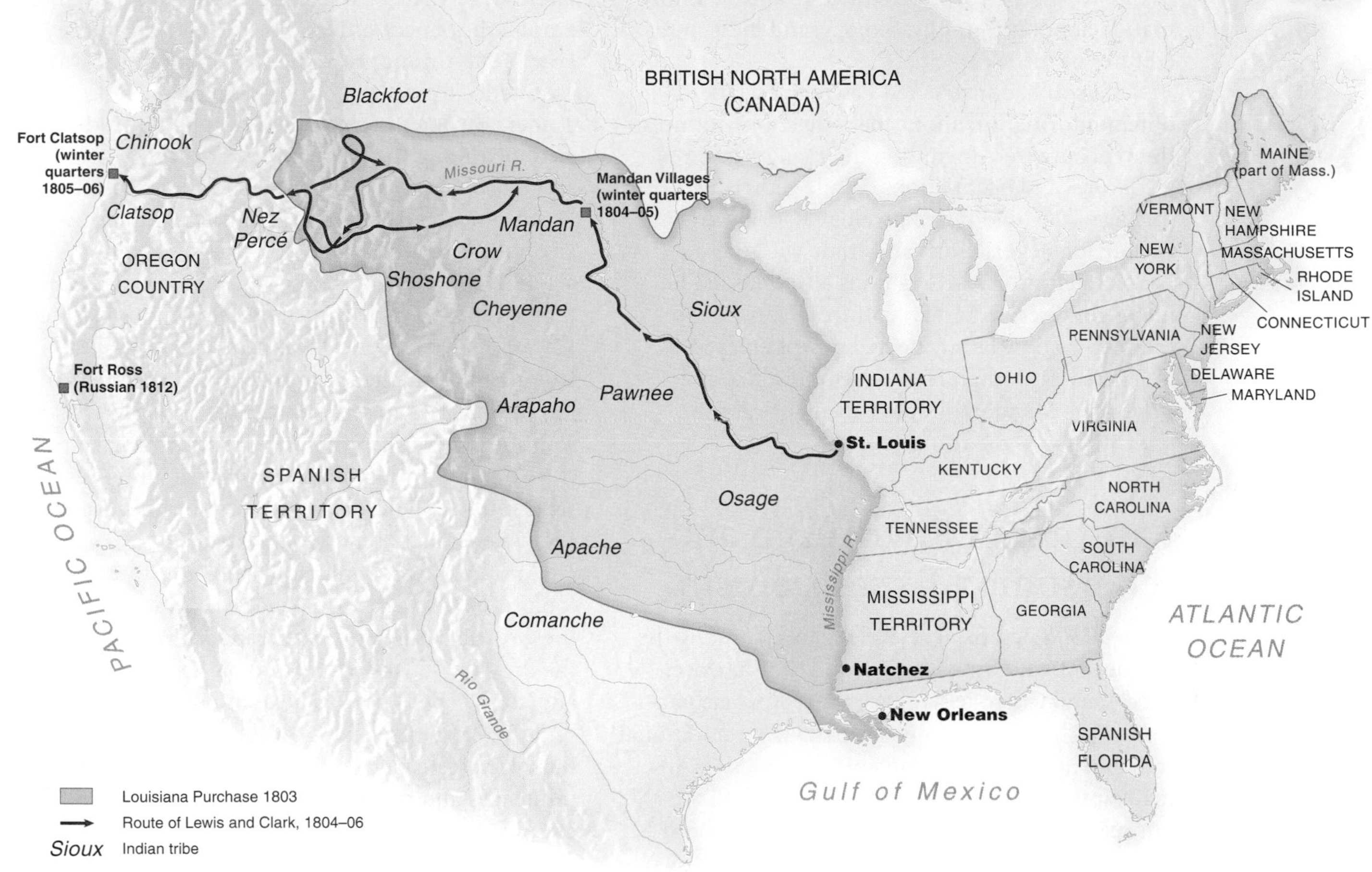

7.5 Louisiana Purchase

Jefferson acquired approximately 827,000 square miles of Western territory, doubling the size of the United States. One of the primary goals of the Lewis and Clark expedition was to map this region.

Western Discovery." Beginning their heroic trek westward in the frontier town of St. Louis, forty-eight explorers set out on keelboats, long narrow boats that could carry as much as 10 tons of supplies. The expedition traveled up the Missouri River. Progress was slow and in some cases the explorers had to wade along the bank to pull the boats forward by ropes. Still, if all went well they were able to travel 14 miles on a good day.

The purchase of Louisiana added a new element to Lewis and Clark's mission. In addition to gathering information about native plants, animals, and geography, Lewis was charged with negotiating with Indian Tribes commercial treaties and informing the European and American traders inhabiting the Louisiana Territory that they were no longer subject to French law, but were now subject to the laws of the United States. Lewis and Clark helped establish official relations with the Indian peoples they encountered.

The mission also included a French interpreter, Toussaint Charbonneau, and his Shoshoni wife, Sacagawea, who served the corps ably as a translator. In addition, her presence signaled the Indians that this group of armed men was not a war party. The inclusion of Sacagawea and her young child—neither being perceived as a warrior—thus helped the Corps of Discovery to avoid conflict. Clark stressed the importance of this when he wrote in his journal, "a woman with a party of men is a token of peace." Enduring incredible hardship, including temperatures as low as 45 degrees below zero, the Corps of Discovery traversed an immense swathe of territory, almost 4,000 miles. The entire trek took more than two years to complete. The map (7.5)

What role did Sacagawea play in the Lewis and Clark Expedition?

shows the path Lewis and Clark took in their voyage of discovery. The corps provided invaluable information about geography, biology, and indigenous cultures of the West.

Jefferson had instructed Lewis and Clark to obtain information about the indigenous cultures they encountered, including their languages, traditions, and occupations. While gathering intelligence would prove invaluable for future diplomatic negotiations and trade with these peoples, Jefferson's instructions also reflected his lifelong interest in Indian cultures. Many items that Lewis and Clark collected were displayed in Jefferson's "Indian Hall" at Monticello. An impressive Mandan buffalo robe hangs above the entrance to the room (**7.6**).

Pan-Indian Revivalism and Jeffersonian Expansionism

In the 1790s a cultural revival occurred among the Iroquois in western New York and the Shawnee, Creeks, and Cherokees on the trans-Appalachian frontier. The revival aimed at revitalizing traditional Indian religious beliefs and cultural practices. In many instances, the revivalists also attacked the European and American practices that had been incorporated into Indian cultures.

One leader in the Indian revival movement was Handsome Lake, who led a revitalization movement among the Seneca of New York beginning in the year 1799. Among the values he championed was abstinence from the consumption of alcohol. Traders during the colonial period had introduced alcohol among Indians peoples, creating a serious social problem for many indigenous communities. Handsome Lake had himself battled with his own alcohol addiction. In addition to abandoning alcohol, he experienced a series of religious visions that led him to revive aspects of the Iroquois Great Law of Peace. This ideal was central to the Great Iroquoian Confederacy, and enjoined members of the confederacy to seek diplomatic, not military, solutions to conflicts. In 1801 Handsome Lake traveled to Washington, D.C., to meet with President Jefferson to defend the land claims of his people against encroachment from settlers.

Another effort at religious and cultural revival took place among the Shawnee and other tribes of the Great Lakes region. The leader of this movement, the Prophet Tenskwatawa, also battled with alcohol addiction. The Prophet's ideas also came to him in a series of religious visions. According to these visions the Prophet instructed his people to reject Western influences and return to traditional Indian ways. In contrast to Handsome Lake's evocation of peace, Tenskwatawa adopted a more militant stance. The Shawnee Prophet joined his brother, the military leader Tecumseh, in organizing rival Indian nations together. This **pan-Indian resistance movement** united six tribes in an effort to repel white encroachments in Ohio and Indiana, thus defending Indian land and culture. Rather than seek peaceful accommodation with the United States, this movement resolved to defend Indian lands by force.

7.6 Jefferson's Indian Hall at Monticello Jefferson's main entrance hall contained a host of Indian artifacts, including a Mandan buffalo-hide robe (far right). The images painted onto these robes often depicted heroic exploits and battles of the warriors who wore them.

What were the central beliefs of Handsome Lake's religious revival?

Dissension at Home

In 1804 Jefferson easily defeated his opponent, the Federalist Charles Pinckney, by a margin of 162 electoral votes to 14 to start a second term as president. The margin of victory in this election was a tribute to the achievements of his first administration, during which he had overseen a peaceful, relatively smooth transition from Federalist to Republican rule. Jefferson had dismantled parts of the government bureaucracy, overseen a robust economy, and preserved the ideal of a nation of yeoman farmers by acquiring the vast new territory of Louisiana. In contrast to the successes of his first term, however, Jefferson faced challenges at home and abroad that marred his second four years in office. Divisions within the Republican movement plagued Jefferson's second term. Meanwhile, his effort to avoid entanglement in European politics and conflicts would lead him to institute an embargo against foreign trade that proved extremely unpopular in New England and seaport cities.

Jefferson's Attack on the Federalist Judiciary

The final element in the Republican strategy to rein in the Federalist judiciary involved the use of the constitutional power of impeachment to remove two of the most controversial Federalist judges from office. Toward the end of his first term Jefferson scored a victory by removing John Pickering of New Hampshire, a notorious drunk. Although he had clearly been unqualified to hold office, many Jefferson supporters were worried about the use of impeachment as a partisan tool. A number of Republicans doubted that Pickering's deplorable behavior qualified as "high crimes and misdemeanors," the Constitution's criteria for removal from office. Republicans managed to persuade enough members of the Senate to convict Pickering.

Buoyed up by his impressive victory in the election of 1804, Jefferson next turned his attention to Samuel Chase, a federal judge who had used the bench as a pulpit to denounce Jefferson and his ideas by delivering longwinded speeches to federal juries. Although Chase had used his position as a judge to denounce Republican ideas, his partisanship seemed even less likely than drunkenness to meet the high standard set by the Constitution for impeachment. Ardent Republicans argued that impeachment was the only tool to check the excesses of unelected judges. More moderate Republicans and Federalists insisted that an impeachable offense had to be a criminal act; ideological bias and partisanship were simply not impeachable offenses. The Senate failed to convict Chase, and the episode drove a wedge between the radical and moderate wings of Jefferson's coalition.

The Controversial Mr. Burr

The tragic duel between Hamilton and Burr ended the latter's public political career, but it did not end his political scheming. Burr was soon embroiled in another controversy, this time charged with conspiracy and treason. The exact details of Burr's plot are sketchy, but he appears to have planned to raise a private army and conquer Mexico. Although ample evidence indicates that Burr had been plotting some type of assault on Mexico, the evidence that he intended to invade American territory is less compelling. In any case Burr was one of the more flamboyant personalities of the early Republic, a quality his friend and protégé, painter John Vanderlyn, captured in this portrait of him (**7.7**).

Jefferson pushed hard to prosecute Burr for treason. Chief Justice John Marshall refused to construe the treason clause in more broad terms, forcing the government to produce two witnesses that could testify to the fact that Burr had waged war against the United States. Under this more narrow definition of treason, the prosecution was unable to convict Burr. Marshall's decision to read the treason clause in such narrow terms infuriated Jefferson, who on this occasion seemed to embrace a theory of constitutional interpretation at odds with his own preferred theory of strict construction. Burr went into temporary exile in Europe after the trial but eventually returned to New York to start a lucrative law practice.

7.7 Portrait of Aaron Burr Artist John Vanderlyn, a protégé of Burr, painted this striking portrait of the controversial politician during Burr's tenure as vice president. [*Source:* Collection of The New-York Historical Society, Acc. #1931.58]

Why did Jefferson target the federal judiciary and seek to limit its power?

America Confronts a World at War

In 1803, within two weeks of its sale of Louisiana, France was again at war with Britain. Although Napoleon's armies dominated the European continent, Britain's navy still commanded the seas and defeated the French fleet at the Battle of Trafalgar in 1805. During the early phases of the European conflict, American merchants reaped enormous profits by trading with both the French and the British. However, both Britain and France, eager to exert economic pressure on their enemies, set out to blockade the ports of their adversaries. The United States argued that neutral nations had a right to carry on nonmilitary trade with both sides in the conflict, but neither Britain nor France honored this idea. The British navy boarded and searched American ships and seized cargoes without providing any compensation. Even more galling to Americans was the British naval practice of **impressment**, forcing merchant seamen to serve in the British navy. Numerous sailors on American ships had once served in the British navy but now claimed American citizenship. The British navy refused to recognize these claims, arguing that the men were deserters and still subject to British law. Between 1803 and 1812 the British navy abducted and impressed as many as 6,000 Americans.

The tense environment on the high seas reached a crisis in 1807, when the British ship the *Leopard* fired at an American navy ship, the *Chesapeake*. In the skirmish three Americans were killed and eighteen wounded. The British abducted four American sailors whom they charged were deserters from the Royal Navy. People in America's seaport towns clamored for revenge for the **Chesapeake Affair**. Citizens of Norfolk, Virginia, were particularly outraged because the *Chesapeake* had been built in the town's shipyards. Norfolk passed a resolution denouncing this outrageous assault on American liberty and honor. One British diplomat noted that "the lowest order of the Americans are much irritated and inclined for violent measures." Cautious, President Jefferson instructed the governors of the states to be prepared to call up as many as 100,000 militia men to defend the nation if war became inevitable.

The Failure of Peaceable Coercion

Hoping to avoid a military conflict with the British and French, Jefferson proposed a policy of "peaceable coercion," ordering an economic embargo prohibiting trade with Britain and France. "Our commerce," Jefferson wrote, "is so valuable to them, that they will be glad to purchase it, when the only price we ask is to do us justice." The **Embargo Act of 1807** became the cornerstone of Jefferson's plan of "peaceable coercion." By keeping America's ships out of harm's way and depriving Britain and France of the economic benefits of trade, Jefferson hoped to exert pressure on both sides to respect the rights of neutrals on the high seas. Smugglers widely flouted Jefferson's policy of peaceable coercion, and it proved unpopular in New England and seaport cities, where the policy hit the shipping business hard. American exports fell from $108 million in 1807 to $22 million in 1808. To enforce the embargo along the Canadian border, Jefferson had to send in troops, a decision he had decried during the Whiskey Rebellion a decade earlier. Federalists in New England, whose political fortunes had been flagging, now regained their voice, rallying against Jefferson and his "dambargo." As this cartoon (**7.8**) lampooning Jefferson's efforts to avoid foreign conflict suggests, the embargo did not intimidate Britain or France, but it weakened the American economy.

Madison's Travails: Diplomatic Blunders Abroad and Tensions on the Frontier

The presidential election of 1808 marked the first time that Republicans split over who should lead them. James Madison, who had been Jefferson's closest advisor during the turbulent 1790s, was Jefferson's choice. Quiet, almost scholarly in temperament, Madison had an impressive list

What was the policy of peaceable coercion?

of accomplishments. He had been an architect of the Constitution, had drafted the Bill of Rights, and had served as Jefferson's secretary of state during the recent conflict with Britain and France. Other choices were former Anti-Federalists George Clinton and James Monroe. Clinton's candidacy quickly fizzled, but Monroe gained some support from Republicans. A caucus of Republican congressmen made the final decision about who would inherit Jefferson's legacy, endorsing Madison.

Jefferson's Embargo Act not only divided Republicans but also strengthened the fortunes of the Federalists in places such as New England, where the economic impact of the embargo hit hardest. The Federalist candidate, Charles Pinckney, received three times as many votes as he had in the 1804 presidential election, doing particularly well in New England. Despite the strong Federalist showing in New England and New York, the Republican Madison handily defeated the Federalist Pinckney by 122 to 47 electoral votes to become the fourth president of the United States.

Unfortunately for Madison he had inherited a major foreign policy crisis from his predecessor Jefferson. The embargo had not forced Britain and France to change their policy. The main casualties from this policy had been Southern agriculture and New England commerce. Madison's faith in a peaceful solution received a boost when Britain's ambassador opened a new series of talks about ending the embargo. Britain appeared conciliatory, even accepting Madison's insistence that Britain pay reparations for the *Chesapeake* incident and offering to end the policy of searching and seizing American vessels in neutral waters. However, the British government repudiated the generous terms negotiated by the British Ambassador, dashing hopes for peace.

Frustrated by the diplomatic impasse, Congress sought another solution to the problem. A House select committee headed by Nathaniel Macon proposed a bill designed to provide much needed customs revenue by allowing British and French goods back into American harbors if they were transported on American ships. Although the measure failed, a second proposal, Macon's Bill No. 2, did pass. Macon's Bill No. 2 stipulated that when either Britain or France repealed its restrictions on neutral trade, America would reinstate sanctions against the other nation. Seizing on this law, Napoleon promised that France would honor the rights of neutrals. However, Napoleon, who had little intention of keeping his word, used Macon's bill to drive a wedge between the United States and Britain.

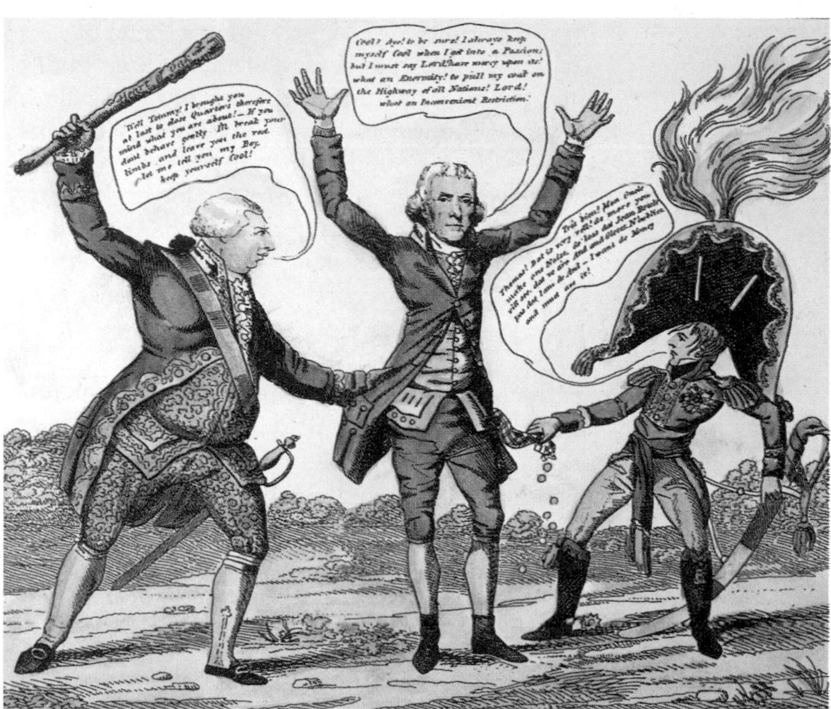

7.8 ***Intercourse or Impartial Dealings*** Jefferson stands helpless, caught between King George and Napoleon.

The British pointed out that Napoleon had reneged on his promise to honor the terms of Macon Bill No. 2 and that the new sanctions levied on British trade were unjustified. Rather than reopen commercial relations with Europe, the new policies only heightened tensions between America and Britain.

The repeated violation of the rights of neutral nations to trade on the high seas was not the only grievance that Americans felt against Britain. As American settlers streamed into the new state of Ohio (1803) and Indiana territory, many of them blamed the British for instigating Indians to attack them. Britain's lucrative trade with these Indians included the sale of firearms, and these weapons proved especially useful to Tecumseh, whose pan-Indian resistance movement was gathering followers as Indians faced further encroachments on their land. Although Tecumseh's brother, the Prophet, exhorted his followers to reject all aspects of white civilization, European military technology proved too useful to abandon. Tecumseh worked to convince various tribes to renounce intertribal warfare and unite to oppose further American expansion.

Indigenous resolve to resist Western expansion intensified after the Treaty of Fort Wayne (1809), in which the United States wrested three million acres of land from the Delaware and Potawatomi in Indiana. To squash resistance, William Henry Harrison led a military expedition against Tecumseh and his supporters in 1811. Harrison's expedition

How did British relations with Indians in the Northwest exacerbate political tensions between America and Britain?

burned the village of Tippecanoe, the center of Tecumseh's pan-Indian movement, to the ground. After this attack Tecumseh entered into a formal alliance with the British, who supplied further arms to the Indians. Confident that their alliance with the British would help defeat American forces, Tecumseh and his allies stepped up attacks on American settlements along the frontier.

The War of 1812

Frustrated by the inability of peaceable coercion to force Britain to respect American rights on the high seas and angered by British support for Tecumseh, Madison began preparations for war. Madison called Congress into an early session in the fall of 1811. Republicans dominated Congress but were divided over the wisdom of going to war against Britain. Many Republicans from the mid-Atlantic, especially New York, were reluctant to endanger their economic fortunes by taking on the most powerful navy in the world. Madison's enemies, particularly those from his home state of Virginia, feared that war would lead t o the creation of a large military establishment and new taxes to pay for a war. Madison drew his strongest support from a group of **War Hawks**, young Republican congressmen from the South and Western regions of the country who were intensely nationalistic, resented British attacks on American rights, and favored an aggressive policy of Western expansion into Indian occupied territory. The two leading voices of the War Hawks were Henry Clay, a first term Congressmen from Kentucky, and John C. Calhoun, an up-country South Carolinian educated at Yale.

7.9 ***Columbia Teaches John Bull His New Lesson*** Columbia, depicted as the goddess of liberty, stands before other symbols of the new American nation, including an eagle and a shield bearing the stars and stripes of the American flag. She warns France's Napoleon and Britain's John Bull to respect American rights.

The House voted to declare war by a majority of 79 to 49. The margin in the Senate was 19 to 13. No single pattern accounts for all the votes, but popular enthusiasm for the war ran high in many parts of America. Regional, economic, and party identities shaped the final vote. The British blockade had hit the South and the West especially hard. British involvement with Western Native American tribes, particularly in the supply of guns, angered Westerners. Northeastern Republicans who favored war were motivated by anger against this latest threat to American freedom from British tyranny. They saw a struggle that had begun during the Revolution and would not end until America was truly free of British power.

Opposed to war, Federalists viewed the vote as another example of the Republicans' distorted vision of the world. For Federalists, France, not Britain, was America's true enemy. Federalists were unanimously opposed to the war, a position that intensified when they learned that the British had been prepared to yield on the vital question of neutral rights. Anger over Federalist opposition to war led to violence. One Baltimore Federalist newspaper editor who attacked the war was targeted by a mob of angry Republicans, who attacked his office and destroyed his printing press. The attempt by the disgruntled editor to resume printing after the incident triggered a full-scale riot that plunged the city into chaos and was put down only when the militia was called out to quell the riot. The resulting destruction of property and loss of life was the worst instance of public unrest in the young nation's short history and earned Baltimore the nickname "Mob Town" for decades.

News of the reversal in the British position, however, arrived too late for America to change course. America, at President Madison's request, finally declared war, which began in 1812. The war pitted the United States against Great Britain for the second time within less than a half century. As this political cartoon shows (**7.9**), the primary justification for the **War of 1812** was Britain's violation of American neutrality and seizure of American sailors. In the cartoon, Columbia, the symbol of America, rebukes France and Britain, reminding them that they both must learn to respect free trade and seamen's rights or face retribution. The other issue, British support for Indian attacks on frontier settlements, also galvanized popular support for the war effort, particularly in the West. For a better understanding of the division over entering the war, see *Competing Visions: War Hawks and Their Critics.*

Who were the War Hawks?

Competing Visions

WAR HAWKS AND THEIR CRITICS

Americans were deeply divided over the War of 1812. One theme that rallied support in the Southwest for the war was Britain's trade relationship with American Indians. Representative Felix Grundy, a prominent War Hawk from Tennessee, charged that the British had instigated Indian violence. Indians killed three of Grundy's brothers in the conflict along the frontier. By contrast, the sharp-tongued, Virginian conservative John Randolph became a vocal critic of the war. Fiercely independent, Randolph dismissed Grundy's suggestion of an Indian–British conspiracy, instead putting the blame for Western conflicts squarely on the settlers who violated Indian land claims. How did Grundy's experiences as a Westerner color his decision to support war? Was Randolph's response likely to attract political support (why or why not)? Why would Randolph opt to frame his opposition in these terms?

In this impassioned speech, Felix Grundy accused the British of arming and inciting American Indians to take up arms against Americans.

"It cannot be believed, by any man who will reflect, that the savage tribes, uninfluenced by other powers, would think of making war on the United States. They understand too well their own weakness and our strength. They have already felt the weight of our arms; they know they hold the very soil on which they live as tenants in sufferance. How, then, sir are we to account for their late conduct? In one way only; some powerful nation must have intrigued with them, and turned their peaceful dispositions towards us into hostilities. Great Britain alone has intercourse with those Northern Tribes."

John Randolph's response to Grundy dismissed the notion of a conspiracy. The source of conflict along America's frontier, Randolph argued, was the greed of Westerners who encroached on Indian lands.

"He [Randolph] was sorry to say that for this signal calamity and disgrace the House was, in part, at least answerable. Session after session, their table had been piled up with Indian treaties, for which the appropriations has been voted as a matter of course, without examination. Advantage had been taken of the spirit of the Indians, broken by the war which ended in the treaty of Greenville [1795]. Under the ascendancy then acquired over them, they had been pent up by subsequent treaties into nooks, straightened in their quarters by a blind cupidity seeking to extinguish their title to immense wilderness, for which (possessing, as we do already, more land than we can sell or use) we shall not have occasion for half a century to come. It was our own thirst for territory, our own want of moderation, that had driven these sons of nature to desperation."

A Scene on the Frontiers as Practiced by the "Humane" British and Their "Worthy" Allies

Why did Westerners believe that the British were encouraging Indian violence against Americans?

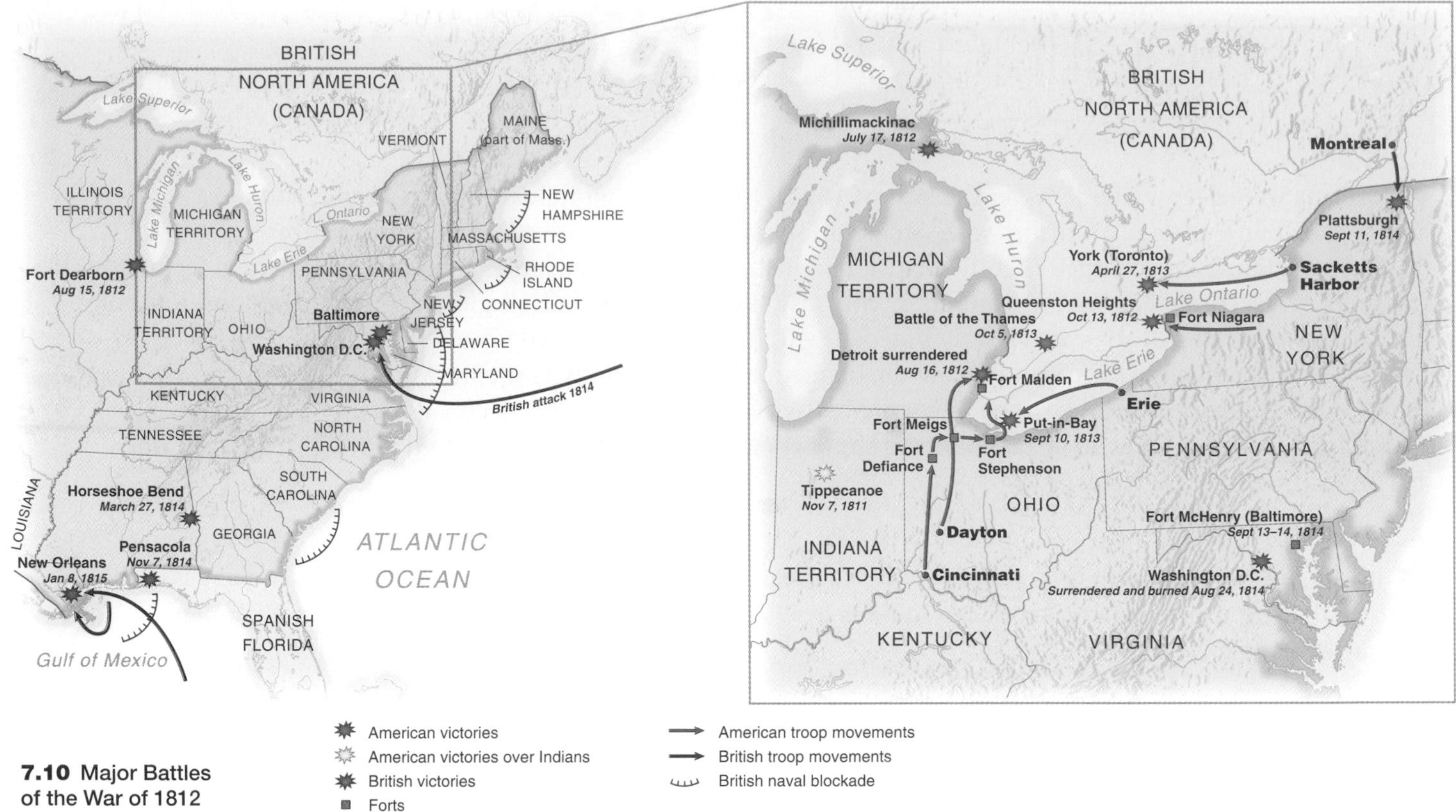

7.10 Major Battles of the War of 1812 America's effort to seize Canada failed, but some of the fiercest fighting occurred along this northern frontier.

Rather than take on Britain on the high seas, the American war effort concentrated on Canada (**7.10**). Attacking the British in Canada appealed to the War Hawks for several reasons. Canada was poorly defended, and Americans mistakenly believed that the province of Quebec's large French-speaking population, with little love for Britain, would eagerly join Americans to expel the British from Canada. An attack on Canada would also deprive Tecumseh of his primary source of arms. Given the power of the British Empire, particularly its naval superiority, the focus on conquering Canada, or at least holding it hostage to force Britain to respect neutral rights on the high seas, seemed a promising strategy.

American efforts to wrest Canada from Britain, however, failed miserably as British troops beat back incursions into Canada along the U.S. border. The British also waged a successful campaign in harassing America's coastal settlements. In the most audacious move of the war, in the summer of 1814, the British attacked Washington, D.C., and burned the capital. The British assault on Washington forced President Madison and his wife Dolley to flee their home. When the British troops finally arrived on the scene, they feasted on an elegant dinner that had been set out for the president and his wife. They took many items from the house, including Madison's personal medicine chest, which the British government returned 125 years later to President Franklin Roosevelt.

The British next attacked Fort McHenry in Baltimore harbor. An eyewitness to the attack, Francis Scott Key, composed a patriotic poem, "The Star Spangled Banner," that became America's national anthem in the 1930s. Although the American navy failed to challenge the British in the Atlantic, it did score impressive victories against the British on the Great Lakes, at Put-in-Bay and at Niagara Falls. While diplomatic efforts to end the war intensified, the British launched an assault on New Orleans. Andrew Jackson, the American leader at New Orleans, commanded a mixture of regular troops, militia, free blacks, and a small body of Indians. Although he had been reluctant at first, Jackson even accepted help from a band of French pirates. As a result of his victory, Jackson became the hero of the Battle of New Orleans. His accomplishments were celebrated in ballads such as the *Hunters of Kentucky*, "Old

> "Nothing was adjusted, nothing was settled—nothing in substance but an indefinite suspension of hostilities was agreed to."
> JOHN QUINCY ADAMS, describing the Treaty of Ghent (1815)

Hickory" (Jackson's nickname) became a symbol of steadfastness and bravery. Newspapers across the nation proclaimed the victory a symbol of the "Rising Glory of the American Republic."

Neither side in this Battle was aware that a peace treaty had already been signed between the two nations. It took two weeks for word of peace to reach Louisiana, arriving after the battle was concluded. The Treaty of Ghent in 1814, named for the city in Belgium where the negotiations were conducted, ended the fighting but failed to resolve the longstanding issues that had divided the two nations. Indeed, if judged by the terms of the peace treaty negotiated in Ghent, the War of 1812 accomplished little. The diplomatic issues at stake at the beginning of the war, including impressments of American sailors and the rights of neutral trade, remained unresolved. In private, some Americans, including John Quincy Adams, one of the diplomats who helped negotiate the treaty, felt it did little but end hostilities. The American public generally regarded the war as a victory, some calling it the Second War for Independence. At least America had defended the nation's honor against Britain, forcing the most powerful nation in the world to treat the new nation with respect, a perception reflected in this symbolic painting celebrating the treaty (**7.11**); America, represented by the goddess of liberty, reaches out the hand of friendship to Britannia, symbol of Great Britain.

While the British and Americans had fought to a draw, the most conspicuous losers in the war were the Indians living along the frontier, who lost an important ally and were forced to make a number of major land concessions to Americans. The goal of pan-Indian nationalists such as Tecumseh suffered a severe set back at the hands of William Henry Harrison and Andrew Jackson, whose military successes secured the trans-Appalachian frontier, the Western territory beyond the Appalachian Mountains, for settlement.

The Hartford Convention

While many Americans celebrated Jackson's victory over the British at the Battle of New Orleans, Federalists in New England convened at the **Hartford Convention** in Hartford, Connecticut, to protest the War of 1812. While some Federalists in New England had flirted with the idea of secession, the delegates to the Hartford Convention stopped well short of advocating the breakup of the Union. Although New England Federalists had denounced the radical states' rights ideas that Jeffersonians had espoused in response to the Alien and Sedition Crisis in 1798, they now echoed many of those ideas. The

7.11 Treaty of Ghent
In this representation of the peace accord worked out between America and Britain at Ghent, Belgium, Columbia and Britannia hold hands. Two sailors unfurl the flags of their nations, proclaiming a new era of harmony.

What were the main goals of the Hartford Convention?

7.12 *The Hartford Convention or Leap, No Leap*
In this cartoon George III beckons to Massachusetts, Connecticut, and Rhode Island to jump off the cliff and join him, promising them "titles, nobility," and other rewards for abandoning their fellow states.

convention delegates proposed a series of constitutional amendments that would strengthen New England's influence in the Union. In particular, they sought to require a two-thirds majority for commercial regulations, declarations of war, and the admission of new states. To weaken the South's influence in Congress, the Hartford Convention also called for a repeal of the three-fifths compromise, which allowed Southerners to count a percentage of their slaves for the purposes of determining a state's representation in the House. The Hartford Convention's proposals were publicized at the same time as news of the Treaty of Ghent and America's impressive victory at the Battle of New Orleans were fueling a new sense of national pride. In this political cartoon ridiculing the Hartford Convention (**7.12**), leading New England Federalists appear ready to leap off a cliff into the welcoming arms of Britain's king. Federalists' narrow sectionalism appeared out of step with the public's new patriotic fervor. Even in their New England strong-hold, Federalists saw themselves irreparably damaged as a movement. The War of 1812 facilitated the demise of the Federalists as a viable political organization.

How are the actions of New England states represented in the political cartoon on the Hartford Convention above?

The Republic Reborn: Consequences of the War of 1812

The War of 1812 transformed America, its politics, economy, society, and relations with other nations. The postwar era inaugurated a period of nationalism that was evidenced in diplomacy, economic policy, and law. There was broad popular support for a stronger central government, one capable of dealing with foreign challenges and spurring domestic economic growth. Thus the partisan squabbling of the Jeffersonian era gave way as the necessities of fighting a war forced leading politicians to unite the best aspects of Jeffersonian politics with Hamiltonian economics. John Quincy Adams, the talented secretary of state under James Monroe, proved to be an effective diplomat, skillfully negotiating a number of important treaties for the United States. The demands of the wartime economy not only spurred economic and technological innovation but also increased demand for manufactured goods, such as firearms and textiles for uniforms. The new nationalist ethos and a more sympathetic attitude toward economic development were evidenced in the decisions of the Supreme Court after the war.

The National Republican Vision of James Monroe

The experience of war radically transformed Republican political and constitutional ideas. In his annual message to Congress in 1815, the first after the Treaty of Ghent, Madison suggested that the nation expand the size of its military and reaffirmed his support for a national bank and for protective tariffs for American industry. Seeking to push beyond this nationalist agenda, Madison floated the idea of chartering a national university and even considered amending the Constitution to give the federal government the power to promote internal improvements such as roads and canals. Madison did cling to one traditional republican idea. He believed that to exercise such powers required a constitutional amendment granting the federal government the power to achieve these objectives. Although on this one point of constitutional theory Madison reasserted the traditional Republican view of the limited scope of federal power, as a practical matter he had aligned himself with much of the old Hamiltonian agenda. Indeed, John Quincy Adams, son of the former president and a staunch Federalist, believed that Madison and "the Republicans had out-Federalized Federalism."

The collapse of Federalists in the aftermath of the War of 1812 led to a shift away from the rancor that had characterized politics during the Jeffersonian era. Following Madison as president, James Monroe sought to unite the political ideals of Jeffersonianism with aspects of Hamiltonian economic theory. For a brief period he managed to create an administration free of the partisan divisions that had characterized American politics since Washington's second term. As a gesture toward nonpartisan politics, the Republican Monroe named the brilliant Federalist John Quincy Adams as his secretary of state. Monroe also appointed individuals from different regions, an effort to heal old sectional tensions. In addition, Monroe took a lesson from Washington, the other president who seemed most successful at rising above party, and embarked on a goodwill tour of the nation. Monroe began his tour in Boston, a city with strong Federalist sympathies. Praising Monroe's gesture, a Boston newspaper proclaimed a new **Era of Good Feelings** to describe the absence of bitter partisan conflict during Monroe's presidency. Monroe also enjoyed some successes in restoring luster to the office of the presidency. He became noted for his stylish mode of entertaining in the executive mansion. To repair the extensive smoke damage to the executive mansion (**7.13**), a result of the British attack on Washington during the War of 1812, Monroe had the house painted a brilliant white. The official residence of the President of the United States has been known as the White House ever since.

7.13 ***A View of the President's House in the City of Washington after the Conflagration of the 24th of August, 1814*** Repairs to the damaged executive mansion included a new coat of white paint. Afterwards, the residence became known as "the White House."

Why was Monroe's presidency described as an "Era of Good Feelings"?

Monroe not only sought to reconcile Federalist and Jeffersonian ideals but he also served as a bridge between the political cultures of two different centuries, the eighteenth and the nineteenth. Monroe was the last president with ties to the founding generation that fought the Revolution and wrote the Constitution. Monroe's roots in the eighteenth century appear in the clothes he wore at his inauguration. Most men by now had abandoned their wigs and replaced breeches and silk stockings with more modern trousers. But Monroe retained the ideals and dress of eighteenth-century gentility. In this portrait, he wears breeches and silk stockings (**7.14**). If Monroe's personal style and values harked back to the eighteenth century, many of his policies as president reflected newer ideas espoused by such young and up and coming leaders as the nationalist War Hawk John C. Calhoun. Monroe endorsed Calhoun's plan for internal improvements, including roads and canals, which together would create "a domestic market" encouraging "an active intercourse between the extremes and throughout every portion of our Union." One aging Federalist remarked that "the Party in Power seems disposed to do all that federal men ever wished."

7.14 Portrait of President James Monroe
This image of Monroe captures his role as a transitional figure between the eighteenth century world of the Founders and a new era in American politics. He appears without the wigs favored by eighteenth-century gentlemen, but his silk stockings and knee breeches reflected the values of the founding generation.

Another portrait of Monroe was painted by Samuel Morse, then a young painter but later to be known as the inventor of the telegraph. While in Washington to paint Monroe, Morse also began to paint a picture of the newly refurbished chamber of the House of Representatives, which, like the White House, the British had damaged during the War of 1812. In this painting, Morse took the opportunity to represent American nationalism and present a vision of politics consistent with Monroe's idea of republican ideals. For more on Morse's work and his representation of Monroe's political vision, see *Images as History: Samuel Morse's* House of Representatives *and the National Republican Vision.*

Diplomatic Triumphs

After the war, John Quincy Adams, Monroe's secretary of state, took an active role in resolving several outstanding border disputes with Britain. In the Rush-Bagot Treaty of 1817, the United States and Britain agreed to limit naval armaments on the Great Lakes. An accord reached the following year set the new boundary between the Louisiana Territory and Canada at the 49th parallel. In this same accord, the British also recognized American fishing rights off Labrador and Newfoundland, and America and Britain agreed to continue to occupy jointly the Oregon Territory in the Pacific Northwest. These diplomatic successes effectively normalized U.S.-Canadian relations and created a peaceful border between the two countries that has persisted for more than two hundred years.

With a successful resolution of America's northern border disputes with Britain, Adams was now free to address America's southern boundary disputes with Spain. For several decades America had been eager to wrest Florida from Spain. In March 1818 General Andrew Jackson led a raid into Spanish Florida to attack the Seminoles. Under the pretext of protecting American frontier settlements against future Indian attack, Jackson mounted a major offensive against Spanish Florida and captured two Spanish forts, thereby further weakening Spain's bargaining position. Rather than risk war, Spain resolved to abandon Florida. In the Adams-Onis Treaty of 1819, Spain ceded all claims to Florida and formally recognized U.S. sovereignty in Louisiana.

Spain's empire in the Americas had been crumbling for two decades. In 1811 Paraguay and Venezuela each declared independence from Spain. In 1818 Chile declared its independence, while Peru followed suit in 1821. Building on the goodwill generated by the successful diplomatic resolution of the northern boundary issue between the United States and Canada, Britain's foreign minister approached the United States in 1823 with the suggestion that the two nations issue a declaration that neither intended to annex these newly liberated states in Spanish America. While Monroe was tempted to accept the British offer, Secretary of State John Quincy Adams advised against it. Instead, Monroe followed the advice of his brilliant secretary of state. In his annual message to Congress in 1823, he presented a general policy for Spanish America.

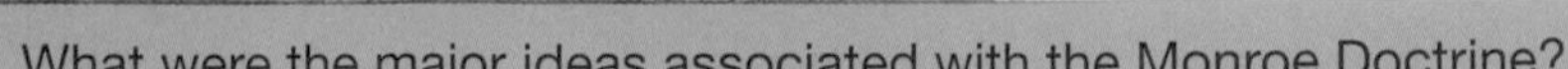
What were the major ideas associated with the Monroe Doctrine?

Images as History

SAMUEL MORSE'S *HOUSE OF REPRESENTATIVES* AND THE NATIONAL REPUBLICAN VISION

In 1819 Samuel Morse began his ambitious painting of the House of Representatives. The painting not only reflected the political ideas of the Era of Good Feelings, it projected a nationalist vision of America's bright future. How did Morse's emphasis on architectural grandeur convey the values of Monroe and Nationalist Republican belief?

Although the crowded chamber bustles with activity, Morse presented a scene of cordiality and harmony. The painting captures the time before formal political business began, a decision that allowed Morse to create a scene free of conflict or tension.

Morse chose a rare evening session of the House to illustrate. This decision allowed him to further shift the focus away from the actions of politicians. Occupying the dramatic center of the painting is the House of Representative's doorkeeper, who is lighting a large chandelier to illuminate the evening's activities. The painting thus pays tribute to America's technological progress. It links America's political institutions symbolically to light and progress.

Benjamin Henry Latrobe, the architect responsible for rebuilding the Capitol after the War of 1812, chose multicolored stones for the columns supporting the roof of the House. This particular architectural element became a visual symbol of the idea of federalism, in which the different states, represented by the stones, blended together in a single harmonious republican structure, a classical column.

A number of distinguished guests are in the House chamber, including the entire Supreme Court, and a number of guests occupy the gallery. The inclusion of the Pawnee chief, Petalesharo, signifies America's inevitable subjection of Indians. Morse's painting idealizes a brief moment in American politics that was already on the wane by the time his painting was displayed. Monroe's vision of a National Republican consensus and the "era of good feelings" was being supplanted by rising sectional tensions over slavery and a new era of partisan conflict.

Morse highlighted the multicolored stone columns, which symbolized the ideal of federalism.

The Indian figure in the gallery symbolized Monroe's diplomatic achievements and the inevitable subjugation of America's indigenous population.

Morse focused on the act of lighting the House's impressive chandelier, a symbol of American progress.

Samuel Morse's *The Old House of Representatives*
[*Source:* Samuel F. B. Morse, "The Old House of Representatives". 1822. Oil on Canvas. 86 1/2 × 130 3/4. Museum Purchase, Gallery Fund. Corcoran Gallery of Art]

Why did Morse highlight architecture and minimize the people in his painting?

This statement, the **Monroe Doctrine**, reiterated the policy outlined in Washington's Farewell Address that America would not meddle in European affairs and expanded upon this policy by warning European powers that the United States would view European intervention in the affairs of any of the newly independent republics of Spanish Americas as a threat to U.S. security.

Economic and Technological Innovation

The War of 1812 not only led to a renewed political commitment to economic development but also spurred a remarkable period of technological development. America's embargo against foreign goods and the demands of the wartime economy provided incentives for economic innovation. Firearms production was improved, steam engines powered new modes of transportation, and new agricultural technology led to a boom in cotton production.

Not surprisingly the war spurred innovation in the production of firearms. The federal arsenals at Springfield, Massachusetts, and Harpers Ferry, Virginia, played a pivotal role in advancing these developments. Indeed, within a decade of the end of the war, Harper's Ferry had pioneered a mass production technique for manufacturing firearms. In place of older artisan methods, in which master craftsmen handcrafted items for production, the system used new power machinery to cut and shape standardized parts. By 1820, John H. Hall had perfected the manufacturing techniques for "fabricating arms exactly alike and with economy by the hands of common workmen." Hall began producing a new breech loading rifle, an improvement over the traditional muzzle loading muskets.

A simple, but far-reaching technological improvement in agricultural production transformed the American economy. The **cotton gin**, an invention by Eli Whitney, an industrious Connecticut Yankee working as a tutor on a Southern plantation, devised a means for removing the seeds that adhered tenaciously to short staple cotton, a hearty variety of plant well suited to Southern climate and soil. Whitney's cotton gin revolutionized cotton agriculture. Before Whitney's invention, an adult slave needed a whole day to clean a single pound of cotton. Whitney's cotton gin allowed a single slave to clean 50 pounds of cotton in a single day. In 1790 the South produced 3,000 bales of cotton. By 1810 the cotton gin facilitated the production of 178,000 bales. Immediately after the War of 1812, cotton production almost doubled again to 334,000 bales. Cotton agriculture would provide huge new economic incentives for slave-based agriculture by making it much cheaper to produce cotton for market.

Although cotton exports to England consumed a high percentage of this new cash crop, some of the cotton produced was purchased for use in domestic textile manufacturing. In 1793 Samuel Slater established a mechanized spinning factory in Pawtucket, Rhode Island. Slater's mill was a relatively modest structure whose size and architectural style fit the scale of a small New England village. The first mills depended on water power and took advantage of natural falls to power water wheels (**7.15**). Slater

7.15 Slater's Mill The earliest factories were not imposing structures belching forth smoke, but small water-powered mill factories. Slater's first water-powered mill resembled the clapboard rural structures that had been used to grind grain or saw logs and that easily blended into their rural settings.

What was the economic significance of Whitney's cotton gin?

pioneered the mill village model of industrial production. Eventually others followed Slater's model, adapting it by creating entirely new mill villages. In these mill villages, the company owned the adjacent farmland and rented it to men whose families worked in the mills. This Rhode Island or "family" model of the mill village was the first successful model of sustained capitalist economic development in manufacturing.

Judicial Nationalism

No figure captured the new nationalist spirit of the nation more fully than the young Supreme Court Justice Joseph Story. A brilliant lawyer, Story was only thirty-two when James Madison appointed him to the Court. Story, an anti-embargo Republican from Massachusetts, was appointed by Madison who hoped the new justice would check the nationalism of Chief Justice John Marshall. Madison would not be the first president to be shocked and disappointed by the behavior of one of his Supreme Court appointments. Story proved to be as nationalistic as Marshall. Story's decisions on the court supported the power of the federal judiciary and limited the power of the states. In a series of landmark decisions, Marshall and Story helped strengthen the power of the federal government and the courts and paved the way of economic growth.

The most famous case dealing with the issues of federalism that came before the court was *McCulloch v. Maryland.* The case arose when the state of Maryland levied a tax on the Baltimore branch of the Second Bank of the United States. Most Republicans had made their peace with the idea of a bank, but some continued to harbor resentment against this highly visible symbol of Hamiltonian federalism. Marshall declared the Maryland state tax unconstitutional and affirmed an essentially Hamiltonian view of the powers of the federal government. According to Marshall the federal government enjoyed broad powers under the "necessary and proper" clauses of the Constitution, which allowed it to charter a bank. Marshall further argued that the power to tax was also the power to destroy and allowing the state to tax a federally chartered institution would have allowed the state of Maryland to undermine an act of the federal government. While Marshall conceded that the powers of the federal government were not unlimited, he affirmed that within its sphere of authority it enjoyed enormous latitude to accomplish any legitimate constitutional objective. In contrast to many Republicans who accepted the Jeffersonian idea that individual states could judge the constitutionality of federal acts, the Marshall Court insisted that it was the sole prerogative of the Supreme Court to determine when the federal government had exceeded its authority.

No other decision rendered by the Supreme Court generated so much controversy as that of *McCulloch v. Maryland.* For some radical opponents of the Marshall Court, *McCulloch* seemed to bring the Anti-Federalists' most dire predictions to pass. Anger over *McCulloch* led many Republicans, particularly in the South, to develop a more aggressive version of the doctrine of states' rights. These Republicans challenged the authority of the Supreme Court to decide arguments about the balance of power between the states and the federal government. For nationalists such as Marshall and Story, however, the creation of a more powerful central government was essential to the survival of American government.

> "The present moment is every way favorable to the establishment of a great national policy and of great national institutions, in respect to the army, the navy, the judicial, [and] the commercial ... interests of the country."
>
> Justice JOSEPH STORY [1816–1820?]

The Marshall Court also decided a number of cases dealing with the law and the economy. One of the most important cases dealing with economic development also greatly expanded the scope of federal power over commerce. In *Gibbons v. Ogden* (1824), a case involving steamboats, the court grappled with the scope of federal powers over interstate commerce. In that case Marshall construed the word *commerce* broadly to encompass "every species of commercial intercourse." The court also held that federal power over interstate commerce did not end at the borders of each state, but extended to within states when that commerce was intermingled with economic activity that crossed state lines. Although in the nineteenth century the federal government did not exploit its power over interstate commerce to the fullest, the power to regulate interstate commerce is currently one of the most far-reaching possessed by the federal government.

Which Marshall Court decisions best illustrate the Court's nationalism?

Crises and the Collapse of the National Republican Consensus

The patriotic sentiments stirred by the War of 1812 and the emergence of a new consensus around a Hamiltonian economic vision contributed to a period of prosperity and optimism. The new consensus, however, proved fragile, and a severe depression soon followed the economic boom of the postwar period. The issue of slavery also vaulted to national attention when Missouri sought admission to the Union as a slave state. The hope that Monroe's creative synthesis of Jeffersonian and Hamiltonian visions might usher in a new Era of Good Feelings proved short lived as economic and political crises once again divided the nation.

The Panic of 1819

The surge in demand for cotton boosted the American economy. Economic expansion, in part driven by cotton, led to a growth in the financial sector of the American economy. States began chartering new banks so that the number of banks doubled in the period from 1815 to 1818, from just over 200 to more than twice that number. In 1816 Congress chartered a Second Bank of the United States, which further fueled economic expansion and land speculation. Because of the combined efforts of the state banks and the Second Bank of the United States, land sales in the brief period between 1815 and 1818 more than tripled.

However the dip in the price of cotton and other agricultural products exported by America dropped in 1819, creating a ripple effect that led to a severe economic downturn that affected nearly every aspect of the American economy. Since much of the expansion in credit by American banks was tied to agricultural production, the crisis spread to America's financial institutions. The value of land purchased on credit dropped sharply, and when these loans came due, speculators were unable to repay the banks that had loaned them the money to purchase these properties. The American economy, now heavily dependent on cotton, sank into depression. As speculators increasingly defaulted on their obligations, one bank after another collapsed. The economic crisis affected nearly every region of the country. The **Panic of 1819**, the economic crisis triggered by the drop in agricultural prices and bank failures, produced economic hardship on an unprecedented scale. While the sudden downturn in the economy hurt Western land speculators and cotton producers in the Deep South, it also devastated the growing urban centers of the Northeast that were also hard hit. In Philadelphia three out of four workers lost their jobs. In New York the number of people classified as paupers increased from eight thousand to thirteen thousand in a single year.

The Missouri Crisis

The economic downturn in 1819 was soon overshadowed by another crisis. In 1819 Missouri applied for admission to the Union as a slave state. Congressman John Tallmadge from New York demanded that Missouri ban further imports of slaves and make a commitment to eliminate slavery before joining. Public meetings across the Northeast protested Missouri's proposed admission as a slave state. The issue of slavery now came to the center of American politics.

The growth of cotton agriculture and the prospect of large new swathes of territory in the western United States entering the Union as slave states prompted a political crisis. While Northern congressmen denounced slavery as a violation of the ideals of the Declaration of Independence and the Constitution, Southerners defended the institution, invoking the language of states' rights developed in 1798 in the Virginia and Kentucky resolutions to support the right of the states to decide the slavery question. A Georgia congressman warned that Tallmadge had "kindled a fire which all the waters of the ocean cannot put out, which seas of blood can only extinguish." The New Yorker's amendment passed the House, where the Northeast enjoyed a numerical majority, but was defeated in the Senate, where the North and South were equally balanced.

To avert a constitutional crisis, Congress worked out a compromise. One of the key players

What was the Missouri crisis?

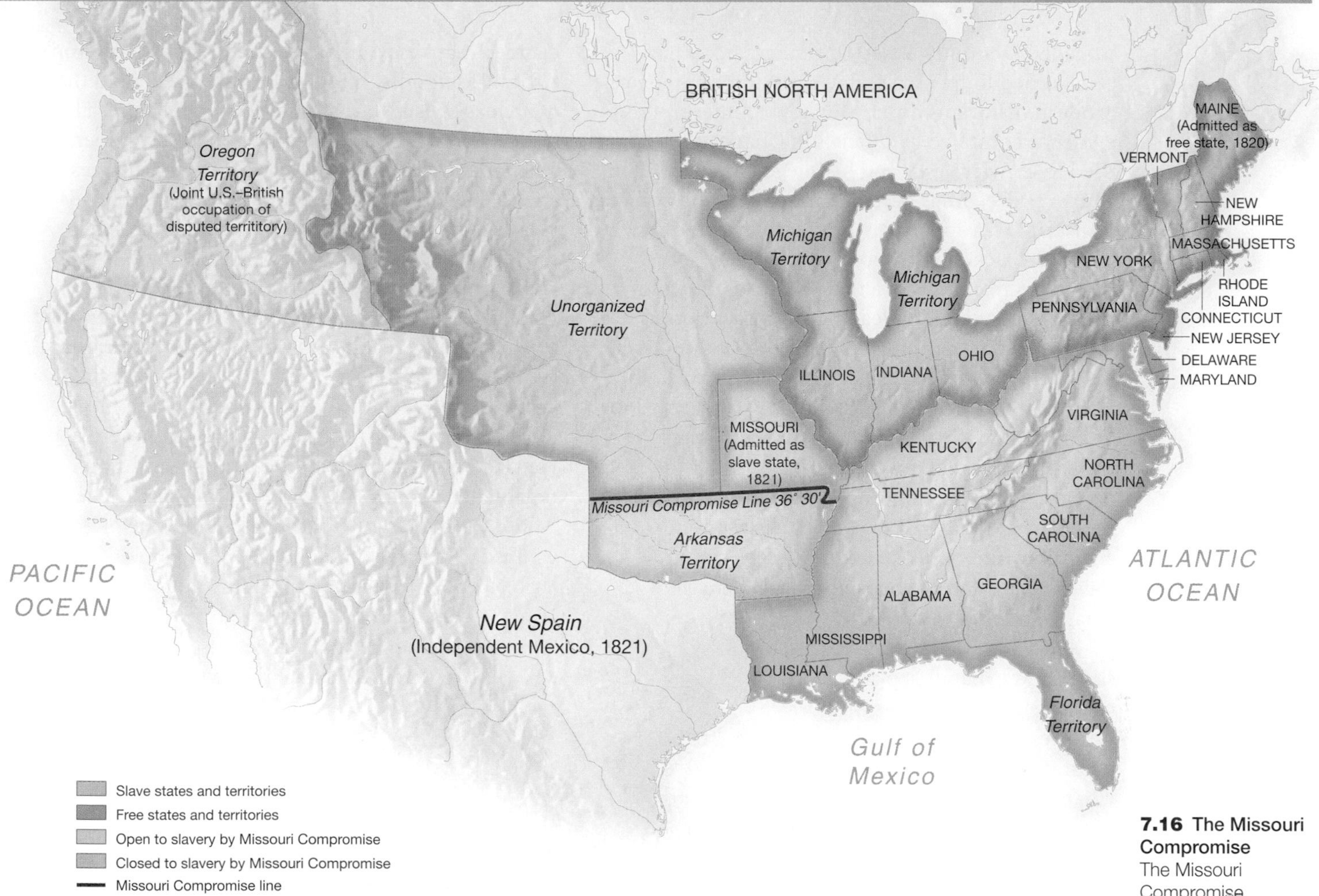

7.16 The Missouri Compromise The Missouri Compromise established a new policy for dealing with slavery in Western territories. The compromise drew an imaginary line across the map of the United States. Land south of this line would be open to slavery, while territory north of the line would be free.

negotiating this solution was Henry Clay, one of the most influential figures in Congress. The **Missouri Compromise** called for the admission of Missouri as a slave state and Maine as a free state, thus preserving the balance between free states and slave states in the Senate. The Missouri Compromise drew an imaginary line across the territory acquired through the Louisiana Purchase at 36° 30' latitude (**7.16**). Land below this imaginary dividing line would be slave territory, while land above the line would be free. When he learned of the outcome of the Missouri Compromise, Thomas Jefferson wrote to a friend that the news struck him as a "fire bell in the night." Being awakened from a sound sleep by a fire alarm, the metaphor chosen by Jefferson evoked the magnitude of the Missouri crisis. For Jefferson the Missouri crisis had etched the issue of slavery onto the map of the United States and would make any resolution of this issue in the future impossible. The debate over Missouri promoted John Quincy Adams to write in his diary that "Slavery is the great and foul stain upon the North American Union." For the moment, however, it seemed that most politicians were unwilling to contemplate erasing the great stain on American society.

Denmark Vesey's Rebellion

The problem of slavery was once again a subject of national concern in the summer of 1822. Newspapers from Charleston to Boston and as far west as the Illinois Territory carried the sensational story of Denmark Vesey, a free African American artisan from Charleston, South Carolina, who had been arrested, tried, and executed for—so the charges went—leading a slave insurrection.

A talented and charismatic figure, Vesey had obtained his freedom when he won a lottery jackpot in 1799 and used his earnings to purchase his freedom and set up his own small carpentry shop. A natural leader, he became a prominent member of a local African American church that became an important meeting place for African Americans. Rumors of a slave revolt led authorities to arrest him and charge him with plotting an insurrection, the

Who was Denmark Vesey?

so-called **Denmark Vesey Uprising**, said to have been aimed to free slaves in Charleston by violence. Modern historians differ over how to interpret the evidence compiled by officials in Charleston that was used to convict Vesey and his alleged followers. The court's proceedings occurred in secrecy, and the trial transcript was apparently produced after the fact. Given the lack of corroborating evidence, some historians reject the idea that Vesey was a revolutionary figure bent on leading an uprising and see him instead as an unfortunate victim, a vocal free black leader who became a scapegoat for paranoid Charleston whites ever fearful of slave insurrection. Others believe that there was a plot, although the scope of it remains uncertain. Whether the proposed insurrection was real or simply imagined, the evidence gathered to convict Vesey provides a window into both the way whites perceived slave culture and the behavior of slaves in the Charleston region.

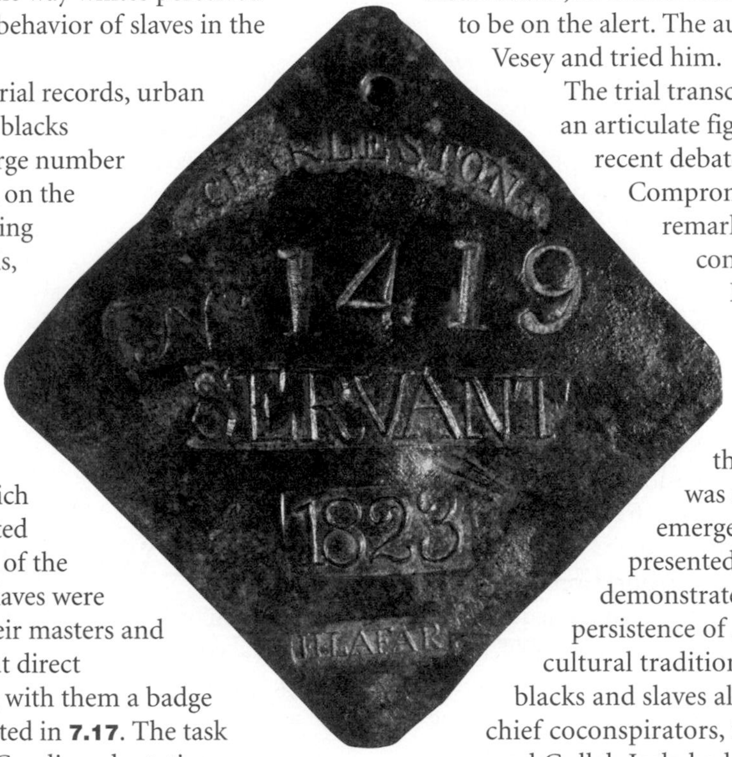

7.17 Slave Badge Badges such as this one were carried by slaves in Charleston when they were hired out to other employers.

According to the trial records, urban slaves and urban free blacks conspired with the large number of slaves who worked on the plantations surrounding Charleston. The rebels, the records suggest, were poised to take advantage of the mobility enjoyed by African Americans in this region, an area in which travel was less restricted than in other regions of the South. Charleston's slaves were often hired out by their masters and often traveled without direct supervision, carrying with them a badge such as the one depicted in **7.17**. The task system employed by Carolina plantation owners also provided slaves with considerable autonomy and some mobility. After finishing their day's tasks, slaves were allowed to work their own plots of land, hunt, or fish. Slaves not only used this surplus food to supplement their meager rations but also often brought this food to Charleston's markets for sale. The ease of travel greatly facilitated communication between slaves and freedmen. Free black churches provided places for African Americans, slaves and free blacks, to meet and discuss ideas, including perhaps revolution. The prosecution claimed that Vesey, an active member of Charleston's African-Methodist Episcopal Church, had used the church as a place to recruit others to his cause. The alleged insurrection was planned for the summer, when many whites left the city for cooler climates.

If Vesey's plan was real and not invented by his prosecutors, his conception was a bold one. After seizing the city arsenal, Vesey and his followers allegedly planned to burn the city and set sail for Haiti. (In 1804 Saint Domingue became the republic of Haiti.) The Caribbean island's own revolutionary experience might have provided an inspirational symbol for Vesey, who saw the uprising as a model for toppling the institution of slavery in America. Haiti therefore provided both a model and a potential haven for Vesey and his followers. When South Carolina's governor heard about the planned insurrection, he ordered five companies of militia to be on the alert. The authorities arrested Vesey and tried him.

The trial transcript portrays Vesey as an articulate figure well aware of the recent debates over the Missouri Compromise, including the remarks of antislavery congressmen from New England. He had also pointed to the rise of abolitionist sentiment in the North as a sign that the time for revolution was ripe. The plot that emerges from the evidence presented at the trial also demonstrates the continuing persistence of African religious and cultural traditions preserved by free blacks and slaves alike. One of Vesey's chief coconspirators, for example, a slave named Gullah Jack, had a reputation as a conjurer who would provide Vesey's followers with magical charms to protect them from harm. There is also evidence that African American culture had developed its own distinctive approach to Christian ideas. African Christianity highlighted certain Old Testament themes taken from the plight of the ancient Israelites. Thus Vesey was said to have reminded his followers that God had delivered the children of Israel out of bondage in Egypt and would surely deliver slaves to freedom now.

How did the Missouri crisis contribute to the climate of fear in Charleston during the Vesey trial?

Before the end of the summer of the trial, Charleston's authorities sent thirty-four blacks, including Vesey, to the gallows. The press widely reported the trial, and a transcript, including the decision and punishments meted out, was published as well. For the Charleston white elite who prosecuted Vesey, one of the lessons of the trial was that "The indiscreet zeal in favor of universal liberty, expressed by many of our fellow-citizens in the States north and east of Maryland; aided by the Black population of those States" posed a serious threat to the institution of slavery. The sectional tensions caused by slavery and the growing animosity between Northern abolitionists, black and white, and Southern defenders of slavery would only turn more bitter in the coming decades.

Conclusion

Jefferson's election in 1800 ushered in a new era in American politics. After a decade of Federalist rule, Republicans now controlled the executive and Congress. Only the judiciary remained in the hands of Federalists. Although Jefferson stopped well short of dismantling the powerful fiscal military state created by Federalists, he did scale back the size of government. By shrinking the government, Jefferson effectively eliminated the threat posed by Hamilton's fiscal and military programs, but without having to repudiate all the accomplishments of the two previous administrations. Nor did Jefferson follow the suggestions of his most radical states' rights supporters who wished him to seriously weaken the powers of the federal government. Although Jefferson did not fully assert all the powers his predecessors had claimed, he did not divest the federal government of power that might prove useful in pursuing his own vision of America's future. Indeed, Jefferson discovered that he could put a powerful federal government to good Republican use. He came to recognize the utility of employing Hamiltonian tools to Jeffersonian ends. The purchase of Louisiana, an action entirely consistent with Hamiltonian loose construction of the Constitution, was difficult to reconcile with Jefferson's own theory of strict construction, but Jefferson put his constitutional scruples aside to make the purchase.

By the time James Madison became president, leading Republicans had adopted much of the Hamiltonian economic agenda. America's difficult experiences during the War of 1812 seemed to underscore the wisdom of many of Hamilton's proposals. The next president, James Monroe, took these lessons to heart; his administration sought a nonpartisan synthesis of Jeffersonian and Hamiltonian values. The press hailed Monroe's presidency as an Era of Good Feelings, a time in which partisan rancor gave way to consensus and a new wave of nationalism. This brief respite from partisanship proved short-lived, however. Within a decade, partisan divisions resurfaced. A new two-party system emerged in which party organization and identity would become central in American culture. This new political culture was more democratic and more aggressive.

If there were conspicuous losers in the Jeffersonian era it was American Indians and slaves. The former faced a more powerful and well-organized American government eager to expand westward. The War of 1812 had a disastrous impact on Western tribes, who lost an important ally, Britain, in their struggles against the United States. Finally the cotton boom and introduction of land well suited to cotton agriculture meant that the institution of slavery became stronger. The struggles over the Missouri Compromise, Jefferson's "Fire Bell in the Night," were prophetic. The issue of slavery, particularly the expansion of slavery, would play an increasingly important role in American public life.

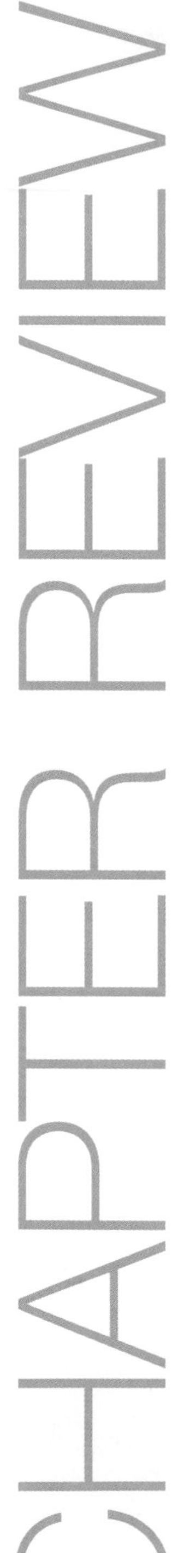

1800–1802

Jefferson elected president
Peaceful transfer of power from Federalists to Republicans

Sally Hemings Scandal
Jefferson is accused of having a slave mistress

1803

Louisiana Purchase
Jefferson acquires Louisiana Territory, doubling the size of the nation

Marbury v. Madison
John Marshall asserts power of Supreme Court to decide constitutionality of acts of Congress (judicial review)

1804–1811

Burr and Hamilton duel
Aaron Burr kills Alexander Hamilton in a duel in 1804

Embargo Act of 1807
Jefferson implements policy of peaceful coercion

Battle of Tippecanoe, 1811
Defeat of Pan-Indian nationalist movement in Ohio and Indiana

Review Questions

1. How revolutionary was Jefferson's revolution of 1800?
2. What role did honor play in the political culture of the new nation?
3. How did Jefferson's home at Monticello express his political ideals? How might critics have seen it as compromising his ideals?
4. Which features of Jefferson's domestic policy agenda were the most successful and why?
5. Why was Jefferson's second term in office more contentious than his first?
6. What were the main causes of the War of 1812? What were its most important economic consequences?
7. What was the "Era of Good Feelings"?
8. Why did Thomas Jefferson describe the Missouri Compromise as a "Fire Bell in the Night"?
9. How did the Marshall Court's decisions contribute to economic growth and development?

1812

War of 1812
United States and Britain go to war

1814–1815

Treaty of Ghent
Britain and America sign a treaty ending the War of 1812

Battle of New Orleans
Andrew Jackson and his troops defeat the British at Battle of New Orleans

1816

James Monroe elected president
Monroe inaugurates the "Era of Good Feelings"

1819–1822

Missouri Compromise
Settles the issue of slavery in the territories by drawing an imaginary line across the map of the United States and creating a permanent division between slave and free territory

Denmark Vesey charged with plotting an uprising
Slaves and free blacks in Charleston, S.C., are captured, charged with plotting an insurrection, tried, and executed

Key Terms

Louisiana Purchase The acquisition by the United States of the Louisiana Territory from France in 1803, thereby securing control of the Mississippi River and nearly doubling the size of the nation. **198**

pan-Indian resistance movement Shawnee leaders Tenskwatawa and Tecumseh's plan to unite Indian tribes to repel white encroachments in Ohio and Indiana, thus defending indigenous lands and reasserting the traditional values of Indian culture. **200**

impressment The practice of forcing merchant seamen to serve in the British navy. **202**

Chesapeake Affair An incident in 1807 when the British ship the *Leopard* fired at an American navy ship, the *Chesapeake*. The British abducted four American sailors, whom they charged were deserters from the Royal Navy. **202**

Embargo Act of 1807 The cornerstone of Jefferson's plan of peaceable coercion that attempted to block U.S. trade with England and France to force them to respect American neutrality. **202**

War Hawks Young Republican congressmen from the South and Western regions of the country who favored Western expansion and war with Britain. **204**

War of 1812 The war fought between Britain and America over restrictions on American trade. British trade with American Indians, particularly trade in weapons, was also an issue. **204**

Hartford Convention A meeting of Federalists in Hartford, Connecticut, to protest the War of 1812. The convention proposed several constitutional amendments intended to weaken the powers of the slave states and protect New England interests. **207**

Era of Good Feelings A term that the press coined to describe the absence of bitter partisan conflict during the presidency of James Monroe. **209**

Monroe Doctrine A foreign policy statement by President Monroe declaring that the Americas were no longer open to colonization and that the United States would view any effort to reassert colonial control over independent nations in the Western Hemisphere as a threat to America. **212**

cotton gin Eli Whitney's invention for removing seeds from cotton. **212**

Panic of 1819 A downturn in the American economy in 1819 that plunged the nation into depression and economic hardship. **214**

Missouri Compromise The congressional compromise in which Missouri entered the Union as a slave state, and Maine was admitted as a free state to preserve the balance of slave and free states in Congress. The law also drew an imaginary line at 36° 30' through the Louisiana Territory. Slavery was prohibited north of this line. **215**

Denmark Vesey Uprising An alleged plot led by a free black man, Denmark Vesey, to free slaves in Charleston and kill their masters. **216**

CHAPTER 8

Democrats and Whigs

Democracy and American Culture, 1820–1840

Democracy in America
p. 222

> "American society is essentially and radically a democracy. . . . In the United States the democratic spirit is infused into all national habits, and all the customs of society."
>
> French traveler MICHAEL CHEVALIER, *Society, Manners, and Politics in the United States* (1839)

George Caleb Bingham's painting, *Stump Speaking or the County Canvass* (1853), captures the drama of a new democratic style of politics that transformed American life starting in the 1820s. The term stump speech referred to politicians' practice in some remote parts of the nation of addressing the electorate by simply finding the nearest tree stump and using it as a rough-hewn platform from which to speak. Bingham, a Whig opponent of the Democratic Party, used the painting to express his reservations about what he considered the dangers posed by too much democracy. Bingham wrote that the politician on the platform was a "wiry" fellow who had "grown grey in the pursuit of office and the service of his party" and literally bends to the popular will in the painting. Across from the speaker, seated amid the crowd, a man in a top hat and light-colored suit listens thoughtfully, refusing to be swayed by the politician's words. Bingham described this figure as an "outstanding citizen" whose noble features not only set him apart from the crowd but also contrast noticeably with the shifty look of the Democratic politician standing at the rostrum. The painting suggests that the "outstanding citizen," a true Whig leader, refuses to pander to the mob.

As this scene reveals, democracy did not yet embrace all Americans; it excluded women, African Americans, and Indians. The crowd Bingham depicts is overwhelmingly male and, apart from a lone African American in the background, all white. While the white men participate in the political life of the nation, the lone black figure labors on a wagon selling refreshments to the crowd.

No figure better personified this new age than Andrew Jackson, the country's leading Democrat. Jackson's 1828 election changed American politics forcing his opponents, the Whigs, to make more effective use of the tools of democratic politics and the symbols of democracy in their campaigns. Indeed in their electoral win in 1840 the Whigs had outdone the Democrats, portraying their candidate William Henry Harrison, as a simple man born in a log cabin who drank hard cider like an ordinary farmer.

Although the Whigs may have learned valuable political lessons from the Democrats about how to campaign, their party steadfastly opposed Jacksonian policies on every major issue of the day. From economic issues to the question of how to deal with American Indians, the two parties battled one another, offering the American people competing visions and clear choices. Political participation in this period rose as Americans responded to the messages of the two parties and turned out to vote in unprecedented numbers.

What elements in the painting *Stump Speaking* illustrate the growth of American democracy?

RIGHTS
OF
MAN

GENERAL HARRISON'S
LOG CABIN MARCH
& QUICK STEP

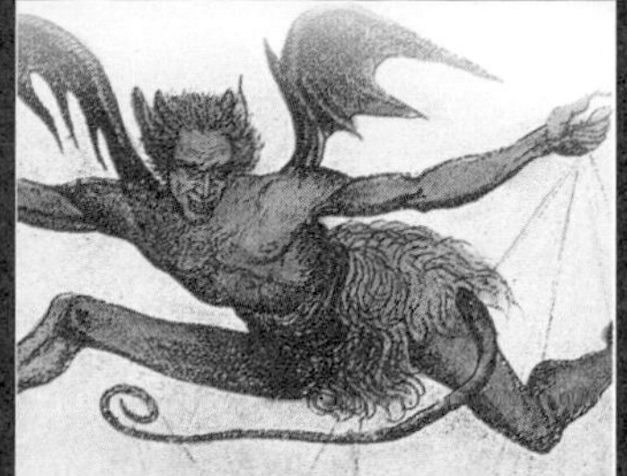

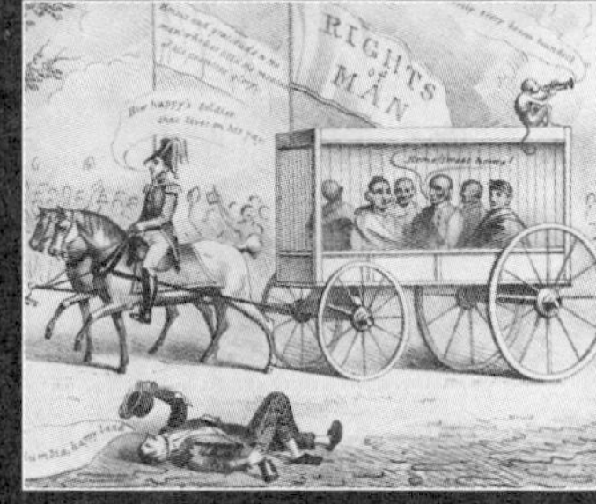

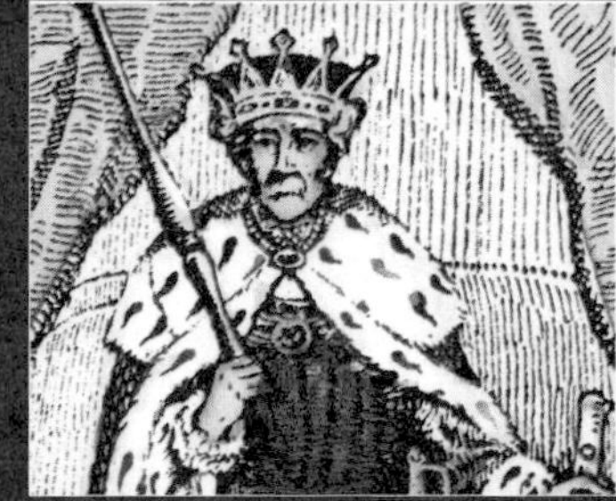

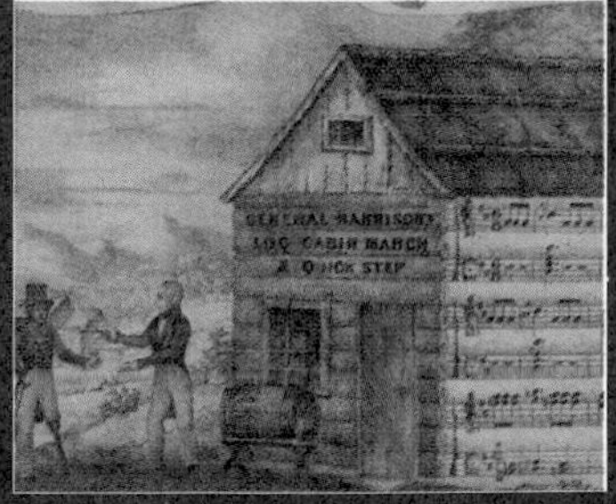

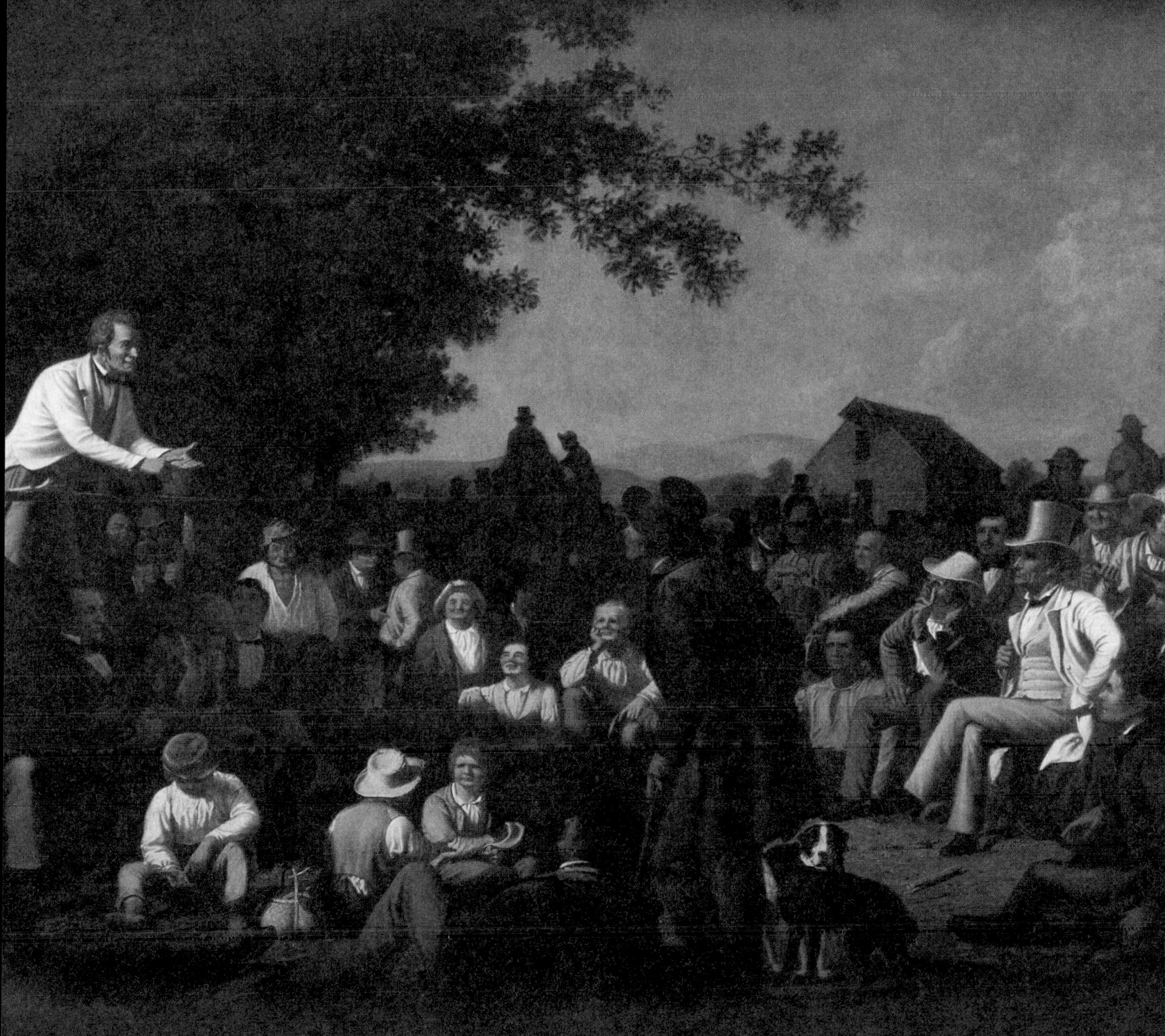

Democracy in America

Between Thomas Jefferson's election in 1800 and Andrew Jackson's victory in his presidential bid in 1828, profound changes transformed American culture and politics. Travelers to America during this period consistently remarked about the democratic character of American society. Democracy appeared to suffuse every aspect of culture and politics. Whereas in 1800 most states had some type of property requirement for voting, within three decades most of these restrictions on the right to vote had been swept aside. Many of the new Western states that entered the Union in the intervening years adopted constitutions with no property requirements. As population shifted westward the center of political gravity of the nation also shifted. Many of the politicians who dominated the national political scene came from Western states such as Tennessee and Kentucky, not the older, settled regions of the nation such as Virginia and Massachusetts.

Democratic Culture

In 1835 a young French nobleman, Alexis de Tocqueville, published an account of his recent trip to America. "No novelty in the United States struck me more vividly during my stay there," he wrote, "than the equality of conditions. It was easy to see the immense influence of this basic fact on the whole course of society." *Democracy in America* (1835), Tocqueville's analysis of the influence of democracy on American life, remains one of the most important books ever written about American society.

The young French aristocrat was hardly the only foreign visitor drawn to America. In the 1820s and 1830s, America attracted the interest of many other foreign visitors who were all impressed by the democratic character of American life. "The term *democrat*, which elsewhere would fill even republicans with terror," Michael Chevalier, a French visitor to America, noted, "is here greeted with acclamations." Francis Trollope, an English observer, was shocked to see Americans talking to complete strangers "on terms of perfect equality." Democracy nurtured a more egalitarian culture that shocked Europeans. In colonial America a bow, courtesy, or doffed hat and lowered head were all signs of deference to one's social betters. Many of these customs persisted in Europe. Americans, however, had abandoned most of them by the 1830s, preferring to shake hands, a form of greeting far more egalitarian in spirit. One English commentator complained that in America he had to "go on shaking hands here, there, and everywhere, and with everybody." Another Englishman confessed his astonishment that travel in America meant mixing with men and women of different classes. "There is but one conveyance, it may be said, for every class of people—the coach, railroad, or steamboat, as well as most of the hotels, being open to all; the consequence is that the society is very much mixed."

A significant political consequence of the growth of democracy was the expansion of suffrage to include virtually all white men. As the maps (**8.1**) show, most of the new Western states that entered the Union after the War of 1812 adopted democratic constitutions that rejected property qualifications for suffrage. The constitutions of the new Western states generally embraced this ideal from the beginning. When older states such as New York revised their constitution in the 1820s, the question of suffrage became one of the most contentious. See *Competing Visions: Should White Men Without Property Have the Vote?*, page 224.

Davy Crockett and the Frontier Myth

The French visitor to America Alexis de Tocqueville commented that "in the Western settlements we may behold democracy arrived at its utmost limits." Tocqueville may well have been thinking of figures like the legendary frontiersmen and politician Davy Crockett (1786–1835) when he made that statement. No figure in American public life did more to help establish the association of the West with democracy than Davy Crockett. Born in Tennessee in 1786, Crockett served under Andrew Jackson during the Creek Wars (1813–1814), where he distinguished himself as a soldier. In addition to putting him in the Tennessee state legislature, his home state elected Crockett to Congress, where he became a supporter of his former commander, Andrew Jackson, another symbol of frontier democracy.

What role did the frontier play in nurturing the growth of democracy?

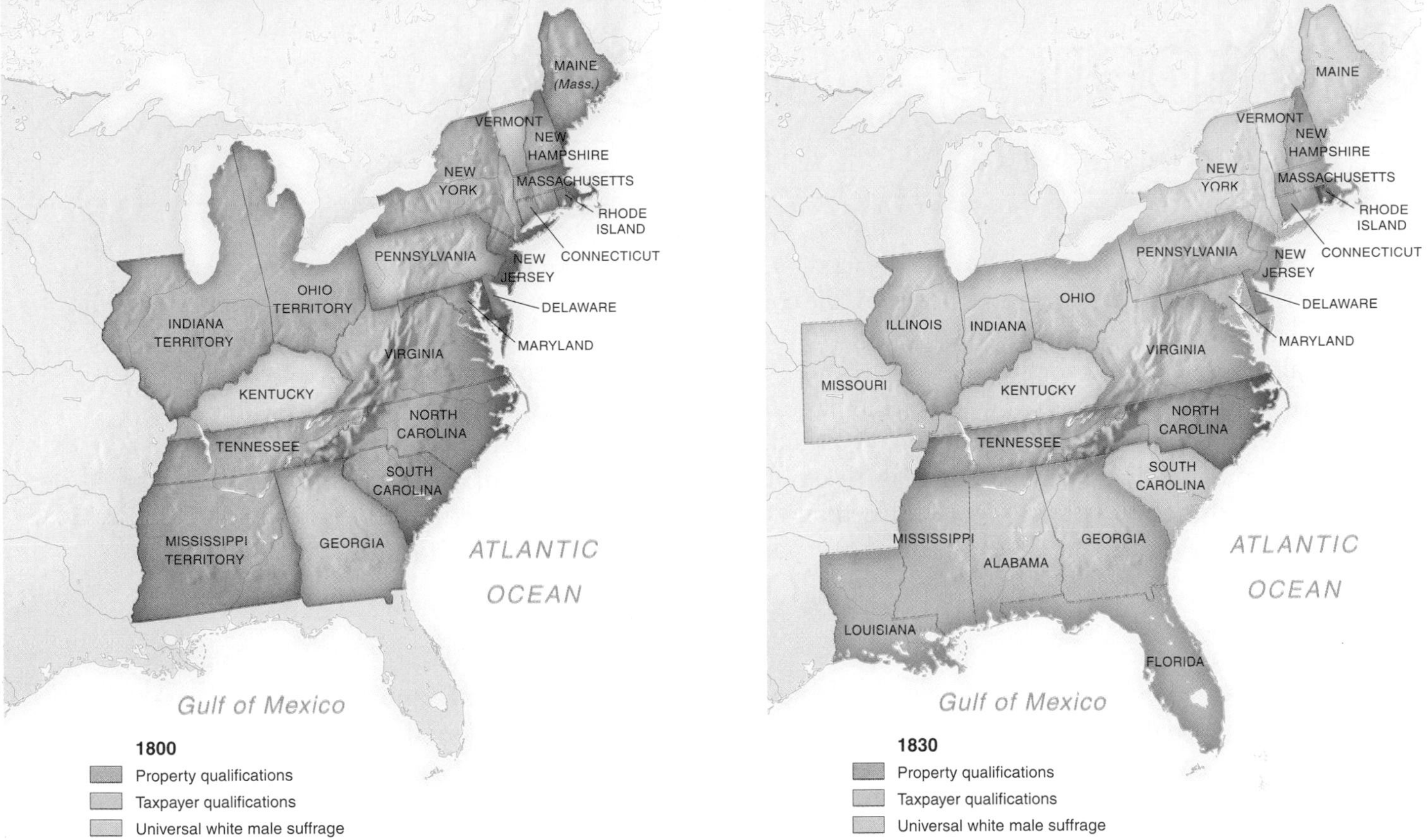

8.1 Changes in Suffrage Requirements between 1800 and 1828
Many of the Western states that entered the Union after 1800 did not impose property requirements for voting. By 1828, most states had eliminated such requirements.

Crockett's achievements inside the chambers of the state legislature and Congress paled in significance to the stories about his exploits as a frontiersmen and Indian fighter, myths that Crockett helped shape and market to a growing audience of readers eager to learn of his daring exploits. As one contemporary English magazine noted: "Democracy and the far west made Crockett: he is a product of forests, freedom, universal suffrage, and bear hunts."

In his own colorful account of his entry into politics, Crockett becomes a politician almost by accident. While coming to town to sell his pelts and furs, he exchanges a few words with local politicians, who immediately recognize him as a natural leader and draft him for the state legislature. Crockett's career in Congress was brief, but his fame grew as literary treatments recounted stories about his exploits. *Crockett's Almanac*, for example, a cheaply marketed magazine-like publication, vividly described the frontiersman-politician, whose honesty as a stump speaker and legendary adventures wrestling alligators, hunting bears, and fighting Indians captivated audiences. For Crockett delivering a stump speech meant literally standing on the nearest tree stump, as shown in this illustration from the *A Narrative of the Life of David Crockett Life* (**8.2**).

Although Crockett was a big hit on the stump and celebrated in the popular literature of the day, the most important political figure to make use of the association of the West with democracy was Andrew Jackson. The Tennessee-born Jackson had distinguished himself as a military leader during the battle of New Orleans and earned a reputation as a fierce Indian fighter during the Creek War (1813–1814). Jackson entered politics, serving as both a member of Congress and a member of the Senate. A supporter of Jackson described his political style as typical of the Western United States, where democratic values and egalitarian ideals flourished: "In Europe" custom "decreed that kings shall rule and the people submit. In this wilderness, as if by magic, a new and different order of things has appeared." Jackson's effort to link his Western origins with his democratic values became a key component of his political message for the rest of his career in public life.

8.2 Crockett as Politician
Crockett the frontiersman-politician addresses a crowd outside a rural tavern. Crockett reflected and helped shape the myth of frontier democracy in the new Republic.

What aspects of Davy Crockett's life made him a good symbol of frontier democracy?

Competing Visions

SHOULD WHITE MEN WITHOUT PROPERTY HAVE THE VOTE?

In 1821 New Yorkers gathered to revise their state's 1777 constitution. The issue of property requirements for elections proved to be one of the most heated in the convention. James Kent, a conservative lawyer and judge who began his career as a Federalist, defended the idea of property requirements. Kent's vision of politics was deeply hierarchical, which led him to oppose an expansion of suffrage. Kent was opposed by a group of younger politicians. Nathan Sanford, a man who entered politics fully a decade later than Kent, began his career as a Jeffersonian democrat. Jefferson's election to the presidency had not ushered in the reign of terror that his Federalist enemies predicted, and Sanford eagerly embraced the growing enthusiasm for democracy that marked politics in the early decades of the nineteenth century. Which man has a more optimistic view of human nature? Which theory of politics seems closer in spirit to the ideas behind the Federal Constitution?

The most eloquent champion of retaining property requirements was James Kent, a former State Supreme Court judge and Chancellor of the State of New York (an English-style judicial office that no longer exists). Kent warned that an unchecked democracy composed of the property-less and working classes would threaten the rights of private property.

The tendency of universal suffrage is to jeopardize the rights of property and the principles of liberty. There is a constant tendency in human society, and the history of every age proves it; there is a tendency in the poor to covet and to share the plunder of the rich; in the debtor to relax or avoid the obligation of contract … there is a tendency in ambitious and wicked men to inflame these combustible materials.

The notion that every man that works a day on the road, or serves an idle hour in the militia, is entitled as of right to an equal participation in the whole power of government is most unreasonable and has no foundation in justice… . Society is an association for the protection of property as well as life, and the individual who contributes only one cent to the common stock ought not to have the same power and influence in directing the property and concerns of the partnership as he who contributes his thousands.

Nathan Sanford was a lawyer from Long Island who entered politics as a Jeffersonian, holding several state offices before being elected as a senator from New York. Rather than focus on the need to protect property, Sanford argued that those who bore the burdens of government had earned a right to have a say in their government.

The question before us is the right of suffrage—who shall, or who shall not, have the right to vote … the principle of the scheme now proposed, is, that those who bear the burthens of the state, [paid taxes, served in the militia, or consented to volunteer to work on public works projects such as roads] should choose those that rule it… . To me, and the majority of the committee, it appeared the only reasonable scheme that those who are to be affected by the acts of the government, should be annually entitled to vote for those who administer it.

***Fourth of July in Center Square* by John Lewis Krimmel, 1819**

Why did James Kent oppose the elimination of property requirements?

Andrew Jackson and His Age

The new democratic spirit of American politics helped elevate Andrew Jackson's political career, and he in turn did everything in his power to promote his particular vision of democracy. Jackson's democratic ideas stopped well short of the most radical egalitarian ideas of his day. Indeed Jackson's vision of democracy had no room for blacks, Indians, or women. Still Jackson's invocation of the will of the people marked a turning point in the history of American political development. After Jackson, politicians from across the political spectrum would outdo each other in affirming their commitment to democracy and lavishing praise on the wisdom of the people.

Jackson's long road to the presidency began with his narrow defeat in 1824, which eventually led to his decisive victory in 1828. In contrast to earlier presidents who were drawn from the ranks of the nation's elite, Jackson was a self-made man. An orphan who rose to become a rich planter and influential political figure in his home state of Tennessee, Jackson became a symbol for American democracy. Indeed one of Jackson's supporters characterized the presidential election of 1828, in which Jackson squared off against John Quincy Adams for the second time, as a struggle in which "the Aristocracy and Democracy of the country are arrayed against each other." Others viewed Jackson's democratic leanings in a less positive light, however, viewing his election as the start of the "reign of King Mob." Jackson's presidency proved to be marred by deep divisions within his own administration and serious challenges from outside. In particular South Carolina's decision to respond to federal tariff policy by calling a convention to nullify federal law forced a showdown between Jackson and states' rights supporters.

The Election of 1824 and the "Corrupt Bargain"

James Monroe, the fourth Virginian to occupy the presidency since the adoption of the Constitution (1817–1825), anointed no political figure to be his successor and carry forward his policies and ideas. Following Washington's model Monroe had sought out a talented but diverse collection of men for his cabinet who represented a broad spectrum of political and economic views. Three of these cabinet ministers sought the presidency in 1824: William Crawford, secretary of the treasury; John Quincy Adams, secretary of state; and John C. Calhoun, secretary of war. A fourth candidate was Henry Clay, Speaker of the House of Representatives (who had turned down an offer to serve as secretary of war in the Adams administration). Andrew Jackson, hero of the battle of New Orleans, also joined the race for president. Jackson had served in Congress, as a judge in Tennessee, and as an appointed governor of the Florida territory.

Crawford, born in Virginia but raised in Georgia, was heir to the old Jeffersonian republican vision of politics with its emphasis on states' rights and strict construction of the Constitution. Crawford opposed Monroe's National Republican synthesis of Jeffersonian politics with Hamiltonian economics (see Chapter 7). In contrast to the other candidates in the crowded field, Crawford clearly opposed using federal power for economic development. Public expenditures for internal improvements, such as roads and canals, and charters for banks were government functions that the Constitution, Crawford argued, had wisely left to the individual states.

John Quincy Adams, the son of President John Adams, was a New Englander who had been a professor at Harvard and spent considerable time in Europe as a diplomat, serving in Holland, Prussia (now part of Germany), Great Britain, and Russia. As secretary of state he had not only successfully negotiated the Treaty of Ghent that ended the War of 1812 but also was largely responsible for formulating the Monroe Doctrine (see Chapter 7). A short,

What were the strengths of John Quincy Adams as a presidential candidate?

Our Country.....Home Industry.

MANUFACTURERS AND MECHANICS,

Your enemies have rallied under the banner of Gen. Jackson—the same man whom they a few days since declared a tyrant and a murderer. One of their avowed objects is a repeal of all the laws which have been enacted for the encouragement of manufactures.

If the Jackson Party prevail, a majority of the next Congress will be opposed to the tariff, to mechanics, manufacturers, and domestic industry. As proof of this, the Jackson papers, nearly one and all, have published articles recommending the repeal of all laws that have been passed to encourage our mechanics and manufacturers. The consequence will be, that the sound of the shuttle will no more be heard. Our stores will be filled with British and Scotch ginghams, shirtings, checks and bedticks; and not a place will be found for a yard of American cloth. British goods, labelled with Jackson's name, and in large quantities, have been sent among us.

The Legislature of Virginia, a majority of whom were Jacksonians, solemnly resolved, that all the laws passed for the protection of mechanics and manufacturers were a violation of the constitution. At a great Jackson meeting, held in South Carolina, a committee, previously appointed to ascertain public opinion, reported that nineteen-twentieths of the southern section of the country were opposed to all laws enacted to encourage manufactures. These are the warm advocates of General Jackson. Will you take away the power from such old tried friends as Henry Clay, who has always been your hearty supporter, and give it to your enemies? If you vote for the Jackson ticket, you will do it. If the Jackson Assembly ticket prevails, they mean to repeal the Electoral law, and appoint Electors that will drive Henry Clay, and all the friends of the American system, from office.

Fellow-citizens, Manufacturers, and Mechanics! be on the look out, or you will be most wofully betrayed. Don't suffer yourselves to be deceived by stories that General Jackson is your friend. He has consented to serve your enemies, and he must be judged by his company. What will his battle of New-Orleans avail you, if you are thrown out of employment and made beggars? Don't fail to go to the polls, and show by your votes that you are not the dupes of such men as Coleman, who has always been your enemy. He tells you to vote for General Jackson: vote directly opposite to his advice, and you will vote for your country. As a proof of this, I ask who has always sided with the British against his country? Will you not answer, Coleman? Who has abused the best patriots America ever produced? Is not Wm. Coleman the man? Who scandalized Madison? Who vilified Jefferson? Who has slandered Henry Clay? Has not Coleman been the man? He now asks you to vote for the party that uphold Jackson, and destroy your best friends; cripple your own occupation; build up England, and ruin the American system. This is the man who exulted when a British fleet lay off the Hook. The Evening Post was received wet from his office on board their ships every day. Nothing but respect for the laws prevented our incensed countrymen from demolishing the press and types that printed the diabolical treason.

Fellow-citizens! Henry Clay was your early friend. He first risked his all to sustain you. His speeches will be read as long as eloquence has admirers. By arguments unanswerable, he brought forward the American system. He has since sustained it; and if he is not sacrificed by those whom he has befriended, he will consummate the system he has begun. If General Jackson's party prevails, a majority of the next Congress will surely turn him, and every friend you have in the Administration, from their places; and the truest, ablest, and best friend you ever had will be destroyed. It is for his friendship to you that Virginia, his native state, has denounced him. It is for this that Georgia and the Carolinas have libelled him. It is for this that the enemies of the American system, the Colemans, Pickerings, and Coopers, whether British by birth or choice, have vilified him, and cruelly endeavoured to blast his character. This is what has made every British agent that lurks in our city the traducer of Henry Clay. The history of depravity affords nothing that exceeds the vileness of their calumny towards him—witness the testimony of their own witness, Buchanan.

Go to the Polls—put down the favorite British candidates—vindicate your friends—and save yourselves and your country.

ON BEHALF OF THE MANUFACTURERS.

8.3 Our Country ... Home Industry This detail of an election broadside links John Quincy Adams with Clay's American System. The images at the top symbolize the way the American system would help manufacturing, commerce, and agriculture.

balding, intellectual figure, Adams was neither charismatic nor politically astute; he even admitted that he could seem dogmatic and pedantic. Before entering the race for president, his primary experience had been in foreign, not domestic, politics.

John C. Calhoun, the other Southerner in the race, had been a prominent War Hawk during the War of 1812. An astute politician Calhoun decided to withdraw from the crowded race. Jackson and Adams each accepted him as their running mate, which virtually guaranteed his election to the office of vice president. Calhoun expected to bide his time until the moment was more auspicious to mount another try for the presidency.

Henry Clay, the vivacious Speaker of the House from Kentucky, began his career as a War Hawk during the War of 1812. On economic issues Clay had the most clearly developed vision of America's future. Clay built on Monroe's neo-Hamiltonian policies, pushing them in a more nationalistic direction. Monroe favored federal support for internal improvements such as roads as a matter of policy, but he maintained some of the same constitutional reservations about such policies that his predecessors Jefferson and Madison had articulated. Clay was an unapologetic champion of aggressive federal involvement in economic development. The **American System**, Clay's plan for using the power of the federal government to encourage American industry, included tariffs to help protect American industry by keeping cheap foreign goods from undermining American producers, continuing support for a national bank, and an ambitious program of federal funding for internal improvements.

Clay's theory sought a harmonious interplay between agriculture, industry, and commerce. John Quincy Adams endorsed the essence of Clay's American system; this election broadside (**8.3**) reflects his support for Clay's economic policies. The central image of a ship symbolizes commerce, while the two smaller vignettes depict a farmer at the plow and a worker at a loom. The name of the ship, *John Quincy Adams*, symbolizes Adams's claim to be a proven leader who could pilot the nation to a prosperous future.

Of the major candidates for the presidency in 1824, Andrew Jackson's agenda was the least defined. Clay and Adams sought to portray Jackson as an opponent of the American System, and Jackson tried to finesse the issue by stressing that he wished to support commerce, agriculture, and industry. Jackson's campaign focused less on issues and more on character and underlying political values. Jackson fashioned himself as a frontier democrat whose honesty and courage were his primary credentials for the presidency.

In the divided field Jackson won 42 percent of the popular vote and the most electoral votes, but he fell short of the majority in the Electoral College necessary to win the election (**8.4**). Under such circumstances the Constitution directed that the House of Representatives choose from among the top three candidates. Henry Clay did not emerge as one of the frontrunners in this tight race, but his powerful role as Speaker of the House made him a key player in determining the outcome. Given the choice among Crawford, an old-style Jeffersonian who opposed Clay's vision for America's future; Jackson, whose support for a more nationalist economic program was lukewarm at best; and Adams, who was sympathetic to Clay's American System, the choice was an easy one for Clay. Adams became president.

Adams chose Clay to be his secretary of state, which in this era functioned as the stepping-stone

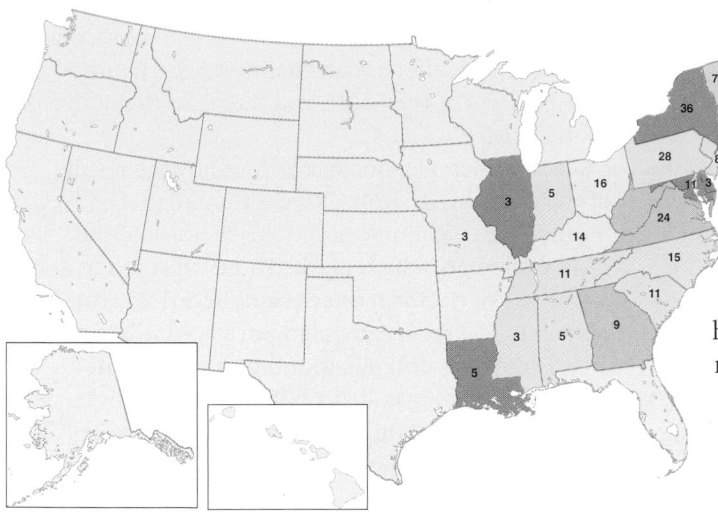

4 Electoral vote by state	Electoral Vote (%)	Popular Vote (%)
John Quincy Adams (Democratic-Republican)	84 (32)	108,740 (31)
Andrew Jackson (Democratic-Republican)	99 (38)	153,544 (44)
William H. Crawford (Democratic-Republican)	41 (16)	40,856 (12)
Henry Clay (Federalist)	37 (14)	47,531 (14)
States that split electoral votes		

8.4 Electoral Votes and Popular Votes 1824
Although Jackson won the most votes, no candidate gained a majority in the Electoral College. After the House of Representatives decided the outcome, Jackson claimed that Adams and Clay had struck a "corrupt bargain" to deprive him of the presidency.

for the office of the presidency. (In the United States today, the vice presidency sometimes functions as the path toward the presidency.) Jackson and his supporters charged that Clay had traded his support for the office of secretary of state in a "**corrupt bargain**" that deprived Jackson of the presidency and gave the election to Adams.

Adams embraced Clay's American system. In addition to supporting Clay's plan for public expenditures on internal improvement projects, including new roads and canals, Adams hoped to create a national university and an astronomical observatory. Yet while he embraced the forward-looking nationalist vision of economic development associated with Clay's American System, Adams was an eighteenth-century politician when it came to thinking about the role of the president as a virtuous leader who stood above partisan bickering. He continued to believe that Monroe's goal of rising above party was not only laudable but also achievable. Rather than use his patronage powers as president to reward his political friends and consolidate his administration's power, Adams appointed individuals on the basis of merit, with little concern for their political loyalties or even their commitment to his agenda or to him personally. Adams proudly proclaimed his intention to "discard every element of rancor" and "yield to talents and virtue." One exasperated supporter of the president complained that "the friends of the administration have to contend not only against their enemies," but "against the Administration itself, which leaves its power in the hands of its own enemies." Adams sought to move beyond partisanship at a time when America was on the verge of becoming more politically polarized.

Adams made another tactical error when he chastised Congress for refusing to embrace his economic agenda. He accused legislators of being hampered "by the will of their constituents." Seen in light of his republican belief in the need for virtuous leadership, Adams's comment invited Congress to lead rather than follow the nation. For his opponents, however, the remark smacked of condescension and elitism. His comments were out of step with the rising tide of democratic sentiment that had swept over American society. For those who supported this new, more democratic ethos, Adams had maligned the people. Andrew Jackson and his supporters exploited Adams's gaffe, using it to highlight their own commitment to democracy. Jackson extolled "the voice of the people" and attacked Adams for his apparent haughty contempt for the popular will.

The Election of 1828: "Old Hickory's" Triumph

The election of 1828, which saw Andrew Jackson squaring off with John Quincy Adams for a second try at the presidency, was a pivotal moment in American politics. Jackson trumpeted his humble origins, military career, and support for democratic values. Jackson's supporters applauded their candidate's commitment to democracy and lambasted Adams's aristocratic pretensions.

8.5 "Some Account of the Bloody Deeds of General Jackson" This pro-John Quincy Adams broadside casts Jackson as a brutal despot whose military record demonstrated that he was unfit to be president. The coffins symbolized the six militiamen Jackson ordered executed for desertion during the Creek War (1813–1814).

Adams's supporters defended his traditional republican ideals and support for the American System and warned voters that Jackson was a demagogue who would undermine America's constitutional system.

At a more fundamental level, Jackson rejected the antiparty sentiments of Monroe and Adams. Jackson set out to win the presidency in 1828, forming an alliance with Crawford and Calhoun to defeat Adams and Clay in the election. The politician who formulated the strategy for this new alliance was New York's Martin Van Buren, an influential Republican figure in New York politics who had served both as a state senator and a U.S. senator. Van Buren's supporters were nicknamed "Bucktails" because they wore buck tails (the tails of a deer) on their hats instead of feathers. Van Buren embraced the idea of party with a passion. His goal was to re-create the old Jeffersonian coalition, which united "the planters of the South and the plain Republicans of the North."

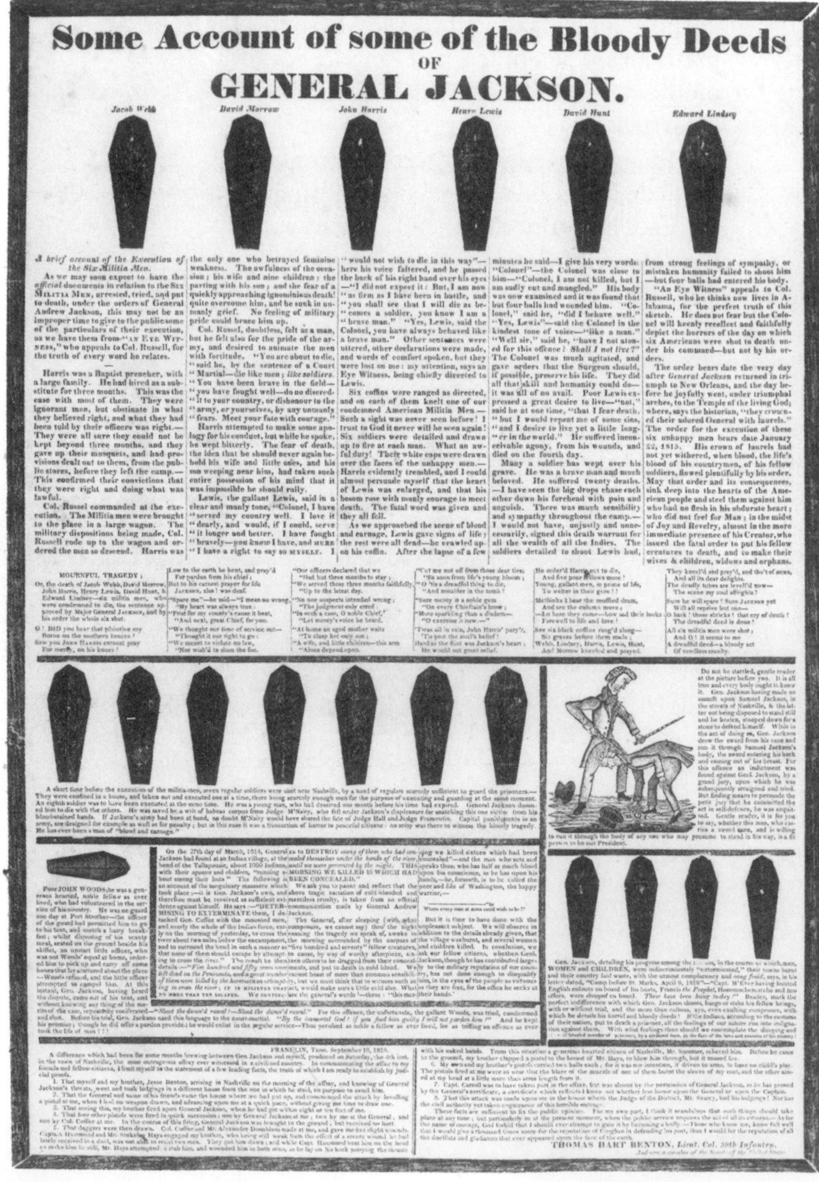
Some Account of some of the Bloody Deeds of GENERAL JACKSON.

Jacob Webb · David Morrow · John Harris · Henry Lewis · David Hunt · Edward Lindsey

Jackson felt personally aggrieved by the result of the election of 1824. Charges that Adams had "stolen" that election colored the rhetoric of the 1828 campaign, which marked a new low in terms of the use of personal attacks and negative campaigning. Jackson's campaign portrayed Adams as an aristocrat of dubious morality, pointing out that Adams had installed a billiard table in the White House. Although now known as a popular recreation, originally billiards was an aristocratic pastime. Perhaps the most sensational claim the Jackson campaign made against Adams was that during Adams's time as a diplomat in Russia he had "made use of a beautiful girl to seduce the passions of the Emperor." The Jacksonians charged that Adams was a licentious aristocrat with perverse sexual values.

The attack on Adams's character was more than matched by the ferocious assaults on Jackson's morality. The smear campaign against Jackson also charged him with sexual immorality, challenging the legality of his marriage. Supporters of Adams claimed that Jackson had seduced a married woman and lived with her in "open and notorious lewdness" before she had legally divorced her first husband. Jackson, they claimed, was a violent, brawling frontiersman who could not be trusted with the nation's highest office. The Adams campaign even attacked Jackson's military accomplishments. Philadelphia printer John Binn's "Coffin Handbill" (**8.5**) detailed the "bloody deeds of General Jackson," who had in fact executed six militiamen during the war against the Creek Indians. The author of the pamphlet warned Americans about the danger of putting "at the head of our government, a man who was never known to govern himself."

In Jackson's defense his supporters cast the general as "**Old Hickory**," a rough-and-tumble democrat and latter-day George Washington whose plain frontier code of ethics contrasted with Adams's elitist eastern values. To call attention to Jackson's reputation as the hero of the battle of New Orleans, his supporters gathered on the anniversary of the victory to plant hickory trees and raise liberty poles made of hickory. They ridiculed Adams's bookish temperament, chanting "Adams can write" but "Jackson can fight." Supporters of Adams answered the smears by praising "his long and varied public

How did the "Coffin Handbill" attempt to discredit Andrew Jackson?

services, his great experience, his talent, his learning."

To get out their message, Jackson's supporters developed a sophisticated and highly organized campaign apparatus. A centralized committee in Nashville directed the actions of local and state Jackson committees, who in turn worked with local "Hickory Clubs." In addition to these innovations in campaign organization, Jackson's supporters created an effective network of pro-Jackson newspapers to get out the word about their candidate. Eighteen new pro-Jackson newspapers sprouted up in Ohio alone. The Jacksonians also pioneered new fundraising tactics to pay for their campaign, including public banquets and other ticketed events in which supporters gathered to celebrate the achievements of their candidate. They developed an astonishing range of campaign knick-knacks and mementos, including badges, plates, sewing boxes, and ceramics. Jacksonians also used rallies and parades effectively to spark enthusiasm for their candidate. The tactics of Jackson and his supporters galvanized the electorate. In 1824 only about one-fourth of the eligible voters had participated; in 1828 more than half of the electorate turned out to vote. In the end Jackson won an impressive victory, garnering more than twice as many electoral votes as Adams.

The Reign of "King Mob"

Andrew Jackson's inaugural in January 1829 captured the new democratic spirit of the age. Jackson's supporters poured into Washington for the event, captured in this contemporary print of the crowds who thronged the White House (**8.6**). Margaret Bayard Smith, a Washington socialite, described the scene in detail. "Thousands and thousands of people, without distinction of rank, collected in an immense mass around the Capitol." Smith was shocked not only by the composition of the crowd but also by its rowdiness. The boisterous attendees, she recounted, broke "glass and bone china to the amount of several thousand dollars." Smith was clearly ambivalent about the inauguration of the "people's president." She was impressed by the "majesty" of the people assembled at the swearing-in ceremony but disturbed by the rude and disorderly behavior of Jackson's supporters at the reception that followed at the White House. This print of the inaugural confirms Smith's impressions that Jackson's inaugural was a popular affair, drawing a much more diverse crowd than previous inaugurals had. Not everyone was as impressed by the people's majesty. Supreme Court Justice Joseph Story complained that Jackson's inaugural had ushered in the "the reign of King Mob."

In contrast to Adams, who refused to use his powers of appointment to reward his political supporters, Jackson was unabashed in appointing his supporters to office. In his first inaugural Jackson defended the need for rotation in government offices. Jackson rejected the traditional republican notion, advanced by John Quincy Adams, that government offices were best reserved for a small elite, typically drawn from the ranks of the wealthy and well educated. "The duties of all public officers," Jackson maintained, were "plain and simple." One Jackson supporter proudly proclaimed that he saw "nothing wrong in the rule that to the victor belong the spoils of the enemy." Opponents mocked Jackson's appointments as "men of narrow minds" who were "hardly gentlemen." Opponents also attacked Jackson's system of replacing government officeholders with those loyal

8.6 "President's Levee, or all Creation going to the White House" This image of the boisterous crowd in front of the White House during Jackson's inaugural captures the fear that his presidency would usher in the "reign of King Mob."

How did the spoils system further Jackson's democratic agenda?

8.7 Office Seekers In this attack on the spoils system, a demonic Andrew Jackson dangles the spoils of victory before eager office seekers.

to him as the **spoils system**. This cartoon (**8.7**) shows Jackson dangling the spoils of victory before eager office seekers. However Jackson's practices were less radical than his rhetoric. Only 20 percent of federal officeholders lost their job because of Jackson's new policy.

Apart from his appointment of Martin Van Buren as secretary of state, Jackson's cabinet comprised undistinguished figures selected for their loyalty to Jackson. Shortly after Jackson had assembled his cabinet, another sexual scandal engulfed his administration. The controversy swirled around his new secretary of war, John Eaton, a close friend of the president. Washington society, prone to gossip, began spreading rumors that Eaton's wife, Peggy, the daughter of a Washington tavern keeper, was a promiscuous woman who had engaged in a clandestine affair with Eaton before their marriage. The fact that Peggy's first husband had committed suicide only further besmirched her reputation. Still angry over the attacks on the legitimacy of his own marriage (his wife died before Jackson took office), the president defended Peggy Eaton's reputation and ordered his cabinet members to do likewise. The Eaton scandal, which some contemporaries described as "Eaton Malaria," consumed Jackson's presidency for months, preventing him from focusing on pressing public matters. Because the wife of the vice president, Floride Calhoun, had been one of the most prominent women to snub Peggy Eaton, the Eaton affair also strained the already tense relations between Jackson and Vice President John C. Calhoun. The disruption to Jackson's administration forced the president to fire most of his cabinet in 1831.

States Rights and the Nullification Crisis

Even if Jackson and Vice President Calhoun had not fallen out over the Eaton affair, the two men were on a collision course. The rift between the two widened as the politics of states' rights divided the nation. Calhoun's home state of South Carolina became a hotbed of radical states' rights doctrine, and Calhoun was forced to carry the banner of states' rights forward or retire from public life. Choosing to take up the cause, Calhoun became one of its leading spokesmen. The issue that vexed South Carolina was federal tariffs on imported goods. In 1828 Congress passed new tariff legislation that enacted high import duties on a variety of goods, including textiles. The South objected to the tariff, believing that Britain would retaliate against America by raising tariffs on imported cotton, a move that would hurt Southern agriculture. John C. Calhoun secretly wrote a manifesto, *Exposition and Protest* (1828), defending South Carolina's right to nullify, or make legally void, the 1828 tariff. Calhoun's

What was the theory of states' rights?

manifesto developed ideas first articulated by Jefferson and Madison in the Virginia and Kentucky Resolutions and fashioned them into a radical theory of states' rights (see Chapter 6). According to Calhoun the Union was a sovereign compact among the people of the states. When the states and the national government disagreed over the constitutionality of a federal law, Calhoun asserted, the states were entitled to judge the constitutionality of federal laws. This position challenged both the supremacy of the federal government and the power of the federal courts to be the final arbiter on the constitutionality of federal laws. Asserting that a state could call special conventions to nullify federal laws, Calhoun's doctrine of **nullification** went further than either Jefferson or Madison's earlier defenses of states' rights.

The issue of states' rights resurfaced in 1830 when Congress debated a proposal to limit sales of Western lands. Samuel Foot, a senator from Connecticut, proposed to slow western expansion by cutting back on the public sale of Western lands, a decision that would have also robbed the government of revenues and made it even more dependent on tariffs. Prompting Foot's resolution was a report from the land office that 72 million acres of land already surveyed remained unsold. Thomas Hart Benton of Missouri and Robert Hayne of South Carolina rose in the Senate to denounce Foot's resolution. Benton and Hayne saw an opportunity to forge a southern and western alliance against New England's commercial interests. Benton saw Foot's proposal as a means for New England's industrialists to maintain their supply of cheap labor by making it harder for laborers to settle on Western lands. Hayne took a different tactic; framing the issue in terms of South Carolina's theory of states' rights, he moved beyond the specifics of Foot's proposal to suggest that federal control over Western lands was itself a source of danger since it encouraged the growth of federal power. Hayne suggested that Western lands be returned to those states in which they were located.

Daniel Webster, senator from Massachusetts, responded directly to Hayne's proposal, attacking the South Carolinian's theory of states' rights. The ensuing debate between Hayne and Webster was a brilliant display of rhetoric and oratory. One contemporary observer recalled: "It was a day never to be forgotten by those who witnessed the scene in the Senate Chamber and a day destined to be forever memorable in the Annals of the Senate." In a riveting speech Webster concluded by denouncing the theory of states' rights and asserting the supremacy of the Union over the individual states: "Liberty and Union, now and forever, one and inseparable." Building on ideas developed by Hamilton and John Marshall (see Chapter 6 and Chapter 7), Webster's constitutional nationalism denied that the states could judge the constitutionality of federal laws and rejected the theory of nullification.

The contemporary press widely reprinted Webster's reply to Hayne. The speech became an instant classic; schoolchildren would recite it throughout the Northeast for generations. This meticulous historical painting by artist George Healy (**8.8**) immortalized the debate. In the painting Webster, pausing for a moment's reflection, stands in

"Every seat, every inch of ground, even the steps, were compactly filled, and yet not space enough for the ladies—the Senators were obliged to relinquish their chairs of the State to the fair auditors who literally sat in the Senate."
MARGARET SMITH'S recollections of the Senate Chamber during Webster's reply to Hayne

8.8 ***Webster Replying to Hayne*** George Healy's painting of Webster's famous speech is reminiscent of Bingham's *Stump Speaking*. Calhoun Is presented as a wiry character, while Webster stands tall, a model of virtue.

How did Webster's theory of the Union contrast with Calhoun's theory of states' rights?

a hushed Senate Chamber. Onlookers crowd the galleries, transfixed by the senator's oratory. Not shown in the painting, a number of senators had given up their Senate seats in the chamber to accommodate the many women who attended to hear the speech. Healey instead placed all the women in the Senate gallery, a decision likely motivated by his belief that this would be less distracting and give the painting a more serious air.

With the Webster-Hayne debate fresh in everyone's memory, supporters of states' rights gathered in Washington to honor the memory of Thomas Jefferson. Hayne and Calhoun both attended this dinner as did President Jackson. When Hayne concluded a long address devoted to defending states' rights, attention turned to Andrew Jackson, who was expected to propose a toast to Hayne's pro-states' rights sentiments. Having always been a moderate supporter of the doctrine of states' rights, Jackson would surely support Hayne, the crowd thought. They were shocked, however, when Jackson lifted his glass and proclaimed, "Our Federal Union. It must be preserved." Rather than echo Hayne, the president appeared to echo Webster. Vice President Calhoun, who had become an outspoken defender of states' rights, responded with his own toast, "The Union, next to our liberties, the most dear." Realizing that he could not effectively defend the interests of South Carolina and promulgate the cause of states' rights from the position of vice president, Calhoun resigned. South Carolina promptly elected him to the Senate.

The issue of states' rights and nullification was once again at the center of American political life as the controversy over tariffs heated up another time. Congress intended the Tariff Act of 1832, which President Jackson signed, to be a conciliatory gesture to South Carolina. Although the new act lowered import duties, South Carolinians continued to view tariffs as an illegitimate effort by one section of the nation to wage economic war against another. The state of South Carolina called a convention and issued a declaration nullifying the tariff. Andrew Jackson denounced Carolina's actions as "subversive of the Constitution." Privately Jackson warned that if South Carolina spilled a drop of blood in "defiance of the laws of the United States," he would, "hang the first man of them I can get my hands on to the first tree I can find." Missouri senator Thomas Hart Benton, warned that when President Jackson "begins to talk about hanging, they can begin to look out for ropes." This contemporary cartoon attacking nullification (**8.9**) highlights Jackson's tough stance toward the nullifiers. The president, restraining one of Calhoun's supporters, declares, "Stop you have gone too far. Or by the Eternal I will hang you all!"

The president persuaded Congress to pass a **Force Bill** that gave him the power to use military force to collect revenues, including tariffs. At the same time that Jackson was adopting a public tough stance, Henry Clay was working behind the scenes to avert a confrontation. On the same day that Congress passed the Force Bill, it also passed a compromise measure that scaled back tariffs. In response to this conciliatory gesture, South Carolina rescinded its act of nullification, but not before issuing another act nullifying the Force Act. Clay's compromise measure had narrowly averted a constitutional crisis in which the states and the federal government had nearly come to blows. For the moment the conflict between states' rights and a more nationalist vision of the Constitution had been settled in favor of the latter theory.

Although Jackson adopted a hard line with South Carolina, he would prove to be far more flexible when federal and state power collided over other issues, notably Indian rights. Jackson's democratic nationalism had little room for anyone but white men. The narrowness of his democratic vision would become increasingly clear during his term as president.

8.9 *Despotism*
In this anti-nullification cartoon Calhoun ascends a platform that leads from nullification to despotism.

How does the political cartoonist represent nullification theory in the cartoon *Despotism*?

White Man's Democracy

The democratic ideas that swept Andrew Jackson into the presidency were premised on a vision of society that was not truly inclusive: it excluded blacks and Indians, and showed little interest in women's rights. The new state constitutions drafted in the Jacksonian era expanded rights for nonproperty-owning white men at the same time that they stripped voting rights from property-owning African Americans. The plight of American Indians also became a major issue during Jackson's presidency. Jackson and his supporters sought to restrict Indians' rights and expropriate their lands.

Although the revised state constitutions systematically stripped away rights from free blacks, African American communities created a network of thriving communities in the free states of the North and the old Northwest (the modern Midwestern states of Ohio, Indiana, Michigan, and Illinois). However, harassment of African Americans in the nation's cities also increased during the Jacksonian era. Indeed the struggles of African Americans to achieve some measure of economic and social respectability prompted vicious attacks in the popular press.

Jacksonian democracy showed little regard for the rights of Indian peoples. The Cherokee fought a valiant effort to defend their rights within the rules established by the Constitution and learned that the rule of law provided scant protection against racism and a rapacious desire for Indian land.

Race and Politics in the Jacksonian Era

While many individual states were expanding the suffrage for white men, many other states were imposing new restrictions on black men. The 1821 New York state constitutional convention that had abolished property requirements for white men adopted a high property requirement for African Americans that effectively disenfranchised most blacks. Thus while the state's African American population numbered some thirty thousand in 1825, fewer than three hundred black men were eligible to vote. New York's actions were part of a broader pattern of racial exclusion that limited the rights of African Americans throughout the North and West. African Americans lost the right to vote in Rhode Island in 1822 and Pennsylvania in 1838. Most of the new states that entered the Union after 1819, apart from Maine, denied suffrage to African Americans.

Many states also passed laws regulating the conduct of free African Americans. In 1831 Indiana passed a law requiring that "Negroes and mulattoes emigrating in the state" post a bond (much like prisoners awaiting trial were expected to do) or be deported. Illinois not only barred blacks from voting but also prohibited them from testifying in court or bringing civil law suits. Ohio barred African Americans from access to the courts in "any controversy where either party to the sale is a white person" and passed a law declaring that African Americans "have no constitutional right to present their petitions to the General Assembly for any purpose whatsoever."

Gradual emancipation schemes in the North increased the number of free blacks in the North and West. In part the intensification of racism reflected concern over economic competition from the rising number of free blacks. Yet despite the legal barriers placed in the way of African Americans' economic progress, vibrant communities grew in many parts of the North. The most obvious measure of the success of these communities was the rise of a rich array of African American cultural and economic institutions, including churches, fraternal organizations, and benefit societies. African Americans published their first newspaper, *Freedom's Journal*, in New York in 1827.

The efforts of free blacks in the North and West to improve their conditions became a subject of widespread comment in the press. Typically the press lampooned the efforts of African Americans to attain some measure of cultural and economic respectability. Exploiting this popular racism, artist

What types of legal disabilities did blacks face outside of the slave South?

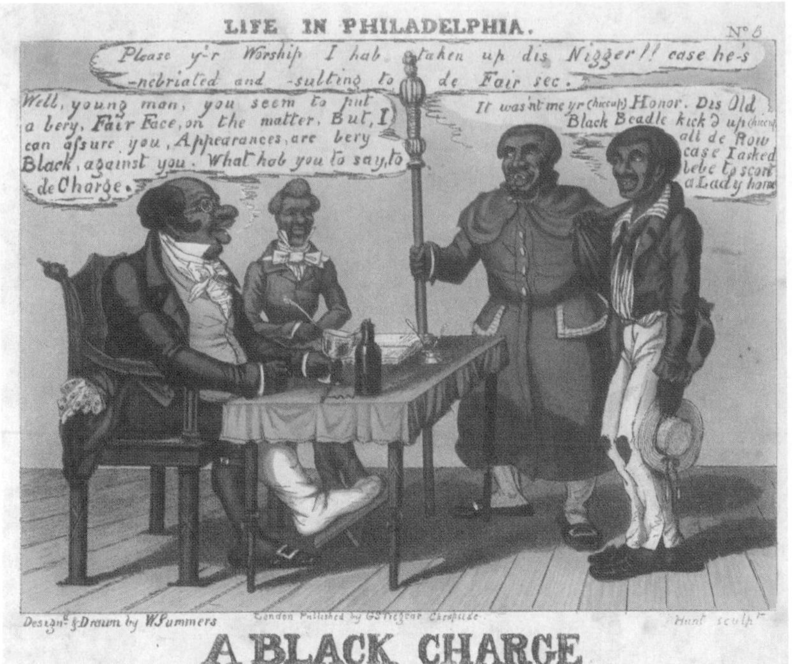

8.10 *A Black Charge*
From a series of racist caricatures of black life in Philadelphia, this image lampoons African American aspirations to respectability. A church official disciplines a church member for alleged misconduct. [*Source:* The Library Company of Philadelphia]

Edward William Clay published a series of fourteen cartoons ridiculing Philadelphia's African American community. For example in *A Black Charge* (**8.10**), Clay mocks a black church official who must attempt to discipline a disorderly member of his community. As was typical in all of the racist caricatures of this era, the artist has exaggerated the physical appearances of African Americans and caricatured their speech patterns, suggesting that blacks could only speak a distorted form of English.

The racism inherent in the notion of a white man's democracy was directed not only at African Americans but also at Indians. Racism played a central role in Jackson's Indian policy. Andrew Jackson's military reputation was closely identified with his role as an Indian fighter. At the conclusion of the Creek War (1812–1813) Jackson had seized 23 million acres of Creek land, more than half of present-day Alabama and part of Georgia. Jackson treated the Indians as conquered subjects, not as a sovereign people. Given this status of the Indians, Jackson did not believe that "treaties with Indians" could be "reconciled to the principles of our government." Jackson's dealings with Indian peoples during his presidency were also consistent with his view that Indians were culturally inferior to whites, and that their civilization was on the path toward extinction. In Jackson's political calculus white settlers' need for land was paramount and the rights of Indians carried little if any weight. These beliefs shaped Jackson's response to the conflict between the state of Georgia and the Cherokee Indians.

The Cherokee were among the Indian peoples that white Americans described as the "Five civilized tribes:" Cherokees, Choctaws, Seminoles, Creeks, and Chickasaws. These five Indian tribes earned this name because to varying degrees they chose the path of cultural assimilation rather than resistance to America's expansionist policies. These tribes together numbered some 75,000 people who were spread out over the Carolinas, Georgia, Alabama, Mississippi, and Tennessee. Adopting the agricultural practices of their white neighbors and converting to Christianity were two major efforts the tribes made to accommodate to American culture.

No tribe was more committed to the strategy of accommodation than the Cherokee. The Cherokee nation took a dramatic series of steps to assert its right to govern itself and exist as a sovereign nation. They converted to Christianity, established schools, and practiced American-style agriculture; a few prosperous Cherokees even kept slaves to work on their cotton plantations, mimicking their white neighbors in Georgia. In addition they abandoned their traditional form of tribal governance, declared themselves an independent republic, and adopted a constitution modeled on the Federal Constitution. As a sovereign nation they claimed to enjoy all the legal privileges that all nations enjoyed and were therefore not subject to the laws of the state of Georgia. However the ideas that the Cherokee wished to enact, such as becoming an independent nation within the territorial confines of Georgia, did not sit well with the government of the state.

When Georgians discovered gold on Cherokee land in 1828, a horde of non-Indian prospectors tried to stake out claims on Indian lands, a clear violation of tribal authority and law. Declaring tribal law null and void, the state of Georgia backed the prospectors and passed a law that stripped the tribe of any legal authority over their lands. Henceforth Georgia law, not Cherokee law, would govern the Cherokee. The state also created a special police force, the Georgia Guard, to patrol Indian territory. The tribe lobbied opponents of Jackson sympathetic to their plight and turned to the federal courts for protection, arguing that Georgia's actions violated treaties between the Cherokee and the United States.

While the Cherokee awaited their day in court, Jackson turned up the pressure on them. The president refused the Cherokee's plea for federal troops to protect them. Since Indians could not testify in Georgia courts, the Cherokee were left without any legal means of defending their rights under the laws of Georgia.

Jackson seized the opportunity provided by the Georgia crisis to advance a plan to remove the Cherokee from Georgia and relocate them to Western lands beyond the Mississippi River. Jackson cast himself as benevolent father, intervening to rescue the Cherokee from certain extinction. Jackson's program would not force Indians to leave, but it made it extremely unattractive for anyone to remain behind. The program would relegate Indians who refused to relocate to the status of free blacks, who had only minimal legal rights under Georgia law. Jackson presented the Cherokee with two equally disastrous choices: accept the legal destruction of their tribal identity and live as second-class citizens in Georgia, or relocate to a distant territory far from their ancestral homes.

Jackson's opponents in Congress, many of whom had close ties to Protestant churches and missionary societies that had helped convert the Cherokees to Christianity, attacked his proposals. New Jersey's senator Theodore Frelinghuysen wondered if "it is one of the prerogatives of the white man, that he may disregard the dictates of moral principles, when an Indian shall be concerned." Others attacked the president's proposal as a sham that offered Indians no legal protections if they stayed and allocated few resources to allow them to make a safe journey west. In this cartoon critical of Jackson's Indian policy (**8.11**), the president leads a parade that includes the devil and a group of caged Indians.

Protestant clergymen who had taken a leading role in converting Indians to Christianity led the opposition to Jackson's Indian policy. However although they valiantly defended Indian rights, religious leaders who opposed removal were not great champions of Indian culture. Indeed the religious defense of Indian rights shared many of the racist assumptions about Indians and their cultures of Jackson and others eager to dispossess Indians. Yet these supporters of Indians' rights believed that the supposed "inferiority" of Indian culture did not sanction unjust treatment or the violation of Indian rights. Women's reformers also rallied to the cause of Indian rights. Women's groups touted themselves as disinterested guardians of public morality who were not subject to the "blinding influence of party spirit." Removal, they argued, threatened the ongoing effort to Christianize and civilize the Indians. Invoking the moral authority of women's own spheres, opponents attacked Jackson's policies as an affront to church, school, and the family. Indeed such appeals were so effective that Martin Van Buren, Jackson's chief lieutenant, was shocked that his own niece opposed Jackson's

8.11 *The Grand National Caravan Moving East*
In this attack on Jackson's Indian policy, the president leads a parade that includes the devil playing a fiddle and a group of caged Indians.

How does the Grand Caravan represent Jackson's Indian policy?

policy and hoped that the president would lose his bid for reelection in 1832!

The Jacksonians defeated the supporters of Indian rights and passed their removal bill by a narrow margin. The **Indian Removal Act of 1830** gave President Jackson the authority to confiscate Indians lands within the borders of the existing states. Although some tribes reluctantly accepted the inevitability of relocation, other resisted. The Cherokee eloquently protested against their forced relocation. Cherokee leaders stated their desire to remain on the land of their ancestors and reminded Americans that their existing treaties with the United States guaranteed them this right.

"We wish to remain on the land of our fathers. We have a perfect and original right to remain without interruption or molestation."

Address of a council of the Cherokee nation to the people of the United States, written in July of 1830.

The Cherokee Cases

The struggle between the state of Georgia and the Cherokee raised important constitutional questions. The Cherokee claimed to be a sovereign nation not subject to the laws of the state of Georgia. As was true of any sovereign nation, they claimed the right to govern themselves by rules that their own legislature enacted and claimed the right to deal with the United States as a sovereign power. Georgia rejected both these claims, arguing that Indians were subjects of the United States and that the idea of an independent Indian state within Georgia was an absurdity. The status of Indian nations in American constitutional law came before the Supreme Court of the United States in two separate cases related to the claims of the Cherokee nation.

In the **Cherokee Cases**, *Cherokee Nation v. Georgia (*1830) and *Worcester v. Georgia* (1832), the Supreme Court determined that Indian nations retained certain rights traditionally associated with sovereign nations, including the right to govern themselves by their own laws, but lacked other rights, such as the ability to sue the state of Georgia. The latter case came to the Supreme Court because Georgia had imprisoned two Protestant missionaries, Samuel Worcester and Elizur Butler, charging them with residing on Indian land without obtaining a license from the state. As both men were citizens of the United States, clearly they were entitled to sue in federal courts. Writing for the Supreme Court, Chief Justice John Marshall found that the missionaries had been wrongly imprisoned and were entitled to protection by the federal courts. Moreover Marshall gave the Cherokee an important victory when he held that "the laws of Georgia can have no force" on Cherokee territory. Although the Cherokee did not enjoy all the privileges accorded foreign nations by U.S. law, they did retain the right to make laws within their own lands.

Some Cherokee leaders, including Elias Boudinot—who believed that with the courts on their side, Georgia would have no alternative but to respect the Cherokee's rights—greeted Marshall's ruling in *Worcester* enthusiastically. Others within the tribe, including Chief John Ross, were more wary of putting excessive faith in the rule of law when Indian rights were at issue. Sadly Ross, not Boudinot, turned out to be right. Georgia refused to accept the high court's ruling and did not release the imprisoned missionaries. President Jackson was unwilling to antagonize Georgia, and was generally ill-disposed to Indians rights. He refused to enforce Marshall's decision. The case might have precipitated a major constitutional crisis: A president refusing to follow an injunction from the court would have challenged the legitimacy of the entire federal judiciary. Jackson decided to avoid such a showdown by persuading the governor of Georgia to simply pardon Worcester and Butler. Once the men were freed, the legal issue vanished, and Jackson and Marshall were no longer pitted against one another.

Resistance and Removal

The release of the two missionaries eliminated any legal issues and cleared the way for the Jackson administration to pursue its policy of removal. The Cherokee now faced the painful choice of accepting the inevitability of removal or continuing to resist Jackson and the state of Georgia. (See *Choices and Consequences: Acquiesce or Resist? The Cherokee Dilemma.*) In 1835 a minority of the Cherokee leadership gave in and signed a treaty agreeing to relocate west of the Mississippi. Many Cherokee denounced the treaty, and many hoped that their leaders could avert relocation. In 1838 federal troops forcibly began rounding up Cherokee and placing them in stockades to await deportation. The squalid conditions in the stockades took a heavy

What do the Cherokee cases reveal about the limits of judicial power?

Choices and Consequences

ACQUIESCE OR RESIST? THE CHEROKEE DILEMMA

Should the Cherokee have resisted Jackson's removal policy? The Cherokee nation faced a difficult decision regarding how to deal with the increasing pressure on them to abandon their land and relocate to Western territory in what is now Oklahoma. The tribal leadership was divided. The majority of the Cherokee supported Principal Chief John Ross, who advised resisting, while a minority of the tribe supported Elias Boudinot, who argued that it was better to relocate than to continue to oppose the inevitable.

Choices

1 Agree to treaty and relocate; seek the best possible terms from the U.S. government to facilitate the removal process.

2 Reject treaty and attempt to rally support and lobby Congress to protect Indian rights against the state of Georgia.

3 Reject treaty and use force to resist removal.

Decision

A small but vocal minority of the Cherokee, including Elias Boudinot, believed that continued residence in Georgia would only result in further harassment. They reasoned that it would be more prudent to try to obtain the best deal from the United States and relocate to Western territories. However the majority of Cherokee supported John Ross, who believed that it was still possible to rally support among religious groups and other whites sympathetic to Indian rights. Influential senators Daniel Webster and Henry Clay opposed Jackson and were eager to use the plight of Indians to attack him. Most Cherokee rejected the treaty requiring them to relocate and refused to participate in the referendum held on it.

Consequences

Bolstered by popular opposition to the treaty among the Cherokee, John Ross lobbied the Senate to reject the treaty as fraudulent and came within one vote of defeating it. Having won a narrow victory, Jackson signed the treaty and the Cherokee were given two years to leave their homes or face military deportation. After relocation, supporters of John Ross assassinated several prominent Indian supporters of the fraudulent treaty, including Elias Boudinot.

John Ross

Continuing Controversies

Was it realistic for the Cherokees to think that they might be able to win support for their cause?

Most scholars agree that Jackson's Indian policy was racist and unethical, particularly the violation of existing treaties. There is, however, some disagreement over the Cherokee response to the dilemma created by Jackson's policy. Supporters of John Ross note that he was an extremely savvy politician whose calculation that opposition to Jackson and sympathy for the plight of Indians was a reasonable gamble. Opponents of Ross argue that Boudinot and others who voted in favor of the treaty were more realistic in their assessment of the political situation.

Elias Boudinot

Was resistance to removal a viable strategy for the Cherokee?

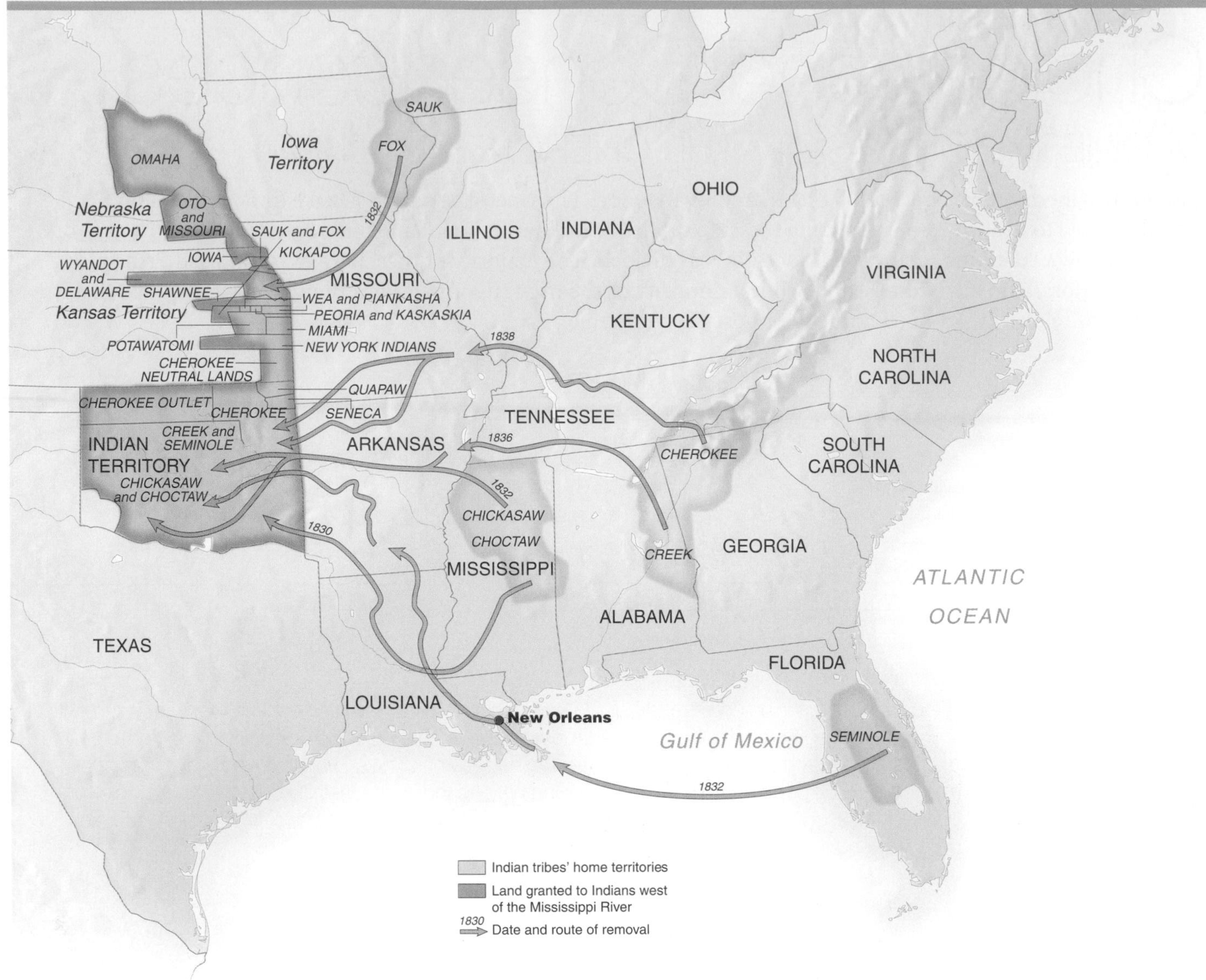

8.12 Cherokee removal
This map shows the path taken by Indian tribes forced to relocate under Jackson's Indian removal plan. Thousands died during the forced migration.

toll, and many of the most outspoken Cherokee opponents of removal now recognized that further resistance was futile.

Indian leaders who had continued to protest were joined in their protest by a broad coalition that included clergymen, women reformers, and constitutional nationalists such as Henry Clay and Daniel Webster, who were horrified at Jackson's behavior toward the Cherokee. The two men were particularly outraged by Jackson's disregard for treaty obligations, and his disrespect for the authority of the federal courts. Opposition to Indian removal provided a rallying point for a diverse collection of opponents who believed Jackson had become a tyrant who showed little regard for justice or the rule of law.

During the long and arduous march westward to what is now Oklahoma (**8.12**), thousands of Cherokee men, women, and children died. Harsh weather, a shortage of supplies, and poor sanitation facilities contributed to a staggering death toll. Estimates vary but as many as four thousand of the twelve thousand Cherokee who were relocated perished in the trip. For the Cherokee and their descendants, the move westward became known as "the Path Where They Cried," or the "Trail of Tears."

Democrats, Whigs, and the Second Party System

Unlike previous partisan movements Jackson's Democratic Party operated as an efficient and nationally integrated political organization. The new party organization called also for a new party name. In the election of 1828, Jackson supporters had described themselves as Democratic-Republicans, while Adams supporters opted for the name National Republicans. These two labels testify to the transitional nature of the election of 1828. Both names harked back to political labels that were associated with the partisan struggles of Jefferson's and Monroe's administrations. By the election of 1832, Jackson supporters were simply calling themselves Democrats.

By contrast Jackson's opposition was still defining itself. A third political party, the Anti-Masonic party, organized in response to the undue influence of the Masonic order—a fraternal organization whose members included many of the nation's most prominent politicians—capturing the imagination of voters briefly, but then disbanded. During Jackson's second term a new political party, the **Whigs**, rose out of the ashes of the old National Republicans, stressing the need for a talented, virtuous elite to shape the nation's future. Evoking the name of the seventeenth-century English opponents of absolute monarchy and the Patriot leaders who had opposed the tyranny of George III during the American Revolution, the Whigs saw themselves as defenders of the Constitution against executive despotism. Opposition to Jackson's Indian policy created one of the essential elements of the coalition that formed the Whig Party. Economic policy, as defined by Clay's American System (which included support for the national bank), and a general opposition to the new vision of executive power personified by Jackson also defined core Whig ideas.

Once voters aligned with one of the two main parties, they tended to remain loyal to it over the course of their lifetime. Rather than seeking votes from an undifferentiated electorate, both sides now concentrated on getting out the vote from their party's constituents and maintaining popular enthusiasm for the party's choices for local, state, and national offices. This further intensified the divisions between the two new parties.

Third Party Challenges: Anti-Masonry and Workingmen's Parties

In the election of 1832, Andrew Jackson, aiming at a second term as president, faced Henry Clay, who still saw himself as the heir to James Monroe and John Quincy Adams's National Republicans. Another candidate, William Wirt, a talented lawyer who had argued the Cherokee cases before the Supreme Court, entered the fray as the choice of the Anti-Masonic party. The presence of a third party complicated the election and worked against Clay, effectively splitting the anti-Jackson vote.

The Anti-Masons emerged in New York state as a reaction against the power of the Masonic order, a secret fraternal organization that included many of the nation's most powerful figures, including Andrew Jackson and Henry Clay. Freemasonry had a long history in America. Many members of America's Founding generation had been Freemasons, including George Washington and Benjamin Franklin. The Freemasons championed Enlightenment ideals, but they also drew some of their rituals and symbols from the mystical

Why did opponents of Jackson call themselves Whigs?

tradition. The best-known Masonic symbol, an eye suspended over an unfinished pyramid, appears on the reverse side of the Great Seal of the United States (and also on the modern dollar bill). Several characteristics of the Freemasons made them a likely target of popular suspicion. Secret handshakes, rituals, passwords, and other Masonic practices were one source of suspicion. The presence in the order of many prominent politicians who were Masons encouraged conspiracy theories about the organization. In addition Freemasonry's support for the Enlightenment angered some religious groups, especially evangelicals, who believed that Masons were anti-Christian.

These suspicions and resentments provided the backdrop to a sensational crime involving the Freemasons. In 1826 a disgruntled ex-Freemason, Daniel Morgan, threatened to expose the order's secret rituals. When this ex-Mason was kidnapped and disappeared, a popular clamor arose against the order. The Anti-Masonic party, capitalizing on this sensational crime, attracted evangelicals to the Anti-Masonic cause. Meanwhile the Freemasons did not remain silent. In this attack on the Anti-Masons, who are cast as the mythical monster the hydra, the Freemasons represent their own Enlightenment values, such as science and equality, as the steps of a pyramid, a common Masonic symbol (**8.13**).

> "As long as property is unequal: or rather, as long as it is so enormously unequal, as we see it at present... those who possess it, *will* live on the labor of others."
>
> THOMAS SKIDMORE, *The Rights of Man to Property!* 1829

8.13 Anti-Masonic Apron This parody of the Anti-Masons contrasts their values, "Persecution, Intolerance, Hypocrisy," with the Masons' Enlightenment ideals: universal benevolence, equal rights, tolerance, and scientific inquiry.

The Anti-Masons proved to be innovative politicians, building an effective popular political movement. Although short-lived, their party, the first third-party movement in American history, helped pioneer several new political techniques that mainstream parties soon adopted. The Anti-Masonic party pioneered the use of a national nominating convention to select a presidential candidate. It was also the first party to adopt an official party platform, published so that voters could judge the party's position on the important questions of the day. This party also energized an important group of religious voters who were drawn into public life and politics as a result of the party's efforts.

At the same time that the Anti-Masonic party was organizing, workers in Philadelphia (1828) and New York (1829) formed their own political parties. The Workies, as they were called, won several seats in the state legislatures. Among the political reforms the Workies managed to achieve was the abolition of imprisonment for debt. In this pro-Workie cartoon (**8.14**), an honest working man exercises the ballot freely, while a corrupt tool of the moneyed interest serves the devil.

What lasting contributions did the Anti-Masons make to American politics?

8.14 ***No More Grinding the Poor—But Liberty and the Rights of Man***
The devil hands money to a rich man in an effort to buy his vote, telling him to "grind the Workies." A virtuous workingman invokes Liberty and the Rights of Man and casts his vote independently, while the goddess of Liberty holds out the ballot box.

The most radical spokesmen among the Workies, men such as the artisan Thomas Skidmore, advocated a comprehensive program to use inheritance taxes to equalize wealth. In his book *The Rights of Man to Property!* (1829) Skidmore proposed to abolish inherited wealth and redistribute wealth to each new generation, who would start life equally and prosper or fall by their own efforts. Although the Workies were unable to turn their successes into the basis for creating a national labor party, their attack on banking had a strong influence on mainstream Democratic politicians, including Andrew Jackson. The class-conscious rhetoric of the workers would influence the way Democrats framed their political message for the American people.

The Bank War and the Rise of the Whigs

Jackson's growing opposition to Clay's American System, including a visceral hatred for the Bank of the United States, emerged as one of the defining features of his presidency. The political war that arose over the bank issue helped Jackson's opponents to define their political identity and to create a new political party, the Whigs.

Henry Clay and Daniel Webster, two very influential figures within the anti-Jackson National Republican party, believed that the president's hatred for the bank could be used to defeat Jackson in the election of 1832. Clay reasoned that Jackson's opposition to the bank would alienate most voters from Jackson because they would recognize the importance of a national bank. Clay approached Nicholas Biddle, the head of the Bank of the United States, with the idea of petitioning Congress for an early renewal of the bank's charter. Clay knew that Jackson was opposed to the bank and might veto the new charter, a move that Clay believed would turn the public against Jackson. Jackson confided to Martin Van Buren his intention to destroy the bank. "The Bank, Mr. Van Buren, is trying to kill me, but I will kill it!" The bank became the central issue of the presidential campaign of 1832.

Although the bank had many supporters, including some figures in Jackson's administration, the veto turned out to be extremely popular. Jackson had managed to convert opposition to the bank into support for democracy itself. In his **Bank Veto Speech**, Jackson not only explained why he opposed rechartering the Bank of the United States but also took the opportunity to lay out his own vision of American democracy and constitutional government. Jackson attacked "the rich and powerful" who "too often bend the acts of government to their selfish purposes." His speech appealed to "the humble members of society—the farmers, mechanics and laborers."

Democratic newspapers echoed Jackson's view of the bank. "The Jackson cause is the cause of democracy and the people against a corrupt and

> "The Bank Veto ... falsely and wickedly alleges that the rich and powerful throughout the country are waging a war of oppression against the poor and the weak."
>
> *Boston Daily Atlas*, editorial, 1832

abandoned aristocracy." Drawing on rhetoric similar to that employed by the Workies, Jackson framed his appeal directly to the "humble members of society."

Opponents attacked the veto as an assault on the Constitution itself. The press hammered away at Jackson, charging that he had become "a DICTATOR." Jackson's veto, one newspaper claimed, was the act of a tyrant who had contempt for Congress. Rather than represent a victory for democracy, Jackson's recklessness was a sign of his corruption. For his opponents Jackson became the embodiment of tyranny.

Jackson's war against the Bank of the United States inspired a rich assortment of political cartoons, both critical and supportive of his policies. Democratic cartoonists cast Jackson as the champion of the common man, while supporters of the bank depicted him as a reckless tyrant. These images are explored in *Images as History: "Old Hickory" or "King Andrew": Popular Images of Andrew Jackson*, page 244.

In the election of 1832, Jackson defeated Clay by 150,000 votes and by a roughly 5-to-1 margin in the Electoral College. Clay's strategy of making the bank the central issue in the campaign had backfired, and Jackson's attack on the bank had actually increased his popularity. Still the Bank War provided Jackson's opponents with an issue that helped them define their own political identity and helped create a new political party, the Whigs.

Having defeated supporters of the Bank of the United States, Jackson might have opted to let the bank die a natural death by simply allowing its charter to expire. However fearing that his enemies would try to revive the bank during the next congressional session and vote it a new charter, he decided to withdraw all federal funds from the bank, a move that would have made its revival financially impossible. Jackson ordered his secretary of the treasury to remove the government's deposits, but even his own minister thought such a move rash and damaging to the economy. The president had to fire two men before he could find one willing to take the job of secretary of the treasury and follow his orders. Jackson justified this unusual step by noting that his reelection had given him a broad popular mandate to destroy the bank. No previous president had ever cast his election in such terms. Even some congressional Democrats believed that Jackson had risked the economic well-being of the country to satisfy his personal vendetta against the bank.

Jackson's enemies in Congress condemned his actions as additional proof that Jackson was a tyrant who sought "a total change of the pure republican character of the Government and the concentration of all powers in the hands one man." In the view of the Whigs, Jackson was little better than George the III, the monarch America's own Whig Patriots had opposed more than fifty years before.

Economic Crisis and the Presidency of Martin Van Buren

Jackson's decision to remove funds from the bank and deposit them into state banks damaged the economy. State banks were far less cautious than the Bank of the United States in loaning money, particularly for speculative land ventures. The resulting expansion of credit led to a speculative frenzy. Between 1832 and 1836 land sales expanded from 2.6 million to almost 25 million. To slow down the overheated economy, Jackson adopted a hard money policy, the Species Circular, which required that land purchased from the government be paid for with hard currency (before this policy individuals had purchased land with bank notes that were not guaranteed by gold or silver). Jackson left office with the nation's economy teetering on the verge of collapse.

Martin Van Buren had become the most influential figure in Jackson's inner circle and would become the Democrats' candidate for the presidency in 1836. In most respects Van Buren was nearly the opposite of Andrew Jackson. Political caricaturists made much of the physical and personality differences between the two. Jackson was tall, thin,

How did Whigs interpret the Bank Veto?

impulsive, and headstrong, while Van Buren was short, stout, cautious, and compromising. The nicknames of the two only underscored the differences. Jackson was the "Hero of New Orleans" or "Old Hickory," while Van Buren was the "Little Magician" or the "Slippery Elm."

Van Buren won by a narrow margin in the election of 1836, garnering 50.2 percent of the popular vote. Making matters worse Van Buren inherited a weak economy. Within a year of taking office, he was forced to deal with the Panic of 1837, an economic crisis that plunged the nation into a serious economic depression. Unemployment rose dramatically, and the number of farm foreclosures and business failures increased. Wages dropped as much as 50 percent, and a third of the workforce was out of work in some hard-hit areas, such as Philadelphia. The cartoon *The Times* illustrates the failure of Jackson's economic policies (**8.15**). The images of idle workers staggering drunk, while a respectable-looking woman and child beg for coins, show the plight of the working class. Although Whigs blamed Jackson's war against the bank, the economic causes of the panic were largely foreign. In 1837 the Bank of England decided to raise its interest rates and restrict the flow of credit to British banks investing in America. This constriction of credit forced American banks to restrict their loans and call in many outstanding debts. Without access to additional credit, many businesses and farms defaulted on their loans. When these loans went bad, many banks, caught short, had to close. These bank failures led to a further constriction of credit, which then triggered another round of foreclosures and business failures. To make matters worse the price of cotton on the world market plummeted in 1837, leaving many cotton speculators without the funds to cover their loans and causing additional bankruptcies. Critics of the president gave him a new nickname—"Martin Van Ruin."

8.15 Panic of 1837
This political cartoon highlights the economic hardships caused by the Panic of 1837. The spirit of Andrew Jackson, symbolized by his hat, glasses, and clay pipe, hovers over the scene of suffering and despair.

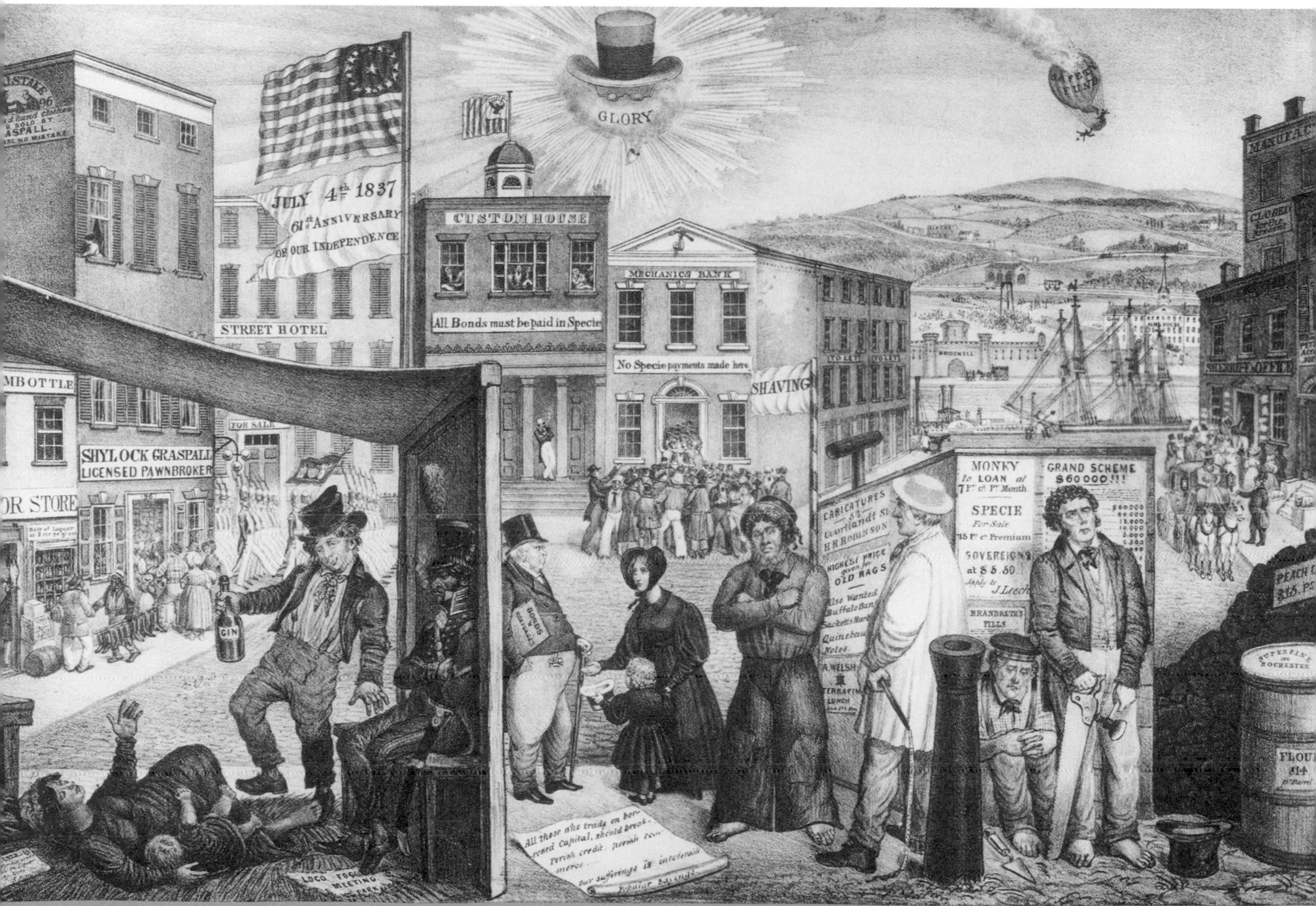

What are some of the signs of economic distress in this political cartoon on the Panic of 1837?

Images as History

"OLD HICKORY" OR "KING ANDREW": POPULAR IMAGES OF ANDREW JACKSON

The controversies swirling around Andrew Jackson's presidency, particularly his war on the Bank of the United States, provided political cartoonists with ample material for parody and praise. The Jacksonian era, riddled with partisan tensions, generated some of the most memorable cartoons in American political history. They portrayed Jackson variously as a rough frontiersman, a spiteful old lady, a tyrannical king, and a heroic statesman.

This pro-Jackson image, *Set To Between Old Hickory and Bully Nick*, produced to defend Jackson's Bank Veto, shows the president boxing with Nicholas Biddle, president of the bank. Jackson's loyal sidekick, Martin Van Buren, urges him on to victory. Jackson is represented as "Old Hickory," a rough-hewn westerner who does not shy away from a good fight. The other figures in the lithograph reinforce the contrast between Jacksonian democracy and the aristocratic bank.

The shirtless Jackson stands firm like an "Old Hickory" ready to stand up to Biddle and the bank.

Martin Van Buren stands behind Jackson, urging him on.

Old Hickory vs. Bully Nick [*Source:* The Library Company of Philadelphia]

Mother Bank, dressed in finery, stands behind Biddle and shouts encouragement.

A buckskin-clad frontiersman urges Jackson to defeat Biddle.

How would you describe the difference between the two images of Jackson in these political cartoons?

Behind Biddle, Mother Bank, clad in a fancy dress, stands with a bottle of port in her hand, a type of alcoholic beverage typically consumed by the wealthy. By contrast, championing Jackson's cause is a backwoodsman clad in buckskin who stands beside a bottle of whiskey, a drink associated with frontiersmen and the working class.

This anti-Jackson cartoon, *King Andrew the First*, portrays the president as a monarch in regal robes. He holds the Bank Veto in one hand and a royal scepter in the other.

Visual images such as these two cartoons helped translate the complex political and legal issues at stake in the controversy over the bank into terms that most Americans could understand. The two radically different visions of Jackson captured the divisive politics of his presidency.

Jackson is clad in the regal robes and crown of a monarch.

In his hand he holds the Bank Veto.

The regal Jackson tramples on the text of the Constitution of the United States, which lies in shreds below his feet.

King Andrew

Why is Jackson portrayed as a monarch in this political cartoon?

Playing the Democrats' Game: Whigs in the Election of 1840

Largely because the Whigs split their vote among different regional candidates in 1836, they lost the election to Van Buren. However the failure of the Whigs also reflected their problem communicating their message to the American people. Millard Fillmore, a young Whig from upstate New York (who would later become president), lamented the "heterogeneous mass" of the Whig Party, which included "old national republicans, and revolting Jackson men, Masons and Anti-Masons, Abolitionists, and pro-Slavery men." Fillmore hoped that his party could find some "crucible ... to melt them down into one mass pure Whigs of undoubted good metal." In 1840 the Whigs did find a route to unification and learned how to frame their message in terms that appealed to the American people. Drafting a popular military figure, William Henry Harrison, the Whigs reshaped their campaign using the tools and rhetoric that had made the Democrats so successful, especially their direct appeals to the people. In brief they learned to play the Democrats' game. In addition the Whigs pioneered new techniques for mobilizing voters and made an unprecedented effort to involve women in their cause.

The Log Cabin Campaign

Democrat Martin Van Buren's supporters derided the Whig candidate in 1840, General William Henry Harrison, as "Old Granny" or "Old Tippecanoe." The nicknames alluded to the general's age—he was almost seventy—and to his role in defeating Shawnee Indians at the battle of Tippecanoe in 1811. One Democratic editor in Baltimore suggested that given his advanced age it might be best to "give him a barrel of hard cider" and let him "sit out the remainder of his days in his log cabin." The effort to ridicule Harrison backfired, however; the Whigs seized on the twin images of hard cider and log cabins as the symbols for their campaign. The new campaign message transformed Harrison's public persona almost overnight: he was no longer the well-educated son of a wealthy Virginia planter (his real background), but was instead William Henry Harrison, a simple farmer born into a log cabin who enjoyed a glass of hard (alcoholic) cider like all common folk. Eager to take advantage of the Democratic mistake, the Whigs plastered log cabins and barrels of hard cider onto an astonishing array of items: badges, banners, buttons, belt bucklers, hair brushes, pewter spoons, lithographed prints, quilts, and song sheets. The Whigs also used miniature wooden log cabins as parade floats, transforming what had been marches into truly festive parades. Two Whig slogans became two of the most successful campaign slogans in U.S. history: "Tippecanoe and Tyler too" to support Harrison, and "Van, Van is a used up man" to taunt their opponent.

8.16 Harrison Log Cabin and Hard Cider Sheet Music This piece of sheet music includes the two most common symbols of Harrison's campaign, a log cabin and a barrel of hard cider. To highlight Harrison's own military accomplishments, the artist shows him greeting a disabled veteran.

The *Democratic Review,* capturing the irony of the election of 1840, noted that "we have taught them how to conquer us." Whigs not only adapted the Democrat's campaign techniques for mobilizing the popular vote but also developed their own innovative campaign style. With parades and campaign music such as "General Harrison's Log Cabin March & Quick Step," one of several popular campaign songs, the Whigs trounced their opponents (**8.16**). One Democratic paper complained: "We could meet the Whigs on the field of argument

What political innovations helped the Whigs out-democrat the Democrats?

and beat them." But, the paper went on to say, how were Democrats to respond when the Whigs "lay down the weapons of argument and attack us with musical notes"?

While Whigs cast Harrison and his running mate John Tyler as men of the people, they made Martin Van Buren out to be a dissipated aristocrat who gorged himself on expensive French cuisine and sipped expensive champagne while Americans suffered economic hardship. Although charges of sexual misconduct were not new in American politics—Jefferson had been tarnished by the Sally Hemmings scandal during his administration (Chapter 7)—the political smears of the Jacksonian era sunk even lower. Eager to discredit him the Whigs spread malicious rumors that Van Buren was a sexual pervert who had instructed the groundskeeper at the White House to create a giant anatomically correct mound in the shape of a women's breast in the back of the White House.

Gender and Social Class: The Whig Appeal

Another especially innovative aspect of the Whig's electoral strategy was their effective mobilization of women to their cause. Although women could not vote, the Whigs hoped to get them to deliver their husbands' votes. The Whig appeal to women relied on two elements: a defense of morality against corruption and an appeal to economic interest. Whig newspaper editor Horace Greeley's description of the choice Americans faced in the 1840 election captures the appeal of the Whigs to many women. The debate, Greeley noted, was one between the Whigs, whom he characterized as supporters of the family and Christian morality, and the Democrats, whom he accused of being atheists and sexual perverts. "Wherever you find a bitter, blasphemous Atheist and enemy of Marriage, Morality, and Social Order, there you may be certain of one vote for Van Buren." Although such appeals to traditional family values and morality motivated some women to devote their energies to the Whig cause, other women were inspired by economic arguments that Whigs directed at male voters. Democratic policies had left the American economy in shambles, and Whig policies promised to bring back prosperity. Taking advantage of women's interest, Whigs sponsored all-female political rallies in support of Harrison, including a meeting in Ohio in which Whig women raised cups of tea in toasts to "Old Tippecanoe." Democrats complained about the Whigs "making politicians of their women," which was "something new under the sun."

Whigs also attacked Democrats for fanning the resentments of class antagonism. Thus one Whig chided the Democrats for their "incessant and unrelenting assaults" that tore "asunder the good feelings which bind men to each other." Rather than highlight the struggle between democracy and aristocracy, a favorite rhetorical theme of Democrats, Whigs stressed the essential harmony of all economic classes. An observer at a Whig rally proudly noted that "all classes" had rediscovered that "their interests were the same." Calvin Colton, a leading Whig, evoked the notion that "This is a country of self-made men, than which nothing better could be said of any state of society." Whig policies would promote prosperity for all hard-working Americans.

> "The ladies they flock'd to their windows,
> In numbers, I say not a few,
> And held out their star-spangled banners
> All to the honor of Tippecanoe."
>
> Harrison campaign lyric, 1840

The election clearly energized the voting population, who turned out in record numbers, nearly four-fifths of eligible voters casting a vote. Harrison defeated Van Buren by 150,000 votes and a 4-to-1 margin in the Electoral College. President Harrison's inaugural speech was the longest in American history, 105 minutes long. His term in office, however, was the shortest. Within a month of becoming president, he contracted pneumonia and died. Harrison's vice president John Tyler became the tenth President of the United States. Some dubbed him "His Accidency" because he inherited his position after Harrison's death.

Democrats and Whigs: Two Visions of Government and Society

The Whigs and Democrats represented opposing political visions. The Whigs favored a strong central government, encouragement for industry, and defense of Indians' rights; in the North and parts of the Midwest they aligned themselves against slavery. Rejecting the views of old-style conservatives such as Chancellor James Kent, an heir to the Old Federalist vision of politics, the Whigs adopted the more popular style of politics pioneered by the anti-Masonic party, using it to reach out to American voters. Whigs embraced Clay's American System, arguing that the rich and poor would each see their fortunes rise. Whigs emphasized the harmonious interaction of different elements of the economy and attacked Democrats for preaching an ideology that fostered class conflict.

The Whig version of democracy was not egalitarian, but rather it recognized the need for a talented and virtuous elite to guide the nation. The Whigs' frank acceptance of inequality allowed them to find a place in their ranks for African Americans, Indians, women, and any other group who needed guidance or protection from an enlightened elite. Although slightly paternalistic in outlook, the Whigs believed they had a duty to protect these groups. Thus Whigs championed the rights of Indians against the efforts of Jackson and other Democrats to forcibly remove them from their lands. Although Southern Whigs supported the institution of slavery, Whigs outside of the South often supported the abolition of slavery. Finally Whigs actively cultivated women's involvement in their campaign efforts.

The Whig Party drew from the Old National Republican Party of John Quincy Adams, adding to their ranks Democrats who opposed Jackson's Bank War. Anti-Masons and the more commercially minded Southern planters were also drawn to the Whig message. Whiggery also had a significant ethnic and religious basis. Individuals of English origin were also more likely than others to be Whig in sympathy, and mainstream Protestant denominations such as the Congregationalists, Presbyterians, and Episcopalians were more likely to vote Whig.

Democrats' vision of white men's democracy was more egalitarian than that of the Whigs, but it was also more exclusive. Although Democrats often couched their appeals in egalitarian terms, this rhetoric was not inclusive when it came to the issue of racial equality. Instead Democrats reached out to workers, small farmers, and members of the planter class. Democrats attracted voters more suspicious of the burgeoning market economy, including those who blamed banks, especially the Bank of the United States, for the economic problems they experienced. They asserted their support for the sanctity of private property and for the doctrine of states' rights, meaning that they were the party best suited to protect the interests of Southern slaveholders. Obtaining more land for white farmers, including Southern planters, was the primary goal of Democrats. Promoting this old Jeffersonian ideal of an expanding nation of yeoman farmers meant having to sacrifice the rights of Indians. From Jeffersonianism, Jacksonian Democrats inherited a strong fear of centralized government and large concentrations of financial power. Thus Democrats opposed Clay's American System and the Whig's emphasis on a powerful federal government involved in economic development. Although not opposed to economic growth, Democrats believed that the individual states, not the federal government, ought to guide economic development.

Rural farmers and urban workers flocked to the ranks of the Democrats. Religious affiliation also dictated Democratic Party affiliation. Democrats were more popular among the less affluent evangelical Protestant sects such as the Baptists and Methodists, who found Jackson's egalitarian message appealing. Democrats also attracted some free thinkers and Catholics who feared that the Whigs were trying to impose Protestant morality on others. For a summary of the ideas of the Democrats and Whigs, see the following chart (**8.17**).

8.17 Democrats and Whigs: Major Beliefs

Democrats
Oppose tariffs
Oppose federal support for internal improvements
Oppose Bank of the United States
Favor Indian removal
States' rights

Whigs
Favor tariffs
Favor federal support for internal improvements
Support the Bank of the United States
Oppose Indian removal
Support strong central government

What were the most important differences between Whigs and Democrats on economic issues?

> "The aristocracy of our country ... continually contrive to change their party name. It was first Tory, then Federalist, then no party ... then National Republican, now Whig. ...But by whatever name they reorganize themselves, the true democracy of the country, the producing classes, ought to be able to distinguish the enemy."
>
> FREDERICK ROBINSON, Democrat, 1834

Conclusion

Between the elections of Thomas Jefferson in 1800 and Andrew Jackson in 1828, American politics and society underwent a gradual democratization. Foreign travelers to the young republic often noted the relatively democratic and egalitarian nature of American society. In part the change in American life reflected the increasing importance of the new Western states. Politicians such as Davy Crockett and Andrew Jackson typified this new type of political leader. Democracy was hardly the exclusive province of the West, however. Many eastern states adopted new constitutions that eliminated property qualifications for suffrage for nearly all white men. While some states were eliminating legal barriers to the participation of white men in politics, they were also erecting new barriers to prevent African Americans from participating fully in the political life of the new nation.

Democrats, led by Andrew Jackson, cultivated white male voters and showed little concern for the rights of blacks, Indians, or women. Jackson's vision of politics was forcefully expressed in his Bank Veto Speech, when he attacked special interests and championed the cause of ordinary Americans. By contrast the Whigs, especially the influential Daniel Webster and Henry Clay, made their Senate careers supporting greater government involvement in the economy. The Whigs also defended the rights of women, blacks, and Indians. Indeed the protests against Cherokee removal galvanized many opponents of Jackson and provided an important core around which the Whigs could later organize. The Whigs were particularly effective at reaching out to women, involving them in the political process. Although the political techniques the Democrats and Whigs employed had become nearly indistinguishable by the pivotal election of 1840, the underlying visions of politics and the policies pursued by the two parties remained radically different. The Democrats defended the idea of states' rights and opposed efforts to use the power of the national government to further economic development. The Whigs, by contrast, became the champions of a stronger activist national government.

The Whigs and the Democrats each grappled with profound changes in American political culture and economic life. Each group not only responded to the democratization of politics but also grappled with major changes in the American economy. Changes in technology, the expansion of the factory system, and expanding market were transforming American life. Taken together these changes helped spread a set of interrelated changes that historians describe as a market revolution. The Whigs championed the market, believing that government could help expand the market economy and promote American prosperity. Democrats accepted the necessity of the market but were more wary of its changes, and were particularly concerned that government not manipulate the market economy to further the interests of a wealthy elite.

CHAPTER REVIEW

1824–1826

Tariff of 1824
Congress adopts protective tariff, a key element of Clay's American system

John Quincy Adams elected president
House of Representatives decides presidential election. Jackson charges Adams and Clay with a "corrupt bargain"

Murder of ex-Mason Daniel Morgan
Morgan's murder spurs rise of anti-Masonry as organized political movement

1828

Andrew Jackson elected president
In a bitter election campaign, Jackson defeats Adams and claims a broad popular mandate for his democratic agenda

Publication of South Carolina *Exposition and Protest* asserting states rights
South Carolina forcefully states the theory of states' rights and nullification

1829–1830

Thomas Skidmore publishes *Rights of Man to Property!*
Skidmore's book energizes Workingmen's movement

Webster-Hayne Debate
In dramatic speech to a crowded Senate chamber, Daniel Webster defends the Union against supporters of states' rights

Review Questions

1. What were the main features of Clay's American System?
2. How did the negative themes of the presidential campaign of 1828 reflect the new, more democratic style of American politics?
3. What role did states' rights play in shaping Andrew Jackson's presidency?
4. Was Jackson's Indian policy consistent with his democratic ideals? How did Jackson's perception of Indians allow him to reconcile his policy with his ideals?
5. Why did Jackson's opponents call their new party the Whigs? What were the Whigs' main beliefs and how did they differ from those of the Democrats?
6. What kinds of images did Democratic and Whig cartoonists use to represent Jackson during the Bank War?
7. Did the Bank War cause the Panic of 1837? How did the Bank War impact subsequent American politics?
8. How did the Whigs out-democrat the Democrats in the election of 1840?

1831–1832

Jackson's Bank Veto
Jackson vetoes renewal of Bank of the United States while attacking privileged elites

***Cherokee Nation v. Georgia* decided by Supreme Court**
Supreme Court rules against Cherokees in the first of two cases concerning their status as a sovereign nation

1833

South Carolina nullifies federal tariff
South Carolina becomes the first state to invoke the doctrine of nullification and resist federal law

1836–1837

Martin Van Buren elected president
Democrats retain control of the White House after Jackson's retirement from office

Panic of 1837
Economic downturn is blamed on Jackson's policies

1838–1840

Cherokee Removal (Trail of Tears)
Jackson's policy of forcing Indians to give up their lands and homes and relocate to Western lands is approved and implemented

William Henry Harrison Elected President
Whigs exploit new methods of democratic politics to elect their candidate to the presidency

Key Terms

American System Henry Clay's comprehensive national plan for economic growth that included protective tariffs for American industry and government investment in roads and other internal improvements. **226**

"corrupt bargain" Term presidential candidate Jackson's supporters used to attack the alliance between John Quincy Adams and Henry Clay that deprived Clay of the presidency. **227**

"Old Hickory" The nickname that General Andrew Jackson earned for seeming as stout as an "Old Hickory tree" in fighting against the British in the War of 1812. **228**

spoils system The name applied to Jackson's system of replacing government officeholders with those loyal to him. **230**

nullification A constitutional doctrine advanced by supporters of states' rights that held that individual states could nullify unconstitutional acts of Congress. **231**

Force Bill A bill enacted by Congress that gave President Jackson the power to use military force to collect revenue, including tariffs. **232**

Indian Removal Act of 1830 Legislation that gave President Jackson the authority to remove Indians tribes to lands west of the Mississippi. **236**

Cherokee Cases *Cherokee Nation v. Georgia* (1830) and *Worcester v. Georgia*, the two cases in which the Supreme Court of the United States determined that Indian nations retained certain rights of sovereign nations, but did not enjoy the full powers of a sovereign nation. **236**

Whigs (American, 19th Century) Anti-Jackson political party; the name evoked the seventeenth-century English opponents of absolute monarchy and the Patriot leaders who had opposed the tyranny of George III during the American Revolution. Whigs supported Clay's American System and a stronger central government. **239**

Bank Veto Speech Jackson's veto of a bill to re-charter of the Bank of the United States, in which he explained why he opposed the bank and laid out his own vision of American democracy and constitutional government. **241**

CHAPTER 9

Workers, Farmers, and Slaves

The Transformation of the American Economy, 1815–1848

> "The greatest want of civilized society is a market for the sale and exchange of the surplus of the produce of the labor of its members.... If we cannot sell, we cannot buy."
>
> HENRY CLAY, 1824

The United States experienced extraordinary economic growth and change in the first half of the nineteenth century. But the economies of the Northern and Southern regions of the nation evolved along very different paths. The North developed a free labor economy marked by rapid industrialization and urbanization as well as massive immigration. Essential to this process was the introduction of new technology like water-powered looms, railroads, steamboats, and the telegraph. By contrast, while the South experienced some industrialization and urban growth, the great majority of its expansion and development focused on raising cash crops by means of slave labor. The huge profits generated by cotton cultivation prompted the expansion of plantations into the so-called Black Belt that stretched from Alabama westward.

By mid-century Northerners and Southerners became increasingly self-conscious about the distinctiveness of the labor system in their own region and more critical of that employed in the other half of the nation. This image, *The Tree of Liberty* (1846), illustrates the radical differences between the vision of liberty defended by Northern proponents of free labor and that of Southern defenders of slavery. On the right side of the tree, a slaveholder reclining in a chair while fanned by a slave announces, "Surrounded by slaves & basking at ease by their labor we can have a clearer conception of the value of liberty." On the other side of the tree, the artist has placed two industrious farmers conversing with one another, and a group of young mill women in front of their factory.

Although North and South had developed different labor systems, each was tied to the expanding market economy that Henry Clay praised in his 1824 address. The expansion of the market economy transformed the countryside in both the North and South and fueled the growth of America's cities. Economic growth was spurred by new technologies that made agriculture more productive and factories more efficient, as well as by improvements in transportation and communication that spurred consumer demand for the latest goods.

How did the dominant labor systems of the North and the South differ from one another?

LOWELL
OFFERING
November, 1845.

The Market Revolution

At the start of the nineteenth century, most rural households produced only a small surplus that was traded locally, often through a system of barter that did not require cash transactions. Most manufactured goods were produced by artisans whose workshops were usually located in their homes. Over the course of the nineteenth century, the American economy became more commercially oriented. Farmers began producing cash crops for sale in distant markets, and a wider range of consumer goods, many of them made in factories, became available. The **market revolution**, the term used by historians to describe this transformation, encompassed several interrelated developments that revolutionized agriculture, industry, technology, transportation, and communications. This market revolution would radically change both North and South in the antebellum period. Improved technology such as iron plows and steam-powered cotton gins enabled farmers to produce more crops, while the development of cheaper, more efficient forms of transportation like the railroad allowed them to deliver these goods to markets. The development of new communication technology, notably the telegraph and steam-powered printing press, increased the speed and volume of news and information available to Americans.

Agricultural Changes and Consequences

Most farmers in both the South and the North before 1815 labored to achieve a "competence," which meant enough food for a family's own consumption and a small surplus to trade locally or barter for goods, such as tools, that could not be produced in the home. But beginning in the early nineteenth century, American farmers began raising crops for an expanding commercial market with an eye toward earning profits and accumulating wealth. Periodicals geared to farmers promoted this new emphasis on commercial farming, touted the latest agricultural theories, and advertised the most up-to-date labor-saving devices. Publications such as *The New England Farmer* warned that "the cultivator who does not keep pace with his neighbors as regards agricultural improvements and information will soon find himself the poorer consequence of the prosperity that surrounds him."

One of the earliest and most important of these "improvements" was an iron plow introduced by Jethro Wood in 1819 that could double a farmer's efficiency. Within a decade John Deere had improved Wood's design, creating a plow that seemed to move through soil so easily that it was dubbed the "singing plow." In the wheat-growing regions of the Midwest, farmers adapted horse-driven machines to tasks such as threshing and raking. Crank-powered churns transformed arduous women's tasks, such as churning butter by hand. The cotton gin (see Chapter 7) transformed Southern agriculture. In 1839 the *Farmers Almanac* proclaimed that "scarcely a tool ... has not been altered for the better in some way or other." The new scientific methods of agriculture included crop rotation and the use of manure for fertilizer.

The creation of a market economy encouraged farmers to concentrate on crops that they could sell for cash in the market place, a trend that caused changes in farming patterns that varied by region. The South concentrated on staples for export such as cotton, while farmers in the Midwest produced grain, particularly wheat. Eastern farmers shifted their efforts to livestock production, dairy goods, fruits, and vegetables.

Market-oriented farming, with its emphasis on efficiency and profit, also transformed social values and communal patterns of life. The new, more commercial approach to farming challenged traditional ideas of neighborliness and community that had been central to rural life. Increasingly farmers began to see harvest parties, husking bees (communal celebrations in which corn was husked), dances, and other ritual communal occasions in which work and leisure were combined as inefficient and wasteful. The *Farmer's Almanac* in 1833 advised that "if you love fun, frolic, and waste and slovenliness, more than economy and profit, then make a husking." In

How did technology change agriculture in the era of the market revolution?

this humorous image of a corn husking (**9.1**), a man finds a lucky ear of red corn that entitles him to a kiss, but his advance is met by a girl holding a corn "smut," a weathered ear of corn that gave her the right to refuse her suitor.

Upcountry Southern farmers continued to concentrate on production of food for personal consumption and devoted a relatively small percentage of their land to commercial crops. While other regions of the country sought to improve every parcel of land for commercial agriculture, parts of the South remained committed to practices that encouraged a more self-sufficient style of agriculture, geared to personal use. Unlike in the North, for example, where extensive land was enclosed behind fences, most Southern states enacted laws against fencing in lands not used for agricultural production so that livestock could roam freely.

A Nation on the Move: Roads, Canals, Steamboats, and Trains

Central to the development of commercial, market-oriented farming were improvements in transportation technology and networks. These changes allowed those previously unable to deliver farm products to the growing cities of the Northeast and Midwest to enter the market. For those already in the market, the costs of business were dramatically lowered. These changes also spread information, including almanacs, books describing the latest agricultural techniques, and advertisements for the latest goods.

The first major development in transportation was the building of a network of roads and turnpikes that by the 1820s helped knit together the major urban areas along the eastern seaboard. New York state embarked on the most ambitious program of road building, adding 4,000 miles of improved road and turnpikes by 1820. The National Road, the first federally funded road in U.S. history, stretched from Cumberland, Maryland, to Wheeling in what is now West Virginia. By the 1830s it would take travelers as far west as Columbus, Ohio. Pennsylvania built the Lancaster turnpike connecting Philadelphia with Pittsburgh and allowing wagonloads of raw materials to travel east while manufactured goods traveled west. By the 1820s 30,000 tons of freight moved by wagon across this route annually.

The new road network dramatically cut travel times: A coach journey from New

9.1 ***Corn Husking Frolic*** Alvan Fischer's 1828 painting captures the festive communal atmosphere of a corn husking. [*Source:* Alan Fisher, "Corn Husking Frolic". 1828. Oil on Panel, 70.8 × 62.23 cm. Museum of Fine Arts, Boston Asso. #62.27 Photograph © 2010 Museum of Fine Arts, Boston]

Why did the *Farmers Almanac* frown on huskings and frolics?

York to Boston that had taken four days in 1800 took half that time in 1824. Even more dramatic was the invention of the steamboat. Navigable rivers such as the Mississippi, Ohio, Missouri, and Hudson had long served as vital arteries for moving agricultural products from the interior to market. This water highway system moved almost exclusively in one direction. Traveling upriver from New Orleans to Louisville, for example, was extremely slow (as long as three to four months) and expensive. As a result few manufactured goods reached the interior regions of the nation. The arrival of the steamboat would revolutionize upriver travel, reducing the same New Orleans to Louisville journey to just over a week by 1826. The rise of the steamboat proved an economic boon to river cities such as St. Louis and New Orleans on the Mississippi and Pittsburgh, and Cincinnati, and Louisville on the Ohio River. Hannah Stockton Stiles, the daughter of a prosperous merchant, stitched this elaborate needlework quilt, capturing the hustle and bustle of Philadelphia's busy waterfront. Stiles included a steam boat, with smoke billowing from its smoke stack (**9.2**).

9.2 Trade and Commerce Quilt In this quilt Hannah Stockton Stiles created images of maritime trade on Philadelphia's thriving waterfront. [*Source*: Fenimore Art Museum, Cooperstown, New York. Photo by Richard Walker. New York State Historical Association]

Canals provided another means of moving goods more cheaply and faster than across roads. Since the 1780s private companies had made modest efforts at building small canals, usually less than 20 miles long. In 1817 America had about 100 miles of canal, with no single canal longer than 30 miles. In that same year, however, New York's governor De Witt Clinton persuaded the state legislature to fund a 364-mile canal linking Buffalo on Lake Erie to Albany on the Hudson River. The Erie Canal, as it was called, was an unprecedented undertaking, both in terms of engineering and state investment. The $7 million in bonds that the New York state legislature approved to fund the project was a huge sum, roughly a quarter of all the money spent by all the states on internal improvements in the 1820s. Although opponents mocked the project as "Clinton's ditch," the Erie Canal was a stupendous success. Before the opening of the Erie Canal, wheat from western New York state took twenty days to reach Albany by wagon and cost almost $100 per ton to transport. After the completion of the canal, the same ton of wheat could be transported all the way to New York City in ten days at a cost of $5. Much as the steamboat fueled the growth of river towns, the Erie Canal fueled the development of new cities such as Rochester, Buffalo, and Syracuse. The canal's success sparked "canal fever" across the country, and more than 3,300 miles of canal were completed by 1840 at a cost of about $125 million.

In 1825, the same year that the Erie Canal was completed, the first railway began operating in England. Americans soon developed their own railroads, and by 1840 railroad mileage surpassed canals. Railroads continued the trend of increasing the speed at which goods and people moved from one part of the country to another. By 1840 the trip between Boston and New York by rail took a mere half day.

Americans greeted with amazement each innovation of the transportation revolution, but the railroad evoked the most powerful responses. "What an object of wonder!" wrote one American in response to his first sight of railroad in 1835. Charles Caldwell, the founder of the University of Louisville in Kentucky, praised the railroad as an agent of civilization that would help spread morality and education by linking people together more effectively. As *Images as History: Nature, Technology, and the Railroad: George Inness's* Lackawanna Valley *(1855)* indicates, railroads were eager to capitalize on the popular fascination with this new marvel.

What impact did the Erie Canal have on New York's economy?

Images as History

NATURE, TECHNOLOGY, AND THE RAILROAD: GEORGE INNESS'S *THE LACKAWANNA VALLEY* (1855)

The president of the Delaware, Lackawanna, and Western Railroad commissioned George Inness to paint the company's impressive new roundhouse, a facility designed to house and repair trains. Inness took the commission but soon found that his artistic vision and the vision of the railroad were in conflict. For the railroad, artistic considerations were less important than advertising the company's achievements. The main point of disagreement between Inness and his patrons focused on the representation of the roundhouse. The artist wished to render the facility accurately, which would have diminished its importance in the painting. Ultimately Inness agreed to make the roundhouse appear larger than it would have had he rendered the scene in actual perspective. He sacrificed some measure of artistic truth to the necessities of the market place.

Inness's painting draws on many of the conventions used to represent nature, but applies them to a scene in which nature and technology coexist harmoniously. Thus Inness includes a reclining youth, a figure often used in landscape paintings. Here, he sits calmly gazing toward the oncoming train. Rather than disrupt the serenity of nature, the train appears to blend harmoniously.

Although Inness portrays the railroad in a positive light, he also suggests the cost of technological progress: A field of tree stumps provides evidence of the negative impact of economic development on landscape. Which aspects of the painting present a positive view of progress? Which aspects suggest a negative view of progress?

The figure of the young boy evokes an ideal of distant building.
Although this distant building should have appeared much smaller, Inness increased the size of the roundhouse to please his patrons.
The prominent stumps suggest that the artist was aware that technological progress came at a cost: the defilement of nature.

George Inness, *The Lackawanna Valley*
[*Source*: George Inness, "The Lackawanna Valley". 1856. Oil on Canvas, 33 7/8" × 50 3/16". Image (c) 2010 Board of Trustees, National Gallery of Art, Washington, D.C.]

How did George Inness view technological progress in his painting of the Lackawanna Valley?

9.3 Time Lag for News 1800–1841 Improvements in communication technology and transportation dramatically reduced the time it took for news to travel from the coastal cities to the interior cities.

Spreading the News

Improvements in roads, canals, and railroads facilitated improvements in communication. The near doubling of the number of post offices and miles of improved postal roads between 1810 and 1820 brought an increase in the number of letters delivered annually from not quite four million to nearly nine million. News traveling from Richmond, Virginia, to New York City in Jefferson's day had taken ten days. By the 1810s this time had been slashed to five days. The advent of the railroad, as the figure (**9.3**) shows, literally accelerated this trend, cutting dramatically the time for news to travel. For example in 1817 it took nineteen days for news to travel from New York to Cincinnati; by 1841 this time had shrunk to seven days.

The most significant advance in communications was the **telegraph**, an invention that used electricity to send coded messages over wires. The telegraph revolutionized communication. In 1844 Samuel Morse, painter turned inventor who had patented the device in 1837, transmitted a message taken from bible verse—"What hath God Wrought?"—along a telegraph line from Washington, D.C., to Baltimore. The message was in code—the Morse code—that he also developed. Contemporary observers predicted correctly that the nearly instantaneous communication of telegraphy would usher in a new age of communications. By the middle of the 1850s, companies such the Western Union Telegraph Company had established offices across the nation, improving communication between major towns and cities as far apart as Boston and New Orleans.

Improvements in print technology sharply reduced the cost of publishing, leading to an enormous increase in the number of newspapers, magazines, and books. In 1801 there were only 200 newspapers in America; by 1835 the figure had jumped to 1,200. The number of magazines also rose dramatically, giving Americans a far greater range of printed materials to read. While most eighteenth-century magazines and newspapers were directed at a broad general audience, many of these new publications were aimed at specific audiences. The *Farmer's Almanac*, for example, dispensed advice about agriculture, while magazines such as *Godey's Lady Book* informed a large and growing group of middle-class women readers of the latest ideas in fashion, literature, and family matters. Also on the rise by the 1830s, American book publishing, with an output of at least a thousand titles a year, nearly

How did the telegraph transform communication?

rivaled that of Britain. Between 1825 and 1840 the value of the American book business doubled to $5.5 million.

Technological improvements in printing also made it possible to produce better and cheaper images. In 1834 Nathaniel Currier began producing cheap colored lithographic images using a new process of making prints that was cheaper than traditional engraving techniques. Rather than aspire to provide high art, Currier set out to provide "cheap and popular pictures" of contemporary events, historical figures, and scenes of everyday life. Touted as "Printmakers to the People," Currier's firm, eventually renamed Currier and Ives, produced images costing as little as 15 cents. These were sold on city street corners, and itinerant peddlers carried them in bags to country stores across the nation. Currier and Ives prints often featured patriotic themes, displaying the wealth, ingenuity, and economic achievements of the nation. Technological progress proved to be a favorite theme. Consumers could choose from an assortment of steamboats and trains. This late nineteenth-century Currier and Ives print (**9.4**), celebrating the technological achievements of the first half of the nineteenth century, features a number of inventions that helped transform the American economy, including steam-powered printing presses, steam-powered boats, the railroad, and the telegraph.

Beyond making it easier and faster to send messages and news, the communications revolution also contributed to economic expansion of the market revolution by fueling the desire for new consumer goods and fashions. Newspapers were filled with advertisements for the latest goods. Lavishly illustrated magazines inspired readers to procure the latest fashions.

9.4 Currier and Ives Lithograph of American Technological Achievements This print celebrates steam-powered printing presses, the steamboat, and the telegraph. These technological innovations made communication cheaper and faster.

What examples of the transportation revolution are evident in this Currier and Ives image of progress?

The Spread of Industrialization

Beginning in the early nineteenth century, the United States began a transition from a predominantly agricultural economy to an industrial one. This process unfolded unevenly across different sectors of the American economy and followed several different models depending on the industry and region. Driven by the introduction of new manufacturing technology and techniques, industrialization led to a vast increase in the number of goods—everything from clothing and shoes to tools and toys—available to the American consumer. But for many workers, especially skilled artisans, the new industrial economy led to a devaluation of their skills and loss of social status. For less-skilled workers industrialization often meant exploitation, long hours, and low pay. For others, however, the new manufacturing economy opened up opportunities for advancement.

From Artisan to Worker

The group of workers most dramatically affected by the onset of industrialization was artisans, or workers who used specialized skills to produce all sorts of consumer goods, from shoes to bread to candles. In the colonial period skilled artisans worked in small shops attached to their homes, using hand tools to produce goods for local consumption. They also employed an apprenticeship system, offering boys training in their skills (until about age twenty) in exchange for their labor. The relationship between artisan and apprentice was close. Typically an apprentice lived in his master's house, receiving food, clothing, and education.

In the new factory system first pioneered by Samuel Slater in Rhode Island (see Chapter 7), the artisan system of small-scale production was replaced with a new set of roles: owners, managers, and wage workers. The owner provided the money for the enterprise, the manager supervised the workers, and the laborers did the actual work, which was usually less skilled than the traditional crafts practiced by skilled artisans. Some industries, such as textiles, shifted relatively rapidly to the use of power-driven machinery. Shoe production, by contrast, continued to employ large numbers of manual laborers into the 1860s. In both cases manufacturers undermined the old craft traditions of artisans by breaking down the productive process into simple steps that could be performed by workers with minimal training.

Factory work forced laborers to give up many aspects of working-class culture. The work rhythm of artisans before the rise of the factory included periods of intense activity followed by slack periods in which artisans might socialize with one another, perhaps meeting in a tavern to drink and discuss politics. Under industrialization the clock ruled. Factory workers were required to follow a strict schedule and perform at a steady pace day in and day out. Beyond the rigid regulations of the workers' day, the factory robbed them of the pride of craft associated with handmade goods. In contrast to **artisan production**, where a skilled craftsman might create one-of-a-kind pieces, factory goods allowed for no originality; goods were designed to be identical.

In addition to creating a labor force of less skilled workers, the new system also led to a sharp separation between home and workplace. Before 1800 most artisans in New York had workshops attached to their homes, but by 1840 two-thirds of them lived in one place and worked in another. The rise of the factory system separated home and work place. The apprenticeship system suffered as well. By 1827 less than a quarter of apprentices lived in the same household as their employer.

If the factory system diminished the control that working people had over their time and work, it increased the goods they could afford to buy. Because factory-made goods cost less to produce, items once available only to the wealthy were now available to families of modest means. Ordinary Americans could now purchase finished furniture, clocks, dishes, silverware, and the latest fabrics.

Women and Work

The growth of the factory system had a tremendous impact on the lifestyle and status of many American women. While men's work increasingly shifted to

How did the factory change the nature of work?

sites outside the home, women's economic activity remained primarily in the home. Nevertheless some women participated more directly in the new manufacturing economy through "outwork." In this system skilled processes were broken down into simpler tasks that could be farmed out to women to perform in their homes. Manufacturers just provided the materials to women with a specified completion date. They saved money because they did not have to provide a workshop or factory, and they paid women a fraction of the wages earned by a skilled male artisan. In New England during the 1830s, some 33,000 women took part in outwork production of palm leaf hats. Among the other goods women produced by this system were paper boxes, hoopskirts, artificial flowers, and cloaks. In urban areas many women depended on the meager earnings of outwork for their economic survival.

In rural areas, such as parts of New England, women might rely on outwork for supplemental income while continuing to perform traditional agricultural work, such as producing milk, butter, and cheese. Women from rural New England would eventually provide the labor force for one of the most ambitious industrial experiments of the day: the Lowell mills.

The Lowell Experiment

In 1814 a group of Boston merchants decided to expand on Samuel Slater's mill village model (see Chapter 7) and create a large-scale planned industrial town. They built a textile factory in Waltham, Massachusetts, and developed the **Waltham System**, a mill town model that relied on highly centralized factories, each one of which united all the distinctive steps of cloth production under a single roof. The system also came to depend on a large labor force housed in company-owned dormitories.

In 1823 the same group of merchants, led by Francis Lowell, opened an even larger factory on a site in Massachusetts adjacent to the Merrimack River. The Lowell mill consolidated all aspects of cloth production. Cotton from the South arrived at the mills, where it was cleaned, carded, spun, and finally woven into a finished fabric. Within a decade the new mill town of Lowell boasted twenty-two mills, and grew to over fifty mills by 1850. Not surprisingly many competing mill towns subsequently cropped up all over New England and upstate New York.

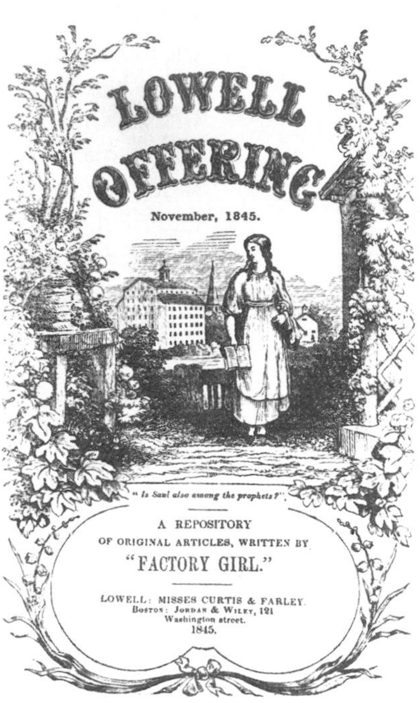
LOWELL OFFERING

November, 1845.

" Is Saul also among the prophets?"

A REPOSITORY
OF ORIGINAL ARTICLES, WRITTEN BY
"FACTORY GIRL."

LOWELL: MISSES CURTIS & FARLEY.
BOSTON: JORDAN & WILEY, 121
Washington street.
1845.

9.5 *Lowell Offering*
The Lowell mill women produced this title page of the final issue of the magazine *Lowell Offering*, presenting an image of industrial harmony. The young mill woman, holding a book in her hand, stands amid symbols of natural abundance.

The mill owners recruited young, single women from rural New England to work at the factory town. To accommodate this workforce and appease their concerned parents, they built dormitories and libraries and provided boardinghouse matrons to supervise the morality of the workers. Each boardinghouse, with up to ten bedrooms per building, housed between twenty and forty women. In some cases two women might have to share a single bed. The boardinghouses also contained a kitchen, a dining room and parlor, and separate quarters for the housekeepers, who were generally older women.

Compared with life in some of the remote New England villages from which most of the women came, Lowell offered many amenities. To begin with Lowell allowed women to earn significantly more money compared with farm labor and domestic service, the two most common occupations for single women. The women operatives in the mills also made friends with their coworkers and enjoyed free time away from the factories to socialize and pursue cultural and educational opportunities not available in their small home towns. As Josephine L. Baker, a mill worker, noted, "there are lectures, evening schools, and libraries, to which all may have access." The mill women even produced their own literary magazine, the *Lowell Offering* (**9.5**). The magazine, nominally independent of the mills, echoed this rosy portrait. Indeed the cover of this 1845 issue shows a mill girl holding a book and adopting a contemplative pose. She stands in a lush natural setting composed of flowers, trees, and vines. In its early years the Lowell experiment was touted as an example of American ingenuity, a popular destination for European visitors eager to see the wonders of the new world. British novelist Charles Dickens visited and later wrote with wonder that that the mill women were not degraded by factory life, but rather retained "the manners and deportment of young women."

Despite the upbeat image portrayed on the cover of the *Lowell Offering*, life in the mills was hard. The women worked thirteen-hour days, six days a week. Furthermore the noise of the machines, the dust and lint generated by the manufacturing processes, and the long hours demanded by the mill owners often overwhelmed women accustomed to working out of their homes. As one young Vermont mill woman noted in a letter home to her family, "It is very hard indeed and sometimes I think I shall not be able to endure it. I never worked so hard in my life."

For a decade the Lowell mill owners enjoyed high profits and peaceful labor relations. But increased competition with other textile producers led them in 1834 to announce a wage cut. Furious, the Lowell mill women went on strike, or "turned out." Critics of the strike saw it as a radical assault on the rights of the mill owners' economic freedom and a display of unseemly behavior for women. The mill women defended their actions as an assertion of their rights as American citizens and wrapped their actions in the ideals of independence and liberty that had inspired the American Revolution (see *Competing Visions: The Lowell Strike of 1834*). The strike failed to block the women's wage cut, but their actions were a milestone in the history of both women's rights and labor organization. Within a decade of this early strike, a new organization, the "Lowell Female Labor Reform Association," would join a large national struggle for a ten-hour working day for all workers.

Urban Industrialization

In contrast to the mill town system developed at Lowell, New York and Philadelphia followed different paths toward industrialization. Metropolitan industrialization was far more diverse than mill town systems. In New York and Philadelphia, factories turned out a multitude of products by using everything from skilled handwork, similar to artisan production, to steam powered machinery run by low-skilled factory operatives. The factories produced an enormous range of goods under this system, including chemicals, paints and varnishes, musical instruments, finished clothing and hats, tools, machines, furniture, and books.

New York's role as the nation's leading fashion and clothing center emerged during this period. Initially the city took a leading role in the production of cheap "Negro cottons," coarse garments assembled for sale in the South to clothe its large population of slaves. By the 1830s elegant tailoring houses such as the venerable firm of Brooks Brothers were offering well-tailored clothes for the members of the upper class and the more prosperous members of the middle class, who sought to emulate the upper class.

The industrial economy that emerged in antebellum America created jobs and opportunity for many workers, as well as a vast array of consumer products. But not everyone benefited equally from these developments. To protect themselves skilled workers built a large labor movement; twenty labor newspapers emerged in this period to champion the workers' cause. In 1835 twenty thousand Philadelphia workers from a dozen trades walked off their jobs to protest working conditions and to demand a ten-hour workday. The strike was the most successful labor action in the nation's short history and made the ten-hour workday the new standard. By 1836 labor councils or federations, a precursor of modern labor unions, had been founded in thirteen manufacturing centers scattered across the nation, as far north as Boston and as far west as Cincinnati. In the largest cities, such as New York and Philadelphia, more than fifty separate trades joined to form the general councils. The movement collapsed in the wake of a severe economic depression that began in 1837. Hard times produced high unemployment and intense job competition, undermining labor's ability to bargain for higher pay and better working conditions.

Worker unrest stemmed in part from their awareness that a small group of Americans were benefiting more than others from the new economic order. The distribution of wealth became less equal. Between 1800 and 1840 the average wealth of Americans increased by almost a third. By 1860 the average wealth of Americans would increase by another 33 percent. Although the wealth of the average citizen grew, the proportion of wealth concentrated in the hands of the nation's wealthiest citizens also increased (**9.6**). In 1800 the top 10 percent of the population owned less than half the nation's wealth. By 1860 the richest 10 percent owned two-thirds of the nation's wealth.

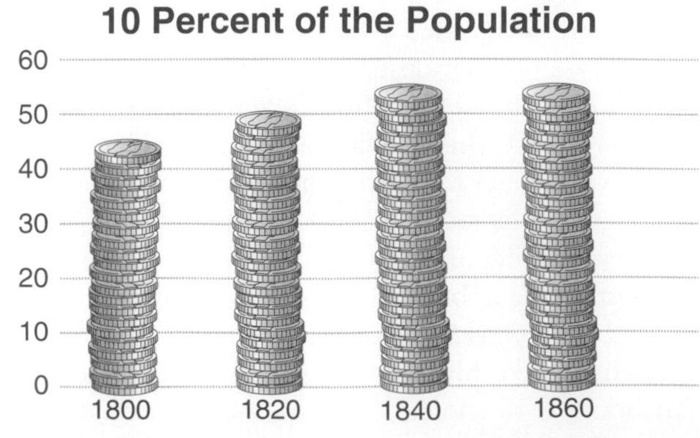

9.6 Wealth Stratification As the nation's wealth grew during the first half of the nineteenth century, it became more concentrated in the hands of a few. The wealthy controlled an even larger percentage of the nation's wealth by the middle of the century.

How did urban industrialization differ from other models of industrialization such as the Waltham (Lowell) model?

Competing Visions

THE LOWELL STRIKE OF 1834

In protesting a proposal to cut their wages, the Lowell mill women looked to the language of the American Revolution. They cast the mill owners as tyrants who sought to rob the workers of their independence and reduce them to economic slavery. For those sympathetic to the mill owners, the strikers were un-American, radical followers of the British thinker Mary Wollstonecraft, the champion of women's equality (see Chapters 5 and 6). Why did the protestors at Lowell seek to wrap their cause in the banner of the American Revolution and its ideals?

The Lowell mill women cast themselves as the heirs to the Patriots who fought the American Revolution. Their appeal for public support focused on issues of rights and independence, themes that echoed the language of the American Revolution.

UNION IS POWER

Our present object is to have union and exertion, and we remain in possession of our unquestionable rights. We circulate this paper wishing to obtain the names of all who imbibe the spirit of our Patriotic Ancestors, who preferred privation [poverty] to bondage, and parted with all that renders life desirable—and even life itself—to procure independence for their children. The oppressing hand of avarice [greed] would enslave us, and to gain their object, they gravely tell us of the pressure of the time, this we are already sensible of, and deplore it. If any are in want of assistance, the Ladies will be compassionate and assist them; but we prefer to have the disposing of our charities in our own hands; and as we are free, we would remain in possession of what kind Providence has bestowed upon us; and remain daughters of freemen still.

"Union Is Power," petition of the striking Lowell women, 1834

In this contemporary report of the Lowell protest, a Boston newspaper highlighted the radical and unladylike behavior of the strikers.

We learn that extraordinary excitement was occasioned at Lowell, last week, by an announcement that the wages paid in some of the departments would be reduced 15 percent on the 1st of March. The reduction principally affected the female operatives, and they held several meetings, or caucuses, at which a young woman presided, who took an active part in persuading her associates to give notice that they should quit the mills.... The number soon increased to nearly 800. A procession was formed, and they marched about the town, to the amusement of a mob of idlers and boys, and we are sorry to add, not altogether to the credit of Yankee girls.... We are told that one of the leaders mounted a stump and made a flaming Mary Wollstonecraft speech on the rights of women and the iniquities of the "monied aristocracy."

Salem Gazette, February 18, 1834

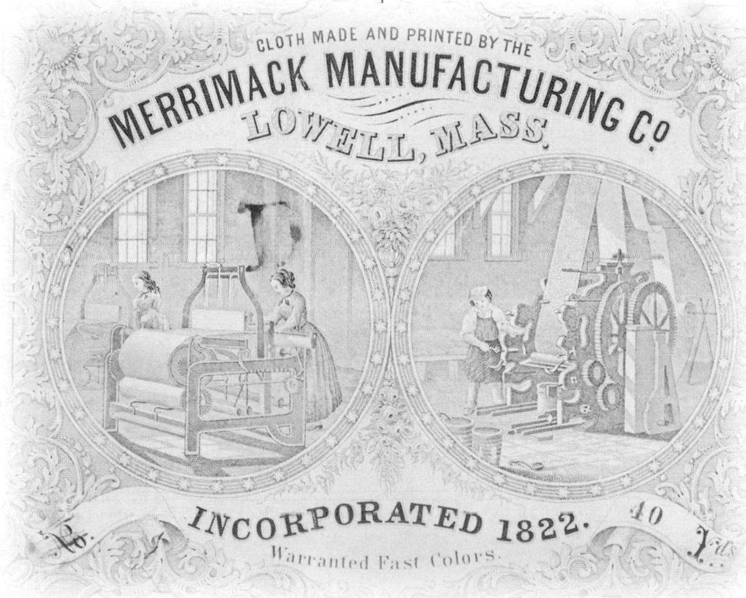

Label showing women at work in the mill

How did ideas about gender shape the response of critics of the Lowell strike?

The Changing Urban Landscape

The rise of industrialization accelerated the growth and changed the nature of American cities. While less than 10 percent of the nation's population resided in cities (areas with population of more than 2,500) before 1820, by 1860 that number had grown to 20 percent. Older cities such as New York, Philadelphia, Boston, and Baltimore grew in population, and a host of new cities in the West such as Pittsburgh, Cincinnati, St. Louis, and Chicago emerged as new urban centers. The population growth in these cities was fueled by migration from the American countryside and foreign immigration, especially from Ireland and Germany. Immigration fostered cultural diversity in cities, but it also led to rising tensions and occasional violence along ethnic, racial, and religious lines. Rising tensions between Protestants and Catholics, and between whites and blacks, led to increasing levels of urban violence. Policing became a far more complex problem in these growing cities.

Old Port Cities and the New Cities of the Interior

With nineteenth-century industrialization and population growth, major changes occurred in American cities. New kinds of neighborhoods developed that reflected the class and ethnicity of their inhabitants. Distinctive working-class neighborhoods, including the first urban slums, formed. This trend reflected the drop in the number of artisans who owned their homes and the rise of multiple-family dwellings, as well as the number of boardinghouses taking in lodgers.

New York's Five Points neighborhood illustrates the profound changes in the urban landscape caused by rapid economic development. To its working-class inhabitants, Five Points was a poor but thriving multiethnic and racially mixed community. To outsiders, however,

9.7 Five Points This image reflects the elite's view of the Five Points neighborhood. The artist has depicted a robbery in progress in the foreground.

What was the Five Points neighborhood and why did it become so well known?

its shabby housing and reputation for crime, especially prostitution, made it a symbol of urban decline. Thus while its inhabitants saw the neighborhood as a vibrant and diverse community, New York's elite viewed it as a notorious slum to be avoided. This contemporary image (**9.7**) captures the multiracial character of the neighborhood, but it also reflects the fears of many New Yorkers that Five Points was crime-ridden and dangerous.

Middle- and upper-class families eager to escape contact with working people, immigrants, and free blacks segregated themselves into new, more exclusive neighborhoods. New York's Gramercy Park, for example, was created in 1831 as a private park surrounded by elegant private homes. Ringed by a tall gated fence, the park was accessible only to the adjacent homeowners who received special keys. This image of a similar exclusive enclave (**9.8**), St. Johns Square in New York, shows a park with a fence that segregates the rich residents from individuals such as the African Americans lampooned in this image for attempting to dress and act above their station in life. The African American figures are caricatures whose physical features are exaggerated to conform to the racist stereotypes of the day.

In 1800 even America's largest urban centers were "walking cities." A person could easily walk around all of New York, Philadelphia, or Boston in just a few hours. By 1820, however, these cities had grown to contain more than half the urban population of the new nation, and by mid-century these once compact walking cities had become sprawling metropolises. Some of this growth came from annexation. Philadelphia in 1854 annexed several of its suburbs, increasing its size from 2 square miles to 129. Much of the growth was driven by advances in mass transportation that allowed city dwellers to live farther and farther away from where they worked, shopped, and visited for entertainment. The first of these modes of transportation, which arrived in 1827, was the "omnibus," an urban stagecoach that carried up to twelve passengers over fixed routes for a flat fee. Expensive, slow, and uncomfortable, it gave way by the 1850s to the horsecar, a twenty-passenger coach pulled on rails by horses. Faster, cheaper, and more comfortable than the omnibus, horsecars, or street-railway lines, spread to virtually every large city by 1860. Philadelphia alone boasted 155 miles of track. At the same time steam-powered locomotives had begun to carry commuters—or people who traveled over a significant distance from home to work—to and from outlying areas.

9.8 **St. Johns Square**
St. Johns Square was one of several gated parks created to keep the poor and working classes separate from upper-class New Yorkers. [*Source*: The Library Company of Philadelphia]

Within the first decade of the nineteenth century, New York surpassed Philadelphia to become the nation's largest city. Central to this development was the city's harbor, the largest on the East Coast and one ideally suited to become a major port. The completion of the Erie Canal in 1825 ensured New York's economic supremacy as it connected the city to the Midwest. It increased dramatically the flow of finished goods from Europe and the rest of the United States into the American heartland and the flow of foodstuffs produced by Midwestern farmers into domestic and foreign markets.

Inland cities such as Pittsburgh, Cincinnati, St. Louis, and Chicago were among the fastest-growing urban areas in the nation. Situated on rivers or lakes and soon connected by railroads, inland cities became manufacturing centers and often served as transportation hubs. Between 1800 and 1840 these new cities saw their populations quadruple. If any city in America fit the modern stereotype of a soot-covered industrial town, it was Pittsburgh. The French traveler Michel Chevalier remarked that "a dense black smoke which, bursting forth in volumes from the foundries, forges, glass-houses, and the chimneys of all the factories and houses, falls in flakes of soot upon the dwellings and persons of the inhabitants. It is, therefore, the dirtiest town in the United States." Cincinnati, a small settlement on the Ohio River in 1800, emerged as a major industrial center by 1840, producing a wide range of manufactured products, including furniture, tools, candles,

What does the creation of gated parks such as Gramercy Park tell us about urban life in this period?

paper, leather, and soap. The soap industry grew out of the city's large number of pig-slaughtering houses (Cincinnati's nickname was "Porkopolis") that produced fat renderings that provided an essential ingredient for making soap. The firm of Procter & Gamble was founded in the city in 1837.

Immigrants and the City

The sharp rise in urban populations in the nineteenth century stemmed from two sources: the migration of Americans from rural areas and immigration from Europe. The latter expanded dramatically after 1830, soaring from 23,000 in 1830 to 428,000 in 1854. Immigrants left their homelands for the United States for many reasons, including poverty, poor harvests, warfare, and political and religious persecution. The most dramatic exodus in this period was triggered in 1845 when Ireland's potato crop failed. The disaster killed more than one million people and spurred more than a million others, mostly poor peasants, to cross the Atlantic to America. Both poor harvests and political turmoil in Europe boosted German immigration to the United States. Besides the Irish and Germans, the other large groups of immigrants came from other parts of Britain, notably Scotland and Wales, and from Scandinavia, such as Danes, Swedes, and Norwegians (**9.9**).

The influx of immigrants from Ireland and Germany between 1830 and 1860 dramatically changed America's ethnic composition. For the first time large numbers of non-Protestants entered American society. Irish immigrants were almost entirely Catholic, while German immigrants included both Catholics and Protestants. Ethnic enclaves with names like *Kleindeutchland* (Little Germany) and Little Ireland, with their own churches, mutual aid societies, theaters, newspapers, restaurants, and social clubs, developed in many cities.

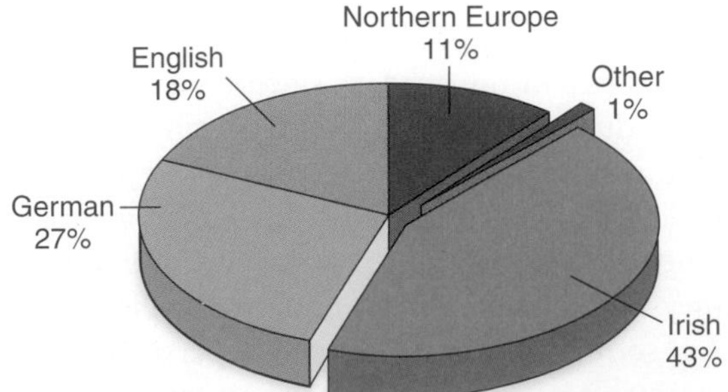

9.9 Sources of European Immigration
A growing number of immigrants from Germany and Ireland changed the population mix in many parts of the nation. The influx of Catholic immigrants in particular resulted in tensions with Protestant groups.

Irish immigrants generally came from the poorest segments of society; they arrived with very little money and few skills needed in an urban economy. They often ended up in slum neighborhoods like Five Points and came to dominate low-skilled jobs such as laborer and domestic servant. Nonetheless many Irish immigrants entered the skilled trades and several became successful entrepreneurs.

German immigration drew from a more diverse population. As with the Irish, German immigration included many poor peasants forced off the land, but it also included large numbers of skilled artisans and even some liberal intellectuals who fled Germany after the political upheavals of 1848 that swept over much of continental Europe. Germans were more likely than the Irish to become farmers, shopkeepers, or skilled tradesmen. Germans also ventured farther inland, settling places such as Cincinnati and St Louis. More skilled on average than their Irish counterparts, Germans transformed a number of fields. Adolph Busch, a skilled brew master, brought German-style beer to America, and skilled musical instrument makers such as Heinrich Steinway helped launch such venerable firms as Steinway and Sons, piano makers.

Free Black Communities in the North

Urban centers in the North and Midwest were home to some of the the largest free African American communities in the nation. Free blacks living in enclaves such as Boston's "New Guinea" or Cincinnati's "Little Africa" were probably the most urbanized subgroup in America. Racial segregation was more pronounced in the urban North than in the cities of the South, where urban slaves were likely to live in their masters' homes. Thus an African American living in Boston was almost twice as likely to live in a segregated neighborhood than was an African American living in New Orleans. African American communities developed a variety of thriving institutions, such as churches, schools, and self-help societies.

Still, life for free African Americans was hindered by racial prejudice and discrimination. In the North and parts of the Midwest, exclusion from many of the skilled trades often forced African Americans into the most menial types of labor. This situation actually worsened in the 1840s and 1850s as immigrants, especially the Irish, took over occupations traditionally dominated by African Americans, such as barbers and cart men. In the cities of the North and West, hostility to African Americans competing for jobs with whites intensified. A drawing from the period (**9.10**) exploits white fears of African American laborers. The racist message of the image is clear: Free blacks will steal the jobs of white workingmen.

9.10 ***The Results of Abolitionism*** This poster warns white laborers that their jobs might be taken by free African American laborers. [Courtesy Library Company of Philadelphia]

Through persistence, talent, and good fortune, some African Americans could surmount the many obstacles they faced in the labor market and achieve financial security or occasionally even prosper. Henry Boyd of Cincinnati provides an example of one such life. Trained as a carpenter while still a slave, Boyd, somehow having managed to obtain his freedom, later began to ply his trade in Cincinnati. Although Boyd was able to find some work, many employers refused to hire him. Yet in 1836 Boyd accumulated enough money to establish his own furniture-making business, and by 1842 his downtown factory was using the latest steam-powered equipment to make furniture. By the 1850s Boyd was employing a mixed-race workforce of some fifty people. Nine years later, however, fire destroyed Boyd's factory. Without insurance Boyd was unable to rebuild his factory, leaving him as he had begun his career—a struggling artisan.

Riot, Unrest, and Crime

Urbanization in the first half of the nineteenth century was accompanied by a sharp rise in crime and disorder. During the 1830s there were 115 incidents of mob violence, a steep rise from previous decades. One newspaper reported that "a spirit of riot" had taken over the nation's cities. Violence increased as growing cities became increasingly divided racially, economically, and ethnically. Anti-Catholic sentiment spurred much of the intensified violence. In 1834 a mob attacked and burned a Catholic convent just outside Boston. Ten years later in Philadelphia, the "bible riots" left twenty dead and two Catholic churches in ashes.

Racial animosity also inspired urban unrest. Cincinnati's African American community faced the ire of white mobs in 1829, 1836, and 1841. A three-day riot in Providence, Rhode Island, in 1831 destroyed most of the African American part of the city. A riot in New York in 1834 destroyed an African American church, school, and a dozen homes. Adding to the tensions of the period and occasionally sparking violence were political battles between Democrats and Whigs, antagonisms between supporters and opponents of slavery, and conflicts over regulating or eliminating behaviors such as gambling and drinking.

Contributing to the rise in urban violence was the steady increase in the number of single men living outside of traditional family units, a trend that arose from industrialization and immigration. In the 1840s and 1850s, at least 30 percent of male urban dwellers lived outside of family units, usually in boardinghouses. Free from the traditional guidance and restraint of adults and family, young men developed a masculine subculture in which alcohol and fighting played a central role.

The masculine subculture also led to a significant rise in prostitution (as did the poverty of many women), a situation that alarmed many officials. Influential minister Lyman Beecher decried the fact that so many young people were "thrown out upon the open bosom of our city" where they were easily "corrupted by sensuality." Beecher's fears were well founded. Theaters encouraged prostitutes to attend their performances as a means of boosting sales, a practice so common that the cheap seats they occupied were dubbed the "guilty third tier." Many Americans became aware of the prevalence of prostitution in American cities through the media sensation that attended the murder of the prostitute Helen Jewett in New York City in 1836. Rival newspapers competed to be the first to publish the latest revelation about the case, and the story dominated headlines for months. The salacious appeal of the murder even produced colorful images such as this scene showing the alleged murderer leaving the scene of the crime (**9.11**). Reflecting the low regard in which prostitutes were held, the man accused of killing Jewett was acquitted despite significant evidence pointing to his guilt.

Most urban crime did not involve sensational tales of murder, but rather petty crimes against property or person. The informal policing mechanisms that cities had relied on in the eighteenth century, including the use of night watchmen and sheriffs who had to rely on community support to quell unrest, proved woefully inadequate to policing a major metropolitan area in the nineteenth century. In 1839 the mayor of New York pushed to create a professional police force, fearing that without strong intervention New York would attain "the character of a riotous city." In 1845 New York created the first modern professional police force in America, modeled on London's Metropolitan Police Force. The city employed eight hundred men organized in a military structure; they carried weapons (but not firearms) and were deployed to keep the peace and apprehend criminals.

9.11 Murder of Helen Jewett Currier's lurid depiction of the murder of the prostitute Helen Jewett was part of the media frenzy surrounding this sensational murder. [*Source*: Collection of The New-York Historical Society, Neg. #40696]

What does the murder of Helen Jewett reveal about nineteenth-century city life?

Southern Society

Even as Northern society changed dramatically between 1815 and 1860 due to immigration, urbanization, and industrialization, Southern society remained committed to slavery and a cash crop economy. The rise of cotton cultivation and the expansion of plantations into the band of fertile land from Georgia to Texas transformed the institution of slavery. Although the vast majority of Southerners did not own slaves, the institution of slavery suffused Southern culture and society. A small minority of planters shaped the political and economic life of the whole South. Addressing a Southern audience in 1850, one Southern leader described slavery as connected with all the South's institutions" and affecting "the personal interests of every white man."

"I could easily prove that almost all the differences which may be noticed between the characters of the Americans in the Southern and in the Northern states have originated in slavery."

ALEXIS DE TOCQUEVILLE, *Democracy in America* (1838)

The Planter Class

Only a few planters lived in the grand luxury many people today associate with the world of nineteenth-century slavery (an image celebrated in the classic 1939 film, *Gone with the Wind*). For example at Nottoway, in Louisiana, John Hampden Randolph built a magnificent mansion that contained 64 rooms, 200 windows, and 165 doors. But the typical planter lived far more modestly in a simple two-story wood-framed house. The planter's home, generally described as "the big house" because it was always the largest domestic dwelling on a plantation, was at the center of a variety of smaller out-buildings, including a kitchen, well, dairy, ice house, smokehouse, and laundry. More substantial plantations included many other types of buildings, such as barns, stables, sheds, and storehouses. Georgia rice planter Henry McAlpin's Hermitage plantation (**9.12**) resembled a small town, with multiple residences, a hospital, and a variety of other buildings. Indeed, the slave quarters constituted an even smaller village within this self-contained community. Most plantations were far more modest. The vast majority of slave owners owned between one and nine slaves. Fewer than 1 percent owned a hundred or more slaves. Thus the typical slaveholder

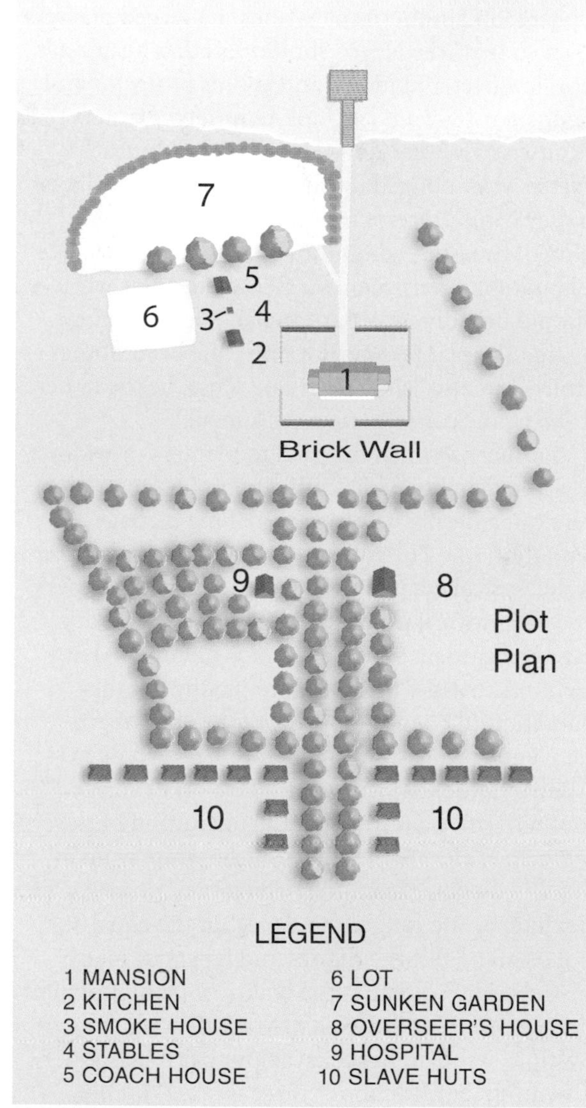

9.12 Schematic Map of Hermitage Plantation Large plantations were like small towns. This planation included a separate overseer's house, hospital, and a collection of slave huts.

worked a small family farm of about 100 acres with fewer than ten slaves.

Planters created something akin to English-style aristocracy. Thomas Dabney, who had migrated to Mississippi from Virginia in 1835 to establish a large cotton plantation, aspired to this kind of aristocratic lifestyle. Dabney tried to emulate the life of an English country gentleman, taking tea in the afternoon and treating his less affluent neighbors as social inferiors.

While industrialization in the North created a sharp divide between work and home, physically separating the two realms, Southern plantations fused the two realms together. A large body of advice literature geared toward plantation management appeared in Southern magazines that urged planters to act so that "the Negro should feel that his master is his lawgiver and judge; and yet his protector and friend." An 1842 advice book reminded planters that because slaves were "placed under our control," masters were obliged to care for and instruct slaves so they could "receive moral and religious uplift." In theory masters sought to "govern absolutely." "Plantation government," a Georgia planter wrote, "should be eminently patriarchal." He went on to say that the planter was not only "the head of the family" but also "should, in one sense, be the father of the whole concern, negroes and all."

Southern women married to planters or widows or eldest daughters in families without a matriarch were often deeply involved in helping manage plantation life. The role of the plantation mistress, as she was called, was to supervise a group of slaves who might work in the kitchen, nursery, laundry, stable, or garden. While husbands often relied on overseers to assist them and frequently left the plantation to attend to business or public affairs, the planter's wife was often left to her own devices to run a home that was more like a small village. Southern men claimed that the institution of slavery had helped elevate the status of the white woman and liberated her from the drudgery of domestic life, making her "no longer the slave, but the equal and idol of man." But the diaries and letters of many mistresses indicate that the reality of plantation life did not meet this lofty ideal. Mary Kendall, for example, wrote in her diary about her loneliness, lamenting that "for about three weeks I did not have the pleasure of seeing one white female face." Although she did possess authority over the slaves, she did so only as the wife or daughter of the master, to whom she was expected to be obedient.

Yeomen and Tenant Farmers

Most Southern whites were not planters but yeoman farmers, independent landowners who worked their own small farms. In 1860 more than three-quarters of Southerners owned no slaves. As a result yeomen farmers were dependent on neighborliness and communal cooperation to complete tasks such as planting, harvesting, or building. Lacking the urban centers and cheap transportation that allowed many small farmers in the North to enter fully into the market economy, many Southern yeomen did not produce large surpluses for market. Instead they devoted most of their resources to producing food for their own families and generally allocated only a small portion of their lands for cash crops that could be sold to purchase seed, sugar, and the occasional manufactured good. Since they could not afford the cost of transporting their surpluses to market, yeoman farmers depended on planters to market their small surpluses. They likewise depended on planters for the use of the plantation mill to grind corn into meal. In many parts of the South where planters and yeomen resided side by side, a complex web of economic, political, and social ties bound these two classes together. At the same time many yeomen living in the upcountry regions of the South were fiercely independent and often resented the more affluent planters who dominated their state's militia, state legislatures, and courts.

Indeed most Southern state legislators and judges were drawn from the ranks of the planter class. The same was true of the officers of the militia. Below the ranks of officers, the yeomanry formed the core of the militia system that had the primary responsibility for catching runaway slaves and guarding against slave insurrection. In this anti-slavery woodcut, the slave patrol is depicted terrorizing a captured slave (**9.13**), found traveling without a pass. Passes were written by owners and were required for any traveling slave.

Many Southerners owned no land and worked as tenant farmers. In some parts of the South, as many as 50 percent of the white population fell into this category. While some of the landless population in the South comprised young men waiting to inherit land from their fathers, a substantial segment of the population rarely entered the ranks of the solid yeomanry. In some parts of the Deep South densely populated with African American slaves, poor whites fraternized with slaves, including engaging in clandestine activities with them: smuggling liquor

What values defined the planter class?

9.13 *A Slave Caught Without a Pass*
In this woodcut from an abolitionist almanac, a slave patrol harasses a slave traveling from one plantation to another.

into the slave quarters, helping runaways, or forming sexual liaisons and permanent relationships with slaves. More often, however, the dominance of a white supremacist ideology overcame the prospects of class solidarity across racial lines.

Free Black Communities

While the vast majority of African Americans in the South were enslaved, some 6 percent of the black population in the South by 1860 lived as free people of color. The vast majority of free blacks resided in the upper South, with especially large communities in border states such as Delaware and Maryland. A third of the free blacks resided in Southern cities, with the largest communities in Baltimore, Richmond, New Orleans, Charleston, Memphis, Mobile, and Natchez. The South's Black Codes were even more restrictive than those in the North (see Chapter 8). Free Southern blacks had to carry identification to prove that they were not slaves. Southern law also barred them from holding office and in some cases even from testifying in court against whites.

Although life for free blacks in the South was difficult, the shortage of skilled artisans in many cities of the South created opportunities for them to enter trades such as cabinet making. Southern cities were also less spatially segregated than Northern cities, and Southern African Americans played a prominent role as domestics and in some fields and trades such as tailoring and hair cutting. The free black community in New Orleans was one of the most affluent in the South. It published its own newspapers and hosted lavish balls each year for its most elite members.

Religious institutions also played an important role in the free African American community. In addition to tending to the spiritual needs of their congregations, ministers were often leaders within the African American community. The size of the membership of Southern churches far exceeded that of similar institutions in the North. Thus the largest

African American church in the North, New York's Abyssinian Baptist, had a membership of 440 at mid-century, a mere fraction of the size of First African Church of Richmond, which counted 3,160 members.

White Southern Culture

Wealthy white Southerners in the antebellum years entertained on a lavish scale, hosting parties, balls, fox hunts, and horse races. Fondness for the aristocratic ideal even led some to sponsor medieval tournaments that included jousting. Southerners took pride in their seaside resorts along the Gulf Coast, gracious vacation spots characterized by a "quiet ease." They expressed disdain for the bustling character of Northern resorts such as Newport, Rhode Island, and Saratoga Springs, New York. New Orleans gradually replaced New York as the horse racing capital of the nation. Traditional blood sports such as cock fighting also continued to be popular, particularly among less affluent Southerners.

Reputation and honor were central values in the male-oriented Southern culture. An "unsullied reputation," one observer of Southern values noted, was all that a man required to be "on a social level with his fellows." A Scottish traveler remarked that Southern men "consider themselves men of honor" and "more frequently resent any indignity shown them even at the expense of their life, or that of those who venture to insult them."

When a gentleman experienced an insult from a social inferior, the appropriate response was to cane or horsewhip the offender. Dueling, by contrast, was reserved for settling matters of honor among gentlemen. In 1838 John Wilson, a former governor of South Carolina, published *The Code of Honor; or the Rules for the Government of Principals and Seconds in Dueling*, which explained such things as the role of seconds and the choice of weapons. The centrality of honor to Southern culture was the chief reason dueling endured in this region long after it had been outlawed in the North. Many of the South's leading politicians, including Andrew Jackson and Henry Clay, had participated in duels at one time or another in their careers. This contemporary drawing by a Northern opponent of slavery (**9.14**) portrays the South as a culture dominated by dueling, brawling, and mobbing. For some Northerners, especially those opposed to slavery, the dueling and other violence they associated with the South was a result of the brutality inherent in the institution of slavery. The connection between slavery and Southern violence figures prominently in the image, which shows a cruel master whipping a young helpless slave child.

9.14 Southern Violence This Northern depiction of Southern violence links the brawling and dueling of Southerners with the brutal labor regime of slavery. References to the pistol and the lash became important in abolitionist attacks on Southern culture.

What role did honor play in Southern culture?

Life and Labor under Slavery

Slavery was a complex institution that took many forms in the South. Some slaves lived on large cotton plantations and worked in gangs under the authority of an overseer, while others toiled beside their master on small farms. Still others lived in cities where, if they possessed skills, they were often hired out. Regardless of these differences the law treated all slaves as property, leaving them entirely at the mercy of their master who had the power to impose punishment and separate slaves from their families by selling them. To protect themselves slaves developed various traditions and strategies. Many turned to religion to provide spiritual comfort and culture resources to resist the domination of their masters. Slaves also developed subtle forms of resistance such as feigned illness, work slow downs, and destruction of tools and other property. Occasionally slaves took more overt measures like running away, either to seek a temporary respite from the harsh labor regime or to escape North to freedom. The most radical and the rarest form of resistance was insurrection, rising up against the established authorities.

Varied Systems of Slave Labor

Slave labor produced a variety of other agricultural products—tobacco, hemp, sugar, and rice. But the leading product was cotton, an enterprise in which more than half of all slaves toiled. By 1840 cotton accounted for more than half the nation's exports with most of it heading for European (especially British) textile mills. The remainder was sent north to American textile mills in places like Lowell, Massachusetts.

Yet even in those regions of the South in which cotton was not the primary crop, the cotton economy influenced economic life. Many farmers who did not produce cotton produced foodstuffs and supplies for consumption on cotton plantations. For instance hemp was turned into rope that was used to bind cotton bales for shipment.

The antebellum South was divided economically into two regions, the lower South and the upper South. The warm climate of the lower South was ideal for cotton cultivation, as was the dark rich soil of the region stretching from Alabama to Texas known as the **Black Belt**. In the decades after 1820, cotton cultivation spread rapidly westward along the Black Belt, propelled by two factors. First the great wealth produced by cotton provided huge economic incentives for bringing new lands under cultivation. Second because cotton exhausted soil of its nutrients, growers constantly sought new lands to bring under cultivation. To grow and harvest this cotton, planters relied on a labor force that was 90 percent enslaved.

The upper South included eight slave states, but it lacked the fertile land and long growing season necessary for cotton agriculture. As a result the upper South embraced agricultural diversification, including grain and livestock. Of the agricultural staples produced in this region, corn, rye, and hemp (used to produce rope) were particularly important. With each passing decade of the antebellum period, slavery became less and less viable in this region and many masters elected to sell their slaves to the lower South where demand for their labor was extremely high.

Most slaves worked as field hands, toiling from sun up to sun down most of the year. On most large plantations slaves worked in the fields in gangs, which gave their masters more control over their labor. Men and women generally worked together, in many cases supervised by a hired white overseer. Masters sometimes employed slaves to act as drivers, or supervisors, a role that required them to discipline other slaves or face severe punishment themselves. In some cases a clever driver might find a way to protect other slaves from more severe punishment at the hands of an overseer. Larger plantations also employed many slave craftsmen as carpenters, blacksmiths, weavers, coopers, and other occupations. Household slaves functioned as cooks and coachmen and in a variety of other domestic duties, such as nannies or cleaning women.

Planters used a system of rewards and punishments to enforce slave discipline. As rewards some planters allowed slaves to maintain a small garden or even sell produce at market. Ultimately,

Where was the Black Belt?

9.15 Broadside with Image of Slave Whipping
To portray the horror of slavery, abolitionists made effective use of the image of slave owners whipping their slaves.

however, labor discipline was enforced by violence. A popular plantation management book that many planters consulted argued that "after reason and persuasion have been exhausted without producing the desired effect, punishment of some sort must be resorted to." As one English observer of the gang system noted, "Absence from work, or neglect of duty, was punished with stinted allowances, imprisonment, and flogging." Northern abolitionist literature made the image of the whip one of their most prominent metaphors of life in the South as this broadside with images drawn from an antislavery almanac reveals (**9.15**).

Beyond physical punishment Southern masters also exerted control over their slaves by threatening to sell them on the slave market. Slaves residing in the upper South feared being sold "down river" to a cotton plantation because it meant separation from family and kin and more than likely a harsher existence. The sale of slaves tore families apart. By some estimates the sale of slaves may have dissolved as many as one-third of all slave marriages and separated close to half of the children living in the older parts of the South from a parent. The British painter Eyre Crowe painted a scene in a Richmond slave market, in which men, women, and children wait their turn on the auction block (**9.16**). Scenes such as this were common throughout Virginia and parts of the Carolinas. One of the largest slave auctions occurred in 1859 when the Georgia planter Pierce Butler sold 450 slaves in a single auction lasting several days. A reporter from the *New York Tribune* described the misery of the slaves whose "brothers and sisters" were to be "scattered through the cotton fields of Alabama." The "expressions of heavy grief," the reporter noted, reflected their horror at having been "torn from their homes" and separated from their loved ones.

9.16 ***The Slave Market, Richmond, Virginia***
An English traveler who accompanied the English novelist William Makepeace Thackeray on a tour of America captured the grim realities of a slave auction.

Although the vast majority of the South's slaves toiled as agricultural laborers, many toiled in some type of

What role did violence play in slave society?

industrial enterprise, primarily those located in the upper South. While the South lagged far behind the North in industrial development, taken on its own it exceeded all but the top five or six industrial nations in production of textiles, iron making, grain and timber milling, sugar refining, and leather tanning. Most of these upper South industries relied on slave labor and by 1850 at least 5 percent (between 150,000 and 200,000) of the South's slaves worked in industry. Employers owned 80 percent of the slaves who worked in industry with the rest hired out on yearly contracts or short-term leases. In some cases enslaved blacks and free whites worked side by side. Richmond's Tredegar Iron Works employed such a mixed labor force until 1847, when a strike by whites prompted the mill owners to turn exclusively to enslaved blacks for all of its labor needs apart from a few white supervisors.

Slaves also worked in nonagricultural enterprises in cities such as Richmond, Virginia, Mobile, Alabama, Charleston, South Carolina, and New Orleans, Louisiana. Slaves worked as domestics, skilled artisans, carriage drivers, gardeners, couriers, and nurses. Southern cities also employed slaves for public works projects, including sanitation, road building, and bridge maintenance. Savannah, Georgia, and Charleston, South Carolina, even used slaves as firefighters.

Life in the Slave Quarters

Compared to Brazil, where living conditions were among the worst in the Americas, American slaves lived under less harsh conditions. This fact contributed to a significant natural increase in the slave population in the United States; the population increased nearly fivefold between 1790 and 1850. Still American slave owners often treated their slaves brutally and provided inadequate food, shelter, clothing, and medical care. As a result infant mortality rates for slave children were twice the rate of white children. Life expectancy for whites in the South was between forty and forty-three years, lower than that in other parts of the country; that of the average slave, however, was only between thirty and thirty-three years.

Fanny Kemble, the wife of planter Pierce Butler, described the slave quarters on her husband's plantation in stark terms. "These cabins consist of one room, about twelve feet by thirteen," and providing extremely cramped surroundings. "Two families (together numbering sometimes eight or ten) reside in one of these huts which are mere wooden frames." Wealthier planters sometimes built sturdier slave quarters that consisted of framed houses with wooden floors or in some cases houses made of brick.

The oppressive nature of slavery also shaped family life. Although Southern law did not recognize the legality of slave marriages, many slave men and women sought to form stable family relationships. Slaves developed their own marriage rituals to seal their unions. The most common was "jumping the broom," a ritual that derived from traditional African marriage practices. Relatives or close friends of the bride and groom held opposite ends of a broom about a foot off the ground, and the couple would jump together over the broom as a symbol of their union. Planters generally encouraged slaves to marry because planters recognized that married slaves were less likely to run away. In addition the offspring of slave marriages provided planters with additional laborers.

On larger plantations a slave family might reside together. In the case of smaller plantations and farms, husbands and wives might reside on neighboring plantations. Such "abroad" marriages were common. Visiting a spouse under these circumstances required obtaining permission, and husbands might see their families only once a week. The slave family included extended kin, such as uncles, aunts, and, most important, grandparents, all of whom took an active role in rearing children.

Slave Religion and Music

During the 1830s Southern churches embarked on a major missionary effort to convert slaves to Christianity. In proselytizing slaves white ministers stressed the conservative elements of Christian theology, often forbidding slaves from dancing during religious services and reminding them of the passages in the Bible that demanded slaves obey their masters. A popular *Catechism for Colored Persons*, for example, instructed slaves to "count their Masters 'worthy of all honour,' as those whom God has placed over them in the world."

Although slave owners hoped to use religion to instill docility in their slaves, these efforts largely failed. Rather than accept their masters' vision of Christianity, African Americans recast Christianity to suit their own needs as slaves and articulate their hopes. The Old Testament story of Exodus, which told of the flight of the Israelites from slavery in Egypt, was particularly popular among slaves. "God was working for their deliverance," a Georgia slave

Why did so many slaves marry slaves living on other plantations?

9.17 ***Plantation Burial***
While a slave preacher leads a funeral service, the plantation master and mistress are visible in the woods in between the two trees in the background, a reminder that slaves were never free from the watchful eyes of their masters.

commented, and "would deliver them from bondage as sure as the children of Israel were delivered from Egyptian bondage." African Americans created covert churches called "brush arbors" or "hush arbors" to practice their version of the faith.

African American slaves also borrowed elements from African religions, creating a distinctive African American religious culture. White observers were perplexed by the "ring shout," an ecstatic form of worship that mixed elements of African religious practice with Christian beliefs, describing its chanting as "weird" or "droning" and its dance as "wild" and "barbaric." Yet to the enslaved the ring shout's rhythmic circle dance involving joined hands, counterclockwise movement to a steady beat, hand clapping, and free-form upper body movements became an important religious ritual.

Slave funeral practices also reflected this fusion of African and Christian rituals. Slaves often scattered broken ceramics over a grave, a practice carried over from African burial practices. A Maryland observer of one funeral noted that the body was interred with a miniature canoe and paddle. The slaves explained that this would allow the spirit to cross the ocean and return to Africa. Because slaves toiled in the fields during the day, their funerals typically took place at night. Torchlight processions to gravesites, accompanied by drumming and other African-inflected music and chants, appeared eerie to many white observers. Still some white observers, as this painting of a slave preacher leading a funeral service (**9.17**) shows, overcame their cultural bias and appreciated the sublime beauty of slave burials. Barely discernible in the space between the two trees in the foreground are the plantation master and mistress. The artist's rendering of the scene provides a visual reminder that slaves were never completely free from the watchful eye of their masters.

Spirituals, a distinctive musical art form created by slaves, drew heavily on biblical themes. The figure of Moses and the plight of the ancient Hebrews who were delivered from slavery were two common themes. The River Jordon also figures prominently in slave spirituals. Images of crossing over the great river to freedom in this life or redemption in the next occur as prominent themes as well.

Music played an important role in aspects of slave culture other than religion. Slaves used song as a means to preserve African traditions, help relieve the monotony of work, entertain, or even communicate cryptic messages intended only for other slaves. When slaves "went around singing 'Steal Away to Jesus,'" a former slave recalled, it not only affirmed the hope of redemption but also often served as practical means of signaling to others that there would "be a religious meeting that night."

Resistance and Revolt

Slaves developed a complex range of behaviors to resist the harsh work discipline forced on them. Many preferred to employ subtle tactics to thwart their owners because they minimized the chances for punishment. Slaves feigned illness, broke tools, and slowed their pace of work as means of fighting back against their economic exploitation.

Another means of resistance available to slaves was flight. Typically runaways left only for short periods of time, seeking a brief respite from servitude, or to visit kin and spouses on neighboring plantations. Less frequently slaves sought to gain their freedom by fleeing to free territory in the

Why did Old Testament themes figure so prominently in slave spirituals?

> "Steal away to Jesus!
> Steal away, steal away home.
> I ain't got long to stay here.
> My Lord calls me,
> He calls me by the thunder;
> The trumpet sounds
> within my soul,
> I ain't got long to stay here."
>
> Spiritual, "Steal Away to Jesus"

North or in Canada. In the Deep South, some slaves fled to Indian territory or to swamps to escape detection. In a few celebrated cases, slaves devised daring methods of escape.

The most extreme form of resistance was insurrection. In 1831 Nat Turner led the largest slave uprising in American history. A lay preacher Turner had a vision of a battle between "white spirits and blacks spirits" that would commence when the "sun was darkened." Turner believed that the solar eclipse in 1831 was a divine sign that the time for insurrection was ripe. **Nat Turner's Rebellion** lasted two days and attracted somewhere between sixty and eighty slaves before authorities were able to subdue the rebels. Before the carnage ended fifty-five whites were killed and as many African Americans. This woodcut from a contemporary account of the rebellion written by a supporter of slavery depicts the rebels unsympathetically, about to attack defenseless women and children, and depicts as heroic the efforts of whites to defend their loved ones (**9.18**). The bottom of the image shows the militia riding to the rescue of these helpless victims. Many opponents of slavery in the North, however, viewed Nat Turner as a righteous and heroic warrior again the evil of slavery.

In the aftermath of the Nat Turner Rebellion, Southern states enacted a new series of repressive laws designed to prevent further rebellions. The new laws prevented African Americans from preaching and limited the access of free blacks to firearms. States also strengthened their militia organizations and stiffened penalties for assaults by slaves, making them made capital offenses. In the aftermath of the rebellion, the Virginia legislature even considered abolishing slavery and debated the issue thoroughly before voting of 73 to 58 against a proposal to end slavery.

Slavery and the Law

Each Southern state passed its own set of laws, or slave codes, governing the institution of slavery. These laws described the property rights of masters (slaves were categorized somewhere between property and people), the duties slaves owed to their masters, and the punishments for rebellion. Although laws varied from state to state, all slave codes accorded slaves minimal rights. These laws curtailed the movements of slaves, forbidding them to travel without written permission from their masters. The law also did not recognize slave marriages and proscribed teaching slaves to read or write. Slaves had no right to testify in court, and planters served as both judge and jury on their plantations, meting out punishment. On rare occasions a slave successfully obtained a day in court, as in the case where a South Carolina court ruled that a slave could not be tried for the same crime twice, an application of the constitutional prohibition on double jeopardy that was a bedrock of American law. In spite of such modest protections, however, slaves still enjoyed only the slimmest legal protection and remained at the mercy of their masters (see *Choices and Consequences: Conscience or Duty? Judge Ruffin's Quandary*, page 278).

9.18 Woodcut Image of Nat Turner's Rebellion This image reflects the views of Southerners who were horrified by Turner's uprising.

Who was Nat Turner?

Choices and Consequences

CONSCIENCE OR DUTY? JUDGE RUFFIN'S QUANDARY

In 1829 Chief Justice Thomas Ruffin of the North Carolina Supreme Court issued his opinion in *State v. Mann*, a case involving an assault on a slave, Lydia, by John Mann. Lydia's owner, Elizabeth Jones, brought the suit against Mann (slaves could not bring suits) for wounding her slave. Mann had rented Lydia from Jones, which gave him temporary ownership of her. During the time he was her master, he had all the legal authority of her owner, including the right to administer punishment for disobedience. When Mann tried to discipline Lydia, she ran off. Mann then shot and wounded her. A lower court convicted Mann of an assault and battery on Lydia, and Mann then appealed the case to the North Carolina Supreme Court. ***State v. Mann*** explored legal questions at the heart of slavery. In deciding whether the domination of the master over the slave was complete, Supreme Court Judge Ruffin faced difficult choices.

Choices

1. Uphold Mann's conviction and affirm that the right of the master to discipline and punish his slaves was limited.

2. Overrule the lower court and assert that the master's power over slaves was unlimited.

3. Order that Mann be retried for attempted murder—one of the few crimes against a slave for which a white person could be prosecuted.

Decision

Ruffin chose to overrule the lower court and asserted that masters possessed total control of their slaves. Although tempted to sympathize with the plight of slaves and offer them some legal protections, Ruffin argued that the law demanded the denial of such protections. "The power of the master must be absolute to render the submission of the slave perfect." To bestow upon slaves basic rights would undermine slavery itself.

Woodcut image of master shooting slave

Consequences

Within five years, in *State v. Will,* Judge Ruffin's fellow justices partially repudiated his decision. In that case the court accepted that slaves' submission stopped short of yielding their right to defend themselves against excessive force. The case did not dispute Ruffin's major premise that a slave must be totally submissive, but it did reject his other claim that the only means to accomplish this goal was to give the master total power. The court accepted that the master's power did not deprive the slave of a basic natural right of self-defense.

Continuing Controversies

What role did ideas of justice play in Judge Ruffin's understanding of the rule of law?

Most modern scholars agree that the decision in *State v. Mann* reflects the fundamentally immoral nature of slavery. The controversy over the decision focuses on a more basic question about law itself. Does law simply reflect the dominant power relations of society? Or, can the law embody ideals of justice or fairness that are not simply a mask to disguise the naked exercise of power? Ruffin's decision reinforced the power of the planter class, and many view it as a vindication of those who believe that the law is a tool that enables the powerful (the masters) to dominate the weak (the slaves). However Ruffin's anguish and the later ruling in *State v. Will* might be seen as proof that law is not simply a tool of the powerful to exploit the weak, but shows that the rule of law does impose constraints on the powerful.

Does the law of slavery support the claim that the law is a tool of the powerful or a constraint on the powerful?

"No one can read this decision, [State v. Mann] so fine and clear in expression, so dignified and solemn in its earnestness, and so dreadful in its results, without feeling at once deep respect for the man and horror for the system."

Abolitionist HARRIET BEECHER STOWE, *A Key to Uncle Tom's Cabin*, (1853)

Conclusion

The market revolution transformed American life, especially in the North. American agriculture became more efficient, allowing fewer farmers and laborers to produce increasing amounts of food. Improved transportation reduced the cost of transporting raw materials to port cities and industrial centers and manufactured goods throughout the nation. Technological developments such as the steam-powered printing press and the telegraph facilitated an enormous expansion in newspapers, which brought the latest news to Americans and advertisements for an ever-expanding variety of products.

The market revolution also transformed work, promoting the production of goods by workers in factories rather than by artisans toiling in workshops. Several different models of industrial development emerged, ranging from small mill villages in New England to sprawling industrial metropolises such as New York. The metropolises were transformed by mass immigration into multiethnic and multiracial urban centers marked by new forms of leisure and politics, but also rising rates of crime and disorder that prompted the creation of modern police forces.

At the same time a very different economic and social system developed in the South, one based on an expanding cotton economy that relied on the labor of a growing slave population (nearly four million by 1860). Southern cotton became the nation's top export, supplying the textile factories of Europe as well as the American North. Although most white Southerners did not own slaves, slavery shaped the politics, economy, and culture of the South.

Although slavery varied by region in the South, most slaves lived lives of hardship, deprivation, and abuse. Despite the horrors of slavery, African Americans managed to preserve their idea of family life and develop a thriving culture that provided important resources to cope with the difficulty of their lives. They also developed tactics that allowed them to resist in subtle but effective ways the authority of their masters.

How did the market revolution change American society in the North and South?

1823–1825

Lowell mill opens
Waltham System at Lowell, Massachusetts, becomes showcase for the new model of industrial production

Erie Canal opens
One of the great public works projects of the early nineteenth century reduces dramatically the cost of transportation

1829

State v. Mann
Decision affirms the idea that the master's control over the slave is absolute

1831

Nat Turner's Rebellion
Virginia slave leads the bloodiest slave uprising in U.S. history

Review Questions

1. What role did technological change play in the improvements in agriculture during the era of the market revolution? What kind of impact on values did such changes foster?
2. What role did the railroad play as a symbol of American progress?
3. How did nineteenth-century ideas about gender roles affect the organization of the Lowell system?
4. How did slavery shape Southern society? In what ways did slavery impact the lives of non-slaveholders in the South?
5. How did slaves modify Christianity to articulate their distinctive religious vision?
6. Why did Judge Ruffin (see *Choices and Consequences: Conscience or Duty, Judge Ruffin's Quandary*) argue that the power of the master must be absolute over the slave?

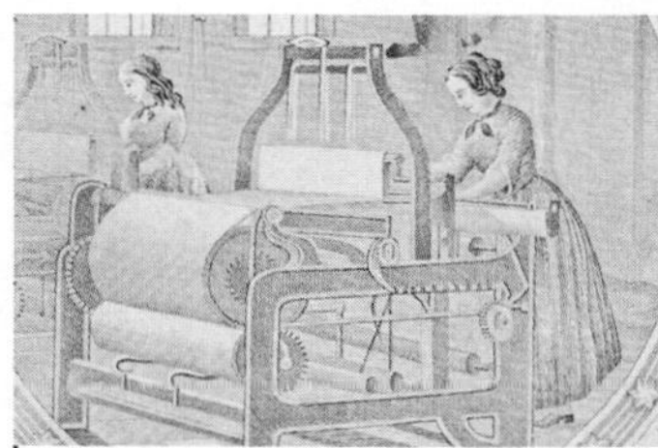

1834

First strike at the Lowell mill
Mill women's strike at Lowell signals the beginning of a new phase of conflict between labor and capital

1836

Helen Jewett murdered
The sensational murder of Helen Jewett shocks the nation and helps spur a huge increase in newspaper circulation

1838

The *Code of Honor* published in South Carolina
Etiquette book for Southern politicians who sought to settle matters on the field of honor

1844

Samuel Morse transmits a telegraphic message from Baltimore to Washington
Telegraph provides near instantaneous communication, vastly improving the speed with which news travels

Key Terms

market revolution A set of interrelated developments in agriculture, technology, and industry that led to the creation of a more integrated national economy. Impersonal market forces impelled the maximization of production of agricultural products and manufactured goods. **254**

telegraph Invention patented by Samuel Morse in 1837 that used electricity to send coded messages over wires, making communication nearly instantaneous. **258**

artisan production A system of manufacturing goods, built around apprenticeship, that defined the pre-industrial economy. The apprentice learned a trade under the guidance of an artisan who often housed, clothed, and fed the apprentice. **260**

Waltham System Also known as the mill town model, a system that relied on factories housing all the distinctive steps of cloth production under a single roof. The Waltham System depended on a large labor force housed in company-owned dormitories. **261**

Black Belt A swath of dark rich soil well suited to cotton agriculture that stretched from Alabama westward, and eventually reached the easternmost part of Texas. **273**

spirituals Religious songs created by slaves. Spirituals' symbolism drew heavily on biblical themes. **276**

Nat Turner's Rebellion The 1831 Virginia slave uprising led by Nat Turner shocked many in the South and led to a host of new repressive measures against slaves. **277**

Steve v. Mann The 1829 North Carolina Supreme Court case that involved a white man's assault on a slave. The case asserted that the domination of the master over the slave was complete. **276**

CHAPTER 10

Revivalism, Reform, and Artistic Renaissance

1820–1850

> "In the history of the world the doctrine of Reform had never such scope as at the present hour. ... We are to revise the whole of our social structure, the state, the school, religion, marriage, trade, science, and explore their foundations in our own nature."
>
> RALPH WALDO EMERSON, *Man the Reformer* (1841)

The expansion of democracy and the changes resulting from the market revolution left Americans concerned about their lives and the nation's future. Rising levels of inequality and a bitter debate over slavery further intensified anxieties. In this popular lithograph, *The Way of Good and Evil,* the artist portrays the social ills facing America, including alcoholism, prostitution, and crime. A tavern, brothel, and prison represent the path of destruction. Images of a different set of buildings—school house, home, and church—anchor the center. The path to salvation leads from these institutions through college and eventually up into heaven. In the artist's view Americans face a clear choice: salvation or eternal damnation.

Americans sought solutions for the nation's social problems and clamored for reforms. Many turned to mainstream religion for guidance. Religious reform movements focused on improving education and prisons or dealing with the danger posed by alcohol. Some religious movements viewed the market economy as the root of America's problems and advocated the abandonment of private property. Several secular utopian movements came to similar conclusions.

Still other reformers adopted a radically different critique of market society. The day's leading thinkers, including Ralph Waldo Emerson and Henry David Thoreau, urged Americans to reject the values of the marketplace and turn to nature or to their individual consciences for inspiration. Other writers grappled with the changes in American society in their writing, exploring America's past and the market revolution and probing philosophical issues.

The rise of a more aggressive abolitionist movement and the development of an equally fervid defense of slavery intensified the public debate over slavery. Abolitionism helped radicalize many women and gave them the opportunity to develop effective organizing skills. Inspired by a more radical theory of equality and equipped with their new skills, women's rights advocates applied their critique of slavery to women's status under American law.

Reform efforts affected architecture as well. Many reformers advocated transforming the American landscape itself, including the built environment, as a means of promoting social reform and spiritual renewal.

How did religious and secular reform movements respond to the market revolution?

EVERLASTING PUNISHMENT
GALLOWS
MURDER
ADULTERY
ROBBERY
FORGERY
SWEARING
CHEATING
STATES PRISON
DUELLING. HYPOCRISY
INTEMPERANCE
IGNORANCE
FIGHTING
VANITY
SCHOOL HOUSE
DISOBEDIENCE TO PARENTS AND TEACHERS
OBEDIENCE TO PARENTS AND TEACHERS
TRUTH
HUMILITY
FAITH IN CHRIST
PURE OF HEART
RIGHTEOUSNESS
AVOIDING EVIL
THE HOUSE OF GOD
THE COLLEGE
Every way of a man is right in his own eyes: but the LORD pondereth the heart.
PEACE
INDUSTRY
HEALTH

Revivalism and Reform

The Cane Ridge revival in Kentucky (1801) was the first stirring of the larger revival movement that constituted America's Second Great Awakening. (For a discussion of the First Great Awakening, see Chapter 3). In the next four decades, this emotional style of evangelical Protestantism attracted large numbers of Americans. For those swept up in the revival, the forces of change transforming American society were seen as a threat to the church and the family. However the most far-sighted proponents of revival, such as Charles Grandison Finney, realized that the power of the market revolution might be turned to good ends and used to promote religion and reform.

By the 1830s Americans began to believe that the economic, political, and social changes sweeping over their society were undermining individual morality, the ability of communities to prosper, and the integrity of the family. This belief drove the push for moral reform. In many cases religious impulse inspired reformers. Finney preached that "true saints love reform" and argued that humankind could create a perfect society here on earth if all Americans made "the reformation of the whole world" their top priority. Not all reformers were religiously motivated, however. Some reform efforts promoted secular goals and drew on the Enlightenment's ideals of reason, science, and faith in humankind's ability to improve and reshape its surroundings (see Chapters 3 and 4). A variety of secular reform movements emerged that led to improvements in schools, care for the mentally ill, and new methods of reforming criminals. Whether religious or secular, reform efforts targeted individual behavior such as drunkenness and prostitution.

Revivalism and the Market Revolution

One way of promoting revivalism was the camp meeting, an outdoor religious revival that lasted for several days. This painting of *Religious Camp Meeting* (**10.1**) by an English artist captures the emotional intensity of these events during which grown men and women swooned and collapsed in response to the fiery preaching of revival ministers. The painting shows overwrought men and women, physically exhausted from the revival, splayed across the ground and on the benches in the foreground. One observer compared the audience's response to the fiery sermons of the camp meeting with the "swelling" of an ocean wave, an awesome spectacle of people "fainting, shouting, yelling, crying, sobbing and grieving." The tents pictured in the background of the painting give only a small sense of the scope of these events. Camp meetings could last as long as a week and attract as many as three thousand individuals and one hundred different preachers.

10.1 ***Religious Camp Meeting*** A contemporary artist captured the intense emotional experience of a revival meeting.

What was the Second Great Awakening?

Revivalists faulted many mainstream ministers for their overly intellectualized approach to preaching. The materialism associated with the market revolution was another cause ministers blamed for America's problems. One minister feared that the same forces that were "increasing the business and moneyed interests in the Nation" would "by spreading vice and irreligion prove its ruin. Those very things which all regard as improvements will be our destruction." For some proponents of revivalism, however, the new methods of communication and wealth generated by the market revolution were tools to press into the service of revivalism. No figure proved more adept at turning the tools of the market to religious purposes than Charles Grandison Finney, a lawyer turned preacher who became a leading spokesman for spreading the revivalist message of the Second Great Awakening to towns and cities. His influence was felt particularly strongly in those towns and cities most closely associated with the market revolution, such as the towns along the Erie Canal.

While walking to his law offices one day, Finney experienced a religious conversion. In a lawyerly manner he declared that from that day on he would be on a "retainer from the Lord Jesus Christ to plead his cause." Drawing on his experience as a courtroom lawyer, he fashioned a forceful and direct style of preaching that cajoled, harangued, and pleaded with his audience to embrace salvation. Finney's theology rejected many of the Calvinist assumptions of non-evangelical churches (see Chapter 3). Where Calvinists stressed predestination, the belief that God predetermined our individual destinies, including who will be saved and who will not, Finney instead stressed free will, the ability of individuals to seek out salvation through their own efforts. Linked to Finney's emphasis on free will was his ideal of perfectionism. By aiming for perfection, Finney preached, human beings could usher in the millennium. In contrast to the pessimistic message of Calvinism, which condemned most people to damnation, Finney emphasized sobriety and hard work along with his religious message. Finney's sermons appealed to the expanding middle class and the wealthy.

Finney found an especially eager audience in men and women in the cities and towns along the Erie Canal in upstate New York. A dramatic revival occurred in Rochester, New York, in 1830–1831. Finney adapted many of the new political techniques associated with Jacksonian democracy, techniques designed to get voters actively involved in politics, to his revivals. Politicians, Finney noted, "get up meetings; circulate handbills and pamphlets; blaze away in the newspapers." The goal of such actions was to stimulate "excitement and bring the people out."

> "Capital is one of the means God uses to convert the world."
> REVEREND DAVID MAGIE, Sermon, 1847

Finney and other evangelicals took advantage of the opportunities provided by the market revolution, particularly the expansion of the publishing industry, to churn out tracts, Bibles, and other evangelical periodicals. Organizations such as the American Bible Society and the American Tract Society led the way in marketing evangelical religion books and pamphlets, making a concerted effort to use high-quality woodcut images in many of their publications.

Temperance

Temperance, the reform movement that developed in response to concern over the rising levels of alcohol consumption in America society, became an unusually effective reform effort. By 1830 consumption of spirits reached an all-time high in American history: almost 7 gallons per person of pure alcohol a year (more than twice the amount that the average American drinks today). Alcohol had always played an important part in many communities in America. Every class in American society imbibed alcohol, and hardly a community function took place without alcohol consumption. Workers on the job often drank alcohol during their midmorning break and with their mid-afternoon break. One social commentator noted that "a house could not be raised, a field of wheat cut down, nor could there be a log rolling, a husking, a quilting, a wedding, or funeral without the aid of alcohol."

Although Western religions had always frowned on drunkenness, Christians had never deemed the consumption of alcohol a sin. The Great Awakening changed this as spokesmen for the revival fastened on intemperance as an issue. At first proponents of temperance merely sought to promote moderation, but by the middle of the 1820s a more radical temperance movement had developed that sought complete abstinence from any consumption of

How did Finney use the tools of the market revolution to spread his revivalist message?

alcohol (see *Competing Visions: Temperance Reform and Its Critics*). The first national temperance organization was founded in 1826, and within three years the number of similar organizations had risen to 222. By the middle of the 1830s, temperance organizations numbered more than 1.5 million members, and more than 2 million Americans had taken the movement's pledge of abstinence. Evangelical religious leaders took the lead in these organizations, delivering sermons with titles like: "The Nature, Occasions, Signs, Evils, and Remedy of Intemperance." Temperance reformers warned Americans that alcohol threatened their souls as well as their bodies. For congregational minister Lyman Beecher, temperance organizations were "a disciplined moral militia," an ironic metaphor given that the real militia had become another illustration of the problem of intemperance. Although militia musters, the practice sessions of the militia, had always been festive occasions that included drinking, by the middle of the nineteenth century they had become drunken revels, as this depiction of a militia-day muster colorfully illustrates (**10.2**). The militiaman in the foreground is so inebriated he cannot stand, and the dancing figure of the African American suggests that the atmosphere is more carnival-like than military.

In addition to forming reform organizations, temperance advocates campaigned for prohibition laws banning the sale of alcohol. The cause of temperance also attracted other reformers such as the young Whig politician Abraham Lincoln. The Whigs helped to secure new laws designed to promote sobriety. Maine adopted the most wide-sweeping law in 1851, prohibiting alcohol. By 1855 thirteen of the nation's thirty-one states had passed "Maine laws" prohibiting the sale of alcohol. The temperance movement did not manage to banish drinking from American life, but it did dramatically reduce alcohol consumption among Americans.

Schools, Prisons, and Asylums

Alcohol consumption was a major concern of many reformers, but hardly the only one. Reformers also turned their attention to education, the criminal justice system, and the treatment of the mentally ill. They founded a variety of new institutions to deal with these social problems and campaigned to change the way Americans thought about these issues.

Education was central to reform efforts. The Reverend Lyman Beecher, a prominent figure in the Second Great Awakening, wrote that "we must educate, or we must perish by our own prosperity." Unfettered growth and expansion, according to such leaders as Beecher, would otherwise subvert America's moral foundations. The leading spokesman for educational reform in America was the Massachusetts Whig politician Horace Mann. As a member of the Massachusetts state legislature, Mann worked tirelessly to create a state board of education that would establish a uniform curriculum for all of Massachusetts and improve teacher training. Mann became the first head of the new state board of education. Massachusetts also became the first state in the nation to pass a compulsory school attendance law. For reformers such

10.2 A Militia Muster Although militia musters had always included some drinking, the scene depicted here shows a militia man too drunk to stand up. Martial virtue is nowhere to be seen.

What does this painting of a militia muster reveal about alcohol consumption in America?

Competing Visions

TEMPERANCE REFORM AND ITS CRITICS

The temperance movement brought an evangelical zeal to its antidrinking cause. The prominent minister Lyman Beecher, like many other leading spokespeople for temperance, took an active role in the Second Great Awakening. But other Americans viewed the zealousness of the reformers as a problem almost as bad as the sins they sought to expunge. The young lawyer Christopher Columbus Baldwin represented the more moderate view. In what way did Beecher's position as a minister inform his views of temperance? How did Baldwin's approach to the issue differ from Beecher's?

The minister Lyman Beecher cast the problem of intemperance in terms of a threat to the spiritual and political welfare of the nation. His religious idiom invoked the language of sin and compared drunkenness to biblical plagues, ranging from floods to fire.

Intemperance is the sin of our land, and, with our boundless prosperity, is coming upon us like a flood; and if anything shall defeat the hopes of the world, which hang upon our experiment of civil liberty, it is the river of fire, which is rolling through the land, destroying the vital air, and extending around us an atmosphere of death.

Lyman Beecher, *Six Sermons on the Nature, Occasions, Signs, Evils and Remedy of Intemperance* (Boston, 1828)

Christopher Columbus Baldwin, a resident of Worcester, Massachusetts, expressed some cynicism and skepticism about temperance advocates. In 1833 the state temperance movement held its annual convention in Worcester, and Baldwin was amused that at least some of the nearly 500 delegates in attendance did not take their vows of sobriety as seriously as their rhetoric suggested. Baldwin made these wry observations in his diary.

I am not a member of a temperance society, contenting myself with the practice of virtue without extra preaching it to others. It is one of the faults of the day to occupy so much of our time in recommending the practice of virtue that we have no time left us to perform it. So true it is that when mankind undertake a reformation they are always running into extremes.

The Diary of Christopher Columbus Baldwin, 1829–1835 (Worcester, 1901)

The MORNING DRAM.

The GROG SHOP.

The CONFIRMED DRUNKARD.

CONCLUDING SCENE.

The Drunkard's Progress

How did critics of temperance respond to this reform movement?

as Mann, the Common School—universal public education—would cure all of society's ills. As Mann wrote, "let the Common School be expanded to its capabilities . . . and nine tenths of the crimes in the penal code would become obsolete; the long catalogue of human ills would be abridged." While many types of reform were "curative or remedial," schools, according to Mann, were "preventive." Mann intended his reforms, like much mainstream educational reform of the day, to make good citizens and workers. This era saw the development of many features of modern schooling. The assignment of students to grades according to age and ability, the use of standardized procedures for promotion, and the notion of uniform textbooks for instruction all emerged out of the Massachusetts model that Mann helped pioneer.

An important new textbook, the popular McGuffey's reader, appeared in 1836. This text went through multiple editions for the remainder of the nineteenth century. The McGuffey readers carried a clear political message well suited to a society in which wealth was become less equally distributed. The readers instructed children not to envy their social betters, but rather to remind them that "it is God who makes some poor, and others rich." A rather different vision of education shaped the agenda of the Working Men's party, which saw education as an invaluable tool in the ongoing political struggle between the people and the aristocratic few. Although they shared Mann's Whig goal of universal education, they intended education to liberate workers, not make them docile workers. Thus a Philadelphia Working Men's party committee declared that "despotism" thrived when the "multitude" is consigned to ignorance, and education and knowledge reserved for the "the rich and the rulers."

Although educational reform attracted a wide range of supporters, including religious leaders, Whigs such as Mann, and the Working Men's party, opposition to such reforms could be equally ardent. A variety of groups feared that government involvement in education would pose a danger to individual freedom. Democrats in Massachusetts, for example, viewed Mann's program as a "system of centralization" that would put "power in a few hands" and would undermine the "spirit of our democratic institutions." Farmers feared that plans for a longer school year would rob them of a valuable source of labor, and feared that increased taxes necessary to fund the new school system would fall heavily on agricultural interests. Finally Catholics feared that the country's Protestant majority deliberately designed the new system as a way of imposing its values on non-Protestants. In response to the rise of the Common School movement, Catholics began creating their own alternative system of parochial schools.

While Mann's utopian vision of education as a cure for society's ills was not realized, the Common School movement did achieve some notable successes. By the middle of the century, over half of the white children in America between the ages of five and nineteen were enrolled in public schools, the highest percentage in the world at that time. Higher education also expanded dramatically. In 1815 there were 33 colleges in America; by 1835 the number had risen to 68 and reached 113 by 1848. The enthusiasm of the Great Awakening inspired much of this growth. Almost half these new colleges were affiliated with denominations that took a prominent role in the Awakening: Presbyterians, Methodists, and Baptists. Among the colleges and universities founded in this period were Amherst and Wesleyan in New England, Earlham in the Midwest, and Emory and Duke in the South. Although most such schools excluded women, whose educational opportunities lagged behind those for men, progress occurred in this area as well. In 1821 Emma Willard founded the Troy Female Seminary in Troy, New York, and in 1837 Mount Holyoke Female Seminary was established in Massachusetts. Oberlin College, founded in 1833 in Ohio, admitted women from its inception. A hotbed of abolitionist sentiment, Oberlin admitted its first African American students two years after opening its doors to white students in 1835. A number of state universities date from this period of educational reform as well, including

> "I believe in the existence of a great, immortal, immutable principle of natural law . . . which proves the absolute right to an education of every human being that comes into the world."
>
> HORACE MANN, 1846

How did Mann's vision of educational reform differ from that of the Working Men's Party?

Louisiana, Missouri, Mississippi, and Wisconsin. Some of the nation's leading Catholic institutions also date from this period, including Fordham, Holy Cross, Notre Dame, Villanova, and Xavier.

Education was not the only area in which reformers worked to transform American society. The new religious emphasis on free will and commitment to moral reform had affected the treatment of criminals. In place of punishment a new reform-based model of incarceration emerged: the "**penitentiary**," a place where individuals were isolated from one another and given a chance to repent and reform. This method departed radically from earlier approaches to crime, which cast behavior in terms of sinfulness, innate depravity, and punishment.

Two different models for implementing this penitential ideal emerged in prisons. The New York State system employed the first at Ossining, a prison in the Hudson River Valley of New York. Prisoners sent "up the river" from New York City to "Sing Sing" were housed in individual cells at night but were organized in communal work details during the day. Inmates worked ten-hour days in local stone quarries; eventually the prisoners manufactured a variety of goods, including barrels, boots and shoes, hats, brushes, mattresses.

Pennsylvania pioneered a different model, which it implemented in Eastern State Penitentiary. Eastern State employed solitary confinement, a system that isolated prisoners from all contact with other prisoners as a means of forcing prisoners to reflect on their criminality and seek repentance. The architecture of Eastern State reflected this new approach to penology. Architect John Haviland's vision of the ideal prison combined elements of a new interest in gothic architecture with an Enlightenment emphasis on geometrical regularity (**10.3**). Thus while the outside of the prison looked like a medieval fortress, the inside consisted of a series of radiating spokes emending from a central watch tower. A guard in the central tower could see the prisoners, who themselves were unable to see the guard. Haviland described his radial design as facilitating "watching, convenience, economy and ventilation." This design, which its inventor, British philosopher Jeremy Bentham, dubbed a panopticon, applied the Enlightenment's ideals of reason to prison reform. Under this system prisoners were potentially under surveillance at all times and could never be sure if the eyes of the state were on them. The goal was to impose discipline on prisoners and have them internalize this discipline as an ideal to be followed. This vision of penal reform fit with the Enlightenment's ideals of reason and control.

Life for the mentally ill was hardly better than that of prisoners. Indeed the two groups were often housed in the same facilities. In 1841 Dorothea Dix, a schoolteacher from Massachusetts, volunteered to provide religious instruction for women in the Massachusetts House of Correction. Shocked by the treatment of the inmates, particularly the mentally ill, who were dressed in rags, confined to one room, and often beaten, Dix embarked on a campaign to change the way mental illness was treated. After visiting a variety of jails and poorhouses where the mentally ill were housed, she compiled a report to the Massachusetts legislature detailing the wretched conditions she discovered in places such as the House of Correction. Dix recommended that criminals be separated from the mentally ill and argued that the latter would benefit from more humane treatment. Other reformers followed Dix's lead, and by 1860, twenty-eight of thirty-three states had public asylums for the mentally ill.

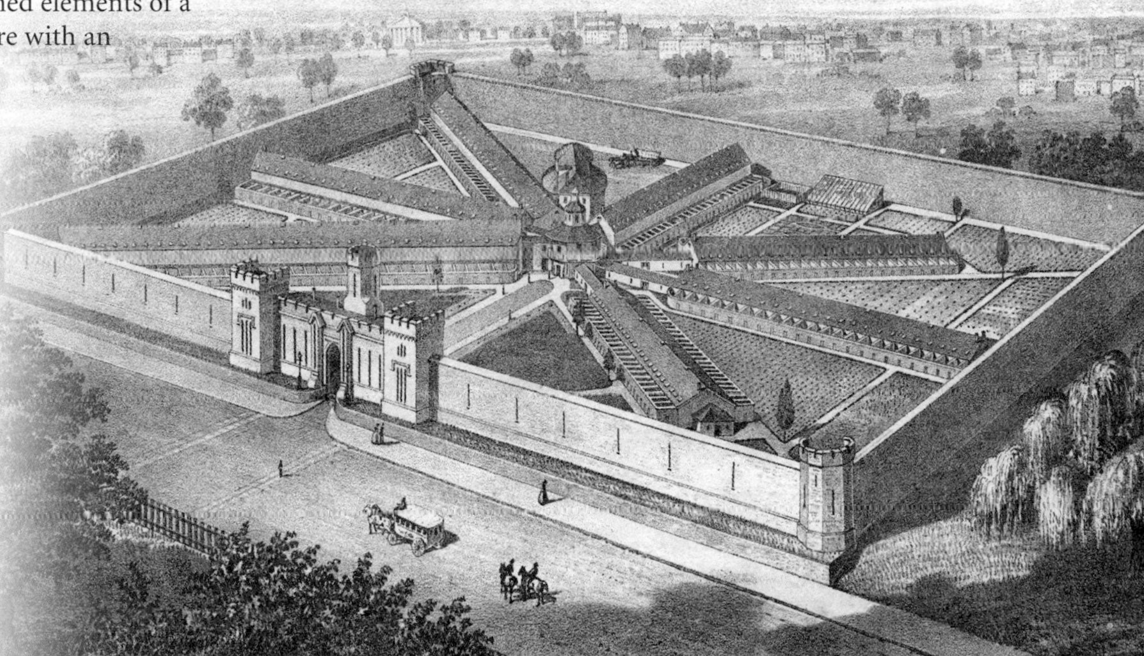

10.3 Philadelphia Penitentiary Architects designed prisons to accommodate the penitential model. Prisoners could be isolated for reflection while still being monitored by prison authorities. [*Source:* The Library Company of Philadelphia]

What was a panopticon?

Abolitionism and the Proslavery Response

The simmering debate over slavery heated up as abolitionists' demands for an immediate end to slavery. Like revivalists abolitionists also took advantage of the new tools provided by the market revolution, particularly communications technologies such as improvements in printing, to bombard Southerners with their message. The rise of a more aggressive style of abolitionism produced a fierce reaction from Southerners, who became increasingly militant in their defense of slavery. Rather than concede that slavery was a necessary evil, as Jefferson and others of the Founding generation had, Southerners developed a new proslavery ideology. They now touted slavery as a positive good that served to reform and uplift slaves. The real evils in American society, they argued, were abolitionism and the factory system. By the middle of the century, the slavery debate created huge divisions within American politics and society.

The Rise of Immediatism

Much of the early opposition to slavery was led by the Quakers. The ideals of the American Revolution also contributed to the rise of abolitionist sentiment, which attracted a number of leading politicians, including prominent Federalists, such as Alexander Hamilton and John Jay. For these abolitionists slavery posed a threat to the republican values of liberty and virtue. Racial equality or justice was not a major concern, and they turned to colonization as a solution to the problem of slavery. James Madison, Henry Clay, and John Marshall championed a plan which included gradually liberating the slaves and returning them to Africa. The American Colonization Society, the organization devoted to implementing this idea, was founded in 1817. The society helped to found the West African colony of Liberia and began transporting free blacks there from the United States. Yet by 1830 only 1,400 blacks had been repatriated to Liberia. Although gradualism and colonization had appealed to many white opponents of slavery, it never attracted much interest among African Americans, who supported a more immediate end to slavery and were committed to remaining in the United States. A convention of free blacks, speaking of the United States, proclaimed these views in forceful terms in 1831, declaring that "this is our home, and this is our country."

> "I shall strenuously contend for the immediate enfranchisement of our slave population. ... I will be as harsh as truth, and as uncompromising as justice. On this subject, I do not wish to think, or speak, or write, with moderation. ... I will not equivocate—I will not excuse—I will not retreat a single inch—AND I WILL BE HEARD."
>
> WILLIAM LLOYD GARRISON, *The Liberator*, 1831

In 1829 David Walker, a free black who had grown up in North Carolina and moved to Boston, published an *Appeal*, which he addressed to the "Coloured Citizens of the World, but in Particular, and Very Expressly, to Those of the United States of America." Walker rejected the ideas of colonization and declared that "America is more our country than it is the whites—we have enriched it with our *blood and tears*." Walker urged slaves to defend themselves, by force if necessary, against their masters. Walker's call for slave insurrection led Southern states to enact legislation that made it illegal to teach slaves to read. It also marked the end of support among many Southern intellectuals for the ideal of colonization. Walker's death in 1830 cut short his career as an abolitionist.

Although Walker's radical, insurrectionary appeal had little impact on mainstream abolitionists, his call for immediate abolition resonated with opponents of slavery. Since the Revolution mainstream abolitionist thought had adopted a gradualist approach,

What was so radical about David Walker's *Appeal*?

preferring to end slavery in a piecemeal fashion. In place of gradual schemes of emancipation, a new doctrine of abolitionism now emerged. Abolitionists rejected gradualism in favor of **immediatism**, a doctrine that advocated an immediate end to slavery. The most forceful spokesman for immediatism was William Lloyd Garrison, who founded the newspaper *The Liberator* in 1831. In the very first issue, Garrison announced that he had recanted the "popular but pernicious doctrine of gradual abolition."

10.4 Abolitionist Puzzle
Abolitionists developed a variety of ways to educate Northern children about the evils of slavery, including jigsaw puzzles. [*Source:* Division of Rare and Manuscript Collections, Cornell University Library]

With the help of other abolitionists, Garrison organized the New England Anti-Slavery Society in 1832. A year later Garrison joined with sixty other delegates, including men, women, whites, and free blacks, to create the American Anti-Slavery Society (AASS). By the end of the decade, more than 1,350 antislavery societies had sprung up in the North with combined memberships of 250,000. The success of British abolitionists, who in 1833 had persuaded Parliament to emancipate West Indian slaves, inspired American abolitionists.

In 1835 American abolitionists, taking advantage of the new opportunities provided by the market revolution to get their antislavery message across, began a vigorous campaign to inundate Southerners with antislavery literature. Abolitionists also worked diligently in the North to raise awareness of the evils of slavery. In addition to using traditional print forms such as newspapers and pamphlets, they developed almanacs, songbooks, children's books, and jigsaw puzzles. This children's puzzle (**10.4**) includes several scenes typical of abolitionist literature, including images of slaves being whipped and brutalized.

Adept at publicizing their cause, abolitionists seized opportunities provided by dramatic events, such as the escape from bondage of Henry "Box" Brown, who had mailed himself from Richmond, Virginia, to Philadelphia in a wooden box. The trip took twenty-six hours, and Brown arrived in his box in Philadelphia a little shaken but unscathed. Abolitionists distributed images of Brown's escape, and he became a prominent spokesman touring the North with a panorama, "The Mirror of Slavery" (**10.5**). Panoramas were large pictures mounted on rollers that, when unfurled slowly, gave the viewer the feeling that the picture before them was moving. Often a narrator accompanied a panorama on tour. Brown's narration complemented the panorama's depiction of the history of slavery in America.

Another event that triggered public interest in slavery was the unveiling of American artist Hiram Powers's sculpture, *The Greek Slave*. Powers's popular work depicted a beautiful Greek woman enslaved by the Ottoman Turks, who were Muslims. The image of a Christian woman degraded and held captive by Muslims captivated American audiences. Displayed in the nude the sculpture also caused something of a sensation in the press. Abolitionists used the attention focused on this sculpture as a means of reminding Americans of the evils of slavery. How they accomplished this—and the opposing views of Southerners—is the subject of *Images as History:* The Greek Slave, page 292.

The antislavery movement attracted a strong following in New England and also drew support among transplanted New Englanders in the

10.5 ***Mailed to Freedom***
This image of Henry "Box" Brown was sold to help finance a speaking tour for Brown, who became an active spokesman against slavery.

Who was Henry "Box" Brown?

Images as History

THE GREEK SLAVE

The Vermont sculptor Hiram Powers's statue, *The Greek Slave* (1844), became one of the most popular sculptures in nineteenth-century America. Powers portrayed the slave stripped naked by her Turkish captors, chained, and placed on the auction block. Religious leaders and even some reviewers had denounced earlier artists who, following European conventions, had portrayed women in the nude, but Powers avoided moral censure by explaining to his audience that by depicting the dignity of the slave in the face of such cruel treatment, he had clothed her in an invisible robe of virtue. How would viewers in different parts of the nation have responded to this work of art? How would abolitionists have interpreted its message? How would defenders of slavery?

Cities across America and small towns in New England and Ohio exhibited *The Greek Slave*. The image here shows a crowded gallery of men, women, and children viewing the work in New York. Besides prompting widespread commentary in the press, Powers's work inspired several poems. A poet in the *Knickerbocker Magazine* described *The Greek Slave* as "Naked yet clothed with chastity." Public reaction to the sculpture became entwined in the larger debate over slavery. While Southerners praised the work, focusing on the theme of Christian virtue, some Northerners compared the slave's suffering to the plight of America's slaves. One New York correspondent wondered how an audience might be driven to tears at the sight of an "insensate piece of marble" and "yet listens unmoved to the awful story of the American slave!" Apologists for slavery mocked such appeals. Noting that many abolitionists had waxed poetic about *The Greek Slave*, one writer wondered why "we have not heard" of a single effort to free her from her chains.

The Greek Slave turns away from viewers, a sign of her modesty.

The chains around her wrists signify her status as a slave.

The Greek Slave [Source: Hiram Powers (1805–1873), The Greek Slave, 1851, after an original of 1844. Marble, 65 1/4 × 21 × 18 1/4 in. (165.7 × 53.3 × 46.4 cm). Olive Louise Dann Fund. 1962.43. Location: Yale University Art Gallery, New Haven, Connecticut, U.S.A. Photo Credit: Yale University Art Gallery / Art Resource, NY]

Although a nude figure would have normally been shocking, *The Greek Slave* attracted huge crowds, including women and children. Exhibition guides reminded viewers that the slave was clothed in Christian virtue.

Viewing *The Greek Slave*

Why was *The Greek Slave's* nudity accepted by the public?

Midwest, particularly those with strong evangelical religious beliefs. Quakers in Pennsylvania and other parts of the country were active members of the abolitionist movement, too. A few prominent Southerners also joined the movement, including Angelina and Sarah Grimké, daughters of a wealthy South Carolina planter, whose conversion to Quakerism facilitated their involvement in abolitionism. The two women eventually left the South to pursue the cause of abolitionism. The antislavery movement galvanized large numbers of women, who became the grassroots activists on behalf of abolitionism. By the end of the 1830s, more than two-thirds of the signers of antislavery petitions submitted to Congress were women.

Anti-Abolitionism and the Abolitionist Response

The rhetoric of proslavery thought intensified as Northern opponents of slavery employed increasingly assertive tactics. Southerners held mass rallies to denounce Northern abolitionists. Garrison's *The Liberator* proved to be especially galling. Within a year of its first issue, the Georgia legislature proposed a $5,000 reward for anyone who would kidnap Garrison and bring him to Georgia for trial. Rewards were posted for bounty hunters to kidnap other prominent abolitionists and bring them to the South for trial. The wealthy New York abolitionist Arthur Tappan had a price of $50,000 on his head at one point. In July of 1835 a steamship arrived in Charleston harbor carrying thousands of anti-slavery tracts and newspapers addressed to Southerners. A crowd of angry residents grabbed the mailbags containing the Northern abolitionist literature; the next night a crowd of three thousand Charlestonians burned the abolitionist literature in a bonfire. This Northern contemporary political cartoon, which captured the antiabolitionist event, ridiculed Southerners' efforts to prevent the distribution of abolitionist materials (**10.6**).

Southern hostility to antislavery publications did not deter abolitionists. They began inundating Congress with petitions calling for an immediate end to slavery. Southerners reacted by passing the "**gag rule**," a procedural motion that required that the House of Representatives automatically table antislavery petitions and not consider them. The gag rule passed with the support of Northern and Southern Democrats. The Senate was unable to pass its own gag rule, but it adopted a practice that produced virtually the same effect. Once the Senate had received slavery petitions, a proslavery senator would simply make a motion to table them. Despite the gag rule abolitionist petitions continued to pour into Congress, especially from women's groups. In 1836–1837 an all-female petition from Massachusetts gathered 21,000 signatures, a record number. Southern efforts to stymie free speech and the right to petition Congress only underscored abolitionists' belief that slavery was incompatible with liberty. To leading abolitionists interference with the U.S. mail and congressional refusal to deal with petitions made slavery a national, as opposed to a local, issue.

The Proslavery Argument

Leading Southerners of the revolutionary era had attacked the institution of slavery even as they continued to profit from it. No member of the Founding generation was more conflicted over the issue of slavery than Thomas Jefferson, who wrote to a friend in 1820 declaring that "we have the wolf by the ears, and we can neither hold him, nor safely let him go. Justice is in one scale, and self-preservation in the other." Jefferson hoped that a new generation

10.6 ***New Method of Sorting the Mail*** The abolitionist mail campaign prompted violent protest in the South. In this drawing Southerners assault the Charleston post office and burn abolitionist mail.

What was the "gag rule"?

> "The peculiar institution of the South—that, on the maintenance of which the very existence of the slaveholding States depends, is pronounced to be sinful and odious, in the sight of God and man; and this with a systematic design of rendering us hateful in the eyes of the world—with a view to a general crusade against us and our institutions."
>
> JOHN C. CALHOUN, speech on abolitionist petitions, 1837

10.7 *Slavery As It Is*
This proslavery cartoon portrays slaves as happy and well cared for by masters who are cast as benign patriarchs.

of statesmen would find a way to eliminate slavery. Such hopes diminished, however, as "Alabama fever" swept across much of the South and cotton agriculture transformed the American economy. To complicate matters further the Denmark Vesey plot and Nat Turner's insurrection (see Chapter 9) frightened many Southerners, who became convinced that Northern abolitionists were stirring up slave insurrections in the South.

In 1832 Thomas R. Dew, a young professor at the College of William and Mary, published his *Review of the Debate in the Virginia Legislature of 1831 and 1832.* Sitting in the aftermath of Nat Turner's Rebellion, the legislature had seriously debated ending slavery, but a narrow majority rejected the idea. Dew repudiated the ideas of Jefferson and others who, agonizing over slavery, considered it unjust and recommended its elimination. Dew defended the property rights of slaveholders and dismissed the impracticality of relocating emancipated slaves outside of Virginia. Dew even went so far as to claim that slavery was a positive good, sanctioned by ancient philosophers such as Aristotle and justified by the text of the Bible.

Proslavery spokesmen championed the religious, philosophical, and economic benefits of slavery in Southern colleges and wrote in the South's leading magazines defending their new proslavery ideology. Southerners took the defense of slavery to new extremes when they argued that slavery was not only good for masters, but also good for slaves. Rather than exploiters of slaves, Southern defenders of slavery cast themselves as benevolent patriarchs; slaves, these defenders argued, were the lucky beneficiaries of this system. This self-serving vision of slavery is reflected in this political cartoon appropriately entitled *Slavery As It Is* (**10.7**). In the cartoon two shocked Northerners express their astonishment that slaves were so well treated and happy. In this particular image the artist singles out the evils of British factory life for condemnation. Southerners often made similar points about Northern industry, which they argued treated its workers more brutally than Southern plantation owners treated slaves.

One of the most influential apologists for Southern slavery was John C. Calhoun, an eminent South Carolina politician. Calhoun argued exuberantly that the South's "**peculiar institution**," which was the term he coined to describe Southern slavery, was not "an evil," a cause of shame, but rather "a good—a positive good," to be championed.

The Cult of True Womanhood, Reform, and Women's Rights

Women took a leading role in reform movements. The most active reformers were members of a growing middle class. Female reformers targeted activities that threatened the family and that demeaned women's role in the family. Prostitution was one prominent target of reformers, but hardly the only social problem that attracted notice from female reformers. A variety of other concerns drew their notice: alcoholism, crime, illiteracy, and even slavery. The social changes brought about by the market revolution, including the rise of the factory system (see Chapter 9), contributed to new ideas about the family and gender roles. The development of a new concept of domesticity and the related notion that men's and women's proper roles lay in separate spheres of activity became the cornerstone of a new middle-class ideal. Society defined the public world of work and politics as male, while the private world of home and family became women's domain. Female reformers defended the new ideal and attacked the social evils that threatened it.

The New Domestic Ideal

Horace Bushnell, an influential New England minister, captured the profound change that transformed American economic and social life when he remarked that the "transition from mother-and-daughter power, to water and steam power, is a great one" and had produced a "complete revolution in domestic life." One consequence of the rise of industry was a growing separation between home and workplace. This change facilitated the rise of a new middle-class ideology that defined women's role as a separate sphere of domesticity. A **"cult of true womanhood"** emerged in which female values were defined in opposition to the aggressive and competitive values of the marketplace. Women were identified with piety, motherhood, and sexual passivity. Although this ideal was largely unattainable for many rural farm women, urban working-class women, and free black women—all of whom had to work to maintain even the most minimal economic subsistence—the rise of this middle-class ideal suffused American culture.

Magazines such as *Godey's Ladies Book*, the growing body of middle-class advice literature such as Catherine Beecher's *Treatise on Domestic Economy*, and the ubiquitous prints produced by Currier and Ives all celebrated the new domestic ideal. Lilly Spenser Martin, the most renowned female artist of her day, made the new domestic ideal a central theme in her paintings. Rather than depict her subjects in the formal settings, garbed in rich velvet clothing and seated in poses borrowed from paintings of royalty and aristocracy, characteristic of the traditional family portraits favored by an earlier generation of artists, Martin often chose intimate scenes of domestic life as her settings. In *Domestic Happiness* she depicts a husband and wife standing before their two sleeping children. The mother's hand gently touches her husband, a gesture symbolizing the new domestic ideal's emphasis on emotional intimacy between husband and wife (**10.8**). At the same time the mother's hand gesture conveys another message. The mother appears to be gently restraining her husband from waking the slumbering children, a subtle reminder that in the domestic sphere, women, not men, were in charge.

10.8 ***Domestic Happiness*** Lily Spenser Martin's painting captures the new ideal of domesticity in which women were assigned the role of instilling the values of piety, family, and sexual passivity. [*Source:* Lilly Martin Spencer, "Domestic Happiness". 1849. Oil on canvas, Spencer, Lilly Martin (1827–1902) / The Detroit Institute of Arts, USA / Gift of Dr and Mrs James Cleland Jr. / The Bridgeman Art Library]

How does *Domestic Happiness* represent the ideal of the family?

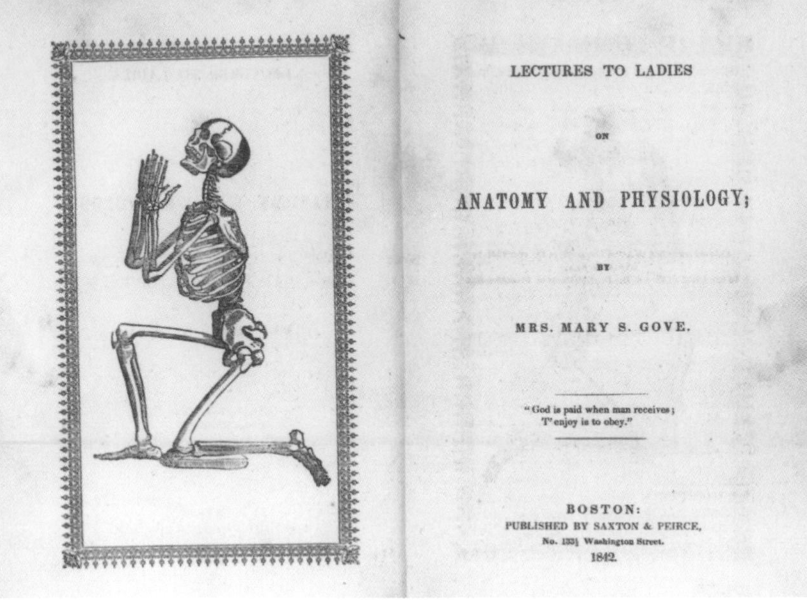

LECTURES TO LADIES

ON

ANATOMY AND PHYSIOLOGY;

BY

MRS. MARY S. GOVE.

"God is paid when man receives;
T' enjoy is to obey."

BOSTON:
PUBLISHED BY SAXTON & PEIRCE,
No. 133½ Washington Street.
1842.

10.9 ***Lectures to Ladies on Anatomy and Physiology*** The image preceding the text of Gove Nichols's book sought to make the idea of a book on female anatomy more acceptable by presenting a skeleton kneeling in prayer. The religious pose and the absence of flesh were calculated to make the book more acceptable to nineteenth-century notions of propriety.

Controlling Sexuality

A key aspect of the new ideal of domesticity was its emphasis on emotional control, including control of sexuality. In 1834 Lydia Finney, the wife of Charles Finney, established the New York Female Moral Reform Society, which sought to champion moral purity. By 1837 the Female Moral Reform Society had fifteen thousand members and branches across New England and New York state. The society focused on the problem of urban prostitution. Estimates vary but in some urban areas such as New York somewhere between 5 and 10 percent of the female population may have been involved in prostitution. The members of the society even visited brothels to try to convert the "fallen women" and urge them to abandon their involvement in commercial sex. Sometimes the reformer tried to shame the male clients of the prostitutes by publishing their names in the press. The society also worked to change laws, lobbying for the criminalization of prostitution.

The reformer Sylvester Graham formulated a far-reaching critique of sexuality. In his widely reprinted lectures on *Chastity* (1834) Graham advised his readers to avoid the dangers of sexual overstimulation, recommending instead that they "Take more exercise in the open air, and use the cold bath under proper circumstances." Graham also believed that diet contributed to overstimulation, producing a variety of physical and psychological ailments. Graham's followers abandoned stimulants such as tea, coffee, and alcohol, replacing them with a bland diet built around whole grain breads and crackers made from whole grains (the forerunner of Graham crackers). Followers of Graham could obtain information about bland diets from the *Graham Journal of Health and Longevity*, or they could attend Graham clubs at college or choose to live in boarding houses committed to Graham's rules.

A follower of Graham's who set off on a different path, Mary Gove Nichols, became interested in the issue of women's reproductive rights and health. She traveled across America lecturing to women about their bodies. Her influential work *Lectures to Ladies on Anatomy and Physiology* (1842) included an image of a female skeleton, kneeling in prayer, on its frontispiece (**10.9**). Nichols argued that the idea of women as passionless was a direct result of her "enslaved and unhealthy conditions." Paulina Wright, another lecturer on women's health issues, actually carried around an anatomically correct female mannequin to help demonstrate issues relevant to sexual and reproductive health. Wright's lectures sometimes proved shocking, causing some in attendance to faint or even "run from the room." The various strains of antebellum reform had forced women to examine the values, institutions, and political forces that justified the oppression and exploitation of women.

The Path toward Seneca Falls

Women had taken an active role in a variety of political and moral reform movements, including opposition to President Jackson's policy of Indian removal (see Chapter 8), temperance, and the crusade against prostitution. Participation in these various reform movements had led women to organize themselves, speak out in public, and begin to question the underlying political, legal, and social values that contributed to the oppression of women. Having taken these steps toward raising their political consciousness, women next turned their attention to the most brutal type of oppression in America—slavery.

Women were drawn to the antislavery movement in large numbers. Of the almost seventy thousand signatures on antislavery petitions submitted to Congress in 1837–1838 more than two-thirds were women's. Organizations such as the Philadelphia Female Anti-Slavery Society (1833) provided women with unprecedented opportunities to become political actors in one of the most important political dramas of the day. Involvement in the antislavery cause could be a harrowing experience. The virulent hatred abolitionists faced, even in the North, did not

What were Sylvester Graham's main beliefs?

make any exemption for gender. In 1838 the Anti-Slavery Convention of American Women refused to comply with a demand that black women be excluded from its meetings. An angry antiabolitionist crowd then stormed the building and later torched it.

Support for abolitionism not only provided many women with practical experience in politics but also led many to question their legal status as women. A major turning point in the relationship between antislavery and women's rights occurred in 1840 when American reformers Elizabeth Cady Stanton and Lucretia Mott attended an international antislavery conference in London. The female delegates were not allowed to speak at the event and were forced to sit behind an opaque screen out of view of the other delegates. Incensed by their treatment in London, Stanton and Mott saw the oppression of women as an evil requiring the same sort of attention as the oppression of slavery.

Stanton was born into a prosperous family, and her father was a prominent lawyer who became a state Supreme Court judge. She spent many hours reading law books in her father's office. The issue that most galled Stanton was the English common law doctrine of coverture, which treated a woman as legally dead once she married. American law had inherited this concept, which meant that a husband would control any property a woman might have owned before her marriage.

In 1837 Thomas Herttell introduced a bill into the New York legislature to give married women more control over their property. Eleven years later the New York legislature passed a landmark married women's property act, which allowed women to retain control of their inherited property. Stanton was among those who helped win approval for this law. The law stopped short of giving married women full control of any wealth or property they gathered during marriage, but it was an important step forward.

The year 1848 proved to be a momentous one in the history of women's rights. In the same year that New York adopted the married women's property act, supporters of women's rights gathered in Seneca Falls, a manufacturing town in New York not far from Rochester, for a historic meeting. The organizers of the convention were Stanton and Mott, two veterans of moral reform and abolitionism. About three hundred men and women, including noted African American abolitionist Frederick Douglass, assembled in a church for the **Seneca Falls Convention**, during which a women's rights manifesto closely modeled on the Declaration of Independence was drafted. The Declaration of Sentiments and Resolutions emphatically declared that "all men and women are created equal." The Declaration of Sentiments noted that women were denied economic opportunities, legal rights, and access to education. The document also asserted that "it is the duty of women of this country to secure themselves their sacred right to the elective franchise." The example of Seneca Falls prompted more than two dozen other such meetings in the next twelve years.

The ardent abolitionist newspaper founded by Frederick Douglass not only applauded the actions of the convention but also exhorted abolitionists to embrace the cause of women's rights alongside their opposition to slavery. The mainstream press, however, was less sympathetic to the cause of women's rights. One newspaper mistakenly concluded that the Declaration of Sentiments was a parody of the Declaration of Independence, not an attempt to appropriate its language on behalf of women. Although 40 percent of American newspapers printed negative accounts of Seneca Falls, 29 percent of American newspapers were favorable. Although still supported by a minority of Americans, the cause of women's rights had become a topic of national conversation for the first time. The Declaration of Sentiments would become a foundational text for all subsequent efforts to promote the cause of equal rights for American women. In Stanton's view the women who gathered in upstate New York in a modest church had instigated "a rebellion such as the world had never seen before."

> "The history of mankind is a history of repeated injuries and usurpations on the part of man toward woman. ..."
>
> "Declaration of Sentiments and Resolutions" of the Seneca Falls, New York, Women's Rights Convention (1848)

The women's rights question caused a major schism in the abolitionist movement. In 1840 delegates to the American Anti-Slavery Society (AASS) debated the issue of women holding office in the organization. William Lloyd Garrison, a supporter of women's rights, outmaneuvered his opponents and emerged victorious on this question. However a number of abolitionists opposed to linking the cause with the women's rights question responded by resigning from the AASS.

How did Stanton's upbringing influence her approach to women's rights?

Religious and Secular Utopianism

As many mainstream religious groups preached the necessity of reform and worked hard to change American society, certain sectarian groups sought a radical transformation of American society. In some cases these groups were attempting to create a heaven on earth, literally preparing the way for Christ's return. A variety of different secular utopian movements also flourished in the middle decades of the nineteenth century. Many groups abolished private property entirely and embraced some form of socialist or communist ideal, in which all goods were collectively owned.

Millennialism, Perfectionism, and Religious Utopianism

Millennialism, the belief that the millennium was imminent and that judgment day would soon follow, attracted many followers in the middle decades of the nineteenth century. Some believers went so far as to name the date of Christ's return to establish the millennium. The followers of William Miller, called Millerites, predicted that Christ would return in March of 1843. When that prediction failed to come true, Miller prophesied a new date, October 22, 1844. The movement collapsed soon after the revised prediction also proved false. Indeed the failure of the Millerites to successfully predict the true date for the millennium inspired a fair amount of humor. This satirical picture of a Millerite depicts a man prepared to lock himself in a trunk together with crackers, cheese, and plenty to drink, which were necessary preparations for the chaos that would precede the apocalypse before Judgment Day. The sardonic image captures some sense of the popular reaction to Miller's failed predictions (**10.10**). Aspects of Miller's teachings survived and were later incorporated into the teachings of the Seventh Day Adventists, another nineteenth-century religious sect, one that celebrated Saturday, not Sunday, as their day of worship.

10.10 Millerite William Miller's prediction that the millennium would arrive in March of 1843 prompted this satirical image of one of his followers preparing for apocalypse by stocking up on cheese and crackers.

The United Society of Believers in Christ's Second Appearing, or Shakers, created a successful religious utopia, establishing settlements across the nation and attracting thousands of followers. Shaker communities practiced a form of Christian communism. The Shaker faith was shaped by the teachings of Mother Ann Lee, an eighteenth-century religious figure who drew on Quaker teachings and adapted them in light of her personal experience and own revelations. The wife of an abusive husband whose four children died

How did the Shakers recast the idea of the family?

during infancy, she experienced a revelation that sex itself was the root of human evil. Her followers became known as Shaking Quakers or Shakers because their religious worship involved an ecstatic form of dance that one contemporary described as involving "extravagant postures" and "fantastic contortions." The sect also adopted a strict rule of celibacy. Mother Ann's vision of Christianity not only transformed ideas about sexuality but also radically recast gender roles. She preached that God was a combination of the masculine and feminine, a radical teaching given the strongly patriarchal character of most Protestant theology in the nineteenth century. Judged by the standards of the day, the Shakers came closer to the idea of equality of the sexes than almost any other group in America. Within the confines of the Shaker community there were only brothers and sisters—neither husbands and wives nor mothers and fathers. Abandoning the idea of procreation, the Shakers grew in numbers by taking in orphans and converting new members. The Shakers radically reconfigured the meaning of the family unit, rejecting the ideal of domesticity and marriage itself.

Shakers not only rejected the values of the domesticity and mainstream attitudes toward family life but they also developed a complex relationship with the growing market economy around them. Thus while Shakers participated in the expanding market economy, they did not internalize its competitive values. Within the confines of the Shaker community, there was no private property. The Shaker collective, however, did not cut itself off from the wider world of the market. Shaker craftsmen developed a reputation for being skilled furniture makers, and Shakers sold a variety of agricultural products to their surrounding communities to help pay the expenses of the community.

The Shakers were hardly the only radical religious experiment that rejected the values of the marketplace and the traditional ideal of the family. One of the most radical utopian leaders was John Humphrey Noyes. A Yale-educated Congregationalist minister, Noyes took the idea of perfectionism, a doctrine that had evolved from Methodism, in a novel direction. Earlier perfectionists had argued that it was possible to attain a perfect state of holiness in one's life. Such a state did not mean that a person was completely free from sin, but rather that one had attained the highest level of spiritual perfection consistent with human nature. In 1840 Noyes created the Putney Association and by 1844 the small group was practicing a form of Christian communism in which all property was commonly owned. The association included thirty-seven who worshiped together in a small chapel, lived in three houses, farmed, and maintained a store. In 1846 Noyes took his theory of perfectionism in a new direction. If one attained a state of religious perfection and could not sin, then he argued one could be free of many government laws enacted to deal with humans' fallen, sinful state. Marriage and monogamy were two such ideals.

Noyes's restructuring of the family and new ideas about sexuality ran afoul of the dominant views of marriage; he was indicted for adultery in Vermont, but fled to upstate New York, to Oneida. At Oneida Noyes instituted the practice of "**complex marriage**," a system where any man or women who had experienced saving grace was free to engage in sexual relations with any other person. Like the Shakers members of the Oneida community also owned all material property in common. Given their commitment to free love, birth control became an important concern of the community. Noyes began to preach the necessity of something he called male continence, a primitive form of natural birth control that required that men engage in sex acts without consummating them. Noyes's views mirrored the views of other nineteenth-century medical reformers such as Sylvester Graham, who believed that it was important for men to conserve their bodily fluids. Eventually the Oneida community embraced a form of eugenics, ways of improving humanity by genetic means in which only the most spiritually perfect were allowed to consummate their sexual unions and produce children. The interior of the Oneida mansion house was organized to facilitate the idea of complex marriage by weakening notions of privacy. The "tent room" on the third floor of the Oneida mansion dispensed with private rooms entirely, replacing them with a series of semiprivate enclosures blocked off by cotton cloth. The "tent room" increased the "sociality" of members and reduced the "cold isolation" of traditional apartments.

Although the practice of complex marriage was radically different from the celibacy practiced by the Shakers, both groups sought to reconfigure the family, sexuality, and their relationship to the market economy. Although each group approached the family and sex from radically different perspectives, the groups shared with one another the practice of communal ownership of property and, although differing in means, they both also attempted to free women from traditional gender

What were the beliefs of the Oneida community?

Choices and Consequences

MARY CRAGIN'S EXPERIMENT IN FREE LOVE AT ONEIDA

Mary Cragin and her husband George were among the many Americans deeply influenced by Charles Grandison Finney's religious leadership in the Second Great Awakening. George found a job in New York working for a reform paper, the *Advocate of Moral Reform,* as an office manager and accountant. George showed his wife a copy of a letter written by Noyes, which introduced Mary to Noyes's ideas of perfectionism. Mary and her husband were both taken with this doctrine and moved to Vermont. Noyes began his experiment in "communism in love" at Putney. As a member of his first perfectionist community at the Putney Vermont community, Mary Cragin faced a choice: either leave the community or participate in its bold new experiment in free love.

Choices

1 Persuade her husband to leave the community with her.

2 Leave regardless of her husband's decision.

3 Stay with her husband and participate in Noyes's system of complex marriage.

Decision

Mary chose option number 3, to stay at Putney with her husband and participate in a complex marriage with Noyes and others.

Consequences

Mary eagerly embraced Noyes's theory and eventually traveled with her husband and others to Oneida, becoming founding members of that community. In the published comments in the "First Annual Report of Oneida Community Association" (1849), she declared that her life at Oneida brought her closer to God than anything else she had ever done. She died a year later when the boat she was traveling on capsized.

Continuing Controversies

Why would a nineteenth-century woman be attracted to utopian movements that rejected mainstream views of the family and marriage? Modern scholars are divided over the impact of "Bible Communism" and "complex marriage" on women's lives. Some scholars argue that compared to the restrictive and oppressive environment most women faced in American society, Oneida provided women with more power, greater control over their sexual lives, and more equality. Although not a feminist utopia, Oneida's system of complex marriage was liberating in many ways for women.

Other scholars view Oneida as just another form of female oppression. According to this view the limited choices granted to women did not end male power and authority. At Oneida men continued to dominate women's lives, controlling their sexual and reproductive choices.

Why might a woman like Mary Cragin have been drawn to the Oneida Community?

roles. See *Choices and Consequences: Mary Cragin's Experiment in Free Love at Oneida* for further discussion of a bold new experiment in women's roles.

Joseph Smith, the founder of the Church of Jesus Christ of the Latter Day Saints, or Mormonism, created another model of a religious utopia. Joseph Smith grew up in western New York, an area in which the fires of the Great Awakening burned hot. In this evangelical milieu Smith had a revelation on which Mormonism was based. According to the Book of Mormon, Smith had a revelation in 1823 prompted by an angel who steered Smith to a set of golden tablets written in an ancient language. With divine help Smith deciphered the tablets, which told of the travails of a lost tribe of Israelites who had settled in America and whom Mormons identified as Native Americans. The book of Mormon was published in Palmyra, New York, in 1830, and this town became the site of one of the earliest Mormon communities. The belief that the Indians were actually descendants of a lost tribe of Hebrews was not a view uniquely held by the Mormons, but this theory attracted considerable attention from a number of prominent religious authors of the time. Smith's treasure hunting was also not that unusual, spurred on by popular stories about buried treasures gathered by ancient Indian civilizations.

An important idea influencing Smith was the widespread belief that the millennium was at hand, bringing with it an end to debt and the return of Christ and a new era of peace, happiness, and prosperity. The revelations detailed by Smith struck a resonant chord with small farmers, tradesmen, and mechanics whose experience with the expanding market economy had been largely negative. Smith's new revelation attracted several thousand followers. Mormons eventually set up their own community in Kirtland, Ohio, and eventually a larger community at Nauvoo, in Illinois. The Mormons did not go as far as the Shakers or Oneidians in embracing communism, but they had a strong communal economic ethic. Smith's 1831 law of consecration urged Mormon's to deed their land to the church, which would distribute it among the faithful, with any surplus being retained by the church.

Secular Utopias

In addition to religious utopian experiments such as the various Shaker communities, Oneida, and the Mormons, a number of socialist utopian communities appeared. Robert Owen's New Harmony, a utopian community in Indiana, was one such ambitious experiment. A successful textile mill owner who began his career in Scotland, Owen was deeply worried about the impact of industrialization on society and hoped to create an ideal community built on a socialist model. The community lasted only three years before disbanding. The French theorist Charles Fourier provided a more popular socialist alternative, including a utopian theory of phalanxes, ideal communities organized around socialist ideals, which gained a considerable following in the 1840s. Indeed between 1841 and 1846, twenty-five of these phalanxes popped up across New England, New York, and the Midwest. Rather than accept the values of the marketplace, Fourier championed the ideas of "association" and "cooperation." Individual communities divided the profits produced by agricultural labor or goods manufactured at the phalanx among the members according to a formula that included the amount invested, the skills of the person, and the amount of his or her physical labor. Fourier's socialist theories also questioned traditional gender roles. In Fourier's view social progress occurred in direct "proportion to the advance of women toward liberty." Women in Fourierist communities enjoyed equal pay and equal opportunities with men and benefited from an egalitarian attitude toward sex that was unusual for its time.

> "Under our system of isolated and separate households, with separate interests and separate pursuits, instead of association and combination among families, there is the most deplorable waste, which is one of the primary sources of the general poverty that exists; and discord, antagonism, selfishness, and an anti-social spirit are engendered."
>
> ALBERT BRISBANE (American Fourierist), *Concise Exposition of the Doctrine of Association*, 1843

Why did Mormon values appeal to farmers in the era of the market revolution?

10.11 Locations of Utopian Communities
The heaviest concentration of these religious and social experiments was in New England, western New York, and the Midwest.

"Although the desire of acquiring the good things of this world is the prevailing passion of the American people ... here and there in the midst of American society ... sects arise which endeavor to strike out extraordinary paths to eternal happiness."

ALEXIS DE TOCQUEVILLE
Democracy in America, (1835)

As the map (**10.11**) shows, utopian experiments, both secular and religious, were scattered across the United States. A host of other smaller utopian experiments were attempted during this period as well. At Brook Farm, a community in Massachusetts near Boston, manual labor was supplemented by activities designed to encourage "intellectual improvement" and "social intercourse, calculated to refine and expand" the mind and soul. When novelist Nathaniel Hawthorne visited Brook Farm, he used his brief residence in the community as the basis for his novel *The Blithedale Romance*. Bronson Alcott's utopian community Fruitlands shared several characteristics with Brook Farm, particularly the emphasis on balancing manual and intellectual labor and its views of communal ownership. In contrast to Brook Farm, dietary restrictions were an important part of this utopia. The members of the community were not only vegetarian but also ate only "aspiring" vegetables—those that grew upward (or reaching up for the supreme truths). Potatoes, beets, and carrots, which grew downward, were forbidden.

A few utopian communities tried to tackle the problem of race in American life. Francis Wright, a Scottish abolitionist, founded Nashoba, an interracial cooperative near Memphis, Tennessee, to demonstrate the potential for blacks and whites to live together as equals. At Nashoba slaves were to be given a formal education and allowed to earn enough to purchase their freedom. However Wright's more radical ideas included the abolition of the nuclear family, religion, and private property. The community lasted only four years before disbanding.

What patterns are evident from this map of utopian communities?

Literature and Popular Culture

The danger posed by the "tyranny of the majority," a subject explored in some detail by Alexis de Tocqueville in *Democracy in America*, attracted the attention of intellectuals and writers such as Ralph Waldo Emerson, a Harvard-trained minister who rejected orthodox religion in favor of philosophical exploration. Emerson's essays, beginning with his manifesto, "The American Scholar," enjoined Americans to wake from their slumbers, reject the latest fashions of the marketplace and instead discover the deeper philosophical truths to be found in nature and self-reflection. Within two decades of Emerson's address, Nathaniel Hawthorne published the *Scarlet Letter* (1850); Herman Melville, *Moby Dick* (1851); Henry David Thoreau, *Walden* (1854); and Walt Whitman, *Leaves of Grass* (1855). The vigorous intellectual and poetic activity of these writers and thinkers constituted a veritable American Renaissance. Some of the best-known works of these literary giants explored the problems of American society in a fictional setting.

While a few literary figures crafted rich and sophisticated works of fiction and poetry, a host of now forgotten writers marketed their books to the growing mass audience of readers. Many popular works depicted lurid tales of city life, including murder and prostitution. The marketplace also adapted to the intellectual ferment of the era by creating new institutions devoted to presenting lectures by leading intellectuals, including Emerson, to the people. In addition to hearing literary figures such as Emerson, one might also learn about the latest intellectual fads, including phrenology, a pseudo-science that focused on the shape of an individual's skull as a means of discerning his or her character and intellect.

Literature and Social Criticism

Emerson's "American Scholar" address marked the beginning of one of the greatest periods of American literary achievement. Emerson became the leading exponent of the philosophy of **Transcendentalism**, a loose set of philosophical and literary ideas that looked to nature for inspiration and philosophical insights. The other leading literary figure associated with this movement was Henry David Thoreau. In his masterpiece *Walden* Thoreau framed his critique of the impact of the market on American society. Ostensibly a tale of Thoreau's effort to get back to nature, *Walden* asserted that "The mass of men lead lives of quiet desperation." Thoreau further declared, "The greater part of what my neighbors call good I believe in my soul to be bad." Only by rejecting the numbing conformity of American society, the tyranny of the majority, and the worldly values of the marketplace could Americans rekindle the divine spark in each person.

Other American literary figures turned a critical eye to American history and society, focusing on different aspects of the age. Nathaniel Hawthorne parodied the excesses of utopian movements in *The Blithedale Romance*. In his 1843 tale "The Celestial Railroad," he took aim at the connections between revivalism and the market revolution. In this tale, an updating of the Christian tale of the religious pilgrim's search for salvation, Hawthorne provided his spiritual seeker with a comfortable seat on a railroad coach. Rather than patiently wait until arriving at the heavenly city, the final stop of the train, most of the travelers in the story prefer to exit at "Vanity Fair," a glittering city that was "an epitome of whatever is brilliant, gay, and fascinating." Although they failed to achieve salvation, the residents of Vanity Fair were well supplied with clergy, churches, and lecturers on the latest topics of discussion, and the stores were stocked with the most fashionable goods.

Novelist Herman Melville's epic novel *Moby Dick* told the story of Captain Ahab's pursuit of the great white whale. A rich and complex novel, Ahab's quest provided another metaphor for the search for meaning, spiritual fulfillment, and truth by those working within an economic system that increasingly treated people as commodities. As was true for Hawthorne, Melville's writing grappled with the alienation of Americans resulting from the economic changes wrought by the market revolution. One

How did Thoreau, Hawthorne, and Melville respond to the forces of the market revolution?

group Melville discussed was the new expanding middle class of clerks for whom "Ocean reveries" provided an escape from their dreary lives. Melville wrote of these cogs in the great machine of industry, "tied to counters, nailed to benches, clinched to desks." In many ways Melville's own experiences at sea not only provided him with details for his tale of the "Great White Whale" but also allowed him to escape the very fate of those clerks trapped at their desks that he chronicled in much of his writing. Indeed one of Melville's most famous literary creations was lowly and alienated clerk "Bartleby the Scrivener," a man drained of all creativity and energy who symbolized the way in which commerce could turn individuals into utterly passive victims of larger social and economic forces. The clerk Bartleby responds to every request from his employer with the same bored refrain, "I would prefer not to."

Domestic Fiction, Board Games, and Crime Stories

Many popular writers of Hawthorne and Melville's day were women, a fact that prompted Hawthorne to lash out angrily at the "damned mob of scribbling women" whose books often sold in the hundreds of thousands. Indeed women had written the top-five bestsellers by the middle of the century. Women favored "sentimental writing" and "domestic fiction," which were immensely popular in the middle decades of the nineteenth century. Susana Warner's *The Wide, Wide World* (1850) sold more than forty thousand copies in its first year and was reprinted sixty-seven times. This tale of an orphaned but resourceful child who must find her way in the wider world recast the traditional tale of the Christian pilgrim on the road to salvation in terms of the ideals of middle-class domesticity. By discovering her inner strength, the heroine is able to demonstrate her talents and virtues. After proving her determination and character, she finds a virtuous man whom she weds, thus fulfilling the ideal of domesticity. This general plotline carries through most of the works of sentimental writing and domestic fiction of the time.

Domestic fiction mirrored the same cultural values that led to the creation of the first popular board game in American history, "The Mansion of Happiness." Ann Abbott, the daughter of a Massachusetts minister, invented the game in 1843. Players in this game traveled along a spiral board that led to the "mansion of happiness" at the center. If they landed on such desirable spaces as "temperance," "piety," and "chastity," they could move forward. Landing on a space such as "idleness" would result in a penalty that sent the player backward. Rather than use dice, which were associated with the evil of gambling, players used a numbered top to determine how many spaces to move on a turn (**10.12.**) The game shared the ideals of popular prints such as *The Way of Good and Evil*, which also imagined life as a journey along a path between piety and sin (see page 283).

10.12 The Mansion of Happiness This popular board game embodied many of the ideals of domestic fiction and prints. Like the current game "Life," the game follows the players' journey along a path between piety and sin.

While domestic fiction and games such as "The Mansion of Happiness" popularized the domestic values esteemed by reformers, there was also a market for stories about the very evils these works advised Americans to avoid lest they wind up in prison or the asylum. The new penny press included a host of papers such as the *National Police Gazette* and the *New York Sun*, whose pages were filled with tales of crime and moral depravity. Literature embraced the sordid as much as the sacred, and an especially popular genre was crime fiction. George Lippard's *The Quaker City, Or, The Monks of Monk*

What ideas about the family and religion are reflected in "The Mansion of Happiness"?

Hall: A Romance of Philadelphia Life, Mystery and Crime (1845) spun a lurid tale that explored the evils of urban life. In contrast to Susana Warner, Lippard imbued his tale of seduction, murder, and intrigue with a subtle class-conscious critique of the debauched elites who gathered in a dilapidated old mansion, Monk's Hall, filled with secret passages and murder victims. The one writer who managed to transform such gothic tales of crime and horror into high art was Edgar Allan Poe. In stories such as the "Tell Tale Heart" and the "Black Cat," Poe explored the psychological dimensions of crime. His taut, gripping stories were models of literary craftsmanship. Poe brought the techniques of high literature to bear on topics that were usually the province of popular writers.

Slaves Tell Their Story: Slavery in American Literature

At the same time that the writers of the American Renaissance were formulating their critique of American society, a variety of other voices were also entering the expanding literary marketplace. Accounts published by runaway slaves provided a graphic description of the brutality of slavery.

The most famous and influential slave autobiography was Frederick Douglass's *Narrative of the Life of Frederick Douglass, An American Slave* published in 1845. The work was a publishing success: More than thirty thousand copies sold within a decade of its initial publication. Douglass awakened Americans to the injustice of slavery by exposing "the cruelties of it as I had myself felt them." The accuracy of his account was a key element of the book's appeal, but critics questioned his work's authenticity. Douglass thus went to great lengths to prove that his book was not an abolitionist hoax. Indeed Douglass worried that his eloquence might itself be used as proof that the book could not have been written by a former slave. To establish his credibility Douglass included a daguerreotype image of himself (a forerunner of modern photography), a copy of his signature (a sign of his literacy), and two testimonials swearing that the narrative was indeed authentic.

Douglass was not the only escaped slave to publish an account of his travails. In 1847 *The Narrative of William Brown* was published and became a bestseller. Douglass and Brown also published fictional accounts of slavery. Brown's novel *Clotel* explored the life of a slave woman, a mulatto daughter of President Thomas Jefferson (for the rumors about Jefferson's slave mistress Sally Hemings, see Chapter 7). The character Clotel ultimately chooses suicide over slavery and leaps off a bridge into the Potomac, a dramatic ending depicted in this woodcut from the book (**10.13**). About a decade after the appearance of *Clotel*, Harriet Jacobs's *Incidents in the Life of a Slave Girl* was published under the pen name Linda Brent. Jacobs had escaped to freedom in 1842, but it took almost another two decades for her to improve her writing to the point where she was able to publish an account of her ordeal under slavery. She described her purpose in writing in forceful terms: "I have not written my experiences in order to attract attention to myself, on the contrary, it would have been more pleasant to me to have been silent about my own history." Jacobs went on to declare her intention to "Add my testimony to that of abler pens to convince the people of the free states what slavery really is." Jacob's account of her life, particularly the firsthand accounts of the sexual predations of white Southerners on black women, exposed the plight of female slaves in a way that accounts by Douglass and Brown could never have done.

10.13 *Clotel* This image from the novel *Clotel* captures the moment in the novel when the heroine throws herself off a bridge rather than suffer enslavement.

Why did Douglas need to prove that he was the author of his autobiography?

Lyceums and Lectures

Josiah Holbrook, a teacher and lecturer, began the Lyceum movement in 1826. Named after the place in ancient Greece where the philosopher Aristotle lectured to his pupils, the Lyceum movement provided a forum for public lectures and debates on a variety of intellectual issues. By 1834 more than three thousand Lyceums appeared in towns and cities across America. As methods of transportation improved with the rise of the railroad, the Lyceum movement created a national market for speakers on a variety of topics of general interest.

An especially popular lecture topic was phrenology, a pseudo-scientific belief that focused on the relationship between the structure of the human head and character and personality. In addition to listening to lectures on the subject, Americans could pay to have their heads analyzed by phrenologists at salons in major cities and towns. By the 1850s the *American Phrenological Journal* had a circulation of more than fifty thousand. Phrenology became an American obsession in the middle of the nineteenth century. Phrenological heads made of plaster or ceramic became common-place decorations in many American homes, prompting the *Boston Christian Examiner* in 1834 to complain that "heads of chalk, inscribed with mystic numbers, disfigured every mantelpiece." Few of these were as striking as this impressive folk sculpture of a young girl's head with the various different zones of the cranium colored according to phrenological theory (**10.14**). Phrenology also attracted the notice of many leading public figures such as Supreme Court Justice Joseph Story, the moral reformer Horace Mann, and the artist Hiram Powers, whose sculpture *The Greek Slave* was the most popular sculpture displayed before the Civil War.

Phrenology affected the lives of many Americans. *Godey's Ladies Book* even advised women to use hats and other head coverings to hide or accentuate certain aspects of their phrenological character. Phrenology appealed to Americans at a time when the nation was experiencing rapid change. In particular phrenology spoke to the fears of urban Americans who increasingly lived and worked in an environment where they dealt with a world filled with strangers. The new market economy opened up countless opportunities for swindlers and rogues of various kinds, prompting a new term, "confidence man," someone who exploited the trust of a stranger to fleece him of his property or money. Although one might dress the part of a member of the respectable middle class, appearances were often deceiving, and the rise of the "confidence man" was symbolic of the danger posed by the anonymous world of the market. Phrenology promised to allow one to see beyond appearances into the true character of an individual and thus see past the masks and disguises of "confidence men."

10.14 Phrenological Head
This colorful folk sculpture of a young girl's head included hand-painted zones that phrenologists believed controlled human emotion and behavior. [*Source:* Asa Ames (1824–1851), "Phrenological Head". Evans, New York. c. 1850, paint on wood. American Folk Art Museum]

Why was phrenology so popular during this period of American history?

Nature's Nation

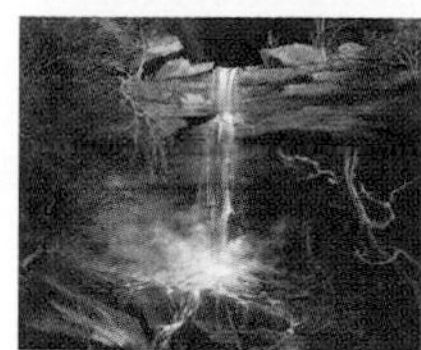

In honor of the opening of the Erie Canal, a young American artist named Thomas Cole staged an exhibition of landscape paintings that became an immediate sensation. Organizers of the show declared that the artist's work "had equaled those works which have been the boast of Europe." Cole's work would "adorn our houses with the American prospects and American skies." While writers such as Emerson and Thoreau extolled nature in prose, painters such as Cole captured its majesty in color on canvas.

The new appreciation for nature influenced the design of urban parks and cemeteries. Reform also prompted Americans to embrace a variety of different architectural styles that would help further the transformation of society. Cemetery designers turned to ancient Egypt for inspiration. The concern for architectural reform even influenced phrenologists, who championed the octagon as the perfect housing form.

Landscape Painting

An exhibition of the work of painter Thomas Cole that was staged at the opening of the Erie Canal in 1825 featured landscape paintings that symbolized a new distinctly American style of art. Americans eager to defend American culture against its European critics took up Cole's cause. An art critic noted that Cole's work proved that American art need not embrace the artificial beauty depicted in so much European art. "Nature needs no fictitious charms," and "the eye requires no borrowed assistance from the memory."

In 1835 Cole articulated his view of nature in his "Essay on American Scenery." He wrote that "the most distinctive, and perhaps most impressive, characteristic of American scenery is its wilderness." Cole realized his vision of nature beautifully in his painting *Kaaterskill Falls* (1826) (**10.15**), depicting a dramatic natural setting in the Catskill Mountains of upstate New York. The scene Cole presents is one of primordial beauty: A dramatic rock outcropping, a tree twisted and broken by nature's forces, and of course the rushing waterfall all reinforce the power and majesty of nature. The only human presence is a lone Indian communing with nature depicted in the center of canvas. Yet even this figure's physical presence is itself dwarfed by the monumental natural landscape, which towers above him.

10.15 *Kaaterskill Falls*
One of Thomas Cole's dramatic landscapes, this painting of a waterfall in New York's Catskill Mountains captures the majesty of nature that Cole so esteemed.

What does Cole's painting reveal about American views of nature?

Parks and Cemeteries

When Cole and other landscape painters were celebrating nature, America was undergoing one of its first great waves of urbanization. As agriculture became more efficient, large numbers of Americans from the countryside streamed into the nation's growing cities. While many urban homes boasted a Currier and Ives print of an idyllic rural setting, a more concrete effort was made to bring nature itself to the city. The creation of urban parks as retreats from the hustle and bustle of city life and a radically new approach to designing cemeteries were two highly visible results of the desire to preserve nature in the midst of rapid urbanization.

New York's Central Park (geographically at the center of Manhattan Island, but originally situated at the edge of the city) was the most ambitious and visible effort to bring the country to the city. Designed by Frederick Law Olmsted and Calvert Vaux in 1857 and officially opened two years later, Central Park sought to bring a varied country landscape, including meadows, rolling hills, lakes, and woodlands, to urban dwellers. To preserve the calming views, the designers sunk roadways beneath the line of sight of most strollers (**10.16**). For many upper-class and middle-class Protestant reformers, Central Park was intended to have a civilizing influence on the city's working-class and immigrant inhabitants. These reformers believed that strolls through the different country settings would exert a spiritually uplifting effect on those whose daily lives were degraded by industrial life and whose private lives were confined to the squalid conditions of areas such as Five Points. Championed by New York's elite and designed with middle-class values in mind, the land for much of the park was acquired by displacing Irish immigrants and destroying one of the city's most long-established African American communities.

Mount Auburn Cemetery, in Cambridge, Massachusetts, just outside of Boston, reflected the new view of cemeteries. The opening of Mount Auburn in 1831 attracted a crowd of two thousand people who were treated to orations by leading ministers and Supreme Court Justice Joseph Story. In contrast to the graveyards or burial grounds of earlier days, designers made the new cemeteries associated with the rural cemetery movement, such as Mount Auburn, places of repose for the living as much as for the dead. As this painting (**10.17**) of a couple strolling through the beautifully landscaped terrain of Mount Auburn suggests, the "repose and sacred loveliness of natural beauty" made the cemetery a destination for nearby city dwellers who wished to experience the ennobling effects of nature. It soon became a major tourist attraction, with as

10.16 Central Park
To maintain its country-like setting, the roads running through Central Park were sunk below the line of sight.

What was the rural cemetery movement?

10.17 Mount Auburn
The "rural cemetery movement" aimed to bring the country to the city and honor the dead by creating places of repose and reflection.
[*Source:* Thomas Chambers, "Mount Auburn Cemetery". Mid-19th C. Oil on Canvas, 14" × 18 1/8". Image © 2010 Board of Trustees, National Gallery of Art, Washington, D.C. Gift of Edgar William and Bernice Chryclor Garbicch]

many as thirty thousand visitors per year traveling to Boston to see Mount Auburn. Its success led to the creation of other cemeteries designed to provide urban dwellers with places of reflection and repose.

The "rural cemetery movement" inspired an important architectural change. Architects looking for inspiration for representing death found it in ancient Egypt's concern for death; Egypt's ancient pyramids and other monumental structures and its funeral practices were extremely elaborate. The image of Mount Auburn shown here (10.18) features one of the most common architectural elements borrowed from ancient Egypt, the obelisk. Mount Auburn and other cemeteries also included Egyptian revival entrances that borrowed architectural elements from ancient Egyptian temples, including the giant pylons that framed ancient temples. The Egyptian revival also inspired architects working on a variety of other public buildings, mostly those with a grim purpose, such as Philadelphia's debtor's prison and New Jersey's state prison.

Revival and Reform in American Architecture

Egypt was not the only ancient culture that American architects and designers turned to in the 1830s for inspiration. Andrew Jackson's rise to power in 1828 had reflected and facilitated a broad democratization of society (see Chapter 8). The democratization of American life coincided with Greece's war for independence from the Ottoman Empire in 1821. The Greek independence movement seemed analogous to America's own struggle against Britain. Not surprisingly American culture

"Nothing has more to do with the morals, the civilization, and refinement of a nation, than its prevailing architecture."
OLIVER P. SMITH, *The Domestic Architect* (1854)

Why did Americans turn to Egyptian architectural styles for inspiration?

10.18 and 10.19 Greek Revival Parlor and Shaker Sitting Room The thick carpets and elaborate decoration and furniture in this Greek Revival parlor contrast sharply with the bare ascetic furnishings of this Shaker sitting room. Shaker furniture were designed to be functional, not fancy. [*Source:* (10.18) Courtesy, Winterthur Museum]; (10.19) The Henry Francis du Pont Winterthur Museum, Inc.]

developed a fascination with Greece, the birthplace of democracy. As a result Greek Revival was a popular style of architecture, interior design, and dress during the 1820s and 1830s. As one contemporary writer noted, Americans had "a perfect mania for the Grecian orders" that pervaded American society and required that "every building from the shop of the tradesmen, to the church and the capitol, must be Grecian." Simple farmhouses were adorned with classical columns and crowned by pediments, giving their doorways the appearance of mini-Greek temples.

The rage for all things Greek not only affected architecture but also shaped the way Americans designed and decorated their homes. Furniture in this period was fashioned to resemble ancient Greek styles, often including decorative motifs drawn from Greece, such as urns and classical pillars. The obsession with ancient Greece literally transformed the map of the United States. Across America cities and towns sprung up with Greek names; western New York alone, along and near the Erie Canal, saw the appearance of cities such as Troy, Ithaca, Utica, and Syracuse. Harriet Martineau, an English traveler who published several accounts of experiences in America, feared that America's youth would grow up thinking that "Utica, Carthage, Athens, Palmyra, and Troy" were simply names of towns in western New York rather than the great cities of antiquity and the cradles of Western civilization. Ohio and Georgia each had its Athens.

While many Americans embraced Greek Revival, many utopian sects rejected mainstream architectural designs and furnishings that accompanied them. No group was more self-conscious about the connection between architecture, furnishings, and reform than the Shakers. The interiors of Shaker buildings were sparsely furnished, and the design of Shaker furniture embodied their ideal of simplicity. The Millennial Law (1823) of the Shakers, a set of rules that governed Shaker communities, actually proscribed the styles of furniture, including permissible colors, and expressly forbade designs that were "merely for fancy." The Shakers's rejection of the values of the marketplace is evident if one contrasts the furnishing and design of a typical Shaker sitting room and a Greek Revival parlor in a prosperous home (**10.18**

What does Shaker furniture reveal about Shaker values?

and **10.19**). Greek Revival architecture and furniture included ornamental designs such as classical columns and urns. The plush cushioned furniture and intricately carved furniture of the Greek Revival room contrast noticeably with the spare ascetic style of the Shaker room. Shaker furniture was devoid of any ornamentation and highly functional, embodying the ideal of simplicity itself.

The power of architecture to transform and uplift individuals inspired several reformers to propose using architecture to mold American character and thereby reform American society. Two of the most influential architectural reformers were Andrew Jackson Downing and Alexander Jackson Davis, who in the 1840s and 1850s helped popularize the Gothic Revival, a style of architecture that looked to medieval Europe for inspiration. Downing authored two popular works on architecture in the early 1840s that went through twenty editions in the three decades following their publication. Downing believed that a properly designed home should serve as a spiritual sanctuary from the commercial world of the market. Downing's Gothic Revival homes, which incorporated medieval architectural elements, such as pointed arches, were meant to be uplifting to those who dwelled in them and inspire those who gazed upon them by literally guiding an onlooker's gaze toward heaven. The Gothic Revival also drew on renewed interest in nature that had inspired painters such as Thomas Cole and the designers of Mount Auburn Cemetery. Rather than embrace the orderly quality of Greek classicism, enthusiasts for Gothic Revival championed a more organic style that shunned regularity in favor of variegated style that closely mimicked the irregularities of nature.

At one level the Gothic Revival was part of the larger reaction against the excesses of Jacksonian Democracy. Leading champions of this style, such as Downing and Davis, also rejected the democratic values of the Greek Revival, believing that architecture should underscore social class position, not seek to erase it. Davis believed that housing ought to announce one's class status, and he envisioned villas for the upper classes, cottages for the middle class, and farmhouses for the working classes. Davis helped plan the nation's first suburbs, including Llewellyn Park in Orange, New Jersey. Lyndhurst in Tarrytown, New York, was an extraordinarily opulent Gothic Revival villa. Compared to the symmetry of Greek Revival buildings, the irregular roofline and different shaped windows of Lyndhurst evoked the unpredictability of nature (**10.20**).

10.20 Lyndhurst
The Gothic Revival mansion, Lyndhurst, embraced elements of medieval architecture. Gothic Revival architecture's soaring arches focused the viewers' attention on heaven above. The angular lines were intended to mirror and evoke the awesome power of nature.

How did religious ideals and views of nature inform Gothic Revival architecture?

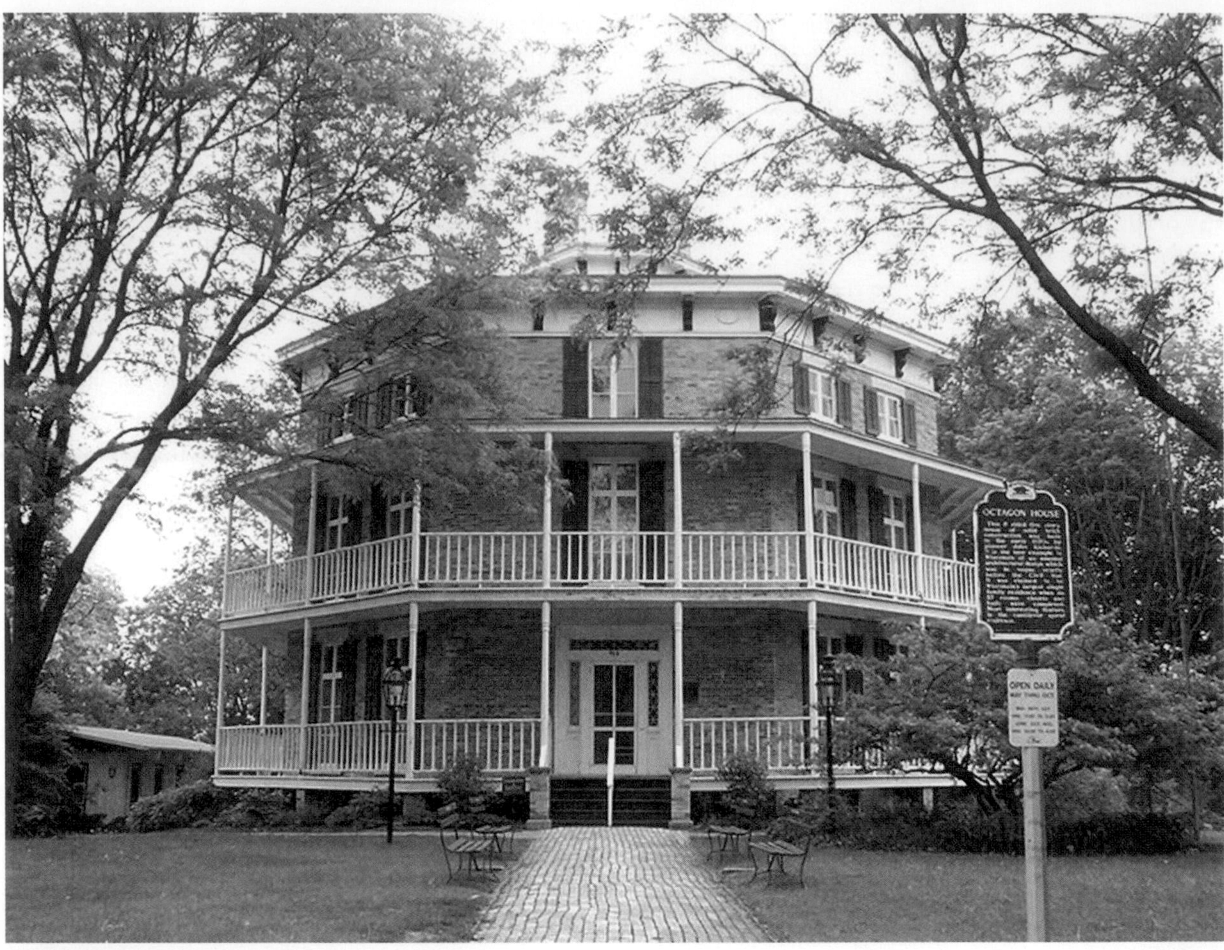

10.21 Octagon House
Phrenologist Orson S. Fowler believed that a balcony on a house corresponded to the upper portion of the skull and would encourage higher mental functions.

The popular phrenologist Orson S. Fowler championed octagon-shaped houses as a cure for America's social ills (**10.21**). Building on his phrenological theories, Fowler attacked box-like homes and argued that by more closely approximating a circle, the octagon encouraged harmony. Although the vast majority of these houses were built in the Northeast, octagon houses dotted the American landscape from Watertown, Wisconsin, in the Midwest to Natchez, Mississippi, in the South. Unlike some reformers who feared progress and believed that the expansion of the market threatened American values, Fowler believed that the march of civilization was inevitable. Americans needed to accept acquisitiveness as crucial to the marketplace, while tempering it with insights gained from new areas of knowledge, such as phrenology. The octagon house, Fowler believed, would serve both goals admirably well. The octagon fad eventually dissipated when phrenology's pseudo-scientific doctrines were themselves discredited.

Conclusion

The force of the market revolution and the democratization of American society transformed American society in the middle decades of the nineteenth century. The rapid pace of social, cultural, and political change left many Americas struggling to deal with

Why did phrenologists favor the octagon as an architectural style?

these developments. The fires of the Second Great Awakening drew many Americans back to religion. Leading revivalists also enjoined Americans to take part in moral reform efforts, such as temperance. The most successful revivalist, Charles Grandison Finney, made use of the tools provided by the market revolution to spread the message of the Second Great Awakening more effectively.

For many Americans the home and family provided a refuge from the aggressive world of the marketplace. A new ideal of domesticity and a cult of true womanhood emerged that defined women's roles and attributes in opposition to the male-oriented values of the marketplace. One of the issues that prompted the greatest concern was sexuality, specifically controlling dangerous sexual impulses and promoting the idea of self-control and middle-class respectability.

In response to the rapid pace of change a host of different religious and secular utopian movements emerged. Older religious groups such as the Shakers attracted new followers, and new groups such as the Mormons attracted a wide following. Virtually all the utopian groups experimented with some type of communal ownership of property, and many also experimented with new models of the family and sexuality. The Shakers did away with the family unit and sex and reconstituted themselves as a brotherhood and sisterhood. The Oneida perfectionists, by contrast, practiced a form of free love and complex marriage in which men and women could each be married to multiple partners.

The middle decades of the nineteenth century saw unparalleled artistic achievement in American art and literature. Novelists such as Nathaniel Hawthorne and Herman Melville published important works in American literature, some of which explored the impact of the market on society. At the same time other popular writers were exploiting the tales of crime and violence reported in the penny press.

Writers such as Henry David Thoreau and Ralph Waldo Emerson explored the mystical truths of nature in their prose. While Thoreau was something of a recluse, Emerson by contrast became one of the leading lecturers in the nation, taking advantage of the Lyceum movement and new developments in transportation to reach a wider audience. A variety of other ideas were marketed through Lyceums and lectures, including phrenology. Painters such as Thomas Cole praised the value of nature and captured its wild beauty on canvas, while others tried to reconcile the growth of civilization and the shrinking wilderness in their art. Reform also influenced American architecture, leading to new designs for prisons, parks, cemeteries, and homes.

The expansion of print material associated with the market revolution facilitated reform efforts. No group made more effective use of this change than abolitionists. The expansion of the literary marketplace also helped former slaves, including Frederick Douglass, find an audience for his firsthand account of the evils of slavery. The effectiveness of the abolitionists' campaign produced a backlash, helping to crystallize a more militant defense of the institution of slavery.

To escape the degradation of the new market society and preserve the traditional agrarian ideal, some Americans found the simplest solution in moving west. This solution, however, created a new set of problems as Americans encountered resistance from Indians and the region's Hispanic population. Westward expansion also fueled the controversy over slavery. Would the new Western lands join the Union as free states or as slave states? The issue of slavery would come to dominate politics in the era of western expansion.

1826

American Society for the Promotion of Temperance founded
Reformers concerned about the dangers of alcohol organize a national movement to promote sobriety

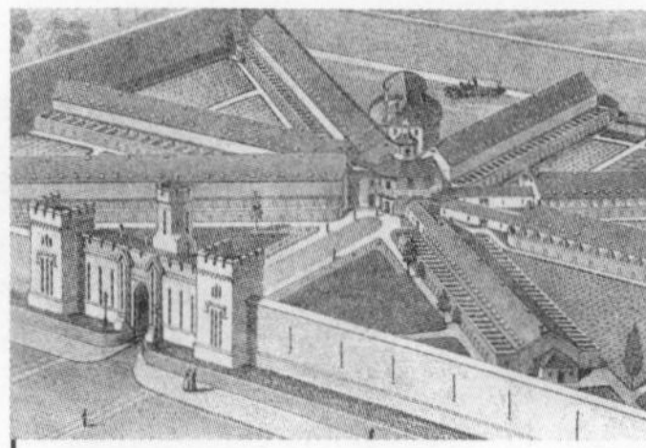

1829

Eastern State Penitentiary opened
Pennsylvania's new penitentiary becomes a model of the new approach to crime suggested by moral reformers

1830

Charles Grandison Finney leads Rochester Revival
The Second Great Awakening targets the towns along the Erie Canal, including the fast-growing town of Rochester

Review Questions

1. How did the Great Awakening minister Charles Grandison Finney use the tools of the market revolution and the new style of Jacksonian politics to spread his religious message?
2. What was the difference between traditional prisons and the new penitentiary favored by reformers? How did prison reformers make use of architecture to implement their new penitential ideal?
3. What was the cult of true womanhood? How did this ideal fit into the new notion of domesticity?
4. What role did the family play in the utopian worlds created by the Shakers, Oneidians, and Mormons? How could the reform efforts of these movements be seen as a response to the social and economic conditions of the era?
5. How did Thoreau's *Walden* embody transcendentalist ideas?
6. Why did phrenology appeal to Americans living during the changes wrought by the market revolution?
7. What was the rural cemetery movement? How did places such as Mount Auburn Cemetery fit within the larger movement of reform?
8. What was the Lyceum movement, and how did it both reflect the values of the market revolution and provide a forum for criticism of American society, including the market?
9. How did architecture reflect the ideals of social reformers in the middle decades of the nineteenth century?

1831

Mount Auburn Cemetery opens near Boston
An expression of the rural cemetery movement's focus on nature, Mount Auburn becomes a major tourist attraction and model for other urban cemeteries

1839–1843

Joseph Smith leads the Mormons to Illinois and founds the Mormon city of Nauvoo
Mormons establish a utopian settlement

Millerite William Miller predicts the end of the world
The Millerites are dispirited and the movement collapses. Elements of their belief are picked up by the Seventh Day Adventists

1845–1847

Publication of Frederick Douglass's autobiography and William Brown's novel *Clotel*
Douglass's popular narrative of his life as a slave and William Brown's novel expose the evils of slavery

1848

Seneca Falls Convention
Women's rights advocates gather to demand legal equality for women

Oneida Community established in New York
Founding of one of the most radical utopian experiments

Key Terms

temperance A reform movement that developed in response to concern over the rising levels of alcohol consumption in America society. **285**

penitentiary A new reform-based model of incarceration that isolated individuals from one another and gave them a chance to repent and reform. This method was a radical departure from earlier approaches to crime, which cast behavior in terms of sinfulness, innate depravity, and punishment. **289**

immediatism Abolitionist doctrine that rejected gradualism and advocated an immediate end to slavery. **291**

gag rule A procedural motion that required that the House of Representatives automatically table antislavery petitions and not consider them. **293**

"peculiar institution" A term that John C. Calhoun coined to describe Southern slavery. In Calhoun's view slavery was not "an evil" or a cause of shame but rather "a good—a positive good" to be championed. **294**

"cult of true womanhood" A set of beliefs in which women's values were defined in opposition to the aggressive and competitive values of the marketplace. **295**

Seneca Falls Convention A convention of women's rights supporters, held in Seneca Falls, New York, whose resolves emphatically declared that "all men and women are created equal." **297**

complex marriage A system developed by John Humphrey Noyes's followers at Oneida, where any man or women who had experienced saving grace was free to engage in sexual relations with any other person. **299**

Transcendentalism A loose set of philosophical and literary ideas focused on the spiritual power of the individual. Transcendentalists looked to nature for inspiration and philosophical insights. **303**

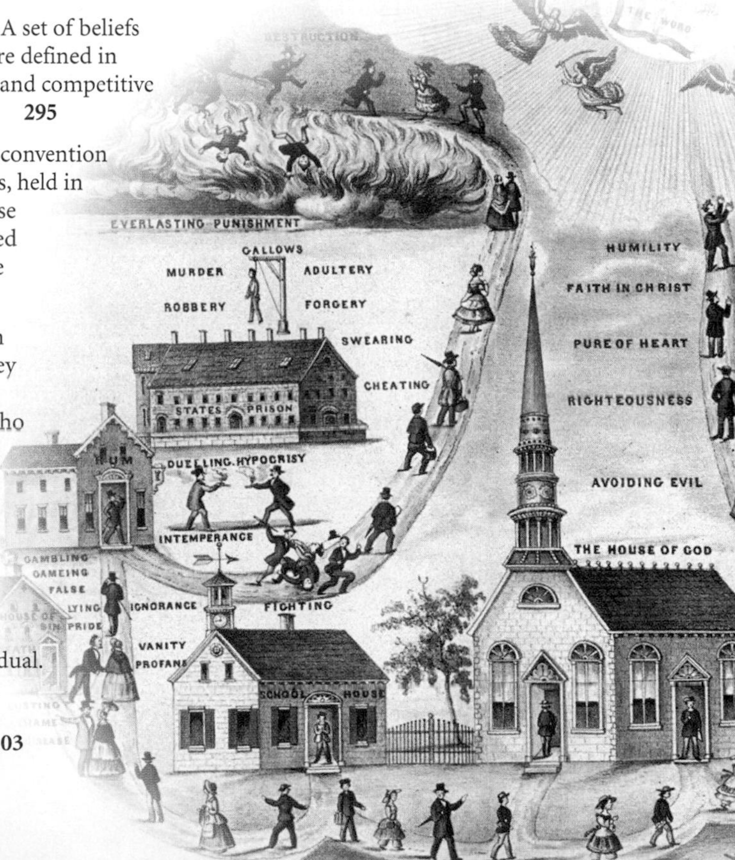

CHAPTER 11

"To Overspread the Continent"

Westward Expansion and Political Conflict, 1840–1848

Manifest Destiny and Changing Visions of the West p. 318

> **"Our manifest destiny [is] to overspread the continent allotted by Providence for the free development of our yearly multiplying millions."**
>
> Newspaper Editor, JOHN L. O'SULLIVAN, 1845

Artist Richard Caton Woodville's painting, *War News from Mexico* (1848), captures the excitement generated by the Mexican War, the first conflict in American history in which news traveled almost instantaneously by telegraph from the frontlines back to Americans. Woodville's painting shows a gathering of white men standing on the front porch of the "American Hotel," a symbol of the American nation. The central figure reads the latest headlines from the war front. The men's faces reveal a range of attitudes, from astonishment to concern, suggesting the diversity of Americans' opinions about the war. A white woman looking out from a window is safely inside the "American Hotel," part of the same nation as the white men but not privy to their political discussion in the public area on the porch. Woodville's painting also shows those excluded from power: A black man sits on the lowest step, and a young African American girl stands entirely outside the building. The Mexican War facilitated westward expansion, bringing new lands into American possession, but it also vastly complicated American politics by making slavery a central issue.

By 1840 all the land east of the Mississippi (excepting the territories of Florida and Wisconsin) had been organized into new states, but Americans remained hungry for land. By this time many had come to believe that America was destined to conquer and settle the entire North American continent, from the Atlantic Ocean to the Pacific Ocean. As a result tens of thousands of Americans migrated west in search of land and opportunity. Some were part of the migration along the Overland Trail to the Pacific Northwest, others came with the large Mormon migration to the Great Salt Lake.

The American defeat of Mexico dramatically increased the size of the nation. The United States incorporated a huge swathe of new territory, stretching from Texas to California. The war was also deeply divisive, exacerbating the divisions between Democrats and Whigs and intensifying the conflict between abolitionists and pro-slavery forces.

What impact did the Mexican War have on American politics?

Manifest Destiny and Changing Visions of the West

During the early decades of the nineteenth century, American fur traders had engaged in a lucrative trade with western Indian tribes. The interactions between the traders and Indians created a "middle ground" (see Chapter 3) in which trade and cultural interaction prospered. By the early 1830s, however, the distinctive multiracial society the Indians and white Americans had created was largely gone. The fur trade went into decline as overtrapping drove down beaver populations and as changing tastes among consumers made them less eager to purchase furs.

By the middle of the 1840s, a new attitude toward the West was emerging in American thought. The world of the fur trappers was gone. Americans began viewing the West as a region that had to be incorporated into an expanding America. Additional land would help preserve the ideal of a yeoman republic of honest and independent farmers that would now stretch from the Atlantic to the Pacific. Americans embraced the idea of westward expansion as both their destiny and a practical necessity given the nation's expanding population. The rights of the indigenous Indian tribes of these regions mattered little to the champions of westward expansion. Even among those who sympathized with the plight of Indians, many believed that Indian civilization was doomed to extinction. The conquest and settlement of the West became an important theme for artists who helped visualize the West for those Americans who did not make the trek westward. In many cases artists memorialized an ideal version of the process of western expansion, helping to forge an important set of American myths about intrepid pioneers taming a frontier wilderness.

The Trapper's World

During the colonial era French and British traders depended on Indians to trap or help them trap fur-bearing animals. American fur traders gradually gained control over this lucrative trade, and by the 1820s they were the dominant fur traders. The key figures in the trade, the trappers, or "mountain men," played an indispensable role in the early exploration and settlement of the West. Between 1822 and 1840 at least three thousand white trappers and traders entered this region.

Many mountain men formed liaisons with, and sometimes married, Indian women. The vast majority of these marriages proved stable despite the long separations that hunting and trapping required. Artist Alfred Miller's 1837 painting, *The Trapper's Bride* (**11.1**), depicts one wedding ceremony, which was a complex economic and cultural transaction. In addition to the mountain man and his bride, the artist shows the woman's father and her tribal chief, who holds the calumet, or peace pipe, in his hand as a symbol of friendship. The particular marriage contract depicted in this painting included a generous payment by the trader to the bride's father of a variety of highly desired goods, including guns, blankets, cloth, and alcohol.

The economic hub of the fur trade was the yearly **rendezvous**, a festive gathering held in the Rocky Mountains in which Indians and mountain men came with pelts to exchange for a variety of goods offered by traders. The system allowed fur trappers, Indians, and traders to remain in the wilderness for much of the year and sell at a specified time and location. With alcohol pouring freely, gambling aplenty, and a relaxed attitude toward sex among the participants, the rendezvous, which could attract as many as a thousand participants, was a carnival-like, often riotous affair.

The fur trade yielded huge profits for some men. The most famous trader, John Jacob Astor, was the son of a German butcher who immigrated to America in 1784. Astor became America's first multimillionaire, amassing by the time of his death in 1848 a fortune of twenty million dollars (more than one hundred billion dollars in today's terms).

What function did the yearly rendezvous play in the culture of fur trappers?

While such traders prospered, their trade had disastrous ecological consequences for otters and beavers. Once numerous, the sea otters off the California coast were nearly extinct by the middle of the century. Only a shift in consumer preferences from fur to silk as the fashionable material for hats in the mid-1830s helped stave off extinction for beavers. While most species avoided extinction, relentless trapping eventually reduced stocks of fur-bearing animals to such an extent that the world of the mountain men and fur traders was largely gone by the 1840s.

The mountain men and their Native American allies had supplied information as well as furs, which generated additional interest in the West. Another important source of information came from expeditions sponsored by the federal government. Following the tradition established with Lewis and Clark's pioneering expedition from St. Louis to the Pacific Coast in 1804–1806 (see Chapter 7) and Zebulon Pike's expeditions in 1806–1807, the federal government underwrote an expedition by Stephan Long in 1819 to explore the Great Plains and the Rocky Mountains. His widely reprinted map, first published in an 1822 atlas, erroneously labeled the southern Great Plains region (western Kansas, eastern Colorado, and New Mexico) as the "Great American Desert." This misleading label likely deterred many potential settlers from migrating westward in the 1820s and 1830s.

Americans gradually developed a more favorable vision of the West, in part due to the explorations of Lieutenant John C. Fremont of the Army Topographical Corps. Fremont published a popular account (largely written by his wife, Jessie) of his expedition in 1845 that not only dispelled the myth of a "Great American Desert" but also provided to those considering the trek westward many invaluable details. Information about weather, terrain, routes, and locations of watering holes and grasslands for pasturing animals was essential for those who made the arduous trek. The collective

11.1 ***The Trapper's Bride*** The arranged marriage between trapper and Indian required the approval of the tribal authorities, symbolized by the chief extending the peace pipe. [*Source:* Alfred Jacob Miller (American, 1810–1874), The Trapper's Bride, oil on canvas, Museum purchase. Joslyn Art Museum, Omaha, Nebraska]

How did exploration of the West both impede and encourage migration?

11.2 Western Trails
This map shows the main trails taken by Western emigrants on the way to Oregon, California, and Santa Fe.

efforts of these explorers (**11.2**) helped America physically map the West and intellectually comprehend its potential for the first time.

Manifest Destiny and the Overland Trail

By the early 1840s, the accumulation of information about the West, and its ever more positive impression, sparked a growing interest in migration beyond the Mississippi. Momentum spiked too as the result of an in increasingly popular notion called **Manifest Destiny**. First coined in the summer 1845 issue of the *Democratic Review* by editor and columnist John O'Sullivan, it gave voice to the belief that God had destined America to spread westward to the Pacific. "Our manifest destiny," wrote O'Sullivan, "[is] to overspread the continent allotted by Providence for the free development of our yearly multiplying millions." Only one year later Senator Thomas Hart Benton of Missouri echoed O'Sullivan's vision of America's future, explicitly framing it in both racial and religious terms: "The White race alone received the divine command, to subdue and replenish the earth!" he asserted. "Civilization or extinction has been the fate of all people who have found themselves in the track of the advancing Whites." Manifest Destiny combined the language of Jacksonian Democracy, stressing opportunity for all white Americans, with a Protestant millennial vision, which defined the nation's future in terms of the progress of "civilization" and the triumph of Christianity over "savagery." Few believed there was room for Native Americans in this vision of geographical expansion and white man's democracy.

Even before O'Sullivan and Benton voiced the doctrine of Manifest Destiny, word of the lush agricultural lands of Oregon had reached east by the early 1840s. The economic dislocations caused by the Panic of 1837 (see Chapter 8) and the absence of cheap land suitable for agriculture in the East and Midwest also sparked interest in Western migration. Propagandists for Western settlement eagerly exaggerated the region's riches to help attract potential migrants to the fertile lands of Oregon. One promoter concluded a rhapsodic description of Oregon by claiming, with a wink to be sure, that "in Oregon the pigs ... [were] already cooked, with knives and forks sticking in them so that you can cut off a slice whenever you are hungry!"

Drawn by these promises many joined an 1843 expedition known as the Great Migration. This 2,000-mile trek along the **Overland Trail** (11.2) consisted of more than one hundred wagons and helped pave the way for subsequent waves of migrants in the coming years. This trail soon became the main route taken by American settlers traveling from the East and Midwest to new settlements in Oregon, California, and Utah. By 1845 at least five thousand settlers had made the arduous five- to six-month-long overland trail journey to Oregon territory.

Migration westward placed an especially heavy burden on women, whose husbands seldom consulted with them before deciding to move. Estimates are that two-thirds of women opposed the idea of relocating to the West. Mary Richardson Walker, the wife of a Protestant missionary who headed to a settlement on the Walla Walla River in what is now Washington, vented her frustration in her diary, confessing about her trying circumstances. "I find it difficult to keep up a usual degree of cheerfulness, " she wrote, "If I were to yield to inclination I should cry half my time." Giving up friends and family and dealing not only with their normal responsibilities of cooking, cleaning, and childcare but also the added burdens of a long and perilous journey made the prospect of moving West terrifying.

"The North Americans will spread out far beyond their present bounds. They will encroach again and again upon their neighbors. New territories will be planted, declare their independence, and be annexed."

DeBow's Commercial Review, 1848

During the move many women were expected to take on traditional male jobs, such as repairing wagons or helping to construct bridges, while carrying on their traditional roles as mothers and wives. In effect the workload of most women doubled during the move westward.

Few Americans, male or female, were aware of this grim reality. Indeed their impressions of the West continued to be shaped by writers, speakers, and a growing host of artists who traveled with the migrants and painted scenes that reflected the rosy vision of Manifest Destiny. This mythic image of the West, created by artists, almost a generation later, was captured by Albert Bierstadt in his 1859 painting, *Emigrants Crossing the Plains* (**11.3**). Bierstadt depicts a group of settlers pausing on their westward journey to allow their sheep and cattle the opportunity to graze and drink. Above them rises a stunning depiction of the Western landscape, while in the foreground Bierstadt places the skeleton of a buffalo. These bones, like the Indian village barely visible in the distance, represent the West's past, while the settlers symbolize the West's future. The sun's location in the Western sky evokes the notion of God's blessing and the optimistic vision of Manifest Destiny—a powerful symbol of both the settler's and the nation's bright future.

The Native American Encounter with Manifest Destiny

One danger associated with western migration that figured prominently in representations of the West, both in paintings and sensational newspaper accounts, was the threat of attack by hostile Indians. Even though such attacks were relatively rare, these representations of Indians came to dominate popular culture. Once again, American artists helped spread a popular vision of the West. Charles Wimar's 1856

11.3 ***Emigrants Crossing the Plains*** In Bierstadt's painting, a caravan passing through Indian-controlled territory on the western trek to Oregon heads toward the bright sun, symbolic of America's Manifest Destiny.

How does the painting of the Oregon trail reflect the ideas of Manifest Destiny?

painting, *Attack on Emigrant Train* (**11.4**), casts the Indians as bloodthirsty savages and accentuates the horror of the emigrants trying to fend off the attack. This painting became a model for later images of Indians and was even used a century later by Hollywood directors as a model for Western fight scenes between Indians and settlers. Americans had been prepared for such a view of Indians by a long tradition stretching back to the earliest European representations of the New World (see Chapter 1) and rendered in paintings such as *The Death of Jane McCrea* (see Chapter 4, Figure 4.16) and in popular literature by *Crockett's Almanac* (see Chapter 8).

Wimar's painting reflected one of two radically different visions of Native Americans that were deeply rooted in American culture. From the very beginning of European contact with the Americas, Indians had been depicted as either bloodthirsty savages or noble savages (see Chapter 1). The image of the noble Indian chief had been propagated by a variety of artists, such as Benjamin West in *The Death of General Wolfe* (see Chapter 3). Artist George Catlin borrowed from this tradition when he set out to capture the culture of Western Indian tribes. After traveling throughout the West and living among several tribes in the 1830s, Catlin returned east and organized an enormously popular traveling exhibit of his paintings and the Indian artifacts he had gathered. Acutely aware that American expansion would likely result in the destruction of much of the Native American societies of the West, Catlin believed that he had a responsibility to future generations to preserve a visual record of Indian culture. These themes are discussed in *Images as History: George Catlin and Mah-to-toh-pa: Representing Indians for an American Audience* page 324.

A small number of Americans rejected both the image of the Native American as a barbaric savage who ought to be exterminated and the noble savage tragically doomed to extinction. A number of Whig and Protestant reformers expressed sympathy for the plight of Native Americans and opposed the forced relocation of Eastern tribes (see Chapter 8). These same groups also opposed the racist and expansionist vision of Manifest Destiny articulated by O'Sullivan and Benton. William Ellery Channing, a Boston minister and reformer, attacked the arrogance and shortsightedness of the ideal of Manifest Destiny: "We are destined (that is the word) to overspread North America; and, intoxicated with the idea, it matters little to us how we accomplish our fate." For Channing and other like-minded reformers, American expansion was not an unqualified good to be obtained at any cost, but something that demanded that Americans act in an honest and respectful manner to Indians and do their utmost to protect them. Yet, despite the qualms of reformers American demand for Western land was nearly insatiable.

11.4 ***Attack on Emigrant Train*** Although Indian attacks on Western emigrants were rare, this image was so powerful that it influenced portrayals of Indians in Western movies made by Hollywood more than a century later. [*Source:* Charles Ferdinand Wimar, "Attack on Immigrant Train". 1856. Oil on Canvas. 139.9 × 200.8 cm. Bequest of Henry C. Lewis. University of Michigan Museum of Art. Acc #1895.80]

Why were tales of Indian attacks on immigrants so popular in American culture?

Images as History

GEORGE CATLIN AND MAH-TO-TOH-PA: REPRESENTING INDIANS FOR AN AMERICAN AUDIENCE

Through his paintings of Western Indians, George Catlin sought to preserve a visual record of their culture and accomplishments. He also believed he had an obligation to portray these "doomed" peoples in a noble light. Capturing the nobility of Indians required representing them in a way that would evoke sympathy and respect from his American audience.

One of the many Indian figures George Catlin painted during his years in the West was the Mandan chief Mah-to-toh-pa, also known as "Four Bears." In the diary he kept of his experiences in the West, Catlin noted that the chief wanted to be painted in a manner that reflected the Mandan notions of beauty and masculinity. Both were closely tied to the ideal of the warrior. Accordingly Mah-to-toh-pa dressed for the painting in all the trappings of a warrior chief. Catlin noted in his journal, "His dress ... was complete in all its parts, and consisted of a shirt or tunic, leggings, moccasins, head-dress, necklace, shield, bow and quiver, lance, tobacco-sack, and pipe; robe, belt, and knife; medicine-bag, tomahawk, and war-club."

Yet Catlin omitted most of these items, believing that they distracted from the chief's "grace and simplicity." The notions of beauty that shaped Catlin's artistic decisions stretched back to antiquity and were different from those of the Mandan chief. In essence Catlin painted his subject as if he were a frontier Cincinnatus, an Indian George Washington. The resulting painting was an idealized version of how an American Indian chief ought to appear to an American audience, not a representation of how a specific Indian chief wished the American people to see him.

How did Catlin fashion his Indian subject and represent him to his American audience? What do these decisions tell us about American attitudes toward Indians in the early nineteenth century?

Catlin's journal informed his viewers that only a warrior of "extraordinary renown" was allowed to wear horns on his headdress.

By omitting the chief's war club, tomahawk, and other objects associated with his prowess as a warrior, Catlin made the chief less frightening to an American audience.

To make Mah-to-toh-pa a great figure in the eyes of his American audience, Catlin painted him as if he were a Roman general or a modern Cincinnatus like George Washington.

Mah-to-toh-pa
[*Source:* George Catlin (1796–1872), "Mah-to-toh-pa, Four Bears, second chief, in full dress (Mandan)". 1832. Oil on fabric; canvas mounted on aluminum, 29 × 24 in. Smithsonian American Art Museum, Washington, DC / Art Resource, NY]

Jean Antoine Houdon, *George Washington*

How did Catlin represent his Mandan subject for an American audience?

The pressure to make more Indian land available for settlement only grew as Americans streamed westward. Following the policy that had been adopted regarding Eastern tribes, such as the Cherokee (see Chapter 8), the federal government forced Midwestern tribes in Iowa territory, including the Sauk and Fox, to relocate to Indian Territory, present-day Oklahoma, Kansas, and Nebraska, after their defeat in the Black Hawk War of 1832. By the early 1840s the massive relocation of American Indians was nearly complete. One of the few tribes to successfully resist removal, at least temporarily, was the Seminole in Florida. The American army fought a long and costly war to force the tribe to relocate. For nearly seven years, from 1835–1842, the Seminoles fought off American forces. In the end, the American government spent ten times the amount of money allocated for all of Indian removal to relocate the Seminole.

While Americans in this era generated many descriptions of westward expansion, there exists relatively little material written from the Indian perspective. One rare and outstanding exception is the memoir of Sarah Winnemucca, a Piute Indian from Nevada who became a champion of the rights of indigenous peoples (see 15.16). Her memoir vividly recounts the full range of experiences with whites, from interactions with "good white people" who traded fairly with her family and her people to traumatic encounters with hostile settlers. In one of the more harrowing episodes, she describes an occasion when a band of white men appeared while the village men were away hunting. Winnemucca's mother and the other women feared that the whites intended to kidnap or sexually assault their children, so she and the other women hid them, burying them in mud and covering their faces with brush. Winnemucca described her anguish—"heart throbbing and not daring to breathe"—as she lay hidden "all day" till the hostile visitors left the village.

The Mormon Flight to Utah

Most of the immigrants streaming into lands once the home of Western Indian tribes went in search of economic opportunities. The members of the Church of Jesus Christ of Latter Day Saints were an exception to this rule. This sect, whose members were popularly known as Mormons, had been founded by Joseph Smith in New York in the early 1830s (see Chapter 10). Smith and his followers had been the victims of violent persecution wherever they settled in the East and later in the Midwest. The Mormon trek westward was the largest organized migration in American history. Nearly sixteen thousand members of the religious group migrated between 1845 and 1847 to the Great Salt Lake in present-day Utah.

Prior to their exodus the Mormons endured a long period of internal dissension and harassment by their non-Mormon neighbors. After leaving New York Joseph Smith established a series of Mormon communities in Ohio and Missouri. In Ohio the Mormons experimented with a variety of communal economic arrangements. The Mormon doctrine of "consecration and stewardship" required individuals to deed their property to the church, which then provided an allotment of land the size of which was tied to the size of the family unit. Mormons also created cooperative agricultural enterprises, pooling their resources and labor. Non-Mormons resented the economic advantages such cooperation brought to Mormon farmers and businesses.

As tensions between Mormons and non-Mormons rose, Smith moved most of his followers to the town of Nauvoo, Illinois, on the Mississippi River. The fastest-growing town in the Midwest in the 1840s, surpassing even Chicago, Nauvoo was a boomtown shaped by a distinctive religious vision. By the end of the 1840s, the Mormon population of this booming city had soared to over ten thousand. The Mormons in Nauvoo replaced the earlier policy of requiring members to donate their property to the church with a system of tithing (required donations to the church). This system of fund-raising built up the financial resources of the church, allowing it to accumulate substantial land holdings and build a monumental temple in Nauvoo. As this contemporary image shows, the Temple (**11.5**) was an imposing structure, that dominated the landscape around it.

As Smith and his followers faced increasing hostility from their non-Mormon neighbors, the church also encountered the problem of internal dissent. When a group of dissident Mormons founded an anti-Smith paper in Nauvoo, Smith took decisive action that set in motion a tragic sequence of events. Outraged by this attack Smith, who was also the mayor of Nauvoo, ordered the city marshal and Nauvoo militia to shut down the paper and destroy its printing press. The governor of Illinois intervened and ordered the state militia to seize Smith and bring him to nearby Carthage, Illinois, for trial. An angry crowd burst into Smith's jail cell and shot him to death.

How did the Mormon immigration differ from other westward migrations?

In response to these tragic circumstances, Smith's successor, Brigham Young, decided to move the entire Mormon community to the West, beyond the reach of the church's critics. Some sixteen thousand Mormons eventually migrated to the Salt Lake Valley of what is now Utah. Young's organizational skills and an almost military-like discipline among his people helped them negotiate the difficult journey westward. It also helped the Mormons adapt to and eventually thrive in their new environment. During the first years of settlement, when food rationing became necessary, Young ordered food surpluses confiscated and distributed to those in need. Once again Mormon communalism helped the community through a difficult time.

Over time, building on the lessons learned at Nauvoo, the Mormons built an economic and religious community that combined elements of communalism and private enterprise. Safely ensconced in the Great Salt Lake Basin, far beyond the control of the federal government, they also began openly to practice polygamy, the practice of men taking more than one wife. Brigham Young himself may have had as many as twenty-seven wives and fathered forty-seven children. Polygamy shocked Americans, particularly in an era when the dominant culture venerated the conventional nuclear family and the cult of true womanhood (see Chapter 10). In striving to remake the conventional idea of the family, the Mormons resembled the Shakers and Oneida perfectionists, two other religious movement of the day that experimented with different models of the family and alternative sexual practices (see Chapter 10). Mormon law required men to provide for their wives and children, which meant that most could not afford to engage in polygamy. So while the Mormon economic and religious elite practiced polygamy, the vast majority of Mormons continued to be monogamous.

11.5 The Nauvoo Temple
The Mormon temple at Nauvoo stood on the highest point of land in the new town, and it towered over the surrounding landscape. The architectural design includes elements of Greek revival architecture, Masonic symbolism, and ideas drawn from Mormon theology.

What role did Mormon communalism play in their experiences at Nauvoo?

American Expansionism into the Southwest

Hoping to stabilize and secure its northern territories that bordered the United States, Mexico adopted a number of new policies that transformed its northern provinces in the West and Texas. Changes were made in the way Indians were treated under the old colonial system in California and New Mexico, and Mexico opened Texas to American settlers in the 1820s. Rather than become integrated in Mexican society and help stabilize the northern provinces of Mexico, the Americans in Texas became a source of discord. Strongly committed to slavery and reluctant to adopt Mexican ways, the Americans eventually fomented an uprising of settlers that resulted in the creation of the Republic of Texas. The subsequent annexation of Texas by the United States only whetted the appetite of proponents of American expansionism. In 1846 the United States declared war on Mexico. The war proved unpopular with many Americans but nonetheless resulted in an American victory and seizure of northern Mexico, vastly increasing the size of the United States.

The Transformation of Northern Mexico

At the start of the nineteenth century, Spain continued to control a huge swath of North America, a holding acquired in the late sixteenth and early seventeenth centuries (see Chapter 1) and constituting all of present-day Texas, New Mexico, Arizona, and California and parts of Nevada, Colorado, and Utah. The Spanish had invested most of their resources in the mineral-rich regions of Peru and Mexico and the sugar islands of the Caribbean (see Chapter 2), and had largely neglected this northern region of their colonial empire. By the middle of the eighteenth century, the Spanish had begun to organize California into four coastal presidios (forts) at San Diego, Santa Barbara, Monterey, and San Francisco.

These administrative and military jurisdictions included twenty-one Catholic Missions run by Franciscans monks and extending as far north as Sonoma California. Under this **mission system** thousands of Native Americans were forced to convert to Catholicism and to labor for the Spanish. Held in an oppressive condition little better than slavery, they were forced to herd livestock, tend crops, and work as skilled and unskilled laborers. Indeed the Russian artist and explorer Louis Choris painted this view (**11.6**) of the Presidio of San Francisco in 1816. This image showing Indian laborers being herded at the point of a lance by a mounted Spaniard illustrates Choris's belief that the Spanish treated Indians little better than cattle.

The economy, politics, and social structure of this region underwent significant change beginning in 1821 when Mexico declared its independence from Spain. Apart from achieving internal political stability, one of the new nation's chief concerns was securing its northern border with the United States. Mexico's northern borderlands were underpopulated and controlled by the Comanches and Apaches. The introduction of horses and guns had allowed the Comanche and Apache tribes to become very powerful, in effect giving them nearly complete control of the trade between Mexico City and its northern provinces. America's westward expansion also posed a threat to Mexico's control of its distant provinces. Mindful of these threats Mexican officials took several steps to gain greater control of the region.

To speed economic development in California, Mexico abolished the mission system and released Indians from their dependent status as bound laborers. In the mission system's place, they adopted the *ranchero* system in California and New Mexico. Huge tracts of former mission-owned land came into the possession of a relatively small number of families. Much of the labor on these rancheros was performed by poorly paid Indians. To encourage population growth and economic development in Texas, the Mexican government took a different approach. In 1824 it enacted a new policy offering land grants to American settlers who agreed to

What was the ranchero system?

"The arrival [of the caravan in Santa Fe] produced a great deal of bustle and excitement among the natives. "Los Americanos!" ... "La entrada de la caravana!" [The Americans! The caravan has arrived!]."

JOSIAH GREGG, *Commerce of the Prairies, or the Journal of a Santa Fe Trader* (1845)

adopt the Catholic religion and learn Spanish. Thousands accepted the offer, and by 1830 almost seven thousand American Texans outnumbered the region's four thousand Hispanic Texans, known as Tejanos. The American settlers were an economic boon to the region. Texans exported an estimated $500,000 worth of goods to the port of New Orleans, mostly cotton and cattle.

Additional trade networks developed elsewhere along the Mexican-American border. In California, New England merchants sought seal and sea otter pelts to sell in China. Beginning in 1821 American traders established a trade route from Missouri to Santa Fe. Far safer and less rugged than the nearly 1,700-mile journey to Mexico City, the Santa Fe Trail soon became a thriving trade route. American traders, whose profits on the sale of goods ranging from cloth to manufactured goods such as umbrellas sometimes reached 40 percent, often received hard currency as payment. Indeed trade with Santa Fe became so crucial to the Western economy that the Mexican silver peso became the unofficial unit of exchange for much of the western United States.

The Clash of Interests in Texas

While Mexico benefited from the increased trade with the United States, the presence of so many American settlers in Texas worried Mexican officials. Three issues were particularly troubling. First, the Americans flouted the laws requiring they learn Spanish and convert to Catholicism. Second, they brought thousands of slaves into Texas at a time when Mexico was heading toward the abolition of slavery (a goal it achieved in 1829). Third, many American settlers did little to conceal their interest in eventually joining the United States.

A small uprising in 1826 of Americans hoping to secede was easily crushed by the Mexican army. The Mexican government reacted to the threat by banning further immigration from the United States. Still Americans came, and Mexico lifted the ban in 1833. Before long the American population in Texas had swelled to more than thirty thousand.

A well-organized effort to separate from Mexico occurred in 1834. This time Americans took advantage of the instability of Mexican politics. In 1834 Mexican General Antonio López de Santa Anna

11.6 View of the San Francisco Presidio
This depiction of the mission system captures the exploitation of the Indian population.

What advantages did Americans have over Mexicans in the lucrative trade with Santa Fe?

11.7 *Fall of the Alamo—Death of Crockett*
The heroism of the Alamo's defenders is captured in this crude woodcut, which shows Crockett's bravery in the face of battle.

staged a coup, set aside the constitution, and assumed dictatorial powers. When American settlers in Texas revolted, demanding a restoration of the constitution, Santa Anna decided to crush the rebellion. The ensuing war between Santa Anna's forces and the American Texans was brutal. One of the bloodiest battles occurred in early 1836 near San Antonio at the Alamo, an old Spanish mission defended by a small body of Texans, including legendary frontiersman and politician Davy Crocket and Jim Bowie (for whom the Bowie Knife was named). When the fierce fighting was over, 187 Americans and more than 600 Mexican troops were dead. Images such as this woodcut of the death of Davy Crockett inspired Americans, whose battle cry for the rest of the war against Mexico became "Remember the Alamo" (**11.7**).

Even as Santa Anna's forces assaulted the Alamo, American Texans declared independence from Mexico (March 2, 1836) and drafted a new constitution. Meanwhile his victory at the Alamo convinced Santa Anna that the Texas forces were no match for his army. Overconfident he recklessly divided his troops, leading to his defeat and capture at the Battle of San Jacinto by the Texans under the command of Sam Houston.

The Republic of Texas and the Politics of Annexation

The citizens of the now independent Republic of Texas expected the United States government to act quickly and annex Texas into the expanding American Republic. They would have to wait nearly a decade, however, as annexation proved to be a controversial issue. Opponents of slavery vigorously opposed annexation of Texas, fearing that it would upset the delicate balance between free states and slave states. Conversely Southerners and others who favored slavery supported Texas annexation. Heated debate in 1836 and 1837 eventually died down as both the Democrats and Whigs sought to avoid the contentious Texas issue. For the moment the bitter dispute between Whigs and Democrats over the Panic of 1837 (see Chap. 8) occupied Americans.

Texas annexation reemerged as a major political issue in 1844, reviving sectional tensions over the issues of slavery and western expansion. It started when President John Tyler, a pro-slavery Whig, began touting his support for annexation in the hopes that it would help him gain the support of Southern Whigs and secure the party's nomination. His strategy backfired, however, when many within

How did Anglo-Texans make use of their defeat at the Alamo to rally support for their cause?

his Whig party opposed his plans for Texas annexation, viewing it as a thinly veiled effort to expand slavery into Western territory. Tyler's pro-slavery stance cost him the nomination for president when the Whigs, seeking to avoid the controversy, chose Henry Clay, perhaps the best-known Whig politician in America, as their candidate.

11.8 Polk Election Banner
Polk welcomes Texas, while Whigs vainly try to hold back the Lone Star Republic from joining the Union.

The Democrats were likewise shaken by the annexation and slavery issues. Although Martin Van Buren was the leading figure in the Democratic Party, Southerners opposed him because of his abolitionist leanings. After nine ballots the Democrats finally settled on a pro-slavery Southerner, James K. Polk, as their candidate. Polk favored annexation of Texas, In this political cartoon from the election of 1844 (**11.8**), the Whigs, including Henry Clay, attempt to block Texas from entering the Union. James K. Polk stands holding an American flag, ready to welcome Texas into the Union. Texans Stephen Austin (left) and Samuel Houston (right) each wave the Lone Star flag of the Texas Republic. Polk's expansionist agenda appealed to Southerners but also struck a resonant chord with Northerners who hoped that westward expansion would mean more land for white farmers.

Polk's strong stance on annexation rattled the Whigs, including Henry Clay, who feared the Democratic Party's aggressive stance on Texas was popular enough to give it an electoral victory. Clay equivocated about opposing annexation, and his flip-flop on Texas drove many antislavery Whigs in the North out of the party and into a small third party, the newly formed **Liberty Party**. The staunchly antislavery, anti-annexation Liberty Party was short-lived, but captured 62,000 votes, a small number but enough to effectively rob Henry Clay of electoral victories in New York and Michigan, thereby handing Polk the presidency in 1844.

Emboldened by Polk's victory the sitting president, Tyler, proclaimed Texas annexation by a joint resolution of both Houses of Congress, a parliamentary maneuver that allowed him to bypass the constitutional requirement that treaties be approved by a two-thirds majority in the Senate. Tyler could have never mustered enough votes to approve a treaty of annexation, so he used his proclamation to effectively bypass the constitutional road block preventing the acquisition of Texas. Opponents of slavery viewed his actions as yet another example of the unscrupulous nature of proslavery forces. In 1845 Texas entered the Union as a slave state.

Polk's Expansionist Vision

A Tennessee lawyer and a protégé of Andrew Jackson, James K. Polk earned the nickname "Young Hickory," which was a reference to his mentor Andrew Jackson's reputation as "Old Hickory" (see Chapter 8) Polk shared Jackson's vision of politics, including his view of the importance of a strong executive and his belief in the necessity and inevitability of western expansion. Polk also shared Jackson's racial views, which included support for slavery and disregard for Native American rights. Indeed former president John Quincy Adams, who became a prominent Whig, denounced Polk as a

11.9 Mexican War Map
The major offensives of the war are depicted in this map.

"Slave-holding exterminator of Indians." Polk wasted very little time in acting on his expansionist vision for America.

Polk first moved to acquire Oregon, an area that the United States and Britain had been wrangling over for decades. In the presidential election of 1844, Polk campaigned on the slogan, "Fifty-four Forty or Fight," a reference to the U.S. demand that the geographical boundary separating Oregon from British Canada be fixed at the latitude 54° 40'. Ultimately Polk settled the issue by agreeing to a border farther to the south that extended across the 49th parallel. This shrewd compromise secured to the United States the most valuable agricultural lands sought by American settlers. The settlement of the Oregon issue in 1846 cleared the way for Polk to focus his attention on Mexico. As the ardently pro-expansion Democratic paper *The New York Herald* noted, "We can now thrash Mexico into decency at our leisure."

The annexation of Texas in 1845 had left open the question of the exact boundary between the United States and Mexico. Seeking to exploit the boundary dispute to exact further land concessions from Mexico, Polk sent John Slidell, a New York City lawyer and Democratic politician on a diplomatic mission to Mexico. Polk charged Slidell with negotiating a settlement to the boundary question and lingering issues about debts that Mexicans owed to Americans. Slidell was also instructed to inquire about the possible purchase of California and New Mexico from Mexico. This aggressive negotiating posture reflected the Polk administration's expansionist desires. Polk and his advisors feared that Mexico might pay off part of its debts to Britain by ceding California to America's chief commercial rival, Britain. By adopting such a belligerent negotiating stance, Polk ensured that the negotiations would fail. Still angry over the loss of Texas, Mexicans were not interested in yielding any further lands to America.

The specific issue dividing the United States and Mexico was the exact boundary between Texas and Mexico. In the view of the Mexican government, the southern boundary of Texas was the Nueces River, not the Rio Grande as the United States claimed (**11.9**). The position of the Rio Grande farther south gave Texas more territory at the expense of Mexico. Polk dispatched American troops under the command of General Zachary Taylor into the disputed zone between the two rivers. When a small group of Mexican forces attacked Taylor's troops on April 25, 1846, Polk called for war, informing Congress that "Mexico has passed the boundary of the United States, and shed American blood on American soil." Congress formally declared war on Mexico on May 13.

The Mexican War and Its Consequences

The Mexican-American War lasted only two years and ended in a resounding victory for the United States. America now controlled most of northern Mexico. Although supporters of Manifest Destiny had seen geographic expansion as a panacea for the nation's economic and social problems, few could foresee how the defeat of Mexico and acquisition of new lands would usher in an era of greater, more intense political conflict. The debate over whether to allow slavery in the territories gained from Mexico would place an enormous strain on the two-party system, splitting Whigs and Democrats into Northern and Southern wings. A new third party, the Free-Soil Party, emerged during this period committed to blocking the spread of slavery.

A Controversial War

The Mexican War divided Americans largely along sectional lines and caused splits in both the Democratic and Whig parties. Southern Whigs supported Polk's efforts. "Every battle fought in Mexico," one South Carolina paper averred, "insures the acquisition of territory which must widen the field of Southern enterprise and power in the future." Northern Whigs, in contrast, denounced the war as an unjust conflict manufactured by Polk to secure California and New Mexico. "This war is waged against an unoffending people, without just or adequate cause," argued one outraged Whig, "for the purposes of conquest; with the design to extend slavery."

The strongest and most stinging criticism emanated from Northern abolitionists who denounced "Mr. Polk's War." William Lloyd Garrison went so far as to welcome "the overwhelming defeat of the American troops, and the success of the injured Mexicans." The most profound critique of the war came from the literary figure and transcendentalist philosopher Henry David Thoreau (see Chapter 10), who defended the ideal of peaceful opposition by citizens to unjust government action. See *Choices and Consequences: Henry David Thoreau and Civil Disobedience* (page 334).

The Mexican War was the first conflict America fought primarily on foreign soil. It was also the most logistically complex war in the nation's brief history, involving multiple fronts, long supply lines, and the complex task of coordinating ground and amphibious assaults. The Mexican War also produced two of the greatest generals in American history, Zachary Taylor and Winfield Scott. Taylor was the common soldier's general, a man without pretensions whose reputation for bravery in the face of enemy fire earned him the nickname among his troops, "Old Rough and Ready." Scott was in many respects the opposite of Taylor. A brilliant tactician and strategist, "Old Fuss and Feathers" was arrogant and fond of pomp and ceremony. The Mexican War also provided a proving ground for a host of future military leaders who later became important generals of the Civil War era, including Ulysses S. Grant, Robert E. Lee, Thomas "Stonewall" Jackson, George McClellan, George G. Meade, and P. G. T. Beauregard.

The United States had clear military superiority over Mexico. American forces under the command of Zachary Taylor scored a notable early victory in May 1846 at the battle of Palo Alto on Mexico's Gulf coast (11.9). General Stephen Kearny then opened a second front by marching from Fort Leavenworth, Kansas, to Santa Fe and then on to California, where he joined up with an army under Captain John C. Fremont. Fremont had already paved the way for the conquest of California by instigating a rebellion against Mexican authority in California known as the "bear-flag revolt." The revolt was named for the emblem that decorated the flag of the rebels, which carried an image of a grizzly bear.

Leading the final phase of the conflict, General Winfield Scott's successful amphibious assault at the coastal town of Vera Cruz established a staging ground for an assault on Mexico City. It took five more months of fierce fighting, but they eventually captured the Mexican capital on May 1, 1847.

What were the most important differences between the leadership style of Generals Zachary Taylor and Winfield Scott?

The Treaty of Guadalupe Hidalgo ended the war between the United States and Mexico (1848). It settled the border dispute between Texas and Mexico and ceded to the United States a vast swath of new territory—some 500,000 square miles—in the Southwest comprising present-day California, New Mexico, Arizona, and parts of Texas, Utah, Colorado, and Nevada. The United States had effectively seized 55 percent of Mexico's territory.

Divided at the outset of the war, Americans remained divided in its aftermath. The treaty arrived in Washington for ratification just as the city was celebrating the dedication of the cornerstone of the Washington Monument. One orator took the occasion to celebrate the victory over Mexico as the triumph of Manifest Destiny. Comparing American liberty to a "locomotive" that was speeding down the "track of human freedom," he declared that "the whole civilized world resounds with American opinions and American principles." Offsetting this ebullient optimism, however, was a sense of foreboding most vividly expressed by Ralph Waldo Emerson, who predicted that expansion and all its attendant political questions, especially those concerning slavery, would prove as much a burden as a blessing: "Mexico will poison us."

Images of the Mexican War

The Mexican War was the first conflict in American history that professional journalists covered and reported to the people directly via the new medium of the telegraph almost daily. Competing for readers newspapers pioneered new techniques for gathering and reporting news, including sending "war correspondents" into battle. This practice freed newspapers from reliance on the military and government, allowing the press to exercise a more independent role. To be sure many papers continued to simply echo the official view of the war provided by the government. But many other editors used their papers to voice dissent. Abolitionists in particular used their antislavery newspapers to challenge the goals of the Polk administration and denounce the war. Indeed one military officer's complaint about the negative impact of a "thousand prying eyes and brazen tongues" was a direct result of "a free and uncontrolled press."

An equally significant innovation in war coverage involved the use of images by papers like *The New York Herald* to explain important events in the Mexican War. The Mexican War was also the first military conflict in America to be captured on film. The daguerreotype, an early form of photography, produced images that seem fuzzy by the standards of modern technology but that seemed miraculous achievements in their day. Americans approached the new technology as if it were an actual facsimile of reality and not merely another artistic representation of it. Indeed the *Herald* proclaimed that it intended its war coverage to be "daguerreotype reports," a term meant to convey unbiased and accurate report of reality in nearly real time. Americans embraced the new pictorial art form enthusiastically. Before shipping off, a soldier might sit for a

What role did images play in shaping American perceptions of the Mexican War?

daguerreotype which he gave to family or loved ones. Soldiers might also carry daguerreotypes of loved ones into battle. Daguerreotypists even followed soldiers into Mexico, setting up temporary studios and recording battle scenes. At least one artist died recording America's war effort. An especially haunting image produced during the war was a daguerreotype of the gravesite of Henry Clay Jr., son of the noted Whig politician, killed at the battle of Buena Vista (**11.10**).

The scene is desolate: a cross, an open grave awaiting a coffin, and an adobe vault over Clay's grave, a necessity that protected the burial site from being attacked by wolves or desecrated by grave robbers. Such an image was likely seen only by a small number of people, but its emotional impact would have been immense.

This sober image contrasts with a heroic representation of Clay's death in a popular print produced for a mass audience (**11.11**). Rather than capture the desolation of a grave in a distant wilderness, the lithograph shows a fallen leader urging his troops on to eventual victory. The artist focuses on Clay's final dramatic gesture with the pistol given to him by his father. "Take these pistols to my father," he tells a comrade, "and tell him I have done all I can with them, and now return them to him." Heroic images of this sort proved the most popular and influential representations of the war. Nathaniel Currier's venerable firm alone produced at least eighty-five different images of the war for an American audience eager to purchase them.

11.10 and **11.11** Clay's Grave and the *Death of Colonel Clay*
These representations of the death of Henry Clay's son capture radically different views of the war. The haunting daguerreotype (left) was a deeply personal artifact, while the more widely distributed lithograph was more inspirational than morbid.

Why did the artist pose Henry Clay in the same posture as General Wolfe and General Warren?

Choices and Consequences

HENRY DAVID THOREAU AND CIVIL DISOBEDIENCE

In 1846 Transcendentalist author Henry David Thoreau refused to pay his poll tax as a protest against the Mexican War. Thoreau's refusal to pay the tax landed him in jail for a night. In Thoreau's view the only place for a just man in an unjust legal and political system was in jail!

Thoreau explored the reasons for his act of defiance two years later. In a lyceum lecture called "The Rights and Duties of the Individual in Relation to Government," he formulated a sketch of this theory of civil disobedience. A year later a small literary journal published a revised version of this lecture, entitled "Resistance to Civil Government."

Thoreau's essay framed the options available to citizens facing government action they believed to be immoral in concise terms. "Unjust laws exist: shall we be content to obey them, or shall we endeavor to amend them, and obey them until we have succeeded, or shall we transgress them at once?" Here are the options as Thoreau envisioned them:

Choices

1 Accept government's decision and refrain from criticism.

2 Obey the law but work to change it.

3 Protest the law by refusing to obey it and suffer the legal consequences for challenging it.

Decision

Thoreau chose the third option and spent a night in the Concord jail.

Consequences

Thoreau's actions had almost no impact at the time, and his essay attracted little attention immediately. It did, however, became one of the most influential political essays ever written. His theory of civil disobedience influenced the twentieth-century Indian political leader Mohandas Gandhi's nonviolent protest movement against colonial British rule in India and mid-twentieth-century American civil rights leader Reverend Martin Luther King Jr.'s campaign against racial discrimination.

Young Texas in Repose

Continuing Controversies

Is the notion of a legal right of civil disobedience a contradiction in terms? Philosophers continue to debate the morality of civil disobedience. If one condones civil disobedience, does this principle invariably lead to anarchy, that is, lawlessness and political disorder, or is it possible to support the rule of law and still accept the moral legitimacy of civil disobedience? Another controversial issue that continues to divide supporters of resistance theory is the role of nonviolence. Must civil disobedience always be nonviolent, or can one legitimately use violence to further the ideals of justice and morality? Abolitionists extensively discussed this latter issue as they pondered what to do about the evil of slavery. The issue continues to divide supporters of the ideal of civil disobedience, many who continue to affirm that the idea can only claim the moral high ground and be effective if it forswears violence.

How significant was Henry Thoreau's essay at the time it was published?

The Wilmot Proviso and the Realignment of American Politics

For a young, up and coming Whig politician from Illinois, the War with Mexico was a decisive moment. Abraham Lincoln opposed the war and viewed further territorial expansion as a threat to America's future. Whigs continued to argue that economic development, not geographical expansion, was the key to America's prosperity. In what would become a hallmark of his distinctive style of rhetoric, Lincoln translated this Whig ideal into a folksy idiom. "[Whigs] did not believe in enlarging our field," Lincoln observed in 1848, "but in keeping our fences where they are and cultivating our present possessions, making it a garden, improving the morals and education of the people." Supporters of slavery held quite a different vision: acquiring a huge new swathe of territory would be a potential boon for slavery. The problem of what to do about slavery in the territories gained from Mexico would place an enormous strain on America's new two-party system, splitting Whigs and Democrats into Northern and Southern wings.

The Wilmot Proviso

In response to concerns that land seized from Mexico would lead to the spread of slavery, Congressmen David Wilmot introduced a measure to stop the spread of slavery. The **Wilmot Proviso** banned slavery from all territory acquired from Mexico. The bill created a political fire storm. The controversy over the Wilmot Proviso ushered in a new era of heightened sectional tensions and conflict over the future of slavery. Southerners denounced it as a thinly veiled attack on slavery, while Northerners denied this charge, insisting that it left slavery untouched where it already existed. The Proviso passed in the House of Representatives, where Northern delegates outnumbered Southern, but it was defeated in the Senate, where the balance between slave states and free states prevented either side from passing legislation objectionable to the other.

The Wilmot Proviso shifted the terms of American political debate to the problem of slavery in the territories, splitting both parties into pro-slavery and free-soil factions. In response a number of politicians tried to find a way to resolve the sectional argument over slavery. President Polk supported a proposal, modeled on the Missouri Compromise (see Chapter 7), to extend the 36° 30' line across the Louisiana Purchase territories separating free states from slave states all the way to the Pacific coast. Northerners opposed this idea because most of the land gained from Mexico lay below this line and seemed likely to enter the Union ultimately as a slave state. Senator Lewis Cass of Michigan suggested another compromise proposal, **popular sovereignty**, a policy that would allow the people in each territory to decide for themselves whether to permit slavery. Hoping to garner both Northern and Southern supporters, Cass intentionally omitted a crucial detail: *when* this decision on slavery would be made. Most Northerners believed this decision would be made when a territorial legislature was established. Most Southerners, however, accepted John C. Calhoun's interpretation that the decision over slavery would not be made until settlers wrote a state constitution, a delay that opponents of slavery feared would allow slaveholders extra time to firmly establish slavery in a territory.

Sectionalism and the Election of 1848

The Wilmot Proviso and the slavery question defined the presidential election of 1848. Both the Democratic and Whig parties tried to downplay the question of slavery in order to attract voters in the North and South. Democrats nominated moderate Lewis Cass, champion of the theory of popular sovereignty, for their presidential candidate. The Whigs had a more difficult time choosing a candidate. Henry Clay had been the clear frontrunner, but his adamant

Why was the Wilmot Proviso so controversial?

11.12 ***The Candidate of Many Parties***
A phrenologist probes General Zachary Taylor's head, looking for some sign of what the presidential candidate thought about the key issues of the day. Taylor's campaign tried to avoid taking stands on issues that might alienate voters.

opposition to the seizure of lands from Mexico was a difficult political position to take. Clay had hoped to avoid having to take a stand on this issue, but the Treaty of Guadalupe Hidalgo undercut his stance: after the Treaty, Clay's policy made no sense. Americans had to decide what to do about slavery in the new lands won from Mexico.

Casting Clay aside the Whigs eventually settled on General Zachary Taylor, a Mexican War hero who cast himself as a "no party man" and a unifier who was above partisanship. Even more useful to the party, because he was a career soldier, Taylor's views on a wide range of political issues were unknown, including his stand on the Wilmot Proviso. This humorous political cartoon from the election of 1848 shows a phrenologist (see Chapter 10) probing the general's skull, supposedly to find some clues to his political beliefs (**11.12**). The title of the cartoon, *The Candidate of Many Parties*, underscores Taylor's attempt to be all things to all people. Indeed the Whigs ran two different campaigns in the two regions of the country. To capture Southern voters they stressed the fact that Taylor owned slaves, asserting that no slaveholder would betray the interests of the South to Northern interests. To appeal to Northerners the Whigs emphasized Taylor's credentials as a Mexican War hero and his support for one of the Whig Party's cardinal principles: opposition to a strong executive, including the use of the presidential veto. By stressing his belief that the veto should only be used in exceptional cases where a law was clearly unconstitutional, Taylor signaled to Northern Whigs that he would not veto a Wilmot Proviso-like law. Embracing this cherished Whig constitutional ideal not only allowed Taylor to underscore his Whig credentials to those who doubted them but also it allowed him to deftly side-step the slavery issue. Taylor's election strategy allowed him to do the seemingly impossible: campaign as a pro-slavery candidate in the South and as a pro-Wilmot Proviso candidate in the North.

The dynamics of the 1848 election were further complicated by the emergence of a third party—the Free-Soil Party. This party brought together disaffected Democrats who supported the Wilmot Proviso and resented the growing influence of Southerners within their party. Led by former president Martin Van Buren, anti-slavery democrats were known as "Barnburners," a nickname that derived from an old Dutch tale about a farmer who burned down his barn to get the rats out. In 1848 the

Why does this political cartoon show a phrenologist examining Taylor's skull?

> "Let the soil of our extensive domains be kept free for the hardy pioneers of our own land, and the oppressed and banished of other lands, seeking homes of comfort and fields of enterprise in the new world."
>
> Free-Soil Party Platform, 1848

"rats" were the proslavery wing of the Democratic Party. A contemporary political cartoon shows Van Buren setting fire to a barn and rats, proslavery Democrats, fleeing the burning building (**11.13**). The Free-Soil Party also attracted disaffected Whigs who, unwilling to support a slaveholder as their party's candidate, came to be known as Conscience Whigs. It also gathered abolitionist supporters of the Liberty Party (the antislavery party founded in 1840). Under the slogan "No more Slave States and no more Slave Territories," the Free-Soil platform took the moderate position of opposing only the extension of slavery into the West.

The Whig, Taylor, won the election handily, but his victory revealed the importance of the slavery issue. See *Competing Visions, Slavery and the Election of 1848*, page 338. He won eight of fifteen slave states, largely because he was a slave owner. The race was much closer in the North, but Taylor prevailed in the key states of Pennsylvania and New York. He owed his narrow margin of victory in the latter state to the Free-Soil Party, which drew thousands of votes away from the Democrats. Overall the Free-Soil Party failed to win a single state, but it polled an impressive 300,000 votes (10 percent of the total) and elected two senators and nine representatives to Congress from states in the Northeast and Midwest.

11.13 ***Smoking Him Out***
In this political cartoon Martin Van Buren is shown in front of a burning barn, while proslavery Democrat Lewis Cass and several rats flee the building. The antislavery democrats were nicknamed "Barnburners."

Who were the Barnburners?

Competing Visions

SLAVERY AND THE ELECTION OF 1848

The problem of what to do with the vast territory acquired from Mexico became a deeply contentious issue in the election of 1848. The two party system fractured, producing a new third party, the Free-Soil Party, which was committed to opposing the spread of slavery westward. The new party met in Buffalo, New York, reflected in the cartoon showing Martin Van Buren, the party's candidate, riding a buffalo. The party platforms of the Democrats, Whigs, and Free-Soil Party each adopted a different approach to the slavery issue.

The Democrat Party Platform reasserted its commitment to the ideal of states' rights and the corollary of this belief: slavery was something that the Constitution had left for the individual states to decide.

The Congress has no power under the Constitution to interfere with or control the domestic institutions of the several states, that such States are the sole and proper judges of everything appertaining to their own affairs, not prohibited by the Constitution; that all efforts of the Abolitionists or others made to induce Congress to interfere with questions of slavery ... are calculated to lead to the most alarming and dangerous consequences.

The Whig Platform avoided mentioning the divisive issue of slavery. Rather than articulate a constitutional theory, the Whig Platform focused on the merits of the Whig candidate for president, Zachary Taylor. Whigs championed Taylor, who was presented as a war hero and a man who put the interests of the nation ahead of any sectional interest.

That we look on General Taylor's administration of the Government as one conducive to Peace, Prosperity, and Union ... we have a candidate whose very position as a Southwestern man, reared on the banks of the great stream whose tributaries, natural and artificial, embrace the whole Union, renders the protection of the interests of the whole country his first trust.

The Buffalo Hunt

What were the most important differences between the strategy of the Whigs and Democrats in the election of 1848?

Conclusion

During the 1840s Americans looked to the West as a land of economic opportunity and in the case of the Mormons a place of religious refuge. Westward expansion was shaped by the idea of Manifest Destiny, a vision of America's future where the nation, with God's blessing, took possession of the entire continent to bring to it the values of the market and American democracy. The establishment of the Overland Trail in 1840 led to rising numbers of whites migrating into the West and the mounting difficulties for Native Americans whose land the settlers coveted. Despite the fact that Indian attacks claimed only a small number of casualties among westward migrants, American popular culture cast Indians as a serious threat to the unfolding of Manifest Destiny.

One area in the West that attracted many thousands of Americans was the region of Mexico known as Texas. At first the Mexican government welcomed the newcomers, but by the early 1830s it became clear that many American settlers in Texas wanted the region to be annexed by the United States. After a revolt by Americans led to the establishment of an independent Texas republic, annexation was stalled for nearly a decade as the fate of Texas became entangled with the deeply divisive issue of slavery. Support for annexation was strongest in the South. Many Northerners opposed annexation because Texas would enter the Union as a slave state, thereby strengthening slavery and harming the interests of free whites. Brushing their opposition aside, President Tyler annexed Texas as a slave state in 1845.

Weeks later the newly inaugurated President James K. Polk entered the White House determined to expand American territory by acquiring a large piece of northern Mexico. When Mexico rebuffed efforts to buy the territory, Polk and Congress seized on a border clash between American and Mexican forces in April 1846 to declare war on Mexico. The Mexican War resulted in the United States acquiring a large swath of new territory. Even before the war was over, however, it reignited and intensified the already contentious issue of slavery. The Wilmot Proviso, a proposal to ban slavery from all of the territory acquired from Mexico, placed the issue of slavery at the very heart of American political debate, vexing the greatest minds of the age and straining the delicate political balance that held the nation together. The election of Zachary Taylor in 1848 provided only a brief respite from the growing conflict over slavery.

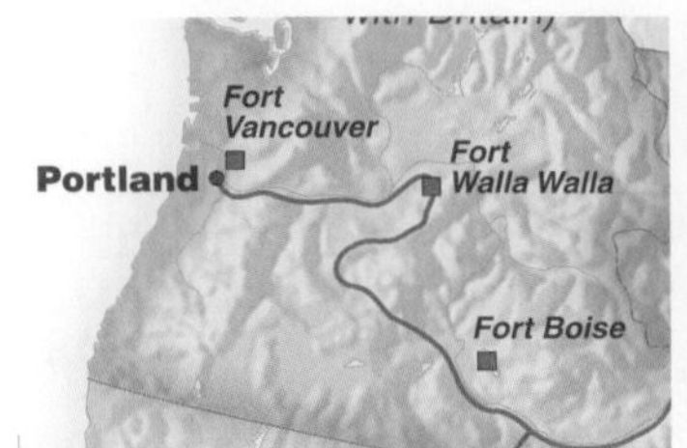

1804–1819

Federal exploration of the West by Lewis and Clark, Zebulon Pike, and Stephan Long
Americans gain accurate information about the West

1821–1825

Mexico declares independence from Spain
Independence ushers in a period of instability in Mexican politics

First fur rendezvous
Indians, traders, and trappers gather to buy, sell, and promote intercultural exchanges

Congress creates Indian territory
An important part of the federal government's policy of Indians approved by Congress

1835–1837

Texas revolts against Mexico
Texans achieve independence

Review Questions

1. What role did ideas of race play in the theory of Manifest Destiny?
2. What symbolic function did Indians play in American artists' representations of the West during the era of expansion?
3. How did the Mormon flight westward differ from the experience of those Americans who headed to Oregon?
4. Why did some Americans oppose the annexation of Texas?
5. How did the representations of the Mexican War in the press and in prints compare with the realities of war?
6. What was the Wilmot Proviso, and why did Southerners react negatively to it?
7. Who were the Barnburner Democrats, and how did they get their name?
8. How did Zachary Taylor's campaign in the election of 1848 deal with the divisive issue of slavery?

1843

Thousands of pioneers trek west to Oregon
First important wave of overland migration begins

1844–1845

Polk elected president
American government pushes Polk's expansionist agenda

John O'Sullivan coins term Manifest Destiny
O'Sullivan helps formulate and promote expansionist agenda for America

1846

Mexican War begins
Armed conflict with Mexico erupts over border dispute

Wilmot Proviso
Provision to ban slavery from any land gained from Mexico heats up the slavery question in American politics

1848

Taylor elected president
Whigs find a candidate able to unite the party across regional divisions

Treaty of Guadalupe Hidalgo
Mexican War ends

Key Terms

rendezvous A festive annual gathering held in the Rocky Mountains in which Indians, mountain men, and traders would gather together to exchange pelts for a variety of goods. **318**

Manifest Destiny A term coined by editor and columnist John O'Sullivan to describe his belief in America's divine right to expand westward. **320**

Overland Trail The 2,000-mile route taken by American settlers traveling to new settlements in Oregon, California, and Utah. **320**

mission system The colonial system devised by the Spanish to control the Indian population, forcing them to convert to Catholicism and work the land. **326**

Liberty Party The staunchly antislavery, anti-annexation, party was short lived, but captured 62,000 votes, a small number, but enough to effectively rob Henry Clay of electoral victories in New York and Michigan thereby handing Polk the presidency in 1844. **329**

The Treaty of Guadalupe Hidalgo This treaty formally ended the war between the United States and Mexico (1848). In addition to settling the border dispute between Texas and Mexico, the United States gained a significant swath of new territory in the Southwest. **332**

Wilmot Proviso Bill introduced by Congressman David Wilmot would have banned slavery from the territories acquired from Mexico. **335**

popular sovereignty An approach to the question of slavery in a newly acquired territory that would have allowed the people in each territory to decide for themselves whether to permit slavery. **335**

CHAPTER 12

Slavery and Sectionalism

The Political Crisis of 1848–1861

> "It is an irrepressible conflict between opposing and enduring forces, and it means that the United States must and will, sooner or later, become either entirely a slaveholding nation, or entirely a free-labor nation."
>
> WILLIAM SEWARD, 1858

The seizure of vast tracts of land from Mexico in 1848 ushered in a period of intense conflict between the North and the South over the question of whether to permit slavery in the territories west of the Mississippi. At the root of these tensions were the starkly different paths of economic and social development being pursued in the two regions. The South prospered in the 1840s and 1850s by expanding its agrarian, slave labor economy; the North, by becoming more urban, industrial, commercial, and multicultural. In the process, the two regions developed divergent visions of the ideal society: The South celebrated the virtues of slavery, states' rights, and white supremacy, while the North touted the benefits of free labor, upward mobility, and equal opportunity.

One of the first and most bitter controversies of the period emerged with the passage of the Fugitive Slave Act in 1850, a law requiring Northerners to assist Southerners in the apprehension of escaped slaves. It produced almost immediately a series of sensational incidents where abolitionists tried, with some success, to thwart the law and spirit escaped slaves to freedom.

Drawn by an abolitionist in the midst of this controversy, this dramatic image seeks to humanize the plight of escaped slaves while at the same time dramatizing the inhumanity of slave catchers and slaveholders. The inclusion of quotations from the Bible ("Thou shalt not deliver unto the master his servant which has escaped from his master unto thee ...") and the Declaration of Independence ("We hold that all men are created equal ...") highlights the fundamental claim of abolitionists that slavery violated both Judeo-Christian morality and republican principles. Southern slaveholders, of course, rejected these claims and asserted their inalienable right to property in all things, including slaves.

This controversy set the tone for a decade that was to be rocked by a series of political, legal, and economic disputes that ultimately led back to the slavery question. By the mid-1850s, each region increasingly came to see the other's system as a threat. Northerners became convinced that Southerners wanted to spread slavery to the West and even to the North, while Southerners believed Northerners sought to destroy slavery and the Southern way of life. When Republican Abraham Lincoln won the presidency in 1860, Southerners declared the Union dissolved, setting in motion events that led to a far more bloody conflict, the Civil War.

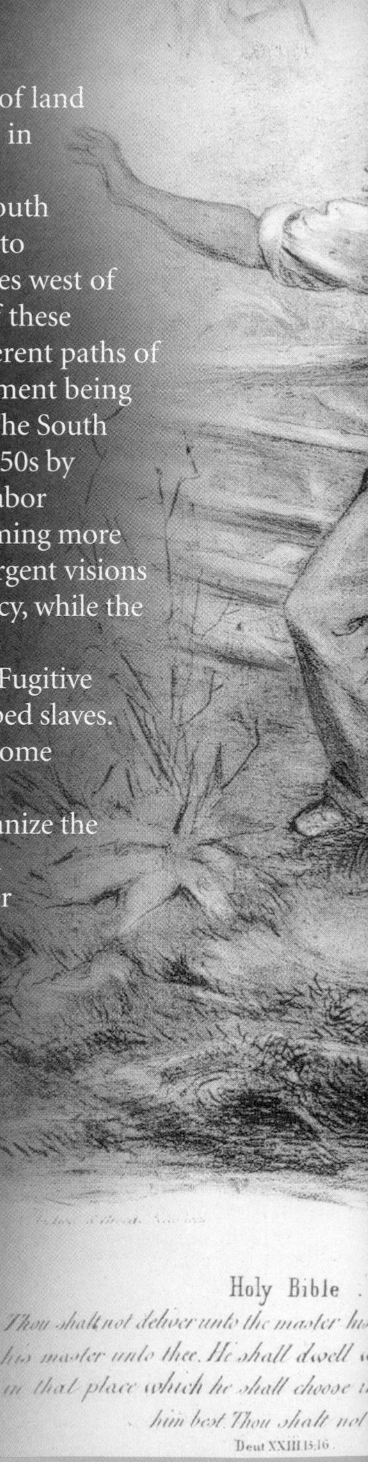

How did the seizure of Western land after the Mexican War fuel a growing controversy over slavery?

130 William Str Corner of Spruce

which has escaped from
Even among you
thy gates where it liketh
him.

Effects of the Fugitive-Slave-Law.

Declaration of independence.
We hold that all men are created equal, that they are endowed
their Creator with certain unalienable rights, that among th
are life liberty and the pursuit of happiness.

Entered according to Act of Congress in the year 1850 by Hoff & Bloede in the Clerks Office of the District Court of the Southern District of New York

The Slavery Question in the Territories

The election of 1848 revealed an emerging sectional divide between the North and South over the issue of slavery. The dispute centered on whether slavery would be allowed in the new territories. Given the small population of white settlers in the West, many politicians hoped that any decision on creating territories and admitting new states would not arise for years. But the discovery of gold in California in 1848 brought tens of thousands of fortune seekers. By late 1849 they constituted a population sufficient to apply for statehood. After much acrimony Congress eventually passed the Compromise of 1850, a set of measures that quieted but did not resolve the fundamental disagreement over the future of slavery in America.

The Gold Rush

Although members of both parties in Congress sought to avoid the contentious issue of slavery and the territories, the discovery of gold in California soon forced them to confront it. In December 1848, following four months of rumors, more than 300 ounces of pure gold arrived in Washington, D.C., sent by the new territorial government of California. The news touched off the Gold Rush: a migration of thousands of gold seekers in 1849 from farms and workshops in the East to northern California on news of the gold strike near San Francisco. California's population exploded as a result, rising from just 14,000 at the start of 1849 to more than 100,000 by year's end. By 1852 it reached 220,000.

Eighty percent of the new arrivals were American-born (including free African Americans), with the rest coming from Mexico, South America, Europe, and Asia. The great majority of arrivals were single white men in their twenties and thirties. They came to California not to settle but rather to strike it rich and return home.

This fortune-seeking spirit of the migrants led to the creation of a rough and raucous society. Mining camps and boomtowns sprang up almost overnight only to be abandoned the moment the gold disappeared or word arrived of a fresh strike elsewhere. Most mining towns lacked any formal government, including sheriffs and judges, leading to high rates of crime and violence.

By 1852 most of the gold that could be easily extracted was gone and with it individual earnings as high as twenty dollars per day in 1849 (compared to less than two dollars per day back east). With much gold remaining embedded in rock deep beneath the earth's surface, mining shifted from independent miners to corporations possessing the capital to pay for the expensive technology required to extract the hard-to-reach gold. Most of the men who remained in mining after 1852 did so as wage laborers. Among them were many thousands of prospectors who had sold their farms and shops in the East in a fruitless quest for easy wealth.

> "I have no pile yet, but you can bet your life I will never come home until I have something more than when I started."
>
> A Gold Rush migrant on his way to California

While many panned for gold, thousands of migrants worked in enterprises that supported the mining industry such as hotels, restaurants, banks, saloons, and laundries. They realized that the surest way to riches lay in selling supplies such as pickaxes, shovels, rope, tents, and clothing at outrageous prices to eager miners. Many women earned high wages working in cooking, cleaning, and health care jobs, but many were forced into prostitution to survive, a practice that flourished in the male-dominated society of California. By one estimate, one out of every five women in California in 1850 worked as a prostitute.

Another group that found its dreams of riches thwarted were the Chinese, forty-five thousand of

What was the fate of most fortune seekers who headed west to mine for gold?

whom arrived in California by 1854. White miners, motivated by racism and greed, used violence and intimidation to confine the Chinese to the least desirable mining areas. The drawing shown here (**12.1**) depicts the segregated world of these Chinese miners. No whites appear in the scene, which shows the Chinese engaged in several activities, primarily mining. In 1852 the state legislature imposed a heavy tax on the Chinese, prompting many to turn from mining to farming, fishing, and operating restaurants and laundries. But increased immigration and job competition with whites in the coming decades would lead to escalating anti-Chinese sentiment and violence in California (see Chapter 16).

Much worse was the fate of the California Indians. The diseases brought by migrants killed tens of thousands, while ruthless bands of miners killed thousands more or drove them off their lands. Of the 150,000 Native Americans who lived in California in 1848, on the eve of the Gold Rush, only 30,000 remained by 1870. Meanwhile, countless *Californios*—Mexicans living in California—lost title to their lands through legal obstacles that the new American government imposed.

The Gold Rush sparked Western development and accelerated the creation of a coast-to-coast American nation. But the immediate consequence of the Gold Rush was not economic or social; it was political. The arrival of tens of thousands of people in 1849 suddenly made California eligible to organize a territorial government as a prelude to statehood. Looming over any discussion of California statehood, however, was the divisive issue of slavery.

Organizing California and New Mexico

Even before the discovery of gold forced national leaders to consider California statehood, the question of the Western territories and the status of slavery there took center stage in Congress. Tempers flared in the House when Northern representatives unsuccessfully attempted to approve a motion upholding the Wilmot Proviso in the Western territories, draft a bill to organize California as a free territory, and pass a bill ending the slave trade in the District of Columbia.

The tension eventually subsided as congressmen decided to wait for president-elect Zachary Taylor to take office and reveal his opinions on the question of slavery and the Western territories. Within weeks of his inauguration in March 1849, Taylor made it clear that while he was a Southerner who did not oppose slavery, he would put national unity above regional loyalty. Instead of creating territorial governments for California and New Mexico that would leave authority over the slavery issue with Congress, he proposed that they be made states immediately and thus have the freedom to decide the slavery question according to popular will. This would remove the

12.1 Racism in the Gold Fields of California Chinese gold-seekers were often confined to segregated encampments and less desirable mining sites.

How did the Gold Rush affect the native Americans of California?

contentious issue from Congress where it sparked bitter debate and increasing sectionalism.

Residents of New Mexico and California responded enthusiastically to Taylor's invitation. By the fall of 1849, California had approved a state constitution prohibiting slavery and applied to Congress for admission as a free state. They also adopted a seal (**12.2**) to symbolize their vision of their state and its future. In the foreground sits Minerva, the goddess of wisdom, while behind her a miner prospects for gold. (The motto, Eureka, is Greek for "I have found it.") Sheaves of wheat at her feet and ships (symbolic of commerce) sailing on the nearby waters indicate their expectations for robust economic growth. Months later, New Mexico's residents also applied for admission.

> "The people of the North need have no apprehension of the further extension of slavery."
>
> President ZACHARY TAYLOR at Mercer, Pennsylvania, July 1849

12.2 The Great Seal of California The inclusion of thirty-one stars indicated the hope that California would be admitted as the thirty-first state.

Taylor's actions touched off a firestorm of protest in the South. State legislatures signed petitions of protest and forwarded them to Washington, while mass meetings across the region denounced Taylor and his Northern supporters. Hard-line defenders of slavery, often called "fire-eaters," then convened a Southern rights convention in Nashville, Tennessee, in June 1850 "to devise and adopt some mode of resistance to Northern aggression."

What angered Southerners most was the threat Taylor's plan posed to the balance of power in Congress. Because of the North's greater population, it sent more representatives to the House. But with the balance of slave and free states standing at fifteen each, Southerners enjoyed equal representation in the Senate, allowing them to block any legislation deemed threatening to slavery or Southern interests (the so-called Southern veto). Admitting California and New Mexico as free states would tip the balance in favor of the North. Under such conditions it would only be a matter of time, warned Southern defenders, before a Congress dominated by Northerners moved to abolish slavery altogether. "For the first time," warned Senator Jefferson Davis of Mississippi, "we are about permanently to destroy the balance of power between the sections."

The Compromise of 1850

As he had done in the Missouri Compromise in 1820 and the Nullification Crisis of 1832–1833, Henry Clay of Kentucky proposed a compromise. His plan admitted California as a free state and organized New Mexico into two territories where the people would eventually vote to decide whether to permit slavery, a principle known as popular sovereignty. It also settled the border dispute between New Mexico and Texas, arranged for the federal government to assume Texas's debt, banned the slave trade in Washington, D.C., and established a stronger federal fugitive slave law.

The speeches inspired by the debate over Clay's bill, among the most famous in the history of Congress, revealed an intensifying clash of visions over the issue of the future of slavery in America. On March 4 John C. Calhoun, near death and too sick to stand, had a colleague read his speech expressing the views of proslavery Southern hard-liners. He demanded that the North stop attacking slavery, uphold the South's rights in the territories (especially the right to own slaves), and enforce the fugitive slave laws.

Three days later the renowned Massachusetts Senator Daniel Webster delivered his famous "Seventh of March Address," an impassioned plea

Why did Southerners react so negatively to President Taylor's plan?

for moderation and compromise, warning that both proslavery and antislavery extremism threatened to destroy the Union. William Seward of New York then rose to voice the views of staunch antislavery Northerners. Rejecting the Southern argument that the Constitution guaranteed the right to extend slavery into the territories, Seward invoked the authority of "a higher law than the Constitution," the law of God under which all people deserved to live in freedom. Congress, he argued, should instead be debating how to eliminate slavery peacefully and gradually.

Debate over Clay's compromise raged for months. The hostility spawned by the differences of opinion over slavery and the Western territories is captured in this 1850 political cartoon, *Scene in Uncle Sam's Senate* (**12.3**). The tone of the cartoon is satirical, but it depicts a real incident in which Mississippi Senator Henry S. Foote pulled a pistol on Missouri Senator Thomas Hart Benton (shown holding his coat open and daring his opponent to shoot). In the end the Senate finally voted it down in July.

Then the unexpected occurred. President Taylor died of severe gastroenteritis on July 9, 1850, and was succeeded by Vice President Millard Fillmore, a moderate Whig from New York. Unlike Taylor, Fillmore was more sympathetic to the South and eager to reach a compromise. With Fillmore's support, a young and ambitious senator from Illinois, Stephen A. Douglas, revived the movement for compromise. He broke up Clay's massive bill into separate pieces of legislation and then, without appeals to patriotism or sectionalism, he assembled enough votes to pass each individually.

> "The South asks for justice, simple justice, and less she ought not to take. … Nothing else can, with any certainty, finally and for ever settle the question at issue, terminate agitation, and save the Union."
>
> JOHN C. CALHOUN, March 4, 1850

12.3 **Tempers Flare During the Debate over Clay's Omnibus Bill**
Reflecting the rising animosity over the status of slavery in the new Western territories, fighting breaks out on the floor of the Senate.

What did Seward mean by a "higher law?"

12.4 The Compromise of 1850
The Compromise attempted to quell the political storm that arose over the slavery question by making concessions to both sides. Free-Soilers gained the admission of California as a free state, while supporters of slavery won a delay in deciding the slavery question in the New Mexico and Utah territories. The Compromise also settled the dispute regarding the western border of Texas, established a Fugitive Slave Act, and abolished the slave trade in Washington, D.C.

As the map illustrates (**12.4**), Douglas's bill, or the **Compromise of 1850**, contained five components, some of which appealed to proslavery Southerners and others to antislavery Northerners. First, California was admitted as a free state. To offset this concession to the opponents of slavery, a second bill created the New Mexico and Utah territories and left the question of slavery to be decided by popular sovereignty when each territory applied for statehood. Left unexplained was the status of slavery in the years leading to statehood. Third, Texas was required to cede disputed territory on its western border to New Mexico (pleasing opponents of slavery by reducing the slave state's size) in exchange for the federal government assuming the $10 million debt Texas had incurred as a republic (pleasing Southerners who held most of the debt). A fourth provision granted abolitionists a partial victory by banning the slave trade—but not slavery—in Washington, D.C. Finally, Congress enacted a strong **Fugitive Slave Act** that greatly increased the federal government's commitment to returning escaped slaves to their owners, something Southern fire-eaters had been demanding for years.

When the bills were all signed by mid-September, joyful crowds gathered in the nation's capital to serenade Congress with song and cheers of "The Union is saved."

But a close examination of the votes on the compromise's bills reveals a weakening of party loyalties and a growing tendency toward voting along sectional lines. Most Northern Whigs, for example, supported the admission of California as a free state and opposed the Fugitive Slave Act. Most Southern Whigs voted in the opposite manner. Only 20 percent of Congress—generally moderates made up of Northern Democrats and Southern Whigs—voted for all five bills. As many antislavery Northerners and Southern hardliners correctly predicted, the question of slavery, whether in the territories or elsewhere, would surface again.

How did the Congressional vote on the Compromise of 1850 reveal growing sectionalism?

Sectionalism on the Rise

One element in the Compromise of 1850—the Fugitive Slave Act—sparked a national controversy that intensified the sectionalism, or hostility between North and South over the slavery question. The act created a force of federal commissioners who possessed broad powers to pursue and return suspected escaped slaves to their owners. It also permitted federal marshals to deputize private citizens to assist in capturing fugitive slaves. Those who refused to help were subject to fines and imprisonment. Once apprehended, an accused fugitive had no right to a jury trial. His or her fate was instead decided by a federal commissioner who stood to earn a fee of ten dollars if he returned the accused to slavery and only five if he released him or her.

Fugitive slaves escaping to the North did not become a major political issue until the 1830s. In that decade the growing abolitionist movement began to encourage and facilitate slave escapes along what came to be known metaphorically as the **Underground Railroad.** It was a network of safe houses and other secret hiding places along a series of routes leading to the North and into Canada where British law prohibited slavery. The existence of such a network is revealed in this page from the 1844 diary of Daniel Osborn, a Quaker living in Alum Creek, Ohio (**12.5**). Between April and September of that year—warm months ideal for travel—Osborn recorded assisting forty-seven escapees. His home

> "The slaves call her Moses."
> THOMAS WENTWORTH HIGGINSON, describing Harriet Tubman, 1859

was situated approximately halfway between the borders of northern Kentucky (where all but three of the fugitives came from) and Canada. Many of his Quaker neighbors also harbored fugitives.

Angry slaveholders and eager abolitionists spread fantastic stories of thousands of slaves being spirited north annually, but the Underground Railroad probably succeeded in bringing no more than several thousand slaves to freedom between 1830 and 1860. Its most famous "conductor" was Harriet Tubman, an escaped slave who made nineteen trips to the South to lead scores of slaves, including many of her relatives, to freedom. Osborn's diary occasionally revealed a similar pattern on a smaller scale. In one eight-day period in August 1844, he recorded that an African American man passed through Alum Creek on his way back to Kentucky where he gathered his wife, child, and sister-in-law and returned safely. He was followed by a woman who came from Canada and successfully brought four of her children and one grandchild to freedom. Most fugitives escaped to the North through less formal arrangements and a combination of perseverance, ingenuity, and luck.

Although the number of escaped slaves remained relatively small, averaging one thousand per year out of a total slave population that approached four million by 1860, Southern slaveholders grew increasingly angry over the unwillingness of Northerners to assist in the return of their "property." Especially galling were the "personal liberty laws" passed by nine Northern states between 1842 and 1850, which prohibited the use of state officials or facilities like courts and jails for the capture and return of escaped slaves.

With these precedents in mind, Southerners made clear in the weeks following the Compromise of 1850 that they expected Northerners to uphold

12.5 Abolitionists Assist Escaped Slaves along the Underground Railroad
This page from the diary of Daniel Osborn, a Quaker living in Alum Creek, Ohio, records the assistance he offered escaped slaves heading for Canada in the spring of 1844.

the Fugitive Slave Act. "It is the deliberate opinion of this Convention," resolved a gathering of Georgia fire-eaters, "that upon the faithful execution of the *Fugitive Slave Law* ... depends the preservation of our much beloved Union." Southern insistence on a new fugitive slave law was full of contradiction. Even though Southern rights advocates consistently celebrated the sanctity of states' rights, they condemned Northern states for enacting "personal liberty laws." States' rights doctrine also opposed any increase of federal power, especially when slavery was concerned, yet Southerners willingly made an exception when it came to using federal authority to capture their escaped slaves.

Abolitionists denounced the new fugitive slave law as "a hateful statute of kidnappers." They soon formed vigilance committees throughout the North and vowed, in the words of one Illinois newspaper, "to trample the law in the dust." Opportunities for resistance soon arose, for unlike the abstract questions raised by Wilmot Proviso and popular sovereignty, the Fugitive Slave Act created a succession of concrete human dramas in dozens of Northern communities (see *Choices and Consequences: Resisting the Fugitive Slave Act*).

Some early and memorable incidents occurred in Boston, the unofficial headquarters of the abolitionist movement. In October 1850, just weeks after the law's enactment, two slave catchers arrived in Boston in pursuit of William and Ellen Craft, who had escaped from Georgia two years earlier. The city's vigilance committee swung into action, hiding the Crafts and posting handbills throughout the city, denouncing the "kidnappers." After five days of sustained harassment and physical threats, the slave catchers left the city. Taking no chances, the Crafts boarded a ship for England.

The controversy over the Fugitive Slave Act played a significant role in popularizing and legitimizing antislavery sentiment—though not necessarily abolitionism—in the North. In the early 1850s only a tiny minority of Northerners were abolitionists. Indeed, many held deeply hostile views of blacks and rejected the idea of racial equality. Other Northerners opposed slavery, but were not willing to jeopardize the national peace achieved by the Compromise of 1850 by supporting abolitionist vigilantism. Nonetheless, the controversial events generated by the Fugitive Slave Act forced Northerners to confront the reality of an institution that had long seemed distant and abstract. The vivid images of Southern agents seizing free people in a community of free citizens and returning them to a life of bondage shocked even the most conservative Northerners. As one conservative Whig wrote after seeing the fugitive Anthony Burns returned to slavery from Boston in 1854, "When it was all over, and I was alone in my office, I put my face in my hands and wept." While these and subsequent events in the 1850s did not convert masses of Northerners to abolitionism, they did move many to see slavery as an evil that at the very least ought to be confined to its present boundaries in order to hasten its eventual demise.

Many Northerners also gradually took a more hostile attitude toward slavery as the result of reading antislavery literature. While the growing number of firsthand accounts of slavery by escaped slaves proved very popular, by far the most widely read and influential book was a work of fiction. First published in installments in an abolitionist newspaper, *Uncle Tom's Cabin* appeared as a novel in 1852. Its author, Harriet Beecher Stowe, came from a prominent abolitionist family. Within a year her novel sold 300,000 copies, making it the best-selling book of the era. Soon thousands of theatrical versions of the story were being performed in cities across the North. Speeches, diaries, letters, and other evidence indicate that Stowe's account of the brutality of slavery and the humanity of the enslaved moved millions of Northerners to take an increasingly hostile view toward slavery, even if they did not necessarily believe in racial equality.

The reaction to the book in the South was very different. Southerners denounced the author as a "wretch in petticoats" and banned the book. They also published several dozen proslavery novels with similar titles. This image (**12.6**) from *Aunt Phillis's Cabin*] *or Southern Life as It Is* (1852), portrays slaves dancing, suggesting they enjoy free time and are happy as slaves.

12.6 Southerners Refute the Antislavery Claims of *Uncle Tom's Cabin* This frontispiece from *Aunt Phillis's Cabin, or Southern Life as It Is* (1852), presents slavery as a happy, carefree existence.

What made *Uncle Tom's Cabin* such an influential piece of antislavery literature?

Choices and Consequences

RESISTING THE FUGITIVE SLAVE ACT

In February 1851 Boston's abolitionists faced a new challenge when federal authorities captured an escaped slave named Shadrach Minkins. As a federal judge ordered a hearing to determine Minkins's status to be held three days later, a large crowd of some two hundred white and black abolitionists gathered outside. Intimidating slave catchers and helping the Crafts avoid arrest had constituted *resistance* to the Fugitive Slave Act, but with Minkins in federal custody the situation raised the question of whether abolitionists were willing to *break* the law to uphold their values.

Choices

1 Drawing upon the civil disobedience tradition (see Chapter 11), declare the Fugitive Slave Act immoral and organize an extralegal effort to free Minkins.

2 Respect the laws regarding fugitive slaves, but wage a legal fight through the courts to prevent the extradition of Minkins and other alleged fugitive slaves.

3 Respect the laws regarding fugitive slaves and accept the likely transportation of Minkins back to slavery, but organize a more effective effort to spirit fugitive slaves out of the country (like the Crafts).

Decision

Convinced that the hearing would result in Minkins's return to slavery, a group of twenty African American men opted for choice 1 and burst into the courtroom, overpowered the guards, and took Minkins to Montreal, Canada. The incident thrilled abolitionists, including Theodore Parker who wrote later, "I think it is the most noble deed done in Boston since the destruction of the tea in 1773." Southerners and conservative Northerners like President Fillmore denounced the mob as lawless.

Consequences

When federal authorities apprehended another escaped slave, Thomas Sims, in Boston two months later, Fillmore sent 250 soldiers to guard the courthouse and escort the captive to a ship bound for Georgia. Nonetheless, similar incidents of extralegal actions by abolitionists occurred elsewhere. In Christiana, Pennsylvania, in October 1851, for example, two dozen armed African American men killed a slaveholder from nearby Maryland in pursuit of two escaped slaves. These events outraged Southerners, especially pro-secessionist fire-eaters. South Carolina, Mississippi, and Georgia held conventions to denounce abolitionism and consider secession. The furor soon quieted down as the number of slave captures decreased sharply, largely the result of thousands of free blacks and escaped slaves fleeing to Canada (Ontario's African American population doubled in the 1850s).

Continuing Controversies

When are acts of civil disobedience and violence to further the cause of justice legitimate?

In the 1850s abolitionists deemed slavery such an outrageous violation of American freedom that acts of resistance—even violence—were justified. This question would reemerge and generate heated debate in every subsequent era in American history, including movements for suffrage in the 1910s and civil rights in the 1960s.

African Americans drive off the slave catchers in Christiana, Pennsylvania

What caused the furor over the Fugitive Slave Act to eventually subside?

Political Realignment

Furor over the Fugitive Slave Act subsided after 1851, and American politics experienced a period of relative calm. Some felt a rising optimism over the prospect of territorial expansion into the Caribbean and Latin America. At the same time, unprecedented levels of immigration spawned a powerful antiforeigner political movement that enjoyed widespread support until eclipsed by the reemergence of the slavery issue. Sectional animosity surged in 1854 as Congress debated whether to allow slavery in the Kansas and Nebraska territories. The resulting Kansas-Nebraska Act prompted the collapse of the Whig Party and in 1856–1857, a violent and protracted conflict between pro- and antislavery forces, known as "Bleeding Kansas."

Young America

By late 1852 a prosperous economy and fear of disunion undermined the appeal of extremists in both sections. Prosperity also helped calm the passions aroused by the Compromise of 1850 and the enforcement of the Fugitive Slave Act. In the presidential election that year, both parties nominated moderate candidates (Democrat Franklin Pierce and Whig General Winfield Scott) and put forth similar platforms pledged to uphold the Compromise of 1850. Pierce won handily, but the most telling aspect of the election was the woeful performance of the Whig Party in the South (**12.7**). Scott, allied with the antislavery wing of his party, won only Kentucky and Tennessee. The Whig Party was falling apart and soon would be gone.

Pierce's appeal lay not in his personality (he was rather dull), but in his credentials as a Northerner with Southern sympathies. He was also a member of a brash movement within the Democratic Party called **Young America**. Enthusiastic about the notion of Manifest Destiny (see Chapter 11), supporters of Young America promoted a nationalist vision of territorial expansion, increased international trade, and the spread of American ideals of democracy and free enterprise abroad. America, they argued, possessed the right, even obligation, to continue its expansion, especially into Latin America and the Caribbean. The Young America program enjoyed broad appeal in both sections of the country and a spirit that found expression in Democratic newspaper editorials, Fourth of July speeches, advertising imagery, and paintings. Among the paintings, Emmanuel Leutze's *Westward the Course of Empire Takes Its Way* depicts a group of pioneers peering out over a vast expanse of Western territory (**12.8**). Native Americans are nowhere to be seen, suggesting that the land is ripe

> "We have a destiny to perform, a 'manifest destiny' over all Mexico, over South America, over the West Indies."
>
> *DeBow's Review*, 1850

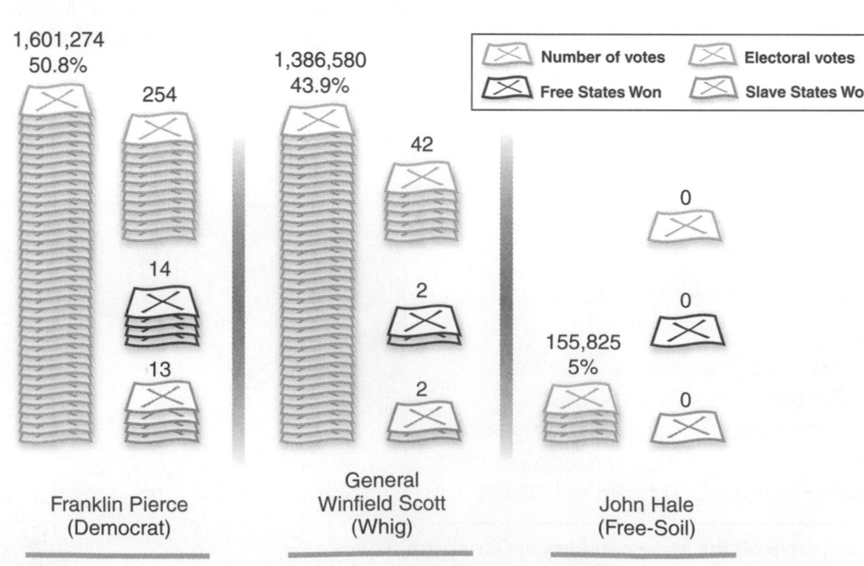

12.7 The Election of 1852 Scott's poor performance in the South (winning only two states) indicated that the Whig Party was fast disintegrating over the slavery issue.

What ideals inspired Young America's vision of westward expansion?

for the taking. By including babies and children, Leutze indicates that generations of future Americans will benefit from the land's bounty. A radiant sunset implies God's blessing is upon the enterprise.

As president, Pierce proved an ardent proponent of expansion, which he believed would strengthen the Democratic Party and unite the nation. Yet his efforts at expansion had nearly the opposite effect. When Pierce entertained proposals to annex Hawaii and purchase Alaska, Southerners in Congress stymied the plans because the treaties would have outlawed slavery. Conversely, Northern representatives denounced Pierce's attempt in 1854 to acquire Cuba—with its plantation economy and 300,000 slaves from Spain. Northerners likewise took a dim view of the invasions of Latin American and Caribbean countries led by small armies of expansion-minded adventurers known as "filibusters" (an English corruption of the Dutch word for pirate). These operations delighted Southern slave owners, however, who viewed these lands as ideal, in the words of Mississippi senator Albert G. Brown, "for the planting and spreading of slavery."

Pierce's support for proslavery expansionism alienated Northern supporters and threatened to upset the sectional peace achieved by the Compromise of 1850. But the controversy over proposed expansion would pale by comparison with that sparked in 1854 over a plan to organize the territories of Kansas and Nebraska.

The Kansas-Nebraska Act

Stephen A. Douglas of Illinois, another leading Young America figure, saw the future development of the United States in the rapid organization of territories and eventually states in the land west of Iowa and Missouri (essentially the northern half of the Louisiana Purchase). He was not alone. Farmers were eager to settle in the region's fertile Kansas and Platte River Valleys, while promoters of a transcontinental railroad hoped to run a northern route through it. Neither settlement nor railroad construction could occur, however, before the federal government negotiated land treaties with Indians and organized the area as a territory.

Douglas faced strong opposition from Southern congressmen who feared the new territories would eventually become two free states. They also had their sights set on a southern route for the transcontinental railroad, from New Orleans through the recently organized New Mexico territory to San Francisco. They told Douglas they would support his plan only if it included a repeal of the ban on slavery north of 36° 30′ that had been a part of the Missouri Compromise in 1820. Promises of popular sovereignty, they warned, would not be enough.

12.8 An Enthusiastic Vision of Westward Expansion This 1861 painting, *Westward the Course of Empire Takes Its Way*, by Emmanuel Leutze, vividly expresses the expansionist spirit of the Young America movement. [*Source:* Emanuel Gottlieb Leutz (1816–1868), "Westward the Course of Empire Takes Its Way (Mural Study, U.S. Capitol)", 1861. Oil on canvas, 33 1/4" × 43 3/8" (84.5 × 110.1 cm). Smithsonian American Art Museum, Washington, DC / Art Resource, NY]

Why did many Southerners support efforts to annex Cuba and seize other Caribbean and Latin American countries?

Fully aware that it would "raise a hell of a storm," but hopeful it would boost his presidential ambitions for 1856, Douglas introduced his **Kansas-Nebraska Act** as a solution to the issues arising over these Western territories. In addition to repealing the ban on slavery north of 36° 30′, the act called for splitting the area into two separate territories, Kansas west of Missouri and Nebraska west of Iowa (**12.9**). He intended this last provision to placate both North and South by allowing the eventual establishment of Kansas as a slave state (since its soil and climate were similar to neighboring Missouri) and Nebraska as a free state.

The Kansas-Nebraska Act touched off a national debate more intense than that of 1850. Most Northerners, both Whigs and Democrats, considered the 36° 30′ line an untouchable agreement that had ensured national peace for more than thirty years. While moderates had been willing in 1850 to allow slavery (via popular sovereignty) into Western territory lying south of the line, they now balked at the prospect of doing so in land north of it. Free-Soilers and abolitionists denounced the bill as "a gross violation of a sacred pledge" and conclusive evidence that the South, now increasingly referred to as the "Slave Power," was bent on spreading the curse of slavery wherever possible. They organized hundreds of "anti-Nebraska" rallies across the North and encouraged speeches, sermons, and petitions to Congress. "Despite corruption, bribery, and treachery," asserted one typical resolution, "Nebraska, the heart of our continent, shall forever remain free."

Undeterred by such opposition, Douglas prevailed, and his bill passed in May 1854. But it was a costly victory that seriously weakened his

12.9 The Kansas-Nebraska Act
The goal of Stephen A. Douglas in gaining passage of the Kansas-Nebraska Act was to open the Great Plains to settlement and facilitate the construction of a transcontinental railroad (ideally running through his home state of Illinois). His repeal of the Missouri Compromise Line and the ensuing vigilante conflict in Kansas reignited the slavery controversy.

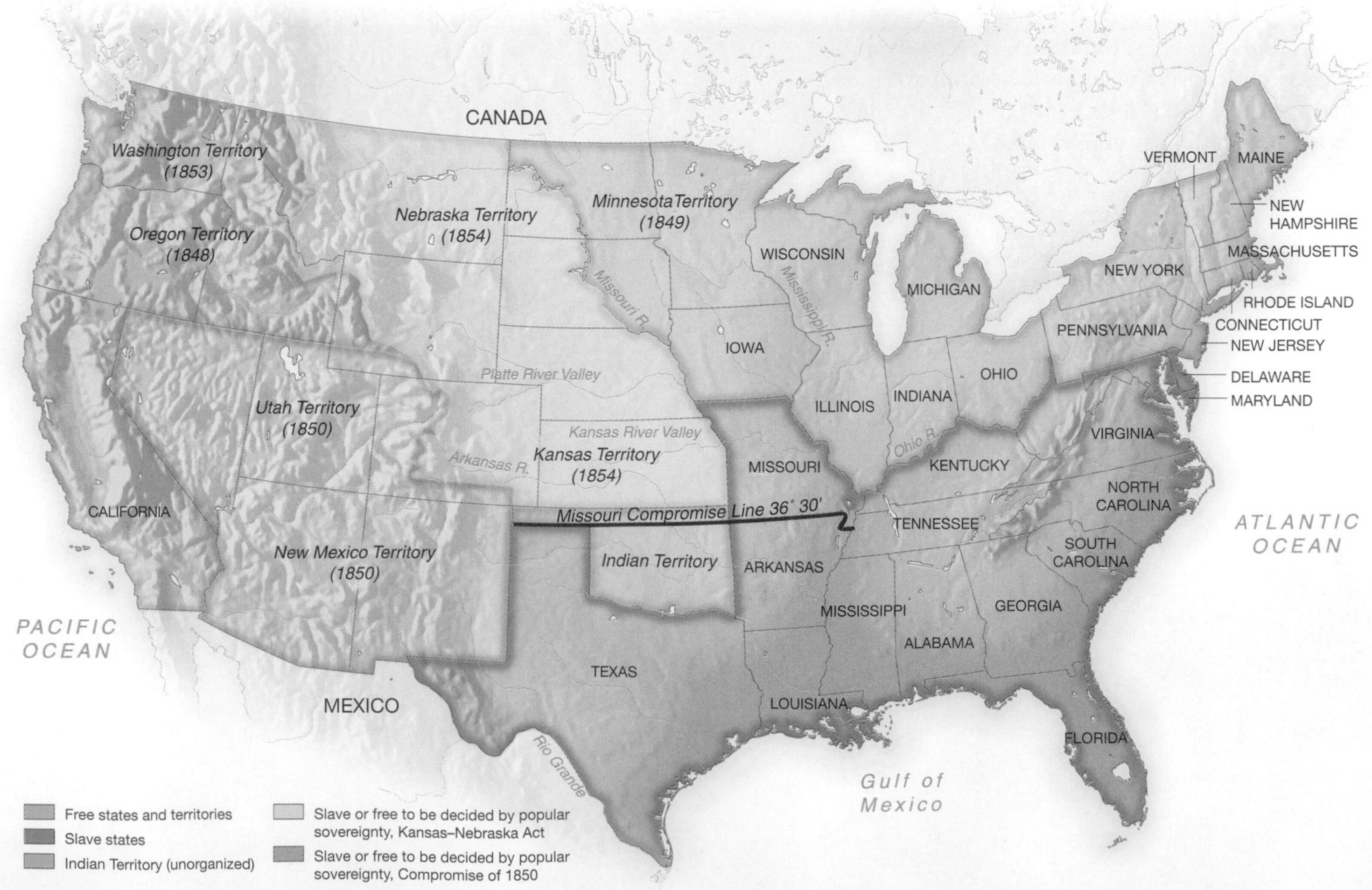

Why did most Northerners oppose the repeal of the Missouri Compromise line of 36° 30′?

Democratic Party and hampered his presidential hopes by associating him with controversy. The impact on the Whigs was even worse, shattering the party along sectional lines. Every Northern Whig in the House and Senate voted against the measure, while most Southern Whigs joined the Democrats in support. More seriously, the death of the Whig Party in the South indicated that the bitter fight over Nebraska had permanently ended the long-standing spirit of accommodation between the sections. Many Northerners resolved to make no more concessions to the Slave Power, while a growing number of Southerners resolved to preserve their rights from attacks by abolitionists.

This intensifying polarization between North and South is depicted in these two sculptures of "Freedom" by noted sculptor Thomas Crawford (**12.10**). Crawford was commissioned in 1854 to create a statue of a monumental figure representing liberty to top the Capitol building in Washington, D.C. One year later he submitted a proposed model for the sculpture to Secretary of War Jefferson Davis, who was overseeing the renovation of the Capitol building. Davis approved of the overall scheme—a large classically robed woman holding a sword and shield—but one detail infuriated the vociferous defender of slavery from Mississippi. Crawford had given "Freedom" a cap that Davis recognized as the one worn by freed slaves in ancient Rome. Sensing an abolitionist plot (Crawford was a friend of leading abolitionist Senator Charles Sumner), Davis threatened to cancel the commission. Crawford quickly reworked the design, replacing the cap with a helmet surrounded by stars and topped by a bald eagle.

Republicans and Know-Nothings

The political impact of the Kansas-Nebraska controversy became clear in the fall 1854 elections. Free-Soilers, ex-Whigs, and antislavery Democrats in the North formed dozens of local parties under names like the Anti-Nebraska or the People's Party. The most popular name, and the one under which they would eventually unite, was Republican. Despite their varied names, the parties shared an overriding commitment to opposing further concessions to Southern slave interests.

As this loose collection of antislavery groups coalesced into the Republican Party, the Democratic Party was transformed. In the midterm elections of 1854, Northern Democrats lost control of the House of Representatives and all but two free-state legislatures. Many of the defeated Democrats lost because they had voted for the Kansas-Nebraska Act. But in the South the Democratic Party actually grew stronger with the addition of proslavery Whigs. From that point the party came under growing Southern, proslavery control.

The nascent Republican Party was not the only movement seeking to succeed the defunct Whig Party. While many Northerners harbored growing concern about the Slave Power, large numbers perceived a greater threat to their way of life: mass immigration. The flow of immigrants into the United States, rising steadily since the 1820s, became

12.10 Slavery and the Republican Image
Crawford's design for a sculpture to top the Capitol's dome included a hat worn by freed slaves in ancient Rome (above). Bowing to pro-slavery objections, Crawford redesigned "Freedom's" hat as a helmet surrounded by stars and topped by a bald eagle.

a tidal wave in the mid-1840s. Industrialization, population growth, and crop failure in Europe led hundreds of thousands of Irish, German, and other western Europeans to seek new lives in America, where industrial jobs and cheap land abounded. Between 1845 and 1855 three million immigrants arrived, often settling in Northern cities.

This surge in immigration caused anti-immigrant sentiment, or nativism—native-born Americans' belief in their superiority to the foreign born—to rise sharply. As *Images as History: The "Foreign Menace"* shows, Americans were upset not merely by the number of immigrants arriving, but also by their perceived character. While most immigrants in previous decades had been Protestants from Britain—many of them with money and skills—a large majority of immigrants in the 1840s and 1850s were poor unskilled Catholics from Germany and Ireland. Anti-Catholicism, with roots in American history going back to the nation's earliest European founders, surged into near hysteria. Some of the best-selling books in the antebellum period were works of anti-Catholic literature that charged Catholicism, with its emphasis on clerical authority and loyalty to the pope in Rome, was incompatible with democracy. Nativists also feared that immigrants took American jobs, drank too much alcohol, refused to assimilate, and increased poverty, disease, and crime.

> "The ill-clad and destitute Irishman is repulsive to our habits and our tastes."
>
> *The Christian Examiner* (N.Y.), 1848

Anti-immigrant sentiment reached a fever pitch in 1854 with the emergence of the American Party. Its core constituents were members of secret anti-immigrant societies founded in cities in the late 1840s. Because secrecy required them to answer "I know nothing" when asked about their organization, they earned the name "**Know-Nothings**." Their political platform condemned both political parties as hopelessly corrupt and called for legislation restricting office holding to native-born citizens, barring the use of public funds for parochial schools, and raising the period of naturalization for citizenship from five to twenty-one years.

With the Whig Party in decline and the Democrats closely associated with the immigrant vote, Know-Nothings achieved stunning success in the 1854 elections, winning control of the state governments in Delaware, Pennsylvania, and Massachusetts. Nationally, about seventy-five Know-Nothing congressmen were sent to Washington. Elections one year later in 1855 saw the party win Maryland and Kentucky, place scores of nativist candidates in office in New York and California, and post impressive tallies in Tennessee, Virginia, Georgia, Alabama, Mississippi, and Louisiana.

In the aftermath of the elections of 1854, the big question was which of these two new political forces—antislavery Republicans or anti-immigrant Know Nothings—would replace the defunct Whig Party. But the American Party disintegrated almost as quickly as it arose, splitting like the Whig Party along sectional lines over the issue of slavery. Most of its members eventually joined the Republican Party. While many former members retained their dislike of foreigners, they grew increasingly concerned about what they perceived as a greater threat to the nation's well-being: the growing aggression of the Slave Power. This threat seemed most menacing in the newly created territory of Kansas.

Ballots and Blood

Even as opponents of slavery denounced Douglas's plan to allow popular sovereignty to decide the status of slavery in the territories, they devised a plan to ensure the results went their way. "We will engage in competition for the virgin soil of Kansas," William Seward warned his Southern colleagues in Congress just before passage of the Kansas-Nebraska Act, "and God give victory to the side which is stronger in numbers as in right." Wealthy New England abolitionists established the Emigrant Aid Company and financed the migration of more than two thousand antislavery settlers to Kansas. Thousands more went on their own.

Proslavery interests, however, proved equal to the task. To offset the soaring numbers of Northern settlers in Kansas, they organized bands of proslavery "border ruffians" to cross into Kansas from Missouri. While some came as settlers, most came as illegal voters determined to see Kansas enter the Union as a slave state. In the spring of 1855, proslavery men from Missouri cast nearly five thousand illegal votes that elected a proslavery territorial government,

What anti-immigrant laws did the American Party propose?

Images as History

THE "FOREIGN MENACE"

From the colonial period up to the present, Americans have held conflicted visions about immigration. On the one hand Americans proudly view their country as a "nation of immigrants" that has incorporated millions of newcomers while fashioning an ethos of tolerance. On the other, periods of virulent anti-immigrant sentiment have punctuated American history. In the 1840s and 1850s, groups of nativists—native-born Americans who believed themselves superior to the foreign born—mobilized to oppose immigration. While they failed to stop the mass influx of foreigners, their movement revealed a vision of immigration as a serious threat to the well-being of the republic.

The cartoon below reflects the belief that immigrants represented a threat to American democracy. The drawing beneath it expresses the fear that Catholic immigrants were part of a conspiracy to claim America for the Pope. What attitudes and actions might these kinds of images have inspired among native-born Americans?

By clothing the Irishman and German in whiskey and beer barrels, the artist reflects the widely held view that immigrants drank too much alcohol.

The brawl at the polling site suggests that immigrants threaten democracy because they use violence rather than persuasion to win elections.

The theft of the ballot box reveals the nativist fear of the rising political power of immigrants in the 1850s.

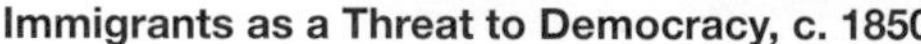

Immigrants as a Threat to Democracy, c. 1850

Borrowed from the Great Seal of the United States this eagle emphasizes the importance of public schools to American democracy.

Placing the Bible under the Pope's foot played upon the belief that Catholic priests and bishops prohibited people from reading the Bible on their own, something Protestants believed essential to Salvation.

Declaring Catholicism un-American, the artist presents the pope as the antithesis of republican authority, a royal figure seated upon a throne.

Alleging a papal plot to overthrow America, the pope points to the public school while a priest in the schoolyard organizes an attack.

***Popery Undermining Free Schools, and Other American Institutions*, 1855**

What caused the sharp rise in anti-immigrant sentiment in the 1850s?

which then gathered in the town of Lecompton, where they voted to legalize slavery.

Antislavery settlers rejected the legitimacy of this "bogus legislature." In the fall of 1855, they drew up a free-state constitution, held elections that resulted in an antislavery legislature and governor located in the town of Lawrence, and asked Congress to admit the territory as a free state. Kansas now had two governments, each bitterly opposed to the other.

Kansas quickly became a divisive issue in Congress. While the Senate (controlled by Democrats) voted to recognize the proslavery government of Lecompton, the House (controlled by Republicans) recognized the free-state government in Lawrence. On May 20, 1856, Senator Charles Sumner of Massachusetts, a rising figure in the abolitionist movement, delivered a speech titled the "Crime Against Kansas," a harsh denunciation of Southern efforts to force slavery into the territory. Days later, South Carolina Congressman Preston Brooks attacked Sumner with a cane in the Senate chamber for his affront to Southern honor. Sumner nearly died from his injuries and never fully recovered his health.

As the image suggests (**12.11**), the antislavery cause in the North hailed Sumner as a near martyr. The artist's emphasis on Brooks's brutality and Sumner's vulnerability (he is armed with only a pen) popularized the abolitionist vision of slavery as an inherently barbarous institution and its supporters, both in Congress and on the plains of Kansas, as violent criminals who did not respect democracy or free speech. In contrast Brooks became a hero in the South for defending Southern rights and dignity. Hundreds mailed him notes of congratulations, while a few even sent canes as a symbol of their support, inscribed with phrases like "Hit Him Again."

Only days after Sumner's speech, a heavily armed band of proslavery vigilantes attacked Lawrence, Kansas, home to the antislavery territorial government. The posse sacked the town, setting fire to the main hotel and destroying its two newspaper presses. An opposing force of antislavery settlers arrived too late to prevent the devastation. Among them was John Brown, a zealous abolitionist who believed himself God's chosen instrument for eradicating slavery, which he ardently believed was a sin. Three days later he led a group of abolitionist avengers in a counterassault at Pottawatomie Creek, Kansas. Falling upon a settlement of proslavery families, the abolitionists pulled five men from their beds and hacked them to pieces with swords.

The violence touched off a wave of vigilante reprisals and counterreprisals by proslavery and antislavery forces. Newspapers began referring to **"Bleeding Kansas"** to describe the quasi-civil war taking place there. The antislavery press in the North, as exemplified by this drawing of the attack on

12.11 The Slavery Controversy Sparks Violence in Congress This lithograph depicting Representative Preston Brooks about to beat Senator Charles Sumner with a cane was circulated throughout the North, where it stoked hostility toward the South and defenders of slavery.

How did events in Kansas expose the flaw in the policy of popular sovereignty?

Lawrence (**12.12**), inflamed abolitionist passions. Note how the artist depicts the "border ruffians," as they were called by opponents of slavery, as the clear aggressors in the clash. These images, along with editorials, sermons, and speeches, inspired some Northerners to send money and guns to aid the Free-Soil cause, or to join groups of Free-Soil settlers heading for Kansas to thwart proslavery efforts. By the time President Pierce sent a new governor and thirteen hundred troops to Kansas in the fall of 1856, two hundred people lay dead, including one of John Brown's sons. The decades-long bitter debate over the status of slavery had disintegrated into armed conflict.

The highly charged events of 1854–1856 proved beneficial to the young Republican Party. Thousands of Free-Soil, Whig, and Democratic voters joined its ranks, making it the largest party in the North. Yet it was also a purely sectional party with no support in the South. Democrats had the advantage of being the only true national party, with strength in both sections.

For the presidential election of 1856, Republicans nominated the famed Western explorer John C. Frémont and waged a campaign likened to an evangelical crusade. Groups calling themselves "Wide Awakes" staged torchlight processions in towns and cities across the North, touting "Free Soil, Free Speech, Free Men, Frémont!" Democrats chose James Buchanan of Pennsylvania, who, like Winfield Scott and Lewis Cass, presidential candidates in elections before him, was a Northerner with pro-South credentials. The centerpiece of Buchanan's campaign was to play on the racism of many Northern voters by branding his opponents "**Black Republicans**," a racist pejorative that Democrats used to suggest that Republicans who opposed the extension of slavery into the Western territories were dangerous radicals who favored abolition and racial equality. The fast-fading American Party nominated ex-Whig and former president Millard Fillmore.

12.12 Bleeding Kansas Determined to make Kansas a slave state, proslavery vigilantes attacked the antislavery stronghold of Lawrence, Kansas.

How did events in Kansas benefit the Republican Party?

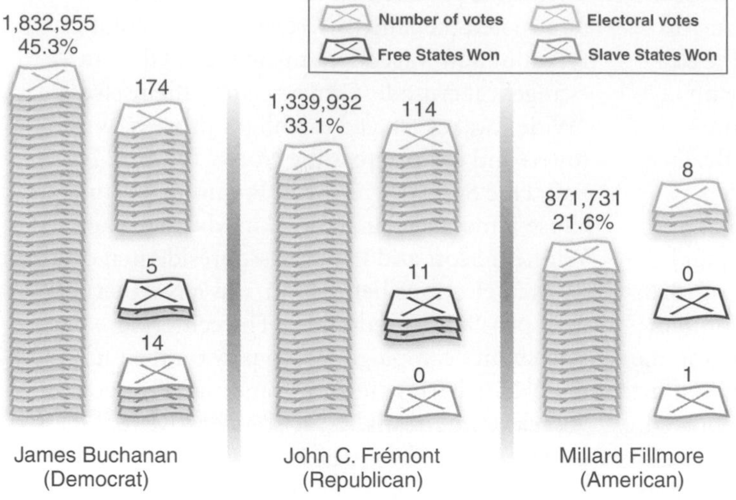

12.13 The Election of 1856 The Republican Party, founded only two years earlier, earned the second-highest vote tally, but its support came almost exclusively from the North.

The three-way contest played out as two distinct sectional elections. As shown in the chart (**12.13**), Buchanan won easily in the South, though Fillmore polled an impressive 44 percent of the vote in the region. In the North the Republican Frémont outpolled Buchanan, but the latter's combined national total won him the overall election.

Deepening Controversy

Buchanan barely had time to settle into the White House in March 1857 when the slavery issue once again seized center stage with a controversial Supreme Court decision. Dred Scott had spent years living in different parts of the country as the slave of army surgeon John Emerson. When he returned to the slave state of Missouri, Scott sued for his freedom, arguing that his years in the free state of Illinois and the Wisconsin Territory (where the Missouri Compromise barred slavery) had made him a free man. The courts in Missouri rejected his suit, but Scott enlisted the help of abolitionist lawyers and appealed to the Supreme Court.

Dominated by proslavery Southerners, including Chief Justice Roger B. Taney, the court ruled in ***Dred Scott v. Sandford*** that slaves were property not people, and as such had no right to sue. Recognizing an opportunity to defend Southern rights and undermine the efforts of abolitionists, the justices also declared that Congress lacked the right to regulate slavery in the territories. In other words, the Court established as the law of the land the extreme Southern position that the right to property in slaves was inviolable and untouchable by any level of American government.

Opponents of slavery denounced the Court's decision as "a wicked and false judgment" and a "willful perversion" of the law. They seized on the decision as an example of the corruption of government by a Slave Power intent not merely on protecting slavery but on spreading it into every corner of the nation, including free states. Already in control of the White House and disproportionately influential in Congress, they argued, slaveholders now controlled the judiciary. Heightening their sympathy for Scott were antislavery publications, such as the widely-read *Frank Leslie's Weekly,* which showed him as a dignified man with a loving family (**12.14**). Some abolitionists declared the ruling "not binding in law and conscience," but most seemed to recognize that the only way to reverse the decision was with new justices named to the Court. That would happen only if the Republicans could win the White House in 1860.

As both North and South considered the meaning of the *Dred Scott* decision, Kansas again became the focus of growing sectional animosity. The introduction of federal troops in 1856 had temporarily ended the spiral of vigilante violence. Tensions reached the breaking point in June 1857

"They [African Americans] had no rights which the white man was bound to respect."

Chief Justice of the U.S. Supreme Court, ROGER B. TANEY, majority of the opinion in the *Dred Scott* case

How did the Supreme Court use the Dred Scott case to expand and protect the rights of slaveholders?

when proslavery Kansans (who controlled the territorial legislature) held a convention in Lecompton and drafted a proslavery state constitution as a preliminary step to applying to Congress for statehood. When these proslavery men put the Lecompton Constitution before the people of Kansas in a referendum, antislavery residents, deeming both the legislature and the convention illegitimate, boycotted it. Because the antislavery residents had excluded themselves from thc approval process, the constitution won approval easily and was forwarded to Congress. To complicate matters, however, in the fall the antislavery party won control of the territorial legislature and immediately authorized a second referendum on the proslavery constitution. This time proslavery residents boycotted, and the antislavery party rejected the constitution by more than two-thirds ofthe voters.

The scene shifted to Washington. President Buchanan gave in under intense pressure from Southerners in his cabinet and in Congress, who threatened secession if the proslavery Lecompton Constitution was not accepted and Kansas admitted as a slave state. Douglas came out against Lecompton because it was unpopular in his home state of Illinois, and it mocked his vaunted principle of popular sovereignty (even as it exposed its weakness). Months of rancorous debate ensued. A brawl broke out in the House, and some members of Congress began to come to the chamber armed. The Senate approved the Lecompton Constitution, but the House narrowly rejected it. Kansas would remain a territory indefinitely.

FRANK LESLIE'S ILLUSTRATED NEWSPAPER

82.—VOL. IV.] NEW YORK, SATURDAY, JUNE 27, 1857. [PRICE 6 CENTS.

OURISTS AND TRAVELLERS.

...e happy to receive personal narratives, ...sea, including adventures and incidents, ...y person who pleases to correspond with ...

...this opportunity of returning our thanks ...merous artistic correspondents through... country, for the many sketches we are ...receiving from them of the news of the ...trust they will spare no pains to furnish ...drawings of events as they may occur. ...also remind them that it is necessary to ...sketches, if possible, by the earliest convey-

...TO DRED SCOTT—HIS FA...Y—INCIDENTS OF HIS LIFE ...ECISION OF THE SUPREME ...RT.

...standing in the Fair grounds at ...uis, and engaged in conversation ...prominent citizen of that enter... city, he suddenly asked us if we ...not like to be introduced to Dred ...Upon expressing a desire to be thus ..., the gentleman called to an old ...who was standing near by, and our ...was gratified. Dred made a rude ...ce to our recognition, and seemed ...y the notice we expended upon ...We found him on examination to ...pure-blooded African, perhaps fifty ...of age, with a shrewd, intelligent, ...atured face, of rather light frame, ...not more than five feet six inches high. After some general ...s we expressed a wish to get his portrait (we had ma le efforts before, through correspondents, and failed), and asked him if he would not go to Fitzgibbon's gallery and have it taken. The gentleman present explained to Dred that it was proper he should have his likeness in the "great illustrated paper of the country," over-ruled his many objections, which seemed to grow out of a superstitious feeling, and he promised to be at the gallery the next day. This appointment Dred did not keep. Determined not to be foiled, we sought an interview with Mr. Crane, Dred's lawyer, who promptly gave us a letter of introduction, explaining to Dred that it was to his advantage to have his picture taken to be engraved for our paper, and also directions where we could find his domicile. We found the place with difficulty, the streets in Dred's neighborhood being more clearly defined in the plan of the city than on the mother earth; we finally reached a wooden house, however, protected by a balcony that answered the description. Approaching the door, we saw a smart, tidy-looking negress, perhaps thirty years of age, who, with two female assistants, was busy ironing. To our question, "Is this where Dred Scott lives?" we received, rather hesitatingly, the answer, "Yes." Upon our asking if he was home, she said,

"What white man arter dad nigger for?—why don't white man 'tend to his own business, and let dat nigger 'lone? Some of dese days dey'll steal dat nigger—dat are a fact."

ELIZA AND LIZZIE, CHILDREN OF DRED SCOTT.

12.14 A Sympathetic Portrayal of Dred Scott and His Family
Frank Leslie's Illustrated, a widely read weekly sympathetic to abolitionism, presented Dred Scott and his family on its cover to emphasize his humanity after a Supreme Court decision that declared him nothing more than property.

Why did Congress reject the Lecompton Constitution?

Two Societies

From an economic standpoint the decade of the 1850s brought stronger bonds of interdependence between North and South. Northern textile manufacturers depended on a steady supply of Southern cotton, while Southerners relied on Northern manufactured goods, credit, and shipping. Yet overshadowing the increased economic integration of North and South was their splitting into two distinct societies. Northeastern and Old Northwest states industrialized at a stunning pace, symbolized by the spread in these regions of the railroad and factory. In much of the South, by contrast, economic growth arose from an ever-expanding system of staple crop production, notably cotton, that depended on the labor of four million slaves. Along with these divergent economies, North and South developed distinct philosophies that defined their vision of the proper social order.

The Industrial North

The North's industrial economy boomed in the 1840s and 1850s, driven by a growing pool of cheap labor swelled by mass immigration and innovations in technology (notably steam power). Manufacturing output soared, and by 1860 the total value of all goods produced in the North reached $1.5 billion (compared to $483 million for the entire nation in 1840). The dynamic and innovative character of the Northern industrial economy was displayed for all the world to see in 1853 at the Crystal Palace Exhibition in New York City (**12.15**). Modeled on a similar exhibition in London in 1851, the "Exhibition of the Industry of the World," as it was officially known, featured more than four thousand exhibits, a majority of them American. Even the building itself, a monumental cast-iron and glass building, reflected the latest trends in architecture, design, and construction materials. Inside, the more than one million visitors saw the latest in modern technology, including Cyrus McCormick's mechanical reaper, Richard M. Hoe's rotary printing press, and Elisha Otis's elevator. Significantly, the only Southern exhibitions of new technology were improved versions of the cotton gin.

Equally important to the emerging industrial economy was the building of a massive railroad network. Total trackage soared from more than 9,000 miles in 1850 to over 30,000 in 1860. Because most of this track lay west of Pennsylvania, it served to bind more closely the states of the Northeast with those in the Midwest, such as Illinois. Trade increasingly moved east to west along railroads and canals rather than north to south along rivers as in earlier decades, accentuating the growing sectional divide.

The growth of the railroads, along with the invention of the mechanical reaper by Cyrus McCormick and the steel plow by John Deere, revolutionized Northern and Western agriculture—still the foundation of the national economy. These new technologies allowed farmers to plow and harvest great expanses of land. The technology also allowed farmers to sell their produce in markets hundreds of miles away and to turn from raising a mixture of animal, fruit, vegetable, and grain products to specializing in single crops such as wheat, corn, or oats. Rising prices and growing demand from abroad for American grain added to this trend.

Industrialization brought rising wages and opportunity to most Northerners, but also new levels of poverty—especially among unskilled and immigrant workers who formed a growing class of urban poor. Wages in many industrializing sectors, such as shoe making and textiles, were too low for one earner to support a family. To increase their family's income, growing numbers of women and children entered factories or performed "outwork" in their homes, often for sixty or seventy hours per week. Many workers became unemployed for long stretches of time, especially in winter, and the number of poor families living in the squalid tenement districts of cities like New York and Boston began to rise.

Cotton Is Supreme

Industry also flourished in the upper South, especially in Maryland, Delaware, Kentucky, Tennessee, and Missouri. But it paled in comparison to industrialization in the North and constituted only a fraction of the overall Southern

How did new technology transform American agriculture?

12.15 The Crystal Palace Celebrates Northern Industry
Hundreds of thousands of visitors flocked to New York City in 1853 to view the "Exhibition of the Industry of the World." The main building itself, made of cast-iron and glass, was an expression of the latest industrial materials and design.

economy. Production of cash crops such as tobacco, sugar, and rice soared, as did prices. Nothing, however, outperformed the South's main staple crop, cotton. Production jumped from 1.35 million bales in 1840 to 4.8 million bales by 1860. Southern cotton by this time accounted for three-fifths of American exports and three-quarters of the world supply of cotton. As one Southern nationalist put it, "Cotton is King."

Most Southern cotton was shipped to Northern factories, indicating a growing economic integration between the two regional economies. But the relationship was by no means equal and Southerners increasingly resented their economic dependence on the North. "We purchase all our luxuries and necessities from the North," lamented a Southern newspaper editor in 1851. "Our slaves are clothed with Northern manufactured goods and work with Northern hoes, ploughs, and other implements. ... The slaveholder dresses in Northern goods. ... In Northern vessels his products are carried to market ... and on Northern-made paper, with a Northern pen, with Northern ink, he resolves and re-resolves in regard to his rights." A vociferous advocate of Southern economic diversification, James D. B. DeBow started a magazine with the motto "Commerce is King" and held commercial conventions throughout the South.

What did Southerners mean by the phrase "Cotton is King"?

By 1860 DeBow and other proponents of greater Southern economic independence could point to substantial progress. Southern railroad mileage had increased fourfold to 9,000 miles, and the number of factories reached eighteen thousand, most in the upper South The only problem for the South was that the economy of the North grew even faster. Even as the South increased its textile manufacture by 44 percent in the 1850s, its share of manufacturing nationwide declined by 2 percent. Indeed, in 1860 the city of Lowell, Massachusetts, operated more textile spindles than all the Southern states combined. The South remained an agricultural society. So long as staple crops brought high prices, no more than a handful of Southerners seemed willing to pursue industrialization.

The Other South

As important as slavery was to the Southern economy and culture, fewer than one-third of Southerners owned slaves. Even fewer owned more than twenty, and as the price of slaves rose in the 1850s the number of slaveholding families decreased. Most white Southerners were modest yeomen farmers who worked small patches of rough backcountry land, often barely at subsistence levels. With no access to capital and few educational opportunities (20 percent of Southern whites were illiterate), few small farmers expected to enter the planter class. In most areas they exerted only limited political power.

Why then did poor Southern whites support a slave society in which they had so little influence and apparently so little stake? Some did so because members of their extended family owned slaves or because they themselves aspired to own slaves, a sign of wealth and status. Others embraced a long-standing Southern doctrine that white freedom depended on slavery. Because slaves performed hard, menial labor, slavery established a floor in the Southern economy below which even the poorest whites could not descend. Above all, poor Southerners supported slavery because they accepted the essential tenets of white supremacy, in particular the notion that blacks were inferior to whites and destined to live under their dominance.

> "There is no such thing as a freeman being fixed for life in the condition of a hired laborer. The *free* labor system opens the way for all."
>
> ABRAHAM LINCOLN, 1860

Divergent Visions

Southern society not only preached the superiority of whites over blacks, but also the superiority of slave labor over wage labor in the North. The most prominent defender of slavery was George Fitzhugh. In several books and pamphlets published in the 1850s, he argued that all great societies in history practiced slavery and that the Southern version was remarkably humane because masters felt obliged to feed, clothe, and shelter their slaves. "The negro slaves of the South," he wrote, "are the happiest, and, in some sense, the freest people in the world." Moreover, argued Fitzhugh and others, such as the artist who drew this image that idealized slavery (**12.16**), slavery rescued Africans from the so-called barbarism of Africa and exposed them to "civilization" and Christianity. Pointing to the North's urban slums swelled with poor industrial workers, Fitzhugh ridiculed the Northern contention that wage labor was morally superior to slavery. Northern factory workers, he asserted, were little more than "wage slaves." Their condition was worse than that of the black slave because factory owners owed them nothing but the lowest possible wage. "Capital exercises a more perfect compulsion over free laborers than human masters over slaves," wrote Fitzhugh, "for free laborers must at all times work or starve, and slaves are supported whether they work or not."

Republicans had an answer for the likes of Fitzhugh: a **free labor** philosophy that celebrated the virtues of individualism, independence, entrepreneurship, and upward mobility. As Fitzhugh did for the slave South, they offered an idealized vision of the industrial North that conveniently ignored the hopeless plight of many poverty-stricken city dwellers. "In the constitution of human nature," wrote New York *Tribune* editor Horace Greeley, "the desire of bettering one's condition is the mainspring of effort." In contrast to the South, which reserved hard labor for slaves, argued Greeley, in the North all

Why did Southern whites who owned no slaves support slavery?

work was noble and moral, no matter how menial. Better still, for the ambitious, wage labor need only be temporary. If a man labored hard, saved his money, avoided drink, and sought opportunity, went the free labor philosophy, he would soon possess his own farm or small business.

A slave-based society, then, for these Republicans, was the antithesis of this dynamic society of democratic opportunity. "Enslave a man," wrote Greeley, "and you destroy his ambition, his enterprise, his capacity." In the view of Northern abolitionists, slavery also stifled the capacity of the majority of poor and middling whites, protecting the privileges of the aristocratic few and leaving the rest with little opportunity for success. Northern writers like Frederick Law Olmsted argued that slavery led to a culture of laziness, luxury, and ignorance as opposed to the capitalist virtues of hard work, thrift, and restraint.

This ideological war of words grew more intense when a financial panic on Wall Street sent the economy plunging into a deep recession in late 1857, bringing unemployment and hard times to the industrial Northeast and agrarian West. But because the Southern economy was so geared toward the export of cotton, it experienced little of the Panic of 1857. Southern nationalists pointed to this as evidence that "cotton is supreme" in comparison to Northern industry. Some Southerners also argued that it proved the South could prosper on its own should the Union ever dissolve.

ATTENTION PAID A POOR SICK WHITE MAN.

ATTENTION PAID A POOR SICK NEGRO.

12.16 Proslavery Propaganda: Slavery and Free Labor Contrasted
This 1852 woodcut captures the argument of George Fitzhugh and other proslavery propagandists, claiming that masters care for their slaves even when sick and unable to work, while cold-hearted Northern factory owners simply dump their sick or injured workers at the poor house.

The development of these divergent philosophies in the 1850s played a major role in creating a climate of extreme mistrust between North and South. Given the moral and social dimension of the proslavery argument, Southerners perceived Northern criticism of slavery and attempts to prevent its spread as attacks on their "way of life." Likewise, Southern celebration of slavery and criticism of capitalist free labor convinced many Northerners that the Slave Power intended to spread slavery everywhere, including into the industrial North. The successful efforts by Southerners in Congress to defeat proposals for higher tariffs to protect Northern industry, land grants to promote a transcontinental railroad, and a homestead act to give 160 acres of public land to Western settlers accentuated hard feelings in the North. A leading ideologue of the Republican Party, William Seward, delivered a speech in 1858 predicting "an irrepressible conflict" between the two societies.

How did the Panic of 1857 strengthen the Southern argument for secession?

A House Divided

By the late 1850s slavery dominated national politics. Nowhere was this more apparent than in the congressional elections of 1858, especially in the state of Illinois where Senator Stephen A. Douglas engaged in a series of famous debates, mostly on the slavery issue, with a little known Republican challenger named Abraham Lincoln. Increasingly, Southerners became convinced that Northerners wanted not simply to exclude slavery from the Western territories but to destroy it completely. John Brown's abolitionist raid on Harpers Ferry in late 1859 only added to this perception. The subsequent election the following year of Abraham Lincoln, whose Republican Party Southern hard-liners believed was committed to abolition, sparked a secession movement that soon brought the nation to the brink of Civil War.

The Lincoln-Douglas Debates

In 1858 national attention turned to Illinois, where Stephen A. Douglas, a leading figure in the Democratic Party and certain 1860 presidential candidate, was running for reelection to the Senate. Many Americans were eager to see which direction he would take on the slavery issue. Opposing him was Abraham Lincoln, a former Illinois state representative and congressman. No abolitionist, Lincoln nevertheless believed slavery was immoral and hoped to prevent its spread to the Western territories. "A house divided cannot stand," warned Lincoln in his speech accepting the Republican nomination to run for senator. "I believe this Government cannot endure permanently half-slave and half-free."

The overwhelming underdog in the contest, Lincoln boldly challenged Douglas to a series of seven debates across the state of Illinois. The ensuing **Lincoln-Douglas debates** focused the fate of slavery, the legal and social status of African Americans, and the viability of popular sovereignty in the wake of the *Dred Scott* decision. Douglas portrayed Lincoln as a radical abolitionist and "Black Republican" whose policies would destroy the Union, elevate blacks to social and legal equality with whites, and promote interracial marriage. Lincoln denied these charges but made clear that a black man was "entitled to all the natural rights enumerated in the Declaration of Independence, the right to life, liberty, and the pursuit of happiness." Lincoln also castigated Douglas for his professed moral indifference toward slavery. "If slavery is not wrong," Lincoln asserted, "nothing is wrong."

Douglas won reelection to the Senate, but Lincoln had forced him to make statements that appeared both indifferent to slavery and willing to let residents in the Western territories ban it, thereby antagonizing both Southern fire-eaters and Northern free soilers. His opponents would use these words against him in the coming presidential campaign in 1860. More important, the debates made Lincoln a national figure and a rising star within the Republican Party.

John Brown's Raid

In 1857, just months after staging the Pottawatomie Creek massacre in Kansas, abolitionist John Brown began plotting an invasion of the South that he hoped would lead to a widespread slave revolt and the end of slavery. A deeply religious man raised from an early age to hate slavery, Brown believed God had called upon him to destroy slavery.

His sense of mission is revealed in this daguerreotype (**12.17**) taken in 1847. In it Brown reenacts a scene from a decade earlier when he stood up in a crowded church, raised his right hand, and pledged to commit his life to abolition. Brown's passion for the cause inspired many supporters and by the summer of 1859, with secret assistance from a number of prominent abolitionists, he had gathered a force of seventeen whites (including three of his sons) and five blacks and moved to a farm in Maryland.

John Brown's raid began at eight o'clock on the evening of October 16. Leading his raiders across the Potomac River to Harpers Ferry, Virginia, Brown quickly took control of the town and seized its federal arsenal full of guns and ammunition. They planned to fan out across the South, arming slaves as they went and touching off a wave of rebellion. But they were quickly cornered, and on October 18 U.S. Marines

How did the Lincoln-Douglas debates harm Douglas's presidential ambitions?

under the command of Colonel Robert E. Lee stormed their stronghold. The soldiers killed ten of Brown's men, including two of his sons, and took Brown and six others prisoner.

Six weeks later a Virginia jury found Brown and his men guilty of treason and sentenced them to hang. When given the opportunity to speak, Brown declared that he had acted in accordance with the Bible's call to fight for justice, a just cause for which he was prepared to die. On the day of his execution, Brown wrote one last note that proved eerily prophetic of the coming Civil War. "I, John Brown, am now quite certain that the crimes of this guilty land will never be purged away but with blood."

If in life Brown had failed to overthrow slavery, in death he furthered the abolitionist cause by becoming an instant martyr to many in the North. On the day of his execution, bells tolled in hundreds of towns from Boston to Chicago. At rallies and church services, Brown was lionized as a righteous instrument of God. Abolitionist William Lloyd Garrison, a life-long pacifist, told an audience in Boston, "I am prepared to say 'success to every slave insurrection at the South and in every slave county.'"

Not all Northerners were so enthusiastic, however; opponents of slavery like Lincoln and Greeley criticized Brown's use of violence to achieve his ends. Still there was no denying, observed one Northerner, that the "death of no man in America has ever produced so profound a sensation."

Sensation struck in the South as well, but it was one of fear and outrage. Brown's audacious act convinced many Southerners that Northern abolitionists would continue to conspire to instigate future slave uprisings in order to destroy Southern society. Increasingly they talked of dissolving their union with the North to protect their property and way of life. Robert Toombs of Georgia voiced the most pressing concern of Southerners: "Never permit this Federal government to pass into the traitorous hands of the black Republican party."

12.17 **John Brown Vows to Destroy Slavery**
In 1847 John Brown stood for this daguerreotype taken by African American photographer Augustus Washington, posing in a reenactment of a pledge he made to destroy slavery ten years earlier at an abolitionist meeting.

The Election of 1860

Throughout the course of the 1850s, the Democratic Party had managed to withstand the strains of sectional discord that demolished the Whigs and created a Republican Party with virtually no support in the South. But when the Democrats met in April 1860 in Charleston, South Carolina, to nominate a presidential candidate, disagreements between Northern and Southern delegates caused the convention to disband, unable to agree upon a nominee. The sectional split became official when a Baltimore convention of mostly Northern Democrats nominated Illinois senator Stephen A. Douglas, a man Southerners had become convinced would not protect slavery. A week later a convention of Southern Democrats also met in Baltimore and nominated John C. Breckinridge, Buchanan's vice president and a staunch proslavery man from Kentucky. To complicate matters further, former Southern Whigs and Know-Nothings formed the Constitutional Union Party and nominated John Bell, a pro-Union slaveholder of moderate views.

The Republicans hoped the split among the Democrats and the emergence of the Constitutional Union Party enhanced their chances for victory. Deeming Seward too controversial on the slavery

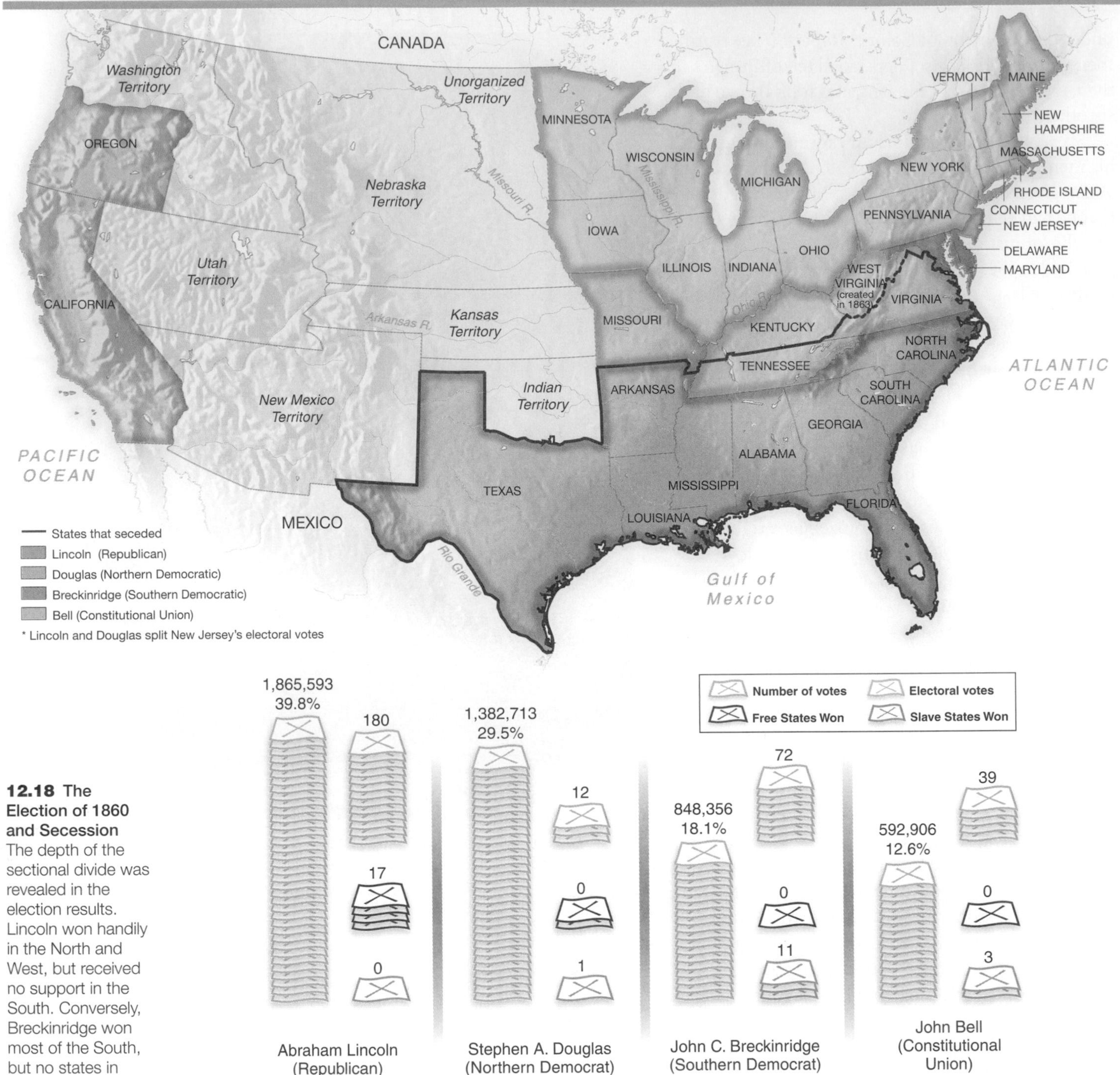

12.18 The Election of 1860 and Secession The depth of the sectional divide was revealed in the election results. Lincoln won handily in the North and West, but received no support in the South. Conversely, Breckinridge won most of the South, but no states in the North.

issue, Republicans selected Abraham Lincoln, a man with few political enemies and an established reputation as a moderate. He won the nomination on the third ballot. The party then adopted a platform touting Republican ideals of free labor, support for a homestead act, and a moderate approach to the slavery question that merely opposed its extension westward.

The national mood grew apprehensive as election day approached. The contest featured candidates who appealed to specific sections rather than to the national electorate. The result of the sectionalism, many observers feared, would be the very thing political leaders had struggled to prevent during the 1850s: disunion.

Lincoln won the four-way election with just under 40 percent of the popular vote. He swept all the states in the North, plus California and Oregon, while Douglas, who won only Missouri, finished second with 29 percent of the popular vote (**12.18**).

What was unique about Lincoln's victory in the election of 1860?

Breckinridge won all the Deep South states but polled just 18 percent of the popular vote. Bell of the Constitutional Union Party finished fourth with 13 percent. For the first time in the nation's history, a purely regional party, the Republicans, had won the White House. It was precisely the scenario Southern extremists had threatened would lead to dissolution of the Union.

> "That the South can afford to live under a Government, the majority of whose citizens ... regard John Brown as a martyr and a Christian hero, rather than a murderer ... is a preposterous idea."
>
> *Baltimore Sun*, November 28, 1859

Secession

Southern fire-eaters, having warned Southerners that the election of a "Black Republican" would lead to the end of slavery and the destruction of their society, wasted no time in calling for secession. Secessionist rallies broke out across the South. On December 20, 1860, a South Carolina convention unanimously passed a resolution declaring that the "union now subsisting between South Carolina and the other States ... is hereby dissolved." In less than two months, six more states—Mississippi, Florida, Alabama, Georgia, Louisiana, and Texas—also seceded (12.18). One by one their representatives in Washington delivered speeches, resigned, and headed home.

Six of the seceded states sent delegates to Montgomery, Alabama, in early February where they organized a government similar to the one they had just left. The major exception, of course, was that its constitution declared slavery legal and protected everywhere in the new nation. They called their new nation the Confederate States of America and elected Jefferson Davis of Mississippi as its first president and Alexander Stephens of Georgia as vice president. They also created a Confederate Seal (**12.19**) that featured George Washington—not only the foremost Founding Father, but also a Virginian and a slave owner—at the center and established his birthday, February 22, as the official birth of the Confederacy. These choices reflected the Confederates' goal to legitimize secession by comparing it to the thirteen colonies breaking away from England during the American Revolution.

Even as the new Confederate government took shape, President James Buchanan, a weak and timid leader with Southern sympathies, did little to avert the crisis, claiming that he lacked constitutional authority to do anything. Moderates mobilized to see if they could, as in previous sectional crises in 1820, 1833, 1850, and 1854, devise a compromise acceptable to both sections. Senator John J. Crittenden of Kentucky put forth the leading proposal. The **Crittenden Compromise**, proposed several constitutional amendments to protect slavery, including one extending the old Missouri Compromise line of 36° 30′ to the Pacific, permitting slavery south of it, prohibiting it to the north. But while president-elect Lincoln expressed a willingness to compromise—including supporting a constitutional amendment protecting slavery where it existed in the South—he made it clear that he could not support the Crittenden Compromise. "On the territorial question," he said in reference to the Republican opposition to extending slavery into the West, "I am inflexible." With that the proposal died.

Newly elected Confederate president Jefferson Davis likewise professed an aversion to conflict, but rejected any prospect of compromise. For the Confederate States of America, the decision to secede was permanent. The citizens of the Confederacy, he argued, asked simply to be left alone.

The impasse left moderates in despair, but Lincoln placed his faith in pro-Union sentiment in the South. He believed that for all their bluster, Southern fire-eaters would eventually pull back from the brink of disunion and civil war as they had so many times before. After all, eight slave states in the upper South still remained within the Union. His inaugural address (see *Competing Visions: Secession or Union?*) emphasized the theme of reconciliation while also declaring the Union indivisible and secession illegal.

Lincoln also asserted his intent to "hold, occupy, and possess" all federal property in the seceded states. Although

12.19 The Confederate Seal: Linking Secession with the Spirit of 1776
By placing George Washington at the center of the Confederate Seal, Southerners sought to legitimize secession by comparing it to the decision of the thirteen colonies to break away from England in 1776.

the seceding states had seized nearly all federal property within their borders, two harbor forts remained in federal control, Fort Pickens in Pensacola, Florida, and Fort Sumter in Charleston, South Carolina.

> "The tea has been thrown overboard; the revolution of 1860 has been initiated."
>
> Charleston (S.C.) *Mercury*, reacting to Lincoln's election

With food and other necessities running low at Fort Sumter, Lincoln informed the South Carolina government of his intention to send a ship with non-military supplies. Confederate General P. G. T. Beauregard decided to force the issue before the ship arrived and ordered Major Robert Anderson, in command of the fort, to surrender. When Anderson refused, Confederate leaders began an artillery assault in the early morning hours of April 12, and by afternoon the next day the Union garrison surrendered. Southerners exulted in their quick victory, and immediately raised the Confederate flag over the ruins as a symbol of their triumph and sovereignty as an independent nation (**12.20**). On April 15 Lincoln declared the lower South to be in a state of "insurrection" and called for seventy-five thousand men to enlist for the purposed of putting down the rebellion. The Civil War had begun.

12.20 The Confederate Flag Flying in Triumph over Fort Sumter Taken the morning following the Fort's surrender, this photograph of Fort Sumter with a Confederate flag snapping defiantly in the breeze neatly captured the exuberance of the Southern victory and grim reality of the Union defeat.

Why did Lincoln attempt to resupply Fort Sumter?

Conclusion

Despite sharing certain aspects of a common heritage, language, and political tradition, as well as increasingly integrated economies, contentious issues in the 1850s, especially slavery, drove North and South apart. Cultural, social, political, economic, and psychological factors contributed to the growing rift, yet all of them, in one way or another, related to the institution of slavery. So too did the controversial events of the decade, from fugitive slave captures to Supreme Court decisions to presidential elections. Half the nation defined itself in terms of slavery, the other half in terms of its absence.

By 1860, the rhetorical references to nation, the Constitution, and Manifest Destiny that once unified the sections carried little weight. Indeed, North and South embraced separate and distinct visions of their destinies. "We are not one people. We are two peoples," argued Horace Greeley. "We are a people for Freedom and a people for Slavery. Between the two, conflict is inevitable." In 1861 these two peoples plunged into war, one in order to gain its independence, the other to deny it and preserve the Union. Neither was prepared for the consequences that war would bring.

Competing Visions

SECESSION OR UNION?

Mississippi's declaration of secession and Abraham Lincoln's inaugural address from March 1861, present opposing views on secession. Observe how both parties invoke the Constitution and other American traditions to justify their positions. What evidence do the secessionists cite to support their claim that the mere election of Lincoln justified secession? How does Lincoln reject the idea of secession and seek to place the burden of responsibility for any hostilities on the seceded states?

Patterned on the Declaration of Independence, Mississippi's declaration of secession sets forth a list of alleged attacks on slavery and states rights by the North.

Our position is thoroughly identified with… slavery—the greatest material interest of the world. Its labor supplies the product which constitutes… the largest and most important portions of commerce of the earth. … These products have become necessities of the world, and a blow at slavery is a blow at commerce and civilization. …

The hostility to this institution commenced before the adoption of the Constitution …

It has grown until it denies the right of property in slaves, and refuses protection to that right on the high seas, in the Territories, and wherever the government of the United States had jurisdiction.

It refuses the admission of new slave States into the Union, and seeks to extinguish it by confining it within its present limits, denying the power of expansion. …

It has nullified the Fugitive Slave Law in almost every free State in the Union …

It advocates negro equality, socially and politically, and promotes insurrection and incendiarism in our midst.

It has enlisted its press, its pulpit and its schools against us, until the whole popular mind of the North is excited and inflamed with prejudice. …

It has recently obtained control of the Government, by the prosecution of its… schemes, and destroyed the last expectation of living together in friendship. …

Utter subjugation awaits us in the Union, if we should consent longer to remain in it. It is not a matter of choice, but of necessity. We must either submit to degradation, and to the loss of property worth four billions of money, or we must secede from the Union framed by our fathers, to secure this as well as every other species of property. For far less cause than this, our fathers separated from the Crown of England.

Our decision is made. We follow their footsteps. We embrace the alternative of separation …

The flag of Mississippi, adopted after the state's secession in January 1861.

Lincoln used his inaugural address in March 1861 to respond directly to the assertions contained in the declarations of Mississippi and other seceded states. He attempted to reassure Southerners that his administration was not hostile to their interests, while rejecting their justification for secession.

Fellow citizens of the United States:

… I hold that, in contemplation of universal law and of the Constitution, the Union of these States is perpetual. Perpetuity is implied, if not expressed, in the fundamental law of all national governments. It is safe to assert that no government proper ever had a provision in its organic law for its own termination. …

It follows from these views that no State upon its own mere motion can lawfully get out of the Union; that Resolves and Ordinances to that effect are legally void; and that acts of violence, within any State or States, against the authority of the United States, are insurrectionary or revolutionary, according to circumstances.

I therefore consider that, in view of the Constitution and the laws, the Union is unbroken; and to the extent of my ability I shall take care, as the Constitution itself expressly enjoins upon me, that the laws of the Union be faithfully executed in all the States. …

In doing this there needs to be no bloodshed or violence; and there shall be none, unless it be forced upon the national authority.

In YOUR hands, my dissatisfied fellow-countrymen, and not in MINE, is the momentous issue of civil war. The government will not assail YOU. You can have no conflict without being yourselves the aggressors. YOU have no oath registered in heaven to destroy the government, while I shall have the most solemn one to "preserve, protect, and defend it."

I am loathe to close. We are not enemies, but friends. We must not be enemies. …

The flag of the United States, updated in January 1861 to include a thirty-fourth star for the new state of Kansas.

How did the slavery issue factor into Mississippi's decision to secede?

1848

Gold discovered in California.
Population boom leads California to apply for statehood, renewing debate over whether slavery would be permitted in the Western territories.

1850–1852

Congress passes the Compromise of 1850.
By offering concessions to both supporters and opponents of slavery, it temporarily calmed sectional tensions.

Fugitive slave Shadrach Minkins is freed by abolitionists.
Similar incidents stoke abolitionist sentiment in the North and anger among Southerners.

Harriet Beecher Stowe publishes *Uncle Tom's Cabin.*
Best-selling antislavery novel converts many Northerners to the abolitionist cause.

1854

Congress passes the Kansas-Nebraska Act.
Allows Kansas and Nebraska to decide the slavery question by popular sovereignty.

Whig Party collapses.
Replaced by the Republican Party.

Know-Nothing movement reaches high point.
Nativist candidates elected throughout Northeast and Midwest, but movement soon fades.

Review Questions

1. Why did slavery emerge as a national political issue in the late 1840s?
2. What led to the rise of the Republican Party? How did the party define its position on the slavery question?
3. What were the sources of nativism that prompted the rise of the Know-Nothings? Why did the American Party fade in significance in the late 1850s?
4. Why was popular sovereignty such an attractive policy for politicians eager to resolve the slavery question in the territories? Why did it fail to accomplish this goal?
5. What led increasing numbers of Northerners to become convinced that Southern slaveholding interests had gained control of the national government?
6. What role did economic development play in the rise of sectional tension?
7. Why did Southern fire-eaters interpret the election of Abraham Lincoln as cause for secession?

1855–1856

Armed conflict between proslavery and antislavery forces in the Kansas territory. The bloodshed lasts into 1857 and discredits the principle of popular sovereignty.

Senator Sumner assaulted for his "Crimes Against Kansas" speech. Increases sectional animosity as Southerners hail Brooks as a hero and Northerners denounce him as a violent villain.

1857–1859

The U.S. Supreme Court decides the *Dred Scott* case. Court rules that slaves are property, not people or citizens, and that the Missouri Compromise prohibition on slavery above 36° 30′ is unconstitutional.

John Brown's failed raid on Harper's Ferry, Virginia. The South vilifies Brown as an abolitionist fanatic; the North hails him as a martyr.

1860

Abraham Lincoln is elected president. Lincoln wins despite receiving no support in the South, revealing the deepening sectional rift over slavery.

South Carolina secedes from the Union. Six more slave states follow suit and unite as the Confederate States of America.

1861

South Carolinians fire upon the Union-held Fort Sumter. First shots of the Civil War prompt the Lincoln administration to issue a call for seventy-five thousand military volunteers. Four more Southern states secede.

Key Terms

Compromise of 1850 An attempt by Congress to resolve the slavery question by making concessions to both the North and South, including admission of California and a new Fugitive Slave Act. **348**

Fugitive Slave Act A component of the Compromise of 1850 that increased the federal government's obligation to capture and return escaped slaves to their owners. **348**

Underground Railroad A network of safe houses and secret hiding places along routes leading to the North and into Canada (where slavery was prohibited) that helped several thousand slaves gain their freedom between 1830 and 1860. **349**

Young America The movement within the Democratic Party that embraced Manifest Destiny and promoted territorial expansion, increased international trade, and the spread of American ideals of democracy and free enterprise abroad. **352**

Kansas-Nebraska Act An 1854 act designed to resolve the controversy over whether slavery would be permitted in the Western territories. It repealed the ban on slavery north of 36° 30′ (the Missouri Compromise) and created two separate territories, Kansas west of Missouri and Nebraska west of Iowa. **354**

Know-Nothings The nickname for the constituents of the nativist, or anti-immigrant, American Party who called for legislation restricting office holding to native-born citizens and raising the period of naturalization for citizenship from five to twenty-one years. **356**

Bleeding Kansas A phrase used to describe the wave of vigilante reprisals and counterreprisals by proslavery and antislavery forces in Kansas in 1856. **358**

Black Republican A racist pejorative that Democrats used to suggest that Republicans were dangerous radicals who favored abolition and racial equality. **359**

Dred Scott v. Sandford The highly controversial 1857 Supreme Court decision that rejected the claim of the slave Dred Scott, who argued that time spent with his owner in regions that barred slavery had made him a free man. It also declared that Congress lacked the right to regulate slavery in the territories. **360**

free labor A procapitalist Northern philosophy that presented an idealized vision of the industrial North, celebrating the virtues of individualism, independence, entrepreneurship, and upward mobility. **364**

Lincoln-Douglas debates A series of high-profile debates in Illinois in 1858 between Senate candidates Stephen A. Douglas and Abraham Lincoln that focused primarily on the slavery controversy. **366**

John Brown's raid A failed assault led by the radical abolitionist on the federal arsenal at Harpers Ferry, Virginia, on October 16, 1859, intending to seize the guns and ammunition and then touch off a wave of slave rebellions. **366**

Crittenden Compromise An unsuccessful proposal by Kentucky senator John J. Crittenden to resolve the secession crisis in the spring of 1861 with constitutional amendments to protect slavery. **369**

CHAPTER 13

A Nation Torn Apart

The Civil War, 1861–1865

> "War for the destruction of liberty must be met by war for the destruction of slavery."
>
> African American leader
> FREDERICK DOUGLASS

The Civil War began in 1861 as a conflict over whether Southern states possessed the right to secede from the Union. But when the Lincoln administration's Emancipation Proclamation took effect on January 1, 1863, it became a war against slavery. The soldiers depicted in this joyous scene were among the 180,000 African American soldiers who contributed to the Union army's successful campaign to defeat the Confederacy. In January 1864, a few weeks after the first anniversary of the Emancipation Proclamation, the popular magazine, *Harper's Weekly,* published this drawing, "Colored troops under General Wild, liberating slaves in North Carolina." The image reflected not merely a growing acceptance of slavery's demise among Northerners, but also the celebration of emancipation as a noble cause, along with restoration of the Union, that helped the North justify the terrible human cost of the war.

Emancipation was but one of the many extraordinary aspects of the Civil War that make it the most written-about event in American history. The war pitted American against American, in some cases brother against brother. Senator John J. Crittenden of Kentucky, for example, saw two sons rise to the rank of general, one Confederate and the other Union. Mary Todd Lincoln, the president's wife, lost three brothers who were fighting for the Confederacy. The Civil War was also, for its time, an unusually bloody conflict. The 618,000 Americans who died in the four years of conflict far outnumber the 115,000 lost in World War I and the 318,000 in World War II. The war also brought to the fore larger-than-life personalities such as Generals William Tecumseh Sherman, Ulysses S. Grant, Robert E. Lee, and Thomas "Stonewall" Jackson, and it produced moments of heroism that would become the stuff of legend.

If these aspects of the war explain its popularity as a historical subject, they also indicate why the Civil War has generated so much heated debate. For generations Americans have argued over the true cause of the war and why the North won (or as some like to put it, why the South lost). They have debated the significance and wisdom of crucial decisions such as Lee's move to attack the North in 1863 or Union general Meade's failure to pursue the weakened Confederates after Gettysburg.

Yet for all this debate, few commentators dispute this fact: the Civil War brought profound social, political, and economic change to the United States. Most also agree that while the war ended the contentious question of slavery, it immediately raised equally challenging questions about racial equality.

Why does the Civil War exert such a hold on the American imagination?

Mobilization, Strategy, and Diplomacy

Neither the North nor the South envisioned the character and course of the war that began with the South's firing upon Fort Sumter in April 1861. Both sides had to hastily mobilize, recruit, train, and outfit modern armies. The North possessed overwhelming advantages in population and industry, but the South enjoyed superior military leadership, a white population to a large degree united against invading Union armies, and a hope that France or England would intervene in the conflict on their behalf.

Comparative Advantages and Disadvantages

As North and South prepared for war, both sides believed they would win and win decisively. Journalist Horace Greeley spoke for many Northerners when, speaking of the president of the Confederate States of America and his administration, he boasted that "Jeff Davis and Co. will be swinging from the battlements at Washington at least by the 4th of July." On paper this confidence seemed justified. As the table (**13.1**) illustrates, the Northern states possessed more than twice the population of the Confederacy, giving the North an enormous advantage in soldiers, farmers, and industrial workers. The North also possessed a vast industrial system nine times greater than that of the Confederacy. Producing 97 percent of the nation's firearms, 94 percent of its cloth, and 90 percent of its shoes and boots, this system would be capable of providing the Union armies with an unlimited supply of materiel. The North also had a modern railroad system twice the size of the Confederacy's and far more integrated.

A final advantage for the North was the firmly held belief among many of its soldiers that they were fighting to uphold the Constitution, the flag, and the Union. This sentiment was stoked by a profusion of speeches, songs, and printed matter like the poster *The Eagle's Nest* (**13.2**), extolling the Union cause. Demonizing secession as treason by invoking the famous 1830 declaration of President Andrew Jackson, a Southerner and slave owner, "The Union! It must and shall be preserved," it also draws on familiar images of patriotism such as the bald eagle and the American flag. Many Northerners shared the belief that they were indebted to the Founding Fathers, whose sacrifices won American independence and established the republic.

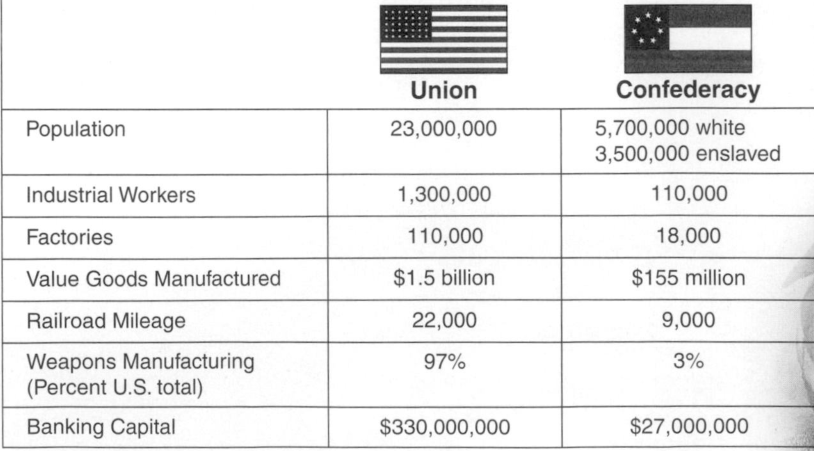

	Union	Confederacy
Population	23,000,000	5,700,000 white 3,500,000 enslaved
Industrial Workers	1,300,000	110,000
Factories	110,000	18,000
Value Goods Manufactured	$1.5 billion	$155 million
Railroad Mileage	22,000	9,000
Weapons Manufacturing (Percent U.S. total)	97%	3%
Banking Capital	$330,000,000	$27,000,000

13.1 Union Advantages on the Eve of War, 1861
The enormous disparities between North and South suggested to many a quick Union victory. But many factors beyond these statistics, notably superior Confederate military leadership, would make for a long and bloody war.

ANNIHILATIO
TO TRAITORS.
THE EAGLE'S NEST.
"THE UNION IT MUST AND SHALL BE PRESERVED"

13.2 *The Eagle's Nest*
Northerners promoted patriotic sentiment in speeches, songs, and printed matter. This poster, "The Eagle's Nest," linked the Union cause to familiar images such as the bald eagle and the American flag.

What significant advantages did the North hold over the South on the eve of war?

Southerners, too, sought to boost their wartime morale. As the song sheet "Secession Quick Step" (**13.3**) shows, they often did so by drawing on the same patriotic images and themes as Northerners. This song and the accompanying image seek to make a connection between the colonists' break from England during the American Revolution and the South's quest for Confederate independence. Note, for example, the reference to "Minute Men" and use of the "Don't Tread on Me" snake, a popular image of defiance used to express colonial resistance to British authority in the 1770s (see Chapter 4).

Southerners also matched Northerners in their confidence about achieving a quick victory. "Just throw three or four shells among those blue-bellied Yankees," boasted one North Carolinian, "and they'll scatter like sheep." Confederates were keenly aware that while they lacked population, industry, and infrastructure, they did possess certain advantages. To begin with, they were fighting a war for independence that carried with it a sense of destiny that would sustain them through the difficult times ahead—just as it had, they reminded themselves, the overmatched colonists in their fight for independence from a superior Great Britain nearly a century earlier.

The South also took heart in its size: to deny Confederate independence the North would have to conquer the South, an area as large as western Europe. Furthermore, this monumental invasion and occupation would very likely unify the South, including poor whites who might otherwise view the conflict as a war to protect the interests of slaveholders. The South could thus fight a defensive war until the North grew tired of the conflict and withdrew, or until a European power, most likely England, which depended heavily on Southern cotton, intervened militarily and forced the North to let the seceded states go.

Finally, whether they knew it or not, in April 1861 Southerners had the upper hand in military leadership. For the first half of the war, generals such as Robert E. Lee and Thomas "Stonewall" Jackson would stymie much larger and better-equipped Northern armies led by inept generals.

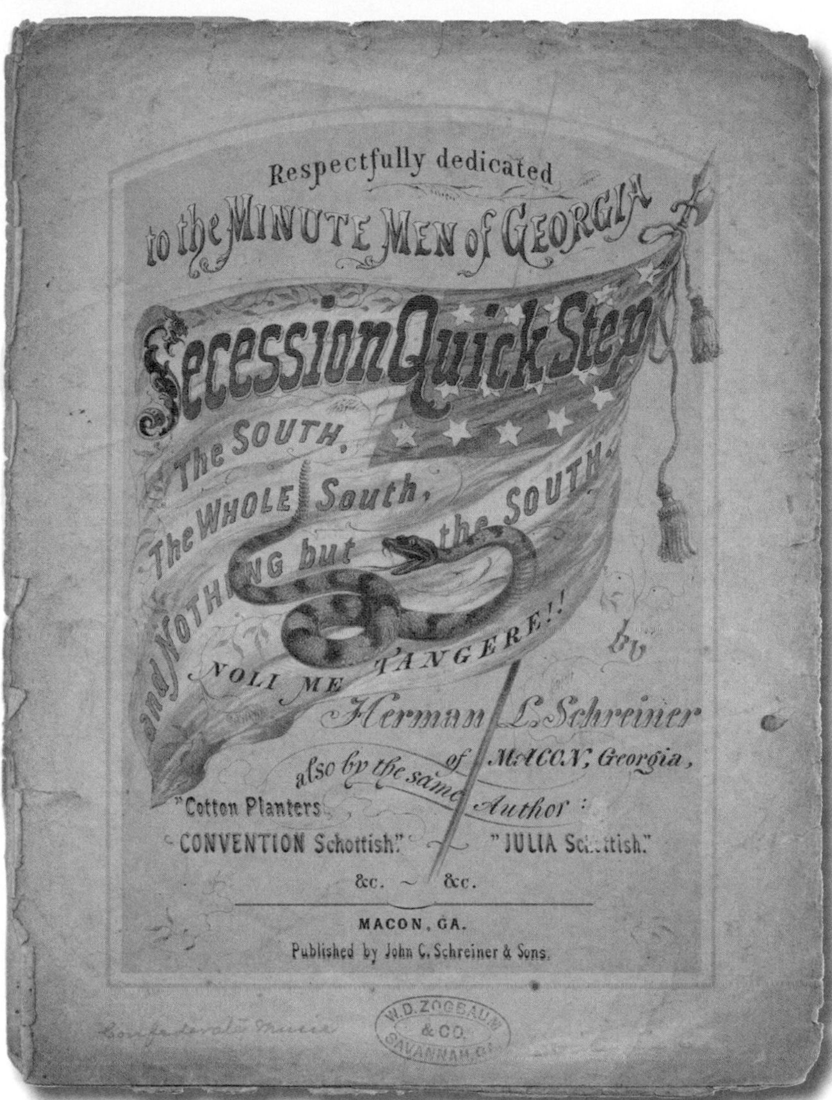

13.3 Connecting to the Colonial Cause
As in the North, Southerners fostered unity, emphasizing the connection between the colonists' revolt against English rule during the American Revolution and the Confederate bid for Southern independence.

Mobilization in the North

Mobilization of the Union Army began days after the firing at Fort Sumter with Lincoln's call for seventy-five thousand volunteers for ninety days' service and the imposition of a naval blockade along the Southern coast. Thousands of eager volunteers jammed recruiting stations, convinced the Union would win quickly and with little loss of life. Among those who clamored to join the Army were thousands of free African Americans anxious to play a role in defeating the slaveholding South. Yet they were turned away because of an overabundance of white volunteers and Lincoln's desire to sidestep issues of slavery and race to avoid provoking the slaveholding states that remained in the Union—Kentucky, Maryland, Delaware, and Missouri—from seceding.

Unfortunately for Lincoln, the Union Army's enthusiasm was no substitute for experience. In 1861 there were only sixteen thousand professional soldiers in the Army, most of them stationed in the West. One-third of the Army's officers quit to join the Confederacy. Of those officers who remained, few possessed any real combat experience. To make matters worse, because state officials named the officers to command the new regiments of volunteers being raised, they invariably chose men whose chief qualifications were their political connections and fondness for parading. One regiment, the 11th New York Volunteer Infantry, was perhaps the most vivid example of this phenomenon. As this print (**13.4**) shows, these volunteers donned flashy uniforms patterned after the Zouaves, France's famous regiments in North Africa, replete with red silk pantaloons and green jackets. The New York Zouaves enjoyed great celebrity at the war's outset, and one of them, Colonel Elmer Ephraim Ellsworth (at right), became the Union's first martyr when he was killed pulling down a Confederate flag in Virginia. Despite their stylishness, however, the 11th New York Zouaves performed disastrously at Bull Run. As the war progressed both armies eliminated special regimental uniforms and replaced them with Union blue and Confederate gray.

13.4 **The Zouaves of the 11th New York**
Many regiments raised to fight for the Union and the Confederacy included inexperienced men whose romantic visions of warfare were expressed in their fanciful uniforms.

Mobilization in the South

Unlike the North, the Confederacy needed to create an Army from scratch. Immediately after seceding Southern states revived, reorganized, and expanded their militias, many of which were more like social clubs than military units. In March 1861 the Confederate Congress established an army of 100,000 volunteers for one-year terms of service, leading to the merging of most state militia companies into the Confederate Army. To thwart the Union's intended blockade of the Southern coastline, the Confederacy commenced creating a navy and authorizing privateers to seize Union ships.

Equipping their soldiers and sailors proved a far greater challenge. Lacking the industrial base of the North, the South built arms factories that eventually turned out some 350,000 rifles. They also managed to import 700,000 more. Nonetheless, throughout the war Confederate soldiers often needed to scavenge battlefields to find weapons and ammunition. The Confederate effort to thwart the Union blockade was similarly hampered by a lack of shipyards.

The Davis administration also confronted the challenge of paying for the war. Possessing few banks and limited reserves of gold and silver, the government tried several schemes, including requiring individual states to pay for the war and imposing an income tax. When none worked, the Confederate government simply printed huge amounts of paper money. With $1.5 billion in circulation by 1864 (twice the amount issued in the North) the citizens of the Confederacy faced punishing inflation, which reached 9,000 percent by 1865 (as compared with 80 percent in the Union).

Another obstacle to Confederate victory was the South's popular doctrine of states' rights. It envisioned the ideal national government as one that left most power and authority to the states. Even though the Confederacy ultimately managed to overcome states' rights opposition and create a centralized national government and military, its efforts were hindered by a number of vociferous critics. Governors Zebulon M. Vance of North Carolina and Joseph E. Brown of Georgia, for example, opposed the incorporation of their state militias' troops into the Confederate army. Later when the Confederacy enacted a military draft, they raised a loud protest and created hundreds of exemptions for friends and state officials.

How did the doctrine of states' rights hinder the Southern war effort?

The Struggle for the Border States

While both sides readied for war, they also struggled for the loyalty of the **Border States**: Missouri, Kentucky, Delaware, and Maryland, the slave states along the border of the Confederacy that had not seceded (see **13.5**). These held enormous strategic value for both sides. Missouri and Kentucky bordered the vital Mississippi River. Kentucky also controlled key sections of the Ohio and Kentucky Rivers. Delaware controlled access to the city of Philadelphia. If Maryland seceded, Washington, D.C. would be surrounded by Confederate territory and the Union's main railroad route west would be lost.

The Davis administration had strong incentive to lure the Border States into joining the Confederacy. These four states contained nearly half the South's white male population and 80 percent of its industry. Given the South's disadvantages in manpower and industry, the loss of these states would seriously weaken the Confederate war effort.

Nonetheless the Union managed to hold all four states. Delaware, where fewer than 2 percent of the white population owned slaves, proved relatively easy to hold. Kentucky was more problematic, as it remained divided between Union and Confederate sympathies. But Lincoln's subtle approach, along with the eventual arrival of federal troops, secured the state for the Union.

Maryland, where pro-Confederate sentiment ran high, presented a far greater challenge. On April 19, 1861, a large pro-Confederate mob attacked the 6th Massachusetts Regiment as it passed through Baltimore on its way to Washington. The inexperienced soldiers panicked and opened fire, killing twelve. The furious mob then destroyed tracks, railroad bridges, and telegraph lines, prompting Lincoln to declare martial law, arrest dozens of Confederate sympathizers, and suspend habeas corpus—the right of a person to petition a judge for release from unlawful imprisonment.

13.5 The Vital Border States
The Border States (Missouri, Kentucky, Maryland, and Delaware) held enormous strategic, military, economic, and symbolic value for both sides. In the end, the Lincoln administration succeeded in keeping them in the Union.

Securing Union control of Missouri likewise required a heavy hand. The situation there resembled that of "Bleeding Kansas" in 1857 (see Chapter 12), with pro-Confederate and pro-Union forces fighting for control of the state. But Union forces under Captain Nathaniel Lyon thwarted the efforts of pro-Confederate state officials to steer Missouri into the Confederacy, allowing pro-Union officials to take control.

The Union's success in preventing the secession of the Border States weakened the Confederate cause in two important ways. First, it deprived the Confederacy of sorely needed soldiers and factories. Second, the retention of four slave states in the Union undermined a primary Confederate justification for secession, namely, that it was necessary to protect the institution of slavery.

What made the Border States so economically and militarily valuable to the Confederacy?

Wartime Diplomacy

Davis hoped to gain from England and France diplomatic recognition for the Confederacy, and perhaps even military intervention. He knew the leaders and aristocracy of both countries sympathized with the Confederate cause and that their economies depended heavily on Southern cotton. Accordingly, Davis sent emissaries to England and France to lobby for recognition.

To increase the chances of foreign intervention, the Confederacy in 1861 also established a **cotton embargo**, a ban on the export of cotton, the South's most valuable commodity. Because the Confederacy wanted to avoid any appearance of blackmailing cotton importing nations like England and France, the embargo was voluntary and unofficial. While the embargo damaged the Southern economy, Confederates believed it a worthwhile risk if it caused enough economic pain in England and France to, in the words of one Charleston newspaper editor, bring about either "the bankruptcy of every cotton factory in Great Britain or France or the acknowledgement of our independence."

Keenly aware that foreign intervention would likely demolish his goal of restoring the Union, Lincoln dispatched his own emissaries to England and France. Shortly after Fort Sumter both nations, seeking to avoid war, declared their neutrality and agreed to honor the Union blockade. Obtaining this latter concession was crucial to the North because had England or France insisted on their right as neutrals to trade with the South, Lincoln would have been forced either to stop their ships—a policy certain to draw them into the war—or allow them to pass and thereby provide the Confederacy with badly needed supplies.

Still, conflict with England did erupt, threatening British neutrality. In November 1861 a U.S. Navy vessel stopped the British ship *Trent* and removed two Confederates heading for Europe to press for intervention. As indicated in this cartoon (**13.6**) from the British magazine *Punch,* England reacted with outrage to the **Trent Affair**, putting its military forces on alert. "You do what is right," Britannia warns a bellicose but smaller America, "or I'll blow you out of the water." Lincoln, unwilling to risk war with England, released the two Confederates, claiming that the captain had acted without authority. The roles were reversed in 1863 when the British government, faced with a Union threat of war, prevented delivery to the Confederacy of two ironclad warships built in a British shipyard.

BRITANNIA
LOOK OUT FOR SQUALLS.
Jack Bull.—"You do what's right, my son, or I'll blow you out of the water."

13.6 A Diplomatic Dust-Up
John Bull (Great Britain) threatens Uncle Sam in the wake of the Trent Affair, an incident that nearly prompted the British to intervene in the war.

Why did Lincoln decide to back down and release the Confederates in the Trent Affair?

The Early Campaigns, 1861–1863

Beginning with Bull Run in July 1861, the Confederacy won repeated victories in Virginia, thwarting Union attempts to seize Richmond, the capital of the Confederacy. The Union found some success in the West and moved closer to its goal of securing control of the Mississippi River. By 1862 new technologies in communications, transportation, and armaments transformed warfare, making it more complex, protracted, and deadly. The war also assumed a revolutionary character, as slaves flocked to invading Union armies, eventually convincing the Lincoln administration to embrace emancipation as a goal of the war.

No Short and Bloodless War

In the weeks following Fort Sumter, pressure mounted in both the North and South for a decisive military victory, despite the disorganized state of their armies. While some argued that given the South's limited resources, their best chance of victory lay with a defensive military posture, most Southerners wanted their military to take the offensive, believing that one or two early victories would bring foreign intervention or prompt Lincoln to abandon efforts to restore the Union by force. Northern leaders faced similar demands. General Winfield Scott had devised a grand strategy called the Anaconda Plan to slowly envelop and strangle the South, but popular sentiment demanded an immediate strike to crush the rebellion.

The highly anticipated first clash, the first Battle of Bull Run, came in mid-July 1861. General Irwin McDowell led thirty thousand Union soldiers of the Army of the Potomac south toward the town of Manassas, Virginia, site of an important railroad junction and a small Confederate force there commanded by General P. G. T. Beauregard. Hundreds of curious and confident spectators from Washington, D.C., followed the army, many with picnic baskets in hand, hoping to catch some of the excitement.

Beauregard positioned his army above Manassas on the south side of a small stream named Bull Run. McDowell attacked and nearly drove the Confederates from the field. Beauregard, however, stabilized his troops, and with reinforcements staged a furious counterassault. Lines of exhausted and undisciplined Union soldiers soon disintegrated into a chaotic, humiliating retreat to Washington.

Victory boosted Confederate spirits and confirmed their belief that one Southerner could whip ten Yankees. For the North the stunning humiliation demolished the notion of a short and bloodless war. Within a week of the debacle, Lincoln authorized the enlistment of one million volunteers for three-year terms of service.

To rebuild the demoralized Army of the Potomac, Lincoln turned to General George B. McClellan. Dubbed the "Young Napoleon" by the press, McClellan was an impressive but supremely arrogant man who treated Lincoln with barely disguised contempt. But Lincoln tolerated these traits because he inspired professionalism among his troops and by the spring of 1862 transformed a mass of inexperienced volunteers into a well-trained army numbering some 150,000.

> "I seem to have become the power of the land. I almost think that were I to win some small success now I could become Dictator or anything else that might please me."
>
> GEN. GEORGE B. MCCLELLAN to his wife, 1861

As the Army of the Potomac regrouped, Union forces in the West gained two desperately needed victories. As indicated in the map (**13.7**), in February 1862 Union forces led by a virtual unknown named Ulysses S. Grant seized Fort Henry on the Tennessee River and, ten days later, nearby Fort Donelson.

The twin victories gave the Union control of vital communication and transportation routes on the Tennessee and Cumberland Rivers and drove the Confederates out of Kentucky and most of Tennessee. They also created an early hero—Ulysses S. Grant—whose initials, the press suggested, stood for "Unconditional Surrender."

Grant continued south along the Tennessee River to seize control of additional railroad lines as part of the larger Union strategy of taking control of the

Why did the First Battle of Bull Run take place before either army was adequately prepared?

13.7 Major Battles in the West, 1862–1863
Grant's army and Farragut's naval force moved swiftly in 1862 to seize control of the Mississippi in order to cut the Confederacy in half.

Mississippi to divide the Confederacy and open the Deep South to invasion. While encamped near Shiloh Church, Tennessee, Confederates under Johnston and Beauregard surprised Grant on the morning of April 6, nearly destroying his army. But timely reinforcements allowed Grant to hold his position. He counterattacked the next day and drove the Confederates off in retreat. Grant's victory secured Union control of the Mississippi River south to Memphis, Tennessee (see **13.7**).

The Confederacy suffered another setback that same month when David G. Farragut's Union fleet of wooden and ironclad vessels forced their way past Confederate forts at the mouth of the Mississippi River and captured New Orleans. This loss deprived the Confederacy of its largest city and chief source of credit and closed the mouth of the Mississippi to Confederate shipping.

The Peninsular Campaign

Lincoln welcomed the successes in the West, but recognized that defeat of the Confederacy required victory over its armies in Northern Virginia. Accordingly, he pressed McClellan to begin an offensive early in the spring of 1862. Despite his gallant image, however, McClellan seemed unwilling to fight, claiming his troops were not yet sufficiently prepared. Only after weeks of goading did he agree to move.

The **Peninsular Campaign**, as his plan was known, reflected McClellan's flamboyant style. Rather than a traditional overland march on the Confederate capital, he designed a complex plan whereby four hundred ships deposited 120,000 soldiers on a long peninsula just east of Richmond at Fortress Monroe, between the James and York Rivers (**13.8**). To Lincoln's frustration it was three weeks before the soldiers were in place. Then McClellan delayed some more.

The Confederates exploited McClellan's delays by sending a force of seventeen thousand under General Thomas "Stonewall" Jackson into the Shenandoah Valley. There between early May and early June he defeated several larger Union forces, raising fears that he would soon take Washington. Lincoln responded by withholding a large force that was scheduled to join McClellan.

When McClellan finally began to inch his army of 110,000 toward Richmond in late May, he confronted Confederate General Joseph E. Johnston in the Battle of Fair Oaks on May 31–June 1, 1862. Although technically a Union victory (since Johnston failed to dislodge McClellan's army), the battle proved inconclusive. Yet it was a turning point in the war because Johnston, severely injured, was replaced by General Robert E. Lee.

Lee proved a brilliant commander and strategist who made the most of the Confederacy's limited resources to bedevil and often defeat much larger Union forces. Often this meant taking the offensive as in the Battle of Seven Days (June 25 through July 1, 1862). Lee attacked with 85,000 troops against McClellan's 110,000 and forced the Union commander to retreat to a secure location on the James River.

The carnage of the weeklong clash was staggering, but McClellan's losses were proportionately smaller than Lee's and his army lay just

Why did the Peninsular Campaign fail?

25 miles from Richmond. He refused, however, to move on Lee's weakened army, claiming inadequate intelligence, supplies, and men. Thoroughly frustrated, Lincoln ordered McClellan to abandon the Peninsular Campaign, remove his forces to northern Virginia, and unite with Pope's army for a traditional overland assault on Richmond. Lee prevented this deadly combination by defeating Pope in the Second Battle of Bull Run (August 29–30, 1862) before McClellan could join him. Lincoln removed Pope from command and, lacking any alternative, placed McClellan in charge of all Union forces in northern Virginia. Vainglorious and ineffective as he was, McClellan still commanded the loyalty of his soldiers.

A New Kind of War

By this time Confederate and Union soldiers had grown accustomed to the rigors of army life. Most of the more than three million who served in the two armies were young men from small farms and towns. One of their first challenges was learning to accept the discipline and authority of military life. They likewise had to set aside their romantic visions of glory and get used to spending most of their time attending to routine duties, drilling, and enduring long periods of inactivity. Soldiers also suffered from bad food and from disease that raged in the camps and claimed three lives for every one lost due to actual combat.

Boredom, disease, and hardship, while difficult to endure, were not new to military life. But certain aspects of the Civil War set it apart from previous wars in ways that have led many historians to declare it the first modern war. While traditional warfare used relatively small armies and emphasized seizing and holding territory, **modern warfare** employed enormous armies that utilized the emerging technologies of the Industrial Revolution. The telegraph allowed for instant communication across vast territory between armies and civilian leaders. Railroads made it possible to shift thousands of reinforcements hundreds of miles in less than a day. Ironclad ships revolutionized naval strategy.

Yet what made this war truly modern was the level of carnage made possible by advances in weaponry. Artillery became more accurate and deadly, while both armies used improved rifled muskets capable of killing a man 400 to 500 yards away (versus 100 yards for traditional muskets).

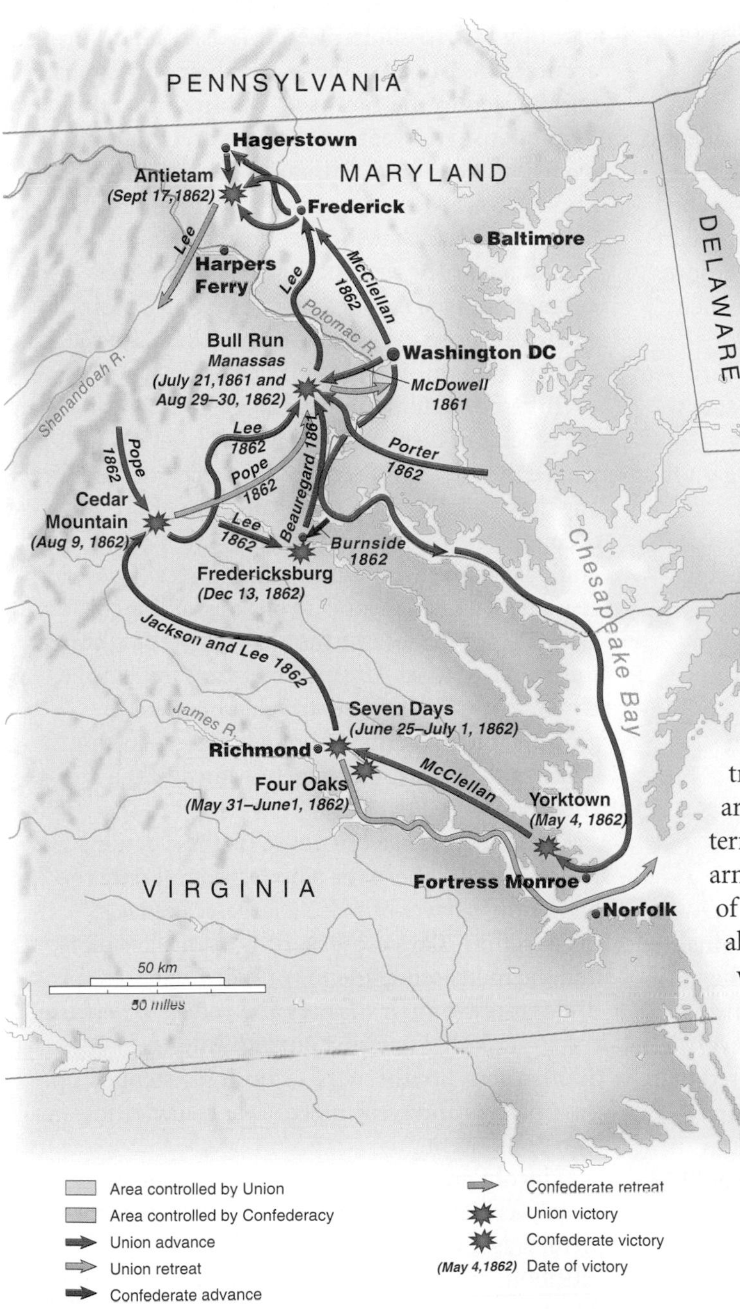

13.8 Major Battles in the East, 1861–1862
McClellan devised an elaborate plan to land his army on the Virginia peninsula below Richmond. But his slowness in moving his army and hesitancy in attacking handed the initiative to the Confederates and led to defeat.

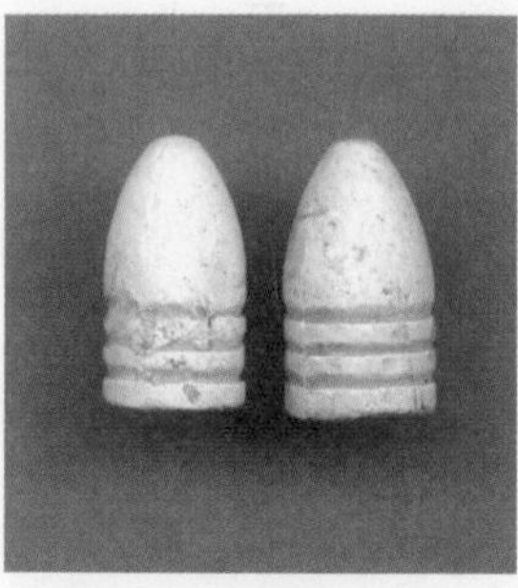

13.9 The Minie Ball
The conical-shaped minie ball (left) replaced round musket balls (right) and greatly increased the accuracy of rifle fire. Its widespread adoption during the Civil War contributed significantly to the high death toll in combat.

The key technological breakthrough for the rifle was the minie ball, invented in France in the 1840s. As these photographs (**13.9**) show, the conical-shaped minie ball (left) replaced round musket balls (right) and were the forerunners of the bullet. The grooves inside the rifle barrel caused the minie ball, when fired, to spiral much like a football, greatly increasing its accuracy. Other aspects of modern war included the emphasis on destroying the enemy's army rather than merely seizing and holding territory and a willingness to inflict suffering on the civilian population.

Military commanders on both sides, however, were slow to adjust to these changes. Schooled in traditional warfare at military academies such as West Point, most were reluctant to abandon the strategy of attacking entrenched enemy positions with massed infantry. When defenders of these positions trained their modern weaponry on charging soldiers, the results were horrific.

Toward Emancipation

The issue of slavery also shaped the Civil War. At the outset of the conflict, moderates like Lincoln insisted the goal of the war was the preservation of the Union, not the abolition of slavery. They realized that many Northerners not only opposed slavery, but also the idea of racial equality. They also feared that talk of emancipation would cause one or more Border States to secede and alienate pro-Union residents of the South who Lincoln hoped would someday overthrow Confederate rule and return their states to the Union. Abolitionists, however, argued that because the Southern states seceded in order to protect slavery, reunion could occur only after slavery was destroyed.

Not content to wait for official word of emancipation, enslaved African Americans took matters into their own hands by taking advantage of the chaos caused by the war and fleeing to Union Army lines. Only weeks after the war began, in May 1861 an angry Virginia slaveholder demanded the Union Army observe the terms of the 1850 Fugitive Slave Act and return his three escaped slaves. General Benjamin Butler refused, declaring fugitive slaves **contraband of war**, or seized property. The Lincoln administration endorsed the contraband policy as a shrewd war tactic likely to cause havoc in the South. As this painting (**13.10**) illustrates, this assessment proved accurate as countless slaves left their white masters and flocked to the camps of Union soldiers. Painted just two years after the war, *On to Liberty*, by artist Theodore Kaufmann, depicts slaves moving toward the smoke of a battle in the distance, aware that the presence of Union forces meant the destruction of slavery. Self-emancipating slaves began arriving at Union Army camps in ever-growing numbers, totaling close to one million by the war's end.

In response to these events, Congress slowly began the process of dismantling slavery. In August 1861 it passed the First Confiscation Act, which declared free any slaves used in the Confederate war effort. A Second Confiscation Act passed in July 1862 empowered the army to seize and render "forever free" the slaves of anyone involved in aiding the Confederacy. That same month Congress authorized the president to let African Americans fight in the Union Army. These measures demonstrated a growing understanding among Northerners that winning the war would somehow involve the abolition of slavery.

The threat to slavery posed by these actions was not lost on Southerners, who feared not only the loss of their slaves but also a large-scale slave insurrection. Slave escapes, rumors of slave plots, and the increased tendency of many slaves to speak disdainfully to their masters and refuse to perform certain tasks led to rising anxiety among Southerners. Southerners accordingly stepped up slave patrols and scrutinized slave behavior for any sign of ill intent.

Lincoln gradually came to see emancipation not merely as inevitable but also as essential for Union victory, as it would "strike at the heart of the rebellion" and prevent British intervention. On July 22, 1862, he informed his entire cabinet of his intent to issue a decree of emancipation. But to avoid the appearance of acting in desperation, Lincoln waited for a Union victory before issuing this decree.

How did the actions of slaves push Lincoln toward emancipation?

It came two months later in mid-September at the Battle of Antietam, in Maryland. Lee, choosing to wage a bold offensive, led his army north into Maryland. McClellan, even after acquiring a copy of the Confederate battle plan, reacted slowly, allowing Lee to consolidate his troops. Finally, on September 17, 1862, McClellan attacked Lee's army and would likely have won a decisive victory but for the last-minute arrival of Confederate reinforcements. The next day, McClellan chose not to attack, despite superior numbers and the shattered condition of Lee's army. The following day Lee led his army back into Virginia, handing McClellan a technical victory. The battle, as discussed in *Images as History: Photography and the Visualization of Modern War* (page 386), claimed six thousand lives and left seventeen thousand wounded, making it the deadliest single day of the war.

Shortly after the victory at Antietam in September 1862, Lincoln issued his preliminary **Emancipation Proclamation.** Unless the seceded states and parts thereof that were not under Union Army control returned to the Union by January 1, 1863, the decree warned, their slaves "shall be then, thenceforward, and forever free." Even though the decree left slavery intact in the Border States and areas held by the Union Army, Lincoln knew conservatives, Northern Democrats, and Border State unionists would react negatively and that Republicans might suffer at the polls that November. Still, he reasoned, the benefits of emancipation far outweighed the risks as it would cause chaos by encouraging slaves to flee their masters and make it highly unlikely that England would intervene in the conflict.

Though some radicals and abolitionists expressed dismay over the fact that the proclamation freed slaves only in the seceded states, they recognized that Lincoln's simple, tersely worded statement of military policy had transformed the meaning of the conflict. If Northerners by late 1862 realized the war was no mere "insurrection," they also understood that its goal was something greater than simply a restored Union. It was now a war of subjugation. Reunion would occur only after the destruction of the fabric of Southern society.

Slaughter and Stalemate

Restoring the Union and abolishing slavery, of course, depended entirely upon victory on the field of battle. But the Army of the Potomac, now commanded by General Ambrose E. Burnside, suffered a devastating defeat at the Battle of Fredericksburg on December 13, 1862. Burnside tried one more offensive on January 22, 1863, a disastrous mid-winter effort that became mired in muddy, impassible roads. The failure of the "Mud March" led a despondent Lincoln to replace Burnside with General Joseph Hooker.

Not all the news from the Union battlefields in late 1862 was negative. On December 31 Union troops under General William S. Rosecrans turned back an attempt by Confederate General Braxton Bragg to regain western Tennessee and Kentucky in the Battle of Murfreesboro. Bragg's retreat on January 2, 1863, left the West firmly in the hands of the Union Army for the rest of the war.

Lee and his Army of Northern Virginia, however, continued to thwart the Union effort to take Richmond. In the Battle of Chancellorsville, April 30–May 6, 1863, despite commanding a force half the size of Union General Joseph Hooker, Lee scored a smashing victory. But it came at a high price: the man Lee had come to count on most, Stonewall Jackson, was killed, accidentally, by his own men.

13.10 **Theodore Kaufmann's *On to Liberty* (1867)** Widespread self-emancipation by slaves in the early years of the war eventually prompted the Lincoln administration to make emancipation official policy. [*Source:* Theodor Kaufmann (1814–1896), "On to Liberty," 1867, Oil on canvas, 36 × 56 in (91.4 × 142.2 cm). The Metropolitan Museum of Art. Gift of Erving and Joyce Wolf, 1982 (1982.443.3) Photograph © The Metropolitan Museum of Art./Art Resource, NY]

How did Lincoln expect the Emancipation Proclamation to benefit the Union War effort?

Images as History

PHOTOGRAPHY AND THE VISUALIZATION OF MODERN WAR

Not all technological innovations that shaped the Civil War were military in nature. Great advances in photography allowed Americans to see what traditionally had been left to the imagination or an artist's pen or brush: actual images of war's carnage and destruction. The first great demonstration of wartime photography came in September 1862 when America's leading studio photographer, Mathew Brady, sent two of his assistants to photograph the aftermath of the Battle of Antietam. Alexander Gardner and James F. Gibson took hundreds of photographs. Most like the one by Gardner shown here focused on the bleak landscape littered with fallen soldiers. Note the contrast with the popular Currier & Ives (right) illustration of the First Battle of Bull Run published one year earlier, when most Americans still believed that the war would be short, glorious, and victorious. How did Gardner's grim image compare to the romantic visions of war Northerners and Southerners expressed at the outset of the conflict? How do you imagine such images shaped the public's attitude toward this and future wars?

Gardner's grim photographs undermined the popular image of war as gallant and exciting.

Gardner's photograph challenged the romanticized visions of war shared by many citizens when the conflict started. It delivers a blunt unambiguous message: the men pictured here may have died gallantly, but they also died in a brutal manner, shredded by cannon fire and pierced by bullets, and then splayed in irregular and undignified poses in the cold dirt.

Including the Dunker church in the background added irony to the scene because the Dunkers were a religious sect that believed in pacifism.

The indignity of the dead soldiers' condition is emphasized by their proximity to the dead horse.

The chaos of battle is conveyed by the intentional placement (probably by Gardner) of a pair of shoes in the foreground. Note the contrast with the artist's imagined scene at Bull Run where even the dead and dying retain their equipment and weapons.

Why did photography have a more powerful impact on the public than artists' depictions of battles?

Currier & Ives's depiction of the Battle of Bull Run showed war as a glorious and seemingly bloodless event.

BATTLE OF BULL RUN, Va July 21st 1861.
Gallant charge of the Zouaves and defeat of the rebel Black Horse Cavalry.

Unlike Gardner's brutal scene of death, the artist's depiction of war shows several Zouaves who have fallen, but their uniforms remain spotless, with no trace of blood.

Note how the caption's reference to the "Gallant charge" emphasizes the image of war as romantic and heroic. An uninformed viewer might be surprised to learn that many Zouaves died that day, and the Union lost the battle.

Brady put the grim collection of photographs on display in his New York gallery under the title "The Dead of Antietam." Tens of thousands paraded by the exhibit in astonishment. For generations people on the home front had relied upon writers and artists like the one employed by Currier & Ives to convey the scenes of conflict and carnage. Now photographers could capture such images in unprecedented detail and realism. "The dead of the battle-field come up to us very rarely, even in dreams," commented the *New York Times*. "We see the list in the morning paper at breakfast, but dismiss its recollection with the coffee … Mr. Brady has done something to bring home to us the terrible reality and earnestness of war. If he has not brought the bodies and laid them in our door-yards and along streets, he has done something very like it."

Behind the Lines

The war brought challenges and hardships to the Union and Confederate home fronts. Civilians faced shortages of goods, soaring inflation, and conscription. These conditions were more severe in the South where civilians in many areas also came under Union military rule. These problems, coupled with mounting death tolls, led to sagging morale and rising criticism of political leaders in both regions. Occasionally discontent exploded into violent riots. The demands of war placed an especially great demand on women, who assumed new occupational and civic roles.

Meeting the Demands of Modern War

While war raged in the East and West, Republicans took advantage of their dominant position in Congress to enact legislation that Southerners had long opposed. Most were policies designed to promote industrialization (a high tariff) and westward settlement (the Homestead and Pacific Railway Acts). Several laws, however, were part of an unprecedented effort to outfit and finance a modern army. The National Bank Acts of 1863 and 1864 established a national banking system whereby member banks could issue treasury notes, or "greenbacks," as currency.

The nation's first income tax, the sale of $400 million in bonds to the public, and the borrowing of $2.6 billion from banks helped pay for the war. The cost of the war increased the federal budget twenty-fold during the war, from $63 million in 1861 to $1.3 billion in 1865. All told, the war effort greatly expanded the size and scope of the federal government.

In contrast to the Union's ability to adopt policies necessary to sustain the war effort, Davis and other Confederate leaders soon discovered that there were limits to how far Southerners were willing to go in adapting to the demands of modern warfare. In response to the need for more soldiers and revenue for the war, the Confederate Congress established a military draft and an income tax in April 1862. Public officials across the Confederacy denounced the measures as gross violations of states' rights. Among the loudest protestors was Alexander Stephens, Davis's own vice president. In the coming years of warfare, Southerners evaded both the draft and income tax to such an extent that neither measure produced the needed men or money. Draft and tax evasion occurred on a large scale in the North, to be sure, but greater supplies of men and money there diminished the significance of their impact.

These limits were compounded by the leadership style of President Davis. Despite his extensive political and military experience, he proved an ineffective leader for a time of crisis. Unlike Lincoln, he selected a weak cabinet to prevent challenges to his authority and bristled when anyone raised the slightest disagreement. He also micromanaged the War Department, successively firing or driving to resignation five secretaries of war in four years. The Confederate Army's success in the war's first two years obscured Davis's leadership flaws, but as the Army's fortunes declined after 1862, the president's leadership style sparked political rancor and disunity.

Hardships on the Home Front

The most apparent impact of the war on the lives of civilians in the North and South came in the form of many hardships. In the North the arms manufacturing, metalworking, boot making, and shipbuilding industries boomed, but the scarcity of cotton caused widespread layoffs and closures in the textile industry. Workers' wages rose by as much as 40 percent, but prices rose even faster as inflation averaged 15 percent annually. In response many workers formed and joined craft unions, but appeals to patriotism and the use of strikebreakers discouraged strikes.

Similar problems plagued the people of the South. The Southern economy was hard-hit by the cessation of trade with the Northern states and Europe due to the Union blockade. Southern industry and agriculture were hindered by both chronic labor shortages due to military service and the flight of slaves, as well as the destruction or seizure of farms and factories by advancing Union armies. As a result the production of goods and agricultural produce in the South decreased by 30

What steps did the Union take to provide funding for the war?

percent during the war. By contrast Northern output increased significantly. These conditions led to shortages of nearly everything in the South, including food, and the emergence of a thriving black market. The cartoon (**13.11**) from a Richmond newspaper captured the rising anger among Southerners directed at speculators and black marketeers. A cold-hearted speculator counts his profits as a hungry mother and child look through his window. "Anathema on him who screws and hoards / who robs the poor of wheat, potatoes, and bread," read the first two lines of the accompanying poem.

New Roles for Women

The war changed the lives of millions of women in both the North and South who remained behind the lines during the conflict. Because so many hundreds of thousands of men left to fight, women assumed new roles running farms and shops and working in factories and offices. Many did so out of a sense of duty to the war effort, while others worked to earn badly needed income, as military pay was low and inflation pushed up the cost of living.

The war also provided women with an opportunity to enter previously male-dominated professions such as teaching, civil service, and nursing. In the case of nursing, the shortage of men and the recruitment efforts by women like Dorothea Dix, head of the U.S. Sanitary Commission, led to thousands of women volunteering to serve as nurses in field hospitals. In so doing they had to overcome opposition from male doctors and others who disapproved of women working in such indelicate situations. Supporters countered by arguing that women brought to the profession nurturing and domestic skills. By 1900 nursing would be an almost exclusively female profession. As Clara Barton, Civil War nurse and future founder of the American Red Cross, put it, at the end of the war the American woman "was at least fifty years in advance of the normal position which continued peace would have assigned her." Many women also joined organizations that actively supported the Union cause, such as the Women's Central Association of Relief, whose seven thousand chapters across the North raised money and sent supplies to the soldiers in the field.

Southern women experienced similar changes during the war. They took on new responsibilities such as running farms and plantations, managing stores, working in government, and serving as nurses. Many worked in factories, including more than five hundred employed by the Confederate Ordnance Department to fill cartridges, dangerous work that killed dozens in explosions. Their jobs grew more demanding as the war demolished the Southern economy and sent food prices soaring. The Union Army's sweep across the South in late 1864 and early 1865 left Southern women and their children destitute and hungry.

Many Southern women also faced the challenge of maintaining the slave labor system, an increasingly

13.11 Anger on the Home Front
Runaway inflation and scarcity of necessities sparked angry accusations that speculators were hoarding supplies and selling them at extortionate prices. Here a speculator counts his profits while a starving mother and child look on.

difficult task as thousands of slaves fled to Union lines, leaving farms and plantations with inadequate labor. Many slaves who did not flee took advantage of the planter's absence and challenged the authority of women unaccustomed to the role of master. As one exasperated wife wrote to her husband, "The Negroes are all expecting to be set free very soon and it causes them to be very troublesome."

"You have given your boys to die for their country, now you can give your girls to nurse them."

MARY STENEBAUGH-BRADFORD, convincing her father to let her care for Union soldiers

Copperheads

One group that stood to benefit from the hard times in the North was the Democratic Party. Even though many Northerners associated it with secession and the Confederacy, it remained a viable political power in the North during the war. After all, it had received 44 percent of the popular vote there in the presidential election of 1860. Many Democrats supported the war against secession, but **Copperheads** (or "peace Democrats") argued in favor of a cease-fire, followed by a negotiated peace settlement even if it resulted in an independent Confederacy. A few Copperheads even expressed support for the Confederacy.

Lincoln viewed the opposition of Copperheads to the Union war effort as seditious, if not treasonous, behavior and he took steps early in his administration to squelch it. In the aftermath of the pro-Confederate rioting in Baltimore in 1861, he suspended habeas corpus, citing the section of the Constitution providing "the privilege of the writ of habeas corpus shall not be suspended, unless when, in cases of rebellion or invasion, the public safety may require it." In so doing, Lincoln established a principle he would follow for the rest of the war. In the name of saving the Union and the Constitution, he would not hesitate to suppress Constitutional guarantees of free speech and the right to a speedy trial. Over the next few years, scores of Copperheads were arrested and jailed for lengthy periods of time without trial. Copperheads initially attracted few followers, but dissatisfaction with the war rose in the winter of 1862–1863 in the wake of repeated Union Army failures and the enactment of the controversial Emancipation Proclamation and military draft. Led by former Ohio congressman Clement Vallandigham, Copperheads denounced Lincoln as a tyrant who abused his power and suppressed free speech by shutting down opposition newspapers and arresting hundreds of people who voiced hostility toward the Union war effort or sympathy for the Confederacy. Copperheads gained support among farmers in the West by claiming the new Republican tariff hurt them economically and among urban workers and immigrants by stoking racial fears of social chaos and job competition that would result from emancipation.

To counter rising Copperhead sentiment, pro-Union speakers, editors, and cartoonists vilified Copperheads as dangerous, disloyal men who threatened the Union. In February 1863, *Harper's Weekly* printed the cartoon shown in *Competing Visions: Civil Liberties in a Civil War*. The cartoonist shows the goddess Liberty, bearing a shield labeled "Constitution" and a drawn sword, being prevented from engaging in battle against the Confederacy by three peace Democrats depicted as copperhead snakes. As part of this effort to squelch Copperhead activism, the Lincoln administration stepped up arrests. On May 5, 1863 a local Union Army commander in Ohio arrested Vallandigham after he delivered a speech denouncing the war and the draft.

Conscription and Civil Unrest

Despite the Lincoln administration's crackdown on Copperhead dissent, opposition to the war among Northerners increased in 1863, especially among those expected to fight. The poor performance of the Union Army in the field, coupled with staggering numbers of killed and wounded, extinguished much of the early enthusiasm for war. Despite offers of cash bonuses and time off in exchange for reenlistment, Union Army soldiers were heading home as their enlistment terms expired and recruitment offices now went begging for new recruits.

To solve the manpower problem, in March 1863 Congress passed the **Conscription Act**, a law that declared all male citizens (and immigrants who had applied for citizenship) aged twenty to forty-five eligible for draft into the Union Army. Each state was assigned a quota of men to fill. If drafted a man had ways to avoid service. He could buy his way out by paying a "commutation fee" of $300 to the

What prompted the Lincoln administration to impose a draft in early 1862?

Competing Visions

CIVIL LIBERTIES IN A CIVIL WAR

The following opinions present opposing views on the constitutionality of Lincoln's policy toward Copperheads. One is a series of resolutions adopted and sent to Lincoln by a group of Democrats. The other is Lincoln's formal response. As you read these excerpts, note what the parties define as the greatest threat to civil liberties and the Constitution. Were Lincoln's actions justified? Are principles such as civil liberties subject to different treatment during times of national crisis such as war?

On May 19, 1863, a meeting of Democrats, including former Congressman Erastus Corning, in Albany, New York, passed and delivered to Lincoln a series of resolutions accusing the administration of having acted unconstitutionally in placing military authority over civil authority.

... Resolved, ... we denounce the recent assumption of a military commander to seize and try a citizen of Ohio, Clement L. Vallandigham, for no other reason than words addressed to a public meeting, in criticism of the course of the administration, and in condemnation of the military orders of that general.

Resolved, That this assumption of power by a military tribunal, if successfully asserted, not only abrogates the right of the people to assemble and discuss the affairs of government, the liberty of speech and of the press, the right of trial by jury, the law of evidence, and the privilege of habeas corpus, but it strikes a fatal blow at the supremacy of law, and the authority of the State and federal constitutions.

Resolved, ... That, regarding the blow struck at a citizen of Ohio as aimed at the rights of every citizen of the north, we denounce it as against the spirit of our laws and Constitution, and most earnestly call upon the President of the United States to reverse the action of the military tribunal which has passed a "cruel and unusual punishment" upon the party arrested, prohibited in terms by the Constitution, and to restore him to the liberty of which he has been deprived.

Northern Unionists depicted Copperheads as traitors who threatened the Republic.

On June 12, 1863, Lincoln sent his reply in which he defended his actions as both constitutional and necessary for the preservation of the Union.

GENTLEMEN: ...Ours is a clear, flagrant, and gigantic case of rebellion; and the provision of the Constitution that "the privilege of the writ of habeas corpus shall not be suspended, unless when, in cases of rebellion or invasion, the public safety may require it," is the provision which specially applies to our present case. ...

... Mr. Vallandigham avows his hostility to the war on the part of the Union; and his arrest was made because he was laboring, with some effect, to prevent the raising of troops; to encourage desertions from the army; and to leave the rebellion without an adequate military force to suppress it. He was not arrested because he was damaging the political prospects of the administration, or the personal interests of the commanding general, but because he was damaging the army, upon the existence and vigor of which the life of the nation depends. He was warring upon the military, and this gave the military constitutional jurisdiction to lay hands upon him.

Long experience has shown that armies cannot be maintained unless desertion shall be punished by the severe penalty of death. ... Must I shoot a simple-minded soldier boy who deserts, while I must not touch a hair of a wily agitator who induces him to desert? ... I think that in such a case, to silence the agitator and save the boy is not only constitutional, but withal a great mercy.

I ... [am un]able to appreciate the danger apprehended by the meeting [in Albany] that the American people will, by means of military arrests during the rebellion, lose the right of public discussion, the liberty of speech and the press, the law of evidence, trial by jury, and habeas corpus, throughout the indefinite peaceful future, ... any more than I am able to believe that a man could contract so strong an appetite for emetics during temporary illness as to persist in feeding upon them during the remainder of his healthful life.

How did Lincoln justify the suspension of habeas corpus?

government or hiring a substitute to serve in his place. Those who lacked such substantial sums of money ($300 was equivalent to a year's pay for a common laborer) could simply disappear—something that more than 20 percent of draftees did.

The first draft held in July touched off widespread protest. Disturbances broke out in Boston; Troy, New York; Wooster, Ohio; Portsmouth, New Hampshire; and other cities. Opposition to the draft was greatest in New York City, where on July 13, 1863, the city erupted in four days of unprecedented violence known as the **Draft Riots**. Mobs of mostly poor, immigrant, and working-class rioters attacked draft offices, Union Army recruiting stations, institutions associated with the Republican Party or abolition, and symbols of wealth and privilege, reflecting animosity toward the inequity of the draft law that allowed the rich to pay a $300 fee to avoid the draft. Rioters also focused their fury against African Americans. As the image (**13.12**) illustrates, they lynched at least eighteen. Rioters blamed blacks as the cause of the war and feared them as potential labor competition.

The riots raged for four days, resulting in at least 119 deaths and $5 million in property damage. In the weeks and months that followed, New York officials defused opposition to the draft by raising money to pay the $300 commutation fee or hire substitutes for draftees not willing to join the Army and allowing easy exemptions for reasons of health or family considerations.

Discontent and unrest also rocked the Confederate home front. In October 1862 the Confederate Congress passed what came to be known as the "Twenty Negro Law." It exempted from the draft one white man per plantation that held twenty or more slaves. Supporters argued that it was a measure vital to maintaining order and productivity on plantations, but to poor white Southerners it engendered similar levels of anger and protest as the commutation provisions in the North. Many cited the law as the reason why they deserted from the Confederate Army.

Another source of discontent was the shortage of food brought about by drought, the blockade, and Union conquest of Southern territory. When shortages and high prices reached critical proportions in 1863, Southern women led food riots in several towns and cities, including most dramatically in the Confederate capital Richmond. "Bread! Bread!" they cried, "Our children are starving while the rich roll in wealth!" The reference to the rich reflected the widespread belief that Confederate leaders and merchants were profiting from the war.

13.12 Opposition to the Draft Turns Violent Poor New Yorkers rioted against the draft in July 1863, venting their anger on army recruiting stations and against African Americans, whom they blamed for the war.

Why did residents of New York riot against the draft?

Toward Union Victory

Despite many setbacks in the early years of the war, by mid-1863 the North's superior industrial strength, large population, and improved military leadership gave the Union the advantage. So, too, did the decision to allow African Americans to serve in the army, for they provided the Union with badly needed manpower at a time of declining enlistments. Military success at Gettysburg, Vicksburg, and Atlanta boosted morale in the North and led to Lincoln's reelection in 1864. Relentless military offensives by General Ulysses S. Grant in Virginia and General William T. Sherman in Georgia led to the Confederate surrender in April 1865. The assassination of President Lincoln, however, quickly dampened the North's joy.

Turning Point: 1863

While the scenes of destruction and antiwar sentiment in New York City shocked Lincoln, events elsewhere in 1863 gave him cause for hope. Back in May, Lee had convinced Davis to approve another invasion of the North. It was risky, but they believed it might cause such alarm in the North as to force Lincoln to pull troops out of the western theater where Grant was threatening to seize the entire lower Mississippi. Even better, a victory on Northern soil would demoralize the Lincoln administration and strengthen the hand of Copperheads and Peace Democrats who were calling for a negotiated settlement. It might even convince France or England to intervene.

In the first week of June, Lee headed north through Virginia's Shenandoah Valley into Maryland and continued north into Pennsylvania. Although slow to react, the Army of the Potomac, now under General George G. Meade, eventually caught up with Lee in central Pennsylvania. On July 1 the two armies collided at Gettysburg, a small town at the junction of several major roads. Although outnumbered ninety thousand to seventy-five thousand, the Confederates made significant advances that day. The following day the battle's momentum swung back and forth all day before Union forces pushed the Confederates back to the previous day's position. On the third and decisive day, Lee recklessly ordered an all-out assault on the heavily fortified Union center. "Pickett's Charge," as it became known, proved gallant, but suicidal. Union forces devastated General George Pickett's twelve thousand men as they tried to cross a mile of open field and ascend Cemetery Ridge. "Picket's division just seemed to melt away," recalled one witness. "Nothing but stragglers came back." With 23,000 Union and 28,000 Confederate soldiers killed and wounded, Gettysburg was by far the bloodiest battle of the war.

The next day, July 4, having lost one-third of his men, Lee removed his tattered army back toward Virginia. Although Lincoln expressed frustration that Meade failed to pursue, he nonetheless recognized that the Union had just won a major victory. Never again would the Confederate Army threaten the North.

That same day Lincoln received news of a vital victory in the West. In May Grant had begun a siege of the town of Vicksburg, the Confederacy's last stronghold on the Mississippi River. It fell on July 4, severing the Confederacy in two and giving the Union complete control over the Mississippi River.

African Americans Under Arms

Despite the twin victories of early July 1863, the Union Army was a long way from ultimate victory. It still faced the big challenge of finding new recruits. Thousands of free African American men already toiled in the service of the Union Army, performing support tasks such as moving supplies and building fortifications. Declining enlistments of whites, however, and steady lobbying by black leaders eventually convinced Union officials to form African American regiments.

One of the first and the most famous of all the African American regiments was the 54th Massachusetts, organized in the spring of 1863 by leading black abolitionists. "I urge you to fly to arms and smite with death the power that would bury the government and your liberty in the same hopeless grave," read a recruitment pamphlet written by another organizer, Frederick Douglass. Among the

Why did Lee decide to invade the North a second time?

13.13 Held Back by Racism Believing African Americans lacked the courage to fight under fire, Union commanders initially relegated them to noncombat roles. Eventually, however, blacks fought in 449 battles, including the Battle of Milliken's Bend on June 7, 1863 (center).

regiment's members were two of Douglass's sons, Lewis and Charles, and the grandson of Sojourner Truth, James Caldwell. Colonel Robert Gould Shaw, son of a leading white Massachusetts abolitionist family, commanded the regiment.

African American soldiers experienced many forms of racism within the Union Army. They served in strictly segregated units under white officers and, as this drawing (**13.13**) indicates, initially served in noncombat duty as guards and laborers. Many also charged that they received substandard medical care in comparison with white soldiers. Most galling, as seen in *Choices and Consequences: Equal Peril, Unequal Pay* (page 396), was that African American soldiers received considerably lower pay than white soldiers.

African American soldiers also faced the prospect of brutal treatment at the hands of Confederate soldiers if captured. The Davis administration announced that African American soldiers taken prisoner would be subject to execution as rebellious slaves. Lincoln's threat of retaliation prevented the Confederacy from carrying out this policy on a wide scale, but acts of murder, torture, and mutilation against African Americans did occur. In the most egregious incident (**13.14**), the Fort Pillow Massacre in Tennessee, Confederate troops murdered dozens of captured black soldiers at Fort Pillow in April 1864. This image, which ran in a popular Northern magazine, was one of many that depicted Confederates as brutal and inhumane. Seeking to influence public opinion, Southern publications ran similar images that alleged Northern atrocities.

"We ... have dyed the ground with blood, in defense of the Union, and Democracy. ... We have done a Soldier's Duty. Why can't we have a Soldier's pay?"

Letter of CORPORAL JAMES HENRY GOODING of 54th Massachusetts to President Lincoln, September 1863

How were African American soldiers treated in the Union Army?

The creation of all-black units in the Union Army raised another critical issue beyond the question of equality of pay or the assignment of white officers to lead. Would these units be sent into actual combat? Racist notions held by whites led them to question whether African Americans possessed the necessary courage to fight. Others cautioned that if black regiments were not used judiciously, critics would charge the army with using them for cannon fodder.

The first well-publicized test of African American soldiers came on July 18, 1863, when the 54th Massachusetts led a nighttime assault on Fort Wagner, a key Confederate outpost that guarded Charleston harbor. The Confederates repulsed their attack. But the courage exhibited by the soldiers under fire—the unit lost 100 dead and 146 wounded—won them universal praise and did much to undermine the racist belief that blacks would not stand and fight.

All told 180,000 blacks, including 144,000 former slaves, served in the Union Army. This number amounted to 10 percent of the total enlisted men even though African Americans comprised only 1 percent of the Northern population. African American soldiers participated in over 449 separate engagements against Confederate troops and 38,000 died in the course of the war. Sixteen black soldiers and four black sailors received the Medal of Honor. "The colored soldiers in this four years' struggle," wrote one African American soldier, "have proven themselves in every respect to be men." Their contribution to the Union war effort proved vital.

Most significant, African American service in the war empowered them to make a claim on full citizenship rights after the war. "Once let the black man get upon his person the brass letters, U.S., let him get an eagle on his button and a musket on his shoulder and bullets in his pocket," said Frederick Douglass, "there is no power on earth that can deny that he has earned the right to citizenship."

The Confederacy Begins to Crumble

News of the losses in the East and West caused dismay across the South. Beyond the setbacks in the field, however, Davis and the Confederate leadership had additional reasons to worry. The immediate problem was a lack of men. A draft instituted in April 1862 failed to attract sufficient numbers of recruits. Protests by poor whites forced the repeal in 1863 of a provision in the draft law that exempted wealthy whites who held twenty or more slaves, but still the numbers of new recruits fell short of the amount needed. The

13.14 The Massacre at Fort Pillow
In April 1864 Confederate soldiers overran Union troops at Fort Pillow in Tennessee and slaughtered dozens of captured African American soldiers.

What role did African American soldiers play in the Union war effort?

Choices and Consequences

EQUAL PERIL, UNEQUAL PAY

In the early stages of enlisting African American soldiers, the War Department planned to pay them the same $13 per month (plus $3.50 for clothes) as white soldiers. Indeed, as the early recruitment poster below shows, many early black recruits received equal pay. But in June 1863 the Lincoln administration, fearing a backlash among white soldiers who did not see African Americans as their equals, adopted a two-tier wage scale that paid black soldiers just $7 per month (plus $3 for clothes). Outraged, African American officers and enlisted men of the 54th and 55th Massachusetts (Colored) Infantry pondered their options.

Choices

1. Quietly accept the lower wages as a regrettable but unavoidable trade-off that allowed them to enlist in the Union Army and fight to end slavery.
2. Accept the unequal wages as better than nothing and necessary to maintain their families, while openly protesting the injustice and lobbying for equal pay.
3. Reject the lower wages on principle, despite the financial hardship on their families, while fulfilling their duties as soldiers, openly protesting the injustice, and lobbying for equal pay.
4. Lay down their arms and refuse to obey orders until they receive equal pay.

Decision

The men of the 54th and 55th Massachusetts (Colored) Infantry chose the third option, rejecting the lower wages on principle, despite the financial hardship on their families. They even rejected an offer by the governor of Massachusetts to pay the six dollars per month difference out of the state treasury, citing the principle of equality that was at stake. Meanwhile they fulfilled their duties as soldiers, openly protested the injustice, and lobbied the Lincoln administration for equal pay.

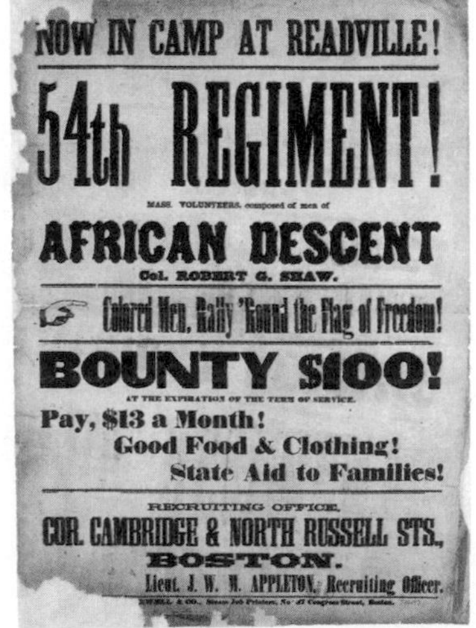

Consequences

The soldiers and their families hung on for more than a year until Congress in June 1864 authorized an equal pay scale for all soldiers regardless of race. By then, given the well-documented professionalism and courage exhibited by black soldiers on the battlefield, the distinction in pay had become an embarrassment to Lincoln's administration. Not all black regiments, however, made the same decision as the Massachusetts 54th and 55th, and the consequences of their actions were starkly different. Sergeant William Walker of the 21st U.S. Colored Infantry had his men lay down their arms in protest over unequal pay. He was convicted of mutiny and executed.

Continuing Controversies

How were African Americans in the military treated after the Civil War?

The U.S. army eradicated the two-tier pay scale, but not racial segregation. African American leaders protested segregation, but for all subsequent wars through World War II, black soldiers and sailors served in segregated units under mostly white officers. President Harry Truman ordered the military desegregated in 1948.

Why did Lincoln initially agree to pay African American soldiers less than white soldiers?

continued loss of Southern territory to the Union Army only exacerbated this trend. So too did a sharp rise in desertions, which topped a hundred thousand by late 1864.

By mid-1863 the inherent weaknesses of the Confederate economy began to show. The Union blockade of the Southern coastline, which had stopped only one in eight Confederate ships in 1862, grew increasingly effective. By 1864 it stopped one out of every three Confederate blockade-runners and half of them by 1865. Increasingly, Confederate blockade-runners were forced to ply ever riskier waters, leading to wrecks such as this one (**13.15**) off the coast of South Carolina. The impact on the import-dependent Southern economy was devastating. Civilians and soldiers alike suffered shortages of food, clothing, and equipment.

The growing success of the Union blockade also exposed a critical miscalculation made by the Davis administration in 1861. The embargo on cotton exports failed because England possessed a surplus of cotton in 1861 and later found alternative sources of cotton in Egypt and India. Moreover English workers, including an estimated 500,000 thrown out of work due to cotton shortages, expressed strong sympathy for the Union and thereby made British intervention on behalf of the Confederacy politically impossible. When the South finally lifted the embargo in 1862, the Union blockade was stronger and the price of cotton had fallen.

The Emancipation Proclamation also shook Southern society, as Lincoln had hoped it would. Inspired by word that freedom was at hand, thousands of slaves left their places of bondage and headed for the Union Army or to the Northern states, exacerbating the Confederacy's labor shortage and further weakening Southern agriculture.

Despite these hardships, the Confederacy remained undefeated. The Confederacy would not likely surrender solely due to hunger, exhaustion, and inflation. Indeed the longer they defended their independence, the greater their chances of success. Even as the Union won major victories at Gettysburg and Vicksburg, discontent and war weariness among Northerners grew. If Lincoln was to preserve the Union, he needed military victories—and soon.

> "The state of despondency that now prevails among our people is producing a bad effect upon the troops. Desertions are becoming very frequent."
>
> ROBERT E. LEE, February 24, 1865

Victory in Battle and at the Polls

The key to winning the war, Lincoln realized, was effective military leadership. After suffering many disappointments and near disasters with a succession of poor generals, Lincoln finally found his man in Ulysses S. Grant who at the end of 1863 delivered yet another badly needed victory for the Union at the Battle of Chattanooga.

On November 23 Grant and the general he increasingly counted on, William T. Sherman, drove General Braxton Bragg's army from Tennessee into Georgia, putting most of eastern Tennessee and the vital Tennessee River under Union control. Already cut in two after the fall of Vicksburg, the Confederates now faced the prospect of

13.15 The Blockade Tightens Ineffective at first, the Union blockade of the Confederate coast eventually grew strong enough to force blockade runners to take risky routes that often ended in disasters like this one off Sullivan's Island in South Carolina in 1865.

What impact did the Union blockade have on the Confederate war effort?

being sliced into thirds. Their main hope was that growing Northerner dissatisfaction with the war might lead to Lincoln's defeat in the election of 1864, or at least force him to accept peace negotiations.

In early 1864 Lincoln named Grant commander of all the Union armies. He did so over the objections of many in the War Department, who argued that the rough-hewn soldier who had left the Army in disgrace in 1854 for heavy drinking was an alcoholic who could not be entrusted with a major assignment. But Lincoln had seen enough of generals with impressive résumés and martial airs. He saw in Grant a commander who understood the key to victory in modern warfare—seek out and destroy the enemy's army.

Grant pursued this policy with single-minded determination. In his Virginia Campaign of 1864, he planned a two-pronged attack to finish off the Confederacy. As shown in the map (**13.16**), he would send the Army of the Potomac, now swollen to nearly 120,000, south to destroy Lee's army of 66,000 and take Richmond. General William T. Sherman, a man who shared Grant's understanding of modern warfare, would take an army of 90,000 from Tennessee and push east to destroy General Joseph E. Johnston's force of 60,000 and seize Atlanta (**13.17**).

The first clash of this campaign, the Battle of the Wilderness, began with Lee attacking Grant on May 5. Over the next two days, aided by the rough, wooded terrain and sluggish Union leadership, the Confederates successfully survived the clash with Grant's vastly superior numbers. The inconclusive battle left eighteen thousand federals and ten thousand Confederates killed, wounded or missing. Normally after so great an engagement Union commanders pulled back and spent weeks, if not months, repairing their armies. But Grant was not like his predecessors. The next day he ordered his army to move against Lee. Possessing total confidence in his overall strategy, he also knew that, unlike Lee, he could replace his fallen soldiers. On May 8 the two armies clashed again, ten miles closer to Richmond in the Battle of Spotsylvania Court House, an epic

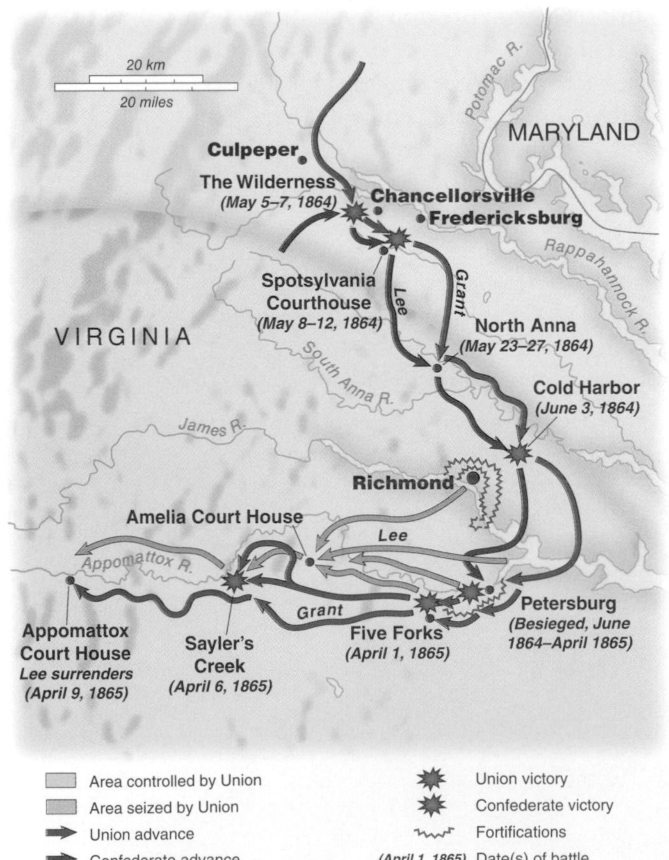

13.16 The Final Battles in Virginia Campaign, 1864–1865
Grant's strategy for defeating Lee was to combine superior strength and a relentless offensive. It resulted in extremely high casualties, but eventually cornered Lee at Petersburg. Lee surrendered at nearby Appomattox Courthouse on April 9, 1865.

13.17 Sherman's March to the Sea, 1864–1865
Sherman dealt a decisive blow to the Confederate cause by waging a scorched-earth campaign across Georgia, destroying vital supplies and weakening Southern morale.

What distinguished Grant's approach to war from his predecessors'?

struggle that played out for days and left another thirty thousand casualties between the two armies.

Still Grant remained resolute, driving the Union Army southward, trying to draw Lee out for a final, decisive battle. Lee kept his army between Grant and Richmond, playing for time and avoiding total defeat. On June 3 at Cold Harbor, Grant again ordered a massive assault against Lee's smaller but heavily entrenched force. The result was the greatest loss of life since Fredericksburg. Many Northerners, appalled at the fifty-five thousand Union casualties (to thirty thousand Confederate) in a single month, questioned Grant's competence; others simply called him a butcher. Peace Democrats renewed their calls for an end to the conflict.

Grant quickly changed his strategy. He moved his army south past Richmond to seize the vital railroad junction at Petersburg and cut Richmond off from the rest of the Confederacy. But Lee kept his exhausted army on the move and managed to dig in around Petersburg just before Grant arrived. By now Grant recognized the futility of staging frontal assaults against entrenched troops and settled down for a prolonged siege. It was not the aggressive form of warfare he preferred, but the fall of Petersburg and Richmond seemed only a matter of time.

Rising popular dissatisfaction with the seemingly endless bloodshed in the summer of 1864, however, imperiled Lincoln's chances for reelection (his counterpart, Davis, was serving a six-year term). Democrats tried to capitalize on the dour mood by nominating former Union General George B. McClellan for president and issuing a platform calling for a cease-fire and peace conference. They also hoped McClellan's outspoken criticism of Lincoln's emancipation policy would draw votes from racist Northerners.

The Republican Party recognized its vulnerability (it lost many seats in the 1862 congressional elections) and took several steps to broaden its appeal heading into the 1864 election. First, Republicans adopted the name Union Party, a symbolic gesture intended to draw support from pro-war Democrats. Second, they replaced Lincoln's vice president with Senator Andrew Johnson of Tennessee, a pro-Union Democrat and the only Southern senator not to resign during the secession winter of 1861. Finally, as this campaign broadside (**13.18**) illustrates, Lincoln's campaign argued that a vote for McClellan was a vote for slavery and military defeat. While Lincoln shakes hands with an artisan (representing the "free labor" North), McClellan shakes hands with Jefferson Davis who stands beneath the flag of an independent Confederate nation. Behind Lincoln white and black children enjoy the benefits of freedom and education, while the background scene to McClellan shows a slave auction. As late as August 1864, however, Lincoln and many of his supporters fully expected him to lose.

In early September 1864, however, Lincoln received welcome news that Grant's counterpart in the West, Sherman, had captured Atlanta on September 2. This crushing blow all but doomed the Confederacy to collapse. It also boosted morale across the North and weakened the peace strategy of the Democrats. Two months later Lincoln soundly defeated McClellan, winning every state except for Kentucky, New Jersey, and Delaware to garner 55 percent of the popular vote. Still his margin of victory—just 10 percent—demonstrated just how essential military success was to political victory.

War Is Hell

Six weeks after Lincoln won reelection, Sherman began to march his army across the state of Georgia (see 13.16b) to deprive the Confederate Army of badly needed supplies and to demoralize the Southern people. Simultaneously, he sent a force under General George H. Thomas that all but destroyed the Confederate army under General John B. Hood at the Battle of Nashville (December 15–16, 1864). One week later, Sherman's army captured Savannah.

Known as **Sherman's March to the Sea**, the "scorched earth" campaign traversed 285 miles

13.18 Lincoln Promises Victory and Union Lincoln's 1864 presidential campaign suggested that while he stood for liberty, his opponent, Democrat George B. McClellan, would make peace with the Confederates and preserve slavery.

What steps did the Republican Party take to improve Lincoln's chances for victory in 1864?

across Georgia. Sherman's soldiers lived off the land, taking what agricultural produce and livestock they could use and destroying the rest. They also destroyed Southern infrastructure, tearing up railroad tracks, burning bridges, and pulling down telegraph wires to impair the Confederacy's ability to move goods, soldiers, and information. Sherman's army caused additional damage to the Southern economy by enticing thousands of slaves to leave their masters and flock to its camps. By the time they reached the coast, Sherman's men left a 60-mile-wide swath of destruction that cost the Confederate army a major source of supplies. More important, the campaign demonstrated the effectiveness of a tactic that would become central to modern warfare in the twentieth century: bringing the conflict to the civilian population to undermine its willingness to continue supporting the war. "We are not only fighting hostile armies," Sherman told his men, "but a hostile people, and we must make old and young, rich and poor, feel the hand of war, as well as their organized armies."

"If slaves make good soldiers our whole theory of slavery is wrong."
CONFEDERATE MAJOR GENERAL HOWELL COBB, Georgia

Sherman compounded the horror felt by the citizens of Georgia with his policy toward the state's freed slaves. After a January meeting with Secretary of War Edwin Stanton and twenty African American ministers to discuss the fate of the freed slaves, Sherman issued **Special Field Order No. 15**. This directive set aside more than 400,000 acres of seized Confederate land for distribution to former slaves in 40-acre plots. Congress soon followed with the Thirteenth Amendment, which abolished slavery everywhere in the United States (it would be ratified eleven months later).

With Georgia now in ashes, the stage was set for the final phase of Grant's plan—the crushing of Lee's army between his and Sherman's forces. On February 1 Sherman left Savannah and headed north into the heart of South Carolina. He faced almost no opposition, a sign Southern resistance had begun to disintegrate. As this photograph (**13.19**) indicates, fire destroyed more than half of Columbia, the state capital of South Carolina. Evacuating Confederates and liberated slaves set some of the fires, but some were also started by Union soldiers motivated by vengeance against the state that for decades leading up to the war represented Southern nationalism and ultimately, secession. Sherman's men kept moving northward into North Carolina where the meager opposition provided by General Joseph E. Johnston's force slowed him only slightly.

As the situation grew critical for the Confederacy, its leaders tried several desperate measures. Among them were secret peace negotiations held in February 1865 at Hampton Roads, Virginia, which failed: Union representatives insisted on unconditional surrender (with gradual and compensated emancipation), while their Southern counterparts demanded recognition of Confederate independence. Confederate officials also began drafting soldiers as young as 17 and as old as 50. The depth of Confederate desperation was revealed in March 1865 when the Confederate Congress authorized a draft of up to 300,000 slaves to serve as soldiers (two regiments raised in Richmond never saw combat).

13.19 Total War and Vengeance Fires set by retreating Confederates, freed slaves, and undisciplined members of Sherman's army left half of Columbia, South Carolina, in ruins.

Why did Sherman deem it necessary to destroy so much property in Georgia?

By now Grant's nearly nine-month-long siege of Lee's army at Petersburg began to take its toll. Cut off from supplies, Lee's men were starving. Thousands had deserted. On April 1 in the Battle of Five Forks, General Philip Sheridan's cavalry and a large force of infantry attacked Lee's right flank and cut off the only remaining railroad line into Petersburg. When Grant attacked all along the Confederate line the next day, he forced Lee to retreat from both Richmond and Petersburg. Lee's remaining hope was to slip his ragged army west and south to join forces with Johnston in North Carolina. To prevent this Grant dispatched Sheridan's cavalry, which headed them off at a small town named Appomattox Courthouse, Virginia. On April 8 Lee made one last attempt to break out, but failed. "There is nothing left for me to do," Lee sadly informed his officers, "and I would rather die a thousand deaths." The next day, April 9, 1865, Lee surrendered.

Lincoln had set a tone of reconciliation in his second inaugural address a month earlier. Accordingly, Grant gave generous terms. The thirty thousand men in Lee's army were permitted to go home, providing they swore never again to take up arms against the federal government. Grant also ordered they be given three days' rations of food and stopped his men from firing their weapons in victory celebration. Over the next few weeks, the remaining armies of the Confederacy would surrender, bringing the Civil War to a close.

Celebrations broke out all across the North as people, weary of four years of war, reveled in both the victory and the peace. The exultation quickly changed to despair. On the night of April 14, just five days after Lee's surrender, Confederate sympathizer John Wilkes Booth shot Lincoln at close range as he watched a play at Ford's Theatre in Washington. Lincoln died in the early morning hours of the following day. The news of the tragedy elicited an enormous outpouring of grief for the martyred president among citizens of the North and freed slaves in the South. After a somber funeral procession in Washington, a train carried Lincoln's body back to Springfield, Illinois, past some seven million people who lined the tracks.

In the coming weeks the last vestiges of the Confederate rebellion ended. On April 26 Sherman accepted Johnston's surrender in North Carolina. Others followed suit, with the last Confederate units laying down their arms on June 23. Lincoln's assassin, John Wilkes Booth, was cornered and killed by federal troops on April 26. On May 10 Jefferson Davis, who had fled hoping to establish a new Confederate government in Texas, was captured and cast in prison. As this image (**13.20**) shows, the popular anger over the war and Lincoln's assassination focused on Davis, with many Northerners demanding his execution for treason. Passions eventually cooled, however, and Davis was released from prison after two years, never to be brought to trial.

13.20 **A Thirst for Vengeance**
In the aftermath of the war many Northerners called for Jefferson Davis and other high-ranking Confederates to be hanged as traitors.

Conclusion

When the Civil War began, both sides expected that they would emerge victorious in a few months. But the conflict lasted four years, claiming more than 618,000 lives, and leaving the South in total subjugation. It also emancipated some four million slaves. Despite these unanticipated outcomes, the war did settle three key long-standing questions. First, it established the supremacy of federal authority over state sovereignty. Second, the war answered with a firm no the question of whether a state possessed the right to secede. Finally, it resolved the question of whether slavery would persist in a nation founded on the principle that "all men are created equal."

But in answering these key questions, the Civil War raised additional ones that would prove equally vexing and divisive. What was the status of the now defeated ex-Confederate states? How would they be restored to full membership in the Union? What was the civil and legal status of the freedmen? How far would the federal government go in protecting their freedom and rights?

What conciliatory measures toward the Confederates did Grant adopt at Lee's surrender?

CHAPTER REVIEW

1861

First Battle of Bull Run
Confederacy wins in a clash of inexperienced armies

Confederate diplomats removed from the British ship *Trent*
Nearly causes a war between the Union and Great Britain

1862

Gen. Grant captures Forts Henry and Donelson in Tennessee
Boosts Union morale and brings attention to Grant's military skill

Lee repulses McClellan's Peninsular Campaign
Exposes again the poor military leadership in the Union Army

1862

McClellan defeats Lee at Battle of Antietam
Victory allows Lincoln to issue the Emancipation Proclamation

Lee defeats Union General Ambrose Burnside at Battle of Fredericksburg
Northern morale, boosted after Antietam, sags once again

Review Questions

1. What advantages did the Confederacy possess that allowed it to enjoy considerable military success in the early years of the war?
2. Why did both North and South consider the Border States vital to their success in the war?
3. What new technologies emerged during the war and how did they affect its character and outcome?
4. How did African Americans contribute to emancipation?
5. What was the basis of the criticisms leveled at Abraham Lincoln by his critics in the North, including the Copperheads? How did he respond?
6. In what ways did the war change Northern society? How did it change the federal government?
7. What approach to warfare set Generals Ulysses S. Grant and William T. Sherman apart from less successful Union military leaders?
8. How did social, economic, and class differences in Southern society eventually contribute to the Confederacy's defeat?

1863

Lee defeats Hooker at the Battle of Chancellorsville
Confederate victory is offset by death of Gen. Thomas "Stonewall" Jackson

Meade defeats Lee at Battle of Gettysburg
Turning point in the war, ends the Confederate gamble of invading the North

Clement Vallandigham arrested
Prompts outrage from Copperheads but Lincoln defends action as necessary to win the war

NOW IN CAMP AT READVILLE!
54th REGIMENT!
AFRICAN DESCENT
Col. ROBERT G. SHAW.

1863

Grant seizes Vicksburg
Entire length of Mississippi River under Union control, severing the Confederacy in two

Bread riots break out in Confederacy. Draft Riots erupt in New York City
Reveal growing discontent over the cost and duration of the war

The 54th Massachusetts participates in attack on Fortress Wagner
Their courage undermines the belief that African Americans will make poor soldiers

1864

Grant defeats Lee in the Battles of the Wilderness, Spotsylvania, and Cold Harbor
Lee's army digs in at Petersburg near Richmond; Grant begins siege

Union General William T. Sherman captures Atlanta
Sherman begins his "March to the Sea," destroying Georgian agriculture and infrastructure

Lincoln wins reelection
Ensures the Union war effort will continue

1865

Thirteenth Amendment passed
Abolishes slavery (ratified late 1865)

Grant captures Petersburg and Richmond
Lee surrenders, ending the war

Lincoln assassinated by John Wilkes Booth
Lincoln becomes a martyr figure

Key Terms

Border States The four slave states, Missouri, Kentucky, Maryland, and Delaware, that bordered the Confederacy. The Lincoln administration succeeded in keeping them in the Union. **379**

cotton embargo A ban imposed by Confederates in 1861 on the export of cotton, the South's most valuable commodity, to prompt cotton-importing nations like England and France to intervene to secure Confederate independence. **380**

Trent Affair A diplomatic incident in November 1861 when a U.S. Navy vessel stopped the British ship *Trent* and removed two Confederates heading for Europe to press for British and French intervention. **380**

Peninsular Campaign The complex plan developed by General George B. McClellan to capture the Confederate capital, whereby four hundred ships deposited 120,000 soldiers just east of Richmond at Fortress Monroe between the James and York Rivers. **382**

modern warfare Military conflict involving enormous armies that utilize the technologies of the Industrial Revolution in the areas of communications, transportation, and firearms. Victory is secured by destroying the enemy's army and inflicting suffering on civilian populations. **383**

contraband of war The term introduced by General Benjamin Butler to justify his refusal to return fugitive slaves to their owners because they were seized property. **384**

Emancipation Proclamation The decree announced by Lincoln in September 1862 and taking effect on January 1, 1863, declaring slaves in the seceded states not under Union army control "forever free." **385**

Copperheads Northern Democrats (sometimes called "Peace Democrats") who opposed the war and the Lincoln administration and favored a negotiated settlement with the Confederacy. **390**

Conscription Act A law passed by Congress in March 1863 to offset declining volunteers to the Union Army. It declared all male citizens (and immigrants who had applied for citizenship) aged twenty to forty-five eligible to be drafted into the Union Army. The rich could pay a $300 fee to avoid the draft. **390**

Draft Riots Four days of rioting in New York City in July 1863 by mostly poor, immigrant, and working-class men who opposed the draft. **392**

Sherman's March to the Sea The 285-mile "scorched earth" campaign of General William T. Sherman across Georgia in late 1864 and early 1865. Sherman's soldiers seized or destroyed $100 million in goods, hurting Southern morale and depriving the Confederate army of supplies. **399**

Special Field Order No. 15 The directive announced by General Sherman in January 1865 during his March to the Sea that set aside more than 400,000 acres of seized Confederate land for distribution to former slaves in 40-acre plots. **400**

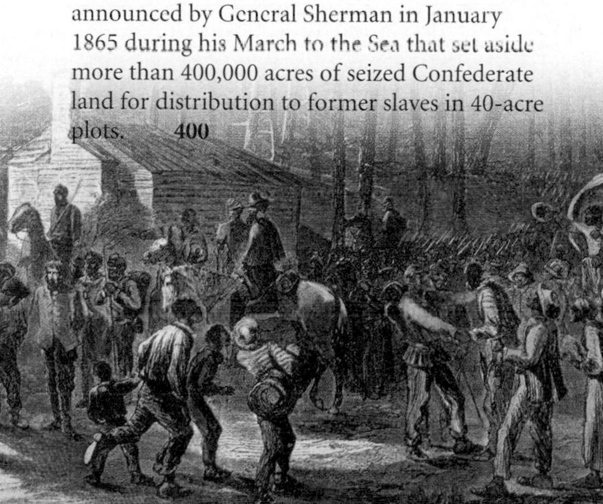

CHAPTER 14

Now That We Are Free

Reconstruction and the New South, 1863–1890

Preparing for Reconstruction p. 406

The Fruits of Freedom p. 409

> "Never before had I a word of impudence from any of our black folk, but they are not ours any longer."
>
> SUSAN BRADFORD, observing the defiant attitude among former slaves on her Florida plantation, 1865

The Civil War ended in April 1865, concluding the bloodiest and most divisive conflict in American history. The period that followed came to be known as Reconstruction for several reasons. Most obviously, the name called to mind the need to rebuild the war-torn South. It also referred to the effort to reestablish the Union torn apart by secession. Finally, it indicated the need to remake Southern society in the wake of slavery's destruction.

The complexities and challenges of this last goal are evident in Winslow Homer's 1876 painting, *A Visit from the Old Mistress,* which depicts ex-slaves being visited by their former owner. The elegant clothing worn by the "Old Mistress" suggests she has money, but clearly the relationship between the women has changed significantly in the wake of emancipation. To begin with, the mistress has come to visit the former slaves in their home, suggesting a diminishing of her status and power relative to them. The scene also lacks any sense of the affection that plantation owners always assured themselves existed between slaves and masters. Indeed, the three African American women eye the mistress warily. One of them even chooses to remain seated in what surely would have been considered a show of contempt. The old order was gone, but what would replace it remained unclear in the aftermath of the war.

Americans entered the Reconstruction period facing the profound questions raised by war and emancipation. Was it possible for whites and former slaves to live together in peace and mutual respect? What rights were the freedmen entitled to and who would guarantee these rights? The different answers articulated by freedmen and white Southerners revealed sharply divergent visions of the future and led to a bitter struggle to define the meaning of freedom. "Verily," observed ex-slave Frederick Douglass, "the work does not end with the abolition of slavery, but only begins."

How does this image reveal the uncertainty of race relations in the postwar South?

The Struggle to Define Reconstruction p. 412

Implementing Reconstruction p. 418

Reconstruction Abandoned p. 423

The New South p. 428

Preparing for Reconstruction

Long before the Emancipation Proclamation took effect on January 1, 1863 countless thousands of enslaved Africans took advantage of the chaos produced by the war to liberate themselves. Their actions raised a host of questions about what rights the freedmen would be entitled to, including land ownership and voting. Lincoln and his advisers preferred to wait until the war's successful conclusion before addressing these questions, but actions taken by the freedmen to assert their rights and secure their liberty forced the Lincoln administration to develop policies during the war that ultimately shaped postwar Reconstruction.

Emancipation Test Cases

Even before the Emancipation Proclamation took effect, the federal government realized that it needed to enact policies regarding the growing numbers of freedmen in areas of the South occupied by the Union army. These policies varied by region and were shaped by local customs and the attitudes of freedmen and white officials. As such, they amounted to test cases for the coming debate over Reconstruction. Three of these test cases revealed both the promise and the contentious conflict surrounding emancipation.

The first test case began when federal forces seized the Sea Islands off the coast of South Carolina in November 1861. They found a vast system of cotton plantations, but no planters. The latter had fled, leaving behind ten thousand slaves, who moved quickly to establish new lives based on their understanding of freedom. While clearly posed, "Planting Sweet Potatoes" (**14.1**), shot by a New Hampshire photographer visiting a regiment from his state stationed on the island, captured one fundamental way in which ex-slaves expressed their freedom. Rejecting cotton, a crop they associated with slavery, they planted crops of their own choosing, such as sweet potatoes and corn for local consumption. Freedom for the African Americans of the Sea Islands meant a future as independent farmers living free of white control.

Many Northern whites who arrived after the military takeover, however, brought with them a very different vision of the future for the Sea Islands. Convinced that Sea Island blacks should resume their labors on cotton plantations—not as slaves but as paid wage earners—federal officials opted not to grant land to the freedmen and instead auctioned it off to the highest bidder. Northern investors bought most of the land, hired freedmen as wage laborers, and resumed cotton cultivation. This vision was

14.1 Freedmen in the Sea Islands Cultivating Sweet Potatoes, 1862
Most freedmen refused to grow cotton, considering it a symbol of slavery. They grew sweet potatoes and other crops, such as corn, primarily for their own consumption. [*Source*: Collection of The New-York Historical Society, [37628]]

How did freedmen define freedom in the Sea Islands?

driven in part by the sincere belief that subsistence farming on small tracts of land was backward, harmful to the long-term interests of the freedmen and also by the racist notion that African Americans were not capable of handling their freedom responsibly and therefore needed white employers to guide them.

A second test case unfolded on Davis Bend, the Mississippi plantations owned by Confederate President Jefferson Davis and his brother Joseph. Before the Civil War, they had tried to make Davis Bend a model slave labor community where slaves received better food and were granted a high degree of autonomy. The Davis brothers hoped other planters would follow their example and thus refute the abolitionist argument that slavery was inhumane. Instead, Davis Bend became a model of a very different sort of ideal, one that vividly demonstrated what freedmen were capable of achieving if granted land and autonomy. When General Ulysses S. Grant arrived and found the former slaves running the plantations, he ordered federal officials to lease land to the freedmen. Unlike the freedmen of the Sea Islands, the African American residents of Davis Bend did not have to contend with Northerners seeking to reassert white control over the land and impose a wage labor system. As a consequence, by 1865 Davis Bend residents had established their own local government and cleared a profit of $160,000 in cotton sales.

A third and far larger test case for emancipation policy began in Louisiana and was eventually extended up the Mississippi Valley affecting some 700,000 former slaves. Soon after Union forces seized New Orleans in April 1862, army officers established a policy to guide the transition from slavery to emancipation. As in the case of the Sea Islands, the policy reflected the racist belief among Northern whites that African Americans could not responsibly handle their freedom and therefore needed strict rules regarding conduct and work. Blacks were required to remain on their plantations, working as wage laborers bound by one-year contracts. Those wishing to travel, even for short distances, required a pass from the plantation owner. Runaways and resisters, as depicted in this 1864 drawing (**14.2**), would be forcibly returned to their plantations. Offsetting these harsh provisions was a ban on the use of corporal punishment for plantation labor. Freedmen bitterly

14.2 Freedmen Forcibly Returned to Their Plantations, 1864 Violators of the Reconstruction plan were deemed "vagrants" and forcibly returned to their plantations.

Why did Union officials define freedom for former slaves so narrowly in Louisiana?

opposed the new system, arguing that it placed them in a nearly powerless position under the authority of their former masters. In New Orleans, home to the South's largest free black population before the war, African Americans began to demand equal rights for all freedmen, including the right to vote and hold office. Although their efforts failed, they sparked a national debate over freedmen's rights that would come to dominate Reconstruction.

The experiences in the Sea Islands, Davis Bend, Louisiana, and elsewhere during the war created a host of conflicting visions regarding the rights of freedmen, land redistribution, and the authority of ex-slave owners. Yet the emancipation experience also revealed the optimism of the freedmen and their commitment to defend their newly won freedom and make the most of it.

Lincoln's Ten Percent Plan

Even as the Civil War raged, President Lincoln had begun to formulate an official Reconstruction policy. A moderate on the big issues before the war, Lincoln proposed a moderate Reconstruction policy. As he suggested so eloquently in his second inaugural address, he intended to deal with the defeated South "with malice toward none" and "charity for all" to "achieve and cherish a just and lasting peace among ourselves. . . ." He believed that extending lenient terms to the South would convince Confederates to surrender sooner and speed the healing process necessary for the good of the Union. Vengeance, he held, would only delay Reconstruction. It might even inspire defeated Confederate soldiers to form renegade bands of insurgents to wage a war of terrorism for years to come.

> "A more studied outrage on the legislative authority of the people has never been perpetuated."
>
> Wade-Davis Manifesto denouncing Lincoln's veto of the Wade-Davis Bill

In December of 1863 Lincoln issued his Proclamation of Amnesty and Reconstruction, also known as the **Ten Percent Plan.** Intended to establish Southern state governments, the plan pardoned all Southerners (except high-ranking military officers and Confederate officials) who took an oath pledging loyalty to the Union and support for emancipation. As soon as ten percent of a state's voters took this oath, they could call a convention, establish a new state government, and apply for congressional recognition.

Radical Republicans Offer a Different Vision

The lenient character of Lincoln's plan enraged many Radical Republicans. In July of 1864 Radical Republican leaders Senator Benjamin Wade of Ohio and Congressman Henry W. Davis of Maryland cosponsored the **Wade-Davis Bill,** a Reconstruction program designed to punish Confederate leaders and permanently destroy the South's slave society. Southerners could reestablish new state governments only after a majority of a state's voters signed an "ironclad" oath declaring they never aided the Confederate army or government. Southerners who did serve as high-ranking army officers or government officials would be stripped of their citizenship, including the right to vote and hold office. The former Confederate states would be readmitted only after a lengthy period of punishment and a clear demonstration of their commitment to the Union, emancipation, and freedmen's rights.

Lincoln quietly pocket vetoed the bill. Undaunted, Wade, Davis, and other Radicals mounted a movement to replace Lincoln as the Republican Party presidential nominee. Although the effort failed, it exposed the deeply divided opinions regarding Reconstruction policy.

Lincoln and his fellow Republicans did manage to find common ground on two issues. In late January 1865, at the urging of Lincoln's administration, Congress passed the Thirteenth Amendment, abolishing slavery. The measure ended any ambiguity that had surrounded the Emancipation Proclamation, abolishing slavery everywhere in the United States and offering no compensation to former slaveholders. Twenty-seven states, including eight former Confederate states, would ratify the amendment by year's end.

In March Congress established the Bureau of Refugees, Freedmen, and Abandoned Lands. Known simply as the **Freedmen's Bureau,** it was to serve as an all-purpose relief agency in the war-ravaged South, providing emergency services, building schools, and managing confiscated lands. It represented the first attempt by the federal government to provide social welfare services and quickly became the bedrock institution for implementing Reconstruction policy.

What advantages did Lincoln see in proposing a moderate Reconstruction policy?

The Fruits of Freedom

Many Southerners were stunned by the response of their slaves to freedom. Clinging to self-serving paternalistic notions of the plantation as one big family under the benign authority of the master and planter, they were taken aback when their slaves refused to obey their orders or exhibited anger or disrespect toward them. Susan Bradford, a young woman living on a Florida plantation, wrote in her diary that she was "hurt and dazed" when one of her former slaves refused to prepare a dinner for her mother. "Tell her if she want any dinner," sneered the free woman, "she kin cook it herself." "I believed that these people were content, happy, and attached to their masters," wrote one South Carolina planter in 1865, unable to comprehend why slaves abandoned their masters "in [their] moment of need." It would be the first of many such shocking experiences for whites, who never imagined that slavery might one day be abolished.

INFORMATION WANTED

OF A MAN BY THE NAME OF ELIAS LOWERY McDERMIT, who used to belong to Thomas Lyons, of Knoxville, East Tennessee. He was sold to a man by the name of Sherman about ten years ago, and I learned some six years ago that he was on a steamboat running between Memphis and New Orleans, and more recently I heard that he was somewhere on the Cumberland river, in the Federal army. Any information concerning him will be thankfully received. Address Colored Tennessean, Nashville, Tenn. From his sister who is now living in Knoxville, East Tennessee.

je24-1m] MARTHA McDERMIT.

SAML. DOVE wishes to know of the whereabouts of his mother, Areno, his sisters Maria, Neziah, and Peggy, and his brother Edmond, who were owned by Geo. Dove, of Rockingham county, Shenandoah Valley, Va. Sold in Richmond, after which Saml. and Edmond were taken to Nashville, Tenn., by Joe Mick; Areno was left at the Eagle Tavern, Richmond

Respectfully yours,

SAML. DOVE.

Utica, New York, Aug. 5, 1865–3m

U. S. Christian Commission,
Nashville, Tenn., July 19, 1865.

14.3 Freedmen Searching for Loved Ones Sold Away during Slavery These classified advertisements in the August 12, 1865 *Colored Tennessean* were just two of thousands published in mainly black-owned newspapers during Reconstruction. They vividly highlight the efforts of freedmen to overcome one of slavery's harshest legacies. [*Source*: Chicago History Museum]

Freedom of Movement

Even before the guns of the Civil War went silent, African Americans had begun to explore the meaning of their freedom and formulate their own vision of a reconstructed postwar South, both of which included unrestricted mobility. Under slavery, movement was sharply limited, and few slaves ventured very far from their plantations. In the chaos of war and later with official emancipation, African Americans hit the road. Many did so to get away from the plantations that were home to their former masters and countless bitter memories. Others simply reveled in the idea of free and unfettered movement. They wandered for the pleasure of it with no particular destination in mind. As these advertisements (**14.3**) from the *Colored Tennessean,* Tennessee's only African American–owned newspaper, indicate, many freedmen also journeyed in search of loved ones sold away years before.

African American mobility led to a sharp rise in the black population of Southern cities. In contrast to rural life, black settlements in cities offered more and varied job opportunities, albeit nearly always menial, difficult, and low paid. Urban life also provided freedmen access to strong black institutions such as churches, charities, and newspapers.

Southern whites reacted to black mobility with a mixture of alarm and disdain. Just as former slaves equated freedom with mobility, their former masters saw in it a shocking reminder that the old order was gone. Not surprisingly, one of the first expressions of white Southern resistance to black freedom was the passage of vagrancy laws intended to restrict African American mobility.

Forty Acres and a Mule

In addition to exercising their right to move about freely, many freedmen also tried to become landowners. If travel was a symbolic expression of their new freedom, land was freedom in concrete form. Land, the freedmen believed, would give freedom meaning by providing an independent living, free of planter control.

The idea that freedmen would receive land in addition to their freedom originated during the war. As Southerners abandoned their plantations before the advance of the Union army, ex-slaves often took control, partitioned land, and planted crops. Freedmen defended these extralegal actions as simple justice, citing the generations of unpaid labor that they and their ancestors had performed on Southern farms and plantations. "The property which they [former slaveholders] hold," asserted a freedmen's convention, "was nearly all earned by the sweat of our brows."

In early 1865 General William T. Sherman issued Field Order No. 15, supplanting these acts of unofficial confiscation. Having laid waste to the Confederate southeast, Sherman announced that 400,000 acres of abandoned land stretching from northern Florida to the South Carolina Sea Islands would be distributed to freedman in 40-acre plots. Weeks later Congress established the Freedmen's Bureau, authorizing it to rent 40-acre plots of confiscated and abandoned land, along with a mule, to freedmen. By June some forty thousand freedmen were living on Sherman lands while thousands more

Why did freedmen believe they were owed land?

> "Give us our own land and we take care of ourselves; but without land, the old masters can hire or starve us, as they please."
>
> A South Carolina freedman speaking to a Northern journalist, 1865

began renting plots under control of the Freedmen's Bureau. African Americans and Radical Republicans hoped to see this program of land redistribution, popularly known as "forty acres and a mule," enacted across the South. Before long, however, their optimism would give way to bitter disappointment.

Regardless of whether they owned or worked their land or worked as farm laborers for wages, African Americans used their freedom to change the way they worked. They often refused to work in gangs under overseers because it reminded them of slavery. Instead they preferred working independently, under the direction of elder family members. Many African American women left work in the field in order to work in their homes and care for children.

Uplift through Education

Along with land, freedmen sought education as a necessary guarantee of their freedom. Laws and customs preventing the education of slaves had left most freedmen illiterate. But with the ability to read and write they could conduct their own legal and business affairs, acquire better-paying jobs, read newspapers, and participate more fully in politics.

14.4 ***The Misses Cooke's School Room, Freedman's Bureau,* 1866** The Cooke sisters moved from the North to Richmond, Virginia to run one of hundreds of Freedmen's Bureau schools established across the South.

General O. O. Howard, the first head of the Freedmen's Bureau, shared the freedmen's belief that education should be an essential goal of Reconstruction. Working with a number of charitable societies and African American leaders, the Freedmen's Bureau helped build three thousand schools across the South that by 1870 served 150,000 students of all ages. By 1875 literacy among freedmen jumped from 10 percent to 30 percent.

Initially, most of the teachers in these schools were educated single white women from the North, like the Cooke sisters (**14.4**). Often sponsored by Northern charitable societies, these teachers saw themselves as missionaries dedicated to the uplift of the freedmen. The journal that published this image in 1866, *Frank Leslie's Illustrated Weekly,* shared this vision. Note how the artist depicted the children in spotless attire with all of them focused on their studies.

That the vision of these teachers and their sponsors went beyond merely teaching ex-slaves to read is shown in this image (**14.5**) of a brief biography of African American poet Phillis Wheatley. Published in 1866 by a Boston Christian organization, it demonstrates their effort to instill in freedmen a pride in African American achievement, believing it would aid them in their quest for education and independence.

Still, educating freedmen was no easy job. Southern whites often put up fierce resistance to African American education, especially in more remote areas. One report in 1865 provided a vivid description of the many hardships teachers faced. "Compelled to live on the coarsest diet . . . subjected

THIRD READER. 75

LESSON XXXIX.

bought	pleas-ant	daugh-ter	ap-pear-ance
chalk	char-coal	learn-ing	ea-ger-ness
health	six-teen	al-though	in-ter-est-ing

PHILLIS WHEATLEY.

PHILLIS WHEATLEY, whose likeness is on this page, was brought to this country from Africa in the year 1761. She was then between seven and eight years old. She was bought by Mrs. John Wheatley, a Boston lady, who chose her from a crowd of robust negroes, although she looked feeble and slender, because of her modest appearance and pleasant face.

14.5 Education and Inspiration Some Northern charitable societies, like the Boston Tract Society, published and distributed books to both teach reading and inspire African Americans.

Why did education become such a priority for African Americans?

to the jeers and hatred of her neighbors . . . swamped in mud—the school shed a drip, and her quarters little better; raided occasionally by rebels, her school broken up and herself insulted, banished, or run off."

The Freedmen's Bureau and Northern aid societies also established more than a dozen black colleges, including Howard in Washington, D.C., and Hampton in Virginia. One of the most immediate goals of these new colleges was to train black teachers. By 1870 African American teachers outnumbered white teachers in freedmen's schools. Many freedmen teachers assumed roles as community leaders and many eventually ran for political office. At least seventy former teachers won seats in Southern state legislatures during Reconstruction.

The Black Church

An even greater source of community leadership came from the vast network of black churches established during Reconstruction. Black churches had existed in the South before the Civil War, but most were part of larger white congregations and subject to strict white control. Southern whites usually insisted that white ministers lead black congregations and made certain that preaching never challenged the system of slavery and white domination.

When the war ended, countless African American congregations of Methodists, Baptists, Presbyterians, and other sects separated from white ones. They resented their inferior status in white-controlled churches and longed to practice a more emotional, expressive worship style disdained by whites. Most important, they wanted black clergymen who could address their spiritual and social needs.

Often churches assumed a central place in the lives of freedmen. Religious services provided spiritual and psychological support for blacks' daily struggles. Churches also ran schools and provided charitable services to the community. As this illustration (**14.6**) of a freedmen community at Trent River, North Carolina, demonstrates, African Americans built a church in the center that doubled as a schoolhouse and meeting place. Churches also offered African Americans a degree of self-government. Members of the congregation were elected to serve as trustees and on committees overseeing many aspects of parish life and budget management. African American women, in particular, filled numerous roles in planning and managing activities, raising money, and running programs such as temperance societies. Like their white counterparts, African American churches also sponsored countless initiatives, such as burial societies, fraternal organizations, drama clubs, and youth groups.

With the church taking so prominent a place in African American life, black ministers, like black teachers, assumed major leadership roles. White hostility convinced most ministers to concentrate on building up their communities from within. Still, many ministers entered politics in an effort to advance the cause of black equality, including more than one hundred ministers elected to Southern state legislatures during Reconstruction. Reverend Richard H. Cain, for example, went to Charleston, South Carolina, in 1865, where he assisted in the reorganization of a black church. Two years later he served as a delegate to the state constitutional convention, followed by terms in the state senate and U.S. House of Representatives.

African Americans' response to emancipation showed that they possessed a clear understanding of freedom. Not simply an end to slavery, freedom meant freedmen's right to free movement and travel, to labor for themselves under conditions of their own choosing, on land granted to them by the government. It meant self-improvement through education and self-help organizations. It meant establishing their own institutions and building their own communities. It also meant full civil and social equality with whites, including the right to vote and hold office.

14.6 ***The Black Church Anchors Freedmen Communities***
African Americans organized thousands of churches across the South to address both their spiritual and their social needs. In the freedmen settlement of Trent River, North Carolina, a simple structure served as a church, school, and meetinghouse (from *Harper's Weekly,* June 9, 1866).

How did the black church become such a vital institution in freedmen communities?

The Struggle to Define Reconstruction

As freedmen in the South worked to define, protect, and extend their freedoms, political leaders in Washington, D.C., debated the best course of action to take in reconstructing the South. The debate revealed sharply divergent visions of the postwar South's social, political, and economic order. Radical Republicans wanted to replace the old slavocracy with a multiracial democracy protected by federal authority. Conservatives sought to limit Reconstruction to granting ex-slaves freedom and opposed proposals to distribute land and to grant full equality to ex-slaves. Moderates held the balance of power in deciding most of these questions, but they lacked a clear vision of the postwar South and made their decisions such as black voting in response to events as they unfolded.

The Conservative Vision of Freedom: Presidential Reconstruction

Andrew Johnson, who assumed the presidency following Lincoln's assassination, was a complicated man. Although he once owned slaves, like many other poor whites from the back country of eastern Tennessee, he grew up deeply suspicious of the planter aristocracy. As a politician, he gained a wide following among poor farmers for his populist criticism of planter power. He opposed secession and was the only senator from a seceding state who did not withdraw from the Senate in early 1861. Lincoln appointed Johnson governor of Tennessee after the state came under Union occupation. In 1864 Republicans sought to appeal to Southern unionism and picked Johnson as Lincoln's vice presidential running mate.

Shortly after assuming the office of president after Lincoln's assassination in April 1865, Johnson indicated that he intended to deal harshly with the South. He spoke of punishing ex-Confederate leaders for their "treason" and indicated an apparent desire to assist the freedmen. Radical Republicans, who shared these views, were thrilled.

Their joy was soon replaced first by despair and then anger. First, despite his harsh antiplanter rhetoric, Johnson held racist views about African Americans and abhorred the notion of black equality. Committed to maintaining white supremacy in the South, Johnson outlined in May 1865 a lenient policy toward the South designed to rapidly reestablish Southern state governments and restore the Union. It offered "amnesty and pardon," including the return of all property, to Southerners who took an oath of allegiance to the Constitution and Union. Former Confederate leaders and wealthy planters possessing more than $20,000 in personal wealth, however, would have to apply to him personally for a pardon.

> "We have turned loose ... four million slaves without a hut to shelter them or a cent in their pockets. ... This Congress is bound to provide for them until they can take care of themselves."
>
> Congressman THADDEUS STEVENS, December 18, 1865

Second, Johnson recognized the reconstructed government of North Carolina and set out the terms for readmitting the remaining ten ex-Confederate states. Johnson would appoint a governor for each state who in turn would call a constitutional convention of elected delegates (chosen by those granted amnesty or pardons). If the convention ratified the Thirteenth Amendment, renounced secession, repudiated all Confederate debts, and held elections for state office and Congress, Johnson would recognize the state as a fully reconstructed member of the Union.

With Congress out of session, Johnson's plan faced little formal opposition. By the fall of 1865, he had granted pardons to all but a small number of planters and high-ranking ex-Confederates. With

What was Andrew Johnson's primary motivation in devising his lenient Reconstruction policy?

these pardons Southerners had restored to them virtually all their lands, including the vast tracts of land that had been set aside in 40-acre plots for freedmen. In December, with all eleven former Confederate states having established new governments under his terms, Johnson announced the Union was restored and Reconstruction was over.

Johnson's actions outraged Northern Republicans, including moderates. In this political cartoon (**14.7**), the artist shows Johnson accepting bags of cash from former Confederates (depicted as the devil) in exchange for a pardon, while a "Pardoned Reconstruction Rebel" in the lower left kills "Union men and freedmen." Three developments in the supposedly "reconstructed" South also stoked Republican discontent. First, many of the state constitutional conventions had failed explicitly to accept the Thirteenth Amendment some even demanded compensation for the financial losses incurred by emancipation. Second, and even more galling, in the state elections in November 1865 Southern voters elected dozens of ex-Confederate officials and army officers. Among them was Alexander Stephens, former vice president of the Confederacy, chosen to represent Georgia in the Senate. Third, new Southern state governments, beginning in late 1865 with Mississippi and South Carolina, passed laws known as **Black Codes** to limit the civil and economic rights of freedmen and create an exploitable workforce. Observing these developments in the eight months since Confederate general Robert E. Lee surrendered, many Northerners wondered if the Civil War had been fought in vain. Had hundreds of thousands died to defeat the Confederacy only to see their leaders quickly resume power? Had slavery been abolished only to be replaced with a similar system of unfree labor?

One of the Mississippi Black Codes of 1865 established the vague charge of "vagrancy"—having

14.7 Johnson's Leniency Angers the North
Johnson's pledge to punish the South ("Treason must be made odious") is ridiculed in this 1866 political cartoon. His sweeping pardons of ex-Confederate leaders and planters and easy terms for readmission of Southern states provoked anger in the North.

Competing Visions

DEMANDING RIGHTS, PROTECTING PRIVILEGE

In the aftermath of the Civil War, one question dominated the minds of Americans North and South: now that slavery was abolished, what would be the status of the freedmen? While newspaper editors, clergymen, and members of Congress debated the issue, white and black Southerners set out to answer the question themselves. As you read the following documents, one from a convention of freedmen and the other from the state legislature of Mississippi, consider the starkly contrasted visions for the future of Southern society. Why do the freedmen feel compelled to say they bear no ill will toward their "former oppressors." Why do Mississippi legislators define vagrancy in such vague terms?

"Address to the Loyal Citizens and Congress of the United States of America," Proceedings of the Convention of the Colored People of Virginia, Held in the City of Alexandria, August 2, 3, 4, 5, 1865.

We, the delegates of the colored people of the State of Virginia … solemnly declaring that we desire to live upon the most friendly and agreeable terms with all men; we feel no ill-will or prejudice toward our former oppressors; are willing and desire to forgive and forget the past, and so shape our future conduct as shall promote our happiness and the interest of the community in which we live …

We must, on the other hand, be allowed to aver and assert that we believe that we have among the white people of this State many who are our most inveterate enemies; who hate us as a class, who feel no sympathy with or for us; who despise us simply because we are black, and more especially, because we have been made free by the power of the United States Government …

We claim, then, as citizens of this State, the laws of the Commonwealth [of Virginia] shall give to all men equal protection; that each and every man may appeal to the law for his equal rights without regard to the color of his skin; and we believe this can only be done by extending the franchise, which we believe to be our inalienable right as freemen, and which the Declaration of Independence guarantees to all free citizens of this Government and which is the privilege of this nation. We claim the right of suffrage:

1st. Because we can see no other safeguard for our protection.

2nd. Because we are citizens of the country and natives of this State.

3rd. Because we are as well qualified to vote who shall be our rulers as many who do vote for that purpose who have no interest in us, and do not know our wants.

Mississippi legislators in December 1865 enacted the first "Black Codes" to limit the freedoms of African Americans. Defining vagrancy in such vague terms allowed white Southerners to arrest freedmen at will and to curtail their freedom of movement. These measures were quickly copied in the remaining ex-Confederate states.

Section 1. All rogues and vagabonds, idle and dissipated persons, … persons who neglect their calling or employment, misspend what they earn, or do not provide for the support of themselves or their families, or dependents shall be deemed and considered vagrants, … and upon conviction thereof shall be fined not exceeding one hundred dollars, with all accruing costs, and be imprisoned … not exceeding ten days. …

Section 5. …In case of any freedman, free negro or mulatto shall fail for five days after the imposition of any or forfeiture upon him or her for violation of any of the provisions of this act to pay the same, that it shall be, and is hereby, made the duty of the sheriff of the proper county to hire out said freedman, free negro or mulatto, to any person who will, for the shortest period of service, pay said fine and forfeiture and all costs …

Colored Men's Convention 1869.

What is significant about the freedmen's use of the term citizen?

no regular home or employment—as a pretext for controlling freedmen. (See *Competing Visions: Demanding Rights, Protecting Privilege.*) Any freedman who hit the road seeking new opportunities could be arrested as a vagrant and fined. If a freedman could not pay his fine, he could be hired out for a period of time to a local plantation owner willing to pay his fine. As this drawing (**14.8**) dramatically shows, in some cases the contracts for such labor were auctioned off to local planters. The artist's intent was to conjure in the minds of Northerners a grim scene reminiscent of a slave auction, suggesting that one of the war's chief accomplishments, emancipation, was being undermined. Some Black Codes required that the children of "vagrant" freedmen be forced to accept apprenticeships that bound them to an employer until age twenty-one. Other stipulations encouraged blacks to sign long-term work contracts as proof of employment. This left them at the mercy of their employers, who were not required to pay them for any work performed if they quit before the contract expired. Other codes included laws restricting freedmen to renting land only in rural areas (to keep them on plantations), prohibiting ministers from preaching without a license, outlawing interracial marriages, and barring blacks from serving on juries.

Congressional Reconstruction and the Fourteenth Amendment

Republicans in Congress, both moderate and Radical, vowed to block Johnson's rapid and lenient Reconstruction program for both idealistic and practical reasons. Excepting emancipation, none of the Republicans' goals for changing Southern society had been accomplished, and the former slavocracy appeared poised to resume power—a result that would lead to the rebirth of the Democratic Party. A slower process of Reconstruction would allow time for the Republican Party to take root in the South, especially if African Americans were granted the right to vote, as many Radicals like Thaddeus Stephens demanded.

The confrontation began in January 1866 when Congress reconvened. Congressional Republicans, led by Sumner and Stephens, refused to admit the senators and representatives from the former Confederate states declared reconstructed by Johnson. Next they established the Joint Committee on

14.8 *The Black Codes in Action* Unable to pay his fine for "vagrancy" as defined in the Black Codes of Florida, a freedman is auctioned off. The high bidder won the right to a freedman's labor for months or years.

How did Black Codes calling for freedmen to sign labor contracts curtail their freedom?

14.9 *Race Riot in Memphis*
White mobs, unrestrained by local police, terrorized the freedmen community in Memphis, Tennessee on May 1–2, 1866, killing forty-six blacks. News of the atrocities, conveyed in images such as this one, stoked Northern public opinion against Johnson's lenient Reconstruction policies.

Reconstruction to investigate conditions in the South. It found widespread evidence of chaos, resistance to Northern authority, and abuse of freedmen's rights.

To counteract Southern resistance and the oppression of freedmen, Congress passed two bills. The first authorized the Freedmen's Bureau to continue operation for two more years. The second, the Civil Rights Bill, went much further. It declared African Americans and all persons born in the United States (except Native Americans) national citizens. It also defined the rights of all citizens regardless of race—for example, the right to sue and to make contracts. Taking direct aim at the Black Codes, the law prohibited state governments from depriving any citizen of these "fundamental rights." Johnson, infuriated at Congress's rejection of his Reconstruction program and determined to thwart efforts to establish racial equality, vetoed both bills.

Although Congress eventually overrode the vetoes and the bills became law, by June 1866 Republicans decided bolder action was necessary. Johnson remained opposed to freedmen's rights, and violence against the freedmen was on the rise in the South. The worst incident, depicted in the image (**14.9**), was a brutal race riot in Memphis, Tennessee, on May 1–2 that left forty-six blacks, most of them Union army veterans, and two whites dead. This drawing appeared in *Harper's Weekly*, a widely read publication that favored freedmen's rights, and was intended to arouse anger in the North over Southern intransigence and support for congressional action. The recently passed Civil Rights Bill was an unprecedented piece of legislation, but its supporters knew that it could easily be overturned by a later Congress. An amendment, on the other hand, became a permanent part of the Constitution.

On June 13, 1866, moderate and Radical Republicans passed the **Fourteenth Amendment** to the Constitution. The Fourteenth Amendment represented a radical redefining of the role of the federal government as the guarantor of individual civil rights. A complex amendment, it contained five

Why did Republicans deem the Fourteenth Amendment necessary so soon after passing the Civil Rights Act?

main provisions. First, it declared all persons born or naturalized in the United States as citizens, a definition that necessarily included all freedmen. Second, all citizens were entitled to "equal protection of the laws" of the states where they lived. Third, states that denied adult male citizens, including African Americans, the right to vote would be penalized by having their representation in Congress reduced. Fourth, all high-ranking former Confederates were prohibited from holding public office, unless pardoned by act of Congress. Fifth, it repudiated the Confederate debt (thus punishing those who lent money to the Confederacy) and denied all claims for compensation by ex–slave owners.

Johnson greeted the unprecedented amendment with an unprecedented response: he went on the campaign trail to urge its defeat. Hoping to make the midterm state and congressional elections in November 1866 a referendum on the amendment, Johnson and his allies played on white racism, conjuring up images of racial equality and racial intermarriage designed to alarm Northern whites. Republicans responded in kind, portraying Johnson and the Democrats as traitors who waged war on the Union. Republicans won a sweeping victory in November. Northern voters, while still leery of racial equality, clearly rejected Johnson's lenient form of Reconstruction because it required too little of Southerners and allowed for the restoration of planter rule.

Radical Republicans Take Control

Emboldened by their legislative and electoral success, congressional Republicans moved to take complete control of Reconstruction policy. In March 1867 Congress passed the first of four Reconstruction Acts. It divided the South (except Tennessee) into five military districts, each governed by a military commander empowered with wide authority to keep order and protect individuals, especially freedmen. As soon as order was established, the ex-Confederate states could begin a new, stricter readmission process. The act called for elections to select delegates to state constitutional conventions—elections that permitted African American men to vote, but barred Southerners who served in the Confederate government and army. The new state constitutions drawn up by these conventions had to allow universal male suffrage, regardless of race. As soon as a state's voters approved the new constitution, the state could hold elections to fill government offices. Finally, if Congress approved the state's constitution and the state legislature ratified the Fourteenth Amendment, the state would be readmitted to the Union.

Fully two years after the end of the Civil War, the federal government had finally adopted a clear Reconstruction plan. The delay was understandable, given Lincoln's assassination and the lack of any precedent. Yet delay granted Southerners time in which to recover from the war and mount an effective resistance to federal intervention.

> "The President has no power to control or influence anybody and legislation will be carried on entirely regardless of his opinion or wishes."
>
> Republican Senator JAMES W. GRIMES, Iowa, January 1867

Passage of the Reconstruction Acts further exacerbated the conflict between President Johnson and congressional Republicans. Johnson promptly vetoed the acts, and Congress passed them again over his veto. Some of the more radical Republicans had grown so embittered by the president's actions and words, they attempted to remove him from office. When Johnson dismissed Secretary of War Stanton in August 1867, Republicans charged him with violating the Tenure of Office Act, a constitutionally questionable measure they had passed back in March. It required the president to seek congressional approval before removing a cabinet official. The House voted to impeach the president, charging him with eleven offenses. The trial began in March 1868 and after two months of heated debate and accusation, the Senate failed—by one vote—to convict Johnson and remove him from office.

Johnson was saved by moderate Republicans who feared that a bad precedent would be set if they supported a largely politically motivated campaign to remove a president from office. They also knew that Johnson had less than a year left in office. Finally, many moderate Republicans had begun to lose confidence in the Radicals' Reconstruction program. Had Johnson been removed from office, the power of the Radical Republicans would have been greatly increased as one of their own, Benjamin Wade, would have succeeded him as president.

Why did moderate Republicans decide not to remove Johnson from office?

Implementing Reconstruction

As Congress engaged in its impeachment struggle with President Johnson in 1867–1868, the Reconstruction Acts took effect. A coalition of African Americans, poor up-country whites, and economically ambitious merchants (many originally from the North) and white planters came together to form the Republican Party in the South. They seized the opportunity presented by the congressional Reconstruction program and dominated the process of electing state governments and gaining readmission to the Union. The task would not be easy, especially as their different goals came into conflict with each other and with those of a majority of white Southerners who would clearly oppose—politically, economically, and violently—any attempt to establish what they called "Negro rule" in the former Confederacy.

14.10 The Hated Scalawag Scalawags became despised figures in the popular Southern mind. Here a scalawag is depicted as an opportunist seeking political power by manipulating the black vote.

The Republican Party in the South

The process of remaking state governments under the Reconstruction Act fell to the Republican Party, an organization comprising three distinct and in some cases antagonistic groups. Northerners who settled in the South after the war constituted one faction. White Southerners derided them as **carpetbaggers**, a term suggesting they were penniless adventurers who came south with all their possessions in a cheap suitcase, or carpetbag, intent on enriching themselves at the expense of Southerners still reeling from the war. In reality most were middle class, often former Union soldiers or merchants, ministers, artisans, and professionals who viewed the South as a region of opportunity and planned to settle permanently. Others came as idealistic relief workers, sent by Northern charitable and religious societies, intent upon aiding ex-slaves in their transition to freedom.

The Republican Party in the South also contained a significant number of white Southerners known derisively as **scalawags**. Most white Southerners considered them traitors to their region and race, men eager to enrich themselves and to garner political power by manipulating black voters (**14.10**). Most scalawags came from the less developed backcountry regions of the South, especially eastern Tennessee and Kentucky, northern Alabama and Georgia, and western North Carolina. They shared the view of carpetbaggers that the Republican Party offered them the best hope for economic betterment. They did not, as a rule, however, share some carpetbaggers' views on freedmen uplift and racial equality.

Former slaves made up the largest, most significant segment of the South's Republican Party. Empowered with the vote by the Civil Rights Act of 1866 and Reconstruction Act of 1867, they moved swiftly to make their political voice heard. In the fall of 1867, as Southern states held elections to select delegates to constitutional conventions, African Americans turned out in huge numbers to exercise their right to vote for the first time. For supporters

What motivated Northerners to move south after the Civil War?

> "But be sure to vote for no Southern men that was a rebel or secessionist; for, if you do, you are pulling them hemp to hang yourself with."
>
> R. I. CROMWELL, advising his fellow freedmen, *New Orleans Tribune,* April 25, 1867

of black suffrage, this extraordinary moment—persons only recently considered property now exercising the right to vote—was captured in this drawing (**14.11**). Published in *Harper's Weekly,* the hopeful, dignified scene depicts three African American voters who symbolically represent a spectrum of blacks that includes common laborers, educated blacks who were free before the war, and Union army veterans. Most of the African American political leaders that soon emerged came from the second group. They tended to come from the North and possessed more wealth and education than the average freedman.

The three factions of the Republican Party—carpetbaggers, scalawags, and freedmen—formed an uneasy alliance as they came together to reestablish Southern state governments. Nonetheless, their combined votes in the fall 1867 elections for delegates to state constitutional conventions led to a sweeping Republican victory. White Republicans won most of the seats, but 265 were won by freedmen. In South Carolina and Louisiana, freedmen constituted a majority of the delegates elected. The number was far below the proportion of African Americans in the South, but it was a striking accomplishment considering that only recently they had been considered property and incapable of citizenship.

14.11 Casting Their First Votes
For supporters of racial equality like the Northern publication *Harper's Weekly,* whose cover featured this drawing, the large turnout of black voters in the fall of 1867 elections was exhilarating.

Creating Reconstruction Governments in the South

In ex-Confederate states delegates drafted new state constitutions according to the guidelines established by the Reconstruction Acts. In a few states, notably Virginia and Texas, conservatives managed to delay the process for more than a year. Nonetheless, by the end of 1868 seven Southern states had ratified new state constitutions, created new state governments, and gained readmission to the Union.

In the coming years these Republican governments achieved remarkable results. To begin with they represented a revolutionary advance in the status of the freedmen. Held as slaves and denied citizenship only a few years before, African Americans now enjoyed the right to vote and to hold office. Between 1869 and 1901 twenty-two African Americans would serve in the U.S. Congress (twenty representatives and two senators). More than six hundred won seats in state legislatures and to other state and local offices.

What impact did African American voting have on the political situation in the South in 1867–1868?

While embittered white Southerners decried what they termed "Negro rule," statistics plainly show that white Republicans held a far greater share of offices than blacks. No African American was elected as governor, and no state legislature ever had a majority of black members (the lower house of the South Carolina legislature briefly had a black majority). What white Southerners really objected to was Republican rule and what it stood for: African American equality and empowerment.

Republican-controlled Southern state governments also achieved several significant reforms. In contrast to the tightfisted governments of the antebellum era, They funded public works projects, established hospitals and orphanages, and built thousands of schools (or took over those created by the Freedmen's Bureau). They also established more equitable tax codes and passed laws to help indebted farmers keep their land. Opponents of Republican rule denounced these initiatives (and the higher taxes needed to fund them) as wasteful and poorly managed. Fundamentally, they objected to their social and racial implications, since many of the projects were designed to aid the poor and freedmen.

But the charges of corruption, mismanagement, and debt lodged by the opponents of Reconstruction governments were not entirely groundless. The rapid expansion of government services and expenditures caused many states to run up huge budget deficits and created opportunities for graft and bribery. Many Reconstruction legislators took advantage.

OUR MOTTO:
THIS IS A WHITE MAN'S COUNTRY;
LET WHITE MEN RULE.

14.12 Campaign of Fear Campaigning against General Ulysses Grant, Democratic presidential candidate Horatio Seymour attempted to exploit Northern racism and anxiety about racial equality with banners such as this one.

Democratic opponents railed against these abuses as alleged evidence that blacks were incapable of holding public office and that their Northern carpetbagger allies were interested only in plunder. In reality the corruption found in Southern state governments paled in comparison to that found in the North. New York's Tammany Hall political machine, for example, under William "Boss" Tweed, stole anywhere between $20 million and $200 million from 1869 to 1871. Moreover, the amount of spending by Southern state governments on social programs looked large only in comparison to the paltry expenditures on education, health care, and public works before the war. Nonetheless, charges of corruption and excess spending, coupled with increased taxes, diminished popular support for the Southern Republican governments and created unfavorable public opinion in the North.

"We cannot vote without all sorts of threats and intimidations. Freedmen are shot with impunity."

Report of a Republican official, 1868

The Election of 1868

By the summer of 1868, there was little doubt whom the Republican Party would nominate for president. General Ulysses S. Grant enjoyed widespread popularity across the North and among Southern Republicans for defeating Robert E. Lee and ending the Civil War. Grant conveyed a tone of moderation in a time of partisan and sectional acrimony. His plea, "let us have peace," from his acceptance of the Republican nomination, became his campaign slogan.

Democrats, still weak in the aftermath of the war and the disenfranchisement of many ex-Confederates, faced an uphill battle against the popular General Grant. As their racist campaign banner makes clear (**14.12**), their nominee, Governor Horatio Seymour of New York, ran an aggressive campaign designed to arouse fears that the Republican Party and black suffrage threatened

Why did Southerners charge that Reconstruction governments were corrupt?

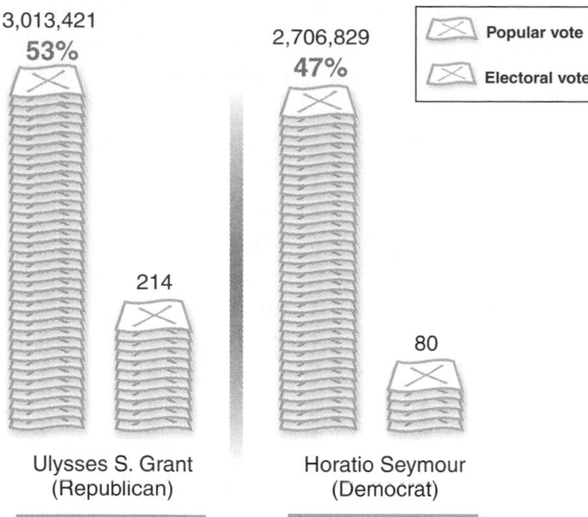

14.13 The Election of 1868
Votes from nearly 500,000 recently enfranchised African Americans proved crucial to Grant's victory in the election. (Several ex-Confederate states not yet reconstructed did not participate.)

the rights of white Americans. Republicans, the campaign claimed, must be defeated to prevent them from spreading the disastrous experiment in black political empowerment into the North.

Projecting an image of moderation, suggesting an even-handed approach to Reconstruction and fiscal responsibility, Grant won the election, garnering 214 electoral votes to Seymour's 80. The popular vote, however, was much closer: 53 percent for Grant, 47 percent for Seymour (**14.13**). This outcome reflected three things. First, it indicated the wide appeal of Seymour's blatantly racist message to conservative whites in both the North and the South. Second, it showed how vital the freedmen vote was to the future of the Republican Party. Grant received 500,000 African American votes, but won by only 300,000 votes. Third, the election outcome revealed the effectiveness of violence as a weapon in electoral politics. The reign of terror unleashed by groups of violent whites in the months before the election, especially in Georgia and Louisiana, kept thousands of black voters away from the polls.

The Fifteenth Amendment

In the wake of the 1868 election, congressional Republicans decided that black suffrage required an explicit constitutional guarantee. Black male suffrage was implied in the Fourteenth Amendment's phrase, "all male citizens," but with Southern resistance on the rise, many Republicans in Congress argued that an additional amendment was necessary to guarantee unequivocally the right of African Americans to vote.

Numerous women's rights activists agreed, but many also argued that the time had come to establish universal suffrage—the vote for all adult citizens regardless of race or gender. Bitterly disappointed over the reference to only "male citizens" in the Fourteenth Amendment, many feminists, such as Elizabeth Cady Stanton and Susan B. Anthony, demanded that any subsequent amendment guarantee universal suffrage.

Their demand was met by strong opposition from former abolitionists and Radical Republicans, including some fellow feminists like Lucy Stone and Frances Harper, who argued that gaining the right to vote for African American men was a higher priority. Extending the vote to women, they argued, would lead to the amendment's rejection because the nation was not ready for such radical change. The cause of women's suffrage could be taken up immediately after black suffrage was secured. Stanton and Anthony rejected this reasoning. Most Republicans in Congress, however, agreed with Frederick Douglass's assertion that this was the "Negro's Hour" and consequently they drafted the **Fifteenth Amendment** to read succinctly: "The right of citizens of the United States shall not be denied or abridged by the United States or by any state on account of race, color, or previous condition of servitude."

Passed by Congress in late 1869 and ratified in 1870, the Fifteenth Amendment presented a striking contradiction. It established a revolutionary experiment in multiracial democracy, something no other slave society, such as those in the Caribbean or Latin America, did so soon and so completely after emancipation. Yet its sparc wording left wide open the possibility that states could devise clever ways to deny blacks the right to vote that did not directly invoke "race, color, or previous condition of servitude."

The Rise of White Resistance

The secret white terrorist organizations that first arose in 1866 and that wrought havoc in parts of the South during the 1868 election grew still bolder and more violent by 1870–1871, especially during

Why did some women's rights activists oppose ratification of the Fifteenth Amendment?

election season. Known by various names, including the White Brotherhood, Knights of the White Camelia, and especially the **Ku Klux Klan**, they functioned in much the same manner. As illustrated in a popular Northern newspaper (**14.14**), Klansmen often operated at night, wearing hoods, robes, and other regalia designed to both hide their identities and overawe the freedmen. Blacks (and occasionally carpetbaggers and scalawags) targeted for "punishment" were beaten and frequently killed. Some had their crops or homes burned or their mules killed. Klansmen also targeted symbols of black self-improvement and independence, such as black churches, businesses, and schools.

Klan terrorism served a number of purposes. For the poor whites who made up the bulk of Klansmen, the violent suppression of African Americans provided them with the psychological reassurance that they were not at the bottom of the social order. For white elites who approved of and often assisted the violence, it prevented a political alliance between poor whites and blacks and maintained a large, exploitable workforce for Southern plantations and industry by keeping African Americans powerless and poor. Klan violence also discouraged African American voting and thus threatened the Republican Party in the South.

In response to surging violence in the South, Republicans in Congress, with strong support from the Grant administration, passed several Enforcement Acts in 1870 outlawing "armed combinations" that deprived anyone of their civil or political rights. Grant's attorney general, Amos T. Ackerman, vigorously enforced these laws across the South, arresting and prosecuting thousands and leaving the Klan and similar organizations decimated by 1872.While it demonstrated that federal authority could effectively protect the rights of freedmen, it also revealed the vulnerability of freedmen should the federal commitment to Reconstruction ever wane.

14.14 ***Another Victim of the Klan*** Terrorist violence by white vigilante groups soared in the early 1870s. In this scene from Moore County, North Carolina, a freedman pleads for his life, surrounded by Klansmen in full regalia.

What was the purpose behind anti-black violence waged by groups like the Klan?

Reconstruction Abandoned

By the end of Grant's first term in office, supporters of Reconstruction and freedmen's rights could look with some satisfaction at the many extraordinary changes that had taken place in the South. Yet ominous signs soon appeared that suggested Reconstruction was in trouble. Despite the crackdown on the Klan, white Southerners increasingly demonstrated their commitment to seizing power and imposing a new form of servitude on African Americans. Northerners, by contrast, seemed less and less willing to support a vigorous Reconstruction policy. Slowly, between 1872 and 1877, the extraordinary experiment in multiracial democracy and progressive government in the South was dismantled in favor of oligarchy and white supremacy.

Corruption and Scandal

A major factor in the pullback from Reconstruction was a series of corruption scandals that plagued the Grant administration. Grant himself was honest, but also politically naive and given to a hands-off style of leadership that gave officials in his administration an unusual degree of independence. Many of them took advantage of Grant's implicit trust to enrich themselves in a variety of illegal schemes.

For example, in 1869 Jay Gould and Jim Fisk, two Wall Street titans, conspired with Grant's brother-in-law in a scheme to corner the gold market. The plan eventually collapsed on September 24, 1869, a day dubbed "Black Friday, but not before hundreds of innocent investors were ruined and countless workers thrown out of work in the ensuing national economic turmoil. Fisk and Gould were pilloried in the press, but emerged unscathed. When the Credit Mobilier scandal became public, it was revealed that Grant's vice president and several high-ranking members of Congress had taken large bribes from the company involved in the completion of the government-subsidized Union Pacific Railroad. Other scandals found that three of Grant's cabinet members used their office for illegal financial gain. In the so-called "Whiskey Ring" scandal, for example, Treasury secretary Orville E. Babcock made a small fortune by illegally allowing whiskey distillers to avoid paying excise taxes. Secretary of War William W. Belknap likewise accepted bribes from companies engaged in corrupt activities on Indian reservations.

The North Retreats

Corruption scandals undermined the authority of Grant's administration. Grant soon found that to secure reelection and keep the Republican Party in power he would have to minimize political controversies. With so much negative publicity stirred up by corruption scandals, Grant's administration took steps to minimize political controversies. To secure his reelection and keep the Republican Party in power, Grant adopted a more conservative approach to Reconstruction, by now a frequent source of rancor in Washington.

In the summer of 1872, for example, Grant lobbied Congress for and then signed into law the Amnesty Act, granting a general pardon to all but a few hundred former Confederate leaders. Now eligible to vote and hold office, these planters, ex-army officers, and ex-Confederate officials wasted little time in reasserting their authority.

> "It seems to me that we are drifting, drifting back under the leadership of the slaveholders. Our former masters are fast taking the reins of government."
>
> GEORGE M. ARNOLD, African American Republican

The retreat from Reconstruction in the 1870s was also hastened by growing dissention within the Republican Party. Many Republicans, including former Radicals, began to question the wisdom of maintaining a strong federal role in the affairs of Southern states. Some Republicans now believed the fundamental goals of Reconstruction—citizenship, civil rights, and suffrage for the freedmen—had been accomplished. There was, they believed, a constitutional and moral limit to what the federal government could do on behalf of the freedmen. Now was the time, they argued, for the freedmen to elevate themselves economically, socially, and politically using their new rights.

What impact did the scandals of the Grant administration have on Reconstruction?

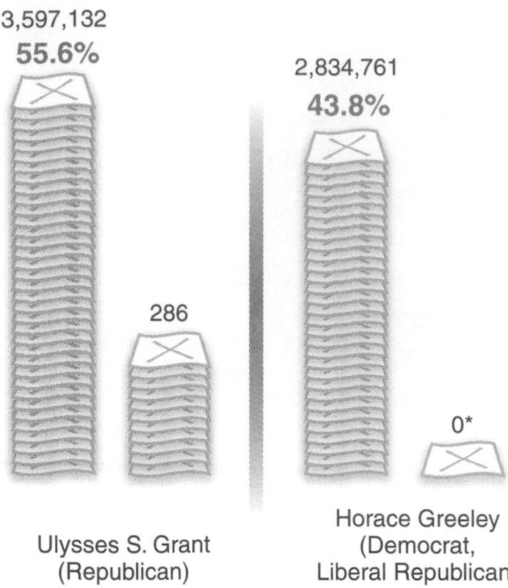

14.15 The Election of 1872 Opposed by a weak candidate, Democrat Horace Greeley, Ulysses Grant easily won reelection. Scandals and economic turmoil soon undermined his popularity and power.

Others, for less optimistic reasons, argued for an end to Reconstruction. Many Republicans, even some of the strongest advocates of abolition before the war and freedmen's rights in the first years that followed, had soured on Reconstruction. These Liberal Republicans, as they came to be called, were tired of the political strife produced by debates over freedmen's rights, concerned about the growing power of the federal government, and disgusted with the effort to impeach Johnson.

They also had grown disgusted by the corruption and mismanagement of Southern Reconstruction governments. They accepted the argument of Southerners that freedmen and their white allies were incapable of honest and effective government. No one embodied this dramatic change of heart more than Horace Greeley, the progressive editor of the *New York Tribune*. Once the outspoken champion of abolition and freedmen's rights, he was by the early 1870s an advocate of returning the South to white rule. Blacks, he wrote in 1870, were a "worthless race," unwilling to help themselves when given the option of accepting charity. Southern Reconstruction governments, as a consequence, were based on "ignorance and degradation." A similar transformation from a progressive to a reactionary view of Reconstruction was revealed in the political cartoons of Thomas Nast (see *Images as History: Political Cartoons Reflect the Shift in Public Opinion*).

The Election of 1872

The dissatisfaction of Liberal Republicans reached full bloom in the summer of 1872. Disturbed by the prospect of Grant being renominated for a second term, they broke from the Republican Party. Liberal Republicans held their own convention in Cincinnati and nominated Greeley as their candidate for president. A divided Democratic Party subsequently endorsed Greeley as well.

The election of 1872 proved disastrous for Greeley and his backers. The public viewed Greeley as an eccentric who during his long career in public life had supported many fringe causes such as vegetarianism, spiritualism, and utopianism. Even his appearance—small eyes set in a round face covered in a tangle of wispy chin whiskers—diminished him in the eyes of the public, especially in contrast to the handsome, noble bearing of Grant. Greeley's call for an end to Reconstruction and reconciliation between North and South also repelled many Northern voters who remained leery of Southerners and the Democratic Party.

In Grant's sweeping victory over Greeley in the November election (**14.15**), Republicans had good reason to cheer. The Democrats' and Liberal Republicans' call for ending Reconstruction and returning the South to white rule had been rejected. Moreover, the Grant administration's crackdown on the Klan had allowed African Americans unprecedented freedom to vote. Still, Northerners and Republicans in Congress were not prepared to support federal intervention in the South indefinitely. As new pressing issues emerged after 1872, support for Reconstruction rapidly eroded.

Hard Times

After a period of readjustment following the Civil War and conversion to peacetime production, the American economy boomed. Hundreds of thousands of new businesses were established. These included a growing number of massive factories that employed hundreds, in some cases thousands, of workers. Aiding this economic growth was the dramatic expansion of the railroad and telegraph systems and increased availability of capital through banks and stock sales.

The booming economy encouraged businesses to expand and investors to take bigger risks. When these trends reached a critical point in the fall of 1873, a panic on Wall Street ensued. Some of the nation's most prominent financial houses and banks went bankrupt. As credit became scarce businesses began to fail. Hundreds of thousands of workers lost their jobs. By early 1874 the nation's economy had plunged into a deep depression that lasted until 1877.

The **Panic of 1873** had a direct impact on Reconstruction. As hard times set in, and hundreds of thousands of workers lost their jobs, the fate of the freedmen became less of a concern to Northerners. Economic issues like currency reform and the tariff took precedence over civil rights and white vigilante violence against freedmen. The public, declared one Republican, is tired of hearing about Southern violence against the freedmen. "Hard times and heavy

Why did Liberal Republicans lose faith in Reconstruction by the early 1870s?

Images as History

POLITICAL CARTOONS REFLECT THE SHIFT IN PUBLIC OPINION

One of the nation's most skilled and popular political cartoonists in the Reconstruction era was Thomas Nast. An immigrant from Germany, he landed a job in 1861 at *Harper's Weekly,* the nation's leading journal of politics and society. Nast's artistic talent, combined with *Harper's* vast circulation, soon turned him into one of the most influential illustrators of his day. As a staunch Republican and Unionist, his drawings during the Civil War were as intensely patriotic and pro-Lincoln as they were anti-Confederate.

After the war, Nast's widely distributed cartoons continued to shape Northern opinion concerning Reconstruction and the issue of freedmen's rights. Cartoons like *And Not This Man?* (August 5, 1865) proclaimed the dignity and humanity of the freedmen and their moral right to full citizenship and suffrage. In others, like *This is a White Man's Government* (September 5, 1868), he stressed the violent intent of white Southerners to reclaim power and the absolute necessity of federal authority in carrying out the goals of Reconstruction.

Nevertheless, Nast's cartoons eventually reflected the growing disillusionment of Northern Republicans regarding Reconstruction. While he rejected the Liberal Republican call for ending Reconstruction, Nast nonetheless expressed the fear that African Americans were incapable of responsible government. Note the contrast between his earlier depictions of freedmen and that in *Colored Rule in a Reconstructed (?) State.*

"Columbia," an early symbol of America and democracy, advocates black suffrage. The globe is actually a nineteenth-century ballot box.

By showing African Americans in Union army uniforms, Nast sought to remind Americans that blacks had earned the right to full citizenship through their service and sacrifice (note the missing leg) in the war.

And Not This Man?

A freedman wearing a Union army uniform is crushed beneath an Irish immigrant (left), a white supremacist ex-Confederate (center), and a Northern capitalist (right). Nast saw these three groups as members of an opportunistic alliance.

A ballot box, representing the freedman's claim on citizenship and voting rights, has been kicked aside.

This is a White Man's Government

Reflecting Nast's disillusionment, "Columbia" chastises African American political leaders.

In 1874, frustrated with what he saw as inept and selfish African American political leadership in the South, Nash changed his depiction of blacks from noble individuals worthy of citizenship to racist caricatures.

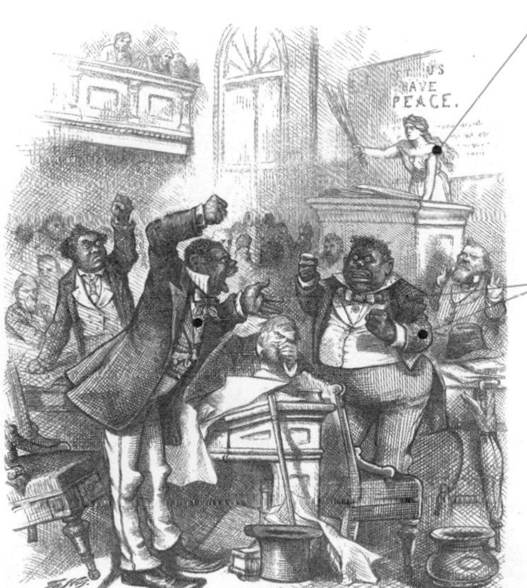

Colored Rule in a Reconstructed (?) State

What makes political cartoons so popular and effective?

taxes make them wish the 'everlasting nigger' were in hell or Africa." The public expressed its discontent in the congressional elections of 1874 by voting in a Democratic majority for the first time since the war.

The Return of Terrorism

Reconstruction was also undone by a resumption of violence waged by white terrorist groups like the Klan. As the Grant administration bowed to political pressure to reduce federal intervention in Southern affairs, advocates of white supremacy seized the opportunity. In one notorious incident in 1873 a large band of heavily armed whites overran Colfax, Mississippi and slaughtered over one hundred African Americans.

As was the case in the late 1860s, white vigilante violence had two goals: to strip away the freedmen's hard-won economic, social, and legal rights and to prevent them from voting and holding office. This effort reached full development in Mississippi in 1875 when armed groups of whites closely allied with the Democratic Party waged a campaign of terror that came to be known as the **Mississippi Plan**. Through threats, beatings, and killings, they delivered an unambiguous message: blacks and their white allies who dared vote Republican risked their lives. But when Mississippi governor Adelbert Ames asked the Grant administration to send troops to keep the peace and protect the polls, his request was rejected.

Not surprisingly, more than sixty thousand Mississippi voters—nearly all black and Republican—stayed away from the polls on election day. Democrats swept to victory and took control of the state legislature for the first time since the Civil War.

"The negroes of the South are free—free as air," says the parliamentary Watterson. This is what the *State*, a well-known Democratic organ of Tennessee, says, in huge capitals, on the subject: "Let it be known before the election that the farmers have agreed to spot every leading Radical negro in the county, and treat him as an enemy for all time to come. The rotten ring must and shall be broken at any and all costs. The Democrats have determined to withdraw all employment from their enemies. Let this fact be known."
"OF COURSE HE WANTS TO VOTE THE DEMOCRATIC TICKET!"
DEMOCRATIC "REFORMER." "You're as free as air, ain't you? Say you are, or I'll blow yer black head off!"

14.16 The Mississippi Plan in Action In many parts of the South, violence kept most freedmen away from the polls. Here a freedman is threatened with death unless he votes for the Democratic Party.

Immediately they threatened Governor Ames with impeachment and forced him to resign.The success of the Mississippi Plan in intimidating black voters and demolishing the base of the Republican Party is indicated in this 1876 image, *Of Course He Wants to Vote the Democratic Ticket* (**14.16**). The artist vividly depicted the ruthless character of the white supremacy movement and the vulnerability of freedmen left without federal protection.

Other Southern states soon employed their own version of the Mississippi Plan. One by one the remaining Reconstruction governments fell to a new class of political leaders known as **Redeemers**. As the name suggests they cast themselves in almost biblical terms as saviors of Southern society. By 1876 only South Carolina, Louisiana, and Florida remained under Republican control—largely because of the presence of federal troops. The removal of these troops in 1877 opened the way for a complete "redemption" of the former Confederacy and the restoration of white supremacy.

Defenders of Reconstruction and the rights of freedmen in Congress were appalled at the rising tide of Redeemer oppression. In response they managed one final measure designed to bolster the rights of freedmen, the **Civil Rights Act of 1875**. Among its several points it required that state governments provide equal access in public facilities such as schools and allow African Americans to serve on juries. The act became law in 1875, but was largely ignored. In 1883 the U.S. Supreme Court ruled it unconstitutional.

The End of Reconstruction

The final blow to Reconstruction occurred as the result of the presidential election of 1876.With the Democratic Party reinvigorated by gaining a majority in the House in 1874 and control of most Southern state governments by 1876, a close election was expected. The Democrats nominated Samuel J. Tilden, governor of New York and a well-known reformer. Republicans nominated Ohio governor and Civil War veteran Rutherford B. Hayes. The issues centered on political corruption, the failed economy, and of course, Reconstruction.

On election day, Tilden received nearly a quarter million more popular votes than Hayes (**14.17**). But the electoral vote—the tally that actually determines the victor—was unclear. Voting irregularities in South Carolina, Louisiana, and Florida left both sides claiming victory—and the twenty electoral votes at stake. Tilden needed to be declared the winner in only one of the three disputed states to win a majority of

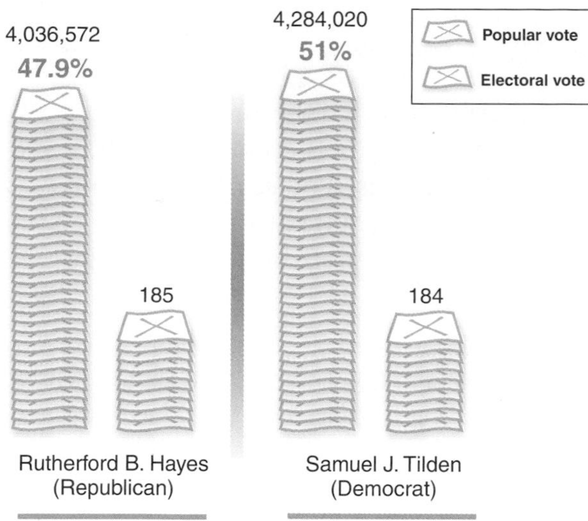

14.17 The Election of 1876
In one of the most controversial presidential elections in U.S. history, Samuel B. Tilden won the popular vote (4,284,020 to 4,036,572), but lost the electoral vote to Rutherford B. Hayes, 185 to 184.

electoral votes and thus the presidency. Hayes needed to win all three states to put him one electoral vote ahead of Tilden and into the White House.

Both sides refused to budge, and a constitutional crisis loomed. Eventually they agreed to abide by the decision of a bipartisan commission. The commission authorized an investigation and heard testimony. Behind the scenes members of Congress and leaders from both parties conducted intense negotiations. On March 2, 1877, the commission issued its decision, known as the **Compromise of 1877**. By a vote of 8 to 7, the fifteen-member commission awarded all 20 disputed electoral votes to Hayes, giving him a 185 to 184 electoral vote victory over Tilden.

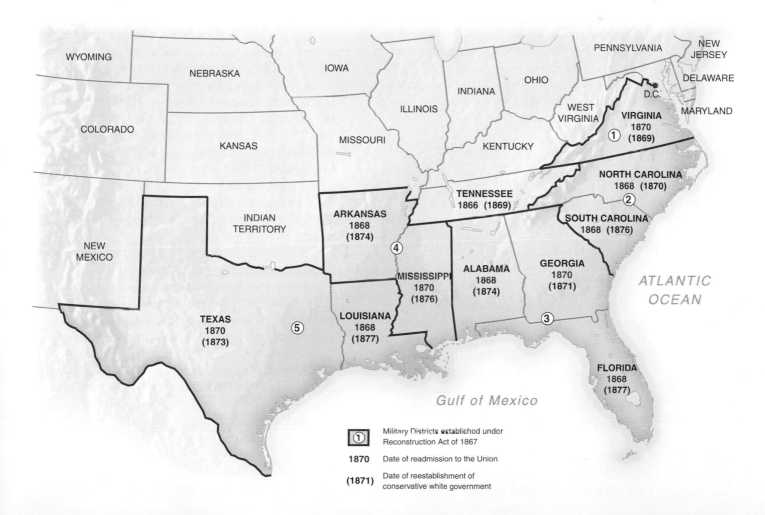

Democrats cried foul and denounced the "stolen election." Yet the election result proved beneficial to the party. Hayes's presidency was weakened by the aura of illegitimacy (detractors referred to him as "his fraudulency"). More important, he oversaw the dismantling of the last remnants of Reconstruction policy. By the end of 1877, the last federal troops were removed from the South, and as the map (**14.18**) indicates, the last Reconstruction governments fell to Democratic redeemers.

14.18 The Readmission of Southern States and Return of White Rule
Most former Confederate states were readmitted to the Union under the direction of Republican-controlled state governments. But as the dates in parentheses indicate, in most cases, conservative white Democratic governments soon seized control.

Why is the eventual result of the election of 1877 considered the end of Reconstruction?

The New South

The optimism with which white Southerners greeted the end of Reconstruction gave rise to the term **New South**. It reflected the South's development of a new system of race relations based on segregation and white supremacy. Even more so, the New South pointed to a profound economic transformation that swept across the region, bringing with it a boom in manufacturing, railroad construction, and urbanization.

Redeemer Rule

The Redeemer governments that took control of Southern states by 1877 represented the arrival of a new ruling oligarchy. Before the war a small and powerful class of planters dominated Southern politics. Now in the aftermath of Reconstruction, a new elite took control. Although some were planters and former planters, most were men who drew their wealth and power from a new Southern economy based on industry, finance, commerce, and railroad construction.

As men of business their politics reflected the dominant economic theory of the era, laissez-faire (from the French "let do," meaning let things alone). It argued that the best form of government was small, frugal, and pro-business. Accordingly, Redeemer governments slashed taxes and spending on social programs and public education created during Reconstruction.

"What I want here is Negroes who can make cotton and they don't need education to help them make cotton."

A Southern planter

Redeemer politics also championed a return to white supremacy. The return of one-party (Democratic) rule in many Southern states resulted in a steady decline in office holding by African Americans and Republicans. Intimidation and violence likewise led to a marked decrease in black voting across the South. Despite these setbacks, however, African Americans in many Southern states managed to vote and hold office in appreciable numbers into the 1880s and 1890s.

Redeemers dominated state politics, but their rule did not go unchallenged. In several Southern states anger among poor farmers coalesced into full-fledged political challenges to oligarchic rule. The insurgents denounced the new elite as "Bourbons" (the name of the French royal family), a derogatory term that implied aristocratic ambitions. In Virginia, for example, a coalition of Republicans and disaffected Democrats called Readjusters turned out the Redeemer government in 1879. All of these challenges to Redeemer rule, however, ultimately failed.

The Lost Cause

Southerners after 1877 embraced not only Redeemer rule, but also an image of the prewar South as an ideal society and the Confederate bid for independence a valiant Lost Cause. Southerners clung to this image because it provided them with a psychologically soothing explanation for why they lost the war. According to the Lost Cause idea, as expressed in poems, plays, songs, speeches, sermons, and books, Confederate society was more virtuous than the North and its soldiers more brave, but the South lost because the Yankees possessed overwhelming advantages in population, industry, arms, and ruthlessness. Defeat, while bitter and painful, was also a glorious martyrdom for a people and a way of life.

The Lost Cause carried with it an obligation to keep alive the memory of Confederate glory. Southerners built elegant battlefield cemeteries to inter the war dead and monuments to celebrate Confederate victories. White Southern women, many widowed by the war, played a major role in these efforts, founding organizations such as the Ladies Memorial Association (1867) and the United Daughters of the Confederacy (1894). Southerners also erected thousands of statues honoring Southern legends like Generals Robert E. Lee, Stonewall Jackson, and Nathan Bedford Forrest. The photograph (**14.19**) vividly demonstrates how enthusiasm for the Lost Cause only grew the further the Civil War receded into history. Lee had discouraged efforts to

Who made up the political leadership of the New South?

raise monuments to the Confederate cause, but soon after he died in 1870 they sprang up all across the South, including this monumental rendering unveiled in Richmond in 1890. Thousands turned out for the dedication of the heroic statue by French sculptor Antonin Mercie and to hear Colonel Archer Anderson laud Lee for his "courage, will, energy . . . fortitude, hopefulness, joy in battle . . . [and] unconquerable soul." Nothing that day, certainly not the speeches or Lee's triumphant pose, recalled the fact that Lee had lost the war.

But the Lost Cause legend served a second purpose beyond helping Southerners cope with their defeat in the war. It celebrated a nostalgic vision of the prewar South that supported their arguments for a resumption of white rule and African American subservience. Through literature, art, and music, Southerners (and some Northerners) fashioned romantic depictions of the "Old South" as a harmonious paradise where benevolent masters treated loyal, contented slaves with kindness, where chivalrous Southern gentlemen protected delicate, charming Southern women, and where everyone revered tradition, family, and the Bible. Yet even as they glorified slavery, the proponents of the Lost Cause downplayed the importance of slavery as a cause of secession. The real issue, they insisted, was "states' rights" and attempts by Northerners to run roughshod over them in the 1850s.

The Lost Cause thus presented Southerners as victims of misguided and unjustified Yankee aggression who, in the wake of devastating war and humiliating Reconstruction, ought to be left alone to run their own affairs. The overt racism and self-serving depictions of slavery in Lost Cause rhetoric and imagery served to justify a resumption of white rule and the return of African Americans to the status of powerless, exploitable laborers.

14.19 Celebrating the Lost Cause As the commemorative ribbon indicates, this monument to Robert E. Lee was erected in the former Confederate capital of Richmond, Virginia in 1890. It was one of thousands of monuments to the Confederacy erected across the South. [*Source*: (ribbon) Lee Monument Unveiling Ribbon Accession #TBMR 277-1 (2). The Museum of the Confederacy]

The New South Economy

Even as Southerners revered the Lost Cause and Old South, their new leadership steered the region's economy into an industrial future. In the 1870s and 1880s, they joined with Northern entrepreneurs who settled in the South during Reconstruction to develop a modern, market-oriented, and diversified economy. This effort entailed not simply the establishment of banks, textile mills, and railroads, but also the celebration and spreading of capitalist values, such as hard work, risk taking, thrift, and the profit motive.

The leading figure in this movement to establish a New South economy was Henry Grady, editor

14.20 Logging Near Laurel, Mississippi Logging became a major industry in the New South, but like mining and cotton cultivation, it was a low-skill industry that produced a raw material rather than a finished product.

of the *Atlanta Constitution*. Beginning in the mid-1870s, he wrote editorials and delivered speeches proclaiming industrialization as the solution to the South's devastated postwar economy. His message appealed to many Southerners, especially those who had never been part of the planter elite. It inspired them to start businesses, invest, and support pro-business policies. Grady also attracted the attention of many Northerners, convincing them to invest in New South enterprises.

The vast expansion of manufacturing represented the most stunning change in the New South. Drawn by low taxes, cheap labor, ample water power, proximity to cotton supplies, and the absence of unions, textile manufacturers moved their operations from New England to the South, especially the Carolinas. By 1900 the South surpassed New England in output to become the nation's leading producer of textiles. A similar transformation occurred in the tobacco industry, as the South went from merely producing raw tobacco to become the nation's leading producer of finished tobacco products like cigarettes.

Another significant aspect of the New South economy was the lumber and furniture industry. As this photograph (**14.20**) of a logging operation near Laurel, Mississippi, in the 1890s indicates, New South entrepreneurs took advantage of the region's tremendous forest reserves and new technologies, such as rotary saws and dry kilns, and an expanded railroad system (shown here), and soon made the South the leading producer of lumber. In Mississippi alone the number of lumber mills jumped from 295 in 1880 to 608 in 1899. The furniture industry likewise boomed in the New South, especially in places like High Point, North Carolina, where a single factory opened in 1889, followed by thirty more over the next decade.

The lower South, especially the city of Birmingham, Alabama, developed into a major iron and steel producer. Birmingham had only a few hundred residents when founded in 1871, but its position at the junction of two major railroads and nearby deposits of coal, iron, and limestone soon attracted iron and steel factories and the nickname, "Pittsburgh of the South." By 1890 the South produced 20 percent of U.S. iron and steel.

> "The growth of the iron interests of the South during the last few years has been the marvel of the age, attracting the attention of the entire business world."
>
> New South booster, M. B. HILLYARD, 1887

As in the North the expansion of industry in the South relied upon the existence of a large pool of cheap labor. But unlike the North, where millions of immigrants and their children made up much of the workforce, the South relied on a rising population of poor white farming families pushed off the land by indebtedness, falling crop prices, and crop failure. In the rare instances where African Americans secured industrial employment, it was usually in the most menial, dangerous, and poorly paid jobs.

What weaknesses limited the success of the New South economy?

The low wages paid Southern workers reveals the limited success of the New South economy in overcoming the region's poverty and social problems. Despite decades of impressive growth in industry, mining, and railroads, the South in 1900 lagged far behind the North in virtually every category of economic and social progress. The majority of Southern industry, for example, was small-scale and focused on low-skill labor. Per capita incomes in the South remained stagnant from 1880 to 1900.

Other indications of backwardness and underdevelopment abounded. The cuts in funding for public education imposed by Redeemer governments reduced per pupil spending to half the average in the North. Rates for illiteracy and infant mortality far exceeded the national average.

14.21 Poverty and Independence
Sharecropping condemned most African Americans to a life of poverty, but it also helped to free them of immediate white control. No longer confined to slave cabins, they also worked on their own, free of white oversight and coercion.

The Rise of Sharecropping

Most revealing about the limitations of the New South economy was the preponderance, even by 1900, of Southern laborers still in agriculture. Only 6 percent of the Southern workforce in 1900 was employed in manufacturing. The region's economy remained fundamentally tied to the production of cash crops, particularly tobacco, sugar, rice, and of course, cotton.

The condition of Southern farmers, both white and black, deteriorated sharply in the last quarter of the nineteenth century. While cotton production soared the price plummeted, from eighteen cents per pound in the early 1870s to five cents per pound in 1894. Shrinking profits forced many Southern farmers to forfeit title to their land and became tenant farmers. Some rented land for a set fee and then were free to grow whatever crops they desired. But most tenant farmers resorted to the sharecropping system, whereby they received the right to farm a plot of land in exchange for rent paid in the form of a share (generally one-third to one-half) of the harvest. By 1900 more than 70 percent of the South's farmers (white and black) earned their living in this manner.

Sharecropping granted African Americans some important measure of independence. White landlords generally left their tenants alone, allowing them to control their own time and to set their own work routines. The people shown in this photograph (**14.21**) are poor and live in a ramshackle house, but like most sharecroppers they work as families free of direct white supervision. Given their slavery experience of gang labor under the brutal control of overseers, freedmen cherished this independence. And yet, as a closer look at this image shows, there is a well-dressed white man in the background—probably the landlord who arranged for the photograph to be taken. Sharecroppers were not slaves, but as this photograph makes clear, they lived under the control of their white landlords.

How did sharecropping provide a limited measure of independence to freedmen?

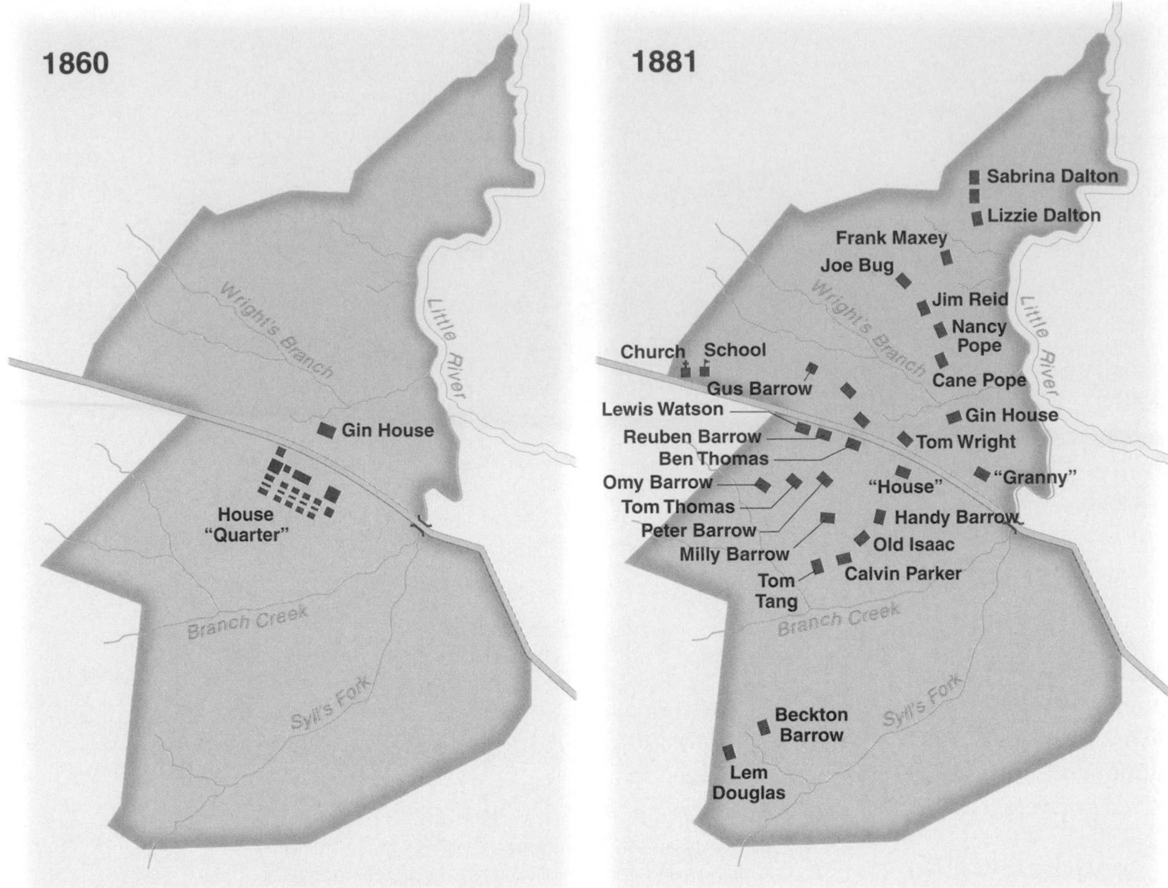

14.22 Moving from Slavery to Freedom: The Barrow Plantation, Oglethorpe County, Georgia, 1860 and 1881 Under slavery the Barrows confined their slaves' housing to a narrow section of the plantation. Sixteen years after emancipation, African Americans on the plantation, living beyond the immediate oversight of the Barrows, established a church and school.

The transformation from the tightly controlled plantation system to the relative independence of sharecropping can be seen in this map (**14.22**) of a Georgia plantation. The 1860 map shows the Barrow Family Plantation before the abolition of slavery. Notice the layout of the slave quarters—in tight rows clustered within sight and earshot of the master. Seeking maximum control over their enslaved laborers, the Barrows kept them close at hand.

Twenty-one years later, many of the Barrow's former slaves and their descendents still lived on the plantation. But as the 1881 map indicates (see 14.22), the relationship between the Barrows and their workers had changed considerably, reflecting a sharp conflict in visions regarding the social order in the postwar South. Initially the Barrows had tried, like so many other former slave owners, to limit the freedom of their former slaves, hiring them as wage workers bound by annual labor contracts and trying to coerce them into accepting gang labor under an overseer. The freedmen, however, refused these demands and eventually negotiated to work as tenant farmers. By 1881 most ex-slaves lived in separate households scattered on the former plantation. They worked as sharecroppers on 25- to 30-acre farms, doing the work as families on their own terms rather than as gang laborers. At harvest they paid a portion of their annual crop as rent. The 1881 map also indicates the presence of two key institutions of African American freedom—a church and a school. Within the narrow limits allowed by hostile whites, freedmen enjoyed privileges they had been deprived of under slavery.

Nonetheless, tenancy exploited the freedmen. Landlords demanded they grow cash crops like tobacco, wheat, and especially cotton. Because they often needed to buy seed, tools, and animals on credit (usually on unfavorable terms) from their landlords or local suppliers, most tenants found themselves in a condition of ever-mounting debt which prevented them from moving to better land or to a landlord offering better terms. It also exposed freedmen to economic reprisals should they try to vote or stand up for their rights.

Jim Crow

While life in the New South for the great majority of African Americans meant poverty and exploitation as sharecroppers, some managed to achieve a remarkable degree of economic success. Despite racism, poverty, and an often hostile white business community they bought property and started small businesses. Some of these endeavors blossomed into large, prosperous enterprises. North Carolina Mutual and Provident Insurance Company, for example, was founded by two African American men in Durham in 1898. By 1907 the company boasted more than 100,000 policy holders. Other African Americans took advantage of the many black schools and colleges established during Reconstruction to enter the professions as teachers, professors, lawyers, doctors, nurses, and ministers. Overwhelmingly, these members of a black middle class worked in segregated settings providing services to their fellow African Americans.

These educated and relatively affluent African Americans provided leadership and direction for their communities, building social networks of churches, fraternal societies, and self-help organizations. The directors of the aforementioned North Carolina Mutual and Provident Insurance Company, for example, used their financial resources to support schools and establish a hospital, bank, and library to serve the black community of Durham. As *Heroes of the Colored Race* (**14.23**) suggests, middle-class blacks also cultivated pride in the accomplishments of African Americans after emancipation. This lithograph was published in 1881 for commercial sale to African Americans. Note its emphasis on the role of African Americans in the Civil War and later as members of Congress, as well as the significance of education.

But in the late 1870s and early 1880s, Southern political leaders began to create a social and legal system of segregation that came to be called Jim Crow (named for a derogatory black character in a popular minstrel show). It reflected their awareness that as long as some African Americans possessed civil, economic, and political rights, especially the right to vote, the idea of white supremacy was called into question. Redeemer politicians also came to recognize the political benefits of stoking racial animosity. It maintained their privileged status as a ruling elite by deflecting the frustration and anger of poor Southern whites away from them and onto African Americans. The ultimate purpose of Jim Crow was to foment racial divisions by segregating African Americans from as many aspects of everyday life as possible. Initial efforts focused on barring African Americans from hotels, restaurants, and railroad cars. Blacks denounced these violations of their constitutional rights and challenged them in court.

But an extremely conservative Supreme Court issued several decisions that sharply restricted the authority of the Fourteenth Amendment and its guarantee of equal protection. In *Hall v. DeCuir* (1878), for example, the Court ruled that a Louisiana law prohibiting racial discrimination on steamboats was unconstitutional because the vessel was engaged in interstate commerce (running routes between

14.23 ***Heroes of the Colored Race***
African Americans kept alive their hopes for a better future by cultivating an appreciation for their history.

Louisiana and Mississippi), a realm of business that only Congress possessed the power to regulate. Five years later, in the Civil Rights Cases, the Court declared the 1875 Civil Rights Act unconstitutional, asserting that the Fourteenth Amendment did not empower Congress to outlaw racial discrimination by private individuals and organizations. The ruling cleared the way for private individuals such as hotel owners and institutions such as men's clubs to bar African Americans, but left standing the right of Congress to prohibit discrimination by state government institutions. As explained in *Choices and Consequences: Sanctioning Separation* (page 434), this matter came before the Court in an 1896 case, ***Plessy v. Ferguson.***

Hand in hand with the spread of segregation came an effort to eradicate the remaining vestiges of black political power by circumventing the Fifteenth Amendment. Violence and intimidation in the 1870s had reduced black voting and office holding significantly, but not completely. In Mississippi, for example, black voter turnout averaged 39 percent in the 1880s. But a rising fear among Redeemer politicians over the voting power of both blacks and disgruntled poor whites led them to commence a program of disenfranchisement.

Given the sparse and direct language of the Fifteenth Amendment, the proponents of disenfranchisement needed to devise laws that deprived African Americans of the right to vote without making specific mention of "race, color, or previous condition of servitude." In 1889 Tennessee became the first of many Southern states to enact a poll tax,

Choices and Consequences

SANCTIONING SEPARATION

In 1890 Louisiana passed a law requiring separate cars for black and white passengers on all railroads in the state. Determined to challenge the law, an African American carpenter named Homer A. Plessy bought a first-class ticket on the East Louisiana Railroad and sat in the whites-only first-class car. As expected he was arrested. Plessy argued before a local judge named John H. Ferguson that the law violated the Thirteenth Amendment's prohibition of slavery and the Fourteenth Amendment's equal protection clause. Ferguson ruled in favor of the railroad, stating that separation did not violate Plessy's rights, a decision subsequently upheld by the state's Supreme Court. When Plessy appealed to the U.S. Supreme Court, the justices considered three major options:

Choices

1 Refuse to hear the case and thus not render a judgment on the constitutionality of segregation, letting stand the Louisiana State Supreme Court decision.

2 Rule in favor of Plessy and declare Louisiana's segregation law unconstitutional.

3 Reject Plessy's appeal and uphold Louisiana's segregation law as constitutional.

Decision

On May 18, 1896, the U.S. Supreme Court by a vote of 7 to 1 chose the third option and rejected Plessy's claim that the law violated his constitutional rights. The Thirteenth and Fourteenth Amendments, argued the majority, were never intended to establish full social equality of the races. Furthermore legal separation of the races, a doctrine subsequently known as "separate but equal," was constitutional so long as states provided equal facilities. The lone dissenting justice, John Marshall Harlan, blasted the majority opinion, declaring the law a racist violation of the nation's "color-blind" Constitution.

Consequences

In sharply limiting the Fourteenth Amendment's equal protection provisions, the court allowed Southern state governments to establish separate schools, hospitals, parks, theaters, restaurants, and public transportation across the South. The decision also opened the way for segregation laws aimed at Mexicans in the Southwest and Asians in California. In practice "separate but equal" proved only half accurate as segregated facilities were indeed separate, but never equal in terms of funding, staffing, and supplies.

Continuing Controversies

How should African Americans respond to the imposition of Jim Crow laws?

Black leaders in the 1890s were divided over the best strategy to oppose segregation. Booker T. Washington, the nation's most prominent African American leader, argued that efforts to overturn segregation were doomed to failure due to black Americans' lack of political and economic power. Instead he recommended blacks focus their energy and resources on self-improvement, especially in education, a strategy that would one day empower them to challenge segregation. Founding member of the National Association for the Advancement of Colored People (NAACP), W. E. B. Dubois, rejected this policy and instead insisted that African Americans keep up a sustained legal and political effort to end segregation. Ultimately it was Dubois's vision and NAACP attorneys that ended legalized segregation. In the 1954 *Brown v. Board of Education of Topeka* decision the Supreme Court overturned *Plessy* and rejected entirely the concept of "separate but equal."

JIM CROW LAW.

UPHELD BY THE UNITED STATES SUPREME COURT.

Statute Within the Competency of the Louisiana Legislature and Railroads—Must Furnish Separate Cars for Whites and Blacks.

Washington, May 18.—The Supreme Court today in an opinion read by Justice Brown, sustained the constitutionality of the law in Louisiana requiring the railroads of that State to provide separate cars for white and colored passengers. There was no inter-

How did the U.S. Supreme Court play a role in the imposition of segregation?

an annual tax imposed on all adult citizens in the state. Those who failed to pay it could not vote. As the image (**14.24**) of a Florida poll tax receipt for 1900 shows, the tax of one dollar was low enough so that most white voters like Henry R. Nicks could pay it, but high enough to disenfranchise thousands of impoverished African Americans. Most states also required that all unpaid poll taxes from previous years be paid off before a citizen could vote, meaning that a black man who had fallen behind in his taxes for five years would need to pay five dollars before entering a polling place.

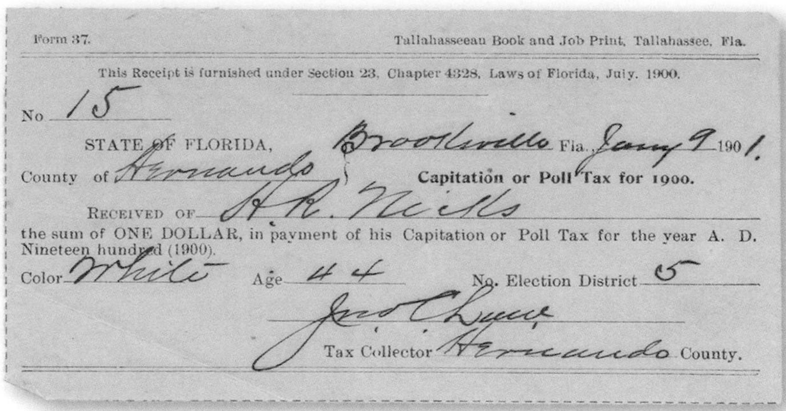

Form 37. Tallahasseean Book and Job Print, Tallahassee, Fla.

This Receipt is furnished under Section 23, Chapter 4328, Laws of Florida, July, 1900.

No 15

STATE OF FLORIDA, Brooksville Fla., Jany 9 1901.
County of Hernando Capitation or Poll Tax for 1900.

RECEIVED OF H. R. Nicks
the sum of ONE DOLLAR, in payment of his Capitation or Poll Tax for the year A. D. Nineteen hundred (1900).

Color White Age 44 No. Election District 5

[illegible]
Tax Collector Hernando County.

14.24 Disenfranchisement through the Poll Tax
Because H. R. Nicks, a white man living in Hernando County, Florida, in 1900, was able to pay his poll tax of one dollar, he was eligible to vote. Mired in poverty, many African Americans could not afford the fee and lost their right to vote.

In 1890 Mississippi enacted a poll tax and an additional measure to facilitate disenfranchisement: the literacy test. It allowed state and local officials to bar from voting anyone who failed a literacy test. The test usually required a potential voter to read a complicated section of the state constitution and explain its meaning—a provision aimed at excluding African Americans given their low levels of education.

In the mid-1890s Southern states added a third disenfranchisement policy, the so-called grandfather clause. It guaranteed the vote to anyone, even if they could not pass a literacy test, if their grandfather had been eligible to vote before 1867. Since no African Americans could vote before 1867, it left them as the only ones subject to literacy tests.

Adding to the effectiveness of the segregation and disenfranchisement movements was a stepped-up campaign of violence against African Americans. Vigilante groups across the South composed largely of poor whites, but often aided by local law officers and prominent citizens, launched an unprecedented wave of beatings, humiliations, and murders intended to intimidate blacks and "put them in their place." Often an unsubstantiated accusation of rape or murder was enough to bring out a community's lynch mob, but many killings were prompted by minor incidents of alleged disrespect such as arguing with a white man. Lynchings in the 1890s soared to an average of 187 per year, or roughly one killing every two days.

By the end of the 1890s, the cumulative effect of these disenfranchisement policies reduced overall black voting in the South by 62 percent. In some states black voting was effectively eliminated. In Louisiana, for example, the number of black voters dropped from 130,334 in 1896 to 1,342 in 1904—a reduction of 99 percent. Disenfranchisement also impacted thousands of poor whites, reducing the total white vote by 27 percent by 1900.White supremacy had triumphed.

Conclusion

Reconstruction was a period of extraordinary contrasts. For the nearly four million former slaves and their supporters, it began as an era full of promise. Despite opposition, often violent, from white Southerners, by 1870 the Fourteenth and Fifteenth Amendments were ratified, declaring African Americans as citizens entitled to full civil rights, including voting, and equal protection before the law. Hundreds of thousands of freedmen joined thousands of Southern whites attracted by the progressive ideology of the Republican Party to build a reconstructed society based on democracy and equal opportunity, and social and civil equality for all. By the late-1870s, however, white Southerners who rejected this vision regained control of their state governments and began to slowly dismantle Reconstruction and impose a new form of white supremacy. Simultaneously, they guided the South toward a dramatic economic transformation. But the boom in industry, railroad construction, and urban growth that characterized the "New South" benefited mainly a small elite, leaving the South mired in poverty, illiteracy, and inequality.

1863–1866

The Ten Percent Plan
Lincoln proposes moderate terms for readmission of Southern states

Thirteenth Amendment (ratified 1865)
Abolishes slavery in every state

Fourteenth Amendment (ratified 1868)
Defines citizenship to include African Americans and guarantees equal protection before the law

1867–1868

The Reconstruction Acts
South placed under military rule and freedmen guaranteed voting rights

Progressive state governments take power in South
Freedmen wield their newly won right to vote and hold office

Republicans impeach Johnson
Reflects the divisive politics of Reconstruction

1869–1871

Fifteenth Amendment (ratified 1870)
Establishes the right to vote for all male citizens regardless of "race, color, or previous condition of servitude"

Enforcement Acts passed
Empowers Grant administration to weaken Ku Klux Klan and like groups

North Carolina elects first Redeemer government
Signals a return to white supremacy in the South; other Southern states soon follow

Review Questions

1. How did white prejudice toward African Americans shape early Reconstruction policy in the Sea Islands and Louisiana?
2. Why did African Americans consider acquiring land so important? How did they justify their claims to plantation lands?
3. How did violence come to play a role in the course of Reconstruction? What measures did Congress and the Grant administration take to curb it?
4. How did some feminists react to the Fifteenth Amendment? What impact did this decision have on the women's rights movement?
5. Who were the "carpetbaggers"? Where did this term originate and what does it tell us about Southern attitudes during Reconstruction?
6. What key factors led to the end of Reconstruction?
7. What was the Lost Cause? What purposes did it serve in the post-Reconstruction South?
8. Who were the "Bourbons" and what was their vision for the New South?

1872–1873

Amnesty Act
Pardons and restores full political rights to most ex-Confederates

Panic of 1873
Begins four years of severe economic depression that weakens Northern support for Reconstruction

1874–1875

The Mississippi Plan
Violence by white terrorist groups keeps thousands of blacks from voting. Restores the Democratic Party to power

Second Civil Rights Act passed
Guarantees equal access to public facilities and affirms the right of blacks to serve on juries

1876–1877

Compromise of 1877
Republican Rutherford B. Hayes becomes president; Republicans promise to remove federal troops from the South. End of Reconstruction

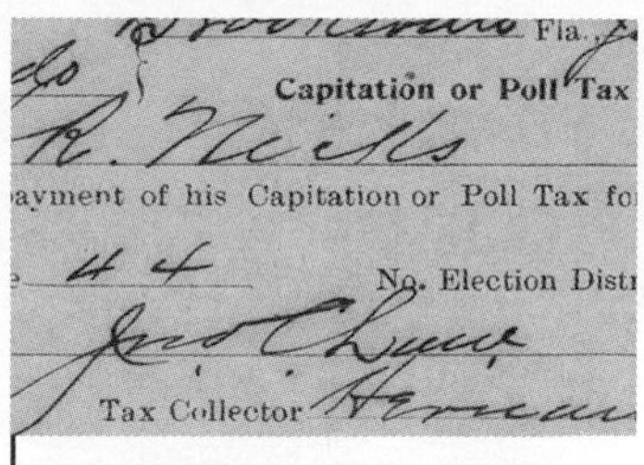

1883–1889

Civil Rights Act of 1875 declared unconstitutional
Clears the way for adoption of Jim Crow policies across the South

Tennessee enacts first poll tax
Sharply reduces black voting; adopted by other Southern states. Followed by literacy test and grandfather clause

Key Terms

Ten Percent Plan Pardoned all Southerners (except high-ranking military officers and Confederate officials) who took an oath pledging loyalty to the Union and support for emancipation. As soon as ten percent of a state's voters took this oath, they could call a convention, establish a new state government, and apply for congressional recognition. **408**

Wade-Davis Bill A Reconstruction program designed to punish Confederate leaders and permanently destroy the South's slave society. **408**

Freedmen's Bureau Relief agency for the war-ravaged South created by Congress in March 1865. It provided emergency services, built schools, and managed confiscated lands. **408**

Black Codes Laws designed by the ex-Confederate states to sharply limit the civil and economic rights of freedmen and create an exploitable workforce. **413**

Fourteenth Amendment Drafted by Congress in June 1866, it defined citizenship to include African Americans, guaranteed equal protection before the law, and established the federal government as the guarantor of individual civil rights. **416**

carpetbagger White Southerners' derogatory term for Northerners who came south after the war to settle, work, or aid the ex-slaves. It falsely suggested they were penniless adventurers who came south merely to get rich. **418**

scalawag White Southerners' derogatory term for fellow whites considered traitors to their region and race for joining the Republican Party and cooperating with Reconstruction policy. **418**

Fifteenth Amendment Constitutional amendment passed by Congress in 1869 providing an explicit constitutional guarantee for black suffrage. **421**

Ku Klux Klan The best-known of the many secret white terrorist organizations that first arose in the South in 1866; they targeted freedmen and symbols of black self-improvement and independence and played a key role in reestablishing white supremacy by the late 1870s. **422**

Panic of 1873 A financial panic on Wall Street that touched off a national economic recession causing financial houses, banks, and businesses to fail. Hundreds of thousands of workers lost their jobs. **424**

Mississippi Plan Campaign of violence and intimidation waged by armed groups of whites closely allied with the Democratic Party that drove Republicans from power in the Mississippi state elections of 1874. Copied by other Southern states. **426**

Redeemers Name for white Southern political leaders who successfully returned their states to white Democratic rule in the mid-1870s. The name was intended to depict these leaders as saviors of Southern society from rule by freedmen, scalawags, and carpetbaggers. **426**

Civil Rights Act of 1875 Passed by Congress in 1875, it required state governments to provide equal access in public facilities such as schools and to allow African Americans to serve on juries. In 1883 the U.S. Supreme Court ruled it unconstitutional. **426**

Compromise of 1877 Resolution of the disputed presidential election of 1876 that handed victory to Republican Rutherford B. Hayes over Democrat Samuel J. Tilden. Democrats agreed to the deal in exchange for patronage and the continued removal of federal troops from the South. **427**

New South Optimistic phrase white Southerners used to describe the post-Reconstruction South, reflecting the South's development of a new system of race relations based on segregation and white supremacy and pointing to a profound economic transformation that swept across the region. **428**

CHAPTER

15

Conflict and Conquest

The Transformation of the West, 1860–1900

> "The destiny of the American people is to subdue the continent—to rush over this vast field to the Pacific Ocean ... to change darkness into light and confirm the destiny of the human race ... Divine task! Immortal mission!"
>
> WILLIAM GILPIN, *The Central Gold Region*, 1859

Most Americans envisioned the conquest and transformation of the West as a tale of triumph. In John Gast's 1872 painting, *American Progress*, the beautiful goddess Liberty glides westward, stringing telegraph wire and holding a book, symbols, along with the distant railroad, of the civilization and new technology that would soon tame the wilderness. Beneath her, Gast depicts farmers and pioneers intent on taking advantage of the West's bountiful resources. Turned into a popular lithograph, it was advertised as worthy of hanging in both "the miner's humble cabin" and the "stately marble mansion of the capitalist." Publishers put the image on the cover of a popular guide to the West, *The New Overland Tourist and Pacific Coast Guide*.

Before 1840 most Americans viewed the lands west of the Mississippi as a great, untamed and dangerous wilderness of rugged terrain, extreme temperatures, wild animals, and hostile Native Americans. But beginning in the 1840s, an ever-growing number of farmers, miners, ranchers, entrepreneurs, and adventurers moved west, aided after 1869 by the completion of the transcontinental railroad and soaring demand for western products and resources.

Gast's celebratory scene reveals, doubtless unintentionally, the bitter conflict that accompanied the transformation of the West. On the painting's left border, a cluster of Native Americans flee before the advancing whites. Above them a herd of buffalo likewise make their escape. Gast's matter-of-fact portrayal of the seizure of Indian land and the near extinction of the buffalo reflected the nation's enthusiasm for "progress" and the inability—or unwillingness—to confront the human and environmental costs associated with it.

By 1900 the West had been radically transformed. Great networks of railroads and telegraph lines crisscrossed the landscape, as did untold miles of fencing that marked the boundaries of millions of farms and ranches. The western landscape also featured cities like San Francisco and Denver that rivaled their eastern counterparts. Perhaps even more remarkable than the appearance of these new aspects of western life was the disappearance of others. By 1900 the American government had confined hundreds of independent Native American tribes that had once lived in virtually every corner of the West to a series of reservations. Gone, too, were the millions of buffalo from the plains and, in areas of intensive mining, large mountain sections of once pristine landscape. The conquest of the West between 1865 and 1900 included many stories of success, achievement, and undeniable progress, but it was far more complex, violent, and tragic than Gast's dreamy vision suggests.

How did the notion of "progress" shape Americans' vision of western settlement?

Natives and Newcomers

Inspired by visions of unlimited opportunity and acts of Congress like the Homestead Act, westward migration increased dramatically after the Civil War. Contrary to the popular notions of a vacant landscape, much of the West was home to hundreds of thousands of Native Americans. Their wide variety of languages, lifestyles, and religious practices made for a rich cultural landscape, but also conflict with the rising numbers of newcomers.

Congress Promotes Westward Settlement

In 1862 Congress passed three major bills designed to facilitate settlement of the **trans-Mississippi West**, the vast region of the United States west of the Mississippi River. The Morrill Land Grant College Act of 1862 created a system whereby funds raised by the sale of public land went toward establishing colleges specializing in agricultural, mechanical, and technological education. Far more significant, however, was the **Homestead Act**. It provided 160 acres of free land to any settler willing to live on it and improve it for five years. Those who took advantage of the program included immigrants, landless farmers from the East, single women, and ex-slaves. Farmers with less patience and more capital could buy the land for a rock-bottom price of $1.25 per acre after living on it for only six months. By making available more than 600 million acres of public land to be settled and farmed, the Homestead Act touched off the largest migration of people ever within the United States.

The actual results of the Homestead Act varied widely by region. On the Great Plains and the lands farther west—regions with a harsh climate, poor soil, inconsistent supplies of water, and limited access to transportation—farmers who participated in the Homestead Act often went bankrupt. By contrast, it worked well in the northern and central portions of the Midwest, where the soil and the climate were favorable to farming.

One of the fortunate beneficiaries was Daniel Freeman, the first person to take advantage of the Homestead Act when it took effect January 1, 1863. Born in Ohio in 1826, Freeman grew up in upstate New York and Illinois. He became a doctor and served in the Union army during the Civil War. While stationed at Fort Leavenworth, Kansas, he picked out a section of land in nearby Nebraska he intended to claim as a homestead. Shortly after midnight on January 1, 1863, he woke up the land office clerk and filed his claim—the first of 417 filed that day. Freeman established a successful farm, and as this image of his certificate indicates (**15.1**), he earned clear title to the land in 1868. In addition to prospering as a farmer, Freeman practiced medicine and served terms as county coroner and county sheriff. He lived on his land until his death in 1908.

Others prospered from the Homestead Act in ways not intended by Congress. Many "homesteaders" were actually speculators who claimed their 160 acres with the intention of selling them for a quick profit in a few years. Larger enterprises like railroads and real estate companies accumulated vast holdings of land

HOMESTEAD.

Land Office at Brownville Neb
January 20th 1868.

CERTIFICATE, No. 1

APPLICATION, No. 1

It is hereby certified, *That pursuant to the provisions of the act of Congress, approved May 20, 1862, entitled "An act to secure homesteads to actual settlers on the public domain,"* Daniel Freeman *has made payment in full for* [illegible] *of Section* [illegible] (26) *in Township* [illegible] *of Range* five (5) E *containing* 160 *acres.*

Now, therefore, be it known, *That on presentation of this Certificate to the COMMISSIONER OF THE GENERAL LAND OFFICE, the said* Daniel Freeman *shall be entitled to a Patent for the Tract of Land above described.*

Henry M. Atkinson *Register.*

15.1 Claiming a Piece of the American West
On January 1, 1863, Daniel Freeman became the first American to file a claim under the Homestead Act. Five years later he received this title, which gave him full ownership of 160 acres of Nebraska farmland. Freeman, shown here more than thirty years after he received a homestead, prospered as a farmer and doctor and served stints as county coroner and county sheriff.

What factors led to the uneven results of the Homestead Act?

by buying out farmers who failed or paying people to file homestead claims and then buying the land from them. The Homestead Act did indeed attract farmers to the West, but by 1900 only 52 percent of original homestead claimants had acquired legal title to the land.

The third major piece of legislation passed by Congress in 1862 to promote western development, the Pacific Railway Act, created two corporations to build the **transcontinental railroad**, a line spanning the continent. The Union Pacific was to build west from Omaha, Nebraska, across the Plains and the Rockies to meet the Central Pacific which was to build from California through the Sierra Nevada Mountains. To help the railroad corporations raise sufficient capital to pay for the road, Congress granted them 10 square miles of land (in a checkerboard pattern with the federal government retaining ownership of the remaining sections) for every mile of track completed. The law also granted the railroads cheap loans and cash subsidies for each mile of track laid.

It took six years of low paid, hard and dangerous (scores were killed) work by huge gangs of workers, especially Irish and Chinese, to complete the project. On May 10, 1869, a grand ceremony marking the union of the two lines took place at Promontory Point, Utah. At the appointed moment, Leland Stanford, president of the Central Pacific, drove a symbolic golden spike into place, joining two rails, one placed by a team of Chinese workers and another by an Irish crew. Telegraph wires attached to the sledge hammer and spike sent a signal out across the nation, announcing to all the long-anticipated news: the continent had been spanned. Keenly aware of the historic nature of the event, railroad officials staged this iconic photograph (**15.2**) showing the workers and locomotives of the Union Pacific and Central Pacific. It soon appeared in numerous publications across the country, often as a lithograph. Conspicuously absent from the photograph, however, are any of the thousands of Chinese workers who labored on the Central Pacific.

15.2 The Continent Spanned Conscious of the historic significance of the event, workers and officials of the Union Pacific and Central Pacific railroads pose for a photograph while celebrating the completion of the transcontinental railroad in 1869.

Why was the federal government so eager to assist the companies that built the transcontinental railroad?

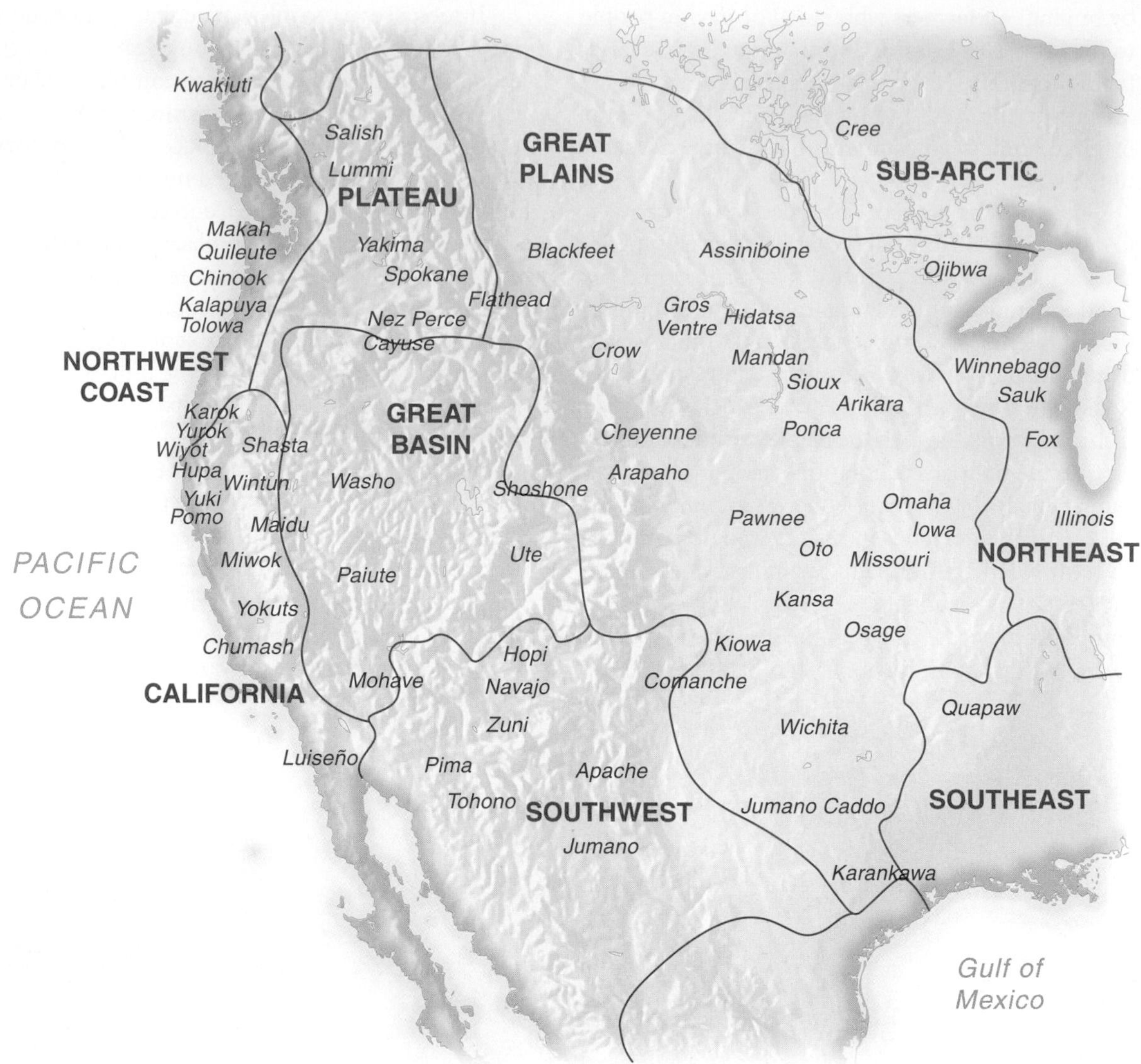

15.3 The Major Tribes of the Trans-Mississippi West
More than 360,000 Native Americans, constituting some five hundred tribes, lived west of the Mississippi River.

The Diversity of the Native American West

As this map of the trans-Mississippi West (**15.3**) shows, white settlers heading west encountered Native Americans belonging to hundreds of different tribes that comprised some 360,000 persons. That number was significantly lower from what it had been a century earlier, reflecting the impact of earlier European contact, starting with the Spanish, French, and Russians, that brought conflict and devastating disease. Most Indians had lived there as far back as anyone could remember, while some had come from the East only decades earlier during the many forced removals (see Chapter 8).

Before the arrival of Europeans, dozens of Native American tribes in what is now California lived in villages as small bands of hunters and gatherers. These include the Hupa, Karok, Northern Paiute, Pomo, Wintun, and Yuki peoples. Their way of life was first disrupted in the late eighteenth century when the Spanish established a line of Christian missions on the Pacific coast running north from San Diego. While thousands of Indians lived independently beyond the reach of the missions, many were subdued by the Spanish and transformed into an exploited class of laborers. Many of them were also converted to Christianity and gradually absorbed into Spanish colonial society. Even greater change followed the discovery of gold in northern California shortly after the U.S. government seized the territory in the Mexican War. Waves of white fortune seekers soon arrived and began violently driving the Native Americans off their lands. This violence, along with the starvation and disease that followed, killed upwards of ten thousand Indians (see Chapter 12).

The region of present-day Arizona, New Mexico, and west Texas likewise fell under Spanish colonial rule in the seventeenth and eighteenth centuries. But because this region was dry and remote, it attracted few Europeans. Native inhabitants, therefore, successfully retained core elements of their culture despite Spanish rule and the presence of Catholic missionaries. Indeed, missionaries managed to gain converts only by conforming their message of Christianity to fit local customs and traditions.

One major group, the Pueblo, descended from the ancient Anasazi people, included the Hopi, Zuni, and Rio Grande Pueblo tribes. They lived in settled farm communities in western New Mexico and eastern Arizona, growing corn and cotton and herding sheep. Neighboring Mexican ranchers, who prized these tribes' rich artistic traditions of decorative pottery and woven cloth, sought these native goods in trade for manufactured goods such as hoes and tools.

Eastern New Mexico and western Texas harbored more tribes, including the Jicarilla Apache and Navajo. Like the Pueblo, they lived in relative isolation from Spanish missions and thus successfully retained much of their traditional religion, language, and culture. Before the sixteenth century they had lived much like the Pueblos, but their adoption of the use of horses, brought to America by the Spanish in the seventeenth century, gradually transformed them into a more migratory people. They hunted, farmed, and tended large flocks of sheep, following them on their seasonal migrations. Sheep provided food, but also wool, which Indian women wove into cloth. The Navajo developed a tradition of silversmithing that produced beautiful jewelry.

The Pacific Northwest, comprising present-day Washington, Oregon, and northern California, was home to thriving native societies. Tribes such as the Chinook, Salish, Yurok, and Shasta lived in settled villages in large houses made from wooden planks. They divided their time between growing vegetables, hunting in the lush forests for bear, deer, and moose, and fishing along rivers and the ocean shore. Highly skilled in woodworking, the men produced excellent canoes for fishing and elaborate totem poles. Women wove intricate baskets that were both beautiful and practical. Many of these tribes enjoyed a rich material life that was offset by their custom of *potlatch*—a ceremony during which rich tribe members gave away many of their possessions as an act of benevolence and a demonstration of superior status.

Native American Tribes of the Great Plains

While Native American tribes could be found in virtually every corner of the West, by far the largest group—constituting nearly two-thirds of all Native Americans in the West—lived on the **Great Plains.** This vast open territory stretched east to west from present-day Missouri to the Rocky Mountains, and north to south from North Dakota to Texas. In the northern half (the Dakotas, Idaho, Minnesota, and Montana) lived tribes such as the Flathead, Blackfeet, Crow, Arapaho, Northern Cheyenne, and Sioux. Tribes in the southern Great Plains (present-day Nebraska, Kansas, Oklahoma, Texas, and New Mexico) included those relocated from the East during the so-called Trail of Tears ordeal (Cherokee, Choctaw, Creek, Chickasaw, and Seminole), as well as Pawnees, Comanches, Kiowas, Southern Arapahos, and Cheyenne (see Chapter 8).

The Plains tribes varied culturally, but many shared a similar tribal structure. Most tribes consisted of bands of about three hundred to five hundred related men and women, each governed by a council and widespread community involvement in the decisions the councils made. The Comanches, for example, divided their population of seven thousand (ca. 1870) into thirteen bands.

Religious beliefs and practices varied among the Plains tribes, but most shared important fundamental elements, beginning with the worship of one primary god whom the Sioux called *Wakan Tanka* (the Great Spirit). Plains Indians also believed in spirits found in everything in creation, from the earth itself, to plants, animals, stars, the moon, and sun, and they considered certain places, such as burial grounds, sacred. A shaman deemed *wakan,* or blessed, led religious ceremonies, healed the sick, and even decided where to hunt.

Many Plains tribes lived in settled villages near rivers where they tended fields of corn, beans, and squash; fished; and hunted a variety of local game, including bear, deer, and buffalo. Trade with white settlers, explorers, and trappers since the eighteenth century had allowed them to procure guns, kettles, and tools. These sedentary tribes included the Wichitas of northern Texas and Oklahoma, Pawnees of western Kansas, the Dakota Sioux of Minnesota, the Mandans of North Dakota, the Omahas of Nebraska, the Osages of western Missouri and Arkansas, and the Arikawas of South Dakota.

Although essential aspects of this Plains lifestyle had changed very little over the centuries, some of

What is significant about the diversity of Native American life in the trans-Mississippi West?

the largest tribes took to using horses (introduced by the Spanish by the eighteenth century) and adopted a migratory lifestyle. These included the Crow, Blackfeet, Cheyenne, Arapaho, Comanche, and Lakota Sioux. The horse allowed the Plains tribes to follow the seasonal migrations of the buffalo, whose population stood at 30 million in 1800. This scene, *Buffalo Chase over Prairie Bluffs*, (**15.4**), painted in 1844 by George Catlin who traveled extensively among Indian tribes in the West from the 1830s to the 1850s, reveals both the drama of the buffalo hunt and the extraordinary horsemanship skills developed by Plains Indians. It also reveals the centrality of the buffalo in Plains Indian culture, for the hunters are shown with clothing, jewelry, spear tips, and bridles made from buffalo parts. Other uses for the buffalo included flesh for food; skin for teepees and blankets; horns and hooves for glue; bones and tendons for weapons; hair for rope; teeth for ornaments; and dung for fuel.

The military advantages of the horse and the material wealth provided by the buffalo led these migratory tribes to become the dominant powers on the Plains, allowing them to oppress weaker sedentary tribes by exacting tribute. But reliance on the huge migratory beasts also meant that tribes, such as the Lakota Sioux in the north and Comanche in the central Plains, traversed enormous tracts of land during the course of their annual migrations, a practice that increasingly brought them into conflict with whites eager to acquire land. It also increased conflict between rival tribes, such as the Lakota Sioux and Crow, as white settlement forced tribes into closer contact.

While not all Native Americans were warlike, the culture of most Plains Indians relished battle. Warriors competed to develop reputations for bravery and skill, both during the hunt and in war. Warfare between tribes to determine control over land and access to game usually took the form of small skirmishes where the goal was not so much to kill their opponents as to steal their horses (a measure of a tribe's wealth and power) and drive them from the field. Individual warriors earned fame and respect by "counting coup," or making contact with an enemy with one's hand or weapon. Respect was also earned through acts of charity. Sitting Bull of the Lakota Sioux, for example, rose to prominence and eventually chief of his tribe both through his success as a warrior and due to his many exhibitions of generosity.

15.4 Plains Indians Hunting the Buffalo This 1844 painting by George Catlin shows Native American hunters pursuing the buffalo, which they relied upon as a major source of food, clothing, tools, and fuel. [*Source*: George Catlin (1796–1872) "Buffalo Chase Over Prairie Bluffs". 1832–33. Smithsonian American Art Museum, Washington, DC/Art Resource, NY]

"I was a famous hunter. . . . I gave the [buffalo] calves that I killed to the poor that had no horses. I was considered a good man."

SITTING BULL

The Great Westward Migration

In the late 1840s, after the Mexican War and the discovery of gold in California, a steady flow of migrant settlers into the trans-Mississippi West commenced. By the mid-1850s, thousands annually traversed the 2,000-mile Oregon Trail that stretched from Missouri to Oregon. What attracted them was a torrent of pamphlets, books, articles, and photographs produced by publicists and boosters, many employed by railroads and land companies, celebrating the virtues of the West as a region of wealth and opportunity.

Several groups led this migration westward. One was the recently freed slaves who hoped to secure new lives as independent farmers, free of the poverty and violence in the South. One of these ex-slaves, Henry Adams, who became a land promoter after emancipation, helped more than twenty thousand "**Exodusters**" on the "Exodus of 1879" from the South to farms in Kansas. This image from *Harper's Weekly* (**15.5**) captures the hopeful quality of this move-

How did the introduction of horses change the lifestyle of some Plains Indians?

ment. Note the contrast the artist draws between the "old style" of African American migration (a desperate escaped slave hiding from a passing steamboat) and "the new" (well-dressed ex-slaves arriving at their destination by steamboat). The name Exodusters reflected the belief that, like the Israelites in the Bible's Book of Exodus, they were heading for a "promised land." The inclusion of a black veteran of the Union army symbolizes the fulfillment of the promise of emancipation won during the war. Unfortunately for many Exodusters, they settled on poor land and lacked the capital necessary to establish successful farms. As a result only about one-third stayed and the rest moved on or returned to the South.

15.5 Seeking a Better Life in the West
In response to poverty and mounting violence in the South, more than twenty thousand African Americans known as "Exodusters" migrated to Kansas in 1879–1880 to acquire homesteads and start new lives as independent farmers.

Native-born whites constituted a second, much larger segment of the westward migration. Many were eastern and midwestern farmers who sought larger plots of land, either through purchase or by the Homestead Act, and opportunities for upward mobility. Others came to work in railroad construction or mining. Still other whites were the large numbers of soldiers in the U.S. Army who had been stationed in the West and elected to stay and settle after their terms of service expired.

One distinct subgroup of native-born whites who relocated to the West were the **Mormons**. Joseph Smith had founded this religious sect in upstate New York in 1830. But persecution, frequently violent—Smith was killed by a mob in Illinois in 1844—prompted the Mormons to head west in 1846 in search of an isolated homeland that could ensure their security and survival. They eventually chose a valley in Utah near the Great Salt Lake, territory then under Mexican rule. After the United States acquired it following the Mexican-American War, Congress created the Utah territory in 1850 (see Chapter 12), and by 1865 some twenty thousand Mormons lived in the region under a form of theocratic local rule. As more non-Mormons moved into Utah, tensions rose, since many other settlers resisted Mormon religious authority and condemned the sect's practice of polygamy (a practice they officially banned in 1896).

Joining Exodusters, Mormons, and native-born Americans in the great migration into the trans-Mississippi West were hundreds of thousands, eventually millions, of immigrants to America. Drawing them were the same desires for free, or at least inexpensive, farmland or opportunities to work in mines, on railroads, or in the rapidly expanding economies of western towns and cities. Over time large concentrations of particular ethnic groups

> "[I]f you strike off into the broad, free West, and make yourself a farm from Uncle Sam's generous domain, you will crowd nobody, starve nobody, and … neither you nor your children need evermore beg for Something to Do."
>
> HORACE GREELEY, Editor, *New York Tribune*, 1867

emerged. In Minnesota, for example, 30 percent of its population in 1880 was foreign-born, including more than 66,000 Germans, over 62,000 Norwegians, and just over 39,000 Swedes. Drawn by jobs in the copper mines, thousands of Irish immigrants settled in Butte, Montana. By, 1900 it was the most Irish city in America.

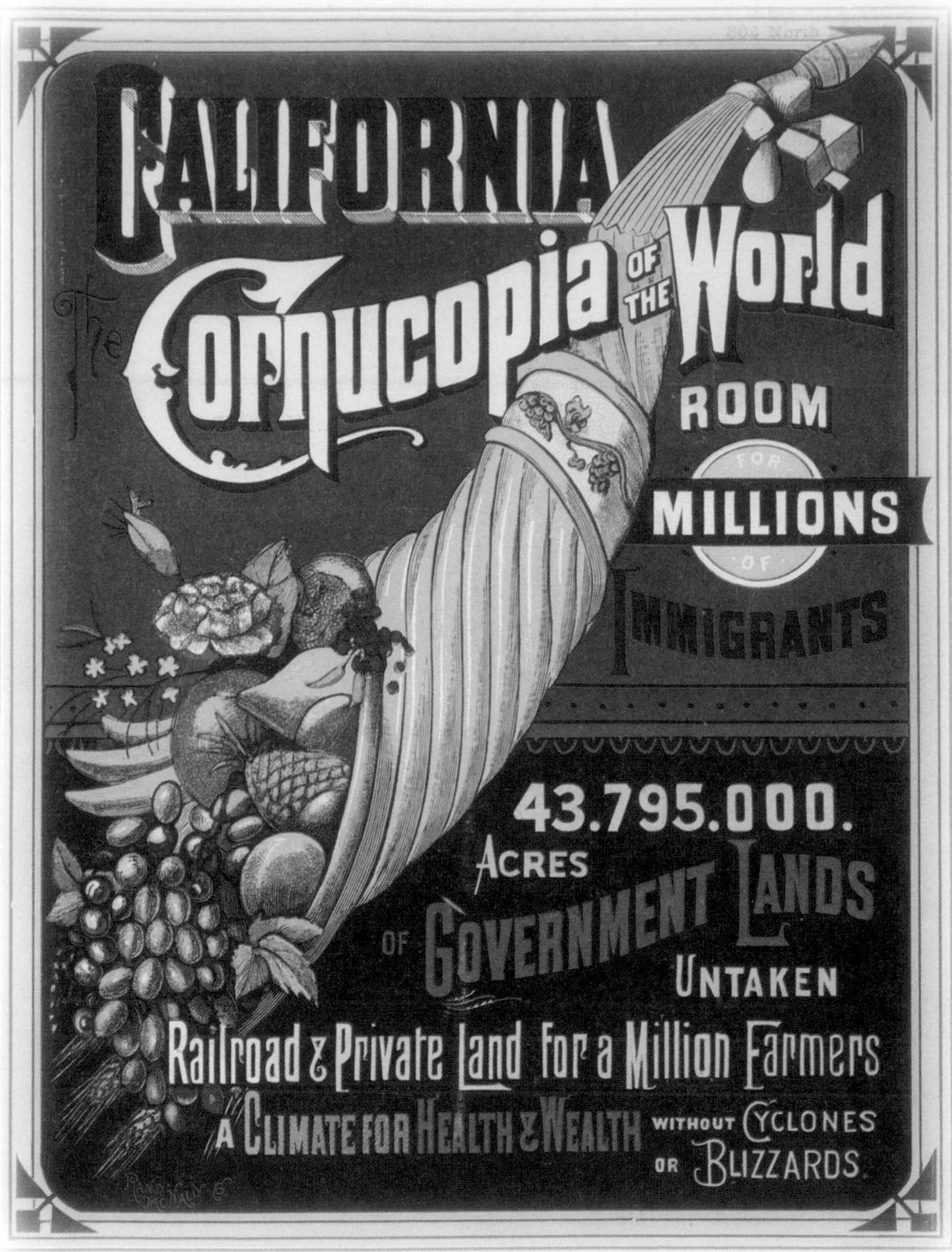

15.6 The Railroads Promote Westward Settlement
Railroads placed promotional posters such as this one from 1883 in eastern cities to entice settlers to head west to settle on land owned by the railroads, much of it acquired in land grants from the federal government.

As in the East, increased ethnic and racial diversity and economic competition in the West led to tension and conflict that occasionally exploded into raw violence. Frequently victims of the violence were Chinese immigrants. By 1880 California was home to 75,132 Chinese while 30,000 more lived elsewhere in the West. But anti-Chinese racism surged in the 1870s and 1880s as white laborers accused the Chinese of taking jobs and lowering wages. One attack in 1885 at Rock Springs, Wyoming, left twenty-eight Chinese miners dead. Two years later white laborers massacred at least thirty-four Chinese miners in Hells Canyon, Oregon.

Railroads and land companies played a key role in promoting immigration to the West, sending agents and advertisements to Europe to encourage migration, sometimes by entire villages, directly to the West. Railroads brought more than two million immigrants to the trans-Mississippi West between 1870 and 1900. “California, Cornucopia of the World” (1883) was one of countless posters that railroads placed in eastern seaports to attract the attention of newly arrived immigrants (**15.6**). The competition between western states for settlers is indicated in the phrase “without Cyclones or Blizzards,” a clear attempt to make California more appealing than the Plains states like Kansas. Also significant is the claim of “Room for Millions of Immigrants,” since only one year earlier Congress, with heavy lobbying from California, passed the Chinese Exclusion Act that barred Chinese immigration to the United States.

Why did railroads promote the migration of immigrants to the West?

The Economic Transformation of the West

While many Americans were inspired to migrate westward by notions of manifest destiny, the primary motivation was economic—a search for land and work. As a result, economic development was the chief driving force behind the profound transformations of the West after 1865. By 1900 four major industries—the railroad, farming, ranching, and mining—had fundamentally reshaped the region. These industries employed millions of workers and supplied some of the essential needs of consumers and industry in the East and internationally. Such progress, however, did not come without a cost as it was accompanied by labor exploitation, lasting environmental damage, and conflict with Indians.

The Railroad Fuels Western Development

Between 1860 and 1900 the country witnessed astonishing growth in agricultural output. The number of farms in the United States grew from two million to six million, with most of the growth taking place in the West. Agricultural output for the nation increased from $1.6 billion in 1860 to $4.3 billion in 1900.

Several factors account for this national boom in agriculture. New technologies such as the steel plow and mechanical reaper dramatically increased the acreage a typical farmer could till. The establishment of many agriculture schools, most funded by state and federal government, led to significant advances in technical knowledge of fertilization, irrigation, crop rotation, and seed selection, and the proper care of livestock.

One of the biggest factors underlying much of this booming growth in agriculture was the spread of the railroad. As the map (**15.7**) shows, the transcontinental railroad was only the beginning of a vast transportation network that spread across the West. In addition to several subsequent major east-west railroad lines, such as the Atlantic and Pacific Railroad and the Northern Pacific Railroad, companies built scores of feeder railroads, smaller lines providing access to a major one. This growing network opened up more and more western lands for farming, allowed farmers in once remote areas to sell their grain in the national market. The railroad also benefited many nonfarmers, beginning with the thousands who built the lines and who later gained employment as firemen, engineers, switchmen, mechanics, dispatchers, and clerks. It also opened up western lands for mining and ranching.

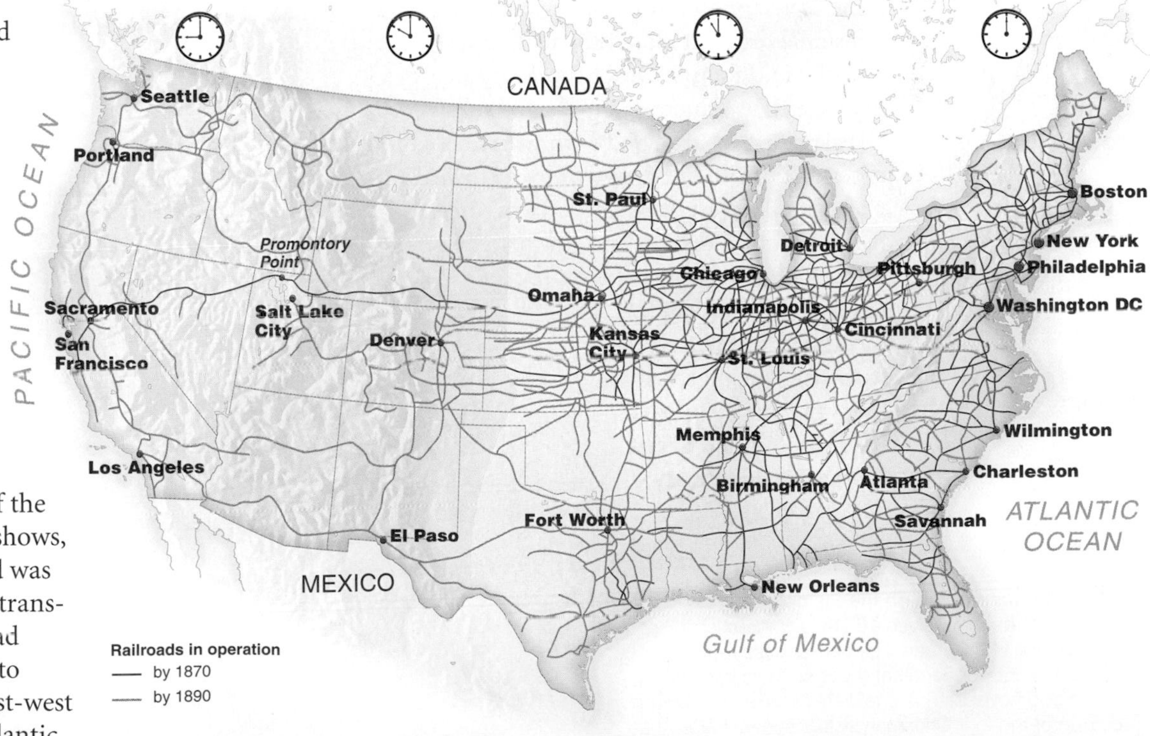

15.7 The Spread of the Railroad
Government loans and land grants helped spread a railroad network across the nation, facilitating economic development and settlement in the West.

How did the railroad shape western economic development?

Railroads also transformed the West by promoting urban growth. Many western cities like San Francisco, California; Portland, Oregon; and Denver, Colorado, had arisen as significant centers of trade before the arrival of the railroad. Once connected to the national rail network, however, they boomed into major metropolises. Their economies diversified as demand for construction, food, transportation, and retail opened up new opportunities for entrepreneurs. By 1890 the West was more urbanized than any region in the United States except the Northeast. Denver's population, for example, rose from 5,000 in 1870 to 100,000 in 1890. The population of Omaha, Nebraska, soared in similar manner, from less than 2,000 in 1860 to 140,452 by 1890. Like their eastern counterparts, western cities struggled with all manner of urban problems, including crime, disorder, corruption, poor public health, inadequate water, and ethnic tensions.

Hard Times for Farmers

While the overall trend in this period was one of expansion and profit, the reality for many farmers was struggle, frustration, and failure. To begin with, farmers faced unpredictable weather patterns. Farmers on the Plains, for example, enjoyed unusually high levels of rainfall between 1878 and 1886, leading them to think this was the norm and encouraging still more farmers to acquire homesteads. But a return to dry conditions and occasional drought after 1886 caused widespread hardship and failure. Other threats came from insects such as grasshoppers that attacked crops.

Farmers also struggled with wild fluctuations in prices paid for their crops from year to year. A plentiful harvest of wheat or corn often meant a glutted market and low prices. In the 1880s wheat farmers on the Plains saw prices fall due to competition with less expensive wheat grown in South America and Australia. Sudden drops in prices pushed many farmers into foreclosure because most carried high levels of debt to finance the purchase of land and equipment such as harvesters, plows, and windmills.

These conditions favored larger farms, revealing a significant flaw in the original Homestead Act: in the more arid regions of the West the 160-acre allotment was not large enough for profitable farming. By the 1880s so-called bonanza farms of 1,000 acres or more became increasingly common in the Dakotas and California. These large enterprises had more capital and thus could better afford expensive equipment needed for plowing, sowing, and harvesting.

On top of all these challenges were the problems of the loneliness and drudgery of life on the Plains. As this photograph (**15.8**) of the four Chrisman sisters standing by their sod house in Custer County, Nebraska, illustrates, life on a western farm was often a Spartan existence. Sod houses and dugouts cut into hills lacked even the most basic amenities like running water and glass windows. Apart from occasional trips to town, church, court sessions, and harvest fairs, opportunities for social interaction were rare since farmers usually situated their homesteads far apart. The Chrisman sisters developed a strategy that diminished their isolation and allowed them to fulfill the Homestead Act's requirement that they live on their land in order to receive full title to it. Beginning with Lizzie's homestead claim in 1887 and Lutie's in 1888, the two younger sisters took turns living on the homesteads, keeping their sisters company, helping on the farm, and waiting until they were old enough to file their own claims. Hattie eventually did, but all the homestead plots were gone by the time Jennie Ruth came of age.

15.8 Homesteading on the Plains
Western farmers received 160 acres of free land through the Homestead Act, but success required years of hard work and sacrifices such as living in crude sod houses. This one, in Nebraska, was owned by one of the four Chrisman sisters shown here.

What challenges did western farmers face?

In 1867, a former clerk in the Department of Agriculture named Oliver H. Kelley founded the Patrons of Husbandry, or **Grange**. This social and educational society was dedicated to alleviating some of the problems faced by farmers by promoting fellowship, fraternity, and education. Grangers, as they were called, shared ideas about farming through a newsletter and attended lectures offered by traveling experts. Local chapters opened all across the nation, and by the early 1870s the organization had several hundred thousand loyal members.

The Grange was transformed into a powerful political movement during the severe economic depression triggered by the Panic of 1873. Hundreds of thousands of farmers faced ruin as prices plummeted, while their creditors demanded payment for loans, and railroads charged high prices to transport their produce to market. In their desperation they created Granger Parties, which in 1874 won control of the legislatures of Illinois, Wisconsin, Iowa, and Minnesota and enjoyed significant influence in several more. They enacted a series of "Granger Laws," some of the earliest regulations of banks and corporations, especially railroads. Granger-dominated state legislatures passed laws setting maximum rates for transporting or storing grain and banning abusive practices such as offering preferred customers special rates. Grangers tried, as this 1873 cartoon (**15.9**) indicates, to convince Americans not involved in farming to recognize the threat posed to them by uncontrolled railroad power. As a "Consolidation Train," a name suggesting monopoly, pulls cars labeled "extortion," "bribery," "usurpation," and "oppression," a Granger warns unsuspecting citizens of their impending doom.

Railroad magnates denounced these limitations on their power and profit as unconstitutional and sued. The Supreme Court, however, in two key cases in 1876 (*Munn v. Illinois* and *Peik v. Chicago and North Western Railroad*) ruled that state legislatures did possess the legal authority under the Constitution to regulate commerce, including especially commerce between states.

Despite this stunning legal victory, the Granger movement faded when the depression lifted and farm product prices rose in the late-1870s, ending the crisis that had produced it. In addition the Democratic and Republican parties added pro-farmer planks to their party platforms that made the Granger parties seem less necessary.

15.9 Warning of the Perils of Monopoly The Grangers saw themselves as reformers trying to warn the American public about the growing danger of powerful railroads to the survival of democracy and individual liberties.

The Cattle Kingdom

Another key emerging sector of the western economy was cattle ranching. When the United States annexed Texas in 1845, millions of longhorn cattle (introduced to Central America in the sixteenth century by the Spanish) roamed the range, raised mainly for their skins and tallow. But as Americans developed a taste for beef in the 1860s, ranchers came to envision the great profits to be made if they could get their cattle to northern markets. A longhorn that cost $4 in Texas could be sold for $40 on the northern market.

Beginning in 1866 and lasting two decades, Texas ranchers began the first of the annual **Long Drives** of more than 1,000 miles to bring the cattle to market. Ranchers Charles Goodnight and Oliver Loving drove several thousand cattle from Texas to Colorado, prompting many imitators, who moved some 260,000 Texas longhorns onto the Great Plains within a year. In 1867 another cattle entrepreneur, Joseph McCoy, established a stockyard, hotel, bank, and office in a small Kansas town along the Kansas-Pacific Railroad. Advertising heavily, he quickly turned Abilene, Kansas for a time into the premier cattle drive destination. By the early 1870s more than 600,000 longhorns arrived per year to be sold and then transported by rail to Chicago and other destinations for slaughtering.

Over time the need for the drives diminished as rail lines were extended from Kansas into Texas and entrepreneurs established large cattle ranches close to railroads in states north of Texas, such as Kansas, Nebraska, Wyoming, and Colorado.

The period of the great cattle drives lasted only twenty years, but it firmly established the cowboy as an enduring icon of the Old West. Nineteenth-century dime novels, paintings, books, and plays (and in the twentieth century, films) traditionally depicted cowboys as paragons of manliness, independence, and courage who spent most of their days battling fierce Indians and driving cattle (see 15.20) and nights in raucous saloons playing poker and engaging in brawls and occasional gun fights. But the life of a cowboy was far more difficult and complicated. Cattle drives exposed them to harsh weather that included searing heat, flash floods, and deadly blizzards. Cowboys' wages averaged only about a dollar a day—or less if the price of beef fell—and they survived on a relentless diet of meat, beans, and coffee. They worked from dawn until dusk and then served a shift guarding the cattle at night against rustlers and hostile Indians.

Moreover, American cowboys were a far more diverse lot than the popular images depicting them as exclusively white men would indicate. Approximately one-third of cowboys in the American West were nonwhite, the largest group being Mexican *vaqueros.* Indeed, much of the equipment, clothing, techniques, and culture of the American cowboy derived from Mexican and Spanish traditions. This borrowing is evident in the many items associated with cowboys that bear names derived from Spanish. For example, the word *cowboy* itself is a direct translation of the Spanish term *vaquero,* while other terms such as lariat (*la reata*), chaps (*chaparejos*), and wrangler (*catallerango*) are anglicized versions of Spanish words.

Native Americans worked as cowboys, as did African Americans who accounted for one in seven cowboys. The eight cowboys shown in this 1880s photograph (**15.10**) worked on the ranch of Thomas Jones (shown standing) in Texas. One of the most famous was Bose Ikard. Born a slave in Mississippi in 1847, he was later taken to Texas where he became a skilled cowboy. Freed by the Civil War, he played a key role in the first Long Drive led by Goodnight and Loving.

Ranching held out the prospect of great profits, but ranchers faced considerable challenges. In the early 1870s the invention of barbed wire effectively ended open-range ranching and the long drives as farmers enclosed their land to protect crops from cattle hooves. Cattle ranchers also clashed with other livestock enterprises, such as sheep herders, over access to water and grazing lands. These conflicts frequently led to violence and on several occasions to widespread hostilities known as "range wars." Ranchers, like farmers, also were vulnerable to extremes of weather, losing cattle in times of scorching heat and drought, as well as freezing cold and snow. Similarly, they suffered from rapid expansion of the ranching industry in the mid-1880s and consequent flooding of the market with cattle that caused a collapse of beef prices, sending many ranchers into bankruptcy.

Fortunes Beneath the Ground: The Mining Booms

While many western adventurers found fortune and failure in railroads, farms, and ranches, still others tried their luck underground in the many mining districts that emerged in the West. The second great western mining boom, after California in 1849 (see Chapter 12), began in 1859 with the discovery of vast silver deposits in Nevada. The Comstock Lode, as the Nevada site was eventually called, yielded an astonishing $300 million to $400 million in silver in the next twenty years.

As was the case in most mining booms, the initial discoverers and nearly all the small-timers who followed garnered only modest profits. The real fortunes came in the succeeding years as heavily

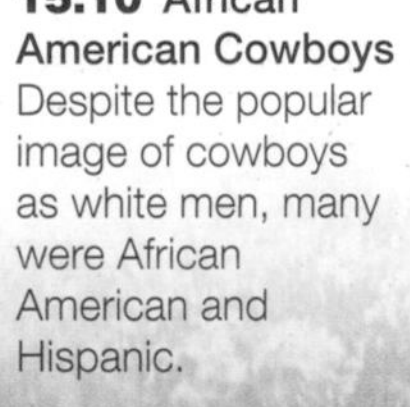

15.10 African American Cowboys Despite the popular image of cowboys as white men, many were African American and Hispanic.

How did the reality of cowboy life differ from that presented in popular culture?

capitalized and incorporated enterprises established mining operations to extract the ore. Among the titans who accrued stupendous fortunes were four Irishmen—John Mackay, Jim Fair, James Flood, and William O'Brien—known collectively as the "Silver Kings." They bought a controlling interest in the Consolidated Virginia Mine, an operation that many declared "spent" and virtually worthless. Yet in 1873 their miners hit the greatest silver vein of them all, the Big Bonanza that eventually yielded more than $100 million. Most fortune seekers, however, earned modest livings as wage earners working in the mines, while others flocked to the resulting boomtown, Virginia City, to work in construction, dry goods stores, and saloons. Thousands of women in Virginia City found work in hotels, laundries, and restaurants. Unfortunately, low wages and a lack of a family network to fall back upon led many women to become prostitutes.

Other mining booms for gold and silver, but also the discovery of such valuable metals as copper, lead, and zinc, followed in Colorado, Montana, Idaho, Wyoming, and the Dakotas. In every case the resulting boom followed the predictable path: the early mining claims gave way to larger, more sophisticated operations. The new corporations had the capital and knowledge to invest in the technology needed to dig deep shafts, extract the ore from rocks, process it on site, and ship it by rail to market. Like eastern industrialists such as Andrew Carnegie and John D. Rockefeller, these corporations often integrated their resources with the means and methods of production to maximize profits (see Chapter 16). The industrial revolution was not merely an eastern phenomenon.

The Environmental Legacy

Economic development in the trans-Mississippi West led to countless success stories of enterprising and risk-taking individuals who established farms, ranches, mines, and small businesses, or who simply found lucrative employment in the region's many urban centers. But such development in many cases carried with it a significant price in terms of the natural environment.

Mining, for example, came in many forms, but in nearly every case it left behind a badly scarred landscape. Open-pit mining of the Mahoning iron ore mine in Minnesota's Mesabi Range eliminated vast tracts of forest and created massive gouges in the land (**15.11**). These changes shattered the local ecosystem and choked surrounding waterways with muddy runoff water. Hydraulic mining, or the use of high-pressure water streams to wash away soil and gravel, created similar problems. Ore processing often used highly toxic chemicals to separate ore from rock or other materials that the miners simply dumped into rivers or open fields, where they eventually seeped into the water table and throughout the ecosystem.

15.11 The Price of Unchecked Economic Development Western states bowed to the powerful and profitable mining industry, leaving its practices unregulated. As a result, methods such as open-pit mining led to serious environmental damage.

The arrival of ever-growing numbers of humans in the West altered the delicately balanced western ecosystems. On the Great Plains, for example, hunting and other human activity led to the eradication or near eradication of elk, bear, wolf, and buffalo populations. Conversely, settlers introduced foreign animals and plants that, lacking natural predators, spread rapidly and disrupted the balance of the ecosystem. For example, cheatgrass, accidentally introduced to the West from Asia in the 1890s, quickly spread over millions of acres, wiping out or diminishing other flora and greatly increasing the incidence of wildfires.

Farming in some arid areas of the West, through the use of deep-cutting steel plows that loosened hard-packed dry soil, contributed to significant topsoil erosion over time. Vast herds of livestock had a similar effect as their grazing eliminated the grass whose roots held the soil in place. Likewise the practices of the timber industry led to deforestation, the loss of habitat for many animal and plant species, and without trees to shield the soil from heavy rainfall, erosion.

As *Competing Visions: Preservation versus Exploitation* (page 452) reveals, some Americans decried this environmental damage, but the great majority of Americans viewed the West through the lens of Manifest Destiny, seeing it as a place of limitless resources provided by God for the enjoyment and enrichment of human beings.

How was the environment of the West altered by human settlement and economic development?

Competing Visions

PRESERVATION VERSUS EXPLOITATION

Much of the economic damage and disruption that resulted from the development of farms, ranches, mines, and other businesses in the West followed from a prevailing attitude among Americans that all of nature was at their service. Lansford W. Hastings, a famous Western explorer, vividly expresses that view in the passage below. Less popular, but nonetheless significant, is the protest over environmental degradation set forth by George Perkins Marsh, a diplomat-turned-environmentalist. How does Hastings invoke the language of Manifest Destiny to justify his vision of the settlement of the West? How does he view the natural resources of the West? How does Marsh challenge the ideas that nature possesses limitless resources and that economic development is glorious progress?

Lansford W. Hastings, *The Emigrant's Guide to Oregon and California* (1846)

This infant country ... is destined, in a very few years, to exceed by far, that of any other country of the same extent and population, in any portion of the known world. ... [T]here is no country ... possessing a soil so fertile and productive, with such varied and inexhaustible resources, and a climate of such mildness, uniformity and salubrity; nor is there a country, in my opinion, now known, which is so eminently calculated, by nature herself, in all respects, to promote the unbounded happiness and prosperity, of civilized and enlightened man. ...

In view of their increasing population, accumulating wealth, and growing prosperity, I can not but believe, that the time is not distant, when those wild forests, trackless plains, untrodden valleys, and the unbounded ocean, will present one grand scene, of continuous improvements, universal enterprise, and unparalleled commerce: when those vast forests, shall have disappeared, before the hardy pioneer; those extensive plains, shall abound with innumerable herds, of domestic animals; those fertile valleys, shall groan under the immense weight of their abundant products: when those numerous rivers shall team [*sic*] with countless steam-boats, steam-ships, ships, barques and brigs; when the entire country, will be everywhere intersected, with turnpike roads, rail-roads and canals; and when, all the vastly numerous, and rich resources, of that now, almost unknown region, will be fully and advantageously developed. ... [W]e are also led to contemplate the time, as fast approaching, when the supreme darkness of ignorance, superstition, and despotism, which now, so entirely pervade many portions of those remote regions, will have fled forever, before the march of civilization ... [These accomplishments] shall forever stand forth, as enduring monuments, to the increasing wisdom of man, and the infinite kindness and protection, of an all-wise, and overruling Providence.

George Perkins Marsh, *Man and Nature*, 1864

Man has too long forgotten that the earth was given to him for usufruct [use without damage] alone, not for consumption, still less for profligate waste. ... But man is everywhere a disturbing agent. Wherever he plants his foot, the harmonies of nature are turned to discords. ... Indigenous vegetable and animal species are extirpated, and supplanted by others of foreign origin ... The terrible destructiveness of man is remarkably exemplified in the chase of large mammalia and birds for single products ... The wild cattle of South America are slaughtered by millions for their hides and horns; the buffalo of North America for his skin or his tongue ... What a vast amount of human nutriment, of bone, and of other animal products valuable in the arts, is thus recklessly squandered! ...

... The ravages committed by man subvert the relations and destroy the balance which nature had established between her organic and her inorganic creations ... When the forest is gone, the great reservoir of moisture stored up in its vegetable mould is evaporated, and returns only in deluges of rain to wash away the parched dust into which that mould has been converted. The well-wooded and humid hills are turned to ridges of dry rock, which encumbers the low grounds and chokes the watercourses with its debris, and ... becomes an assemblage of bald mountains, of barren, turfless hills, and of swampy and malarious plains.

Albert Bierstadt, *Among the Sierra Nevada Mountains, California,* 1868 [*Source:* See Credits section]

Why did few people heed the warnings of writers like Marsh?

Native Americans Under Siege

Westward expansion benefited many Americans, but it proved a devastating fate for Native Americans. They faced a relentless tide of white settlers who possessed both superior weaponry and a belief that they had a higher claim to western land. White settlers also enjoyed the support of the federal government and army. The result for Native Americans in the last third of the nineteenth century was broken treaties, devastating wars, relocation to reservations, and a policy of forced assimilation.

Mounting Problems for Native Americans

In 1851, as it became clear that the traditional government policy of simply forcing tribes into the West was no longer viable because of increased white migration into the region, Congress passed the Indian Appropriations Act. It set aside vast tracts of the Oklahoma Territory as reservations for dozens of Native American tribes. That same year the U.S. government, the Sioux, and several other Plains tribes signed the first Treaty of Fort Laramie. In exchange for declaring nearly all of the central and northern Great Plains off limits, the tribes agreed to allow white settlers to pass unmolested along the Oregon Trail as they moved westward. But the lasting peace that government officials and tribal leaders hoped the treaty would secure did not materialize. Tension and violence between white settlers and Native American tribes only increased in the coming years.

Native Americans faced a series of problems that ultimately doomed their efforts to resist Euro-American incursion onto their lands. Chief among these were the racist attitudes of white Americans that characterized Indians as backward, pagan, violent savages. who lacked a rightful claim to the lands they occupied. Many Americans believed their own culture was vastly superior and considered Native Americans obstacles to national progress that must be removed. "The Red Men are a doomed race," claimed one writer in 1877, for "the savage is giving place to a higher and more civilized race." These notions originated in the colonial period, but greater contact and conflict between whites and Indians after 1850 led to a proliferation of largely negative depictions of Native Americans in newspapers, magazines, songs, plays, and works of art like *The Rescue*, by sculptor Horatio Greenough (**15.12**). Comissioned by the federal government and placed at the entrance to the U.S. Capitol in 1853, the scene drew upon the many sensationalized stories and paintings of white settlers, especially women, being kidnapped, raped, and murdered by Native Americans. But Greenough departed from the traditional depictions and introduced a towering, dominant white settler. Notice the contrasts in the men's size, demeanor, and clothing. "I have endeavoured," Greenough explained, "to convey the idea of the triumph of the whites over the savage tribes." By 1874, the scene had merged with the life of the famous pioneer and icon of frontier masculinity, Daniel Boone (**15.13**). Both images proclaim Indian savagery and justify white domination, a message that eventually resulted in the sculpture's removal from public view in 1958.

15.12 **Promoting an Image of Indian Savagery** This 1853 sculpture by Horatio Greenough promoted the idea among white Americans that Native Americans were violent savages.

15.13 **Seeing Savagery** Greenough's image became so widely known that a dime novel artist easily adapted it to a Daniel Boone story.

What did the government hope to accomplish by signing treaties with Native American tribes?

White hostility to Native Americans shaped government policy, especially when it came to signing and honoring treaties. Invariably, it seemed, federal officials negotiated treaties with tribes that promised to permanently fix the boundaries of their hunting grounds and places of habitation, only to find soon thereafter that whites, hungry for land, had begun settling there. Rather than enforce the terms of the treaty and force the removal of white settlers, the government inevitably revised the treaty to further shrink designated Native American lands.

This combination of white settlers' desire for land and disregard for Native Americans' rights, and the efforts of Native Americans to resist white encroachment, led to repeated outbreaks of violence. one of the most egregious incidents was the **Sand Creek Massacre**. Angered by sporadic attacks on settlers by some Native American tribes in Colorado, a military outfit under Colonel John M. Chivington raided on November 29, 1864 a peaceful encampment of eight hundred Cheyenne at Sand Creek. With most of the Cheyenne men off hunting, Chivington's force slaughtered more than two hundred Indians, mostly defenseless women and children, mutilated their bodies, and returned to Denver with their scalps.

Native Americans also confronted epidemics of diseases such as smallpox and measles—diseases that Native Americans possessed little or no resistance to. While the worst devastation had taken place in previous centuries during initial European contact (see Chapter 1), epidemics of smallpox continued to erupt, killing thousands. For example, a smallpox outbreak in the Pacific Northwest in 1862 killed some twelve thousand Indians. The widespread abuse of alcohol, a commodity obtained through trade with whites, further compromised Native American health.

Additionally, long-standing animosities among tribes prevented Native Americans from developing a united front against the U.S. Army. White officials took advantage of these divisions to obtain help from one tribe, in the form of guides and even soldiers, against another. Disunity *within* tribes also contributed to this problem, as individual bands guarded their autonomy and resisted the idea of centralized authority. For example, in 1863 leaders of the Nez Perce tribe split over whether to sign a treaty that would confine them to a reservation. There were exceptions, of course, and some tribes managed to overcome this problem, at least temporarily.

The Plains tribes' dependence upon the buffalo left them particularly vulnerable in the 1870s. Railroad companies, disdainful of the large herds that occasionally disrupted the passage of trains, hired gunmen to kill buffalo. Entrepreneurs presently made buffalo robes fashionable in the East, thereby encouraging hunters to kill still more buffalo. The U.S. Army soon recognized the strategic value of wiping out the great herds as a means of undermining the independence of the Plains tribes and forcing them to stay on reservation lands. The scale of extermination was staggering. In this photograph (**15.14**), workers at the Michigan Carbon Works prepare thousands of skulls for processing into fertilizer, glue, and other products. The buffalo

15.14 Evidence of Extermination This mountain of buffalo skulls gathered by a fertilizer company attests to the scale of wanton killing of buffalo in the 1870s and 1880s.

How did negative stereotypes of Native Americans influence government policy?

population, estimated at thirty million in 1800, plunged to only a few thousand by the early 1880s creating a major crisis for the Plains Indians who depended on them.

The technological disparity between white settlers and Indians gave the former an enormous advantage. Euro-American settlers and army soldiers alike were heavily armed with modern rifles. The army also possessed early machine guns (called Gatling guns) and heavy artillery. While many Native American tribes had long ago acquired firearms, they never produced guns and ammunition and they remained dependent on whites for them. The U.S. Army also benefited from the telegraph, which allowed them to communicate over great distances about troop movements and Native American military activity, and to request supplies and reinforcements as needed.

> "Women and children were killed and scalped, children shot at their mothers' breasts, and all the bodies mutilated in the most horrible manner. ... Colonel J. M. Chivington all the time inciting his troops to their diabolical outrages."
>
> MAJOR EDWARD WYNKOOP, testimony before congressional committee investigating the Sand Creek Massacre

Wars on the Plains

Despite its lack of commitment to honoring them, the federal government nonetheless signed many treaties in the late 1860s hoping to bring peace to the West and allow continued settlement by whites. Treaties were drawn up and signed with the Apache, Cheyenne, and Arapaho in 1865, the Kiowa, Comanche, and Apache in 1867 (the Medicine Lodge Treaty), and the Sioux (the second Fort Laramie Treaty) in 1868. The latter treaty ended Red Cloud's War (1866–1868), a conflict that erupted when the army announced plans to build forts along the Bozeman Trail in the Wyoming and Montana territories to protect white migrants drawn by the discovery of gold in Montana. It guaranteed to the Sioux ownership of the Black Hills and land and hunting rights in South Dakota, Wyoming, and Montana. It also explicitly barred white people from these lands. "From this day forward all war between the parties to this agreement shall for ever cease," declared the treaty in words that would soon prove false. "The government of the United States desires peace, and its honor is hereby pledged to keep it."

Despite these measures, continued violation of treaties by white settlers who ventured onto Indian lands and bands of Indians who refused to accept confinement on reservation lands led to increased bloodshed. The Red River War broke out in 1874 on the southern plains in present-day Texas, Oklahoma, and Kansas when bands of Kiowa, Comanche, southern Cheyenne, and southern Arapaho Indians, angered over the federal government's failure to uphold its obligation to provide adequate supplies and keep whites off the reservation land (the army actually organized buffalo hunting parties that devastated local herds), left the reservation and launched raids against white settlements. Led by Lieutenant General Philip Sheridan, the army crushed the rebellion by the spring of 1875, thereby ending any future Native American resistance on the southern plains.

By then the primary scenes of conflict had shifted to the northern plains. The discovery of gold in the Black Hills of South Dakota in 1874 touched off a flood of white fortune seekers into the region that was indisputably (as stipulated in the 1868 Fort Laramie Treaty) territory granted exclusively to Native American tribes. Rather than keep white trespassers out, however, the federal government demanded the Sioux vacate their Red River hunting grounds and return to their reservations. When the tribes refused to comply, the army launched an offensive.

In the late spring of 1876 the Seventh Cavalry, led by a young and vainglorious lieutenant colonel named George Armstrong Custer, closed in on a large band of Cheyenne, Sioux, and Arapaho warriors,

How did the dependence of the Plains Indians on the buffalo weaken their ability to resist the loss of their lands?

including the well-known Crazy Horse and Sitting Bull, near the Little Bighorn River in Montana. Eager to earn fame and believing there were only a few hundred Indian warriors when in fact the number was closer to four thousand, Custer attacked before the rest of the army (and other officers who might overshadow him) arrived. The **Battle of Little Bighorn** quickly disintegrated into one of the most devastating defeats ever suffered by the U.S. military as Custer and 257 of his men were killed.

Although the Battle of Little Bighorn was an overwhelming triumph for the Sioux, Cheyenne, and Arapaho, it quickly proved a hollow victory. As this cartoon (**15.15**) published in the *New York Graphic* a few weeks after the battle vividly demonstrates, the eastern media ignored Custer's blundering and instead depicted him and his men as valiant victims and demanded vengeance. Notice the artist's blunt depiction of Indians as savage, semianimal beings in stark contrast to the two white soldiers, one a heroic victim and the other a coolheaded executioner. The caption, "The Right Way to Dispose of Sitting Bull and His Braves—What the Country Expects of General Sheridan," was a not-so-subtle assertion of the popular belief that the government was showing too much leniency toward Native Americans who resisted white expansion into the West. Responding to this pressure, the U.S. government expanded military action in the Black Hills, forcing the Sioux and other defiant tribes onto reservations.

15.15 The Negative Fallout from Little Bighorn
After the Sioux, Cheyenne, and Arapaho Indians defeated Custer and the Seventh Cavalry in the Battle of Little Bighorn, negative press coverage hardened white attitudes toward Native Americans. This image appeared in the *New York Graphic* (August 15, 1876).

War and Conflict in the Far West

Farther west, native tribes encountered similar problems. During the final third of the nineteenth century, the states and territories west of the Rockies also were growing. The mining and railroad industries, the economic centerpieces of that region, required a great deal of land—land long occupied by Native Americans. Just as they were on the Great Plains, the tribes on the West Coast and in the intermountain West

How did the victory over Custer and his men ultimately prove very costly to the Plains Indians?

faced an encroaching white population that considered the land theirs for the taking.

In 1876, following the massacre of Custer and the Seventh Cavalry, army and government officials increased pressure on tribes to move to reservations. One such group targeted was a portion of the Nez Perce tribe that lived on the northwestern plateau of Idaho, Oregon, and Washington. In 1863 most of the Nez Perce tribe had agreed to move onto a reservation, but about a quarter had refused. Led by Chief Joseph, about 750 Nez Perce (500 of them women, children, and elderly non-combatants) fled the region to escape the army. Over the ensuing four months, they engaged in an epic flight of 1,500 miles, hoping to cross into Canada. Despite their small numbers and dwindling supplies, they defeated the army in several battles and came within 40 miles of the Canadian border before they were forced to surrender to the army and to life on a reservation.

> "Hear me, my chiefs! I am tired. My heart is sick and sad. From where the sun now stands, I will fight no more forever."
>
> CHIEF JOSEPH, shortly after his surrender in 1877

Similar scenes of final military resistance played out in the Southwest. An Apache warrior named Geronimo had emerged in the 1860s and 1870s as a fearless opponent to encroaching Euro-American and Mexican settlers. Eventually captured by federal authorities in 1874, Geronimo and some four thousand Apaches were sent to a reservation at San Carlos, Arizona. The grim life on the reservation led him to escape and resume his campaign of resistance. In the face of mounting pressure from the army, he surrendered again in 1884. In 1885 and again in 1886, Geronimo escaped with a small band of warriors and their families and eluded capture for months. These escapades added to his already legendary status, but he eventually surrendered for good in 1886, ending the last significant Native American resistance.

Resistance to exploitation and abuse also erupted in the Southwest among Hispanos (descendants of Spanish colonists) and Mexicans in the 1880s and 1890s. Euro-American settlers who arrived in New Mexico in the mid nineteenth century eventually gave rise to a powerful ruling class of politicians, landowners, and ranchers. Many allied themselves with powerful gangs that provided protection and intimidated (and sometimes killed) their rivals. Poor Hispano and Mexican farmers often bore the brunt of these ruling Euro-Americans' ruthless tactics and hunger for land. When officials began to sell off to speculators and ranchers what had long been used as common grazing lands, the poor farmers resisted. The most famous of these resistors were *Las Gorras Blancas*, or The White Caps, a secret militant vigilante group of Mexican men who in the late 1880s and early 1890s wore white masks and cut fences on lands taken over by speculators. They also destroyed railroad bridges, buildings, and crops.

In Pursuit of a Solution

While most Americans expressed little concern over the fate of Native Americans in the West, a notable few did raise their voices in protest. One of the first was Helen Hunt Jackson. Inspired by an 1879 lecture by Susette La Flesche and her uncle, Chief Standing Bear, relating the plight of the Ponca tribe to an audience in Connecticut, she began speaking and lobbying on behalf of Native Americans. In 1881 she published *A Century of Dishonor*, a book that chronicled in searing detail the misguided and murderous treatment of Native Americans by the U.S. government. The book prompted Congress to appoint a commission to study Indian affairs and seek a new and more humane policy.

Another influential reformer garnered a wide audience as an authentic spokesperson for the Native Americans. Sarah Winnemucca, the granddaughter of a Northern Paiute chief, had received some education from white families in Nevada and California and worked as a translator for the army. In the late 1870s she began lecturing in the East demanding more humane treatment of the Paiutes and other tribes that brought her to the attention of eastern and western reformers. Winnemucca tried to gain credibility among whites by presenting herself as an "Indian Princess," an image firmly

Why were Native Americans so resistant to the government's demand that they settle on reservations?

established in American popular culture by the mid-nineteenth century, notably in the story of Pocahontas (see Chapter 2). In her posed portrait (**15.16**), hardly anything in her costume, especially the crown and bag embroidered with a cupid and bow and arrow, resembles traditional Paiute clothing and jewelry. Nonetheless, in an era when the political and social opinions of women, especially Native American women, were largely ignored, Winnemucca's strategy succeeded for a time in bringing extensive and respectful press coverage of her speeches and eventually her book, *Life Among the Paiutes: Their Wrongs and Claims* (1883). "In the history of the Indians," wrote one reporter in 1885, "she and Pocahontas will be the principal female characters."

"For shame! For shame! You dare to cry out Liberty, when you hold us in places against our will, driving us from place to place as if we were beasts."

SARAH WINNEMUCCA, *Life Among the Paiutes: Their Wrongs and Claims* (1883)

Both Jackson and Winnemucca promoted education for Native Americans, but with very different goals in mind. Jackson represented the reformers who believed it the duty of the government to elevate Native Americans from "savagery" by educating and assimilating them into white Euro-American society. In particular they advocated the establishment of boarding schools for Indian children and the eventual dissolution of reservations (see *Choices and Consequences: Forced Assimilation versus Cultural Preservation*). In contrast Winnemucca believed in formal education, but not at the expense of eliminating Native American culture. She believed it was possible for Indian children to become educated and productive Americans, while retaining the core of their culture and traditions.

Jackson's ideas prevailed among reform-minded legislators in Congress, especially Senator Henry L. Dawes. He had long taken a sincere interest in the plight of Native Americans during nearly three decades in Congress. In 1887 he wrote and Congress passed the **Dawes Severalty Act**, a measure designed to break up the reservations and assimilate Native Americans into the dominant white Christian American culture.

Specifically, the plan offered Native American heads of households allotments of 160 acres of reservation land (with smaller amounts going to those unmarried or under age eighteen) to encourage them to become independent family farmers. Remaining reservation lands would be sold off and the profits set aside for tools and education. Native Americans who accepted these terms then could apply for U.S. citizenship. To prevent speculators from defrauding Indians, land allotments would be held in trust for twenty-five years before full ownership was conferred.

The Dawes Severalty Act was born of high ideals and good intentions, but it nonetheless proved devastating to the Native Americans it was intended to help. The program was rife with flaws, beginning with the allotment of land that, in many cases, was of poor quality, making successful farming difficult if not impossible. It also included restrictions on hunting, further limiting options for participants. Despite safeguards, white speculators and scammers found ways to con Native Americans out of

15.16 Speaking Out for Native American Rights Sarah Winnemucca, a member of the Paiute tribe in California, drew attention to the injustices being suffered by Native Americans through a speaking tour of the eastern United States and the publication of a book.

What led reformers like Dawes to believe the break up of reservations would be beneficial to Native Americans?

Choices and Consequences

FORCED ASSIMILATION VERSUS CULTURAL PRESERVATION

The Dawes Severalty Act of 1887 stipulated that revenue generated from the sale of reservation lands be applied to the education of Native American children. As with the land allotment plan, the principal motivation of people like Dawes and reformer Helen Hunt Jackson was to assimilate Indians into American society, which they believed would be facilitated by providing vocational training to enhance their job prospects. But the act did not specify what kind of education ought to be provided, and so Congress and the Bureau of Indian Affairs faced a choice.

Choices

1 Establish reservation-based schools offering a traditional public school curriculum, while allowing Native Americans to maintain their culture, including their language.

2 Establish reservation-based schools offering a traditional public school curriculum, while requiring a higher degree of assimilation (especially learning English).

3 Establish off-reservation boarding schools committed to eliminating all vestiges of Native American culture.

Decision

The federal government chose to promote the establishment of off-reservation boarding schools. The model was the Carlisle Indian School in Carlisle, Pennsylvania. Established in 1879, it operated on the simple, but brutal principle of "kill the Indian, save the man." As the "before and after" photographs indicate, Native American children sent to boarding schools were required to cut their hair, wear American clothing, take an American name, and speak only English. Some schools made conversion to Christianity a top priority.

Consequences

Removal from families and fellow Native Americans on their reservations caused many children to suffer psychological trauma. Many also suffered from physical abuse, malnutrition, and poor health care. About one in seven ran away, and an unusually high number committed suicide. Still, by 1902 twenty-five federally funded boarding schools, and many more private ones, operated in fifteen states with an enrollment of six thousand students.

Continuing Controversies

What was the long-term impact of the boarding schools?
Along with the trauma inflicted on generations of children, it hastened the demise of Native American culture, including the disappearance or near disappearance of many languages. Several Native American groups have filed lawsuits against the U.S. government and the churches that ran the schools and demanded formal apologies.

Before-and-after photos of Chiricahua Apache children at the Carlisle Boarding School, circa 1890.

What assumptions about Native American culture influenced the boarding school program?

> "The Indians must conform to "the white man's ways," peaceably if they will, forcibly if they must. They must adjust themselves to their environment, and conform their mode of living substantially to our civilization. ... They can not escape it, and must either conform to it or be crushed by it."
>
> THOMAS J. MORGAN, Commissioner of Indian Affairs, 1889

15.17 Selling off Reservation Lands
This advertisement issued by the federal government in 1911 vividly illustrates the Dawes Severalty Act in action as it exuberantly proclaims a sale of 350,000 acres of Indian land.

their allotted land long before the twenty-five-year term. The act also allowed, as indicated by the poster (**15.17**), for the government to sell land deemed "surplus" to white settlers. This poster touts the high quality of the estimated 350,000 acres being offered for sale in 1910. As the map (**15.18**) shows, by the time the Dawes Act was replaced in 1934, two-thirds of Native American reservation land had been lost.

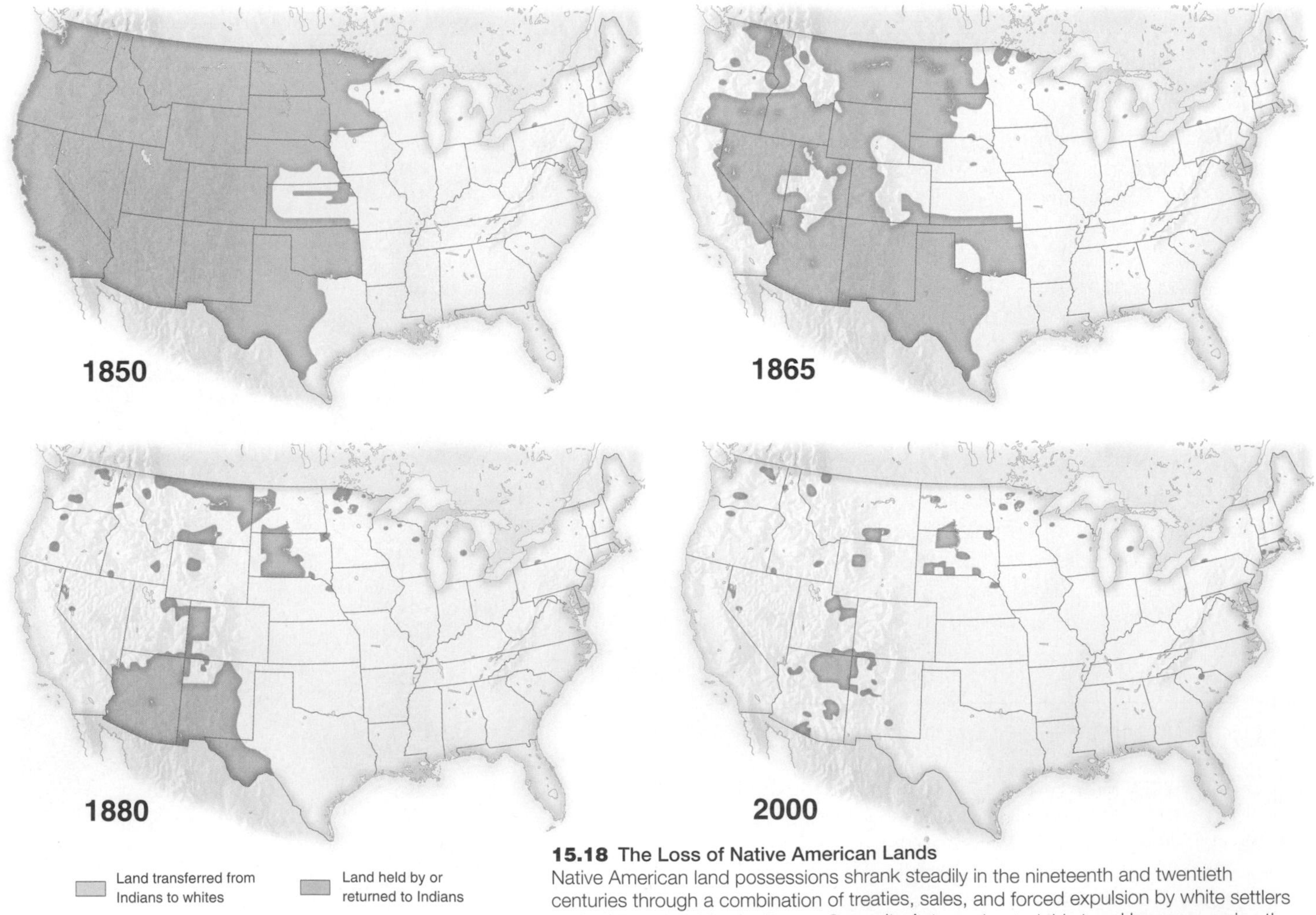

1850

1865

1880

2000

Land transferred from Indians to whites

Land held by or returned to Indians

15.18 The Loss of Native American Lands
Native American land possessions shrank steadily in the nineteenth and twentieth centuries through a combination of treaties, sales, and forced expulsion by white settlers and soldiers. In 1887 the Dawes Severalty Act accelerated this trend by encouraging the breakup of reservations.

How did the Dawes Act play a key role in the loss of Native American land?

Resistance and Romanticism

The surrender of Geronimo in 1886 symbolized the end of any significant armed resistance by Native Americans to the Euro-American settlement of the trans-Mississippi West. Nonetheless, a revival movement called the Ghost Dance, soon arose to offer one final attempt to reverse the fortunes of Native Americans. When that effort ended in brutal suppression at the hands of the army at a place called Wounded Knee, Native Americans turned to more subtle and enduring efforts to preserve their tribes, families, and culture.

At the same time, white Americans continued to fashion a pleasing image of the West as a place of adventure, heroism, individualism, and opportunity. This image found its way into art, literature, music, and innumerable aspects of popular culture in the twentieth century. Yet in recent decades, historians and activists have offered a corrective to this romantic image that takes into account the experiences of Native Americans, Mexicans, and women, as well as the impact on the environment.

Persecution and Persistence

The last major form of resistance to the Euro-American conquest of the West emerged in the late 1880s. The Ghost Dance movement originated in the 1870s, but did not become widely popular until a Northern Paiute shaman named Wovoka began preaching a message of Native American revival based on a vision he had experienced during a total eclipse of the sun in 1889. In this vision, which he related to his followers, he saw a great flood that scoured the land clean of all white settlers, leaving behind Indians who had remained true to traditional teachings and a renewed herd of buffalo. Wovoka told his followers to perform the Ghost Dance, a ritual ceremony where participants donned special shirts and danced in a circle until gradually brought to an ecstatic state that they believed drew to them the spirits of ancestors who would protect them from the white man's bullets.

The hopeful message of the Ghost Dance spread rapidly among Native Americans from the Rocky Mountains to the Great Plains, alarming federal officials who feared it contained the seeds of rebellion. They were especially concerned about its popularity among the Sioux and tried to curb it. After they moved a large group of Sioux Ghost Dancers to Wounded Knee Creek in present-day South Dakota, the army attempted to disarm them on December 29, 1890. When one of the Indians accidentally fired his gun, the soldiers attacked. The clash quickly turned into a massacre, and although estimates vary widely, between two hundred and three hundred Sioux were slaughtered. This photograph (**15.19**), titled "The Medicine Man Taken at Wounded Knee, S.D.," conveyed some of the brutality of the event. The date of January 1, 1891, on the photograph indicates that bodies were left unattended for days before being interred in a mass grave. Note the rifle placed on the body by a soldier or the photographer to present an image of a hostile Indian. It was not the bloodiest clash between Native Americans and the U.S. Army, but the **Wounded Knee Massacre** came to symbolize the brutality associated with the conquest of the West.

The end of armed conflict did not mean an end to resistance for Native Americans. In the coming decades, as they struggled with the loss of tribal lands, the cultural erosion caused by the boarding schools,

15.19 Massacre at Wounded Knee In an incident that came to symbolize American brutality toward Native Americans, U.S. soldiers killed between two hundred and three hundred Sioux at Wounded Knee, South Dakota, after a tense standoff over the Ghost Dance movement. [*Source*: © Nebraska State Historical Society Photograph Collections]

What made Wovoka's message so appealing to Indians and so frightening to military officials?

and high levels of poverty and alcoholism, Native Americans found ways to preserve their culture, including many languages, artistic forms, and religious beliefs. They did so by maintaining traditions within families and establishing informal methods of passing on traditions from one generation to the next. As a result, when a Native American rights movement emerged in the 1960s and 1970s, it included a commitment to reaffirming and strengthening traditional Native American cultures.

Creating Mythical Heroes and Images

The story of the American West has long been the object of romanticism and myth. The image of the West as a place of high adventure, heroism, rugged individualism, and endless opportunity developed with the very first enthusiastic reports of Western explorers such as Lewis and Clarke (see Chapter 7). But this image really flourished after 1850 as greater numbers of people headed west and sent back to loved ones in the East countless letters describing the marvels and perils of the frontier. Increasingly journalists sent back dispatches from the West describing wide-open lands, roaring rivers, majestic mountains, and the heroic struggles of pioneers against weather and hostile Indians. Eventually writers turned to fiction, especially a new genre known as the "dime novel."

The first Western dime novels appeared in the 1860s, and their subjects soon became pop heroes. Two early heroes were "Deadwood Dick," a cowboy dressed in black, and his girlfriend "Calamity Jane," who could handle not only her rifle and six-shooter, but also anything else that came her way. Another wildly popular Western character was Buffalo Bill. Based on the legendary exploits of a real Western scout, William "Buffalo Bill" Cody, stories about him first appeared in a newspaper and then in dime novel form as "Buffalo Bill, King of the Border Men." When it sold well its author, Ned Buntline, wrote a steady stream of Buffalo Bill stories. So, too, did other authors who flaunted copyright laws (eventually fifty thousand dime novels were published from the 1850s to the 1920s).

Cody grew famous but he earned no royalties from the novels. Seeking a way to capitalize on his fame, he created in 1883 "**Buffalo Bill's Wild West**," a circus-like production that purported to show audiences the thrilling and harrowing life on the frontier, replete with huge reenactments of cattle drives and clashes between Indians and cowboys, as well as exhibitions of marksmanship, cattle roping, and riding. The show proved hugely popular and it grew more elaborate every year, eventually topping out at 400 horses and 650 cowboys, Indians, musicians, and support staff. Over time Cody added big-name stars like the famous sharpshooter Annie Oakley and even the Sioux chief Sitting Bull.

Most Americans, indeed, much of the Western world, viewed the West, through Buffalo Bill's performances, as a place of heroism, optimism, gallantry, and success (see *Images as History: Annie Oakley*).

The West in Art and Literature

Western imagery and ideas also shaped American art and literature. Mark Twain, whose real name was Samuel Langhorne Clemens, emerged in the late nineteenth century as one of the first authentically American novelists generally unaffected by European mores. Twain headed west in the early 1860s when his older brother Orion became secretary of the Nevada territory. He had hoped his brother could provide him with a government job, but he also wanted to find his share of the gold and silver associated with the Comstock Lode. Accordingly, he headed west. The result was his classic book *Roughing It* (1872), which fit in with the evolving Western tradition of the yarn or tall tale, and the beginnings of a literary career informed by his experiences with the wild life of Virginia City. His subsequent major works, *The Adventures of Tom Sawyer* (1876) and *The Adventures of Huckleberry Finn* (1885), while not especially "Western" in that they were set along the Mississippi River, both contained Western themes of adventure, individualism, and a desire to escape the constraints of modern society for a purer, more authentic world. In keeping with this theme, when Huck Finn sets out at the end of the book to start life anew, he heads for the West.

Just as Twain's stories crackled with the realism of life on the Mississippi and in the West, Western art found its realist in Frederic Remington. Remington's background prepared him perfectly: after attending Yale's art school, he visited Montana, worked as a sheep herder and bar owner in Kansas, and started following the army, sketching battle scenes. Drawing upon earlier Western artists like George Catlin (see 15.4), he painted, drew, and sculpted vivid scenes of Western life. Most were vignettes of the lives of unknown cowboys, Native Americans, and soldiers.

Why did the West become such a popular topic in entertainment and literature?

Images as History

ANNIE OAKLEY

Two years after William Cody launched his Wild West show, he hired a woman who went on to become one of his most celebrated performers. Annie Oakley was a gifted sharpshooter, born and raised not in the West, but in Ohio. Taught to shoot at a young age, she killed game to earn money for her struggling family. At age sixteen she beat a professional in a sharpshooting match. She soon married the man and joined him on stage. In 1885 they joined Buffalo Bill's Wild West.

For sixteen seasons Oakley stunned and thrilled audiences with her marksmanship. She shot cigarettes from her husband's mouth and coins from his fingers. She blasted an endless succession of glass balls thrown in the air. She hit a target behind her by holding a mirror in one hand and shooting over her shoulder with the other. No one could match the "peerless lady wing shot."

But as this photograph and virtually every one she posed for shows, an essential part of Oakley's appeal lay in her image as an ideal frontier woman who combined Victorian femininity and rugged, almost masculine, strength.

Oakley's adoring public was not put off by her entry into the traditionally male world of guns and horses because she presented a pleasing and reassuring feminine persona. In so doing Annie Oakley, the woman from Ohio, played a key role in shaping the evolving mythical image Americans held of the Old West.

Oakley's dual image as both feminine and tough is captured in her facial expression. In all of her studio portraits, she presents herself as beautiful and composed, but unsmiling, to emphasize her grit and fearlessness.

While Oakley radiated a beguiling feminine charm (she entered the show ring skipping and blowing kisses to the audience), this hand-on-hip pose was very masculine and expressive of manly self-assuredness that audiences associated with cowboys.

Conforming to Victorian mores about proper behavior for women, Oakley always wore a dress and rode side saddle.

Her many medals were intended to lend her authenticity, as if to say that although she was a performer, her skills as a shooter were real.

Oakley's outfit was modeled on the cowboy's, but with exceptions to emphasize her femininity. Unlike the oblong cowboy hat, hers had a broad round brim. She set it on the back of her head to reveal her face and ladylike curls.

She always appeared with a gun, a central icon of how Americans in the late nineteenth century understood the West. It was a symbol they associated almost entirely with men.

Annie Oakley poses for one of her many studio portraits depicting an idealized image of a frontier woman.

What traits did Annie Oakley portray to present an ideal woman of the West?

One exception was Lt. Col. George A. Custer, whom Remington helped make into a hero after the Battle of Little Bighorn. Charles Russell, a cowboy-turned-artist, also emerged as leader of Western art, producing works that often depicted more sensational and imaginative scenes than Remington. Both men played a central role in creating the iconic image of the American cowboy. Russell's 1897 painting (**15.20**) is typical of most depictions, showing skilled and fearless cowboys roping a bull.

Historians Reinterpret the American West

Another key influence on the way Americans came to develop a particular image of the West was the work of historian Frederick Jackson Turner. In 1893 he published an essay, "The Significance of the Frontier in American History," that took as its starting point the recent announcement by the Census Bureau based on data compiled from the recent 1890 census that the American frontier was "closed," that is, for all practical purposes the United States was essentially "settled" from coast to coast. In the essay he set forth what historians long have called the Turner Thesis or the **Frontier Thesis.** According to Turner, the frontier had played a vital role in shaping the American character and consequently American institutions. The frontier's importance began with the first settlers during the colonial period along the eastern seaboard and continued in every succeeding generation as it pushed farther and farther west. This seemingly endless supply of land created widespread opportunity for upward mobility. The tough demands of the frontier, Turner argued, forced Americans to develop a spirit of rugged individualism and innovation. Frontier life also fostered values such as equality and democracy because success was determined not by one's background but rather by one's ability to work hard, sacrifice, and command the respect of others.

15.20 The Making of an American Icon Artists such as Charles Russell, who painted this scene, *The Herd Quitters,* in 1897, played a central role in promoting the cowboy as a symbol of the West as a place of heroism, daring, and manly individualism. [*Source*: Montana Historical Society, Helena]

Turner's thesis proved enormously influential. Several generations of Western historians based their writing and research on his ideas about the frontier. His influence also spread well beyond Western history—indeed, well beyond the study of history itself. Some American politicians and policy makers reacted to the apparent closing of the frontier in the 1890s by embracing imperialism to acquire new lands and markets that might make up for the absence of new places to conquer within the United States.

During the second half of the twentieth century, a new generation of historians reexamined Turner's thesis. In 1987 Patricia Nelson Limerick published *The Legacy of Conquest: The Unbroken Past of the American West.* Just as Turner's article was a product of the optimism and anxiety of late-nineteenth-century American society, Limerick's book offered an interpretation that reflected the fact that she was a woman raised in the 1960s, a time of social ferment, when historians began to focus more on racial, ethnic, and gender issues. Consequently she brought a far more critical eye to her study of the West than Turner.

That awareness was clear in one of the words in Limerick's title: *conquest.* Turner had seen white Euro-American settlers as triumphing over such "obstacles" as a stubborn landscape and "a fierce race of savages." Limerick and other writers, known as "new Western historians," presented a far more complicated story. While not dismissing Turner entirely they emphasized, for example, that Native Americans had inhabited the West for thousands of years before the arrival of Europeans and thus had a legitimate claim to the land. Viewed from this perspective, the story of westward migration was one of violence, exploitation, and conquest. Limerick and other historians also stressed the diversity of the West, seeing it as a meeting place of a wide array of Native American tribes, Euro-Americans, European and Asian immigrants, African Americans, Mexicans, and Hispanos that contributed to and shaped a Western culture that was not simply "white." Finally, the more critical approach of new Western historians has taken into account the environmental impact of westward economic development.

This new way of seeing the history of the West in recent years has had an impact beyond the history books. Hollywood films on Western themes began to change as well. In the classic Western epics of the

How have new Western historians changed the way many Americans understand the history of the West?

15.21 Reinterpreting the History of the West After more than 125 years of only commemorating Custer and his men, in 2003 the site of the Battle of Little Bighorn added an Indian Memorial to honor the Native Americans who fell in the battle. [*Source*: Colleen Cutschall, "Spirit Warriors". Bronze sculpture, 34 ft. × 14 ft. in an arc. Little Bighorn Battlefield National Monument, Montana. Brandon University, Canada]

1940s and 1950s, cowboys were heroes, fighting Indians who terrorized innocent white settlers. Beginning in the 1990s filmmakers began to present a more complicated view of the story of westward settlement, lawlessness, and white-Indian conflict. *Dances with Wolves* (1990), for example, presented Native Americans in very sympathetic terms. *Unforgiven* (1992) presented the West as a place of violence, lawlessness, failure, desperation, and corruption, where the line between good and evil is not at all clear. Many more such films followed.

This reassessment of the West's history has also brought significant changes in the way museums and public memorials present key chapters in American history. Nowhere is this more apparent than at the site of the 1876 Battle of Little Bighorn. For more than a century following the battle, the site was maintained as a memorial that depicted Custer and his men as heroic martyrs who died in the cause of Western settlement. The site was named for Custer (Custer Battlefield National Cemetery) and featured a memorial to the Seventh Cavalry and some Indian scouts on Last Stand Hill. Native Americans, who, of course, won the battle, were simply ignored. But the influence of new Western history and Native American activism led to the renaming in 1991 of the site Little Bighorn Battlefield National Monument and in 2003 the unveiling of the Native American memorial shown here (**15.21**). Located only 100 yards from the Seventh Cavalry monument, it features three bronze outline sculptures representing Sioux, Cheyenne, and Arapaho warriors who participated in the battle. Its official theme is "Peace through Unity," but it also represents a growing awareness that for far too long Americans relied upon an incomplete and overly simplistic understanding of the history of the American West.

Conclusion

The second half of the nineteenth century brought extraordinary changes to the United States as a whole, but especially in the trans-Mississippi West. In 1850 the primary occupants of the region were Native Americans. Most had lived there for thousands of years and developed an extraordinary diversity of lifestyles, traditions, and religious practices. White settlers, spurred on by manifest destiny, enthusiastic reports of open land, and measures such as the Homestead Act, soon began pouring into the region. They established milions of farms, founded countless towns and cities, and developed thriving railroad, ranching, and mining industries. But this rapid settlement and economic development came with a cost, most especially for Native Americans who were eventually forced onto reservations. Despite subsequent federal policies that emphasized forced assimilation and the breakup of reservations, Native Americans worked to retain essential elements of their culture in the twentieth century. Even as the final phases of western settlement and Native American defeat were playing out, Americans began to develop a mythical image of the West that, despite corrective efforts by activists and historians in recent years, remain alive and well in the American imagination.

Why are Native Americans so committed to reshaping the interpretation of historic sites like Little Bighorn?

1862–1866

Homestead and Pacific Railway Acts passed
The first distributes millions of free land to settlers; the second starts construction of the transcontinental railroad

George Perkins Marsh publishes *Man and Nature*
A widely read book that warns of environmental damage due to unrestricted exploitation of western resources

Sand Creek Massacre
Soldiers in Colorado massacre two hundred Indians

First "Long Drive" of cattle from Texas to the Great Plains
Leads to the rapid expansion of the ranching industry in the West

1867–1874

The Grange movement founded by Oliver Kelley
Becomes a powerful pro-farmer political movement by 1874 in western states

Second Fort Laramie Treaty signed
Guarantees the Sioux ownership of the Black Hills and additional land and hunting rights in South Dakota, Wyoming, and Montana

Gold discovered in Black Hills
Leads to escalating conflict as white miners move onto land reserved to Native Americans in the Second Fort Laramie Treaty

1876–1877

The Battle of Little Bighorn
Defeat of Lt. Col. Custer and Seventh Cavalry hardens white attitudes toward Native Americans

The flight of the Nez Perce fails
Symbolizes both Native American resistance to reservation policy and its ultimate failure

Review Questions

1. How was the development of the American West linked to the economy of the eastern United States?
2. What was the significance of railroad building to the West as a region and to its peoples?
3. What challenges did American farmers face in their attempts to establish successful farms in the West?
4. What significant industries, other than agriculture, developed in the West?
5. What were the critical factors that led to the conquest of Native American tribes and their forced relocation to reservations?
6. Why did U.S. government officials embrace a policy of forced assimilation for Native Americans in the late nineteenth century? How did they implement it?
7. Why did Americans develop and embrace a romanticized vision of the American West in the late nineteenth century? How close was this image to reality?
8. In what ways did the New Western History differ from traditional accounts of the settlement of the West?

1879–1881

Exoduster movement begins
To avoid violence in the South, thousands of ex-slaves migrate to Kansas, Nebraska, and Colorado to take up homestead farming

Helen Hunt Jackson publishes *A Century of Dishonor*
Brings national attention to the brutal and dishonest treatment of Native Americans

1883–1886

William Cody launches "Buffalo Bill's Wild West"
This hugely popular traveling show romanticizes the story of westward settlement

Apache resistance leader Geronimo surrenders
Ends the last major Native American military opposition to the U.S. military

1887

Dawes Severalty Act passed
Begins breakup of reservations and promotes boarding schools to encourage farming and assimilation

1890–1893

Wounded Knee massacre
Soldiers open fire on a gathering of Sioux, killing as many as three hundred

Frederick Jackson Turner publishes his frontier thesis
Bemoans the closing of the frontier, arguing that it had exerted a major influence on American values, ideals, and institutions

Key Terms

trans-Mississippi West The region of the United States west of the Mississippi River. **440**

Homestead Act Passed in 1862, it provided 160 acres of free land to any settler willing to live on it and improve it for five years; promoted massive westward migration. **440**

transcontinental railroad A line spanning the continental United States. Congress helped the Union Pacific and Central Pacific railroads build it by providing land grants, cash incentives, and loans.. **441**

Great Plains Vast open territory stretching east to west from present-day Missouri to the Rocky Mountains, and north to south from North Dakota to Texas. **443**

Exodusters More than twenty thousand ex-slaves who in 1879 left violence and poverty in the South to take up farming in Kansas. **444**

Mormons A religious sect founded in upstate New York in 1830. Driven by persecution they headed west in 1846 and settled in a valley in Utah near the Great Salt Lake. **445**

Grange Originally founded in the fall of 1867 by Oliver H. Kelley as a social and educational society for farmers, it became a major political force in the Midwest in the mid-1870s. **449**

Long Drive The annual cattle drives of more than 1,000 miles from Texas to the Great Plains that started in 1866 and established the ranching industry in the West. **449**

Sand Creek Massacre A massacre of some two hundred Cheyenne Indians on November 29, 1864, in Colorado by a military outfit known as the Colorado Volunteers under Colonel John M. Chivington. **454**

Battle of Little Bighorn Lt. Col. George A. Custer and the Seventh Cavalry are wiped out by a force of Cheyenne, Sioux, and Arapaho warriors on June 25, 1876; hardens white attitudes toward Native Americans. **456**

Dawes Severalty Act 1887 law that started the breakup of reservations by offering Native Americans allotments of 160 acres of reservation land to encourage them to become independent farmers. **458**

Wounded Knee Massacre U.S. soldiers open fire on a group of Sioux Indians on December 29, 1890, killing between two hundred and three hundred. **461**

"Buffalo Bill's Wild West" A circuslike production begun in 1883 that helped create a romantic and mythological view of the West in the American imagination. **462**

Frontier Thesis Historian Frederick Jackson Turner's 1893 theory that extolled the positive role the frontier had played in shaping the American character and consequently American institutions. **464**

CHAPTER

16

Wonder and Woe

The Rise of Industrial America, 1865–1900

> "This association of poverty with progress is the great enigma of our times.... It is the riddle which the Sphinx of Fate puts to our civilization, and which not to answer is to be destroyed."
>
> HENRY GEORGE, *Progress and Poverty*, 1879

This scene of industrial discontent, *The Strike* (1886) by artist Robert Koehler, was inspired by the great railroad strike of 1877. Set in an unidentified industrial town, it captures a moment of confrontation as workers pour out of a factory to gather outside the office of their employer. Unlike most scenes of labor unrest painted or drawn in the late nineteenth century, Koehler presented these workers as sympathetic characters, painting each as an individual rather than as nondescript members of a mob. Many wear square hats popular among various skilled trades, suggesting that these are more established workers. They appear as hardworking and hard-pressed men voicing their anger to the employer, perhaps over a wage cut or a round of layoffs, through the spokesman at the bottom of the stairs.

Yet the painting is fraught with tension and an atmosphere suggestive of impending violence. Notice, for example, the worker in the foreground stooping to pick up a rock. Maybe he is doing this merely as a dramatic show of anger, but perhaps he fully intends to throw it. Note also the scene to his left where a woman tries to calm down another angry worker. Again, it is not clear that she will succeed. And what about the employer? He appears to be listening patiently to the workers' representative, but whether he will accede to their demands is unclear (his stiff, emotionless bearing suggests he will not).

The uncertainty in the painting over both what is about to happen and which side—workers or employer—is in the right illuminates a central theme in American society as it experienced rapid industrialization in the late nineteenth century. The last third of the nineteenth century saw the United States thoroughly transformed by the Industrial Revolution, from a predominantly agricultural nation that ranked well behind England, Germany, and France to the world's most formidable industrial power by 1900.

While many Americans celebrated the Industrial Revolution for the unprecedented material wealth and progress it brought to American society, others grew disturbed by some of the grim consequences of industrialization, especially the immense power accrued by big businesses and capitalists and the growing number of workers living in squalid slums. The result of these conflicting visions was an intense debate—much of it vividly captured in Koehler's painting—over the proper role of government in regulating the economy, the rights of workers to form unions and strike for better wages and working conditions, and the impact of growing disparities of wealth on America's republican traditions.

What aspects of industrialization worried Americans in the late nineteenth century?

MONOPOLY

The Emergence of Big Business p. 470

The
LIGHT-RUNNING
NEW
HOME

Creating a Mass Market p. 478

The World of Work Transformed p. 483

Conflicting Visions of Industrial Capitalism p. 489

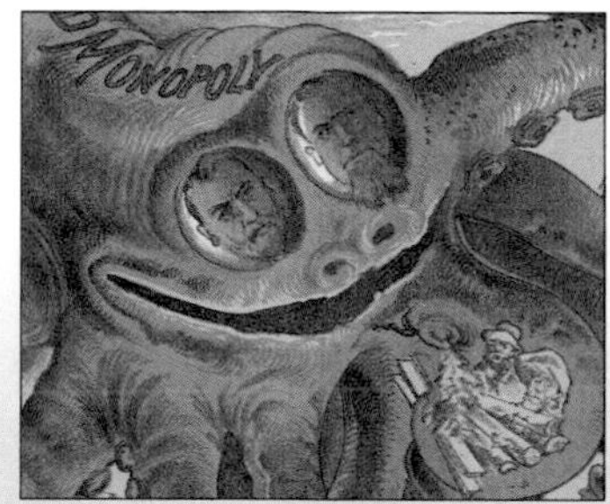

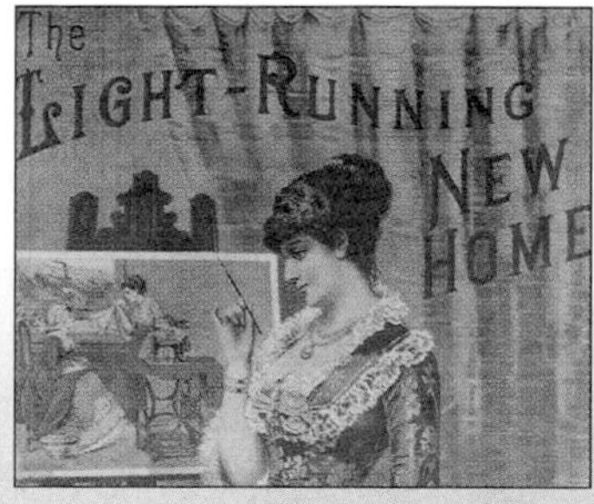

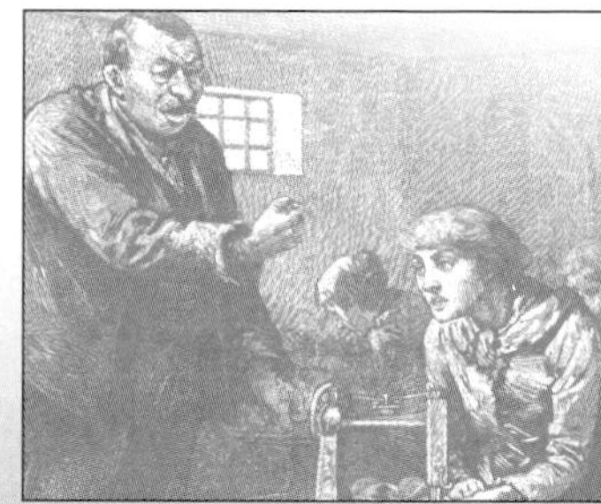

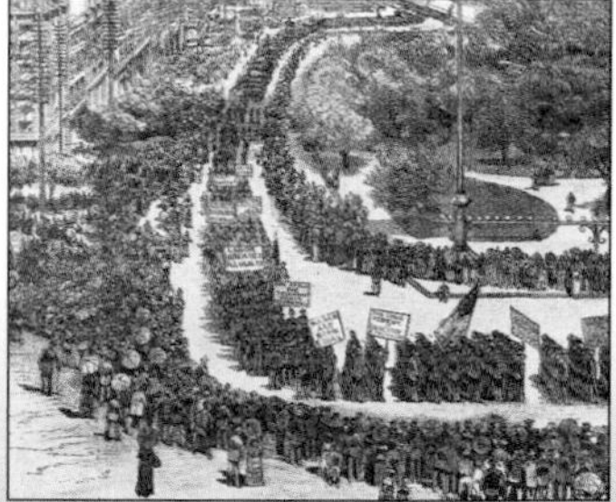

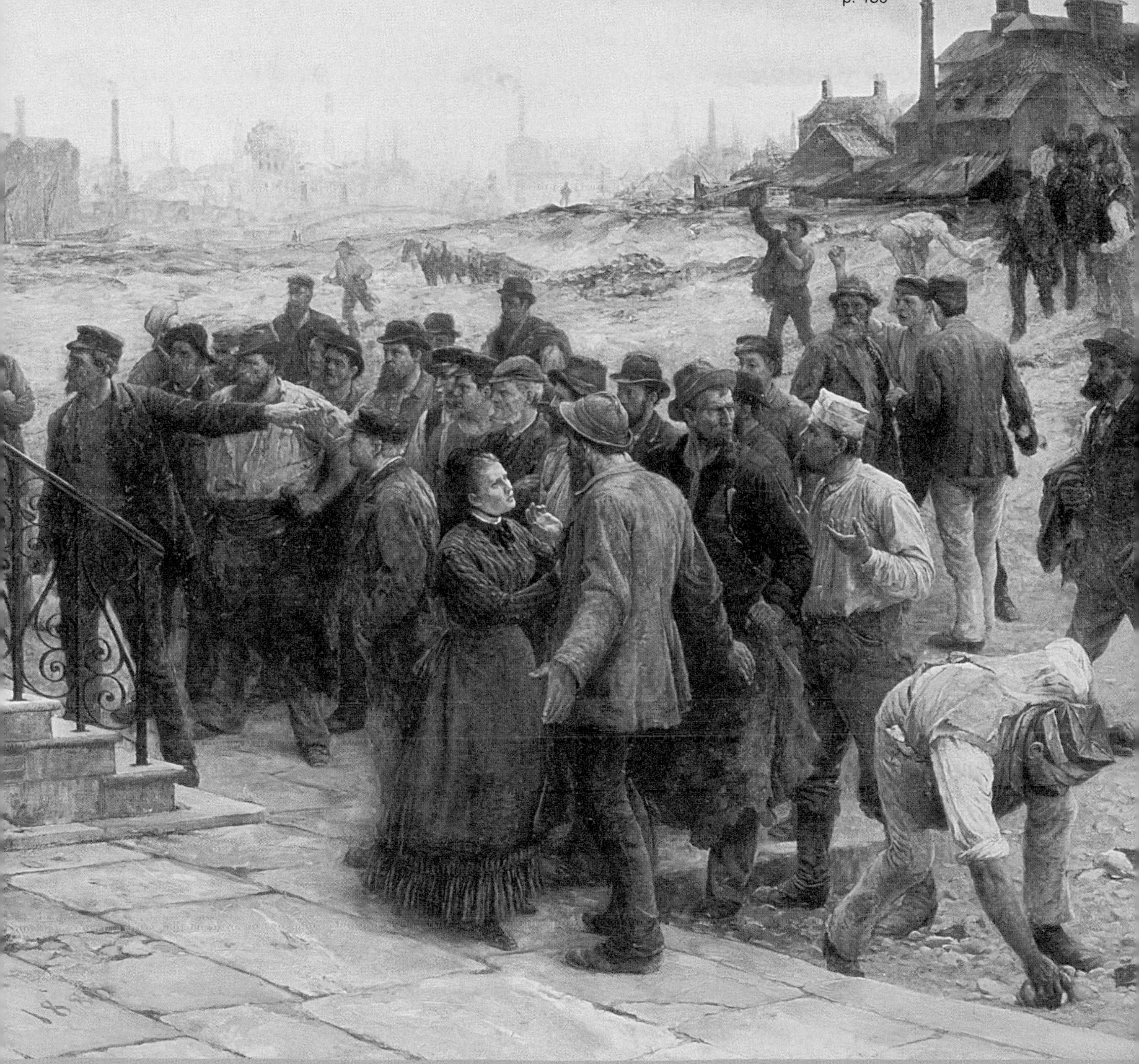

The Emergence of Big Business

America's huge supplies of key raw materials, its rapidly growing urban workforce, and its tradition of imposing few restraints on business enabled the explosion of industrialization after the Civil War. The railroads quickly emerged as the first big business, followed by steel and petroleum. All three industries pioneered in establishing modern business practices, but they also drew increasing criticism as Americans worried about their extraordinary power.

Sources of the Industrial Revolution

Compared to most of Western Europe, the United States was a relative latecomer to the Industrial Revolution, which made its rise to industrial supremacy by 1900 even more astonishing. Every statistical comparison between 1860 and 1900, from factory production to railroad mileage, told the same story of phenomenal growth that saw the Gross National Product rise 171 percent (**16.1**).

Several crucial factors combined to allow the United States to surpass all other industrialized countries by 1900. First, the nation possessed enormous quantities of two essential ingredients for rapid industrialization: raw materials and cheap labor. Vast deposits of bituminous coal in Pennsylvania and Kentucky, for example, provided a seemingly inexhaustible supply of inexpensive fuel to fire steam locomotives and factory machinery. Other plentiful resources included iron, lead, copper, silver, and gold, as well as wood, cotton, and oil. Cheap labor came from two sources. Record levels of immigration (see Chapter 17) in the late-nineteenth century pushed the number of foreign-born to one in five American workers (two in five in manufacturing and mining) by 1910. Likewise millions of American-born workers moved from rural settings to manufacturing centers in search of new opportunities. Women and children, both immigrant and native-born, also entered the workforce in growing numbers.

The incessant development and widespread

16.1 The Industrial Revolution by the Numbers
During the second half of the nineteenth century, every area of the economy produced enormous increases in output and value. Huge population increases helped to drive industrial and farm output.

	1860	1900	% Increase
Population	31,450,000	76,212,000	142.3
Farms	2,044,000	5,737,000	180.7
Value of Farms	$6.64 billion	$16.60 billion	150.0
Factories	140,500	510,000	263.0
Value Factory Production	$1.9 billion	$13 billion	584.0
Industrial Workers	1.3 million	5.1 million	292.3
Patents Issued	4,589	95,573	1982.7
Coal	20 million tons	270 million tons	1250
Lumber	10 billion board ft.	40 billion board ft.	300
Cotton	3.8 million bales	10.1 million bales	165.8
Oil	500,000 barrels	45,824,000 barrels	9064.8
Railroads	30,000 track miles	193,000 track miles	543.3
Steel	13,000 tons	10,382,000 tons	79,761.5
Gross National Product	$7 billion	$19 billion	171.4

What role did human migration play in fostering American industrialization?

adoption of new technology, a reflection of what many called the inventive spirit of the age, also furthered industrialization in the United States. Inventors flooded the U.S. Patent Office with applications, raising the number from an average of 1,000 per year in the 1850s to 20,000 per year in the 1890s.

Some notable inventors, such as George Eastman (Kodak camera), William S. Burroughs (adding machine), Isaac Singer (sewing machine), Alexander Graham Bell (telephone), and Thomas Edison (incandescent light bulb, phonograph, motion picture camera, mimeograph machine, and more) went on to become business giants. Less well known were the many women, immigrant, and African American inventors who filed thousands of patents in this period. For example, Jan Matzeliger, an immigrant of African and Dutch heritage from South America, invented a machine that simplified the most difficult and time-consuming step in the making of shoes (**16.2**). While much of shoemaking had become mechanized by the 1880s, the difficult "lasting" process—attaching the upper portion of a shoe to the sole—could only be done by hand. Matzeliger's lasting machine (patented in 1883) was a remarkably complex device, yet was easy for unskilled workers to operate, allowing manufacturers to greatly boost production while slashing costs.

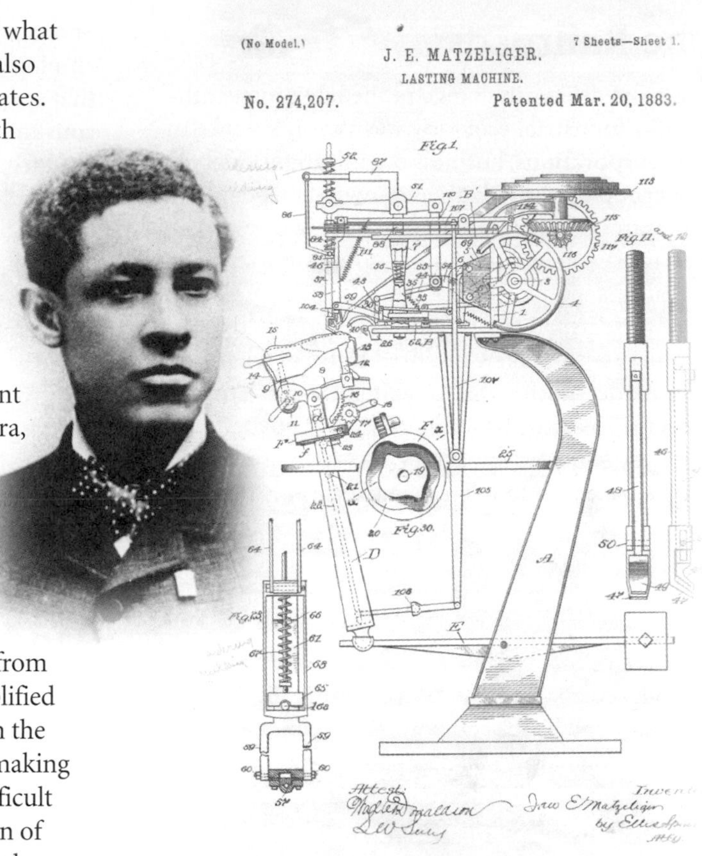

16.2 The Matzeliger Lasting Machine
Jan Matzeliger's complex sewing machine wiped out jobs for skilled shoe "lasters," who had hand-stitched shoe tops to soles, but allowed for a huge increase in mechanized shoe production.

Government policy likewise played a key role in furthering American industrialization. The federal government and the states extended substantial support to railroad projects that totaled almost 180 million acres in land grants and $500 million in loans and tax breaks (see Chapters 13 and 15). Public officials, in an argument later used to justify government support for the Interstate highway system and the Internet, defended this largess by arguing that railroads generated economic growth that benefited everyone from travelers to farmers to manufacturers. High federal tariffs that raised the price of imported goods, thereby helping domestic manufacturers, represented another government policy that promoted industrialization.

Yet the government also promoted industrialization by inaction. Public officials, business leaders, and conservatives subscribed to the philosophy of **laissez-faire** (French for "let do" or leave alone), which argued that the government should impose no restraints on business, including workers' demands for laws to regulate the hours of work, safety conditions, and wages. Government officials also ignored reformers' demands for statutes curbing cutthroat business practices and the establishment of an income tax. As Thomas Nast's political cartoon vividly shows (**16.3**), business and government leaders argued government interference harmed the American economy, depicted here as a woman weighed down by government-imposed burdens such as income taxes, laws (regulations), and "ideal" money (money not backed by gold). The closed shop and idle ship in the background and the vulture circling overhead all suggested these policies would kill the economy. Widespread support for laissez-faire among lawmakers left capitalists to operate in a market free of the restraints of government regulation.

16.3 Defending Laissez-Faire
This 1878 cartoon warns that government interference with the economy threatens the well-being of the nation.

How did government officials defend the practice of making huge land grants to the railroads?

The Railroads

The most dramatic change in the late nineteenth-century industrial economy was the emergence of large **corporations**, business organizations established by a group of individuals and owned by people who buy shares of stock in the company. Before the Civil War, most American manufacturers were small-scale operations with fewer than twenty-five employees. They were usually privately owned and sold their products within a few hundred miles of where they were made. All this changed after 1865, as entrepreneurs, seeking bigger markets and greater profits that they could now reach thanks to the railroad and telegraph, began to form massive corporations that boasted thousands of employees in a single factory complex, operations in several states, and millions of dollars of investment capital raised from the sales of stock.

The original big businesses were railroads, and they played a key role in transforming the United States into an industrial power. In 1865 there were scores of small railroad companies scattered throughout the Northeast and Midwest and, to a lesser extent, the South. Comprising 35,000 miles of track, they serviced small areas and established their own standards for things such as track gauge (the distance between the rails). Nearly all suffered from financial instability and poor management. But by 1900, this haphazard system had developed into a massive, consolidated, and integrated national railroad network of 193,000 miles dominated by just seven large corporations.

Railroads grew at such a ferocious pace because they could be built almost anywhere, creating a transportation network no longer confined to meandering rivers and expensive, slow-to-construct canals that often froze in winter. The railroad also offered another great advantage: speed. People, mail, and goods traveling by stagecoach might, on a good day, cover 50 miles. A steam locomotive pulling many times more people, mail, and goods could cover the same distance in less than two hours. And after the completion of the first of several transcontinental lines in 1869 (see map 15.7) the railroad offered service from coast to coast.

The railroad meant more quick and cheap transportation, both boosts for the national economy. Wherever railroads were built new areas of settlement opened. Farmers settled on nearby land, often sold to them by the railroad company, confident that they could get their agricultural produce to market. Shopkeepers, artisans, laborers, and railroad employees (one million by 1900) settled in towns that sprang up along the tracks. In turn they became consumers of finished goods brought by the railroad from eastern manufacturers. The railroad industry also contributed to the national economy by consuming large quantities of iron, steel, coal, and wood.

Fierce competition among railroads initially led to the rapid expansion of lines. By the 1870s, many railroads tried to diminish competition by buying out rival railroads, leading to the creation of giant corporations such as the Pennsylvania Railroad and the New York Central Railroad. Both owned thousands of miles of track in many states, employed tens of thousands of workers, and handled millions of dollars in investment capital and revenue.

Modern Business Practices

The success of the large railroad corporations led to the modernization of business practices in two important ways. First, railroad corporations allowed other types of businesses to see the advantages of incorporating and issuing stock. Stock sales allowed corporations to raise capital to expand the business (for example, to buy new and more efficient equipment, or to buy a rival company). If the company earned a profit, stockholders benefited from an increase in the value of the stock (which they could sell for a profit) and sometimes by earning dividends. Stockholders played no direct role in running a company; a professional management team performed that function. But stockholders also enjoyed "limited liability": If the company failed they were not liable for any of its debts or obligations, but they stood to lose only their shares. By the 1870s increasing numbers of companies involved in manufacturing, mining, communications, and finance had incorporated.

Second, the sudden emergence of huge railroad corporations operating in many states, employing thousands of workers, and handling millions of dollars encouraged the development of modern, sophisticated management practices. Chief among these practices was standardization. For example, in 1883, the nation's major railroads established the four time zones that are still in use today. This decision helped to combat the problem of irregular "local time" (for example, when local time in New York City was 12:00 p.m., it was 11:55 a.m. in Philadelphia and 11:47 in Washington, D.C.) that

How did railroad grants both reflect and promote national economic growth?

> "Railroad time, it appears, is to be the time of the future. And so, people will now have to marry and die by railroad time. Ministers will preach by railroad time, and banks will be required to open and close by the same time. The sun is no longer the boss of the job."
>
> *Indianapolis Sentinel,* 1883

often led to costly accidents between trains sharing a single track or crossing at a junction.

Similarly, the development of standardized equipment like couplers, signals, and brakes allowed for easier operation and maintenance of a railroad's growing fleet of rolling stock. In 1886 the railroads also established a standard gauge for track of 4 feet 8.5 inches, thereby eliminating costly delays caused by the need to transfer cargo from one train to another wherever tracks of two different gauges met. As this drawing (**16.4**) indicates, many Americans viewed standard gauge as bringing both economic and political benefits to the nation, since it promised to create both a more efficient railroad system and greater unity between the less developed South (see Chapter 14) with the rapidly industrializing North. The banner "The Last Spike in Our Commercial Union" likens the event to the 1869 completion of the transcontinental railroad.

To oversee these vast commercial operations—the largest in the world—executives of the major railroads, such as Jay Gould, Tom Scott, and Collis B. Huntington, developed complex hierarchies of superintendents, managers, and clerks and new systems of accounting, advertising information management, and pricing. Other big businesses, such as steel, oil, manufacturing, and retailing, soon copied these organizational practices, making them the norm in most large corporations.

16.4 Celebrating the Standard Gauge, 1886
In this imagined scene Northerners and Southerners celebrate the adoption of a standard rail gauge as a measure destined to bind the country together economically.

Rising Concern over Corporate Power

Americans greeted the astonishing spread of the railroad with mixed feelings. Many agreed with poet Walt Whitman, who celebrated the railroad as "the modern emblem of motion and power—the pulse of the continent." They delighted in the benefits of inexpensive and speedy travel and increased access to finished goods in new mail order catalogs.

16.5 Demonizing the Monopoly Americans grew increasingly worried about the rising power of railroads, the largest of which were often criticized as monopolies that strangled their competition.

Yet many Americans worried about the larger implications of the railroad. The cartoon depicting the Southern Pacific Railroad as a ravenous octopus (**16.5**) expressed their concern. The railroads and the fabulously wealthy men who ran them (shown in the eyes of the octopus) wielded immense power. The artist labeled the octopus a **monopoly**, a popular term to describe the control of an industry or market by one corporation. Was such unchecked power vested in the hands of so few people, worried the critics, compatible with the nation's republican principles? Many feared it was not—especially when it became clear that railroad executives routinely used their wealth to bribe state legislatures, members of Congress, and cabinet officials. Additional revelations of stock manipulation, price gouging of farmers and manufacturers, exploitation of workers, and shoddy construction and unsafe operation added to the railroad's tarnished image and fueled concerted efforts to curb its power. Although few critics raised the issue at the time, later generations decried the railroad for its role in hastening the defeat of the Plains Indians and the near extermination of buffalo upon which they depended (see Chapter 15).

Growing anxiety and anger over the abusive practices of many large railroads eventually compelled reformers to seek tighter regulation of the industry. Given the immense power and wealth of the railroad and a general reluctance among politicians to regulate business, reform faced many setbacks. Farmers, bitterly opposing the high rates charged by railroads to transport and store agricultural commodities, led the first significant effort to curb laissez-faire business practices. Known as the Grange (see Chapter 15) it led a successful political movement in the 1870s to pass numerous laws regulating prices and outlawing unfair business practices.

Andrew Carnegie: Making Steel and Transforming the Corporation

Of all the new things produced by the explosion of industrial output after 1865, none was more important than steel. Many times stronger than iron, steel became the essential ingredient in the transformation of America into an industrial society, allowing for the construction of the railroad and telegraph networks and tall buildings called "skyscrapers." Steel also allowed for the construction of huge factories, filled with powerful manufacturing machinery—made from steel, of course. Steel likewise accelerated the commercialization of American agriculture as the material that made possible sharp, durable, and deep-cutting plows and mechanical reapers. It also altered modern warfare, enabling the development of more accurate, powerful, and thus more deadly weapons. Steel, in short, was as influential and revolutionary a substance in the late nineteenth century as silicon (used to make computer chips) was to become in the late twentieth.

Steel was important in still another way, for it brought to prominence the single most influential big business man of the era, Andrew Carnegie.

Why did many Americans come to see railroads as potential threats to democracy?

Carnegie's success was all the more remarkable because of his humble origins. Born in Scotland in 1836, he immigrated to America with his family at the age of twelve. Settling in Pittsburgh they struggled to earn a living. Young Carnegie dropped out of school and took a job in a textile factory where he earned just $1.20 per week. Bright and ambitious, Carnegie took night classes in accounting, taught himself telegraphy, and went to work for Western Union. In 1853 Pennsylvania Railroad regional supervisor and future company president, Thomas A. Scott, hired the seventeen-year-old to serve as his personal telegrapher and eventually private secretary. In this capacity, Carnegie learned every detail of modern business practices that the railroad was developing. With his higher salary, he invested in railroads, factories, and, increasingly, the iron and steel industries.

In 1870 while running a very successful company that built steel bridges, Carnegie decided to move entirely in steel production. He built his own steel works and, drawing upon his knowledge of railroad management, he followed obsessively one fundamental business principle: reducing production costs to the lowest possible level.

To achieve this goal, Carnegie hired the brightest executives, accountants, managers, scientists, and engineers. He also invested heavily in the latest technology. He was the first to invest in the breakthrough Bessemer-Kelly process, a method of making exceptionally strong steel quickly and at low cost (in part due to reducing the need for skilled metalworkers).

Carnegie's focus on cost control led him to pioneer what is in the business practice known as **vertical integration**, the organization of a business by which one company controls all the main phases of production, from acquiring raw materials to retailing the finished product. Other industrial magnates who came to dominate their industries opted for a **horizontal integration**, a model where they bought out many companies producing the same product to eliminate competition and achieve greater efficiency (**16.6**). To provide a steady supply of cheap coal, iron, and other essential raw materials that steel production depended on, Carnegie bought mines, smelting operations, railroads, and ships.

Finally, Carnegie pursued cutthroat practices to battle rival steel producers. To drive smaller rivals out of business, Carnegie slashed his prices to levels that bankrupted his competitors, allowing him to buy them out and gain a greater share of the market.

VERTICAL INTEGRATION Seeking to bring under one company the many different products and processes that go into the making of paper, Company A has acquired forests, logging companies, railroads, and chemical companies, as well as paper manufacturing plants. The advantages in this system are lower prices for and greater control over supplies of essential materials (such as wood pulp from trees).

Paper Company A Acquires

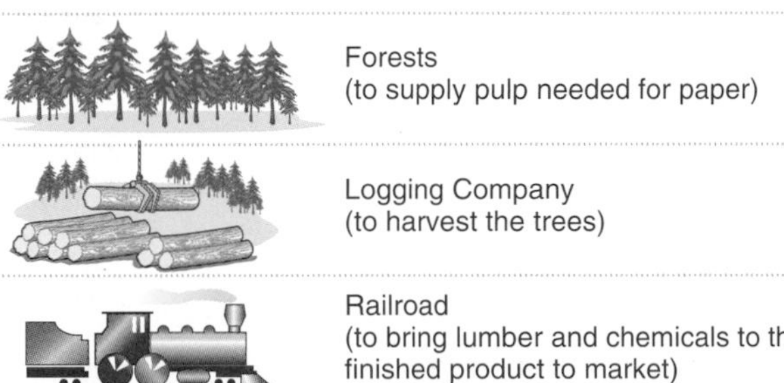

HORIZONTAL INTEGRATION Seeking to gain the largest share of the market for paper products, Company B has acquired five more paper manufacturing companies. The advantage of this system is that Company B can generate more revenue from the added production and sales of paper products. It can also lower costs by eliminating redundant operations like advertising, marketing, and accounting in the acquired companies in favor of single operations covering these functions. Because of its increased size, the company can also lower costs by striking deals with suppliers (wood pulp, chemicals, etc.) eager for its business.

Paper Company B Acquires

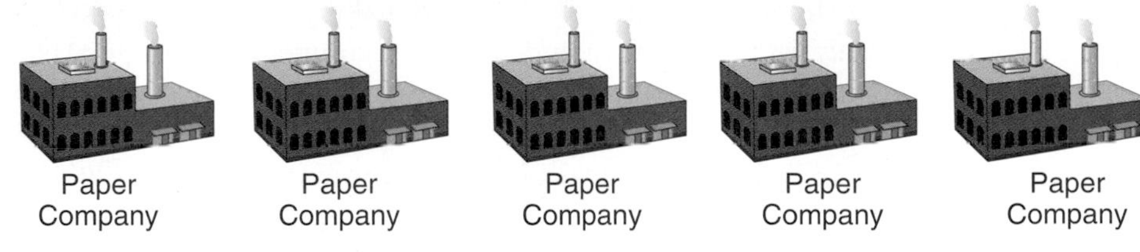

16.6 Horizontal Integration versus Vertical Integration
Industrialists pursued two strategies when seeking to expand the size of their corporation. With vertical integration they sought to minimize costs and increase control of production by acquiring different kinds of companies involved in the chain of production. Through horizontal integration they attempted to reduce competition by acquiring their competitors.

Like many other industrialists, he also signed secret deals with railroads, securing lower transportation rates for his steel than that charged by his competitors. Most of these tactics were legal at that time, but many critics considered them abusive.

The result of Carnegie's business policies was astonishing, bringing annual profits to $40 million by 1900. By then Carnegie Steel was the largest corporation in the world, with more than twenty thousand employees and related operations in many countries. Carnegie's success was part of the much larger story of the "age of steel." By 1900 the U.S. steel industry employed 272,000 workers who that year produced 10.4 million tons of steel—an output more than twice that of its nearest rivals, Germany and Great Britain.

Rockefeller and the Rise of the Trust

Carnegie was the most famous industrialist in the late nineteenth century, but countless others similarly led the way in developing key parts of the American economy. These included entrepreneurs like Philip Armour and Gustavus Swift (meatpacking), James B. Duke (tobacco products), George Eastman (Kodak camera) and Cyrus McCormick (farm equipment). Like Carnegie these industry leaders and thousands more succeeded by combining vision and ruthlessness, leading the public to both laud them as "captains of industry" who offered an ever-growing number of new products and services and denounce them as "**robber barons**," greedy capitalists who grew rich by devious business practices, exploitation of workers, and political manipulation.

The industrialist most frequently denounced as a robber baron was John D. Rockefeller. In many ways his rise to dominance in the oil industry resembled that of Andrew Carnegie. Through relentless cost-cutting, acquisition of new technology, hiring top-notch managers and scientists, and making secret deals with railroads to undermine his competition Rockefeller's Standard Oil company controlled more than 80 percent of the nation's oil-refining capacity by 1879. Unlike Carnegie, Rockefeller initially expanded his interests via horizontal integration (**16.6**), focusing almost exclusively on buying or building oil refineries. Later he followed Carnegie's vertical integration model as well, purchasing oil fields, railroad cars and warehouses, pipelines, and barrel factories.

Rockefeller's chief contribution to the rise of big business was the invention of two new forms of corporation management: the trust and the holding company. Like many industrial magnates, Rockefeller upheld the ideal of competition, but privately he believed competition between rival companies merely created waste and instability in the market. When so-called pools—secret deals between ostensibly rival companies to set production limits to keep prices high and award each participant a certain share of the market—inevitably failed, Rockefeller devised the trust.

Unlike pools, which lacked any legal basis and thus carried no penalty for cheating, **trusts** were legally binding arrangements that brought many companies in the same industry under the direction of a single board of "trustees." To join a trust, a company turned over to a board a majority of its stock in exchange for trust certificates, which guaranteed it a share of the profits. Rockefeller's Standard Oil Trust, for example, consisted of forty companies under the direction of a nine-member board of trustees selected by Rockefeller himself. As profits soared, dozens of trusts in other industries, such as sugar, lead, cotton, and oil, were formed, although not all successfully.

> "Honest labor never rusts: up with labor down with trusts."
>
> Banner in 1889 Boston Labor Day Parade

The rapid emergence of giant trusts, as with the rise of large railroads, alarmed many Americans. Fueling this rising concern was the unwillingness of Congress and the Supreme Court to curb the power of big business. In 1886 the very conservative Supreme Court declared that state railroad commissions did not have the authority to impose regulations on railroads because only Congress had the right to regulate interstate commerce (*Wabash, St. Louis & Pacific Railway Co. v. Illinois*, 1886). In a separate case (*Santa Clara County v. Southern Pacific Railroad*, 1886), the court also declared that corporations were "de facto persons" and thus subject to all the protections under the Fourteenth Amendment. No state or local government, therefore, could impose limits on corporations "without due process of law"—in other words, approval by conservative federal courts.

Why did big business find trusts so useful and attractive?

The next year in 1887 Congress attempted to curb the power of the railroads by establishing the Interstate Commerce Commission and making pools and rebates (special discounts by railroads to favored customers) illegal. But the ICC proved weak and ineffective, especially in the face of a conservative Supreme Court. Of the sixteen cases when railroads challenged a ruling by the ICC between 1887 and 1905, the Supreme Court sided with the railroads fifteen times.

Big business also benefited from enormous political influence in Congress. In this damning 1889 cartoon, *The Bosses of the Senate* (**16.7**), from the popular magazine *Puck*, the bloated trusts are clearly in charge. Congress was all too willing to do the bidding of corporate interests. Note that the doorway marked "People's Entrance" is boarded shut while a much larger "Entrance for Monopolists" is wide open. Note too the bitter conclusion that big business has subverted American democracy: "This is a Senate of the monopolists, by the monopolists, and for the monopolists."

The fate of the **Sherman Anti-Trust Act** of 1890 seemed to verify this conclusion. It was originally proposed as a law that empowered the Justice Department to prosecute any illegal contract, combination, or conspiracy among corporations that was designed to eliminate competition or in any way restrain free trade. In other words the act made trusts illegal. But months of lobbying by corporate interests influenced Congress to word the final version of the act so vaguely that it was essentially unenforceable. As a result, the Justice Department prosecuted only eighteen antitrust cases between 1890 and 1904.

Rockefeller's other major corporate management innovation—the **holding company**—replaced the trust in the 1890s as the preferred big business model. The holding company was a huge corporation that bought and ran other corporations by purchasing their stock. Rockefeller's idea caught on immediately because it offered protection from the Sherman Act and allowed for the creation of enormous corporations, many of which exercised near monopoly control of the market. Corporate mergers occurred at an astonishing pace in the 1890s, so that by 1900 a mere 1 percent of corporations controlled 33 percent of the nation's manufacturing output, a figure that rose to 44 percent by 1910. The same was true of the railroads. In 1900 seven colossal railroads controlled two-thirds of the nation's track mileage. Big business, despite the best effort of reformers, was here to stay.

16.7 The Political Power of the Trusts Reformers criticized trusts for their power to bribe and bully Congress to pass favorable legislation. Here, a meek-looking Congress sits under the domineering gaze of the bloated trusts.

Why did efforts to curb the power of trusts fail?

Creating a Mass Market

Railroads, oil refineries, textile factories, and steel mills were the most vivid symbols of the industrial era, but production was only one part of the story. Equally important was consumption—getting the public to purchase the growing array of the national economy's new products. The development of advertising would play a crucial role in creating a consumer culture, as would the department store and mail order catalogs.

The Art of Selling

To promote consumption, businesses developed sophisticated advertising techniques and marketing strategies. Many hired psychologists and other experts to develop advertising campaigns that appealed to both consumers' fears and their desires. Ads for toothpaste and deodorant, for example, stoked the public's fears of bad breath and body odor, while those for pianos and fine clothing played to desires to appear sophisticated and wealthy. Advertisers also cultivated brand loyalty through catchy slogans and impressive claims. The makers of Ivory Soap, for example, touted their product's healthful qualities with the impressive, but ridiculously exaggerated, claim that it was "99 44/100% Pure." Recognizing the value of celebrity, some manufacturers hired famous entertainers and athletes to endorse their products and allow the use of their pictures in ads. The underlying idea of advertising—spending a portion of a business's profits to generate more profit—soon became a standard business principle. Spending on advertising jumped accordingly, from $50 million in 1867 to more than $500 million by 1900.

As advertising caught on among manufacturers and retailers, competition led to increasingly complex and sophisticated advertisements. Gone were the days from before the Civil War when advertisers relied exclusively on a few bold headlines in a newspaper or magazine and some accompanying text touting a product's quality and price. With so many advertisements jamming the pages of these media, and adorning roadside signs, sides of buildings, and grocery store windows, a product's advertisement had to be eye-catching, convincing, and memorable. Advertisers began experimenting with new styles and sizes of type, developed catchy slogans, and enlisted celebrities and "experts" like doctors to vouch for their product. Once developments in print technology made it possible and affordable, they focused increasingly on images to sell their products. (See *Images as History: Advertising and the Art of Cultivating Anxiety and Desire,* page 480.)

Shopping as an Experience: The Department Store

With the emergence of advertising came the development of the department store. Irish immigrant Alexander Turney Stewart established the first in New York City in 1846. Stewart and the entrepreneurs who copied his idea built giant stores that offered a huge selection of goods, usually organized into different "departments." Customers also found a small army of clerks ready to assist them and fixed prices that eliminated uncomfortable negotiations. Retailers also offered attractive policies such as the money back guarantee and free delivery.

By the 1870s customers, increasingly called "shoppers," flocked to department stores not only for the selection, price, and convenience but also for the experience. Retailers had discovered that it was not enough to offer the finest products at good prices. Shopping had to be a pleasurable experience, so merchants built palatial, richly decorated "emporiums," an impressive Latin term meaning a

> "You can now buy your pins, your outing shirts, your wines, your prayer books, your Indian clubs, your pianolas, your false teeth, your automobiles, … [and] your spectacles … in the same place."
>
> *The Wall Street Journal,* 1903

Why did advertising become so important to business success?

store that displayed a large variety of merchandise. One of the first merchants to do so was John Wanamaker, who took over a Philadelphia railroad depot and in 1876 opened a massive and opulently decorated store he called the Grand Depot.

In the coming decades rival stores sought to outdo each other in size and splendor, and customers came to look forward to store openings. On September 12, 1896, for example, 150,000 New Yorkers paraded through the new Siegel Cooper store on opening day. This new "shopping resort," as the *New York Times* called it, employed eight thousand clerks and cashiers and one thousand drivers and packers. The store offered not only a huge selection of merchandise but also conveniences such as telegraph and long-distance telephone services, offices for foreign currency exchange and stock trading, and a dentist office. As this photograph (**16.8**) of the central lobby shows, the store also wowed shoppers with its lavish interior. Note the marble columns and high, decorative ceilings, as well as the statue at right of "The Republic," a copy of the one recently designed by the renowned American sculptor Daniel Chester French for the 1893 World's Fair in Chicago. It rested in a large fountain where streams of water illuminated by colorful lights flowed over it.

The success of the department store led some retail entrepreneurs to expand their operations to large regions or even the whole country. The most noted figure in this field was Frank W. Woolworth, whose "five and dime" stores specialized in low prices rather than opulence. He opened his first store in Utica, New York, in 1879. By 1900 he owned fifty-nine stores, a number that eventually topped six hundred nationwide by 1911. Like their big business counterpart in manufacturing, Woolworth and other national retailers found that with size came certain advantages. Because they bought huge quantities of goods, Woolworth received big price discounts from wholesalers and manufacturers that in turn allowed him to sell his merchandise at low prices.

Bringing the Market to the Frontier

Some entrepreneurs realized that in spite of advertising and the growth of department stores, a massive retail market remained untapped: rural America. Living on farms or in small towns far from cities, these potential customers had money and desire but lacked access to consumer goods. In 1872 Montgomery Ward set out to change that. If rural

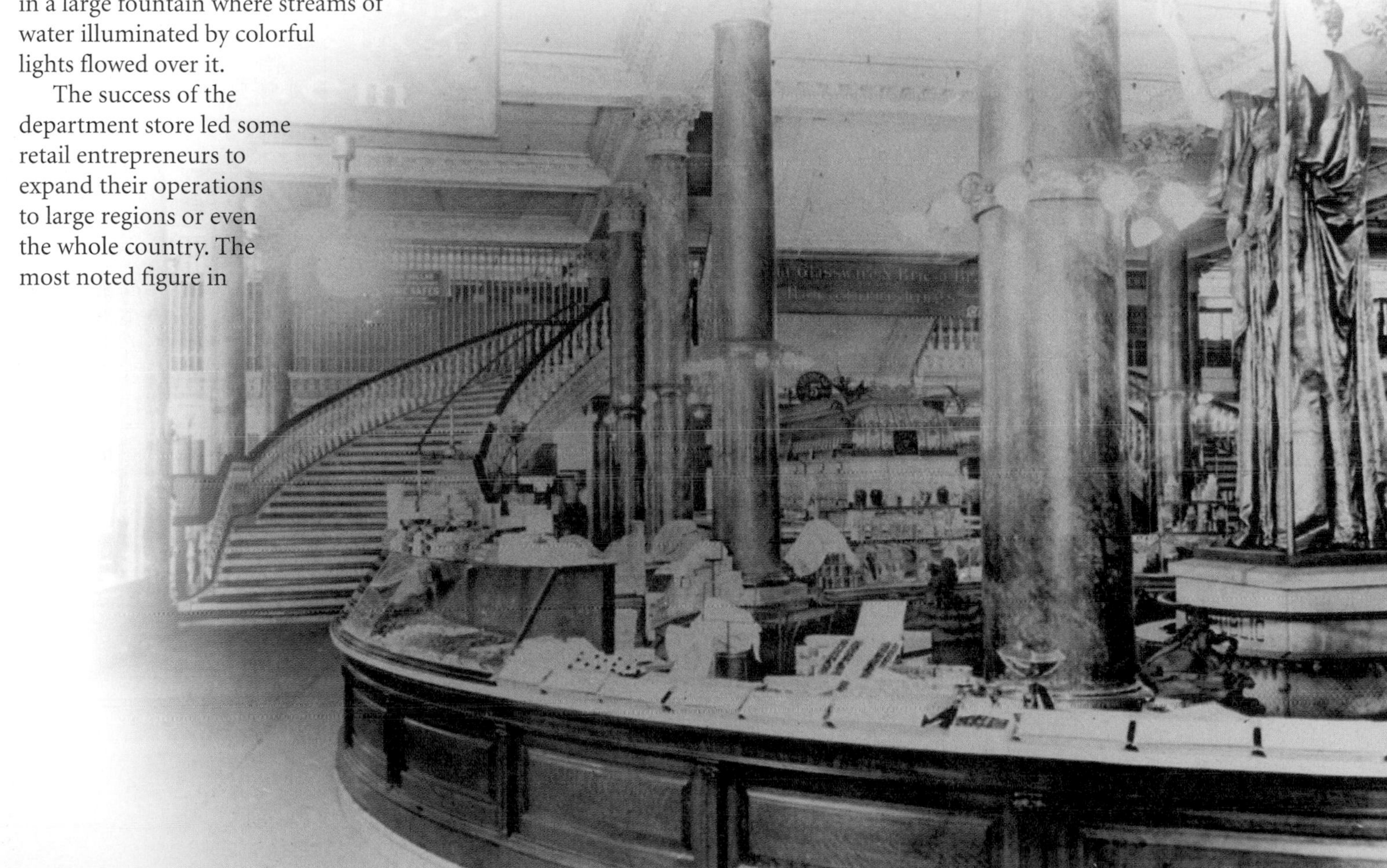

16.8 Shopping as an Experience
Large retailers in cities built lavishly appointed shopping palaces to attract customers. The Siegel-Cooper store in New York City opened with great fanfare in 1896.

How did retailers justify spending so much money to build lavish stores?

Images as History

ADVERTISING AND THE ART OF CULTIVATING ANXIETY AND DESIRE

At first advertisers used images simply to display their product, both to show potential buyers what it looked like and to convince them of its quality. But by the 1880s advertisers began to take literally the old maxim, "a picture is worth a thousand words." They began using images to link certain powerful ideas, sentiments, values, and aspirations with the product. Often advertisers used images without ever showing the product itself. This 1887 advertisement for the Williams' Shaving Stick, a four-inch cylinder stick of shaving soap, that appeared in *Century Magazine* provides a vivid example of this new approach. There was a growing trend among American men in the late 1880s toward a clean-shaven look (or at the very least to confining facial hair to a mustache), a

Nude imagery was considered scandalous and unacceptable in late nineteenth century society. The use of a widely respected religious image, however, allowed the advertisers to grab readers' attention while not offending the public.

By asserting that "Shaggy, unkempt beards were common among the fallen, barbarous nations," the ad suggests that America's rising status in the world depends on its men taking up the razor (and Williams' Shaving Stick, of course).

This full-page advertisement omits an image of the product being sold. Instead it devotes half the page to a religious image and the rest to cleverly crafted words.

All the relics of antiquity, both in art and sculpture, prove the idea of the ancients to have been that

ADAM WAS CREATED WITHOUT A BEARD.

Shaggy, unkempt beards were common among fallen, barbarous nations, until the time of the EMPEROR JULIAN, who was the FIRST to denounce them.

For HALF A CENTURY **WILLIAMS' SHAVING SOAPS** have been the delight of Gentlemen who shave themselves. Eminent Physicians recommend their healing properties as preventive and curative of cutaneous diseases. Their extreme richness and creaminess of lather, rare delicacy, and exquisite fragrance have established them as the favorites of those who are MOST PARTICULAR in regard to toilet requisites.

WILLIAMS' SHAVING STICK.

THIS EXQUISITE TOILET ARTICLE contains all of those rich and lasting qualities which have made our "GENUINE YANKEE" SHAVING SOAP famous for fifty years. Delicately scented with finely selected Attar of Roses. Each Stick in a neat Wood Case, covered with Red Morocco Leatherette. VERY PORTABLE. INDISPENSABLE TO TRAVELERS.

A CONVENIENCE AND LUXURY FOR ALL WHO SHAVE.

If your Druggist does not keep Williams' Shaving Soaps, they will be sent, post-paid, to any address upon receipt of price in stamps or currency, as follows: WILLIAMS' SHAVING STICK, **25** cents; GENUINE YANKEE SOAP, **15** cents; WILLIAMS' CELEBRATED BARBERS' SOAP—FOR TOILET USE—a Pound Package—6 cakes—by mail, **40** cents. Registered Packages, **10** cents extra.

Address THE J. B. WILLIAMS CO. Glastonbury, Connecticut, U. S. A.

(Formerly Williams & Bros., Manchester.) Established 1840.

For Half a Century Manufacturers of the "GENUINE YANKEE" SHAVING SOAP.

The Williams' Shaving Stick
This full-page ad ran in the November 1887 issue of *Century Magazine*.

Instead of using the image of an anonymous man sporting a whisker-free face and a smile of contentment, the advertisers opted for Michelangelo's *Adam at the Time of Creation*, an image most of their target audience—educated middle- and upper-class men who read *Century Magazine*—would recognize and respect.

Note the religious and moral imperative in this phrase: If God created Adam without a beard, the advertisement implies, then God must want all men to be clean-shaven!

How did advertisers cultivate anxiety to generate sales of their products?

trend that benefited manufacturers like J. B. Williams Co. To lure existing shavers to the Williams' Shaving Stick and to convince more men to shed their beards, the company used religious imagery and text to generate anxiety among men over their appearance. What other associations and messages do advertisers often try to convey through images?

This 1885 advertisement poster for the New Home Sewing Machine, designed to hang in a public space such as a train station or store, represents a different use of visual imagery in advertising. Unlike the Williams' Shaving Stick advertisement's effort to instill anxiety, it appeals to the consumer's desire for a more refined and wholesome life.

So central is this machine to creating a "new home" of middle-class tranquility that this woman has included it in the scene she is painting, suggesting that it is part of the family.

Liberated from the dismal, time-consuming task of sewing by the "Light-Running New Home Sewing Machine," this middle-class housewife is free to pursue more refined activities such as painting.

The quality of the sewing machine is taken for granted, for it sits in the background.

The happy child in the picture suggests that women who buy the machine will have more time to devote to the well-being and proper rearing of their children.

Even though this intricate and expensive-looking dress would most likely have been made by a professional and sold in a store, the ad implies that it is easily made with the New Home Sewing Machine.

NEW HOME
SEWING MACHINE CO
30 Union Square, N.Y.

The New Home Sewing Machine
The New Home Sewing Machine Company created this poster in 1885 to promote their product as beneficial to the American family.

America could not get to a department store, he would bring it to them—in the form of a single broadsheet offering two dozen items for sale by "mail order."

Ward's idea proved so successful he steadily expanded his list of offerings. By 1884 Ward presided over a thriving enterprise based on a catalog of 240 pages featuring some 10,000 items. By this time a rival mail order company run by Richard W. Sears and Alvah C. Roebuck had begun operation. Eager to reach this new market, established department stores like Macy's in New York, Jordan Marsh in Boston, and Marshall Field in Chicago followed the trend and brought out their own mail order catalogs.

The reach of corporate retailing beyond urban centers and into rural America (where most Americans lived until 1920) marked the emergence of a mass market. Whereas Americans had long shared a common language and republican political culture, they now developed a shared consumer culture. Exposed to the same advertising images and appeals, millions of Americans in different parts of the country began to adopt the same fashions, develop the same habits (cigarette smoking, for example), and purchase the same newfangled contraptions, including more than one million bicycles a year in the 1890s.

Selling to the World

As the nation's industrial production soared to unprecedented heights, manufacturers began to look for new markets for their goods. The United States had long been an exporter of agricultural products like cotton and wheat, but the leading trend after the Civil War was the export of manufactured goods. The total value of exports rose between 1870 and 1900 from $450 million to $1.5 billion, with the percentage of manufactured goods rising from 15 to 32 percent.

In addition to selling produce and goods overseas, American business interests also began to invest heavily in business ventures in foreign countries. By 1897 Americans had invested $635 million in mines, plantations, oil wells, and increasingly, manufacturing plants ($94 million). By the 1890s the Singer Sewing Machine Co. was an international corporation (**16.9**). With a factory in Kilbowie, Scotland, as well as in the United States, Singer sold its machines throughout the world. Note how the advertisement's text, "The Singer Seam unites Two Continents," and angelic female figures suggest that the company is pursuing humanitarian as well as capitalist goals. Farm equipment giant, International Harvester, likewise opened factories in Canada and Norrkoping, Sweden.

The globalization of the American economy brought many benefits to workers, consumers, and investors. But it also contributed to the growing sentiment in the 1890s that the United States needed to become an imperial power to protect overseas investments and ensure that markets in Asia, Africa, and Latin America remained open.

16.9 The Globalization of American Industry Like many large American corporations, the Singer Sewing Machine Co. became an international corporation by the 1890s, selling its machines throughout the world.

How did advertising promote the development of a national consumer culture?

The World of Work Transformed

The huge industrial enterprises built by Carnegie, Rockefeller, and others ultimately depended not on their individual genius but on the collective labors of American workers. As the number and size of factories grew in the late nineteenth century, the size of the industrial workforce expanded rapidly, from 1.3 million workers in 1860 to 5.1 million in 1900. Many of them faced hardships: long hours, low pay, dangerous conditions, and frequent downturns in the economy. Workers responded by forming unions, staging strikes, and protesting the surging power of business as a threat to democracy.

The Impact of New Technology

The constant introduction of new technology that marked the Industrial Revolution resulted in much more than increased manufacturing output. Even more important was its impact on the status of industrial workers. New machines produced more goods in less time and usually required only low-skilled labor to operate. Machinery transformed shoemaking, for example, from a skilled trade in the 1820s to a low-skill factory occupation by the 1860s. The same was true in the garment and textile industries. Because they could easily replace low-skilled labor, employers could pay them low wages and demand long hours. They could also simply fire or replace workers who complained or failed to keep up the pace with other unskilled workers.

This trend occurred unevenly across industrial America. For example in building trades like carpentry and bricklaying, new technology did little to undermine the position of skilled craftsmen. In other settings new technology created new opportunities for some workers. Some found well-paid skilled work as mechanics, while others became foremen and floor managers who oversaw the work of unskilled operatives. These more fortunate workers often enjoyed far higher wages, shorter hours, and better treatment compared to the unskilled.

Nonetheless for many workers new industrial technology eliminated their skilled jobs in favor of unskilled ones. Just as shoemaking changed from a skilled trade in the 1820s to a low-skill factory occupation by the 1860s, so did the garment and textile industries. In these settings, employers enjoyed increasing power over their employees for the simple reason that unskilled workers were easily replaced.

Hard Times for Industrial Workers

New technology was but one of many difficulties confronting industrial workers in the age of industrialization. Most workers complained about long hours and low wages. Although averages for both varied by industry and region, workers often toiled twelve hours each day, six days a week, for wages that barely covered weekly basic living expenses. By some estimates the average wage earner in the late nineteenth century made $400–500 per year, when living decently required a minimum of $600–800. Working-class families made up the difference by sending their children to work, taking in boarders, and bringing in "home finishing" work, performed by women, such as sewing buttons on new shirts.

Compounding the precarious economic position of wage earners was the "boom and bust" character of the industrial economy. Severe depressions (1873–1877 and 1893–1897) and recessions interrupted periods of prosperity and economic growth. Each **depression**, or "bust" as it was called, involved a contraction of economic growth, widespread business failure, and high rates of unemployment lasting several years. The severe depression of the 1870s, for example, resulted in the loss of more than a million jobs and nearly fifty thousand businesses. Those who did keep their jobs often found their wages slashed and hours increased by employers desperate to remain solvent or ruthless enough to take advantage of rising job competition between the employed and the unemployed. The monotony of industrial work likewise added to the difficulties wage earners faced. Many did work that forced them to perform the same task repeatedly, such as pulling a lever on a metal stamping machine. Workers felt, in the words of one machinist in 1883, that they were

How did new technology weaken the independence of skilled workers?

becoming "part of the machinery," a state of affairs they found "very demoralizing."

The industrial workplace was also extremely dangerous. Every year between 1880 and 1900, 35,000 workers (on average) were killed on the job and another 500,000 injured. This carnage resulted in part from the monotony of factory work, which led mind-numbed workers to make mistakes or fall asleep. But most injuries stemmed from the factory owners' negligence. With no laws compelling them to make their workplaces less lethal, few industrialists were willing to incur the expense of installing safety devices or procedures. Not until the early twentieth century did most states begin enacting laws requiring compensation be paid to injured workers or the families of killed workers.

Another disturbing trend in this era was the sharp rise in child labor. Before the Industrial Revolution children of farmers and artisans performed all sorts of work that contributed to the family economy—but always under the supervision of a parent or relative. Children working in industry, however, left their homes to work in factories and mines under the supervision of a manager rather than a parent. Between 1880 and 1900 the number of children younger than sixteen years of age working for wages—usually a fraction of those paid adults—skyrocketed from 180,000 to 1.7 million. Children as young as seven toiled long hours in dangerous conditions in mines and factories, working at jobs that exposed them to dangerous and unhealthful conditions. The boy in this photograph (**16.10**) lost his arm while operating a power saw in a box factory. Many states passed laws prohibiting child labor, but they rarely enforced them.

16.10 The Price of Child Labor Because they could pay children less than one-half the wages of an adult, employers hired increasing numbers of child laborers in the late nineteenth century, depriving them of education and often exposing them to industrial hazards.

Exploitation, Intimidation, and Conflict

Central to the transformation in the lives of workers ushered in by industrialization was the increasing power exercised by employers in the workplace. Since profit was their paramount goal, employers imposed strict discipline on their industrial workers. The clock came to dominate the workplace, as employers demanded workers begin and end their day (with a few short scheduled breaks) at precise times. Workers who arrived late or took unauthorized breaks were fined or fired. Some factories forbade workers to talk to one another—or worse, to whistle.

> "I make about three dollars a week, and my sister—she is only six years old—she does not make as much, sometimes a dollar a week, sometimes more."
>
> An eight-year-old child laborer, New York, 1871

Enforcing these new rules was an increasingly important figure in the industrial workplace: the manager or foreman. In sharp contrast to the early nineteenth-century preindustrial economy, few workers now ever saw, let alone spoke to, their employer. Instead, they dealt with managers or foremen hired to run a factory as efficiently and profitably as possible. This meant pushing workers to meet production goals and firing those who were unable to keep up or who caused trouble. Many foremen came from working-class backgrounds and treated workers fairly, but others could be abusive, especially those overseeing workers of a different ethnic background. Female workers were particularly vulnerable to abuse. In this drawing from 1888, the foreman in a garment factory shakes his fist at a weary female worker, urging her to work faster (**16.11**). In the larger inset, the overworked woman sprawls on a bed in a dingy tenement. That this image ran under the sensational title *The Female Slaves of New York* in a popular newspaper that often expressed hostility toward workers indicates the notoriety the foreman had achieved in the garment industry by the late nineteenth century.

Workers also found it difficult to organize labor unions. The first major effort to build a national labor movement after the Civil War began in 1866 when William Sylvis, a charismatic iron molder, founded the National Labor Union (NLU). A federation of independent craft unions, the NLU sought to unite skilled workers nationwide to secure demands such as a federal law establishing the eight-hour day and a federal department of labor. Its membership topped 300,000 (nearly all native-born white men in skilled trades) by 1869. But Sylvis's

What factors made industrial workplaces so dangerous?

16.11 Exploiting Female Workers
Shop floor foremen and managers became increasingly important as the size of workplaces grew. As demands for greater productivity grew, female workers were especially vulnerable to abusive foremen. The threat of overwork to the health of women is emphasized in the two insets. One depicts workers carrying heavy bundles of work home while another shows an exhausted laborer collapsed on her bed.

sudden death that year weakened the NLU, and the depression of the 1870s wiped it out completely.

Most employers saw unions as threats to their profits and freedom to run their businesses as they wanted. Many hired spies to expose labor organizers so they could fire them and put them on **blacklists**, lists of workers that employers in a particular town or industry refused to hire because they were considered trouble-makers. During strikes, employers routinely resorted to replacement workers. In this effort they usually enjoyed the cooperation of local officials, who ordered policemen to drive away or arrest pickets gathered outside a workplace. If a labor dispute went to court, an employer could more often than not count on a favorable ruling by a judge or jury. On top of all this, workers faced one over-riding problem—few unions had the financial resources to support striking workers for more than a few weeks. Strikers, one worker attested, "have had nothing to combat capital with except their empty stomachs, while the capitalists have had unlimited financial resources and have been able to starve the workingmen into submission."

Not surprisingly, rising worker frustration and anger led to an increasing number of strikes and violence. Between 1881 and 1905 American workers staged 36,757 strikes that involved more than six million workers. One particularly bitter incident took place in Pennsylvania. In response to the abusive labor policies of coal mine bosses in the 1860s, miners had formed a union called the Workingmen's Benevolent Association (WBA). Many of its members were Irish immigrants some of whom, drawing on the tradition of secret societies that resisted oppressive landlords in Ireland, formed a clandestine labor organization known as the Molly Maguires that carried out acts of intimidation, vandalism, violence, and occasionally, murder against foremen and managers. In 1874 mining interests set out to destroy the WBA by convincing the public that it was one and the same as the Molly Maguires. Within a year this campaign resulted in more than fifty arrests and numerous convictions—many on questionable testimony and with little or no evidence. In all, twenty alleged Molly Maguires were hanged for murder, including ten on a single day, June 21, 1877. Note how in this drawing (**16.12**) public officials created a powerful public spectacle designed to emphasize the men's guilt and, aware that a majority of the region's miners were Catholic, to emphasize their sinfulness.

16.12 The Pageantry of Execution
On June 21, 1877, "Black Thursday," Pennsylvania officials staged carefully planned executions of ten convicted miners known as Molly Maguires.

Why were employers so hostile to labor unions?

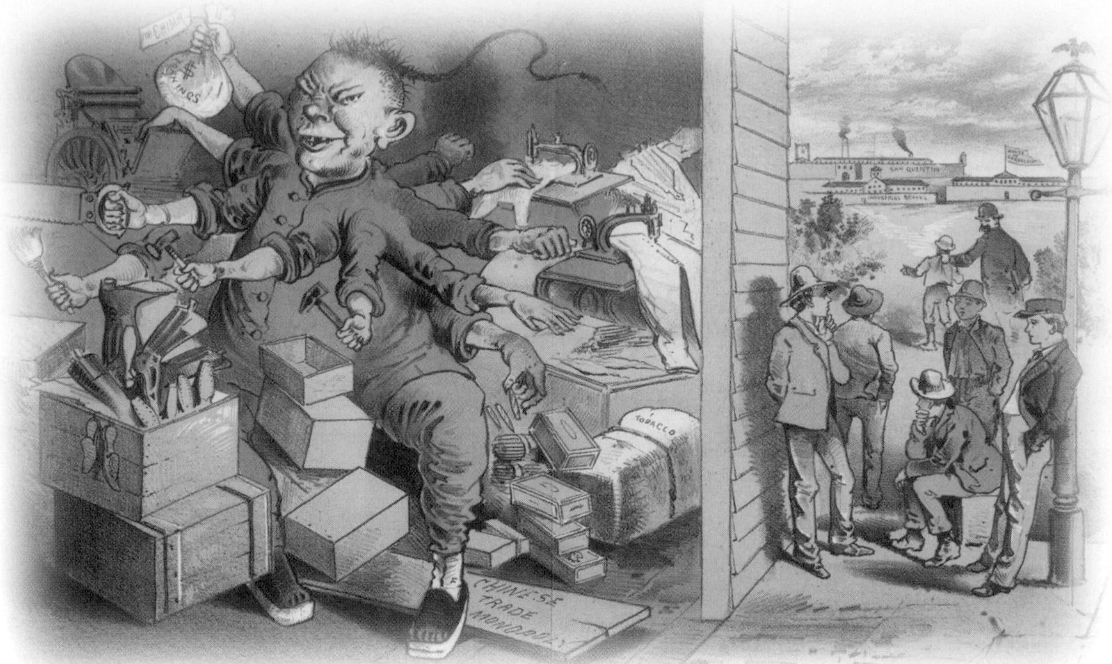

16.13 Hard Times Fuel Anti-Chinese Racism
During the depression of 1873–1878, workers blamed high levels of unemployment on Chinese immigrants, whom they accused of working long shifts for low wages.

Three weeks later, on July 14, 1877, the largest strike in the world in the nineteenth century erupted. The "Great Uprising" of railroad workers began in Martinsburg, West Virginia, and quickly spread to Baltimore, Philadelphia, Pittsburgh, St. Louis, Chicago, and other cities. The strike involved thousands of workers, and violence emanated from both sides. In Pittsburgh, for example, soldiers opened fire on striking workers and their families, killing twenty and wounding twenty-nine. Enraged by the killings, strikers and their supporters attacked the troops and the Pennsylvania Railroad stockyards, resulting in the destruction of all the terminal's buildings and other property.

The mainstream press expressed some criticism of the railroads for slashing workers' wages, but most dismissed labor activism as illegal, ill-informed, and un-American. (See *Competing Visions: The Legitimacy of Unions.*)

While workers in this period faced hostility from employers, politicians, and journalists, they also had to contend with animosity within the ranks of labor that often hindered their ability to organize. Deep hostility often existed between skilled and unskilled workers, who frequently viewed each other as having little in common. Workers were also riven by disputes arising from different ideologies, including several varieties of **socialism**, a theory that rejected capitalism and advocated common ownership of private property and greater social and economic equality. They also argued the persistent question of whether workers' interests were best served by pressuring the major political parties or by forming an independent labor party.

Perhaps the most significant divisions among workers centered on race and ethnicity. A rising tide of immigration in the late nineteenth century brought greater ethnic, racial, and religious diversity to an already diverse workforce, making more difficult the task of uniting them in common cause. For example, when hard times hit during the depression of the 1870s, anti-Chinese sentiment among American workers soared, ultimately leading to the **Chinese Exclusion Act**, a law enacted in 1882 barring Chinese immigration to the United States. As the cartoon (**16.13**) from *The Wasp* demonstrates, Chinese workers were blamed for taking jobs from Americans. The artist depicts a twelve-armed Chinese worker, drawn in racist caricature, laboring maniacally at a dozen tasks while young American-born workers stand idly near a factory. One of the workers is being hauled away by a policeman, implying that unemployment has led him to a life of crime.

African American workers also faced racist hostility from white workers, especially as they began moving to Northern cities in increasing numbers in the 1890s. Much of this hostility stemmed from the widely held racist beliefs of the day that told white workers they were superior to blacks. But it also emanated from the fear that African Americans would take jobs from white workers—a fear exacerbated when employers occasionally used black workers as strikebreakers.

Competing Visions

THE LEGITIMACY OF UNIONS

While conflict between workers and their employers often centered on wages and hours, it also occurred over the legitimacy of labor unions. Many Americans denounced unions as illegal, foolish, and un-American. The editor of *Scribner's Monthly*, writing in the aftermath of the 1877 Great Uprising of railroad workers, reflects this view as does the accompanying image from *Puck*. Workers and their advocates like John Swinton, editor of a pro-labor newspaper in New York, offered a very different vision of labor unions as vital organizations that protected workers from the most extreme forms of exploitation. Why did employers find unions so objectionable, even dangerous? What benefits did workers see in unions?

Scribner's Monthly (October 1877)

And now that it is over, it is a good time to ask once more what good has come from this strike, and what good has come of any strike. The laws of nature which, after all, govern the laws of trade ... can never be overcome or circumvented by a strike. Labor will always command its value—no more, no less. ... Strikes are always mistakes; they are often crimes.

The day of the inauguration of trades unions and labor organizations in this country was a day the blackest and fullest of menace to the popular prosperity and peace that ever dawned upon the nation. They have been an unmitigated curse to employers and employed alike. The nature and purpose of these organizations are simply outrageous. They have been despotic toward their own members, oppressive toward the class in whose interest they pretend to have been established, impertinent and intermeddling. They have assumed the right to control property and business in which they had no more right than if they lived in the moon. There should be in the good sense of the great mass of laborers a reaction against this wretched crime, and this stupendous foolishness.

This Puck magazine cartoon from the mid-1880s portrayed labor union officials as tyrants who hurt the interests of workers

John Swinton's Paper (January 27, 1884)

There are many who cannot understand why Trades Unions exist here. They have heard them described as alien to the American craftsman, causing strikes, and raising ill-feeling generally between... employer and employe[e].

In the present state of industry, Trade Unions are a necessity, recognized as such by the great majority of intelligent workmen, ... and securing for their members a partial degree of protection without which they would sink into depths as yet unfathomed.

There is a hue and cry against the Unions as agencies that provoke strikes. In nine cases out of ten, strikes are made necessary by circumstances over which the Unions have no control whatever; sometimes they are a protest against unendurable reductions in wages ... sometimes by unjust conduct on the part of bosses or corporations. No Union to-day orders a strike that can be avoided by reasonable means; no Union orders a strike without full consideration of the subject and after a fair vote. ...

But we are told that no strike ever brings any advantage to the strikers ... This is a mistake that cannot be made by any one who has observed the results of strikes either in the United States or in any other country. ...

But strikes often fail,—yes, it is true. Capital often triumphs in the conflict with labor,—true again. Yet capital would be even harsher and more exacting than it is, if it were not for the protest of the strike, and the warning that it gives. The wages which, in many industries, are but little above the living point, would be put down and kept down to the starvation point, if the men accepted with submissive spirit every reduction of wages, and all the severe terms that capital tries to enforce.

Why do labor activists argue that unions are defensive in nature?

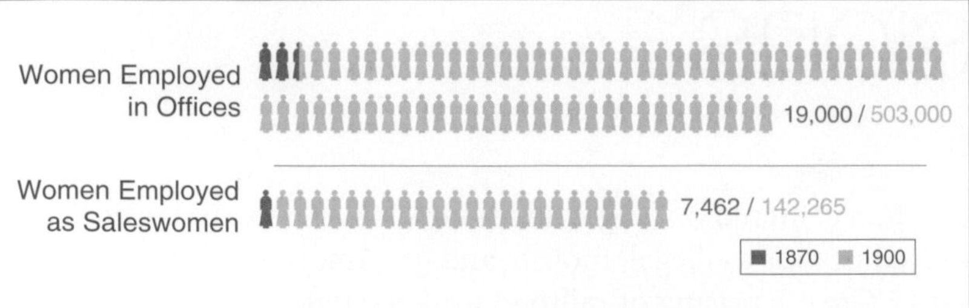

16.14 Rising Numbers of Women in the Paid Workforce Economic necessity and a desire for greater independence brought millions of women into jobs outside the home.

New Roles and Opportunities for Women

Economic necessity brought millions of women into the paid workforce. Whereas just 13 percent of women worked outside the home in 1870, 20 percent did so by 1900. Nearly all these women were single and younger than twenty-five years of age. Domestic service (cooking, cleaning, and childcare in the homes of middle- and upper-class families) remained the leading occupation for wage-earning women in this period, but increasing numbers also took on factory work, especially in the garment and textile industries. Like their male counterparts, these women factory workers labored at repetitive tasks for long hours and in unsafe conditions—but for only half (or less) the wages of men. Employers justified this disparity by claiming women worked merely for extra money whereas men worked to support whole families and therefore deserved higher pay. In fact, many working-class families depended for their survival on the earnings of their sixteen- to twenty-five-year-old daughters. Factory owners simply paid them less because women were powerless to prevent it.

While increasing numbers of women took jobs in factories, the Industrial Revolution also produced a vast array of other kinds of jobs that women came to fill. The emergence of modern corporations requiring armies of secretaries, clerks, and stenographers, combined with the invention of the telephone, adding machine, and typewriter, created new opportunities for educated, native-born, white women (**16.14**). Teaching, social work, and, as indicated in the graduation photograph of the Philadelphia School for Nurses (**16.15**), nursing emerged in the late nineteenth century as an almost exclusively female professions. These fields, even though they represented new opportunities for women, were deemed appropriate because they drew on what was widely believed to be women's "natural" role as nurturers. The pageantry evident in this photograph, especially the bright white and highly professional uniforms, the elegant setting of the Philadelphia Academy of Music, and the presence of Red Cross founder Clara Barton (seated at center), indicates the high reputation the profession had achieved by the turn of the century.

Regardless of the level of work, social custom dictated that women leave the paid workforce soon after they married (only 5 percent of married women worked outside the home in 1900). Of necessity, working-class women continued to earn money to support their families. Only now they did so from within the home by taking in boarders, laundry, and "piece work," which paid by the piece rather than by the hour.

Far larger numbers of African American women, more out of economic necessity than custom, remained in the paid workforce even after marriage. In urban areas in both the North and South, many worked as domestic servants in white middle- and upper-class homes, providing cooking, cleaning, laundry, and childcare services. These jobs required long hours and paid low wages, but racist hiring policies in industry and other sectors of the economy left African American women with few options.

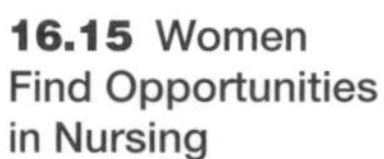

16.15 Women Find Opportunities in Nursing These graduates of the Philadelphia School for Nurses, with Red Cross founder Clara Barton at center, were among the thousands of young women in the late nineteenth century who flocked to the nursing profession.

What factors explain the surge in the numbers of women entering the paid workforce?

Conflicting Visions of Industrial Capitalism

As the Industrial Revolution unfolded in the late nineteenth century, Americans of all classes, occupations, and regions felt its impact. For many it was an age of wonder, marked by a steady succession of new inventions, ideas, and possibilities. Yet one did not have to look far for signs of anxiety, fear, and discontent. Numerous critics in the last decades of the nineteenth century offered a different vision of society, emphasizing the growing poverty, gaps between the rich and poor, and inequality.

Capitalism Championed

The late nineteenth century witnessed an enthusiastic celebration of industrial capitalism and the many benefits it brought to American life. Proponents noted that every year American industry produced more consumer goods, ranging from inexpensive clothing in a dizzying array of colors and styles to exciting new products like phonographs and bicycles. It also generated new forms of transportation that allowed people, including the poor, to travel to new and different places. The introduction of industrial technology to farming led to stupendous annual harvests, falling food prices, and a more varied diet for the average American, who saw life expectancy rise from a mere 38.3 years for white men in 1850 to 50 years by 1910. Industrial technology such as the telegraph, telephone, and steam-powered printing press allowed for the unprecedented spread of information and literacy (aided by an expanded public school system). And in spite of unrest, depressions, and strikes, real wages for the average worker rose 50 percent between 1860 and 1900 (74 percent for skilled workers and 31 percent for unskilled). To these optimists industrial capitalism meant progress.

Of the enthusiastic champions of the new industrial order, none was more fervent and influential than Andrew Carnegie. He offset his hard-driving corporate style with a carefully constructed public image designed to set him apart from many of his fellow industrialists who angered the public with arrogant pronouncements. William K. Vanderbilt, for example, once brushed aside the suggestion that his business practices violated the law by saying, "Law! What do I care about the law? Hain't I got the power?"

In countless speeches and in articles in prominent magazines, the nation's most famous industrialist defended the status quo and emphasized its virtues. He argued that men of industry like him were not, as critics charged, greedy, abusive monopolists. Rather they were visionaries who built key industries that brought immeasurable benefits to Americans, including thousands of jobs for workers and countless products that improved the quality of life. Granted, Carnegie explained in what he came to call the "Gospel of Wealth," he and other entrepreneurs had grown fabulously rich, but this was a necessary and beneficial result of a free economy. Without the hope of future riches, business leaders would not have the incentive to seek new opportunities, take risks, and develop new products.

> "I can hire one half of the working class to kill the other half."
>
> Financier and railroad magnate
> JAY GOULD

Carnegie and other champions of big business also emphasized that industrial fortunes could be—and increasingly were—used to fund philanthropic projects such as schools and libraries. Carnegie was already the nation's most ostentatious philanthropist in 1901, the year he sold his steel empire to financier J. P. Morgan for $400 million. He donated millions to various causes, but most famously to his program of funding public libraries. For a man who was both conservative and optimistic, libraries appeared the perfect form of charity because they provided the

How did business leaders like Carnegie defend industrial capitalism?

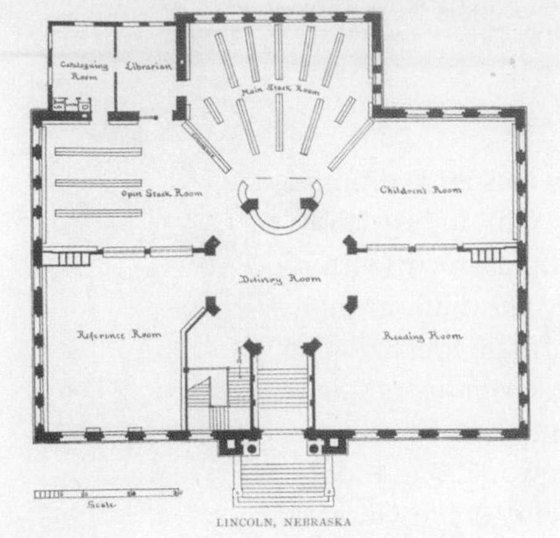

16.16 The Carnegie Library and Floor Plan in Lincoln, Nebraska As a symbol of the virtue of industrial capitalism and the spirit of individual uplift, steel magnate Andrew Carnegie funded nearly 1,700 public libraries in America. The exterior designs reflected the popularity of classical styles circa 1900. The design of the interiors emphasized the industrial values of order and efficiency.

ambitious, hard-working, and intelligent not with a handout, but rather an opportunity to better themselves. This Carnegie library (**16.16**), built in Lincoln, Nebraska, in 1901, typified the more than 2,500 (1,689 in the United States) libraries funded by Carnegie between 1886 and 1929. Communities awarded a library were allowed pick their own architectural style. Most, like Lincoln, opted for some variation on the widely popular neoclassical style. But Carnegie and his staff that oversaw the program insisted that library interiors follow a general design that stressed efficiency and order—similar to the values reflected in the design of his steel factories. Note how the floor plan allowed for a single centrally located librarian (seated at the curved desk in the center) to monitor all the neatly organized spaces devoted to reading, children, reference, and stacks.

When Carnegie and other defenders of industrial capitalism were asked about the growing problem of poverty amid such progress, they pointed to what they claimed was the greatest virtue of a capitalist economy: the idea of the self-made man. As Carnegie's own life story seemed to attest, anyone, regardless of birthplace, family, education, or poverty, could rise up the ladder of success. Success was by no means guaranteed, noted Carnegie. But for those who possessed self-discipline, intelligence, frugality, and diligence and who avoided liquor, and debt, the future was bright.

Aiding Andrew Carnegie and other optimists in spreading this ideal of the self-made man was Horatio Alger. A former minister, Alger wrote more than one hundred young-adult books, beginning with *Ragged Dick* in 1868, all with similar plotlines, featuring a young boy, often a bootblack or a delivery boy, who lived a life of poverty and irresponsibility on the mean streets of a big city. Through the intervention of a "respectable" man, the boy eventually discovers that he need only end his prodigal ways and pursue education and opportunity to enjoy the good life. Alger sold millions of books and his success inspired imitators who churned out similar books and magazines, including the popular *Fame and Fortune* magazine (**16.17**). As this cover shows, each weekly installment offered dramatic "stories of boys who make money" by exhibiting honesty, diligence, and courage.

Not all conservative defenders of industrial capitalism shared Alger's rosy vision of a society where anyone willing to work hard, save money, and avoid liquor could find success. They subscribed to a theory known as **social Darwinism**, a corruption of British naturalist Charles Darwin's theory of natural selection (later termed "evolution"). Popularized by British philosopher and sociologist Herbert Spencer, he took Darwin's central idea that in evolution, plants and animals that are able to adapt to changing conditions survive while others become extinct,

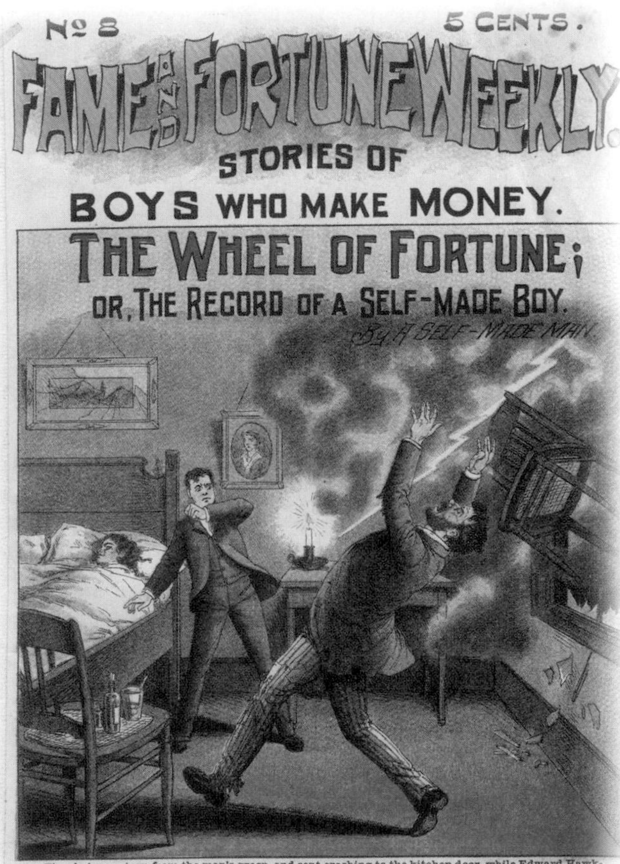

16.17 The Promise of Success
Taking their cue from the success of Horatio Alger's success in writing scores of young adult novels, many imitators published similar books and magazines preaching that reward and respectability could be had if only one worked hard, told the truth, and helped the less fortunate.

Why was the self-made man idea so popular in the age of industry?

tailoring it to fit his idea of modern industrial society as "survival of the fittest." The wealthy and powerful in society were the "fittest," people endowed with innate characteristics of intelligence, strength, and the adaptability that enabled them to succeed in the competitive world of business. And the poor? They were the "unfit," men and women consigned by nature to failure, misery, and early death. To impose government regulation on corporations, proponents argued, was both immoral and impractical, an affront to the laws of nature and God. Equally important, social Darwinism argued against any initiatives public or private to alleviate the plight of the poor, which would lead to the survival and growth of the unfit population with devastating consequences for society.

> "What a blessing to let the unreformed drunkard and his children die, and not increase them above all others. . . . How wise to let those of weak digestion from gluttony die, and the temperate live. What benevolence to let the lawless perish, and the prudent survive."
>
> *The Christian Advocate* (N.Y.), 1879

Capitalism Criticized

Despite these confident assertions on the morality and virtue of laissez-faire industrial capitalism, a host of critics decried the widening chasm between the rich and poor. While some four thousand had become "millionaires" by the early 1890s, millions of Americans lived in poverty, or perilously close to it. A tour of any city provided ample evidence of what some called the "haves and the have nots," people who dwelled in "sunshine and shadow." This cover drawing for Mathew Hale Smith's popular book of the same name from 1869 contrasts the two extremes found in New York City: merchant A. T. Stewart's Fifth Avenue mansion, and a brewery-turned-mission in the notorious Five Points district downtown (**16.18**).

In the former neighborhood were the homes of the Stewarts as well as the Vanderbilts, Astors, Morgans, and Carnegies. They attended opera at the opulent Metropolitan Opera House, entertained each other at lavish balls and dinners, and summered in their fifty-room "cottages" in coastal retreats like Newport, Rhode Island. A few miles downtown in Five Points and the surrounding Lower East Side district, nearly one million people lived in tiny, airless tenement apartments with no running water or toilets. Their neighborhoods had no parks, and their streets were filled with filth due to irregular street cleaning in poor neighborhoods.

A growing number of reformers, ministers, and social critics began to question whether American democracy, with its ideals of equal rights and individual freedom, could endure under such conditions of inequality and enslaving poverty. A self-taught political economist named Henry George, troubled by the growing social inequality and rising class conflict in the mid-1870s, wrote an influential book, *Progress and Poverty*. As the title suggested, George addressed one of the central questions of the age: Must increased poverty accompany industrial and technological progress? If so, he warned, American democracy was doomed. George claimed that the monopolization of resources, especially of land, by powerful elites was to blame for the looming social crisis. Few people understood or supported George's unorthodox solution (a "single tax" on land values), but his vivid diagnosis of the rising clash between labor and capital and his vision of a more equitable social order gained him an enormous following in the 1880s and turned *Progress and Poverty* into a bestseller. In 1886 the United Labor Party nominated George to run for mayor of New York City. He lost the contest but polled 68,000 votes—in an era when labor candidates typically only received a few hundred.

Edward Bellamy achieved a similar level of fame as a critic of laissez-faire capitalism with his

16.18 The Growing Gap between the Haves and Have-Nots The cover of Matthew Hale Smith's book about New York City, *Sunshine and Shadow*, captured the fascination and the fear with which Americans regarded growing poverty amid rising levels of wealth.

novel *Looking Backward, 2000–1887*. Published in 1887, it told the story of Julian West who, like Rip Van Winkle in another era, falls asleep in 1887 and awakens in the year 2000. To his astonishment he finds American society transformed into a socialist utopia. The class conflict, poverty, and economic inequality of the late nineteenth century are gone. The government controlled the economy, eliminating destructive competition and providing a comfortable living for all citizens. Bellamy's book became a bestseller and his largely middle-class followers established nearly five hundred clubs to spread its message.

Power in Numbers: Organized Labor

Less famous, but in many ways far more influential than critics like George and Bellamy, were the protests of those most buffeted by the Industrial Revolution: workers. Through the pages of labor newspapers and in speeches at worker rallies—and in actions such as strikes—American workers articulated a sharp critique of the new industrial order. A small percentage were socialists, but most supported the broad ideals of a free market economy. Their protest stemmed from the growing conviction that greedy monopolists, in league with unscrupulous politicians, had seized control of the economy and bent it toward their own advantage. As a result, argued workers, they received a shrinking portion of the wealth they created, while working longer hours in increasingly inhumane conditions. Try as they might, these workers claimed, the upward mobility celebrated by Andrew Carnegie and Horatio Alger was less and less attainable.

Unsettled and angered by their declining power in the face of big business, American workers

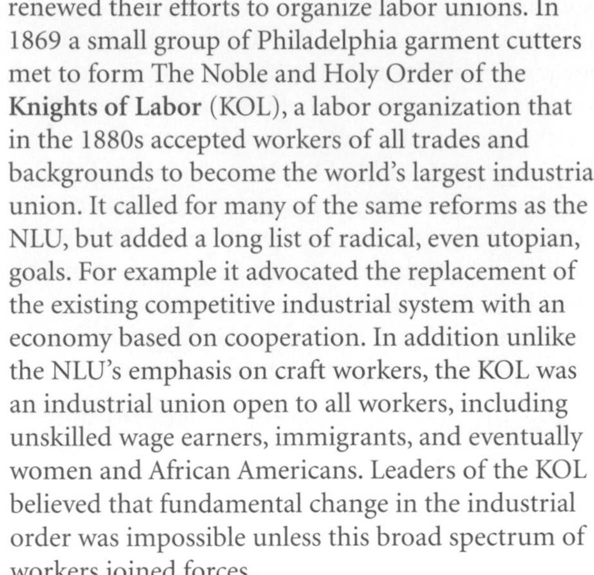

renewed their efforts to organize labor unions. In 1869 a small group of Philadelphia garment cutters met to form The Noble and Holy Order of the **Knights of Labor** (KOL), a labor organization that in the 1880s accepted workers of all trades and backgrounds to become the world's largest industrial union. It called for many of the same reforms as the NLU, but added a long list of radical, even utopian, goals. For example it advocated the replacement of the existing competitive industrial system with an economy based on cooperation. In addition unlike the NLU's emphasis on craft workers, the KOL was an industrial union open to all workers, including unskilled wage earners, immigrants, and eventually women and African Americans. Leaders of the KOL believed that fundamental change in the industrial order was impossible unless this broad spectrum of workers joined forces.

To ensure success in the face of employer hostility, the organization adopted a policy of strict secrecy that necessitated holding meetings in clandestine locations. This requirement, however, combined with the severe economic depression of 1873–1877, hindered its growth. By 1879 it counted just ten thousand members, most in Pennsylvania. Two key developments that year soon propelled the KOL into the national spotlight as the world's largest industrial union. First the national economy recovered from the depression of the mid-1870s, providing wage earners with a measure of economic security that allowed them to form and join local unions in huge numbers. Second, a young machinist named Terence Powderly became the KOL's leader, or Grandmaster Workman. Powderly was a superb organizer and gifted orator who in 1882 abolished the KOL's secrecy rule, a decision that made it possible to recruit thousands of new members and fend off accusations from employers, politicians, and religious leaders that the KOL was a sinister and conspiratorial organization.

Membership soared from 10,000 in 1879 to 42,000 in 1882 (on its way to an eventual peak of more than 700,000 in late 1886). What drew many workers to the organization was the KOL's sharp critique of laissez-faire capitalism and emphasis on economic justice and democracy. Its constitution decried, "the recent alarming development and aggression of aggregated wealth" by industrialists, bankers, and stock speculators, warning that it would soon lead "to the pauperization and hopeless degradation of the toiling masses."

These sentiments and spirit of protest inspired workers in New York City, many of them KOL members, to establish the Labor Day holiday in

16.19 Establishing Labor Day
In 1882 workers in New York City held the first Labor Day celebration. It soon became a national holiday.

Why did so many workers find the Knights of Labor so appealing?

September 1882. The organizers took great care to present workers as orderly and dignified, marching in almost military fashion (**16.19**). Yet they also held aloft signs voicing their grievances ("Abolish Contract Labor" and "8 Hours to Constitute A Day's Work") and announcing their intent to reclaim their influence in the political system ("Vote for the Labor Ticket"). Others proclaimed the importance of workers ("Labor Creates All Wealth" and "Labor Pays All Taxes") and in an age of growing economic inequality, reminded the spectators of key American principles ("All Men Are Created Equal"). The annual Labor Day holiday quickly gained popularity. By 1886 it was a national event, and in 1894 President Grover Cleveland signed into law a measure establishing Labor Day as a holiday for all federal workers.

Another significant aspect of the KOL's vision, albeit one that was not embraced in every part of the country, especially the South, was its inclusion of African American workers as members. Many in the KOL's leadership argued that the union must include all workers, including blacks, because employers would inevitably use them against organized labor to break strikes and lower wages. This same argument for inclusion led the KOL to allow women members. As a result, in an era when labor unions were almost exclusively the domain of white men, the KOL garnered a membership by 1886 that was 10 percent women and 10 percent African American.

Many workers also joined the KOL because of its emphasis on practical goals. Its constitution called for the eight-hour workday, equal pay for men and women, the establishment of state bureaus of labor, and the prohibition of child and convict labor. The KOL also gained enormous support among workers for their successful leadership in strikes. But the decision to strike was difficult and carried great risks. (See *Choices and Consequences: To Strike or Not to Strike?*, page 494).

Most strikes in this period were small and local like the one at Mundell, but on several occasions the Knights of Labor enjoyed success on a grand scale. In 1885 railroad workers affiliated with the KOL won a strike against the Wabash Railroad, owned by financier Jay Gould, a man widely despised and feared by workers. Elsewhere the KOL popularized the boycott, the organized effort to discourage customers from patronizing a business engaged in anti-labor activity, as a very effective labor tactic less costly and risky than a strike.

As the Knights of Labor grew larger in membership and influence in the mid-1880s, it alarmed employers, politicians, and conservatives, who feared its radical rhetoric of class conflict and demands for economic reform. They denounced Powderly and other KOL leaders as radical socialists bent on promoting violence and class warfare. Although neither accusation was true, they made many Americans, including many wage earners, leery of the KOL union and organized labor in general.

The Great Upheaval of 1886

Fear of the KOL in particular and the labor movement in general peaked in 1886. On May 1, 340,000 workers across the country staged a one-day work stoppage to bring attention to their demand for the eight-hour day. Three days later a far more serious incident occurred that would negatively affect the labor movement for years to come. Outraged by the killing of a striking worker outside the McCormick Reaper Works in Chicago, the city's radical labor leaders called for a mass meeting in Haymarket Square on May 4. When three hundred Chicago policemen moved in to violently disperse the crowd, a bomb exploded amid their ranks. The enraged police attacked the crowd with guns and batons. In less than twenty minutes, seven policemen lay dead (most, an investigation would show, from shots fired by fellow police officers) along with four workers. The press quickly dubbed the incident the **Haymarket Incident**, and especially when accompanied by images such as this one (**16.20**), stoked vehement opposition to organized labor. Note the placement of the dead policemen in a sort of martyrs' pantheon above a riot scene depicting "murderous rioters" being gunned down.

16.20 The Haymarket Incident, 1886 The Haymarket incident sparked a nationwide backlash against organized labor. Newspapers ran images like this one, in which martyred policemen hover over a scene where, "murderous rioters" are gunned down.

What role did the press play in promoting a negative impression of labor unions?

Choices and Consequences

TO STRIKE OR NOT TO STRIKE?

Most strikes in the late nineteenth century failed, but the surge in labor activism and the emergence of the Knights of Labor in the 1880s boosted confidence among workers that strikes could succeed. In the summer of 1881, the hundreds of male shoemakers in the Knights Local Assembly 64 successfully opposed a wage reduction by the Mundell Company in Philadelphia. Management then imposed a rate cut on its female shoemakers. One of the workers, Mary Stirling, urged the workers, men and women, to strike until the company rescinded the wage cut. The workers at the Mundell Company considered essentially three major options:

Choices

1. Fearing for their jobs male and female workers refuse to strike.
2. Seeking to protect their recent victory, the men remain on the job while the women walk out.
3. Recognizing their mutual interests in opposing wage cuts for all workers, the male and female workers agree to strike together.

The Mundell Shoe Company was one of the nation's leading manufacturers of footwear in the late nineteenth century

Decision

Inspired by the Knights of Labor motto, "an injury to one is an injury to all," the seven hundred men and women of the Mundell factory decided on option 3, walking out at Mary Stirling's urging. The strike lasted several weeks, during which time the female workers formed their own KOL local assembly—even though the union did not yet allow for female members. Strikers organized pickets, rallies, and fundraisers to help pay for food and rent.

Consequences

The Mundell Company, facing lost profits and pressure to settle from other factory owners who feared worker unrest, rescinded the wage cut. The victory boosted the confidence of the workers and the reputation of the Knights of Labor locally. Within three years the shoe industry alone had eleven local assemblies that managed to win many struggles with employers over wages, firings, and work rules. Even more important, later in 1881 Mary Stirling attended the national convention of the KOL and convinced the organization to admit women. By 1887, 10 percent of the KOL's 700,000 members would be women.

Continuing Controversies

How should organized labor deal with the rising number of women in the workforce?

The admission of women into the KOL did not end the longstanding opposition of many American workers to the rights of women to work and to join unions. They continued to argue that keeping women out of the workforce would open up jobs for men and raise overall wages. When the KOL fell apart in the 1890s, so did the status of women in the labor movement. The American Federation of Labor, the organization that succeeded the KOL, admitted few female members until well into the twentieth century.

What made strikes so risky for workers?

The next day, as hysterical headlines across the nation proclaimed that revolution was at hand, Chicago police arrested eight men, all self-proclaimed anarchists, and charged them with murder. After a hasty trial in which even the prosecution conceded that no one had seen the men throw a bomb, all were convicted. Seven were sentenced to death and one to life imprisonment. Four were subsequently hanged, a fifth committed suicide in his cell. In 1893 Illinois elected a pro-labor governor who pardoned the remaining three, declaring they had not received a fair trial. Haymarket created a climate of fear and provided justification for public officials across the nation to crack down on the labor movement. Throughout the spring and summer of 1886, hundreds of labor activists were arrested—one hundred alone in New York City. In response workers in cities and towns across the nation formed labor parties and ran candidates for offices ranging from city councilor to governor. Most candidates lacked the money or experience to win, but there were some notable surprises. For example Chicago's United Labor Party polled 25,000 votes (of 92,000 cast) and elected a state senator and seven state assemblymen. In Milwaukee, the People's Party elected a mayor, a state senator, six state assemblymen, and one congressman. In one of the most widely watched contests, Henry George, the reformer and author of *Progress and Poverty,* finished a close second in the mayor's race in New York City—out polling Republican Theodore Roosevelt, who finished a distant third.

Several divisive developments, however, soon overwhelmed the unity and hope expressed by workers at the polls in November 1886. First the tumult of 1886 brought to the fore the dissatisfaction of many skilled workers within the KOL. Deeming the organization too strike prone and too influenced by socialists and radicals (who after Haymarket brought organized labor unwanted criticism), twenty-five unions of skilled workers convened in Columbus, Ohio, in December 1886 and founded the American Federation of Labor (AFL). At the same time the more radical activists within the KOL grew dissatisfied with the leadership of Powderly, decrying his growing opposition to strikes and political action. Further weakening the labor movement was a continued atmosphere of anti-labor hysteria in the press and legal repression following Haymarket. Membership dwindled rapidly, falling from its high of 700,000 in 1886 to only 100,000 by 1890.

National leadership of the labor movement after 1886 fell to the newly formed AFL. Comprised exclusively of unions of skilled workers and led by cigar-maker Samuel Gompers, the AFL shunned the KOL's idealistic vision of cooperation. Instead it accepted capitalism and the wage system and focused on what it termed "pure and simple" goals: higher wages, shorter hours, and job security.

The AFL also rejected the idea of organizing unskilled workers, arguing that they were too weak and unreliable. They similarly excluded (with a few exceptions) women, African Americans, and recent immigrants. The AFL would grow to 1.6 million members by 1904. However its narrowed vision and conservative approach to the labor question would leave the growing numbers of less skilled industrial workers without a national voice until the 1930s.

Conclusion

The United States industrialized at a rapid pace after 1865, becoming the world's most formidable industrial power by 1900. For many Americans, especially those who prospered as a result of this transformation, industrial capitalism ushered in an era of progress. But others, especially workers struggling in dangerous factories for long hours and meager wages, industrialization raised troubling questions about economic justice, social equality, and democracy. Thousands joined labor unions and participated in an unprecedented number of strikes. Many middle- and upper-class Americans also worried about the growing gap between the rich and poor and expressed anxiety over the future prospects of America's republican traditions. As a result, this period of industrialization touched off a debate over the proper role of government in regulating the economy and protecting the rights and well-being of its most vulnerable citizens—a debate that would continue into the twenty-first century.

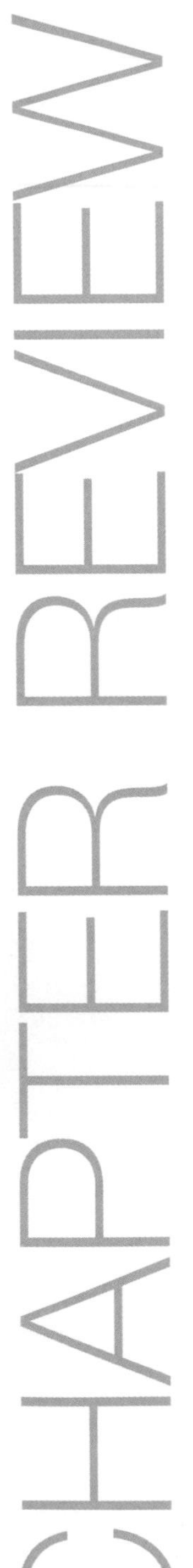

CHAPTER REVIEW

1866–1868

William Sylvis founds the National Labor Union

First significant effort to organize workers nationally

Horatio Alger publishes *Ragged Dick*

First of one hundred "rags to respectability" novels popularizing the ideal of the self-made man

1873–1876

The Panic of 1873

Begins four years of severe economic depression

Wanamaker opens Grand Depot in Philadelphia

Sets standard for lavish department stores in an era of increasing consumerism

1877–1878

The "Great Uprising" railroad strike

Massive strike spreads to several cities. Clashes between workers and police and soldiers leave dozens killed and millions of dollars in damage

Terence Powderly elected Grandmaster Workman of the Knights of Labor

Transforms KOL into a powerful industrial union with 700,000 members by 1886

Review Questions

1. What advantages did the United States possess in terms of resources, culture, technology, and public policy that facilitated industrialization after 1865?
2. Why were the Supreme Court and Congress so slow to take steps to curb the power of big business?
3. How was advertising transformed after 1865? What impact did it have on the Industrial Revolution?
4. Why did American workers have such a difficult time uniting to oppose abusive and exploitative employers?
5. In what ways did industrialization create new opportunities for women? How and why were these opportunities limited?
6. What events, ideas, and policies explain the sudden rise of the Knights of Labor in the 1880s? Why did it collapse almost as suddenly?
7. What was social Darwinism, and why did many business leaders and wealthy Americans embrace it?
8. What was the "self-made man" ideal, and why was it so popular in the late nineteenth century? On what basis did some Americans begin to challenge its validity?

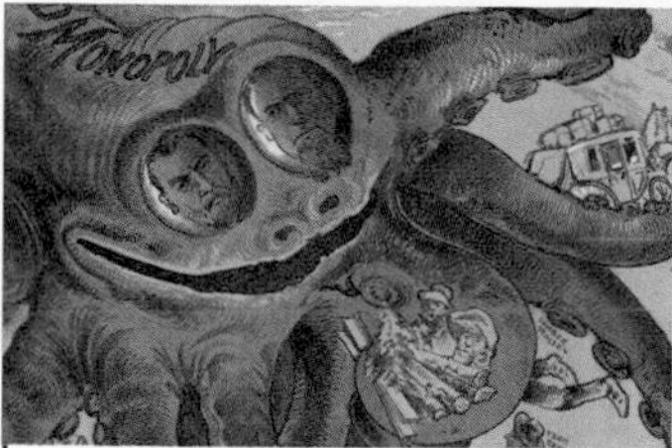

1879–1882

Henry George publishes *Progress and Poverty*
The bestseller gives voice to the growing anxiety over growing social inequality

John D. Rockefeller creates the first trust
Becomes a key feature of modern business organization and target of social critics

1882–1883

Workers in New York City establish Labor Day
Reflects strengthening of labor movement and protest against growing inequality and exploitation

Railroads establish Standard Time zones. In 1886 they establish a standard track gauge
Reflects power of railroads and the trend of standardization in business

1884–1886

Knights of Labor wins strike against Wabash Railroad
Gains publicity and credibility for the KOL, leading to a surge in membership

Police and workers clash in Haymarket
Leads to nationwide crackdown on labor union activism

The American Federation of Labor founded
Workers in skilled trades separate from Knights of Labor

1889–1890

Andrew Carnegie publishes "The Gospel of Wealth"
Popularizes the belief that opportunity and upward mobility are available to all in an industrial society

Sherman Anti-Trust Act passed
Reflects popular mood that big business must be restrained; weak and ineffective

Key Terms

laissez-faire (French for "let do" or leave alone) A philosophy that argued that the government should impose no restraints on business. 471

corporation Businesses owned by people who buy shares of stock in the company. 472

monopoly The control of an industry or market by one corporation. 474

vertical integration Business organization where one company controls the main phases of production of a good, from acquiring raw materials to retailing the finished product. 475

horizontal integration Business organization where one company buys many other companies producing the same product to eliminate competition and achieve greater efficiency. 475

robber barons A pejorative name for big business leaders that suggested they grew rich by devious business practices, exploitation of workers, and political manipulation. 476

trust A legally binding deal bringing many companies in the same industry under the direction of a board of "trustees." 476

Sherman Anti-Trust Act Authorized the Justice Department to prosecute any illegal contract, combination, or conspiracy among corporations that eliminated competition or restrained free trade. 477

holding company A huge corporation that bought and ran other corporations by purchasing their stock. 477

depression A contraction of economic growth, widespread business failure, and high rates of unemployment lasting several years. 483

blacklist A list of workers that employers in a particular town or industry refused to hire because they were considered troublemakers. 485

socialism A theory that rejected capitalism and advocated common ownership of property and social and economic equality. 486

Chinese Exclusion Act An 1882 law barring Chinese immigration to the United States for ten years. Renewed several times. It remained in effect until 1943. 486

social Darwinism The belief that the principles of evolution, which Darwin had observed in nature, also applied to society. Advocates argued that individuals or groups achieve advantage over others as the result of biological superiority, an idea expressed as "survival of the fittest." 490

Knights of Labor A labor organization founded in 1869 that in the 1880s accepted workers of all trades and backgrounds and became the world's largest industrial union. 492

Haymarket Incident A violent incident touched off when a bomb exploded amid a group of policemen as they broke up a peaceful labor rally in Chicago's Haymarket Square on May 4, 1886. 493

CHAPTER 17

Becoming a Modern Society

America in the Gilded Age, 1877–1900

"The day seems brought distinctly nearer when the nation, equipped with the latest implements furnished by science, shall master and use as never before its rich domain."

REV. RICHARD STORRS, speech at the opening of the Brooklyn Bridge

Hundreds of thousands of people, including President Chester A. Arthur and countless dignitaries, participated in the joyful ceremonies marking the opening of the Brooklyn Bridge on May 23, 1883. As this painting of the event demonstrates, Americans in the late nineteenth century celebrated the onset of the urban age. An astonishing sight and the very embodiment of the modern age, it was the world's largest suspension bridge, a style made possible by the one product that in many ways defined the industrial revolution—steel. The bridge's designer, German immigrant John Roebling, emphasized this transition to the modern age by using a stark contrast: he constructed the bridge's twin towers out of the ancient building material (stone) and formed them into gothic archways, a style reminiscent of the great medieval cathedrals of Europe.

The Brooklyn Bridge embodied the new urban and industrial era in ways beyond its cutting-edge technology and symbolic design. Workers who were either immigrants or the children of immigrants constructed the bridge. By connecting the nation's largest city (New York) and third largest city (Brooklyn), a prelude to their consolidation into one city in 1898, the new bridge also symbolized rapid urban growth. Finally the bridge hinted at the emergence of a new, more independent American woman. When Washington Roebling (who succeeded his father as chief engineer) fell gravely ill in 1872, his wife, Emily Warren Roebling, spent the next eleven years as the project's onsite manager.

The enthusiasm that attended the bridge's opening masked the grave problems that attended rampant urban growth. Indeed the era's name, the **Gilded Age**, reflected this notion that the amazing achievements of the period were like a thin gold layer that covered many unresolved social problems. The sections of New York and Brooklyn connected by the bridge, for example, were vast working-class immigrant districts beset by high rates of poverty, crime, and disease. Equally unseen in the immediate glow of the fireworks was the rising discontent among American workers over exploitation at the hands of employers and alienation from an unresponsive political system. Indeed dozens of men had died during the bridge's construction, and on several occasions workers went on strike. These sentiments and those of hard-pressed American farmers in the heartland would explode in the 1890s, leading to the emergence of the People's Party. The party eventually faded away, but not before establishing a reform agenda that would shape the Progressive Era (1900–1920).

How did the term Gilded Age reflect both the optimism and anxiety of the late nineteenth century?

The Rise of the City
p. 500

A Search for Solutions
p. 506

Ride a
STEARNS
and be
content

New Habits, Roles, and Lifestyles p. 512

The Challenge from Below p. 518

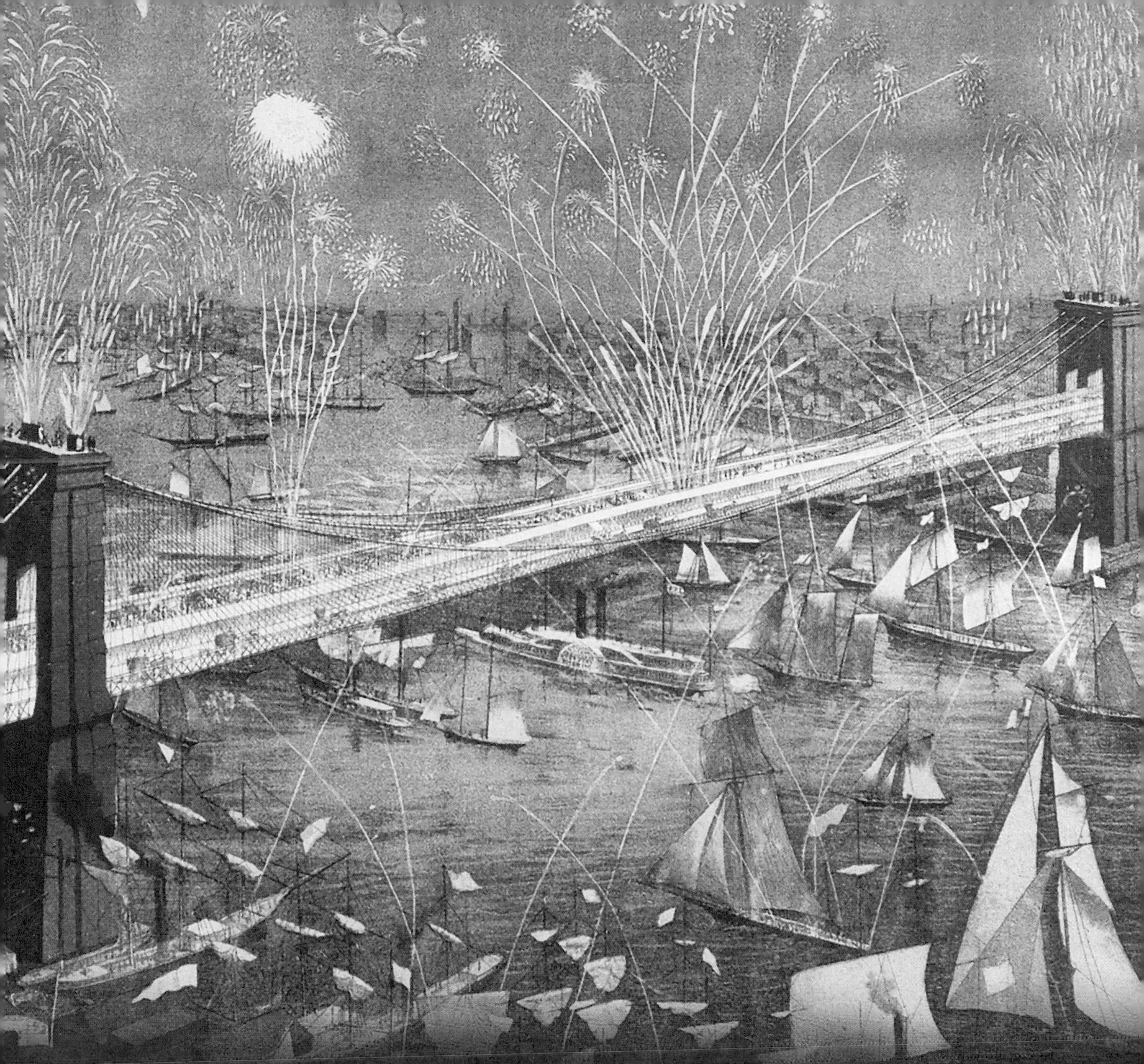

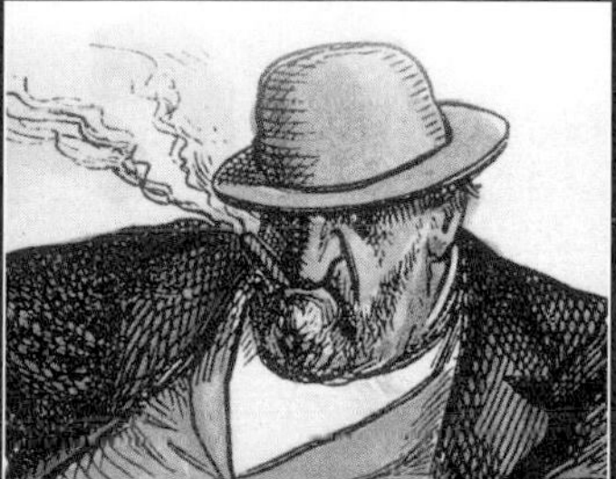

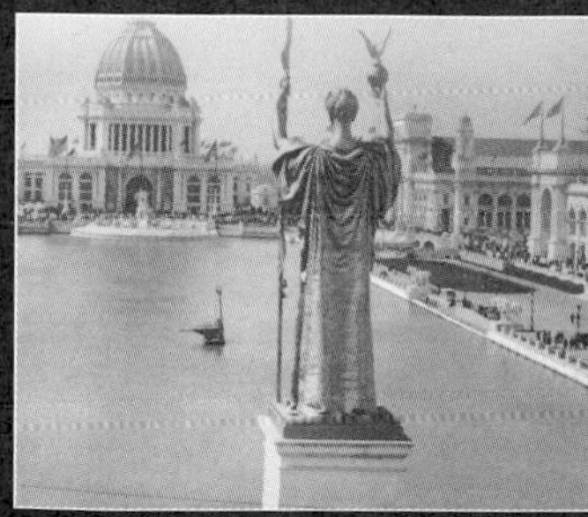

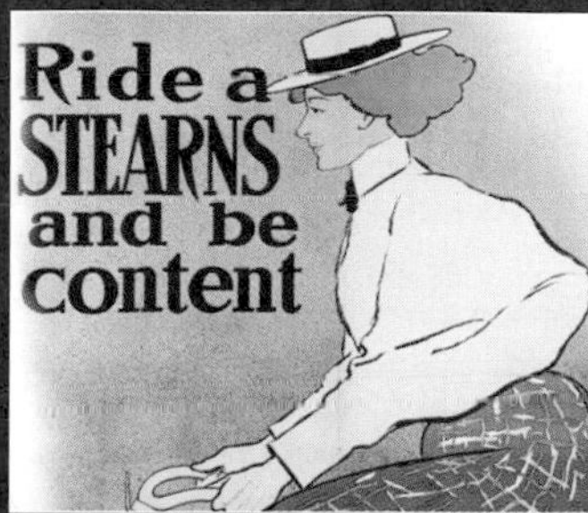

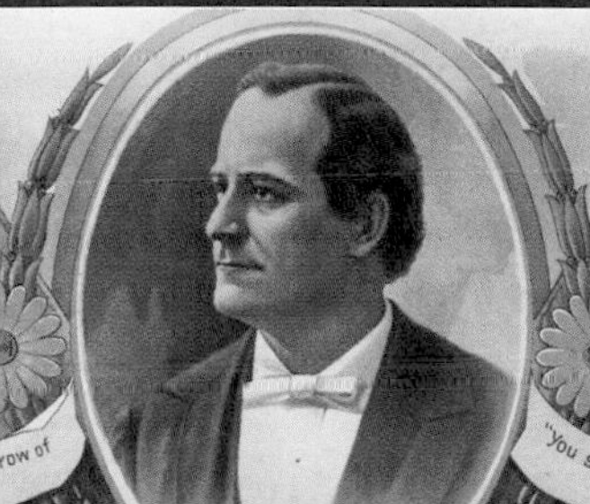

The Rise of the City

The United States experienced explosive urban growth in the second half of the nineteenth century. Industrialization and mass immigration transformed both older cities, such as New York and Philadelphia, and newer ones, such as Denver and Chicago, into major metropolises. Their growth was often chaotic and attended by significant increases in crime, poverty, and disease epidemics. City political machines emerged in this period and grew powerful, providing relief to the vulnerable and promoting urban growth, but in the process earning a reputation for corruption.

To the Cities

The urban population of the United States grew at an astonishing rate between 1860 and 1900. In 1860 one in five Americans lived in urban areas. Forty years later the figure had doubled to two in five. In that same period the number of cities with populations greater than 100,000 jumped from nine to thirty-eight. Among these were New York (3.4 million), Chicago (2.7 million), and Philadelphia (1.3 million). Joining these cities in 1900 were seventy-eight more with 50,000 or more inhabitants.

A significant portion of this new urban population came from rural areas within the United States. As agriculture became more mechanized (see Chapter 15), thereby lowering demand for farm labor, increasing numbers of men migrated to urban areas. Similarly the rise of American manufacturing eliminated the need for rural women to make clothes and other household goods, leading many to seek economic opportunity in cities. These men and women found a wide array of job opportunities in the city, ranging from low-paid work as factory operatives, laborers, and domestic servants to more desirable positions as skilled artisans and clerks. They also faced a significant challenge in adjusting to an utterly new lifestyle.

Another rural-to-urban internal migration involved African Americans leaving the Jim Crow South. Seeking to escape the poverty, racism, and violence of the South (see Chapter 14), a growing stream of African Americans began moving to northern cities. Drawn by word of better jobs and greater freedoms, some 300,000 migrated to northern cities between 1890 and 1910. Chicago's African American population jumped from 15,000 in 1890 to 110,000 in 1920. This trend marked the beginning of what became known as the Great Migration, the relocation of some 7 million African Americans from the South to the North between 1890 and 1970.

By far, however, the greatest source of urban population growth was mass immigration from Europe, with significant numbers also from Latin America, the Caribbean, and Asia. Before 1880 the majority of immigrants to the United States came from England, Ireland, Germany, and Scandinavia. But after 1880 the sources of immigration shifted to nations in southern and eastern Europe such as Russia, Italy, Greece, and Austria-Hungary (**17.1**).

17.1 Immigration to the United States, 1880–1920 Before 1880 the majority of immigrants to the United States came from northern and western Europe, but after 1880 most were from southern and eastern Europe.

Source: U.S. Bureau of the Census.

	1880-1889	%	1890-1899	%	1900-1909	%	1910-1919	%
Austria-Hungary	314,787	6.0	534,059	14.5	2,001,376	24.4	1,154,727	18.2
German Empire	1,445,181	27.5	579,072	15.7	328,722	4.0	174,227	2.7
Greece	1,807	.1	12,732	.3	145,402	1.8	198,108	3.1
Ireland	764,061	12.8	405,710	11.0	344,940	4.2	166,445	2.6
Italy	276,660	5.1	603,761	16.3	1,930,475	23.5	1,229,916	19.4
Russia	182,698	3.5	450,101	12.7	1,501,301	18.3	1,106,998	17.4
Scandinavia	761,783	12.7	390,729	10.5	488,208	5.9	238,275	3.8
United Kingdom	810,900	15.5	328,579	8.9	469,578	5.7	371,878	5.8
Totals	5,248,568		3,694,295		8,202,388		6,347,380	

Why did so many people flock to American cities?

All told the United States accepted fourteen million newcomers between 1860 and 1900, followed by another fourteen million between 1900 and 1920.

As with all immigrants before and since, some of these newcomers chose immigration to escape problems ranging from poverty, warfare, political and religious persecution, and natural disasters. But most were drawn by the promise of economic opportunity and upward mobility in America. Some migrated to rural areas and became farmers, but the great majority headed for America's cities and the ever-expanding number of jobs in industry, construction, service, and entrepreneurship found there.

Cities already characterized by ethnic, racial, and religious diversity brought by earlier arrivals of Irish, German, and other immigrants, as well as African Americans, now saw their diversity reach unprecedented levels. By 1910 immigrants or the American-born children of immigrants comprised an astonishing 78.6 percent of New York's population of 4.8 million residents. Chicago (77.5 percent), Milwaukee (78.6 percent), San Francisco (68.3 percent) and most medium to large cities boasted similarly astounding numbers of immigrants and American-born children of immigrants. Overall the foreign-born comprised 14.8 percent of the national population in 1910.

The Emergence of Ethnic Enclaves

These new immigrants spurring the growth of cities, like the Irish and Germans before them, soon formed concentrated **ethnic enclaves** in the cities. Often they moved into neighborhoods previously dominated by immigrants who had arrived before the Civil War. As a result in New York, for example, the Lower East Side enclaves of Little Ireland, Little Germany, and Little Africa became by the 1890s Little Italy, Chinatown, and the Jewish East Side. This process of ethnic succession is captured in a World War I memorial plaque affixed to the façade of the Church of the Transfiguration on New York's Lower East Side (**17.2**). A community of native-born Americans built the church in 1801 as the English Lutheran First Church of Zion, but they sold it in the 1840s to Irish Catholics who renamed it Church of the Transfiguration. In the 1890s a massive influx of Italians and outflow of Irish to other parts of the city turned the neighborhood into Little Italy and Transfiguration into a mostly Italian Catholic church. (Mother Cabrini, later canonized a saint, worked in the church caring for Italian immigrants.) The plaque provides a snapshot of the transformation from Little Ireland to Little Italy. Of the twenty names of parishioners who died in World War I, seventeen are Italian and only three—Donahue, Durkin, and Kane—are Irish. Today the neighborhood is part of Chinatown and most of the parishioners are Chinese.

Immigrant groups formed ethnic enclaves in part because they faced hostility and discrimination from Americans and other immigrant groups. But the primary cause was their recognition that grouping together created important advantages that enhanced their chances of success in America. Italian immigrants living in Chicago's Little Italy, for example, enjoyed the comfort and practical benefits of residing among people who spoke their language. There they could find help getting a job from an immigrant aid association, fellowship in an Italian fraternal society, or solace in an Italian Catholic church. They also found things that reminded them of home: Italian food, books, newspapers, churches, theaters, and opera houses.

A closer look at these enclaves revealed that they usually comprised smaller units composed of people from a particular region or village of their home country. New York's Jewish East Side, for example, included large concentrations of Jews from Hungary, Romania, Galicia, Russia, and Levantine.

17.2 **Evidence of Ethnic Succession**
This 1919 plaque lists seventeen Italian and three Irish names, indicating that the neighborhood once known as Little Ireland had become Little Italy.

Why did immigrants form ethnic enclaves in cities?

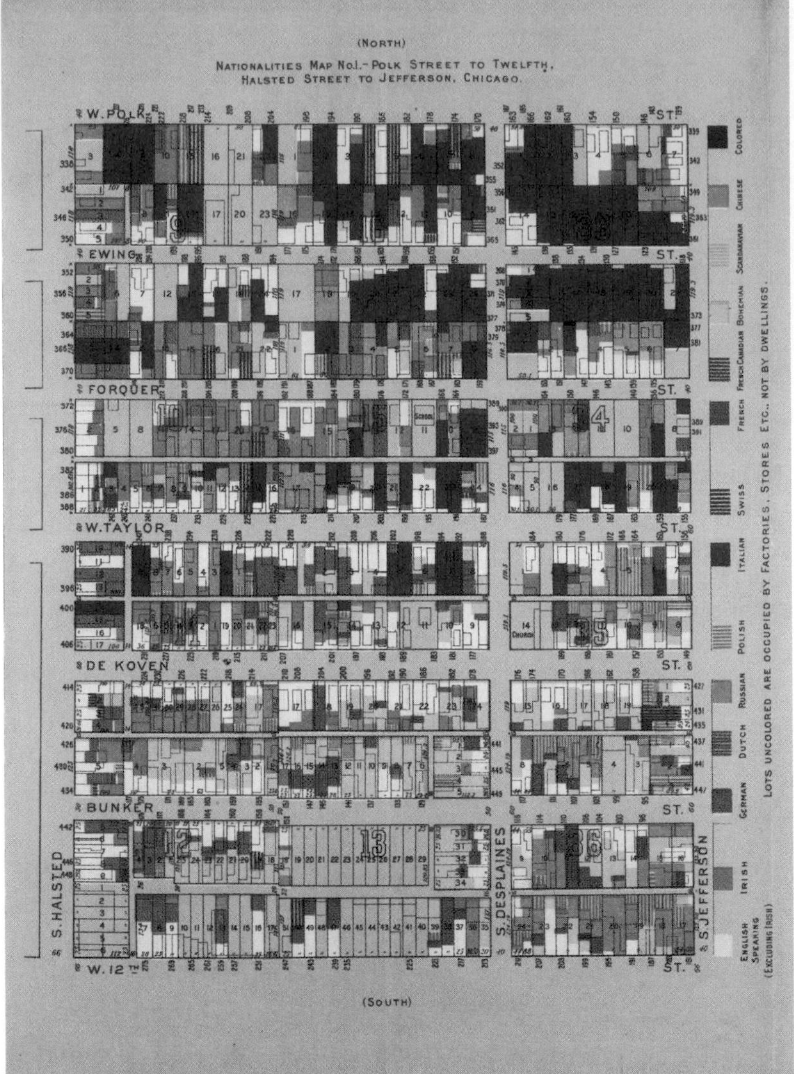

17.3 Mapping the Diversity of Ethnic Chicago
This 1895 map of the twelve-block area surrounding Hull House demonstrates the diversity of the immigrant neighborhood.

Italians living in Boston's North End clustered on certain streets depending on whether they came from Sicily, Campania, Abruzzi, or Liguria. Yet as this 1895 map (**17.3**) of the neighborhood surrounding Chicago's famous Hull House, which provided that city's immigrants with social and educational services, vividly demonstrates, immigrants—even those in ethnic enclaves—shared their neighborhoods with people of diverse origins. This twelve-block section of the city included immigrants from Ireland, Germany, Italy, Russia, Poland, Switzerland, France, Canada, Bohemia, Scandinavia, China, and the Netherlands, not to mention African Americans.

The Troubled City

Many Americans in the late nineteenth century saw cities as exciting places filled with opportunity, cultural diversity, entertainment, and new technology such as electric lighting and skyscrapers. Yet many more viewed cities as places of crowding, turmoil, filth, and despair. Both images were accurate, but the latter generated the most commentary and concern. One of the most striking features of modern urban life was the emergence of densely-packed "slums." In one ward on New York's Lower East Side in 1890, population density reached 334,000 people per square mile, numbers never seen before in history. Most of the people living in these densely packed districts were immigrants who labored for low wages as day laborers and factory operatives. Few men earned enough money to support their families and so they relied on their wives and children to produce additional income (see Chapter 16).

Squalid housing exacerbated the poverty of urban workers. **Tenements**, or multiple family dwellings of four to six stories housing dozens of families, became the most common form of housing for poor city dwellers by the 1860s. Most tenement apartments consisted of just two or three dimly lit and poorly ventilated rooms.

Tenement districts in every city suffered from high rates of disease and death, much of it caused when drinking water became contaminated by disease-causing bacteria due to primitive systems for removing sewage waste. Another source of disease were horses. In 1900 New York's 120,000 horses dropped six million pounds of manure on the city's streets every day! In most cities, as shown in this photograph (**17.4**), street cleaning was inadequate in working-class neighborhoods. Note that in this filthy working-class street in New York, vendors sell all manner of goods on the sidewalks, including food. These conditions contributed to frequent epidemics. In Chicago in 1891, for example, 2,000 people died from typhoid fever and 4,300 from bronchitis and pneumonia. Annually in the same city in the early 1890s some 10,000 to 12,000 children under the age of five died.

Despite the dreadful condition of many tenements, the surging population of American cities kept the demand for housing high, causing rents to rise continually. In New York an 1883 survey of bricklayers, among the city's best-paid wageworkers, determined that they paid 28 percent of their annual income to their landlords. Another survey a few years later revealed that cloakmakers devoted 38 percent of their income to rent. As a result evictions for falling behind in rent occurred frequently. New York averaged more than 16,000 evictions per year in the early 1880s and more than 23,000 by 1892.

> "Thousands of small houses and cottages arranged for one family are now packed with a family in each room."
> Chicago Board of Health report

Late-nineteenth-century cities also suffered from high rates of crime, especially in the tenement districts. Some crime was driven by poverty or despair. Women, for example, usually turned to prostitution as a last resort means of survival. Immigration also played a role as it resulted in a disproportionately high population of young single men (typically an age cohort with higher than average crime rates). The overall growth, diversity, and mobility of urban populations also contributed to the rising crime rate because these populations fostered a greater sense of anonymity and undermined the ability and will of communities to keep a watchful eye on potential criminal activity.

"Boss Rule": The Political Machine

Another unsettling feature of urban life, in addition to poverty, crime, and disorder, was the emergence of **political machines**. Most often associated with the Democratic Party, these organizations became powerful in nearly every large American city by mobilizing large blocs of working-class and immigrant voters while developing favorable relationships with real estate and business interests. Some machines controlled small sections of big cities. Martin Lomasney, for example, was "boss" of Boston's Eighth Ward in the West End. Others, such as New York's Tammany Hall came to rule the entire metropolis by the 1860s. By the late nineteenth and early twentieth centuries, several machines extended their power to the state level.

Several trends coincided to account for the rise of political machines in American cities. First the spread of universal white male suffrage in the 1820s (see Chapter 8) meant that political success depended less on a candidate's family name or wealth and more on his ability to whip up popular

17.4 Mired in Muck Late-nineteenth-century American cities, especially in working-class neighborhoods, suffered from inadequate street cleaning, leading to public health problems.

What factors contributed to high rates of crime in cities?

enthusiasm for candidates and get out the vote on election day. Rapid urban growth also produced unprecedented opportunities for politicians and their machines to reward supporters with construction contracts and jobs such as police officers and building inspectors. Machines also garnered support from immigrants by denouncing nativism and stymieing anti-immigrant legislation such as proposals to deny public jobs to the foreign born. Finally, the growing numbers of the poor provided a needy constituency for which the machines supplied not only jobs but also a whole range of services and favors including cash handouts, payments for funerals, legal assistance, and seasonal giveaways of turkeys at Thanksgiving and bags of coal in winter. Recipients of machine largesse were expected to vote for its candidates in the coming election.

> "Tammany Hall bears the same relation to the penitentiary as the Sunday-school to the church."
>
> A reformer, 1876

The emergence of political machines horrified many wealthy and native-born Americans. They found rule by the foreign-born threatening and the rough and corrupt style of bosses offensive. One aspect of machine politics, however, aroused especially bitter criticism: the no-questions-asked charity. (see *Competing Visions: How Best to Help the Poor?*).

Political machines acquired and retained power not only by providing services to their constituents but also, as suggested by this political cartoon of boss William Tweed, the notoriously corrupt head of Tammany Hall, by engaging in voter intimidation and election fraud (**17.5**). This image shows that the ballot "box" in many cities was actually a transparent glass ball that allowed the political machine's "shoulder hitters" to intimidate voters by letting them know they were watching to see how they voted. The motto "In Counting There Is Strength" refers to the tactic of political machines to use their influence with the police department and local boards of elections to manipulate the vote count to ensure a victory for their party. Equally important was the enormous amount of money machines garnered by selling patronage jobs, demanding kickbacks from city contractors, and collecting protection fees from a vast economy of vice the machine-controlled police allowed to flourish. Reformers railed against the machine, but consistently failed to defeat it.

THE BALLOT
IN COUNTING THERE IS STRENGTH
Th. Nast
"THAT'S WHAT'S THE MATTER."
Boss Tweed. "As long as I count the Votes, what are you going to do about it? say?"

17.5 Winning By Any Means
Political machines often resorted to voter intimidation and election fraud. As the motto "In Counting There Is Strength" suggests, vote counts were manipulated to ensure victory.

How did political machines gain the support of working-class and immigrant voters?

Competing Visions

HOW BEST TO HELP THE POOR?

The following documents by George Washington Plunkitt, a member of New York's Tammany Hall machine, and Josephine Shaw Lowell, founder of the Charity Organization Society, offer sharply contrasting views on how best to help the urban poor. How do they differ in their understanding of the causes of poverty? How do these views shape their approach to helping the poor?

In *Plunkitt of Tammany Hall* (1905), George Washington Plunkitt explains the many kinds of aid he dispensed to his mostly poor, working-class constituents in the course of a typical day.

2 a.m.: Aroused from sleep by the ringing of his doorbell; ... found a bartender, who asked him to go to the police station and bail out a saloon-keeper who had been arrested. ... Furnished bail and returned to bed at three o'clock.

6 a.m.: Awakened by fire engines passing his house. Hastened to the scene of the fire.... Met several of his election district captains who are always under orders to look out for fires, which are considered great vote-getters. Found several tenants who had been burned out, took them to a hotel, supplied them with clothes, fed them, and arranged temporary quarters for them...

8:30 a.m.: Went to police court to look after his constituents. Found six "drunks." Secured discharge of four by a timely word with the judge, and paid the fines of two.

9 a.m.: Appeared in the Municipal District Court. Paid the rent of a poor family about to be dispossessed [evicted] and gave them a dollar for food.

11 p.m.: At home again.... Spent nearly three hours fixing things for four men [looking for jobs], and succeeded in each case.

3 a.m.: Attended the funeral [procession] of an Italian as far as the ferry. Hurried back to make his appearance at the funeral of a Hebrew constituent...

7 p.m.: Went to district headquarters and presided over a meeting of election district captains...

8 p.m.: Went to a church fair. Took chances on everything, bought ice cream for the young girls and the children. Kissed the little ones, flattered their mothers and took their fathers out for something down at the corner [at a saloon].

9 p.m.: At the clubhouse again. Spent $10 on tickets for a church excursion and promised a subscription for a new church bell.... Listened to the complaints of a dozen pushcart peddlers who said they were persecuted by the police and assured them he would go to Police Headquarters in the morning and see about it.

10:30 P.M.: Attended a Hebrew wedding reception and dance.

12 P.M. [*sic*]: In bed.

In "The Bitter Cry of the Poor in New York," (1885), Josephine Shaw Lowell explains her belief that excessive charity harms the poor.

[I]t appears that there have been, during the past three years, in New York, 220,976 *persons* who have asked for *outside* charity in one form or another.... What, then, is the secret of this ... disgraceful showing? ...

One ..., is that instead of having been encouraged and helped to be honest, upright, independent, noble, they have been tempted to lie, to cheat, to cringe, to beg; and by whom has this cruel wrong been done? By the churches, by the benevolent people of this city. It is the work of those who think and say that they want to help the poor, but ... [t]hey forget the horrible temptations they are presenting to their fellow creatures. They give, without consideration, one dollar, two dollars, five dollars, never stopping to think how many hours' *work* it takes to *earn* such sums. Imagine how utterly discouraged and disgusted must be the woman who brings home her dollar earned by a hard day's work over the washtub, when her neighbor shows her an order for a dollar's worth of groceries obtained by a trip to ... the office of some relief society. She naturally will cease to struggle so hard to earn her pittance, and will take her neighbor's advice and seek the next dollar she wants where her neighbor has found it so easy to get one.... It is like a contagion.... [H]ere is a neighbor who tells them they can get their rent, can get city coal, can get grocery orders, by going to the right sources of supply. Who could resist the temptation? And so they give up their work, and set forth on their degrading journey.... [T]hey learn to be idle, to be beggars.

Out on the Sidewalk Eviction was an ever-present fear for many poor and working-class city dwellers.

Why did many Americans worry that the poor were receiving too much charity?

A Search for Solutions

The dark side of urbanization in the late nineteenth century prompted a wide range of competing views and responses. Some Americans concluded that the problem of urban poverty and all the troubling crime, disease, disorder, and corruption that accompanied it was the urban poor, in particular, the foreign-born. Their solution was heightened nativism and a demand for immigration restriction. Other Americans, however, worked to develop government agencies to address the emerging challenges of urban life. Still others established private institutions like settlement houses that reflected a new attitude toward the immigrant poor.

The Nativist Impulse

The rise of the modern American city was accompanied by a revival of nativism, or anti-immigrant views and sentiments. Suspicion of and hatred for the foreign-born had flared up during the Know-Nothing movement (see Chapter 12) in the 1850s, which targeted Irish and German immigrants. In the Gilded Age nativism took aim primarily at the so-called new immigrants, or those coming from southern and eastern Europe. As this 1899 image (**17.6**) illustrates, opponents of immigration in this period decried the newcomers as bearers of a wide range of unwanted habits and ideas. The immigrant, show here in racist caricature of eastern Europeans, carries according to his labels poverty, anarchy, superstition, intemperance, and Sabbath desecration (working or recreating on a Sunday). Note further Uncle Sam's disdainful reaction, but also the sarcastic inscriptions on the gateway—"admittance free," "walk in!" and "welcome"—meant to convey nativists' anger over what they considered lax immigration laws. As slums grew larger and strikes (often involving large numbers of foreign-born workers) became more violent, nativists like Josiah Strong called all the more loudly for the sharp restriction of immigration.

> The city has become a serious menace to our civilization.... It has a peculiar attraction for the immigrant.... Here is heaped the social dynamite; here roughs, gamblers, thieves, robbers, lawless and desperate men of all sorts, congregate; men who are ready on any pretext to raise riots for the purpose of destruction and plunder.
>
> — JOSIAH STRONG, *Our Country: Its Possible Future and Its Present Crisis* (1885)

In 1882 Congress responded to pressure by American workers and passed the Chinese Exclusion Act (see Chapter 16), a law that barred Chinese immigration to the United States. Five years later in 1887 a group of nativists who were especially fixated on the dangers posed by the rising immigration of Catholics formed the American Protective Association (APA) to lobby for immigration restriction. The organization grew to 500,000 members by the end of 1893. Its main base of strength lay in middle-class Protestants in the Midwest, but chapters also sprang up in most cities in the east.

Rising concerns over immigration led Congress to enact legislation in 1890 making oversight of immigration a federal responsibility and establishing immigration depots in most major port cities to screen all immigrant arrivals to weed out and deport those with incurable diseases, radical beliefs, criminal backgrounds, or so little money and skills they seemed likely only to add to the ranks of the urban poor. The largest and most famous of these facilities, Ellis Island, opened in 1892.

Many nativists, considering this new system too lenient, called for additional restrictions on immigration. In 1894 three Harvard graduates founded the Immigration Restriction League, an organization dedicated to lobbying for a literacy test for all would-be immigrants (requiring they demonstrate the ability to read and write in any language). Presidents Cleveland, Taft, and Wilson vetoed the immigrant literacy test bill, but Congress overrode the veto and it became law in 1917.

What fears about immigrants fueled nativist sentiment?

A Different View: Urban Reforms

While some Americans believed urban poverty, crime, disease, and overcrowding could be eliminated simply by restricting immigration, others developed a wide range of innovative policies and institutions to solve, or at least minimize, these problems. To meet the problem of rising crime, most cities followed the lead of New York when in 1845 it replaced the traditional night watch of a few untrained and unarmed men and established a paid professional police department. Similarly large cities disbanded their volunteer fire companies and invested in new technology, such as steam pumpers, and adopted tougher building codes.

More dangerous to a city than fire—at least to its inhabitants—were the frequent outbreaks of cholera, diphtheria, typhoid fever, and other maladies. Drawing on increasing knowledge about germ theory, cities established boards of health and took steps to improve water quality, waste removal, and street cleaning.

The latter half of the nineteenth century also witnessed a movement to build urban parks to provide the beauty and serenity of nature and to offer wholesome and healthy recreation space (as opposed to alleys and saloons) for all. New York City's Central Park, built in the 1850s and 1860s, proved so successful that nearly every large city commenced its own park projects. Because most of the grand parks were located far from the slums, however, reformers in the 1890s pushed urban governments to condemn whole blocks of tenements and build parks within working-class neighborhoods.

17.6 **Fear of Foreigners on the Rise** Decrying the so-called "new immigrants" from southern and eastern Europe as bearers of a wide range of unwanted habits and ideas, nativism surged in the Gilded Age.

Urban reformers also expanded public education. Compulsory education laws (usually requiring schooling until age fourteen) and a massive building campaign saw the number of public school enrollments surge from 6.9 million to 17.8 million between 1870 and 1910. Millions more students attended parochial schools established by the Catholic church. This effort reflected the traditional belief that education made for a productive and informed citizenry. But as the photograph (**17.7**) of children reciting the Pledge of Allegiance illustrates, advocates saw expanded urban public schooling as a means of Americanizing the immigrant masses, teaching them English and respect for democracy and the law. The pledge was first published in a youth magazine in the fall of 1892 as part of an effort to promote patriotism and civic pride among school children on the eve of the four hundredth anniversary of Christopher Columbus's arrival in the New World. Educators quickly adopted the pledge, making its recitation a daily ritual in schools across the country. This earlier style, which required people to end the pledge by extending their arms out straight, was done away with in the 1930s because of its similarity to salutes used in fascist Germany and Italy.

What steps did urban reformers take to improve the safety and liveability of cities?

17.7 Promoting Loyalty and Patriotism
Advocates of public education viewed it as a means of Americanizing the urban immigrant masses. Soon after its introduction in 1892, educators quickly made the Pledge of Allegiance a daily ritual in schools.

Capturing a New View of Poverty

Reformers in the Gilded Age also developed a new way of thinking about poverty and its causes. Most Americans at this time held to the traditional view that poverty was caused by personal or moral failures such as laziness or drunkenness. The poor, as Horatio Alger and others argued so persuasively in popular literature (see Chapter 16), needed only to abandon their dissolute ways and seize the opportunities for success that abounded in American life.

But toward the end of the nineteenth century, reformers began to challenge this view of poverty by arguing that factors beyond the control of the poor caused a significant portion of poverty. A key figure in this new outlook was photojournalist Jacob A. Riis, who emigrated from Denmark to New York in 1870. After spending his first years in America struggling in poverty, he gained a foothold in journalism. By the mid-1880s he had earned a reputation as a reporter covering the city's crime beat. But Riis was deeply troubled by the poverty and suffering he saw and decided to publicize the problem in the hopes of gaining public support for reform measures. In 1887 he started taking photographs of slum life to spark public awareness, and by 1888–1889 he began showing his photographs while giving lectures before reform societies and church groups. Spurred by the positive reaction to these talks, especially to the photographs (see *Images as History: Seeing the Poor*), he wrote the book *How the Other Half Lives: Studies among the*

Why was the Pledge of Allegiance adopted in the 1890s?

Images as History

SEEING THE POOR

Riis presented a shocking exposé account of the dreadful conditions in which the poor lived. But unlike most Americans writing about urban poverty in that era, who attributed these problems to the moral failures of the poor, Riis argued that the poor were *victims* of unhealthy and unregulated tenements for which they were forced to pay most of their earnings. Adding to the book's impact were his photographs and drawings made from photographs. His carefully composed photograph, "An Italian Rag-Picker in Jersey Street," shows the viewer her desperate situation.

Riis convinced many of his readers that the growing numbers of impoverished slum dwellers were trapped in circumstances beyond their control largely due to unhealthy and expensive tenement housing. He called for improved tenements that would free the poor from their debilitating circumstances and allow them the chance to succeed. As a result of *How the Other Half Lives* and several more books, not to mention many magazine articles and speeches, Riis's work led many cities to launch investigations and eventually pass tougher laws regarding room size, windows, running water, and toilets.

Filippo Lippi, *Madonna and Child* (1445) [*Source:* Filippo Lippi, "Madonna and Child," 1440/1445. Tempera on panel, .797 × .511 (31 3/8 × 20 1/8); framed: 1.172 × .854 × .095 (46 1/8 x 33 5/8 × 3 3/4). Samuel H. Kress Collection, Photograph © 2001 Board of Trustees, National Gallery of Art, Washington. 1939.1.290.(401)/PA]

The ladder suggests her "apartment" is little more than a dingy, windowless basement room with only one piece of furniture (the chair on which she sits).

Riis presents her not as filthy or drunk; despite the dreadful circumstances, she and her baby are dressed in clean clothes.

Riis often included babies and innocent-looking children in his photographs to prompt the viewer to wonder—and worry—about their fate if action is not taken to alleviate the plight of the poor.

The man's hat on the wall prompts the viewer to wonder if this desperate woman has a husband, or if she's been abandoned.

Although poor this woman is a hard worker. A rag-picker collected discarded rags and other fabric (see sacks), laundered them on a stovetop tub, and then sold them to paper manufacturers for pennies per pound.

The mother's heavenward gaze was intended to spur sympathy in the minds of middle- and upper-class viewers by conjuring up the familiar religious imagery of the Madonna and Child.

Jacob A. Riis, "Italian Mother and Her Baby in Jersey Street" (1889) [*Source:* Jacob A. Riis "Italian Mother and Her Baby in Jersey Street", in the home of an Italian rag-picker, Jersey Street, circa 1890. Museum of the City of New York, The Jacob A. Riis Collection (#157)]

How did Jacob Riis's portrayal of the poor differ from traditional notions of poverty?

Tenements of New York, which he published in 1890. Books providing shocking accounts of prostitution, drunkenness, and violence in America's slums had appeared as early as the 1840s. Riis's book was different and it caused a sensation.

Living among the Poor: Settlement Houses

Riis was not alone in promoting a more progressive and sympathetic view of poverty and remedies to it. In the early 1880s middle-class and college-educated women began establishing in immigrant neighborhoods **settlement houses**, or institutions dedicated to helping the urban poor by providing a wide range of social and educational services. Jane Addams and Ellen Gates Starr founded the most famous and influential settlement house, Hull House, in Chicago in 1889. Born to wealthy Illinois families, they had met in college and toured Europe together in 1888, where they were inspired by a visit to Toynbee Hall, a settlement house in London's poor East End. There they saw highly educated and wealthy young men from Oxford enter the East End to offer direct assistance to the poor. They vowed to establish a similar institution in Chicago upon their return.

With financial backing from wealthy reformers, Addams and Starr rented an old mansion on Chicago's Near West Side. The neighborhood was overwhelmingly foreign born, with immigrants from dozens of countries and regions. Most lived in poverty in dreary, run-down tenements. The neighborhood also suffered from poor sanitation and high rates of crime. Unlike socially conscious elite women of earlier generations who simply raised money for the poor or lobbied the state legislature for laws against child labor, Addams, Starr, and the many women workers they subsequently attracted to Hull House consciously chose to live among the poor to get to know them and understand their needs—even learn from them.

The staff at Hull House first offered educational classes in literature and art. When these proved popular they began to offer classes on more practical subjects, such as cooking, sewing, hygiene, civics, the English language, and vocational training. They also opened their doors to fledgling labor unions, recognizing the vital role unions could play in elevating the earnings of workers, especially the foreign born.

Within a decade Hull House was a flourishing institution offering a wide array of services to the poor of Chicago. Addams and other Hull House workers like Florence Kelley also became activists to prod city authorities to improve tenement laws, increase street cleaning and garbage removal, and expand public education. They also lobbied state officials for laws against child labor and for improved factory safety. Hull House was not the first settlement in America, but it soon became its most famous, inspiring hundreds of successful imitators, including Denison House in Boston (1889) and Henry Street Settlement in New York (1893).

The White City

The optimistic vision of modern urban life articulated by reformers like Jane Addams and Jacob Riis found vivid expression in the **City Beautiful Movement**. Taking form in the late 1880s, it brought together architects, landscape architects, and urban planners who believed the many problems afflicting American cities could be ameliorated, even eliminated, through the comprehensive planning and grand redesign of urban space. City Beautiful proponents like Daniel Burnham and Frederick Law Olmsted argued for the creation of large parks and public squares linked by grand boulevards. Equally important was their emphasis on classical architectural styles for both public and private buildings.

Burnham, Olmsted, and others first demonstrated these ideas at the 1893 Chicago World's Exposition, an extraordinary event planned as a grand celebration of the four hundredth anniversary of Christopher Columbus's arrival in the New World in 1492 and of Chicago's recovery from its devastating fire in 1871. Like the many world's fairs that preceded it, the Chicago Exposition was a celebration

What services did settlement houses provide the urban poor?

of technology, culture, and commerce. It contained thousands of exhibits on science, machinery, art, history, ethnic heritage, music, and theater. But its greatest significance was its impact on architecture, design, and urban planning. Given nearly 700 acres of waterfront property along Lake Michigan, Burnham and the extraordinary team he assembled, including landscape architect Frederick Law Olmsted and architect Louis Sullivan, eventually developed a master plan that called for beautifully landscaped grounds featuring waterways and reflecting pools.

Around the waterways, (**17.8**), Burnham placed fourteen main buildings designed in the Beaux-Arts architectural style, which emphasized logic, harmony, and uniformity. The Court of Honor buildings, shown in the image, lined the Grand Basin that formed the centerpiece of the exposition grounds. Covered in bright white stucco that gave them a shimmering whiteness, the buildings of the White City astonished the estimated 27 million visitors who entered through the main gates.

Yet as this image indicates, Burnham and his team sought not simply to wow the public with grand architecture. They wanted to make a statement on the potential glory of the modern city. All cities could be—should be—as impressive as the White City. All that was needed was strong civic leadership and enlightened urban planning. This grand vision never fully caught on, but many of the City Beautiful ideals and concepts exhibited in the White City influenced a generation of urban planners and architects committed to making American cities more beautiful, healthy, and efficient.

17.8 The White City Designed by some of the nation's leading architects and landscape architects, the White City consisted of fourteen main buildings designed in the Beaux-Arts style, set in beautifully landscaped grounds featuring waterways and reflecting pools.

How did the White City reflect an optimistic vision of the future of urban life?

New Habits, Roles, and Lifestyles

The development of vast working-class districts was but one aspect of a broad trend that reshaped urban life in the late nineteenth century. Urban and subsequent suburban growth also led to the development of middle-class and elite residential neighborhoods, as well as urban central business districts dedicated almost exclusively to commerce. Middle-class neighborhoods increasingly reflected the new values of the urban middle class, including a growing interest in leisure activities. The growth of leisure time allowed women to take on increasingly significant roles in public life through memberships in socially and politically active clubs.

The New Urban Landscape

The evolution of mass transit systems like horsecars, steam railroads, and trolleys, led to explosive urban growth and the formation of specialized districts dedicated to specific functions. Most cities, for example, developed **central business districts** where almost no residents lived. Instead the high-value real estate in downtowns from Baltimore to Chicago to San Francisco was dedicated to commerce: banks, department stores (see Chapter 16), and the offices of corporations, accountants, lawyers, and other professions. Each day mass transit systems carried thousands of shoppers and workers to central business districts from sections of cities now dedicated almost exclusively to residential use, or from residential neighborhoods just beyond the city limits.

17.9 **Reaching for the Sky**
The completion of the Home Insurance Building in Chicago in 1885 marked the arrival of the skyscraper. Designed with an internal steel skeleton, it rose ten stories high and led to a boom in tall building construction in downtowns across the country.

Soaring real estate values and new technology led to another distinct feature in central business districts: skyscrapers. Before the Civil War few buildings exceeded six stories, but the invention of the elevator and new building materials like cast iron led to ten- and twelve-story buildings by the early 1880s. The big breakthrough in tall building construction came in 1885 with the completion of the Home Insurance Building in Chicago (**17.9**). It was remarkable not for its height (ten stories), but for its internal steel skeleton that allowed for thin walls and large windows. The first true skyscraper led to a boom in tall building construction in downtowns across the country. By 1900 lower Manhattan alone featured twelve buildings of 300 feet or more in height.

Equally significant, although less dramatic, than the upward reach of city skylines was the outward sprawl of urban areas due to mass transit. **Suburbs**, or residential communities established just beyond a city's boundary but connected to the urban center by mass transit, attracted middle-class families that could afford to buy a house and pay the cost of commuting to the city for work. Middle-class families found suburbs attractive for their serenity, cleanliness, and greenery—aspects that stood in sharp contrast to the crime, disease, violence, and

How did new modes of transportation promote the development of specialized urban and suburban districts?

noise of the inner city. Given the prevalence of racist and nativist attitudes in Gilded Age American society, suburbs also attracted people unwilling to live with newly arrived immigrants and African Americans.

The creation of middle-class communities of like-minded people of similar ethnic and religious backgrounds fostered the development of new middle-class values, tastes, and social patterns. Middle-class families had fewer children and higher incomes than their working-class counterparts. Greater wealth and fewer mouths to feed allowed them to purchase an ever-increasing array of consumer products, most often by women who rode trolleys or commuter lines to the central business district. Many of these products were everyday items that came with increasingly recognizable names like Ivory Soap and Coca-Cola. Others were more substantial, such as small pianos that could be purchased on credit. The great popularity of pianos in the late nineteenth century reflected not merely the rising wealth of middle-class families, but also the significant amount of leisure time they enjoyed and their desire to develop refined tastes.

> "Since water hems in the business center on three sides and the nexus of railroads on the south, Chicago must grow upward."
>
> Real estate columnist, *Chicago Tribune*, 1888

New Roles and Expectations for Women

Lower birth rates and a growing trend of hiring servants to perform duties like cooking, cleaning, and laundry left middle-class women with more free time. The dominant notions about gender roles, however, emphasized the need for women to remain in the home, focusing on creating a moral and nurturing environment for their husbands and children. According to this view the outside world of business and politics was the male sphere, full of corruption, dishonesty, immorality, and violence that threatened virtuous womanhood.

Yet two trends in the late nineteenth century led directly to new, more public roles for middle-class women. The first was a significant rise in education, especially at the college level. By 1900 women constituted nearly 20 percent of college graduates, up from just 13 percent in 1890. Education allowed women, if only temporarily, to leave the domestic sphere to interact with other young women and encounter emerging ideas of women's rights. Not surprisingly nearly every leader in the women's rights movement in the late nineteenth century had received at least some college education.

A second significant trend that reshaped the outlook, expectations, and public influence of American women in the period was their increased involvement in a growing number of clubs dedicated to charity and social reform. The General Federation of Women's Clubs, established in 1890, counted 160,000 members in more than five hundred clubs by 1900. The largest and best known organization was the Women's Christian Temperance Union (WCTU). Activism in clubs gave women the opportunity to exert political influence, build leadership skills, and learn from networks of activist, reform-minded women.

By the 1890s many of these activist women joined the **women's suffrage** movement, or the effort to obtain voting rights for women. The movement had split into rival factions in 1869 in the debate over the Fourteenth Amendment (see Chapter 14), but in 1890 they reunited to form the National American Woman Suffrage Association (NAWSA). It helped win suffrage in Colorado in 1893 and Idaho in 1896 (Utah and Wyoming had previously approved it), but voting rights for all women would not occur until ratification of the Nineteenth Amendment in 1920 (see Chapter 18).

Racism led white women to exclude black women from their clubs and the suffrage movement. Nonetheless African American women established their own clubs to pursue goals such as temperance and women's suffrage. Most of these clubs affiliated with the National Association of Colored Women, an umbrella group. Some black women pursued goals of particular concern to African Americans. Ida B. Wells launched a national campaign against lynching in the 1890s

What trends contributed to a growing public activism among women?

that drew many African American women and men into public activism for reform, especially civil rights.

By the 1890s Americans had begun to use the term "**New Woman**" to describe middle-class women who pursued higher education, engaged in political activism, delayed marriage, and bore fewer children. The New Woman had a distinct look, donning the clothing, hair style, and air of the so-called Gibson Girl. A creation of illustrator Charles Dana Gibson in 1890s popular magazines, the Gibson Girl was tall and beautiful, with a tightly cinched waist that accentuated her bosom and hair piled high on her head.

Offsetting these traditionally feminine characteristics, however, was an outgoing, even mischievous spirit that reflected the greater independence and activism of younger American women. Symbolic of this attitude was the degree to which young women took part in the great national enthusiasm for bicycling in the 1890s. Note the striking contrast between these two images. The first from 1886 (**17.10**) shows a traditional Victorian-era wife in formal attire being carried as a passenger by her husband. The second image, an 1896 advertisement poster for the Stearns Bicycle Company (**17.11**), shows a self-confident and carefree woman drawn in the Gibson Girl style breezing along on her own bicycle. Many conservative Americans condemned the bicycling craze as unnatural and immoral because it allowed young women and men the freedom to pedal off unchaperoned, away from the watchful eyes of parents and other guardians of respectability.

17.11 The New Woman
Many Americans saw a connection between the growing independence, activism, and outgoing spirit of young women and their participation in the great national enthusiasm for bicycling in the 1890s.

17.10 The Traditional Woman
Reflecting Victorian values, this conservatively dressed woman in 1886 enjoys a bicycle ride only as the passenger of her husband.

> "Bicycling has done more to emancipate women than anything else in the world. I stand and rejoice every time I see a woman ride by on a wheel. It gives women a feeling of freedom and self-reliance."
>
> SUSAN B. ANTHONY, 1896

New Forms of Leisure and Popular Culture

As industrial life created sharp distinctions between time spent at work and time doing everything else, Americans in the Gilded Age developed the concept of leisure time. This trend was at the heart of the labor movement's persistent demand for the eight-hour day as both a call for shorter hours of toil and an insistence on the right to leisure time. Many city dwellers spent their leisure time in informal activities in their neighborhood such as walking about, playing games in streets and local parks, and socializing with their neighbors. For many working-class men, the local saloon was the preferred place of leisure.

Increasingly popular, however, were more formal leisure opportunities such as amusement parks and organized spectator sports. Amateur, semiprofessional, and professional baseball teams, for example, drew large crowds. Entrepreneurs soon came to see baseball as a business, despite its popular reputation as the "national pastime." They built large baseball stadiums near one or more streetcar lines and sold patrons not merely tickets but also food, beer, trinkets, and scorecards. By the 1880s baseball stars like Mike "King" Kelly and Adrian "Cap" Anson had emerged as high-paid celebrities. Corporations, especially true of the booming tobacco industry, quickly realized the value of celebrity endorsements for their products and in the 1880s created the original baseball cards like the one shown here (**17.12**). To legitimize tobacco use companies such as Old Judge portrayed players like Kelly as ideal men—the perfect blend of athletic masculinity and refined, almost gentlemen-like bearing. In an era when the press rarely reported on the bad behavior of athletes or politicians, few Americans could have known that the real Mike Kelly was a violent alcoholic who would drink himself to death in 1894 at the age of thirty-seven.

Other spectator sports likewise enjoyed great popularity in the late nineteenth century. Professional boxing, horseracing, track and field competitions, and bicycle races drew large crowds to venues such as Madison Square Garden in New York City, the Chicago Coliseum, and the Boston Arena. By the 1890s college football games in Boston, New York, Philadelphia, and Chicago often drew more than fifty thousand fans. Baseball, football, and other urban spectator sports proved consistent money-makers for promoters, but they also attracted criticism from ministers and some public officials who decried the violence, alcohol consumption, and gambling associated with them and the increased tendency to play them on Sundays.

Competing for the attention of the American with increased leisure time on his or her hands was a burgeoning theatrical entertainment industry. By the late nineteenth century, the typical city resident could choose from a vast array of entertainment forms on stage. In ethnic neighborhoods, for example, Old World productions like Italian melodramas based loosely on operas and Yiddish comedies drawn from eastern European traditions flourished.

Elsewhere in the city in more mainstream venues, people flocked to musical comedies, a distinctly

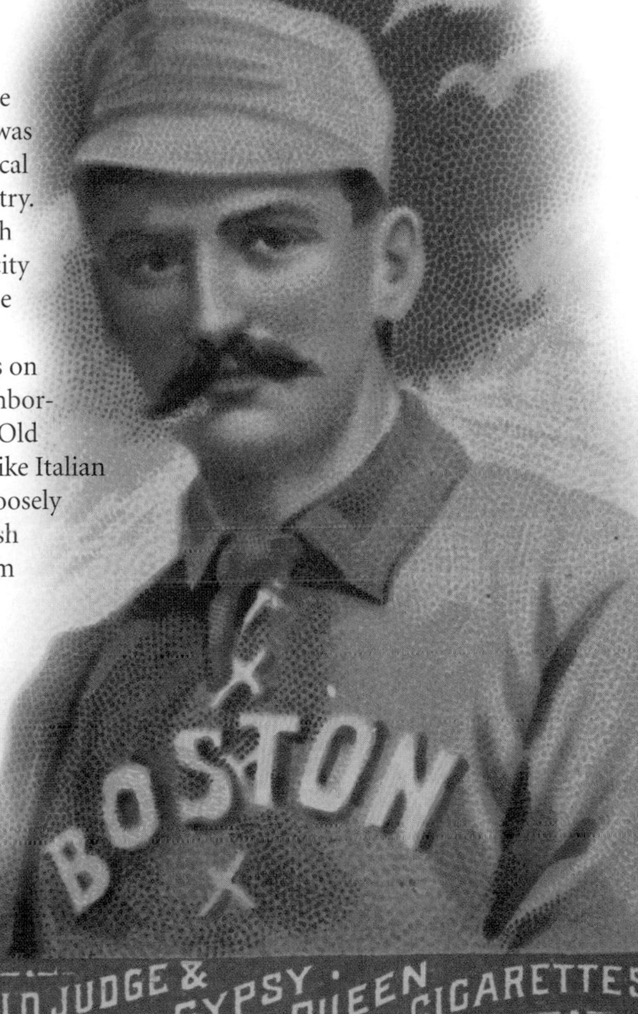

17.12 Selling Celebrity
The booming tobacco industry created the original baseball cards to capitalize on the value of sports celebrity endorsements for their products.

How did commercial interests shape the new forms of leisure in the Gilded Age?

American innovation pioneered by the duo of Edward Harrigan and Tony Hart. They were succeeded by others such as George M. Cohan and Irving Berlin, whose popular songs like "Give My Regards to Broadway" and "Alexander's Ragtime Band" became enduring hits.

Also popular was vaudeville, a kind of variety show featuring acts from jugglers, musicians, acrobats, and family routines, to singers, wild animal acts, ribald comedians, and scantily clad women and aimed at a working-class audience. With its low admission fees and democratic approach, vaudeville was geared for the masses. A typical vaudeville production featured a series of acts by entertainers—anything. At its peak circa 1900, vaudeville shows drew two million patrons a day. Many of the great American stage and film performers from the early twentieth century, such as James Cagney, Mae West, and Al Jolson, began their careers in vaudeville.

Wealthier and better-educated city residents rejected vaudeville and the more raucous forms of musical comedy as undignified and coarse. Instead they went to opera houses to hear European classics and to what they considered legitimate theater to see productions of Shakespeare and the classics.

While these varied forms of entertainment were developed and popularized in America's large cities, they quickly spread via published sheet music and touring companies to communities of every size across the nation. The result was the beginning of a national popular culture, one that would flourish more fully with the arrival of movies, radio, and television in the twentieth century.

17.13 Imagining an American Aristocracy Wealthy Americans in the Gilded Age competed to throw the most expensive and decadent ball, wedding, or party. At Mrs. William K. Vanderbilt's 1883 ball, New York's elite arrived in costumes depicting figures of European royalty. [*Source:* Collection of The New-York Historical Society, Box1.f 10. Negative no. 80433d]

How did varied forms of leisure reflect class differences?

Lifestyles of the Rich and Famous

Another feature of urban life that became a defining feature of the Gilded Age (so much so that it informed the era's name) was the advent of lavish displays of wealth by the rich. Dubbed "**conspicuous consumption**" by sociologist Thorstein Veblen in 1899, this trend involved most prominently the construction of opulent mansions in elite urban districts such as New York's Fifth Avenue, Chicago's Lake Shore Drive, and San Francisco's Nob Hill, as well as in exclusive summer retreats like Newport, Rhode Island. Wealthy families like the Vanderbilts and Astors competed to see who could throw the most extravagant ball, weddings, and parties.

"There is many a palace in Europe that would hide its diminished roof beside the sheer luxury of Fifth Avenue homes."

EDGAR SALTUS

One of the most famous was a ball hosted by Alva Vanderbilt, wife of tycoon William K. Vanderbilt, on March 26, 1883, to celebrate the opening of their new $3 million mansion on upper Fifth Avenue. The elite of New York arrived in costume (**17.13**).Many dressed as Marie Antoinette, Queen Elizabeth, and Louis XV. This choice of an ostentatious theme of royalty reflected the widely shared belief among the nation's wealthy elite that they constituted an American aristocracy—a notion that ran counter to the longstanding American tradition of fear and loathing for such undemocratic pretensions (see Chapters 4 and 5). Some labor activists and social critics castigated the ball and high society's rejection of republican simplicity, but Mrs. Vanderbilt's guests paid no heed. They reveled past dawn in a party that cost $250,000—that in an age when an average worker could expect to earn less than $700 per year. By the mid-1880s most newspapers featured "Society" columns that devoted extensive coverage to the lives of the wealthy.

While Americans followed the exploits of the rich with a certain level of wonder, the public would accept only so much extravagance before expressing revulsion. That finally occurred in February 1897, when the Bradley Martin family hosted a $400,000 party in which eight hundred society guests arrived in costumes depicting European royalty. One society reporter described "a gorgeous, superb, and wonderful spectacle." But in 1897, when the nation was suffering from a severe economic depression, public criticism of the ball poured in from all quarters, including public officials, clergymen, and workers. The Bradley Martins fled to Europe and settled permanently in England, ending the days of diamond-necklace party favors.

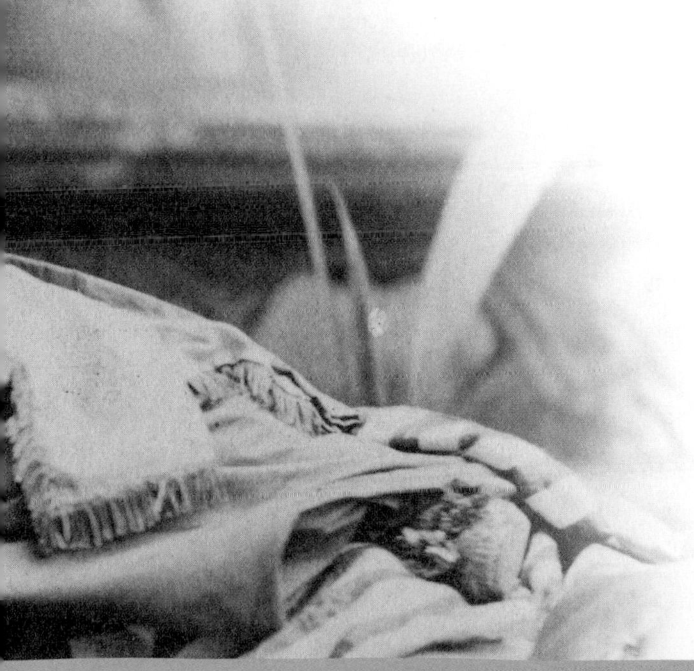

"[Y]ou rich people put next to nothing in the collection plate, and yet you'll spend thousands of dollars on Mrs. Bradley Martin's ball."

Sermon of a minister outraged over the Bradley Martin Ball

How did the great displays of wealth in the Gilded Age represent a break with America's republican traditions?

The Challenge from Below

The revulsion expressed over the Bradley Martin Ball in 1897 reflected the rising discontent of the era. Many farmers and industrial workers felt increasingly exploited by powerful corporations. When they turned to elected officials to address these problems, they found them unresponsive. Most politicians remained committed to a laissez-faire philosophy, which argued against government intervention in the economy. As a result the period was marked by some of the most bitter and violent strikes in American history and the rise of a third party comprised mainly of farmers, workers, and reformers—the **People's Party**—to challenge the two major parties, the Republicans and Democrats.

"The popular mind is agitated with problems that may disturb social order, and among them all none is more threatening than ... the concentration of capital into vast combinations. ... Congress alone can deal with them and if we are unwilling or unable there will soon be a trust for every product and a master to fix the price for every necessity of life."

Senator JOHN SHERMAN of Ohio, introducing his anti-trust bill, 1888

17.14 **Deadlocked Presidential Politics in the Gilded Age** With an electorate evenly divided between the two parties, Gilded Age politics were often marked by stalemate and inaction on key social and economic issues.

Year	Candidate	Party	Popular Vote	Electoral Vote
1876	**Rutherford B. Hayes***	Republican	4,036,298 (48%)	185
	Samuel J. Tilden	Democrat	4,300,590 (51%)	184
1880	**James Garfield**	Republican	4,454,416 (48.5%)	214
	Winfield S. Hancock	Democrat	4,444,952 (48.1%)	155
1884	**Grover Cleveland**	Democrat	4,874,986 (48.5%)	219
	James G. Blaine	Republican	4,851,334 (48.2%)	182
1888	**Benjamin Harrison***	Republican	5,439,853 (47.9%)	233
	Grover Cleveland	Democrat	5,540,309 (48.6%)	168
1892	**Grover Cleveland**	Democrat	5,556,918 (46%)	277
	Benjamin Harrison	Republican	5,176,108 (43%)	145
	James B. Weaver	People's	1,041,028 (9%)	22

Winner in bold

* = winner despite losing popular vote

Why were election results in the Gilded Age so close?

Out of Touch Politics

Popular enthusiasm for politics reached extraordinary heights in the Gilded Age. Indeed American voters turned out in astonishing numbers, averaging 72 percent between 1876 and 1896 (as compared with between 50 and 60 percent in recent decades). Despite such intense interest and participation in politics, politicians made little progress in resolving the major issues that dominated national politics in this period. This political stalemate stemmed from several factors. First, as indicated in (**17.14**), the electorate was evenly divided between the two parties, resulting in remarkably close elections. For example, the five presidential elections between 1876 and 1892 were decided by razor-thin margins. Indeed the contests in 1876 and 1888 saw the candidate with the highest popular vote total lose because his opponent tallied more electoral votes. No incumbent president won reelection, and only twice (each time for just two years) did one party control both houses of Congress and the presidency.

Political inaction in the Gilded Age also reflected the conservatism of most politicians who clung to longstanding political traditions that celebrated small, nonintrusive government, especially at the federal level. For many leaders government regulation of business appeared socialistic and potentially harmful to both the economy and republican principles. Political paralysis stemmed from the power of corporate interests to stymie legislation they deemed harmful to their financial interests. They did so through huge donations to political parties and outright bribery. To cite but one example, big business interests succeeded in maintaining a very high tariff, which protected their manufactures from foreign competition.The record for 1890, the year Congress took up the big issues of tariff, currency reform, and corporate regulation, provides a particularly vivid example of this ineffective political system. Support for corporate regulation reflected rising concern from many corners of American society. Industrial workers saw themselves as victims of corporate power that demanded long hours of dangerous toil for low wages. Many other Americans, as suggested by this 1889 Thomas Nast cartoon, *The Rising of the Usurpers and the Sinking of the Liberties of the People* (**17.15**), viewed trusts as a threat to the principles of democracy and equality. By monopolizing the necessities of life, trusts literally threatened to smother American liberty. The Sherman Anti-Trust Act of 1890 promised to empower the federal government to crack down on business practices that diminished competition (see Chapter 16), but opposition among pro-business legislators weakened the law to such a point that it did little in the coming years to slow the growth of big business. Indeed the 1890s saw record numbers of mergers and big business used the Sherman act to weaken labor unions by arguing that strikes amounted to restraint of trade.

Similarly, Congress also took up the contentious issue of currency reform to determine what constituted the proper basis for American currency. Advocates of "hard money," a group that included most Republicans, businessmen and the wealthy, argued for basing currency on actual gold and silver in the U.S. Treasury. They opposed the issuance of paper money, popularly known as "greenbacks," arguing that it contributed to inflation and lowered interest rates. "Soft money" proponents like farmers, workers, and Democrats, however, argued that the supply of currency in the Gilded Age was insufficient to meet the needs of an expanding commercial economy. They advocated the issuance of greenbacks and expanded coinage of silver. More money in circulation would lead to inflation, but debtors, especially farmers, welcomed inflation because it promised to raise the prices of their goods and diminish the burden of their debts. In 1890 they supported the Sherman Silver Purchase Act of 1890. It required the U.S. Treasury to purchase

17.15 Liberty Suffocated by Big Business This 1889 Thomas Nast cartoon captured the concerns of many, that trusts threatened American principles of democracy, equality, and liberty by monopolizing the necessities of life.

Why did Congress in this period fail to address major social issues?

4.5 million ounces of silver every month and issue notes (paper money) redeemable in either silver or gold.

Republicans opposed the bill but wanted to enact a higher tariff. Democrats opposed a higher tariff, arguing that it amounted to a huge subsidy paid by American consumers to business, so both sides compromised and the bills became law. Neither bill, however, had the desired effect. The higher tariff caused a surge in consumer prices, producing a widespread discontent. The silver program caused the price of silver to fall and so most of the people holding the notes redeemed them for gold, a trend that caused a severe depletion of the nation's gold reserves, which in turn contributed to the Panic of 1893 and subsequent four years of severe economic depression.

The one notable exception to the politics of stalemate was the passage of a civil service law to make certain government jobs open only to people who demonstrated their competency on a civil service exam rather than people who merely possessed strong political connections. Neither political party favored the law since it threatened to undermine their ability to reward friends and campaign contributors. It took the assassination of President James A. Garfield in 1881 by a frustrated and apparently deranged office seeker to gain passage of the Pendleton Act in 1883, a law that placed 10 percent of federal jobs under civil service.

The People's Party

Anger and resentment against the mainstream political system over its corruption and failure to act on critical issues like corporate regulation and currency and tariff reform gradually produced a popular reaction. In the late 1870s **farmers' alliances,** successors to the Granger movement (see Chapter 15), formed to alleviate the plight of farmers beset by rising costs and falling prices for their products. The Southern Farmers' Alliance (established in 1877) and Northern Farmers' Alliance (1880) grew steadily in the 1880s to a combined membership of more than 5 million. Excluded by the segregationist doctrines of the post-Reconstruction South (see Chapter 14), black farmers formed the Colored Farmers' Alliance in 1886 and soon drew a membership of more than 1.25 million.

The alliances argued that the economic woes of the American farmer were due to exploitive bankers who charged farmers exorbitant interest rates for farm mortgages, railroads that charged them extortionate rates to transport farm produce to market, and commodity brokers on Wall Street who bought their crops at rock bottom prices and then turned around and resold them at many times the original price paid. To combat this injustice the alliances promoted the establishment of cooperatives that combined the buying and selling power of farmers to gain them better prices for their produce and lower rates for loans and crop insurance. They also promoted education on agricultural topics.

In 1889 the Northern Farmers' Alliance and Southern Farmers' Alliance united to form the National Alliance. One year later, convinced that they only way to combat the power of the monopolies and trusts was to transform the National Alliance into a political movement to put pro-farmer candidates into office, delegates gathered in Ocala, Florida, and drew up a manifesto listing their grievances and proposed reforms. That fall National Alliance–backed candidates won complete or partial control of twelve state legislatures and elected six governors. They also sent fifty representatives and three senators to the U.S. Congress. Because most were Democrats, Republicans lost control of the House. These positive electoral results convinced many National Alliance activists like Ignatius Donnelly of Minnesota and Tom Watson of Georgia that they needed to form a third party and run a slate of candidates in the upcoming 1892 presidential contest.

A National Alliance convention held in St. Louis in early 1892 led to the formal creation of the People's Party (its followers would be known as "Populists") and the adoption of a preamble to the party's platform that set forth the plight of the American farmer and worker in forceful prose:

> [W]e meet in the midst of a nation brought to the verge of moral, political, and material ruin.... The fruits of the toil of millions are boldly stolen to build up colossal fortunes for a few ...

By now the strength of the People's Party movement had begun to alarm the leaders of the mainstream political parties. Worried about its potential to win enough votes in the upcoming 1892 election to determine the winner by taking votes from the major parties, they launched a campaign to discredit the Populists. In this political cartoon (**17.16**), which appeared on the cover of *Judge*, a pro-Republican magazine, the artist tries to

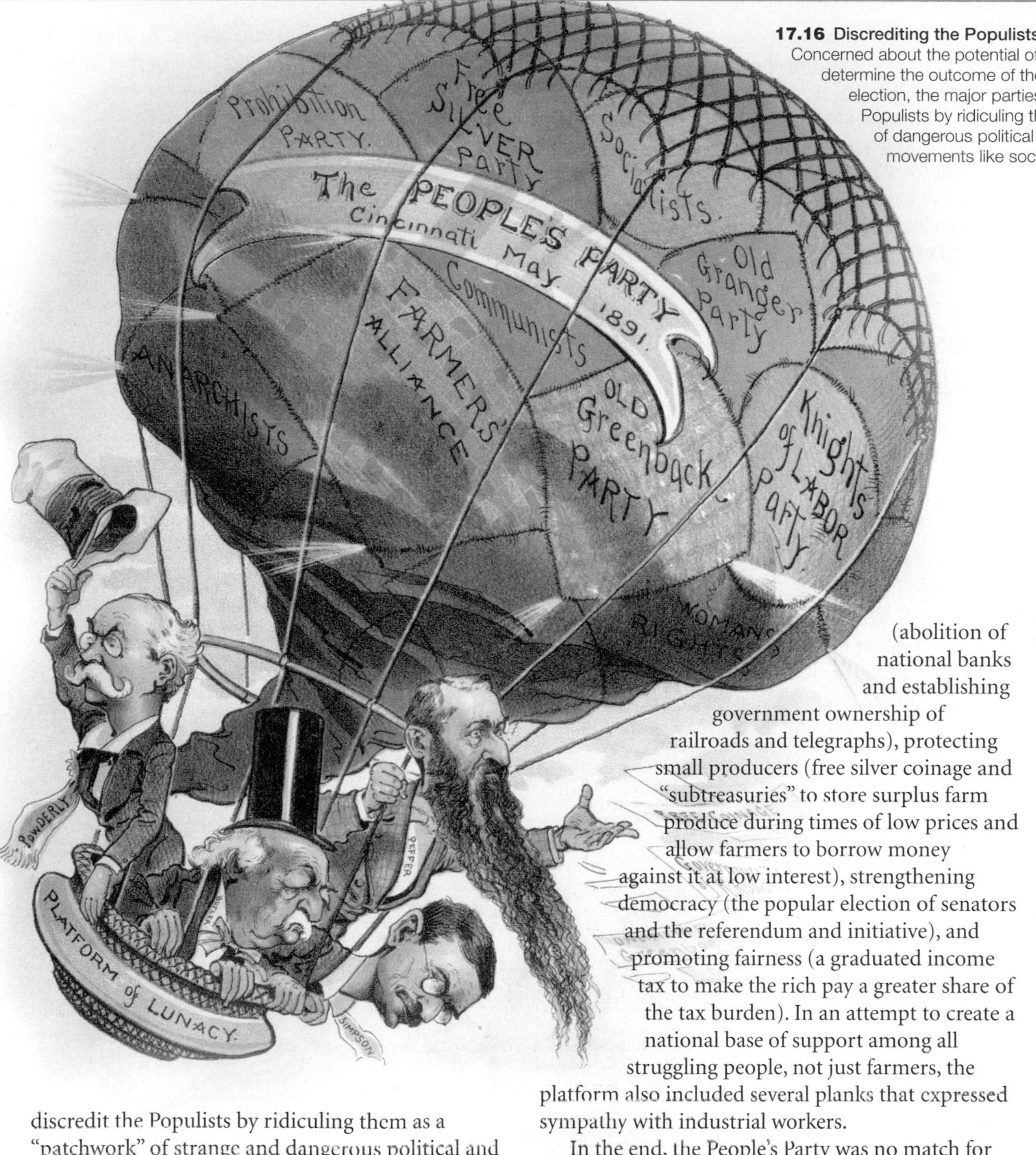

17.16 Discrediting the Populists
Concerned about the potential of the People's Party to determine the outcome of the 1892 presidential election, the major parties tried to discredit the Populists by ridiculing them as a "patchwork" of dangerous political and ideological movements like socialism and prohibition.

discredit the Populists by ridiculing them as a "patchwork" of strange and dangerous political and ideological movements like socialism and prohibition. The balloon's basket, labeled "Platform of Lunacy," carried the party leaders, depicted as eccentric fools.

Populists gathered for a national convention in July 1892 in Omaha and nominated Union Army veteran James B. Weaver for president and Confederate veteran General James G. Field of Virginia for vice president. The convention adopted a platform aimed at eliminating monopolies (abolition of national banks and establishing government ownership of railroads and telegraphs), protecting small producers (free silver coinage and "subtreasuries" to store surplus farm produce during times of low prices and allow farmers to borrow money against it at low interest), strengthening democracy (the popular election of senators and the referendum and initiative), and promoting fairness (a graduated income tax to make the rich pay a greater share of the tax burden). In an attempt to create a national base of support among all struggling people, not just farmers, the platform also included several planks that expressed sympathy with industrial workers.

In the end, the People's Party was no match for the established parties. Democrat Grover Cleveland won the election with 46 percent of the vote to Republican incumbent, Benjamin Harrison's 43 percent. Yet the Populists polled more than one million votes (9 percent) and Weaver won Kansas, Colorado, Idaho, and Nevada. Results on the local and state levels were even more impressive, as Populists elected fifteen hundred candidates to state legislatures, three governors, and five senators and ten representatives to Congress.

How did the People's Party platform reflect the concerns of farmers and industrial workers?

People's Party leaders hoped to build on this achievement, but defeating the major parties in 1896 would depend on the party's ability to overcome several challenges. Election results showed that it had performed poorly among midwestern farmers and industrial workers who opted to stay with either the Republican or Democratic parties. Finally, a successful campaign by conservatives to equate support for the People's Party with attacking white supremacy severely weakened the party in the South.

Industrial Conflict and Depression

Several events soon transpired that highlighted the unchecked power of big business and the severe consequences of a laissez-faire economy. Many People's Party activists hoped the anger and suffering produced by the Homestead strike and Panic of 1893 would prompt workers and farmers to reject the mainstream political parties and join the Populists. Workers at the Homestead Steel Works, a mammoth plant near Pittsburgh and owned by Andrew Carnegie, for years enjoyed a strong union (the Amalgamated Association of Iron and Steel Workers), high wages, and decent living conditions. But in 1892 Carnegie decided to rid the company of the union to allow him to cut costs by introducing the labor-saving machinery and reducing wages. To protect the public persona of a benevolent capitalist that he had worked for years to develop (see Chapter 16), Carnegie left the country for a vacation in Scotland, leaving his hard-nosed business partner, Henry Clay Frick, behind to take care of the dirty work.

On June 29 Frick announced a lockout and closed the mills. After a week the standoff turned violent when workers exchanged gunfire with a group of heavily armed professional strikebreakers of the Pinkerton Detective Agency, whom Frick had brought by boat to the Homestead complex. The clash claimed the lives of six strikers and five Pinkertons. The national press gave extensive coverage to the strike, and its tone in many instances was surprisingly pro-worker, probably due in part to the negative reputation of the Pinkertons. Carnegie, despite his attempt to separate himself from the conflict, drew some of the harshest criticisms. Carnegie's critics challenged his reputation as the great philanthropist who handed out libraries to communities in the United States and Europe by depicting him as a two-faced hypocrite who funded his philanthropic largesse by grinding down his workers with wage cuts (**17.17**).

But the tide of public opinion soon shifted against the strikers, for on July 23 anarchist Alexander Berkman burst into Frick's office and shot him several times. Remarkably Frick survived the assassination attempt. Even though Berkman had no

17.17 Carnegie's Reputation Takes a Hit
The Homestead strike tarnished Carnegie's image as a benevolent capitalist and friend of labor. This cartoon from the July 9 issue of the Utica, New York, *Globe* accuses him of being a two-faced hypocrite who funded his philanthropy by cutting his workers' salaries.

Why did Carnegie's actions in the Homestead strike prompt critics to accuse him of hypocrisy?

17.18 **Coxey's Army Emphasizes Its Patriotism** Aware that critics denounced them as violent radicals, Coxey and his "army" of protesters emphasized their patriotism and moderation by marching with American flags.

connection to Homestead workers, his actions brought widespread condemnation down upon the strikers. In September state officials arrested thirty-three members of the union's leadership and charged them with treason against the state. Two months later, on November 20, 1892, with nearly all the jobs at Homestead filled by replacement workers, the union formally ended the strike.

Six months later, on May 5, 1893, a financial crisis rocked the nation, leading to the most severe economic depression in American history to that time. Within a year the Panic of 1893 led to the failure of thousands of farms and businesses, including seventy-four railroads, and six hundred banks closed, throwing millions out of work and pushing the unemployment rate to 20 percent. The depression produced two vivid images of the widespread suffering endured by millions of Americans and the seeming indifference of public officials to do much about it. The first came from an Ohio Populist named Jacob Coxey who advocated that the government abandon its commitment to laissez-faire and create public works projects such as road building to alleviate mass unemployment and stimulate the economy (programs that the federal government adopted in the Great Depression of the 1930s). To draw attention to this idea, he organized one hundred unemployed men in Massillon, Ohio, to march to Washington, D.C. (the first such march on the capital). Setting out on March 25, 1894, they were joined by various groups along the route. As this photograph (**17.18**) and nearly every other one taken of the march shows, Coxey and his followers sought to portray an image of patriotism, earnestness, and moderation. Dressing as decently as their poverty permitted and marching with dozens of American flags, Coxey and his men rejected the accusations of their critics that they were violent radicals determined to attack the government. Rather, they asserted, theirs was a campaign to save the republic from the clutches of trusts and laissez-faire policies.

Coxey's Army, as it came to be known, numbered about five hundred by the time it reached Washington on April 30, 1894. Denied entry into the Capitol, Coxey delivered an impassioned address on the building's steps.

> We stand here to-day in behalf of millions of toilers whose petitions have been buried in committee rooms, whose prayers have been unresponded to, and whose opportunities for honest, remunerative, productive labor have been taken from them by unjust legislation, which protects idlers, speculators, and gamblers.

Coxey and several other activists were arrested for "disturbing the peace," but eventually they were convicted only for walking on the lawn of the

What did Coxey and his followers want from the federal government?

Capitol grounds. Other groups of unemployed workers staged similar protest marches, but all met with frustration and inaction.

A second image of government indifference in the face of widespread suffering arose in Chicago. The World's Columbian Exposition had opened on May 1, 1893, just four days before the panic on Wall Street. The fair's emphasis on American progress and prosperity, symbolized by the opulence and beauty of its huge complex of white neoclassical buildings, soon stood in stark contrast to the growing despair of the city's tenement districts a few blocks away. When the fair closed in October, thousands of homeless people moved into the vacant buildings that had only recently housed elaborate displays of prosperity. That winter of 1893–1894, as many as sixty thousand Chicagoans per day received a free meal from soup kitchens and missions.

> "We are born in a Pullman house, fed from the Pullman shop, taught in the Pullman school, catechized in the Pullman church, and when we die we shall be buried in the Pullman cemetery and go to the Pullman Hell."
>
> Pullman worker

Some of the hardest hit workers during the depression were employees of the Pullman Palace Car Company, located just outside Chicago. Founded by George Pullman in 1867, the company flourished as a manufacturer of luxury railroad cars. Pullman was an idealist who believed that workers and employers could work together in harmony for mutual benefit. Acting on this idea he established the town of Pullman in 1880, a **company town** built and owned by the Pullman corporation for its employees, who rented homes and patronized stores owned by the company. As this 1881 depiction of the town demonstrates (**17.19**) Pullman, like Carnegie, prided himself on being a model capitalist who earned a vast fortune but still managed to provide a decent living for his workers. This sensibility informs this drawing of Pullman's vision of the future town (since it was still under construction in 1881) as a model community of neat houses, schools, churches, stores, open spaces, and, of course, the factories that made it all possible.

So long as Pullman remained profitable, its employees considered themselves fortunate. But the depression in 1893 hit the railroad industry especially hard, and Pullman laid off hundreds of workers and announced to the rest a wage cut of 30 percent. On top of this devastating news, workers learned that Pullman would not reduce their rents, which were deducted automatically from their paychecks. Some workers soon began receiving checks for less than one dollar per week to cover the cost of food, heat, and clothing.

On May 11, 1894, Pullman's hard-pressed workers went out on strike. After a six-week standoff during which Pullman refused to negotiate, Eugene Debs, the leader of the American Railway Union (ARU) announced all of the union's 125,000 members across the country, as an act of solidarity with the Pullman workers, would refuse to handle Pullman cars. Within days of the start of the boycott, the **Pullman strike** caused the nation's railroad system to slow to a crawl.

The heads of more than two dozen railroads moved to support Pullman and break the ARU by hiring thousands of strikebreakers, pressuring the governor of Illinois, Richard Altgeld, to send in the state militia. When he refused out of sympathy for the strikers and a desire to avoid violence, the railroads turned to Washington, D.C., for help, asking President Grover Cleveland to send in federal troops (see *Choices and Consequences: The Pullman Strike*).

17.19 Capitalism and Community George Pullman's vision of himself as an enlightened and benevolent capitalist was captured in these plans for Pullman, a company town of neat houses, schools, churches, stores, open spaces, and factories.

What actions by Pullman prompted his workers to strike?

Choices and Consequences

THE PULLMAN STRIKE

Grover Cleveland was not the first president to face the choice of whether to send federal troops to quell a labor dispute. President Andrew Jackson dispatched troops in 1834 to end a strike by canal workers. President Rutherford B. Hayes had sent troops to crush the great railroad strike of 1877. Despite these precedents, however, Cleveland was aware that many considered the use of the army against American citizens a violation of the key republican principles of sharply limited federal power. Cleveland also worried that the public would condemn such use of federal power if violence ensued as it did in 1877. He spent several days in late June and early July of 1894, consulting with advisors and mulling over his options.

Choices

1 Take no action, allowing the state of Illinois and its pro-labor governor to handle the matter.

2 Intervene as a neutral and insist that both sides negotiate an equitable settlement.

3 Send in the U.S. Army to break the strike and allow the railroads to use strikebreakers to operate the trains.

Decision

Despite some misgivings Cleveland was a pro-business conservative. He authorized his attorney general, Richard Olney, a man with extensive ties to the railroad industry, to obtain a court injunction declaring the ARU boycott of Pullman cars a "conspiracy in restraint of trade" that unlawfully blocked the U.S. mail. When the ARU defied the injunction, Cleveland ordered the army in to end the boycott and get the trains moving again. Eugene Debs and several other ARU leaders were arrested and the boycott ended by mid July.

Federal troops sent by President Cleveland to break the Pullman strike escort the first meat train out of the Chicago stockyards.

Consequences

Cleveland's decision touched off extensive violence as workers destroyed railroad property and soldiers responded with rifle fire that left thirteen workers dead and scores wounded. The boycott collapsed in mid-July and with it the ARU. The Pullman strike ended in early August in complete defeat for the workers. Public opinion, however, turned against Pullman for his obstinate refusal to negotiate with his workers. A government investigation later criticized Pullman and argued that labor unions and government regulation were needed to curb the power of corporations. Yet in 1895 the Supreme Court (*In re Debs*) upheld the use of injunctions to end strikes.

Continuing Controversies

When is the use of federal troops in a strike compatible with republican principles?

Subsequent presidents, including President Woodrow Wilson, ordered military intervention during labor disputes. In 1916 the National Security Act included a provision empowering the president to federalize a state's national guard to quell a disturbance like a natural disaster, riot, or strike. The two most notable uses of this law, however, came in 1957 (Little Rock, Arkansas) and 1963 (Tuscaloosa, Alabama) to enforce federal desegregation orders.

How did President Cleveland justify using federal power to break the Pullman strike?

The Election of 1896 and Political Realignment

The turmoil caused by the economic depression and Pullman strike greatly affected the outcome of the 1894 off-year elections. Dissatisfaction with President Cleveland's administration hurt the Democrats, who lost their brief hold on both houses of Congress. The shift in power meant more stalemate for the next two years, with a Republican Congress opposed by a Democratic President.

The election of 1896 proved one of the most significant in the nation's history as it led to a major realignment in political affiliations among the American people. Republicans that year nominated former congressman and governor of Ohio William McKinley for president and affirmed their conservative commitment to the gold standard and a high tariff. The Democrats nominated a young and dynamic congressman from Nebraska, William Jennings Bryan. Just thirty-six years old, Bryan had earned a reputation for stirring oratory against the high tariff and in support of free silver. The latter issue came to hold great symbolic importance in the middle of the depression years. Silver was the metal of the common man, argued its supporters, while gold was the metal of elites. In speeches, pamphlets, songs, and images, People's Party activists had convinced millions of Americans that free coinage of silver would both end the depression and curb the power of monopolies and trusts. Recognizing the popularity of this policy, delegates at the Democratic Party convention made free silver a key plank in the party platform.

Bryan then delivered one of the most famous speeches in American history in which he argued that average Americans were being held down by a "cross of gold," forced upon them by Wall Street and big business. Capturing this theme this campaign poster (**17.20**) included the text of the famous speech (framed by silver coins) and ribbons bearing two of its most memorable lines: "You shall not press down upon the brow of Labor this Crown of

17.20 For Silver and the People The Democratic Party emphasized Bryan's commitment to workers and farmers through his advocacy of free silver and his promise to protect Americans from being crushed by a "Cross of Gold."

Why did silver hold such political significance in the late nineteenth century?

Thorns" and "You shall not crucify mankind upon a Cross of Gold." A youthful Bryan flanked by his wife and children tops the poster, while images of a worker and farmer flank the speech text.

That left the People's Party facing a huge dilemma. Most of its activists had expected the Democrats to follow the Republicans and support the gold standard, leaving the silver issue to the Populists. Now the People's Party had to decide whether to nominate their own candidate and divide the rising support for the silver issue with the Democrats, or, as was common practice among small parties in the nineteenth century, to nominate Bryan as their candidate, a move that would diminish their standing as an independent party concerned with other issues beyond silver. In July the People's Party chose the latter option and nominated Bryan. But their ticket differed from the Democrats in choice of vice president, Populist leader Tom Watson of Georgia.

Despite longstanding tradition in American politics that argued that it was unseemly for presidential candidates to campaign, Bryan embarked on one of the remarkable campaigns in American history, traveling more than 18,000 miles through twenty-seven states and delivering more than six hundred stump speeches to audiences totaling three million people.

Bryan's campaign generated a lot of commentary and excitement, but not enough votes on election day. McKinley won with 51 percent of the vote to Bryan's 47 percent (17.15). The most significant outcome of the contest was a new and enduring political alignment. The Republican Party became strongest in the Midwest and Northeast and dominated national political power for the next three decades. Republicans would portray themselves as the party of economic prosperity (the economy recovered under McKinley) and international power. The Democrats became the party of the South and West. They would retain the Populist belief that government needed to do more to secure the well-being of the average citizen and to limit the power of big business. Given its base in the South, however, the Democratic Party also upheld a states' rights philosophy that protected white supremacy.

The People's Party disintegrated after 1896, but many of their core ideas, such as the graduated income tax and the direct election of senators, remained popular and eventually gained adoption during the next two decades, a period known as the Progressive Era.

Conclusion

The period 1877–1900 came to be known as the Gilded Age because in part it was a golden era of tremendous economic growth and dazzling innovations, such as skyscrapers and electricity, and exciting new developments in popular culture and leisure. Yet many Americans perceived these trends as superficial—just as a gilded piece of jewelry has only a thin layer of gold on its surface. Beneath the wealth and excitement that marked the rise of modern America, they argued, lay the harsh realities of urban squalor, political corruption, and worker and farmer exploitation. These problems explain the many strikes that rocked the era, as well as the emergence of the People's Party and efforts to alleviate poverty, improve public health, and curb corruption, efforts that would later form the basis of the Progressive Era.

How did the election of 1896 lead to a major political realignment?

1871

Boss Tweed's corruption ring exposed
Showed the rising influence of political machines in cities and efforts to limit their power

1874–1877

Women's Christian Temperance Union established
An early indication of growing women's activism in the Gilded Age

The Southern Farmers' Alliance established in Texas
Reflects growing discontent of American farmers that eventually leads to the formation of the People's Party

1882–1883

Charity Organization Society founded
Founded by wealthy reformers who feared that too much charity was actually harming the poor

The Vanderbilt Ball
A lavish exhibition of "conspicuous consumption" attended by the richest families in America

The Pendleton Act becomes law
Intended to diminish nepotism and corruption, it required Civil Service exams for 10 percent of federal jobs

Review Questions

1. What factors led to the dramatic growth of cities in the late nineteenth century?
2. In what ways did ethnic enclaves benefit immigrants?
3. Who supported political machines and why? Why did reformers dislike political machines so much?
4. How was the nativist movement of the late nineteenth century similar to that of the Know-Nothings in the 1850s?
5. How did the approach to poverty by reformers like Jacob Riis and Jane Addams differ from traditional approaches?
6. How did the roles and expectations for middle-class women change in the Gilded Age? What social and economic developments made this possible?
7. How did people in the Gilded Age use their leisure time? How did their choices reflect class differences?
8. What were the primary grievances of people who supported the People's Party? How did they propose to resolve them?
9. What did the outcomes of the Homestead and Pullman strikes reveal about the power of big business and the attitude of the government toward workers?
10. What was the long-term impact of the 1896 election on American politics?

1887–1889

American Protective Association founded
Signals a rise in anti-immigrant sentiment

Hull House founded in Chicago
Settlement house movement provides a wide range of social services to poor and immigrants city dwellers

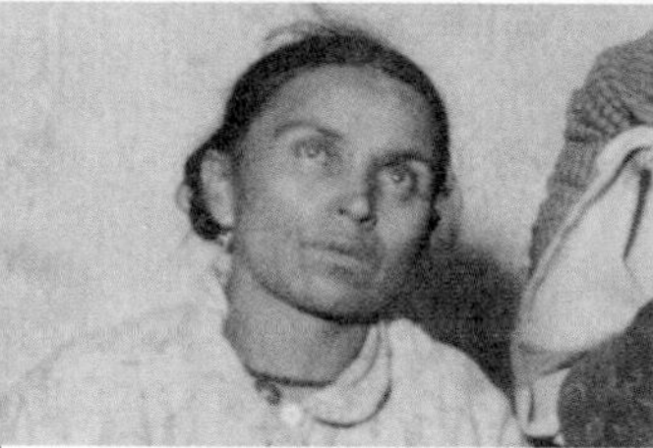

1890

Women's suffrage activists form NAWSA
Brings together two separate women's organization to concentrate on securing the vote for women

Jacob Riis publishes *How the Other Half Lives*
A shocking exposé of urban poverty that builds support for reform measures

Sherman Anti-Trust Act passed
Reflects growing concern over corporate power, but fails to curb it

1892–1893

People's Party established
A coalition of farmers, workers, and reformers committed to curbing the power of big business

The Homestead strike
A bitter and highly publicized defeat for workers

Columbian Exposition opens in Chicago
Celebrates American progress and promotes cleaner, healthier, and more beautiful cities

1894–1896

Coxey's Army marches on Washington, D.C.
Economic depression prompts many to demand relief by the federal government

The Pullman strike
President Cleveland breaks the strike by sending in federal troops

Election of 1896
Republican William McKinley defeats Democrat William Jennings Bryan

Key Terms

Gilded Age The name for the period 1877–1900 that suggested the amazing achievements of the period were like a thin gold layer that covered many unresolved social problems. **498**

ethnic enclaves Urban neighborhoods dominated by one particular immigrant group, often leading to names such as Little Germany and Little Italy. **501**

tenements Multiple family dwellings of four to six stories housing dozens of families that became the most common form of housing for poor city dwellers by the 1860s. **502**

political machines Powerful urban political organizations that mobilized large blocs of working-class and immigrant voters and often engaged in corrupt and illegal activity. **503**

settlement houses Institutions established in cities beginning in the 1880s and dedicated to helping the poor by providing a wide range of social and educational services. **510**

City Beautiful Movement A movement begun in the 1880s that advocated comprehensive planning and grand redesign of urban space to eliminate pollution and overcrowding. **510**

central business districts Sections of cities devoted exclusively to commercial enterprises such as banks, department stores, and the offices of corporations, accountants, lawyers, and other professions. **512**

suburbs Middle- and upper-class residential communities established just beyond a city's boundary but connected to the urban center by mass transit. **512**

women's suffrage The effort to obtain voting rights for women that eventually gained passage of the Nineteenth Amendment (1920). **513**

New Woman A phrase used to describe young women in the 1890s and early 1900s that reflected their rising levels of education, economic independence, and political and social activism. **514**

conspicuous consumption A term used to describe lavish displays of wealth by the rich, including construction of opulent mansions and hosting lavish balls. **517**

People's Party A third party effort launched in 1890 by a coalition of farmer organizations, reformers, and labor unions and dedicated to curbing corporate power and increasing the voice of the masses in politics. **518**

farmers' alliances Organizations in the 1870s and 1880s dedicated to helping farmers struggling with rising costs and falling crop prices by advocating farmer cooperatives and laws to regulate banks and railroads. **520**

Coxey's Army A protest march from Ohio to Washington, D.C., in 1894 organized by Jacob Coxey to publicize demands for the federal government to alleviate the suffering brought on by the Panic of 1893. **523**

company town A town built and owned by a corporation and rented to its employees, reflecting both the corporation's desire to help their workers and to control them. **524**

Pullman strike A bitter strike that began on May 11, 1894, at the Pullman Palace Car Company and soon spread nationwide, paralyzing the railroad system. President Cleveland sent in federal troops and broke the strike. **524**

CHAPTER 18

Creating a Democratic Paradise

The Progressive Era, 1895–1915

> "We have reached the point in our history when we realize that the nation has tremendous social, economic, and industrial problems."
>
> THEODORE ROOSEVELT, 1912

Female employees of the Triangle Shirtwaist Factory, many recently arrived from Italy and eastern Europe, worked on sewing machines six days a week, twelve hours a day, making blouses. On March 25, 1911, a fire engulfed the top floors of the building that housed the factory in New York City's Lower East Side. As bundles fell to the street, onlookers below assumed that workers were throwing their best cloth out the window to save it. They soon realized their mistake. Female workers were jumping by twos and threes to escape the flames. In the end, 146 women and men perished.

The memories of this horrific scene never left eighteen-year-old Victor Gatto, who stood on the corner and watched as women plunged directly onto the pavement. In 1944 Gatto, a self-taught artist, painted *Triangle Fire: March 25, 1911.* His painting depicted unprepared firefighters atop ladders too short to reach the victims above and indifferent police officers carrying a shroud-covered corpse to join a neat row of bodies that lined the street.

By the time Gatto provided this visual indictment of the government's inability to protect workers, Americans' expectations of their government had radically changed. This new vision took hold during the Progressive Era, partially in response to events like the Triangle Shirtwaist Factory Fire. In Gatto's painting the immense stone buildings tower above the lifeless workers, the artist's way of representing the complete domination of big business over labor at the beginning of the twentieth century. On the day of the fire, employers had locked the workshop doors from the outside to prevent the women from stealing materials or leaving early. With the doors bolted and flimsy fire escapes collapsing under the weight of fleeing workers, the windows offered the only means of escape for the rest.

To many Progressive Era reformers, the Triangle Shirtwaist Factory Fire illustrated the tragic consequences of capitalist exploitation and the government's lack of interest in the plight of workers. Middle-class activists championed an array of reforms that envisioned using local, state, and federal governments to protect Americans from the greed and indifference of big business. Their agenda aroused considerable criticism but Progressives, aided by three reform-minded presidents, found enough common ground to construct cross-class alliances that sought to end exploitive business practices and class conflict. Progressive-led coalitions also tackled pressing political and social issues. From the mid-1890s to mid-1900s, Progressives transformed the role of government in American society and laid the foundation for the liberal reform movements of the twentieth century.

What interpretation did this painting offer of the 1911 Triangle Shirtwaist Factory Fire?

The Progressive Impulse

The tide of reforms that swept across America at the turn of the twentieth century had its roots in a range of middle-class concerns. Middle-class dismay over the dismal living and laboring conditions for most working-class people turned to alarm as strikes and the appeal of socialism increased. The Progressives had unprecedented success building alliances that transcended class and political party affiliation, winning the support of three consecutive presidents. Their vision of an activist government that used regulation to safeguard the public challenged the prevailing laissez-faire notion that the government should not interfere with market forces, dramatically reshaping the nation within a decade.

The Angst of the Middle Class

At the dawn of the twentieth century, middle-class Americans looked around the nation and did not like what they saw. The upper 2 percent of the population controlled the nation's banks and industry. Even worse during the Gilded Age (Chapter 17) they openly flaunted their prodigious wealth by leading pleasure-filled lives replete with mansions, yachts, and private art collections. The upper class embraced an ethos of individualism that made each man responsible for his and his family's wealth or poverty. "Failures which a man makes in his life are due almost always to some defect in his personality, some weakness of body, mind, or character, will, or temperament," proclaimed John D. Rockefeller, the billionaire titan of Standard Oil. In the nineteenth century many middle-class Americans had uncritically echoed these same sentiments. Increasingly, however, these words rang hollow as the middle class watched the rich discard the tenets of self-discipline, frugality, and charity that had previously prevented individualism from turning into outright selfishness.

Big business came of age at the turn of the century as huge conglomerates began to dominate the economy. Smaller businesses, many run by middle-class proprietors, found it increasingly difficult to compete with these immense corporations. From 1897 to 1904 a wave of business mergers reduced 1,800 firms to just 157 in key economic sectors. Leading captains of industry vertically integrated businesses to control the production and distribution of their products from start to finish (see Chapter 16). Industrialists also integrated horizontally to eliminate competition from companies manufacturing similar items. Through such measures Rockefeller created the Standard Oil Trust and eventually produced and distributed 90 percent of refined oil in the United States, giving him the sole power to set prices for consumers and making him the richest man in the country.

American factories employed a large wage-earning working-class population that had little chance of improving their circumstances, no matter how hard they worked. More than half (**18.1**) of the nation's population toiled at manual labor in mines, factories, docks, and farms owned by others. Low wages, seasonal layoffs, sickness, and workplace accidents created a life filled with insecurity for most workers. "Father, does everyone in America live like this?" asked an eleven-year-old Russian Jewish immigrant, "Go to work early, come home late, eat and go to sleep? And the next day again work, eat, and sleep?" For the majority of the nation, the answer was a painful "yes."

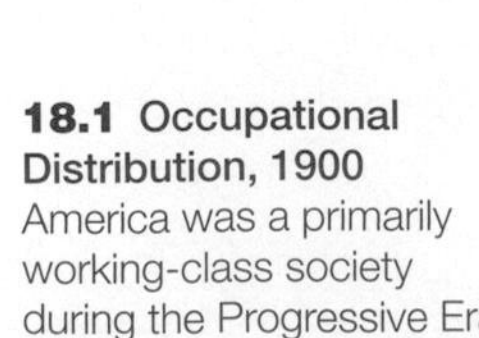

18.1 Occupational Distribution, 1900
America was a primarily working-class society during the Progressive Era.

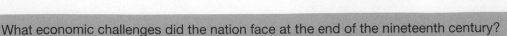

What economic challenges did the nation face at the end of the nineteenth century?

Large corporate bureaucracies also employed a growing number of middle-class clerks whose ranks grew from 4 percent of the working population in 1900 to 8 percent by 1920. Most earned enough to maintain an acceptable middle-class lifestyle, but the middle class worried that the growing divide between the "haves" and "have-nots" put them in a precarious position. Press reports focusing on the dire living and working circumstances of the working class aroused middle-class sympathies, but fear motivated them to act as well.

The popularity of radical political ideologies, unions, saloons and dancing halls within working-class neighborhoods—each in its own way offering the promise of a better, easier life—alarmed the middle class. The classless paradise without private property championed by working-class radical leaders horrified most middle-class professionals who owned their own homes and businesses. This 1912 image of state militia confronting a parade of striking textile workers in Lawrence, Massachusetts, underscored the reality that strikes often turned violent (**18.2**). This photo's suggestion of an imminent clash between the state militia troops enforcing martial law and defiant workers offered visual evidence to middle-class Progressives that class tensions were tearing the nation apart. While sympathetic to labor unions' demands, middle-class Progressives valued law and order as well. They wanted to find a way to end both industrialist exploitation and the steady stream of strikes that disrupted their daily lives.

18.2 Troops and Striking Workers Face Off, Lawrence, Massachusetts 1912 When the governor proclaimed martial law to prevent mass union rallies, protesting workers took to the streets carrying large American flags. Middle-class Progressives hoped their reforms would end strike-related violence, like the mayhem about to unfurl in this scene.

Progressives aspired to change other aspects of working-class culture as well. They deplored what they saw as the twin evils of drink and prostitution rampant in working-class neighborhoods. In the Progressive imagination the relentless pursuit of pleasure by both the upper class and the working class signaled the overall moral decay of American society.

The Progressive Vision

Glaring problems on both sides of the class divide—an idle and exploitive upper class on one side and an increasingly radicalized and impoverished working class on the other—threatened the middle-class vision of what they felt life in America should offer. *Progressivism*, a broad term used to describe a shared philosophical approach rather than a formal organized movement, provided an answer to this threat.

Unlike Populists (see Chapter 17) or Socialists, Progressives did not form their own political party to advance their agenda. The one exception was Theodore Roosevelt's failed attempt to regain the presidency by organizing the short-lived Progressive (Bull Moose) Party in 1912. Instead Progressives built cross-class political coalitions that transcended party lines. Lacking the wealth that the upper class possessed, or the sheer numbers that gave the working class tremendous economic clout, the middle class needed the support of other classes for their reforms to succeed.

Women played a particularly visible and active role in Progressive causes. Female settlement house workers and women's civic club members, usually white, middle class, and college educated, embraced the notion of "municipal housekeeping," the Progressive conviction that women could not adequately protect their children without help from the government. Female trade unionists agreed, but they also wanted to empower female workers by organizing unions to improve wages and working conditions. Tragedies like the Triangle Shirtwaist Factory fire brought these diverse female factions together, even winning support from appalled upper-class women. In the wake of the fire, this cross-class female coalition focused on bolstering city safety regulations, but only the labor activists emphasized the need for unions to end employer exploitation.

One particularly effective cross-class female alliance lobbied for legislation to ensure that mothers had clean, disease-free milk for their children. These women succeeded in their quest for local laws that prevented distributors from using chalk to make dirty milk appear white. They successfully rallied for mandatory pasteurization to kill germs, and for milk to be transported in refrigerated containers. Female-led reform campaigns also injected new energy into the suffrage movement.

> "Children need pure milk and good food, good schools and playgrounds, sanitary homes and safe streets."
>
> A female trade-union activist on why women needed the vote

Many middle-class female Progressive reformers and working-class labor organizers became convinced that without the right to vote, women lacked an essential tool they needed to keep themselves and their families safe. The National Woman Suffrage Association (NWSA) achieved some notable successes between 1910 and 1917, winning the right to vote in Washington, California, Arizona, Kansas, Oregon, and New York. Defeats in other states, however, convinced the NWSA to seek a constitutional amendment guaranteeing all women the right to vote, a campaign that succeeded in 1920 (see Chapter 20).

In a general sense the Progressives wanted to turn America into a middle-class paradise where economic security, education, health, and civility flourished. The tradition of Christian charity also helped shape the Progressive agenda. In the 1880s Protestant ministers like Josiah Strong began preaching the **Social Gospel**, the religious belief that Christians had a responsibility to create an ethically sound and morally upright society. The settlement house movement (see Chapter 17), begun in the spirit of Christian charity, became the incubator for strategies Progressives developed to attain these goals. As they confronted the problems of the poor at Hull House, a settlement house in a Chicago immigrant neighborhood, Jane Addams and Florence Kelley articulated the middle-class values that would form the cornerstone of the Progressive ethos.

Foremost among these was an emphasis on how the environment, as well as individual traits, shaped the lives of the poor. Progressives argued that poor living and working environments created many of the social problems troubling the nation. Exhibiting a typical Progressive faith in the scientific method, Addams and Kelley compiled a statistical portrait of disease, over-crowding, and crime in their Chicago neighborhood that helped Hull House devise solutions to these problems.

Improving sanitation and garbage collection, creating playgrounds for children, eliminating saloons, limiting the hours spent at work, reducing workplace accidents—these were all ways to improve the environment in working-class neighborhoods so that individuals could flourish. Personal responsibility also remained a bedrock principle for Addams and Kelley. While offering more respect for immigrant cultures than many past reformers, Addams and Kelley still believed strongly in teaching immigrants the importance of thrift, temperance, and self-discipline—lifestyle changes that some immigrants resisted.

Finally, Progressives embraced a new vision of governmental power, one that Americans from many different walks of life challenged. Their notion that governmental regulation should protect workers and curtail the excesses of big business put them at odds with industrialists and unions. Industrialists embraced the laissez-faire ethos that they had the right to control their businesses as they saw fit without government interference. Unions also viewed potential government intervention with unease, mindful that during labor conflicts the government usually sided with industrialists. Labor leaders preferred using collective action, including strikes, to win concessions from industrialists. To socialists, who wanted to nationalize all major industries, the Progressive emphasis on regulation was too timid. Essentially the Progressives sought the middle ground between these competing views. They wanted to establish a balance that avoided the excesses of unfettered laissez-faire economics, unending class conflict, or complete government control of the economy. Their aim was notable—the creation of a socially just, capitalist America.

Reining in Big Business

When three consecutive presidents—Theodore (Teddy) Roosevelt, William Taft, and Woodrow Wilson—embraced components of the evolving Progressive reform agenda, Progressivism entered the mainstream with a vengeance. What to do about big business aroused considerable debate within Progressive circles. Progressives held competing visions of whether to regulate, dismantle, or accept the trusts, making it hard to rally public opinion around one clear solution. Presidents Roosevelt, Taft, and Wilson devised differing regulatory and antitrust strategies to reform business practices, and openly disagreed on how to tackle the problem. Curtailing big business's access to the nation's environmental riches also provoked debate. Did business have the right to fully exploit the country's forests and water, or should these resources be preserved?

Roosevelt's Trust-busting

Roosevelt enthusiastically supported turning the government into a "steward of the public welfare." While serving as New York City police commissioner from 1895 to 1897, Roosevelt had become friendly with pioneering photojournalist Jacob Riis (Chapter 17). "The midnight trips that Riis and I took" to the tenements, Roosevelt later acknowledged, showed him "what overcrowding means, some hot summer night." Roosevelt's subsequent feats during the 1898 Spanish-American War made him a national war hero, catapulting him into winning the New York governorship. In 1900 President William McKinley selected Roosevelt as his running mate for his successful reelection bid.

On September 5, 1901, anarchist Leon Czolgosz shot President McKinley with a pistol wrapped in a handkerchief while the president was shaking hands at the Pan-American Exposition in Buffalo, New York. When McKinley died eight days later, the forty-two-year-old Roosevelt became the youngest president in American history. A robust man who appeared forever in perpetual motion dictating letters, lecturing visitors, playing tennis, or having pillow fights with his younger children in the White House, Roosevelt captured the public's affection. When Teddy Roosevelt saved a bear cub during a 1902 hunting expedition, a toymaker felt inspired to name a new children's toy after him, and so the teddy bear was born.

Like many Progressives Roosevelt believed that the country stood at a crossroads—either reform or face the end of democracy. He established his credentials as a Progressive reformer, and won public approval, by mediating the 1902 coal strike and filing suit against the Northern Securities and Standard Oil Trusts.

On May 12, 1902, 140,000 northeastern Pennsylvanian miners walked off their jobs. They demanded an eight-hour day, a 20 percent wage increase, and recognition of their United Mine Workers union. The mine owners refused to negotiate. "'The public be damned,' appears to be their motto," decried one Illinois newspaper as coal shortages forced factories to close and the poor began cooking food with oil-soaked asbestos.

President Roosevelt viewed the miners' predicament sympathetically. "I strongly favor labor unions," he declared. "If I were a wage worker in a big city I should certainly join one." Fearing widespread suffering and possible urban riots, Roosevelt threatened to use troops to take over the mine unless the owners agreed to let a government commission fashion an agreement. For the first time a president had stood up publicly against big business, winning him accolades in union circles. The resulting resolution reduced miners' hours from ten to nine and awarded them a 10 percent pay hike without forcing the owners to recognize the union. "I wish the capitalists would see," the president privately remarked, that the government-ordered compromise "is really in the interest of property, for it will save it from the danger of revolution."

Roosevelt also joined the Progressive campaign to remove the stranglehold that some trusts had on parts of the economy. In 1902 journalist Ida Tarbell began publishing a multipart series, "The History of the Standard Oil Company," in *McClure's Magazine*, a popular and influential middle-class news periodical. In her scathing critique Tarbell detailed the illicit deals that John D. Rockefeller had made with

Why did Roosevelt's personality and behavior captivate the public?

railroad companies to build his oil trust. Secret rebate agreements meant that Rockefeller paid considerably less than his competitors to ship oil. Many could not even get the railroads, which feared incurring Rockefeller's wrath, to transport their oil. Tarbell had firsthand experience with Rockefeller's cut-throat practices: They had bankrupted her father's oil business. She was convinced that Rockefeller's tactics would drive other small producers out of business, leaving a handful of industrialists in control of the entire economy.

The titans of industry offered a competing vision. There was nothing wonderful about economic competition, Rockefeller contended. Destructive price-cutting drove down wages, overproduction created regular depressions, and duplication of services wasted valuable resources. Rockefeller defended his railroad agreements as beneficial to all concerned. Standard Oil got lower rates while the railroads received guaranteed freight. Preventing too much oil from flooding the market stabilized prices and kept men in all oil-related industries profitably employed. The richest man in America also disputed claims that trusts made economic advancement impossible for average Americans, noting that he needed intelligent and skilled men to run his subsidiaries.

President Roosevelt agreed with much of Rockefeller's assessment. "The corporation has come to stay," he conceded, acknowledging that the entire nation benefited from the economies of scale that "good" trusts offered. Nonetheless, Roosevelt maintained, the government needed to break up "bad" trusts when consolidation threatened the public interest. The president soon singled out the Northern Securities Trust for dissolution, earning a reputation for **trust-busting** by taking steps to break up the monopoly.

In 1901 the financier J. P. Morgan had joined with two other powerful trust-builders, James J. Hill and E. H. Harriman, to form the Northern Securities Trust. The new transportation conglomerate meant "that you can ride from England to China on regular lines of steamships and railroads without once passing from the protecting hollow of Mr. Morgan's hand," announced journalist Ray Stannard Baker. With his eye on the 1904 presidential election, Roosevelt filed an antitrust suit charging the Northern Securities Trust with violating the 1890 Sherman Anti-Trust Act. A shocked Morgan rushed to the White House to broker a deal with the president. "If we have done anything wrong, send your man to my man and they can fix it up," suggested Morgan, an offer for a backroom deal that Roosevelt refused. In 1904 the Supreme Court upheld a Justice Department order to dissolve the Northern Securities Trust into independent railroad companies, earning Roosevelt public acclaim. One newspaper called him "the most popular man that has come into public life within recent times," after Roosevelt easily defeated the lackluster Democrat Alton B. Parker to win reelection in 1904. Roosevelt carried the Electoral College 336 to 140, the largest margin of victory in a presidential contest to date.

Standard Oil was next. In 1906 the Justice Department filed suit again, claiming that the trust had violated the Sherman Anti-Trust Act. This political cartoon (**18.3**). depicts Standard Oil as a frenzied octopus that has consumed the entire oil industry. Tentacles grasp overweight steel and copper businessmen in suits on one side and steamboats on the other, symbolizing how Standard Oil's control of the supply and price of oil strangled transportation and manufacturing industries. In the caricature state legislatures and Congress have succumbed to the monster's strength, and a leg now reaches for the White House.

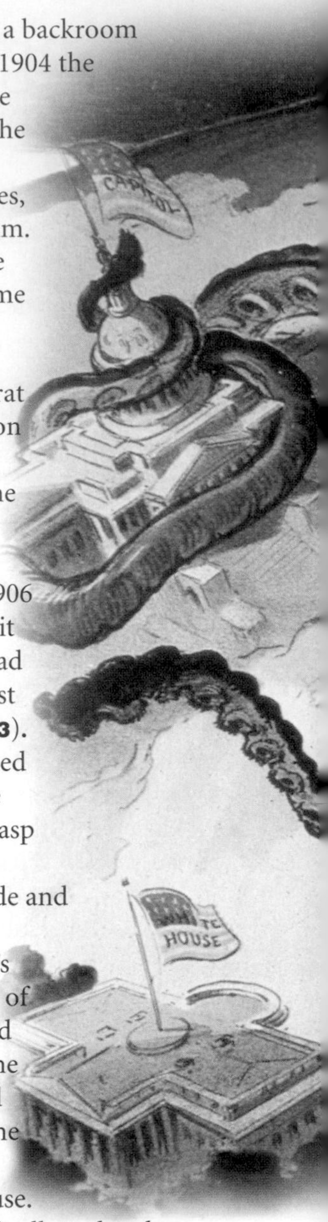

When the Supreme Court finally ordered Standard Oil to dissolve in 1911, the justices avoided a blanket ruling that all trusts were illegal. The Court instead invoked a "rule of reason," stating that only unreasonable restraints of interstate trade violated the law. The Court's ruling aptly described ex-president Roosevelt's own trust-busting philosophy. Roosevelt launched highly visible assaults on the Northern Securities and Standard Oil Trusts. He did nothing, however, when Morgan bought Carnegie's steel empire in 1901 to create U.S. Steel, a trust that employed nearly one million workers.

Roosevelt balanced trust-busting with regulation to ensure that big business behaved responsibly. He strengthened the Interstate Commerce Commission (ICC), created in 1887 to address Populist Party criticism of high railroad freight rates and rebates

18.3 Standard Oil's Tentacles In this political cartoon Standard Oil is an octopus, consuming everything in its path.

(see Chapter 17). By 1900 a series of sympathetic Supreme Court cases had essentially stripped the ICC of any real authority. During his second administration Roosevelt reinstated the power of the ICC to regulate railroad monopolies, convincing a reluctant Congress to pass the 1906 Hepburn Act. Four years later the Mann-Elkins Act further bolstered the rate-setting powers of the ICC and put the telegraph and telephone communication industries under its purview as well.

Taft and Wilson: Competing Progressive Visions

Having promised not to run again for president in 1908, Roosevelt helped his secretary of war, William Howard Taft, secure the Republican nomination. Roosevelt believed that Taft would continue his efforts to create a stronger, regulatory federal government. The Democrats countered by nominating the fiery William Jennings Bryan for a third time (see Chapter 17), trying to siphon Progressive votes away from a tepid Taft. Roosevelt's tireless campaigning for his chosen successor undercut Bryan's claim that he was the only real Progressive in the race. The Republican campaign slogan, "Vote for Taft now, you can vote for Bryan anytime," reminded voters of Bryan's two previous attempts to win the presidency and portrayed him as a perennial loser. Taft won easily, handing Bryan his worst electoral defeat.

Once Taft became president important philosophical differences between Roosevelt and Taft emerged. Like Roosevelt Taft had to work with a divided Republican party that controlled Congress. Roosevelt had sided with the Progressive faction, while

How did exposés and caricatures in the popular media shape public views of Standard Oil?

Taft gravitated to the conservatives. Unlike Roosevelt Taft viewed the president as an executor of law and protector of existing social institutions, not someone who spearheaded new reforms. A stickler for the law, Taft proved less willing than Roosevelt to make any distinction between good and bad trusts, filing more antitrust cases over four years than Roosevelt had in eight. Taft's decision to file charges against U.S. Steel enraged Roosevelt, who saw it as a personal attack on his earlier choice to leave this "good" trust alone.

Unhappy with his successor Roosevelt decided to run for president again in 1912. When Roosevelt's bid for the 1912 Republican nomination failed (the party nominated the incumbent Taft), Republican Progressives bolted and formed the short-lived Progressive (Bull Moose) Party, which nominated Roosevelt as their presidential candidate. The split in Republican ranks offered the Democrats an opportunity to capture the presidency for the first time since 1892. They nominated New Jersey Governor Woodrow Wilson, a Virginia-born politician with Progressive ideals. In contrast to the divided Republican Party, Wilson's candidacy kept the Southern base happy and prevented Progressively inclined Northern Democrats from joining the Progressive Party.

Taft, Roosevelt, and Wilson supported different degrees of federal activism, competing views that gave voters a clear choice in the election of 1912.

18.4 1912 **Presidential Election Results** Strong third-party challenges from the Progressive Party and Socialists split the national vote four ways, but Democrat Wilson prevailed to win the presidency in 1912.

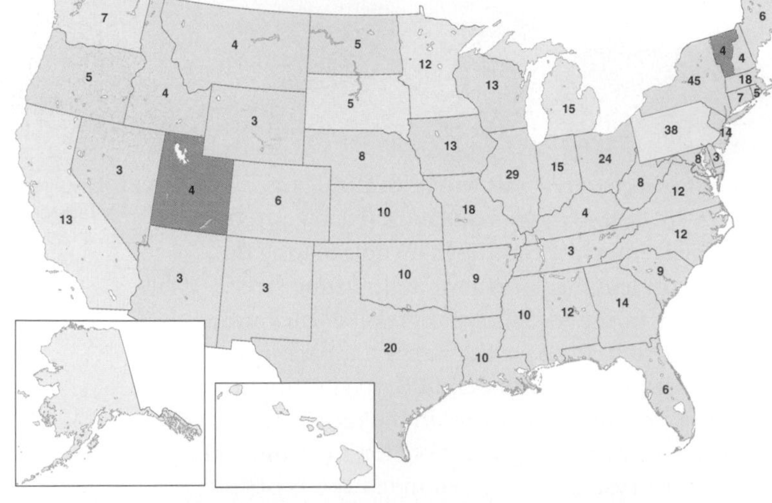

4 Electoral vote by state	Electoral Vote (%)	Popular Vote (%)
Woodrow Wilson *(Democrat)*	435 (82)	6,296,547 (41.9)
Theodore Roosevelt *(Progressive)*	88 (8)	4,118,571 (27.4)
William H Taft *(Republican)*	8 (0)	3,486,720 (23.2)
Eugene Debs *(Socialist)*	0 (0)	900,672 (6.0)

Taft was willing to zealously enforce existing Progressive reforms but had no intention of initiating any new ones. Roosevelt embraced a governing philosophy that he called "New Nationalism," a vision that emphasized increased federal regulation and widespread political reform. In contrast to Roosevelt, who wanted to regulate but not destroy big business, Wilson's "New Freedom" promised to restore a competitive marketplace where small businessmen and farmers thrived.

The 1912 slate also included Socialist Party candidate Eugene V. Debs, a railway trade union leader who had become a socialist after being jailed during the Pullman Strike of 1894. Formed in 1905 the Socialists had won numerous local elections and grown to over 100,000 dues-paying members. Roosevelt, Taft, and Wilson believed that with regulations in place (although each favored different amounts), capitalism would operate more fairly. Debs offered a competing view. He proposed transferring ownership of existing railroad, oil, and steel trusts to the government to ensure fair prices and wages. Government-run monopolies would be the first step toward ending the free-market system altogether.

The vast majority of voters agreed that the time had come to reform how the economy operated, but they overwhelmingly chose Progressivism over Socialism. Wilson won the presidency in 1912 (**18.4**) by a landslide in the Electoral College, while receiving only 41.9 percent of the popular vote. Roosevelt came in second with 27.4 percent of the popular vote, followed by Taft's 23.2 percent. Over 900,000 Americans, 6 percent of the electorate, voted for Debs. Nearly 70 percent of the country voted for Wilson or Roosevelt, an overwhelming public endorsement of Progressive principles and reforms.

Once he entered the White House President Woodrow Wilson went beyond trust-busting to weaken monopolies. He accepted the Democratic orthodoxy of cutting the tariff so foreign businesses could market lower-priced goods in the United States, thereby creating a more competitive marketplace where smaller businesses could thrive. By 1913 most industrialists had dropped their longstanding opposition to lowering the tariff. The heads of Singer Sewing Machines, Eastman Kodak, and U.S. Steel believed that other nations would reciprocate, allowing American captains of industry to conquer foreign markets as well. Wilson offset the lost tariff revenue (which the government needed to fund its operations) with the first federal income taxes, now constitutional thanks to the newly ratified **Sixteenth Amendment** (1913). Only people making more than

What clear philosophical differences separated the four candidates in the 1912 presidential election?

$4,000 a year paid federal income taxes (less than 1 percent of the population) at a time when most workers felt lucky to make $1,000 a year.

Wilson also tried to help small businesses by improving the flow of credit. Most small and big businessmen agreed with Wilson that the time had come to reform the country's chaotic banking system. They vividly remembered the Panic of 1907 when financial giant J. P. Morgan had used his own funds to shore up the national banking system. The nation's seven thousand banks operated with complete independence, issuing all forms of currency, some backed by gold and silver, others backed by government bonds. No centralized authority existed to expand or contract the currency supply as the economy demanded, or to move money throughout the country to stave off panics.

Conflicting visions soon arose over whether private financiers or the government should control the nation's financial institutions. Southern and Western populists wanted a federally run banking system that would destroy the Wall Street "money trust." Eastern bankers likened any government oversight to socialism. After much debate Congress passed the **Federal Reserve Act** (1913), creating a federally run Federal Reserve to serve as a "banker's bank" that held a portion of bank funds in reserve to help member banks in time of crisis. The Federal Reserve also set rates for business loans and issued a new national paper currency.

Wilson beefed up federal regulation of trusts as well. In 1914 the **Clayton Anti-Trust Act** prohibited interlocking directories, the practice of setting up shadow companies that appeared to compete but were actually run by the same board of directors. The law exempted trade unions from prosecution under the 1890 Sherman Anti-Trust Act, eliminating a tactic that businessmen had successfully used to undercut the labor movement. The **Federal Trade Commission** (1914) had the power to order companies to cease unfair trading practices, although its decisions were subject to court review.

Preservation versus Conservation

Roosevelt, Taft, and Wilson prescribed differing amounts of regulation and federal activism to rein in the trusts. Business's access to the nation's forests, water, and minerals provoked another set of competing visions within Progressive circles. In 1867 John Muir suffered a blinding eye injury while working as a mechanic. After his eyes healed Muir walked 1,000 miles from Indianapolis, Indiana, to the Gulf of Mexico to rejuvenate his spirit. Like Muir Roosevelt had turned to the revitalizing power of nature while recovering from personal tragedy when he retreated to his North Dakota ranch in 1884 after both his mother and twenty-two-year-old first wife died on the same day in their New York City home. In 1903 President Roosevelt went camping with Muir in Yosemite, an area of the California Sierra Nevada filled with spectacular waterfalls, massive rock formations, and Giant Sequoia trees nearly 200 feet high and three thousand years old. A photo of the pair on Glacier Point (**18.5**) before Yosemite Falls, the largest waterfall in North America, commemorated the trip. The two men dominate the frame, suggesting the power they had to decide the fate of such national treasures. This moment of unity was fleeting. Despite their mutual love of unspoiled forests, Muir and Roosevelt became formidable opponents who embraced different environmental visions.

Muir was a **preservationist** who championed preserving nature in its unspoiled state as a refuge for a "tired, nerve-shaken, over-civilized people." He accused businessmen of ravaging forests, polluting water, and destroying meadows with little regard for the long-term social costs of ruining the environment. Muir's condemnation resonated well with members of the middle class, who wanted to periodically escape the stress of urban life with holidays in the pristine wilderness. His influential writings led to the establishment of Yosemite as a national park in 1890 and the creation of the Sierra Club, an environmental group dedicated to preserving wilderness, in 1892.

18.5 John Muir and President Roosevelt in Yosemite, 1903 Despite their camaraderie during a shared camping trip, Muir and Roosevelt embraced competing environmental visions.

18.6 "The Vanishing Race," 1904
This blurry image of Navajo men riding away captured the prevailing sentiment that Indian cultures were on the verge of disappearing.

Muir's antibusiness message fit well with the Progressive determination to put the social good ahead of individual self-interest. Roosevelt agreed that a few unscrupulous entrepreneurs should not unfairly consume what belonged to the entire nation. To this end Roosevelt created five national parks, eighteen national monuments, and bird reserves that placed millions of acres off limit to development. The president parted company with Muir, however, by choosing to regulate, not ban, public access to other federally controlled lands, waterways, and mineral deposits. Roosevelt embraced a **conservationist** vision that tried to balance two goals: meeting present economic needs and conserving natural resources for future generations. When the U.S. Forestry Service director Gifford Pinchot allowed timber companies to harvest trees in designated areas, the new regulations enraged both preservationists, who wanted all economic development to cease, and Western businessmen, who demanded unfettered access to federally controlled forests.

Taft was sympathetic to Western complaints that Roosevelt had overstepped his authority. When Taft fired Pinchot, Roosevelt and his Progressive followers took it as a sign that Taft had abandoned conservation, deepening the split between the two former colleagues.

Environmentalists expressed great admiration for Native Americans' ecologically friendly farming and hunting practices, fueling mainstream curiosity about Indian cultures at the turn of the century. In 1900 photographer Edward Curtis began a thirty-year multivolume ethnographic project entitled *The North American Indian*, which recorded images of eighty different Indian civilizations. Many Indians willingly participated in Curtis's photography project, proud of the beautiful portraits he took of them in their best festive dress. Curtis wanted to capture the variety and richness of Native American cultures before they completely disappeared. Considering himself a friend to the Indian, Curtis believed (like most of his generation) that to survive Native Americans needed to assimilate into mainstream American society. The road ahead would not be easy for Native Americans, he felt. An intentionally blurred focus created a wistful aura to one of his most famous images, "The Vanishing Race" (**18.6**), which showed a line of Navajos riding off as one looks regretfully back. "The thought which this picture is meant to convey is that the Indians as a race, already shorn in their tribal strength and stripped of their primitive dress, are passing into the darkness of an unknown future," Curtis wrote.

Neither preservationists nor conservationists had any interest in reversing official policies of forced assimilation that divided collective reservation lands into individual farms, banned native languages, and sent Indian children to boarding schools (see Chapter 15). Preservationists inadvertently hastened the demise of some Indian cultures by enticing Americans to visit national forests. Tourism undercut Indians' access to traditional hunting grounds so that their economic survival increasingly depended on selling crafts to tourists and charging them to see performances of native dances.

Compare Progressive-Era debates over the environment with attitudes about disappearing Indian cultures.

Competing Views on Transforming the Workplace

In 1900 the United States earned the questionable distinction of being one of the most strike-torn nations in the world. To end class conflict and introduce more social harmony, Progressives wanted to transform the workplace into an environment where workers labored a reasonable number of hours in safe conditions for decent wages. Industry and labor each presented a competing view that challenged the Progressive vision as they sought the upper hand in their decades-long class struggle.

Capitalist Visions of Industrial Harmony

Industrialists differed on how to rid the workplace of labor conflicts that interfered with the smooth operation of their businesses. The National Civic Federation brought together moderate industrialists and labor union leaders dedicated to seeking industrial peace through compromise. Ohio senator Mark Hanna, who made his fortune in coal, argued that industrialists should turn labor into "the ally of the capitalist, rather than a foe." In return for a few minimal concessions, factory owners could demand that union leaders discipline their membership and keep workers on the job, thus ending the constant strife that permeated the industrial sector.

Hanna's voice was a decided minority. Most industrialists refused to compromise any of their authority. Staunchly antiunion they employed a host of methods to undercut unions. If forced to accept a union, they insisted upon an "open shop" that let workers choose whether to join a union, then used intimidation to stop workers from enrolling. Industrialists fired identified union members, hired private security forces to spy on workers, and created lists of fired workers, known as blacklists. Once listed a worker could not find another job. During strikes factory owners expelled families from company-owned housing and hired substitute workers (called scabs) to replace striking workers. To protect union members from these discriminatory industrialist policies and build strength, labor organizers fought to establish a "closed shop," which required all workers in the same company to join the union.

Other industrialists embraced benevolence as a way to dissuade workers from organizing. **Welfare capitalism**, the notion of using benefits to gain workers' loyalty, aimed to improve worker morale and weaken interest in unions. Some large firms instituted free medical care, pensions, kindergartens, and even baseball leagues, but these services typically evaporated at the first sign of economic downturn. Unions did not want to leave it up to the employer to decide whether to offer benefits. They preferred using collective bargaining to negotiate a contractual agreement between workers and their employers that established such benefits as a permanent right.

The drive for efficiency, a goal that many Progressives shared, was another way that industrialists undercut workers' collective power. Henry Ford's innovations in automobile manufacturing demonstrated how industrialists could boost profits by reducing manufacturing costs. The son of a prosperous Irish immigrant farmer in Dearborn, Michigan, Ford built his first car in 1896 in a shed behind his Detroit home. Forming the Ford Motor Company, Ford introduced the Model T in 1908, a moment when 515 separate companies were manufacturing automobiles. Ford standardized parts, constantly improved machinery, and used conveyor belts on his assembly line—innovations that let him produce more cars for less money. Ford passed these savings onto consumers, lowering the price of his "car for the great multitudes" from $825 in 1908 to $345 in 1916. By then Ford had captured half the market for new cars.

In 1914 Ford created headlines by offering workers a five-dollar daily wage for eight hours of work. Ford paid twice the standard wage rate because he recognized that the common practice of paying workers subsistence wages limited the markets for many consumer goods. Ford wanted his workers to be able to afford his automobiles. Working eight instead of ten hours a day, Ford reasoned, reduced fatigue-induced mistakes and worker turnover, giving the company a loyal and

What different ways did industrialists try to end labor conflict?

> "The men do their work and go home—a factory is not a drawing room."
>
> HENRY T. FORD on his rule prohibiting workers from talking to each other as they assembled automobiles

experienced workforce.The moving conveyor belt in Ford's assembly lines (**18.7**) meant that workers no longer had to lift or move the chassis as they assembled a car. Ford admitted that he "could not do the same thing day in and out," but he condescendingly believed that the average worker "wants a job in which he does not have to think." To keep workers focused and productive, Ford prohibited sitting, talking, singing, or whistling in his factories. Fearful of losing their jobs, workers only dared to criticize Ford's iron control over the production process in private.

Ford's five dollar/eight hour day came with strings attached. Ford instituted many reforms that Progressives sought because they made business sense, but he staunchly resisted government regulation and attempts to organize a union, retaining the right to make his own factory rules. Ford also firmly subscribed to industrialists' long-standing belief that they had the right, and the duty, to interfere in the private lives of their employees. For Ford this meant offering benefits only to employees who met certain moral criteria. Married men, for instance, had to live with their families. Thirty investigators working for Ford's Sociological Department visited workers' homes and sometimes imposed other requirements, such as mandatory English classes for immigrants. Gambling, excessive drinking, or having sexual relations with a prostitute were all grounds for dismissal. A Ford Motor Company investigator had to verify that a worker was morally upright (and not trying to organize a union) before he and his family could move into a spacious two-story home built by the company.

Progressives valued efficiency and expertise, and Frederick Winslow Taylor took the drive for

18.7 The Assembly Line
Ford's innovative mass production techniques included a well-lit and ventilated environment that relieved workers of backbreaking tasks. The assembly line also deadened the mind, as constant routine movements eliminated the need for any decision making. [From the Collection of the Henry Ford, THF23871]

How much did Ford's innovations and paternalism benefit workers?

efficiency further than Ford by popularizing **scientific management**, the effort to use scientific knowledge for maximizing output and profit. Taylor used stopwatches to evaluate how long each part of the manufacturing process should take. He then outlined the steps laborers should replicate to lay bricks without any wasted energy, and determined the perfect shovel size and the exact amount of rest workers needed to lift the maximum amount of pig iron each day. After establishing the optimal time and method for a specific task, Taylor argued, industrialists could then fine or fire unproductive workers who failed to maintain an acceptable pace. Taylor admitted that his system, dubbed "taylorism," intentionally eliminated workers' independence and creativity. Each man, he asserted, must "grow accustomed to receiving and obeying directions covering details, large and small, which in the past have been left to his individual judgment."

Working-Class Labor Activism

The working class had long fashioned their own solutions to surviving difficult living and working conditions. Fraternal associations assisted those who lost their jobs or needed to bury a loved one, while urban political machines (see Chapter 17) secured voters' loyalty by helping families endure personal tragedies such as fires or illness. Meanwhile unions tried to negotiate better wages and shop floor rules for dues-paying members, but organizing the working class so it could speak with one voice proved impossible. Ethnic and racial prejudices kept the working class fragmented. Italian strikebreakers, for instance, had few qualms about walking across a picket line manned by Slavic strikers. The craft-based American Federation of Labor (AFL), led by Samuel Gompers, only organized skilled, mostly white workers, refusing to let unskilled laborers, women, or blacks into their unions. Only a handful of industrial unions like the United Mine Workers and International Longshoreman's Union adopted a big umbrella approach that organized all workers in one industry into the same union.

Middle-class Progressives supported many union goals but deplored their methods. Strikes continually disrupted normal life by shutting down railroad lines, street cars, and coal mines. Government regulation, they maintained, would improve workers' lives and ensure that the economy functioned smoothly. Nevertheless many unions remained skeptical about relying on the government to solve their conflicts. The AFL preferred using its collective economic power to force industrialists to negotiate. Its members had unhappy memories of what happened when state or federal officials intervened in labor conflicts, as during the 1894 Pullman Strike (see Chapter 17).

The Roosevelt administration occasionally chose to aid labor, but Progressive Era court decisions nearly always favored industrialists. In 1908 the Supreme Court stopped workers from launching sympathy strikes or boycotts to support fellow workers, labeling them "restraints of trade" barred under the 1890 Sherman Anti-Trust Act, a law originally intended to curtail the creation of business monopolies. Another 1908 decision allowed employers to fire workers who joined unions. Reducing government interference in labor conflicts therefore remained the AFL's primary goal.

Radical trade unionists rejected the AFL vision of working within the free market system. The **Industrial Workers of the World** (IWW), formed in 1905, envisioned "one big union" that welcomed all workers regardless of sex, race, ethnicity, or skill, which would one day take over all means of production in the United States. "It is the historic mission of the working class to do away with capitalism," declared the founders of the IWW, whose members were nicknamed "Wobblies." The founding group included seventy-five-year-old Mother Mary Jones, a tireless white-haired organizer for the United Mine Workers, and William D. "Big Bill" Haywood, an organizer for the Western Federation of Miners. Their drive to abolish private property and formal government struck many Progressives as anarchy. Government harassment of the IWW limited its formal membership to around ten thousand.

The Progressives' Limited Progress

Employers had traditionally held employees responsible for workplace accidents, maintaining that workers knowingly accepted all job-associated risks. Personal carelessness caused most mishaps, they argued. Progressive organizations undertook detailed sociological studies to refute these self-serving generalizations. Lewis Hine's photographic investigation into the lives of injured Pittsburgh workers suggested that few were responsible for

18.8 An Injured Pittsburgh Worker Portraits of maimed workers helped generate a groundswell of support for state workers' compensation laws.

their accidents. This young man (**18.8**) had his leg crushed when he fell under a coal car in a Pittsburgh coal mine. The company paid the hospital expenses for his amputation, but nothing else. In the image a nicely dressed passerby avoids making eye contact with the injured boy who stands idle on the street, suggesting that the well-off preferred to ignore the plight of disabled workers. The boy's tidy appearance reveals an effort to maintain some personal dignity while relying on private charity to survive. Studies like Hine's convinced many states to establish worker compensation programs that provided employer-funded disability payments and medical care to injured workers. As a result employers began paying more attention to workplace safety.

The drive to limit hours for male workers was less successful. Employers had traditionally maintained that as property owners they had the sole power to decide the terms of employment. In the 1874 Slaughterhouse cases, the Supreme Court had ruled that a state could not deny individuals control over their own labor. Industrialists claimed that this decision granted individual workers the constitutionally protected right to negotiate wages, hours, and workplace rules. According to this line of reasoning, state laws or unions that tried to impose restrictions on individual workers violated their right to control their own labor.

The Supreme Court, however, proved willing to abridge this right to protect public health and safety. In 1898 the Court upheld an eight-hour day for Utah miners, deciding that guarding the health of workers engaged in a dangerous occupation served the public interest. Progressives failed in their efforts to extend these protections to the entire workforce. In ***Lochner v. New York*** (1905), the Court ruled that unless long work hours directly jeopardized workers' health, the government could not abridge an employee's freedom to negotiate his own work schedule with his employer. This decision is explored more fully in *Choices and Consequences: Regulating Workers' Hours.*

Miserable and unsafe working conditions also persisted. The Colorado mining town of Ludlow sat along the Purgatory River, a telling name that suitably described what working in a mine was like. In Ludlow, the Rockefeller-owned mining company paid miners $2 a day in company-issued currency (called scrip) redeemable only in the company-run store. The mining company required that workers live in company-owned housing, and claimed no responsibility for accidents that killed two hundred miners between 1904 and 1914.

In 1913 twelve thousand miners, mostly Italian, Greek, and Serbian immigrants, went on strike to protest these conditions and demand company recognition of their United Mine Workers union. When the company expelled the strikers and their families from their homes, the workers erected a series of tent cities in the nearby hills. After armed company detectives failed to dislodge the miners, the Colorado governor sent in state troops, whose wages Rockefeller agreed to pay. The **Ludlow Massacre** ensued on April 20, 1914 when troops set fire to one striking miners' camp, and thirteen women and children suffocated to death in a shallow underground shelter where they had sought refuge.

Throughout the nation outraged laborers temporarily put their ideological divisions aside to stage protest marches in every major city. The United Mine Workers issued "a call to arms," and hundreds of neighboring miners flooded into Ludlow to defend their comrades against the state militia. Faced with the prospect of all-out class war, the Colorado governor requested federal troops and President Wilson immediately complied. Federal intervention left the union in tatters and Rockefeller free to run his mining town as he saw fit. Incidents like these convinced many unions that the Progressive proposal to rely solely on the government to solve their problems was not the answer. Throughout the twentieth century union folklore and songs used the memory of Ludlow to inspire workers to organize.

How effective were the different strategies that Progressive and unions employed to reform the workplace?

Choices and Consequences

REGULATING WORKERS' HOURS

Most city residents, especially tenement-dwellers who did not have ovens, bought their bread from bakeries. Bakers worked long hours in hot and poorly ventilated kitchens, sleeping and washing where they baked bread. In 1895 New York passed a law that set sanitary standards and limited bakers to ten hours of work per day, sixty hours per week. Joseph Lochner, a bakery owner in Utica, challenged the law after New York fined him $50 for making an employee exceed these limits. The Supreme Court faced several choices when it heard the case in 1905.

Choices

1 A state could use its police powers to protect workers' health and safety.

2 A state could not limit an individual's right to buy or sell labor in nonhazardous occupations such as baking.

3 States had the right to enact any laws not expressly forbidden in the Constitution to promote the general well-being of society.

Decision

The Court ruled 5 to 4 that the Fourteenth Amendment, which declared that "no state shall ... deprive any person of life, liberty, or property without due process of the law," prevented states from using their police powers to regulate work that did not imperil the health or safety of the public.

Consequences

The decision curtailed Progressives' attempt to use regulation to transform the workplace. During the subsequent thirty-two-year "Lochner" era, the Court struck down maximum hour, minimum wage, and child labor laws if no clear risk to the public existed. Dismayed Progressives noted that many state laws restricted an individual's ability to buy or sell labor, such as mandatory school laws or Sunday closures, to promote the general welfare. They also accused the Court of ignoring the disproportionate power that employers wielded over workers to set the terms of employment.

Continuing Controversies

Should the government limit work hours or set a minimum wage?

Lochner remained the law of the land until 1937, when the Supreme Court ruled that it was "reasonable" for Washington State hotel owners to pay female hotel maids the state-mandated minimum wage because the state had a right to protect its residents. Defining an acceptable standard for work and pay has been controversial ever since. Is a reasonable day's work six, eight, ten, or twelve hours? Does it matter if the work involves strenuous physical labor or sedentary work? Is it better for unions to negotiate the terms of employment or for the government to step in? How does regulating hours of work or setting a minimum wage hurt or benefit the general public? These are questions that Americans have debated for the last seventy years.

Lochner bakery

What competing views existed concerning a state's right to regulate the workplace?

Protecting Women and Children

Progressives never convinced unions to give up strikes, but together they demanded laws protecting women and children. Relying on mountains of sociological data and heart-rending photographs, female activists helped secure protective legislation that reduced the hours women worked and kept children in school longer. Working-class men offered more resistance when female reformers tried to make temperance the law of the land.

Women at Work

In 1908 Curt Muller, a laundry owner in Portland, Oregon, challenged a recent state law granting a ten-hour workday for female laundry workers. In making his case before the Supreme Court, Muller followed the same line of reasoning used in the *Lochner* case, arguing that the law deprived his workers of their right to control their own labor. He disputed the reformers' claim that scrubbing all day in a hot, wet workplace posed a serious risk to laundry workers' health. In its unanimous affirmative 1908 ***Muller v. Oregon*** ruling, the Supreme Court upheld maximum hour laws for female workers, accepting lawyer Louis Brandeis's argument that protecting women's reproductive health served the public good. "As healthy mothers are essential to vigorous offspring, the physical well-being of woman becomes an object of public interest and care in order to preserve the strength and vigor of the race," the Supreme Court declared.

Reactions to the ruling among women were mixed. Middle-class Progressive reformers and female trade unionists celebrated the ruling as a victory for female workers, unperturbed by the Court's emphasis on the biological inferiority of women to men. Feminists who believed in total equality were disappointed with the ruling, creating a fissure in the women's movement that widened into an open split within the next few years. The male-dominated AFL embraced the decision, believing it reduced employers' incentive to hire women instead of men. As if to prove this point, Muller responded by firing his female workers and hiring Chinese men to take their place.

Cross-class alliances between middle-class and working-class women flourished around other efforts to help working women. In 1898 the National Consumers' League (NCL) formed to coordinate local consumer boycotts of department stores that mistreated their female clerks. The NCL made the long hours and low pay endured by female working-class clerks the responsibility of every middle-class female shopper. The group soon expanded their boycotts to include stores that sold clothing made in sweatshops or with child labor. Compiling "blacklists" of stores to boycott was illegal, so the NCL instead worked with female garments' unions to create "white lists" of shops with equitable labor policies, places where socially conscientious women could shop without remorse.

18.9 Carry A. Nation Portrait and Hatchet Pin
Carry A. Nation cultivated her notoriety as a Bible-toting, ax-wielding saloon smasher by selling portraits and pins to her admirers.
[*Source* (pin): Kansas State Historical Society]

Stamping Out Vice

Local and state reformers also took aim at alcohol, believing that prohibition would improve women's lives by reducing domestic violence and bolstering family income. The Woman's Christian Temperance Union (WCTU; see Chapter 17) viewed the saloon as a haven for gambling, prostitution, corrupt city political machines, and excessive alcohol consumption. The WCTU crusade took a surprising turn on June 6, 1900, when a deeply religious

Why did the campaign for maximum work hour laws succeed for women, but fail for men?

sixty-four-year-old woman named Carry A. Nation strode into a southwestern Kansas bar with a bag of bricks and smashed the liquor bottles, glassware, and mirrors, then calmly left. Nation's tactics were extreme, but many Progressives shared her sense of urgency. Drinking was on the rise in America. From 1885 to 1900 beer consumption nearly doubled from 590 million to 1.2 billion gallons. Hundreds of inspired "Home Defenders" throughout the nation organized similar attacks on neighborhood bars, hoping to convince their communities to go dry. As her fame grew Nation raised funds by selling miniature hatchet pins, her new weapon of choice (**18.9**), along with photos of herself holding her bible and hatchet. She spent time in jails from New York to Los Angeles publicizing the temperance cause before collapsing on a stage in 1911 and dying shortly thereafter.

Working-class men resolutely defended their freedom to drink, and many upper-class men were reluctant to give up a pleasure-based lifestyle that included ready access to alcohol. Attacking on multiple fronts the nonpartisan Anti-Saloon League, founded in 1893, and the WCTU established an effective coalition that included Progressives, rural Americans, and industrialists. Prohibitionists linked ridding the nation of alcohol to the broader Progressive desire to eliminate the corrupting influences of big-city political machines. Saloons, temperance advocates maintained, served as the headquarters where dishonest city politicians paid immigrants for votes and dispersed favors to supporters. Temperance advocates drew rural folk into the movement by addressing their concerns about the growing cultural influence of urban pleasures and the beer-drinking immigrants who lived in the cities. Molding their message to appeal to industrialists, temperance advocates blamed saloons for contributing to the nation's labor troubles by giving unions a place to meet and recruit.

> "You refused me the vote and I had to use a rock."
>
> CARRY A. NATION explains her saloon-smashing ways

Working through churches in the South and the West, the Anti-Saloon League and WCTU urged supporters to focus on making their state or county "dry" by banning the sale of alcohol. The "Prohibition 1904 and 1917" map (**18.10**) traces the rapid success of this strategy as the number of dry states grew from three to twenty-three. Many Western women had already secured the right to vote, and they flocked to approve prohibition in large numbers.

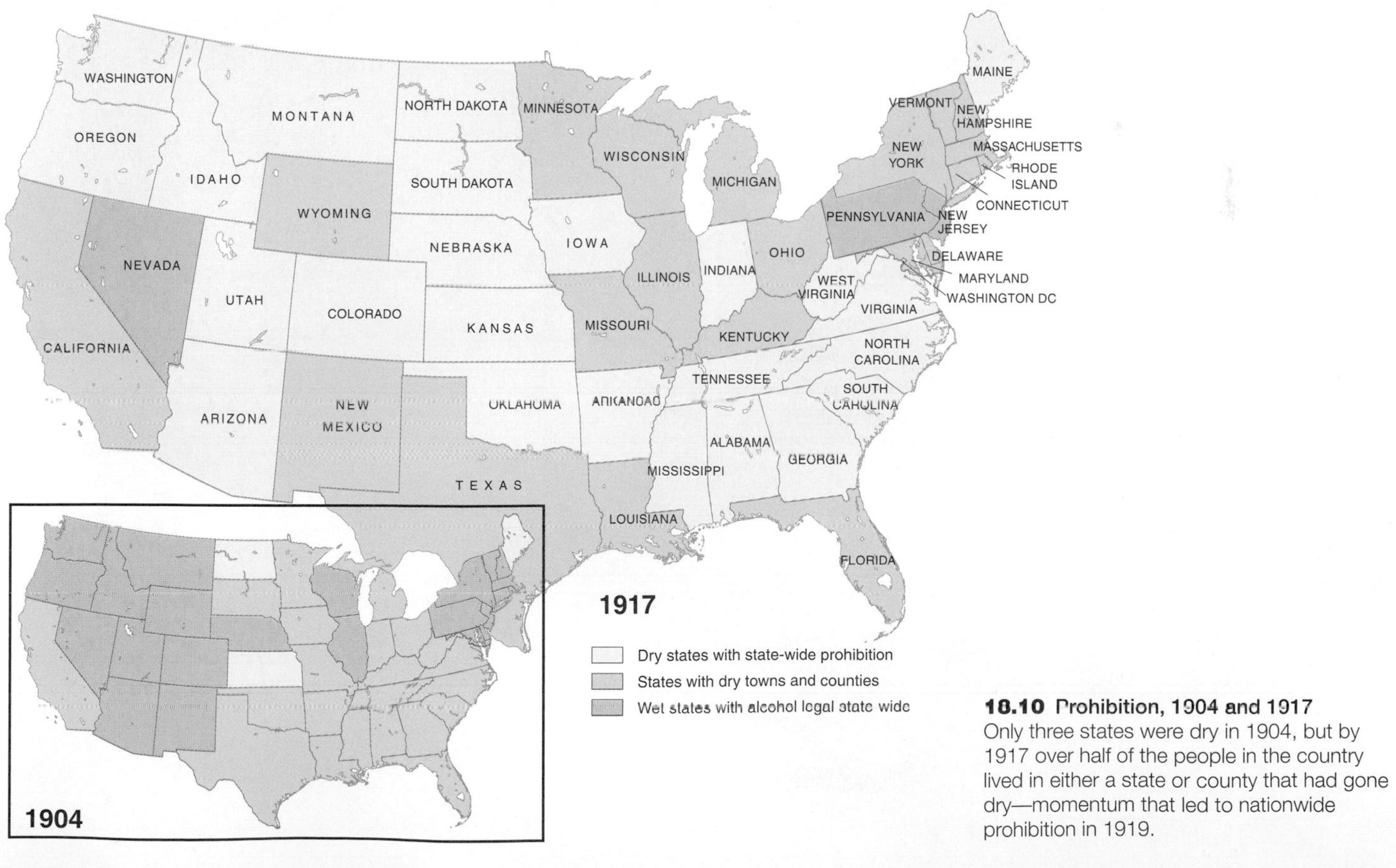

18.10 Prohibition, 1904 and 1917 Only three states were dry in 1904, but by 1917 over half of the people in the country lived in either a state or county that had gone dry—momentum that led to nationwide prohibition in 1919.

What diverse concerns about alcohol helped the temperance movement gain momentum?

Restoring Childhood

Middle-class Americans believed that childhood should be devoted to education and play, not work. This advertisement (**18.11**) from an 1898 Sears and Roebuck catalog portrayed the type of idyllic childhood that many middle-class families tried to give their children. In the ad an immaculately dressed young girl rides joyfully in the sunshine on a new bicycle, a portrait of health and happiness. The reality for working-class children offered a stark contrast. Census records revealed nearly 1.75 million children ages ten through fifteen worked in factories full time, a figure that did not include children employed in home sweatshops or on family farms.

To Progressives child labor epitomized the greed of employers who eagerly sent children into mining crevices where adults could not fit, used children to harvest crops in the Midwest, or dispatched an army of small boys to hawk newspapers in Northern cities. Organized labor joined this crusade, certain that child labor drove down adult wages. Industrialists offered a competing vision, arguing that jobs provided valuable training for working-class children who

18.11 "Models of 1898"
The middle class believed that children should engage in healthy and creative play, not work in dangerous and dreary factories.

What does this advertisement reveal about middle-class ideals of childhood?

needed to learn the importance of punctuality and hard work to become successful adult workers.

Many working-class families shared employers' beliefs that their children should work. In Chicago Hull House cofounder Jane Addams discovered that most immigrants, having worked themselves as children, found nothing wrong with putting their own children to work. "A South Italian peasant who has picked olives and packed oranges from his toddling babyhood, cannot see at once the difference between the outdoor healthy work which he has performed in the varying seasons, and the long hours of monotonous factory life which his child encounters when he goes to work in Chicago," she noted, adopting the Progressive tendency to gloss over the drudgery of farm work.

Most working-class families depended on their children's meager wages to survive. Child labor provided one-tenth of family income in the early twentieth century. Recently arrived immigrant men, especially unskilled, non-English speakers, realized with dismay that their English-speaking children were more apt to be hired than they were. Children in these families became the breadwinners, while their fathers stayed at home. This reversal of normal family relations often created tensions within working-class households. "I left Europe and I was a man, and here I am a what?" lamented one Russian Jewish immigrant. Idle men, frustrated over their inability to provide for their families, sometimes turned to drink, depleting the family's income even further.

The drive to end child labor gained momentum when the National Child Labor Committee formed in 1904 to lobby for state and federal laws prohibiting child labor. The group hired photographer Lewis Hine to help them build a scientific, legal, and moral case against child labor. In one photo-story, Hine paired images of children who worked in two textile mills owned by the same company. The company's mill in Huntsville, Alabama, hired children as young as eight years old, Hine noted, while Massachusetts law prohibited the Lowell factory from employing children under the age of fourteen. The National Child Labor Committee presented such regional discrepancies as evidence that the nation needed a federal child labor law. *Images as History: Exposing Child Labor*, page 550, explores Hine's images more fully.

The pervasiveness of child labor in the South particularly troubled him. In 1900 nearly 25 percent of the workers in textile factories and cotton mills were white children ages ten to sixteen. Some reformers viewed child farm work as a healthier alternative to long days in a factory. Hine disagreed. "The sunshine in the cotton fields has blinded our eyes to the monotony, overwork and the hopelessness of their lives," he wrote.

In 1916 President Wilson signed a law banning the interstate sale of products made by child labor that protected only about 150,000 industrial child laborers out of nearly 1.75 million. Two years later the Supreme Court sided with a father who argued that the law deprived him of his parental right to control his sons' labor and declared the law unconstitutional. Progressives responded by trying to amend the Constitution. In 1924 Congress approved an amendment giving the federal government the power to regulate child labor, but Southern opposition to any curtailment of states' rights prevented its ratification. A nationwide ban on child labor did not come until the 1930s, when the Court upheld a New Deal federal child labor law.

Ultimately child labor declined as states began to mandate school attendance. Embracing the notion that all children had the right to an education, local women's groups pushed hard to ensure that their neighborhood schools received appropriate funding, provided free books, offered kindergarten, paid teachers adequately, and were equipped with satisfactory fire escapes. Throughout the Progressive Era school enrollments, the number of days in a school year, and money spent per pupil all rose.

Several other Progressive endeavors also aimed to improve the lives of working-class children. The allure of pleasure and hunger at home sometimes became too strong for children, who resorted to stealing to meet their needs. "Most of these premature law breakers are in search of Americanized clothing and others are only looking for playthings," Jane Addams maintained. Some, she pointed out, were simply "eager to take home food or fuel which will relieve the distress and need they so constantly hear discussed." Reformers spearheaded the creation of a juvenile criminal system that focused on rehabilitating young offenders.

To keep young children safely off the streets when their parents went to work, Progressive activists established urban playgrounds with adult supervisors. To divert female teenagers from tempting dance halls and male adolescents from saloons or brothels, Progressives created a wide array of local boys and girls clubs that included organized sports teams and art classes. Not every child appreciated becoming the object of reform. "I can't go to the playgrounds now," complained one eleven-year-old boy. "They get on me nerves with so many men and women around telling you what to do."

What obstacles did reformers face while trying to eliminate child labor?

Images as History

EXPOSING THE EVILS OF CHILD LABOR

Trained as a sociologist, photographer Lewis Hine took nearly five thousand photographs as a staff photographer for the National Child Labor Committee from 1908 to 1918. Hine visited factories, canneries, textile mills, farms, and mines snapping photos and recording the life stories of each child, evidence the National Child Labor Committee used to argue that full-time work damaged children's health, deprived them of an education, and ruined their childhood. Hine often posed as a factory inspector or salesman to gain access to factories or mines. When a factory owner guessed his real purpose and refused to let him in, Hine took pictures of child laborers arriving at daybreak or leaving covered in grime. He carefully recorded the children's names, ages, and stories to counter industrialists' accusations that he staged his photos.

His notes for this image of a young girl tending machines in a South Carolina cotton mill read, "Sadie Pfeifer, 48 inches high, has worked half a year. One of the many small children at work in Lancaster Cotton Mills." Are Hine's photographs best understood as historical evidence or propaganda, or both?

Sadie Pfeifer was a spinner in a South Carolina cotton mill, charged with repairing breaks or snags as the machines spun the cotton into yarn or thread.

The electric lights indicate her long hours, beginning before daybreak and extending after dark.

The closed windows helped the factory maintain the hot and humid conditions that prevented thread from breaking.

The long row of machines underscores how much work she had to manage on her own, dangerous work that could cost her a finger.

The photograph does not convey the deafening noise that left some workers partially deaf.

The adult supervisor in the background represented Sadie's future and underscored her subservient position in the mill.

Lewis Hine, "Sadie Pfeifer, Lancaster Cotton Mills, South Carolina"

How did the composition of this photograph reinforce Hine's message about child labor?

Wise beyond their years, these tough-looking newsboys emulate their elders by learning to enjoy pipes and cigarettes. Newsboys also gambled, swore, and began visiting houses of prostitution at a shockingly young ages.

Camaraderie among newsboys helped make a difficult and lonely job more enjoyable.

This photo of hardened newsboys warned that without a proper education, these boys contributed to the moral breakdown of society.

By innocently buying a daily paper from one of the hundreds of newsboys who hawked newspapers on city corners from dawn to dusk, the middle class helped perpetuate an insidious form of child labor.

Lewis Hine, "Newsies Smoking on a Monday Morning, St. Louis, Missouri, 1910"

MAKING HUMAN JUNK

SMALL GIRLS AND BOYS WANTED

GOOD MATERIAL AT FIRST

THE PROCESS

THE PRODUCT

No future and low wages

"Junk"

SHALL INDUSTRY BE ALLOWED TO PUT THIS COST ON SOCIETY?

The National Child Labor Committee distributed Hine's "Making Human Junk" poster nationwide to send the message that child labor ruined individual lives and hurt the entire society.

The poster showed a group of healthy children entering a harsh and dangerous factory environment where they were powerless to control their own fates.

Appealing to middle-class self-interest, this poster suggested that sickly child workers contaminated the materials used to make clothing for the middle class.

Hine directly refuted industrialists' claims that work benefited children. "The object of employing children is not to train them, but to get high profits from their work," he wrote.

Long days in the mill turned children into broken pieces of industrial "junk" that factory owners discarded, burdening society with their care.

Lewis Hine, "Making Human Junk"

Did these images offer similar or different reasons to oppose child labor?

Reforming the Government

Progressives recognized that passing laws governing the workplace or protecting women and children was not enough. Ensuring their enforcement through the establishment of regulatory agencies required reforming how local, state, and federal governments functioned. Only then could the government become a positive force in workers' lives. Socialists agreed that the government should act, but ultimately wanted to give state and national governments control of all major industries.

Containing Socialism

Progressives discovered an unexpected ally in their drive to turn the government into a guardian that actively protected the public. Both Progressives and socialists championed the creation of city-run utilities to provide streetcar service, gas, water, and electricity. Progressives viewed such arrangements as an efficient way to deliver reliable, fairly priced public services to city residents, prevent disruptive strikes, and improve conditions for utility workers. Socialists believed that municipal-run utilities would become the opening wedge that led to eventual public ownership of railroads, mines, and banks.

In 1904 the novelist and socialist Upton Sinclair lived with workers in Chicago for nearly two months, learning firsthand about their work in the meatpacking industry. This experience became the basis for Sinclair's novel, *The Jungle*, which told the story of a Lithuanian immigrant family who came to America full of hope only to discover crushing poverty and horrific working conditions. The novelist wanted his exposé to convince Americans that socialism offered the only way to end the rampant capitalist exploitation that ground down the working class. Instead readers focused on his vivid descriptions of rotten meat, workers' fingers, and rat excrement all being tossed into the hopper to produce the sausage that Americans enjoyed each morning for breakfast. When a federal investigation confirmed Sinclair's account, the public demanded federal regulation to ensure that the nation's meat supply was safe. Faced with plummeting meat sales, packinghouse owners understood that government certification of their meat as disease-free could help them regain consumer confidence. The **Meat Inspection Act** (1906) gave federal inspectors the authority to condemn meat unfit for consumption and established federal sanitary standards for meatpacking plants.

> "I aimed at the public's heart, and by accident I hit it in the stomach."
>
> UPTON SINCLAIR laments America's reaction to his novel, *The Jungle*

Reformers also wanted manufacturers of patent medicines to list their ingredients. Lydia E. Pinkham's Vegetable Compound, a widely popular patent medicine, circulated advertising cards (**18.12**) with images of rosy-cheeked children to create the impression that the company used the purest ingredients in its syrup. The flipside of this card touted the medicine as "a positive cure for all those painful complaints and weaknesses so common to our best female population," including headaches, depression, ovarian troubles, and menopause. In 1906 the **Pure Food and Drug Act** levied fines for mislabeling food or medicine. To their dismay many female temperance advocates who had avidly consumed Lydia E. Pinkham's Vegetable Compound discovered that the serum contained 15 percent alcohol.

Ultimately the Progressive vision of government oversight prevailed over the socialist view of complete government control. Most cities balked at direct ownership of public utilities, preferring to create regulatory boards that set rules for the private companies that continued to run streetcars or gas lines. The subsequent improvement in city services reduced the appeal of socialism in many working-class neighborhoods.

Ending Government Corruption

Progressives knew that meaningful regulation required eliminating corruption within all levels of government. For an enticing bribe, city officials often

What importance did the socialist movement have during the Progressive Era?

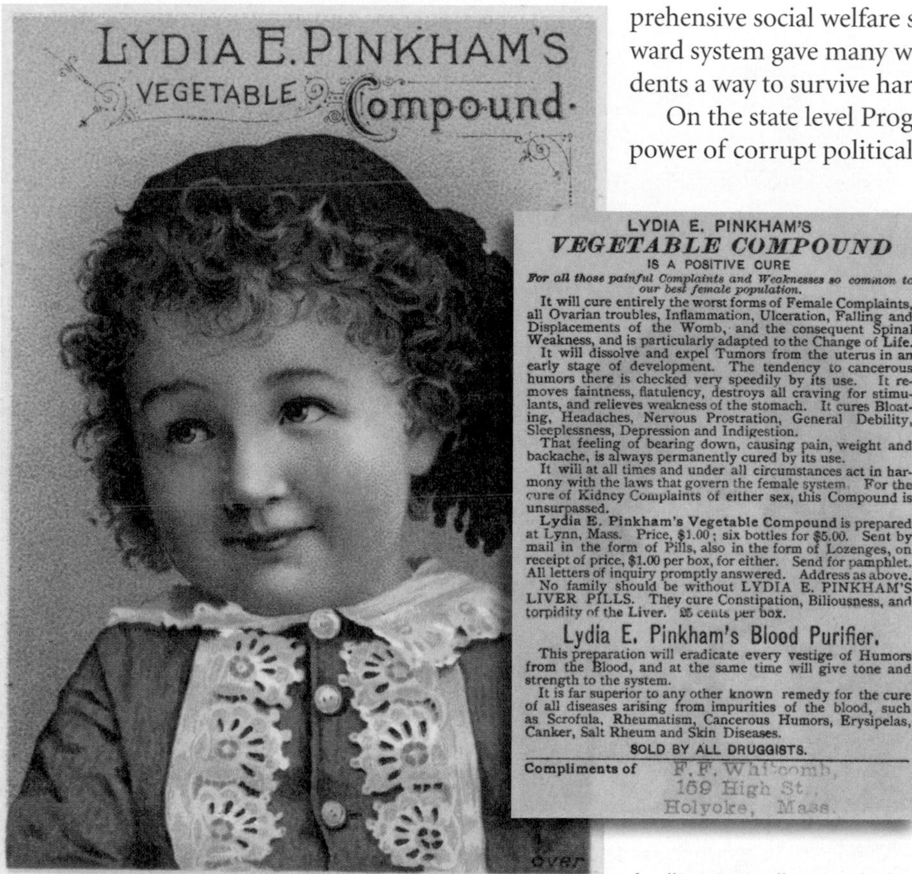

18.12 Marketing Lydia E. Pinkham's Vegetable Compound
Ads for the patent medicine promised to cure practically every ailment and restore youthful vigor.

proved willing to look the other way when businesses broke the law. Political parties sometimes stole elections as well, creating fictitious lists of voters that let individuals use multiple aliases to vote as often as they liked.

Progressives disagreed over how to eliminate corruption. One answer was to get rid of politicians and instead rely on nonpartisan commissions of experts or city-managers to run city services. Over four hundred municipalities turned to commission-style governance, an approach that reflected the broad faith placed in expertise during the Progressive Era. Other Progressives replaced the ward system that let each neighborhood select its own councilman with city councils elected at large. Voters expected their ward representative to "bring home the bacon," patronage that Progressives felt encouraged parochialism and corruption. Impoverished working-class residents offered a competing vision. Their ward representatives provided needed job opportunities or relief. In the absence of a comprehensive social welfare system, the patronage-based ward system gave many working-class urban residents a way to survive hard times.

On the state level Progressives tried to reduce the power of corrupt political parties. Many states eliminated the previous practice of handing voters different colored ballots marked "Republican" or "Democrat" to stuff into the ballot boxes as party officials looked on. The secret ballot removed the threat of payback or shunning if one broke with the neighborhood party boss. Instead of letting party leaders chose candidates, some states introduced direct primaries that allowed party members to pick the candidates. A reform measure called the "**initiative**" provided a way, usually by gathering signatures on petitions, for the electorate to introduce legislation before state legislatures. The **referendum** put legislative proposals on the ballot, letting the voting public decide whether a measure became law. Finally the **recall** used special elections to remove unpopular or corrupt officials from office before their term expired. Wisconsin, one of the most Progressive states in the nation, adopted all these measures under the leadership of Governor Robert Lafollette.

In 1906 journalist David Graham Phillips detailed the close ties between big business and federal senators in a series of magazine articles entitled "The Treason of the Senate." Phillips viewed this alliance as threatening to "the American people as any invading army could be." Roosevelt charged Phillips with overexaggerating the extent of corruption and urged the "men with the muck-rakes" to avoid stirring up needless controversy. Roosevelt's rebuke gave investigative journalists a new nickname, "**muckrakers**." Subsequent corruption scandals solidified public support for the **Seventeenth Amendment** (1913), which allowed voters, rather than state legislatures, to elect federal senators.

18.13 Hampton Institute Students Building a Staircase, 1900 Black educators distributed images of tidy black students working industriously to counter stereotypes that portrayed blacks as lazy or dangerous.

Accepting Separate but Equal

The Progressive campaign to remake the government into a champion of the common man did not include challenging the legal edifice constructed in the wake of the Supreme Court's 1896 "separate but equal" ruling in *Plessy v. Ferguson* (see Chapter 14). At the turn of the century, Southern states rushed to pass laws that formally segregated every public facility from railroad waiting rooms to water fountains. Use of poll taxes and literacy tests to disenfranchise blacks also exploded. When Southern-born Woodrow Wilson took office in 1913, he let the heads of federal agencies segregate their offices.

Few white Progressives spoke out against the onslaught of discriminatory laws. They convinced themselves that segregation would quell racial conflict, essentially choosing social peace over racial justice. "Good fences make good neighbors," asserted Southern Progressive leader Edgar Gardner Murphy. Jane Addams was a notable exception. She disagreed that segregation benefited the black middle class by giving black doctors and businessmen a ready clientele. Most other Northern Progressives remained content to let the South handle the "race problem" as it saw fit.

African American leaders cultivated their own reform impulse during the Progressive Era. Unlike white Progressives black leaders had little faith that government would solve their social problems. The most prominent African American leader of the Progressive Era, Booker T. Washington, instead embraced self-help as the best way to end poverty among African Americans. Born a Virginia slave in 1859, after the Civil War Washington moved with his family to West Virginia where he worked in a coal mine. As a child Washington developed an almost fanatical desire to get an education, arriving penniless

How does this photograph convey the Hampton Institute's educational philosophy?

at the doorstep of Virginia's Hampton Institute, a vocationally oriented high school founded in 1868 to educate freed slaves and Indians. He passed his entrance exam—sweeping a floor—with flying colors. Hampton taught practical skills such as brick-making, blacksmithing, and shoemaking along with more traditional academic subjects like reading and math. This staged photograph (**18.13**) of a Hampton Institute carpentering class, taken twenty years after Washington attended, encapsulated the school's educational philosophy. The photo underscored that these perfectly groomed, hard-working, and well-trained students had the skills they needed to advance step-by-step up the ladder (in this case staircase) of success.

Washington followed the Hampton model when he established his own school in 1881, the Tuskegee Institute in Tuskegee, Alabama. A captivating orator Washington popularized the notion that blacks should focus on economic advancement first, politics and civil rights later. Washington's apparent willingness to accept social segregation, as long as blacks and whites worked together toward their common economic goals, won him a large white following. Roosevelt even invited him to dine in the White House, the first African American to ever receive this honor—an invitation that provoked howls of protest throughout the South. Washington's private behavior, however, was often at odds with his public persona. Publicly he reassured whites that most blacks had little interest in demanding equality as long as they could prosper economically. Privately Washington helped fund court challenges to *Plessy v. Ferguson* and sent his own children to Northern white colleges.

Washington believed that American race relations would gradually improve. Methodist minister Henry McNeal Turner offered a competing vision, telling blacks to leave the country and immigrate to Africa. Black journalist Ida B. Wells-Barnett also disagreed with Washington. Rather than striving to prove their economic worth to whites, Wells-Barnett urged African Americans to use boycotts to win equal treatment from white-owned railroads. She also advocated armed resistance to lynch mobs. "A Winchester rifle should have a place of honour in every black home, and it should be used for that protection which the law refuses to give," she declared. Wells-Barnett began lobbying for a federal anti-lynching law after a white mob in Memphis, Tennessee, lynched three friends of hers who had opened a grocery store that drew customers away from white businesses. With her life threatened Wells-Barnett moved to Chicago where she worked with Jane Addams to prevent the segregation of city public schools and continued her anti-lynching campaign.

The most powerful challenge to Washington's vision came from the Northern-born sociologist W. E. B. Du Bois, the first African American to attend Harvard University. Du Bois argued that individuals should receive the education that best suited them, regardless of their race. He emphasized that the African American community needed educated professionals and teachers, the so-called "Talented Tenth." Economic progress was not possible without the right to vote, Du Bois contended, pointing out that discriminatory laws made it difficult for black sharecroppers or craftsmen to get ahead. *Competing Visions: Seeking Racial Uplift* (page 556) offers more detail on the debate between Washington and Du Bois. In 1909 Du Bois joined with Wells-Barnett and Addams to establish the National Association for the Advancement of Colored People. The interracial civil rights organization demanded an immediate end to all forms of racial discrimination, beginning a decades-long struggle for racial justice that would eventually overturn Jim Crow laws in the 1950s and 1960s.

> "No white American ever thinks that any other race is wholly civilized until he wears the white man's clothes, eats the white man's food, speaks the white man's language, and professes the white man's religion."
>
> BOOKER T. WASHINGTON, explaining why black students needed to learn middle-class habits of dress and decorum

What alternatives did critics of Booker T. Washington offer to improve life for African Americans?

Competing Visions

SEEKING RACIAL UPLIFT

In 1895 Booker T. Washington delivered his most famous speech, "The Atlanta Exposition Address," to an audience of Northern and Southern whites and blacks. The speech proposed a compromise that accepted social segregation in return for white support of blacks' economic advancement. In 1903 W. E. B. Du Bois accused Washington of sending blacks down a path that ensured their permanent enslavement to white America. How does Washington take into account the racially hostile climate that prevailed in the South during the Progressive Era? Is Du Bois's criticism of Washington accurate?

In this passage from his 1895 "Atlanta Exposition Address," Washington outlines his plan for racial progress and peaceful race relations.

Our greatest danger is that in the great leap from slavery to freedom we may overlook the fact that the masses of us are to live by the productions of our hands, and fail to keep in mind that we shall prosper in proportion as we learn to dignify and glorify common labour and put brains and skill into the common occupations of life. . . . No race can prosper till it learns that there is as much dignity in tilling a field as in writing a poem. It is at the bottom of life we must begin, and not at the top.

In all things that are purely social we can be as separate as the fingers, yet one as the hand in all things essential to mutual progress. . . . Nearly sixteen millions of hands will aid you in pulling the load upward, or they will pull against you the load downward. We shall constitute one-third and more of the ignorance and crime of the South, or one-third its intelligence and progress.

The wisest among my race understand that the agitation of questions of social equality is the extremest folly, and that progress in the enjoyment of all the privileges that will come to us must be the result of severe and constant struggle rather than of artificial forcing. No race that has anything to contribute to the markets of the world is long in any degree ostracized. It is important and right that all privileges of the law be ours, but it is vastly more important that we be prepared for the exercises of these privileges. The opportunity to earn a dollar in a factory just now is worth infinitely more than the opportunity to spend a dollar in an opera-house.

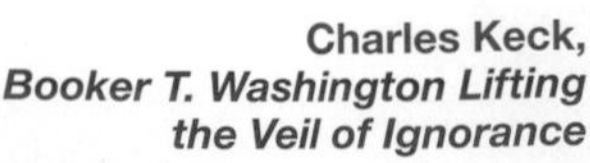

Charles Keck, *Booker T. Washington Lifting the Veil of Ignorance*

In this excerpt from his book, *The Souls of Black Folk* (1903), Du Bois explains why Washington's ideas would not work.

Mr. Washington distinctly asks that black people give up, at least for the present, three things,—

First, political power,
Second, insistence on civil rights
Third, higher education of Negro youth,
—and concentrate all their energies on industrial education, the accumulation of wealth, and the conciliation of the South.

Is it possible, and probable, that nine millions of men can make effective progress in economic lines if they are deprived of political rights, made a servile caste, and allowed only the most meager chance for developing their exceptional men? If history and reason give any distinct answer to these questions, it is an emphatic *No*. And Mr. Washington thus faces the triple paradox of his career.

1. He is striving nobly to make Negro artisans business men and property-owners; but it is utterly impossible, under modern competitive methods, for workingmen and property-owners to defend their rights and exist without the right of suffrage.
2. He insists on thrift and self-respect, but at the same time counsels a silent submission to civic inferiority such as is bound to sap the manhood of any race in the long run.
3. He advocates common-school and industrial training, and depreciates institutions of higher learning; but neither the Negro common [elementary] schools, nor Tuskegee itself, could remain open a day were it not for teachers trained in Negro colleges, or trained by their graduates.

His doctrine has tended to make the whites, North and South, shift the burden of the Negro problem to the Negro's shoulders and stand aside as critical and rather pessimistic spectators; when in fact the burden belongs to the nation.

Was Washington a sell-out, as Du Bois implies, or a master strategist?

> "This country will not be a permanently good place for any of us to live in unless we make it a reasonably good place for all of us to live in."
>
> THEODORE ROOSEVELT summarizes the Progressive ideal, 1912

Conclusion

The origins of twentieth century liberal reform movements such as the Civil Rights Movement and the New Deal lay in the Progressive Era. During this time, reformers first articulated the liberal vision that the government needed to play an active role in securing social, political, and economic justice. Progressives were reformers, not revolutionaries. They embraced capitalism and democracy, believing that a reformed economy and government could serve the interests of all, not just the wealthy few. The Progressives proved remarkably adept at creating coalitions that overcame class divisions and political party affiliations to advance reform causes that ranged from abolishing child labor to protecting the environment. From the mid-1890s to the mid-1910s, most Americans came to accept that it was the government's responsibility to regulate the economy, control destructive capitalistic practices, and stabilize the nation's financial system.

Using governmental power to protect workers and the environment proved more contentious. Americans debated how to balance individual freedom with social responsibility; private property with governmental action. Within a short period Progressive initiatives substantially reshaped industrial relations. States adopted varying degrees of protective legislation for female and child laborers and workers injured on the job. Federal regulators curtailed industrial access to federal forests, managed collective water resources, and became the caretakers for new nationally designated wilderness areas.

Progressives wanted to imbue Americans with a new sense of collective responsibility for their fellow citizens. Middle-class reformers worked particularly hard to create cross-class alliances to rein in exploitive capitalism and prevent workers from embracing socialism. Fissures nonetheless remained. The slew of social problems that Progressives addressed did not include the racial segregation and disenfranchisement recently sanctioned by the Supreme Court. Reformers also failed to question the prevailing "Vanishing Race" notion that Indian cultures would soon disappear.

Using regulation to transform the workplace and control big business required reforming the government as well. At the local and state level, Progressives employed a myriad of approaches to try to break the corrupt ties between businessmen and politicians and make the government more directly accountable to the voting public. Ultimately Progressives transformed the ways that American democracy and capitalism functioned. Not every Progressive reform succeeded, but the failures provided a blueprint for the next wave of social reform during the 1930s New Deal.

The link between democracy and capitalism that Progressive reformers cultivated at home influenced American foreign policy as well. The desire to achieve lasting social peace, shared prosperity, and true democracy—the heart of the Progressive reform impulse—shaped the path that the nation pursued as it stepped out in the world. The activist federal government that the Progressives had helped create set an ambitious international agenda for America at the turn of the century.

1901–1903

McKinley assassinated, Roosevelt becomes president
Progressivism gains presidential advocate

Ida Tarbell published "The History of the Standard Oil Company"
Exposé of oil trust stokes interest in trust-busting

Roosevelt and Muir camp together in Yosemite
They later champion competing preservationist and conservationist visions.

1905

Lochner v. New York
Stymies Progressive effort to mandate set working hours and wages

Socialist Party of America and IWW formed
Unlike Progressives, Socialists and IWW emphasize working-class solidarity over reform

1906

Pure Food and Drug Act and Meat Inspection Act passed
Establishes new regulatory role for the federal government

Roosevelt files suit against Standard Oil
"Trust-busting" president distinguishes between good and bad trusts

Review Questions

1. What factors led to the emergence of Progressivism?
2. What social problems did middle-class Progressives identify at the beginning of the twentieth century? How did their solutions differ from the ones embraced by the Socialists and laissez-faire industrialists?
3. What principles unified Progressives? How did they disagree?
4. Why did the Progressive notion of an activist, regulatory government create controversy on both the right and the left?
5. Evaluate the Progressive strategy for reform, giving examples of successful cross-class or bipartisan alliances they constructed.
6. How did visual images and investigative journalism transform Americans' views of poverty and corruption?
7. What role did government, including presidents, the Supreme Court, and state and local governments, play during the Progressive Era?
8. In what ways did the Progressive reform agenda succeed? How did it fail?

1908–1909

Lewis Hine begins photographing child laborers
Nationwide campaign to ban child labor fails

Muller v. Oregon
Upholds maximum work hour laws for women

National Association for the Advancement of Colored People formed (NAACP)
Seeks immediate end to segregation

1911–1912

Triangle Shirtwaist Factory Fire
Shocking tragedy confirms need to reform workplace

Supreme Court announces "rule of reason" in breaking up trusts
Makes distinction between good and bad trusts

Republican Party splits into progressive and conservative factions
Democrat Woodrow Wilson elected president

1913

Wilson allows federal agencies to racially segregate their offices
Reflects lingering impact of *Plessy v. Ferguson*

Federal Reserve Act
Creates a federally controlled currency and banking reserve system

Sixteenth Amendment ratified
Congress authorizes first federal income taxes

Seventeenth Amendment ratified
Popular election of senators intended to diminish big business's influence in politics

1914

Ford announces eight hour/five dollar workday
Secures competitive advantage through benefits and assembly lines

Ludlow Massacre
Reveals potency of class conflict during Progressive Era

Key Terms

Social Gospel Thebelief that Christians had a responsibility to create an ethically sound and morally upright society. **534**

trust-busting Governmental action to dissolve monopolies. **536**

Sixteenth Amendment (1913) The constitutional amendment authorizing federal income taxes. **538**

Federal Reserve Act (1913) The act creating a federally run Federal Reserve to serve as a "banker's bank" that held a portion of bank funds in reserve to help member banks in time of crisis, set rates for business loans, and issued a new national paper currency. **539**

Clayton Anti-Trust Act (1914) The act prohibited interlocking company directories—the practice of setting up shadow companies that appeared to compete but were actually run by the same board of directors—and exempted trade unions from prosecution under the 1890 Sherman Anti-Trust Act. **539**

Federal Trade Commission (1914) A federal agency with the power to order companies to cease unfair trading practices whose decisions were subject to court review. **539**

preservationist An environmentalist who championed preserving nature in its unspoiled state. **539**

conservationist An environmentalist who wanted to meet present economic needs and conserve natural resources for future generations. **540**

welfare capitalism The notion of using benefits to gain workers' loyalty, improve worker morale, and weaken interest in unions. **541**

scientific management The effort to use scientific knowledge to secure maximum output and profit. **543**

Industrial Workers of the World (IWW) This group envisioned "one big union" that welcomed all workers regardless of sex, race, ethnicity, or skill, which would one day take over all means of production in the United States. **543**

Lochner v. New York (1905) A Supreme Court ruling that unless long work hours directly jeopardized workers' health, the government could not abridge an employee's freedom to negotiate his own work schedule with his employer. **544**

Ludlow Massacre (1914) Colorado state troops set a striking miners' camp ablaze, killing thirteen women and children, an act that outraged laborers throughout the nation. **544**

Muller v. Oregon (1908) The Supreme Court upheld maximum hour laws for female workers because protecting women's reproductive health served the public good. **546**

Meat Inspection Act (1906) Law gave federal inspectors the authority to condemn meat unfit for consumption and established federal sanitary standards for meatpacking plants. **552**

Pure Food and Drug Act (1906) Law levied federal fines for mislabeling food or medicine. **552**

initiative Provided a way, usually by gathering signatures on petitions, for the electorate to introduce legislation before state legislatures. **553**

referendum Put legislative proposals on the ballot, letting the voting public decide whether a measure became law. **553**

recall Used special elections to remove unpopular officials from office before their term expired. **553**

muckrakers Progressive Era term for investigative journalists who wrote exposés on government and business corruption. **553**

Seventeenth Amendment (1913) A constitutional amendment that allowed voters, rather than state legislatures, elect federal senators. **553**

CHAPTER 19

Imperial America

The United States in the World, 1890–1914

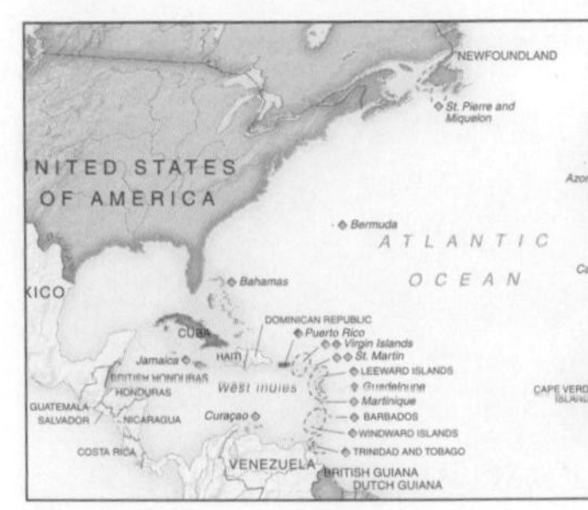

Becoming a World Power p. 562

> **"Remember the *Maine* and to hell with Spain!"**
>
> Newspaper slogan urging war with Spain in the wake of the *Maine* explosion

On February 15, 1898, a naval officer awoke President William McKinley in the middle of the night with the stunning news that the American battleship the *Maine* had exploded in Havana, Cuba, killing 266 of the 354 crew members. The explosion turned the battleship into a hunk of molten steel. This illustration depicted the blast propelling bodies and debris sky-high in Havana Harbor. Americans also read moving firsthand accounts in the press, including one from survivor James R. Young. "I was feeling a bit glum," Young recalled, "and in fact was so quiet that Lieutenant J. Hood came up and asked laughingly if I was asleep. I said, 'No, I am on watch.' Scarcely had I spoken when there came a dull, sullen roar. Would to God that I could blot out the sounds and the scenes that followed."

The United States and Spain had long been at odds over the question of independence for Cuba, then a Spanish colony. McKinley had sent the *Maine* to Havana to stop Spanish-instigated attacks on American-held property in Cuba. Many Americans suspected that Spanish saboteurs had blown up the ship to protest the U.S. incursion into Spanish territorial waters. The shocking images and accounts of the *Maine* explosion fueled public anger against Spain for its supposed attack on the U.S. Navy, creating a moment of crisis between the two nations. An official investigation confirmed these widely held views, blaming the *Maine* explosion on a Spanish mine in the harbor. The exact cause of the blast, however, remained a mystery. Some experts now cite a spontaneous combustion from the coal stored alongside ammunition as the most likely culprit, a misfortune shared by thirteen similar American naval vessels between 1895 and 1898. Others suggest that Cuban revolutionaries may have planted the explosives, expecting the United States to blame Spain and declare war.

The *Maine* explosion ignited a short, four-month war between the United States and Spain in 1898. This "splendid little war," as one official called it, ended with an overwhelming American victory. The overseas possessions that the United States gained from Spain, including Puerto Rico and the Philippines, gave the nation a new formal colonial empire. The United States simultaneously constructed an informal economic empire throughout the Caribbean and East Asia at the turn of the century. As the United States established itself as a budding world power, Americans offered conflicting visions of how the United States should behave outside its borders.

How has the meaning of this image changed since 1898?

IGNORANCE
ROBBERY

Becoming a World Power

Throughout the nineteenth century the Atlantic and Pacific oceans provided Americans with a sense of security and detachment from world affairs. By the 1880s, however, advancements in transportation and communication suddenly made the world seem smaller and more dangerous to Americans. Fear alone, though, did not explain Americans' growing interest in venturing overseas. Americans looked outside their borders to find markets for U.S. goods and the raw materials needed to fuel a growing industrial economy. International recognition as a world power and spreading American values also appealed to the country's growing sense of national greatness.

European Imperialism

In the seventeenth and eighteenth centuries, Britain, France, and Spain had based their world prominence on far-flung colonial empires, places that they populated with settlers and soldiers to exploit economic resources and protect ocean trade routes. In the eighteenth and nineteenth centuries, these settler communities launched a slew of successful revolutions that liberated colonies in North and South America from European rule. With the "old" colonial empires now defunct, European nations and Japan sought places to build new ones. As Britain, France, Belgium, Germany, Italy, Portugal, Spain, Russia, the Netherlands, and Japan discovered vulnerable areas around the globe to colonize, they developed a new style of empire building. **Imperialism**, the late nineteenth-century term for colonizing foreign nations and lands, relied primarily on business, political, and military structures rather than settlers to rule colonized peoples and exploit their resources. Europe's drive to create colonial empires in Africa and Asia in the late nineteenth century provided a model to either emulate or reject as the United States embarked on its campaign to become a world power.

Besides exploiting colonies for economic gain, Europeans also drew satisfaction from fulfilling a self-imposed "civilizing" mission to spread Western culture and values to nonwhite and non-Christian populations throughout Africa and Asia. The drawbacks to empires, however, included the need to defend widely dispersed territories and suppress popular uprisings against colonial rule. Americans,

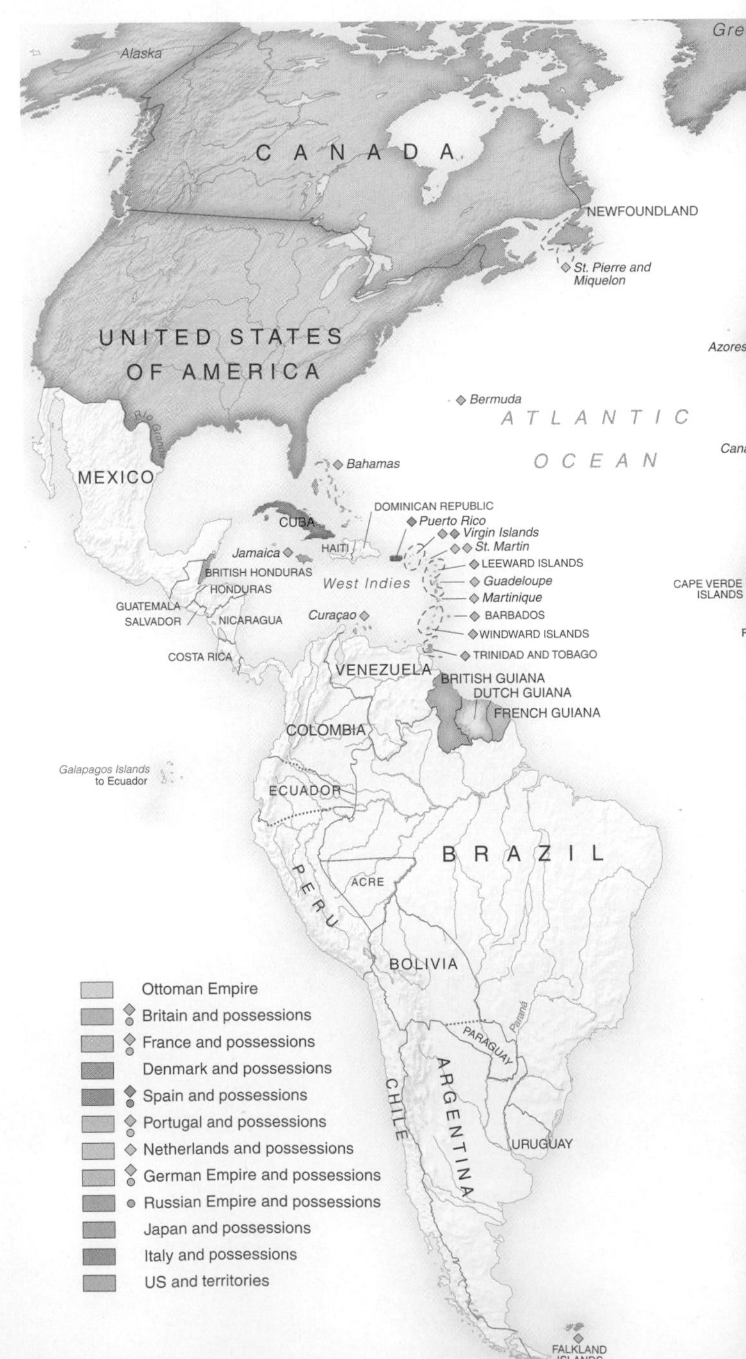

How did European imperialism affect the U.S. effort to create a formal empire?

therefore, developed conflicting visions from the lessons that they drew from the European experience. Some saw it as an inspiration; others, a cautionary tale.

As the map (**19.1**) indicates, the world situation in 1898 affected where the United States could hope to expand its influence. By the time the United States began exploring opportunities for expansion beyond the North American continent, Britain, France, Germany, and the Netherlands had already established colonial empires throughout Africa, East Asia, and South Asia. Great Britain exerted the greatest reach, making it the world's preeminent imperial power. This left the Western Hemisphere and China as possibilities for U.S. colonial expansion.

The Impulse for Expansion

Throughout American history territorial expansion played an important role in defining national identity and providing economic opportunity to Americans. In the early nineteenth century, manifest destiny, or the belief that Americans had a divine right to land in North America, fueled expansion across the continental United States. Imbued with a sense of cultural and racial superiority over the

19.1 Map of the World, 1898
The creation of far-flung European empires at the end of the nineteenth century limited opportunities for the United States to establish its own colonies or new overseas markets.

Which characteristics defined a nation as a world power in the late nineteenth century?

indigenous peoples who inhabited these lands, Americans felt justified in taking away land from Indians. In their view, Native Americans had failed to make the land commercially productive. The government relocated many Indian tribes onto reservations, where officials and missionaries embraced the goal of "civilizing" Indians by teaching them Western capitalist and Christian values (see Chapter 15). The same belief in manifest destiny, quest for economic opportunity, and ideas of racial superiority that had fueled American expansion across North America throughout the nineteenth century spurred interest in expanding American influence and trade overseas.

Many prominent businessmen, commercial farmers, and politicians urged the country to seek territory and markets outside the United States. In the 1890s American companies and farmers sold 90 percent of their goods to other Americans. The time had come, these critics argued, to develop global markets and even colonies to ensure continued prosperity and economic opportunity at home. When the country suffered a devastating economic depression from 1893 to 1897, these calls crystallized into a resolve within some quarters to build a commercial and colonial empire overseas.

Technological innovations also encouraged Americans to look beyond their borders. The laying of transatlantic telegraph cables increased both the speed and the volume of information sent throughout the world. The telegraph in many respects served as the Internet of the nineteenth century. Telegrams accelerated the exchange of diplomatic notes between governments, while dispatches from journalists overseas connected Americans on a daily basis to happenings around the world.

If the telegraph hastened the flow of information, the advent of steam-powered ships dramatically reduced the time needed to move people and goods throughout the world. In his seminal 1890 work, *The Influence of Sea Power on History, 1660–1783*, U.S. Navy Captain Alfred T. Mahan traced a direct correlation between a powerful navy and world power. In the new age of steam-powered battleships, the navy's outdated wooden sailing ships, described by one congressman as "floating washtubs," were ill-suited for advancing U.S. interests in the world. From 1890 onward the United States built battleships to match its growing economic power and its expansionist ambitions, and it soon boasted the second most powerful navy in the world after Great Britain. In 1907 President Theodore "Teddy" Roosevelt sent the nation's sixteen battleships and four destroyers on a global tour to show off America's world-class steam-powered navy, a trip that took two years to complete.

Americans' growing pride in their nation's economic might and technological prowess encouraged the United States to seek international recognition as a world power. So did the ideological vision encapsulated by social Darwinism, an ideology that applied nineteenth-century naturalist Charles Darwin's theory of biological evolution to human society through the notion of "survival of the fittest." At home Americans often used social Darwinism to justify the dominance of the wealthy and powerful, considered "the fit," over the poor and weak, or "the unfit." These ideas also shaped the way that Americans viewed the world. In the social Darwinist view, the "racial superiority" of Northern European populations explained why Britain, France, and Germany were world powers that easily colonized nonwhite peoples throughout the world. To take its rightful place alongside, or even above, these world powers, the United States needed to demonstrate its fitness by entering the global competition underway for colonies.

In making a case for expansion, the congregational minister Josiah Strong linked older ideas of manifest destiny with this newer emphasis on survival of the fittest. "It seems to me that God, with infinite wisdom and skill, is training the Anglo-Saxon race to prevail" in the competition to control lands throughout the world, Strong wrote in his influential book, *Our Country: Its Possible Future and Its Present Crisis* (1885). In Strong's view the United States risked losing its chance for global eminence if it failed to join the scramble for colonies already underway worldwide.

Driven to perfect democracy at home, many Progressives found the call to spread American values abroad appealing. Their reform impulse extended beyond U.S. borders to imagine a world freed from tyranny and injustice. In many respects the strong, activist government that Progressives helped construct at the turn of the century made it possible for the United States to extend its imperial reach during the Progressive Era. Progressives never spoke with one voice on domestic matters, and they also offered competing visions on expanding U.S. influence in the world. Progressives who opposed the nation's overseas forays feared strengthening big business at the expense of exploited foreign peoples and American workers. They also believed that imperial ventures drew attention away from Progressive reform projects at home.

How did European imperialism affect the U.S. effort to create a formal empire?

The Spanish-American War

The first significant opportunity to expand U.S. influence overseas came when Cuba rose in revolt against Spanish rule. Extensive press coverage of Spanish atrocities and U.S. economic interests in Cuba prompted the nation to take note of this colonial struggle for independence. After a mysterious explosion sank the *Maine* battleship and killed hundreds of American sailors, many Americans accused Spain of deliberately attacking the ship. Fearing that Congress might declare war on its own, a reluctant President William McKinley finally agreed to an armed intervention. The war with Spain was short, but the outcome was dramatic. The peace treaty with Spain granted the United States island possessions in the Caribbean and Pacific that became the territorial foundation for the new U.S. colonial empire.

The Growing Conflict with Spain

In the early nineteenth century, when Spain's other Western Hemisphere colonies successfully fought for independence, Cuba remained loyal to Spain. By 1868, however, oppressive Spanish rule provoked a rebellion in Cuba that ended ten years later with Spain's pledge to grant the island increased autonomy. Failure to fulfill this promise, economic hardships inflicted by the 1890s depression, and continued agitation by exiled Cuban rebels living in the United States fanned the flames of rebellion once again in 1895. By the time the second revolt began, the United States and Cuba had established strong commercial ties. Cuba sent over 90 percent of its exports to the United States, and American investment totaled nearly $50 million in Cuban sugar, cattle, mining, and tobacco industries.

Spain paid a heavy price to maintain this last symbol of its imperial past. Of the 278,000 Spanish troops sent to Cuba to suppress the revolt, nearly 50,000 had died of yellow fever or malaria by 1898, and an equal number lay too sick to fight. A much smaller force of 20,000–30,000 Cuban rebels drew on their knowledge of the terrain and support from civilians to fight an effective guerrilla war that ravaged tobacco and sugar plantations to deprive the Spanish government of revenue. Rebels purposefully steered clear of American-owned plantations to avoid antagonizing the United States.

Cuban exiles in the United States drew appealing analogies between their struggle for independence and the American Revolution, highlighting the similar desire of Cuban and American colonists to free themselves from an exploitive ruler and establish democratic self-rule. If any uncertainty existed among the American public over which side they supported, Spanish General Valeriano Weyler's infamous reconcentration policy ended those doubts. Through **reconcentration** Spanish soldiers tried to crush the Cuban rebellion by herding Cuban peasants off their farms into heavily fortified cities and then systematically destroying the crops that fed the rebel armies. This policy created a humanitarian crisis in Cuba as famine and disease ravaged the civilian population, killing nearly 100,000. Outraged Americans denounced reconcentration as uncivilized and illegal warfare.

The **yellow press**, tabloid journalists and newspapers that reported sensationalist stories with a strong emotional component, fueled public anger against the Spanish. This unique name for nineteenth-century tabloid journalism derived from competing "Yellow Kid" comic strips in leading New York newspapers that portrayed the antics of a precocious boy living in the city's tenements. Yellow journalism emerged in the 1880s when Joseph Pulitzer began using melodramatic, partly fictionalized stories to bolster sales of his newspaper, the *New York World*. After William Randolph Hearst took over the *New York Journal* in 1895, the two newspapers waged daily battles over who could print the most lurid tales.

In the Cuban crisis both papers saw a chance to report the kinds of scandal-driven stories guaranteed to sell newspapers. Exiled Cuban rebels living in the United States provided a steady supply of atrocity stories (some fabricated, some true) to the yellow press, and the vivid illustrations accompanying these accounts helped the public visualize Spanish brutality.

Why did Americans take an interest in the Cuban rebellion against Spain?

Images as History

ATROCITY STORIES AND PUBLIC OPINION

Ever since the yellow press helped raise American ire against Spain in the years leading up to the Spanish-American War, Americans have pondered the power of the press in the United States. How much power do atrocity stories and pictures have to shape public opinion? Can the press convince the public to fight a war?

On February 12, 1897, the *New York Journal* published a story by Richard Harding Davis about a young Cuban woman whom Spanish authorities had expelled for carrying secret messages between Cuban rebels. Davis reported that "Spanish officers" followed Clemencia Arango and her companions onto an American ship. The Spanish officers "demanded that a cabin should be furnished to them to which the girls might be taken, and they were then undressed and searched" for messages to exiled Cuban rebels living in the United States. Frederic Remington's illustration "Spaniards Search Women on American Steamers" accompanied Davis's story.

Hearst next took up the cause of Evangelina Cisneros. Sentenced to twenty years in prison for trying to lure a Spanish officer into a rebel death trap, Cisneros was awaiting deportation to an African penal colony. According to the *New York Journal*, her only crime was calling for help from nearby Cuban rebels to stop a Spanish officer, "a beast in uniform," from raping her. On October 10, 1897 the paper stunningly announced that a *New York Journal* reporter had helped Cisneros break out of jail and sail to the United States. The yellow press presented Clemencia and Evangelina as symbols for the virtuous and victimized Cuban people, fueling public sympathy for the Cuban rebellion.

Frederic Remington (who was in the United States when this incident occurred) drew a beautiful naked white woman standing defiantly before the three overly curious and swarthy-looking Spanish officers who had undressed her. In fact, female prison matrons performed the search.

"There are things more dreadful than even war and one of them is dishonor," the *New York Journal* editorialized about the Clemencia Arango incident.

This 1897 illustration of dark-skinned men viewing and touching the body of a white woman resonated powerfully with many white Americans because it aroused their racial prejudices.

"Spaniards Search Women on American Steamers."
***New York Journal*, February 12, 1897.**

Press coverage of Cisneros's escapades generated so much interest that huge crowds gathered to hear of her adventures when she appeared in New York and Washington, D.C., where President McKinley received her in the White House.

The headline criticized diplomatic inaction and suggested that only heroic, manly military-style action could save Cuban rebels.

NEW YORK JOURNAL
AND ADVERTISER.

EVANGELINA CISNEROS RESCUED BY THE JOURNAL.

An American Newspaper Accomplishes at a Single Stroke What the Red Tape of Diplomacy Failed Utterly to Bring About in Many Months.

MISS CISNEROS BEFORE AND AFTER THIRTEEN MONTHS' INCARCERATION.

THE PETITION TO THE QUEEN.

New York Journal accounts exaggerated Cisneros's light-skinned beauty, noble birth, and prison sufferings.

Nearly fifteen thousand women, including President William McKinley's wife, signed the newspaper's petition to Spain's Queen María Cristina demanding Cisneros's release.

"Evangelina Cisneros Rescued by the Journal."
***New York Journal*, October 10, 1897.**

Why did popular media accounts depict the Cubans as light-skinned and the Spanish as dark-skinned?

The importance of illustrations to the yellow press became clear in a fabled exchange between Hearst and the artist Frederic Remington. Remington, already famous for his portraits of the American West, went to Cuba to draw illustrations for the *New York Journal.* Tiring of the rebellion's slow pace, Remington told Hearst he was leaving Cuba. Hearst supposedly replied, "Please remain. You furnish the pictures, and I'll furnish the war." This exchange passed quickly into American folklore as proof of Hearst's determination to use shocking images, real or staged, to provoke a war with Spain. No evidence exists, however, that Hearst ever wrote or sent this reply. *Images as History: Atrocity Stories and Public Opinion* examines how yellow press illustrations shaped American public opinion.

The Decision to Intervene in Cuba

With the yellow press clamoring for military action, President William McKinley turned to diplomacy to end the impasse over Cuba peacefully and repeatedly asked Spain to grant Cuba more autonomy. In 1897 the Spanish government ended reconcentration by recalling Weyler and allowing Cuban peasants placed in reconcentration compounds to return to their homes. Spain also announced a plan for limited Cuban self-government, inviting protests from all sides. Cuban rebels urged Americans to help them attain complete independence. Meanwhile Cubans still loyal to Spain reacted angrily to the limited autonomy plan and rioted in the streets of Havana. An alarmed McKinley decided to send the *Maine* battleship to Havana to deter loyalists from organizing attacks on Americans or their property. Acting within the boundaries of acceptable international practice, McKinley expected the battleship's presence (with the implied threat of bombardments) to restore calm to Havana. Events in February, 1898, however, conspired against McKinley's effort to resolve the crisis peacefully. First Hearst's *Journal* published a private letter written by the Spanish ambassador, which described McKinley as "weak and a bidder for the admiration of the crowd." Although tame compared with the vicious statements American newspapers routinely made about the president, the published letter outraged the public.

> "Worst Insult to the United States in Its History."
>
> Yellow press headline regarding Spanish ambassador's disparaging comments about McKinley

Next the *Maine* exploded in Havana Harbor. After a month of press speculation about the cause of the explosion, an official naval investigation erroneously blamed a Spanish harbor mine for the disaster, rather than the real culprit: faulty ship design that caused an internal explosion, or perhaps sabotage by Cuban rebels who wanted the United States to declare war on Spain. In the weeks immediately following the sinking of the *Maine*, McKinley tried unsuccessfully to convince Spain to grant Cuba independence and to calm calls for war from Congress. "I have been through one war," McKinley told a friend, referring to his military service in the Civil War. "I have seen the dead piled up, and I do not want to see another." For many other Americans, however, memories of brutal Civil War battles had faded. They enthusiastically viewed war as a manly adventure that would instill discipline and vigor in American men. The assistant secretary of the navy, Theodore Roosevelt, championed this competing view, writing to a friend in 1897, "I should welcome almost any war, for I think this country needs one."

With the Democrats championing war, Republicans feared that McKinley's resistance to fighting might hurt the party at the polls. Some senators even suggested that Congress declare war whether McKinley agreed or not. The pressure on McKinley increased when Senator Redfield Proctor, several days before the navy released its findings on the *Maine* attack, gave the Senate a grim accounting of the appalling effects of Spain's reconcentration policy on the Cuban people. "I went to Cuba with a strong conviction that the situation had been overdrawn," Proctor noted, then went on to detail the starvation, squalor, and sickness he had seen. This sober address from a conservative Republican and stalwart friend of McKinley's convinced many wavering congressmen and Americans that the country had a humanitarian duty to save Cuba.

To head off a war, Spain made one last offer to grant Cuba increased autonomy, rejecting McKinley's call for total independence. "Mr. President, I can no longer hold back the Senate," Vice President Garrett Hobart told McKinley. "They will act without you if you do not act at once." Accepting that he had failed to negotiate an acceptable settlement to the crisis, McKinley asked Congress to

Why was McKinley unable to avoid war with Spain?

authorize an armed intervention to end the civil war in Cuba without declaring war on Spain. Congress complied. On April 24, 1898, however, Spain declared war on the United States. The next day Congress responded with its own declaration of war, dating it retroactively to April 21, 1898. The United States was now officially at war with Spain.

To underscore the nation's altruistic motives in declaring war, Colorado Senator Henry M. Teller added an amendment to the war resolutions that specifically disavowed any intention of annexing Cuba. The **Teller Amendment (1898)** promised "to leave the government and control of the [Cuban] Island to its people" at the end of the Spanish-American War. Congress made no such promise to other colonized peoples under Spanish control in the Caribbean and Pacific.

> "I could not have told where those darned islands were within two thousand miles."
>
> President McKINLEY on the location of the Philippines before the Spanish-American War

Fighting the War against Spain

America's victory in the Spanish-American War, which lasted from April to August 1898, paved the way for U.S. territorial expansion in the Caribbean and Pacific. One week after the war began, American Commodore George Dewey sailed into Manila Harbor, in the Spanish colony of the Philippines, (**19.2**) and destroyed the Spanish Pacific fleet. Why, Americans wondered, did the navy fight the first battle to liberate Cuba halfway around the world in the Philippines, an archipelago of seven thousand islands in the Pacific Ocean? By eliminating the Spanish Pacific fleet, Dewey prevented it from sailing to Cuba. Losing its Pacific fleet also put added pressure on Spain to sue for peace. Dewey's stunning victory at Manila catapulted the Philippines into the spotlight, and Americans learned that the Filipinos were in the midst of their own rebellion against Spain. At first the Filipino rebels, who controlled the interior, welcomed the Americans as liberators. "I have studied the Constitution of the United States, and I find in it no authority for colonies and I have no fear," rebel leader Emilio Aguinaldo told one American general. Time would prove Aguinaldo wrong.

Besides securing the Philippines the McKinley administration also used the war against Spain as a pretext for settling the festering question of annexing Hawaii that had divided Americans for nearly a decade. Americans had a long history of

19.2 The Spanish-American War, 1898
The U.S. Navy first attacked the Spanish in the Philippines, and then blockaded Cuba as U.S. forces invaded.

Why did the United States first attack Spain in the Philippines?

involvement in Hawaiian affairs. By the 1880s American-owned sugar plantations dominated the Hawaiian economy, American missionaries had waged a successful campaign to eradicate native religions, and the U.S. Navy had established a permanent naval station at Pearl Harbor on the island of Oahu. Responding to popular discontent over the erosion of native Hawaiians' economic standing and cultural traditions, when Queen Liliuokalani assumed the throne in 1891 she promised to curtail U.S. dominance over Hawaiian politics and agriculture. Within two years, however, American businessmen and missionaries working on the islands (representing 5 percent of the islands' population) overthrew Queen Liliuokalani. U.S. Marines sent to protect American property ensured the revolution's success. Thousands of Hawaiians took to the streets to protest the coup, to no avail.

The new Hawaiian government requested annexation by the United States, a request that President McKinley endorsed to foster U.S. commercial interests in the Pacific. In 1897, however, the Hawaiian Patriotic League successfully blocked a formal U.S. takeover by presenting the Senate with a 556-page anti-annexation petition signed by over half of the native-born Hawaiian population. Faced with Hawaiians' overwhelming opposition to annexation, the Senate voted the measure down. A year later, however, with the Spanish-American War underway, the Senate reversed course. Supporters of annexation successfully argued that U.S. ships headed to the Philippines needed guaranteed access to the naval way-station in Pearl Harbor. Deciding to put its own strategic and economic needs ahead of Hawaiians' desire to remain independent, the United States assumed sovereignty over Hawaii on July 7, 1898, when McKinley signed a congressional joint resolution authorizing annexation. The president appointed a territorial governor to head the Hawaiian government, and in 1900 Congress granted Hawaiians the right to elect the territorial legislature.

Meanwhile military planners focused on defeating the Spanish in Cuba. The accompanying map, "Spanish-American War, 1898" (19.2) illustrates how the navy immediately blockaded Cuba, trapping the Spanish Atlantic Fleet in Santiago. America's traditionally small peacetime army, however, was woefully unprepared to train and equip the thousands of volunteers enlisting

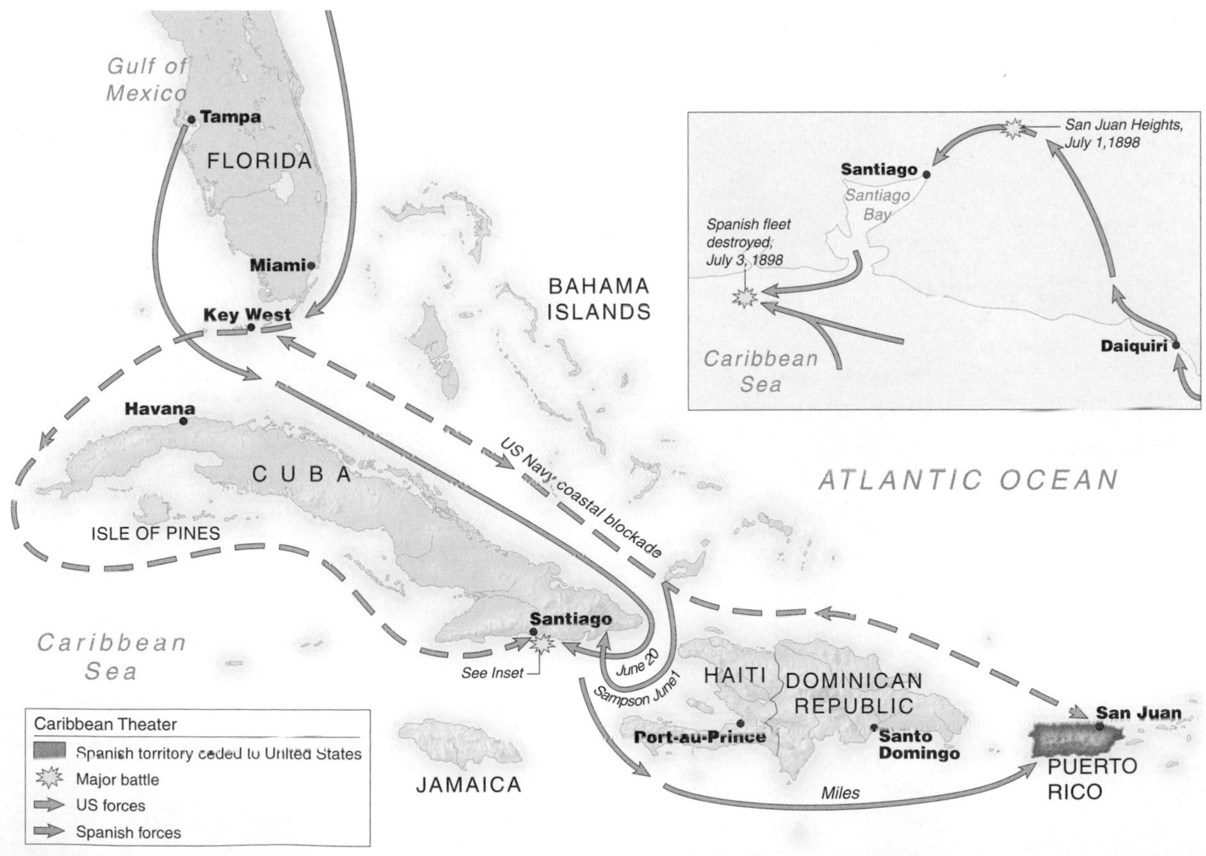

Why did Hawaii lose its independence in a war to liberate Cuba?

throughout the country. Theodore Roosevelt resigned as assistant secretary of the navy and formed the First U.S. Volunteer Calvary by recruiting Americans from wildly diverse backgrounds. Many of the recruits had personal connections to Colonel Roosevelt, a result of his eclectic lifestyle that included attending Harvard, hunting expeditions in the West, and a stint as police commissioner in New York City. Dubbed the **Rough Riders**, this collection of cowboys, Ivy League athletes, city police officers, and Pawnee scouts was one of the few volunteer units that fought in the war. Although American forces swelled from 28,000 to 275,000, the vast majority never left the United States.

On June 22, seventeen thousand U.S. troops landed in Cuba to join Cuban rebels on a slow march through heavy jungle to the port city of Santiago, which contained the bulk of the Spanish navy and army. Hidden Spanish sharpshooters harassed U.S. soldiers as they made their way to the San Juan Heights, the outlying hills that encircled Santiago. On July 1, the Americans, under the command of General William Shafter, attacked 750 Spanish soldiers along the San Juan Heights.

"I have seen many illustrations and pictures of this charge on the San Juan hills, but none of them seem to show it just as I remember it," recalled journalist Richard Harding Davis, who watched the charge from the sidelines. Like most illustrations of the battle seen in newspapers at the time, this painting (**19.3**) shows waves of eager American soldiers advancing with the flag flying, suggesting "an invincible overpowering weight of numbers," Davis noted. Yet, he continued, "I think the thing which impressed one the most, when our men started from cover, was that they were so few. It almost seemed as if someone had made an awful and terrible mistake. One's instinct was to call to them to come back." Roosevelt led the Rough Riders to the top of the San Juan Heights, a feat that garnered Roosevelt and the unit much acclaim. They stood alongside African American troops from the Ninth and Tenth Calvary who had actually reached the top first, a fact that Roosevelt and the mainstream media failed to mention when celebrating the victory.

The battle provided another opportunity for the yellow press to whip up war fervor on the home front. Responding to (false) rumors that Spanish soldiers had mutilated the corpses of American servicemen killed during the clash, a *Judge* magazine cover (**19.4**) pictured a Spaniard drenched in the

19.3 Charge up the San Juan Heights, 1898 This painting depicted the charge up the San Juan Heights as glorious and heroic, with the flag flying and no casualties. Illustrations like this contributed to the image of the Spanish-American War as a "splendid little war."

How accurate were the legends that surrounded the charge up the San Juan Heights?

blood of American soldiers who lay at his feet. In one hand the ape-like figure holds the bloody knife responsible for the recent atrocity. His other hand rests on the gravestone of U.S. sailors whom he allegedly killed by exploding the *Maine*. A brute that trampled on the American flag, the image reinforced earlier yellow press portrayals of Spain as a beast that the United States needed to subdue. The caricature also fed into racist notions of white supremacy—just like African Americans at home, and soon the Filipinos abroad, the dark-skinned Spanish posed a threat to the civilized world. In future conflicts American wartime propaganda used strikingly similar images to arouse passionate hatred of the nation's German and Japanese enemies.

Legendary accounts attributed the American success in charging up the San Juan Heights to heroic frontal charges; in fact, the Americans' three Gatling machine guns made the decisive difference. Believing his exhausted troops could go no farther after reaching the top, General Shafter decided to lay siege to Santiago instead of attacking the city directly. While American troops encircled the city atop the surrounding hills, U.S. naval ships blocked the port, thus trapping the bulk of the Spanish navy and army in Santiago. When the Spanish fleet made a dash to leave the harbor on July 3, American ships sank or beached every Spanish vessel. On July 17, Spanish troops surrendered the city and Cuba to the Americans. After defeating the Spanish in Cuba, U.S. forces landed in Puerto Rico, also a Caribbean Spanish colony, where they encountered only token opposition. American troops fought one more battle to take Manila on August 13, having not yet received word that the war between the United States and Spain had ended the day before.

19.4 *The Spanish Brute,* 1898
This wartime caricature portrayed the Spanish as bloodthirsty beasts who murdered and mutilated American servicemen.

The war concluded on a sour note, however, as the high costs of fighting in the tropics without adequate preparations became clear. With a limited understanding of how malaria, yellow fever, and typhoid spread among humans, U.S. Army physicians could not stop these tropical diseases from ravaging the soldier population that occupied Cuba during the summer of 1898. Victory celebrations among U.S. troops soon gave way to panic when hundreds of soldiers fell ill and healthy young men became hollow-eyed, walking skeletons. It was "a heartbreaking sight" to see her husband, a yellow fever victim whose weight had dropped from 165 pounds to 89 pounds, Grace Paulding recalled. He needed a year's nursing before he could work again.

Despairing over the lack of qualified hospital attendants, the Surgeon General turned in desperation to the female nurses offering their services to the military. Eventually, 1,500 professional and Red Cross female nurses worked side by side with army doctors at home and overseas. Overall the Americans counted 385 officers and soldiers killed in combat (excluding those killed on the *Maine*), and nearly 2,000 deaths from disease.

The peace treaty, signed on December 10, 1898, ended the Spanish-American War and set the terms of the U.S. victory. In the **Treaty of Paris**, Spain relinquished its claim to Cuba, and the United States received Puerto Rico, some smaller Caribbean islands, and the Pacific island group of Guam. In return for $20 million, Spain turned the Philippines over to the United States. How this territorial transfer would affect the political future of the Philippines remained in doubt. Did the United States intend to grant the Philippines independence or keep the territory as a colony? Americans soon offered competing visions on how to resolve this question.

Despite the idealistic guarantees given in the Teller Amendment, Cuba became an independent nation in name only. The United States linked the withdrawal of American occupation troops to several concessions from Cuba. The **Platt Amendment (1901)** required Cuba to give the United States the right to maintain a naval base at Guantánamo Bay and to intervene militarily in Cuba to protect "life, property, and individual liberty." Besides granting the United States a privileged trading relationship with Cuba, the Cuban government also needed permission from the United States before entering into treaties with other nations. The former Spanish colony essentially became a U.S. protectorate, a relationship in which a superior power assumes authority over a weaker country or territory to protect it from invasion and to share in managing its affairs. The United States took advantage of these rights and occupied Cuba numerous times until Congress repealed the Platt Amendment in 1934. The United States continued to maintain a naval base at Guantánamo Bay, using it to jail and interrogate foreign prisoners captured during the wars in Afghanistan and Iraq that began in 2001 and 2003, respectively.

In his successful 1900 reelection bid against Democrat William Jennings Bryan, McKinley made a strong connection between events at home and abroad. One campaign poster (**19.5**) featured portraits of the president and his war hero running mate, Theodore Roosevelt. The individual vignettes reminded Americans of the devastating 1890s depression and Cuban suffering under Spanish rule. It then noted that domestic prosperity returned and social justice prevailed overseas once the United States stepped out into the world. The claim that American intervention improved life for both U.S. and world citizens became a powerful argument in favor of constructing an American empire. Bryan focused his campaign on the evils of imperialism, but McKinley carried the election with a "full dinner pail" slogan that emphasized restored prosperity.

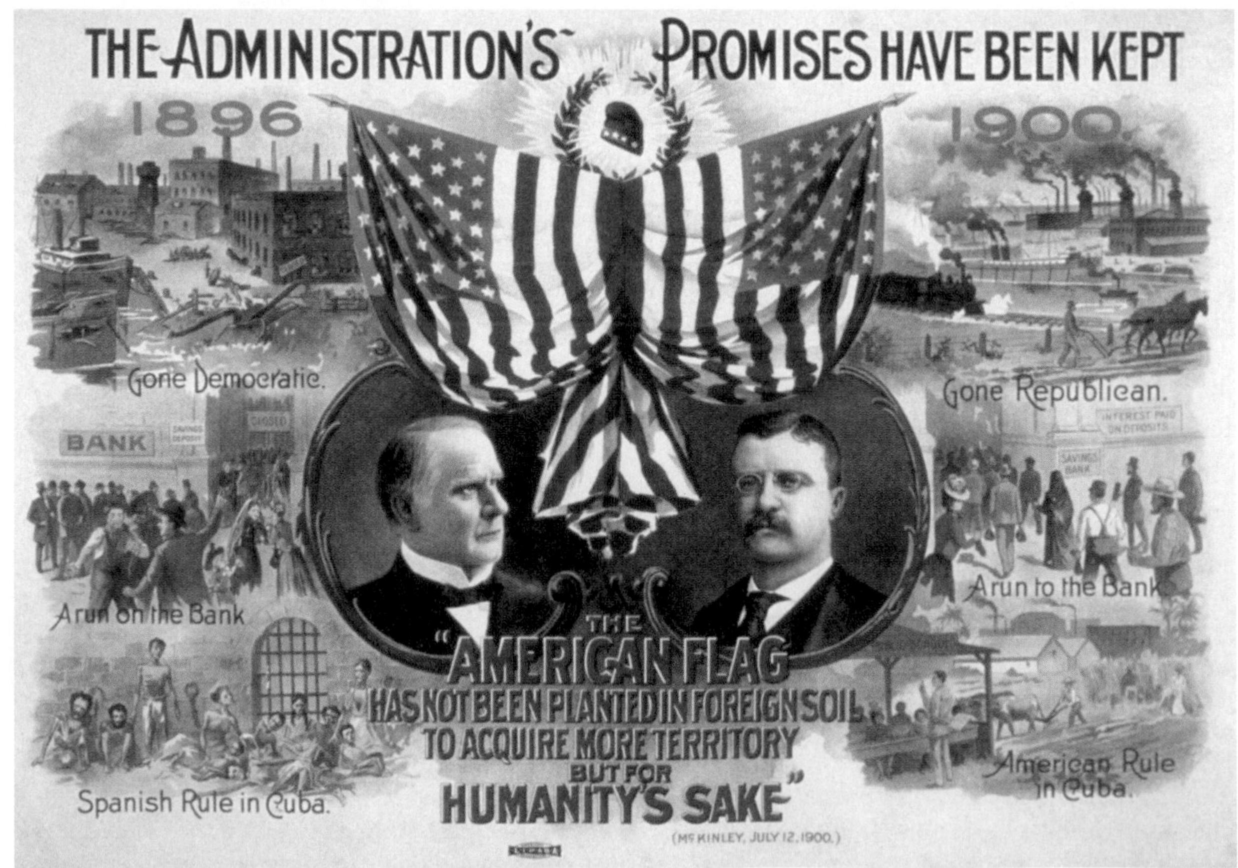

19.5 McKinley Campaign Poster, 1900
This poster helped voters visualize how expanding the nation's global influence created trading opportunities that made the whole country more prosperous. Emphasizing the American humanitarian mission abroad resonated with Progressive reformers and religious groups dedicated to spreading American values and institutions.

What steps did the United States take to construct a formal and informal empire after its victory over Spain?

Creating an American Empire

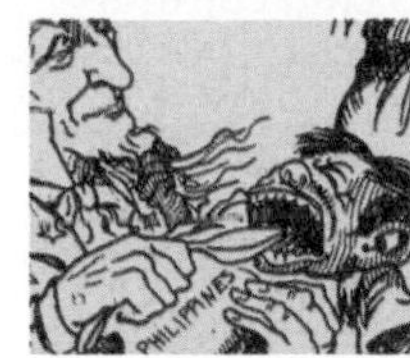

The Senate's razor-thin ratification of the Treaty of Paris, with just two votes to spare, ignited a strident internal debate over whether the United States should annex or free the Philippines. In the wake of ratification, both imperialists and anti-imperialists offered competing economic, political, and racial arguments about the wisdom of colonizing the Philippines. Unwilling to simply leave their fate in the hands of American politicians, Filipinos revolted against U.S. forces. The rebellion soon evolved into a vicious all-out war with high casualties on both sides.

The Debate over Colonies

In a risky strategic move that divided Democrats, party leader William Jennings Bryan had urged anti-imperialist Democratic senators to support ratification of the Treaty of Paris so that the United States could grant the Philippines independence once Spain relinquished control. But after the Senate had ratified the treaty, the majority of Republicans fought to keep the Philippines as a colony. Maps in the popular press helped Americans visualize the strategic and commercial importance of the nation's new island possessions. The "Map of the China Seas ... Under the National Flags, 1898" (**19.6**), published in *Harper's Weekly*, portrayed key parts of the imperialist argument for building an American empire in East Asia. By showing the proximity of the Philippine islands to European colonial possessions in East Asia, the map reinforced President McKinley's claim that another European power would certainly colonize the islands if the United States withdrew. The map also illustrated the imperialist slogan, "trade follows the flag." The closeness of the Philippines to China, for example, underscored the usefulness of the colony for developing a strong trading relationship between the United States and China.

A competing economic argument came from the Anti-Imperialist League, an organization that attracted a broad cross-section of politicians, Progressive reformers, writers, industrialists, and labor activists who opposed overseas colonial expansion. How would markets for American industrialized goods suddenly materialize in undeveloped Asian countries, the league asked. Anti-imperialists had a point, as the notion of a vast, untapped China market proved to be a seductive myth. Europe, not China, remained the most important overseas market for American goods throughout the twentieth century. Instead of economic gains anti-imperialists foresaw decades of costly expenses to maintain colonial outposts.

Debate also centered on the ability of the Filipinos to govern themselves. On the imperialist side,

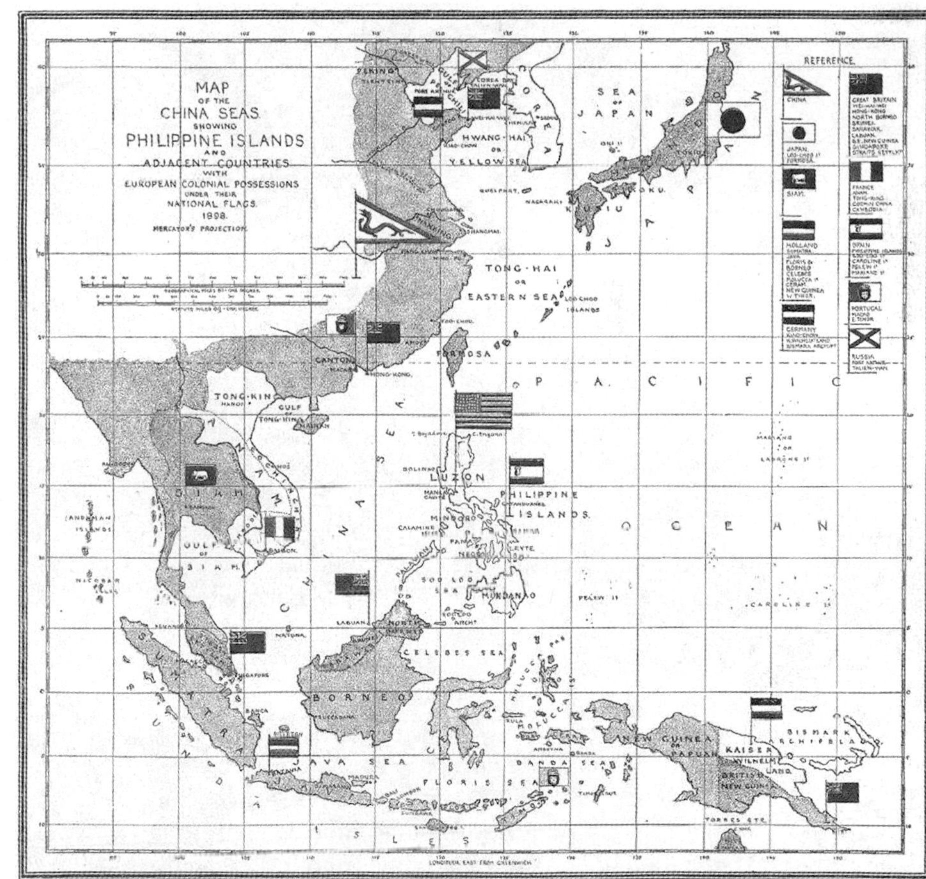

19.6 **"Map of the China Seas ... Under the National Flags, 1898"**
This *Harper's Weekly* map depicted the United States taking its rightful place alongside other world powers with colonial empires in East Asia.

What competing economic arguments did imperialists and anti-imperialists offer about colonies?

19.7 ***Give the Child Over to the Nurse, Uncle, and It Will Stop Crying***
Uncle Sam protects a Filipino child from ignorance and crime, portrayed as a savage black nurse, by feeding him education and civilization. This 1899 pro-expansionist political cartoon accused anti-imperialists like Hoar of failing to realize that the racially inferior Filipinos were too immature to rule themselves, no matter how much the Filipinos protested.

President McKinley adopted a strong paternalistic stance, arguing that "We could not leave them to themselves—they were unfit for self-government, and they would soon have anarchy and misrule worse then Spain's was." Caricatures helped imperialists publicize their case, incorporating popularly accepted notions of Americans' racial and moral superiority to so-called uncivilized peoples. This political cartoon contained strong racial undertones (**19.7**), depicting Uncle Sam as a nurturing white father who protects the wailing savage Filipino child from Independence (pictured as a depraved mammy-like figure) and from anti-imperialists like Senator George Hoar, a Republican from Massachusetts. The majority of Filipinos had converted to Catholicism under Spanish rule, a religion that most Americans distrusted. Besides spreading Anglo-Saxon cultural and political values, McKinley called upon Americans to take control of Filipinos' spiritual lives by turning them into Protestants.

Anti-imperialists viewed the question of governing the Filipinos differently. They claimed that subjugating the Philippines to imperial rule violated the principles of representative government outlined in the Constitution. Their slogan, "the Constitution follows the flag," conveyed their belief that Congress could not withhold constitutional rights, including the right to self-government, from colonial subjects.

In the 1900–1904 Insular Cases, the Supreme Court affirmed Congress's authority to govern the Philippines, Hawaii, and Puerto Rico as colonies. The court upheld the acquisition of colonies as constitutional and ruled that colonial populations did not become American citizens until the United States incorporated the colonies as territories. The justices offered a more mixed response on the question of extending constitutional rights to colonial subjects. In these cases the court denied colonial subjects some constitutional protections, such as procedural rights that guaranteed a fair trial, but held that Congress could not abridge the "natural rights" of free speech and religion. Recognition of these limited rights did not appease anti-imperialists, however. "Yes, as near as I can make out the Constitution follows the flag—but doesn't quite catch up with it," quipped Secretary of War Elihu Root. In 1900 Congress granted inhabitants of Hawaii and Alaska American citizenship, making them eligible for full protection under the Bill of Rights. Puerto Ricans had to wait until 1917. Filipinos never held American citizenship.

Finally some anti-imperialists envisioned that the burden of colonies would detract from solving racial problems at home. In the political cartoon *Civilization Begins at Home* (**19.8**), a woman symbolizing justice tries to draw McKinley's attention away from the map of the Philippines to the problems of racial injustice just outside his window. Other anti-imperialists, however, had racist reasons for opposing colonies. "Why do we as a people want

How did white Americans' racial views influence the debate over colonizing the Philippines?

> "[T]here was nothing left for us to do but to take them all, and to educate the Filipinos, and uplift and civilize and Christianize them."
>
> President McKINLEY explaining the imperialist vision for annexing the Philippines as a colony

to incorporate into our citizenship ten millions more of different or of differing race?" asked Senator Ben Tillman (D-SC) on the floor of the Senate.

In 1899 the British poet Rudyard Kipling entered the American debate over colonizing the Philippines when the popular magazine *McClure's* published his poem, "The White Man's Burden—The United States and the Philippine Islands." Kipling pictured Americans embracing "**the white man's burden**," the Anglo-Saxon quest to better the lives of so-called racially inferior peoples by spreading Western economic, cultural, and spiritual values and institutions. To Kipling, the term *white man* referred to more than skin color. It served as a symbol for people who embraced Anglo-Saxon moral standards and values. Theodore Roosevelt described the poem as "rather poor poetry, but good sense from the expansionist standpoint" when he sent it to Massachusetts's Republican senator Henry Cabot Lodge, who shared Roosevelt's views on expanding U.S. global influence. Black newspapers offered a competing vision, publishing an array of poems and editorials that detailed "the black man's burden" of living in a country that accepted Jim Crow practices in the South. The poem is reprinted, along with the satirical response from an anti-imperialist activist, in *Competing Visions: The White Man's Burden* (page 576).

19.8 *Civilization Begins at Home*
In this 1898 illustration, a woman holding the scales of justice tries to draw President William McKinley's attention away from the Philippine-American War to the grisly lynchings of blacks at home.

Competing Visions

THE WHITE MAN'S BURDEN

For American imperialists, Rudyard Kipling's 1899 poem "The White Man's Burden" offered a strong justification for annexing the Philippines. The poem's title became synonymous with the imperialist civilizing mission. Some disagreed, suggesting that Kipling portrayed colonies as burdens rather than assets. Others saw the poem as rife with irony. Social reformer and poet Ernest Crosby, president of the Anti-Imperialist League of New York, offered a competing vision of "the white man's burden" in his 1899 poem "The Real 'White Man's Burden.'" What views do these poems offer on the benefits and drawbacks of colonization?

Rudyard Kipling, "The White Man's Burden"

Take up the White Man's burden—
Send forth the best ye breed—
Go bind your sons to exile
To serve your captives' need;
To wait in heavy harness,
On fluttered folk and wild—
Your new-caught, sullen peoples,
Half-devil and half-child.

Take up the White Man's burden—
In patience to abide,
To veil the threat of terror
And check the show of pride;
By open speech and simple,
An hundred times made plain
To seek another's profit,
And work another's gain.

Take up the White Man's burden—
The savage wars of peace—
Fill full the mouth of Famine
And bid the sickness cease;
And when your goal is nearest
The end for others sought,
Watch sloth and heathen Folly
Bring all your hopes to nought.

Take up the White Man's burden—
No tawdry rule of kings,
But toil of serf and sweeper—
The tale of common things.
The ports ye shall not enter,
The roads ye shall not tread,
Go mark them with your living,
And mark them with your dead.

Take up the White Man's burden—
And reap his old reward:
The blame of those ye better,
The hate of those ye guard—
The cry of hosts ye humour
(Ah, slowly!) toward the light: —
"Why brought he us from bondage,
Our loved Egyptian night?"

Take up the White Man's burden—
Ye dare not stoop to less—
Nor call too loud on Freedom
To cloke your weariness;
By all ye cry or whisper,
By all ye leave or do,
The silent, sullen peoples
Shall weigh your gods and you.

Take up the White Man's burden—
Have done with childish days—
The lightly proferred laurel,
The easy, ungrudged praise.
Comes now, to search your manhood
Through all the thankless years
Cold, edged with dear-bought wisdom,
The judgment of your peers!

Ernest Crosby, "The Real 'White Man's Burden'"

With apologies to Rudyard Kipling

Take up the White Man's burden.
Send forth your sturdy kin,
And load them down with Bibles
And cannon-balls and gin.
Throw in a few diseases
To spread the tropic climes,
For there the healthy niggers
Are quite behind the times.

And don't forget the factories.
On those benighted shores
They have no cheerful iron mills,
Nor eke department stores.
They never work twelve hours a day
And live in strange content,
Altho they never have to pay
A single sou of rent.

Take up the White Man's burden,
And teach the Philippines
What interest and taxes are
And what a mortgage means.
Give them electrocution chairs,
And prisons, too, galore,
And if they seem inclined to kick,
Then spill their heathen gore.

They need our labor question, too,
And politics and fraud—
We've made a pretty mess at home,
Let's make a mess abroad.
And let us ever humbly pray
The Lord of Hosts may deign
To stir our feeble memories
Lest we forget—the *Maine.*

Take up the White's Man's burden.
To you who thus succeed
In civilizing savage hordes,
They owe a debt, indeed;
Concessions, pensions, salaries,
And privilege and right—
With outstretched hands you raised
 to bless
Grab everything in sight.

Take up the White Man's burden
And if you write in verse,
Flatter your nation's vices
And strive to make them worse.
Then learn that if with pious words
You ornament each phrase,
In a world of canting hypocrites
This kind of business pays.

Is Kipling's poem best understood as imperialist propaganda or a satire of the civilizing mission?

The Philippine-American War

On January 20, 1899, the rebel Filipino leader Emilio Aguinaldo declared the Philippines independent of the United States. He formed a provisional government that concentrated power in the hands of elites from the main island of Luzon to rule the ethnically and religiously diverse societies that inhabited the archipelago. Fighting began a few weeks later on February 4, 1899, when U.S. and Filipino patrols clashed in the darkness, igniting a full-scale battle on the outskirts of Manila. The U.S. government called the conflict the Philippine Insurrection, using *insurrection*, a term used to describe an illegitimate revolt against an established government, to underscore that the Philippines was a U.S. colony, not an independent nation capable of waging war. The conflict nonetheless soon assumed the scope of a full-fledged war. In the Philippine-American War, fought from 1899 to 1902, the United States eventually defeated Filipino rebel forces. The cost of the two-and-a-half-year war in human lives differentiated it immediately from the quick American victory in Cuba. Between 1899 and 1902, 70,000 U.S. soldiers (nearly 70 percent of the army) fought a grueling war against the insurrectionists, and 4,234 lost their lives. Estimates place the number of Filipino soldiers and civilians killed as high as 220,000.

The rebels used conventional warfare tactics at first, but eventually turned to ambushes, sniping, and sabotage to drive out U.S. occupying forces. American soldiers called the Filipino way of war "amigo warfare" (amigo being the Spanish word for friend) because the guerilla fighters posed as friendly peasants during the day, then fought for the rebel army at night. The logistical difficulties of supplying troops with food and adequate medical care as they marched through the jungle in search of insurgents contributed to American soldiers' miseries. To uproot the guerilla forces, the U.S. Army adopted a mix of persuasive and coercive tactics. In many villages the army built roads, improved sanitation, vaccinated civilians, and created schools. Tens of thousands of Filipinos aided the U.S. Army during the rebellion by providing information and supplies, a sign of their gratefulness for American-engineered improvements in their daily life and their own religious, class, or ethnic disagreements with the Aguinaldo-led independence movement. Rebel soldiers, however, dealt harshly with civilians who refused to supply them with food or told the Americans where to find insurgent hideouts.

Benevolent policies won over only half of the archipelago, however. In provinces where these reforms failed to curtail guerilla attacks, U.S. troops lashed out with increasing brutality. "With an enemy like this to fight, it is not surprising that the boys should soon adopt 'no quarter' as a motto, and fill the blacks [Filipinos] full of lead before finding out whether or not they are friends or enemies," a soldier from Utah wrote home. American soldiers burned villages and crops to deprive rebels of shelter and food, tactics that created a starving civilian refugee population and encouraged resentful peasant men to join Aguinaldo's rebel force. Exposés in the American press and Senate investigations revealed the inventive tortures the army used to extract information from captured Filipino rebels, fueling the ongoing debate over whether the United States was civilizing or conquering the Philippines. In the "water cure," for example, interrogators shoved a bamboo shoot down a victim's throat to keep his mouth open while they poured water into his throat and nose until his stomach swelled and he could not breathe, and then pushed on the stomach to expel the water. The victim had a few minutes to release the desired information before his interrogators repeated the entire process.

> "Every tree seemed to shoot at us!"
>
> An American soldier confronting Filipino rebel guerilla tactics

Justifying annexation of the Philippines as part of the "white man's burden" posed a particularly thorny dilemma for the six thousand African American soldiers fighting in their own segregated regiments to subdue the Filipino rebels. White soldiers constantly referred to Filipinos as "niggers," the same derogatory term they used when speaking about their African American comrades. Knowing that many African American civilians opposed the war as "an unholy war of conquest," a term coined by activist minister Henry M. Turner, black soldiers nevertheless hoped that their honorable military record would help create more opportunities for African Americans at home and in the military. Filipino rebels posted signs on trees that chastised African Americans for fighting "against people who are struggling for recognition and freedom, [while] your people in America are being lynched and disfranchised by the same who are trying to compel

What tactics did the U.S. Army adopt to fight the Filipino rebels?

us to believe that their government will deal justly and fairly by us." Yet these Filipino appeals to lay down their arms had little effect on most African American troops, who focused instead on avenging the lives of comrades killed by Filipino rebels. One exception was Corporal David Fagan, a black soldier who had fought in Cuba and defected to the Filipino army shortly after arriving in the Philippines. He was one of five black soldiers who deserted to the other side. Fagan's reputation grew to mythic proportions as he eluded capture and successfully organized guerilla raids on his former comrades-in-arms.

Rebel leader Emilio Aguinaldo was not so fortunate. In March 1901 a captured messenger revealed the location of Aguinaldo's hideaway 50 miles into the jungle. To capture Aguinaldo General Frederick Funston assembled a group of Macabebe scouts, a Philippine ethnic group that had traditionally rendered military service to Spain and now joined the U.S. fight against the rebels. Posing as reinforcement rebel troops, the Macabebe soldiers entered Aguinaldo's camp accompanied by five American soldiers pretending to be prisoners. The group arrived as a birthday celebration for Aguinaldo was under-way, and when the infiltrators reached for their weapons, Aguinaldo's guards assumed they were preparing to fire an honor salute. Instead the Macabebe scouts began shooting, the signal for the rest of Funston's men, who were waiting on the perimeter, to invade the camp. Aguinaldo's guards fled in panic, leaving the rebel leader in the hands of the Americans.

A chastened Aguinaldo called on his followers to lay down their arms and accept U.S. rule. One by one Aguinaldo's generals surrendered, and the war ground to a halt. Theodore Roosevelt, who became president after McKinley's 1901 assassination (see Chapter 18), declared the war over on July 4, 1902. American troops nonetheless remained in the Philippines for another eleven years to subdue separate revolts by Muslim Moro tribal leaders in remote islands of the Philippines.

In 1900 William Howard Taft became the first civilian Governor General of the Philippines. When the war ended he expanded humanitarian efforts to build roads and schools, and improve sanitation. Taft also convinced Congress to purchase church-held land from the Vatican, which the colonial administration then helped peasants purchase with low-cost mortgages. To put the debate over annexing the Philippines to rest, the government sponsored exhibits at the 1904 St. Louis World's Fair that championed the imperialist vision of colonization. In the Philippine Reservation display, visitors walked through six reconstructed Filipino villages and watched partially clothed members of remote Filipino tribes demonstrate native practices that included feasts of dog and headhunting. By inviting tribes with the most exotic customs to participate, organizers intended to juxtapose the primitiveness of Filipino culture with the civilizing influence of U.S. rule. Photographs such as this (**19.9**) captured the U.S. effort to provide illiterate, nearly naked Filipinos with a Western education. The curious American visitors in the gallery observing a white female instructor teaching her pupils appear unconcerned about putting these people on display as a tourist attraction. Instead Americans who talked with Filipinos at the exhibit quickly "disabused themselves of any impression that the natives could take care of themselves," one newspaper reported. Other displays at the World's Fair championed America's scientific, economic, and cultural achievements. Collectively these exhibits suggested that as a leading nation in the civilized world the United States had the duty and right to become a colonial power.

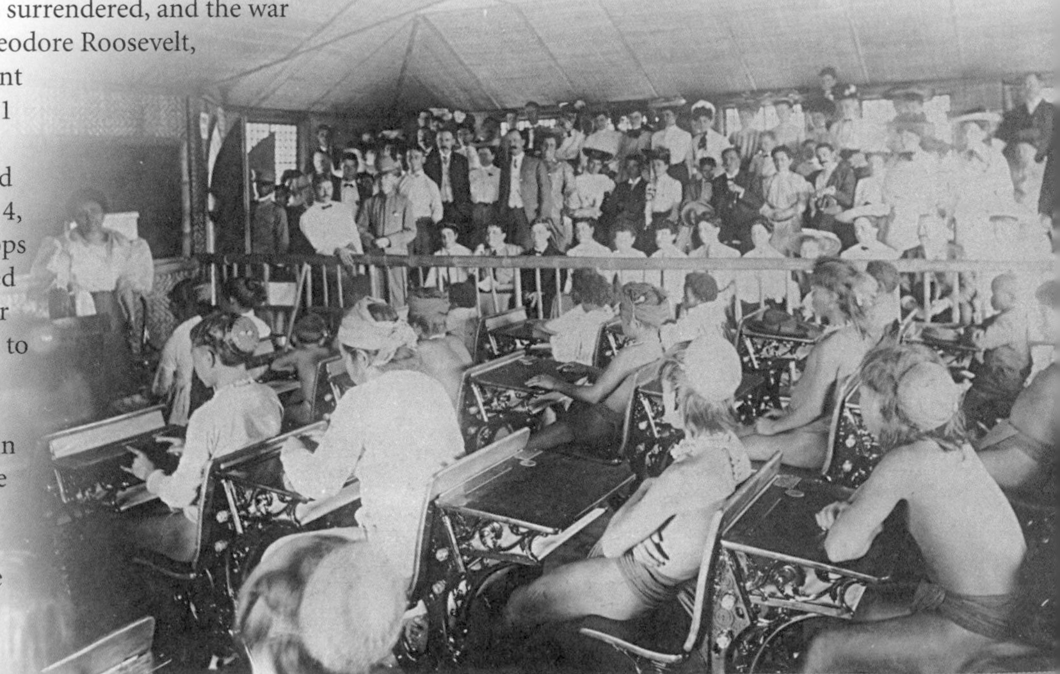

19.9 American Rule in the Philippines
The 1904 St. Louis World's Fair included exhibits on American efforts to school native tribes in the Philippines, turning these exotically dressed people into tourist attractions.

How did imperialists try to quell debate over colonizing the Philippines?

America and East Asia

The United States fought a war of conquest in the Philippines to secure an independent trade route to East Asia only to discover that the coveted China market was in danger of disappearing. To prevent the world's leading powers from carving China up into formal colonies at the turn of the century, the United States turned to diplomacy, scoring an impressive victory when it convinced these nations to keep Chinese trade open to all. Americans also viewed their nation's role in negotiating an end to the Russo-Japanese War in 1905 as an additional sign of America's growing world stature. Not all international conflicts in this period originated outside the United States, however. In 1907 President Roosevelt used diplomacy to smooth over the crisis that arose in Japanese-American relations when California initiated a campaign to segregate and ban Japanese immigrants.

The Open Door in China

Throughout the nineteenth century China granted most-favored trading status (commercial privileges) to every world power that asked. This strategy prevented any one foreign nation from gaining too much power over the Chinese economy and helped China remain independent in an age when Europe and Japan colonized many Asian lands. Any nation contemplating a campaign to colonize China risked provoking the wrath of angry competitors eager to protect their own access to Chinese trade.

In the 1880s and 1890s, American Protestant missionaries began venturing forth into the interior of China, away from the ports where foreign businessmen concentrated their commercial activity. In their letters to American churches, missionaries exaggerated Chinese interest in Western agricultural crops such as wheat and cotton. By whetting public curiosity about a vast Chinese market, missionaries hoped to bolster domestic support for their religious work in China. The debate over colonizing the Philippines also heightened the allure of an untapped Chinese market for U.S. goods.

> "There are 400,000,000 active stomachs in China, and each cries for food three times a day."
>
> A New York newspaper extolling the opportunities to export American crops

American access to these potential customers, however, appeared in danger of evaporating at the turn of the century. The world's leading nations descended on China to each claim a **sphere of influence**, the term used to describe the exclusive political and trading rights that a foreign nation enjoyed within another nation's territory. American missionaries continued their religious activities in these new spheres of influence, areas that American businessmen also coveted as future markets for U.S. goods. At this point the involved nations only demanded a monopoly over trade in a specific region, but the U.S. government feared that an outright division of China into formal colonies would soon follow. "All Europe is seizing on China and if we do not establish ourselves in the East that vast trade, from which we must draw our future prosperity" would close to the United States forever, Senator Henry Cabot Lodge warned.

Already stretched to the limit in the Caribbean and Philippines, and facing strong anti-imperialist sentiments at home, McKinley never considered sending troops to China to seize a port or territory. Instead Secretary of State John Hay circulated a carefully worded set of notes that laid the foundation for the **Open Door Policy**, a U.S.-sponsored nonbinding international agreement that kept the Chinese market open to all foreign nations. The first set of Open Door Notes asked France, Italy, Japan, and Russia to allow other nations to trade freely within their respective spheres of influence, refrain from imposing arbitrary duties on foreign goods, and allow Chinese officials to collect customs fees (thereby recognizing China's continued political control). By January 1900 Hay reported that all nations with a sphere of influence in China had

Why did Americans develop a strong interest in China at the turn of the century?

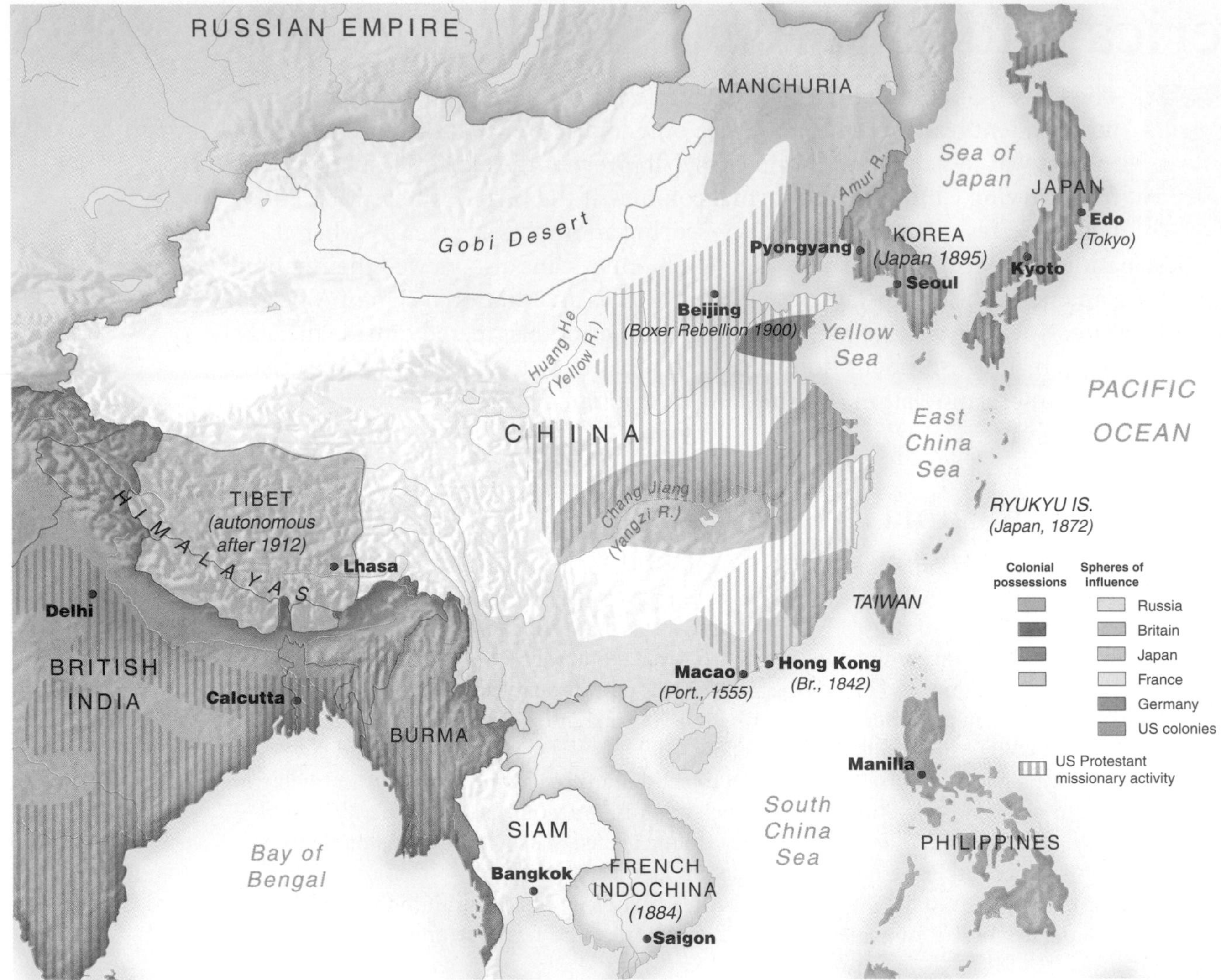

19.10 Foreign Activity in China, 1901 American missionaries and businessmen established a presence in China that the U.S. government tried to protect by negotiating with nations that had spheres of influence there.

agreed to abide by these terms. For the time being the allure of trading opportunities in the spheres of others outweighed the desire for full-fledged colonies in China. China was the only nation Hay neglected to consult in his diplomatic negotiations.

Angry over the humiliating foreign domination of China, a group of Chinese militants vowed to restore Chinese sovereignty over its land and economy. In 1900 a secret society called the Righteous and Harmonious Fists initiated a terrorist campaign to drive the "foreign devils" out of China, a crusade that some members of the Chinese imperial government secretly funded. Westerners called this group the Boxers because of the clenched fist the rebels adopted as their emblem and the militants' martial arts training. When thousands of Boxers began roaming the countryside and attacking foreigners at will, an international force of ground troops and battleships assembled to crush the insurgency. Tensions escalated dramatically when the Boxers took foreign diplomats and businessmen hostage in Beijing.

Throughout the crisis Secretary Hay worked frantically to prevent the involved nations from using the Boxer Rebellion as an excuse to colonize China. In a second round of Open Door Notes, Hay asked the same nations that had accepted the first Open Door Notes to respect the "territorial and administrative integrity" of China. To avoid any negative responses, Hay did not ask for a formal reply to his request. To further protect American missionary and economic interests in China (pictured on **19.10**), McKinley sent 2,500 U.S. soldiers to join the multinational force in freeing the foreign hostages and ending the Boxer Rebellion. As punishment for the imperial government's support of the Boxers, the international coalition demanded $333 million in indemnities from China. The United States used its share to provide scholarships for Chinese students studying at American universities.

What does this map reveal about relations between China and the world's leading powers, including the United States?

Relations with Japan

Despite the Open Door Policy, the competition for rights to control railroads, mines, and ports in China continued, and within a few years Japan and Russia fought to control the resource-rich Manchurian province of China. The Russo-Japanese War of 1904–1905 threatened to topple the careful balance of power that the United States was trying to maintain in China. Concerned that too overwhelming a Japanese victory "may possibly mean a struggle between them and us in the future," President Roosevelt offered to negotiate a peace settlement. In August 1905 a financially exhausted Japan and a militarily defeated Russia came to the peace table in Portsmouth, New Hampshire. Many Americans delighted at the sight of their president mediating a conflict between two world powers. In 1906 Roosevelt received the Nobel Peace Prize for his role in ending the Russo-Japanese War.

No sooner had Roosevelt negotiated a settlement between Japan and Russia than he faced the possibility of losing the Japanese friendship he had worked so hard to protect. In 1905 California legislators, newspapers, and labor leaders joined hands to mount a strident campaign to halt Japanese immigration. Japanese and Korean exclusion leagues urged Congress to follow the precedent established with the 1882 Chinese Exclusion Act and prohibit all Asians from entering the nation. These groups denounced Asians as a degenerative element who threatened American culture and unfairly competed for jobs that rightfully belonged to native-born white workers.

California legislators lumped all Asians together when they spoke about defending the nation from the "Yellow Peril," but Roosevelt understood the vast difference between a weak, humiliated China and a powerful, proud Japan. "If we show that we regard the Japanese as an inferior and alien race, and try to treat them as we have treated the Chinese; and if at the same time we fail to keep our navy at the highest point of efficiency and size—then we shall invite disaster," Roosevelt wrote privately. In 1906 the San Francisco Board of Education decided to send Japanese, Chinese, and Korean children to one set of segregated schools. With Japan bristling at the insult of Americans lumping Japanese together with other Asian peoples whom they viewed as inferior to themselves, Roosevelt intervened to control the damage to U.S.-Japanese relations. California agreed to revoke the segregation order in return for an end to Japanese immigration, but Hawaiian sugar planters protested that they needed Japanese workers. As a compromise Roosevelt issued an executive order that allowed Japanese workers into Hawaii. The president then negotiated a reduction in Japanese immigration to the mainland through a series of diplomatic notes between Japan and the United States. In the **Gentleman's Agreement** (1907–1908), the Japanese government agreed to deny passports to Japanese workers intending to immigrate to the United States. This informal agreement helped Japan escape the indignity of joining China as the only other nation legally banned from sending immigrant workers to the United States.

Angel Island

In the Gentleman's Agreement Japan reserved the right to issue passports to professionals and to the relatives of Japanese migrants or citizens already living in the United States. Until the United States closed this loophole in 1921, Japan gave passports to Japanese wives so they could join their husbands in the United States. Americans called these women "picture brides" because couples often exchanged photos of each other through the matchmaker who arranged long-distance marriages for Japanese men residing in the United States. The three hundred to five hundred Japanese "picture brides" who immigrated annually to the United States met their new husbands for the first time when they arrived.

The United States also experienced a surge in Chinese immigration during this period. The 1906 earthquake in San Francisco destroyed the city's birth records and without any way to prove otherwise, hundreds of Chinese men successfully claimed that they were American-born. As citizens they asserted their right to bring their families to the United States. Many brought in "paper sons," boys whose families paid a fee to Chinese men already in the United States to fraudulently claim to be their fathers.

In 1910 U.S. authorities opened up an immigration processing station on **Angel Island** in the San Francisco Bay to verify the identities of Japanese and Chinese immigrants claiming the right to enter the United States. Chinese "paper sons" endured long periods of detention on Angel Island while authorities investigated their background. Before leaving China "paper sons" memorized details about their "father," including descriptions of relatives, houses, and key events in a family's history. Once they arrived at Angel Island, inspectors quizzed sons and fathers separately and refused entry to those whose answers failed to match. Chinese men detained on Angel Island sometimes passed the time

How did domestic racial prejudices affect diplomatic relations with Japan?

by etching poetry onto the barrack walls, including one anonymous poet who expressed his angst by writing, "who was to know two streams of tears would flow upon arriving here?"

In 1919 California politicians reignited their campaign against the Japanese, successfully passing laws that made it illegal for Japanese immigrants to own property. Naturalization laws allowed just people of white or African ancestry to become citizens, preventing Japanese immigrants from seeking U.S. citizenship to circumvent these restrictions. In *Takao Ozawa v. United States* (1922), the Supreme Court held that Japanese immigrants were indeed ineligible for citizenship because they were not white. *Choices and Consequences: The Legal Construction of* "*Whiteness*" explores this decision.

The fact that Japanese picture brides bore children who were U.S. citizens, and therefore eligible to own property, did not escape the notice of those campaigning for a ban on Japanese property ownership. Senator James D. Phelan (D-CA) led the campaign to stop admitting picture brides to the United States, ominously predicting that a booming birthrate in the Japanese immigrant community would lead to Japanese dominance of California agriculture. To garner publicity for their anti-Japanese crusade, a congressional delegation traveled to Angel Island in 1920. The legislators invited news photographers to take photos (**19.11**) as they sternly examined the passports of bewildered, frightened young women, dressed in their best clothes to meet their new husbands. Fearful that rising anti-Japanese prejudice might lead to a Japanese exclusion law, Japan agreed to stop issuing passports to picture brides in 1921. Congress banned all immigration from Asia in 1924 (see Chapter 21).

19.11 **Japanese Picture Brides, 1920**
To rally public support for their drive to cut off the flow of Japanese women coming to the United States, a delegation of congressmen posed for the cameras as they examined the passports of these shy, pretty Japanese picture brides, whose ethnicity made them unwelcome.

What insights does this photo offer into issues of ethnicity and gender in the early twentieth century?

Choices and Consequences

THE LEGAL CONSTRUCTION OF "WHITENESS"

Takao Ozawa was a Japanese immigrant who lived in California and Hawaii for twenty-eight years before he applied to become a citizen of the United States. Aware that naturalization laws allowed only Caucasians and people of African ancestry to become citizens, Ozawa argued that he was white. He emphasized his complete assimilation into American society and the lightness of his skin. When the Supreme Court heard his case in 1922, the justices faced several options about how to define "whiteness."

Choices

1. Differing physical features divided the human species into white, black, and yellow races.
2. Skin color established racial identity.
3. Whiteness was a socially constructed notion with no scientific basis.
4. Assimilating into American culture made one "white."

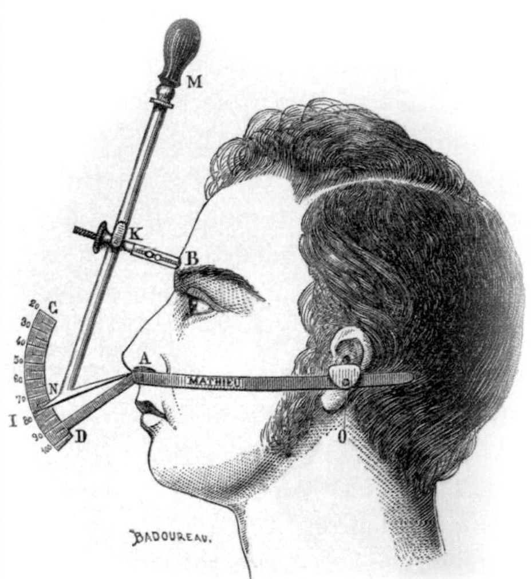

Measurement of the Head and Face, 1883

Decision

The Court rejected Ozawa's contention that skin pigmentation signified whiteness and his claim of complete assimilation. In a unanimous decision the justices ruled that "the words 'white person' are synonymous with the words 'a person of Caucasian race.'" This decision accepted contemporary anthropologists' assertions that measurements of facial features provided scientific evidence to classify the Japanese as members of the "Mongolian race."

Consequences

Within three months the court unanimously reversed its reasoning, deciding instead that whiteness was a socially, not scientifically, constructed category. When Indian immigrant Bhagat Singh Thind applied for citizenship, he argued that anthropologists categorized Asian Indians as Caucasians. In rejecting Thind's claim of whiteness, the Supreme Court now ruled that "the words 'free white persons' are words of common speech, to be interpreted in accordance with the understanding of the common man." Deciding who was legally white now depended on the whims of the larger culture, not the claims of scientists.

Continuing Controversies

What determines racial identity?

Well into the twentieth century, many Americans continued to believe that biologically based racial differences existed, even within the Caucasian race. In the 1920s the United States severely curtailed immigration from eastern and southern Europe, viewing northern Europeans as racially superior (see Chapter 21). The fear that light-skinned blacks were "passing" as whites caused many Southern states to bar individuals with any African ancestry, the so-called "one-drop" of blood rule, from using "whites-only" facilities. The view of racial identity as a social construct also drew adherents. Radical black civil rights leaders tried to cultivate a racial identity based on African Americans' cultural distinctiveness, while others sought a color-blind society that did away with racial identities completely.

What differing ways have Americans defined racial identity?

In America's Backyard

Establishing a U.S. presence and maintaining favorable relations in East Asia became key aims of American foreign policy at the turn of the century. Americans also, however, explored opportunities to expand closer to home. The government focused in particular on constructing an isthmian canal through Central America to facilitate U.S. trade with China and better protect the nation's coastlines. Earlier transportation breakthroughs such as the Erie Canal, National Road, and transcontinental railroad quickened the movement of people and goods and helped the United States expand across the continent. The Panama Canal secured U.S. dominance of the Caribbean, and the government resolved to keep other foreign powers out of the region.

The Panama Canal

At the end of the nineteenth century, American canal advocates emphasized increased trade and better defense as reasons for building the **Panama Canal**, a manmade waterway through Panama completed in 1914 to link the Pacific and Atlantic oceans. The canal project received a boost when one of its strongest advocates, Theodore Roosevelt, assumed the presidency. Roosevelt took up the canal project immediately. "No single great material work which remains to be undertaken on this continent is of such consequence to the American people," Roosevelt told Congress the first time he addressed the legislators.

Roosevelt intended to take up where Ferdinand de Lesseps, the French mastermind who built the 1869 Suez Canal in Egypt that linked the Mediterranean and Red seas, had left off. In the 1880s de Lesseps had begun building a canal through Panama (then part of Colombia). Battling mudslides and earthquakes de Lesseps eventually abandoned the project and sold his concession from the Colombian government to the New Panama Canal Company, a French company headed by Philippe Bunau-Varilla, a longtime engineer on the project.

In 1902 the United States offered the New Panama Canal Company $40 million for its concession and assets, a sum that Bunau-Varilla eagerly accepted. Colombia, however, rejected Roosevelt's offer of $10 million to secure the rights to maintain a U.S.-controlled canal in Panama indefinitely. The Colombian government knew that the New Panama Canal Company's concession expired in 1904, and by stalling Colombia expected to pocket the $40 million earmarked for the company. "Those contemptible little creatures in Bogotá [the capital of Colombia] ought to understand how much they are jeopardizing things and imperiling their own future," Roosevelt wrote in frustration to his secretary of state John Hay.

In 1903 Panama revolted against Colombia. The timing was not coincidental. Fearing it would lose everything, the New Panama Canal Company encouraged and financed the rebellion by Panamanian business and political elites who did not want to share revenue from the projected canal with the rest of Colombia. Bunau-Varilla not only set the date for the revolution but also provided its leader, Manuel Guerrero Amador, with money, defense plans, a declaration of independence, and even a flag. Roosevelt never gave Bunau-Varilla any direct promises of U.S. support but, the president later recalled, it was Bunau-Varilla's "business to find out what he thought our Government would do . . . in fact, he would have been a very dull man had he been unable to make such a guess."

Once the Panamanian revolt began, Roosevelt acted immediately to ensure events turned in favor of the United States. The difficult mountain terrain separating the rest of Colombia from Panama forced Colombian troops to come by sea. When they arrived U.S. naval ships patrolling both coasts prevented them from landing in Panama. Roosevelt claimed that an 1846 agreement with Colombia gave the United States the authority to control transit across Panama. The nineteenth-century pact, however, envisioned using U.S. forces to protect, not destroy, Colombian sovereignty in Panama. In the 1920s Congress apologetically sent Colombia $25 million for Roosevelt's transgression.

With America's help the revolution in Panama succeeded. The United States immediately received its reward from Bunau-Varilla, the newly appointed

How did U.S. intervention in Panama compare with its colonization of the Philippines?

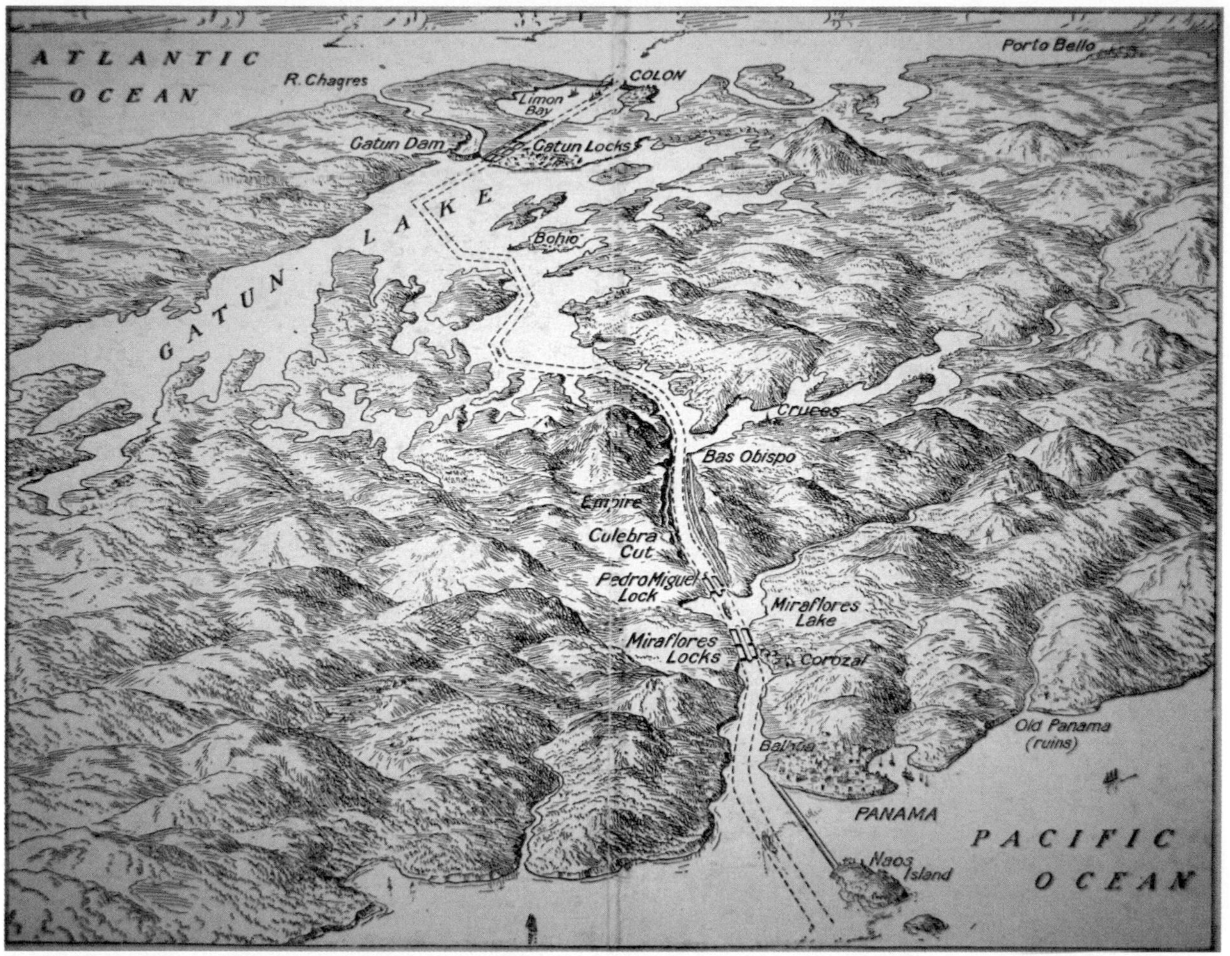

19.12 **Building the Panama Canal**
The Americans used a system of locks and dams to construct the waterway through a mountainous terrain subject to flooding and mudslides.
[*Source:* Map of the Panama Canal from the Atlantic to the Pacific Ocean, 1913 (litho), American School, (20th century) / Private Collection / Peter Newark American Pictures / The Bridgeman Art Library International]

minister to the United States for the Republic of Panama. The Hay–Bunau-Varilla Treaty (1903) gave the United States perpetual control over a strip of land 10 miles wide that included the Panama Canal for $10 million and an annual rent of $250,000. These terms remained in effect until December 31, 1999, when the United States turned control of the canal over to Panama.

When American engineers took over building the Panama Canal in 1904, they confronted a host of geological challenges. At several points the Chagres River crisscrossed the route selected for the canal. Tropical rains regularly poured down the mountains into the Chagres, which, if not diverted, would dump floodwaters and huge silt deposits into the planned canal. By damming the Chagres River, U.S. engineers created the artificial Gatun Lake that ships reached through a stairway of locks on either side. This approach used water rather than shovels to create a large portion of the waterway. The accompanying map (**19.12**) shows the 164 square miles of rain forest that construction crews flooded to create Gatun Lake. The five thousand American engineers, skilled workers, and foremen at the construction site relied on thousands of foreign workers, mostly blacks from the British West Indies, to dig the rest of the canal.

President Theodore Roosevelt shared the public's fascination with the feat of building the canal, and visited the site in 1906. His two-week trip made Roosevelt the first American president to leave the country while in office. Not content merely to watch the huge steam shovels through the window of the train bringing him to the Culebra Cut, the project's largest excavation site, Roosevelt tramped through the mud to reach one and climbed into the driver's seat. As photographers snapped away Roosevelt

> "It is an epic feat, and one of immense significance."
>
> President ROOSEVELT, after visiting the Panama Canal construction site

How did U.S. engineers overcome the geological obstacles to building the Panama Canal?

> "You had to pray every day for God to carry you safe, and bring you back."
>
> A black worker on felling giant trees and surviving mudslides while building the Panama Canal

learned that the Bucyrus steam shovel picked up 8 tons of dirt in a single scoop, required a crew of ten, and dug five times more than older machines.

This photo of Roosevelt sitting at the controls of a Bucyrus steam shovel (**19.13**) captured the adventurous spirit of an era dedicated to overseas economic expansion, technological innovation, and world prominence. "The real builder of the Panama Canal was Theodore Roosevelt," wrote Major George W. Goethals, chief engineer on the project. Americans usually saw photos of their formally dressed presidents standing on podiums, sitting at desks, or posing with visiting dignitaries. In this photograph Roosevelt appears as the larger-than-life personality he was, literally building the canal he played such a large part in securing for the United States.

Americans solved more than the engineering riddle of constructing the canal. They also conquered the disease-carrying mosquito. Guided by the recent discovery that mosquitoes transmitted malaria and yellow fever among humans, Dr. William C. Gorgas undertook a relentless fumigation campaign that

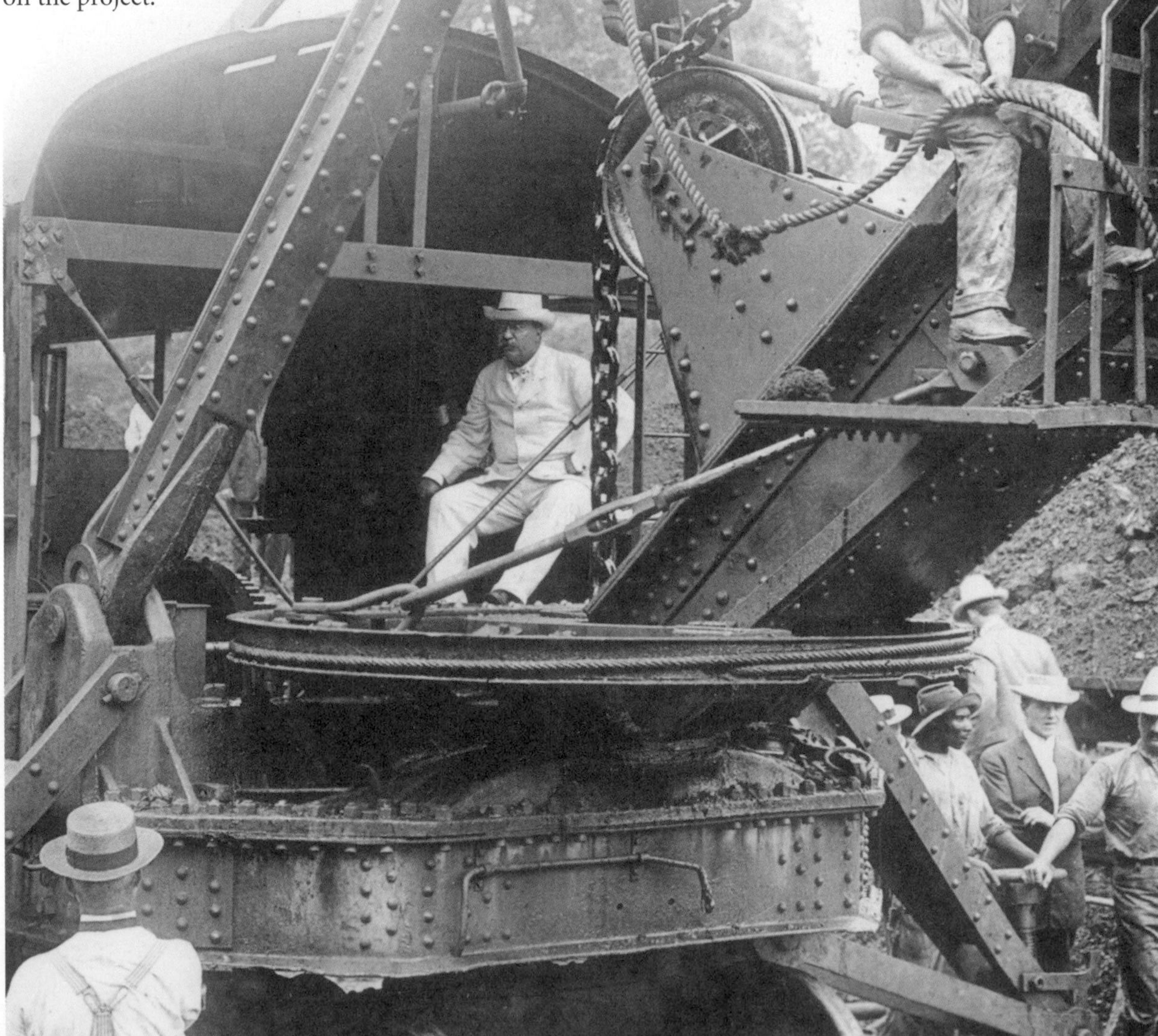

19.13 Theodore Roosevelt Visits the Canal Zone
Instead of observing construction of the Panama Canal from a safe distance, Roosevelt climbed into the seat of a steam shovel to work its controls.

What does this photograph convey about Roosevelt and the feat of building the Panama Canal?

saved thousands of lives. Nonetheless poor sanitary conditions in the black workers' laboring camps (which Roosevelt criticized during his visit) and the dangers posed by mudslides and working with dynamite still exacted a toll. Nearly 4,500 foreign black workers and 500 white Americans died during the American phase of construction.

The Roosevelt Corollary

The completed Panama Canal stood as a symbol for U.S. technological achievement, naval power, and economic strength. The canal also increased the importance of the Caribbean to U.S. national security. "America's interests in this hemisphere are greater than those of any European power," Roosevelt stated, therefore the United States intended to "police and protect" the canal alone. Roosevelt had reason to worry about European naval incursions into the region. Anxious about overdue debts, Britain and Germany blockaded Venezuela in 1902 and two years later several European nations threatened to intervene with force in the Dominican Republic for the same reason. To head off a European invasion, the Dominican Republic asked Roosevelt to accept the nation as a protectorate. Roosevelt privately remarked he had "about the same desire to annex it as a gorged boa constrictor might have to swallow a porcupine wrong-end-to." He nonetheless agreed to help the Dominican Republic, but only after deciding to use the incident to establish a new principle in U.S. foreign policy.

19.14 ***Theodore Roosevelt's Big Stick***
In this cartoon illustrating the impact of the Roosevelt Corollary, the president pulls a line of naval vessels around the Caribbean to keep nearby nations in line and prevent the creation of European empires too close to U.S. shores.

To prevent European military incursions into the Western Hemisphere, Roosevelt announced a corollary to the 1823 Monroe Doctrine (see Chapter 7), which had declared the Western Hemisphere off-limits to further European colonization. The **Roosevelt Corollary** of 1904 stated that when confronted with "flagrant cases" of wrongdoing by Latin American nations, such as not paying their debts to Western nations, the United States intended to act as an "international police power" in the region. In this political cartoon (**19.14**), a gigantic Roosevelt, dressed as a Rough Rider, holds a big stick as he pulls U.S. ships labeled "sheriff" and "debt collector" around the Caribbean. Americans dubbed the Roosevelt Corollary the "big stick" policy in reference to a West African proverb that Roosevelt favored: "Speak softly and carry a big stick, and you will go far." The corollary exempted Argentina, Brazil, and Chile because Roosevelt considered them civilized nations capable of meeting their international commitments and running their own domestic affairs. Satisfied that the United States would help Europe recoup its loans to Central and South American nations, European nations reacted positively to the Roosevelt Corollary.

Roosevelt's successor in the White House, William Howard Taft, further expanded U.S. influence over Latin America. Not content to simply ensure that Caribbean nations paid their debts, Taft initiated a policy of Dollar Diplomacy that encouraged U.S. investment in Latin America to ensure U.S. economic dominance over the region.

How did the Roosevelt Corollary bolster U.S. stature as a world power?

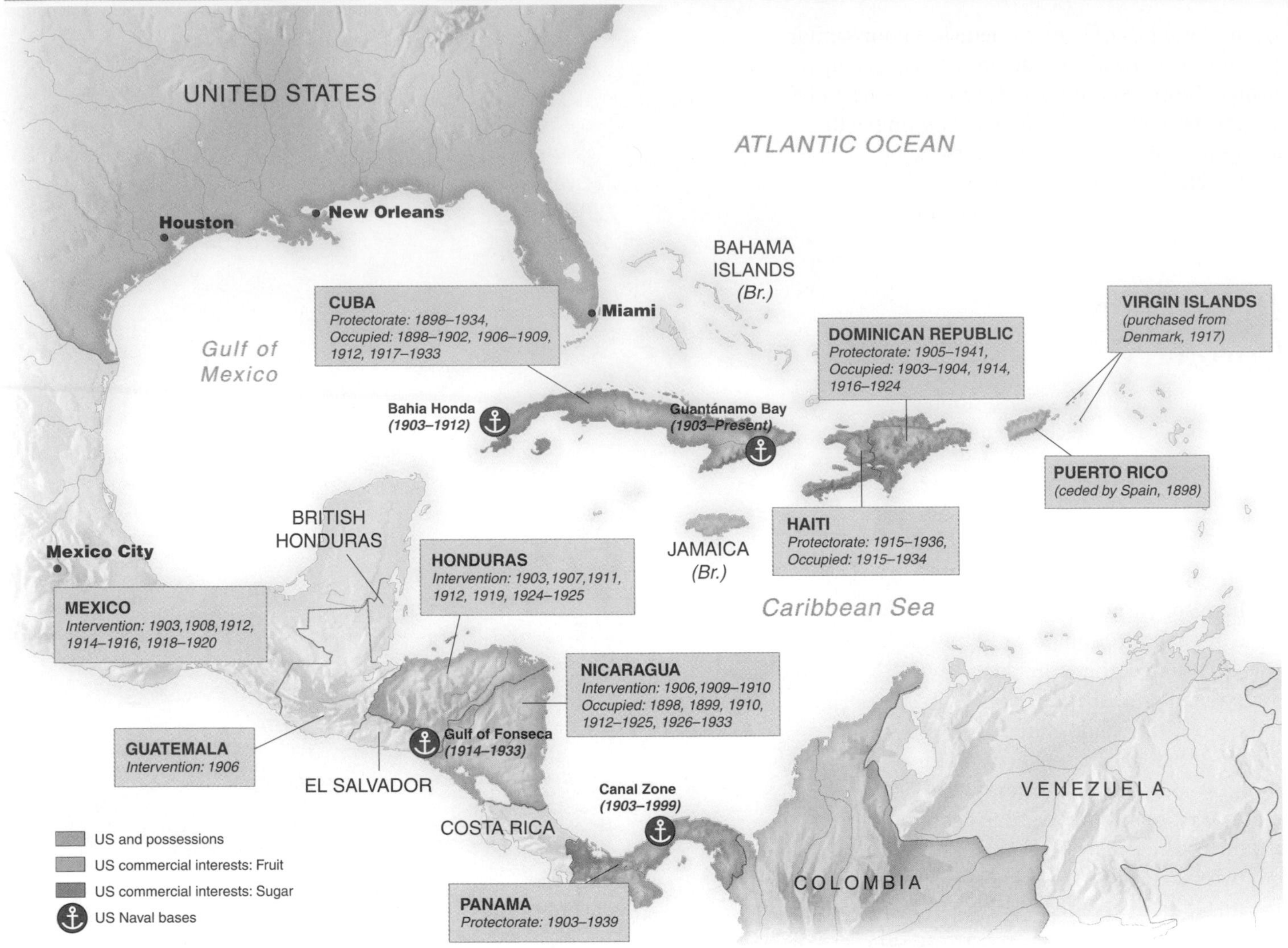

19.15 American Involvement in Latin America, 1898–1939
The United States intervened continually in the domestic affairs of its southern neighbors to protect the area as a U.S. sphere of influence.

Hoping to substitute "dollars for bullets," Taft shared Roosevelt's desire to turn the Caribbean into an American lake. When Democrat Woodrow Wilson became president in 1912, he followed in Roosevelt and Taft's footsteps by acting aggressively to protect U.S. business interests and curtail European access to the Western Hemisphere. The map, "American Involvement in Latin America, 1898–1939," (**19.15**) lists the many U.S. military incursions that occurred in areas where American businessmen had invested heavily in fruit and sugar industries. During this period U.S. troops invaded Mexico, Guatemala, Honduras, Nicaragua, Haiti, the Dominican Republic, and Cuba for a variety of strategic, commercial, and humanitarian reasons. American occupying armies often stayed for years, and in 1915 Haiti joined Cuba, the Dominican Republic, and Panama as a U.S. protectorate. Exerting influence over the domestic affairs of its Caribbean neighbors, through military invasions and protectorships, became a mainstay of twentieth-century U.S. foreign policy.

America's emerging role as a mediator in international disputes also included sending delegates abroad to resolve conflicts among European nations, including an agreement that partitioned Morocco in North Africa between Spain and France in 1906. Many congressional leaders feared that this diplomatic intervention represented a dangerous precedent. They made clear their refusal to support any departure from the traditional U.S. policy of

What steps did Taft and Wilson take to protect the Caribbean as a U.S. sphere of influence?

neutrality in the precarious game of European geopolitics. Their concerns proved well founded. On August 15, 1914, the Panama Canal officially opened. Newspapers buried this news about America's crowning achievement of the imperial age in their back pages, instead devoting their headlines to the eleven-day-old war sweeping through Europe. The beginning of World War I ushered in a new era in world history, one of global warfare made possible by the powerful empires constructed in the late nineteenth century. Now actively engaged in the world, the United States would find it difficult to stay out of this spreading conflict.

Conclusion

From 1890 to 1914 U.S. imperialists identified key commercial, strategic, and moral reasons for the United States to play an active role on the world stage. Americans increasingly saw expansion overseas, through war or trade, as the answer to its domestic and foreign concerns. Opportunity for expansion came first in Cuba. Shocked by stories of Spain's reconcentration program and worried about U.S. business interests in Cuba, Americans agreed to help Cuba liberate itself from Spain when the *Maine* exploded in Havana Harbor. After its victory in Cuba, the United States established a protectorate there, acquired Puerto Rico and Guam, and purchased the Philippine islands. These territorial possessions in the Caribbean and Pacific formed the basis of the U.S. empire for the next forty years.

Americans offered conflicting visions over the virtues of creating a U.S. colonial empire. Imperialists asserted that acquiring colonies would enhance the prestige of the United States, provide valuable economic resources, and help establish a trade route to China. Advocates also viewed imperialism as a mission to improve the lives of native peoples. Anti-imperialists voiced concern over subjugating people against their will and the costs of maintaining an empire. As Americans argued, Filipino rebels took up arms against the American occupying force. The costly Philippine-American War cooled American enthusiasm for using military conquest to acquire more colonies.

Establishing a strong trading relationship with East Asia also required diplomacy. The implementation of the Open Door Policy guaranteed American businessmen unfettered access to China by preventing other foreign nations from colonizing China. To maintain the balance of power in East Asia, President Roosevelt took a leading role in negotiating the peace treaty that ended the Russo-Japanese War. Roosevelt also forged the Gentleman's Agreement, which limited Japanese immigration to the United States.

In return for helping Panama win independence from Colombia, the United States received permission to build and control a canal across Panama. The construction feat evoked pride in the nation's industrial achievements. The Roosevelt Corollary announced the U.S. intention to police the Western Hemisphere to ensure that the region remained an American sphere of influence. By building the Panama Canal, establishing protectorates in Central America, acquiring territory in the Pacific, and authoring the Open Door Policy in China, the United States emerged as a world power at the turn of the century. With the American economy increasingly dependent on overseas markets, the United States would find it difficult to ignore the threat that World War I posed to its trade, and eventually to its borders.

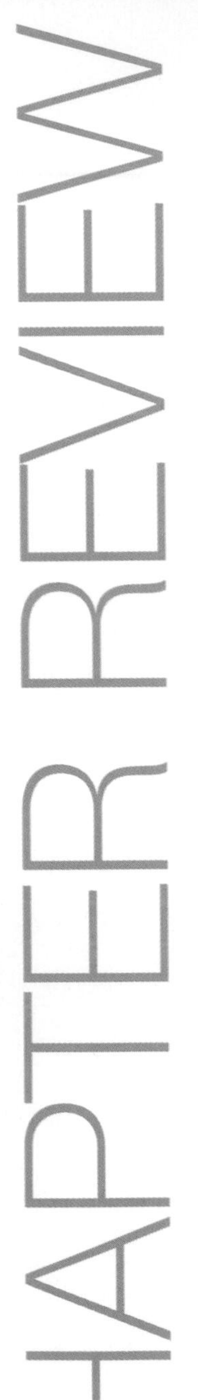

1893

Four-year depression begins
Intensifies interest in finding foreign markets for American goods

1898

The *Maine* explodes in Havana Harbor
Major cause of Spanish-American War

Spanish-American War
United States defeats Spain in four months

Treaty of Paris signed
Ends war with Spain; United States gains Caribbean and Pacific islands

1899

Philippine-American War begins
Ignites debate within United States over keeping Philippines as a colony

Rudyard Kipling publishes "The White Man's Burden"
Imperialists believe it articulates the civilizing mission; others see it as a parody

Review Questions

1. What concerns and fears encouraged the United States to look outside its borders in the 1890s?
2. How did Americans' longstanding interest in Cuba become a full-blown crisis in 1898? What image did Americans have of Spanish rule in Cuba and the American war against Spain?
3. How did the United States benefit from its victory against Spain?
4. What conflicting visions did imperialists and anti-imperialists hold toward colonizing the Philippines? How did each reconcile their ideas with traditional American values and ideals?
5. How did American views about race and racial identity shape the nation's development as a world power?
6. What different tactics did the United States use to protect its economic and strategic interests in East Asia versus those used in the Caribbean at the turn of the century?
7. How did the United States overcome political, engineering, and medical challenges to build the Panama Canal?

1900–1901

Open Door Notes
Protects American access to China market

Platt Amendment
Cuba becomes a protectorate of the United States

1904

Roosevelt Corollary
Establishes United States as international police presence in the Caribbean

St. Louis World's Fair
Exhibits highlight industrial progress and "civilizing" mission in colonies

1907–1908

Gentleman's Agreement
Limits Japanese immigration

1914

Panama Canal opens
Symbol of U.S. technological, military, and economic might

World War I begins
Global war engulfs Europe and its empires

Key Terms

imperialism The late nineteenth-century term for colonizing foreign nations and lands, relying primarily on business, political, and military structures rather than settlers to rule colonized peoples and exploit their resources. **562**

reconcentration Spanish policy that herded Cuban peasants off their farms into heavily fortified cities followed by systematic destruction of the crops that fed the rebel armies. **565**

yellow press Tabloid journalists and newspapers that reported sensationalist stories with a strong emotional component. **565**

Teller Amendment Congressional promise "to leave the government and control of the [Cuban] Island to its people" at the end of the Spanish-American War. **568**

Rough Riders A volunteer unit of cowboys, Ivy League athletes, city police officers, and Pawnee scouts led by Theodore Roosevelt that gained fame by charging up the San Juan Heights during the Spanish-American War. **570**

Treaty of Paris Agreement that ended the Spanish-American War with Spain relinquishing its claim to Cuba and the United States receiving Puerto Rico, some smaller Caribbean islands, and the Pacific island group of Guam. In return for $20 million, Spain turned the Philippines over to the United States. **571**

Platt Amendment Law linking U.S. withdrawal from Cuba to Cuban government granting the United States the right to maintain a naval base at Guantánamo Bay, to intervene militarily in Cuban domestic affairs, and to establish a privileged trading relationship with Cuba. The Cuban government also needed permission from the United States before entering into treaties with other nations. **572**

"the white man's burden" The Anglo-Saxon quest to better the lives of so-called racially inferior peoples by spreading Western economic, cultural, and spiritual values and institutions. **575**

sphere of influence The term used to describe the exclusive political and trading rights that a foreign nation enjoyed within another nation's territory. **579**

Open Door Policy A U.S.-sponsored nonbinding international agreement that kept the Chinese market open to all foreign nations. **579**

Gentleman's Agreement (1907–1908) Japanese agreement to deny passports to Japanese workers intending to immigrate to the United States. **581**

Angel Island Immigration processing station in the San Francisco Bay for Asian immigrants. **581**

Panama Canal A manmade waterway through Panama completed in 1914 to link the Pacific and Atlantic oceans. **584**

Roosevelt Corollary (1904) Corollary to the 1823 Monroe Doctrine that announced the U.S. intention to act as an "international police power" in Latin America. **587**

CHAPTER 20

The Great War

World War I, 1914–1918

> "The world must be made safe for democracy."
>
> President WOODROW WILSON, 1917 War Address

On May 7, 1915, Ernest Cowper was chatting with a friend aboard the *Lusitania*, a British passenger ship traveling from New York to the British Isles, as it passed the lush, green coast of Ireland. Looking into the water, Cowper suddenly felt a stab of terror when he spotted a German torpedo just seconds before it hit the ship. Peering through the periscope the German submarine captain watched hundreds of people jumping into the water in a desperate attempt to reach empty lifeboats. The ship sank within eighteen minutes, killing 1,198 passengers, including 128 Americans. Cowper was one of the lucky survivors, a Toronto newsman whose vivid recollections soon appeared in American newspapers.

The sinking of the *Lusitania* was a defining moment for the United States during World War I, often also called the Great War. The nation had remained neutral when the war began nine months earlier in August 1914, refusing to chose sides among the European powers involved, led by Great Britain and France on one side and Germany and Austria-Hungary on the other. When, however, the war spread to the high seas and American business initiated a lucrative arms trade with Great Britain, Americans increasingly found themselves in the line of fire.

American newspapers highlighted the tragic deaths of innocent women and children on the *Lusitania*, stirring outrage against Germany. One U.S. news report described the corpse of a mother embracing her three-month old baby, noting that "her face wears a half smile. Her baby's head rests against her breast. No one has tried to separate them." This description inspired the first American war-era propaganda poster, pictured here. The image, by artist Fred Spear, showed a mother and her baby sinking into the depths of the sea accompanied by one word—"Enlist."

Not all Americans, however, blamed Germany for the attack. German Americans pointed out that the *Lusitania* was secretly transporting munitions from New York to Britain. Rural Americans castigated Northeast business interests for trading primarily with Britain, fearful that favoring Britain and its allies would draw America into the war. President Woodrow Wilson offered a competing vision of the *Lusitania's* importance. Through increasingly strident diplomacy Wilson decided to defend the rights of neutrals to travel wherever they liked. This stance put the United States on a collision course with Germany that resulted in America entering the war two years later. Once America entered the war, President Wilson gave the country a larger purpose than defeating Germany. Introducing a new, and controversial, vision of American world leadership, Wilson promised to achieve a lasting peace by spreading democracy throughout the world.

To mobilize the nation's economic and manpower resources to fight the grim trench warfare underway along the Western Front, the government unfurled a far-reaching propaganda campaign, offered unprecedented support to labor unions, and raised a mass army through conscription. Americans suffered severe casualties in a short time, and their war effort helped the Allies defeat Germany by November 1918. The nation expected a peace treaty that embodied Wilson's promise to make this conflict "the war to end all wars." Americans held conflicting visions, however, over how to achieve this goal.

What meaning does this poster attach to the sinking of the *Lusitania*?

NOTICE!

TRAVELLERS intending to embark on the Atlantic voyage are reminded that a state of war exists between Germany and her allies and Great Britain and her allies; that the zone of war includes the waters adjacent to the British Isles; that, in accordance with formal no-

ENLIST

The Decision for War

NOTICE!
TRAVELLERS intending t
embark on the Atlantic voyag
are reminded that a state o
war exists between German
and her allies and Great Britai
and her allies; that the zone o
war includes the waters adja
cent to the British Isles; that

In the summer of 1914, Europe ignited as war swept across the continent (**20.1**). Instead of the easy victory that many Europeans expected, the war turned into a prolonged global struggle that took the lives of millions of men. World War I pitted the **Allies**, initially composed of Britain, France, Belgium, and Russia, and eventually totaling eighteen nations including Italy and the United States, against the **Central Powers** of Germany and Austria-Hungary, expanding by 1915 to include the Ottoman Empire and Bulgaria.

Europeans rushed into battle without taking the time to pause and consider what a general war would mean. Americans, however, followed a completely different road to war, openly debating whether this was their war to fight. It took two and a half years for the United States to enter the war. By then few illusions remained about the horror of modern warfare. Unlike Europeans in 1914 Americans knew they were committing to total war—and that winning would require the complete economic and psychological mobilization of the home front.

The War in Europe

On June 28, 1914, a nineteen-year-old Bosnian Serb named Gavrilo Princip arrived in Sarajevo, the capital of Bosnia, as part of a terrorist band that intended to assassinate the heir to the Austro-Hungarian throne, who was also visiting the city. Princip belonged to the Black Hand, a Slavic nationalist group based in the neighboring independent country of Serbia that longed to free Bosnia, then part of the Austro-Hungarian Empire. The group's first attempt to assassinate Archduke Franz Ferdinand failed when the bomb that one of Princip's coconspirators threw at the archduke's motorcade bounced off the side of the car carrying him, injuring two Austrian officers instead. Eluding the police Princip disappeared into the crowd. Later in the day the archduke made a fateful decision to visit his injured staff members. On the way to the hospital, the driver made a wrong turn down a narrow street and began slowing down to put the car in reverse. Standing at the end of the street was Princip, who could barely believe his good fortune as he saw the archduke and his pregnant wife coming toward him. Seizing the opportunity he stepped forward, pulled a pistol from his pocket, and fired, killing them both.

> "Mr. Mayor, it is perfectly outrageous! We have come to Sarajevo on a visit and have had a bomb thrown at us."
>
> ARCHDUKE FRANZ FERDINAND after surviving the Black Hand's first assassination attempt

World War I began with these two deaths and ended four years later with more than nine million more. In responding to the assassination, Austria-Hungary, Russia, and Germany all tried to leverage the crisis to fulfill longstanding territorial ambitions, events summarized on the timeline, "Countdown to War, 1914" (**20.2**). Austria-Hungary and Russia vied for control of the Balkans, which offered ready access to the Mediterranean Sea and the Middle East. Germany hoped to become the dominant power in Europe and had recently challenged the world dominance of France and Britain by building a strong navy, acquiring colonies, and winning the Franco-Prussian War in 1871.

Austria-Hungary held Serbia responsible for the assassination and demanded that the Serbian government make amends. In response Serbia chose appeasement over confrontation. Serbia accepted all of Austria-Hungary's demands except the one insisting that Austro-Hungarian judges participate in the trials of any Black Hand terrorists captured in Serbia. Without actually reading the Serbian response, German Kaiser Wilhelm II encouraged Austria-Hungary to quickly invade and annex Serbia. The next day, when the Kaiser read the Serbian statement, he jotted in the margins: "a great moral victory for Vienna; but with it every reason

What role did nationalism and imperialism play in bringing about World War I?

- Central powers
- The Allies
- Neutral nations
- The Western Front, March 1914
- The Eastern Front, 1914–1917
- Territory lost by Russia, Treaty of Brest-Litovsk 1918
- Allied blockade
- German unrestricted submarine warfare zone
- British-mined areas of the North Sea

20.1 World War I in Europe, 1914–1918
Miscalculations led to a two-front war for Germany and the creation of the Western Front in 1914, while the war at sea eventually drew the United States into the conflict.

Countdown to War, 1914

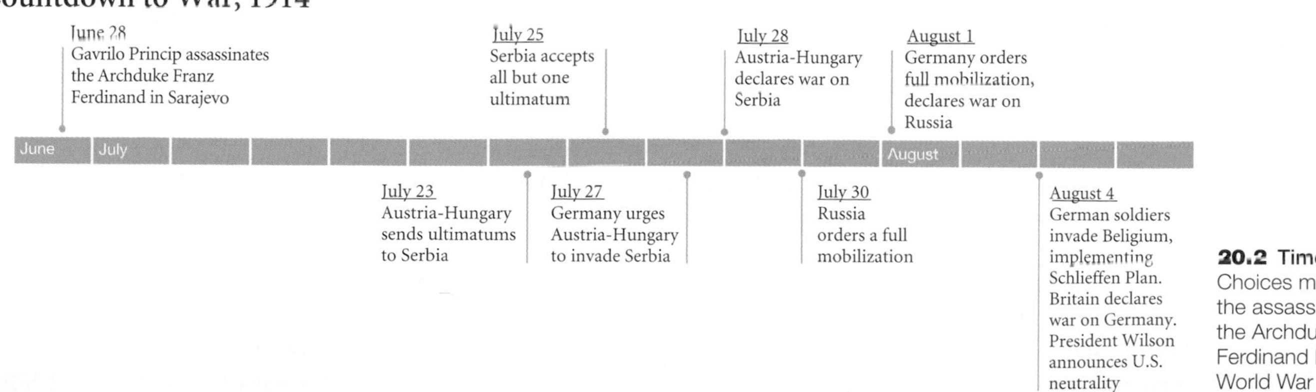
June 28
Gavrilo Princip assassinates the Archduke Franz Ferdinand in Sarajevo
July 23
Austria-Hungary sends ultimatums to Serbia
July 25
Serbia accepts all but one ultimatum
July 27
Germany urges Austria-Hungary to invade Serbia
July 28
Austria-Hungary declares war on Serbia
July 30
Russia orders a full mobilization
August 1
Germany orders full mobilization, declares war on Russia
August 4
German soldiers invade Beligium, implementing Schlieffen Plan. Britain declares war on Germany. President Wilson announces U.S. neutrality
June
July
August

20.2 Timeline, 1914
Choices made after the assassination of the Archduke Franz Ferdinand led to World War I.

Why did the assassination of Archduke Franz Ferdinand spark a general European war that soon spread to the world?

for war is removed." His comments came too late. An hour later, on July 28, 1914, Austria-Hungary declared war on Serbia.

As Austro-Hungarian naval artillery bombarded Belgrade, Serbia's capital city, Russia resolved to stand by Serbia and defend its own interests in the Balkans. Russian Tsar Nicolas II made a momentous decision when he ordered a general mobilization of his army on July 30, 1914. Germany viewed the Russian mobilization as a direct threat. Ever since the 1894 alliance between Russia and France, Germany had worried about fighting a two-front war sometime in the future. In 1905 the German chief of staff Alfred von Schlieffen developed a plan that called for Germany, in the event of war, to attack and quickly defeat France while the cumbersome Russian army mobilized. **The Schlieffen Plan** avoided the well-defended border between France and Germany and instead sent German troops on a northward arch. Passing quickly through Belgium German troops would enter France through the undefended northern border and encircle Paris within six weeks. Germany could then turn its full forces against the much larger Russian army.

For the Schlieffen Plan to work, Germany needed to strike first. With Russia refusing to halt its mobilization, Germany declared war on Russia on August 1, 1914, and put a modified version of the Schlieffen Plan into motion. Two days later Germany declared war on France. When German troops crossed into Belgium on August 4, Britain declared war on Germany, fulfilling its 1839 pledge to guarantee Belgium independence.

The Schlieffen Plan quickly unraveled. German troops encountered unexpected resistance from the Belgian army and had difficulty resupplying a mass army on the move, giving the French and British time to mobilize. In the east Russia attacked with its partly mobilized army sooner than Germany expected, prompting German Chief of Staff Helmuth von Moltke to divert some troops from France to defend Berlin. At the Marne River, 35 miles northeast of Paris, the French and British successfully stopped the German drive toward Paris. Instead of defeating France quickly, Germany's attack ignited a general European war. As each army dug defensive trenches in France and Belgium, the trench deadlock of the **Western Front** took shape. For nearly four years men would live and die in the complex system of earthworks that ran for 550 miles from the North Sea to Switzerland. To bolster their forces Britain, France, and Germany began immediately enlisting men and resources from their colonies. When the Ottoman Empire (which ruled Turkey and most of the Middle East) joined the Central Powers and Italy joined the Allies, the conflict became a true world war.

American society contained many first- and second-generation immigrants from both the Central Powers and the Allied nations who disagreed over which nation had started the war. In 1914 President Woodrow Wilson believed that all belligerents shared collective responsibility for the war. Wanting to both stay out of the war and prevent bitter divisions from ripping America apart, Wilson proclaimed the United States neutral.

The Perils of Neutrality

As war engulfed Europe Wilson advised Americans to avoid "passionately taking sides" and to "remain impartial in thought, as well as action." Neutrality, however, turned out to be a difficult concept for Americans to define and maintain. Did neutrality mean trading with both sides selectively, or with no one? Did Americans have the right as members of a neutral nation to travel wherever they liked without coming under attack? The conflicting visions that emerged as Americans confronted these questions created a strident debate as the war wore on.

The dilemma was how to remain neutral without inflicting serious damage on the American economy. Since the 1890s American foreign policy had focused on protecting American business interests abroad (see Chapter 19). Cutting off trade completely with Europe would have had severe consequences for American citizens. At first Wilson tried to limit America's financial involvement in the war by banning private American bank loans to the belligerent nations. Secretary of State William Jennings Bryan believed the loan ban would "hasten a conclusion to the war" by making it impossible for the countries at war to buy the arms that they needed to continue fighting. Wilson, however, lifted the ban in 1915. The Allies were running short of cash, and Wilson feared a widespread U.S. recession if these nations stopped buying American goods.

Trading with or loaning money to both sides was another possible way to stay neutral. In theory American manufacturers and banks were free to do business with both Britain and Germany. In practice, however, the chart of U.S. Exports to Europe, 1914–1917 (**20.3**) reveals that they chose primarily to help the Allies. By 1917 American banks were loaning Britain an average of $10 million a day. In contrast American trade with Germany had dropped

What miscalculations stymied German expectations of a short war?

U.S. Trade with Nations at War

	1914	1915	1916	1916 Figure as a Percentage of 1914 Figure
Britain	$594,271,863	$911,794,954	$1,526,685,102	257%
France	$159,818,924	$369,397,170	$628,851,988	393%
Italy*	$74,235,012	$184,819,688	$269,246,105	364%
Germany	$344,794,276	$28,863,354	$288,899	0.08%

*Italy joined the Allies in April 1915.

20.3 U.S. Exports to Europe, 1914–1917
The nation's robust trade with Britain, France, and Italy—allied nations fighting Germany—provoked debate among Americans holding conflicting visions of neutrality.

to less than 1 percent of what it had been in 1914. Even if American manufacturers and banks had wanted to help Germany, trade became nearly impossible when Britain used its navy to blockade waterways leading to Germany and cut the international cable between the United States and Germany. The country's financial elite, however, had no desire to trade with both sides. Many upper-class Americans revered British culture and had warm feelings towards the French. Widespread publicity of German atrocities against Belgian civilians also fanned anti-German sentiment. Newspapers published vivid accounts of German soldiers burning homes, ransacking museums, and executing random Belgian civilians in retaliation for guerilla attacks against the German army. The press embellished these stories with fabricated tales of German soldiers cutting off women's breasts and children's hands.

Some Americans remained skeptical of such reports, seeing them as little more than British propaganda. America's disproportionate aid to the Allies alarmed the sizable German American and Irish American communities (the latter hated British rule of Ireland). People in the Midwest and South accused Eastern banks of violating the principle of neutrality, thereby pulling the nation slowly into a war most Americans did not want to fight. These critics embraced a strict vision of neutrality and wanted the government to announce an arms embargo that would prevent American companies from trading with nations at war.

When the war spread to the high seas, these conflicting visions provoked heated debate over America's role in the war. Facing a trench stalemate on the Western Front, Britain used its superior navy to establish a blockade around the Central Powers that included mining the North Sea. The blockade immediately affected American trade. American ships could not sail through the North Sea to Germany without first allowing the British to search their cargo for contraband, merchandise such as guns or ammunition that Britain wanted to stop from entering Germany. In mounting its blockade Britain soon violated international law by adding cotton and food to the contraband list. The 1915 political cartoon, *Britannia Must be More Careful How She Waves the Rules* (**20.4**), inverted the traditional motto associated with British naval dominance, "Britannia Rules the Waves," to criticize the blockade's effect on neutral countries, especially the United States. The cartoon depicts American shipping as a crying child that Uncle Sam is trying to comfort. Other neutral countries affected by the blockade (Norway and Sweden) bawl inconsolably, while John Bull, the symbol of Great Britain, tells Uncle Sam that "I'm trying to hit him," pointing to the German Kaiser, who raises a menacing sword at his foe. In March 1915 Wilson formally protested British blockading

Copyrighted, 1914, by John T. McCutcheon.

20.4 ***Britannia Must Be More Careful How She Waves the Rules***
This 1915 political cartoon criticizes Britain for mining the North Sea and preventing American ships from trading with Germany.

What competing visions did Americans offer on the question of trading with warring Europeans nations?

> "The American people do not want to go to war to vindicate the right of a few people to travel or work on armed vessels."
>
> Missouri Senator WILLIAM J. STONE to President Wilson, 1916

> "I cannot consent to any abridgement of the rights of American citizens in any respect. The honor and self-respect of the nation is involved."
>
> WILSON'S reply

practices. The British eventually agreed to buy enough American cotton to offset the loss of the German market.

The president proved less accommodating when Germany declared all the waters around Britain a war zone and threatened to attack any ship that entered the area. To combat the British blockade Germany turned to a new weapon, its **U-boat**, or submarine, to launch surprise torpedo attacks against Allied merchant and naval ships. International law recognized a naval blockade as a legal weapon of war, but required that the attacking ship give the merchant vessel's crew time to evacuate, and if necessary, take them aboard before sinking the ship and cargo. These pre-war customs rendered the U-boat useless, removing the element of surprise that made it such an effective weapon. Once spotted, armed merchant vessels did not hesitate to attack fragile U-boats.

20.5 German Warning to Travelers in the War Zone When Wilson criticized Germany for sinking the *Lusitania*, German Americans pointed out that the German government had published warnings like this ahead of time urging Americans to stay off ships headed to the war zone.

NOTICE!

TRAVELLERS intending to embark on the Atlantic voyage are reminded that a state of war exists between Germany and her allies and Great Britain and her allies; that the zone of war includes the waters adjacent to the British Isles; that, in accordance with formal notice given by the Imperial German Government, vessels flying the flag of Great Britain, or of any of her allies, are liable to destruction in those waters and that travellers sailing in the war zone on ships of Great Britain or her allies do so at their own risk.

IMPERIAL GERMAN EMBASSY
WASHINGTON, D. C., APRIL 22, 1915.

On May 7, 1915, a German U-boat sunk the *Lusitania*, a British passenger ship sailing off the coast of Ireland. Calls for war swept through the press. "Germany must surely have gone mad," surmised one Richmond newspaper. Wilson sent a series of notes demanding that Germany pay reparations and accept the right of Americans to travel on any ship they wished. The Germans defended the sinking, pointing out that they had published warnings to passengers in American newspapers (**20.5**) and that the *Lusitania* was carrying munitions as part of its cargo.

The *Lusitania* sinking was an ideological turning point for the United States. In reaction to the crisis, Wilson redefined the meaning of neutrality, thus putting the United States on an eventual collision course with Germany. The president moved away from his initial definition of neutrality as remaining "impartial in thought, as well as action." The president now embraced neutrality as a concept that first and foremost gave neutral nations the irrevocable right to trade and travel wherever they liked. Secretary of State Bryan urged Wilson to ban Americans from traveling on ships headed to the U-boat–patrolled waters around Great Britain. Wilson refused. Convinced that the president's preoccupation with the rights of neutrals would lead to war, Bryan resigned in protest.

As the United States and Germany argued over the *Lusitania*, a German U-boat sunk another British passenger ship, the *Arabic*, in August 1915, leaving two Americans among the dead. Worried about further provoking the United States, Germany stepped back. On September 1, 1915, Germany issued the *Arabic* Pledge, promising not to sink passenger ships without warning. Germany renounced surprise attacks on merchant ships in May 1916 following another controversial sinking. For the moment Germany's pledges averted war with the United States.

The debate deepened when prominent pro-Ally political, business, and financial leaders formed the National Security League and began lobbying for universal military training to give all men of fighting age instruction in drilling and marksmanship. In response Progressive reformers formed the American Union Against Militarism to denounce any preparations for war. The appeal of the pacifist

Why was the sinking of the *Lusitania* a turning point in the neutrality debate?

vision made the 1916 song "I Didn't Raise My Son to be a Soldier" a hit. Taking stock of the controversy swirling around the preparedness versus peace debate, Congress authorized only a modest, but still controversial, increase in the size of the peacetime army.

Recognizing the potency of antiwar sentiment, Wilson ran for reelection in 1916 on the slogan "He Kept Us Out of War." The banners covering a Wilson reelection campaign truck (**20.6**) revealed the strong connections that Wilson drew between domestic and foreign issues. Wilson reminded voters of his Progressive reform agenda, which included a Federal Reserve System that "broke the money trust" and passage of an eight-hour day for railroad workers (see Chapter 18). The slogan "Peace with Honor" referred to Wilson's success in securing pledges from Germany that respected America's right to trade with the Allies. This overseas commerce created the prosperity that Democrats boasted about on the same sign. During the campaign Wilson noted that twice he had sent his trusted advisor Colonel Edward House to Europe to negotiate a peace settlement, lamenting that House had returned home empty-handed each time. At the same time he campaigned on the slogan of preparedness to underscore his commitment to defending the country if necessary.

20.6 Wilson Campaign Slogans
In a tight race for reelection in 1916, Woodrow Wilson emphasized his progressive legislative agenda and championed his success at keeping the nation out of the war without sacrificing national honor or economic prosperity. [*Source* (buttons): Cornell University, Carl A. Kroch Library, Division of Rare and Manuscript Collections]

In contrast to the Wilson campaign, the Republican challenger Supreme Court Justice Charles Evan Hughes never developed an effective slogan or theme. The Hughes campaign believed that Woodrow Wilson had won the presidency in 1912 because progressive Republicans had supported Theodore Roosevelt's run as a third-party Progressive Party candidate over the incumbent Republican president William Howard Taft (see Chapter 18). With the conservative and progressive factions of the Republican Party now reunited, Hughes tried to avoid controversy with vague calls "for law and liberty" and "undiluted Americanism." On election night, with returns from California still uncounted, Wilson went to bed certain that he had lost the election. He awoke to discover that he had won reelection by only 23 electoral votes, 277–254.

After the election Wilson tried once again to negotiate a settlement. On January 22, 1917, he outlined a plan for "peace without victory" based on "American principles, American policies." Democracy, freedom of the seas, no entangling alliances, and equality of rights among nations were, Wilson asserted, "the principles and policies of forward-looking men and women everywhere, of every modern nation, of every enlightened community." Wilson's desire to export democracy overseas while simultaneously protecting American access to foreign markets promised to greatly expand America's imperial reach. No longer limiting American intervention to its Pacific colonies or nearby Latin American countries (see Chapter 19), Wilson proposed remaking Europe in the image of America.

Wilson's words had little effect on European leaders. Unbeknownst to the president Germany had already decided to resume unrestricted submarine warfare. Having staked everything on Germany's willingness to let Americans travel unmolested in the war zone, Wilson's neutrality policy collapsed.

America Enters the War

Germany expected the Allies to capitulate quickly once German submarines cut off the lifeline between the United States and Britain. Even if the resumption of unrestricted submarine warfare brought the United States into the war, Germany knew that it would take at least a year for the American government to raise, train, and equip an overseas force. By then Germany would have won the war.

To further hamper the deployment of American troops to France, the German government tried to distract the U.S. government by provoking a border conflict between the United States and Mexico. Throughout 1914–1917, German spies had spent nearly $12 million to support rebel factions in Mexico hostile to the United States who resented the U.S. government's active involvement in Mexican domestic politics. In 1916 Francisco "Pancho" Villa raided American border towns, hoping to draw U.S. troops into Mexico and destabilize the new U.S.-backed constitutional government headed by Venustiano Carranza. Much as Villa anticipated, Wilson sent a twelve thousand–troop punitive expedition under the command of Brigadier General John J. Pershing into Mexico in 1916 to arrest Villa. Carranza angrily denounced the American expedition as an invasion of Mexico. Tensions between the two countries escalated dramatically after a deadly clash in Carrizal on June 21, 1916. Wilson began planning for war with Mexico, but just in time learned that American troops had attacked first at Carrizal. After months of talks between U.S. and Mexican negotiators, American troops left Mexico in January 1917.

That same month the German foreign minister Arthur Zimmermann sent the **Zimmermann Telegram** to Mexico stating that in the event of war with the United States, Germany would help Mexico recover Texas, New Mexico, and Arizona (territory lost in the nineteenth century) if Mexico started a borderland war with the United States. Zimmermann also asked Mexico to mediate between Germany and Japan (which had joined the Allied side in 1914), hoping to entice Japan into attacking America's Pacific colonial possessions. Carranza had no interest in fighting the United States after the American withdrawal from Mexico, and Germany had no men or munitions to offer. Carranza, however, never had a chance to respond. In one of the war's greatest intelligence coups, British intelligence agents intercepted and deciphered the secretly coded telegram. When the State Department released the Zimmermann Telegram to the press six weeks later, many Americans viewed it as evidence that Germany had hostile intentions against the United States. Antiwar activists denounced the telegram as a forgery, but Zimmermann confessed to sending the note. With war between Germany and the United States growing more likely, Zimmermann wanted the United States to believe the threat was real so they would keep troops at home to protect the border.

Despite the public outcry over the Zimmermann Telegram, Wilson still hesitated. The president broke off diplomatic ties with Germany, but still no declaration of war came. German submarines began sinking over half a million tons of Allied shipping per month, and the Allies warned Wilson that without these supplies they were doomed. Finally, on April 2, 1917, Wilson went before Congress to ask for a declaration of war, laying out war goals that went far beyond simply defeating Germany. "We are glad, now that we see the facts," Wilson proclaimed ". . . to fight thus for the ultimate peace of the world and for the liberation of its peoples . . . for the rights of nations great and small and the privilege of men everywhere to chose their way of life and of obedience."

> "It is a fearful thing to lead this great peaceful people into war."
>
> President WILSON, 1917 war address before Congress

Congress declared war with a vote of 90 to 6 in the Senate and 373 to 50 in the House, but a vocal minority opposed going to war. Republican Senator George W. Norris from Nebraska expressed the "rich man's war, poor man's fight" sentiment that ran deep in rural America. Only four days into her term as the first female member of Congress, Jeannette Rankin (R-Montana) caste her maiden vote against the war. She lost her reelection in 1919, but returned to Congress in 1940. Sticking to her pacifist principles, she was the only legislator who voted against entering World War II after the Japanese attacked Pearl Harbor. Critics expressed their opposition freely during the debate over declaring war, but once the nation was officially fighting Germany, most Americans rallied behind the flag.

Why did the United States finally decide to fight Germany?

Conflicting Views among the Allies on the War's Purpose

Wilson claimed that the United States "had no selfish ends to serve" by going to war. Skeptical voices from revolutionary Russia soon prompted Wilson to defend this claim. On November 7, 1917, seven months after the United States entered the war, the Bolshevik revolutionary Vladimir Lenin seized power in Russia with promises of peace, land, and bread. Lenin's Communist government immediately published secret Allied treaties, revealing that Tzarist Russia, Britain, and France had agreed to enlarge their empires at the expense of Germany, Austria-Hungary, and the Ottoman Empire if they won the war. This disclosure exposed evident competing visions on the Allied side: Wilson's vague promises that the war was about democracy and the now-revealed territorial ambitions of the Allies.

Trying to bridge this gap, Wilson outlined a broad statement of Allied war goals in his **Fourteen Points** speech to Congress on January 8, 1918. In the Fourteen Points Wilson envisioned a world dominated by democracy, free trade, disarmament, self-determination, resolved territorial disputes in Europe, and a league of nations to mediate future international crises. He explicitly linked the spread of democracy with the expansion of capitalism, a position that gained new urgency as Russian Communists began confiscating private property and promising to redistribute wealth throughout the population. Whether spreading democracy meant increasing political rights and free trade or reallocating wealth became a cornerstone of the ideological debate between the United States and the newly formed Soviet Union throughout the twentieth century.

> "God gave us his Ten Commandments and we broke them. Wilson gave us his 14 points—well, we shall see."
>
> French Prime Minister GEORGE CLEMENCEAU, 1918

Free trade and freedom of the seas offered more than an antidote to communism, however. These principles also advanced American economic interests at the expense of major imperialist powers like Britain and France. The Fourteen Points speech revealed some contradictions in Wilsonian idealism. Like other world leaders Wilson advanced principles that protected the interests of his own country. Yet Wilson also demanded some sacrifices from Americans to make this "the war to end all wars." Once they joined the general association of nations that Wilson proposed, Americans faced modifying their traditional desire to act unilaterally in the Western Hemisphere.

Wilson's Fourteen Points further declared that all peoples should enjoy **self-determination**, or a voice in selecting their own government. Using this principle Wilson proposed redrawing the map of Eastern and Central Europe along ethnic lines and even proposed extending this right to colonial populations. Robert Lansing, who replaced Bryan as secretary of state, remained dubious. The principle of self-determination "is simply loaded with dynamite," Lansing noted. "It will raise hopes which can never be realized."

Shortly after Wilson issued his Fourteen Points, another model emerged for how the war might end when Lenin negotiated a separate peace with Germany. The Treaty of Brest-Litovsk officially ended the war between Russia and Germany on March 3, 1918. This treaty reflected Germany's complete victory over Russia and exposed the full imperialist thrust of German war goals. The treaty made Ukraine, parts of Poland, Finland, Lithuania, Estonia, and Latvia satellite states of Germany. Map 20.1 illustrates Russia's territorial losses in 1918. With these gains Germany intended to eliminate Russia as a future rival and expand its empire into resource-rich eastern lands.

The Brest-Litovsk treaty gave the Allies an idea of the terms that a victorious Germany might impose on them. This knowledge hardened the British and French resolve to achieve total victory and inflict equally punitive terms of their own. The treaty even convinced Wilson that maintaining peace in Europe would require weakening Germany militarily and economically.

With Russia out of the war, Germany finally had the opportunity to fight the one-front war it had sought in 1914. Now holding a clear manpower advantage, Germany prepared to strike along the Western Front. As the American government raced to mobilize the nation's men and industry for total war, many in Europe feared that the United States had entered the war too late to save the Allied side.

How did the Fourteen Points lay the foundation for future domestic and international debates?

The War at Home

America could not mobilize, supply, and feed an army without granting new powers to the federal government. The federal government used a mix of incentives, threats, and patriotic appeals to negotiate the preexisting class, gender, and racial conflicts that threatened to make wartime cooperation difficult. Official propaganda urged unity, but Americans retained conflicting visions about regulating big business, unionizing, female suffrage, and racial equality.

Gearing Up for War

Wilson's democratic rhetoric convinced many Progressive reformers that they could count on the president to use his wartime powers to rein in big business (see Chapter 18). The president, however, feared that the war would make corporations more powerful than ever. "We shall be dependent upon the steel, oil, and financial magnates," Wilson privately worried. "They will run the nation." Wilson's concerns were well-founded. Increased wages and federal protections for unions improved the lives of many workers, but the resurgent power of big business prevented Progressives from making these wartime reforms permanent.

20.7 "Little Americans Do Your Bit!" This propaganda poster showing a three-year-old saluting a bowl of corn-based porridge underscored the total mobilization of American society.

In the winter of 1917, gridlock paralyzed the railroad system. Blizzard conditions, fuel shortages, and poor coordination among private railway companies prevented trains from delivering tons of war-related freight. Labor unrest also created havoc as skilled railway workers left in droves for better-paying factory jobs and railway unions prepared to strike. To sort out this mess, the federal government took over management of the railroads for the duration of the war. The Railroad Administration met union demands for high wages, standardized equipment, and coordinated the use of tracks. To improve the flow of needed materials, the newly created War Industries Board (WIB) ranked industries so that those most critical to the war effort received raw materials ahead of nonessential wartime businesses. Steel, for example, went first to manufacturers producing guns and ships, while factories making civilian cars, freezers, and corsets (they needed steel for the inner stays) had to wait. The government paid railroad companies handsomely for wartime use of their trains and track to mute their objections to government management of the railroads. When private companies regained control of railroad lines in 1920, the nation's railroad network lay in shambles, a victim of heavy wartime traffic and the government's failure to properly maintain the lines.

Food Administration director Herbert Hoover chose a different path to ensure that the country produced enough to feed civilians at home, soldiers, and refugees overseas. Congress had given the president near dictatorial powers to regulate the food and fuel industries in the 1917 Lever Food and Fuel Act. Hoover, however, opted to use high prices and patriotic appeals to control the nation's food supply rather than rationing. To stimulate production Hoover had the American and Allied governments pay high prices for agricultural goods. To curb civilian demand Hoover organized a massive propaganda campaign around the slogan "food will win the war." Citizens signed pledge cards vowing to observe wheatless Mondays, meatless Tuesdays, and porkless Saturdays. Urging Americans to conserve wheat for shipment overseas, the Food Administration plastered the country with posters that tried to popularize cornmeal, which did not transport well, as a tasty and acceptable substitute for wheat flour. The agency offered housewives cornmeal recipes and cooking classes, and even tried to enlist the

What varying strategies did the government use to mobilize economic resources?

cooperation of finicky toddlers (**20.7**) by urging them to eat cornmeal instead of oatmeal.

Americans responded well to Hoover's patriotic appeals to conserve food, but whether the government could quell labor unrest for the duration of the war remained questionable. Wilson quieted industrial class conflict by throwing money at the problem. The steel, copper, petroleum, and meatpacking industries enjoyed a healthy increase in profits once they began selling their products to the government. Wilson also offered industrialists, still bristling over Progressive-era laws that curtailed monopolies and regulated working conditions (see Chapter 18), an olive branch by giving them a role in setting the government's wartime price, wage, and production codes.

Labor benefited during the war as well. The government built high wages and union protection into its wartime contracts in exchange for a no-strike pledge from labor. The National War Labor Board (made up of representatives from government, business, and labor) required industries that accepted government contracts to honor the eight-hour day and forty-hour week. These companies also had to pay a living wage, maintain high safety standards, and recognize a union's right to recruit members at work. Not all labor groups benefited equally from the sudden government attention. Official support for collective bargaining helped the more moderate unions that formed the American Federation of Labor. Radical labor groups that continued to oppose the war suffered when the government arrested their leaders and members for sedition.

Even the gains for moderate labor unions proved fleeting, however. Workers received higher wages, but after adjusting for the considerable wartime inflation, real wages only increased 4 percent. When the war ended and the government canceled its contracts, workers lost federal protection for organizing unions. Without the government stopping them, many manufacturers quickly returned to their old union-busting ways (see Chapter 21).

Black Migration

Immigrants had long provided American industry with a source of inexpensive labor. The war disrupted the flow of immigrants to the United States at the exact moment that the demand for industrial goods exploded. In 1914, 1.2 million immigrants entered the country. In 1917 only 110,618 arrived. Labor recruiting agents soon turned to white and black Southerners to fill the void. During the war over half a million African Americans migrated from Southern farms and cities to the North, lured by offers of high-paying industrial jobs. The African American painter Jacob Lawrence celebrated this mass exodus in a series of paintings he completed in the 1940s. His first painting showed brightly dressed streams of families preparing to board trains through doors marked "Chicago," "New York," and "St. Louis" (**20.8**). Many migrants exalted at their newfound freedom in the North. "I can quit any time I want," noted one migrant, without forfeiting a year's pay as in the sharecropping system. Another man realized that in Chicago he was no longer afraid "to rub up against a white person" accidentally on the street or sit down next to one on a streetcar. In the South he had constantly feared the consequences of an unintended breach of Southern racial etiquette. Migrants also discovered, however, that despite the absence of overt segregation or intimidation, racial prejudice existed in the North as well.

20.8 The First Wave of the Great Migration (1916–1919) "Around the time of WWI, many African-Americans from the South left home and traveled to cities in the North in search of a better life," wrote artist Jacob Lawrence to explain this 1940 painting.

The migration of Southern blacks northward also unveiled regional and class tensions within the black community. Working through organizations like the Urban League and the Young Men's Christian Association, paternalistic Northern middle-class blacks tried to help Southern migrants adjust to the rhythms of industrial jobs and urban life. Besides wanting to genuinely assist recent arrivals, middle-class blacks worried that migrants' rural customs might harm the reputation of the entire Northern black community. A list of dos and don'ts published by the *Chicago Defender*, a newspaper serving the African American community, entreated migrants to watch their language, mind their manners, respect the law, keep their houses clean, and send their children to school.

The Urban League had reason to fear that racial rioting might accompany the arrival of black workers from the South. The explosive combination of economic competition, housing shortages, and latent racial hostility triggered a series of racial riots in Northern cities during the war. The most deadly one occurred in East St. Louis, Illinois, in July 1917. In East St. Louis companies intentionally recruited immigrants and Southern blacks to undermine union activism. Company owners knew that racial and ethnic prejudices would prevent native-born whites from allowing these new workers to join their unions, which in turn undermined the union's ability to mount a strike. Viewing black migrants as potential strikebreakers, white workers initiated a series of minor attacks on black workers that escalated into a full-fledged racial riot on July 2, 1917. The anti-lynching crusader Ida B. Wells-Barnett interviewed over fifty black eyewitnesses for a report that she submitted to Congress, including one witness who recalled seeing black men exit homes with their hands raised. As they pled for their lives, mobs stoned them to death. Overall the riot left nine whites and thirty-nine blacks dead and hundreds wounded on both sides. The subsequent congressional investigation held white employers, labor leaders, and politicians responsible, but six thousand African Americans left the city anyway.

Female Suffrage

The war inadvertently provided an opportunity for women to gain suffrage and for the temperance reform movement (see Chapter 21), where women held leading roles, to build momentum. Mobilizing the home front meant securing the active cooperation of women. Over the course of the war, savvy female leaders successfully parlayed their newly recognized economic clout into a demand for political power.

Women did the shopping and cooking in most homes, so the Food Administration needed their full support for its food conservation efforts to succeed. "Will you have a part in Victory?" queried one propaganda poster above the image of a young woman in a stars and stripes gown scattering seeds in a "victory garden" to provide vegetables for her family. Over eight million women volunteered for Red Cross work, producing surgical dressings, sweaters, socks, and mittens for soldiers and refugees. With workers in short supply, companies increasingly recruited women to fill positions in factories, and the government hired many as clerks. In desperate need of laborers, companies in Bridgeport, Connecticut, even hired airplanes to scatter leaflets throughout residential neighborhoods that urged housewives to apply for jobs in munitions factories. Overall, however, few homemakers entered the workforce. Instead, the eight million women already at work shifted positions, taking advantage of new, albeit temporary, opportunities to work at better paying and higher skilled jobs.

Suffragists wanted the nation to thank women for their war work by giving them the right to vote. The vision of an engaged female citizenry working actively to defend the nation reduced the appeal of longstanding arguments against votes for women. In the past the close ties between female suffragists and the temperance movement had led some urban and midwestern male residents to resist enfranchising women because so many women supported prohibition. The South feared that female suffrage meant extending the right to vote to black women. Other opponents argued that the male head of the household adequately represented his family's interests in the public domain, holding fast to a vision of women as primarily domestic, not public, figures.

In the 1910s the middle- and upper-class women leading the suffragist movement had divided into radical and conservative factions (see Chapter 18) and each offered a competing vision of how to obtain the vote for women. For months members of the militant National Woman's Party stood outside the White House with banners asking "how long must women wait for liberty?" Once the United States entered the war, militant suffragists turned Wilson's democratic rhetoric against him. They erected a sign (**20.9**) intended to embarrass Wilson as he greeted a Russian delegation from the parliamentary government that ruled Russia for a short time in 1917 before Lenin seized power. Wilson hoped to convince the delegates to keep Russia in the war so democracy could triumph over autocracy in Europe. The suffragists instead focused on the recent introduction of female suffrage in Russia, urging the envoys to "help us make this nation really free" by convincing Wilson to support female suffrage.

Daily scuffles broke out between outraged war supporters and the picketing suffragists, whom the press vilified as unpatriotic. After the police arrested the suffragists, the women initiated a hunger strike to protest their poor treatment in prison. After news accounts of prison guards forcing feeding tubes down the throats of suffragists leaked out, Wilson pardoned them. Unbowed the female militants returned to the White House gates, where they burned Wilson in effigy.

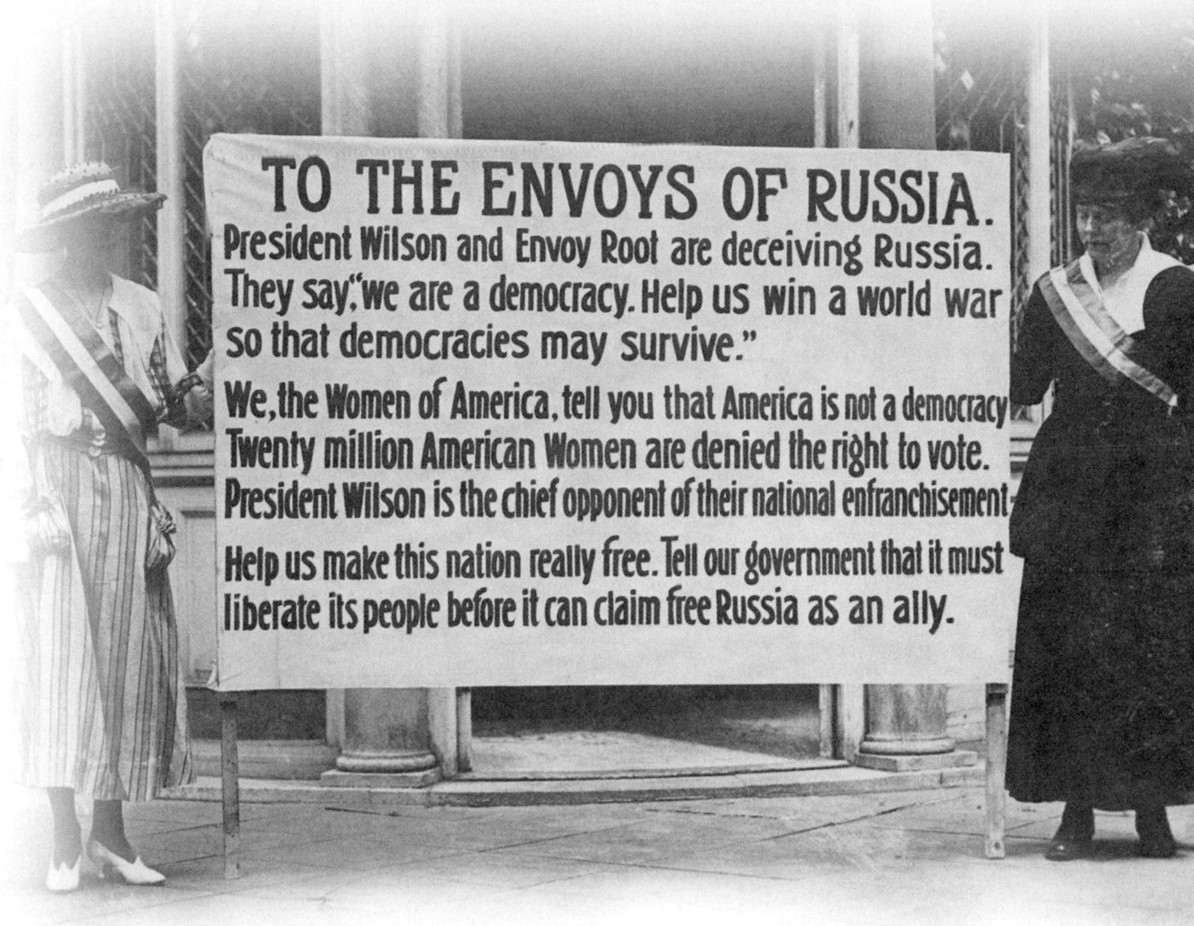

TO THE ENVOYS OF RUSSIA.
President Wilson and Envoy Root are deceiving Russia.
They say,"we are a democracy. Help us win a world war so that democracies may survive."
We, the Women of America, tell you that America is not a democracy
Twenty million American Women are denied the right to vote.
President Wilson is the chief opponent of their national enfranchisement
Help us make this nation really free. Tell our government that it must liberate its people before it can claim free Russia as an ally.

20.9 Suffragists Picket the White House The radical wing of the suffragist movement criticized Wilson, who claimed that an Allied victory would spread democracy, for refusing to support female suffrage.

The more moderate National American Woman Suffrage Association (NAWSA) followed a different tack. The NAWSA presented the vote, not as a question of equality or democracy, but as a way to reinforce the traditional desire of women to protect their families (see Chapter 18). The NAWSA also seized upon wartime prejudices against German Americans, whose loyalty many Americans increasingly questioned. "It is a risk, a danger to a country like ours to send 1,000,000 men out of the country who are loyal and not replace those men by the loyal votes of the women they have left at home," NAWSA president Carrie Chapman Catt proclaimed. All these arguments eventually swayed Wilson. In September 1918 he became the first president to endorse national female suffrage, convinced that the female pacifist nature could help secure his postwar goals for a lasting peace. Congress sent the **Nineteenth Amendment**, a constitutional amendment that granted women the right to vote, to the states on June 4, 1919, seven months after the war ended. Final ratification came on August 26, 1920.

Rallying the Public

To control the flow of information and shape public opinion about the war, Wilson formed the **Committee on Public Information** (CPI). Headed by George Creel, a Progressive muckraking journalist, the CPI disseminated propaganda posters, pamphlets, and films. The CPI translated its pamphlets into multiple languages to reach the nation's huge immigrant population. The agency also recruited so-called Four-Minute Men to speak before audiences in movie halls, markets, fairs, and churches. The CPI limited each speech to four minutes to fill the time that it took to change the reels for silent films in movie theatres. Creel estimated that 75,000 Four-Minute Men gave nearly seven million impassioned speeches during the war on topics such as German submarine warfare and German espionage. Hollywood helped the official propaganda effort by making movies like *To Hell With the Kaiser*, a film that depicted the German leader as a depraved lunatic who receives a much-deserved punch in the mouth from the American soldier who captures him.

The government also used war bond campaigns to win over hearts and minds. Rather than angering the public with higher taxes to pay for the war, the government financed two-thirds of the war's costs with **war bonds**, short-term loans that individual citizens made to the government. Secretary of the Treasury William G. McAdoo believed that Americans who bought a fifty-dollar liberty bond, a five-dollar war savings certificate, or a twenty-five cent thrift stamp felt personally connected to the war. "Any great war must necessarily be a popular movement," McAdoo noted. Financing the war through war bonds, however, made the war more expensive because eventually the government had to pay interest to each bondholder.

With the government reaching out to immigrants from Russia, Poland, and Italy through war bond campaigns and military recruitment, the war gave many immigrants a chance to feel American for the first time. Recent arrivals often lived in ethnic neighborhoods and worked alongside their compatriots, circumstances that had made assimilation difficult. Rather than having to choose between their homelands and their new country, these immigrants could openly support both during the war. "By Helping the American Red Cross You are Helping Italy," read an ad in one Italian American newspaper.

Immigrants from the Allied nations thrived during the war, but for German-Americans the war years were bleak. Wartime propaganda accentuated Americans' sense of duty, concern for troops in the field, and fears of a German invasion. *Images as History: Propaganda Posters* discusses the impact of this anti-German imagery more fully. Propaganda posters whipped up patriotic fervor and hate for the enemy to justify the war and motivate young Americans to fight. To their dismay, Progressive reformers soon realized that the same publicity techniques they had perfected to expose corrupt business practices and spur interest in reform during the Progressive Era (see Chapter18) could also incite war hysteria. Wartime propaganda ultimately served its purpose. Americans spent nearly $21.4 billion on war bonds purchases.

German Spies and Civil Liberties

Throughout the period of U.S. neutrality, German spies and saboteurs in the United States tried to disrupt the munitions trade between the United States and Britain. Spies planted tiny egg-shaped bombs on ships carrying munitions and detonated dynamite in several munitions factories. The most spectacular prewar strike by German saboteurs occurred at a munitions depot in Black Tom, New Jersey, on the Hudson River. Citizens as far away as Philadelphia, Pennsylvania, heard the huge explosions on the morning of July 30, 1916. Shrapnel left holes in the Statue of Liberty, and shock waves shattered thousands of windows in lower Manhattan. Anxious to keep the country neutral, the government labeled each incident an accident despite clear evidence of sabotage. The government could not explain away the actions of Eric Muenter, a German American professor who planted a bomb that exploded in an empty U.S. Senate reception room on July 2, 1915. Muenter then broke into the house of financier J. P. Morgan, whose bank acted as the purchasing agent for the British government, where he shot and wounded Morgan.

> "When the nation is at war many things that might be said in time of peace ... will not be endured so long as men fight."
>
> Supreme Court Justice OLIVER WENDELL HOLMES Jr., upholding the constitutionality of the Espionage Act

Once the country entered the war, government propaganda urged the public to stay alert for "spies and lies" and report "the man who spreads pessimistic stories, divulges—or seeks—confidential military information, cries for peace, or belittles our efforts to win the war." The 1917 **Espionage Act** made it a crime to obstruct military recruitment, to encourage mutiny, or to aid the enemy by spreading lies. These prohibitions had a chilling effect on speech. The **Sedition Act**, passed in 1918, went even further by prohibiting anyone from uttering, writing, or publishing "any abusive or disloyal language" concerning the flag, constitution, government, or armed forces. Civil liberties and antiwar advocates challenged both laws in court, but the Supreme Court upheld the Espionage Act and Sedition Act as constitutional.

What effect did revelations of German spying and wartime propaganda have on the public?

Images as History

PROPAGANDA POSTERS

In his war address Wilson told the American people that "we have no quarrel with the German people." But Wilson also privately predicted that "a nation couldn't put its strength into a war and keep its head level; it had never been done." The government soon plastered the nation with propaganda posters that relied on negative images of Germany and Germans to rally the public to support the war. Teaching Americans to despise anything German had negative consequences on the home front, where German Americans went from being one of the most respected immigrant groups to one of the most hated. Wartime propaganda also questioned the patriotism and masculinity of men who refused to serve. What made these wartime posters effective propaganda?

This 1917 army recruiting poster depicts the Germans as savage beasts who raped, pillaged, and killed.

In 1939 Adolf Hitler rallied German opinion against the former Allied nations by reprinting this poster with the caption: "When they assaulted us 25 years ago, they wrote on their rotten slanderous poster: 'Destroy this mad beast'—they meant the German people!"

The gorilla carries the club of culture, alerting Americans to reject the contaminating influences of Germany's culture. Nearly half of the states banned or restricted the teaching of German, and Americans renamed the hamburger a "liberty sandwich."

Europe lays in ruins behind the gorilla-like German soldier who carries his limp female victim, a ravaged Lady Liberty, as he makes his way to American soil.

The image of Germany threatening the American coastline reminded viewers that German U-boats patrolled the Atlantic coast looking for troop and merchant ships to sink.

"Destroy this Mad Brute"

The poster shows a fearful man hiding shamefully in the dark with his back turned against the bright, vibrant scene of virile men marching proudly under a large flag.

This man's wistful look implies that he will regret his decision to stand apart from his countrymen.

This loner is a man of privilege, reflecting concerns about the emasculating effect of urban life on middle- and upper-class American men.

Several cities held "slacker raids" where policemen stormed into movie theaters and arrested those who could not produce a draft registration card.

"On Which Side of the Window Are You?"

How did visual depictions of the Germans compare to media images of the Spanish during the Spanish-American War?

TEN LITTLE HYPHENS

Ten Lil Hyphens sitting on line, Uncle Sam jailed one and then there were nine.

Nine Lil Hyphens hiding among freight, one dropped a great big bomb and that left eight.

Eight Lil Hyphens talking war and heaven, one cheered for Faderland and that left seven.

Seven Lil Hyphens full of spying tricks, one had his nose bumped hard so that left six.

Six Lil Hyphens trying to connive, one was caught in the act so that left five.

Five Lil Hyphens feeling very sore, one faked his passport and that left four.

Four Lil Hyphens of very high degree, one joshed the President and that left three.

Three Lil Hyphens with very much ado, one skipped to Mexico and that left two.

Two Lil Hyphens fooling with a gun, the gun was marked U. S. A., so that left one.

One Lil Hyphen sitting all alone, believed the German war news and then there was none.

20.10 *Ten Little Hyphens*
Capturing the public's fears of German espionage, this caricature implied that "hyphenated Americans" retained dangerous loyalties to their homelands. This song identified blowing up a munitions factory and criticizing the president as equal threats to national security.

Some Americans decided to take matters into their own hands, attacking German Americans and their businesses. In the war's most infamous incident of vigilante justice, a mob murdered German American Robert Prager in Collinsville, Illinois. When the first attempt to hang Prager failed, the assailants granted his request to write a letter, expecting him to detail a plot to dynamite a mine. Instead Prager wrote a letter to his mother and father who still lived in Dresden, Germany. "Dear parents," he wrote in German, "I must on this fourth day of April, 1918, die. Please pray for me, my dear parents." The murder went unpunished. To protect themselves from similar assaults, many German American families changed their names, stopped teaching German to their children, and purchased multiple war bonds.

The caricature *Ten Little Hyphens* (**20.10**) captured the growing sense that dual loyalty meant disloyalty. The lyrics in the ditty refer to real incidents of German espionage in the United States, including German agents who blew up munitions, assumed false identities by faking passports, or fled to Mexico. The caricature also referenced the demand from some patriots that "German-Americans," so-called "hyphenated Americans," drop their allegiance to their native lands and become 100 percent American. "We can have no fifty-fifty allegiance in this country," proclaimed Theodore Roosevelt.

This caricature underscored another dilemma facing the nation: how to protect itself from terrorist attacks without denying residents the right to free speech. The lyrics reveal that during the war, officials considered words as dangerous as acts of sabotage, punishing German Americans who "cheered for Faderland," or their fatherland.

Besides routing out suspected spies the Espionage and Sedition acts also helped the federal government suppress pacifists who refused to give up opposition to the war and radical political groups like the Socialist Party and Industrial Workers of the World that had long opposed capitalism. "The master class has always declared the wars; the subject class has always fought the battles," declared Eugene Debs, the leader of the Socialist Party. During the debate over declaring war, before passage of the Espionage Act, members of Congress had uttered similar denunciations of the rich and powerful. But as punishment for uttering these words in 1918, a federal judge sentenced Debs to ten years in prison. Debs became a hero in some quarters for his steady opposition to the war. In 1920, two years after the war ended, Debs made his fifth and final bid for the presidency from his jail cell and received one million votes. President Warren Harding pardoned Debs in 1921.

How does this song capture the tension between preventing espionage and protecting civil liberties?

Fighting the War

Germany had good reason to assume that it would take time for the United States to pose a threat on the Western Front. The country confronted significant challenges raising and training an army quickly. In 1917 the American armed forces numbered just over 300,000. Over the next nineteen months, however, the military grew to over four million and managed to arrive overseas just in time to prevent a German victory.

Raising an Army

When the nation entered the war, the government faced the choice of raising its armed forces with volunteers, instituting conscription immediately, or waiting until enlistments began to flag before turning to a draft. In previous wars the government had selected the third option. Wilson, however, chose to implement conscription immediately. Wilson knew that the United States needed to supply the Allies with troops, munitions, and food. The draft gave the government the power to decide who stayed at home to work in essential wartime industries and who went into the army. Letting individuals decide might deprive industry of its best workers or leave the military understrength once the initial enthusiasm for enlisting subsided. To combat the impression that conscription forced reluctant men to fight, the government renamed the draft "selective service." Selective service, the government repeatedly told the American public, placed men where they could best serve the war effort.

To offer the public a visible demonstration of male patriotism, all men registered publicly for selective service on the same day. On June 5, 1917, ship horns, church bells, and factory whistles rang out and crowds gathered to cheer for men filling out their draft registration cards. Three million men, or 11 percent of the draft-eligible population, refused either to register or to serve. Some went to jail; others managed to elude authorities by changing jobs often. The Selective Service Act allowed **conscientious objectors** from recognized pacifist sects to apply for noncombatant duty. Those who opposed fighting for philosophical or political reasons had no legal way to stay out of fighting units. The most famous conscientious objector of the war was Sergeant Alvin C. York who, like 80 percent of drafted conscientious objectors, eventually agreed to fight. *Choices and Consequences: Alvin York, Deciding to Serve* (page 610) explores York's decision to serve in the army. Conscripts ultimately accounted for 72 percent of the four million men in the wartime army. Overall, 20 percent of the draft-eligible male population (ages 18–45) served in the wartime military, 15 percent of the adult male population overall.

"You're in the Army Now"

In makeshift training camps across the country, soldiers trained (sometimes with wooden rifles) and spoke eagerly of getting to France before the "big show" ended. The army reflected the diversity of the American population. Approximately 18 percent of the entire force, or one in five, were foreign-born. Nearly twelve thousand Native Americans served, composing only a small fraction of the total military force, but representing nearly 25 percent of the Native American male population. Sixteen thousand women went overseas as nurses, telephone operators, or welfare workers working in army canteens.

African Americans made up 13 percent of the military, though they were only 10 percent of the country's population. The wartime army remained strictly segregated. Black soldiers received few chances to demonstrate bravery or leadership since 89 percent served as labor troops under mostly white officers. Although they received little recognition from white authorities, these troops performed important logistical services by constructing the roads and bridges required to keep a modern army in the field. In France many black troops discovered a more racially tolerant environment where white French had no qualms socializing with African American soldiers. "You now know that the mean contemptible spirit of race prejudice that curses this land is not the spirit of other lands," noted the African American minister Francis J. Grimké to a group of returning black soldiers. The fear that black servicemen intended to bring the fight for democracy home provoked numerous postwar riots and lynchings that often targeted black veterans in uniform. Determined to fight back against white supremacists, black veterans helped forge a more

Why did the government choose to draft the wartime army?

Choices and Consequences

ALVIN YORK, DECIDING TO SERVE

Alvin York grew up poor in the Tennessee Appalachian Mountains, where he became an expert marksman hunting wild turkeys in the forests. He spent his youth carousing, gambling, and drinking. As an adult he underwent a religious conversion and joined the Church of Christ in Christian Union, a pacifist Christian sect. Drafted six months before his thirtieth birthday, York faced an agonizing decision on whether or not to fight. "I believed in my Bible," he said. "And it distinctly said. 'THOU SHALT NOT KILL.'" But, York acknowledged, "I wanted to be a good Christian and a good American too."

Choices

1 Request noncombatant duty as a conscientious objector.

2 Refuse to serve in any form of military duty.

3 Agree to serve and fight.

Decision

Like many men claiming conscientious objector status, York faced intense pressure to fight once he entered a training camp. After several conversations about the Bible with his commanding officers, York eventually decided that the biblical injunction "Blessed are the peacemakers" overrode the Sixth Commandment prohibiting killing because the war promised to be "the war to end all wars." York agreed to fight.

Consequences

York became the most celebrated American hero of the war for his feats on the battlefield in France. On October 8, 1918, York was credited with killing 24 German soldiers, silencing 35 machine guns, and capturing 132 enemy soldiers during the Meuse-Argonne campaign. Surviving combat without a scratch reaffirmed York's faith in God, but on his deathbed he still wondered whether God would punish him for killing men in battle.

Continuing Controversies

What is the ultimate meaning of York's experience? Some historians note that York's transformation from pacifist to warrior demonstrated that Wilsonian ideals inspired many American soldiers to fight in World War I. With Americans divided in 1941 (before the Japanese attacked the American naval base in Pearl Harbor, Hawaii) over the merits of entering World War II, the Hollywood film *Sergeant York* sent the message that fighting to defend the country was a citizen's Christian and patriotic duty. Others note that York personified the poorly educated and underprivileged conscript who did the bulk of the fighting along the Western Front. Some believe that the army exaggerated York's feats to boost morale. Rather than a cause for celebration, his experience reveals the difficulty of becoming a conscientious objector during the war—an experience repeated in future conflicts, especially the Vietnam War.

Sergeant Alvin C. York, with his mother in front of his home in Tennessee

What factors constrained or influenced York's choice to serve?

militant postwar civil rights movement (see Chapter 21).

To help the army turn this polyglot force into a functioning military force, civilian psychologists administered intelligence tests to soldiers in the training camps. Quickly assessing a recruit's intelligence could help the army immediately identify whether a man was officer material or better suited for unloading boxes of supplies off ships in France. To their surprise 25 percent of the soldier population had to take the test designed for illiterates. The majority of native-born white soldiers had completed only 7 years of school, while foreign-born men averaged 4.7 years and Southern black men 2.6 years of schooling.

Psychologists claimed their intelligence tests measured native intelligence, but the test questions suggest they primarily assessed level of education, economic background, and familiarity with mainstream American culture (**20.11**). Tabulated exam results claimed that the white American soldiers had a mental age of 13, while the average mental age was 11.01 for Italians, 11.34 for Russians, 10.74 for Poles, and 10.41 for American-born blacks. Some critics argued that the tests only showed that immigrants and blacks needed more comprehensive schooling. Social Darwinists, who used Charles Darwin's ideas of survival of the fittest to establish a racial hierarchy of superior and inferior human races, believed these figures validated existing ideas of white northern European superiority. After the war public schools began administering intelligence tests to determine the aptitude of their pupils, a trend that continues today.

On the Western Front

The United States entered the war at a critical moment. The peace with Russia gave Germany a clear manpower advantage on the battlefield. As U-boats began sinking Allied shipping indiscriminately, the Germans transferred over one million men from the Eastern Front with Russia to the Western Front in France. In March 1918 the Germans accomplished what many had thought impossible: They broke through the trench stalemate

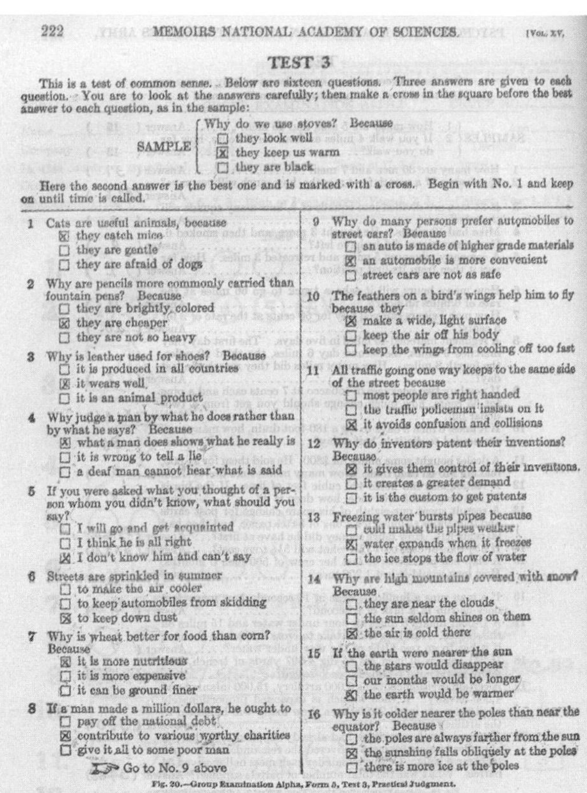

222 MEMOIRS NATIONAL ACADEMY OF SCIENCES. [Vol. XV.

TEST 3

This is a test of common sense. Below are sixteen questions. Three answers are given to each question. You are to look at the answers carefully; then make a cross in the square before the best answer to each question, as in the sample:

SAMPLE: Why do we use stoves? Because
☐ they look well
☒ they keep us warm
☐ they are black

Here the second answer is the best one and is marked with a cross. Begin with No. 1 and keep on until time is called.

1 Cats are useful animals, because
☒ they catch mice
☐ they are gentle
☐ they are afraid of dogs

2 Why are pencils more commonly carried than fountain pens? Because
☐ they are brightly colored
☒ they are cheaper
☐ they are not so heavy

3 Why is leather used for shoes? Because
☐ it is produced in all countries
☒ it wears well
☐ it is an animal product

4 Why judge a man by what he does rather than by what he says? Because
☒ what a man does shows what he really is
☐ it is wrong to tell a lie
☐ a deaf man cannot hear what is said

5 If you were asked what you thought of a person whom you didn't know, what should you say?
☐ I will go and get acquainted
☐ I think he is all right
☒ I don't know him and can't say

6 Streets are sprinkled in summer
☐ to make the air cooler
☐ to keep automobiles from skidding
☒ to keep down dust

7 Why is wheat better for food than corn? Because
☒ it is more nutritious
☐ it is more expensive
☐ it can be ground finer

8 If a man made a million dollars, he ought to
☐ pay off the national debt
☒ contribute to various worthy charities
☐ give it all to some poor man

Go to No. 9 above

9 Why do many persons prefer automobiles to street cars? Because
☐ an auto is made of higher grade materials
☒ an automobile is more convenient
☐ street cars are not as safe

10 The feathers on a bird's wings help him to fly because they
☒ make a wide, light surface
☐ keep the air off his body
☐ keep the wings from cooling off too fast

11 All traffic going one way keeps to the same side of the street because
☐ most people are right handed
☐ the traffic policeman insists on it
☒ it avoids confusion and collisions

12 Why do inventors patent their inventions? Because
☒ it gives them control of their inventions.
☐ it creates a greater demand
☐ it is the custom to get patents

13 Freezing water bursts pipes because
☐ cold makes the pipes weaker
☒ water expands when it freezes
☐ the ice stops the flow of water

14 Why are high mountains covered with snow? Because
☐ they are near the clouds
☐ the sun seldom shines on them
☒ the air is cold there

15 If the earth were nearer the sun
☐ the stars would disappear
☐ our months would be longer
☒ the earth would be warmer

16 Why is it colder nearer the poles than near the equator? Because
☐ the poles are always farther from the sun
☒ the sunshine falls obliquely at the poles
☐ there is more ice at the poles

Fig. 20.—Group Examination Alpha, Form 5, Test 3, Practical Judgment.

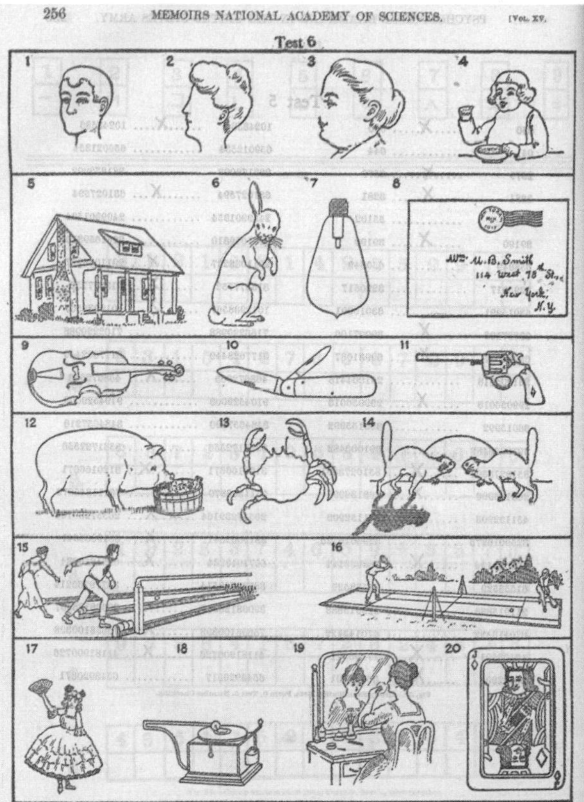

256 MEMOIRS NATIONAL ACADEMY OF SCIENCES. [Vol. XV.

Test 6

1 2 3 4 5 6 7 8 9 10 11 12 13 14 15 16 17 18 19 20

20.11 Intelligence Tests for Soldiers
These questions come from an intelligence test on logic given to literate soldiers in training camps. The pictorial exam for illiterates and non-English speakers required that soldiers draw in the missing item.

Take these intelligence tests yourself. Who would fare well on these tests and why?

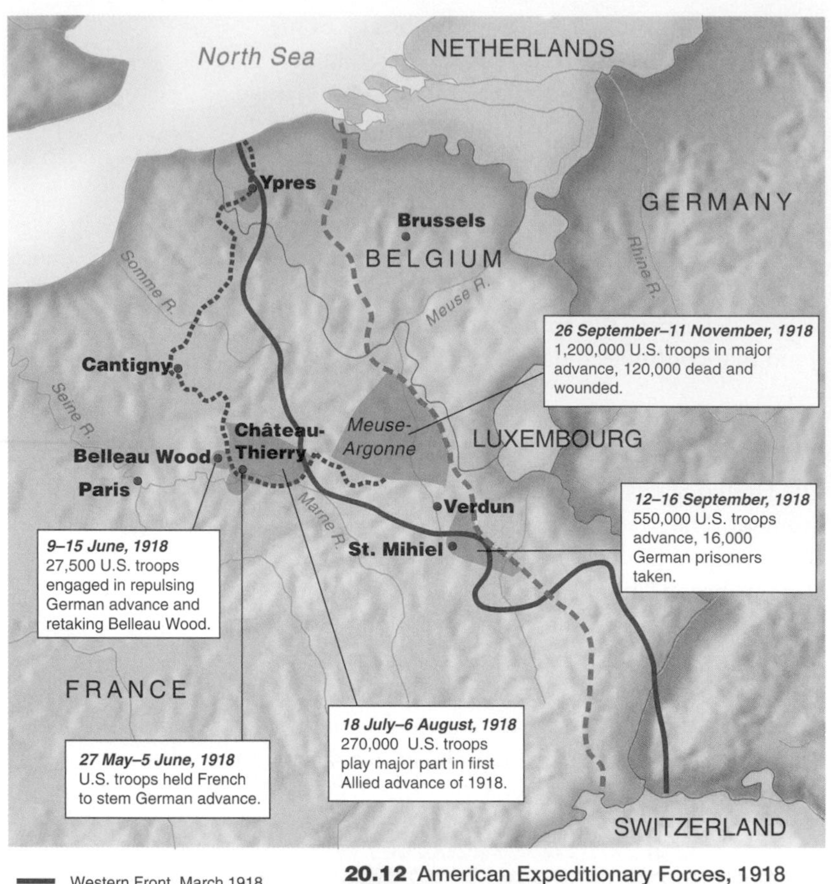

20.12 American Expeditionary Forces, 1918
U.S. troops fought hard for six months along the Western Front, winning key victories at Chateau-Thierry, St. Mihiel, and during the Meuse-Argonne campaign.

> "I hope that you have not arrived too late."
>
> The American ambassador to General JOHN J. PERSHING upon his arrival in France

and began marching once again toward Paris. The map (**20.12**) reveals how much French territory the Germans captured during their spectacularly successful spring offensives against the British and French armies.

As in 1914, however, the pace of the offensive exhausted German troops, who quickly outran their supply lines. The arriving **American Expeditionary Forces**, the American soldiers who fought overseas under the command of General John J. Pershing, played a critical role in stopping the German drive toward Paris in battles at Cantigny, Belleau Wood, and Chateau-Thierry. In July American soldiers fought with the French in a successful six-week counteroffensive that pushed the German army back to where it had begun the spring offensives. These campaigns initiated American soldiers to the reality of fighting along the Western Front. Men collapsed from the strain of continuous artillery bombardments and the sight of bodies blown to bits. Soldiers diagnosed with shell shock suffered from panic attacks, and some could not sleep or speak. Private Duncan Kemerer arrived at a military hospital in such poor condition that the sound of a spoon dropping sent him frantically searching for cover under his bed.

American soldiers soon settled into the predictable routine of trench warfare. The three-dimensional trench shown in the *World War I* special feature portrays the different components of a working trench. A strip of land known as No-Man's Land separated the Allied and German trench systems. The actual distance between the two lines averaged 250 yards. Scores of barbed wire covered this barren strip of land, which was filled with huge craters formed by artillery shells.

The U.S. Army rotated soldiers, putting them in the trenches for twenty-one days, with a week to recuperate in the rear before their next rotation. Each day just before sunrise, the men assembled and went on alert. If dawn passed with no enemy attack, then the men spent the day trying to stay out of sight from enemy snipers and airplanes that strafed troops with machine gun fire. By feasting on corpses rats grew to gigantic proportions and multiplied by the thousands. Adding to the misery of trench life was the constant rain in northern France, which created a thick, gooey mud. At night, No-Man's Land came alive as small patrols scrambled out of the trenches to repair damaged wire or raid enemy lines for prisoners who might reveal valuable military information.

German artillery bombed the Allied lines, day and night. "To be shelled is the worst thing in the world," noted one American soldier. "It is impossible to adequately imagine it." Troops developed an array of superstitions to try to make sense of who lived and who died in the trenches. "They claim that a man's shell has his name on it, if it's for him," joked Sergeant Harry Weisburg. "But it is the part of a wise man to keep his nose out of the way of another man's shell." By 1918 one of every four shells fired on the Western Front contained poison gas. Troops especially feared odorless, colorless mustard gas, which caused painful burns on any exposed skin and was deadly if inhaled. Slow-moving tanks also made their first appearance on the battlefield, but the war ended before either side could exploit their full potential as an offensive weapon.

World War I

The trenches along the Western Front were intricate defense systems that both protected soldiers and added to their misery in the front lines. As a straight line, the trenches ran for 460 miles from the North Sea to Switzerland. The network of trenches, however, encompassed nearly 35,000 miles, disfiguring the Belgian and French countryside. France suffered the heaviest casualties of the Allied nations: On the whole, the number of Frenchmen who died each day (900) was twice as high as the number of British (457) and more than four times higher than the number of Americans (195). But in the last six months of the war, the American death rate jumped to 820 a day as U.S. troops experienced their share of brutal fighting. Overall fewer American soldiers perished, but the cost to the United States was still high. More Americans died on the battlefield in World War I than in Korea or Vietnam, both much longer wars.

No-Man's Land.
The desolate strip of land that divided opposing trench lines was covered with huge shell craters, corpes, and barbed wire.
Communication trenches.
Messages, supplies, wounded men and replacement troops funneled through these passages.
Listening post.
Men in this trench sent up warning flares if the enemy attacked.
Support and reserve trenches.
The bulk of troops remained here unless attacking.
Front-line Trench.
Men climbed "over the top" when making an attack.
Sandbags.
Absorbed enemy bullets.
L-shaped pattern.
This prevented enemy troops from breaking through and firing machine guns straight down the trench.
Wooden planks.
Covering the trench floor, these kept soldiers from sinking into the mud.
Dug-outs.
Underground quarters protected troops from artillery shells.

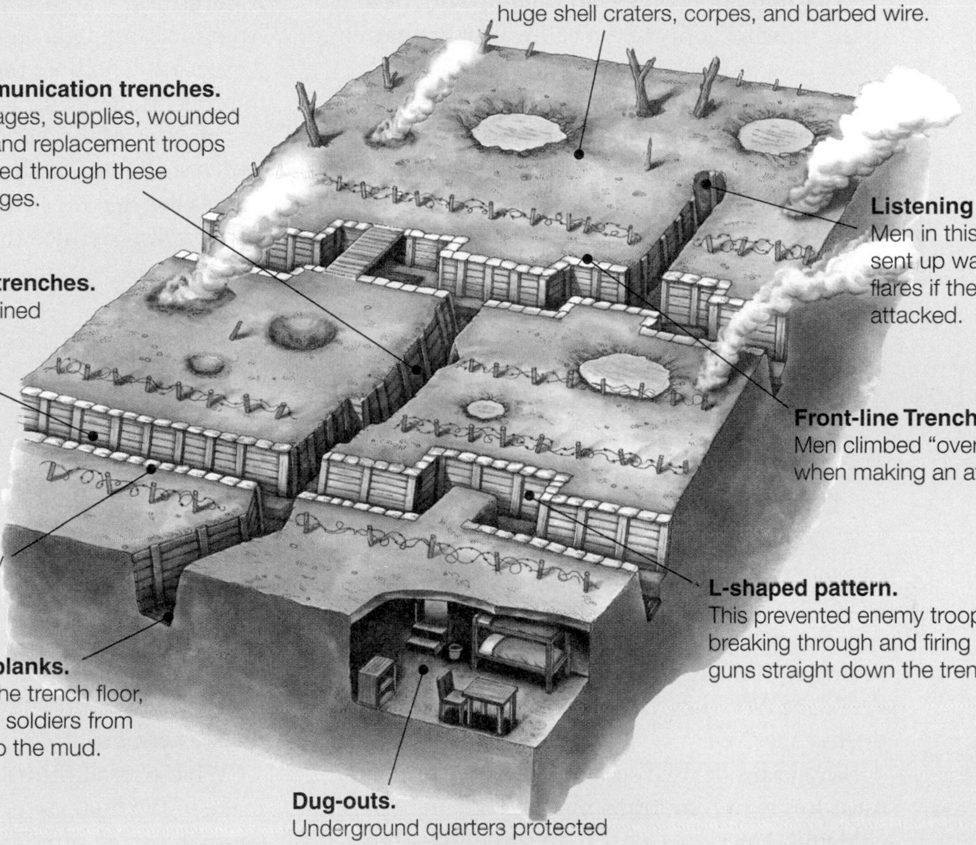

	Deaths	Wounded
France	1.3 million	3.0 million
Britain	950,000	2.1 million
Germany	1.8 million	4.2 million
Russia	1.7 million	4.9 million
United States	116,000	204,000
Austria-Hungary	1.2 million	3.6 million

World War I Casualties

Conflict	Total Serving	Battle Deaths	Other Deaths	Wounded
Civil War (1861–1865)				
Union	2,213,363	140,414	224,097	281,881
Confederate	600,000 – 1,500,000	74,524	59,297	—
World War I (1917–1918)	4,734,991	53,402	63,114	204,002
World War II (1941–1945)	16,112,566	291,557	113,842	670,846
Korean War (1950-1953)	5,720,000	33,741	2,833	103,284
Vietnam War (1964–1973)	8,744,000	47,355	10,796	153,303

America at War: Battlefield deaths, deaths by disease, and wounded

What differing perspectives do these charts and trench diagram offer on the U.S. battlefield experience?

Flu Epidemic

In 1918, in the midst of mounting battlefield casualties, the world suddenly encountered a new vicious killer. Without warning a particularly lethal strain of influenza traversed the globe. The virus became known as **Spanish Influenza** because the Spanish press first reported its outbreak. Biologists speculate that the influenza germ began as a mutated version of avian (bird) flu in the American Midwest in March 1918. American soldiers carried the germ to France, and the virus spread rapidly from Europe to Africa, Asia, and Central America. Nearly twenty-five million Americans fell ill, a quarter of the entire population, and 675,000 died.

Anecdotes of people who went to work healthy in the morning, only to die before dinnertime, illustrated how suddenly the lethal virus could strike. Influenza was usually the most severe for children and the elderly, segments of the population with weak immune systems. This flu virus attacked young adults especially hard—making it particularly unique and terrifying.

Public officials closed movie houses, schools, churches, and office buildings in an effort to contain the epidemic. Nearly one million American soldiers also fell ill, further hampering an overseas military campaign that already faced considerable challenges fighting with an inexperienced force. General John Pershing, Assistant Secretary of the Navy Franklin D. Roosevelt, and President Woodrow Wilson all suffered from the flu, but survived.

> "I had a little bird/Its name was Enza/I opened up the window/And in-flu-enza."
>
> A children's rope-skipping rhyme inspired by the 1918 influenza epidemic

Physicians devised some useless precautionary measures to prevent transmission. Throughout the epidemic Americans wore masks in public (the microscopic virus passed easily through the fabric), boiled their dishes, and sprayed public areas with disinfectants. In mid-1919, as suddenly as it had come, the virus disappeared, having run out of susceptible human beings to infect.

The Spanish Influenza pandemic had a catastrophic effect worldwide. From 1918 to 1919, the disease killed thirty million people. Nine million men died in battle from 1914–1918. The bloodiest war to date thus coincided with the deadliest influenza epidemic yet recorded.

The Final Campaigns

In September 1918 the American army attacked at St. Mihiel (20.12). The battle successfully reduced a bulge in the lines (called a "salient"), thereby weakening German defenses. Two weeks later, the Allies began a massive coordinated assault along the entire Western Front. The Americans hit the Germans hard in the Meuse-Argonne region of France, while the British and French struck farther north and west. Advancing in heavily wooded and hilly terrain against dense German fortifications, the American effort stalled. Regrouping, the Americans began pushing the Germans back in October. Battle casualty rates averaged 2,550 a day, with 6,000 Americans dying each week of the 47-day Meuse-Argonne campaign. "It was most assuredly the Americans who bore the heaviest brunt of the fighting on the whole battle front during the last few months of the war," the German General Erich Ludendorff later recalled.

Besides making headway on the battlefield, Allied convoys also stymied the German unrestricted submarine warfare campaign. Instead of letting individual ships take their chances at sea, British and American naval vessels began escorting groups of Allied merchant vessels across the Atlantic. At the beginning of November, the German military high command requested an armistice. On the eleventh hour of the eleventh day of the eleventh month of 1918, the Armistice went into effect and guns fell silent along the Western Front.

What overall contribution did American troops make to the final victory? At key moments in the German spring offensives in 1918, American soldiers helped stop the Germans from taking Paris. American divisions provided key strength for the French-led counteroffensives over the summer, and in the Meuse-Argonne campaign American soldiers leveled a devastating blow to the German army that helped make British and French advances to the north possible. Also important, the prospect of fighting a million more fresh American recruits in 1919 convinced Germany to seek a negotiated peace.

Did the Allies win the war, or did Germany lose it?

Peace

The Armistice ended active fighting, but the details of the peace settlement took months to negotiate. Twenty-seven nations and four British dominions sent delegates to the Paris Peace Conference. Germany expected to join the negotiations, but instead the terms of peace were determined in secret by the Big Four: Wilson, Clemenceau, the British Prime Minister Lloyd George, and the Italian Premier Vittorio Orlando. The **Versailles Peace Treaty** required Germany to pay reparations and disarm. Germany signed the treaty under protest on June 28, 1919, the same date of Archduke Franz Ferdinand's assassination five years earlier. In the end the flawed and controversial Versailles Peace Treaty laid the groundwork for future conflict in Europe and raised questions at home about the future role America wanted to play in the world.

The Paris Peace Conference

Woodrow Wilson enjoyed worldwide popularity on Armistice Day. Throughout the United States and Europe, Wilson's idealistic pronouncements had raised hopes that the war's slaughter might pave the way for a lasting peace. Wilson broke with tradition and decided to travel overseas to negotiate the peace treaty himself, rather than sending representatives to hash out the details. As Wilson toured Paris, London, Rome, and Milan, papers greeted him as "The Savior of Humanity." British and French leaders, however, knew that four years of suffering had created a deep-seated desire for revenge against Germany within their nations. The war had hardened Wilson's view of Germany as well, and he agreed to weaken postwar Germany by eliminating its navy and colonies. He disagreed, however, with the French insistence on eviscerating the German economy and military permanently.

Certain that America had played a vital role in winning the war, Wilson felt confident asserting his equal right, along with Britain and France, to shape the terms of peace. British and French leaders, however, publicly downplayed America's contribution to defeating Germany, hoping to limit Wilson's say in the peace treaty. At the request of Allied leaders, the British and French press began printing increasingly disparaging reports about the American army's inexperience and leadership. Resentful over the Allies' apparent ingratitude for their wartime sacrifices, Americans' postwar disillusionment only grew as the treaty-making process got underway.

Wilson's domestic political problems weakened his negotiating position. In November the Republicans won control of Congress despite Wilson's plea to voters to return a Democratic majority as a vote of confidence for his peace proposals. The reasons for the Republican victory were complex, a result of unease with conditions at home as well as concern about Wilson's ideals. The Democrats' loss energized opponents of the **League of Nations**, a Wilson-supported collective security organization where member nations agreed to mediate future international disputes to prevent wars and work together to improve global human conditions.

Domestic opponents of the League of Nations worried that by joining the international organization America would lose control over its own foreign policy and invite international meddling in the Western Hemisphere. They also doubted that the League could successfully maintain world peace. League critics divided into two camps, each offering conflicting visions of America's role in the postwar world. Isolationists, led by Republican Senator William E. Borah from Idaho, preferred adopting an official policy of neutrality. The isolationists believed that if the United States kept out of all foreign disagreements, the country could avoid going to war in the future. By contrast the faction headed by Massachusetts Senator Henry Cabot Lodge, the Republican majority leader and chairman of Senate Foreign Affairs Committee, favored a return to the former balance of power system in Europe. Lodge wanted the United States to help rebuild, and perhaps join, a strong alliance among democratic European nations that could contain Germany indefinitely.

Eager to shore up support for the League of Nations at home, Wilson briefly sailed home to

What opposition did Wilson face overseas and at home to his peace plan?

confer with Republican leaders who were still upset that Wilson had not invited any leading Republicans to join his Paris negotiating team. The possibility of compromise appeared slim. Lodge had an intense personal dislike for Wilson, whom he regarded as sanctimonious. Wilson returned the distain, viewing Lodge as narrow-minded. Discussion soon stalled. On the day before Wilson left to return to Paris, Lodge handed the president a pledge signed by thirty-nine senators who vowed to reject the League covenant in its present form.

Hoping to appease his Republican critics, Wilson managed to incorporate key Republican demands in the final League covenant. The League of Nations now agreed to respect the Monroe Doctrine, the 1823 American pronouncement that the Western Hemisphere was off-limits to other world powers, and to allow nations to withdraw from the League. Wilson also tried outmaneuvering his domestic critics. He opted against creating two international agreements, a peace treaty and a covenant creating the League of Nations, that would each require a separate Senate ratification. Instead Wilson decided to incorporate the League covenant into the peace treaty. The Senate, Wilson gambled, would never refuse to ratify the peace treaty, even one that contained a controversial League of Nations.

> "With his mouth open and his eyes shut, I predict that he will make a Senator when he grows up."
>
> WILSON'S joke about his infant grandson touched upon his political troubles with Republican Senators

Allied leaders pressured Wilson to compromise as well. To get them to accept the League of Nations, Wilson gave up his idea of peace without victory. When Supreme Commander of Allied Armies Ferdinand Foch read the harsh demands of the Versailles Peace Treaty, he accurately predicted, "this isn't a peace, it's a twenty year truce." The treaty required that Germany pay reparations to French and Belgian civilians for the coal mines, factories, and fields its troops had destroyed during "the war imposed upon them by the aggression of Germany." This war guilt clause held Germany alone responsible for starting World War I. The treaty also forced Germany to disarm. The Reparations Committee set Germany's initial bill at $33 billion in gold, although commissions in the 1920s significantly reduced the amount owed. The United States accepted no reparation payments, and in the 1920s even loaned Germany money to help it pay this debt. The war guilt clause and the reparations bill created tremendous resentment in Germany. In the 1930s the German chancellor Adolf Hitler cultivated this anger to fuel a resurgent national fervor dedicated to restoring German economic and military strength.

The Versailles Treaty settled old territorial disputes in Europe, but the dismemberment of the Russian, German, and Austro-Hungarian empires created new sources of tensions. The redrawn map of eastern Europe reflected Wilson's principle of self-determination, fulfilling the ambitions of ethnic groups in Czechoslovakia, Poland, Yugoslavia, Croatia, Latvia, Lithuania, and Estonia to create their own nations (**20.13**). To limit Germany's postwar strength, the Allied side disregarded the desires of German-speaking peoples in Poland, Czechoslovakia, and Austria to unite with Germany. These three weak independent states remained vulnerable to future German and Soviet expansionist schemes. Twenty years later, Hitler justified his invasions of Austria (1938), Czechoslovakia (1938), and his joint invasion of Poland with Soviet leader Josef Stalin (1939) as a drive to reunite the German-speaking world separated by the terms of the Versailles Treaty (see Chapter 23).

Other nations also left the conference feeling slighted. Italy resented the Allies for denying it Austrian territory, a humiliation that the fascist leader Benito Mussolini vowed to avenge when he seized power in 1922. Japan protested the failure to incorporate into the League Covenant a statement protecting the rights of nonwhite nations, helping breed Japanese resentment against the West. In the Middle East, Africa, and Asia, the peace treaty transferred colonial possessions from the losers (the Ottoman and German empires) to the victors under a mandate system. In theory the mandate system named a Western nation as a League of Nation trustee for territories in need of political instruction before they assumed the responsibilities of self-government. In reality the mandate system simply cloaked old-style imperialism in the new rhetoric of

20.13 Europe and the Middle East after the War. The victorious Allies dismantled the German, Austro-Hungarian, and Ottoman empires to create independent nations in Central Europe and colonies for themselves in the Middle East.

self-determination. By redrawing the map of the Middle East to expand their global influence, Britain and France set in motion political, religious, and cultural conflicts in the region that created tremendous strife throughout the century. Denying Arab nationalist demands for independence, France took control of newly created Lebanon and Syria. Britain ruled Transjordan (present-day Jordan) and brought together three distinct ethnic groups—the Kurds, Sunnis, and Shiites—who had previously lived in autonomous regions to form the country of Iraq. When the British took over Palestine, they kept wartime promises to open up part of the territory to Jewish immigration, angering Arab residents in the process. Competing claims to this territory continue to this day.

The Treaty Fight at Home

Wilson saw the flaws in the final treaty, but he hoped that over time the League of Nations could modify the treaty's worst excesses. To counter the initial burst of public enthusiasm for joining the League of Nations, Republicans challenged Wilson's idealistic pronouncements promising world peace. "Are you ready to put your soldiers and your sailors at the

What significance did the re-drawn maps of Europe and the Middle East have?

disposition of other nations?" Senator Lodge asked the American people. The political cartoon *Looking a Gift Horse in the Mouth* (**20.14**) captured the public's mounting concern about the League. While Wilson tries to assure Uncle Sam that the League is better than nothing, the Senate carefully examines the mule. Wary of going against public opinion too strongly, Lodge did not urge outright rejection of the Versailles Treaty. He instead proposed adding fourteen American reservations. The most important one required explicit congressional approval before American troops went overseas. Wilson refused to accept modifications. Instead Wilson tried to create a groundswell of public support for the League that would force the Republicans to accept the treaty as written.

To reignite public enthusiasm for the League of Nations, the president traveled 10,000 miles in three weeks and made forty speeches to hundreds of thousands of people. The political cartoon *Ratification Rapids* (**20.15**) offered a sympathetic portrayal of Wilson, shown here using all his strength to steer the treaty and League Covenant to safety. In the cartoon a young woman clutches both documents to her breast, symbolizing both the besieged nation and innocent victims of war. In his speeches Wilson dismissed Republican concerns about sending American troops throughout the world as impractical. "If you want to put out a fire in Utah, you don't send to Oklahoma for the fire engine. If you want to put out a fire in the Balkans, if you want to stamp out the smoldering flames in some part of Central Europe, you don't send to the United States for troops," Wilson told an audience in Salt Lake City. *Competing Visions: Joining the League of Nations* further explores the debate between Wilson and Lodge.

20.14 *Looking a Gift Horse in the Mouth*
This political cartoon expresses skepticism about the League of Nations. By taking a closer look, the Senate realizes that the League (represented here as a broken-down mule) is not strong enough to handle the hard work of keeping the peace.

20.15 *Ratification Rapids*
This sympathetic portrait of Woodrow Wilson trying to steer the Versailles Treaty through the ratification process illustrates how contentious the treaty debate became.

What competing views do these political cartoons offer on the question of ratifying the Versailles Treaty?

Competing Visions

JOINING THE LEAGUE OF NATIONS

In 1919 President Woodrow Wilson and Senator Henry Cabot Lodge debated the wisdom and value of joining the League of Nations. Consider the exact wording of Article X, and then the differing interpretations of it offered by Lodge and Wilson. What changes in American foreign policy does each foresee arising from the League? Are there any points of agreement between the two about the future world role of the United States?

Article X of the League Covenant ignited tremendous controversy over whether the United States should join the League of Nations.

The Members of the League undertake to respect and preserve as against external aggression the territorial integrity and existing political independence of all the members of the League. In case of any such aggression or in case of any threat or danger of such aggression the Council shall advise upon the means by which this obligation shall be fulfilled.

Republican senator Henry Cabot Lodge contended that the League Covenant stripped Congress of its power to declare war in this August 12, 1919, congressional address.

We should never permit the United States to be involved in the internal conflict in another country, except by the will of her people expressed through the Congress which represents them.

With regard to wars of external aggression on a member of the league, the case is perfectly clear. There can be no genuine dispute whatever about the meaning of the first clause of article 10. In the first place, it differs from every other obligation in being individual and placed upon each nation without the intervention of the league. Each nation for itself promises to respect and preserve as against external aggression the boundaries and the political independence of every member of the league. ... It is, I repeat, an individual obligation. It requires no action on the part of the league, except that in the second sentence the authorities of the league are to have the power to advise as to the means to be employed in order to fulfill the purpose of the first sentence. ...

We may set aside all this empty talk about isolation. Nobody expects to isolate the United States or to make it a hermit Nation, which is a sheer absurdity. But there is a wide difference between taking a suitable part and bearing a due responsibility in world affairs and plunging the United States into every controversy and conflict on the face of the globe.

Wilson defended the League in a speech on September 25, 1919, in Pueblo, Colorado, that recalled the sacrifices of soldiers during the war, bringing many in the audience to tears.

But you will say, "what is the second sentence of article 10? That is what gives very disturbing thoughts." The second sentence is that the Council of the League shall advise what steps, if any, are necessary to carry out the guaranty of the first sentence, namely, that the members will respect and preserve the territorial integrity and political independence of the other members. I do not know of any other meaning for the word "advise" except "advise." The Council advises, and it can not advise without the vote of the United States [as a member of the Council]. ... Whether we use it wisely or unwisely, we can use the vote of the United States to make impossible drawing the United States into any enterprise that she does not care to be drawn into...

My friends, on last Decoration Day I went to a beautiful hillside near Paris, where was located the cemetery of Suresnes, a cemetery given over to the burial of the American dead. ... I wish some men in public life who are now opposing the settlement for which these men died could visit such a spot as that. I wish that the thought that comes out of those graves could penetrate their consciousness. I wish that they could feel the moral obligation that rests upon us not to go back on those boys, but to see the thing through, to see it through to the end and make good their redemption of the world. For nothing less depends upon this decision, nothing less than the liberation and salvation of the world.

Who has the more compelling argument regarding the League of Nations, Wilson or Lodge?

Pushing himself to the limit to defend the League of Nations, an exhausted Wilson paid the price. On September 25, 1919, hours after he reminded a Pueblo, Colorado, audience that American soldiers had died to protect "the liberty of the world," the president fell ill. His personal physician rushed a twitching and nauseated Wilson back to Washington, D.C., where two days later he suffered a stroke. His life in the balance and permanently paralyzed on his left side, Wilson spent the rest of his presidency hidden in the White House. Wilson, the British Prime Minister Lloyd George remarked, was "as much a victim of the war as any soldier who died in the trenches."

The White House kept the president's illness a secret, issuing a vague statement that he was recovering from exhaustion. For weeks, however, Wilson only spent three hours a day out of bed and saw no one except his physician, Dr. Cary Grayson, and his family. His wife carefully controlled all correspondence reaching the president and helped compose his replies. Critics later accused her of serving as a shadow president during Wilson's convalescence, but Edith Wilson steadfastly maintained that Wilson made every decision himself. Wilson rejected all private suggestions that he resign, and still refused to accept any reservations to the Versailles Treaty.

With Wilson absent from the public stage, opposition to the League of Nations spread. Wilson's refusal to compromise doomed the treaty to defeat. The Senate rejected both the original treaty and one with Lodge's reservations attached. The Senate therefore never ratified the Versailles Treaty. It took two more years for the war to end officially for the United States. In October, 1921, the Senate finally ratified separate peace treaties with Germany, Austria, and Hungary.

Nations that ratified the Versailles Peace Treaty also agreed to join the League, with the exception of Germany, which was not allowed to join until 1926. The League remained headquartered in Geneva, Switzerland, from 1920 until 1946, when the United Nations took its place. Wilson won the Nobel Peace Prize for his efforts to establish the League of Nations, but without American membership the League became little more than a place to air grievances.

Wilson never regained his health, and he died in 1924. The war altered countless other lives as well. Most American families of fallen soldiers opted to have their remains returned from France at government expense. John Steuart Curry's painting, *The Return of Private Davis from the Argonne* (**20.16**) captured the mixture of commemorative ritual and private mourning that accompanied the reburial of his friend in a small Kansas town. The flag-draped

20.16 ***The Return of Private Davis from the Argonne*** John Steuart Curry's 1940 painting of gathered mourners burying a fallen soldier reflected Americans' ambiguity over how to remember World War I. The artist juxtaposed the intense personal grief of the soldier's family and community with a vast void behind them. [Property of the Westervelt Company and displayed in The Westervelt-Warner Museum of American Art in Tuscaloosa, AL]

coffin, wreaths, and honor guard offer official assurances that Davis died in service to his nation and humanity, but the emptiness of the landscape behind the mourners suggests that nothing constructive resulted from his death. Like Curry, the nation remained undecided over whether to remember the war as a great victory or tragedy.

Conclusion

Conflicting visions over America's role in the world shaped both the American road to war and the outcome of World War I. From 1914 to the spring of 1917, the nation debated whether neutrality required ending trade with Europe, trading equally with all sides, or instead gave Americans the right to trade and travel wherever they liked. When Wilson embraced the last definition of neutrality in 1915, he managed to keep the country out of the war only by convincing Germany to curtail submarine attacks on passenger and merchant ships. When Germany resumed unrestricted submarine warfare in 1917 and sent Mexico the Zimmermann Telegram, Wilson decided that German aggression now threatened the nation's economic and territorial interests and asked Congress to declare war.

The war left a lasting imprint on the nation. Leading a divided nation into war, the Wilson administration quickly rallied pubic support through a massive propaganda drive, a complete mobilization of the industrial and agricultural economies, conscription, espionage and sedition laws, and war bond campaigns. All these efforts greatly extended the reach of the federal government into the private lives of American citizens. The home front experience during World War I set the precedent for how the United States would marshal its resources to combat the Great Depression and fight a much longer World War II.

After the war women had the vote and African Americans continued their migration northward. The wartime coalition had included a place for labor, but the government abandoned its support of unions when the war ended. Progressive faith in expertise and efficiency infused some parts of the war effort, such as relying on experts to manage governmental wartime agencies and embracing conscription as the most efficient way to mobilize the armed forces. However, the Progressive drive to regulate big business languished as the war strengthened industrialists' influence within governmental circles, and the Progressive Era came to an end.

World War I shaped the twentieth century. Fledgling democratic nations replaced the former German, Russian, and Austro-Hungarian empires, redrawing the map of Central Europe. The war laid the foundation for World War II, and gave the world an ideal of self-determination that helped encourage colonized peoples to seek independence. The creation of the Soviet Union in 1922 would also have severe consequences for future generations.

Americans went to war to stop German aggression and make the world safe for democracy. The country remained divided, however, over what role America should have in the postwar world. The domestic debate over the League of Nations revealed strong conflicting visions—isolationism, balance of power, collective security—over how to maintain peace. Although the nation never joined the League of Nations, Wilson's democratic ideals inspired American foreign policy for decades to come. The United States continued to mold its own distinct imperial tradition—eschewing the addition of formal colonies, but continuing to extend its economic and ideological reach throughout the world.

1914

Archduke Franz Ferdinand assassinated in Sarajevo, Bosnia
Triggers breakdown of European balance of power system

Germany invades Belgium and France
World War I begins; Wilson declares United States neutral

1915

Britain mines the North Sea; German U-boats patrol British waters
Incites domestic debate over how to stay neutral

German U-boat sinks *Lusitania*
Wilson asserts rights of neutrals to travel unmolested

1916

Villa raids American bordertowns
U.S. troops sent to Mexico; war narrowly avoided

Germany renounces unrestricted submarine warfare
Wilson wins reelection, promising "peace with honor"

Review Questions

1. Was any one nation primarily responsible for starting World War I or did Europe share collective responsibility?
2. Why was neutrality so difficult to define and maintain for the United States?
3. How did the government rally public support for the war? Consider the various types of approaches taken in presidential speeches, in propaganda posters, and by wartime governmental agencies. What were the positive versus negative consequences of these various approaches?
4. How well did the government balance the need to uncover German espionage with protecting civil liberties during the war?
5. How did women and African Americans fare during the war? Which changes were temporary? Which were more permanent?
6. What challenges did soldiers face in the trenches? How was fighting this war different from previous American wars such as the Civil War or Spanish-American War?
7. Evaluate the key flaws of the Versailles Treaty. What concerns did Americans raise about the League of Nations? In what ways did the treaty create the groundwork for future world problems?

DESTROY
THIS MAD BRUTE

1917

Germany resumes unrestricted submarine warfare; Zimmermann Telegram sent to Mexico
Congress declares war against Germany

Race riot in East St. Louis, Illinois
Racial animosities intensify as Southern blacks migrate north

Bolsheviks seize power in Russia
Communist victory sets the stage for future conflicts

1918

Wilson gives Fourteen Points Speech
Establishes democracy, free trade, and collective security as key postwar goals

Congress passes Sedition Act
Dilutes civil liberties and freedom of speech

Peak of influenza pandemic
Deadly flu virus kills 675,000 Americans; 30 million worldwide

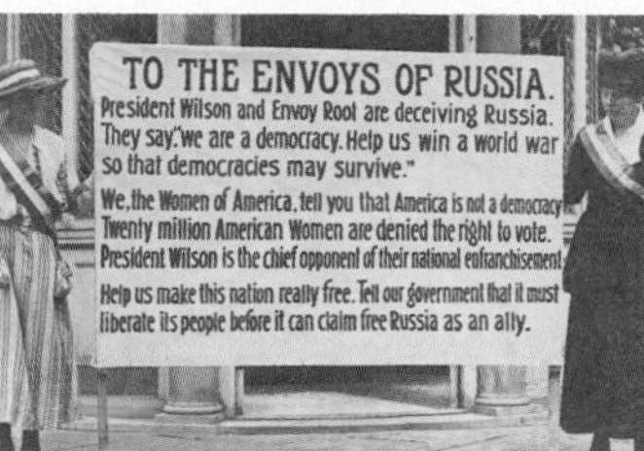
TO THE ENVOYS OF RUSSIA.
President Wilson and Envoy Root are deceiving Russia. They say "We are a democracy. Help us win a world war so that democracies may survive."
We, the Women of America, tell you that America is not a democracy. Twenty million American Women are denied the right to vote. President Wilson is the chief opponent of their national enfranchisement.
Help us make this nation really free. Tell our government that it must liberate its people before it can claim free Russia as an ally.

1918

Wilson supports female suffrage
Ends picketing outside White House by suffragists

Armistice between Allies and Germany
Germany capitulates before Allies cross into Germany

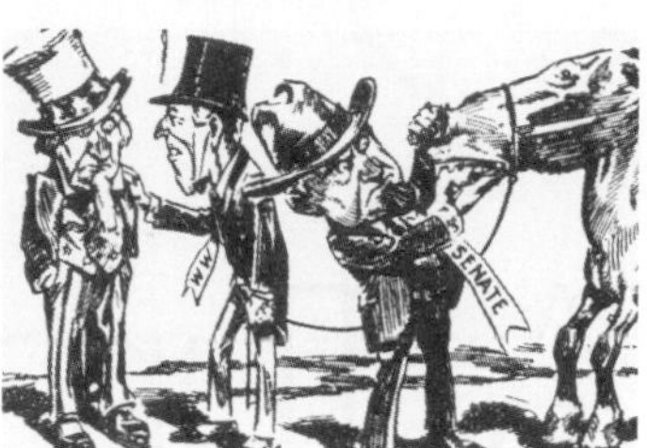
SENATE

1919

Germany signs the Versailles Treaty
Punitive terms create resentments Hitler will later exploit to rise to power

Senate rejects the Versailles Treaty
Ends strident debate on the merits of joining the League of Nations

Key Terms

Allies (World War I) Initially composed of Britain, France, Belgium, and Russia, and would eventually total eighteen nations, including Italy and the United States. **594**

Central Powers Initially Germany and Austria-Hungary, expanded by 1915 to include the Ottoman Empire and Bulgaria. **594**

The Schlieffen Plan A military plan that called for Germany to attack and quickly defeat France while the cumbersome Russian army mobilized. **596**

Western Front Complex system of trenches and earthworks that ran for 550 miles from the North Sea to Switzerland that pitted Germany against Belgium, France, Britain, and the United States. **596**

U-boat German submarine, a new weapon that launched surprise torpedo attacks against Allied merchant and naval ships. **598**

Lusitania British passenger ship sunk by a German U-boat on May 7, 1915, an attack that killed 1,198 passengers, including 128 Americans. **598**

Zimmermann Telegram German foreign minister Arthur Zimmermann offered to help Mexico recover Texas, New Mexico, and Arizona if Mexico would start a borderland war with the United States and ask Japan to join them. **600**

Fourteen Points Speech by Woodrow Wilson to Congress on January 8, 1918, that outlined a postwar world dominated by democracy, free trade, disarmament, self-determination, the settlement of territorial disputes in Europe, and a league of nations to mediate future international crises. **601**

self-determination Giving people a voice in selecting their own government. **601**

Nineteenth Amendment Constitutional amendment that granted women the right to vote; it was ratified August 26, 1920. **605**

Committee on Public Information Government agency that controlled the flow of information and shaped public opinion about the war with posters, Four-Minute Men, pamphlets, and films. **605**

war bonds Short-term loans that individual citizens made to the government that financed two-thirds of the war's costs. **606**

Espionage Act (1917) Legislation that made it a crime to obstruct military recruitment, to encourage mutiny, or to aid the enemy by spreading lies. **606**

Sedition Act (1918) Legislation that went even further than the Espionage Act by prohibiting anyone from uttering, writing, or publishing "any abusive or disloyal language" concerning the flag, constitution, government, or armed forces. **606**

conscientious objectors Those who opposed participating in military service because of religious, philosophical, or political belief. **609**

American Expeditionary Forces Two million American soldiers who fought overseas under the command of General John J. Pershing. **612**

Spanish Influenza A lethal flu virus that killed millions worldwide. **614**

Versailles Peace Treaty The controversial treaty that required Germany to pay reparations and disarm. **615**

League of Nations An international collective security organization composed of member nations where member nations agreed to mediate future international disputes to prevent wars and work together to improve global human conditions. **615**

CHAPTER 21

A Turbulent Decade

The Twenties

> "Was every decent standard being overthrown?"
>
> Journalist FREDERICK LEWIS ALLEN, commenting on youthful rebellion in the twenties

On a cold December afternoon in 1926, two young women posed for the camera as they danced on the ledge of a Chicago hotel. With their short skirts, bobbed hair, and heel-kicking dance steps, they displayed a carefree lifestyle that defied the stricter morals embraced by their mothers' generation. The pair embodied the high spirits of a generation ready to put the tragedy of World War I behind them and move forward into the modern era. Novelists and journalists referred to these women as flappers, a decades-old slang term for young girls. Now it was used to describe independent young women who smoked, drank, danced to jazz, and flaunted their sexual liberation by wearing revealing clothes. Rebellious postwar writers made flappers a cultural icon. Their youthful exuberance and daring behavior excited some Americans and created a sense of moral outrage in others.

The flapper controversy was one of many cultural conflicts that turned political in the turbulent twenties. Flappers and the equally controversial birth control movement championed the right of women to take control of their bodies. Other Americans preferred using the government to control behavior. Prohibition of the manufacture and sale of alcoholic liquors became the law of the land, promising to rid the nation of poverty, crime, and disease. To prevent the communist-inspired Russian Revolution from spreading to the United States, the government arrested suspected political radicals and drastically reduced the flow of European immigration. Meanwhile religious Fundamentalists argued that the country was morally adrift and launched a well-publicized crusade against teaching evolution in public schools. African Americans, too, played an important role in changing America's cultural landscape, creating new artistic centers and political movements that challenged the methods of established civil rights leaders.

Putting the Progressive-era faith in trust-busting aside, the government allowed large industrial conglomerates to dominate key industrial sectors, such as steel and automobiles. Still staunchly antiunion, some factory owners nonetheless became more responsive to workers' grievances to reduce labor strife. Mass production, accompanied by mass consumption, spurred the decade's economic prosperity. Cars, suburbs, and asphalt highways soon dotted the American horizon, changing the living habits of millions.

Domestic cultural conflict dominated political discourse in the twenties, yet a distinct foreign policy also took shape during the decade. Despite its refusal to join the League of Nations, the country remained active in world affairs. By exerting rising international influence through diplomacy and foreign aid, Republican presidential administrations offered an alternative way to maintain world peace.

How much of the old order would America jettison or protect as it entered the postwar age? Throughout the twenties Americans held competing visions of what modernity had to offer.

What qualities define the women in the photo as flappers?

Cars and Planes: The Promise of the Twenties

During the twenties America became a car culture. Car registration jumped from 9.2 million in 1920 to 26.5 million ten years later. By 1927 the United States contained 80 percent of the world's cars. Conflicting ideas soon emerged, however, over how much car-based commerce should transform the American landscape and whether all Americans could be trusted with the new freedom their cars bestowed.

The push to produce cars and other consumer goods more efficiently caused industrialists to change how they treated their workforce. Competing visions of industrial work culture between industrialists and workers emerged alongside ongoing clashes over wages and hours. Did America's increased reliance on machines render individual skill or initiative irrelevant? When aviator Charles A. Lindbergh made his historic solo flight across the Atlantic Ocean, he became an instant hero to a society needing reassurance that people and machines could coexist harmoniously.

The Car Culture

At the turn of the century, cities were smelly, dirty places. In New York City alone, horses dumped 2.5 million tons of manure and 60,000 gallons of urine on city streets yearly. The car seemed to offer a clean, flexible solution to city transportation problems. Paving the streets with asphalt would remove the dust that often forced dwellers to keep their windows shut. No one foresaw that a fleet of privately owned cars would soon clog city streets, or that their exhaust would become a serious public health hazard.

Although initial expectations focused on the improvements that cars would make in cities, farmers also benefited significantly from the new technology. Tractors made plowing easier, while trucks transported produce more quickly to market. Whole families piled into cars on Saturday morning to head into town, ending the isolation that had previously characterized farm life.

A car represented a significant purchase for a family. Cars cost between 20 and 45 percent of a non-farm family's annual income, and between 50 and 100 percent of a farm household's yearly earnings. Credit plans required that purchasers pay one-third in cash as a down payment and spread the remaining payments over one year. Most plans also came with hefty interest rates averaging around 16 percent.

Besides enriching automobile manufacturers the explosion in car ownership meant boom times for numerous other industries. To satisfy the unquenchable thirst for gasoline, the petroleum industry underwent a major expansion with new oil wells appearing daily in Texas and California. The building trades saw their business take off when millions took advantage of the mobility that cars afforded and moved to the suburbs. An acute need soon developed for tunnels and bridges to link cities by car to ever-dispersed commuter suburbs. In 1927 the Holland Tunnel, the nation's first underwater motor vehicle tunnel, opened between New York City and New Jersey. On its first day of operation, nearly fifty thousand people paid fifty cents to drive through the tunnel that ran under the Hudson River.

21.1 Cottage Gas Station
Many businessmen built gas stations that looked like country cottages to assure passing motorists that their establishments were safe and clean.

How did cars transform urban and rural lifestyles?

On the Road

Many Americans took vacations away from home for the first time, and to satisfy their wanderlust, the public demanded good roads through rural areas. The government responded with a massive road-building and paving program. Following the precedents set in the nineteenth century when the federal government had funded canal construction and given railroad companies huge land grants to build railroads (see Chapter 15), the federal government now helped states build a new national highway system.

Car travelers also needed food, lodging, and gas. To entice tourists to stop at their establishments, rural businessmen erected eye-catching signs and buildings. A revolution in commercial roadside architecture was soon underway. Small clusters of cottages where tourists could spend the night on long road trips, forerunners of today's motels, appeared in remote areas. The miniature house (**21.1**) emerged as the most popular type of commercial roadside building in the twenties, a way to assure passersby that the restaurant, store, or gas station was a safe and respectable establishment.

Other retailers used surreal images to entice motorists to stop. An array of giant milk bottles, toads, and hot dogs soon lined the highways of America. The Teapot Dome Service Station (**21.2**), built in 1922 along a highway in Zillah, Washington, humorously reminded patrons of the Teapot Dome political scandal that rocked the Harding White House in the early twenties. The Republicans had selected Warren Harding, an unassuming senator from Ohio, as their 1920 presidential candidate because his easygoing nature and call for "a return to normalcy" presented the electorate with a welcome respite from the sternness of Democrat Woodrow Wilson's wartime leadership. Winning 60 percent of the popular vote, Harding easily defeated Democrat James Cox, who suffered when he stood by Wilson and his failed League of Nations crusade (see Chapter 20). Harding's two years in office (he died of a heart attack in 1923, making his vice president Calvin Coolidge president) were, however, tarnished by scandal. The largest scandal involved Secretary of the Interior Albert B. Fall, who went to jail for accepting bribes from two wealthy businessmen to lease government-controlled oil reserves in Teapot Dome, Wyoming. The enterprising owner of this service station gave his customers a laugh at the president's expense by selling oil and gasoline in a teapot-shaped gas station.

21.2 Teapot Dome Gas Station, Zillah, Washington Roadside architecture in the twenties often included whimsical structures designed to entice passing motorists to stop. This gas station shaped like a teapot made a joke of the Teapot Dome scandal.

What messages did the architecture of roadside gas stations convey?

Throughout the twenties Americans embraced conflicting visions of the architectural merits of such buildings. Some celebrated them as a vernacular form of pop art, while others dismissed them as eyesores. The controversy surrounding America's nascent car culture extended beyond competing aesthetic ideals of roadside architecture. Some traditionalists also lamented Americans' changing recreational habits. Ministers complained that instead of spending Sundays in church, many families chose instead to take all day drives. Cars let teenagers take their courting out of the family parlor and into the backseat of the family automobile, to the dismay of parents everywhere. "The best way to keep children home is to make the home atmosphere pleasant—and let air out of the tires," quipped author Dorothy Parker. Automobiles also made it harder for town officials to regulate red-light districts, causing one judge to declare that "the automobile has become a house of prostitution on wheels."

Welfare Capitalism and Consumer Culture

During World War I the government had mandated that industrialists with wartime contracts pay high wages, provide clean and safe working conditions, and allow unions to organize within their factories (see Chapter 20). In return for this official protection, the government demanded a no-strike pledge from unions. When the war ended in 1918, the government abruptly canceled its orders and withdrew from managing worker-industrial relations. The government's hands-off attitude emboldened many industrialists to reinstate low wages, long hours, and blacklists for union members. To protect their wartime gains, unions orchestrated the greatest wave of strikes in American history in 1919. Although they rallied millions of workers to the picket lines, outmatched unions lost this battle.

Industrialists accused unions of following in the footsteps of the recent Russian Revolution and trying to spread communism in the United States. These accusations won industrialists the support of local governments, who once again forcefully broke up many picket lines. Defeated steel, coal, and garment unions, however, did not give up organizing and continued to attract members. In the early 1920s union ranks grew to five million, the largest to date. When faced with the dismal vision of unending labor strife, Progressives had crafted government regulation to rein in business and improve working conditions (see Chapter 18). In the 1920s industrialists used the guarantee of government noninterference to pursue a different vision.

Throughout the decade the Harding and Coolidge administrations left industrialists free to fashion their own solutions to such labor troubles, adopting an openly pro-business stance. *The Wall Street Journal* exulted that "never before, here or anywhere else, has a government been so completely fused with business," referring to Commerce Department workshops that helped businesses eliminate wasteful practices, a Justice Department that largely stopped enforcing anti-trust laws, and a high protective tariff that made imported goods more expensive than American industrial products.

Progressive-era innovations aimed at improving industrial efficiency, however, remained popular. Scientific management and welfare capitalism gained even more adherents in the twenties. Mirroring how army psychologists had used intelligence tests to rank the aptitudes of different racial and ethnic groups in World War I (see Chapter 20), the Central Tube Company in Pittsburgh devised a chart (**21.3**) assessing the abilities of various nationalities to perform skilled and unskilled jobs. The new profession of psychology accepted pseudoscientific social Darwinian ideas that "race" determined aptitude, and the factory owner used this "scientific" information to organize and run his business more efficiently. Unsurprisingly, given this racial climate, white Americans topped the list as good at all types of tasks. Jews were considered bad at every job and American blacks were listed as only suited for unskilled jobs. There were some surprises on the chart, however. While social Darwinists usually viewed northern Europeans as superior to southern and eastern Europeans, in the factory's ethnic hierarchy Italians and Poles actually outscored Germans and French as desirable skilled workers.

Some innovative industrialists tried to put aside the prevailing idea that the interests of capitalists and workers inevitably clashed. Rather than driving their workers relentlessly to secure a profit, advocates of welfare capitalism suggested that industrialists offer a wide range of benefits such as medical insurance, pensions, and stock ownership plans to create a loyal workforce.

As the vogue for welfare capitalism spread, many industrialists began to change their management practices. To develop a stable, well-trained workforce, industrialists introduced fringe benefits (including paid vacations and sick pay), created industrial committees where workers could air grievances,

How did ethnic profiling and welfare capitalism promise to help industrialists run their factories more efficiently?

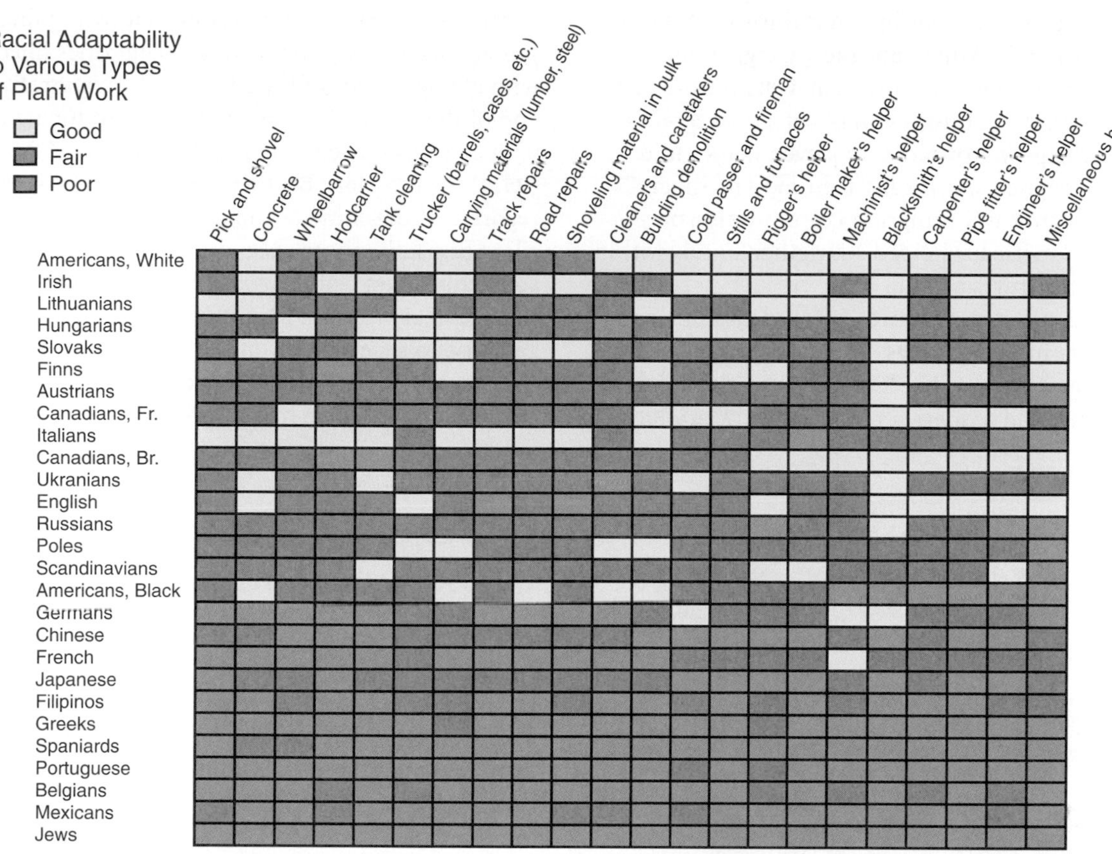

21.3 Employment Chart of the Central Tube Company, Pittsburgh, 1925 Social Darwinian ideas about the innate abilities of different racial and ethnic groups determined where individuals could work in this factory.

and offered bonuses for workers who exceeded production quotas. A worker usually needed at least twenty-five years with one company to qualify for a pension, so this policy alone could potentially keep workers from leaving to pursue other job opportunities. Industrialists also experimented with offering employees stock options, hoping to dilute class antagonism by making each worker an investor who would share in the company's profits.

Despite workers' enthusiasm for welfare capitalism, the reality rarely matched the rhetoric. Seasonal lay-offs continued, wage rates fluctuated constantly, and long hours in unhealthy factories persisted. As one worker complained, "we had to wait five years for one week's vacation. And I've seen men work four and one-half years and then get laid off." Industrialists' promises ended up simply whetting workers' appetites for stable well-paid jobs with benefits. During the Great Depression in the 1930s (see Chapter 22), the labor movement would demand that the government fulfill the hopes that industrialists had raised in the twenties.

Increased industrial productivity and efficiency created an unprecedented abundance of affordable goods in the twenties. Blue-collar workers toiling in dead-end jobs in factories staffed with salaried white-collar employees performing unsatisfying clerical tasks produced these items. Frustrated at work, many working- and middle-class Americans used their growing leisure time and access to material goods to create more fulfilling lives. A modern consumer culture arose that deemphasized traditional Victorian values of thrift and restraint. Americans instead increasingly relied on credit to buy cars, radios, and household appliances.

Radio played a key role in forging a national mass culture. Over 60 percent of American homes acquired radios in the twenties, which until 1924 required headphones. Americans from all walks of life now simultaneously gathered around their radios to learn election results. Baseball fans throughout the nation listened to the play-by-play of the World Series, radio broadcasts that made New York Yankee player Babe Ruth a national sports hero. Farmers closely followed weather reports, and bankers digested the day's financial news. "There is radio music in the air, every night, everywhere," one newspaper observed. Big companies like Walgreen Drugs and Palmolive Soap started sponsoring nationally syndicated radio shows to boost sales of their products. These weekly comedies and dramas, filled with plugs for the sponsor's merchandise,

What job could you have gotten in this factory?

cultivated shared tastes in entertainment and brand-name products. Americans increasingly bought the same brand-name toothpaste at a chain store like Woolworths. Big business was not alone in recognizing the power of radio, however. Local radio shows designed specifically for union members, religious groups, immigrant communities, or African Americans helped strengthen bonds within these subcultures as well.

Movie stars and athletes enjoyed nationwide adulation in the twenties. Silent-film actors like the comedian Charlie Chaplin, the sex symbol Rudolph Valentino, and "America's Sweetheart" Mary Pickford became household names among a movie-going public that avidly purchased fan magazines filled with glossy photos of their favorite film stars. By the end of the decade Hollywood began producing films with sound, a novelty highlighted in this 1929 poster (**21.4**) for the Marx Brothers' first film. The verbal repartee of the comedy trio delighted audiences. As silent films disappeared, so did the careers of many silent-film stars whose artistic talents lay in physical, not vocal, expression. Meanwhile professional sports gave rise to a slew of national sports heroes, such as the boxer Jack Dempsey. In an era dominated by cultural heroes, none rose to greater prominence than the pilot Charles A. Lindbergh.

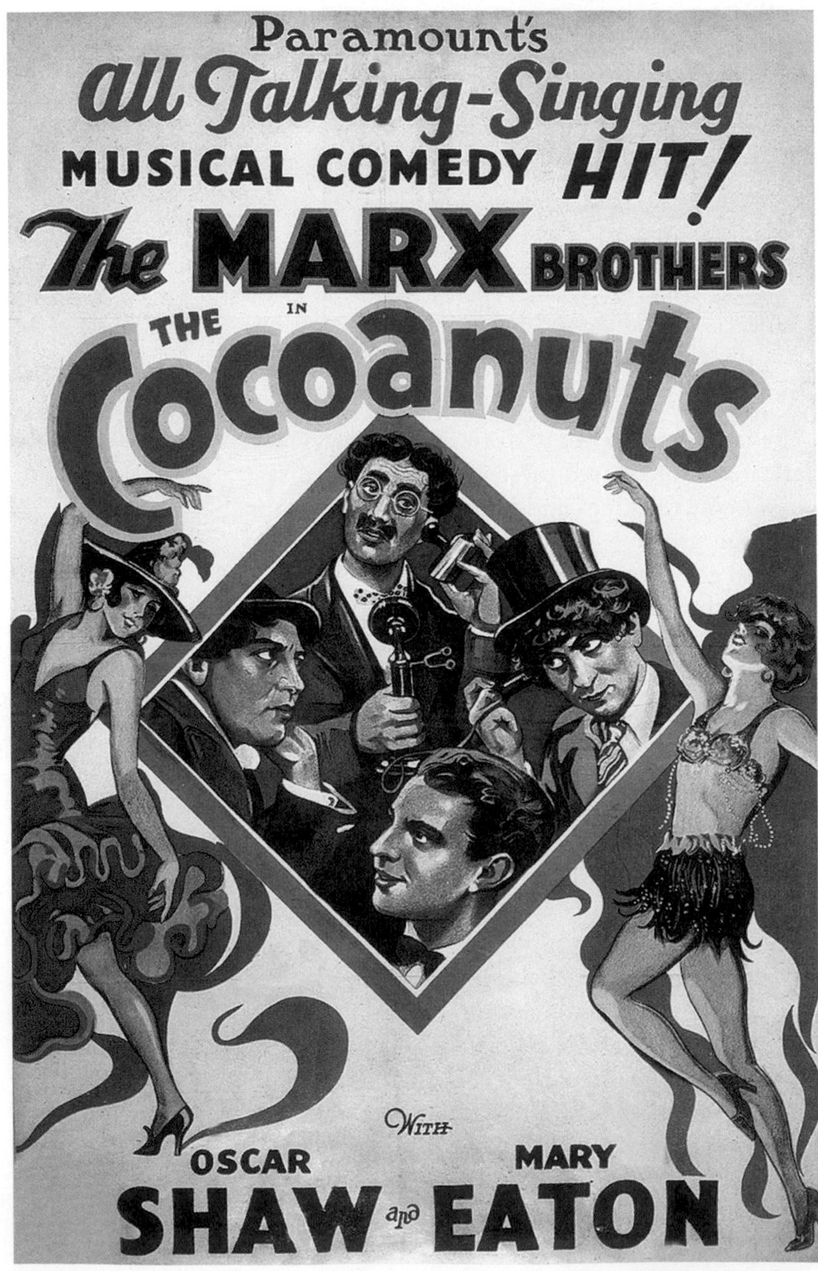

21.4 The End of Silent Films
By the end of the decade Hollywood began advertising "all talking-singing" movies like "Cocoanuts."

The Age of Flight: Charles A. Lindbergh

The feats of pilot Charles A. Lindbergh ushered the nation into the age of flight. Commentators called the sky the new frontier, a label loaded with potent historical significance for Americans. By the late twenties, a time when machines seemed to matter more than people, the image of the lone pilot against the vast blue sky recalled the pioneer spirit of the nineteenth century.

Lindbergh piloted his plane, the ***Spirit of St. Louis,*** on the first-ever nonstop solo flight from New York to Paris on May 21, 1927. Flying without the radio or radar that help modern pilots navigate, Lindbergh relied on a few navigational instruments and looking out the window to locate his position on a paper map as he flew. Sitting in a wicker chair with sandwiches and water under it, Lindbergh had a rubber raft on board in case he was forced to land in the cold Atlantic and a flashlight to examine his wings for ice.

Lindbergh's flight lasted 33.5 hours, enough time to make him the hero of the decade. This photomontage (a composite photo made by pasting together separately taken images) of the *Spirit of St. Louis* (**21.5**) passing by the Eiffel Tower combined the signature symbol of Paris with the image of Lindbergh's iconic plane. "Had we searched all America we could not have found a better type than young Lindbergh to represent the spirit and high purpose of our people," the jubilant American ambassador to France wired President Coolidge amid the celebrations that followed Lindbergh's landing in Paris. Lindbergh's triumph assured Americans that individual initiative still mattered and that technological advancement benefited humankind at a time when the recent industrialized

> "The *Spirit of St. Louis* is a wonderful plane. It's like a living creature, gliding along smoothly, happily, as though a successful flight means as much to it as to me."
>
> CHARLES LINDBERGH, evoking the perfect symmetry between man and machine

slaughter on the Western Front (see Chapter 20) suggested otherwise. The vision of planes serving a peaceful purpose by transporting mail and tourists replaced wartime images of aerial dogfights. Lindbergh toured the nation tirelessly to promote commercial air travel, and also flew flood relief missions in China with his wife, the author Anne Morrow Lindbergh, in 1931 to demonstrate the humanitarian good that planes made possible.

In exalting Lindbergh's achievement Americans channeled their own conflicting visions of the modern age. Some praised Lindbergh for exhibiting the same adventurous spirit that had propelled American pioneers across the West in the nineteenth century, values that seemed increasingly at risk in a machine-dominated age. "Charles Lindbergh is the heir of all that we like to think is best in America," opined *Outlook* magazine. Others, including Lindbergh, rejected the idea that his flight epitomized a return to the past. Lindberg asserted that his flight illustrated the nation's industrial march forward, "the culmination," he said, ". . . of all that was practicable and best in American aviation." Although differing on whether the flight represented the revival of traditional values or the modern ethos of industrial might, Americans agreed that his flight renewed faith in the benefits of technology.

Lindbergh suffered, however, in the public spotlight. The 1933 kidnapping and murder of his firstborn son became the most reported tabloid story of the day. Later in the decade Lindbergh tarnished his image by expressing admiration for Nazi Germany and joining with those who initially argued against American intervention in World War II. After Japan's bombing of Pearl Harbor in 1941, Lindbergh changed his position. He went on to fly combat missions against the Japanese, and his reputation recovered when he took a strong anti-communist stand during the Cold War in the 1950s.

21.5 Photo Montage of the *Spirit of St. Louis* Flying Near the Eiffel Tower
In this imagined scene an unnamed photographer celebrated the moment that pilot Charles Lindbergh arrived in Paris by pasting an image of his famous plane flying past Paris's most recognized monument.

Why did Americans celebrate Lindbergh's solo flight to Paris?

Cultural Unrest

Celebrating Lindberg's achievement was a unique moment of national unity in a decade dominated by cultural turbulence and strife. During the 1920s Americans initiated a series of societal-wide debates that reflected competing visions over what values the nation should embrace as it entered the modern age. Cultural conflict turned political in the twenties as Americans debated the need for legislation to protect the nation's morals, ethnic purity, and capitalist economy.

The Lost Generation

"I've kissed dozens of men. I suppose I'll kiss dozens more," declared the flapper heroine of F. Scott Fitzgerald's novel *This Side of Paradise* (1920), announcing a new attitude of living for the moment that defined the era's youth culture. With his wife Zelda by his side, Fitzgerald put this philosophy into practice, moving from party to party in his fast-paced life as an expatriate in Europe. The Paris-based American writer Gertrude Stein coined the term "the Lost Generation" to describe white intellectuals and artists like Fitzgerald who rebelled against Victorian values in the twenties and lived primarily overseas.

Lost Generation writers used Austrian psychologist Sigmund Freud's theories to justify their revolt against "repressive" codes of conduct. Freud believed that subconscious sexual impulses drove human behavior and that repressed desires sometimes found expression in dreams. Fitzgerald was one of a host of writers including Ernest Hemingway, e. e. cummings, and John Dos Passos who championed sexual liberation as one way to escape the sterile and deadly confines of modern life. Men and women "spend their lives going in and out of doors and factories ... they live their lives and find themselves at last facing death and the end of life without having lived at all," asserts a character in Sherwood Anderson's *Many Marriages* (1923) who, in the throes of a passionate extramarital affair, is preparing to end his marriage and leave his job.

The hedonistic lifestyles depicted in many Lost Generation novels, while rarely bestowing lasting happiness on the protagonists, still rankled more traditionally minded Americans. Agreeing that modern culture was flawed, these Americans wanted to bolster, rather than reject, traditional values. These clashing cultural visions had strong political overtones. Alcohol remained central to the Lost Generation ethos of pleasure-seeking, an indulgence that became illegal in the twenties thanks to temperance reformers who felt that drinking threatened the moral fabric of American society.

Prohibition

Temperance, one of the nation's longest lasting reform movements (see Chapters 17 and 18), took on a new life during World War I. Wartime temperance propaganda claimed that "German brewers in this country have rendered thousands of men inefficient." Organized "wet" opposition to the dry campaign materialized slowly, partly because critics of the temperance movement could not easily counter its emphasis on health, thrift, and morals. Some wets focused on personal freedom. Senator James Wadsworth contended that it seemed unfair to tell exhausted workers at the end of the day "you shall not have a glass of beer." Other critics felt uneasy about increasing the power of the federal government so it could enforce prohibition. Once the debate centered on a possible constitutional amendment prohibiting alcohol, they argued that such an amendment would violate states' rights. The middle-class Anti-Saloon League's highly structured propaganda and lobbying campaign, however, easily overpowered this disjointed wet response on the local, state, and national level.

Evangelical preacher Billy Sunday converted many churchgoers to the temperance cause, delivering impassioned sermons on the evils of alcohol. Sunday, a former professional baseball player turned preacher, littered his sermons with slang, winning a large following among the rural poor and urban working class who flocked to his revival meetings throughout the Midwest. The political elite also embraced the preacher. Sunday often dined at the White House and considered the oil tycoon John D. Rockefeller a friend. In his most famous temperance speech, Sunday urged his listeners in 1908 to "get on the water wagon; get on for the sake of your wife and babies, and hit the booze a blow."

What critique did the Lost Generation offer of American society?

On December 18, 1917, Congress approved the **Eighteenth Amendment**, which banned the sale, manufacture, and transportation of intoxicating liquors. By January 16, 1919, the required thirty-six states had ratified the amendment. By the time every state had voted, only Rhode Island and Connecticut had rejected it. When prohibition went into effect in 1920, Congress clarified what constituted an intoxicating beverage in the **Volstead Act (1919)**, a law that defined any beverage with more than 0.5 percent alcohol as intoxicating liquor and established criminal penalties for manufacturing, transporting, or possessing alcohol.

Congress never appropriated enough money for wide-scale enforcement, hampering Justice Department efforts to curb illegal drinking. The police raided working-class neighborhoods to shut down illegal distilleries, but the well-to-do drank their bathtub gin or homebrewed beer without interference. Many reform goals of the temperance movement remained unmet. Belying the expectation that prohibition would create a more virtuous, law-abiding society, prohibition gave birth to a much more insidious form of crime. Organized crime syndicates ran profitable bootlegging operations that financed beer breweries and liquor distilleries, bribed cops, and stocked the shelves of illegal bars throughout major metropolitan areas. Trafficking in forbidden alcohol, the publicity-crazed gangster Al Capone became a powerful figure in the Chicago underworld, a position he maintained with unprecedented violence. In the 1929 St. Valentine's Day Massacre, Capone's men, posing as cops, pretended to arrest rival gang members and then lined them up against a wall and used submachine guns to mow them down. Tabloid papers vividly recounted every detail of Capone's "new technique of wholesale murder" to a shocked American public. Suffering from syphilis that he contracted from a prostitute in one of his own brothels, Capone became increasingly unstable and violent before he went to prison for tax evasion in 1931.

Secret bars called speakeasies proliferated. To demonstrate Americans' widespread disrespect for prohibition, federal agent Izzy Einstein timed how long it took him to find alcohol in most major cities. It took him 21 minutes in Chicago, and only 31 seconds in New Orleans when he asked a taxi driver where he could get a drink and the man replied, "right here," as he pulled out a bottle. Einstein personally shut down over four thousand speakeasies nationwide, prompting bartenders to post his picture with the caption "watch for this man."

21.6 Well-Dressed Trio Entering a Speakeasy Frequenting speakeasies, which patrons entered by giving a secret password to the doorman, became fashionable for women during prohibition. Gone was the stigma that had stopped respectable women from drinking in public.

Illicit drinking became fashionable among the young urban elite, whose escapades Lost Generation writers helped glamorize. This image of a well-dressed woman barhopping with her male companions (**21.6**) revealed new social acceptance for public drinking by respectable middle- and upper-class women. Americans had previously viewed saloons as male establishments that only women of low moral character, like prostitutes, dared to enter.

The competing visions of whether illegal drinking was harmless fun or a vice that destroyed families kept the political debate over prohibition alive throughout the 1920s. "Drys" credited prohibition for the prosperous economy. By putting alcohol aside, they claimed, workers had become more productive, could afford to buy cars and furniture, and had more savings. Critics of prohibition argued that the amendment generated disrespect for the law as it became socially acceptable for Americans to commit a crime by purchasing alcohol. States' rights advocates increasingly resented the arrival of federal officials trying to track down local bootleggers. Picking up the Anti-Saloon League's longstanding emphasis on protecting women and children, the wet lobby emphasized the dangers of teenagers drinking contaminated "moon-shine" (a slang term for illicitly manufactured alcohol) in speakeasies run by the mob. Better to have them drink safely in public cafes, the wets argued.

The beginning of the Great Depression in 1929, which thrust the nation into an unprecedented financial crisis, undermined the dry claim that prohibition brought prosperity. Wets made headway with the argument that enforcing the law drained the federal treasury. When Democrat Franklin D. Roosevelt entered the White House in 1933, he immediately asked Congress to repeal prohibition. With lightening speed the states ratified the **Twenty-First Amendment** (1933), which repealed the

Eighteenth Amendment. The temperance vision remained regionally popular, however, especially in Southern and Midwestern rural areas that continued to enforce local prohibition statutes. A few states also passed minimum-age drinking laws in the 1930s to curtail alcohol consumption, but most states did not enact such laws until the 1980s.

The First Red Scare and Immigration Restrictions

The vision of America as the land of opportunity for peoples worldwide came under severe attack in the 1920s. Debates over immigration were not new (see Chapter 17), but for the first time the nativist vision prevailed. In the early twenties the United States underwent a historic shift, changing from a nation that admitted over 1 million immigrants a year in the decade leading up to World War I to one that grudgingly allowed fewer than 200,000 to enter the country annually.

World War I was the catalyst that turned longstanding nativist attacks against immigrants (see Chapter 17) into a mandate for dramatic change. Alarm over German Americans' continued ties to Germany linked concerns about assimilation to the more potent political question of national security. After the war Congress passed the 1921 Emergency Immigration Act. This law temporarily allowed a total of 350,000 European immigrants to enter the country each year and set limits on how many immigrants could come from each European nation. Three years later Congress made these quotas permanent. The **Immigration Act of 1924** allowed unrestricted immigration from the Western Hemisphere, curtailed all Asian immigration, and used quotas to control how many immigrants emigrated from individual European nations. The law authorized a total of 165,000 immigrants from Europe, a figure that Congress reduced to 150,000 in 1929 at the start of the Great Depression.

Assumptions about the racial superiority of northern European races strongly influenced the new national quotas portrayed on the "Immigration Act of 1924" chart (**21.7**). In this new quota system, Germany received the highest quota. If Americans no longer feared German immigrants, then why did the country feel compelled to adopt immigration restrictions? The answer: The Communist-inspired Russian Revolution, a critical wartime event that some Americans envisioned politically radical immigrants from Russia and Eastern Europe recreating in the United States. To meet this threat the Justice Department arrested and deported alien anarchists and Communists suspected of trying to destroy American democracy and capitalism during the **First Red Scare (1919–1920)**.

Like Communists, anarchists believed that capitalist exploitation of the working class created widespread social suffering. While Communists wanted to create a workers' government that controlled property, anarchists viewed all governments as corrupt. The anarchist movement's most famous spokesperson was Emma Goldman, an eloquent speaker who had emigrated from Russia as a young girl. Anarchism, she wrote, "stands for the liberation of the human mind from the dominion of religion; the liberation of the human body from the dominion of property; liberation from the shackles and restraint of government." Some radical anarchists felt justified using violence to advance their cause (one had assassinated President William McKinley in 1901, see Chapter 18). Goldman, however, disavowed armed conflict and instead tried to popularize the anarchist philosophy through lectures and the magazine that she founded, *Mother Earth*.

In 1919 post office clerk Charles Kaplan helped avert disaster after reading a newspaper account of two anarchist mail-bomb attacks, one against the mayor of Seattle and another against a senator from Georgia, as he rode the subway home. Kaplan realized that the description of the booby-trapped packages matched that of sixteen parcels he had recently set aside for insufficient postage, including one addressed to oil tycoon John D. Rockefeller. Kaplan's discovery triggered a nationwide investigation that netted eighteen more mail bombs.

As anxiety over national security mounted, terrorists exploded dynamite outside the home of Attorney General A. Mitchell Palmer, the man heading the Justice Department's hunt for Bolshevik and anarchist terrorists. Palmer warned that "on a certain day which we have been advised of," radicals were planning "to rise up and destroy the Government at one fell swoop." To head off this revolutionary uprising, Palmer raided the homes and offices of suspected radicals and deported a few hundred immigrants with ties to radical organizations, including Emma Goldman.

While the government focused on the need to ensure public safety, radicals asserted their right to freedom of speech and peaceful assembly. Without concrete evidence of their participation in any criminal activity, they argued, the government was prosecuting them merely for their beliefs. Coming

Why did the nation enact strict immigration restrictions in the twenties?

Northwest Europe and Scandinavia		Eastern and Southern Europe		Other Countries	
Country	**Quota**	**Country**	**Quota**	**Country**	**Quota**
Germany	51,227	Poland	5,982	Africa (other than Egypt)	1,100
Great Britain and Northern Ireland	34,007	Italy	3,845		
		Czechoslovakia	3,073	Armenia	124
Irish Free State (Ireland)	28,567	Russia	2,248	Australia	121
Sweden	9,561	Yugoslavia	671	Palestine	100
Norway	6,453	Romania	603	Syria	100
France	3,954	Portugal	503	Turkey	100
Denmark	2,789	Hungary	473	Egypt	100
Switzerland	2,081	Lithuania	344	New Zealand & Pacific Islands	100
Netherlands	1,648	Latvia	142		
Austria	785	Spain	131	All others	1,900
Belgium	512	Estonia	124		
Finland	471	Albania	100		
Free City of Danzig	228	Bulgaria	100		
Iceland	100	Greece	100		
Luxembourg	100				
Total (Number)	142,483	**Total (Number)**	18,439	**Total (Number)**	3,745
Total (%)	86.5	**Total (%)**	11.2	**Total (%)**	2.3

21.7 Immigration Act of 1924
The United States enacted a quota system in the 1920s that allotted most slots for immigrants from northern Europe.

on the heels of wartime arrests under the Espionage and Sedition acts, the government's harassment of radical activists during 1919–1920 made it practically impossible for radical groups to organize, distribute literature, or give public speeches championing their political ideals.

Radicals tried to fight back by taking up the cause of anarchists Nicola Sacco and Bartolomeo Vanzetti, two Italian immigrants arrested in Massachusetts for the robbery and murder of a payroll guard in 1920. Poor Italian immigrants and left-leaning union members made numerous small donations to the Sacco-Vanzetti Defense Committee, which sponsored picnics and wrestling matches to raise funds for their defense. Many intellectuals also supported the pair, including Roger Baldwin, who had recently founded the American Civil Liberties Union (ACLU), an organization dedicated to protecting constitutional liberties. Foreign-born, openly radical, in possession of guns and anarchist pamphlets when arrested: The portrait that prosecutors painted of Sacco and Vanzetti epitomized the terrorist threat many Americans feared. Sacco and Vanzetti's radical and liberal supporters embraced a competing vision, blaming growing xenophobia for the pair's conviction and 1927 electrocution. Recent findings suggest that Sacco and Vanzetti were indeed dedicated anarchists with close connections to those who planned the spate of 1919 bombings, but no conclusive evidence ties them to the 1920 murder.

The First Red Scare ended quickly. As the anarchist attacks ceased, the press began to poke fun at Palmer's "hallucinations" of a mass uprising and accused him of exaggerating the "revolutionary menace" as part of a failed campaign to win the Democratic Party presidential nomination in 1920. Although the arrests and deportations stopped, the First Red Scare gave credence to the anti-immigration argument that the country needed protection from foreigners who might import dangerous radical political theories.

Other arguments also helped tip the balance in favor of immigration restriction. Urban elites and rural folk worried about protecting the "racial purity" of American stock, while unions and African Americans feared economic competition from immigrant laborers. By the early twenties industrialists had dropped their complaint that immigration restrictions would deprive business of a traditionally inexpensive labor source. Many now believed that machines would increasingly replace unskilled immigrant workers in factories, and felt confident that there were enough African American or Mexican workers readily available to alleviate any labor shortage. With the consensus in the nation moving toward immigration restrictions, immigrant associations focused their lobbying efforts on ensuring that their nationality received the highest quota possible.

Official quotas, however, do not reveal the exact numbers of immigrants who entered the country. If denied entry under the quota system, which remained intact from 1924 through 1965, determined immigrants found loopholes to exploit. The 1924 law contained two key provisions that have remained staples of American immigration legislation since the 1920s: the principle of family reunification, which let resident immigrants bring in members of their immediate families, and the desirability of certain skills. The law, for example, established exemptions for trades facing worker shortages in the United States, such as domestic service. Other savvy European immigrants simply entered the country illegally, often by way of Mexico or Canada, two nations that still enjoyed unrestricted immigration to the United States.

Fundamentalism

The cultural debates surrounding prohibition and immigration restrictions assumed a decidedly political edge in the 1920s. Christian Fundamentalists added to the decade's cultural turbulence when they initiated a campaign to stop the teaching of biologist Charles Darwin's views on evolution. Religious conservatives felt that Darwin's theories contradicted the Bible's depiction of God creating the world and humankind in seven days. They instead subscribed to the tenets of **fundamentalism**, an evangelical Christian theology that viewed the Bible as an authentic recounting of historical events and the absolute moral word of God. By critiquing Darwin Fundamentalists offered a conservative alternative to **modernism**, a liberal Christian theology embraced in many urban areas that emphasized the ongoing revelation of divine truth. Offering competing religious visions Fundamentalists accepted the Bible as errorless, while Modernists reinterpreted the Bible when confronted with new scientific knowledge (such as fossil evidence of evolution).

Believing that "monkey men mean monkey morals," the World Christian Fundamentals Association lobbied for state laws that prohibited teaching evolutionary ideas in public schools. In 1925 Tennessee passed a law making it a punishable crime to teach "any theory that denies the story of the Divine Creation as taught in the Bible, and to teach instead that man has descended from a lower order of animals." Passed mostly to make sweeping school reforms more palatable to Fundamentalist voters, the state made no effort to enforce the law and even adopted a biology textbook that included an extended discussion of Darwin's ideas.

The ACLU viewed the law as a violation of the First Amendment's guarantee of free speech. Hoping to test the law's constitutionality, the ACLU offered to help any teacher in Tennessee who wanted to challenge the law in court. A group of civic boosters in Dayton, Tennessee, responded to the offer. A trial highlighting the clash between science and religion was bound to attract huge crowds, they reasoned, and by hosting this national extravaganza Dayton expected to draw an influx of visitors with cash to spend. The boosters approached twenty-four-year-old John Scopes, a science teacher and part-time football coach, who agreed to step forward so officials in Dayton could arrest him. The infamous Scopes trial was underway.

Interest in Scopes, the ACLU, and Dayton faded once William Jennings Bryan agreed to prosecute the case and the attorney Clarence Darrow arrived to defend Scopes. Bryan was the former leader of the Democratic Party who had unsuccessfully run for president three times and resigned as secretary of state when President Woodrow Wilson abandoned complete neutrality during World War I. The devout Bryan blamed Germany's embrace of evolutionary notions like "survival of the fittest" for causing the brutal global war. Darrow was an acknowledged agnostic, famous for defending both radical labor leaders, such as the socialist Eugene Debs, and wealthy murderers.

Hundreds of journalists descended on the town to observe the courtroom confrontation between Bryan and Darrow. Their dispatches helped build publicity for the "monkey trial," a reference to evolutionists' claim that humans had descended from apes. Urban-based reporters billed the case as a conclusive struggle between modern America and the ignorant rural masses (few of whom shared in the general prosperity of the 1920s) whose alleged backward thinking threatened to impede the country's progress. In his widely read reports, nationally syndicated columnist H. L. Mencken regularly referred to Fundamentalists as hillbillies and yokels. Fundamentalists fought back. The carnival-like atmosphere outside the courtroom soon included Fundamentalist revival meetings and performances by trained chimpanzees that mocked evolutionists. Vendors did a brisk business selling monkey dolls, like the one held by Lena Ruffner

Why did Fundamentalists object to teaching evolution in public schools?

Dueling newspaper headlines during the Scopes Trial:
"'They Call Us Bigots When We Refuse to Throw Away Our Bibles,' Bryan says."

"We say 'Keep Your Bible,' but keep it where it belongs, in the world of your conscience."

(**21.8**), who announced her support of Bryan by pinning a sign "they can't make a monkey out of me" to her dress.

Both Bryan and Darrow argued that they were protecting American democratic institutions. Bryan maintained that the Tennessee legislature had the right to pass any law that the majority wanted; Darrow contended the state had violated the constitution by establishing Christianity as an official religion and limiting freedom of expression. The mainstream press viewed the trial as a showdown between science and religion, with science winning a decisive victory. In their account, the climatic moment came when Darrow called Bryan to the witness stand and trapped him into confessing he did not accept the entire Bible as the literal truth. "We have the purpose of preventing bigots and ignoramuses from controlling the education of the United States," Darrow declared in court, expressing Modernists' view of fundamentalism. The national press labeled Bryan a broken man when he passed away in his sleep five days after Scopes was found guilty and fined. The courtroom, however, had burst into applause when during his cross-examination Bryan had thundered, "I am simply trying to protect the word of God against the greatest atheist or agnostic in the United States." Southern folk songs popularized this competing heroic image of Bryan among his supporters, viewing him as someone who "fought for what was righteous and the battle it was won / Then the Lord called him to heaven for his work on earth was done."

After Scopes's conviction the ACLU appealed to the Tennessee Supreme Court, which upheld the law's constitutionality and then overturned the verdict because the judge rather than the jury had imposed the fine. Scopes's acquittal meant that the ACLU had to find a new case to take before the U.S. Supreme Court. After the ridicule heaped on Dayton, however, no town or teacher was willing to help the ACLU try again. The Tennessee state legislature did not repeal the law until 1967. A year later the U.S. Supreme Court declared anti-evolution laws unconstitutional.

Although soon forgotten by mainstream America, throughout the twentieth century Fundamentalists created a thriving minority subculture of churches, schools, universities, publishing houses, radio ministries, and missionary societies. Fundamentalists rejoined the cultural and political mainstream in the 1970s and are generating headlines once again with their challenges to teaching evolution in public schools. In one striking break from the past, Fundamentalists now use Darrow's line of reasoning to argue that keeping the biblical theory of creation out of high school biology classes violates the constitutional guarantee to freedom of expression.

21.8 **Young Woman Holds Monkey Doll during the Scopes Trial** A supporter of prosecutor William Jennings Bryan wears a sign ridiculing the theory of evolution and displays the monkey doll she bought from a vender outside the courthouse.

Racial Violence and Civil Rights

Advocates of prohibition, immigration restrictions, and fundamentalism had varying degrees of success reshaping American society after the war. Throughout the twenties African Americans were also active, employing new strategies to advance their vision of racial equality. Continued lynchings and a resurgent Ku Klux Klan in the South and Midwest exposed the willingness of many whites to use violence to maintain their competing vision of white supremacy. A new generation of black political activists emerged, determined to fight back when whites attacked. Jamaican immigrant Marcus Garvey won both praise and criticism within the African American community by calling for black economic self-sufficiency at home and the creation of a homeland in Africa. The **Harlem Renaissance**, an outpouring of African American artistic expression in the 1920s and 1930s also stirred debate within the African American community over the best way to improve the lives of African Americans.

Lynching, Racial Rioting, and the Ku Klux Klan

Lynch mobs tortured and killed nearly five thousand victims between 1880 and 1930, roughly two per week. The souvenir postcard (**21.9**) depicting the lynching of Thomas Shipp and Abram Smith is a disturbing relic from this grisly past. Professional photographers often attended lynchings and sold hundreds of picture postcards to perpetrators and witnesses, who put them in family scrapbooks or sent them to friends and relatives. Besides buying souvenir postcards whites sometimes took other relics from the victim, including hair, clothing, fingers, and ears. Both the existence of this postcard and the scene it depicts raise chilling questions about the ritual of lynching. Rather than viewing their murder as a shameful act or believing that they needed to conceal their identities to avoid prosecution, these participants smile openly for the camera. Local and state police rarely arrested anyone for committing a lynching, preferring instead to claim that the victims died "at the hands of persons unknown."

Trumped-up accusations that the victim had raped or murdered a white person usually fueled a lynching frenzy. Local police had arrested Shipp and Abram for robbery, murder, and rape. The purpose of lynching, however, went beyond simply administering extralegal justice. Lynching also created a climate of terror that helped whites maintain social control over all blacks, not just the ones killed. James Weldon Johnson, a well-regarded poet who served as director of the National Association for the Advancement of

21.9 Souvenir Postcard, Thomas Shipp and Abram Smith Lynching, Marion, Indiana After witnessing the lynching of two black men, smiling men and women had their pictures taken as a memento. The two girls to the left clutch pieces of the victims' hair.

What does this souvenir postcard reveal about the ritual of lynching?

Colored People (NAACP) in the twenties, coined the term "The Red Summer of 1919" to describe the wave of vicious assaults against black communities that left at least forty-three African Americans dead. Some whites also used organized violence to prevent blacks from competing with whites economically. Mobs intentionally attacked thriving black business centers and middle-class homes in Tulsa, Oklahoma, in 1921, and in Rosewood, Florida, in 1923. A headline in a local Tulsa newspaper even helped mobilize whites by issuing the call "To Lynch A Negro Tonight."

In both the Tulsa and Rosewood race riots, African Americans fought back against their attackers, but enraged white crowds still burned both communities to the ground. Officials in Tulsa declared martial law and imprisoned one-half of the city's black population in internment camps. After gaining their freedom a few weeks later, one thousand families spent the winter in tents before beginning the huge task of rebuilding their community. In 1994 the Florida state government awarded survivors of the Rosewood race riot $150,000 each in monetary reparations. For the first time African Americans received compensation for past racial injustices, raising the question of whether victims of other racially motivated attacks deserved financial settlements.

With the states unwilling to prosecute the members of lynch mobs, the NAACP lobbied to make lynching a federal crime. Hoping to shock the rest of the nation into supporting an anti-lynching law, the NAACP used graphic images of lynchings in their pamphlets, parades, and posters. Southern congressmen, however, successfully blocked the passage of a federal anti-lynching bill by claiming that it violated the constitutional right of states to police themselves.

The lynching documented by this souvenir postcard reveals another key aspect of racial violence in the twenties. Although most lynchings took place in the South, the attack pictured here actually occurred in Marion, Indiana. Indiana was home to the largest chapter of the Ku Klux Klan in the 1920s, enrolling nearly one-half of the state's white male population even though only 3 percent of the state's population was black. The federal government had suppressed the original Ku Klux Klan during Reconstruction (see Chapter 15). The Klan revived in the 1910s, and in its second incarnation became a national organization that drew members from all parts of the country with membership fluctuating between three and six million throughout the twenties.

21.10 Ku Klux Klan in Washington, D.C., 1925
Klan members unfurl a giant American flag on the steps of the Capitol, equating patriotism with their call for white supremacy.

The new Klan organized their call for white Protestant supremacy under the banner of 100 percent Americanism, and their list of enemies included any group that threatened the traditional order. Anxieties aroused by blacks' wartime migration to Northern and Midwestern industrial centers, the Red Scare, women's suffrage, mass immigration, prohibition, and postwar strikes caused many conservative whites to listen sympathetically to Klan outbursts against blacks, Jews, Catholics, immigrants, radicals, feminists, and bootleggers. The 1925 Klan march in Washington, D.C. (**21.10**), exposed the group's national appeal. City officials required the forty thousand assembled Klan members to march from the White House to the Capitol without their masks. Like lynch mobs these Klan members were unafraid to reveal their identities as they proudly unfurled an American flag that championed the Klan's "patriotic" slogan of "native, white, Protestant supremacy." The march represented the high tide of Klan power in the twenties. As fears of social upheaval diminished, Klan membership rolls also decreased.

Marcus Garvey

The African American community had long debated how to end racial attacks and segregation. In the 1890s Booker T. Washington squared off against W. E. B. Du Bois over whether blacks should focus first on improving their economic position or demanding political rights (see Chapter 18). Washington died in 1915 and in the 1920s Jamaican immigrant Marcus Garvey took up Washington's idea of empowering blacks economically. Garvey founded the **Universal Negro Improvement Association (UNIA)** to encourage economic self-sufficiency by creating black-owned businesses. The UNIA organized the Black Star Line, a short-lived capitalist venture that sold $5 stock certificates to finance the world's only black-owned and staffed fleet of steamships. Garvey's working-class followers, native-born African Americans and recently arrived immigrants from the West Indies, purchased stock enthusiastically. Poor management, however, forced the Black Star Line to dissolve in 1922.

Despite their shared message of economic empowerment, the black nationalist Garvey was much more militant than Washington. There was nothing shameful in being black, Garvey told his audiences, criticizing African Americans who used skin lighteners and hair straighteners to make themselves appear more white. God, Garvey said, "made no mistake when he made us black with kinky hair. We have outgrown slavery, but our minds are still enslaved to the thinking of the Master Race. Now take these kinks out of your mind, instead of out of your hair." Like Washington, Garvey rejected the political goal of dismantling Jim Crow that dominated other civil rights organizations. But unlike Washington, who wanted to improve life for blacks within the United States, Garvey spoke often of acquiring enough economic power to establish an independent African nation that could reunite the world's dispersed black peoples.

21.11 Marcus Garvey The leader of the UNIA often appeared in full military dress to project an image of strength and racial pride. He challenged prevailing racial stereotypes of black subservience by adopting regalia usually worn by kings.

Pageantry was a hallmark of the UNIA. The group's meetings often included a uniformed male African Legion dressed in blue and female Black Cross Nurses in white. To give these gatherings an official air, participants waved flags that were "black for our race, red for our blood, and green for our hope," Garvey said. Black middle-class detractors ridiculed Garvey's tendency to appear, as pictured here (**21.11**), wearing a plumed hat and military regalia. These critics called him "a clown" in a "gaudy uniform" who led "big parades of ignorant people down the street selling pie in the sky." Garvey, however, believed that seeing a black man dressed as an aristocrat inspired confidence among his followers and challenged the stereotype of black subservience perpetuated by white America. The Justice Department took notice of Garvey's theatrics. Worried that his movement was sowing the seeds of a violent black rebellion, government spies monitored his activities.

Competing Visions: Debating Garveyism explores Marcus Garvey's vision for black America and the criticism he received from W. E. B. Du Bois, a leader in the NAACP who supported immediate integration. Some of Garvey's other black critics organized a "Garvey Must Go" campaign and helped the government convict him of fraudulent use of the mails in 1923. He served four years in prison and upon his release immigration authorities deported him. Without Garvey the UNIA collapsed. Garveyism, however, offered African Americans an important alternative to the integrationist vision of the NAACP and introduced separatist ideas that Black Power advocates would resurrect in the 1960s (see Chapter 27).

The Harlem Renaissance

Garvey based the UNIA in Harlem, a thriving African American neighborhood in New York City that became the hub of black politics and culture in the 1920s during the **Harlem Renaissance.** African

Why did Garvey elicit such strong emotions among both followers and critics?

Competing Visions

DEBATING GARVEYISM

Many of the traditional civil rights elite despised Marcus Garvey, whom they accused of swindling the poor of their hard-earned money and stirring up racial animosity within the United States. Garvey in turn accused light-skinned African American leaders of racial prejudice, arguing that they could not accept the dark-skinned Garvey as their equal. In the following excerpts Garvey lays out his reasons for urging black Americans to go "Back to Africa," while W. E. B. Du Bois, one of the light-skinned elites Garvey attacked, criticizes Garvey's vision. How does Garvey propose to stop "crimes against the race"? What portrait does Du Bois offer of Garvey?

In "The True Solution of the Negro Problem" (1922) Marcus Garvey argued that creating a homeland in Africa could solve the problem of racial violence in the United States.

We cannot allow a continuation of these crimes [lynching and disenfranchisement] against our race. As four hundred million men, women and children, worthy of the existence given us by the Divine Creator, we are determined to solve our own problem, by redeeming our Motherland Africa from the hands of alien exploiters and found there a government, a nation of our own, strong enough to lend protection to the members of our race scattered all over the world, and to compel the respect of the nations and races of the earth.

Do they lynch Englishmen, Frenchmen, Germans or Japanese? No. And Why? Because these people are represented by great governments, mighty nations and empires ... ever ready to shed the last drop of blood and spend the last penny in the national treasury to protect the honor and integrity of a citizen outraged anywhere. Until the Negro reaches this point of national independence, all he does as a race will count for naught, because the prejudice that will stand out against him even with his ballot in his hand, with his industrial progress to show, will be of such an overwhelming nature as to perpetuate mob violence and mob rule. ...

If the Negro were to live in this Western Hemisphere for another five hundred years he would still be outnumbered by other races who are prejudiced against him. He cannot resort to the government for protection for government will be in the hands of the majority of the people who are prejudiced against him, hence for the Negro to depend on the ballot and his industrial progress alone, will be hopeless as it does not help him when he is lynched, burned, jim crowed and segregated. The future of the Negro therefore, outside of Africa, spells ruin and disaster.

Button won by Marcus Garvey supporters

In this 1923 biographical sketch, "Marcus Garvey," W. E. B. Du Bois views Garvey as misguided and inept.

Garvey soon developed in America a definite and in many respects original and alluring program. He proposed to establish the "Black Star Line" of steamships under Negro ownership and with Negro money, to trade between the United States, the West Indies, and Africa. He proposed to establish a factories corporation which was going to build factories and manufacture goods both for local consumption of Negroes and for export. ... When Mr. Garvey brought his cohorts to Madison Square Garden, and when, ducking his dark head at the audience, he yelled, "We are going to Africa to tell England, France and Belgium to get out of there," America sat up, listened, laughed, and said here at least is something new. ... Thus the Black Star Line arose and disappeared, and with it went some $800,000 of the savings of West Indians and a few American Negroes. ...

His African program was made impossible by his own pigheadedness. He proposed to make a start in Liberia with industrial enterprises. From this center he would penetrate all Africa and gradually subdue it. Instead of keeping this plan hidden and working cautiously and intelligently toward it, he yelled and shouted and telegraphed it all over the world. Without consulting the Liberians, he apparently was ready to assume partial charge of their state. ... [H]is talk about conquest and "driving Europe out," aroused European governments. ...

The present generation of Negroes has survived two grave temptations, the greater one, fathered by Booker T. Washington, which said, "Let politics alone, keep in your place, work hard, and do not complain," and which meant perpetual color caste for colored folk by their own cooperation and consent ... and the lesser, fathered by Marcus Garvey, which said, "Give up! Surrender! The struggle is useless; back to Africa and fight the white world."

How did Garvey and Du Bois link the U.S. Civil Rights Movement to international politics?

Claude McKay
"If We Must Die"
(1919)

If we must die, let it not be like hogs
Hunted and penned in an inglorious spot,
While round us bark the mad and hungry dogs,
Making their mock at our accursed lot.
If we must die, O let us nobly die,
So that our precious blood may not be shed
In vain; then even the monsters we defy
Shall be constrained to honor us though dead!
O kinsmen we must meet the common foe!
Though far outnumbered let us show us brave,
And for their thousand blows deal one deathblow!
What though before us lies the open grave?
Like men we'll face the murderous, cowardly pack,
Pressed to the wall, dying, but fighting back!

Countee Cullen
"Incident"
(1924)

Once riding in old Baltimore,
Heart-filled, head-filled with glee,
I saw a Baltimorean
Keep looking straight at me.
Now I was eight and very small,
And he was no whit bigger,
And so I smiled, but he poked out
His tongue, and called me, "Nigger."
I saw the whole of Baltimore
From May until December;
Of all the things that happened there
That's all that I remember.

In these poems how do responses to racism vary?

American artists, photographers, musicians, and writers openly celebrated the distinctiveness of black culture. Many writers published their works in black magazines such as *The Crisis* and *The Messenger*. White literary figures like Carl Van Vechten also became patrons of the Harlem Renaissance, helping black writers publish their works with commercial presses that exposed white America to black artistic endeavors for the first time. The African American philosopher Alain Locke captured the creative impulse of the Harlem Renaissance in 1925 when he published *The New Negro*, an anthology of essays and poems by emerging literary voices. According to Locke the **New Negro** embodied a spirit of black racial pride and militancy that set a younger generation of African American artists and civil rights leaders apart from their predecessors, who had emphasized assimilating into white culture.

Harlem Renaissance writers took up themes previously absent from serious works of literature. Poet Langston Hughes discussed black Americans' aspirations; Jean Toomer's novel *Cane* explored the rhythms of working-class life in the countryside and city; Zora Neale Huston exposed the power of female sexuality in her novel *Their Eyes Were Watching God*; poet Countee Cullen confronted the psychological impact of racism; and Claude McKay celebrated manly violence in his poems and novels. The poems displayed here show how McKay, Cullen, and Hughes protested racial discrimination through their poetry.

The Harlem Renaissance also included the jazz music innovations of trumpeter Louis Armstrong, pianist and arranger Fletcher Henderson, and pianist and composer Ferdinand "Jelly Roll" Morton. Jazz was an original American musical style that melded African American and European musical traditions. White and black patrons flocked to Harlem jazz clubs to listen to black bands at venues like the Cotton Club and the Savoy, while white musicians nationwide formed jazz bands of their own. Thanks to new commercial radio stations and the growing phonographic record industry, jazz became so popular that Americans began calling the twenties **"The Jazz Age."** Jazz music, the white conductor Leopold Stokowski rejoiced, was "an expression of the times, of the breathless, energetic, superactive times in which we are living."

James Weldon Johnson's poem "The Prodigal Son" highlighted the dangers awaiting new arrivals unschooled in big-city ways, who flocked to Harlem's jazz clubs. In the two-dimensional drawing by African

American artist Aaron Douglas that accompanied the poem (**21.12**), female dancers surround a young man and gyrate to the music provided by a hovering jazz trombone. The fragments of a dollar, playing card, and gin label evoke the temptations confronting this young man. Johnson's poem echoed the rhythms of sermons that folk preachers delivered to their Southern congregations who might be planning to go to Harlem, warning that these "sweet-sinning women stripped him of his money / And they stripped him of his clothes / And they left him broke and ragged / In the streets of Babylon."

As Johnson's poem suggested African Americans expressed conflicting views about jazz. Many artists celebrated the music's originality and exuberance. Like Southern preachers, however, the urban black middle class viewed jazz as "the devil's music," believing that its syncopated rhythms aroused sexual impulses and encouraged lewd behavior. Jazz clubs often served illegal alcohol purchased from organized crime rings, linking jazz music to the immoral lifestyle that many black middle-class prohibition advocates wanted to eradicate. The middle class preferred religious spirituals, a distinctive African American musical tradition that they felt projected a more respectable image of black culture to mainstream America.

Langston Hughes

"I, Too, Sing America"

(1925)

I, too, sing America.

I am the darker brother.
They send me to eat in the kitchen
When company comes,
But I laugh,
And eat well,
And grow strong.
Tomorrow,
I'll be at the table
When company comes.
Nobody'll dare
Say to me,
"Eat in the kitchen,"
Then.

Besides,
They'll see how beautiful I am
And be ashamed—

I, too, am America.

The literature of the Harlem Renaissance drew fire as well. Du Bois criticized novelist Claude McKay for depicting black working-class culture as a collection of pimps, petty criminals, drunks, and whores in his novel *Home to Harlem*. Du Bois lambasted McKay for reinforcing the negative stereotypes that white America held of African American culture, thereby undermining the possibility of using art to challenge the racial status quo. Defending New Negro aesthetics and the principle of artistic freedom, Langston Hughes countered, "We younger Negro artists who create now intend to express our dark-skinned selves without fear or shame. If white people are pleased we are glad. If they are not, it doesn't matter. We know we are beautiful."

21.12 ***Prodigal Son,*** **1927**
Aaron Douglas's innovative angular style evoked the fast pace of modern life in an illustration that both portrayed and epitomized the artistic innovations of the Harlem Renaissance.

What competing views arose over the purpose of art during the Harlem Renaissance?

The New Woman

Women began the decade with a significant political victory when the Nineteenth Amendment gave them to right to vote in 1920. Female reformers expected newly enfranchised women to care deeply about issues affecting their gender, but the much-anticipated "women's vote" never materialized. Throughout the twenties Americans offered competing visions of women's proper place in American society. Former suffragists envisioned modern women playing an active role in politics. Popular culture, however, consistently defined the "new woman" as someone who kept herself thin, pretty, and lively for her husband.

Women in the Twenties

When women got the right to vote nationwide, an aging generation of feminists tried immediately to organize the female vote behind causes that particularly affected women. Black women had actively supported suffrage as a step toward politically empowering the African American community. Throughout the South, however, authorities used poll taxes, literacy tests, and intimidation to stop black women from registering to vote. The League of Women Voters, created by the National American Women Suffrage Association in 1920, drew up a list of issues that it expected to resonate among female voters including child labor, protective legislation for female workers, and cleaning up city politics. This list did not include demanding that the Nineteenth Amendment be enforced for black and white women alike.

Responding to studies that revealed high rates of infant mortality and women dying in childbirth, the League of Women Voters successfully lobbied Congress for the nation's first major social welfare measure to help impoverished women and children. The Sheppard-Towner Act (1921) offered eight years of matching funds to states for classes that taught poor mothers about nutrition, hygiene, and prenatal care. It also provided visiting nurses for low-income pregnant women and new mothers.

By 1929, however, it became clear that women did not vote as a bloc. Therefore despite evidence of the law's success, Congress did not renew the program. Rather than rallying to gender-specific causes, the best predictor of how a woman would vote was how her husband voted.

Feminists also failed in their effort to amend the constitution by adding an **Equal Rights Amendment (ERA)**, a proposed constitutional amendment which stated that "equality of rights under the law shall not be denied or abridged by the United States or by any State on account of sex." The radical National Women's Party, chaired by Alice Paul, argued that such an amendment would eradicate in one fell swoop all the legal barriers that a dizzying array of archaic state legislation created for women. These laws, advocate Elsie Hill noted, denied a woman "control of her children equal to the father's; they deny her, if married, the right to control her earnings; they punish her for offenses for which men go unpunished," such as adultery. The moderate Progressive reformers who dominated the League of Women Voters, like future first lady Eleanor Roosevelt, worried that the Equal Rights Amendment might endanger the protective legislation for women that they had so carefully crafted in recent years, such as the maximum hour laws designed to shield mothers from overwork (see Chapter 18). They opposed the amendment, arguing that it was better to remove troubling laws individually, like the ones that prevented women from serving on juries or inheriting property.

Over the course of the decade, younger women displayed little interest in the social movements championed by their elders. Instead many women in their twenties and thirties focused on their economic prospects. Women made up 23.6 percent of the workforce by 1920, although they remained restricted to professions considered appropriate for their gender. During the decade clerical work as secretaries and telephone operators became primarily female occupations. Rapid expansion of corporate bureaucracies created a new need for office workers, a demand that the growing numbers of white female high school graduates filled. Women earned less than men, but companies were certain that married women made most of the purchasing decisions in American households. Product advertising in the 1920s, therefore, carefully targeted female consumers. *Images as History: Advertising the New Woman* explores how advertisements in the popular media also helped define the feminine ideal in the twenties.

What different strategies did women develop to improve their lives in the twenties?

Images as History

ADVERTISING THE NEW WOMAN

Popular advertising characterized the "new woman" as an efficient homemaker, devoted mother, high fashion sophisticate, and engaging spouse with the time and energy for a dizzying circle of friends and club activities. Manufacturing discontent about a woman's lifestyle and insecurity about her looks was another advertising strategy designed to get women to purchase products.

Advertisements that featured attractive women to entice potential customers, as in the Fisher car ad pictured here, reflected changing ideas about the ideal female body type. In the nineteenth century upper-class women proudly displayed their corpulence as evidence of their wealth and health. In the twenties, the popular media depicted the vigorous, alert modern woman as thin. But according to a 1928 study, only 17 percent of American women were both slender and over 5 feet 3 inches tall. How does this Fisher car ad both celebrate the new freedoms that women enjoyed in the twenties and perpetuate traditional stereotypes about women?

"Body by Fisher"

How did the popular media define "the new woman"?

Margaret Sanger and the Fight for Birth Control

Advertisers promised that modern electrical appliances would give women more time to spend with their children, and women's popular magazines offered a plethora of articles on how to use this additional time to raise children properly. Birth control advocate and trained nurse Margaret Sanger viewed the mother's plight somewhat differently. Too many children, Sanger argued, ruined women's health and relegated them to the ranks of the poor. In her view providing women with information on safe and reliable contraception was more important than dispensing advice on how to raise children.

"No woman can call herself free who does not own and control her own body."

Birth control advocate MARGARET SANGER

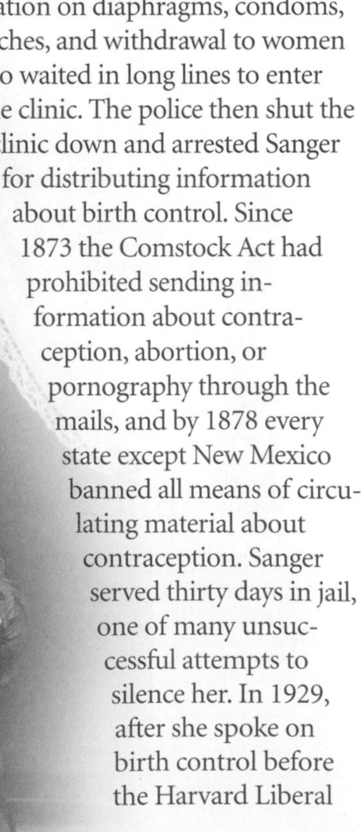

21.13 Margaret Sanger Protests When officials in Boston refused to let Margaret Sanger speak publicly about birth control, she appeared before a crowd with her mouth bandaged to protest their censorship. Her ploy garnered headlines across the nation, giving the birth control cause a boost.

In 1916 Sanger opened the nation's first birth control clinic in Brooklyn, New York, where she passed out flyers to advertise the benefits of contraception over illegal and dangerous back-alley abortions. For nine days Sanger dispensed information on diaphragms, condoms, douches, and withdrawal to women who waited in long lines to enter the clinic. The police then shut the clinic down and arrested Sanger for distributing information about birth control. Since 1873 the Comstock Act had prohibited sending information about contraception, abortion, or pornography through the mails, and by 1878 every state except New Mexico banned all means of circulating material about contraception. Sanger served thirty days in jail, one of many unsuccessful attempts to silence her. In 1929, after she spoke on birth control before the Harvard Liberal Club in Boston, the outraged mayor threatened to revoke the license of any hall that allowed her to speak again. In response Sanger appeared with her mouth bandaged before an audience in Boston's Ford Hall Forum (**21.13**). Her silent protest won headlines across the nation, helping Sanger publicize her cause even more widely.

By openly discussing birth control, Sanger made public the private contraception practices of middle-class couples. Poor mothers, she said, pleaded for her to share "the secret the rich have." Studies suggested that at least twice in their lifetimes, women living in poverty pulled their shawls over their heads to visit the five-dollar abortionist down the street. Sanger often told the story of Sadie Sachs (whose authenticity was never verified), a woman whom Sanger, as a young nurse, met when she accompanied a physician into the tenements to care for Sadie after she fell ill from a botched self-induced abortion. When Sadie begged the middle-class doctor to give her the information she needed to avoid another pregnancy, he replied, "Tell Jake to sleep on the roof." The next time Sanger saw Sadie, she lay in a coma dying from another abortion. Sanger used the story to personalize the extent of the abortion problem (nearly one million abortions that resulted in fifty thousand female deaths each year) and to dispel the misguided belief that no "decent" woman needed information about contraception.

Rather than counseling women to avoid sex, Sanger asserted that women had as much right as men to enjoy sexual intercourse without fearing for their lives. Contraception would not make women more promiscuous, she predicted. Once freed from the constant strain of childbearing, women would become more interesting spouses by developing their intellectual, political, and cultural interests much as popular advertising encouraged them to do.

Through her arrests, clinics, and public lectures, Sanger gradually helped change attitudes toward birth control. Although laws censoring information about birth control remained part of the legal code until the 1970s, enforcement became rarer and rarer. By the late 1920s thirty birth control clinics operated nationwide. **Eugenicists**, who wanted to improve the human race by controlling its hereditary qualities, also developed a strong interest in birth control. For Eugenicists contraception could prevent those they viewed as "unfit" from reproducing. Under their influence many states authorized compulsory sterilization of the institutionalized mentally handicapped, criminals, and epileptics until the 1960s.

What arguments did Sanger make to support her campaign for legal contraception?

Ensuring Peace: Diplomacy in the Twenties

Leaders in the birth control movement developed close ties with women's right groups in other countries, just one example of the global presence that Americans maintained throughout the twenties. Although the nation focused mostly on domestic concerns, international issues sometimes dominated the headlines. In 1920 the Senate refused to ratify the Versailles Treaty, which officially ended the war with Germany, or to join the League of Nations, which President Woodrow Wilson had championed to protect world peace. Rejection of Wilson's vision of collective security through the league did not signal a withdrawal from world affairs. American presidents Warren Harding and Calvin Coolidge tried instead to use disarmament and dollars to prevent armed conflict.

Disarmament

The high point of the disarmament movement came when Republican President Warren Harding convened the **Washington Conference (1921–1922)** in Washington, D.C., to negotiate a set of agreements that would limit naval arms. The conference also reaffirmed America's Open Door Policy (see Chapter 19) that kept Chinese trade open to all and secured pledges of cooperation among the world's leading military powers, including Britain, Japan, Italy and France.

Through the Washington Conference, Harding reshaped the political vision of his Democratic predecessor, Woodrow Wilson. Harding rejected Wilson's idea of using an open-ended commitment to the League of Nations to ensure world peace. He agreed with other Republicans who felt membership in this world body would unduly restrict America's ability to set its own foreign policy. Harding instead sought to prevent another war by convincing all major powers to disarm and to agree to mediation when disputes arose. Harding knew that Congress's penny-pinching mood meant certain rejection of any administration proposal to maintain a large military or embark on a major shipbuilding campaign. What better way to balance this domestic reality with the need to protect American shores from heavily armed naval competitors than by negotiating multinational disarmament treaties?

The White House and press referred to the meetings in Washington as a "peace conference" to cultivate the image that the negotiations would correct Wilson's blundering in Paris during the Versailles Treaty proceedings (see Chapter 20). The opening ceremonies underscored the symbolic comparisons that the Harding administration wanted to draw between the two international conferences. Delegates first attended the solemn burial in Arlington National Cemetery of an unidentified American soldier who had fallen on the battlefields of France. The Tomb of the Unknown Soldier was a memorial to all deceased soldiers who went missing or unidentified during the war. Next, Secretary of State Charles Evans Hughes opened the conference with a detailed public statement of his objectives, putting into practice the open diplomacy that Wilson had called for in the Fourteen Points and then quickly abandoned for closed door sessions in Paris.

Japan's 1905 victory in the Russo-Japanese War had signaled its emergence as the premier military power in East Asia. To contain Japan and Britain, which still controlled the world's greatest navy, Hughes proposed scrapping thirty American, twenty-three British, and seventeen Japanese battleships. One thrilled observer noted that Hughes had single-handedly sunk more British battleships "than all the admirals of the world had destroyed in a cycle of centuries." The Japanese, who unlike the British and Americans had only one ocean to patrol, accepted a naval tonnage ratio of 5:5:3 between the United States, Great Britain, and Japan. This meant that for every 5 tons of naval shipping that America and Great Britain maintained, Japan retained 3. Besides arms limitation, negotiations focused on settling potentially explosive issues in the Pacific. There American objectives included curtailing Japanese expansion in East Asia and preserving the Open Door in China. The American delegation met these goals, but at some cost. Japan accepted a smaller navy in

How did Harding's foreign policy vision differ from Wilson's?

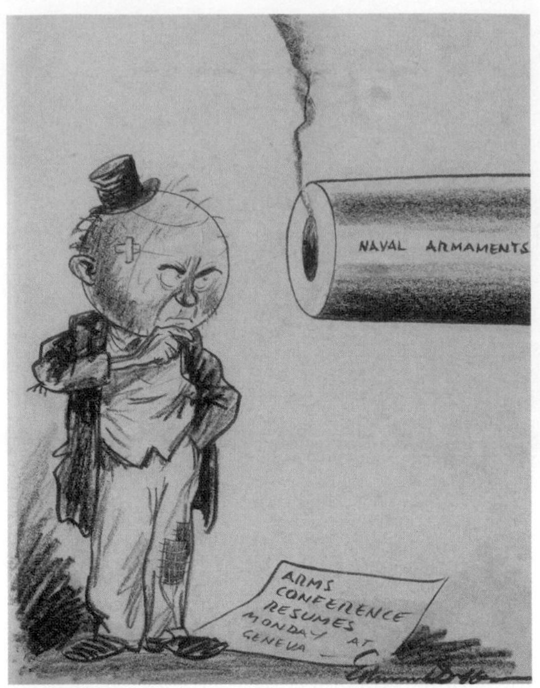

21.14 ***Looking into the Black Hole of Ruin***
This 1927 political cartoon forecasts disaster if the world powers failed to reach a second naval disarmament agreement. In the cartoon the world is in disarray after a naval gun showers it with gun powder.

return for a pledge that the others would refrain from improving their naval bases or fortifications in the western Pacific. American naval experts warned that this concession would leave American Pacific possessions vulnerable to a future Japanese attack. Hughes, who doubted that Congress would approve funds to improve naval defenses, accepted the deal. The resulting Five Power Treaty (which included smaller tonnage limits for France and Italy) set a ten-year moratorium on battleship construction and limited the number of guns that ships could carry. The treaty, however, made no mention of limits for submarines, light cruisers, aircraft, or land forces.

The Washington Conference also negotiated an accompanying Four Power Treaty, in which France, the United States, Britain, and Japan agreed to respect one another's Pacific possessions and to consult if any dispute arose. The Nine Power Treaty was the conference's final achievement. In this agreement the above five nations and Portugal, the Netherlands, Belgium, and China all agreed to respect the Open Door in China, a policy advocated by the United States since the turn of the century (see Chapter 19).

The resulting agreements essentially protected the United States, Britain, and Japan from an aggressive naval attack on their borders. They left Britain in control of the European seas, gave the United States charge of the Americas, and recognized Japanese predominance in East Asia. For the time being, avoiding an arms race and maintaining the status quo served the interests of the world's major powers.

Calvin Coolidge, Harding's successor in the White House, continued the Republican effort to find alternative ways to maintain world peace. Leading powers met again in Geneva in 1927 to broker another disarmament pact. This 1927 political cartoon (**21.14**) offered support for the proceedings by showing a disheveled world covered with gunpowder from a recently fired naval gun. This time, however, the leading powers failed to reach an agreement. Coolidge's secretary of state Frank Kellogg had more success negotiating the **Kellogg-Briand Pact (1928)**, whose signatories renounced aggressive war as an instrument of national policy and agreed to resolve their disagreements through peaceful means. *Choices and Consequences: Preventing War in Europe* examines why President Coolidge chose to support a multinational treaty that outlawed war.

Wartime Debts

World War I revealed the importance of European trade to American prosperity, but in the twenties the politically sensitive question of securing repayment from Allied nations for American wartime loans threatened to undermine Europe's economic recovery. From 1914 to 1925 the United States had loaned the Allies nearly $10 billion to finance wartime purchases of American goods and to help rebuild war-torn Europe (**21.15**). In the 1920s the Allied governments urged the United States to cancel the loans. How, they asked, could America insist on repayment when the Allies had sacrificed a whole generation of men to the joint cause of defeating Germany? Americans had supplied money while the Allies gave their blood, they argued. The United States, the Allies claimed, could easily afford to cancel the loans as the country had profited enormously from the war.

Americans remained vehemently opposed to canceling the debt. "They hired the money, didn't they," retorted President Calvin Coolidge in the mid-twenties, expressing a common American view that Europe had a moral obligation to repay its debts. Coolidge did, however, agree to lower the interest rate on the loans, which reduced the total amount due by 43 percent. Further complicating the debate, the high American tariff enacted in 1922 made it difficult for Allied nations to sell manufactured goods in the United States, revenue that they needed to repay their war loans. Using a high tariff to protect American industries from foreign competition had tremendous domestic appeal and the United States refused to lower it.

The Allies consequently relied on reparation payments from Germany (authorized in the Versailles Treaty) to repay their U.S. war loans. This punitive aspect of the Versailles Treaty troubled many Americans, who viewed the $33 billion reparation bill imposed on Germany as excessive. The United States denied any connection between war loans and reparation payments, seeing the first

What benefits and drawbacks did the Washington Conference agreements offer the United States?

Choices and Consequences:

PREVENTING WAR IN EUROPE

In 1928 France invited the United States to sign a treaty renouncing war between the two nations, hoping to coax the American government into playing a more active peacekeeping role in Europe. President Coolidge faced several choices about how to respond. Americans had conflicting visions of the best way to avoid another war, and vocal supporters backed each option.

Choices

1 Adopt a non-interventionist policy that kept the United States out of European affairs.

2 Sign a nonaggression pact with France as the first step toward creating a formal defensive alliance that rebuilt the pre-WWI balance of power system in Europe.

3 Reject bilateral agreements and instead join the League of Nations.

4 Negotiate a multinational nonaggression pact.

Decision

Coolidge rejected any suggestion that the United States join the League of Nations but knew that the idea of outlawing war had strong appeal at home. Consequently he agreed to let Secretary of State Frank Kellogg meet with French Foreign Minister Aristide Briand to fashion a multinational nonaggression pact. By opening the treaty up to other nations, Coolidge avoided the impression that the United States was allying itself with France. The resulting Kellogg-Briand Pact was eventually signed by sixty-three nations, including Germany and Japan.

Consequences

The Kellogg-Briand Pact proved popular with Americans because its vagueness allowed it to be all things to all people. Non-interventionists saw the pact as insulating the country from ever fighting another war overseas. They liked that the United States resolved to stay peaceful yet made no binding commitments to defend other nations. Internationalists, who wanted the United States to play a more active role in maintaining world peace, saw the treaty as the first step toward creating an American presence in international arbitration bodies like the World Court and the League of Nations.

"A Christmas Carol: Peace on Earth, Good Will Towards Man"

Continuing Controversies

What value did the Kellogg-Briand Pact have?

Critics called the treaty a "letter to Santa Claus" and dismissed it as "not worth a postage stamp," pointing out that the world's major powers signed the agreement but continued to arm their nations for war. The Kellogg-Briand agreement still allowed for wars of "self-defense," a slippery term that nations could easily manipulate. As if to prove the point, when the Senate enthusiastically ratified the treaty with only one dissenting vote, it added a reservation stating that preserving the Monroe Doctrine constituted self-defense. Others acknowledge that the treaty did not prevent World War II but point out that it gave the victorious nations a legal way to punish Nazi officials who were convicted of violating the Kellogg-Briand Pact in postwar war crimes trials.

Did the Kellogg-Briand Pact represent a new path in American foreign policy?

21.15 American Loans to Europe, 1914–1925
The United States demanded that Europe repay loans given to help nations defeat Germany and rebuild after World War I.

as an honest debt and the latter as blood money. The Allies, however, refused to reduce the reparation bill as long as the United States insisted on collecting Allied war loans.

In 1923 skyrocketing inflation caused Germany to miss a reparation payment, and in retaliation France and Belgium occupied the Ruhr Valley, a German industrial center. This crisis threatened to undermine American economic interests abroad by thrusting Europe into recession. Having ruled out lowering the tariff or canceling Allied war loans as ways to foster Europe's economic recovery from the war, the United States resolved to help Germany make its reparation payments. Twice in the decade international committees of experts convened to discuss reparations. In 1924 Secretary of State Hughes sent Chicago banker General Charles G. Dawes and General Electric Company head Owen D. Young to Europe. The resulting **Dawes Plan (1924)** loaned Germany $200 million in gold to pay a reduced reparation bill and gave Germany more time to meet its debt. Certain that a German recovery was imminent, American bankers eagerly provided half the funds for the Dawes Plan, and made private loans and investments that helped Germany even more. Dawes went on to become vice president during Coolidge's successful reelection bid in 1924 and won the Nobel Peace Prize in 1925. In 1929 the Young Plan further reduced Germany's final bill to $8 billion and restructured the payment schedule once again.

American money kept the whole system afloat. Between 1923 and 1930 American banks loaned $2.6 billion to Germany; Germany made $2 billion in reparation payments; and the Allies repaid $2.6 billion of their American war loans (one-fifth of the amount owed). The "Global Flow of Reparation

How did lingering financial issues from World War I shape relations between the United States and Europe?

Payments" (**21.16**) details the journey that American money took around the world through Germany, France, and Great Britain until it landed back in American coffers. When the stock market crashed in 1929, American bankers drastically reduced their overseas loans. The withdrawal of American funds caused the whole arrangement to collapse. First Germany, then the Allied governments defaulted on their payments. In 1931 President Herbert Hoover successfully called for a one-year moratorium on all international debts. With the connection between reparation payments and war loans now formally acknowledged by the United States, the Allied governments canceled most of Germany's remaining reparation payments. By 1934 all governments except Finland defaulted on their wartime American loans. Finland was the only nation that finally repaid its entire debt of $8 million to the United States by 1969.

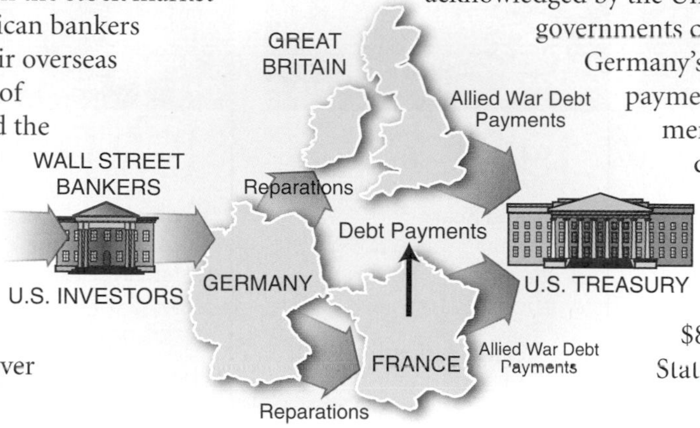

21.16 The Global Flow of Reparation Payments American capital kept the reparation system created by the Versailles Treaty afloat in the twenties.

Conclusion

The 1920s proved a pivotal decade for the United States, a period when Americans both embraced and resisted modernity. The health of the automobile industry became essential to the country's economy, and cars refashioned daily life, inner cities, and the rural landscape. Welfare capitalism offered the promise of better industrial working conditions. Lindbergh's solo flight across the Atlantic captured the public's imagination and provided evidence of American technological prowess. Meanwhile multinational agreements that limited armaments and outlawed war promised to keep the world peaceful without entangling America in defensive alliances or the League of Nations.

In the twenties Americans embraced conflicting visions over what values should dominate the nation in the modern era. The Fundamentalist-Modernist cultural divide fueled the controversy that surrounded the Scopes Trial over teaching evolution in public schools. Temperance advocates viewed alcohol as a scourge that increased vice and corrupted politics. They led the nation into a thirteen-year experiment with prohibition that ended when the increase in organized crime and widespread flouting of the law convinced Americans that prohibition was unenforceable and misguided.

The birth control movement and Lost Generation writers challenged traditionally accepted notions of female sexuality in the twenties, but a consumer culture focused on improving appearance urged the "new woman" to continue thinking of her husband and children first. Fearing that unchecked immigration would infect American culture with foreign ideologies, especially communist ideals, the nation supported drastic immigration restrictions. Meanwhile the desire to protect a racial status quo based on white, Protestant supremacy fueled a resurgence of lynchings and the Ku Klux Klan. Embodying a new militant spirit, the New Negro clashed with traditional civil rights leaders over whether the solution to breaking down the barrier of racial discrimination lay in demonstrating artistic merit, economic self-help, or leaving the United States altogether.

Blinded by prosperity in the industrial sector, few Americans focused on farmers' difficulties or the growing concentration of wealth at the top in the twenties. All this changed quickly when the stock market crashed in 1929. Suddenly the plight of the common people became the nation's top concern.

Why did the United States intervene to settle European financial crises in the 1920s?

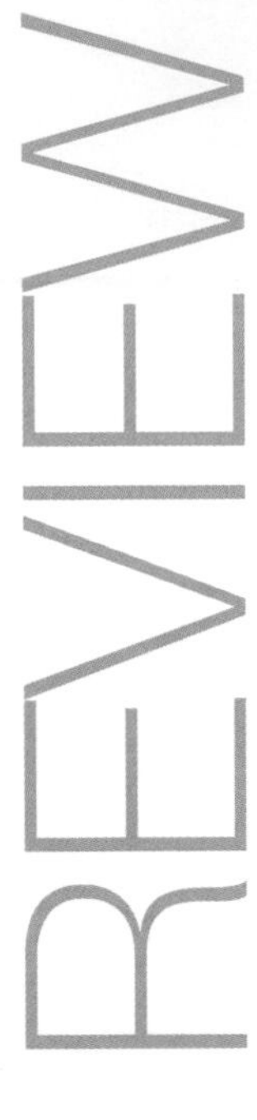

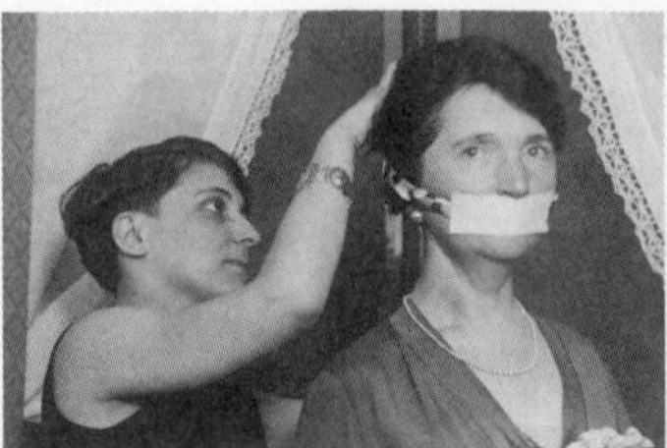

1916

Margaret Sanger opens first birth control clinic
Sanger champions birth control to improve female health and eliminate poverty

1919

First Red Scare
Anti-communist campaign destroys radical political organizations

Eighteenth Amendment ratified
Initiates era of national Prohibition

1921–1922

Washington Conference held
Disarmament becomes a major goal of American foreign policy

UNIA Black Star Line founded
Short-lived black-run steamship operation line embodies Marcus Garvey's ideal of economic self-help

Teapot Dome Scandal
Corruption weakens Harding's presidency

Review Questions

1. What features and controversies characterized America's transformation into a car culture in the 1920s? How did lifestyles and labor relations also change during the decade?
2. What symbolic significance did Americans attach to Charles Lindberg's solo flight across the Atlantic?
3. Compare the various manifestations of cultural conflict in the twenties. What similar impulses motivated Americans to enact prohibition, immigration restrictions, and laws prohibiting the teaching of Darwin's theory of evolution? What differing impact did these various reforms have on American society?
4. Why were the Harlem Renaissance and Marcus Garvey controversial?
5. Were the 1920s a time of political, economic, and social liberation for women? What traditional concerns or ideas remained intact?
6. How did the United States fashion a new role for the nation in world affairs in the twenties? What ideals informed American foreign policy in this era?

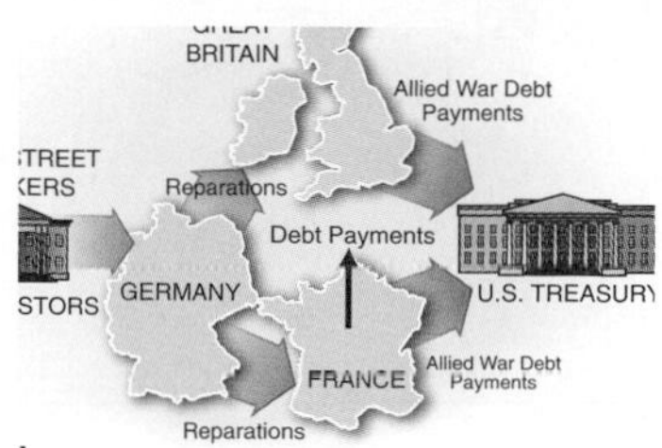

1924

Immigration Act of 1924
Severely reduces immigration and establishes nationality-based quota-system

Dawes Plan
United States uses financial aid to stabilize postwar European economies

1925

Scopes Trial
Highlights cultural conflict between religion and science

Ku Klux Klan marches in Washington, D.C.
White-instigated racial violence surges as the Klan becomes national organization

Publication of *The New Negro*
Harlem Renaissance gives rise to African American artistic outpouring

1927

Charles A. Lindbergh flies nonstop from New York to Paris
Reassures Americans that man and machine can coexist harmoniously

1928

Kellogg-Briand Pact
America uses world influence to secure global pledges of peace

Key Terms

Spirit of St. Louis The plane that Charles Lindbergh piloted on the first-ever nonstop solo flight from New York to Paris on May 21, 1927. **630**

Eighteenth Amendment (1919) Constitutional amendment that banned the sale, manufacture, and transportation of intoxicating liquors. **633**

Volstead Act (1919) Law that established criminal penalties for manufacturing, transporting, or possessing alcohol. **633**

Twenty-First Amendment (1933) Constitutional amendment that repealed the Eighteenth Amendment. **633**

Immigration Act of 1924 Law that allowed unrestricted immigration from the Western Hemisphere, curtailed all Asian immigration, and used quotas to control how many immigrants emigrated from individual European nations. **634**

First Red Scare (1919–1920) Period when the Justice Department arrested and deported alien anarchists and Communists suspected of trying to destroy American democracy and capitalism. **634**

fundamentalism An evangelical Christian theology that viewed the Bible as an authentic recounting of historical events and the absolute moral word of God. **636**

modernism A liberal Christian theology embraced in many urban areas that emphasized the ongoing revelation of divine truth. **636**

Harlem Renaissance An outpouring of African American artistic expression in the 1920s and 1930s. **638**

Universal Negro Improvement Association (UNIA) Organization founded by Marcus Garvey to spread his message of racial pride, economic self-sufficiency, and returning to Africa. **640**

New Negro Spirit of black racial pride and militancy that set a younger generation of African American artists and civil rights leaders apart from their predecessors. **642**

The Jazz Age Nickname for the twenties that reflected the popularity of jazz music. **642**

Equal Rights Amendment (ERA) A proposed constitutional amendment, which stated that "equality of rights under the law shall not be denied or abridged by the United States or by any State on account of sex." **644**

Eugenicists Those who wanted to improve the human race by controlling its hereditary qualities. **646**

Washington Conference (1921–1922) Meeting of world powers that resulted in agreements that limited naval arms, reaffirmed America's Open Door policy that kept Chinese trade open to all, and secured pledges of co-operation among the world's leading military powers. **647**

Kellogg-Briand Pact (1928) Treaty that renounced aggressive war as an instrument of national policy. **648**

Dawes Plan (1924) International agreement that loaned Germany $200 million in gold to pay a reduced reparation bill and gave Germany more time to meet its debt. **650**

CHAPTER 22

A New Deal for America

The Great Depression, 1929–1940

The Early Days of the Depression p. 656

A New President and a New Deal p. 662

> "I pledge you, I pledge myself, to a new deal for the American people,"
>
> FRANKLIN D. ROOSEVELT, 1932

When Franklin D. Roosevelt accepted the Democratic nomination for president in 1932, he promised to remember "the forgotten man at the bottom of the economic pyramid." FDR won the election and took office in the throes of the Great Depression, the most devastating and longest economic crisis in American history. Four years later the photographer Walker Evans traveled to Alabama to document the hardships of three struggling sharecropping families. While there he photographed Floyd Burroughs, who spent his days toiling in the cotton fields alongside his wife and children. For seven years, through the worst of the Depression crisis, Burroughs had struggled to provide the minimal basics for his family without any government help.

To gain public support for new government programs designed to help sharecroppers, the Farm Security Administration had commissioned this and photos like it to show Americans the faces of poverty-stricken farmers. Evans's portrait of the "forgotten man" aroused more than sympathy, however.

Americans had different visions of how the government should respond to the crisis, and throughout the decade political debate centered on whether and how much the government should intervene. Presidents Herbert Hoover and Franklin D. Roosevelt both championed initiative, freedom, and opportunity. They disagreed, however, over what government action preserved or destroyed these values. In the early thirties President Herbert Hoover, who preferred minimal government intervention in the economy, took a few historic steps by lending money to banks and businesses and helping farmers. More attuned to the mood of the public, Roosevelt initiated a broad array of public works programs and social reforms to satisfy the demand for direct government intervention in the economy.

Taken together, policy initiatives by Hoover and Roosevelt paved the way for a complete transformation of the role that the federal government played in American society. The New Deal did not end the Depression; that honor belonged to World War II. It was, however, one of the most important periods of legislative activity in American history.

Farmers, migrants, and industrial workers did not just passively wait for help during these hard times. They demanded a "new deal" from the federal government that alleviated the sufferings of common people. Organized labor and charismatic populist politicians on the left helped create a groundswell of support for active government intervention in the economy. The decade, therefore, was not just the story of unrelenting hardship. The era also had moments of triumph for ordinary Americans, like Burroughs, who found their political voice.

What emotions does Walker Evans's portrait of the "forgotten man" arouse?

AIR
THIS IS YOUR COUNTRY DONT LET THE BIG MEN TAKE IT AWAY FROM YOU

The Early Days of the Depression

In 1928 the future looked rosy to most Americans, and even President Herbert Hoover believed that permanent prosperity was at hand. Americans venerated Hoover as the "Great Humanitarian" when he began his term. He left four years later amid bitter denunciations that he cared more for banks than for people, earning him the new nickname of the "Great Scrooge." The causes of the Depression were complex, giving rise to competing visions over what action, if any, the government should take and how far it should go to engineer an economic recovery. Hoover went further than any other president to date in offering federal assistance to businesses and farmers, but his awkward manner along with his refusal to approve direct governmental relief made him appear uncaring to most Americans by 1932.

Herbert Hoover

Herbert Hoover's personal story was a classic rags-to-riches tale that reaffirmed faith in the American Dream. Orphaned at nine years old, he later recalled that "my boyhood ambition was to be able to earn my own living, without the help of anybody, anywhere." This personal ethos shaped his lifelong political views.

Starting as a mine laborer working for $2.50 a day, by the age of forty Hoover was a respected engineer with millions in the bank. During World War I Hoover became the country's most famous humanitarian when he served as food administrator and organized relief missions to help feed a starving post-war Europe. Hoover's organizational talents and dedication to good works inspired such awe that the first time his name ever appeared on a ballot in 1928, he won, becoming president of the United States. Hoover was a poor public speaker, lacked charisma, and closely guarded his private life. But when he became president, he enjoyed immense popularity. After all, Hoover was a success in business, he had fed starving people, and he believed that people would do the right thing once the government showed them the way.

Like most Americans, Hoover believed that able-bodied individuals should make their own way in the world. He maintained that if the government stepped in too often to manage the economy, individuals and businesses lost their initiative. For Hoover individualism meant more than individuals selfishly pursuing their own well-being. He felt that Americans and American business also had a responsibility to serve the community; like Progressive reformers he believed that self-interest often caused great harm to others (see Chapter 18). Hoover, however, did not share the Progressive desire to use government regulation to solve economic problems. Hoover envisioned a more cooperative, voluntary approach. Instead of passing more laws, Hoover wanted the government to organize meetings so industrialists, labor, and farmers could craft their own agreements to address issues such as overproduction, price wars, low wages, and strikes. The beginning of the Depression gave the country a chance to see if Hoover's voluntary and cooperative approach to economic problems could stem the crisis.

> "Just making money isn't enough."
>
> HERBERT HOOVER, explaining his decision to leave a lucrative engineering career for public service

Economic Weaknesses in a Time of Prosperity

The economic downturn in 1929 took the country by surprise. However, a hard look at the twenties reveals that problems in the nation's economy existed even during the boom years, both in large-scale industries and on family-run farms.

Some industries, especially textiles and mining, suffered throughout the decade from overproduction and falling demand. By the end of the twenties, even

What qualities made Hoover a popular president when he was first elected?

automobile, construction, and appliance industries found it difficult to turn a profit. Cooling demand for automobiles soon rippled outward to industries such as steel and rubber. Some of the reasons for the slump lay in the unequal distribution of income in American society. From 1923 to 1929 corporate profits rose 62 percent, while workers' hourly wages increased by only 8 percent. With economic growth now linked to consumer spending, the limited purchasing power of working-class Americans contributed to the growing financial crisis.

High tariffs (taxes levied against imported products) kept the prices of foreign-made goods high, protecting American companies from overseas competition. Foreign countries responded by levying high tariffs against American goods, reducing overseas markets for U.S. companies. When demand for American-made goods declined at home, American companies were slow to lower prices. By the time they did, demand had fallen so dramatically that massive layoffs were inevitable. As the chances for making money in manufacturing lessened, investors stopped buying industrial stocks. This loss of capital further dampened manufacturers' efforts to recover their earlier momentum. Together, these problems revealed an ailing industrial sector.

More evident problems existed in the farming sector. Farmers' boom times had come during World War I, when high demand, generous prices, and easy access to credit induced many to expand their crop production. When the war ended and demand fell, farmers were left with debts, large farms, and falling crop prices. The long-term trend toward mechanized farming also contributed to the country's looming agricultural crisis. With tractors, farmers could plow and harvest more land on a daily basis. The ability to grow more crops, more easily, paradoxically hurt farmers because overproduction drove prices down even further.

Even before the Depression officially began, Hoover had devised a plan to help farmers escape the vicious cycle of overproduction and low prices that kept them from sharing in the prosperity of the twenties. The Agricultural Marketing Act (1929) created a Farm Board with the power to buy and store crops to reduce the harvest-time market glut, which lowered crop prices. In keeping with his ethos of self-help, Hoover expected farmers to do their part to keep agricultural prices high by growing less. These measures, however, were too little, too late. Unsure about what his neighbors would do, no farmer wanted to be the only one to reduce his crop and then suffer both low prices *and* a small harvest. The nation's farmers continued to plant crops in record numbers.

"In the 93 years of my life, depressions have come and gone. Prosperity has always returned and will again."

Oil Magnate J. D. ROCKEFELLER, doubting the need for government action

The Stock Market Crash of 1929

These underlying problems all laid the foundation for an economic downturn, but by themselves did not predict a worldwide depression. Any chances for a mild recession disappeared in the **stock market crash of 1929**, a ten-day period beginning on October 20, 1929, when the value of stocks plummeted as panicked investors sold off their stock in droves. This moment is usually considered the official start of the Depression.

Before the crash the stock market promised investors easy profits. When investors buy stock they own pieces of the company and receive dividends (their share of the profits). Normally the price of a share fluctuates in relation to the expected profitability of the company. By the late 1920s, however, speculators had taken over the stock market. Speculators did not care about holding on to their share purchases to earn dividends. Instead, they sold their shares as soon as the share price rose.

The epidemic of speculation created three key financial problems:

1. The influx of money into the stock market inflated share prices to such an extent that a stock's price soon bore little relation to the actual worth of a company.
2. Many speculators bought on margin, the name given to the short-term loans used to purchase stock, and planned to cover these loans by quickly reselling their shares at a higher price. When stock prices began to fall, too many investors could not pay these debts.

Why did farmers fail to prosper in the 1920s?

3. Many investors were speculating with other people's money, funds from ordinary Americans' savings accounts that banks used to finance speculative stock market purchases. That explains why, although only 10 percent of Americans actually owned stock, the life savings of millions disappeared in October 1929.

On Monday, October 20, 1929, the downward spiral began. Stock prices plummeted three days later on Black Thursday when a record 12.9 million shares changed hands. On Black Tuesday the following week, October 29, 1929, 16 million shares were traded and losses totaled $14 billion. That evening James Rosenberg, a Wall Street bankruptcy lawyer who was also a trained artist, etched an expressionist portrait of the chaotic scenes he had witnessed. Rosenberg's *Day of Wrath 1929* (**22.1**) captured the panic that swept Wall Street as

22.1 ***Oct. 29 Dies Irae (Days of Wrath) 1929***
James Rosenberg used apocalyptic biblical imagery of God's wrath as the world comes to an end to convey the panic that swept Wall Street after the stock market crashed. The photo shows investors racing to the New York Stock Exchange. [*Source* (left): James N. Rosenberg, American, (b. 1874). Oct 29 Dies Irae, 1929, Lithograph. Philadelphia Museum of Art, Lola Downin Peck Fund]

What factors led to the stock market crash in 1929?

investors raced to the New York Stock Exchange. In the lithograph the nation's financial institutions teeter on the verge of collapse, frightened crowds gather in the streets, and dark clouds hover over a sky filled with stockbrokers jumping to their deaths. Throughout the crisis rumors circulated about ruined investors committing suicide from the city's skyscrapers and ambulance sirens wailed continually as crews responded to false alarms.

Hoover's Response to the Depression

When the stock market crashed, no one knew that this was the beginning of a ten-year ordeal. The **Great Depression** lasted from 1929 to 1939, the most devastating and longest economic crisis in American history. In the 1920s the federal government played a relatively minor role in the economy, and conservative businessmen urged Hoover to keep it that way. Do nothing, the laissez-faire capitalists told the president, setting in motion a political debate over government intervention that would dominate the Depression era.

Rejecting the laissez-faire suggestion, Hoover envisioned the government fostering a spirit of teamwork that encouraged Americans to work together as the nation weathered the economic downturn. In keeping with his ideas of service-minded individualism, he brought the leaders of banking, industry, and labor to the White House and urged them to do their bit to keep the economy afloat. Responding to Hoover's plea, industry agreed not to lay off workers or cut wages, and labor leaders accepted a shorter workday to create more jobs. Hoover asked state governments to accelerate their road and public building projects to add jobs in their communities.

Hoover also stepped up hiring for long-planned federal construction projects including the Hoover Dam and asked Congress to extend the already existing tariff on manufactured goods to agricultural imports. Congress complied in 1930, raising tariffs to their highest level ever. When other nations retaliated with their own high tariffs, American companies and farmers lost overseas markets. As a result the world and the United States plunged deeper into economic depression.

In orchestrating this unprecedented federal response to an economic depression, Hoover stayed within limits acceptable to most conservatives. Most fiscal conservatives wanted government-built roads and a high protective tariff and preferred non-governmental solutions to economic problems. When it came to helping needy citizens directly, Hoover went no further than asking local governments and charities to assume their traditional role of distributing food and clothing to the poor. This stance surprised Hoover's Progressive supporters, given the president's previous triumph organizing a massive international relief effort to feed hungry Europeans after World War I. It was not a question of helping people, Hoover asserted. "It is solely a question of the best method by which hunger and cold shall be prevented," he explained. To Hoover the American tradition of self-help made relief the responsibility of local governments and charities.

How did Hoover respond to the initial economic crisis?

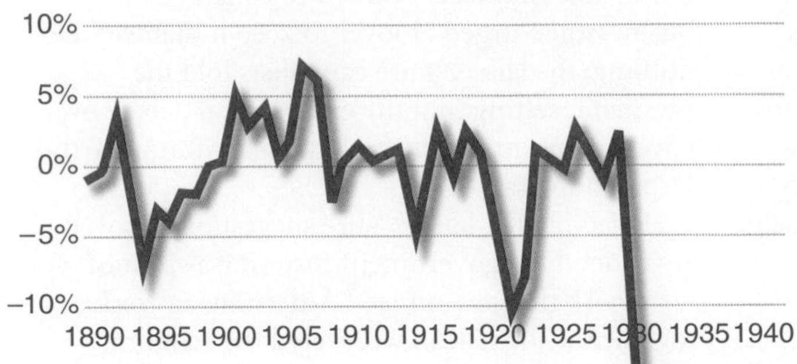

22.2 Economic Trends in the Depression
This graph shows the sharp dip in the nation's gross national product during the Depression, a result of reduced productivity and consumption.

Hoover's approach began to unravel as the Depression worsened. The chart "Economic Trends in the Depression" (**22.2**) reveals the severity of the historic financial crisis.When the crisis entered its second year, U.S. Steel announced a 10 percent wage cut. Other companies followed suit, and within ten days American business had slashed millions of workers' wages and begun massive layoffs. The nation's deepening financial woes convinced Hoover to lend federal money to businesses and states. This decision was a dramatic break from past practice. In previous financial panics and depressions, private bankers had put up the money needed for recovery and presidents had cut federal spending to ensure a balanced budget. In 1932, by proposing a direct economic role for the government in ending the Depression, Herbert Hoover—the man who wanted to decrease Americans' reliance on the government to solve their problems—went further than any previous peacetime president in similar circumstances.

By providing money to banks, insurance companies, farm mortgage associations, and railroads through the Reconstruction Finance Corporation (RFC) Act of 1932, Hoover helped institutions that were vital to the prosperity of any community. In its first year the government loaned more than $1.5 billion to these businesses, but little relief trickled down to workers. When critics pressured the president to provide direct help to those without work or food, Hoover responded with the Emergency Relief Act (1932), which lent money to the states for public works programs. Although his farm program, the RFC, and state loans failed to bring about recovery, Hoover had unknowingly set a precedent for direct governmental management of the economy that Franklin D. Roosevelt would continue and expand.

With the unemployment rate hovering around 20 percent in 1932, Hoover's popularity declined steadily. Shantytowns constructed by the homeless became known as "Hoovervilles" and people waved "Hooverflags" (empty pockets turned inside out) during their street protests. A well-circulated joke began with Hoover asking an aide for a nickel to call a friend from a public telephone. "Here," said the man, tossing him a dime, "call them both."

In the 1932 presidential campaign, Hoover faced off against Franklin D. Roosevelt (commonly referred to as FDR), a fifth cousin of Theodore Roosevelt. In sharp contrast to how he would govern, Franklin D. Roosevelt ran a fairly conservative campaign and let Hoover's missteps win him the election. One of those mistakes was the violent eviction of a group of war veterans from the nation's capital. Throughout the summer of 1932 the **Bonus March**, a two-month-long demonstration by forty thousand impoverished World War I veterans in Washington, D.C., transfixed the nation. The Bonus March ended violently when the army expelled the protesters, further damaging Hoover's popularity at a key moment during the 1932 presidential campaign. *Choices and Consequences: Evicting the Bonus Marchers* explores how Hoover lost control of the decision to evict the Bonus Marchers from the city and paid the consequences.

"We didn't admit it at the time, but practically the whole New Deal was extrapolated from programs that Hoover started."

REXFORD TUGWELL, key advisor to FDR

What innovative solutions did Hoover propose as the economic crisis continued?

Choices and Consequences

EVICTING THE BONUS MARCHERS

In 1924 World War I veterans had received a federal bond certificate (worth an average of $1,500) set to mature in 1945. In May, 1932, veterans arrived en masse in the nation's capital to demand immediate payment of this bonus. They set up a huge "Hooverville" of makeshift shacks and tents and staged continuous demonstrations on the Capitol steps. Hoover faced several choices about how to deal with the demonstration, depending on what interpretation of the protest he embraced.

Choices

1 Accept the veterans' argument that the government should pay the bonus immediately to alleviate their Depression-caused suffering.

2 Accept his advisers' view that the Bonus March was a communist-inspired plot to incite revolution and use force to thwart it.

3 Reject their claim but treat the veterans as essentially harmless, if misguided, citizens in desperate financial straits.

Decision

While many in the general public and press viewed the Bonus Marchers as down-on-their-luck citizens, Hoover grew convinced that they were a dangerous, radical force. After a skirmish between veterans and the local police in August, Hoover opted to send in troops with instructions to restore order.

Consequences

Once the troops were deployed, Chief of Staff General Douglas MacArthur exceeded Hoover's orders and decided to drive the veterans out of the city using tear gas and bayonets. Hoover never publicly revealed MacArthur's insubordination. When Democratic presidential candidate Franklin D. Roosevelt heard of the violent eviction, he reportedly told an adviser, "Well, Felix, this will elect me."

Continuing Controversies

Was the government right to use force to evict the Bonus Marchers?

To justify the eviction the White House mounted a furious public relations campaign that included false accusations of discovering dynamite in the main veterans' encampment. Some upper-class Americans applauded the government's actions, hoping to dampen any revolutionary impulse brewing among the poor. Many working-class and middle-class Americans saw their own destroyed lives in the smoldering ruins of the veterans' shantytown and turned against Hoover for refusing to aid men who had served the nation loyally.

The ruins of a Bonus Army encampment

Why was Hoover's choice to evict the bonus marchers significant?

A New President and a New Deal

FDR became president in 1933 during the lowest moment of the Depression with 25 percent of the workforce unemployed. Half of those with home mortgages had defaulted on their loans, and the entire banking system appeared ready to collapse. Empathy for the common people encouraged FDR to act, but so did fear that a social revolution might result if Washington did nothing for them. "I pledge you, I pledge myself, to a new deal for the American people," FDR had proclaimed during his campaign. FDR entered office dedicated to protecting America as a capitalist society, and his vision of government activism came under severe scrutiny from both sides of the political spectrum.

FDR: The Politician

"Only a foolish optimist can deny the dark realities of the moment," noted FDR upon taking office in 1933. If FDR had a mandate for anything, it was bold action. He met that expectation with the **New Deal**, an avalanche of legislation from 1933 to 1938 intended to promote economic recovery, reform American capitalism, and offer security to ordinary Americans. The chart "Key New Deal Legislation" (**22.3**) shows the most significant laws passed under Roosevelt's watch.

22.3 Key New Deal Legislation

Year	Legislation
1933	**Reconstruction Finance Corporation** continued Businesses and banks receive federal loans
1933	**National Industrial Recovery Act** Allows business to set price, wage, production codes
1933	**Agricultural Adjustment Act** Paid farmers to plant less to raise crop prices establishing key precedents in government farm policy
1933	**Civilian Conservation Corps** Employed young men in reforestation and construction
1933	**Public Works Administration** Construction projects provide work relief to poor
1933	**Glass-Steagall Act of 1933** Insures bank deposits; separates commercial and investment banking
1933	**Tennessee Valley Authority** Brings electricity to rural areas, stops devastating floods
1935	**Social Security Act** Guaranteed eligible workers a pension, unemployment insurance, aid to disabled and widows with dependent children
1935	**Wagner Act** Offers government protection to unions
1935	**Works Progress Administration** Extensive public works program employed 8 million ranging fromartists to construction workers
1938	**Fair Labor Standards Act** Established federal minimum wage and maximum hours per week

Having campaigned as a fiscal conservative who would balance the budget, FDR did not have a blueprint for ending the Depression when he came into office. He did, however, have a fairly well-shaped social philosophy. "He had a profound feeling for the underdog, ...a very keen awareness that political democracy could not exist side by side with economic plutocracy," according to one of his key advisers. "We are going to make a country," the president told a Cabinet member, "in which no one is left out." FDR sought advice for specific programs and regulations from the Brain Trust, a group of leading academics who served as presidential advisers in the early years of the New Deal. The Brain Trust wanted to revive the Progressive-era practice of using government regulation to solve economic problems and protect the common good (see Chapter 18). Brain Trust members Raymond Moley, Rexford Tugwell, and Adolf Berle diagnosed underconsumption as the main cause of the Depression, blaming the unequal distribution of income, the farm crisis, the rigidity of prices, and low wages as the key culprits. This cartoon (**22.4**) depicts the conservative complaint that the Brain Trust hurt the country with New Deal programs intended to correct these economic problems. Posing as doctors, these professors have anesthetized the country with propaganda. Now the patient lies on an operating table oblivious to the knives and drills about to destroy his body. Besides attacking the New Deal as a set of unwise experiments, the cartoon touches on conservatives' concern that too much government involvement in the economy (like too

22.4 Conservatives Attack the New Deal
This 1934 cartoon mocks the Brain Trust for experimenting with the nation's well-being, implying that New Deal policy initiatives did more harm than good.

many pointless operations) would result in more harm than good.

In formulating his policies FDR leaned on another critical adviser: his wife. Eleanor Roosevelt served as the president's "eyes and ears" by traveling around the country and reporting to him what she observed. In her first year Eleanor Roosevelt traveled 30,000 miles visiting Americans where they worked and lived. In 1935 the Washington *Star* felt it newsworthy to print the headline "Mrs. Roosevelt Spends the Night at the White House."

Over time Eleanor Roosevelt became more outspoken in advancing causes dear to her heart concerning racial injustice and poverty. She invited prominent African Americans to the White House to talk directly to the president on civil rights matters. Eleanor Roosevelt's visible participation in political affairs set her apart from former First Ladies, who had mostly served as official hostesses at White House functions. Her activism opened up political opportunities for other women. There were many firsts for women in the thirties: first ambassador, first judge on the Court of Appeals, and first cabinet secretary, Secretary of Labor Frances Perkins.

Americans differed in their reactions to Eleanor Roosevelt's left-leaning political activities. Conservative detractors advised her to "stay at home and make a home for your husband." Her civil rights

> "If it fails, admit it frankly and try another. But above all, try something."
>
> FDR's approach to shaping the New Deal

activism particularly upset southern Democrats in Congress. She had equally ardent supporters, and consistently won a two-thirds approval rating in Gallup polls—often bettering her husband. Thousands of Americans wrote to her each week, to ask for financial help, or to praise her work.

Like his wife, FDR connected well with the public. Throughout his presidency FDR used weekly radio addresses that he called "fireside chats" to speak directly to the nation. After the president's death in 1945, people stopped Eleanor on the street to tell her how much "they missed the way the President used to talk to them," she recalled. "They'd say, 'He used to talk to me about my government.' " FDR was often photographed smiling and smoking from an elegant-looking cigarette holder (**22.5**), and the public found his visible cheerfulness refreshing.

FDR infused hope into a time of trouble and confusion. Yet little in his background suggested that he would understand the plight of common people. The only son of doting, wealthy parents who imbued him with tremendous self-confidence, the athletic, charming, and brilliant FDR attended Harvard and passed the New York State bar exam after just one year at Columbia Law School. In 1929 he became governor of New York. A personal tragedy in FDR's life, however, convinced the public that he understood what it meant to overcome adversity. In 1921 at the age of thirty-nine, FDR contracted polio. It left him partially paralyzed for the rest of his life, and in pain much of the time. His disability "made it possible for the common people to trust him to understand what it is to be handicapped by poverty and ignorance, as well as by physical misfortune," Secretary of Labor Frances Perkins noted.

22.5 FDR's Trademark Cigarette Holder and Smile
Most Americans found FDR's cheerfulness reassuring, and he inspired confidence in America's security and future prosperity.

What role did Eleanor Roosevelt play during her husband's administrations?

Managing Appearances

22.7 FDR Running
Political cartoons never showed the president's physical disabilities. [Reproduced with permission of *The Kansas City Star* © Copyright 2007 *The Kansas City Star*. All rights reserved. Format differs from original publication. Not an endorsement.]

Although FDR benefited from people knowing that he had overcome a misfortune, he also believed that visual images of his handicap would convey the impression that he was weak and physically unfit for his responsibilities. FDR made a personal and political decision to conceal his paralysis. To hide his heavy leg braces, he wore extra long pants and had the visible portion painted black to blend with his shoes. He learned to stand upright by holding onto a cane with one hand and the arm of an aide, usually his son, with the other (**22.6**). He would then use his hips to swing his legs forward in a semiarch to give the illusion of walking. All of this required tremendous physical exertion. James Roosevelt later noted that he often had bruises on his arms from the force of his father's grip. Father and son disguised their physical effort by smiling and joking as they "walked" together before audiences.

Away from the crowds, aides carried FDR up stairs or from the car to a wheelchair. In public he often used his automobile as a prop to hide his disability, and by holding a bar installed in the backseat of an open touring car, he could pull himself up to address crowds. At one stadium rally a ramp was constructed so that the president's car could be driven onto the stage in the center of the field. FDR gave his speech without leaving the car.

The press obeyed White House rules that prohibited taking photos of the president in a wheelchair or being carried. As a result there are only two known photographs of FDR in a wheelchair. This self-censorship even extended to political cartoons, which never once depicted the president as incapacitated. Instead, these caricatures usually portrayed an energetic FDR running or jumping like this 1936 caricature from the *Kansas City Star* (**22.7**), in which a running FDR replicates Benjamin Franklin's kite-flying experiment to bring electricity to the rural poor.

22.6 FDR Walking
Shunning his wheelchair, candidate FDR holds onto his son's arm as the two greet supporters during his first presidential campaign in 1932.

The Temper of the Poor: Passivity and Anger

Hoover kept his distance from common people and paid the price. FDR was a more astute politician. But what was the temper of the people he needed to help? Two competing images of the poor soon emerged. One emphasized their helplessness and suffering; the other saw them as teetering on the brink of revolt.

> "There is something about the first anniversary of your layoff which makes you feel more hopeless."
>
> A worker during the Great Depression

How and why did FDR manage his political image?

Countless government investigators detailed the plight of hardworking family men suddenly without jobs. "I find them all in the same shape—fear, fear driving them into a state of semi-collapse; cracking nerves; and an overpowering terror of the future," reported one social worker. Many Americans chose to suffer silently, making their own decisions about how to cope, sometimes blaming themselves rather than the Depression for their troubles. This portrait by Dorothea Lange (**22.8**) conveys this "quiet desperation" of the poor. In Lange's image an unemployed man grasps his empty tin cup and leans over the rail as if he is kneeling at a church altar praying for salvation. The man's plight is moving, but his passivity is also vaguely reassuring to those who feared angry demonstrations or social revolution.

As the Bonus March revealed, however, not all Americans were waiting patiently for conditions to improve. Federal investigator Lorena Hickok feared that a social revolution was brewing. "I still feel that vast numbers of unemployed in Pennsylvania are 'right on the edge,' so to speak—that it wouldn't take much to make Communists out of them," she concluded. The Communist Party hoped that she was right. Unlike Roosevelt and his conservative critics, Communists had no interest in saving capitalism. They instead hoped that the crisis would provoke a social revolt that ended all forms of private property. The 1930s are sometimes referred to as the "heyday of American Communism," as the party grew from seven thousand members in 1930 to a hundred thousand in 1939. Across the country Communists organized unemployed councils that blocked evictions from city apartments, mounted hunger marches, and reconnected gas and electricity lines for workers who had fallen delinquent in their bills.

Grocery store robberies were also common, although newspapers rarely reported these events. When the manager of a grocery store in Detroit denied a group of men credit, they ransacked his store. Witnessing the food riot, the novelist John Dos Passos wondered why the manager did not call the police. "If more people heard about affairs like this, there would be more trouble," the manager replied.

While the urban poor stole food, farmers organized public demonstrations to demand higher prices for their crops. Across the Midwest farmers disrupted food shipments by blocking highways with logs and pouring milk onto roads. When banks seized land, cattle, or farm machinery from farmers who defaulted on their loans, the police stood guard to ensure that public sales of the seized property went smoothly. At some farm auctions farmers devised an effective strategy to help their neighbors by offering only a penny for the property on sale. Nooses hung on barn doors at penny auctions warned prospective buyers that bidding on a farm family's possessions would not be a wise thing to do. "If anyone in the farmyard might be so ignorant of what was going on as to put in a serious bid, a suitably burly man would be likely to step up and put a hand on his shoulder with the words, 'That bid's a little high, ain't it?'" one farmer recalled.

22.8 **"Breadline," San Francisco, 1933**
The man's empty cup symbolized his pervasive hunger. His unthreatening pose created sympathy for his plight, while the militant poor provoked fears of social revolution.

Recovering from the Depression

"First of all," FDR stated in his inaugural address, "let me assert my firm belief that the only thing we have to fear is fear itself." These courageous words inspired confidence in the country's new leader at a time when financial institutions were on the brink of collapse. Jump-starting the economy involved restoring confidence in the banking system, putting people to work and keeping businesses afloat. Following Hoover's lead, FDR established a cooperative relationship between the government and business and provided federal money for banks and businesses. But FDR differed from Hoover in a major way: he was willing to provide jobs through extensive public works programs and to fund temporary direct relief to average citizens.

Revamping Banking and Financial Institutions

By the time FDR took office, Americans had lost nearly $2.5 billion in nine thousand bank failures. The new president declared an immediate bank holiday on March 6, 1933, that closed the nation's banks for a week. An obedient Congress quickly passed emergency banking legislation that allowed only banks with the Federal Reserve's stamp of approval to reopen. "I can assure you that it is safer to keep your money in a reopened bank than under the mattress," FDR told the public in his first fireside address. When the "holiday" ended, millions of Americans demonstrated their faith in the president by depositing more money than they withdrew in the weeks that followed. "Capitalism," a FDR adviser said later, "was saved in [those] eight days."

"It was the Government's job to straighten out this situation," FDR told radio listeners. His administration soon proposed more reform measures intended to inspire public confidence in the nation's banks. The Glass-Steagall Act of 1933 created the Federal Deposit Insurance Corporation (FDIC), insuring the accounts of small depositors in member banks. The FDIC still exists. The same legislation protected the deposits of ordinary Americans by separating investment and commercial banking so bank officials could no longer make speculative loans or stock purchases with depositors' money. This provision was repealed in 1999.

Finally, the New Deal tackled the problems caused by an unregulated stock market that had contributed to the crash of 1929. A series of laws established the Securities and Exchange Commission (SEC) and reformed the practices of buying and selling stock. The SEC required companies to disclose financial details to potential investors so they could make an informed stock purchase. The SEC also regulated the practice of buying stocks on margin.

Reforms in home mortgage lending practices probably had a more immediate impact on the lives of ordinary Americans than stock market reform. In 1933 forty percent of homeowners were on the brink of losing their homes to bank foreclosures. In response FDR created a program that refinanced one out of every ten home mortgages and spread the payments out over twenty years instead of the usual five. Designed to encourage Americans to purchase homes (and thereby give the construction industry a boost), the Federal Housing Authority (FHA), founded in 1934, offered insurance to private lenders who financed home mortgages for new homes. FHA backing allowed creditors to reduce the amount of the down payment required, lower interest rates, and lengthen the life of the loan. These government-supported initiatives helped form the modern mortgage lending practices that enabled the percentage of Americans who owned their own homes to increase by one-third over the next forty years.

Father Charles Coughlin

Many businessmen and bankers supported these reforms because they renewed public faith in the basic structures of capitalism. With internal battles dividing members, the Communist Party never mounted an effective challenge to the New Deal. Instead, the most influential dissenter on the left who challenged New Deal banking reforms was Father Charles Coughlin.

A popular "radio priest" from Detroit who spoke with an Irish brogue, Father Coughlin gave sermons

How did FDR reform the nation's banking and financial institutions?

on a weekly radio program that drew audiences of thirty to forty million. In 1934 Coughlin received more mail than anyone in the United States, including Roosevelt, most of it from adoring fans making donations to advance Coughlin's cause. Coughlin singled out financiers and international bankers as the culprits who caused the Depression. The popularity of Father Coughlin's relentless attacks on the elite helped push FDR increasingly to the left over the course of his first administration.

Following the lead of the Populists of the nineteenth century (see Chapter 17), Coughlin focused on how existing currency and banking arrangements helped bankers but hurt the common people. With currency in short supply, average citizens had to work harder to pay off their debts. Putting more money into circulation made sense in the midst of a depression, but bankers held firm to their old orthodoxy that all sound economies were based on the gold standard. Coughlin proposed a revaluation of the price of gold and the monetization of silver to allow the government to put more dollars into circulation. He also wanted to nationalize the banks to take money lending out of the hands of private bankers.

Coughlin initially supported the New Deal in sermons like "The New Deal Is Christ's Deal" and praised the president when he took the country off the gold standard in 1933. The president welcomed Coughlin's support at first but eventually grew tired of the priest's impromptu visits to the White House. As their relationship soured Coughlin began criticizing the administration for doing too little to rein in powerful banking and capitalist interests. Many of his followers begged him to reconsider his break with FDR, then withdrew from the short-lived third party that he headed. By 1938 Coughlin's star was in decline. His broadcasts became increasingly strident, filled for the first time with anti-Semitic diatribes against an imagined international Jewish banking conspiracy. He stayed on the air until 1942, when his bishop ordered him to cease all political activities.

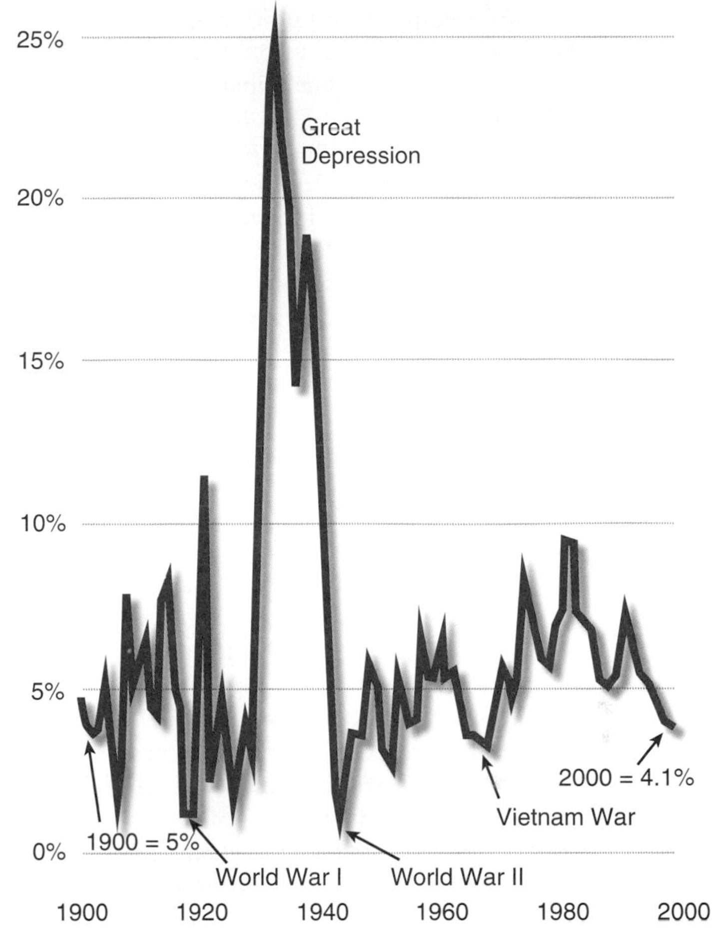

22.9 **Soaring Unemployment** This graph reveals the historically high unemployment rate during the Great Depression.

Helping Industry and People

Besides shoring up banks, FDR also immediately sought ways to get people back to work. As the graph (**22.9**) reveals, FDR faced the most severe jobs crisis in American history. At first FDR followed in his predecessor's footsteps. The Reconstruction Finance Corporation, begun under Hoover's watch, continued to make loans and began buying bank stocks to help banks acquire the liquid capital needed to stay open. The National Recovery Administration (NRA), established by the 1933 National Industrial Recovery Act, was the cornerstone of FDR's efforts to devise a Hoover-like cooperative solution to the crisis. Temporarily suspending antitrust laws, the NRA established industrial boards for each sector of the economy that brought competitors together to set prices, production quotas, and wages. Architects of the NRA believed these industrial codes would stop manufacturers from cutting wages to subsidize lower prices, a practice that reduced the purchasing power of workers, contributing to overproduction and underconsumption.

When prices rose without any corresponding increase in wages, however, many Americans became unhappy with the NRA. Even the larger corporations that benefited from the price codes remained leery of the NRA, fearful that the agency might force them to negotiate with labor unions. To everyone's relief the Supreme Court declared the NRA unconstitutional in 1935, ruling that it delegated too much power from the legislative to the executive branch and regulated more than interstate commerce.

FDR's reading of the public mood quickly encouraged him to depart from the policies of his predecessor and offer direct financial relief to individuals out of work. FDR encouraged Americans to write to him, and in their correspondence destitute Americans bared painful details of their poverty and often asked for specific items, such as a coat or shoes. Attuned to the widespread misery, FDR created the Federal Emergency Relief Administration (FERA), a federal agency that distributed more than $1 billion in three years.

Although many Americans were grateful for this help, applying for federal relief or a "dole" was a humiliating experience for previously self-sufficient working people. Even at the height of the Depression, accepting relief carried the stigma of personal failure. Conservatives felt that laziness, alcoholism, lack of ambition, and a poor work ethic created a class of indigent poor that would likely always exist. Progressives believed that dismal living and working conditions deadened workers' spirits, encouraging them to turn to drink or crime. Although they envisioned the roots of poverty differently, both conservatives and Progressives viewed relief with suspicion, fearful that handouts might discourage workers from trying to support themselves in the future. One could feel sympathy for the poor, therefore, and still worry about the negative consequences of distributing charity or relief.

Like many of his contemporaries, FDR disliked using federal monies to fund direct relief. FDR always preferred federal programs that employed the poor over those that simply handed out food or money. In 1935 he decided to stop providing direct cash grants to the needy. "To dole out relief in this way is to administer a narcotic, a subtle destroyer of the human spirit," FDR told Congress. From this point on the states handled relief while the federal government tackled the problem of putting "employable" persons to work.

Putting People to Work

To the dismay of conservatives and gratitude of the unemployed, the New Deal created a variety of programs, each administered by a different agency, which provided 15 million jobs over the course of the Depression. The Civil Works Administration (CWA), Civilian Conservation Corps (CCC), and Public Works Administration (PWA) were all founded in 1933. During its four-month existence, the CWA provided jobs that helped more than 4 million workers survive the winter of 1933–1934 and stemmed growing unrest among the unemployed. The CCC (which lasted until World War II) focused on giving economically disadvantaged young men a chance to gain work experience. It undertook major reforestation projects, constructed campgrounds, restored historic battlefields, and stocked rivers and lakes with fish. The PWA, run by Harold Ickes, funded public works projects, especially roads and buildings, to help revive the construction industry.

After deciding in 1935 to fund only work relief programs, Roosevelt created the Works Progress Administration. The WPA, managed by Harry Hopkins, was a major public works program that employed more than 8 million workers from 1935 to 1943, one-fifth of the workforce. Over the course of its existence, the WPA constructed 200,000 buildings and bridges along with 600,000 miles of roads. The agency also funded the arts, subsidizing painters and writers. Thanks to massive New Deal government spending on work-relief, and the subsequent strengthening of consumer spending power, the economy began gradually recovering in the mid-thirties.

> "I gave the best part of my life to the American country, and I spent every cent I made here. They owe it to me to take care of me."
>
> A worker, happily accepting a WPA job

> "I wouldn't plow nobody's mule from sunrise to sunset for 50 cents per day when I could get $1.30 for pretending to work on a DITCH."
>
> A Georgia farmer, criticizing the WPA work ethic

Who was helped by the wide range of New Deal work relief programs?

22.10 *Turning a Corner*
Like most Depression-era post office murals, this one celebrated workers as the backbone of the nation. "My interest," artist Joe Jones noted, "was in portraying man at work—his job before him—and how he goes about it with his tools—man creating."

Even permanent government agencies put Americans to work during the Depression. The Treasury Department, for instance, hired artists to decorate post offices throughout the nation. Edward Bruce, who directed the Treasury Department program, wanted to "enrich the lives of all our people" by making "beauty part of their daily lives" when they visited the post office. Post office murals celebrated Americans and their communities. In rural areas these murals projected images of prosperous farmers running family farms. Joe Jones painted *Turning a Corner* (**22.10**) for the Anthony, Kansas, post office, a mural that showed a farmer using a tractor to harvest a beautiful field of golden wheat before an approaching storm damaged his crops. The mural made no reference to the drought or dust storms that ravaged farms during the thirties, nor criticized farmers for overproducing and causing crop prices to fall. Instead, the artist celebrated the farmer for growing the food that fed the nation and romanticized his relationship with the land.

Americans had different visions of work relief, disagreeing over whether it was ruining or saving the country. For critics of work relief, the sight of WPA construction crews workers standing around talking instead of working led to jokes that WPA stood for "We Piddle Around." Farmers looking for day laborers also complained bitterly that federal work relief often paid more than working in the fields. Many WPA employees, however, saw government-provided jobs as a right that they had earned.

In a 1935 *Fortune* magazine survey, nearly 90 percent of lower-middle-class and working-class respondents answered yes when asked "Do you believe that the government should see to it that every man who wants to work has a job?" Roosevelt agreed to a point. FDR consistently tried to terminate these programs at the slightest sign of recovery in an effort to balance the federal budget, remaining true to his conservative fiscal values. The government reduced funds to the WPA when unemployment dropped in 1937 to 7.7 million from a high of 12.8 million in 1933. However, the sharp reduction in government spending, combined with new taxes and higher interest rates, all caused the fledgling recovery to grind to a halt. During the 1937 recession automobile production declined by 50 percent, steel by 70 percent, rubber by 40 percent, and the unemployment rate rose to 9.5 million (17 percent of the working population). With no federal funds for new relief projects available, New Jersey responded by issuing licenses to beg on the streets. The next year FDR restored public works funding.

A New Deal for Farmers

New Deal public works programs dotted the American landscape with new roads, murals, and dams, a lasting legacy of Depression-era recovery efforts. Reforms in the agricultural sector also outlived the immediate crisis, part of FDR's commitment to save American capitalism and create "greater security for the average man than he has ever known before in the history of America." Americans from all walks of life, however, questioned the government's desire to help displaced farm workers.

Handling the Farm Crisis

Assisting farmers protected an American way of life with strong mythic connections to the nation's beginnings as a land of opportunity. Farmers received more direct aid than any other group during the Depression. The Agricultural Adjustment Act (AAA) of 1933 tried to ensure that farmers earned an adequate income by paying them to take land out of cultivation, which the administration hoped would cause crop prices to rise. When reducing acreage failed to sufficiently lower output, FDR approved a series of laws that established marketing quotas for each commodity. If farmers tried to sell more than their allotted quota, they were hit with a heavy fine.

The administration departed temporarily from this approach when the Supreme Court ruled the AAA unconstitutional in 1936. The Court decided that the tax on food-processing plants used to finance the acreage-reduction program was an illegal sales tax because the plants passed the cost of the program on to consumers. Congress passed a second AAA in 1938, but in the midthirties the problems facing farmers in some parts of the country had changed.

In the **Dust Bowl** drought and soil erosion caused massive dust storms across southern and plains states throughout the thirties. During one storm in May 1934, experts estimated that the winds transported 350 million tons of soil from the West to the East. Dust fell like snow on Chicago, the sun was obscured in Washington, D.C., and ships 300 miles out to sea reported dirt settling on their decks. This photo (**22.11**) captures an approaching dust storm carrying deadly amounts of dirt. Each storm left piles of dead cattle and wildlife in its wake as

22.11 "Approaching Dust Storm" Ominous clouds of dirt descend on a small town in Colorado during one of the dust storms that plagued the plains states and the southwest in the thirties. The storms killed livestock and kept people inside for days.

How did FDR tackle the problems of rural America?

residents barricaded themselves inside their houses with damp towels over their mouths to avoid suffocation or wore Red Cross-provided gas masks. But even these precautions did not completely prevent deaths from occurring when a duster hit.

To encourage better farming practices, the government began paying farmers in the Dust Bowl to plant soil-improving crops like legumes instead of traditional cash crops such as wheat, cotton, and tobacco that exhausted the soil. In one innovative program the government planted 220 million trees in a 100-mile-wide swath from Childress, Texas, to the Canadian border. These trees stopped western dust from traveling east by cooling the air and reducing the wind velocity of dust storms.

Bringing electricity to rural areas was another way the New Deal improved the quality of life for the rural poor. Most of the urban population had electricity to ease the daily tasks of pumping water and washing clothes, advantages available to only one in ten rural families in 1930. Begun in 1933, the Tennessee Valley Authority (TVA) was a government-owned utility company that provided thousands of jobs as it built a series of dams that generated power, provided flood relief, and created recreational lakes throughout the seven states (Tennessee, Alabama, Mississippi, Kentucky, Virginia, North Carolina, and Georgia) serviced by the Tennessee River. These areas soon enjoyed good fishing, cheap electricity, and relief from debilitating floods.

Government-sponsored low-interest loans enabled rural cooperatives to string electrical lines and manufacture power. "The women went around turning the switches on and off," noted an observer after one home received its hookup. "The light and wonder in their eyes was brighter than that from the lamps." By 1941 almost half of all American farms had access to electricity, a figure that rose to 90 percent by 1950.

Native Americans were another rural population aided by New Deal policies. Commissioner for Indian Affairs John Collier pressed successfully for passage of the 1934 Indian Reorganization Act that ended the land allotment policies sanctioned under the 1887 Dawes Act (see Chapter 15) and returned a degree of self-government to Indian reservations. The stage was set for a gradual rebirth of Native American cultures in the twentieth century.

Overall, New Deal subsidies succeeded in improving farm owners' lives. Farm income doubled from $2 billion in 1929 to $4.6 billion in 1939. Although farmers still made only 37.5 percent of what nonfarm workers made, farming had become a much more profitable business. These agricultural policies created some unexpected problems, however, by helping landowners at the expense of tenant farmers and farm laborers whose services were no longer needed once the government began paying farm owners to take land out of cultivation. The Farm Security Administration helped a small number of tenants purchase land, offering sharecroppers a way to break out of the traditional cycle of debt that bound them to landowners. But millions of tenant farmers and farm laborers, white and black, had to find their own way out of the crisis.

Hitting the Road

Nearly 2.5 million farmers hit the road in search of work in the thirties. Besides families traveling together in cars, nearly 250,000 teenagers, usually young men, "rode the rails" by hopping into empty railroad freight cars. Constantly on the move, these wandering youths found companionship in "hobo jungles" (homeless encampments) as they looked for jobs, lived off handouts, and sometimes stole to get by. Nearly 400,000 Americans left farming areas in the middle of the country and headed to California. Old trucks piled high with personal belongings flooded western highways, demonstrating how completely the United States had become a car culture. The United States was "the only Nation in the history of the world that ever went to the poor house in an automobile," quipped the cowboy humorist Will Rogers.

California state officials tried to discourage migrants. A billboard on Route 66, the main highway that migrants took west, near Tulsa, Oklahoma, proclaimed: "NO JOBS in California, If YOU are looking for work—KEEP OUT, 6 men for Every Job, No State Relief Available for Non-Residents." The signs did little to discourage families from heading to California.

The majority of new California arrivals settled into the nomadic life of the migrant worker, traveling an average of 516 miles during the six-month harvest season. Despite their dependence on migrant workers to pick the crops, native Californians did not welcome "Okies," the pejorative term for Dust Bowl refugees, with open arms. "Okies" were now subject to the same kinds of discrimination that migrant workers of Mexican, Chinese, Japanese, and Filipino descent had suffered for

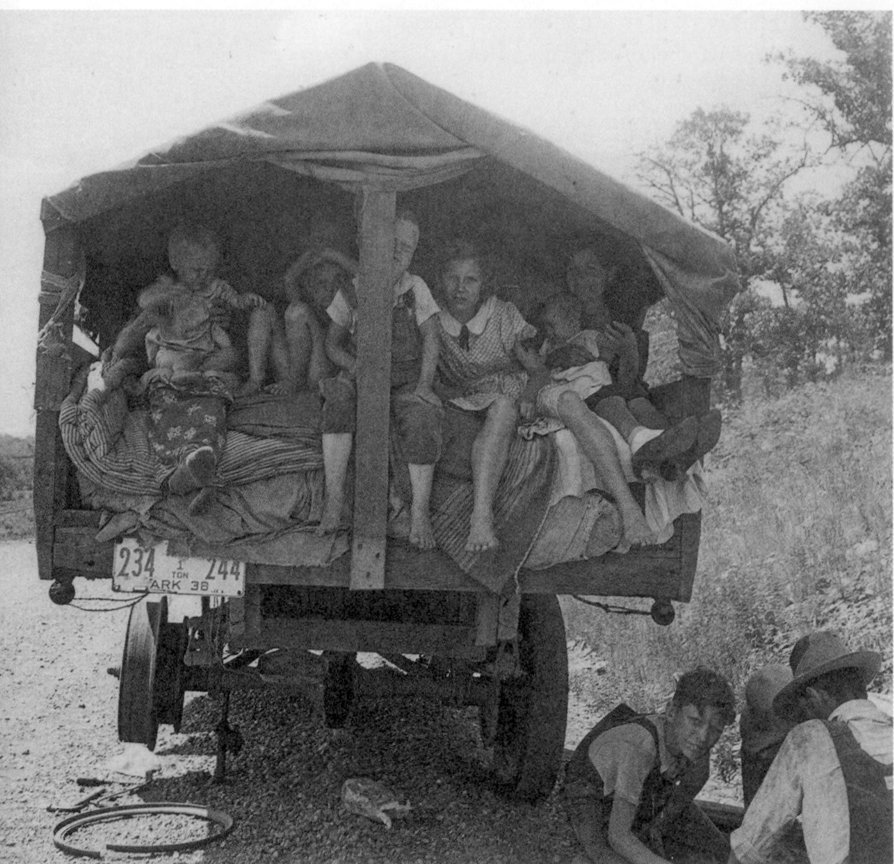

22.12 Migrants Hit the Road Rickety trucks piled high with possessions and children filled western highways as families fled the Dust Bowl in search of employment elsewhere.

years in California. Migrant workers often lived in makeshift roadside camps near disease-ridden water ditches. When the government tried to create camps that offered migrants better and cleaner facilities, some Californians objected. Growers worried that concentrating migrant workers in government-run camps would make it easier for them to organize unions and strikes. Other Californians believed that improving living conditions would draw even more displaced farmers to their state.

In 1935 California-based photographer Dorothea Lange began taking photographs for the Resettlement Administration to document the extent of migrant workers' suffering and arouse the public's sympathy. This photo (**22.12**) shows a father from Arkansas changing the tire on his truck as he and his seven children followed the crops in Oklahoma and Texas. "We'll be in California yet," he proclaimed. Lange was renowned for her ability to take photographs that revealed her subjects' true feelings. Left lame by polio, Lange believed that her own disability made strangers trust her. Her photographs, discussed more fully in *Images as History: Migrant Mother, an American Icon*, had a distinct political purpose: to cement public support for migrant worker aid programs.

Repatriating Mexican Immigrants

Reducing competition from immigrants seeking work was another way that the government tried to help native-born farm workers. In 1929 the government effectively ended legal immigration from Mexico for the duration of the Depression to protect jobs for American citizens. Foreshadowing today's debate over the benefits and drawbacks of immigration, California officials argued that alien workers held jobs that should rightfully go to native-born Americans. Large-farm owners disagreed, predicting that they would face a serious labor shortage if they lost their traditional workforce since few Americans wanted these jobs.

Anti-immigration forces prevailed. Faced with the offer of a free trip back to their original homes (financed by the United States and Mexico) or the option of staying in a country where employment options had dwindled, thousands of Mexican workers accepted repatriation. Local and federal officials arrested and then deported others who had entered the country illegally. With the advent of the New Deal, immigrants' interest in voluntary repatriation dwindled. New Deal agency regulations made legal aliens eligible for food relief, although most public works programs gave jobs only to citizens. The deportation of undocumented workers continued. Overall approximately 415,000 Mexicans left the United States during the 1930s, both voluntarily and involuntarily.

"Social change is a difficult thing in our society unless you have sentiment."

President FRANKLIN D. ROOSEVELT

What happened to Mexican immigrants during the Depression?

Images as History

"MIGRANT MOTHER," AN AMERICAN ICON

In March 1936 the photographer Dorothea Lange entered a makeshift migrants' camp and saw a thirty-two-year-old woman sitting with four of her seven children and all the family's possessions. Taking six quick pictures, she jotted down a few notes about the family: "Destitute in pea pickers' camp, Nipomo, California, because of the failure of the early pea crop. These people had just sold their tires in order to buy food. Of the 2500 people in this camp most of them were destitute."

Lange's final portrait, "**Migrant Mother**," was a masterpiece. The viewer has the sense of intruding on an intensely personal moment, but Lange made no apologies for invading this woman's privacy. "She asked me no questions," the photographer later recalled. Instead, she "seemed to know that my pictures might help her, and so she helped me." When these photographs appeared in the *San Francisco News* in 1936, relief authorities immediately sent food to the entire camp of starving pea pickers. In later years Florence Thompson, the subject of "Migrant Mother," tried to suppress the diffusion of this photograph because she felt that it stigmatized her as poor. As she lay dying of cancer in 1983, however, her children successfully used the image to raise funds for their mother's medical expenses.

This initial photograph did not send the clear message that Lange wanted. In subsequent photos she focused on the despair of the mother and her small children rather than their general poverty.

The father was nowhere in sight, conveying either the comforting possibility that he was out looking for work or the discomforting suggestion that he had abandoned the family.

"Migrant Mother series, no. 2"

The presence of an older daughter raised potentially troublesome questions about when the woman began having children, why she continued to have so many, or why the teenager was not working to help the family.

In her next shots, Lange carefully framed out the open luggage and trash to erase any suggestion that the family lacked discipline.

Because they wanted their photographs to arouse public sympathy, government photographers always depicted the migrants as heroic victims. They were never shown smiling, angry, or in any way responsible for their misery.

The mother clearly wants to love and care for the children who lean on her, but her anxiety severs her from them emotionally and leaves her alone with her thoughts.

Lange's composition suggests "a sort of anti-Madonna and Child," wrote one critic.

"Migrant Mother series, no. 6"

What was the purpose and impact of Dorothea Lange's migrant farmer photographs?

Reforms to Ensure Social Justice

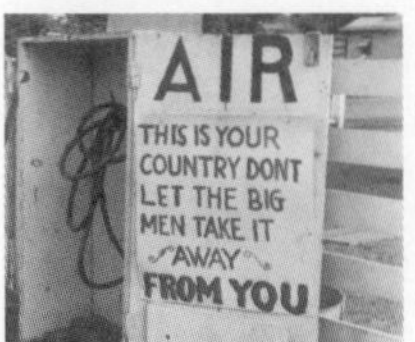

In 1935 the New Deal moved beyond measures intended to help the nation recover from the Depression to policies designed to correct basic inequities in American society and provide security to ordinary Americans. Reforms protected unions, guaranteed many elderly a government pension, established a minimum wage for factory workers, and abolished child labor. The momentum for these New Deal reforms came from the growing strength of left-leaning politicians, unions, and senior citizens who were unafraid to press the popular president to adopt their vision of a more just society.

The Challenge from Huey Long: "Share Our Wealth"

Roosevelt's move to the left toward the end of his first administration was partially a response to the combined popularity of Father Coughlin (see page 000) and Senator Huey Long. Before he became a senator, Huey Long was an adored, although corrupt, governor of Louisiana who provided free school textbooks, built much needed roads and hospitals, and curbed the power of the state's oil industry. "They do not merely vote for him," a reporter wrote of Louisianans in 1935, "they worship the ground he walks on."

Long supported the New Deal at first, but his dissatisfaction with the pace of change and his own political ambitions caused a break with FDR. As an alternative to the New Deal, Long proposed a **share our wealth** plan to redistribute money from the rich to the poor. Long wanted to limit every person to $1 million in income and $8 million in capital investments each year. The government would confiscate all other personal income and corporate profits and redistribute $2,000 annually to every American family. Besides offering Americans a guaranteed income, Long also championed old-age pensions, expanded veterans' benefits, a shorter working day, and government support for education. He created a Share Our Wealth Society and claimed a membership of 5 million, promising to make "every man a King."

Long argued that under his plan the rich would still enjoy a life of luxury, and even published a budget for a family of four on $1 million a year to show that they could easily afford $10,000 of jewelry each season and a new $100 suit a day. Yet even the great fortunes amassed by the richest Americans were too small to support the kind of program Long proposed. Despite the flaws in his plan, Long successfully tapped into public anger at the rich, whom many blamed for causing the Depression, and long-standing resentments about the concentration of wealth in the hands of a few. Long never had a chance to challenge FDR as a third-party candidate, however, because a disgruntled man who detested Long assassinated him on the steps of the Louisiana state capital in the fall of 1935. "I wonder why he shot me," Long asked before he died, a question the assassin, killed on the spot by Long's bodyguards, could never answer. *Competing Visions: Sharing the Wealth* explores the Depression-era debate over redistributing income.

Social Security

Alongside the larger-than-life personas of Huey Long and Father Coughlin stood Dr. Francis Townsend, an unassuming sixty-six-year-old physician who organized a campaign for old-age pensions in 1933 after seeing three old women outside his house in Long Beach, California, rummaging through the trash. The combined activism of these three men helped push FDR to the left in 1935. The outpouring of support each enjoyed convinced FDR that the time was right to create a comprehensive social-welfare system that protected the aged, the unemployed, and those unable to care for themselves.

Townsend's call for government pensions for the elderly struck a nerve, setting in motion a powerful

> "It is hard to be old and not have anything."
>
> A woman from North Dakota, writing to Roosevelt

How did critics from the left shape the social justice programs of FDR's second administration?

Competing Visions

SHARING THE WEALTH

Should money be redistributed from the haves to the have-nots? During the Depression, many Americans answered a resounding "yes." Below are two views, reflecting different visions of how income redistribution might affect the future of American capitalism and democracy. What justification or objection does each give for redistributing wealth throughout the population?

In this 1935 radio address, Senator Huey Long outlines his proposal to redistribute wealth from the rich to the poor.

We find not only the people going further into debt, but that the United States is going further into debt.... And with it all, there stalks a slimy specter of want, hunger, destitution, and pestilence, all because of the fact that in the land of too much and of too much to wear, our president has failed in his promise to have these necessities of life distributed into the hands of the people who have need of them....

But we have been about our work to correct this situation. That is why the Share Our Wealth societies are forming in every nook and corner of America ...

Here is what we stand for in a nutshell:

Number one, we propose that every family in America should ... have a home and the comforts of a home up to a value of not less than around $5,000 or a little more than that.

Number two, we propose that no family shall own more than three hundred times the average family wealth, which means that no family shall possess more than a wealth of approximately $5 million—none to own less than $5,000, none to own more than $5 million.

Number three,... We propose that no family will have an earning of less than around $2,000 to $2,500 and that none will have more than three hundred times the average less the ordinary income taxes, which means that a million dollars would be the limit on the highest income.

We also propose to give the old-age pensions to the old people, not by taxing them or their children, but by levying the taxes upon the excess fortunes to whittle them down, and on the excess incomes and excess inheritances, so that the people who reach the age of sixty can be retired from the active labor of life ... We also propose the care for the veterans, including the cash payment of the soldiers' bonus. We likewise propose that there should be an education for every youth in this land and that no youth would be dependent upon the financial means of his parents in order to have a college education.

In the following letter to Eleanor Roosevelt, a woman from Columbus, Indiana, protests that government-distributed relief robbed hardworking honest men to help "good-for-nothing loafers."

Dec. 14, 1937

Mrs. Roosevelt: ... We have always had a shiftless, never-do-well class of people whose one and only aim in life is to live without work. I have been rubbing elbows with this class for nearly sixty years and have tried to help some of the most promising and have seen others try to help them, but it can't be done. We cannot help those who will not try to help themselves and if they do try a square deal is all they need and by the way that is all this country needs or ever has needed: a square deal for all and then, let each one paddle their own canoe, or sink .... As for the old people on beggars' allowances: the taxpayers have provided homes for all the old people who never liked to work, where they will be neither cold nor hungry: much better homes than most of them have ever tried to provide for themselves. They have lived many years through the most prosperous times of our country and had an opportunity to prepare for old age, but they spent their lives in idleness or worse and now they expect those who have worked like slaves, to provide a living for them and all their worthless descendants.... There is many a little child doing without butter on its bread, so that some old sot can have his booze and tobacco: some old sot who spent his working years loafing around pool rooms and saloons, boasting that the world owed him a living..... During the worst of the depression many of the farmers had to deny their families butter, eggs, meat, etc. and sell it to pay their taxes and then had to stand by and see the dead-beats [who qualified for relief] carry it home to their families by the arm load, and they knew their tax money was helping pay for it.... Is it any wonder the taxpayers are discouraged by all this penalizing of thrift and industry to reward shiftlessness, or that the whole country is on the brink of chaos?

What competing images of the poor do Long and this Indiana woman offer?

22.13 Three Steps to Security
This 1936 poster deliberately emphasized the monthly check workers would receive during retirement, not the payroll deductions that would reduce their take-home pay to help finance immediate pensions for the elderly.

grassroots movement. For many working-class Americans their final years had always been a steady decline into poverty. Unable to work due to age, illness, or the unwillingness of employers to hire them, most relied on family members or charities to survive. The plight of the aged assumed crisis proportions when Depression-era bank failures swept away the savings of many older Americans. Townsend clubs, formed to promote government pensions for the elderly, barraged Congress with petitions signed by 10 million supporters, sending a clear message to the president and legislators in Washington, D.C.

Roosevelt responded. In drafting the bill that provided pensions for the elderly, he attached some controversial measures. Unwilling to take the political risk of voting against extremely popular pensions for the elderly, many conservative congressmen ended up grudgingly voting for a law that also provided unemployment benefits, assistance to the disabled, and aid for dependent children.

FDR wanted to help the "**deserving poor,**" needy Americans legitimately entitled to public support, a category open to differing interpretations. What made someone deserving of aid in the new social security system? This poster (**22.13**) urging Americans to apply for their old-age benefits clearly noted that only industrial workers working for a salary or wage were eligible for the new pension program. The system did not cover agricultural and domestic workers until 1950, a concession to southern and agricultural business interests who claimed they could not afford the mandatory employers' contribution to their employees' Social Security accounts (employers paid half). The Social Security Act of 1935 also set the following criteria for its other categories of aid: being laid off (not fired for cause) from an industrial job and being physically disabled or a widow (not an unwed mother) with children to raise.

The Social Security pension system operated along the same lines as private insurance by collecting premiums from individual subscribers in the form of payroll taxes. The public embraced Social Security as a system that simply returned these earlier deposits to retirees. Retired workers, however, began receiving checks in 1940, clearly too soon for these recipients to have paid enough to cover the costs of their pension benefits. Ida May Fuller, a retired legal secretary, received the nation's first Social Security check for $22.54 after paying a total of $24.75 in payroll taxes. She lived until the age of one hundred, collecting more than $22,000 in Social Security checks before she died in 1975.

Supporting Unions

Political pressures from the left and empathy for the poor had encouraged Roosevelt to create the Social Security system. These same forces influenced the president as he faced a different set of choices concerning the standoff between business and labor. His desire to curtail political challenges from the left and solidify his voter base by building a new coalition that included unions encouraged Roosevelt to choose the side of labor in this simmering industrial dispute. Business leaders' open hostility to

Who was considered part of the "deserving poor" in the new Social Security system?

New Deal relief and public works programs also prompted FDR to ally himself with labor in 1935. When FDR proposed a heavy tax on the rich (again inspired by Long), the business elite denounced the wealthy president as "a traitor to his class."

FDR openly mocked his opponents when running for reelection in 1936. "I should like to have it said of my first Administration that in it the forces of selfishness and of lust for power met their match. I should like to have it said of my second Administration that in it these forces met their master," declared Roosevelt in his last campaign speech before defeating the Republican candidate, Kansas governor Alf Landon. The general public's antipathy to the rich was captured perfectly in this photo (**22.14**) by Dorothea Lange of a gas station in Kern County, California, which displayed a sign declaring "This is your country, don't let the big men take it away from you" next to the free air pump.

Roosevelt's actions matched his antibusiness rhetoric. Throughout the great strikes of the nineteenth century, the federal government had usually sided openly with industrialists to break workers' movements. Thanks to important legislation passed during the New Deal, the federal government suddenly became labor's friend.

The National Industrial Recovery Act (1933), the same law that created the NRA, provided the first hint of things to come by declaring that workers had the right to organize and bargain collectively. Labor officials often referred to this section of the law, 7a, as the "Magna Carta" of organized labor because it recognized a right that many industrialists still refused to acknowledge. When the Supreme Court declared the National Industrial Recovery Act unconstitutional, FDR took a historic step by signing the Wagner Act (1935), a law sponsored by Senator Robert Wagner (D-NY) to increase the purchasing power of workers by giving them the power to negotiate for higher wages. The Wagner Act created the National Labor Relations Board (NLRB) to supervise unions' elections for their collective bargaining agents. The law prevented employers from firing or blacklisting workers who joined a union, or infiltrating unions with spies. With this government protection, the union movement exploded. Between 1933 and 1941, union membership rose from 2.9 million to 8.7 million workers.

In 1938 FDR went even further with the Fair Labor Standards Act, which established a national minimum hourly wage (set initially at twenty-five cents, rising gradually to forty cents), set maximum hours for the workweek (forty-four hours), and outlawed labor by children under sixteen (with some exemptions, such as newspaper carriers). Aimed at industrial workers, the act excluded agricultural and domestic workers. FDR again demonstrated political savvy in maneuvering the bill through Congress. FDR attached the controversial wage and hours measures to a bill prohibiting child labor, knowing that few congressmen would vote against such as a popular measure.

22.14 This Is Your Country
This sign reflected the general resentment toward the rich that encouraged Roosevelt to attack business and support unions in 1935.

How did government support of unions change during the 1930s?

The Resurgence of Labor

Government regulation gave crucial support to unions, but the task of building a successful labor movement lay with workers. Overcoming workers' fears that they would lose their jobs if they joined a union posed a significant hurdle for all organizers. When the United Auto Workers (UAW) took on Henry Ford, a strident opponent of unions, organizers passed out handbills assuring workers that "the Wagner Bill is behind you! Now get behind yourselves!" Ford had offered the best terms of employment with his five-dollar-a-day wages and eight-hour workdays in the 1910s and revolutionized American industry with his introduction of the assembly line (see Chapter 18). By the thirties, however, workers in unionized auto plants had much higher wages and guaranteed benefits.

Ford ruled his plants with an iron fist, and when five labor organizers tried to pass out handbills to workers entering the Ford motor plant in Dearborn, Michigan, in 1937, forty members of the company's private security force attacked them. As seen in this photo (**22.15**), the Ford guards unleashed a flurry of punches and kicks, throwing each man face first onto the pavement before tossing him down a set of stairs. One man's back was broken, and another recounted how two men held his legs apart while the security guards kicked him repeatedly in the groin.

A few news photographers managed to smuggle out photographs of the attacks, thwarting the attempt by Ford's security force to confiscate their film. The shocking images caused a public outcry. The NLRB ordered Ford to stop interfering with union organizing, but securing industry-wide recognition of the UAW required more dramatic action at Ford Motor Company and elsewhere. Ford's antiunion intimidation had worked in the past, but by the midthirties, many workers were ready to fight back. In 1934 alone 1.5 million workers participated in eighteen hundred strikes.

Support from the government helped the labor movement grow but so did a new vision of who could join a union. The **American Federation of Labor (AFL)** was a craft-based organization that accepted only skilled workers, like carpenters or cigar makers, who practiced a trade. Excluding unskilled workers from the labor movement made little sense once assembly-line mass production began to dominate the manufacturing process. John L. Lewis, head of the United Mine Workers, argued that unions needed to find room for unskilled workers, no matter their race or ethnicity, to become truly powerful. When the AFL

22.15 Ford Security Guards Attack Labor Organizers
Ford's guards pull a labor organizer's jacket over his head to immobilize his arms as they pummel him. Signaling new support for the labor movement, the federal government intervened after these photos were published.

expelled Lewis for trying to organize these groups, he formed the **Congress of Industrial Organizations (CIO)**, a new type of labor organization that organized workers within an entire industry rather than by their trade orientation.

The AFL and CIO offered competing visions of how to construct a successful union. The CIO organized all workers in the automobile industry into one union, rejecting the AFL idea of creating separate unions for auto mechanics, welders, and so on. The CIO warned workers not to fall for their employers' old tricks. "The man working beside you, be he Negro, Jew or Pollock [Polish] is a working man like yourself ... You work together—FIGHT TOGETHER," one CIO labor organizer told steelworkers. "We were making a *religion* of racial unity," noted another CIO official. In sharp contrast to its enlightened racial views, the CIO made no effort to recruit women. The CIO instead joined with the AFL in urging women to voluntarily leave their jobs so men could have them. Within two years of its founding, the CIO boasted 3.7 million members as compared to the 3.4 million workers who belonged to the AFL.

Besides recruiting unskilled and minority workers into its ranks, the CIO reversed the labor movement's indifference to electoral politics. Now that the government was actively supporting unions, keeping sympathetic officials in public office became a major CIO goal. "Every worker owes it to himself, his family, his union and his country to go to the polls himself, and to see that his fellow workers go too, to cast their votes in organized fashion for the labor-endorsed candidates," a CIO newsletter told meat packinghouse workers in 1938. Recruiting members became easier when the CIO devised new methods of collective action that bore results. Automobile workers seized the spotlight when they pioneered a new and effective tactic: the sit-down strike. During a **sit-down strike** workers occupied a factory to paralyze production lines and prevent strikebreakers or management from entering the building. Because sit-down strikes caused the employer, as well as his striking employees, to lose money, this tactic brought employers to the negotiating table more quickly than traditional picket lines. Nearly 400,000 workers participated in sit-down strikes in 1937 alone, causing *Time* magazine to comment that "sitting down has replaced baseball as the national pastime."

When the UAW took over the main General Motors plant in Flint, Michigan, in 1937, the governor of Michigan and FDR (who had just received 84 percent of the votes cast by organized labor and 81 percent from low-income voters in the 1936 presidential election) refused to authorize the use of troops to retake the plant. By standing with the strikers, FDR solidified his support among the working class. Within six weeks General Motors capitulated and recognized the union. Ford held out until 1941, when he finally recognized the UAW. Having lost the battle on the ground, the automobile companies fought back through the courts. In 1939 the Supreme Court ruled that sit-down strikes were illegal seizures of property.

The union movement's successes in the automobile, steel, and textile industries markedly improved the daily lives of workers, but even with these gains, workers had few material comforts in comparison to laborers today. By 1941 factory workers earned an average of $1,449 a year, enough for a married father with two children to buy two dresses for his wife every year, shoes for his children every other year, and a coat for himself every six years while living in a five-room apartment and driving a used car.

A New Deal for African Americans

FDR's turn to the left also included a new willingness to advance the cause of civil rights. As late as 1932 the majority of black northern voters (few African Americans could vote in the South) remained loyal to the Republican Party and Herbert Hoover. Four years later Gallup polls estimated that 76 percent of northern blacks had voted for FDR. What had FDR done to deserve this newfound loyalty among black voters? At first glance it seemed very little.

During his first administration, the power that southern Democrats held in Congress prevented FDR from proposing any civil rights legislation or guaranteeing equal treatment by New Deal agencies. He knew Congress would never approve such measures, and he needed southern legislators' support to pass New Deal legislation. Still, New Deal programs offered African Americans more federal and state aid than they had ever received before. Southern blacks usually received smaller relief payments than whites, but before 1933 most state agencies had given them nothing. In the 1936 presidential election, Democratic campaigners emphasized the benefits that the New Deal had brought to the African American community, proclaiming on billboards: "Do not bite the hand

Why did many African Americans switch their allegiances from the Republican to the Democratic Party in the 1930s?

WORLD'S HIGHEST STANDARD OF LIVING
There's no way like the American Way

22.16 **"There's No Way Like the American Way"** The photo captured the irony of trumpeting America as the land of opportunity for whites, while needy black citizens stood in line at a soup kitchen in 1937.

that feeds you." An African American preacher offered the same message to his congregation, telling them, "Let Jesus lead you and Roosevelt feed you." Eleanor Roosevelt's well-known interest in civil rights also helped draw many black voters to FDR.

When black voters abandoned the Republican Party for the Democratic Party, they joined the **New Deal coalition**, a political partnership formed in the midthirties among liberals, trade unionists, Catholics, and northern blacks that redrew the nation's political map. The strength of the New Deal coalition increased the president's freedom to pursue his legislative agenda. In the newly elected 75th Congress, the president did not need a single southern or Republican vote to pass New Deal legislation.

As the black vote gained new importance to the Democratic Party, the administration became more responsive to African American demands. During FDR's second term public works projects hired more black workers. FDR also appointed the first black federal judge and convened an unofficial Black Cabinet to investigate civil rights abuses and advise him on racial matters. Nonetheless, racial discrimination continued to plague the lives of African Americans in the thirties. In Margaret Bourke-White's 1937 photo (**22.16**), black residents wait for emergency relief during the Louisville, Kentucky flood, while above them, a billboard poster shows a carefree well-dressed white family driving a car. The image symbolically showcased the racial divide that remained intact throughout the decade.

The Supreme Court Weighs In

FDR's popularity made it difficult for opponents to organize a sustained campaign against him. In 1936 he won reelection with 61 percent of the popular vote, carrying every state except Maine and Vermont in the Electoral College. Clearly the majority of Americans supported the New Deal. The same could not be said of the Supreme Court. Of the nine justices, four consistently opposed New Deal legislation and two remained unpredictable. By 1937 the Court had declared two major pieces of early New Deal legislation, the NRA and AAA, unconstitutional. With lawsuits against the Wagner Act and Social Security Act on the Court's docket, Roosevelt decided to act.

Suggesting that advanced age (rather than conservative ideology) was hampering the work of the Supreme Court, FDR proposed increasing the number of justices to a maximum of fifteen by adding one new justice for every one over seventy who had served more than ten years on the Court. With the conservative bloc all over seventy, Roosevelt's plan would either increase the size of the court or force the older justices to retire. Either way FDR would have a chance to appoint judges who were sympathetic to the New Deal.

The campaign to expand the size of the Court soon exposed the limits of FDR's power. Dubbed the "Court-packing scheme" by detractors, the clash consumed a whole session of Congress and ended

What role did the Supreme Court play during the New Deal?

with a resounding defeat for FDR. FDR always maintained that though he lost the battle, he won the larger war with the Court. As Congress debated his proposal to add more justices, the Supreme Court surprised everyone by upholding the constitutionality of the Wagner Act and the Social Security Act. Over the next few years, deaths and retirements gave FDR the chance to appoint seven justices.

The fallout from the Court struggle had some negative repercussions for the president, however. Although the Court began upholding New Deal legislation, the battle alienated progressive Republicans who had previously supported the president and pushed conservative Democrats into an alliance with like-minded Republicans. In 1938 Republicans narrowed the Democratic majority in Congress. The bipartisan conservative coalition was now strong enough to thwart any new reform initiatives and to begin cutting expenditures for New Deal recovery programs. The New Deal thus ground to a halt in 1938, after five years of public policy initiatives, experiments, and reforms.

What did the New Deal accomplish over those five years? It alleviated much human suffering, fashioned an institutional apparatus that strengthened the capitalist market structure, and provided economic security to ordinary Americans where none had existed before. New Deal reforms bolstered financial institutions, protected the housing market, kept farmers afloat, improved industrial wages, and created old-age pensions. This legacy outlived the Depression crisis, shaping the lives of countless Americans for decades to come. FDR's legislative program reached workers, farmers, African Americans, and migrant workers, forging a new, permanent relationship between the federal government and common people. Despite the New Deal's accomplishments, the nation's financial crisis continued. It took unprecedented government spending during World War II to end the Depression.

Conclusion

The New Deal was one of the most important periods of legislative activity in American history. Before 1932 a stroll down Main Street or a visit to a private home would have uncovered little evidence of the federal government. The situation by the end of the decade could not have been more different. By 1940 the American landscape was dotted with the highways, campgrounds, tunnels, and bridges constructed by government-sponsored work relief projects. The federal government subsidized farmers, guaranteed pensions, regulated the stock market, insured the life savings of small bank depositors, gave industrial workers unemployment insurance, protected unions, and for the first time, set a federal minimum wage. The federal government was now an active presence in the lives of millions, provoking a debate that continues into the twenty-first century over the proper role of the government in the economy and who is deserving of help.

Clashes that pitted unions against industry, Mexican immigrants against government officials, and migrant farmers against native Californians roiled the nation during the Depression. The decade was more than unrelenting hardship or confrontation, however. The era also had moments of triumph for ordinary Americans. African Americans were now valued members of the New Deal coalition. Industrial unions attracted many new members and won benefits with their new tactic of sit-down strikes.

By the late thirties international affairs began to intrude on the mostly insular vision that Americans had maintained throughout the decade. The outbreak of war in Europe helped the American economy recover, but forced the country to confront the question of whether to join another overseas war. Eventually, Japan's attack on Pearl Harbor in 1941 made this decision for the United States. For the next four years Americans would focus on winning World War II.

Why did the New Deal end in 1938?

CHAPTER REVIEW

1929

Stock Market Crashes
Signals beginning of Depression

1932

Reconstruction Finance Corporation established
Hoover's effort to help businesses and banks with federal loans

Bonus March
Public outrage over army's eviction of protesting veterans from Washington, D.C.

1933

FDR inaugurated president
Restores faith and confidence in government and capitalism

Review Questions

1. What were the causes of the Great Depression?
2. What groups of people did the New Deal help? What new role did the New Deal establish for the federal government in their lives?
3. How did the government publicize the plight of farmers and Dust Bowl refugees in the thirties? Why did these images become an enduring symbol of Depression-era suffering?
4. What factors account for labor protests in the thirties, a time when one might expect workers simply to be grateful for any job on any terms?
5. What conflicting visions prompted the right and left to criticize the New Deal?
6. What was the short-term versus long-term significance of the New Deal?

1933–1938

New Deal created
Slew of federal agencies, laws, and reforms restructure American capitalism and provide economic security to citizens

1935

Share Our Wealth Movement
Senator Huey Long's proposal to redistribute wealth pushes FDR to the left

CIO founded
Organizes workers by industry rather than by trade

1936

Dust Bowl crisis worsens
Drought, soil erosion result in major ecological disaster

FDR wins reelection
New Deal coalition formed

CIO begins sit-down strikes
Wins union recognition, but later ruled unconstitutional

1937

FDR tries to reform Supreme Court
Proposal failure exposes limits of FDR's power

Social Security payroll taxes begin
Establishes funding mechanism for federal pensions

Key Terms

stock market crash of 1929 A ten-day period beginning on October 20, 1929, when the value of stocks plummeted as panicked investors sold off their stock in droves. This moment is usually considered the official start of the Depression. **657**

Great Depression The most devastating and longest economic crisis in American history that lasted from 1929 to 1939. **659**

Bonus March A two-month-long demonstration by forty thousand impoverished World War I veterans in Washington, D.C., that ended violently when the army expelled the protesters. **660**

New Deal An avalanche of legislation from 1933 to 1938 intended to promote economic recovery, reform American capitalism, and offer security to ordinary Americans. **662**

Dust Bowl Drought and soil erosion caused massive dust storms across southern and plains states throughout the thirties. **670**

"Migrant Mother" Dorothea Lange's 1936 photograph of a destitute woman, which became an iconic portrait of Depression-era suffering. **673**

share our wealth Louisiana Senator Huey Long's plan to redistribute money from the rich to the poor. **674**

deserving poor Needy Americans who were legitimately entitled to public support, a category open to differing interpretations. **676**

American Federation of Labor (AFL) A craft-based organization that accepted only skilled workers, like carpenters or cigar makers, who practiced a trade. **678**

Congress of Industrial Organizations (CIO) A brand-new type of labor organization that organized workers within an entire industry rather than by their trade orientation. **679**

sit-down strike Workers occupy a factory to paralyze production lines and prevent strikebreakers or management from entering the building. **679**

New Deal coalition A political partnership formed in the mid-thirties among liberals, trade unionists, Catholics, and northern blacks that redrew the nation's political map. **680**

CHAPTER

23

World War II

Fighting the Good War, 1939–1945

"Yesterday, December 7, 1941—a date which will live in infamy—the United States of America was suddenly and deliberately attacked by naval and air forces of the Empire of Japan."

President FRANKLIN D. ROOSEVELT

In early December 1941 a Japanese naval convoy secretly traveled toward Hawaii, stopping within 250 miles of the Hawaiian island of Oahu. At 6:00 a.m. on December 7, Admiral Chuichji Nagumo launched two consecutive attacking waves of bombers, torpedo planes, and dive-bombers. As Japanese pilots approached Pearl Harbor, a naval station on Oahu, they saw a line of American battleships parked in a neat row. Moments later those battleships were on fire.

Before Pearl Harbor debate raged over how to respond to the growing threat of war in the Pacific and Germany's conquest of Europe. Non-interventionists and interventionists offered competing visions of how to protect America's vital interests in a world torn apart by war. Now Americans needed no other explanation than this photo of a battleship engulfed in flames to understand why they were at war. Questions instead arose over why the United States had given the Japanese such an inviting target. Hoping to pressure Japan into withdrawing from China, President Franklin D. Roosevelt had sent the U.S. Pacific Fleet to Hawaii. There, he believed, the battleships were far enough away from Japan to escape attack but close enough to convince Japan to end its expansionist drive into East Asia. Roosevelt erred on both counts. Instead, Japan resolved to drive the Western powers out of East Asia.

In their attack on Pearl Harbor, the Japanese sank or damaged eighteen American ships and killed 2,405 Americans. Congress declared war on Japan the day after the attack. On December 11 Germany and Italy declared war on the United States, and Romania, Bulgaria, and Hungary quickly followed suit. The United States now faced the challenge of fighting resolute and capable enemies in Europe and the Pacific against whom victory was not certain.

The attack on Pearl Harbor silenced all political debate about whether America needed to fight, but were all the war-generated changes in American society positive ones? World War II thrust the United States into a new position of global leadership. Mobilizing the nation's resources to fight also created vast economic and social changes at home. The United States eventually prevailed against its enemies, but the cost of victory was high on the battlefield and on the home front.

How did the attack on Pearl Harbor compare to the sinking of the *Maine* in 1898?

The Approaching War

From 1939 to 1945 war engulfed nearly the entire globe, as shown on the map (**23.1**). Huge areas fell under German and Japanese control, naval battles occurred on vast stretches of sea, and colonies provided key materials needed by warring nations. Until 1941, however, the United States remained on the sidelines as Germany attacked continuously in Europe, and Japan launched steady invasions throughout East Asia. As long as the fighting remained far from their shores, Americans disagreed over whether these wars were theirs to fight. Still coping with the social and financial problems created by the Great Depression, **non-interventionists** urged the nation to put "America First" and stay out of overseas conflicts. By the late thirties, however, **interventionists** increasingly challenged this view, arguing that only direct engagement could prevent the world conflagration from reaching American shores.

Fascism and Appeasement

In the midst of the Depression, the United States had to formulate responses to Adolf Hitler's rise to power in Germany in 1933, Italy's invasion of Ethiopia in 1935, and the Spanish Civil War in 1936–1939.

Appointed chancellor in 1933, Hitler immediately began turning Germany into a **fascist state** under Nazi control, a dictatorial form of government that glorified the state over the individual. Widespread economic suffering, lingering resentments against the harsh terms of the Versailles Treaty (see Chapter 20), and virulent anti-Semitism created fertile ground for Nazism to flourish. Stripped of their German citizenship, Jews could not practice medicine or law, attend public school after the age of fourteen, or enter public parks and libraries. Promising to restore Germany's economic and military prowess and protect the presumed "racial superiority" of the German people, Hitler rearmed the country and sought allies.

In formulating their response to the rise of fascism in Europe, non-interventionists in Congress sought to avoid repeating the mistakes of the past that had led to involvement in the bloodbath of

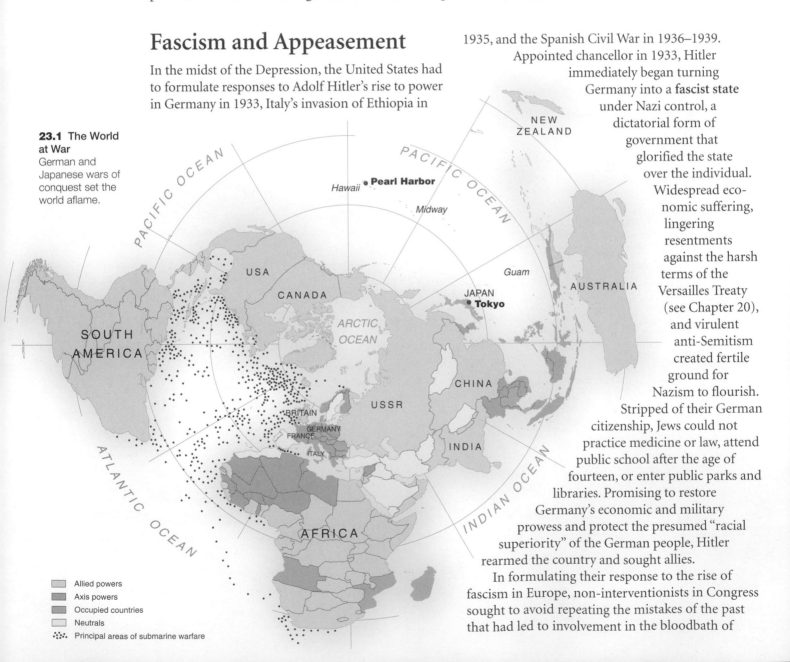

23.1 The World at War
German and Japanese wars of conquest set the world aflame.

Allied powers
Axis powers
Occupied countries
Neutrals
Principal areas of submarine warfare

What does this map convey about the scope of World War II?

World War I. Senator Gerald P. Nye, a Republican from North Dakota, chaired a series of Senate investigations in the midthirties into the role that American arms manufacturers had played in the nation's decision to enter World War I. Although the investigations unearthed little hard evidence of a conspiracy, they did buoy the consensus that the United States had entered that war to continue profitable arms sales and to guarantee that the Allies, the powers who had fought Germany, repaid their war loans to private banks. When these European countries defaulted on their loans during the Depression, public sentiment hardened against helping foreign nations.

To ensure that trading with belligerent nations did not drag the country into another war, Congress passed the **Neutrality Acts**, a series of laws from 1935 to 1939 that restricted arms sales, loans, and transport of goods with nations at war (see U.S. Countdown to War timeline, **23.2**). These popular laws encapsulated the widespread non-interventionist vision of avoiding involvement in an overseas conflicts that did not directly threaten U.S. territory. Depending on the official policy pursued, the Atlantic and Pacific Oceans could serve as buffers protecting the nation or as pathways to war. Trying to ensure the former, the 1935 Neutrality Act prohibited the sales of arms and ammunition to nations at war. In 1936 Congress barred all loans to warring nations. The 1937 Neutrality Act allowed belligerent nations to purchase non-war-related goods if they paid cash for them and transported them on their own ships, a policy known as "**cash and carry.**"

FDR momentarily challenged the non-interventionist vision with his 1937 Quarantine Speech which urged peace-loving countries to isolate aggressor nations and actively seek peace. Outraged non-interventionists accused FDR of trying to turn the United States into the world's policeman. "It's a terrible thing to look over your shoulder when you are trying to lead – and find no one there," the president remarked to an aide before he publicly reaffirmed his support for the Neutrality Acts. The zenith of non-interventionist sentiment was reached in 1938 when Congress considered a constitutional amendment that required public approval through a national referendum for any declaration of war, except in the event of an enemy invasion. The amendment was debated, but never approved by Congress.

The United States was not alone in its desire to remain at peace. Eager to avoid war with Germany, Britain and France recalled how a relatively minor incident (the assassination of Archduke Franz Ferdinand) had become the catalyst for war in 1914 (see Chapter 20). Instead of mobilizing their armies when Germany violated the terms of the Versailles Treaty by rearming and threatening its neighbors, France and Britain turned first to negotiation. In 1938 Germany annexed Austria and then demanded the Sudetenland, a German-speaking province made part of Czechoslovakia against its will when the Allies dissolved the Austro-Hungarian Empire at the end of the World War I. By the thirties many Europeans felt that the Versailles Peace Treaty had punished Germany too severely, creating the widespread impression that Hitler's actions and demands were reasonable. Taking Hitler at his word that he was interested only in reuniting German-speaking peoples into one nation, Britain and France agreed at the **Munich Conference** in 1938 to let Germany occupy the Sudetenland.

Instead of dampening Hitler's ambitions, the Munich Conference convinced the dictator that the Western democracies were too weak to oppose him militarily. Arguing that Germany needed "living space" in the East for its people, Hitler initiated his master plan to displace what he demeaningly called the "inferior" Slavic "races," the peoples living in Eastern Europe, and to exterminate the European Jews. Intent on avoiding the mistakes of World War I, when Germany had fought a two-front war, Hitler resolved to fight one war at a time. To accomplish

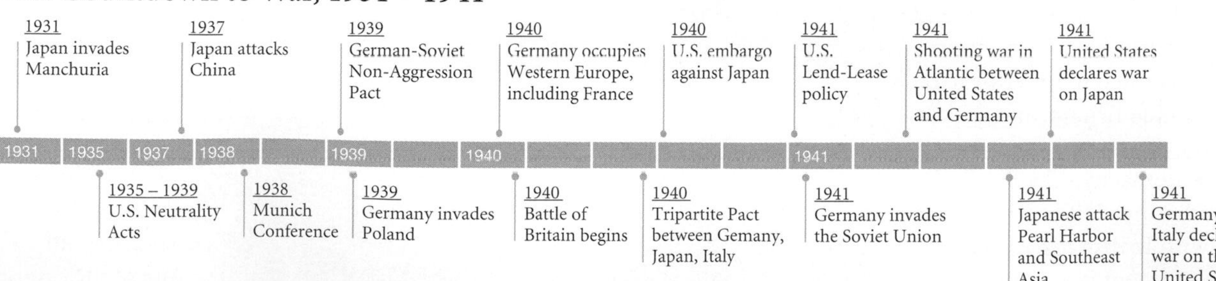

23.2 Origins of World War II
The United States remained neutral until the Japanese attacked Pearl Harbor.

What different lessons did America and other world powers draw from World War I?

this, in the late summer of 1939 Hitler signed a non-aggression pact with Josef Stalin, the dictator of the Soviet Union (USSR). In this agreement Germany and the Soviet Union agreed to jointly partition a defeated Poland and other parts of Eastern Europe, and the USSR offered Hitler supplies for his pending attack on France and Britain. The non-aggression pact ensured that Germany's eastern border remained peaceful when it attacked western and southeastern Europe. Only days after signing the pact, Hitler invaded Poland, bringing a declaration of war from Britain and France and the official beginning of World War II.

In the spring of 1940, Hitler began his massive assault on Western Europe by invading Norway and Denmark. He then marched through Luxembourg, Holland, and Belgium to invade France. Unlike in 1914, when Germany's broad attack against French lines ended in a trench stalemate, in May 1940 Germany's Blitzkrieg (lightning war) punched holes in the French defense system and then sent tanks, infantry, artillery, and aircraft through these openings to disrupt communications and threaten the French army from the rear. When German troops entered Paris, Hitler underscored his triumph by visiting Paris's Eiffel Tower. In this photograph (**23.3**) Hitler is posing before the landmark monument, transforming a banal tourist excursion into an act that, by symbolizing his control of Western Europe, carried sinister and tragic overtones. With France under Nazi domination, Italy formally entered the war on the side of Germany. Through a combination of alliances and force, the **Axis**, those nations fighting on the German side, quickly took control of the rest of Eastern Europe and the Balkans.

As German troops were rolling toward Paris, the British army had escaped capture at the French port town of Dunkirk. For a full year Britain fought Germany alone, surviving a massive bombing campaign known as the Battle of Britain. That changed in June 1941, however, when Hitler invaded the Soviet Union. Frustrated in his efforts to subdue Britain, and without the means to launch an invasion across the English Channel, Hitler decided that with British forces off the continent it was time to conquer Russia. Up until this point Hitler had successfully fought a series of isolated wars, but he made his first major strategic error when he invaded the Soviet Union. Instead of advancing quickly to Moscow, German troops found themselves bogged down in a massive battle along a far-flung Eastern Front.

23.3 Hitler in Paris Adolf Hitler's quick subjugation of Western Europe brought him to Paris by June 1940. Hitler posed in front of the city's most recognizable monument, the Eiffel Tower, to underscore France's defeat and his power over Western Europe.

The Arsenal of Democracy

As these events developed in Europe, both President Franklin D. Roosevelt and the majority of the American people opposed going to war. Publicly embracing non-interventionists measures during his first two terms, Roosevelt adopted an officially neutral stance as the war spread. Unlike Wilson in World War I, however, Roosevelt did not ask Americans to remain impartial in thought. Immigration restrictions had limited the number of first-generation immigrants from Europe, and Roosevelt had few concerns that well-assimilated Americans of German ancestry might retain strong loyalties to Germany. Indeed public opinion polls in 1939 revealed that nearly 84 percent of Americans supported the **Allies**, the powers fighting Germany, with only 2 percent expressing pro-German views.

Despite FDR's public declaration of neutrality, in private the interventionist argument that inaction would invite catastrophe increasingly influenced the president's thinking. For the time being Roosevelt tried to satisfy both non-interventionists and interventionists by finding a way to ensure the defeat of Hitler without actually declaring war. "Our national policy is not directed toward war," Roosevelt assured Americans. "Its sole purpose is to keep war away from our country and our people." In an effort to help Britain and France without risking the direct involvement that non-interventionists opposed, the Neutrality Act of 1939 revised the "cash and carry" policy to include munitions as well as non-war-related goods.

Breaking with the self-imposed two-term limit set by George Washington and respected by every other subsequent president, Roosevelt made the unprecedented decision to run for a third term in 1940. Roosevelt, who typically kept even his closest advisers guessing before he reached an important

How did Hitler accomplish his rapid conquest of Eastern and Western Europe?

decision, surprised everyone, even his wife, with his announcement. FDR never explained his decision to anyone, but the shock of France falling to Nazi control undoubtedly influenced his decision to run again. Roosevelt's candidacy and his selection of a liberal New Dealer, Henry Wallace, as his vice president caused some grumbling among conservative Democrats, who nonetheless rallied around Roosevelt in the general election. The Republican challenger Wendell Willkie and Roosevelt each argued that the nation should offer all the help it could to the Allies short of entering the war. Willkie tried to paint Roosevelt as bent on direct intervention, but this charge and Willkie's anti-New Deal rhetoric resonated poorly with voters. Roosevelt easily won a third term as president.

FDR saw his task as satisfying "the wish of 70% of Americans to keep out of the war" and "the wish of 70% of Americans to do everything to break Hitler, even if it means war." To accommodate the public's conflicting emotions, Roosevelt proposed turning the nation into a "great arsenal of democracy." By telephone and telegraph British Prime Minister Winston Churchill pressed FDR continually for aid. Stressing America's vulnerability, Churchill warned that "overwhelming sea power would be in Hitler's hands" if Germany defeated Britain. FDR responded as Churchill hoped. Besides selling Britain arms, FDR agreed to trade fifty old American destroyers for ninety-nine-year leases on seven British air and naval bases in the Western Hemisphere. Britain needed these ships to transport weapons overseas. He also supported the introduction of a peacetime draft and invited a leading interventionist, Republican Henry Stimson, to join his cabinet as secretary of war.

Interventionists countered the non-interventionists' slogan of "America First" with Churchill's argument that a Nazi-controlled Europe directly threatened America's well-being. As part of the heated exchange between non-interventionists and interventionists, Dr. Seuss (the alias used by Theodore Geisel, who was to gain fame in the 1950s as the author-illustrator of *The Cat in the Hat* and many other children's books) drew editorial cartoons for *PM*, a short-lived left-wing New York magazine, that denounced non-intervention as folly. Dr. Seuss depicted non-interventionists as ostriches with their heads in the ground, anti-Semites, and appeasers. This Seuss cartoon (**23.4**) shows a non-interventionists wearing an "America First" hat in a bathtub that is jumping with predatory sea creatures adorned with swastikas, the symbol of the Nazi Party. His eyes closed tight, the man ignores the lurking danger, saying with a satisfied smile, "The old Family bath tub is plenty safe for me." This cartoon challenged the non-interventionists' belief that the Atlantic Ocean would protect the United States from a Nazi attack. As he moved closer to the interventionist position, FDR voiced similar concerns about the vulnerability of the American coastline.

By 1941 Britain had run out of cash, and neutrality laws still prohibited the United States from loaning the British the money they needed to buy munitions. FDR circumvented these restrictions with a policy called **Lend-Lease** that loaned rather than sold arms to Britain. The United States would "say to England, we will give the guns and ships that you need, provided that when the war is over you will return to us in kind the guns and ships that we have loaned you," Roosevelt told Secretary of the Treasury Henry Morgenthau. Lend-Lease, FDR explained to the nation, was simply one neighbor helping another to put out a fire. No one would say, FDR noted, "Neighbor, my garden hose cost me $15; you have to pay me $15 for it . . . I don't want $15—I want my garden hose back after the fire is over." As the

23.4 Dr. Seuss Lampoons Non-Interventionists Dr. Seuss lampooned non-interventionists for closing their eyes to the threat that Hitler's navy (depicted here as swastika-marked monsters) posed to American shores.

The old Family bath tub is plenty safe for me!
AMERICA FIRST
AMERICAN HEMISPHERE

Did the competing visions of non-interventionists and interventionists influence FDR's rhetoric and actions?

> "Some of our people like to believe that wars in Europe and in Asia are of no concern to us. But it is a matter of most vital concern to us that European and Asiatic war-makers should not gain control of the oceans which lead to this hemisphere."
>
> President FRANKLIN D. ROOSEVELT, radio "fireside chat," December 29, 1940

Lend-Lease bill worked its way through Congress, however, non-interventionists successfully attached an amendment that prohibited the U.S. Navy from escorting British convoys carrying American goods across the Atlantic. Fittingly, given the analogy that FDR used to explain Lend-Lease, one of the first shipments to Britain contained boxes of fire hoses.

When Hitler attacked the USSR in 1941, the United States extended Lend-Lease aid to the Soviets as well. FDR had formally recognized the Soviet Union in 1933, hoping to find another overseas market for American goods. Trade with the Soviets remained minimal during the Depression, but exploded during the war. By 1945 the United States had provided $50 billion of materiel to the Allies under this program. No one, however, expected Britain and the Soviet Union to return "loaned" ammunition or arms to the United States. Instead, the law left it up to the president to decide what form repayment would take. After the war President Harry Truman accepted favorable postwar trade relations as repayment from Britain and demanded $2.6 billion from the Soviet Union for nonmilitary lend-lease goods. Russia did not pay its debt until after the fall of communism in 1991.

Securing American guns and ammunition solved only half the problem for Britain. Because of the number of German submarines patrolling the Atlantic, Secretary of War Henry Stimson warned, sending arms to Britain was like pouring water into a leaky bathtub. When the American destroyer *Greer* gave chase and exchanged fire with a German submarine, FDR used the incident to invoke his authority as commander in chief by ordering U.S. naval ships to escort all ships headed to Britain and "shoot on sight" any German submarine or ship. Although it remained unclear whether the Germans knew that the *Greer* was an American ship, FDR denounced the skirmish as a deliberate attack in American waters. "We have sought no shooting war with Hitler. We do not seek it now," FDR declared in September 1941. "But when you see a rattlesnake poised to strike, you do not wait until he has struck before you crush him. These Nazi submarines and raiders are the rattlesnakes of the Atlantic." Three months before Japan's attack on Pearl Harbor, the United States was fighting an undeclared naval war with Germany.

War with Japan

The catalyst for America's formal entry into the war did not come in the Atlantic, however, but on the other side of the globe when Japanese pilots attacked **Pearl Harbor**, a naval base in Hawaii, on December 7, 1941. The attackers discovered a neat line of battleships, reproduced in this miniature version of Pearl Harbor (**23.5**) that Japanese filmmakers constructed for a wartime propaganda film that reminded Japanese audiences of their nation's great victory against the United States.

The Japanese attack on Pearl Harbor was the culmination of two decades of tension and growing mistrust between the two nations. Japan's desire to establish itself as the major power in the Pacific alarmed the United States, which maintained an array of island possessions and a strong naval presence in the Pacific to support its trading relationship with China. Access to Chinese markets had been a cornerstone of American foreign policy since the Spanish-American War. From the Japanese perspective, claiming East Asia as Japan's proper sphere of influence was no different from the United States declaring the Western Hemisphere off-limits to foreign powers through the 1823 Monroe Doctrine and 1904 Roosevelt Corollary. Japan aimed to build the Greater East Asia Co-Prosperity Sphere, creating satellite states throughout Asia that would free Japan from dependence on Western-controlled resources like oil. In the twenties the United States and Japan successfully mediated their differences, with Japan agreeing to reduce the size of its navy and renouncing war as an instrument of foreign policy (see Chapter 21). The Japanese army's 1931 invasion of Chinese-held Manchuria (land long disputed by China, Russia, and Japan), however, signaled the

Were there significant differences between FDR's version of neutrality and Wilson's in World War I?

beginning of a direct confrontation between Japan and the United States. Claiming that Manchuria rightfully belonged to Japan, the Japanese army assumed control of all raw materials and industry to support Japan's military endeavors.

In July 1937 Japan attacked China. The Japanese unleashed a brutal war of conquest; during the infamous Rape of Nanking, a Chinese city, over 350,000 Chinese perished, including 20,000 women, who were raped, tortured, and then executed. "Soldiers impaled babies on bayonets and tossed them still alive into pots of boiling water," a Japanese soldier later admitted. More than 6 million Chinese died at the hands of Japanese soldiers over the next eight years.

Growing American sympathy for Chinese victims and concern over protecting American economic interests in Asia coincided with rising tensions in Europe. By 1940 aiding Britain had become President Roosevelt's foreign policy priority. Containing Japan with a series of escalating economic sanctions and warnings, FDR reasoned, was the best way to defuse the situation in the Pacific so the nation could focus on problems in the Atlantic and Europe. Hoping that a show of force would convince Japan to abandon its imperialist ambitions, the United States embarked on a naval building program and stationed the Pacific Fleet in Pearl Harbor, on the Hawaiian island of Oahu, 2,500 miles from California (see 23.1). Roosevelt also sent aid to China and in July 1940 imposed a limited embargo on scrap iron and high-octane aviation fuel to Japan.

Japan was not deterred. Instead of withdrawing from China, Japan seized parts of French Indochina, a French colony in Southeast Asia, the site of present-day Vietnam. In response, on September 26, 1940, the United States announced a total embargo on scrap metal shipments to Japan. The following day Tokyo signed the Tripartite Pact with Germany and Italy, an agreement dedicated to "the establishment of a new order" in East Asia and Europe. Aimed at offering mutual aid in the event that the United States attacked, the pact did not envision any strategic coordination between the European and Asian theaters of war. Japan and Germany shared mutual enemies during the war, but little else.

When Japan increased its incursions into French Indochina in the summer of 1941, the American government froze Japanese assets in the United States and stopped oil shipments (which accounted for four-fifths of Japan's oil supply). Diplomatic

23.5 Japanese Model of Pearl Harbor
This mock-up of Pearl Harbor, constructed for a Japanese wartime film of the attack, showed American battleships lined up in a row, making them easy targets for aerial bombs.

> "The United States was in the war, up to the neck and in to the death. ... Being saturated and satiated with emotion and sensation, I went to bed and slept the sleep of the saved and thankful."
>
> British Prime Minister WINSTON CHURCHILL, upon learning of the 1941 Japanese attack on Pearl Harbor

exchanges continued until the eve of the attack on Pearl Harbor, even though Japan decided in September to launch an expansionist war into resource-rich Southeast Asia to push the United States and Britain out of the region.

The Japanese calculation that the United States would withdraw from East Asia after a devastating attack on Pearl Harbor proved as faulty as the American belief that sanctions were the best way to prevent a war with Japan. The Japanese assault on Pearl Harbor ended all debate over entering the war. Having agonized over how far to pull the country toward war, Roosevelt reportedly told an aide that the attack took the matter "entirely out of his hands, because the Japanese had made the decision for him."

Despite catching the Americans by surprise, the Japanese victory at Pearl Harbor was far from complete. Although the attack prevented the United States from interfering with Japan's subsequent invasion of Southeast Asia, Japan failed to destroy America's Pacific Fleet. Fearing a counterattack Nagumo, on the day of the attack, called off a third air strike on storage tanks containing millions of gallons of fuel oil and repair facilities. Most American sailors in Hawaii survived the attack, and the navy eventually repaired six of the eight damaged battleships. In another stroke of luck, the Pacific Fleet's two aircraft carriers were at sea and escaped the attack. The navy also had eleven battleships and two aircraft carriers stationed elsewhere to defend the nation from further attack. Nonetheless the short-term damage was severe. Over the next twenty-four hours, Japan attacked American territory and countries throughout Southeast Asia. While the attack on Pearl Harbor horrified Americans, it brought hope to the British. Churchill knew immediately that the United States would soon be in the war against Germany.

After Pearl Harbor some die-hard noninterventionists immediately questioned whether the Japanese attack could have been prevented. Charges of dereliction of duty against the commanders of Pearl Harbor and suspicions that Roosevelt had allowed the attack to take place in order to enter the war against Hitler (through the back door) surfaced. By early December, American commanders expected a Japanese attack against American Pacific possessions. Most intelligence data, however, indicated that the Japanese would invade the Philippines and mainland Southeast Asia, as they subsequently did. American officials simply overlooked the few bits of information indicating that Hawaii was both a possible and a probable first target. The extent to which the Japanese took the Americans by surprise is reflected in this telegram (**23.6**),which alerted all ships in Pearl Harbor to take the air sirens seriously. American radar had picked up the waves of aircraft approaching the naval base, but officials assumed these were American planes arriving from the mainland. The telegram, therefore, was not sent until the bombs had already started falling.

23.6 Pearl Harbor Under Attack
Caught off guard, the navy rallied their defenses against the Japanese attack on Pearl Harbor with this telegram.

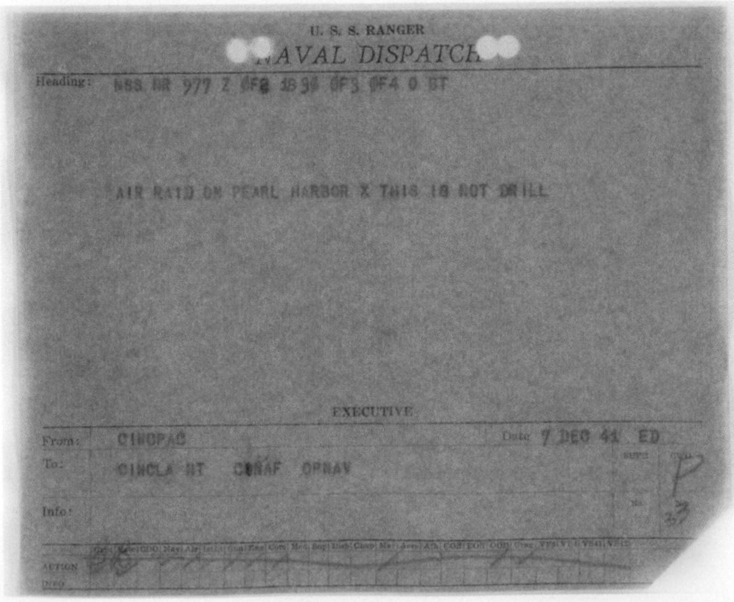

U. S. S. RANGER
NAVAL DISPATCH

AIR RAID ON PEARL HARBOR X THIS IS NOT DRILL

EXECUTIVE

From: CINCPAC
Date: 7 DEC 41
To: CINCLANT COMAF OPNAV
Info:

How significant was the attack on Pearl Harbor in the short and long run?

On the Home Front

The U.S. government made the formal declaration of war, but winning it required the active participation of the American people. Americans remember World War II as the "good war" not only because it ended the Depression but also because it united the nation against its enemies. While unified in the desire to prevail on the battlefield, Americans embraced conflicting visions that kept ethnic, gender, race, and class divisions intact. Motivating the country to fight the Japanese was easy after the attack on Pearl Harbor, but cultivating hatred of the enemy had direct consequences for Japanese immigrants and Japanese Americans. The wartime economic boom ended years of financial struggle and hardship, but prosperity brought its own share of strains. Cities with major defense industries found themselves inundated with migrants from rural areas and struggled to contain rising racial and ethnic tensions between white inhabitants and black and Hispanic communities.

Images of the Enemy

Americans had long exhibited disdain for Asian immigrants and Americans of Asian descent. Before the war localities and the federal government had passed a series of discriminatory laws that targeted Asian immigrants generally and their American-born children. These laws segregated swimming pools and dance halls, denied Asians the right to own land, prohibited intermarriage with whites, and prevented Asian immigrants from becoming citizens. The attack on Pearl Harbor provoked more virulent expressions of hatred for the Japanese, leading to even greater discrimination.

In the opening days of the war, *Life* and *Time* magazines offered the nation a crash course in "how to tell a Chinese from a Jap." Understanding the difference was crucial, *Life* magazine asserted, to protect the Chinese Americans, "whose homeland is our staunch ally," from unwarranted attacks. As the Chinese embassy prepared to hand out identification buttons for Chinese immigrants and Chinese Americans to wear, *Life* and *Time* instructed the nation in distinguishing pseudoscientific, stereotypical "racial" characteristics. *Life* magazine used photos (**23.7**) to compare the facial features and expressions of a Chinese civil servant with those of General Hideki Tojo, the minister of war who ruled Japan during the war. The magazine called on readers to note Tojo's heavy beard and cheekbones and humorless expression, all supposedly key traits of Japanese physiognomy. *Time* and *Life* were not alone in feeling a sudden need to distinguish members of the "yellow race." Congress lifted the ban on Chinese naturalization and granted China an annual quota of 105 immigrants a year. This act symbolically differentiated the Chinese from the Japanese (banned as immigrants in 1924 and prohibited from becoming naturalized citizens, see Chapters 19 and 21), but protected the nation from any substantial increase in Chinese immigration.

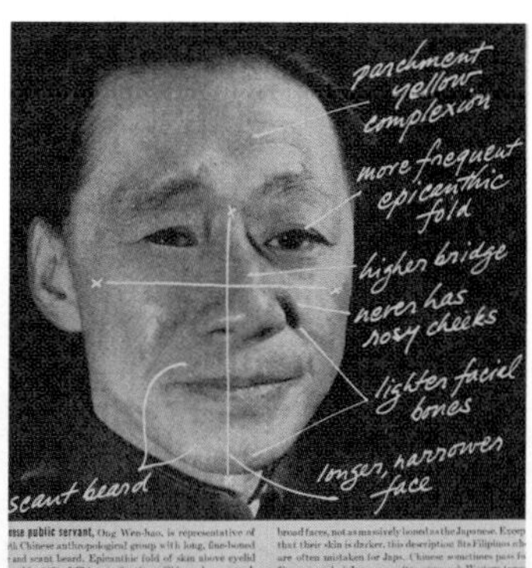

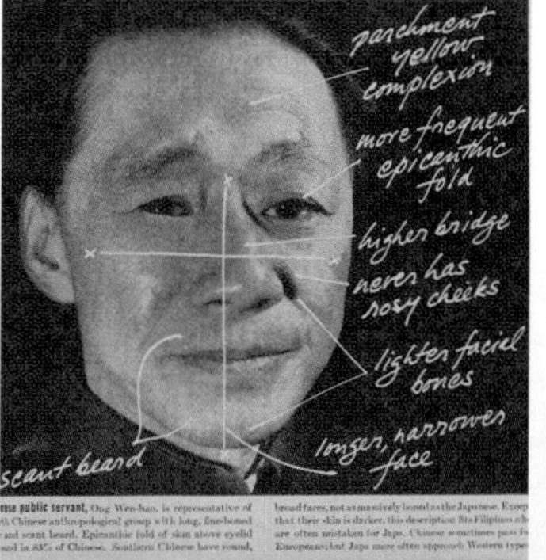

23.7 "How to Tell Japs from the Chinese" Lamenting the American tendency to lump all Asians together, *Life* magazine analyzed the facial features of Chinese and Japanese men to instruct readers in the difference between the two groups—one an ally, the other the enemy.

Renewed outrage against Japan greeted news of ongoing atrocities in the Pacific war, such as the April 1942 Bataan Death March. When American and Filipino soldiers finally surrendered their position on the Bataan Peninsula in the Philippines, their Japanese captors forced the sick, starving troops to walk almost 90 miles through the intense heat and jungle to a prisoner of war camp. Out of 76,000 men who began the trek, 22,000 succumbed to illness, starvation, and severe beatings from Japanese soldiers.

Still these horrors were not enough to explain Americans' deep-seated hatred for the Japanese. "In Europe we felt that our enemies, horrible and deadly as they were, were still people," Ernie Pyle wrote in one of his newspaper columns toward the end of the war. "But out here I soon gathered that the Japanese were looked upon as something subhuman and

What distinctions did Americans now make between the Japanese and Chinese?

repulsive; the way some people feel about cockroaches or mice." As Pyle noted, general views toward the Germans were decidedly different. Remembering the vigilante attacks against German Americans in World War I (see Chapter 20), government propaganda took great care to focus on Hitler and Nazism as the enemy, not the German people.

Internment Camps

In the immediate wake of the attack on Pearl Harbor, Americans were eager for explanations. Rumors circulated that Japanese American farmers on Hawaii had plowed arrows in their fields to show Japanese pilots the way to military installations. Yet no evidence of internal spying ever surfaced, and suggestions that the government round up and quarantine these Hawaiian residents went nowhere. Composing one-third of Hawaii's population, people of Japanese descent were too important to the local economy to deport, and there were no ships available to transport replacement workers to the islands.

The 110,000 Japanese and Japanese Americans who lived in California, Oregon, and Washington, where they were not so vital to the economy, met a different fate. The day after the attack on Pearl Harbor, air raid sirens wailed in San Francisco. Then, when a Japanese submarine torpedoed an American ship off the California coast, Americans feared that the West Coast would soon be under attack. Frenzied officials instituted blackouts; Coast Guard units patrolled the seas. Throughout the war West Coast defense factories camouflaged their plants, as illustrated in these "Plant Camouflage, Before and After" photos (**23.8**). This aircraft factory in Burbank, California, stretched a tarp over its facilities to make it look like a suburban housing development from the air. The camouflagers hoped that an attacking Japanese pilot would pass over the site in search of a more recognizable military target.

Within this atmosphere of heightened anxiety, Japanese immigrants and Japanese Americans on the West Coast found themselves targeted as potential enemy agents. Increasingly the larger public and the government embraced a vision that viewed their presence near vital ports and military bases as a threat to national security. On February 19, 1942, President Roosevelt signed Executive Order 9066, giving the military the ability to declare certain areas off-limits to any or all persons. Lieutenant General John L. DeWitt, head of the Western Defense Command, immediately declared the entire West Coast a military zone closed to "all persons of Japanese ancestry, both alien and non-alien." The order called for the evacuation of anyone of Japanese descent; even orphanages had to comply by relocating Japanese American babies.

In mid-March 1942 Roosevelt created the War Relocation Authority to oversee the forced removal of 38,000 Japanese immigrants and 72,000 Japanese American citizens to **internment camps** where they were held under armed guard in isolated areas. Posted "Instructions to All Persons of Japanese Ancestry" (**23.9**) informed Japanese inhabitants that they had only a few days to sell their belongings and settle their affairs. "It is difficult to describe the feeling of despair and humiliation experienced by all of us," one internee later said, "as we watched the Caucasians coming to look over our possessions and offering such nominal amounts knowing we had no recourse but to accept whatever they were offering." Evacuees were allowed to take only what they could carry. With numbers pinned on their coats, they

23.8 Plant Camouflage, Before and After This aircraft factory in Burbank, California, camouflaged its facility with a painted tarp and cardboard houses to create the facade of a suburban housing development, in the hopes of deceiving Japanese pilots on the lookout for military targets.

What do these photos reveal about American fears of a Japanese attack?

rode trains to recently abandoned stables or stockyards to await transport to one of ten internment camps scattered in remote areas throughout the interior West.

Offering a conflicting vision that emphasized their loyalty to the United States, the overwhelming majority of Japanese and Japanese Americans complied quietly with the evacuation order. A few, however, found ways to register their protest against this wholesale violation of their civil rights. For propaganda purposes the Office of War Information hired photographer Dorothea Lange to document that the government was treating evacuees humanely as it contained this suspect population. Sympathetic to the plight of Japanese Americans, Lange managed to capture this scene (**23.10**) of a Japanese American veteran reporting to a Santa Anita assembly center in his old military uniform, a silent demonstration of his long-standing loyalty to the country.

In January 1943 the army decided to recruit Nisei men, the American-born children of Japanese immigrants. While their parents remained in the camps, these men joined with Japanese Americans from Hawaii to form the 442nd Regimental Combat Team, a unit that became the most decorated American unit in the nation's history. These men opted to prove their loyalty by fighting for their country. Other Japanese Americans sought redress in the courts, but the Supreme Court upheld the government's evacuation policy in 1944. *Competing Visions: Civil Liberties and National Security Clash* (page 696) examines this controversy in more detail.

As the tide of the war began to turn in America's favor, the military justification for interning people of Japanese descent weakened. In 1945 the government let inmates return to their West Coast homes. Three years later the federal government offered some restitution to those who had lost homes or businesses. It took until 1988, however, for Congress to offer an apology and reparation payment of $20,000 to each of the 60,000 surviving internees.

Prosperity, Scarcity and Opportunities for Women

Japanese Americans were among the few to suffer financially from the war. For most Americans jobs were plentiful and wages high. Over the course of the war the nation's gross national product rose 60 percent, and 17 million new jobs were created. To mobilize the economy the government quickly established a slew of agencies to allocate scarce resources, help business convert their factories to a wartime footing, and enlist the public's full support for the war. After the difficult years of the Depression, the war-fueled economic boom came as a welcome relief. "People are crazy with money," one store owner exclaimed. "They don't care what they buy. They purchase things . . . just for the fun of spending." Madison Avenue advertising firms assured the public that consumerism was essential to the American way of life. "Will you ever own another car?" asked one ad. "Another radio? Another gleaming new refrigerator? Those who live under dictators merely dream of such possessions."

Concerns over unemployment gave way to worries about inflation as the additional money flowing into the economy sent prices soaring. The government tried to curb inflation by instituting price and wage controls. Because the nation's

WESTERN DEFENSE COMMAND AND FOURTH ARMY
WARTIME CIVIL CONTROL ADMINISTRATION
Presidio of San Francisco, California
April 1, 1942

INSTRUCTIONS
TO ALL PERSONS OF
JAPANESE
ANCESTRY

Living in the Following Area:

All that portion of the City and County of San Francisco, State of California, lying generally west of the north-south line established by Junipero Serra Boulevard, Worchester Avenue, and Nineteenth Avenue, and lying generally north of the east-west line established by California Street, to the intersection of Market Street, and thence on Market Street to San Francisco Bay.

All Japanese persons, both alien and non-alien, will be evacuated from the above designated area by 12:00 o'clock noon Tuesday, April 7, 1942.

No Japanese person will be permitted to enter or leave the above described area after 8:00 a. m., Thursday, April 2, 1942, without obtaining special permission from the Provost Marshal at the Civil Control Station located at:

1701 Van Ness Avenue
San Francisco, California

The Civil Control Station is equipped to assist the Japanese population affected by this evacuation in the following ways:

1. Give advice and instructions on the evacuation.
2. Provide services with respect to the management, leasing, sale, storage or other disposition of most kinds of property including: real estate, business and professional equipment, buildings, household goods, boats, automobiles, livestock, etc.
3. Provide temporary residence elsewhere for all Japanese in family groups.
4. Transport persons and a limited amount of clothing and equipment to their new residence, as specified below.

The Following Instructions Must Be Observed:

1. A responsible member of each family, preferably the head of the family, or the person in whose name most of the property is held, and each individual living alone, will report to the Civil Control Station to receive further instructions. This must be done between 8:00 a. m. and 5:00 p. m., Thursday, April 2, 1942, or between 8:00 a. m. and 5:00 p. m., Friday, April 3, 1942.

23.9 "Instructions to All Persons of Japanese Ancestry" This poster illustrates the hasty pace of the evacuation of Japanese Americans. They had just seven days to leave their homes.

23.10 A Japanese American Protests Internment Government officials censored this photograph of a Japanese American veteran who reported to the evacuation center in his old uniform. He gave his name to a Japanese-American staff member who decided instead to cooperate openly with authorities.

What competing responses did Japanese Americans have to internment?

Competing Visions

CIVIL LIBERTIES AND NATIONAL SECURITY CLASH

In *Korematsu v. United States* (1944), the Supreme Court upheld the constitutionality of relocating and interning Japanese Americans as a justifiable military measure. Three Supreme Court justices dissented from the majority opinion, concluding that internment violated the constitutional rights of Japanese American citizens. Which side made the stronger argument? How has America resolved a similar dilemma over national security versus civil rights in the aftermath of the 9/11 attacks (see Chapter 29)?

Justice Hugo Black wrote the majority opinion that upheld the constitutionality of interning Japanese Americans.

Exclusion of those of Japanese origin was deemed necessary because of the presence of an unascertained number of disloyal members of the group, most of whom we have no doubt were loyal to this country. ... We are not unmindful of the hardships imposed by it upon a large group of American citizens. ... But hardships are part of war, and war is an aggregation of hardships. All citizens alike, both in and out of uniform, feel the impact of war in greater or lesser measure. Citizenship has its responsibilities as well as its privileges, and in time of war the burden is always heavier. Compulsory exclusion of large groups of citizens from their homes, except under circumstances of direct emergency and peril, is inconsistent with our basic governmental institutions. But when under conditions of modern warfare our shores are threatened by hostile forces, the power to protect must be commensurate with the threatened danger. ...

Regardless of the true nature of the assembly and relocation centers—and we deem it unjustifiable to call them concentration camps with all the ugly connotations that term implies.... Korematsu was not excluded from the Military Area because of hostility to him or his race. He was excluded because we are at war with the Japanese Empire, because the properly constituted military authorities feared an invasion of our West Coast and felt constrained to take proper security measures, because they decided that the military urgency of the situation demanded that all citizens of Japanese ancestry be segregated from the West Coast temporarily, and finally, because Congress, reposing its confidence in this time of war in our military leaders—as inevitably it must—determined that they should have the power to do just this. There was evidence of disloyalty on the part of some, the military authorities considered that the need for action was great, and time was short. We cannot—by availing ourselves of the calm perspective of hindsight—now say that at that time these actions were unjustified.

Justice Frank Murphy disagreed with the majority opinion, arguing that internment was racially motivated.

This exclusion of "all persons of Japanese ancestry, both alien and non-alien," from the Pacific Coast area on a plea of military necessity in the absence of martial law ought not to be approved. Such exclusion goes over "the very brink of constitutional power" and falls into the ugly abyss of racism ... it is essential that there be definite limits to military discretion, especially where martial law has not been declared. Individuals must not be left impoverished of their constitutional rights on plea of military necessity that has neither substance nor support. ...

No one denies, of course, that there were some disloyal persons of Japanese descent on the Pacific Coast who did all in their power to aid their ancestral land. Similar disloyal activities have been engaged in by many persons of German, Italian and even more pioneer stock in our country. But to infer that examples of individual disloyalty prove group disloyalty and justify discriminatory action against the entire group is to deny that under our system of law individual guilt is the sole basis for deprivation of rights. ... To give constitutional sanction to that inference in this case, however well-intentioned may have been the military command on the Pacific Coast, is to adopt one of the cruelest of the rationales used by our enemies to destroy the dignity of the individual and to encourage and open the door to discriminatory actions against other minority groups in the passions of tomorrow. ...

I dissent, therefore, from this legalization of racism. Racial discrimination in any form and in any degree has no justifiable part whatever in our democratic way of life.

Japanese American girl saying the Pledge of Allegiance

Did a legitimate military reason exist to place Japanese Americans in internment camps?

resources were now being poured into producing military equipment and supplying the troops, consumers faced shortages of all kinds. To deal with the scarcity of resources, the government rationed many goods, including gas and sugar, by distributing coupon books that allotted families a set amount of each item. In an effort to save wool, cotton, and nylon, the War Production Board (WPB) dictated fashion trends by forbidding tailors to make cuffs, vests, or double-breasted jackets for men. The WPB's demand that bathing suit manufacturers use 10 percent less material meant that skintight one-piece bathing suits soon took the place of billowing bathing costumes on America's beaches. Hemlines on ladies' skirts also rose to save fabric.

The government spent as never before, expanding the federal budget from $9 billion in 1939 to $100 billion by 1945. As in World War I, the nation used conscription to fill the ranks and enlisted the help of big business to provide the masses of guns, tanks, ships, and bullets that a modern army needed. Numbers help convey the immensity of the American war effort. The military grew from 227,000 to 16 million, of whom 10 million were conscripted. American industry produced 77,000 ships, 300,000 airplanes, 2.5 million trucks, and 20 million small arms for the American and Allied armed forces. Nearly 15 million civilians relocated during the war to take advantage of opportunities in cities with booming wartime industries such as Los Angeles, New Orleans, Seattle, Detroit, and Philadelphia. The sudden growth of many cities forced hundreds of thousands of recent migrants to live in "the backs of stores, in public buildings, warehouses, and garages," the Bureau of Labor reported.

To combat the growing labor shortage, the War Manpower Commission, a wartime agency charged with keeping American workers on the job, tried to lure "Mrs. Stay-at Home" into the wartime workforce. Whether swayed by wartime propaganda or attracted instead by new employment opportunities and higher wages, droves of married women entered the workplace. Nearly 19 million women held jobs during the war, for the moment a record high. Many of these women would have worked anyway. Only 3 million new female workers entered the wartime workforce. Not all Americans supported this change in the domestic life of the nation, however. Male workers resented competing with women for desirable positions. Many mothers also expressed mixed feelings about leaving their children in day care.

Over 350,000 women served in the armed forces, including 150,000 in the Women's Army Corps (WAC). The majority of women in uniform served as nurses and clerks, fulfilling vital communication and record-keeping services. Many men and the media found these clerical roles easy to deride. The press nicknamed the WACs the "Petticoat Army" and their quarters "Fort Lipstick." The recruiting slogan for the WACs—"Release a man for combat"—publicly underscored the different risks faced by women and men in the military.

> "Instead of cutting the lines of a dress, this woman cuts the pattern of aircraft parts."
>
> 1943 newsreel, *Glamour Girls of '43.*

Female soldiers also performed more traditionally "male" tasks, serving as gunnery instructors, mechanics, and truck drivers, and 1,000 women even flew combat aircraft from domestic manufacturers to overseas bases. General Douglas MacArthur called female troops "my best soldiers." At least one congressman, however, offered a competing vision, wondering "what has become of the manhood of America?" now that women had a formal place in the armed forces.

Once victory seemed ensured in 1944, government-sponsored propaganda reversed course, embracing a vision that emphasized women's domestic responsibilities instead of their public duties. Toward the end of the war, the *Saturday Evening Post* carried this "Mothers at Work" ad (**23.11**) that urged women to consider the toll that working outside the home had on their children. The ad also emphasized this woman's imminent postwar need for new appliances. As expected the overall percentage of women working returned to 28 percent (from a wartime high of 36 percent) in 1947 as women quit their

23.11 "Mothers at Work"
As the war drew to a close, official posters and private advertisements encouraged women to revert to their traditional roles as homemakers.

What competing visions of working women emerged over the course of the war?

jobs to raise families or employers fired them to free up positions for returning veterans. Similarly, only a few thousand women remained in uniform as the military cut slots reserved for female troops. Their position within the armed forces rebounded a bit, however, when an act of Congress in 1948 gave women a permanent, though segregated, place in the army, navy, and air force. The debate over whether to limit female soldiers to support tasks or use them in active operations was only just beginning.

Even children pitched in to help the war effort. To encourage children's active participation, the government released photographs of small girls and boys doing their bit (**23.12**). This young boy takes care of the family shopping while his parents work in war-related jobs, handing the family's ration card to the merchant. At home this little girl carefully saves tin and foil in separate jars for the local scrap drive, all scarce materials needed by the military. Classrooms across the nation collected pennies and nickels for war bonds, which the federal government sold to Americans to help finance the war. The remoteness of the war often made it seem like a great adventure to children, who enthusiastically scoured their neighborhoods for aluminum, rubber, and tin foil, sometimes banging pots and pans outside homes until residents came forth with a donation. War games gained popularity on the nation's playgrounds, and some children joined the Junior Commandos, a group that let young uniformed recruits, only a few years away from qualifying to fight in the army, train on a rugged obstacle course.

With the wartime economy booming, many Americans concluded that wars, by nature, were good for the economy. However, a set of unique factors made World War II particularly beneficial for the American economy.

- The war effort withdrew 16 million servicemen and women from the workforce just as millions of new positions were created, absorbing all surplus labor and creating a labor shortage.
- Massive government spending on the war, not the war per se, ended the Depression. If the government had been willing to spend $323 billion (the total cost of the war) on New Deal programs, then the economy would likely have rebounded earlier.
- The wartime boom years came at the expense of future generations. Direct taxation paid for less than half of the war's cost. It took until 1970 for the government to finish paying off its war debts.

During the war, prosperity and unity of purpose failed to guarantee tranquility in labor relations on the home front. Competing visions on the meaning of wartime sacrifice emerged immediately. The chairman of the National War Labor Board dramatized the difficulty of asking unions for wage

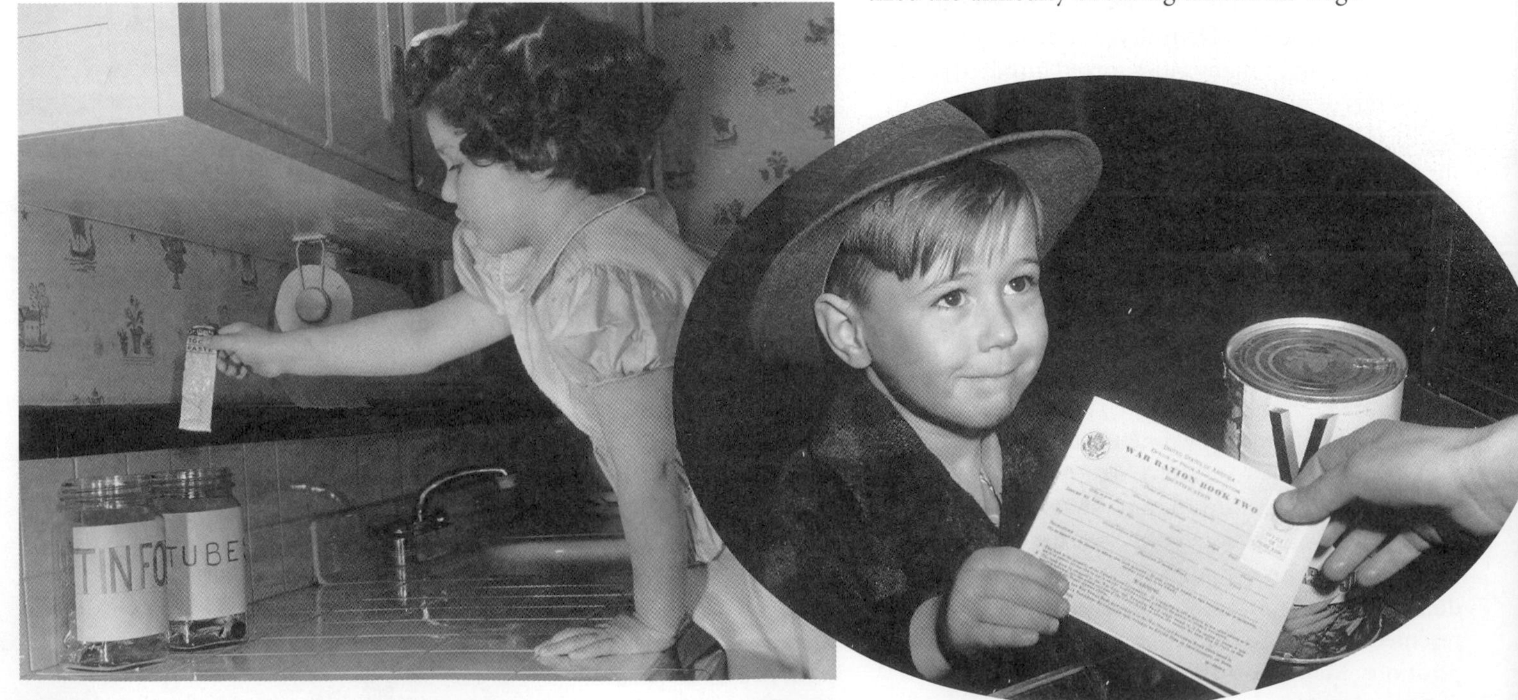

23.12 Children and War
Children helped in the war effort by collecting metal for neighborhood scrap drives and by shopping with a ration card while their parents worked.

concessions by noting, "If you say to the boys, 'Why don't you make a sacrifice for your country?' they are going to say, 'That is fine. I am making a sacrifice for my country, but I am not going to make it to increase the profits of General Motors.'" Workers were right to suspect that big business profited tremendously from the war. Government contracts with generous profit margins, federal loans for factory conversion or expansion, and tax write-offs went overwhelmingly to the nation's one hundred largest companies. Even companies that at first glance appeared peripheral to the war effort prospered. Both Coca-Cola and Wrigley's Gum, for instance, managed to get their products declared essential war commodities, thus gaining access to carefully rationed sugar and shipping space. By following American servicemen around the globe, Coca-Cola cultivated a worldwide taste for its beverage. Wrigley's Gum convinced the War Department that gum reduced stress in war workers and combat troops. The company provided a free stick for every soldier's combat rations.

> "If you are going to ... go to war ... in a capitalist country, you have to let business make money out of the process or business won't work."
>
> Secretary of War HENRY L. STIMSON

During the war, labor's clout, like that of big companies, also expanded. Union rolls swelled from 8.7 to 14.7 million thanks in part to supportive War Labor Board policies. Industrialists tried to use the wartime rhetoric of sacrifice to rein in these growing unions. In one published advertisement, for example, the Jenkins Valve firm linked work slowdowns (used to pressure a company to agree to labor's demands) to the unnecessary deaths of American sailors. The ad showed a small child staring at a sailor's cap that had washed up along the shore; above ran the caption "Is a Plant Slow Down Worth It?" Unions did not completely abandon strikes, but overall the war ushered in a less militant era of collective bargaining.

Racial Discord

The war provided many opportunities for racial minorities to assert their claims for equal rights in all aspects of American social and political life. These groups offered a strikingly different view of the war's ultimate purpose. Unlike the majority of white Americans who confined their thoughts to the struggle against fascism abroad, many civil rights leaders championed a competing vision that sought to eradicate discrimination at home. Using the war to promote a **double-victory campaign** against both fascism overseas and racial prejudice at home, these activists promoted a vision of an egalitarian and color-blind society.

At first the wartime boom threatened to leave African Americans behind because many essential wartime industries refused to hire blacks. In 1941, the African American labor leader A. Philip Randolph threatened to assemble 10,000 blacks in front of the Lincoln Memorial in Washington, D.C., to "demand the right to work and fight for our country." Nationally known for successfully organizing a union for black railroad porters, Randolph realized that FDR's lock on the black vote gave him little reason to offer more than sympathy in private meetings with black leaders about rampant racial discrimination. To pressure FDR to act on blacks' behalf, a step certain to anger the president's white Southern supporters, Randolph resolved to publicly protest employment discrimination.

Randolph's idea for a march on Washington immediately attracted the support of civil rights groups and the ire of the White House. When FDR tried to convince Randolph to call off the march, Randolph stood firm, telling the president, "We feel as you have wisely said: 'No people will lose their freedom fighting for it.'" Seeking to avoid an embarrassing demonstration that highlighted racial problems at home, FDR agreed to issue an executive order that forbade discrimination in the defense industry and government if Randolph canceled the march. Roosevelt's order also established the Fair Employment Practices Committee to handle complaints of discrimination. For the first time since Reconstruction, the period following the Civil War, the federal government was intervening directly to protect the civil rights of African Americans. Randolph's aborted demonstration later inspired the 1963 march on Washington, where black civil rights leader Martin Luther King Jr. delivered his "I Have a Dream" speech standing before the Lincoln Memorial (see Chapter 27).

Interest in direct action grew throughout the war. The Fellowship of Reconciliation's Committee on Racial Justice initiated a wave of sit-ins where groups of blacks and whites entered segregated restaurants together and refused to leave when denied service. In Washington, D.C., Howard University students successfully picketed segregated restaurants with signs that read "We Die Together. Let's Eat Together" and "Are You for Hitler's Way or the American Way? Make Up Your Mind."

Nearly 1 million blacks served in the armed forces during the war, including Brigadier General Benjamin O. Davis, the first African American general in the U.S. Army. The War Department finally agreed to train African American pilots, and the Tuskegee Airmen (who received their stateside training at Alabama's Tuskegee Institute) amassed an admirable war record in Europe. The military remained segregated, however, and the overwhelming majority of black soldiers served in noncombatant units where they cleared beaches in France of mines, manned supply lines transporting food and ammunition to front-line troops, and built roads and railroads for the advancing army.

Within the United States black servicemen continued to receive daily reminders of their second-class status. When a group of black soldiers entered a whites-only restaurant in Salina, Kansas, the owner stopped them. We "just stood there inside the door, staring at what we had come to see—the German prisoners of war who were having lunch at the counter. . . . This was really happening. It was no jive talk. The people of Salina would serve these enemy soldiers and turn away black American G.I.'s," one soldier recalled. The proper epitaph to mark each black soldier's grave in the Pacific, African Americans sarcastically told one another, would be "here lies a black man killed fighting a yellow man for the protection of a white man."

The double-victory campaign laid the groundwork for the postwar civil rights movement by pioneering new strategies that would later prove extraordinarily successful. The accelerated migration northward also created new bases of political power that would aid the civil rights movement in the 1950s and 1960s. Throughout the war hundreds of thousands of African American civilians hit the road in search of job opportunities in midwestern and western cities. In 1943 Los Angeles welcomed 10,000 black migrants a month, most from Texas and Louisiana. Overcrowding and changing demographics created explosive racial situations in many urban areas. The most serious wartime race riot took place in 1943 in Detroit, Michigan. Home to the nation's largest automobile manufacturers, Detroit became the leading producer of military goods when these companies began manufacturing jeeps and tanks for the military. Plentiful jobs drew thousands of migrants to the city, including African Americans, who had trouble finding adequate lodging in the strictly (albeit unofficially) segregated city housing market. White workers, resentful at working next to black workers, staged work slowdowns in the city's wartime defense plants. To protest racial discrimination some black residents initiated a "bumping campaign," purposefully nudging whites off sidewalks. The anticipated confrontation finally came on a warm spring afternoon when several groups of black and white teenagers tussled at a crowded amusement park located on Belle Isle. As the violence escalated, a mob of 5,000 whites formed to attack blacks as they crossed the bridge back to the mainland. Racial rampaging soon engulfed the entire city. Hundreds of African Americans were injured and twenty-five were killed before state and federal troops restored order. Nine whites also died in the rioting.

Horace Pippin, a self-taught African American painter who rocketed to fame in the late thirties, took note of the racial discord on the home front in his 1943 painting *Mr. Prejudice* (**23.13**). Pippin's composition expressed doubt that the double-V campaign would succeed. In the painting a racist white worker, backed by a Klansman, hammers a chisel down the center of a V, the symbol of victory. A fellow worker stands to his left, holding a noose—a reference to lynching. The Statue of Liberty, portrayed as an African American woman, is toppling down as the dream of racial unity unravels. The fractured V threatens to crack into two, permanently dividing the friendly white soldiers reaching out to their black comrades in arms—a doctor, sailor, aviator, and soldier who are all serving loyally during the war.

African Americans were not the only targets of racial violence, however. The same summer that racial violence rocked Detroit, white sailors and soldiers on leave in Los Angeles began a ten-day rampage against Mexican American **zoot-suiters**, youths who wore baggy pants, long oversize coats, and broad-brimmed hats. The zoot-suit was a fashion trend established by African American men in the thirties. By the war years white Americans viewed zoot-suiters at best as juvenile delinquents who refused to dress and act properly, and at worst as marauding criminal gangs bent on robbery and rape. Some *pachucos*, as zoot-suiters called themselves, engaged in criminal activity, but most limited their adolescent rebellion to wearing different clothes from adults.

The explosive growth in the Mexican American community, coupled with a general intolerance for any nonconformity in time of war, set the stage for the conflict in Los Angeles. Street fights between sailors and Mexican American men escalated into full-scale rioting when organized groups of servicemen began attacking boys as young as twelve and Mexican American businesses. Local white civilians joined in the rioting, and when a mob came upon a zoot-suiter, they often beat and stripped him and sometimes even burned his clothes. The casualties included more than a hundred seriously injured Mexican Americans, and at least a hundred more who refused hospital care. Newspapers in Los Angeles egged on the white crowds by praising their efforts to rid the city of the "hoodlums" and "gangsters." Federal investigators cited racial prejudice as the cause of the riots, but Los Angeles nonetheless passed an ordinance that prohibited wearing zoot-suits on city streets. The image of Mexican Americans as disaffected youths belied the reality that 500,000 Latinos served alongside whites in the armed forces during the war, playing a large role in the doomed defense of the Philippines and heavily represented among Medal of Honor winners.

23.13 Horace Pippin, *Mr. Prejudice* (1943)
The fractured V in Pippin's painting suggested that the African American vision of using the war to secure democracy at home and abroad was in jeopardy. [*Source:* Horace Pippin (1888–1946), "Mr. Prejudice," 1943. Oil on canvas, 18 × 14 inches. Philadelphia Museum of Art, Gift of Dr. and Mrs. Matthew T. Moore. Photo by Graydon Wood. 1984-108-1]

Perceived as natural-born warriors, Native Americans encountered less hostility within the armed forces than blacks or Latino Americans. More than 25,000 Native Americans served, including the famed Navajo code talkers who transmitted secret messages between units in their native language, baffling the Japanese, who never deciphered it. Military service offered many young Native Americans their first decent wages and a chance to leave the reservation. Government officials expected military service to hasten the process of assimilation, since Native American soldiers lived among whites. Yet sending men into combat also gave some tribes a reason to resurrect rituals surrounding battle, such as requiring returning soldiers to spend time in a sweat hut to cleanse themselves of the evils associated with war. Serving in the military, therefore, became a catalyst that both expanded veterans' knowledge of the wider world and reinforced their own cultural traditions, helping them to see themselves and mainstream society in a different light.

How did the wartime experiences of African Americans compare to those of Latino Americans?

On the Front Lines

No bombs fell on American cities and no occupying armies marched through the streets, but with 16 million men in the armed forces, nearly everyone knew someone who might not make it home. The United States essentially fought two separate wars in World War II, one against Germany and its allies in Europe; the other against Japan in the Pacific. The initial news from the battlefront was not good, as the American armed forces encountered one setback after another. America had determined foes in Japan and Germany, and defeating them required time and patience. Important first victories finally came, but the closer the Allies got to Japan and to Germany, the harder their enemies fought. Initially leery of exposing Americans to blood and gore, over time magazines and newspapers began to publish photographs that registered the rising toll of death at the front. The public welcomed photographs of enemy destruction as evidence that the nation was nearing victory, but reacted strongly to any sign of suffering by American soldiers. Nothing prepared the public, however, for the shocking details that emerged from liberated Nazi concentration camps in 1945.

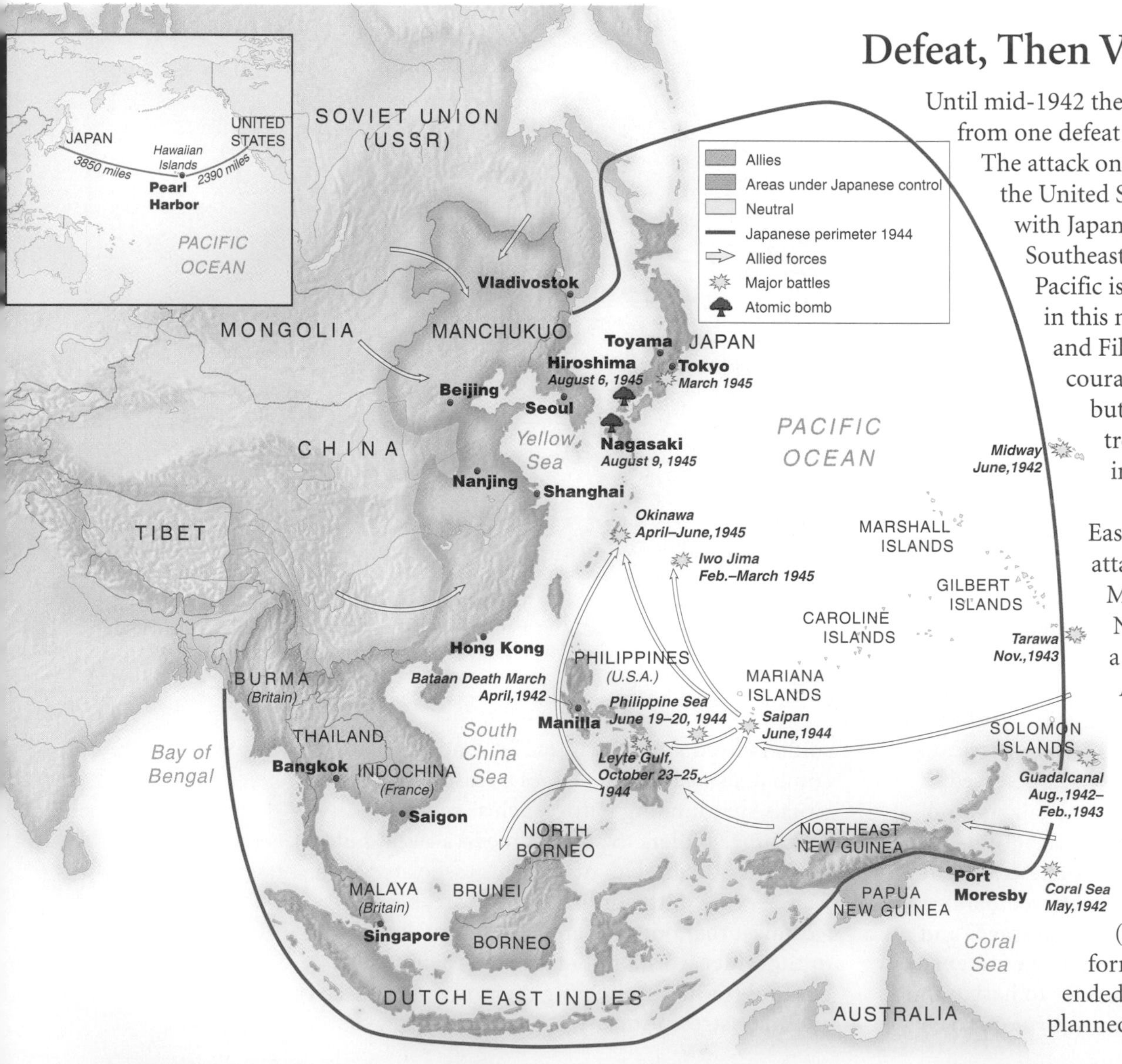

23.14 War in the Pacific
Allied victories at Guadalcanal, the Coral Sea, and Midway halted the Japanese expansionist drive, preparing the way for the Allied island-hopping campaign in 1944–1945.

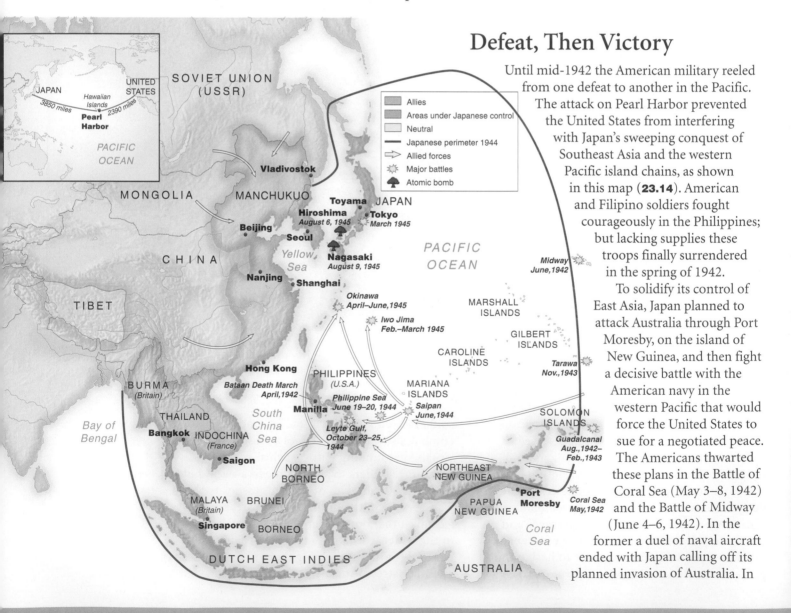

JAPAN
UNITED STATES
Hawaiian Islands
3850 miles
2390 miles
Pearl Harbor
PACIFIC OCEAN

Allies
Areas under Japanese control
Neutral
Japanese perimeter 1944
Allied forces
Major battles
Atomic bomb

SOVIET UNION (USSR)
MONGOLIA
MANCHUKUO
Vladivostok
CHINA
TIBET
JAPAN
Toyama
Hiroshima August 6, 1945
Tokyo March 1945
Beijing
Seoul
Yellow Sea
Nagasaki August 9, 1945
Nanjing
Shanghai
PACIFIC OCEAN
Midway June, 1942
Okinawa April–June, 1945
Iwo Jima Feb.–March 1945
MARSHALL ISLANDS
GILBERT ISLANDS
CAROLINE ISLANDS
Tarawa Nov., 1943
Hong Kong
PHILIPPINES (U.S.A.)
Bataan Death March April, 1942
Philippine Sea June 19–20, 1944
Manilla
MARIANA ISLANDS
Saipan June, 1944
BURMA (Britain)
THAILAND
Bangkok
INDOCHINA (France)
Saigon
South China Sea
Bay of Bengal
Leyte Gulf, October 23–25, 1944
SOLOMON ISLANDS
Guadalcanal Aug., 1942–Feb., 1943
NORTH BORNEO
NORTHEAST NEW GUINEA
Port Moresby
Coral Sea May, 1942
PAPUA NEW GUINEA
MALAYA (Britain)
BRUNEI
Singapore
BORNEO
Coral Sea
DUTCH EAST INDIES
AUSTRALIA

Defeat, Then Victory

Until mid-1942 the American military reeled from one defeat to another in the Pacific. The attack on Pearl Harbor prevented the United States from interfering with Japan's sweeping conquest of Southeast Asia and the western Pacific island chains, as shown in this map (**23.14**). American and Filipino soldiers fought courageously in the Philippines; but lacking supplies these troops finally surrendered in the spring of 1942.

To solidify its control of East Asia, Japan planned to attack Australia through Port Moresby, on the island of New Guinea, and then fight a decisive battle with the American navy in the western Pacific that would force the United States to sue for a negotiated peace. The Americans thwarted these plans in the Battle of Coral Sea (May 3–8, 1942) and the Battle of Midway (June 4–6, 1942). In the former a duel of naval aircraft ended with Japan calling off its planned invasion of Australia. In

What does this map reveal about the military challenges facing the United States in the Pacific?

the latter American dive-bomber squadrons surprised a convoy of Japanese aircraft carriers in the midst of refueling their planes. Japan's heavy losses at Midway prevented Japan from launching any major naval offensives for the rest of the war. Midway was a crucial turning point that put Japan permanently on the defensive.

America adopted a "Europe First" strategy, but the war in the European theater began equally poorly for the Allies. Initially the United States wanted to get needed supplies across the Atlantic and open up a second front against Germany in Western Europe. Meeting the first goal required winning the Battle of the Atlantic. For eighteen months the Allied cause looked grim as German submarines controlled the seas and sank an average of one hundred ships a month. The extensive submarine activity on Map 23.1 illustrates the ferocity of the struggle to control the Atlantic. Finally, in the summer of 1943, the tide began to turn in the Allies' favor. Better air surveillance, improved radar, the discovery that the Germans had broken the convoy-routing code, and breaking the German submarine code all contributed to Allied success in the Atlantic.

The issue of opening a second front in Europe remained. Roosevelt was reluctant to commit large numbers of American land forces until he could field an army that was better equipped and supplied than those of its adversaries. But he recognized that committing American ground troops to the war in Europe would build morale at home; it would also prevent the Russians from seeking a separate peace with Germany.

Soviet leader Joseph Stalin urged Britain and the United States to invade Nazi-occupied France in 1943. Churchill and FDR refused. Britain worried about repeating the trench stalemate of World War I, while the Americans doubted that their inexperienced army could prevail against the first-rate German troops stationed in France. As an alternative FDR and Churchill decided to attack through "the soft underbelly of Europe" by first establishing supply and air bases in North Africa and then attacking Italy. Despite some American blunders on the battlefield, by the summer of 1943 the Allies had gained control of North Africa and invaded Sicily, as shown in the map "The European Theater" (**23.15**).

Italy's surrender on September 8, 1943, meant little, however. German forces invaded the Italian peninsula, saving Mussolini's regime and keeping Allied troops bogged down in a bloody campaign that lasted until the spring of 1945. When Mussolini tried to escape in 1945 with the retreating Germans, Italian resistance fighters captured him and his mistress, shot them, and strung them upside down in a

23.15 The European Theater The Soviet army fought alone in Europe until the United States invaded Italy in 1943 and joined with Great Britain to launch the D-Day invasions in 1944.

Why did the United States attack the Axis powers first in Italy, rather than France?

public square in Milan where resistance fighters had been executed.

In 1943 the Allies launched the first major incendiary attack of the war. The bombing raids on Hamburg, a major industrial German city, ignited a firestorm in the hot, dry conditions that killed 45,000 and wounded nearly 40,000. Germany's aerial attacks during the Battle of Britain in 1940–1941 had hardened British views about bombing civilians in Germany, while the Americans preferred trying to hit actual military and industrial installations. Dresden, home to key railroad lines, was the site of another devastating incendiary bombing raid in February 1945, which killed approximately 35,000 Germans. Although many American bombs failed to hit their precisely designated industrial or military targets, in fighting Germany, the United States never formally adopted terror bombing, the strategy of dropping high concentrations of bombs on civilian populations to create panic and misery.

In late November 1943 FDR and Churchill met with Stalin for the first time in Tehran, the capital of Iran, to discuss Allied strategy for the coming year. During the conference FDR privately described Stalin as "altogether quite impressive," and the president purposefully stayed in the Soviet Embassy to build a good rapport with the Soviet leader. Churchill remained more leery of Soviet intentions to expand its influence into Eastern Europe after the war. The Soviet's victory at Stalingrad (January–February 1943), a pivotal battle that put the Allies on the path to victory, buoyed optimism that the tide had turned in Russia's favor on the Eastern Front. Within a few months, the Soviets would also prevail in Leningrad, ending a 900-day German siege of the city that lasted from September 1941–January 1944. Churchill wanted to join the fight in the East by launching an Anglo-American invasion of the Balkans through the Adriatic Sea. FDR doubted that Americans would support a sustained campaign in Eastern Europe when the nation's traditional interest lay in defending Britain and France. In addition the president was reluctant to send American troops into a region that the USSR clearly intended to dominate after the war. The president was wary of antagonizing the Soviet Union when he still hoped to convince Stalin to declare war against Japan once the European war ended. Instead, the United States persuaded Britain to join the United States in an invasion of France in 1944.

The campaign in the Pacific followed a similar strategy of attacking Japan in the "soft underbelly" of its empire in the South Pacific. The Allies opened this campaign with successful, but difficult attacks on Guadalcanal in the Solomon Islands and on New Guinea. In early 1943 Japan accepted its defeat in the South Pacific by withdrawing its fleet and aircraft to a new defensive line that extended through Southeast Asia, the Philippines, and the Mariana Islands.

To keep up the pressure on Japan, the Allies decided to launch a two-pronged attack on Japanese forces in the Central and South Pacific. From the Central Pacific the Americans hoped to establish a naval blockade that cut Japan off from supplies in the south. The United States quickly took the Gilbert and Marshall Islands. During the subsequent invasion of the island of Saipan in the Marianas, the Americans destroyed so many Japanese naval aircraft in the Battle of the Philippine Sea (June 19–20, 1944) that the battle became known as "the Great Marianas Turkey Shoot." The final capture of the Mariana Islands in August 1944 put the United States, armed with massive and heavily-loaded B-29s that could travel up to 2,000 miles, within striking distance of Japan.

"I shall return," General Douglas MacArthur had proclaimed when FDR ordered him to head to Australia and leave his embattled troops on the Philippines in 1942. On October 20, 1944, he fulfilled this promise by wading ashore in the Leyte Gulf four hours after the first American force

23.16 General MacArthur's Return to the Philippines MacArthur used the press to publicize his return to the Philippines in 1944. Military photographers captured his purposeful stride ashore, and that evening MacArthur proclaimed in a radio address, "People of the Philippines: I have returned ... Rally to me."

How did the tide gradually turn in favor of the Allies in Europe and the Pacific?

23.17 **"A Wartime Souvenir"**
In 1944, *Life* magazine chose this photo as its picture of the week. The young woman's fiancé sent her a Japanese skull with an inscription that read: "This is a good Jap—a dead one picked up on the New Guinea beach." Collecting enemy body parts as war trophies was common among American troops fighting in Japan, but not in the European theater.

landed in a carefully choreographed act that MacArthur insisted on filming several times to get just right. To build morale and enhance his reputation as a fearless leader, MacArthur presented himself as part of the invasion force, a general who was willing to get his boots wet and resolutely press forward, as seen in this photo (**23.16**). The Battle of Leyte Gulf (October 23–25, 1944), the largest naval battle in history, ended with an American victory. It took until July 1945, however, to completely liberate the Philippines from isolated infantry garrisons.

With the war advancing well in the Pacific, Americans began to feel optimistic about achieving a swift victory. These hopes faded, however, when Japan switched from fighting a strategic war to waging a war of attrition. Mounting losses, Japan's leaders reasoned, would force the United States to the negotiating table. With conventional weapons like ships, guns, and planes in short supply, Japan introduced a set of suicidal battlefield tactics on land and sea in the fall of 1944 that dramatically intensified the struggle. In the western Caroline Islands, Japanese soldiers resolved to fight to the last man. Forcing the Americans to rout out every enemy soldier from an interlocking system of caves and bunkers prolonged the battle and raised American casualties. During the Battle of Leyte Gulf, the first kamikaze pilots plowed their planes into the decks of six American ships, setting off a cascade of explosions from the ships' gasoline and ordnance that damaged five and sank one.

A month later seaman James Fahey was on a ship under attack. He and the sailors battled for hours, shooting down a steady stream of incoming aircraft. "The explosions were terrific as the suicide planes exploded in the water . . . the water looked like it was on fire," Fahey wrote in his diary. Parts of the destroyed planes fell onto his ship, and during a lull in the action, the sailors went sifting through the debris for souvenirs. "The deck near my mount was covered with blood, guts, brains, tongues, scalps, hearts, arms etc. from the Jap pilots," Fahey recalled. Fahey watched men select body parts to preserve in alcohol and send home to relatives. Soldiers involved in the Pacific island–hopping campaigns exhibited a similar macabre interest in collecting Japanese soldiers' body parts. In May 1944 *Life* magazine published "A Wartime Souvenir," showing an attractive young woman writing a thank-you note to her fiancé for sending her a souvenir Japanese skull (**23.17**). "The armed forces disapprove strongly of this sort of thing," *Life* noted. Yet the image of this woman calmly contemplating her war trophy elicited no controversy. Instead, many Americans exorcised their own desire for revenge against Japan through such images. The press had to handle photographs of American war dead more carefully (see *Images as History: Combat Photography*, page 706).

The Final Push in Europe

On June 6, 1944, the Allies launched the D-Day invasion, their long-anticipated invasion of Normandy, a region of northern France, under the command of General Dwight D. Eisenhower. "The eyes of the world are upon you," the popular leader told his troops. Eisenhower, raised in a poor Jehovah Witness Kansas family, became a national hero for his successful planning and execution of the D-Day invasions and subsequent offensives through France and Germany. His achievements and sunny personality would make him an appealing postwar presidential candidate in 1952 (see Chapter 24).

Images as History

COMBAT PHOTOGRAPHY

War photography brings the realities of combat into the homes of ordinary citizens. How do pictures of combat force viewers to think about the overall meaning and worthiness of the conflict?

For the first year and a half of American involvement, when there was little good news to report, the military believed that photographs of dead American soldiers would weaken morale on the home front. In 1943 Allied victories in the South Pacific and North Africa raised spirits at home—perhaps a bit too much in the eyes of some officials. Aware of the long road ahead and the need for continued sacrifice on the home front, the War Department now approved the dissemination of bloody battlefield photographs.

In September 1943 *Life* magazine published a photograph of three American soldiers lying partially buried in the sand in New Guinea. In the accompanying editorial *Life* anticipated the public's shock at seeing the first photograph of American war dead. "Why print this picture, anyway, of three American boys dead upon an alien shore? Is it to hurt people? To be morbid?" *Life* editors wrote. "Those are not the answers. The reason is that words are never enough."

Magazine editors chose their images from an ever-increasing supply of casualty pictures. Two-thirds of the 291,557 American troops killed in battle during the war died in 1944–1945. Photographer Joe Rosenthal's "Old Glory Goes Up on Mt. Suribachi, Iwo Jima," a candid shot of five marines and one navy corpsman raising a flag on the Pacific Island of Iwo Jima on February 23, 1945, remains the most famous image from World War II. Rosenthal's Pulitzer Prize–winning photograph would inspire a Marine Corps statue, erected in Washington, D.C., in 1954.

Military censors forbade publication of photographs containing identifiable war dead or badly mutilated corpses, worried that such pictures might depress morale on the home front.

"Publication of photos showing some of our boys killed in action had a sobering effect on people and brought the realities of war closer to home," a satisfied War Department official noted.

"Here Lie Three Americans"

The image of six men working together to push the flag upright conveyed the teamwork necessary to defeat Japan, and that the uphill struggle to victory was not quite completed.

Critics later accused Rosenthal of staging this photo, a charge that he denied.

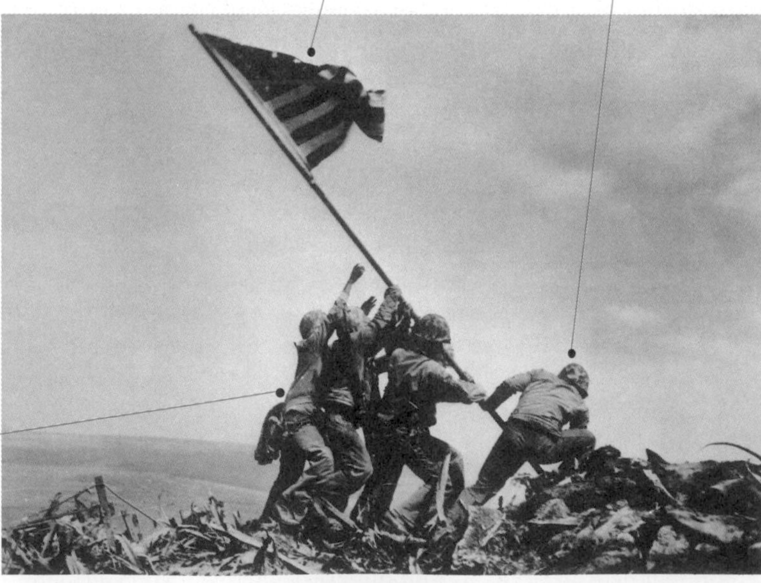

Three of the marines in Rosenthal's photograph died in the ensuing battle. The others returned home and toured the country in an overwhelmingly successful war bond campaign.

"Old Glory Goes Up on Mount Suribachi, Iwo Jima"

How did the political and military situation influence the way Americans viewed these photographs?

Although stormy weather made traversing the English Channel treacherous, and the Americans faced fierce resistance on Omaha Beach, the D-Day invasion was an overwhelming success. The heavy buildup for the attack, involving 175,000 troops, 6,000 aircraft, and 6,000 naval vessels, made complete surprise impossible. But the Allies had dramatically increased the invasion's chances of success by deceiving the Germans into expecting the attack to come farther north. Diversionary bombing, false agent reports, and misleading radio communications convinced the Germans to station the majority of their first-rate infantry divisions farther north. Hitler continued to hold these units in reserve even after the D-Day invasion began, certain that the Normandy landings were just a diversion. The German delay in responding gave the Allies the time they needed to establish a beachhead that stretched for 55 miles by the end of the first day.

Life photographer Robert Capa hit the beaches with the troops, living up to his famous statement, "If your pictures aren't good enough, you aren't close enough." Anxious to see Capa's photographs, a rushing darkroom technician used too much heat to dry the film and inadvertently melted nearly all his images. The excessive heat blurred the remaining few, creating a surreal aura to this instantly iconic image (**23.18**) of an American soldier struggling through the turbulent surf to reach the shore. Capa put down his camera long enough to pull this soldier to safety after a bullet struck him in the right shoulder.

It was still a long way from Normandy to Berlin, however. After two more months of hard fighting, the Allies finally began to push forward. On August 15, 1944, the Americans launched a second invasion through the south of France. Within a month these troops had joined with the Normandy invasion forces to establish a continuous Allied front from the English Channel to the German frontier. Hitler had no intention of going down without a fight. In December 1944 the Germans launched a massive counteroffensive. The Battle of the Bulge, so named for the Germans' pocket of penetration into Allied lines, was the largest battle fought by the American Army in Europe. Fighting in the snow and bitter cold, the Allies suffered 77,000 casualties before finally halting the German counterattack a month later.

"Two kinds of people are staying on this beach, the dead and those who are going to die."

Colonel GEORGE TAYLOR, urging his dazed troops forward on Omaha Beach during the D-Day invasions

When Roosevelt, Churchill, and Stalin met in February 1945 at Yalta, a town in the Ukraine, to discuss their next step, Roosevelt was fresh off an unprecedented fourth-term victory in the 1944 presidential election. The Republican candidate Thomas Dewey, a popular New York State governor, had attacked Roosevelt as a "tired old man" no longer up to the challenge of running the war. Roosevelt solidified support within the Democratic Party by replacing the controversial liberal Henry Wallace with Harry S Truman, a straight-talking moderate senator from Missouri, as his vice-presidential candidate. The selection of an acceptable vice-presidential candidate was important to Democratic Party bosses who feared that the ill Roosevelt might not live to complete a fourth term in office. Suffering from advancing heart disease and the strain of war, Roosevelt nevertheless managed to display renewed energy during the campaign, convincing Americans not to "change horses in mid-stream." He won 432 to 99 votes in the Electoral College, receiving 54 percent of the popular vote.

23.18 D-Day Invasion, 1944 Robert Capa's grainy photograph conveyed the chaos and danger American soldiers faced when they hit the beaches in Normandy, France.

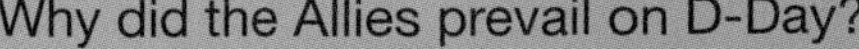

Why did the Allies prevail on D-Day?

At the Yalta Conference the larger question of how to defeat Germany was behind the Allies. The issues now on the table included governing postwar Germany, ensuring victory over Japan, and maintaining peace in the postwar world. At the conference FDR secured a Soviet promise to enter the war against Japan three months after Germany capitulated. In return Stalin wanted the United States and Britain to grant the Soviet Union territorial concessions in Japan and China. For the moment FDR acceded to Soviet control of Eastern Europe, but secured a pledge from Stalin to hold free elections in a liberated Poland.

The decision at the Yalta Conference to name the United States, Britain, France, China, and the USSR as permanent members of the proposed United Nations Security Council, each with the power to veto any resolution, cleared the way to officially create a United Nations (UN) to replace the now-defunct League of Nations. Delegates from fifty nations met in San Francisco between April 25 and June 26, 1945, to found the UN, an international organization that offered nations a place to discuss their differences and collectively promote economic development and peace throughout the world. To ensure that the United States joined the UN, its creators made participation in UN peacekeeping missions voluntary. In addition the Security Council veto gave the United States (and other major powers) a way to control UN activities. Unlike after World War I, when the United States failed to join the League of Nations, the United States was one of the first countries to join. The UN subsequently built its headquarters in New York City.

Now unstoppable in Europe, the Allies crossed the Rhine River into Germany in March. On April 30, 1945, Hitler committed suicide in a bunker 55 feet under the ground in Berlin. After dictating his will and marrying his longtime companion Eva Braun, Hitler bit into a cyanide capsule and shot himself in the head. Two days later Russian soldiers entered Berlin, where they destroyed the bunker and took Hitler's burned remains so an autopsy could confirm he was dead. Germany surrendered unconditionally on May 7, 1945.

America's Response to the Holocaust

In the spring of 1945, Allied troops began liberating the concentration camps holding Jews, Poles, prisoners of war, and a host of other groups that the German state considered enemies or racially inferior. News of the Final Solution, Hitler's plan to systematically murder the Jews and other "lesser" peoples, first reached the West in August 1942. Along with ten other nations, the United States condemned "in the strongest possible terms this bestial policy of cold-blooded extermination." During the war mainstream American newspapers, fearful of reporting falsified atrocity stories amid a glut of war news, had published little about the **Holocaust**, the term used to describe this Nazi-engineered extermination. The United States did little initially to aid European Jews. In January 1944, however, the Secretary of the Treasury, Henry Morgenthau, who was Jewish, protested to FDR that anti-Semitism within the State Department had thwarted a plan to ransom 70,000 Rumanian Jews with private funds, leaving the United States open to charges that it was acquiescing to the "murder of the Jews." FDR immediately issued an executive order establishing the War Refugee Board (WRB). Over the next year the WRB saved approximately 200,000 lives by convincing Rumania and Hungary to stop deportations and helping Jews and other victims of Nazi persecution escape or survive in hiding. *The Holocaust* special feature depicts both the response of the United States to the Holocaust and the scope of German atrocities.

Pressed by some Jewish groups to undertake a dramatic rescue of Europe's Jews by bombing either the concentration camps or the railroads leading to them, Roosevelt demurred. He argued that any diversion of military resources from the ultimate goal of winning the war would only prolong the Jews' suffering. In February 1944 the War Department decided not to send armed forces to rescue "victims of enemy oppression unless such rescues are the direct result of military operations conducted with the objective of defeating the armed forces of the enemy." Bombing Auschwitz, the main Nazi extermination camp in Poland, became a real possibility only in the summer of 1944. In August Allied planes dropped more than 1,000 bombs on synthetic-oil plants less than 5 miles from Auschwitz.

Whether the Allies should have also targeted the gas chambers has provoked heated debate since the war. Advocates of bombing the camps argue that destroying the railroad lines leading to Auschwitz or its gas chambers would have slowed down the killing as liberating Allied troops approached the camps, perhaps saving as many as 100,000 Jews. These would have included Anne Frank, a thirteen-year-old German refugee who was sent to Auschwitz after her

What significant decisions were reached at the 1945 Yalta Conference?

The Holocaust

> "I have gotten rid of the Jews."
> ADOLF HITLER, 1944

The United States reacted slowly to Hitler's persecution of Jews in the Depression-plagued thirties. Strict immigration quotas and anti-Semitism limited visas for Jewish refugees fleeing Nazi persecution. After Kristallnacht, a 1938 German rampage against Jewish businesses and homes, FDR granted more Jews asylum, but acceded to public concern over increasing immigration dramatically. In 1939 the United States turned back the *St. Louis*, a ship carrying Jewish refugees who did not have visas to enter the country. Of all nations, the United States, despite its strict immigration quotas, accepted the largest number of Jewish refugees fleeing Nazi persecution. Once at war FDR refused to bomb the concentration camps from the air, worried that any diversion from attacking the German military would lengthen the war. Instead, American ground troops liberated major concentration camps in Western Europe, including Buchenwald, Dachau, and Mauthausen. The Germans killed over 6 million Jews, 3 million Soviet prisoners of war, 2 million non-Jewish Poles, nearly 200,000 disabled individuals, 10,000 Jehovah Witnesses, and an undetermined number of homosexuals.

German-run Concentration Camps in World War II

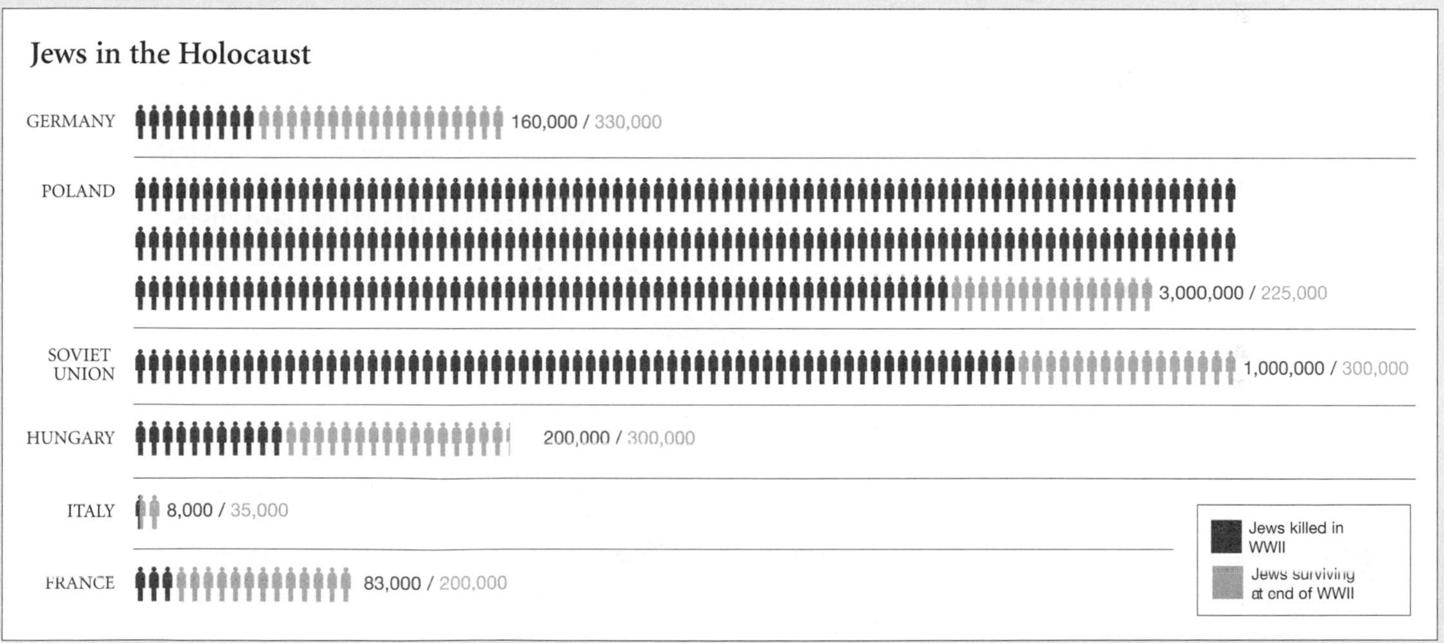

America and the Holocaust

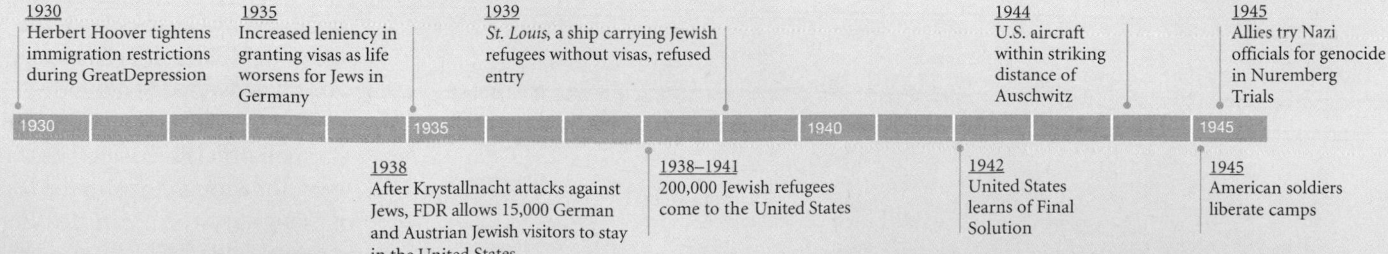

What insights does this data offer on the scope of the Holocaust and the American response?

> "The wrongs which we seek to condemn and punish have been so calculated, so malignant, and so devastating, that civilization cannot tolerate their being ignored, because it cannot survive their being repeated."
>
> American prosecutor, Supreme Court Justice ROBERT JACKSON, in opening the Nuremberg War Crimes Trials

family's capture in Amsterdam and whose journal of her experience in hiding, *The Diary of Anne Frank*, became a postwar literary classic. Detractors note the determination of the Nazis to use any means possible to slaughter the Jews, including mass executions by firing squads and forced marches, until the very end of the war.

As the camps were liberated, reporters tried through words and pictures to convey how 6 million Jews had met their deaths. Even though Americans had grown accustomed to seeing photos of war dead, nothing prepared them for images from the concentration camps. American commanders invited the press into the camps to head off any possible denials over the scope of the Holocaust. Photographs of concentration camps were, one reporter wrote, "so horrible that no newspaper normally would use them, but they were less horrible than the reality." Soldiers set themselves up as witnesses (a term used to describe both survivors and liberators) who could personally vouch for the extent of the horrors by posing in photographs before piles of corpses, next to the ovens used to cremate bodies, or in showers that dispersed cyanide gas instead of water to asphyxiate victims. "You can photograph results of suffering but never suffering itself," observed one British politician.

By documenting the act of discovering Nazi atrocities, witness photographs helped Americans share the horror that soldiers felt. The American military also posted photographs of concentration camp atrocities in German towns and villages for civilians to see, but many American commanders went further. In the photo shown here (**23.19**), American soldiers assembled German civilians before a truckload of corpses to listen to a lecture on the barbarity. Forcing German civilians to view the carnage with their own eyes, and in some cases bury the bodies, was part of a deliberate Allied campaign to make all Germans accept responsibility for their nation's war crimes.

After the war the Allies jointly tried twenty-two Nazi leaders in the Nuremberg War Crimes Trials. In these trials individual Germans were charged with starting the war, authorizing the killing of prisoners of war, and orchestrating the wartime genocide against victims who mostly came from nations occupied by Germany (see the "Jews in Holocaust" chart, page 709). The United States independently tried thousands of other German officials as well. These trials were not enough to calm the fears of many survivors. Many left Europe to resettle elsewhere.

23.19 German Civilians Viewing Corpses in a Concentration Camp Photographs from liberated concentration camps, like this one from Buchenwald, Germany, shocked the world. American military commanders forced German civilians, who professed ignorance about the Final Solution, to view and bury the dead.

How did images instruct Americans about the meaning of the Holocaust and their role as liberators?

Ending the Pacific War

Germany was now under Allied control, but in the Pacific the war raged on. There the fighting took a desperate turn in 1945, and each victory cost the United States dearly. Despite a mounting death toll, American troops edged closer to Japan and officials began planning an invasion of the mainland. News of a successful atomic bomb test detonation in the New Mexico desert dramatically altered existing political and military calculations on how to achieve victory. Employing this new, terrible weapon eventually generated conflicting views within the United States over the ethics of atomic warfare.

Edging Closer to Japan

Japan's use of "cave and bunker" tactics on land and kamikazes at sea dramatically raised the cost of capturing Iwo Jima (February 19–March 26, 1945) and Okinawa (April 1–June 21, 1945), the last two islands that remained before the United States could launch an invasion of the Japanese homeland. Battles on Iwo Jima and Okinawa produced some of the toughest fighting of the war.

The Americans coveted the 7-mile pork–chop–shaped island of Iwo Jima for its airstrips, both to stop Japanese fighter planes from harassing B-29s headed to Japan and to provide emergency landing fields for crippled B-29s returning from mainland bombing raids. In their conquest of Iwo Jima, the Americans took only 216 prisoners out of 21,000 enemy troops, the rest perishing in the fighting. As the marines shot flamethrowers into caves to extract hiding enemy soldiers, "the scene became wild and terrible," one correspondent recalled. "More Japs rushed screaming from the caves. They tumbled over the rocks, their clothes and bodies burning fiercely." The capture of Okinawa, needed as a staging area for the actual invasion of Japan, was equally bloody. Weeks of kamikaze attacks alone took the lives of 5,000 sailors, while ground troops squared off against an entrenched enemy determined to fight to the last man.

As on Iwo Jima vast numbers of Japanese soldiers (70,000) perished. In this battle, however, an equal number of Japanese civilians either took their own lives (they had been told of mass rape and torture if taken prisoner) or were killed by Japanese soldiers if they tried to surrender. The Americans suffered 75,000 casualties in capturing Okinawa. With the actual invasion of the Japanese homeland up next, the Americans feared facing, in the words of Harry Truman, "an Okinawa from one end of Japan to the other."

Meanwhile American pilots brought the war home to the Japanese people from newly established air bases in the Marianas. When the bombing campaign began in earnest in the Pacific theater in 1945, the United States quickly abandoned efforts to differentiate between civilian and military targets as it had in Germany. "There are no civilians in Japan," declared one air force official. "We are making War and making it in the all-out fashion which saves American lives, shortens the agony which War is, and seeks to bring about an enduring peace." The United States targeted sixty-seven Japanese cities for incendiary bombing in 1945, resulting in the destruction of 187 square miles and approximately 300,000 deaths. During one night-time raid the entire city of Toyama burned to the ground. The most destructive air attack of the war came on March 9–10, 1945, when incendiary bombs dropped on Tokyo ignited fires that American bombers kept going by spreading gasoline and chemicals over the city. This attack destroyed 16 square miles and killed nearly 90,000 Japanese—more than would perish from the atomic bomb blast over Hiroshima five months later.

Dropping the Atomic Bomb

Franklin D. Roosevelt died at the age of 65 of a cerebral hemorrhage on April 12, 1945, while at his cottage in Warm Springs, Georgia. Throngs of mourners lined railroad tracks and city streets as the casket holding FDR's remains traveled first to Washington, D.C., for funeral services in the White House and then to his final resting spot at his home in Hyde Park, New York. Throughout the grieving nation many Americans could barely remember a time when FDR had not been president.

FDR's firm grip on power had kept his vice president Harry Truman in the dark about the four-year, $20 billion **Manhattan Project**, the code-named secret government research program established to

What new tactics raised the death toll in the Pacific war?

produce the atomic bomb. Thrust overnight into the presidency, Truman faced a host of critical strategic decisions in Europe and the Pacific, none more important than what to do with the newly developed atomic bomb. In mid-July 1945 the United States exploded its first atomic bomb in the New Mexico desert. *Choices and Consequences: How to Use the Atomic Bomb* traces Truman's options and the consequences of his decision to use the bomb against Japan.

> "The crux of the matter is whether total war in its present form is justifiable, even when it serves a just purpose."
>
> German Jesuit Priest in Nagasaki, when the atomic bomb was dropped

On August 6, 1945, a B-29 bomber christened the *Enola Gay* dropped an atomic bomb on the Japanese city of Hiroshima. As pilot Captain Paul Tibbets turned the *Enola Gay* away from Hiroshima, Sergeant George Caron snapped several photographs, giving Americans their first look at the telltale mushroom cloud formation that came to signify nuclear annihilation.Three days later, acting on a standing order to use the atomic bomb "as made ready," an American plane dropped a second atomic bomb on Nagasaki.

Saved from firebomb attacks because of their minimal military value, Hiroshima and Nagasaki presented virgin ground for a clear demonstration of the bomb's force. The United States wanted to make a profound impression on the Japanese. Secretary of War Stimson believed "the atomic bomb was more than a weapon of terrible destruction; it was a psychological weapon." The firebombed ruins of cities like Tokyo, therefore, presented a much less appealing target for demonstrating the full power of a nuclear bomb.

American soldiers scheduled to take part in the planned invasion gave little thought to civilian victims on the ground. "When we learned to our astonishment that we would not be obliged in a few months to rush up the beaches near Tokyo assault-firing while being machine-gunned, mortared, and shelled, for all the practiced phlegm of our tough facades we broke down and cried with relief and joy. We were going to live. We were going to grow to adulthood after all," recalled literary critic Paul Fussell in a 1988 essay, "Thank God for the Atom Bomb."

The Final Surrender

Truman and his advisers recognized that American possession of the atomic bomb was certain to reshape postwar relations between the United States and the Soviet Union. In the minds of several key presidential advisers, America's nuclear monopoly increased the chances of limiting Soviet influence over Eastern Europe and ending the Pacific war without any Soviet help. Soviet spies in the Manhattan Project had already alerted Moscow of the bomb's existence when Truman finally told Stalin in July 1945 at the Potsdam Conference, held near Berlin, that the United States had developed a potent new weapon. When the first bomb destroyed Hiroshima, the Soviets quickly invaded Manchuria on August 8 to seize their planned territorial objectives before the war ended.

By August 10 the combination of two atomic bomb blasts and the Soviet entry into the war caused Japanese Emperor Hirohito to take the unprecedented step of imposing his own views on official policy. Traditionally the emperor simply approved decisions taken by his cabinet. With the peace and militarist factions within his government still strongly divided over whether to make one last stand against the Allies, Hirohito pleaded for peace. After several key military leaders accepted the emperor's wishes, Japan sued for peace with the condition that the Imperial Institution remain. Truman agreed, thereby modifying the original goal of unconditional surrender. Could a Japanese surrender have come sooner if the United States had guaranteed the emperor's office earlier? Before August 6 Truman likened keeping Hirohito to allowing Hitler to remain in power, and he believed that the American people would never accept these terms for peace. In mid-August, however, Truman concluded that letting Hirohito tell the Japanese people to lay down their arms would facilitate the occupation of Japan. Hirohito paved the way for a peaceful surrender when he addressed the Japanese people on the radio for the first time ever, calling on them to accept his decision. The formal surrender took place on September 2 aboard the battleship *Missouri* in Tokyo

How did the war against Japan finally end?

Choices and Consequences

HOW TO USE THE ATOMIC BOMB

President Harry Truman considered the bomb a legitimate weapon to use alongside the more conventional tactics of terror bombing, an economic blockade, and a planned invasion of Japan. He did, however, face some choices over how to exploit this new weapon to meet his goals of securing an unconditional surrender from Japan, saving American lives, and establishing American postwar supremacy over the Soviet Union.

Choices

1. Demonstrate the bomb's destructive power in a trial demonstration on an uninhabited area to convince Japan to surrender.
2. Drop one atomic bomb and give Japan time to react.
3. Drop the two atomic bombs in American possession.
4. Inform the Soviet Union of the bomb's existence before dropping it.

Decision

Truman chose to drop both atomic bombs on virgin sites to magnify the psychological shock of one bomb causing so much destruction. Senior advisers rejected a test demonstration of the bomb as impractical. Truman vaguely informed Stalin of "a new weapon of unusual destructive force," unaware that spies in the Manhattan Project had already alerted Stalin of the bomb's existence.

Consequences

On August 6, 1945 "Little Boy," the atomic bomb dropped on Hiroshima, destroyed three-fourths of the city and killed 80,000 people instantly. "Fat Man" destroyed two-fifths of Nagasaki and killed 35,000 people on August 9. The Emperor announced Japan's surrender on August 14. Truman's attempted secrecy increased Soviet distrust of the United States and unleashed a nuclear arms race between the two nations.

Continuing Controversies

Should the United States have dropped the bomb?

Supporters of Truman's decision claim that dropping the bomb ended the war. It saved 1 million American lives by making an invasion of Japan unnecessary and convinced the Japanese government to end the war. Not all supporters, however, agree that the second bomb on Nagasaki was militarily necessary. Critics counter that the bomb was not needed to end the war. Traditional bombing, the blockade, and Soviet invasion of Manchuria would have ended the war without the planned invasion, critics claim. Because the United States accepted a modified surrender that allowed Japan to retain the Emperor, abandoning the demand for unconditional surrender earlier may have convinced Japan to surrender sooner. Finally, some detractors accuse Truman of using the bomb mainly to curtail Soviet territorial ambitions in postwar Europe and Asia.

Bomb over Nagasaki

Why does so much controversy surround the dropping the atomic bomb and not conventional weapons?

Bay, attended by delegates from Japan and the Allied nations. The deadliest war in human history, whose death toll is charted in "The Human Cost of Global War" (**23.20**), had finally ended.

When news of the Japanese surrender hit the United States, Americans swarmed into the streets to celebrate the good news. "Every female was grabbed and kissed by men in uniform," recalled one woman who joined the crowd in Times Square, New York City. The celebrants included a sailor whose impromptu kiss with a passing nurse was captured in *Life* photographer Alfred Eisenstaedt's candid "Kiss in Times Square" photograph, known as "the smack seen round the world"(**23.21**). Eisenstaedt never revealed the identity of the kissing couple, preferring to let their shielded faces symbolize the exuberance of young men and women who had survived the war. In the ensuing years three nurses and eleven sailors stepped forward to claim that they were the individuals in the photograph.

Hirohito escaped facing trial as a war criminal, but the Allies intended to punish other Japanese leaders for their part in the war. In the few weeks between the Japanese surrender and the Allied occupation of Japan, more than 1,000 officials and officers committed suicide and others destroyed thousands of documents concerning Japanese mistreatment of prisoners of war and massacres of civilians in occupied countries. Nonetheless the Allies convicted thousands of Japanese in a series of war crimes trials throughout East Asia, including twenty-eight major Japanese leaders in Tokyo.

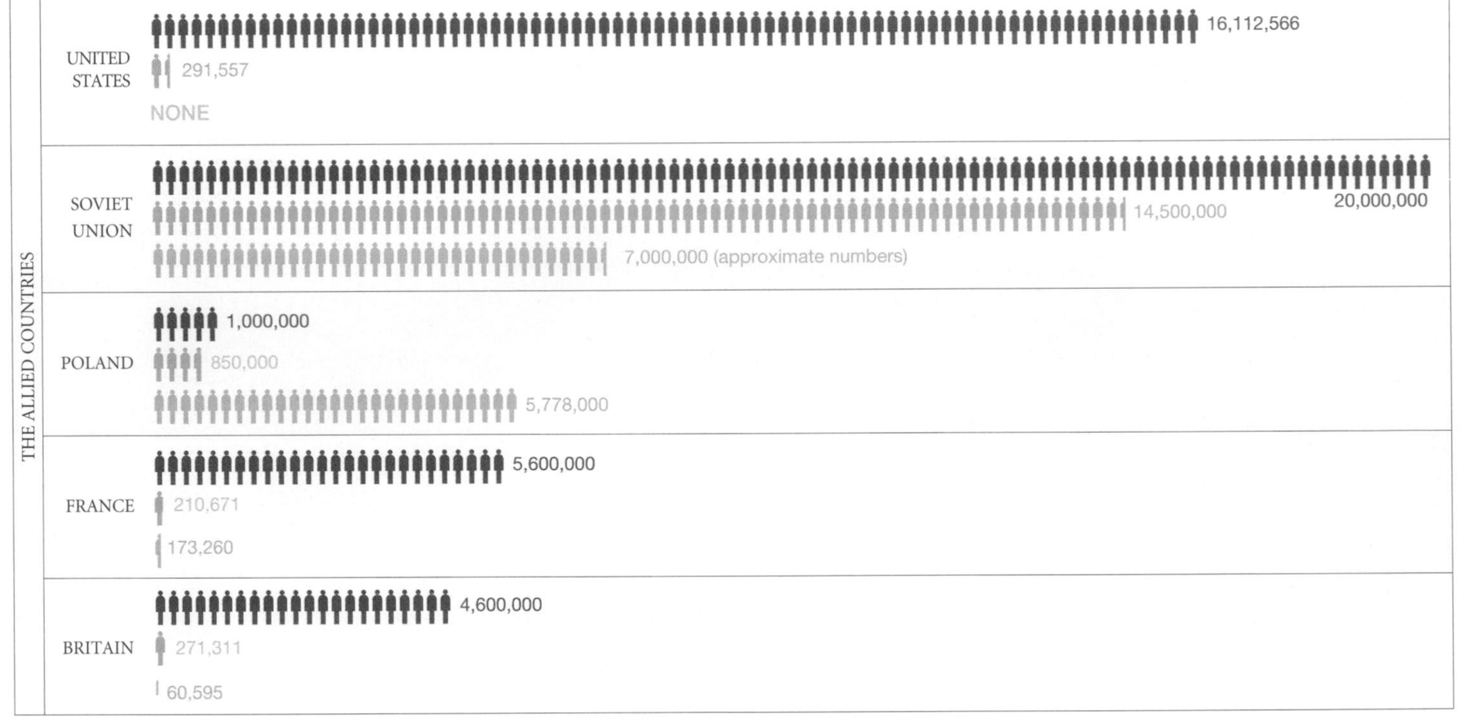

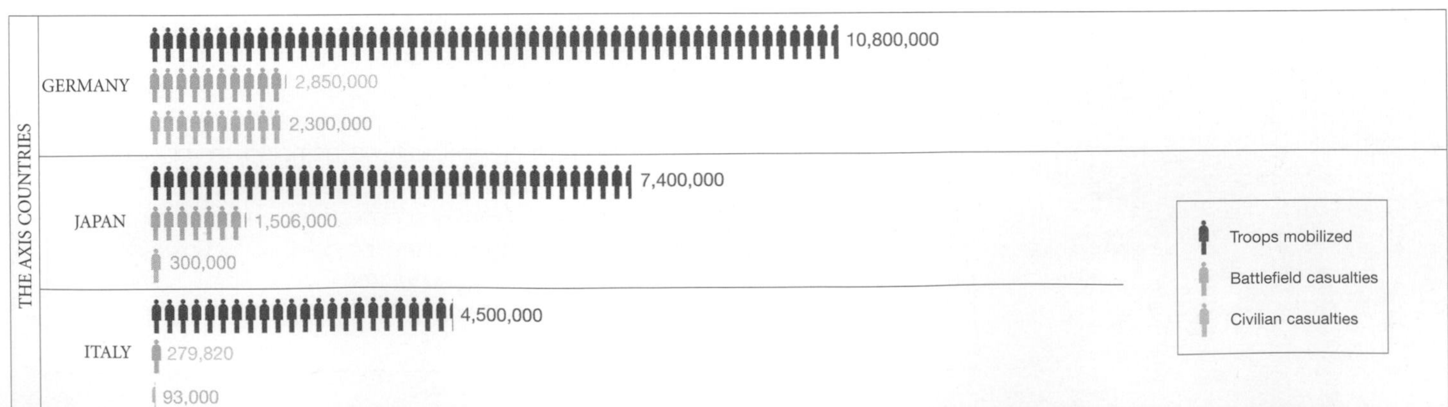

23.20 The Human Cost of Global War Worldwide wartime casualties, those killed and wounded, numbered in the millions.

How might this distribution of wartime casualties shape the postwar world?

23.21 Kiss in Times Square
Jubilation greeted the news that Japan had surrendered. Two strangers shared a passionate kiss in Times Square, conveying the life-affirming energy that filled the air.

Conclusion

Combat, genocide, and terror bombing took millions of lives during World War II. Americans could rightly see themselves as having both suffered and caused the war's deadly violence. After two years of debating conflicting visions of how best to help Britain defeat Germany in Europe, the impetus for war came from the other side of the globe when Japan attacked Pearl Harbor. Fighting on multiple fronts, against enemies that took modern warfare to a new level of brutality, the United States eventually found itself willing to adopt an ends-justifies-the-means approach to winning the war.

At home the U.S. government placed Japanese Americans in internment camps, mounted a massive propaganda campaign to rally support for the war, and took control of the economy by rationing scarce commodities. Americans became accustomed to seeing photographs of death and destruction, but nothing prepared the public for the shock of the Holocaust. The cruelty unleashed during the war and the deadly power of the atom bomb changed the position of the United States in the world, giving the nation new moral and strategic reasons to stay engaged in world affairs after its victory against Germany and Japan.

During the war millions of rural Americans moved to cities, married women entered the workplace in record numbers, and civil rights activists scored significant victories. As men came home from war and Americans rushed to spend their wartime savings, the expected period of peace failed to materialize. Instead, the United States became immediately embroiled in a Cold War with the Soviet Union. For the second time in the same decade, Americans confronted the challenges of exercising world leadership. This time, however, Americans faced the threat of nuclear annihilation.

CHAPTER REVIEW

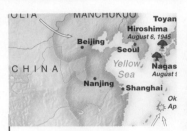

1937

Japan attacks China
Initiates Japan's expansionist drive in East Asia

1939

Germany invades Poland
Beginning of World War II

Neutrality Acts completed
Restrictions on arms sales reflected strong non-interventionist sentiments

1940

France falls to Germany
Completes Hitler's conquest of continental Europe

Economic sanctions against Japan
FDR attempts to halt Japanese aggression

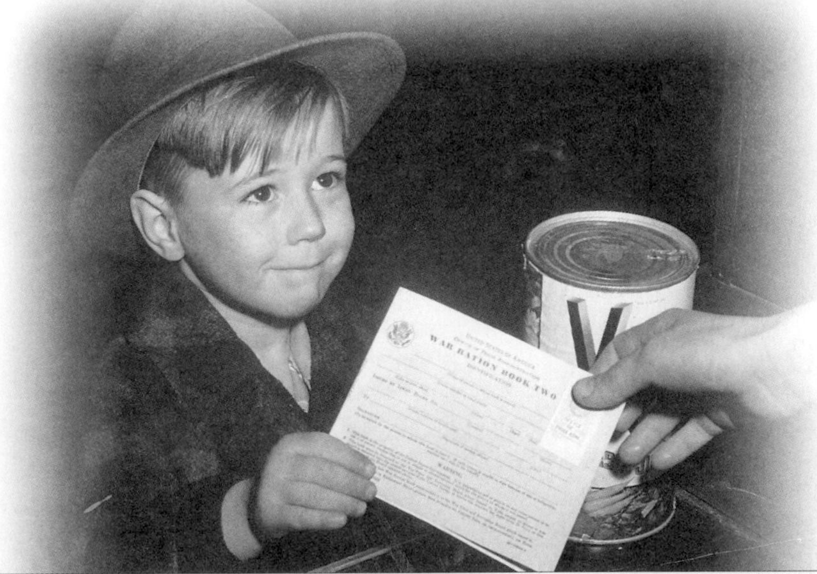

Review Questions

1. What conflicting visions did Americans offer in response to the expansionist drives of Germany and Japan? How did they influence the American path to war?
2. How did visual images influence Americans' views of the war and their enemies?
3. How did the war affect racial, labor, and gender relations on the home front? What conflicting visions emerged?
4. What distinct strategic challenges and battlefield conditions did the United States face in the Pacific and European theaters? How did the United States prevail against Japan and Germany?
5. Why did the United States drop the atomic bomb?

1941

Lend-Lease begins
Interventionist vision prevails as America offers economic aid to Allied side

U.S. ships exchange gunfire with German U-boats
Beginning of unofficial shooting war with Germany in the Atlantic Ocean

Japanese attack Pearl Harbor
United States officially enters World War II

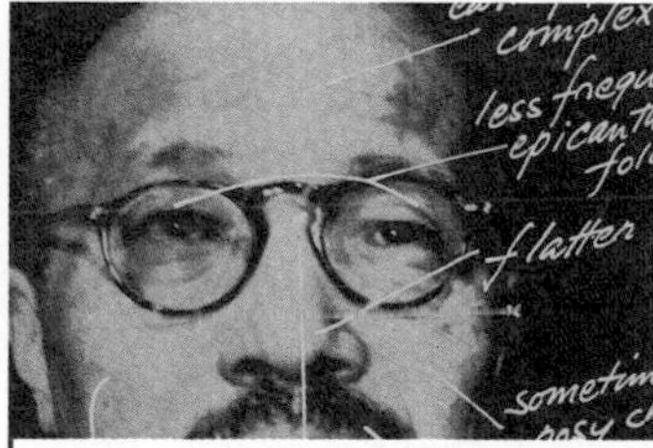

1942

FDR issues Executive Order 9066
Creation of Japanese American internment camps

Battle of Midway
Puts Japan on defensive in Pacific naval war

U.S. government learns of Final Solution
Limited exposure of Hitler's plan to exterminate the Jews

1944

D-Day landings
Beginning of Anglo-American march to Berlin

Supreme Court upholds constitutionality of internment camps
Rules that national security outweighs civil rights

1945

American troops enter concentration camps
Published images confirm German atrocities

FDR dies
Harry Truman assumes presidency

Germany surrenders
End of European war

United States drops atomic bomb on Hiroshima and Nagasaki
Ends war in Pacific, initiates nuclear arms race

Key Terms

non-interventionists Those urging the nation to stay out of overseas conflicts. **686**

interventionists Those advocating direct engagement in overseas conflicts. **686**

fascist state A type of dictatorial regime that arose in Germany, Italy, and Spain that glorified the state over the individual. **686**

Neutrality Acts A series of laws from 1935 to 1939 that restricted arms sales, loans, and transport of goods with nations at war. **687**

"cash and carry" A policy that required belligerent nations to pay cash for goods and transport them on their own ships. **687**

Munich Conference (1938) Hoping to avoid war, Britain and France agreed to let Germany occupy the Sudetenland, a German-speaking part of Czechoslovakia. **687**

Axis Name for nations fighting the Allies, including Germany, Italy and Japan. **688**

Allies (World War II) Name for powers fighting Germany, eventually including the United States, Britain, France, and the Soviet Union. **688**

Lend-Lease A 1941 policy that circumvented "cash and carry" by loaning rather than selling arms to the Allies. **689**

Pearl Harbor A U.S. naval base in Hawaii that the Japanese attacked on December 7, 1941. **690**

internment camps Camps in the United States that held people of Japanese descent under armed guard in isolated areas. **694**

double-victory campaign Civil rights call for victory against both fascism overseas and racial prejudice at home. **699**

zoot-suiters Name given to Mexican American youths who wore oversize suits. **700**

Holocaust German-engineered wartime extermination of Jews and other peoples that Germans considered inferior. **708**

Manhattan Project Secret U.S. wartime project to develop an atomic bomb. **711**

CHAPTER

24

A Divided World

The Early Cold War, 1945–1963

Origins of the Cold War p. 720

"Communism is on the march on a worldwide scale, which only America can stop."

Senator ARTHUR VANDENBERG, April 26, 1946

As World War II ended, Soviet and American troops, converging from different directions, met and shook hands on a bridge spanning the Elbe River in Germany. Each side was pleasantly surprised by this first encounter with their wartime ally. "They looked like ordinary people. We had imagined something different," recalled one Soviet soldier of American troops. "I guess we didn't know what to expect from the Russians," an American soldier said after the meeting. "If you put an American uniform on them, they could have been American!" Within two years the lost promise of this friendly encounter was obvious to all. A 1947 U.S. propaganda film replayed footage of this historic meeting and struck a lightning bolt across the frozen image of Soviet and American soldiers shaking hands. "Here two worlds actually met," the narrator thundered, "but this coalition was to be torn asunder" by Soviet postwar incursions in Eastern Europe that the United States viewed as part of a Soviet plan for global conquest.

In the decade after the Allies' victory against Hitler, relations between the United States and the Soviet Union soured dramatically. As the contours of the Cold War between the United States and the Soviet Union took shape, two competing ideological visions, an escalating nuclear arms race, and confrontations in Europe and Asia, including a war in Korea, heightened fears that another world war was in the making.

From 1946 to 1965 most Americans viewed the world as sharply divided into free and totalitarian societies. American leaders proclaimed that the United States was engaged in an epic struggle with the Soviet Union over the future of humankind. Protecting the world from the menace of Soviet-led communism became a key American foreign policy goal in this era. Americans fought the Cold War at home as well, where citizens expressed differing views on whether government tactics in rooting out Soviet spies undermined American democracy or saved it. On the other side of the ideological divide, Soviet leaders developed an abiding distrust of Western motives as they sought to counter the American nuclear advantage with territorial and technological gains. As each nation struggled to extend its world influence, Americans once again confronted the crucial question of defining their nation's role in the world.

What was the significance of this brief 1945 encounter between U.S. and Soviet soldiers?

Fighting Communism: Cold and Hot War p. 729

BURN
ALL
REDS

Spies in Our Midst p. 737

ACHTUNG!

Averting Nuclear War p. 742

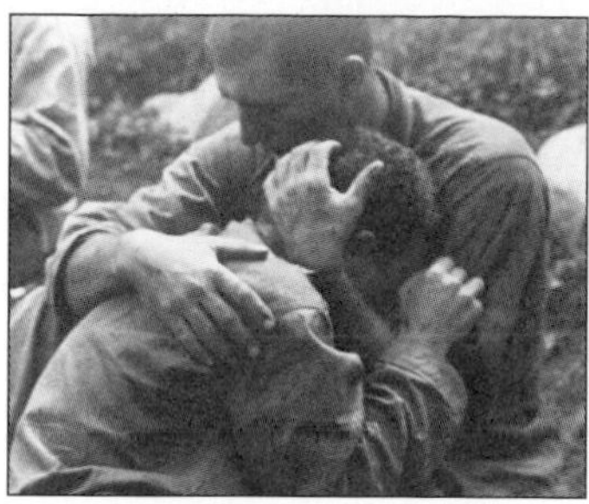

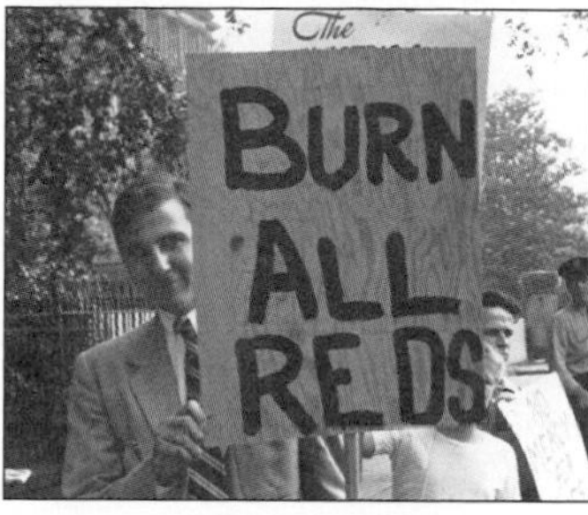

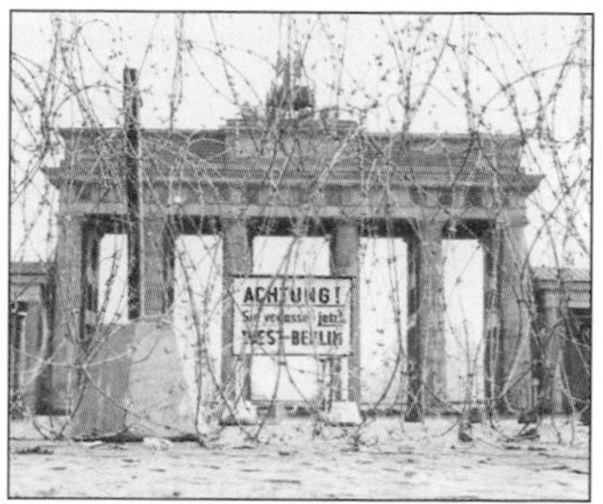

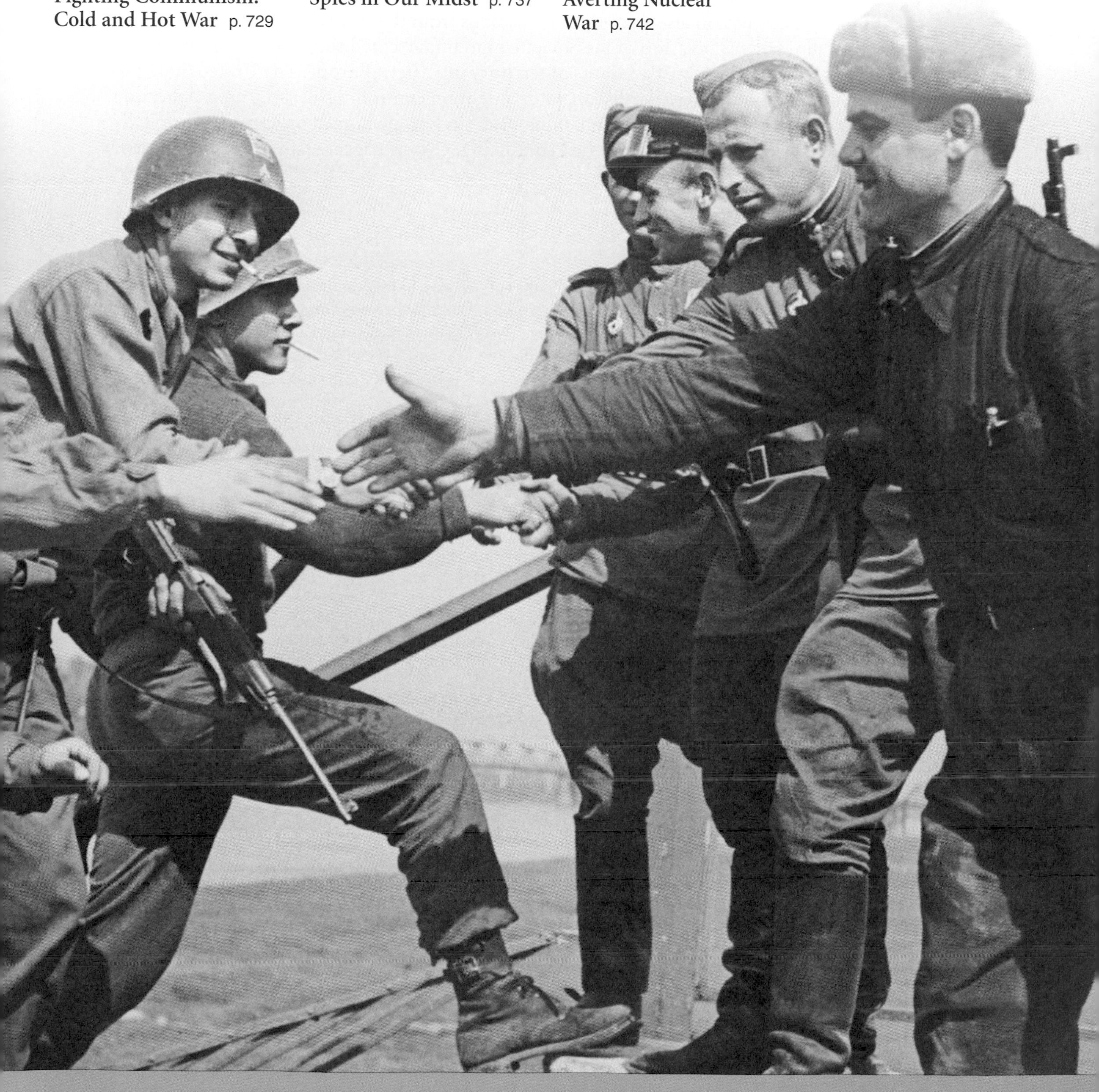

Origins of the Cold War

The United States and the Soviet Union worked effectively together in World War II to defeat Adolf Hitler, but each nation had dramatically different visions of the postwar world. The United States remained dedicated to free markets and democracy, while the Soviet Union embraced a Marxist vision that eschewed private property ownership and celebrated concentrated state authority. Each nation also drew different lessons from the recent war. For the Soviet leader Josef Stalin, Hitler's invasion of the Soviet Union underscored the need to secure his nation's borders by controlling vast amounts of territory in Eastern Europe. The United States feared that Stalin was another Hitler-like dictator, intent on controlling all of Europe. American political leaders believed that maintaining peace in Europe hinged on spreading capitalism and democracy. These differing, often conflicting, visions triggered an immediate postwar clash between the former allies.

Differing Goals in the Postwar World

The origins of the Cold War hark back to World War II. The victory against Hitler came at a huge cost for the Soviet Union. An estimated twenty-five million Soviet soldiers and civilians died, almost ninety times the 291,551 Americans who perished in combat. Germany had attacked the Soviet Union twice in the last thirty years, a fact that contributed to Stalin's obsession with protecting his nation from future attack. Stalin also suspected that the Americans and British had delayed opening up a second front in Europe (see Chapter 23)

24.1 Soviet Soldier Raises Flag over Reichstag, 1945
The Soviet triumph over Germany in World War II came at a high cost for both nations. Stalin sought future security for his nation by keeping war-destroyed Germany weak and installing friendly regimes throughout Eastern Europe.

What important symbolism does this photograph contain regarding the Soviet victory over Germany?

> "I have never been talked to like that in my life,"
> Soviet foreign minister VYACHESLAV MOLOTOV to Truman
>
> "Carry out your agreements and you won't get talked to like that."
> TRUMAN'S retort, angered over the Soviet's refusal to hold Democratic elections in postwar Poland

to further weaken the Soviet Union, causing him to distrust of the United States. This photo (**24.1**) of a soldier waving the Soviet flag from the roof of the Reichstag, the German parliament building, above the ruins of Berlin, illustrated Germany's complete defeat at the end of World War II. It also represented a past that the Soviet Union had no intention of repeating. To protect his nation's borders, Stalin installed friendly Communist governments throughout Eastern Europe to create a buffer zone between Germany and the Soviet Union. He also tried to keep Germany as weak as possible by carting off German heavy machinery to the Soviet Union, disarming the Germany military, and requiring large reparation payments.

In the postwar era Stalin fully expected to retain his firm grip on power within the Soviet Union. Standing only 5 feet tall with a thin mustache, yellowed teeth, and a pockmarked face, Stalin was not physically imposing. In this case, however, images were deceiving. "An unforewarned visitor would never have guessed what depths of calculation, ambition, love of power, jealously, cruelty and sly vindictiveness lurked behind this unpretentious façade," one American diplomat noted. Stalin had been responsible for the deaths of nearly ten million Soviet citizens before World War II, a result of failed agricultural policies that created widespread famine and relentless executions of all suspected political opponents. The Soviet dictator was willing to sacrifice the lives of countless others to achieve his new territorial objectives.

The postwar goals on the American side reflected lingering dismay over the nation's failure to prevent the rise of expansionist regimes in Japan and Germany during the 1930s. Before his death in April 1945, President Franklin D. Roosevelt had argued that American leadership in the newly formed United Nations (UN) could promote a peaceful future by deterring and punishing any aggression before it spun out of control. Roosevelt also stressed the importance of preventing another global depression like the one that had helped bring Hitler to power and had fueled non-interventionist sentiment in the United States.

By themselves these differing ideas on how to maintain peace in Europe did not necessarily guarantee a future clash between the United States and the Soviet Union. During the war the United States and Britain had accepted that the Soviet Union would exert considerable postwar political influence over Eastern Europe. FDR and British Prime Minister Winston Churchill, however, had tried to rein in the Soviet dictator by making him promise to hold free elections in the region. Stalin had offered some backing for Western postwar schemes as well, agreeing to support the United Nations and to a joint occupation of a defeated Germany. When Harry Truman assumed the presidency after Roosevelt's death, even the first signs of Soviet intransigence on fulfilling its wartime agreements failed to produce a permanent rift. To put pressure on Stalin to hold free elections in Soviet-occupied Poland, Truman abruptly canceled Lend-Lease payments, thereby denying much needed aid to the war-torn Soviet Union. When the Soviet foreign minister Vyacheslav Molotov called on the new president in the White House, Truman went even further, personally berating Molotov for Stalin's failure to schedule the promised elections. The long-term impact of this heated exchange was minimal, however. Truman quickly sent an emissary to Moscow to patch things up with Stalin. As a gesture of goodwill, he also reversed his initial decision to suspend Lend-Lease shipments to the Soviet Union.

The American Vision Takes Shape: Kennan's Long Telegram

Over time, however, these initial skirmishes between the United States and the Soviet Union developed into the **Cold War**. This intense ideological conflict between the United States and the Soviet Union and their allies led to several hot wars around the globe, although the Americans and Soviets never fought each other directly. In the opening phases of the Cold War, each side focused on defining the exact threat that the other posed. At the heart of this clash lay both conflicting visions of the future and a mutual distrust that only deepened whenever the balance of power threatened to shift dramatically in favor of one nation or the other. To Stalin the American monopoly on nuclear weapons placed the Soviet Union at a distinct strategic disadvantage that he intended to remedy as quickly as possible. For the United States Stalin's attempt in 1946 to use military force to extend his reach into the Middle East and Mediterranean raised concerns that the Soviet leader sought world domination.

Tensions mounted further in 1946 when Stalin gave a belligerent speech predicting the inevitable triumph of communism over capitalism. U.S. State Department officials were now concerned enough to ask the American embassy in Moscow for more information about Stalin's intentions. The response was the "**long telegram**," an influential five-thousand-word missive in which diplomat George F. Kennan outlined why America needed to develop an aggressive foreign policy aimed at containing Soviet expansionist impulses. Kennan concluded that Stalin needed an outside enemy to keep himself in power because an external threat kept the Soviet public from focusing on his ruthless dictatorship. Stalin, Kennan also explained, believed that conflicts between capitalist societies would lead to their demise, thus allowing communism to triumph when capitalist societies collapsed. Given this Soviet mindset, negotiations to resolve differences between the two nations would be fruitless, Kennan advised. Kennan suggested strengthening Western-style capitalist and democratic structures to foil communist efforts to woo impoverished peoples. He predicted that Stalin would moderate his ambitions only if he encountered strong and steady resistance from the West each time he tried to expand beyond the Western-accepted Soviet sphere of influence in Eastern Europe. "It is clear that the main element of any United States policy toward the Soviet Union must be that of a long-term, patient but firm and vigilant *containment* of Russian expansive tendencies," Kennan wrote in a version of the telegram that he published in 1947 under the pseudonym Mr. X in *Foreign Affairs* magazine. With this one statement Kennan articulated the philosophical foundation for **containment**, the label affixed to multiple American foreign policy initiatives meant to prevent the Soviet Union from increasing its influence around the globe. Kennan had economic and political policies in mind when he penned these words, but hard-liners in the Truman administration seized on his analysis to craft a new vision of U.S. military engagement in the world.

A month after Kennan sent his long telegram, the former British prime minister Winston Churchill visited Westminster College in Fulton, Missouri, where he used Kennan's words to underscore that a military, not just ideological, standoff lay ahead. In his speech Churchill declared that there was nothing the Soviets "admire so much as strength, and there is nothing for which they have less respect than for military weakness." Stalin accused Churchill of trying to provoke a war with his comment that an "**iron curtain**," Churchill's characterization of the military and ideological barrier erected by the Soviet Union, separated Western and Eastern Europe into free and unfree halves. Many American newspapers agreed, denouncing Churchill's speech as too belligerent.

The Truman Doctrine and the Marshall Plan

Turning the principles of containment into concrete action that had public approval took another year. By the end of 1947, the Truman Doctrine and the Marshall Plan established containment as the new course of American foreign policy, a direction strengthened even further in 1949 with the creation of a post-World War II military alliance between the United States and Western European powers through the **North Atlantic Treaty Organization**(NATO). These initiatives evolved in response to a series of crises in Europe, portrayed in **24.2**.

In 1947 Truman briefly returned to FDR's notion of working through the UN to resolve international disputes. That year the UN successfully pressured Stalin into removing Soviet troops from northern Iran. At the same time Truman stationed the American Sixth Fleet in the Mediterranean to prevent the Soviets from seizing Turkish-controlled shipping lanes through the Dardanelles. Stalin accepted the setback in oil-rich Iran without fanfare, but he continued to demand unrestricted naval access through the Dardanelles passage, the only way for Soviet military and commercial vessels to travel

What analysis did Kennan's Long Telegram offer of Stalin's beliefs and behavior?

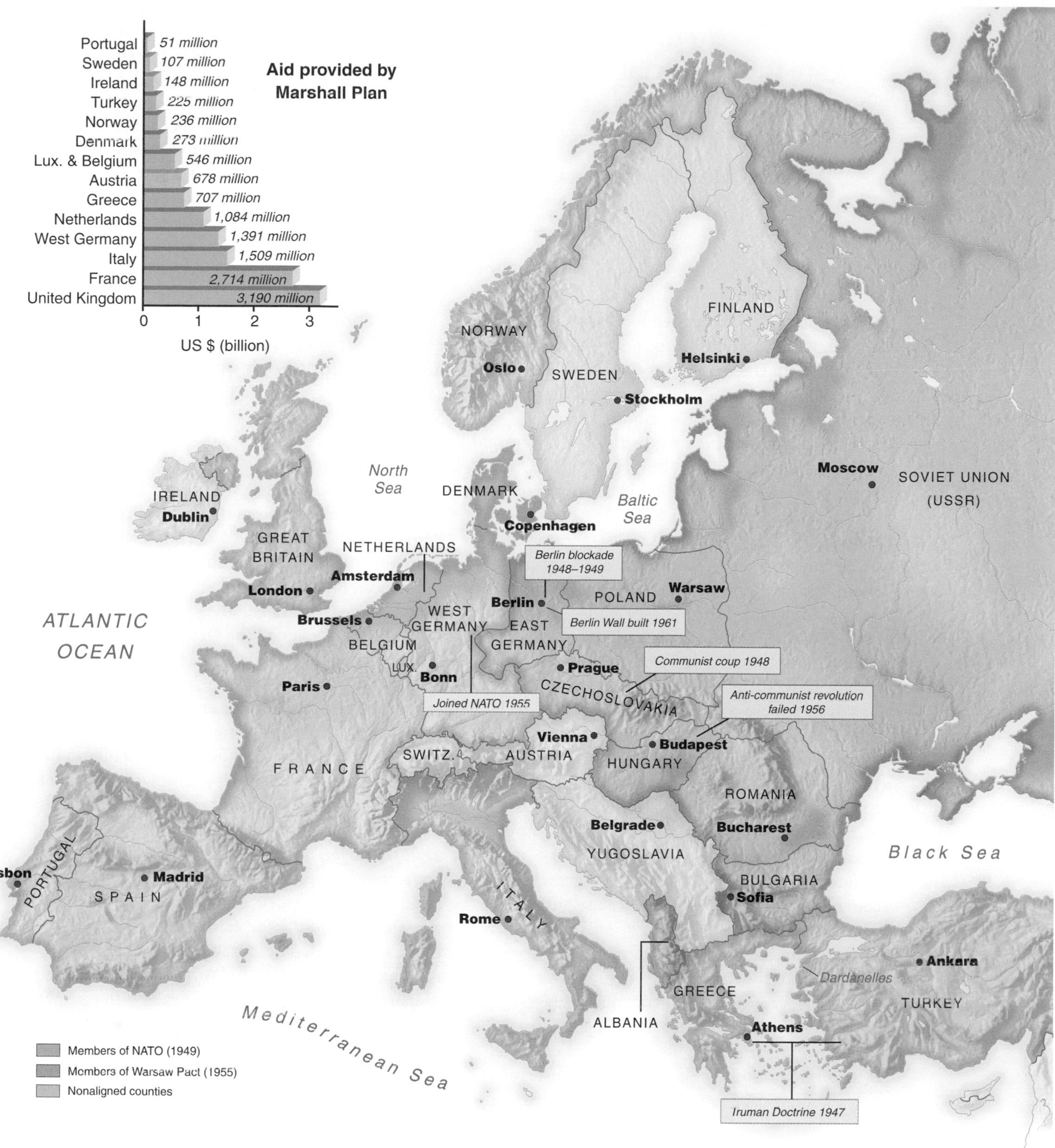

24.2 The Cold War in Europe
Europe divided into two competing alliance systems after World War II. The United States used the NATO alliance and Marshall Plan aid to strengthen ties with Western Europe.

What new role did the United States play in Western Europe after World War II?

> "From Stettin in the Baltic to Trieste in the Adriatic, an iron curtain has descended across the continent."
>
> Former British Prime Minister WINSTON CHURCHILL in Fulton, Missouri, March 1946

from the Black Sea to the Mediterranean. In 1947 Stalin sent troops to the Turkish-Soviet border to force Turkey to keep the passage open.

The sense of crisis in the eastern Mediterranean soon deepened, encompassing both Turkey and Greece. Throughout 1946 the British had supported the Greek monarchy in its efforts to subdue Greek Communist rebels and sent aid to Turkey to help the country stand firm against the Soviet Union. In 1947 as part of a general decision to renounce its world-wide imperial role, a financially strapped Britain informed the United States that it could no longer give economic or military aid to Greece and Turkey. Fearing that the British withdrawal meant certain Communist success in Greece and Turkey, Truman asked Congress to grant American assistance to these countries. Secretary of State Dean Acheson outlined the threat to America in a meeting with congressional leaders. "Like apples in a barrel infected by one rotten one," Acheson explained, "the corruption of Greece" would "carry the infection" of communism to Western Europe, Africa, and the Middle East.

In preparing his speech before Congress in 1947, Truman pondered how to convince the public that events in far-off Greece and Turkey necessitated an unprecedented peacetime interference in European affairs. "Scare [the] hell out of the American people," Republican senator Arthur Vandenberg suggested. Truman followed this advice. Dividing the world into "us" and "them," Truman told Americans that "at the present moment in world history nearly every nation must choose between alternative ways of life. The choice is too often not a free one." The Western side of the divide championed democracy and freedom. On the other were Communist states where "terror and oppression, a controlled press and radio, fixed elections, and the suppression of personal freedom" were parts of daily life. Drawing a line in the sand to stop the spread of communism was the nation's responsibility to the world and the only way to protect the American way of life at home. While asking specifically to help Greece and Turkey, in this speech Truman set forth a more expansive view of America's global responsibilities, asking the country to abandon its traditional non-interventionist stance. Instead the president proposed the **Truman Doctrine**, a foreign policy initiative that gave the United States an active role in stopping the global spread of communism by supporting "free peoples who are resisting attempted subjugation by armed minorities or by outside pressures."

The administration almost immediately used the principles articulated in the Truman Doctrine to justify extending a helping hand to Western Europe as well. In the eastern Mediterranean the United States wanted to prevent Communist armies from taking over the region. In war-torn Western Europe, the American government feared that hungry, exhausted citizens might voluntarily turn to communism, which promised bread for all, out of despair. Free elections in Western Europe offered the grim possibility that Communists might be voted into power. Embracing Kennan's vision, Secretary of State George C. Marshall, the former army chief of staff who had designed the victorious American strategy in World War II, suggested offering massive amounts of financial aid to help European capitalistic economies recover. **The Marshall Plan (1948–1952)** aimed to restore Europeans' faith in capitalism by sending $13 billion ($119 billion in today's dollars) overseas to rebuild Europe's ruined roads, bridges, factories, and farms. "Our policy is directed not against any country or doctrine but against hunger, poverty, desperation, and chaos," the secretary of state claimed, avoiding the dualistic "us" against "them" rhetoric of the Truman Doctrine. Certain that widespread economic suffering in the thirties had caused desperate people to embrace fascism, which then led to World War II, the Marshall Plan explicitly linked peace with prosperity. All European nations (including the Soviet Union) were invited to submit proposals for aid. Stalin briefly entertained the idea of applying for American funds to rebuild his devastated nation, but as Marshall and Truman expected, he quickly abandoned this idea. Instead the Soviets publicly denounced the plan as an American plot to colonize Europe and refused to allow Eastern European nations to participate. Besides cash, the Marshall Plan offered European nations technical and management advice that helped spread American farming

How did the Truman Administration convince the public to accept a new direction in U.S. foreign policy?

24.3 **American View of the Marshall Plan**
The Marshall Plan is portrayed as a lifeline offered by the United States to help a desperate Western Europe pull itself out of war-inflicted misery and away from the powerful influence of the Soviet Union, seen in the distance.

techniques, labor policies, and manufacturing practices.

The recovery of Western European markets under the Marshall Plan furthered the ideological divide between the United States and the Soviet Union. These conflicting political cartoons (**24.3** and **24.4**) reflected the American view that free markets fostered independence and the contrasting Soviet critique of capitalism as an exploitive, class-based system that enriched some at the expense of others. In his illustration (24.3) the American cartoonist Daniel R. Fitzpatrick viewed the Marshall Plan as a lifeline to Western Europe pulling people out of war-inflicted misery and away from the looming Soviet menace in the distance (represented in the cartoon by the distant towers of the Tsar's former palace in Leningrad, a readily recognizable symbol of the Soviet Union to Americans). Americans took pride in the wave of Western European prosperity that resulted from the Marshall Plan, making it one of the great economic success stories of the Cold War. In sharp contrast the Soviet magazine *Krokodil* showed European leaders groveling at the feet of their American lord, depicted in the cartoon (24.4) as a paunchy Uncle Sam relaxing with his feet on their backs. This cartoon implied that the Marshall Plan, rather than fostering recovery, enslaved Western Europe to the United States, which grew richer by the day. There was some truth to the Soviet claim that the Marshall Plan, which ran from 1948 to 1952, strengthened the American economy. Western European nations spent most of their funds in the United States on raw materials, food, machines, and fuel, creating a taste for American goods that continued even after the Marshall Plan ended.

The Berlin Airlift and NATO

The American policy of containment quickly evolved into more than a vision of financial assistance for struggling governments and economies overseas. By 1949 containment also meant a firm military commitment from the United States to come to the defense of Western European nations that allied themselves with America. Almost overnight the United States shed its traditional reluctance to intervene militarily in European affairs as Americans became convinced that they were the only ones who could stop Stalin from controlling Europe.

In 1948 Stalin supported a coup by Czech Communists that overthrew the only democratic government in Eastern Europe. The quick demise of democracy in Czechoslovakia caused the West to fear that an emboldened Stalin might

24.4 **Soviet View of the Marshall Plan**
In this Soviet cartoon, European leaders grovel at the feet of their American capitalist master, who has used the Marshall Plan to conquer Europe.

What conflicting views of the Marshall Plan are presented in these two cartoons?

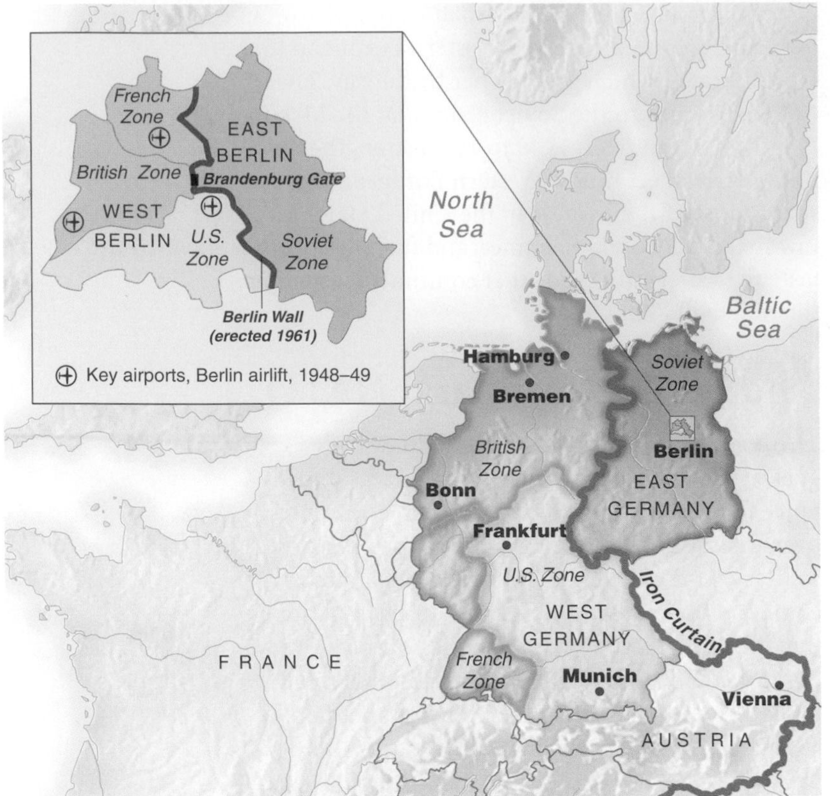

24.5 A Divided Berlin
Key showdowns during the Cold War took place in Berlin, including the Berlin airlift in 1948–1949 and the construction of the Berlin Wall in 1961.

have Germany, with its wrecked economy and nonexistent military, in mind as the next target for a Soviet-inspired communist revolution. With the country still divided into four occupied zones, the German economy was in shambles. Keeping Germany weak to punish it for World War II, initially a shared American and Soviet objective, increasingly made little strategic sense as the Soviet menace grew. By 1948 the United States saw strengthening Germany as a way to halt the Soviet expansionist drive across Europe. With this goal in mind, the United States, Britain, and France began discussing the possibility of consolidating their separately occupied sections of Germany to form a new democratic German government and offering it Marshall Plan funds to bolster the economy. The Soviet Union firmly opposed any plan for rebuilding Germany and protested that its former allies were violating the 1945 Yalta agreement that all four nations had to agree before any restructuring of Germany could occur.

As the West and the Soviet Union argued over how to deal with Germany, the stakes rose precipitously. Trying to pressure the United States, Britain, and France to abandon either their plan to reunify Germany or their stake in Berlin, Stalin ordered his army to stop all road, railroad, and canal traffic between the Western and Soviet zones of Germany. Berlin lay in the heart of the Soviet-occupied sector, but at the end of World War II the Allies had agreed to divide the German capital into four zones of occupation, portrayed on the map (**24.5**). To supply and reach their respective zones in Berlin, the Americans, British, and French needed to travel on roads, rail lines, and waterways that ran through the Soviet sector of Germany. Stalin now barred them from using these transportation facilities, setting in motion the first direct military confrontation of the Cold War between the United States and the Soviet Union.

The United States faced a set of difficult choices. One option was to try to breach the blockade by sending an armed convoy down the autobahn (the German name for freeway) with permission to fire back if attacked by Soviet forces. In the midst of a difficult reelection campaign, Truman doubted Americans' willingness to fight the Soviet Union to help a recent enemy. The other option was to try to circumvent the blockade by supplying the Western-occupied sectors of Berlin from the air. The chances of an airlift working appeared slim since each plane could carry only 3 tons of supplies and the West normally sent an average of 12,000 tons of supplies a day to sustain a combined population of 2.3 million in their three zones. Faced with two unappealing choices, Truman gambled on the airlift and won.

> "The situation was dark and full of danger."
>
> State Department official GEORGE F. KENNAN on the Soviet blockade of Berlin in 1948

In the **Berlin airlift (1948–1949)**, American and British planes resupplied West Berlin for nearly a year to stymie the Soviet blockade of the city. It was a brilliant success, both a spectacular logistical feat and a propaganda coup for the United States worldwide. In sharp contrast to dour Soviet soldiers turning away convoys carrying needed food and medicine, the world saw photographs of German

Which international disputes led to the 1948–1949 Soviet blockade of Berlin?

children cheering the arrival of American and British planes. This photo (**24.6**) underscored how much the world had changed in a mere three years. The children stood on the rubble from a building destroyed by Allied bombers during the war. Instead of fleeing for their lives as American planes approached, they now welcomed the Americans as saviors for a city where strict rationing meant most children received only gruel (hot milk and flour) for their noontime meal. One American pilot was so touched by the sight of children scanning the skies for food planes that he attached miniature parachutes to candy bars and gum to drop to them when he flew by. "The spectacle of the British and Americans trying to feed the 2,000,000 Germans in Berlin, while the Soviet Union was trying to starve them, has been an object lesson to the German people far beyond anything that words could convey," Churchill noted.

Images like these convinced Americans that their help was both welcome and needed overseas. They also boosted Truman in the 1948 presidential campaign as he squared off against the Republican challenger, Thomas Dewey, who led in the polls, and two other third party candidates. Faced with public dissatisfaction over rampant inflation at home and a badly divided Democratic Party, these photos bolstered Truman's image as a resolute leader.

Truman could not correct all his political problems with photographs, however. The 1948 presidential campaign presented voters with sharply competing visions of what direction the country should take. Angry over Truman's proposal that the federal government investigate racial discrimination in voting and employment, many conservative Southern Democrats supported Strom Thurmond, the governor of South Carolina, in his presidential bid as a segregationist candidate for the States' Rights Party. Meanwhile liberal factions of the Democratic Party, upset with Truman's tepid reform agenda (see Chapter 25), formed the Progressive Party and nominated Henry A. Wallace who championed national health insurance. The former vice president's downplaying of the Soviet threat brought charges that Wallace had communist sympathies. Dewey, who had run against FDR in 1944, was a moderate Republican who, like Truman, supported civil rights and containing communism. Many believed that the president's unpopularity and the three-way split within the Democratic Party assured Dewey's election. Determined to "give them hell," Truman traveled nearly 32,000 miles during the campaign, appealing to the New Deal coalition of farmers, Northern blacks, Catholics, unions, and

24.6 The Berlin Airlift, 1948–1949 Photographs of waving German children welcoming American food planes convinced Americans that their help was both needed and welcomed overseas.

What political impact did this photo have?

24.7 Truman's Triumph
On election night in November 1948, Truman celebrated his reelection by holding the *Chicago Daily Tribune,* with its mistaken headline, from his campaign train.

liberals that had secured FDR's victory in 1936. Dewey's unwillingness to attack the president's foreign policies during this time of international crisis also helped Truman. In the summer of 1948, Truman issued an executive order desegregating the military to prevent the defection of black voters to Wallace, who called for an immediate end to Jim Crow. Thanks to votes from African Americans and labor, Truman won a second term, with 303 electoral votes and 49.5 percent of the popular vote, defeating Dewey who received 189 electoral votes and 45.1 percent of the popular vote, Thurmond (39 electoral votes; 2.4 percent of the popular vote), and Wallace (no electoral votes; 2.4 percent of the popular vote). This victory came as a surprise to many, including the *Chicago Daily Tribune,* which tried to get a jump on the competition by declaring Dewey the victor on election night before all the votes were counted. In a photo (**24.7**) that became an instant classic, a jubilant Truman held the paper and its erroneous headline "Dewey Defeats Truman" above his head the next morning when his victory was confirmed.

Besides helping Truman win reelection, the sight of wave after wave of planes arriving twenty-four hours a day in Berlin also demonstrated America's strength and resolve to the Soviet Union. After nearly a year, Stalin finally admitted defeat and revoked the blockade on May 12, 1949. The capitalist enclave in the heart of the Soviet sector of Germany had survived. By that time the Americans, British, and French had merged their zones within Berlin and the rest of Germany to create the Federal Republic of Germany, or West Germany. In response the Soviets organized a Communist-led German government in their sector, the German Democratic Republic, or East Germany. Germany was now formally divided into two separate nations.

In the wake of the Soviet-backed coup in Czechoslovakia and the blockade of Berlin, the United States refined its policy of containment even further. These events had shattered any chance of creating consensus within the Truman administration around Kennan's vision that economic aid through the Marshall Plan was enough to safeguard democracy and prosperity in Western Europe. If peace were to prevail, it would be an armed peace. Western European nations took the first step by allying themselves in the Brussels Pact in 1948. This alliance blossomed into the American-led NATO alliance in April 1949. The Soviet Union responded with their own alliance, the Warsaw Pact, among Eastern European nations. The map of the Cold War in Europe portrays the two alliance systems that formally divided Europe into capitalist and communist camps (see 24.2).

By joining NATO the United States created its first formal military alliance since the Revolutionary War. There would be no repeat of World War I or World War II, when the United States had waited over two years each time before declaring war. As a member of NATO, the United States was obligated to come immediately to Western Europe's defense in the event of a Soviet attack. Besides putting American bases and soldiers permanently in Europe, NATO extended the protection of America's atomic shield to its NATO partners.

Like the Marshall Plan NATO was designed to do many things at once. Besides creating a permanent role for the United States overseas and containing communism, NATO also helped keep peace among European nations that had clashed repeatedly in the last hundred years. A popular saying claimed that NATO kept "the Soviets out, the Americans in, and the Germans down" by ensuring that West Germany remained friends with Western democracies even after the nation regained its economic vigor.

Why was NATO an important development in the Cold War?

Fighting Communism: Cold and Hot War

As the Cold War took shape, the United States did not gain any noticeable advantage from its atomic monopoly in dealing with Stalin. Losing it, nonetheless, caused great angst in the United States. In 1949 the Soviet Union successfully tested its own atomic bomb, challenging Americans' view of their own nation as the world's dominant military power. Suddenly the chances of an international crisis escalating into nuclear war appeared greater. As Americans digested this news, the epicenter of the Cold War shifted to Asia. By 1950 a Communist government controlled China, and the Korean War had begun. In the **Korean War (1950–1953)**, the United States fought Communist North Koreans and Chinese to a stalemate, frustrating Americans.

Communism Rising: 1949

The United States did not have long to celebrate its achievements during the Berlin airlift. Three months after Stalin admitted defeat in Berlin, an American spy plane detected a large amount of radioactive fallout in the desert of Kazakhstan, a Soviet republic. This unusual finding could mean only one thing: the Soviet Union had successfully tested its own atomic bomb. This news shattered the American certainty that it would retain a nuclear monopoly for at least ten years. Waiting impatiently for a formal announcement from the Kremlin, Truman finally broke the news to the world in September 1949. The Soviet Union confirmed the American report, but gave no other information about Stalin's plans for his nuclear-building program.

Fearful that Stalin might use nuclear weapons to expand beyond the iron curtain, the Truman administration broadened the scope of America's containment strategy beyond NATO and the Marshall Plan. Truman decided to station American troops in Western Europe permanently to both deter and, if necessary, respond to a nuclear attack. At the same time the United States began stockpiling atomic bombs to gain a numerical advantage over the Soviet Union. Finally Truman authorized the development of a "superbomb," a thermonuclear hydrogen bomb that was a thousand times more powerful than the uranium-enriched atomic bomb dropped on Hiroshima and the plutonium one that destroyed Nagasaki.

Americans were still recovering from the shock of the Soviet bomb when they received more bad news. The twenty-five-year-old Chinese Civil War had finally ended with the Communist Mao Zedong victorious over the Nationalist leader Jiang Jieshi (Chiang Kai-shek), who fled with his government to Taiwan, an island off the southeast coast of mainland China. Mao was an avid swimmer who refused even as an old man to be deterred by the human waste floating in China's polluted rivers. A master of staying afloat in water and in politics, Mao adopted Stalin and Soviet-style policies as his model, inflicting similarly painful waves of famine and political oppression on the Chinese people that killed more than twenty million. Fearful that the United States intended to attack China and restore Jiang to power, Mao immediately reached out to Stalin. "There should be some division of labor between us," Stalin suggested, with the Soviet Union furthering the communist cause in Europe and Mao doing the same in Asia. Accepting Stalin's offer Mao spent two months in Moscow devising a joint strategy that resulted in the 1950 Sino-Soviet Treaty, which pledged mutual assistance in the event of an enemy attack. This alliance created a second front in the Cold War that forced the United States to divide its attention between Europe and Asia.

> "There is only one thing worse than one nation having the atomic bomb—that's two nations having it."
>
> American physical chemist HAROLD ULREY, September 1949

In light of these new threats on the world stage, Truman ordered a full review of American foreign

How did the USSR acquiring nuclear weapons and the rise of communist China change the contours of the Cold War?

policy. The State Department responded with a document known as National Security Council Memorandum 68, or NSC-68. Not mincing words NSC-68 declared that "the issues that face us are momentous, involving the fulfillment or destruction not only of this Republic but of civilization itself." Secretary of State Acheson later admitted that NSC-68's cataclysmic vision of a Soviet enemy "animated by a new fanatic faith" and bent on worldwide domination was meant to convince the president to use all means "short of war" to halt the apparent Soviet drive for world conquest. NSC-68 crystallized the piecemeal developments of the last four years into one clear vision: The United States must build up "the political, economic, and military strength of the free world to frustrate the Kremlin design of a world dominated by its will." This message was transmitted to the public not only through political speeches but also through films and novels. Perhaps no writer better encapsulated the public's fears of worldwide communist domination than George Orwell in his classic novel *1984,* which hit bookstores in 1949. In the novel Orwell envisioned a future where totalitarianism has triumphed and the people's loyalty to a Stalin-like dictator "Big Brother," who watches over everyone and censors their behavior, is ensured by a cycle of endless wars and torture. As the main character Winston Smith undergoes another round of torture, his tormentor tells him, "Imagine a boot stamping on a human face—forever." This image neatly encapsulated the American public's view of communism in the Cold War.

The Korean War

At the end of World War II, the United States and the Soviet Union had agreed to divide the former Japanese colony of Korea, a peninsula along the Asian Pacific Coast, into two zones of occupation. The country was split along the 38th parallel, with the USSR occupying the north and the United States in the south. In 1945 partitioning the country seemed like a good way to both deprive Japan of Korean resources and prevent the Soviet Union from completely taking over the peninsula. When the Soviet Union organized a Communist government under Kim Il-sung in North Korea and the United States selected Syngman Rhee to head a capitalist government in the south, the previously unified nation appeared permanently divided.

By 1949, however, the United States had begun to reevaluate its military commitment in South Korea. The military occupation was expensive to maintain, and Pentagon officials increasingly doubted the strategic importance of the peninsula. The State Department agreed, believing that economic aid and political reforms could strengthen South Korea enough to discourage a North Korean attack. In January 1950 Secretary of State Acheson openly questioned the importance of South Korea to the overall defense of American interests in East Asia. In a speech before the National Press Club, Acheson outlined a defensive perimeter in the Pacific that the United States would defend against Communist incursions that included Japan, Okinawa, Formosa, and the Philippines, but not South Korea. Accordingly Truman began withdrawing American soldiers from South Korea. To deter North Korea from attacking, the United States left a stockpile of conventional weapons and promised continued financial aid.

Yet when North Korea launched a surprise invasion of South Korea in June 1950, Truman dramatically reversed course. Within days Truman decided to send American ground troops to help roll back the offensive. The speed and success of the North Korean attack alarmed Truman. Within two days North Korean troops had entered Seoul, the capital of South Korea (**24.8**), and by the end of one week North Korea had pushed the bulk of the South Korean army into the toe of the Korean peninsula around Pusan. Viewing this overpowering offensive as confirmation of the vision encapsulated in NSC-68, Truman immediately suspected that the USSR was behind the attack. Truman was partly right. Kim Il-sung had secured reluctant support from Stalin and Mao Zedong for the invasion by promising an easy victory. In the event that the United States intervened in Korea, Stalin saw advantages to diverting American attention away from Europe.

Other global and domestic events by June 1950 left many Americans feeling that the West was losing the Cold War. Worldwide these events included China falling to communism and the explosion of a Soviet atomic bomb. At home sensational spy trials fueled continued doubts about Truman's leadership. In this political climate doing nothing was hardly an option for Truman.

Truman's intimate understanding of World War I (he had served as an artillery captain in France) and World War II encouraged him to break with the precedent set by these recent conflicts. In each of these wars, Americans had debated the merits of fighting for more than two years before declaring war. "I remembered how each time the democracies

Why did the United States decide to fight in Korea?

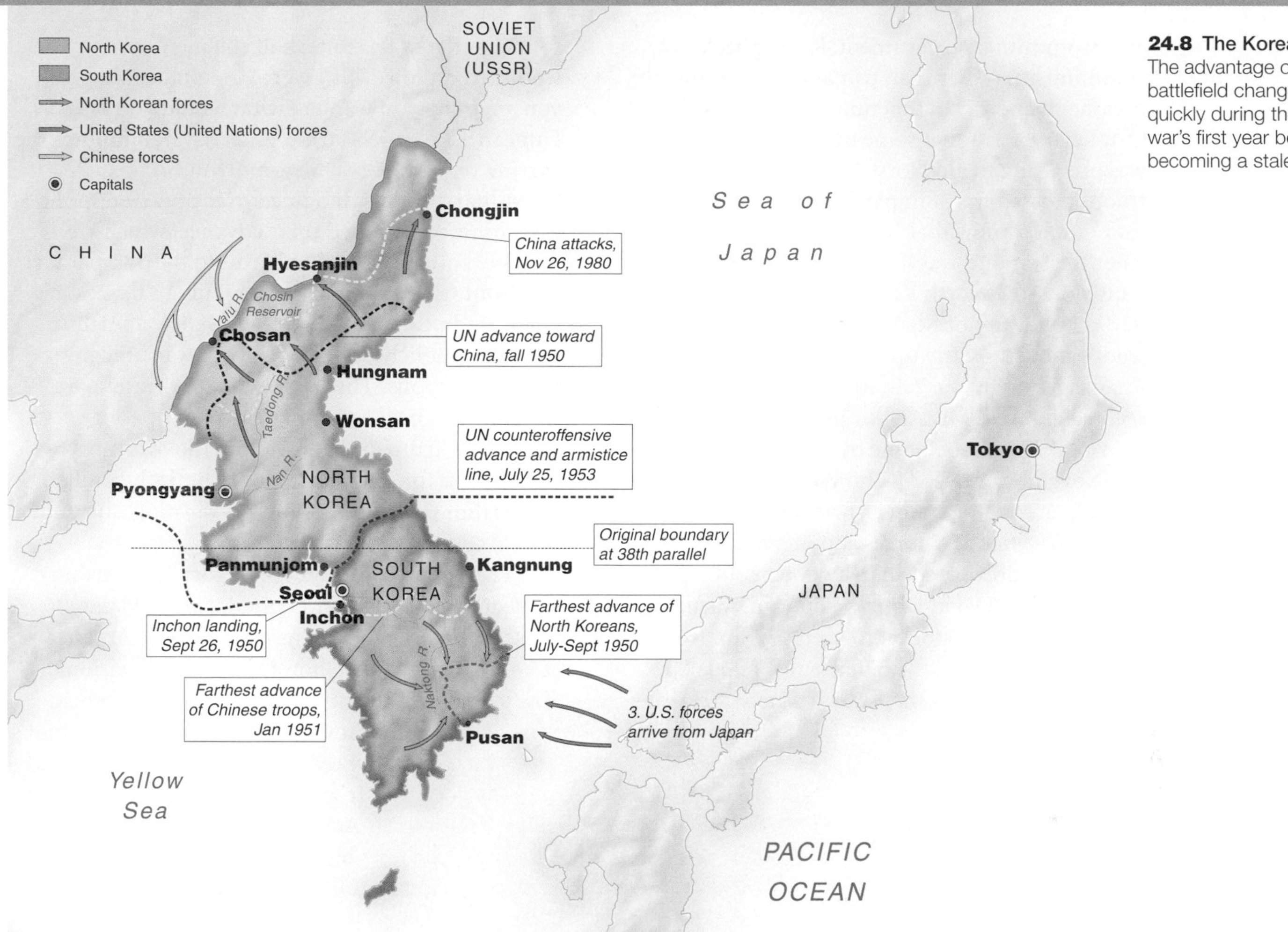

24.8 The Korean War
The advantage on the battlefield changed quickly during the war's first year before becoming a stalemate.

failed to act it had encouraged the aggressors to keep going ahead," Truman noted. Determined to respond quickly this time, Truman committed American troops to combat within a matter of days. Although Truman consulted Congress, he never asked for a declaration of war against North Korea. Truman instead decided to work through the UN, which authorized the use of force to restore the original 38th-parallel boundary between North and South Korea. Sixteen nations sent troops to Korea to serve in the UN police force, but the United States provided the bulk of troops and commanded military operations. When polled three-quarters of Americans approved of Truman's decision to send military aid to South Korea. Americans, for the time being anyway, subscribed to Truman's vision that "the future of civilization depends on what we do."

The situation on the battlefield, however, was grim, with South Korean soldiers holding on precariously around Pusan. To reverse the situation General Douglas MacArthur, the Supreme United Nations commander, devised a dramatic and risky strategy. Rather than simply confronting the North Koreans head-on, MacArthur decided to stage an amphibious landing at Inchon, a port city near Seoul. This attack on the North Koreans' rear would cut their supply lines and force them to fight on two fronts. The tides at Inchon, however, were the second highest in the world, varying twenty-nine feet between high and low tides. Within a matter of minutes, the quickly receding tide could mire a boat in mud. Inchon, MacArthur reasoned, was the right place to attack precisely because it was so uninviting and would take the enemy by surprise. As he predicted the North Koreans had stationed only 2,000 troops there, and the UN force of 70,000 encountered little resistance in taking the city. The success of this operation turned MacArthur, already famous for his feats in World War II, into a national hero. Following the Inchon invasion UN forces quickly drove North Korean troops out of South Korea.

In the wake of this victory, Truman pondered giving the war a new purpose. Instead of simply restoring the status quo of a divided Korea, Truman now decided to try to reunify Korea under an

What accounted for America's initial successes on the battlefield?

anti-Communist government. Rolling back communism, rather than containing communism, became the new goal sanctioned by the UN in October 1950. At that same moment, however, China was preparing to aid North Korea. When American troops crossed the 38th parallel into North Korea, they did not know that Mao had already resolved to enter the war and was massing Chinese troops and guns along the North Korean-Chinese border.

Still unaware of Mao's intentions, American troops moved swiftly up the peninsula to celebrate Thanksgiving by the Yalu River. Imminent victory seemed assured: MacArthur promised Truman that the troops would be home by Christmas. Then in late November waves of Chinese troops began pouring across the border, shrieking and blowing bugles. Terrified UN forces suffered heavy casualties as they withdrew in the harsh winter cold. *Life* photographer David Douglas Duncan, warming his camera in his coat pocket to keep the film from breaking, chronicled the bitter retreat of 10,000 Marines who fought their way to safety. Nearly every soldier suffered frostbite; half the men were wounded or killed. "If I were God and could give you anything you wanted, what would you ask for?" Duncan asked one Marine. After several minutes the Marine replied, "Give me tomorrow."

Military leaders disagreed over how to respond as the Chinese continued their advance, which UN forces eventually contained around the 38th parallel. The Joint Chiefs of Staff urged Truman to seek a negotiated peace, advice he followed. MacArthur, however, publicly endorsed all-out war utilizing nuclear weapons. The president and theater commander now began to pursue two competing visions. As Truman made diplomatic overtures to the Chinese for a ceasefire along the 38th parallel, MacArthur issued the Chinese a warning: surrender or face complete destruction.

"There is no substitute for victory," MacArthur wrote to Congressman Joseph Martin of Massachusetts, echoing the feelings of countless Americans at home. This was not, however, Truman's vision of how to end the war successfully; when Martin read these words on the House floor, he sealed MacArthur's fate. Truman fired MacArthur the next week, triggering, as Secretary of State Acheson had predicted, "the biggest fight of your administration."

MacArthur came home, not in disgrace, but to great acclaim. Many Americans shared MacArthur's frustrations with the stalemate on the battlefield. Six years after defeating two great military powers in World War II, the United States found itself unable to reunify Korea under an anti-Communist government. Responding to MacArthur's vision of total victory, huge crowds greeted the general when his ship docked in San Francisco, and he reveled in a ticker-tape parade held in his honor in New York City. Congress debated impeaching Truman but then opted instead to hold hearings into MacArthur's removal. During the hearings MacArthur's critics interrogated the general about the possibility

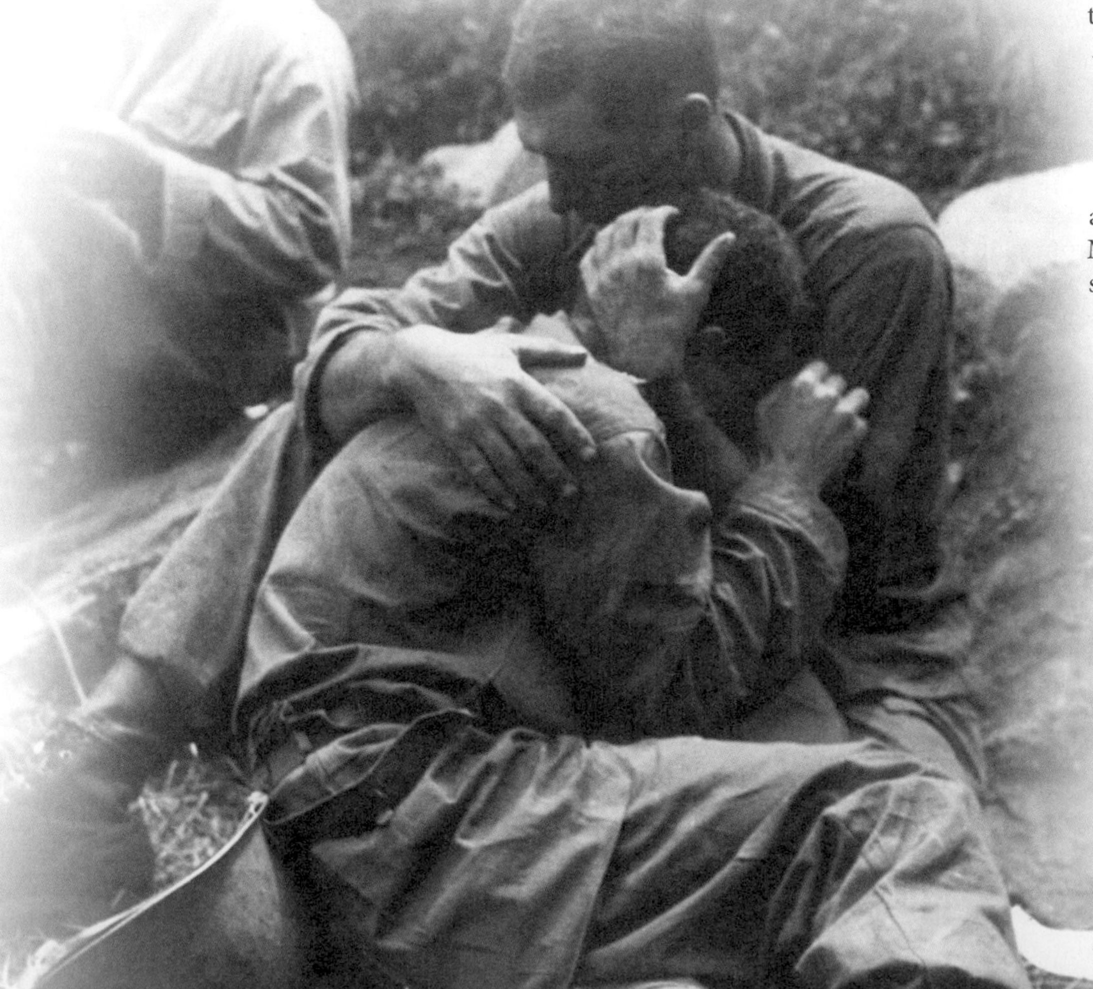

24.9 "The Price of Victory: A Soldier Grieves for His Lost Buddy" An American soldier comforts a comrade distraught over the death of a friend during the Korean War in the fall of 1950.

How did the entry of the Chinese into the Korean War affect political and military debates within the United States?

that using nuclear weapons in Korea might lead to a global nuclear war. MacArthur's response, "that doesn't happen to be my responsibility," caused the general's popularity to plummet. The cooling enthusiasm for MacArthur's vision of all-out war did little to bolster public confidence in Truman, however. In public opinion polls only 24 percent of Americans approved of how Truman was handling the presidency, reflecting public disappointment over the situation in Korea, continued anger at Truman over "losing China," and several well-publicized Soviet spy scandals that together revived the image of Truman as an ineffectual leader. Truman's aggressive support for civil rights and his domestic reform agenda (see Chapter 25), too much for conservatives and too little for liberals, also contributed to his poor rating.

Korea was the last American war that the public viewed primarily through photographs. Only 34 percent of American homes were equipped with television sets in 1952, rising to 86 percent by 1960. In 1950 *Newsweek* published the photograph "The Price of Victory: A Soldier Grieves for His Lost Buddy" (**24.9**). One reader's suggestion that this image should serve as the iconic photo of the Korean War, just as "Old Glory Goes Up on Mt. Suribachi, Iwo Jima" had served to represent World War II, revealed a significant shift in the public's attitudes over the last five years (see *Images as History: Combat Photography,* Chapter 23, page 706). The World War II image of five marines and one navy corpsman raising the flag suggested teamwork, victory, and the triumph of democracy. In sharp contrast "The Price of Victory" looked at the personal cost of war—the sorrow and compassion that drew men together on the battlefield—even as the photograph reaffirmed the willingness of soldiers to die for their country. Photographers and the public were beginning to probe the impact of fighting on the ground soldier, stoking the ambivalence that the country increasingly felt about the war.

With MacArthur out of the picture, General Matthew Ridgway took over command of UN operations in 1951 and armistice negotiations began. Talks were still underway two years later when a new president, Dwight D. Eisenhower, took office. Eisenhower's sunny demeanor offered a sharp contrast to Truman's more combative and coarser personality. Whereas Truman cussed, told off-color jokes, and picked fights with reporters, Eisenhower was gregarious and friendly to all. Some Democrats had tried to draft Eisenhower as a presidential candidate in 1948. Four years later the Republican "We Like Ike" campaign finally convinced Eisenhower to seek office. The young women adorned here (**24.10**), with "Ike" dresses and umbrellas, illustrate Republicans' enthusiasm for Eisenhower on the eve of the nominating convention where delegates enthusiastically selected him as their presidential candidate.

Admired by Americans for his command of the D-Day invasion in World War II, Eisenhower's military experience convinced Americans that he would be a capable leader in a time of war. The negotiations remained deadlocked, however, until Eisenhower threatened to reconsider the question of employing nuclear weapons. Finally the two sides agreed to a permanent ceasefire in July 1953.

The war was costly on all sides. More than 600,000 Chinese soldiers and nearly two million North and South Koreans perished. For the first time in its history, the United States could not claim outright victory over its opponent despite nearly 33,000 men killed in combat and 103,000 men wounded. "What the hell is there to celebrate?" remarked one soldier when news of the armistice reached the front. The silence at home offered a marked contrast to the jubilant demonstrations that had filled the streets

24.10
"We Like Ike"
The enthusiasm for his candidacy displayed by Republicans in 1952 convinced Eisenhower to run for president.

eight years earlier when Japan surrendered. China embraced a competing vision of the stalemate, reveling in their ability to hold their own against the United States.

The Korean War had major geopolitical consequences by turning the Cold War into a global conflict. The war tied South Korea and Japan, economically resurgent thanks to American aid, even more closely to the United States, and these two nations became staunch allies in creating a defensive perimeter against communism in East Asia. Holding the line against communism in Korea increased America's interest in other regional civil wars, including one underway in Vietnam. The war poisoned relations with China, and the two nations did not reestablish diplomatic relations until 1979. Pledged to defend South Korea, the United States to this day maintains a large military presence along what continues to be the most heavily armed border in the world.

24.11 Godzilla
A 1954 Japanese horror film used the ravages of a nuclear-spawned dinosaur named Godzilla to criticize American use and testing of its nuclear arsenal. This political message was edited out of the version shown in the United States.

INCREDIBLE, UNSTOPPABLE TITAN OF TERROR!
GODZILLA
It's Alive!
KING OF THE MONSTERS!
CIVILIZATION CRUMBLES as its death rays blast a city of 6 million from the face of the earth!
RAYMOND BURR
MIGHTIEST MONSTER! MIGHTIEST MELODRAMA of them all!

Nuclear Fallout and Fear

While soldiers fought and died on the battlefield, Americans at home waged their own defensive war against nuclear weapons. The government sponsored atmospheric and underwater tests of nuclear bombs in the 1940s and 1950s both in the United States and on the Bikini Atoll in the Marshall Islands in the Pacific. Even when the United States had a secure monopoly on nuclear weapons, many Americans expressed concern about **nuclear fallout**, the deadly pollution that descends through the air after a nuclear bomb explosion.

Over the course of the decade, popular science fiction writers and filmmakers tapped into this preoccupation with nuclear fallout. In the Japanese film classic *Godzilla,* for example, a nuclear explosion awakes a fire-breathing monster who, as the film's promotional poster (**24.11**) illustrated, terrorizes Tokyo. Like the atomic bomb that ravaged Hiroshima and Nagasaki, Godzilla is an unstoppable nuclear force that obliterates everything in his path. Americans, however, saw only a carefully edited version of the film, with all critical commentary on America's ongoing nuclear testing program in the Pacific carefully excised. In a similar vein two popular Marvel comic book characters, the Incredible Hulk and Spiderman, were spawned by contact with radioactive material. In the *Incredible Hulk*, a scientist exposed to gamma rays is transformed into a green, 300-pound giant, while a bite from an irradiated spider turns nerdish lab assistant Peter Parker into Spiderman.

Teaching Americans how to live with the constant threat of nuclear war meant convincing citizens to remain vigilant and calm. To combat both indifference and panic, governmental propaganda underscored the seriousness of the threat, while also reassuring the public that they could survive an atomic bomb blast if they took precautionary measures such as building fortified fallout shelters or remembering to "duck and cover." *Images as History: Surviving an Atomic Bomb Blast* explores how government-generated images presented competing visions that both reassured and frightened Americans about the likely effect of a nuclear bomb attack.

What insights does popular culture offer into Americans' concerns about nuclear weapons?

Images as History

SURVIVING AN ATOMIC BOMB BLAST

Controlling how people react to advice or propaganda can be difficult to predict. What was the government's purpose in disseminating images of a possible nuclear attack? What were the possible unintended effects that these images could have on the Americans viewing them?

By 1950 schoolchildren throughout the nation had learned to jump out of their seats and under their desks with their hands clasped firmly over their heads when their teachers shouted "Drop!" during civil defense drills. In government-produced civil defense films and comic books distributed to schools, a cartoon character named Bert the Turtle instructed children to "duck and cover" during a nuclear attack. Advocates of the "duck and cover" approach argued that flying debris and shattered windows had killed many victims in Hiroshima and Nagasaki; therefore, teaching children to "duck and cover" was practical advice.

To ensure that Americans remained vigilant in preparing for a nuclear attack, the government also released "before" and "after" photographs from a test explosion in the Nevada desert on March 17, 1953. *Time* magazine estimated that nearly three-quarters of the nation saw these pictures.

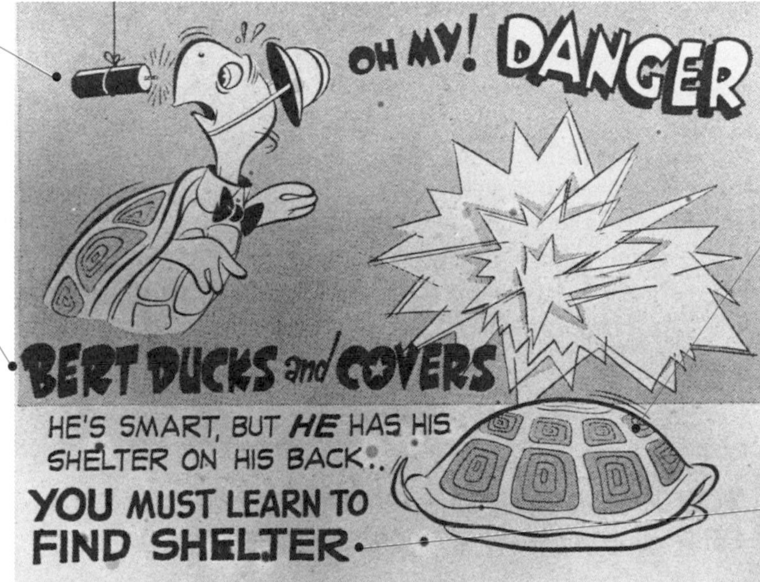

The stick of dynamite dangling from a stick symbolized a nuclear attack, exactly the kind of danger children needed to learn to recognize.

A catchy jingle accompanied this lesson in civil defense: "There was a turtle by the name of Bert, and Bert the Turtle was very alert / When danger threatened him he never got hurt / He knew just what to do / He'd Duck and Cover / Duck and Cover."

The intact shell implies that one could safely survive a nuclear attack by hiding under something.

Authorities advised children—who did not carry their shelters on their backs like Bert—to seek protection behind walls and trees or under tables if an atomic bomb hit.

The "before" blast images portrayed a normal middle-class suburban home and yard.

The "after" blast photographs showed these suburban houses engulfed in flames and blown to bits within two seconds of being hit with a nuclear bomb.

This image directly contradicted the vision that one could survive a nuclear attack by seeking shelter under a bed as "Bert the Turtle" advised.

Did these images offer competing or complimentary visions of the nuclear threat?

Fallout Shelters

With the successful test explosion of the hydrogen bomb in 1954, the Eisenhower administration embraced mass evacuation from city centers as the best civil defense against nuclear attack. The president's decision to construct an interstate highway system changed official policy "from 'Duck and Cover' to 'Run Like Hell,'" the *Bulletin of the Atomic Scientists* concluded. Multilane highways served peacetime needs by linking cities to suburbs and military needs by making the evacuation of civilians and the mobilization of the military easier if the United States was attacked. Practice evacuation runs were not encouraging, however. "Operation Kids," for example, an effort to move 37,300 schoolchildren in Mobile, Alabama, out of the city without warning resulted in heavy traffic jams.

Eisenhower also urged Americans to build private family shelters at their own expense. The government distributed pamphlets with suggested floor plans, and advised women to store enough food and medical supplies to sustain their families if a nuclear attack contaminated water supplies or destroyed grocery stores. "Grandma's pantry was ready" whenever guests unexpectedly arrived; "is your 'pantry' ready in event of emergency?" one government pamphlet asked.

Given their high cost (even a barebones shelter cost $1,000, about one-fifth an average family's annual income) only a small number of Americans could afford to construct their own fallout shelters. At a moment of crisis in 1961 when the United States and the Soviet Union clashed once again over the fate of Berlin, Eisenhower's successor, John F. Kennedy, dedicated some public funds to preparing mass underground shelters in schools and public buildings. Signs with three yellow triangles superimposed on a black circle (**24.12**) that pointed toward underground public fallout shelters now became ubiquitous in schools and government buildings throughout the country.

In 1956 the government began constructing secret centers scattered throughout the nation to house officials in the event of a nuclear attack. The government did not make these preparations public, avoiding uncomfortable questions about what would happen to the rest of the country. These secret plans sought to ensure the continued functioning of Congress by transporting legislators and some staff members (without their families) to an underground shelter in White Sulphur Springs, West Virginia. As part of its preparations, the Treasury Department put an eight-month supply of one-dollar bills and a two-year supply of five-, ten-, and twenty-dollar bills in bombproof shelters. The military scattered mini-Pentagons throughout the country, including underground facilities for the president and his cabinet near Gettysburg, Pennsylvania. Plans to whisk the government to safety during a nuclear attack remained in place until 1995.

24.12 Fallout Shelter Sign
In the early 1960s, fallout shelter signs posted in neighborhoods, schools, and public buildings were daily reminders of the nuclear threat that hung over the nation.

What defensive measures did the public and government take against a possible nuclear attack?

Spies in Our Midst

Recently released documents from the Soviet Union suggest that as many as three hundred Americans spied for the USSR during the 1930s and 1940s. Does this reality justify the attack on civil liberties that occurred during the anti-communist crusade that swept across the country during the 1940s and 1950s? During the Cold War many Americans believed that this anti-communist campaign made the country safer and freer; a minority voiced the competing vision that the government was using spy investigations to limit the scope of legitimate political discourse by eliminating the radical left. The government's crusade against communism in the First Red Scare (1919) after World War I lasted only a few short months. The widespread effort to root out Communist spies after World War II lasted for nearly a decade.

The Second Red Scare

To a country reeling from the loss of China to communism and the detonation of a Soviet bomb, the suggestion that the government was rife with Communist spies offered a simple explanation for these complex events. The House Un-American Activities Committee (HUAC), which had investigated fascist activities in the United States during World War II, now probed the communist threat. Other World War II–era measures also took on new life during the **Second Red Scare**, including the Smith Act (1940), which outlawed advocating the forceful destruction of the government. Acting on a precedent set by Franklin D. Roosevelt in World War II, Truman created a federal employee loyalty program in 1947 that gave the Federal Bureau of Investigation (FBI), the police arm of the Justice Department, the right to investigate the backgrounds of federal workers. In 1950 Congress tightened restrictions on radical political activity even further by passing the McCarran Act, which stopped Communists from entering the country and required Communist or Communist-front organizations to register with the attorney general.

Most of the individuals investigated by HUAC and the FBI had once belonged to the Communist Party, which had attracted many new members during the labor unrest of the 1930s (see Chapter 22). Whether past or even present membership in the Communist Party made one a traitor was another question. When David Wellman was a young boy, his family was under constant police surveillance. Two unmarked cars sat outside their Detroit home and followed him and his sister to school, ball games, and the store. "Trying to turn fear into fun, we made shaking them a game," he later recalled. Wellman maintained that his father, a wounded World War II veteran and leader in the Michigan Communist Party, and his mother, a communist active in trade unions, were not traitors but people who believed that revolution was an American ideal.

The constant surveillance took a toll on the family. "It felt as if the government penetrated the deepest recesses of our lives every minute of the day," Wellman recalled. Paranoia caused the family to censor speech within the home and on the telephone, certain that the police were always listening. As an adult Wellman got access to his family's police file and was stunned to learn that the actual reports contained almost no information about his parents' political activism. The police had discovered very little through this constant surveillance, succeeding mostly in terrorizing the family, which, Wellman suspected, was their true intent all along.

> "They were trying to put the fear of police power in the minds of the people they spied on. To a large degree, it worked."
>
> DAVID WELLMAN, whose family was under police surveillance during the Second Red Scare

The two biggest spy cases of the era involved Alger Hiss and Ethel and Julius Rosenberg. In 1948 Whittaker Chambers, a *Time* magazine editor and former member of the Communist Party, accused Alger Hiss, a high-ranking official during the

What insights does Wellman's story offer into the Second Red Scare?

Roosevelt administration, of being a communist. Hiss denied the charge before HUAC, announcing under oath that "I am not and never have been a member of any Communist-front organization." Chambers responded by charging that Hiss spied for the Soviet Union in the 1930s and as proof produced several rolls of microfilm that Chambers had hidden in a hollow pumpkin in his garden. The "pumpkin patch" microfilm contained copies of secret State Department papers from 1938 regarding the Soviet Union, Nazi Germany, and the Spanish Civil War that had been typed on Hiss's typewriter. The "pumpkin patch" papers corroborated Chambers's account, and recently declassified intelligence documents have confirmed that Hiss worked as a Soviet spy through at least 1945. Because the statute of limitations on espionage had expired, a federal court convicted Hiss of perjury for lying to HUAC about his communist ties. Hiss served four years in jail. Congressman Richard Nixon, a member of HUAC, believed that the "Hiss case, for the first time, forcibly demonstrated to the American people that domestic communism was a real and present danger to the security of the nation." Nixon's leading role in the Hiss investigation catapulted him into the national spotlight. His prominence increased even further when he ran successfully for vice president on the Republican ticket with Eisenhower in 1952.

24.13 The Rosenbergs Spy Case, 1953
Protesters urge the government to execute convicted spies Julius and Ethel Rosenberg, reflecting the fury many Americans felt toward anyone believed to have betrayed the United States.

In 1953 another spy case involving Ethel and Julius Rosenberg, the Jewish parents of two young boys, captivated the nation. The federal government charged Julius with passing atomic bomb secrets to the Soviet Union during World War II, information he had supposedly gathered from his brother-in-law, a Soviet spy working for the Manhattan Project who later testified against the couple. Although Julius's wife Ethel was never personally implicated in the spy ring, the government charged her with knowing of her husband's involvement. Arrested to spur her husband into confessing, both went on trial for espionage. They each maintained their innocence even when convicted and sentenced to death by electric chair.

As the execution date neared, demonstrators from the right and the left took to the streets, offering the public two competing visions of the Rosenbergs and the government's anti-communist investigations. Men carrying signs that read "Burn All Reds" and "No Mercy for Spies" picketed before the White House (**24.13**). Supporters who believed that the Rosenbergs were being persecuted for their radical beliefs organized marches for clemency. Radio and television reporters witnessing the execution shared intimate details with a nation riveted on the couple's final moments, including Ethel's botched electrocution on June 19, 1953, when it took three tries to kill her. Their two young sons, aged ten and six, endured intense media scrutiny as well. Relatives put them in an orphanage, and New Jersey revoked their right to attend public school. Two of their parents' supporters eventually adopted the boys and changed their names. As adults they were active in leftist causes and until recently steadfastly maintained their parents' innocence. For decades the right and the left embraced two competing visions of the Rosenbergs case. The right viewed the couple as traitors whose cooperation with the Soviet Union demonstrated the clear internal threat that the nation faced from Soviet spies. The left, believing the Rosenbergs innocent, felt that mainstream politicians exaggerated the Communist menace to gain public support for eradicating all left-leaning political groups from American society. In some respects both portraits were accurate. Newly released Soviet documents reveal that Julius did indeed pass valuable atomic data to the Soviet Union, but it appears that Ethel knew nothing of her husband's espionage activities, making her, along with countless others in the 1950s, a victim of overzealous investigators who equated leftist politics with treason.

What competing visions arose over the Hiss and Rosenbergs spy cases?

HUAC against Hollywood

The effort to expose the evildoings of communists went far beyond punishing government officials who spied for the Soviet Union. In 1947 HUAC began an investigation into alleged communist activities in Hollywood. Over the next few years, hundreds of screenwriters, producers, directors, and actors were called to testify in Washington, D.C. Initial hearings focused on the supposedly subversive plotlines and imagery of selected motion pictures, such as *Mission to Moscow,* a World War II–era film that presented the Soviet Union as paradise on earth. Jack Warner, the head of Warner Studies, had produced *Mission to Moscow* after the Roosevelt administration requested a film that would improve the public's impression of the nation's wartime ally. This episode in producing left-wing political propaganda was the exception rather than the rule in Hollywood. Most studio heads subscribed to Sam Goldwyn's view that "if you want to send a message, use Western Union." The iron grip of the Hollywood studio system allowed directors little independence to include political content in their films that was not approved by the studio bosses. As a result HUAC could find little evidence of "subversive" content in Hollywood films. Rather than abandoning its investigation of Hollywood, however, HUAC shifted focus to the political affiliations and beliefs of the individuals involved in making movies.

After ten screenwriters, dubbed the "Hollywood Ten," were convicted of contempt of Congress for refusing to cooperate and sentenced to a year in prison, studio executives announced the creation of a **Hollywood blacklist**, a list of individuals with suspected past or present communist ties whom film studios refused to hire. The FBI had already infiltrated the Communist Party and provided HUAC with the names of all those in Hollywood with present or past communist affiliations. HUAC nonetheless pressured subpoenaed witnesses to publicly name names, not to gain information, but to test witnesses' loyalty. Many cooperated with HUAC to salvage their film careers. The vast majority who refused to testify or to name names never worked in films again. Others, like future president Ronald Reagan, then the president of the Screen Actors Guild, joined the anti-communist crusade by privately providing the FBI with the names of individuals in Hollywood with potential communist connections. Reagan testified before HUAC as a liberal Democrat (his shift to the right came a few years later), where he denied that communists "have ever at any time been able to use the motion-picture screen as a sounding board for their philosophy."

Director Elia Kazan and playwright Arthur Miller used their artistic work to explain the different choices they made when asked to testify by HUAC. Kazan's film *On the Waterfront* (1954) starred Marlon Brando as an ex-prizefighter turned longshoreman who overcomes his aversion to "ratting on your friends" and testifies against his corrupt union bosses. Kazan, who had been a member of the Communist Party in the 1930s, intended for the film to justify his own decision in 1952 to provide HUAC with the names of eight former Communist Party colleagues (see *Competing Visions: Naming Names in Hollywood,* page 740). *On the Waterfront* won Academy Awards for Best Picture, Best Director, and Best Actor. Conversely Miller refused to testify when called before HUAC in 1956 and criticized the hysteria created by the Second Red Scare in his play *The Crucible,* which likened the HUAC investigations to the 1692 Salem witch trials in colonial Massachusetts.

> "We will not knowingly employ a Communist nor a member of any party or groups which advocates the overthrow of the Government of the United States by force or by illegal or unconstitutional methods."
>
> Studio executives' statement announcing the creation of a Hollywood blacklist, 1947

McCarthyism

The government's anti-communist crusade during the Second Red Scare also became known as **McCarthyism**, named for the media-savvy Republican senator Joseph McCarthy from Wisconsin, who, along with HUAC, spearheaded numerous governmental investigations into communist activities, many of them spurious. Anti-communist spy investigations predated McCarthy, but his flair for the dramatic made the senator an instant media sensation. McCarthy burst onto the scene after waving around a piece of paper during a speech before the Women's Republican Club in Wheeling, West Virginia, on

What was the purpose and impact of HUAC's Hollywood investigations?

Competing Visions

NAMING NAMES IN HOLLYWOOD

The following opinions, one from former first lady Eleanor Roosevelt who wrote a syndicated magazine column, "My Day," and the other from film director Elia Kazan, offer opposing views on aiding the HUAC investigations. Consider how Roosevelt and Kazan defined the threat to American democracy in this period. What risks were involved in following the different suggestions each made? Could their two views be reconciled in any way?

In a 1947 "My Day" column, Eleanor Roosevelt expressed concerns that HUAC was creating a police state atmosphere that would squash artistic creativity and freedom of expression.

I have waited a while before saying anything about the Un-American Activities Committee's current investigation of the Hollywood film industry. I would not be very much surprised if some writers or actors or stagehands, or what not, were found to have Communist leanings, but I was surprised to find that, at the start of the inquiry, some of the big producers were so chicken-hearted about speaking up for the freedom of their industry.

One thing is sure—none of the arts flourishes on censorship and repression. And by this time it should be evident that the American public is capable of doing its own censoring.... The film industry is a great industry with infinite possibilities for good and bad. Its primary purpose is to entertain people. On the side, it can do many other things. It can popularize certain ideals, it can make education palatable. However, in the long run, the judge who decides whether what it does is good or bad is the man or woman who attends the movies. In a democratic country I do not think the public will tolerate a removal of its right to decide what it thinks of the ideas and performances of those who make the movie industry work.... What is going on in the Un-American Activities Committee worries me primarily because little people have become frightened and we find ourselves living in the atmosphere of a police state, where people close doors before they state what they think or look over their shoulders apprehensively before they express an opinion.... If you curtail what the other fellow says and does, you curtail what you yourself may say and do. In our country we must trust the people to hear and see both the good and the bad and to choose the good. The Un-American Activities Committee seems to me to be better for a police state than for the USA.

Many people in Hollywood never forgave Elia Kazan for cooperating with HUAC. In his 1988 autobiography Kazan refused to apologize for his actions. Instead he asserted his right to protect his career and the need to defend the country.

I believed it was the duty of the government to investigate the Communist movement in our country. I couldn't behave as if my old "comrades" didn't exist and didn't have an active political program. There was no way I could go along with their crap that the CP [Communist Party] was nothing but another political party, like the Republicans and the Democrats. I knew very well what it was, a thoroughly organized, worldwide conspiracy. This conviction separated me from many of my old friends ...

Did I really want to change the social system I was living under? Apparently that was what I'd stood for at one time. But what s**t. Everything I had of value I'd gained under that system ...

Why had I taken so long to even consider telling the country—that's what it amounted to—everything I knew? Was it because of the moral injunction against "informing," which was respected only depending on which side you were on? ... If the situation were reversed, wouldn't the "comrades" protect themselves without hesitation and by any means? Including naming me.... I began to measure the weight and the worth of what I was giving up, my career in films, which I was surrendering for a cause I didn't believe in. It seemed insane. What was I if not a filmmaker? ... If you expect an apology now because I would later name names to the House Committee, you've misjudged my character.... The people who owe you an explanation (no apology expected) are those who, year after year, held the Soviets blameless for all their crimes.

Hearings before the House Committee on Un-American Activities during the Second Red Scare

What different perspectives do Roosevelt and Kazan offer on protecting the right to freedom of expression?

February 9, 1950, thundering that he had a list of 205 known communists who worked in the State Department. (The paper turned out to be just a prop.) When pressed for the names of the individuals on his list, McCarthy stalled and announced that he would only show their names to Truman, which he never did. In each subsequent speech the number cited by McCarthy dropped until he finally settled on fifty-seven.

"When a great democracy is destroyed, it will not be from enemies from without, but rather because of enemies from within."

Senator JOSEPH R. MCCARTHY, Wheeling, West Virginia, 1950.

As a Republican attacking a Democratic administration, McCarthy's accusations had a distinctly partisan ring. Taking advantage of the media spotlight, McCarthy issued new charges against an assortment of State Department officials, ruining the careers of numerous individuals who could not mount an effective defense against his bullying. Reveling in the press attention that every new allegation brought, McCarthy sought increasingly bigger targets, even attacking Secretary of Defense George C. Marshall, who had authored the Marshall Plan while secretary of state, for having joined "a conspiracy so immense and an infamy so black as to dwarf any previous such venture in the history of man."

A year after the Rosenbergs were executed, the personal career of Joseph McCarthy as an anti-communist crusader ended when the senator began investigating the army for subversion. National television broadcast the hearings, and Americans watched aghast for thirty-six days as McCarthy intimidated witnesses, ignored facts, and made ludicrous charges. The climactic moment in the hearing came when the army's attorney Joseph Welch rebuked McCarthy, telling him, "You have done enough. Have you no sense of decency, sir, at long last?" Public approval ratings for McCarthy plummeted from 50 percent to 35 percent in Gallup polls.

The public unraveling of support for McCarthy mirrored growing concerns among his fellow Republicans in Congress. By 1954 Eisenhower and former HUAC member Richard Nixon were in the White House. Attacking a Republican-controlled administration yielded fewer political benefits, and some Republicans privately urged Eisenhower to rein in McCarthy. Leary of having his own anti-communist credentials challenged, Eisenhower refused to confront McCarthy directly. Instead the president tried to take the high road. "I will not get down in the gutter with that guy," Eisenhower vowed, reasoning that if he gave McCarthy enough rope, he would eventually hang himself. This hands-off approach allowed McCarthy to run wild until 1954, when, as Eisenhower predicted, he went too far. Eventually it was the mainstream press, not the president, who denounced McCarthy. In the wake of the Army-McCarthy hearings, the esteemed television journalist Edward R. Murrow exposed McCarthy's slander and lies in a television documentary. McCarthy, Murrow pointedly told his audience, "didn't create this situation of fear; he merely exploited it." However when the Senate censured McCarthy on December 2, 1954, for violating Senate rules, the legislators chose to depict McCarthy as solely responsible for the excesses of anticommunism. McCarthy left the Senate in disgrace, and died from liver failure caused by alcoholism four years later at the age of forty-nine.

"No one man can terrorize a whole nation unless we are all his accomplices."

Journalist EDWARD R. MURROW during a 1954 television exposé on McCarthy

As Murrow suggested the end of McCarthy's career as a red-baiter did not stop the government's anti-communist crusade. Republicans and Democrats alike took their cue from McCarthy and freely attacked any suspected radical working in local or state governments, public schools, or universities. The Smith Act remained in place, as did loyalty oaths, Hollywood blacklists, and police surveillance of suspected radicals. By the 1950s using the charge of communism to discredit political opponents or liberal activists (such as Martin Luther King Jr.) was commonplace in American politics.

Is the term McCarthyism a useful or misleading way to characterize the Second Red Scare?

Averting Nuclear War

The worldwide ideological, political, and military struggle between the United States and the Soviet Union fueled Americans' abiding fear of communism, both at home and throughout the world. The vision of fighting a nuclear war continued to haunt Americans even after the ceasefire in Korea. Technological advances in long-range ballistic missiles and satellites provoked a new moment of crisis in the Cold War standoff between the United States and the Soviet Union. A missile fitted with a nuclear warhead could now travel through space to reach the United States within half an hour from the Soviet Union. A series of armed uprisings in Eastern Europe, renewed Soviet demands that the West abandon Berlin, and the Cuban Missile Crisis combined to create a climactic moment when the world teetered on the edge of all-out nuclear war.

Sputnik

On October 4, 1957, the Soviet Union successfully sent the world's first satellite, nicknamed Sputnik ("fellow traveler"), into outer space. The size of a basketball and weighing just 183 pounds, Sputnik (**24.14**) nonetheless became a symbol of Soviet technological superiority, a satellite that could orbit the earth in ninety-eight minutes. Today satellites serve a host of peaceful functions, transmitting television images and telephone calls throughout the globe. In 1957, however, Americans focused primarily on the new strategic advantage that satellite technology gave the Soviets. The Soviets could easily fit a missile that sent Sputnik into orbit with a nuclear warhead and launch it at the United States. Fearing that the United States was in danger of losing the "space race," the government created the National Aeronautics and Space Administration (NASA) to launch America's own investigation of space, and the Defense Department scrambled to develop American satellite technology.

24.14 Sputnik, 1957
For Americans this small satellite symbolized Soviet technological superiority over the United States, fueling the ongoing arms race between the two nations.

Predicting how the Soviet Union's volatile new leader might use this technological breakthrough kept Americans on edge. In the power struggle that followed Stalin's death from a brain hemorrhage in March 1953, Nikita Khrushchev emerged as the new Soviet premier. A poorly educated peasant who rose through the ranks to become a Stalin protégé, Khrushchev reveled in rhetorical excess. He proclaimed that the USSR was producing missiles "like sausages," and enjoyed keeping his American visitors off-balance. During a visit by Minneapolis senator Hubert Humphrey to Moscow, Khrushchev stopped his threatening tirade long enough to ask Humphrey where he was from. "That's so I don't forget to order them to spare the city when the rockets fly," he said good naturedly.

Eager to catch up with the Soviet Union in missile technology and cut the defense budget (conventional military forces cost more than building nuclear weapons), Eisenhower oversaw a tremendous increase in American nuclear weaponry, which grew from eight hundred to nearly eight thousand warheads between 1953 and 1960. This nuclear arms build-up was part of a strategic vision called the "New Look." In 1954 Eisenhower's tough-talking secretary of state John Foster Dulles announced that the United States would focus on developing "massive retaliatory power" to deter Soviet aggression. The National Security Council agreed with Dulles that the country would go bankrupt trying to develop adequate defenses against Soviet nuclear weapons and policing the world with ground troops. Dulles maintained that building a strong arsenal of intercontinental missiles armed with nuclear warheads would allow the United States to "retaliate, instantly, by means and at places of our choosing" when the Soviets stepped out of line. Eisenhower particularly liked the New Look because it offered a way to counter the Soviet manpower advantage while maintaining a small peacetime army at home. The appeal of "massive retaliation" was simple—it provided "more bang for the buck," some commentators noted.

Getting accurate data on the Soviet arsenal became critical once the United States embraced the doctrine of massive retaliation. The year before the Soviets launched Sputnik, the Americans began

What caused the nuclear arms race to escalate in the late 1950s?

using a new spy plane, the U-2, to take photographs of Soviet military installations. Soviet radar could detect the U-2, but the plane flew at altitudes out of range for Soviet fighter pilots or antiaircraft missiles. For four years the United States used U-2 missions to collect intelligence about the number of Soviet long-range missiles before turning to spy satellites. The photographs were reassuring. At the end of 1959, the United States learned, the Soviet Union had only six intercontinental ballistic missile (ICBM) sites, which were places to launch a missile carrying a nuclear warhead. Because it took twenty hours to fuel each missile, which could travel through space to reach targets 5,000 to 6,000 miles away in half an hour, the United States would have ample time to respond if the Soviet Union launched a first strike with six missiles. Despite Khrushchev's claims that the Soviets possessed a huge nuclear arsenal, in fact American stockpiles of nuclear warheads and ICBMs far exceeded those of the Soviet Union.

Having made much of the claim that the Soviet Union possessed more ICBMs than the United States in his successful 1960 presidential campaign against Richard Nixon, newly elected Democratic president John F. Kennedy waited a few months before revealing the truth. Calling Khrushchev's bluff Kennedy announced to the world that the United States had a "second strike capability which is at least as extensive as what the Soviets can deliver by striking first. Therefore, we are confident that the Soviets will not provoke a major nuclear conflict." The gap only kept growing in America's favor. Continuing the policy of massive retaliation, Kennedy oversaw an increase in the American ICBM stockpile from 63 to 424 from 1961 to 1963.

The attention given to the missile gap during the 1960 presidential campaign revealed the constant pressure that Americans felt to retain the upper hand in the ever-evolving nuclear arms race. The chart (**24.15**) lists the key developments in early Cold War nuclear weaponry, illustrating the intense competition between the United States and Soviet Union to develop nuclear weapons, including nuclear-powered submarines that could stay submerged for two months and fire nuclear-fitted missiles.

INNOVATION	USA	USSR
Nuclear-powered submarine	1954	1958
First Trial of ICBM	1958	1957
ICBM operational	1960	1959
Submarine-launched ICBM operational	1960	1957

24.15 Nuclear Arms Race, 1950s The United States and Soviet Union tried to best each other by developing more sophisticated nuclear weapons.

The Berlin Wall

Americans weighed Kennedy's reassuring words about the missile gap against recent events that once again demonstrated the heavy hand of Soviet authority in Eastern Europe. In 1956 Khrushchev publicly denounced Stalin's crimes against the Soviet people. Khrushchev's speech, taken as a cue that the new Soviet regime would be more open and tolerant, set off rebellions in Poland and Hungary. Soviet troops immediately rolled into Hungary to crush the rebellion, revealing that Khrushchev intended to retain Soviet control over Eastern Europe.

Khrushchev also moved to consolidate Soviet power over Berlin, twice issuing ultimatums to the West to vacate its territory in the divided city. The stark differences between life in East and West Berlin had become a public embarrassment to the Soviet Union. Lavishly rebuilt by West Germany and the Marshall Plan, West Berlin teemed with new housing, industry, and commerce. Moving freely between the more prosperous western half and the areas under Communist control, many Berliners voted with their feet. Nearly a million East Germans defected in 1956, traveling easily from West Berlin into West Germany to start new lives.

Khrushchev viewed the forty-four-year-old Kennedy as an inept, inexperienced leader whom he could easily intimidate. A botched U.S. invasion of Cuba in 1961 (discussed more fully later) only reaffirmed Khrushchev's low opinion of Kennedy. Believing that Kennedy would crumble under pressure, Khrushchev demanded that the West leave Berlin when the two met for the first time in Vienna. To Khrushchev's surprise the president stood firm. Kennedy left the summit "shaken and angry," one reporter claimed. He never met with Khrushchev again. Instead he returned home and requested funds for additional nuclear and conventional forces. The public fully supported their president. More

24.16 Brandenburg Gate, 1961 For Americans the desolate scene before the Brandenburg Gate, the traditional entry point into the city of Berlin, symbolized the heavy hand of Soviet oppression as the Berlin Wall went up.

than 82 percent favored maintaining American, French, and British forces in Berlin, even if it meant war with the Soviet Union.

With Kennedy unwilling to abandon the city, Khrushchev resisted the temptation to erect another blockade. Instead of revoking permission for the West to use roads through East Germany to supply the city, as Stalin had in 1948, he made the controversial decision to build a wall between East and West Berlin. In the twilight hours of August 13, 1961,

> "Freedom has many difficulties and democracy is not perfect, but we have never had to put a wall up to keep our people in, to prevent them from leaving us."
>
> President JOHN F. KENNEDY, in a speech before the Berlin Wall, 1963

construction of a barbed wire fence began. East German tanks and troops rolled up to the monumental Brandenburg Gate, the traditional entry point into the city of Berlin, to prevent a popular protest from breaking out in front of this symbol of German nationhood. East German workers quickly laid a thin line of barbed wire in front of the Brandenburg Gate, turning the popular square into a desolate no-man's land (**24.16**). As tensions mounted the British strung a second line of barbed wire on the western side as a safety measure to prevent irate West Berliners from instigating a shooting war between the two sides. The sign initially placed at the site, "Attention—You Are Now Leaving West Berlin," was hardly necessary now.

Photos put a human face on the suffering. In one (**24.17**) two young girls, standing on the western side, chat with their grandparents over the makeshift fence that now divided them. East Germany eventually replaced the barbed wire with 12-foot-high concrete walls that ran for nearly 30 miles, and was dotted with guard towers, spotlights, guard dogs, and minefields. West Germans flocked to the construction site, curious and in shock. Some East Germans made desperate last-minute escapes, jumping from the windows of buildings that straddled the boundary into nets held by West German firefighters. East German soldiers first bricked up the windows, then demolished the buildings to create 100 yards of empty space between the wall and any other structure. The "dead zone" on the eastern side made it impossible for people to approach the wall. Guards along the wall had strict orders to shoot anyone who tried to cross it. Nearly a thousand people died trying to escape to West Berlin during the wall's twenty-eight-year existence.

The wall succeeded in stopping the flow of people from East to West Berlin without provoking a major confrontation with the United States. As the wall went up in 1961, Kennedy remarked to his aides that "a wall is a hell of a lot better than a war." The Soviet success came at a cost, however. For over two decades the Berlin Wall served as the most visible symbol to the world of Soviet oppression. When Kennedy finally visited the wall in June 1963, he expressed

24.17 Berlin Wall
Two sisters living in West Berlin chat with their grandparents across the barbed wire that divided East and West Berlin. Before East Germany replaced the barbed wire with a concrete wall, many East Germans escaped to the West by jumping over the flimsy barricade.

What meaning did photographs of the Berlin Wall have for Americans?

solidarity with the people on both sides of the divided city by announcing, "Ich bin ein Berliner" (which Kennedy thought meant "I am a Berliner," not realizing that *ein Berliner* was the name for a popular German doughnut). Over the years the wall on the western side became covered in graffiti and required continual repair from saboteurs' efforts to destroy parts of it.

Bay of Pigs and the Cuban Missile Crisis

Americans viewed Communist activities in Germany with dismay, but the prospect of a Communist Cuba alarmed the government more: Cuba lay just 90 miles south of Florida. In 1959 Fidel Castro had emerged as the victor in the Cuban Revolution, overthrowing the dictator Fulgencio Bastista y Zaldívar. Castro moved quickly to consolidate his power. He declared himself a communist, confiscated a billion dollars in American property, and accepted aid from the Soviet Union. In response an alarmed Eisenhower broke off diplomatic relations and imposed economic sanctions, including an embargo that banned the export of American goods to the island. The Central Intelligence Agency (CIA) urged more forceful action and began planning the covert **Bay of Pigs operation**, a failed amphibious invasion by Cuban exiles in 1961 to overthrow the Cuban dictator Fidel Castro.

Eisenhower left office before the scheduled invasion, but Kennedy quickly gave his blessing to the plan. Problems arose immediately. Two days before the ground attack, American planes (painted to look like stolen Cuban aircraft) bombed Cuban air defenses. On April 17, 1961, fourteen hundred exiles landed and were all immediately killed or captured. Kennedy's unconvincing public statement that the United States was not involved in this "struggle of Cuban patriots against a Cuban dictator" hurt his credibility at home and overseas.

The Bays of Pigs fiasco hardened the resolve of Kennedy, Khrushchev, and Castro to gain the upper hand in this new Cold War hotspot. The CIA devised various schemes for overthrowing Castro that involved sabotage and terrorism. In November 1961 CIA agents and Cuban exiles formed attack squads that covertly traveled in speedboats from Florida to Cuba, where they burned sugar plantations and blew up factories and oil depots. The CIA also plotted to assassinate Castro by trying to poison his ice cream and cigars and enlisting Mafia crime bosses to kill him. Castro complained to Khrushchev about America's murderous intentions, and in return received an influx of Soviet economic and military aid. Protecting communism in Cuba now became a major goal for the Soviet Union.

On October 22, 1962, President Kennedy appeared on national television to deliver the stunning news that the Soviet Union was building missile launching pads in Cuba for short- and intermediate-range nuclear missiles. The United States maintained bases in Italy, Britain, and Turkey that housed nuclear missiles aimed at the Soviet Union. Putting Soviet missiles in Cuba, a mere 90 miles from the American coast, would teach Americans "just what it feels like to have enemy missiles pointing at you," Khrushchev told his advisors. The **Cuban Missile Crisis**, a showdown in 1962 between the United States and the Soviet Union over Khrushchev's decision to place Soviet missiles in Communist Cuba aimed at America, was underway.

Instead of accepting the Soviet view that missiles in Cuba simply leveled the playing field, Kennedy responded with a competing vision that the Soviet actions represented "a provocative change in the delicate status quo both countries have maintained." Short- and intermediate-range Soviet missiles in Cuba threatened to reduce the strategic advantage that America held with its larger long-range nuclear arsenal. This was unacceptable to Kennedy. Intelligence officials estimated that the missile sites would become operational in two weeks, giving Kennedy only a small window of time before the Soviets would double their ability to launch a devastating nuclear strike against the United States.

Kennedy ultimately decided to use a naval blockade to prevent Soviet ships from arming the launching sites with nuclear missiles. (Only later would Kennedy discover that missiles were already in Cuba. The president never learned that the estimate of 10,000 Soviet troops in Cuba was wrong—there were actually 42,000).

How did the United States respond when communism took hold in Cuba?

Choices and Consequences

THE CUBAN MISSILE CRISIS

Long-range Soviet missiles (4,000–5,000 miles) launched from the USSR could already reach America, but short-range (1,100 miles) and intermediate-range (2,200 miles) nuclear-armed missiles in Cuba helped close the missile gap by giving the Soviets more weapons to use against the United States. Determined to get Soviet missiles out of Cuba, Kennedy and his advisors debated how to respond on October 16, 1962.

Choices

1. Use air and ground forces to attack Cuba and destroy the missile sites.
2. Follow up an attack on Cuba with a full-scale invasion to depose Castro.
3. Negotiate with the Soviet Union and Cuba.
4. Enact a naval quarantine to prevent Soviet-supplied missiles from reaching Cuba.

Distance between Cuba and Major U.S. Cities, 1962

Decision

Kennedy opted for the quarantine. He sent the American navy 500 miles offshore of Cuba to intercept Soviet vessels carrying missiles, and threatened a nuclear attack on the Soviet Union if missiles were launched from Cuba.

Consequences

For two tense days Soviet ships steamed toward American naval vessels. At the last minute Khrushchev called the ships back and offered to negotiate by removing the missiles if Kennedy pledged not to attack Cuba and the United States dismantled its missiles in Turkey. Kennedy privately agreed to these terms. By deciding against an air strike, Kennedy may have unknowingly averted a nuclear war. Unbeknownst to the president nuclear warheads were already in Cuba. Soviet commanders on the ground had permission to use them if the United States attacked and considered using them against the blockade.

Continuing Controversies

Did Kennedy react correctly during the Cuban Missile Crisis?

Supporters argue that Kennedy effectively used the threat of an American nuclear attack, traditional naval tactics, and old-fashioned diplomacy to end the crisis without resorting to war. By doing so he maintained America's strategic advantage against the Soviet Union and improved the nation's image worldwide after the Bay of Pigs fiasco.

Detractors claim that Kennedy provoked a crisis where there was none. Short- and medium-range missiles in Cuba did not alter the ability of the Soviets to attack with long-range missiles or of the United States to respond. Supporters counter that the improved accuracy of shorter-range missiles fired from Cuba posed a real threat. Critics also point out that because Kennedy made concessions privately to Khrushchev, the crisis gave rise to the myth that "brinkmanship," or threatening nuclear war, rather than diplomatic negotiations, caused the Soviets to back down. American overconfidence in the wake of the Cuban Missile Crisis would lead to missteps in America's growing military involvement in the Vietnam War and elsewhere in the next few years.

What political and military considerations influenced Kennedy during the Cuban Missile Crisis?

Choices and Consequences: The Cuban Missile Crisis, outlines the options facing Kennedy during this tense fortnight, the closest that the world ever came to fighting an all-out nuclear war. The world waited for thirteen days as Soviet ships steamed toward the American fleet guarding Cuban ports. American pilots sat in planes loaded with nuclear weapons, waiting to take off for Cuba at a moment's notice. Finally Khrushchev called Soviet ships back and offered to negotiate. The public breathed a collective sigh of relief that nuclear war had been averted, but the crisis lingered on behind closed doors for another month. As Soviet engineers continued to work on the missile sites, Kennedy and Khrushchev debated the exact terms of an agreement. In the end the American navy won the right to inspect ships carrying dismantled missiles out of Cuba. In return the United States agreed to dismantle its missiles in Turkey and pledged to respect Cuban independence by not launching another Bay of Pigs–type invasion. Over the next few years land-based missile sites lost significance as more American and Soviet submarines equipped with nuclear missiles began patrolling the world.

> "We're eyeball to eyeball, and I think the other fellow just blinked."
>
> Secretary of State DEAN RUSK, upon receiving word that Soviet ships had turned back during the Cuban Missile Crisis in 1962

Having teetered on the brink of nuclear war, both the United States and the Soviet Union opted to deescalate tensions. Kennedy and Khrushchev agreed to establish a hotline connection between Washington and Moscow so the two leaders could speak directly in the event of another crisis. In June 1963 Britain, the Soviet Union, and the United States also signed the Limited Test Ban Treaty, which banned atmospheric and underwater testing of nuclear weapons.

Conclusion

By 1950 conflicting visions within the U.S. government over how to respond to Soviet aggression gave way to an American strategy focused on containing communism. The United States sent financial aid to Western Europe, offered assistance to nations resisting Communist aggression, and stationed American soldiers permanently overseas. When the Soviet Union acquired the atomic bomb and China fell to communism, the United States responded by building a hydrogen bomb and stockpiling an enormous arsenal of nuclear weapons. The Cold War turned hot when North Korea invaded South Korea and the United States decided to intervene. After three years of fighting, a ceasefire ensured South Korean independence.

At home some Americans built bomb shelters to protect themselves from radioactive fallout, and civil defense drills taught schoolchildren to "duck and cover" during a nuclear bomb attack. Fears that Soviet spies were infiltrating the military, government, and film industry led to the Second Red Scare.

After a brief lull Cold War tensions reignited when East Germany built the Berlin Wall in 1961 and the Soviets attempted to place missiles in Cuba in 1962. The Cuban Missile Crisis passed without either side launching a nuclear strike, but this was the closest the world came to nuclear annihilation during the Cold War.

Throughout the Truman, Eisenhower, and Kennedy administrations, America made critical choices about how to handle the new threat that the Soviet Union posed to the nation's economy, global influence, and national security. Eschewing diplomacy three presidents chose instead to contain communism with a mix of international aid, military alliances, and direct fighting with Communist nations presumably financed and controlled by Moscow. In the early 1960s American policymakers decided that defeating the North Vietnamese Communist regime was essential for America to win the Cold War, a strategic vision that the peace movement soon challenged.

What was the ultimate significance of the Cuban Missile crisis?

CHAPTER REVIEW

1946

Kennan's Long Telegram
Makes containing communism a key American goal

1947

Truman Doctrine
Gives United States a role in helping other nations resist communism

HUAC begins investigating Hollywood
Leads to establishment of blacklist

1948

Marshall Plan
Grants U.S. aid to rebuild war-torn Europe and prevent spread of communism

Berlin airlift
Highly visible Cold War victory for the United States

Review Questions

1. In the postwar period, the United States assumed the role of global protector against Communist aggression. What competing visions did policymakers offer on the role that the United States should play in world affairs? How did the Truman Administration justify its foreign policy decisions from 1945–1950?
2. Evaluate the impact that international crises had on domestic politics from 1945 to 1963. Consider the reverse as well: How did domestic politics affect foreign policy during the early Cold War?
3. How did images and popular culture shape Americans' ideas about the Soviet Union and the atomic bomb?
4. What factors contributed to the Second Red Scare? What differing views did Americans have about its impact on American society?
5. Compare how Truman and Kennedy each handled a Soviet-instigated crisis over Berlin. Why did Americans consider West Berlin so important? What key decisions and risks did each leader take in resolving the crisis?
6. What key contributions did Truman, Eisenhower, and Kennedy make to the strategy of containment?

1949

NATO formed
First formal American military alliance since the Revolutionary War

Soviet Union acquires atomic bomb
United States loses atomic monopoly

China falls to communism
Provokes fears that communists are winning the Cold War

1950

Joseph McCarthy gives Wheeling, West Virginia, Speech
Begins career as major figure in Second Red Scare

Korean War begins
United States enters fighting; Cold War extends into East Asia

1953

Stalin dies; Khrushchev assumes power
Ruthless dictator replaced by brash and unpredictable one

Armistice announced in Korea
Limited victory that restores initial boundary between North and South Korea

Julius and Ethel Rosenberg executed
Spy case fuels Second Red Scare

1961–1962

Bay of Pigs invasion
Failed attempt to oust Castro in Cuba embarrasses the United States

Berlin Wall built
Becomes symbol of communist oppression

Cuban Missile Crisis
Nuclear showdown between the United States and the USSR prompts fears of nuclear war

Key Terms

Cold War A full-scale ideological and military conflict between the United States and the Soviet Union and their allies that led to several hot wars around the globe, although the Americans and Soviets, fearful of a nuclear showdown, never fought each other directly 721

"long telegram" An influential five-thousand-word missive by diplomat George F. Kennan that outlined why America needed to develop an aggressive foreign policy aimed at containing Soviet expansionist impulses. 722

containment The label affixed to multiple American foreign policy initiatives meant to prevent the Soviet Union from expanding its influence around the globe. 722

iron curtain Churchill's characterization of the military and ideological barrier erected by the Soviet Union that separated Western and Eastern Europe into free and unfree halves. 722

North Atlantic Treaty Organization (NATO) A post-World War II military alliance between the United States and Western European powers. 722

Truman Doctrine A foreign policy initiative that gave the United States an active role in stopping the global spread of communism by supporting "free peoples who are resisting attempted subjugation by armed minorities or by outside pressures." 724

Marshall Plan (1948–1952) Aimed to restore Europeans' faith in capitalism by sending $13 billion ($119 billion in today's dollars) overseas to rebuild Europe's ruined roads, bridges, factories, and farms. 724

Berlin airlift (1948–1949) Americans and British used planes to resupply West Berlin to stymie the Soviet blockade of the city. 726

Korean War (1950–1953) The United States fought Communist North Koreans and Chinese to a stalemate, frustrating Americans who had to learn to accept only a partial victory. 729

nuclear fallout The deadly pollution that descends through the air after a nuclear bomb explosion. 734

Second Red Scare Widespread effort to root out Communist spies after World War II that lasted for nearly a decade. 737

Hollywood blacklist A list of individuals with suspected past or present communist ties whom film studios refused to hire. 739

McCarthyism The government's anti-communist crusade named for Senator Joseph McCarthy from Wisconsin, who, along with the House Committee on Un-American Activities (HUAC), spearheaded numerous governmental investigations into communist activities, many of them spurious. 739

Bay of Pigs operation (1961) Failed attempt to use an amphibious invasion by Cuban exiles to overthrow the Cuban dictator Fidel Castro. 745

Cuban Missile Crisis (1962) A showdown between the United States and the Soviet Union over Khrushchev's decision to place Soviet missiles in Communist Cuba aimed at America. 745

CHAPTER

25

In a Land of Plenty

Contentment and Discord, 1945–1960

> "It was the longest block I ever walked in my whole life."
>
> ELIZABETH ECKFORD, confronting a mob as she walked from the bus stop to school in Little Rock, Arkansas

On September 3, 1955, a young black teenager, Elizabeth Eckford, walked past an angry mob after state troopers refused to let her enter the all-white Central High School in Little Rock, Arkansas. This photo captures her harrowing ordeal as a young white woman, her face contorted with rage, screamed at Eckford. In the days that followed a sympathetic white man put an ad in the local newspaper featuring this photograph. "Study this picture and know shame," he told his neighbors. Instead for years Hazel Bryan received congratulatory letters from diehard segregationists for her verbal assault on Eckford that day. Five years later Bryan tracked down Eckford in Little Rock to apologize. Eckford went on to graduate from college, served in the army, and then started a career as a probation officer.

This photograph challenges the traditional image of the fifties as a tranquil period of material contentment and ideological consensus. Americans did enjoy unprecedented prosperity during the decade. They also, however, experienced a fair amount of domestic discord along racial, generational, and political lines. New energy surged into the Civil Rights Movement in the 1950s. Acts of extraordinary bravery by Elizabeth Eckford and others like her took on new significance in an era of favorable Supreme Court rulings that pushed the federal government to take an active role in protecting the civil rights of African Americans. Leadership from black churches and black students infused the movement with an ethos of nonviolent direct action that forced white America to see the injustice of Jim Crow, the southern legal structure that relegated African Americans to second-class citizenship.

A different type of discord permeated American home-life throughout the 1950s. In many respects families were the focus of American society from 1945 to1960. Enjoying a rising standard of living in generally prosperous times, American families grew at an unprecedented rate. Lured to fast-growing suburbs by low-cost loans and affordable housing prices, an exploding middle class filled their homes with an array of possessions previously out of reach for most Americans. The baby boom generation, those 76.4 million Americans born between 1946 and 1964, now coming into adolescence, embraced new standards in dress, music, and movies that distinguished the "teen" generation from their parents. Some teenagers rebelled against authority in more overtly political ways. High school and college students, for instance, were the ground troops in many civil rights demonstrations. Others joined the counterculture beat movement to express their rebellion against social norms through poetry, novels, and art.

From 1945 to 1960 Americans debated the divergent political paths that the country could take domestically during the Cold War era. They pondered the effects of New Deal programs, unions, suburbs, civil rights, and consumption on American society. Altogether the changing American way of life created a sense of both contentment and crisis for the nation.

What symbolism made this photograph an icon of the Civil Rights Movement?

Don't INFLATE
THE PRICES
Just DEFLATE
the PROFITS
USA-CIO

Securing the New Deal Legacy

Once prosperity returned after World War II, Republicans launched a campaign to undo the New Deal, arguing that these Depression-era laws and benefits programs hampered the free market and deprived industrialists of the freedom to run their companies as they saw fit. Moderate Democrats, like President Harry Truman, focused on ensuring the permanency of past reforms. When labor unions launched a series of unpopular postwar strikes, Republicans joined with conservative Southern Democrats to successfully roll back New Deal legislation that had benefited the labor movement. The victory over labor, however, did not provide enough momentum for conservatives to achieve their ultimate goal: the entire dismantlement of the New Deal.

The Labor Movement Curtailed

In 1945 the labor movement enjoyed unparalleled strength. Government support for union organizing during the New Deal and World War II, combined with a wave of successful sit-down strikes in the 1930s, had made labor a powerful force in American society. This was the high point of the labor movement in American history. Over fourteen million workers belonged to unions, nearly 35 percent of the industrial workforce. Labor flexed its muscle in 1946, when the lifting of wartime price controls sent prices skyrocketing. Nearly 4.6 million

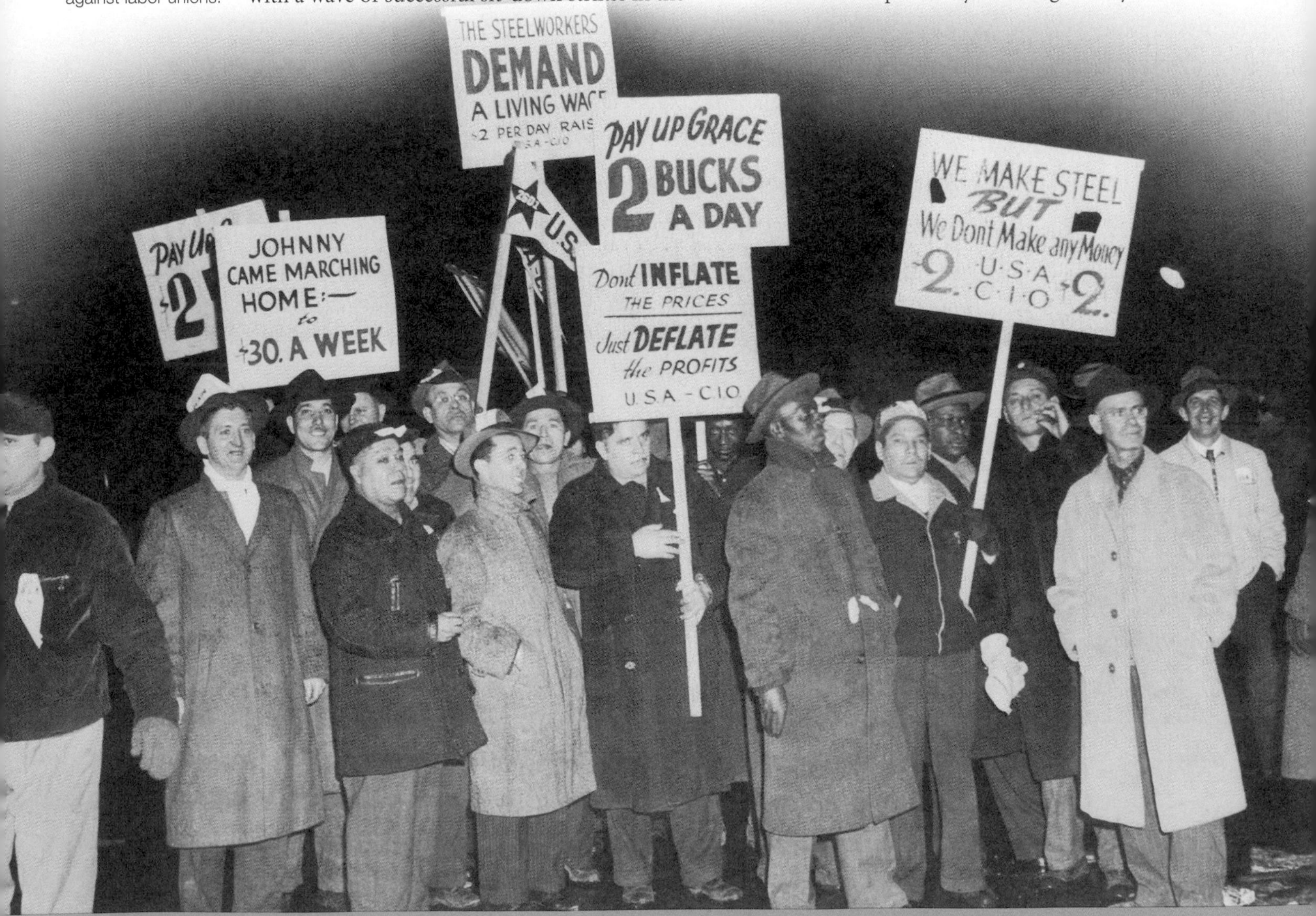

25.1 Striking Steel Workers, 1946 Picketing steel workers carried signs with slogans meant to win sympathy from ordinary Americans, but widespread strikes caused a public backlash against labor unions.

What overall arguments do these signs make in favor of labor's demands?

workers participated in five thousand strikes nationwide in 1945–1946, demanding not just higher wages and benefits but also the right to participate in management decisions regarding investments, product lines, production methods, and plant locations. The signs held by striking steelworkers in this photo (**25.1**) outside a Bethlehem Steel Plant were intended to mobilize public support. The slogans demanded fairness to returning veterans, gave assurances that higher wages would not lead to higher prices, and proposed a living wage for workers who made such a valuable commodity. Black and white steelworkers manned this picket line together, reflecting the success of the Congress of Industrial Organizations (CIO) in mending racial divisions that had previously weakened the labor movement (see Chapter 22).

As the scale of labor unrest widened, popular support for strikes diminished. The public had little sympathy for threats to shut down the steel and car industries, which formed the core of the national economy. Strikes in the coal and meatpacking industries also caused public dismay by making it more expensive for Americans to heat their homes and eat meat. When railroad workers went on strike, Truman intervened. The railroad strike "threatens to paralyze all our industrial, agricultural, commercial, and social life," leading to potential starvation at home and abroad, the president proclaimed. Although supportive of New Deal labor legislation, Truman announced he would use the army to run the railroads and draft striking workers into the military if they did not return to work. Moments before he was scheduled to address Congress to ask for authorizing legislation, Truman received word that the strikers had returned to work.

Workers in other industries fared a bit better. Negotiated settlements in the steel and auto industries set the benchmark for wages, benefits, and shop floor practices that other companies, even nonunionized ones like the general merchandiser Sears Roebuck, adopted to maintain peaceful labor relations. Industrialists gained as well in these agreements. Longer contracts ensured a lengthy period of tranquility with no strikes, and in all settlements company owners maintained control over management decisions.

The Republicans' successful mid-term campaign slogan, "Had Enough? Vote Republican," capitalized upon voters' dismay over labor conflicts and higher prices. For the first time since 1933, the Republican Party won majorities in both the House and the Senate in the 1946 congressional elections. Republicans hoped to use this victory as a springboard for unseating Truman from the White House in 1948. The Eightieth Congress immediately passed strong anti-labor legislation over Truman's veto. Although dismayed with the strikes of 1946, Truman knew that he would need labor's vote in the upcoming presidential contest. The **Taft-Hartley Act (1947)** abolished the closed shop, a practice that required all workers who benefited from a union-negotiated contract to join the union. The law also banned so-called sympathy boycotts, strikes by workers who wanted to support another union's protest. Finally the law's requirement that all union officers sign affidavits certifying that they were not members of the Communist Party encouraged unions to purge its most radical members, often those who had pioneered new tactics, like the sit-down strike in the 1930s. The Taft-Hartley law was a serious blow to the labor movement. The merger in 1955 between the CIO and the more conservative American Federation of Labor (AFL) ushered in a more cautious era of labor organizing that mostly ignored unskilled and southern workers.

Presidential Agendas: Truman and Eisenhower

Conservative Republicans hoped that the Taft-Hartley law would spearhead a drive to dismantle the New Deal. Instead the curtailment of labor removed the most visible symbol of what was supposedly "wrong" with the New Deal just as the 1948 presidential campaign got underway. To win Truman decided that the votes of labor and northern African Americans were more important than retaining the solid South. The Democratic Party adopted the slogan "Don't let them take it away," referring to the minimum wage, unemployment insurance, and Social Security that the New Deal granted to industrial workers. Liberals in the Democratic Party successfully pushed Truman to take a stronger stand on civil rights. In July 1948, for both principled and pragmatic reasons, Truman ordered the desegregation of the armed forces, an important civil rights milestone.

Truman's embrace of civil rights caused Southern conservatives to bolt from the Democratic Party; his earlier confrontations with labor convinced social progressives to leave the party as well. Vowing to preserve segregation conservative Southern Democrats formed the States Rights Party and nominated South Carolina governor Strom Thurmond to run against Truman and the Republican candidate, Thomas Dewey. On the political left former Vice President Henry Wallace ran on the Progressive Citizens of America ticket, representing a coalition of liberals and radicals upset about the assault on civil liberties at home and the nation's aggressive foreign policy as the Cold War took shape. Truman's campaign assault on big business as "gluttons of privilege," strong support from labor and blacks, and the success of the Berlin airlift (see Chapter 24) propelled him to a clear victory in the Electoral College (303 to 189), but he led Dewey by just 2 million in the popular vote. The concentrated segregation and states' rights vote in the South garnered Thurmond 39 electoral votes in return for the 1.2 million popular votes he received. Wallace received nearly the same number of votes as Thurmond nationwide, but won no electoral votes.

> "The time has come to walk out of the shadow of states' rights and into the sunlight of human rights."
>
> Minneapolis Mayor HUBERT HUMPHREY, urging Democrats to adopt a strong civil rights stance in the 1948 presidential election

For much of his second term, Truman focused on managing foreign affairs and fending off assaults on his administration from Senator Joseph McCarthy (see Chapter 24). Abandoning his earlier stance of merely sustaining the New Deal, Truman advanced the **Fair Deal**, proposals for national health care, public housing, education, and public works projects. The Democratic majority that controlled the Eighty-First Congress funded state school systems and urban public housing, increased the minimum wage, and continued bringing electricity and telephones into rural areas. Proposals for national health insurance stalled, but Congress did vote to build more hospitals and expanded public health facilities for the poor.

In June, 1950, North Korea invaded South Korea and political debate shifted to the Korean War (see Chapter 24). Truman, wary of undermining bipartisan support for his Cold War policies and the Korean War, did not push hard for highly controversial Fair Deal initiatives such as repealing the antiunion Taft-Hartley Act, price and wage controls, or universal health care. Only a fraction of Truman's Fair Deal proposals became law, but his program foreshadowed the more successful and extensive liberal agendas of future presidents John F. Kennedy and Lyndon B. Johnson, both Democrats.

By the end of the Truman administration, most Americans could not imagine a society without Social Security or a minimum wage, expectations that shaped the political vision of the nation's next president. In 1952 and again in 1956, the Republican candidate Dwight Eisenhower won in landslide elections, both times defeating Democrat Adlai E. Stevenson, the governor of Illinois. The virtually unknown Stevenson faced the daunting challenge of overcoming southern anger at Truman's civil rights reforms (which Stevenson supported) and America's affection for Eisenhower, a World War II hero. A gifted orator Stevenson stuck to traditional stump speeches, while Eisenhower became to the first presidential candidate to use televised political ads. He honed his folksy image in short television ads that aired during the commercial breaks of popular nighttime programs. America voted overwhelmingly for the man they knew and liked, with Eisenhower defeating Stevenson by 422 to 89 electoral votes. In 1956, running on a slogan of "peace and prosperity" that noted his success in ending the Korean War, Eisenhower polled even higher numbers, receiving 457 electoral votes to Stevenson's 73.

Republican critics like Senator Robert Taft attacked the Fair Deal as "creeping socialism" because these expensive programs required high taxes and, in Republicans' view, gave the government too much power. The 1953 editorial cartoon *Who Said 'Creeping Socialism'* (**25.2**) reflected the conservatives' fear that Eisenhower would have trouble taming New Deal and Fair Deal programs. The congressman, a symbol of runaway big government, holds a briefcase labeled "Govt. in Business, Housing, Power, Transport," and his running head start makes it impossible for Eisenhower to catch up. In fact, though, the cartoon misrepresented Eisenhower's intentions. The president liked to say that he was "conservative when it comes to money and liberal when it comes to human beings." To appeal to the moderates in each party, Eisenhower announced that he had no intention of

25.2 *Who Said 'Creeping Socialism,'* 1953
During the 1952 presidential election, conservative Republicans criticized the New Deal and Fair Deal as "creeping socialism." This caricature portrays the newly elected Republican President Dwight Eisenhower struggling to catch a runaway congressman who clutches onto programs enacted during previous Democratic administrations.

dismantling popular New Deal programs. "Should any political party attempt to abolish social security and eliminate labor laws and farm programs, you would not hear of that party again in our political history," Eisenhower concluded, to the dismay of conservatives in the Republican Party. His "victory of the moderates," as some commentators termed it, underscored that New Deal reforms were here to stay. Eisenhower did curb the Fair Deal by vetoing new public housing and public works projects and never offered any new social welfare measures of his own.

Fiscally conservative, Eisenhower believed that balancing the budget and limiting government expenditures created a favorable business environment that promoted jobs and prosperity. He worked hard to foster strong ties between government and the defense industry as the Pentagon amassed a huge nuclear arsenal. In the president's view a nuclear shield protected the nation more cheaply and effectively than conventional arms or troops, which were expensive to maintain. But Eisenhower expressed misgivings about the domestic costs of a large defense budget as early as 1953: "Every gun made, every warship that is launched, every rocket fired, signifies, in the final sense, a theft from those who hunger and are not fed, those who are cold and are not clothed." Nine years later, as he prepared to vacate the White House, Eisenhower suggested that he had gone too far in promoting the convergence of military and industrial interests. In a well-remembered speech, he urged Americans to monitor vigilantly the growth of the "**military-industrial complex**," Eisenhower's term for the close ties between the defense industry and the Pentagon that might influence government policy. "We must never let the weight of this combination endanger our liberties or democratic processes," Eisenhower warned.

"I have always assumed that what was good for the United States was good for General Motors, and vice versa."

Secretary of Defense CHARLES E. WILSON, when asked about a possible conflict of interest between his government position and his former job as the head of General Motors, 1953

What significance did Eisenhower's "victory of the moderates" have?

A Middle-Class America

By any measurement the 1950s was a prosperous decade. From 1945 to 1960 per capita consumption rose 50 percent, wages grew by one-third, and unemployment averaged 4.6 percent. American productivity boomed as well. Inhabited by only 6 percent of the world population, the United States produced half of the world's manufactured goods in the 1950s. The 1950s gave the generation raised in the austerity of the Great Depression something they had never known: prosperity. For the first time many Americans enjoyed the trappings of middle-class life—a suburban home filled with modern appliances and a car in the garage—previously available only to a small segment of the population. By 1960 the nation crossed a significant historic threshold when 60 percent of Americans were classified as middle class. The United States was no longer a primarily working-class society.

Postwar Prosperity

In 1948 Vernon Presley brought his family to Memphis, Tennessee, hoping to escape the grinding poverty of Mississippi. Gladys Presley later recalled that her son, Elvis, "would hear us worrying about our debts, being out of work and sickness and he'd say, 'Don't you worry none, Baby. When I grow up, I'm going to buy you a fine house . . . and get two Cadillacs—one for you and Daddy, and one for me." Elvis Presley fulfilled this promise to his parents when he became the most famous rock-and-roll star of the era. For the rest of his life, Elvis, an extreme example of the era's conspicuous consumption, gave away cars to friends and family.

Few Americans enjoyed this level of financial success, but the kind of deprivation that Elvis experienced as a child became a relic of the past for millions in the 1950s. The typical American "has access to amenities—foods, entertainment, personal transportation, and plumbing—in which not even the rich rejoiced a century ago," economist John Kenneth Galbraith noted. Having discretionary

25.3 and 25.4 Buying on Credit "What They Have" vs. "What They Own." The before and after photos of this *Life* magazine spread demonstrated Americans' heavy reliance on credit to accumulate the trappings of middle-class life in the fifties.

What factors caused standards of living to improve for many Americans in the 1950s?

income for things such as a television, vacations, or sending a child to college transformed the lives of American workers. "If what we lived through in the 1950s was not liberation," Jack Metzgar, the son of Pennsylvania steelworkers, noted, "then liberation never happens in real human lives."

An aggressive union movement seeking higher wages and benefits and the New Deal safety net of guaranteed pensions and unemployment insurance helped fuel this leap into the middle class for many industrial workers. Other government initiatives also helped transform the way Americans lived. In 1944 just 44 percent of Americans owned their homes. By 1960 this figure had risen to 60 percent thanks to the 1944 GI Bill of Rights that offered returning veterans low-interest loans and a tax code that provided incentives for homeowners. In addition state and federal governments constructed the roads, schools, bridges, and sewers that new suburban developments required.

During World War II production of consumer goods was scant, and many Americans had accumulated savings that they were now eager to spend. In 1950 alone Americans snatched up 6.2 million refrigerators, 14.6 million radios, and 6.2 million automobiles. This represented three-quarters of the appliances purchased worldwide. Installment plans helped millions of Americans purchase these key consumer items. Consumer debt rose from 8.3 billion in 1946 to 56.1 billion in 1960, a trend that caught *Life* magazine's attention in 1953. To illustrate the newly affluent lifestyle of middle-class Americans, *Life* photographer Loomis Dean put a couple with their two children in front of their Los Angeles suburban home alongside all their furnishings and car. The first picture (**25.3**) showed "what they have": an oven, refrigerator, two television sets, car, and furniture. The second photograph (**25.4**), "what they own," put the family in front of the foundations of a house and a pair of wheels to reflect how far along they were in their mortgage and car payments. The refrigerator, couch, stove, and one television set—all bought on credit—were missing. By purchasing so heavily with credit, this family risked losing nearly everything if a recession hit and the father lost his job.

American leaders felt that their nation's material abundance clearly demonstrated the superiority of the capitalist societies over communist ones, where basic consumer items were often in short supply. Others condemned American materialism. In his biting social commentary *The Status Seekers*, Vance Packard criticized Americans for jettisoning the frugality of the past in favor of status-seeking conspicuous consumption. Manufacturers played an active role in creating this new consumerist

Compare this family's possessions and home life to those of previous generations.

orientation. One executive conceded that it was the advertisers' job to "see to it that Americans are never satisfied." A middle-class family now considered their car or refrigerator "obsolete after two or three years even though it works well," financial columnist Sylvia Porter noted.

The Move to the Suburbs

Suburbs built in the 1920s ringed major cities and remained connected to the metropolitan core by streetcars or rail lines. In the 1950s suburbs moved farther away from cities, becoming insular communities that depended increasingly on cars to transport people. The roads Eisenhower built to help evacuate urban areas if the nation came under nuclear attack (see Chapter 24) were now filled with suburbanites running errands and commuting to work. Of the thirteen million new homes constructed between 1948 and 1958, 85 percent were built in suburban neighborhoods. By 1960 thirty-seven million Americans lived in suburbs.

When developer William Levitt erected thousands of mass-produced homes on the former potato fields of Long Island, New York, he pioneered building techniques that transformed the housing market. Applying Henry Ford's automobile assembly line–style innovations to the housing industry, Levitt built "**Levittowns**,"—planned suburban communities where developers standardized every part of the construction process. Levitt claimed that his crews could assemble a house in fifteen minutes, while it took only three minutes to complete the paperwork to purchase one. Levitt passed these savings onto home-buyers, dropping the prices of new homes from $14,000 to $8,000. When other developers copied his techniques nationwide, the low price of suburban homes, coupled with readily available government-backed financing, brought home ownership within reach of millions of Americans.

These new suburban homes typically contained living room picture windows that developers installed to make their 1,000-square-feet houses feel more spacious. When the curtains were open, these large windows also displayed a family's possessions and prosperity to the neighborhood. Suburban homes had "living kitchens" where families both prepared and ate their meals and "family rooms" to accommodate the television, toys, and games that brought the family together at the end of the day. A garage sheltered the automobile that every suburban family needed to own.

Americans offered competing visions on whether suburban living improved daily life or encouraged mindless conformity. Conflicting interpretations greeted images of idealized suburban life. "For literally nothing down" Americans could purchase a "box" in a suburban development "inhabited by people whose age, income, number of children, problems, habits, conversation, dress, possessions and perhaps even blood type are also precisely like [theirs]," wrote John Keats in *The Crack in the Picture Window* (1957). Abraham Levitt, the son of developer William Levitt, fought back against these charges. "Houses are for people, not critics . . . — and the people for whom we do it think it's pretty good." This debate is explored in *Competing Visions: Suburbs—American Dream or Nightmare?*

The move to the suburbs converged with an explosion of childbearing among couples who had put off having children during the Depression and World War II and younger couples encouraged by boom times to start their families immediately. Between 1935 and 1955 the birth rate jumped nearly 40 percent. Levittown's nickname, "Fertility Valley," underscored this link between the suburbs and the **baby boom generation**, the 76.4 million Americans born between 1946 and 1964.

The baby boom generation shaped American society for decades to come. As babies and children they helped stimulate a huge industry devoted to diapers, baby formulas, and toys. Teenagers, a term coined after World War II to describe adolescents, formed the backbone of fifties popular culture and the antiwar movement and cultural upheavals of the sixties. In the twenty-first century, as the baby boomers begin to retire, the imperative to care for a large aging population poses significant challenges for American society.

The fifties ushered in other key lifestyle changes besides suburban living and an emphasis on family life. As more Americans entered the middle class, they increasingly worked at white-collar jobs ranging from clerks to professionals to corporate executives. The effect of corporate culture on American society was as hotly debated as the impact of suburban life. In an era when McCarthyism eliminated radical discourse as a legitimate form of political expression, social critics worried that suburbs and corporations were bleaching individuality and innovation out of the national character. "When white-collar people get jobs, they sell not only their time and energy but their personalities as well," sociologist C. Wright Mills contended. Others, including *Fortune* magazine, regularly defended corporations for extending job security and prosperity to millions.

Why did suburbs boom in the 1950s?

Competing Visions

SUBURBS—AMERICAN DREAM OR NIGHTMARE?

As the suburbs grew social critics debated whether suburban life represented the epitome of the American dream or a nightmarish existence that isolated Americans from one another. To challenge historian Lewis Mumford's assertion that the suburbs were cultural wastelands, sociologist Herbert J. Gans moved his family into a Levittown to study the habits and behaviors of its residents. As you read the following excerpts from Mumford and Gans, consider how each links the suburbs to changing lifestyles. What positive and negative changes do these writers attribute to suburban life? What different futures do they envision for a suburban-based American culture?

Lewis Mumford in *The City in History* (1961) contended that suburban life bred conformity, loneliness, and alienation.

In the mass movement into suburban areas a new kind of community was produced … a multitude of uniform, unidentifiable houses, lined up inflexibly, at uniform distances, on uniform roads, in a treeless communal waste, inhabited by people of the same class, the same income, the same age group, witnessing the same television performances, eating the same tasteless pre-fabricated foods, from the same freezers, conforming in every outward and inward respect to a common mold …

The town housewife, who half a century ago knew her butcher, her grocer, her dairyman, her various other local tradesmen, as individual persons, with histories and biographies that impinged on her own, in a daily exchange, now has the benefit of a single weekly expedition to an impersonal supermarket, where only by accident is she likely to encounter a neighbor. …

The cost of this detachment in space from other men is out of all proportion to its supposed benefits. The end product is an encapsulated life, spent more and more either in a motor car or within the cabin of darkness before a television set.

Levittown Street Scene

Herbert J. Gans defended suburbanites in *The Levittowners: Ways of Life and Politics in a New Suburban Community* (1967).

[Levittowners] are not apathetic conformists ripe for takeover by a totalitarian elite or corporate merchandiser; they are not conspicuous consumers and slaves to sudden whims of cultural and political fashion. … even though Levittowners and other lower middle class Americans continue to be home-centered, they are much more "in the world" than their parents and grandparents were. Those coming out of ethnic working class backgrounds have rejected the … ethnocentrism which made other cultures and even other neighborhoods bitter enemies. This generation trusts its neighbors, participates with them in social and civic activities, and no longer sees government as inevitably corrupt. Even working class Levittowners have begun to give up the suspicion that isolated their ancestors from all but family and childhood friends. Similarly, the descendants of rural Protestant America have given up the xenophobia that turned previous generations against the Catholic and Jewish immigrant, they have almost forgotten the intolerant Puritanism which triggered attacks against pleasure and enjoyment, and they no longer fully accept the doctrine of laissez-faire that justifies the defense of all individual rights and privileges against others' needs.

These and other changes have come about not because people are now better or more tolerant human beings, but because they are affluent. For the Levittowners, life is not a fight for survival any more; they have been able to move into a community in which income and status are equitably enough distributed so that neighbors are no longer treated as enemies, even if they are still criticized for social and cultural defiance. By any yardstick one chooses, Levittowners treat their fellow residents more ethically and more democratically than did their parents and grandparents. They also live a "fuller" and "richer" life. … superior to what prevailed among the working and lower middle classes of past generations."

Popular Culture in the Fifties

The introduction of television sets into family living rooms transformed the home life of millions of Americans. So did the emergence of an autonomous youth culture, with its own slang, rock-and-roll music, and modes of dress. Were these harmless expressions of adolescent rebellion or signs of the disintegration of American culture? These stirrings of generational conflict in the 1950s exploded a decade later into full-fledged revolt.

The Television Age Arrives

The first commercial television transmission occurred in 1939 when President Franklin D. Roosevelt visited the New York World's Fair. The war slowed the introduction of televisions into the consumer market, but by the 1950s, the television age had arrived. In 1948 just 178,000 homes had televisions. Seven years later three-quarters of American households owned one.

President Dwight Eisenhower set the tone for the decade with the widely publicized image of the president and his wife, Mamie, eating dinner each night off tray-tables set up in front of a television in their private White House parlor. Whereas in the forties Americans had flocked to movie theaters for entertainment, now they stayed home. "Don't be a Living Room Captive—Step Out and See a Great Movie," film studios urged Americans. Many Americans, however, appeared to agree with President Eisenhower, who wrote in his diary, "If a citizen has to be bored to death it is cheaper and more comfortable to sit at home and look at television than it is to go outside and pay a dollar for a ticket." Throughout the nation movie theaters closed and the studios made fewer films. Only drive-in theaters in suburban towns, where customers sat in their cars next to individual speakers to watch a movie on a giant outdoor screen, thrived. Drive-in theaters appealed to young parents who could pile their children into the car for a night out and teenagers who could escape the watchful eyes of adults for a few hours.

What were Americans watching at home? Many early television shows dealt with the social conditions and cultural values of the day, paying particular attention to family and consumerism. In *The Honeymooners*, the working-class Kramdens lived in a sparsely furnished apartment and often clashed, particularly when one of the get-quick-rich schemes devised by bus driver Ralph (played by comedian Jackie Gleason) started to unravel. His wife Alice always stood her ground, even when Ralph threatened her with one of the show's trademark lines: "One of these days, Alice . . . one of these days . . . POW, right in the kisser." By the end of each episode, the couple had reconciled, with Ralph often telling his wife, "Baby, you're the greatest."

I Love Lucy began in a small Manhattan apartment, but eventually Lucy Ricardo (played by Lucille Ball) and her Cuban husband Ricky (Ball's real-life husband Desi Arnez) relocated to suburban Connecticut to raise their son. Lucy's farcical adventures to get a job, enter show business, or best her husband always ended with Lucy realizing that being a wife and mother was fulfilling enough. Situation comedies like *Father Knows Best* and *Leave it to Beaver* focused on the roles that each member of an ideal white suburban family played: Father worked hard and came home in time to resolve the minor crises of the day; mother kept a spotless home, volunteered, and supported her husband's career; and children learned to tell the truth, work hard, and obey their parents. These television shows mirrored the general preoccupation with child-rearing during the baby boom, a time when family and religion were at the center of white middle-class suburban life. Yet because plotlines never involved the working class, people of color, politics, or domestic discord, these shows offered little insight into the social realities that shaped family life for millions of Americans during the 1950s.

Television programming in the 1950s provided plenty of escapist fare. Nightly news broadcasts, however, brought glimpses of the wider world into American homes and played an increasing role in politics. Politicians quickly learned to use the new medium to their advantage. Republican vice presidential candidate Richard M. Nixon was the first politician to give a televised speech to defuse a political scandal. During the 1952 presidential election, the press revealed that Nixon had a secret fund financed by California businessmen. Hoping to stem the damage, Nixon appeared on television

What insights do 1950s television shows offer into American culture?

to refute charges that the money was for his personal use or that these businessmen were buying "secret favors" from him with their donations. Laying out the details of his personal finances, Nixon defiantly told viewers that without campaign donations only the rich could run for office. In the speech's most famous passage, Nixon mentioned one personal gift that he would not return. "A man down in Texas heard Pat [his wife] on the radio mention the fact that our two youngsters would like to have a dog" and surprised the family with the gift of a black-and-white cocker spaniel. "And our little girl Tricia, the six year old, named it 'Checkers.' And you know, the kids, like all kids, love the dog, and I just want to say this, right now, that regardless of what they say about it, we're gonna keep it," Nixon declared.

In the aftermath of the speech, Nixon posed with his family and Checkers in this photo (**25.5**). The Checkers speech saved Nixon's place on the Republican ticket alongside Eisenhower. Like Nixon, John F. Kennedy also astutely used posed photographs, like this one with his attractive young family (**25.6**). By creating such images Kennedy hoped to distract attention from his inherited wealth and Catholicism, long considered an undesirable religious affiliation for a politician.

On September 26, 1960 in the **Kennedy and Nixon debate**, the two candidates faced off in the first televised presidential election debate. Nearly 77 million Americans, or 60 percent of the adult population, watched this historic event. Nixon, still pale and underweight from a recent two-week stint in the hospital, squared off against a tan and fit Kennedy, who impressed viewers with his comfortable presence before the cameras. By contrast Nixon refused to wear make-up, looked like he needed a shave, wore a poorly fitted shirt, and was visibly sweating throughout the exchange. The majority of Americans who watched the debate felt that Kennedy had won, while most Americans who listened on the radio gave the edge to Nixon. Kennedy went on to narrowly win the election, revealing the power of images to sway political judgments.

Teen Culture and Rock-and-Roll

Teenagers came into their own in the 1950s. Their parents remained haunted by visions of Depression-era deprivation and the life-and-death struggle of World War II. By contrast in the fifties many middle-class teenagers grew up with an abundance of material possessions. Most teenagers agreed with their parents when it came to politics, sharing their concern about communist expansion throughout the world and the growing Soviet nuclear threat. Many however adopted

25.5 and 25.6 Two candidates, one family portrait Throughout their political careers, Richard M. Nixon and John F. Kennedy used portraits of their family life to connect with voters. These images fit with the era's idealized image of the perfect American family, which included a supportive wife, two children, and at least one dog.

How did politicians use television and photographs to shape their public image?

an ethos of pleasure-seeking that often put them at odds with their parents who emphasized thrift and self-discipline. Unlike their parents' generation teenagers were no longer expected to earn money to help support their families. Millions of young people experienced unprecedented leisure time, longer schooling, and were free to spend money earned from after-school jobs as they liked.

Teenagers flocked to buy record players and radios to play music marketed specifically to them. In 1958 the Coasters scored a number-one record with their song, "Yakety Yak," which depicts a teenager rebelling against household chores. In one refrain, the parent orders the teenager to "Take out the papers and the trash / Or you don't get no spendin' cash," to which the teenager replies "yakety yak," with the parent then retorting: "don't talk back."

> "Teenagers are my life and triumph. I'd be nowhere without them."
>
> ELVIS PRESLEY, whose stardom demonstrated the strength of teen culture in the 1950s

Teens' freedom to create their own social world filled with slang and fads that adults did not understand disturbed some critics. By the end of the decade, sociologist Edgar Friedenberg noted that "the 'teen-ager' seems to have replaced the Communist as the appropriate target for public controversy and foreboding." In this cultural clash traditionalists lambasted horror comic books and teen films for encouraging teenagers to revolt against their parents and social norms. But rock-and-roll music and musicians provoked the most outrage.

Rock-and-roll burst onto the national scene when Bill Haley and the Comets recorded "Rock Around the Clock" in 1955, the first rock-and-roll tune. The following year Chuck Berry thundered "Roll over, Beethoven, and tell Tchaikovsky the news!" proclaiming rock-and-roll the music of choice for this teenage generation. It took Elvis Presley, however, to make rock-and-roll (which got its name from a rhythm and blues slang term for sexual intercourse) a phenomenon. Exposed to the raw sexuality and powerful rhythms of African American rhythm and blues music as a young boy growing up in Mississippi, Presley also sang gospel and country music in church. Melding the sounds and explosive delivery of these musical traditions with catchy pop lyrics, Presley developed his own highly eroticized dancing style. "If I could find a white man who had the black sound and the black feel, I could make a billion dollars," predicted record producer Sam Phillips, the owner of Sun Records, a small recording company in Memphis, Tennessee. Philips found his man when Presley walked into Sun Records to record a song as a gift for his mother.

Americans embraced competing visions over whether the growing popularity of rock-and-roll meant the triumph of consumer tastes or the downfall of American civilization. Nicknamed "Elvis the Pelvis" for his suggestive hip thrusts while dancing, partially captured in this photograph (**25.7**), Presley became a lightening rod for critics who denounced rock-and-roll from the pulpit, in the press, and even in congressional hearings. When teenager Ron Kovic's family watched Presley on television's *Ed Sullivan Show*, his sister went "crazy in the living room jumping up and down," his mother sat "on the couch with her hands folded in her lap like she was praying" and his dad shouted from the other room that "watching Elvis Presley could lead to sin." In introducing Presley the affable TV host Sullivan assured parents that the twenty-two-year-old Presley was "a real decent, fine boy." To avoid controversy, however, Sullivan ordered camera crews to frame out Presley's legendary pelvic thrusts and gyrations, showing only his head and chest. It took the draft to tame Elvis. "Presley wriggled off to military service," one newspaper columnist wrote, "but comes marching home . . . shorn of his sideburns and behaving the way a sedate, serious-minded youngster should." The new "clean-cut" Presley kept his original fan base but had limited appeal to the teenage generation coming of age in 1960.

Ed Sullivan showcased a range of music, skits, and comedy acts designed to keep the whole family watching together during the hour-long show. Dick Clark, however, helped pioneer television programming exclusively for teenagers with his daily afternoon show *American Bandstand*, which featured Philadelphia high-school students dancing to the latest hits. The advent of pocketsize transistor radios meant that teenagers could listen to radio stations broadcasting the top forty best-selling records or independent rhythm and blues stations in the privacy of their bedrooms, away from critical adult ears.

Hollywood also catered to teenage tastes with films like *The Wild Ones* (1953), which featured Marlon Brando as part of a rebellious motorcycle gang, and *Rebel Without a Cause* (1955). In the latter

How did larger economic and technological changes make a mass teen culture possible?

frightened some adults but thrilled teenagers. Embracing the persona of an angry youth discontented with mainstream society, Dean (who died at the age of twenty-four in a car accident) became an icon of teenage rebellion in the fifties.

Parental norms often prevailed in the end. Teenagers in the fifties grew up quickly. Students who dated a lot in high school tended to marry within a few years of graduation. As much as they may have rebelled as adolescents, once married, they quickly started families, conforming to the lifestyle standards set by their parents.

25.7 Elvis Presley Nicknamed "Elvis the Pelvis," Elvis Presley's suggestive dancing enraged parents but earned the singer thousands of adoring teenage female fans.

The Beats

Teens in the fifties used their purchases—of music, clothes, cars—to define their generational identity, while their parents announced their newly acquired middle-class status by buying cars and suburban houses. **Beats** or beatniks, members of the bohemian communities of poets, novelists, and artists that flourished in New York's Greenwich Village and San Francisco's North Beach, offered an alternative vision. The Beats rejected home ownership, career, and marriage in favor of individual freedom and immediate pleasure (including drugs and casual sex).

The national spotlight briefly shined on City Lights Bookstore in San Francisco when it published the controversial poem "Howl" (1955) by then-struggling Beat poet Allen Ginsberg. "I saw the best minds of my generation destroyed by madness, starving hysterical naked, dragging themselves through the negro streets at dawn looking for an angry fix," began the opening stanza of "Howl." The poem sent readers on a journey into the underground lives of the drug addicts, musicians, artists, radicals, and homosexuals who lived on the margins of mainstream society. In the 1950s most states had so-called antisodomy laws that criminalized same-sex intercourse. Ginsberg's open celebration of gay sex in "Howl" offended anti-obscenity crusaders in San Francisco. The police arrested the owner of the City Lights Bookstore for selling the poem, but a judge

film James Dean and Natalie Wood played teenagers from upper-middle-class suburban homes; unsure how to handle their racing hormones, the two become defiant. Dean's character tries to prove his masculinity by drag racing, while Wood's character uses promiscuity to rebel against an overprotective father. This view of the suburbs as hotbeds of intergenerational conflict and alienated youth

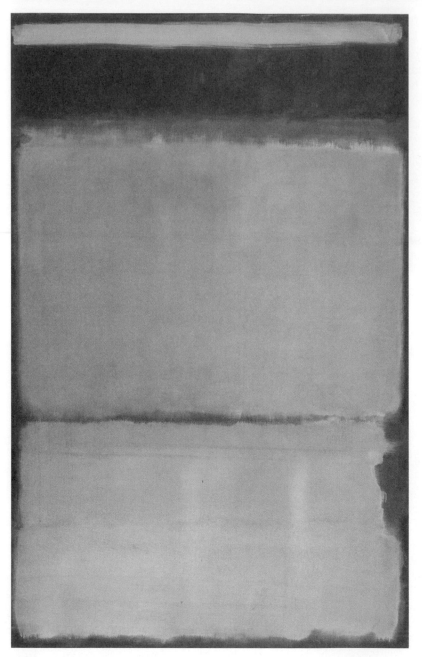

25.8 Mark Rothko, *Number 10*
The Abstract Expressionist painter Mark Rothko expressed his personal feelings rather than reproducing objects or addressing politics in his paintings. Refusing to title or explain his paintings, Rothko wanted viewers to interpret his work freely. [*Source*: Mark Rothco (1903–1970), "Number 10". 1950. Oil on canvas. 7' 6 3/8" × 57 1/8". Gift of Philip Johnson. (38.1952) Location:The Museum of Modern Art, New York, NY, U.S.A. Digital Image © The Museum of Modern Art/Licensed by SCALA / Art Resource, NY. Estate of Mark Rothco © 2010 Artists Rights Society (ARS), NY]

dismissed the charge, arguing that "Howl" was a socially significant artistic work.

In his novel *On the Road* (1955), the Beat novelist Jack Kerouac celebrated the spiritual quest for a meaningful life away from the suffocating materialism and conformity of middle-class society. Guilty at times of over-romanticizing working-class life for its "authenticity" without appreciating the deadening effects of poverty, the Beats nonetheless laid the foundation for the youth protests of the sixties (see Chapter 27).

Most Americans never read "Howl" or *On the Road*. They instead formed their impressions of the Beats from watching *The Many Loves of Dobie Gillis*, a television series that showcased a beatnik best friend who urged Dobie to reject his father's single-minded drive to make money and instead enjoy life to the fullest. This televised depiction of Beat culture helped interject new words, such as "dig it," "cool," and "man" that the Beats took from African American culture, into the vocabulary of white teenagers.

> "What sphinx of cement and aluminum bashed open their skulls and ate up their brains and imagination?"
>
> Beat poet ALLEN GINSBERG, critiquing suburban life in "Howl"

Beat poets and novelists were not the only artists rebelling against received traditions in the fifties. American modern artists formulated a new mode of visual art called Abstract Expressionism that broke with the predominant painting styles of the previous generation. Before World War II leading artists included the Cubist painter Pablo Picasso who reordered the physical world in his paintings and American social realist painters who captured the lives of ordinary people during the Depression. Politics informed much artistic work in the 1930s and 1940s. In the fifties a restless generation of new artists chose instead to emphasize personal expression over politics. "The big moment came when it was decided to paint. . . . Just TO PAINT. The gesture on the canvas was a gesture of liberation, from Value—political, aesthetic, moral," wrote art critic Harold Rosenberg in 1952. American painters such as Jackson Pollock, who dripped paint on the canvas, and Mark Rothko, who painted fields of color, created signature styles that epitomized the rebellious nature of Abstract Expression (**25.8**). Young artists idolized these painters for refusing to represent reality or use their art to send a message. More tradition-bound artists denounced their work as trivial. Like James Dean in films and Elvis Presley in music, the painters Pollock and Rothko embodied the rebellious streak of fifties youth culture.

How does Rothko's painting compare to social realist paintings in the 1930s (see Chapter 22)?

Freedom Now: The Civil Rights Movement

The Civil Rights Movement entered a pivotal phase in the 1950s. Key Supreme Court rulings, new leadership, and innovative strategies emboldened thousands of black and white people to demand the end of racial segregation in the South. The National Association for the Advancement of Colored People (NAACP) successfully challenged the constitutionality of segregated public schools. Martin Luther King Jr. emerged as a major leader, alongside a generation of activist black and white college students who employed new nonviolent strategies to compel white Americans to confront the harsh realities of Jim Crow. Favorable decisions from the Supreme Court pressured the federal government to intervene on behalf of African Americans. Meanwhile television and news magazines transmitted shocking images of racial violence that made it impossible for the nation to ignore the demands of civil rights activists.

Separate and *Unequal*: Challenging Segregated Schools

"Tastes the same to me, Mom."

LEO LILLARD, after secretly sampling water from "white" and "colored" fountains as a boy in Nashville

Black and white southern children, as this photo of a street scene in a small southern town suggests (**25.9**), grew up in two separate worlds. They lived in different parts of town, went to segregated schools, drank from separate water fountains, ate in different restaurants, waited for buses in different waiting rooms, sat in separate sections of movie theatres, and often shopped in different stores. For many black children segregation meant daily humiliation and unanswered questions. "I guess if you are from a small Georgia town, as I am," one black college student recalled, "you can say that your first encounter with prejudice was the day you were born. . . . My parents never got to see their infant twins alive because the only incubator in the hospital was on the 'white' side."

After World War II ethnic and racial minorities successfully challenged the legality of segregated schools. In 1947 the Supreme Court ruled that educating children of Mexican ancestry in separate California schools was illegal because state law only authorized segregated schools for children of Asian decent. In the wake of this ruling, California repealed this discriminatory law. Ending legalized racial segregation came next.

In 1954 the Supreme Court overturned the 1896 *Plessy v. Ferguson* "separate but equal" ruling that had allowed the South to maintain segregated schools from elementary school to graduate school. In *Plessy v. Ferguson* the Court had concluded that separate facilities (schools, waiting rooms, railroad cars) for whites and blacks were constitutional as long as they offered each race similar amenities. (See *Choices and Consequences,* Chapter 14.) In practice legalized segregation usually resulted in inferior

25.9 A Southern Town
On their visit to town, these white and black children carefully avoided mixing, demonstrating how early children in the South learned to respect their region's racial customs.

In what ways did racial discrimination shape southern children's lives?

25.10 Emmett Till and his mother
"If you have to get on your knees and bow when a white person goes past, do it willingly," Emmett's mother told her northern-raised son before he left to visit relatives in Mississippi, instructions that the teenager tragically disregarded.

accommodations and schools for black citizens. The Supreme Court ruled in ***Brown v. Board of Education*** **(1954)** that segregated schools indeed violated the equal protection clause of the Fourteenth Amendment.

The *Brown* case concerned seven-year-old Linda Brown, whose parents wanted to send her to an all-white school closer to their home. In mounting the case NAACP lawyer Thurgood Marshall (who later became the first African American appointed to the Supreme Court) and his team based their argument on more than the law. To convince the public and the Supreme Court that segregation was wrong, they needed to dramatize the effects of segregation. "To show damage and a violation of equal protection under the Fourteenth Amendment, you had to show that being segregated actually damaged children," psychologist Kenneth Clark asserted.

To demonstrate the irreversible effects of segregation on African American children, the NAACP cited Clark's controversial research. In a series of studies, Clark asked white and black children whether they liked a white or black doll best. The majority of children picked a white doll because it was "nice" and rejected the black doll as "bad." Clark next asked the children to identify the doll that was the most like them. The black children now had to pick the doll that many of them had just rejected as "bad." In the North black children often burst into tears rather than respond. In the South, however, reactions like the one from a young boy in Arkansas, who laughed, "pointed to the brown doll, and said, 'That's a nigger. I'm a nigger,'" convinced Clark that segregation taught African American children to accept their inferiority to whites.

Not everyone agreed with Clark's methodology, so the NAACP relied heavily on his findings in preliminary court challenges and then mentioned them only briefly in their Supreme Court filing. The wording of the *Brown v. Board of Education* decision, however, revealed that the NAACP had guessed right in emphasizing the impact of segregation on the self-esteem of black children. In reaching their unanimous decision, the Court noted that "to separate [black children] from others of similar age and qualifications solely because of their race generates a feeling of inferiority as to their status in the community that may affect their hearts and minds in a way unlikely ever to be undone."

Emmett Till

In 1955 Emmett Till was just another fourteen-year-old posing for the camera with his mother. Their portrait reveals a boy with a beaming smile and a mother's pride in her growing son (**25.10**). That summer Mamie Till-Bradley sent Emmett from his home in Chicago to visit relatives in Mississippi. To prepare her northern-raised son for the racial customs of southern society, his mother warned him to think of his safety when encountering southern whites. One morning at a country store in Money, Mississippi, Emmett forgot his mother's warning. While playing with some black teens on the porch of the store, Emmett bragged that he had a white girlfriend in Chicago. "Hey, there's a [white] girl in that store there," one of the boys retorted, "I bet you won't go in there and talk to her." Responding to the dare Emmett walked into the store, bought some candy, then grabbed the arm of Carol Byrant, who ran the store with her husband, and allegedly asked, "How about a date, baby?" Till's aghast cousin ran in and pulled him out of the store.

Three days later a car pulled up to Emmett's granduncle's house in the middle of the night. Two white men burst into the house and dragged Emmett out of bed. The husband of the young woman in the store, Roy Bryant, and her brother, J. W. Milam, threw a terrified Emmett into their truck and drove away. This was the last time his relatives saw him alive. The white men drove to an abandoned shed on a nearby plantation where they beat Till severely, then drove to the Tallahatchie River and forced Emmett to strip before they shot him in the head and tossed his body into the river. With his mother's permission, *Jet* magazine and the *Chicago Defender*, stalwarts of the black press, published the grisly photos of the corpse. *Images as History: Inspiring a New Generation to Act* discusses the transforming effect that images of Emmett Till's murder had on the Civil Rights Movement.

Why did the Supreme Court rule that segregated schools were unconstitutional?

Images as History

INSPIRING A NEW GENERATION TO ACT

The photo of Emmett Till's broken body, printed in African American newspapers and magazines, became the wake-up call for a group of young people destined to play major roles in the future Civil Rights Movement. The Emmett Till case gave the nation more than a clear image of the victim. It also provided a snapshot of the killers and the vigilante justice dealt out in many small towns across the Deep South. At first, some southern officials and citizens denounced the murder. But when the northern press castigated the entire South for the crime, southerners fought back with competing claims that Emmett Till was alive and in hiding or that the NAACP had set up the murder to embarrass the South. Why are these images important for understanding the history of race relations and the Civil Rights Movement?

Deciding that "the world is going to have to look at this," Mamie Till-Bradley took her son's body back to Chicago where she insisted on an open casket funeral that thousands attended.

The black northern press provoked outrage over the killing by pairing this gruesome image of Emmett's battered corpse with the photograph of him smiling with his mother (25.10).

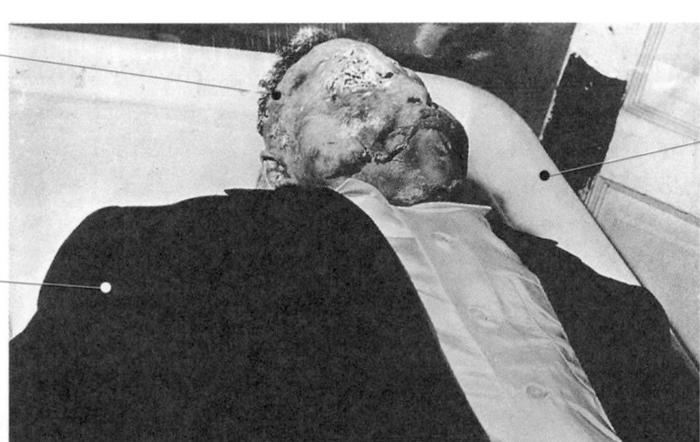

Emmett Till's corpse

After seeing these photos future civil rights activist Julian Bond "felt vulnerable for the first time in my life—Till was a year younger—and [I] recall believing that this could easily happen to me—for no reason at all."

The accused men's nonchalance in the courtroom and the show of support from the white observers sent a warning to the African American witnesses who testified against the pair, illustrating how communities like Money, Mississippi, at that time preserved the racial status quo.

Bringing their children into the courtroom bolstered the accused men's image as upstanding family men and helped teach white youth about the importance of maintaining white supremacy.

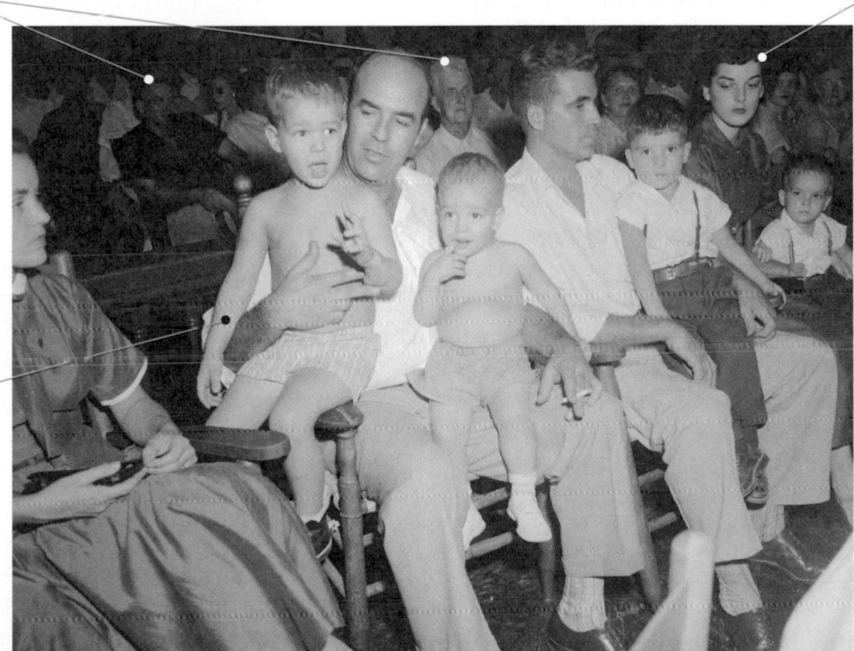

Men on trial for Emmett Till's murder, sitting with their families.

For many of his neighbors, Roy Bryant's defense of his wife protected her honor, his reputation, and fulfilled his duty to help the white community keep the color bar intact.

How do these photos compare to postcards of lynchings (see Chapter 21)?

What made Emmett Till's murder different from previous racially inspired killings of African Americans in the South was the courageous decision of his family to fight back. Ignoring the kidnappers' warnings to keep quiet (so Emmett would become yet another black boy who went mysteriously "missing"), Emmett's cousin called the sheriff and Emmett's mother the next day. The sheriff found Emmett's body and three days later arrested Roy Bryant and J. W. Milam. When Mamie Till-Bradley saw her son's tortured body, a sight that would have caused many mothers to fall apart, she instead vowed that "here's a job that I got to do now."

Emmett's granduncle, Moses Wright, had begged the white men to just whip Emmett, while his wife offered them money to leave Emmett alone. Now Moses Wright decided to seek justice by testifying against the pair when they went on trial for murder. The sixty-four-year-old Wright later recalled that as he entered the courtroom he could "feel the blood boil in hundreds of white people as they sat glaring." When the prosecutor asked him to identify Milam as one of the men who took Emmett, Wright stood up, pointed his finger, and said, "Thar he." News of Wright's testimony emboldened other black sharecroppers to step forward and testify about hearing Emmett crying for his mother as he was beaten. Fearing for their lives all of these sharecroppers left town after appearing in court.

At first it seemed they had risked everything for naught. The all-white male jury took less than an hour to proclaim the men not guilty. They would have returned the verdict sooner, the jury foreman bragged, "If we hadn't stopped to drink pop." A second jury acquitted the men on the charge of kidnapping. Two months after their murder trial, Bryant and Milam sold their story to an Alabama journalist for $4,000 and admitted killing Emmett. Double jeopardy, a legal concept that prevents authorities from retrying someone for the same crime, protected the pair from prosecution after their confession. Nonetheless the sight of ordinary black citizens standing up in court to accuse their white oppressors electrified a generation ready to strike back. Four months later, partly because of the Emmett Till case, the Montgomery Bus Boycott began.

Montgomery Bus Boycott, 1955

The *Brown v. Board of Education* decision was a milestone in the fight for racial equality, but by the mid-1950s civil rights activists were no longer content simply to fight for justice through the courts. Many resolved to use economic boycotts, picketing, and mass demonstrations to force white America to take notice of the injustice and violence experienced daily by African Americans. Courageous men and women, ordinary people who took extraordinary risks, set this new direction in civil rights protest.

On December 1, 1955, Rosa Parks, a forty-three-year-old black seamstress, boarded a bus in downtown Montgomery, Alabama, and selected a seat. She was one of forty thousand blacks who paid a dime twice a day to the white driver, then stepped down and entered the bus through the rear door. When a white man demanded her seat, Parks had to decide whether or not to comply. *Choices and Consequences: Rosa Parks Makes History* explores her decision to stay seated.

As soon as English professor Jo Anne Robinson heard of the arrest, she mimeographed 35,000 handbills urging black citizens to stage a one-day bus boycott on the day of Parks' trial. Robinson was president of the Montgomery Women's Political Council, which had been planning a one-day bus boycott for months. The Parks' arrest offered a perfect moment to act. Two of her students helped Robinson distribute the handbills to black schools, businesses, and churches. "Negroes have rights, too, for if Negroes did not ride the buses, they could not operate," the handbill read. When the day-long boycott succeeded, community leaders decided to continue it indefinitely.

The **Montgomery Bus Boycott (1955–1956)** was a year-long boycott that brought a new leader, Martin Luther King Jr., and a new strategy of nonviolent protest to the forefront of the Civil Rights Movement. The boycotters' initial demands were moderate: courteous treatment from bus drivers, first-come-first-served segregation so no one would have to give up a seat, and the hiring of some black bus drivers. The city administrators and bus company executives refused. The Montgomery Improvement Association (MIA) now prepared for a lengthy boycott. Mass meetings twice a week kept boycotters' spirits high and helped disseminate accurate information within a black community that had no radio station or newspaper. The MIA also set up an elaborate carpool system to transport black workers to their jobs and back home. Volunteers picked up passengers from one of forty-two collection points throughout the city, which became the target of terrorist bombings on several occasions. Images of black workers waiting peacefully for carpools contrasted with the burnt remains of

Which individual choices mattered in the Till case?

Choices and Consequences

ROSA PARKS MAKES HISTORY

Unlike the signs above water fountains or posted in waiting rooms, there was no clear section marked "colored" on Montgomery city buses. Instead as more white passengers boarded the bus, black passengers had to vacate their seats for them. When three other black passengers heeded the white driver's request to move on the afternoon of December 1, 1955, Rosa Parks faced a set of choices over how to respond.

Choices

1 Move to the back of the bus.

2 Refuse to give up her seat.

3 Vacate her seat but express her outrage by participating in a planned one-day bus boycott.

Decision

Rosa Parks refused to give up her seat. When the driver threatened to call the police, Parks quietly replied, "You may do that." She was arrested.

Consequences

On the day of Parks's trial (she was found guilty and fined), the Montgomery Women's Political Council organized a one-day boycott that it had been planning for months and nearly all Montgomery's black citizens stayed off the buses. That evening the city's black male clergy met and formed the Montgomery Improvement Association (MIA), which voted to continue the boycott. The group chose Martin Luther King Jr., a twenty-six-year-old Baptist minister who headed the church that Rosa Parks attended, as their president. When the Supreme Court ruled that bus segregation was unconstitutional in 1956, the year-long boycott ended.

Continuing Controversies

Who was the real Rosa Parks?

The folklore is that Parks was simply a tired seamstress who impulsively decided to stay seated. This narrative leaves out key details. Parks was also secretary of the Montgomery chapter of the NAACP and had attended the left-leaning Highlander Folk School in Tennessee where civil rights and labor leaders trained. She knew that the NAACP wanted to test the bus segregation law in the courts and had recently participated in a mass meeting protesting Emmett Till's murder. Boycott leaders played down Parks's activist past, worried that it would diminish her "everyman" appeal and that moderates might view her as a radical agitator. Some activists later suggested that this simplified tale sent the wrong message about how to initiate social change. Rosa Parks's bravery mattered, they agreed, but so did careful preparation, organization-building, and ideological dedication.

What is the enduring legacy of Rosa Parks's decision?

bombed cars provided good television footage for the national television networks that covered the boycott extensively. Television interviews with King, a twenty-six-year-old Baptist minister, turned him into a celebrity overnight and allowed him to appeal directly to moderates throughout the nation. To raise money and garner publicity for the boycott, King also toured the country giving speeches.

> "If Martin Luther King had never been born this movement would have taken place. I just happened to be there."
>
> MARTIN LUTHER KING JR., commenting on his role in the Montgomery Bus Boycott.

Instead of discouraging the protesters, white resistance convinced the MIA to broaden its demands to include the complete desegregation of the buses. The violence now threatened to spiral out of control. When King's house was bombed, a crowd of supporters arrived carrying knives and guns. "If you have weapons, take them home," King told the crowd as news cameras rolled. Publicizing the new civil rights ethos of nonviolence, King declared, "'He who lives by the sword will perish by the sword.' . . . We must meet hate with love."

Over time white opposition to the boycott began to fracture. Some whites had been openly sympathetic to the boycott from the beginning, even though their businesses and social life suffered as a result. Others had more pragmatic reasons for helping black workers reach their jobs. When the mayor chastised white women for chauffeuring their black maids to and from work, one defiant white woman wrote to the newspaper: "If the mayor wants to do my wash and wants to cook for me and clean up after my children let him come and do it."

After nearly a year the boycott was victorious. In November 1956 the Supreme Court ruled that segregated buses were unconstitutional. On December 21, 1956, Martin Luther King Jr. boarded the first integrated bus in Montgomery with the African American minister Ralph Abernathy and the white Reverend Glenn Smiley, both key leaders in the boycott. In their carefully choreographed ride, pictured here (**25.11**), all three followed the guidelines that the MIA had established for integrating buses. An MIA pamphlet advised: "For the first few days try to get on the bus with a friend in whose non-violence you have confidence. You can uphold one another by a glance or a prayer." The MIA cautioned black riders not to respond to curses or shoves. When King entered the bus, the presence of newspaper reporters and cameramen protected him from violence. "We are glad to have you here this morning," the bus driver cordially greeted King as he climbed aboard. The ride was not so smooth for other Montgomery citizens. In the weeks to come, snipers fired into buses and Abernathy's house was bombed.

Two months later King met with ministers from eleven other southern states to form the **Southern Christian Leadership Conference** (SCLC). Black churches, they decided, could help the Civil Rights Movement devise a new nonviolent strategy of direct action that challenged segregation and discrimination throughout the South. At first King saw nonviolence mostly as a way to gain sympathy and to prevent authorities from using violence against demonstrators. King employed a bodyguard throughout the boycott and had applied for a permit to allow him to carry a gun (which the police refused). "King sees the inconsistency, but not enough. He believes and yet he does not believe . . . if he can *really* be won over to a faith in nonviolence there is no end to what he can do," Smiley noted privately.

Over the next few years, King would develop that faith. King's social justice fundamentalism evolved from his reading of Jesus's biblical "Sermon on the Mount" that urged Christians to create "a beloved community" by winning over enemies with love and humility rather than seeking to punish or defeat them. King was also influenced by activists like Reverend James Lawson who had traveled to India to study the Hindu religion's version of nonviolence pioneered by the Indian activist Mahatma Gandhi in the 1930s to win independence from Britain. Lawson was in India during the Montgomery Bus Boycott but returned in time to instruct members of the SCLC and university students as they broadened their attack on Jim Crow in the early 1960s.

The Little Rock Nine, 1957

The *Brown v. Board of Education* case launched a decades-long struggle to integrate public schools. Many white southerners had grown up without ever questioning segregation. The Brown ruling now forced them to either formulate a defense and

Why was the Montgomery Bus Boycott a turning point in the Civil Rights Movement?

rationale for segregation or consider changing generations-old habits. Throughout the South diehard segregationists dug in. "The Negro race, as a race, plainly is not equal to the white race, as a race," asserted James Jackson Kilpatrick, the editor of a Richmond newspaper. Segregationists also advanced a states' right argument, arguing that the federal government had no right to dictate racial policies to the South. Sympathetic to claims that it would be difficult to change ingrained habits overnight, the Supreme Court issued only a vague directive for school systems to desegregate "with all deliberate speed" in 1955. This ruling encouraged entrenched segregationists to try to delay integration indefinitely.

In a scattering of southern cities, moderate whites proved willing to accept the piecemeal dismantlement of Jim Crow. Little Rock, Arkansas, for instance, had desegregated its parks, buses, and libraries with little controversy. After the Brown decision the school board made plans to integrate slowly by inviting nine black teenagers to attend high school alongside two thousand white students. Nicknamed the **Little Rock Nine**, the nine teenagers who integrated Central High School in Little Rock, Arkansas, in 1957 became the focus of a national crisis that required the intervention of federal troops to resolve.

Segregationists quickly organized statewide opposition to the planned integration of Central High School. Concern about states' rights and segregationists' claims that integration would lead to white and black students dancing together at school social functions won over some moderates. Two weeks before the school year started, the threats began. One night a rock shattered the living room window of Daisy Bates, secretary of the local NAACP chapter. The note tied around the rock read "stone this time. Dynamite next."

Influenced by poll numbers showing 85 percent of white Arkansans opposed school integration, Arkansas governor Orval Faubus, who faced a

25.11 First Ride on an Integrated Montgomery Bus, 1958 Martin Luther King Jr., seated on the left, rides with other activists on the first day that buses were integrated in Montgomery after a year-long bus boycott. Fearing vigilante attacks from angry whites, King urged all black bus riders to exude steely resolve and to ride in pairs.

What messages did this planned scene send to whites and blacks?

difficult reelection campaign, declared he would not "force acceptance of change to which the people are so overwhelmingly opposed." In September 1957 Faubus decided to ring Central High with state troops on the first day of school to stop the black students from entering the high school. Using state troops to defy a federal mandate fit well with the desire of moderate whites and die-hard segregationists to protect the sanctity of states' rights.

To protect the black teenagers, Daisy Bates asked parents to drop the students off at her house so they could go to school together. However Elizabeth Eckford, whose family did not have a telephone, never received the message. Instead she took a bus to the school by herself and confronted the angry mob alone. At first she felt reassured when she saw the troops, whom she assumed were there to protect her. She quickly realized her error. When she tried to squeeze past a guard, "He raised his bayonet, and then the other guards moved in." As she stood there confused, the crowd started to chant "Lynch her! Lynch her!" Television cameras, tempering the crowd's enthusiasm for a lynching, likely saved Elizabeth's life. Also a godsend Grace Lorch, a white woman, came out of the crowd to help Elizabeth flag down a city bus and escape.

Over the next few days, as the crowds in front of the high school grew, attacks against news photographers and cameramen became more common. The television footage coming out of Little Rock, reporter David Halberstam noted, "made it hard for people watching at home not to take sides" as they saw "orderly black children behaving with great dignity" being assaulted by a "vicious mob of poor whites." Outrage outside of the South over such images put pressure on President Eisenhower to act, as did the negative worldwide attention that the Little Rock incident garnered. "Our [Communist] enemies are gloating over this incident and using it everywhere to misrepresent our whole nation," Eisenhower warned the country.

Resistance to Supreme Court–mandated integration created more than a racial crisis. It also led to a showdown between the federal government and the state of Arkansas. Under pressure from the White House, Faubus withdrew state troops. It was the president's responsibility to enforce federal law, Eisenhower told the American people, announcing his decision to send federal troops to Little Rock to ensure that Arkansas obeyed the Supreme Court's ruling. With paratroopers from the 101st Airborne Division ringing the school, the Little Rock Nine walked up the front steps surrounded by armed guards.

This was the first time that the federal government had used troops to protect the civil rights of African Americans since the Reconstruction era. The troops, Melba Pattillo Beals recalled, meant a "declaration of war" in the hallways of Central High where white teenagers insulted, kicked, shoved, and ostracized the Little Rock Nine, who were each sent to different classrooms. Eight of the nine finished the year. (Minnijean Brown was expelled for dumping chili on a white student's head after he insulted her in the cafeteria line.) The following year Faubus defied the order to integrate by keeping the schools closed all year. In 1959 Central High reopened with one black student in attendance; in 1960 there were five; then eight in 1961. The small numbers of black students in Central High signified the long, slow road to complete the process of school integration.

The Sit-ins

By the end of the fifties, with the nonviolent Civil Rights Movement in full bloom, the movement's attention shifted from schools to segregated lunch counters. In 1958 James Lawson began conducting SCLC workshops for local college students in Nashville to prepare them for a sit-in campaign to desegregate the city's lunch counters. At these meetings students studied Christian pacifist principles, Gandhi's theories of nonviolence, and the nineteenth-century philosopher Henry David Thoreau's ideas on civil disobedience. During **sit-ins** protesters occupied seats at whites-only lunch counters and remained there even after they were refused service, sometimes for hours. The sit-ins employed the tactic of **civil disobedience**, breaking the law in a peaceful way to call attention to an unjust law, and replicated a tactic used successfully by the CIO in the 1930s when workers had occupied factories during strikes (see Chapter 22). Sit-ins, like sit-down strikes, disrupted business, making it impossible for white businessmen to ignore the protesters' demands. Highly visible sit-ins in downtown Nashville department stores were also guaranteed to attract press attention.

Lawson warned the students that their anger over Jim Crow was not enough to sustain them through the challenges ahead. Instead they needed to truly embrace nonviolence as the governing principle of their lives. They were fighting back, he assured his students, but in a way that broke the cycle of violence. Armed resistance was not only morally wrong, Lawson argued, but it was also futile to believe that blacks could take on the police and army with guns.

Why did Eisenhower send troops to integrate Central High School in Little Rock?

> "Do show yourself friendly on the counter at all times. Do sit straight and always face the counter. Don't strike back, or curse if attacked. Don't laugh out. Don't hold conversations. Don't block entrances. ... Remember the teachings of Jesus, Gandhi, Thoreau, and Martin Luther King, Jr."
>
> Instructions to sit-in demonstrators in Nashville, Tennessee, 1960

Students learned how to ignore the taunts and blows that whites would heap on them during a sit-in, to go limp when pulled from the seats, and to curl into a protective fetal position if attacked with blows. Lawson's Nashville workshops identified and trained students who would become major leaders in the Civil Rights Movement, including John Lewis, Diane Nash, and Jim Bevel.

Black civil rights protesters had intermittently organized sit-ins since 1942, but it was the spontaneous decision in 1960 of four freshmen from the all-black North Carolina Agricultural and Technical College to request service at a Woolworth's lunch counter in Greensboro, North Carolina, that ignited the national sit-in movement. By acting on impulse these four teenagers ignored SCLC rules, which emphasized careful preparation and planning before launching any civil rights protest. The evening television news broadcast images of their defiance throughout the nation, demonstrating that the actions of ordinary people could make a difference. In this posed photo taken of the four when they returned to the lunch counter the following day, the young men "had a certain look on their faces, sort of sullen, angry, determined. Before, the Negro in the South had always looked on the defensive, cringing," Bob Moses later recalled (**25.12**). Their courage inspired Moses to leave his job teaching math in Harlem and head south to join the movement. He would go on to spearhead the 1964 voter registration drive in Mississippi known as "Freedom Summer" (see Chapter 27).

25.12 Second Day of Woolworth's Lunch Counter Sit-In, 1960
These freshmen from the North Carolina Agricultural and Technical College ignited the southern sit-in movement when they decided to request service at a whites-only lunch counter in Greensboro. They sat unmolested day after day for a week, until the store shut down the lunch counter.

25.13 Mississippi Sit-In, 1963
Assaults on sit-in protesters grew more vicious as the demonstrations moved into the Deep South.

Over the following weeks churches and students worked together to unleash waves of sit-ins throughout the South. In Nashville Lawson's group unfurled the longest and most sustained series of sit-ins. After a month of letting roving gangs of thugs punch and kick the students, the Nashville police tried to end the sit-ins by arresting the demonstrators for "disorderly conduct." The students responded with a "jail-no bail" strategy. "Only so many can fit into a cell; if you remain here, there can be no more arrests! Imprisonment is an expense to the state; it must feed and take care of you. Bails and fines are an expense to the movement, which it can ill afford," SCLC organizer Bayard Rustin told the students. With the jails full and the sit-ins continuing, the SCLC increased the pressure with a successful boycott of the downtown stores.

The standoff came to a head when the home of a prominent black lawyer (who had represented the students in court) was bombed. Marching to city hall the students demonstrated the power of nonviolence to change minds. Confronting the mayor, Diane Nash asked: "Mayor West, do you feel it is wrong to discriminate against a person solely on the basis of their race or color?" Answering as "a man had to answer, not a politician," Mayor Ben West, a moderate on racial issues, agreed it was wrong. Three weeks later the lunch counters in Nashville were desegregated. Energized by their success the Nashville group staged "stand-ins" in the city's segregated movie theaters and "sleep-ins" in the lobbies of whites-only hotels.

Throughout the upper South photographs of the sit-ins provoked a similar awakening among moderate whites. The contrast between "the colored students, in coats, white shirts, ties" quietly requesting service at a lunch counter and the ragtag gangs of "white boys come to heckle" was hard to ignore, noted the *Richmond News Leader* when sit-ins hit the capital of Virginia. Resistance to sit-ins in the Deep South proved more formidable and vicious. In 1963 Tougaloo College student Anne Moody sat at a Woolworth's lunch counter with two white activists in Jackson, Mississippi. As this photo shows (**25.13**) a lunchtime crowd of high school students ferociously assaulted the three and poured condiments on their heads. Egging them on was the older man in the picture, who urged the mob to get the demon-

Why were sit-ins successful in the upper South?

strators off the stools and pour salt on their wounds. The crowd's heated anger convinced Moody that "many more will die before it is over with."

By the spring of 1960, Jim Lawson and SCLC organizer Ella Baker saw that students had emerged as a powerful force within the Civil Rights Movement. The two leaders urged university students to form their own civil rights organization. Students, they realized, were willing to take more risks than were many adult activists. Employing the lyrics of a movement song that urged protesters to "keep your eyes on the prize," Baker told the students that their goal needed to be "bigger than a hamburger." The students responded by forming their own civil rights organization, the **Student Nonviolent Coordinating Committee**, or SNCC (pronounced Snick) in 1960.

In the struggles ahead SNCC and SCLC often forged a crucial partnership between black churches and university students. Idealistic and enthusiastic college students, white and black, eagerly put themselves in the frontlines during civil rights demonstrations. Black churches provided the experienced organizers, meeting spaces, and funds necessary to organize successful protests. Often SNCC acted alone. Commenting on the importance of SNCC to the modern civil rights crusade, Diane Nash noted that "the media and history seem to record it as Martin Luther King's movement, but young people should realize that it was people just like them, their age, that formulated goals and strategies, and actually developed the movement."

The Civil Rights Movement brought together many critical features of the 1950s. While print media remained important, film footage shown on evening television news broadcasts of confrontations between racist whites and nonviolent protesters forced the rest of the nation to confront the realities of Jim Crow and racial violence in the South. Thanks to television what happened in the South no longer remained in the South. The rise of a distinctly teenage culture within the baby boom generation also helped to create a strong generational bond among those young adults who joined the movement. Finally the ideological overtones of the Cold War that pitted democratic capitalism against communism helped civil rights protesters focus attention on the inherent contradictions between America's self-proclaimed goal of spreading democracy throughout the world and visible racial discrimination at home.

Conclusion

Americans enjoyed unprecedented prosperity from 1945 to 1960. A strong labor movement, readily available credit, and generous veterans' benefits fueled a booming consumer and housing market. Growing American families headed to the suburbs, where cars and televisions played prominent roles in their daily lives. Americans debated the meaning of their newfound prosperity throughout the decade. For some this wealth offered a clear demonstration of the superiority of capitalism over communism and made people more tolerant. To others the suburbs were places where all people learned to think and act alike. Conflict also followed Americans into their homes, where parents railed against teenage tastes in music and films.

In the realm of politics, the federal government made only minor adjustments to the New Deal reforms inherited from the Roosevelt administration. The Supreme Court issued path-breaking rulings on the unconstitutionality of segregated schools and buses. In the wake of Emmett Till's murder and Rosa Parks's arrest, a new generation of civil rights activists fought back against racial injustice by employing the tactics of nonviolent direct action and civil disobedience. The publicity given to individual acts of tremendous bravery demonstrated the ability of ordinary Americans to ignite extraordinary changes in the American polity. Overall the fifties planted the seeds for the cultural conflict that traversed the nation in the sixties, a time when youth culture, civil rights, the television age, and an unpopular war in Vietnam created division and discord.

What different strengths did students and churches bring to the Civil Rights Movement?

CHAPTER REVIEW

1945–1946

Five thousand labor strikes sweep the country
Creates public backlash against unions

Baby Boom begins
Generation sets cultural trends from cradle to grave

1947–1948

Taft-Hartley Act
Puts restrictions on labor unions

First Levittown built
Mass migration to suburbs begins

Truman desegregates the armed forces
First major U.S. institution to integrate in the twentieth century

1952

Nixon's "Checkers" speech
First use of television to diffuse a political crisis

Review Questions

1. How did efforts to undo the New Deal and curtail the Fair Deal fare from 1945 to 1960?
2. How did Americans react to rising prosperity in the United States? What internal debates arose over suburbanization and teen culture?
3. Consider the role of the media in the 1950s. How did the media affect intergenerational conflicts? What role did the media play during the Civil Rights Movement? How did activists, both conservative and liberal, use the media to sway opinions?
4. What key social conditions and events triggered the modern Civil Rights Movement?
5. What means were available to African Americans to fight against Jim Crow?
6. Why was the Civil Rights Movement successful in the fifties? What role did ordinary citizens play? How important were its leaders?

The Long Road to War

From 1945 to 1965 America gradually shifted its Cold War focus from Europe to Asia. The United States first supported French efforts to recover Vietnam as a colony, and then sustained an independent anti-communist South Vietnam with financial aid. At home some American policymakers envisioned the war as part of the worldwide struggle between democracy and communism. In Vietnam, however, Americans confronted a country torn apart by a civil war that reflected long-standing religious and political divisions within the nation. No American president sought a war in Vietnam, and key presidential advisors offered competing assessments of America's chances for victory. Yet at critical moments when the intractable political and military situation called for a response, each president chose to bolster the American commitment rather than turn back.

The Escalating Importance of Vietnam

America first became involved in Vietnam during World War II, when Japan took over the French colony of Indochina (present-day Laos, Cambodia, and Vietnam). In 1945 U.S. intelligence operatives worked with Ho Chi Minh, the leader of an underground Vietnamese communist resistance movement that launched guerilla attacks against the Japanese occupiers. When the war ended Ho Chi Minh and his rebel force formed a provisional government in Hanoi and declared independence from France. Eager to reestablish its position as a world power after the humiliating occupation by Germany in World War II, France sent in troops to crush the Vietnamese independence movement.

In search of international support for Vietnamese independence, the Western-educated Ho Chi Minh turned to the United States. Ho Chi Minh had previously tried to interest the United States in the cause of Vietnamese independence by submitting a petition to the American delegation at the Paris Peace Conference in 1919 after World War I that called for democratic reforms in French-held Indochina. The American delegation ignored Ho Chi Minh's request, mindful that his proposal would anger the French, whose support President Woodrow Wilson needed to create the League of Nations (see Chapter 20). After the rebuff in Paris, Ho Chi Minh became a communist, attracted by communism's revolutionary promise to free colonized peoples. "It was patriotism, not communism, that inspired me," he later claimed. In 1941 after nearly three decades abroad working as a Soviet spy, Ho Chi Minh returned to Vietnam to help organize a communist resistance to the Japanese occupation. Despite this revolutionary background Ho Chi Minh held out hope that the United States would support Vietnamese independence when Japan withdrew in 1945. Ho Chi Minh's communist credentials, however, tainted him in the eyes of President Harry S. Truman, who remained unmoved by Ho Chi Minh's truthful assurances that the Soviet Union did not control or finance him.

In the 1940s the Americans saw Ho Chi Minh as a communist puppet doing Moscow's bidding. His Vietnamese followers, however, viewed him as a charismatic leader ignited with a patriotic desire to free his nation from French colonial control. As one disciple recalled, the fifty-five-year-old "Uncle Ho" spoke with an "ardent and idealistic nationalism" that encouraged many Vietnamese to join the **Vietminh**, the term initially used to describe all Vietnamese communists, and used after 1954 solely for North Vietnamese communists. This photograph (**26.1**) of Ho Chi Minh sitting with a group of children reinforced his reputation in Vietnam as a beloved, wise elder. The image tapped into prevailing Confucian ideals, including filial piety (respect toward living and dead relatives), loyalty, and humane treatment of others. Ho Chi Minh broadened his appeal by eschewing personal luxuries and living simply in a small cottage. By the time American troops arrived in the late 1960s, an ailing Ho Chi Minh played almost no official role in the conflict. He nonetheless remained the face of Vietnamese communism for supporters and opponents throughout the war.

Who was Ho Chi Minh to his supporters and foes?

Cold War geopolitics consistently influenced how Americans reacted to the Vietnamese Communist revolt. As the emerging Cold War with the Soviet Union in the 1940s made containing communism in Europe a national obsession, Vietnam took on new political significance for the United States. The United States needed help from a vigorous and cooperative France to defend Western Europe from Soviet incursion. To rebuild the French economy and build goodwill, the United States gave France arms and funds beginning in 1947 (see Chapter 24). The French government used some of this aid to finance the war in Vietnam. The United States also agreed to support French efforts to regain control of its Vietnamese colony.

In 1950 the strategic importance of Vietnam for the United States also changed dramatically. The fall of China to communism in 1949 and the outbreak of the Korean War in 1950 when Communist-led North Korea invaded the anti-communist South Korea created fears that all of Asia might fall to communism. The "who lost China" debate severely hurt Truman politically, and no subsequent president wanted to be the one blamed for Vietnam falling to communism. Containing communism in both Europe and Asia became cornerstones of American foreign policy from this point on, requiring the United States to maintain military bases throughout Western Europe and along a string of Pacific islands from Japan to the Philippines.

As the Cold War spread to Asia, key presidential advisors insisted on seeing the hand of the Soviet Union behind every communist victory. By the early 1950s National Security Council Memorandum 68, or NSC-68, a document that described a global communist monolith, set the tone for U.S. foreign policy (see Chapter 24). Any more territory "under the domination of the Kremlin," the National Security Council warned, would make the Soviet Union invincible in any future military conflict. The threat would deepen if the Soviets gained control of resource-rich Southeast Asia, whose rubber, rice, tin, and oil were important economically to the United States. These resources were even more for vital for Japan, now a key American ally in the struggle against communism, and the United States wanted to ensure Japanese access to these materials by preventing them from falling into unfriendly communist hands.

Hardliners in the Truman and Eisenhower administrations embraced the **domino theory**, the fear that a communist Vietnam would open the door to a complete communist takeover of Southeast Asia, with communists repeating how Japan had conquered the region in World War II. Announcing the domino theory President Dwight D. Eisenhower explained in a 1954 press conference: "You have a row of dominos set up, you knock over the first one, and what will happen to the last one is the certainty that it will go over very quickly. So you could have a beginning of a disintegration that would have the most profound influences." Key events in the 1950s gave credence to these fears. Josef Stalin's success in pressuring China and North Korea to accept an

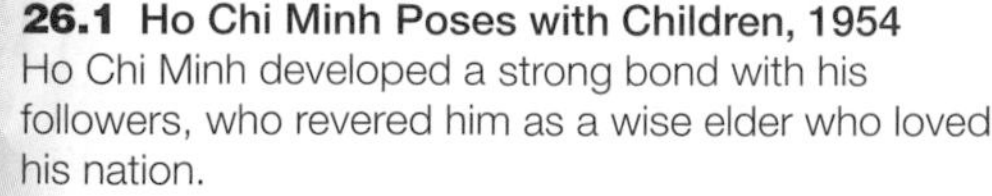

26.1 Ho Chi Minh Poses with Children, 1954
Ho Chi Minh developed a strong bond with his followers, who revered him as a wise elder who loved his nation.

What political and strategic importance did Vietnam assume in U.S. foreign policy by the mid-1950s?

26.2 ***How About the Other Buttons?*** This 1953 illustration shows Soviet leader Josef Stalin pressing his finger on a button labeled "Korea" to end the Korean War. This cartoon suggested that Stalin had the power to stop other conflicts that he had initiated throughout the world, including the war in Indochina.

armistice to end the Korean War strengthened the American conviction that the Soviet Union had the power to start or stop communist insurgencies around the globe. This political cartoon (**26.2**) by illustrator Marcus Edwin showed Stalin pressing the stop button for Korea, and suggested that he could also stop the conflict in Indochina (Vietnam) if he wished. Indeed Stalin had encouraged the Chinese leader Mao Tse-tung to take the lead in promoting communist revolution throughout Asia. The immediate influx of Communist Chinese advisors to train Vietminh officers, plus mountains of Chinese-manufactured vehicles, arms, and ammunition, seemingly confirmed that the Vietminh were part of an international communist conspiracy masterminded in Moscow.

American policymakers failed to appreciate, however, that a shared belief in communism did not override the nationalistic ambitions of the Soviet Union, China, or Vietnam. Ho Chi Minh accepted help from the Chinese, but remembering the Chinese ancient colonization of Vietnam, he remained suspicious of their ulterior motives and had no intention of turning Vietnam over to them. "It is better to sniff French dung for a while than eat China's all our life," warned Ho Chi Minh. In an American worldview that saw every communist revolution as part of the Soviet Union's master plan, however, the specific grievances or goals of the Vietminh became irrelevant.

Taking Over from the French

To hold the line in Vietnam, the American government was willing to foot the bill but wanted the French to do the actual fighting. The United States upheld its end of the bargain. By 1954 the United States was paying for 80 percent of the war's costs, money used to both purchase arms and fund humanitarian projects including free health clinics, food for refugees, and seeds for farmers. Increasingly, however, the United States doubted, in the words of Truman's outgoing secretary of state Dean Acheson, the "French will to carry on." As Acheson anticipated, the incoming Eisenhower administration soon faced a crisis in Vietnam. In 1954 the Vietminh defeated the French at Dien Bien Phu, in the northwest corner of the country, prompting the French to seek an international agreement with the Vietminh. The resulting **Geneva Accords (1954)** called for a temporary partition of Vietnam along the seventeenth parallel, with the Vietminh in the north and the French in the south, and a general election in two years to reunify the country under one government. Refusing to sign the Geneva Accords, the Eisenhower administration instead resolved to use the two-year period to ease the French out of South Vietnam and create a new government capable of raising and training a strong military to resist communist aggression.

To head the new South Vietnamese government, the United States selected Ngo Dinh Diem, a wealthy Catholic who had served as minister of the interior in the French colonial administration before resigning when the French refused to enact reforms he proposed. A staunch nationalist Diem moved to the United States, where he became well known to American policymakers. Neither Diem nor the United States intended to let the scheduled election take place, certain that Ho Chi Minh's authoritarian government would use force and fraud to ensure victory in the north and perhaps in the south as well. Instead the United States tried to destabilize Ho Chi Minh's fledgling Communist government by creating political turmoil in North Vietnam. Central Intelligence Agency (CIA) operatives destroyed government printing presses, contaminated the oil used in bus engines, sabotaged railway tracks, and planted rumors of Chinese troops raping North Vietnamese women.

Eisenhower supported the creation of an anticommunist South Vietnam to stem the tide of communism in Southeast Asia. As an additional defense against communism, the United States

What key choices did Eisenhower make in 1954 that increased U.S. involvement in Vietnam?

formed the **Southeast Asian Treaty Organization (SEATO)** in 1954. Through SEATO the United States, Britain, France, Australia, New Zealand, Thailand, the Philippines, and Pakistan pledged to "meet common danger" in Southeast Asia together. A separate agreement identified Vietnam, Laos, and Cambodia as areas that would endanger the "peace and security" of SEATO members if any of these three nations came under attack. Unlike the North Atlantic Treaty Organization (NATO), which guaranteed the mutual defense of member nations in Europe, the SEATO treaty left each nation's exact commitment vague. Secretary of State John Foster Dulles wanted it that way, reluctant to overextend American military responsibilities around the world by guaranteeing the borders of SEATO members. Even if this loosely worded pact failed to deter communist aggression, Dulles reasoned, it would provide a justification for direct American involvement in Vietnam to protect SEATO members if the United States decided to escalate its involvement in the future. An important development in America's ever-increasing involvement in Vietnam, SEATO illustrated how completely the United States linked the civil war in Vietnam to the global crusade against communism.

With the United States poised to embark on a major campaign to create an independent South Vietnam, dissenting voices within the government urged the president to pull back. Secretary of Defense Charles E. Wilson warned that he could "see nothing but grief in store for us if we remained." The joint chiefs of staff complained it would be impossible to build a capable South Vietnamese army without a "reasonably strong, stable civil government in control." This "chicken and egg" argument over which needed to come first, a strong South Vietnamese government or a strong military, divided American policymakers for the next fifteen years.

With Diem the United States got neither. A short, stocky man who always dressed in white, Diem's stiff and privileged appearance contrasted poorly with the plain dress and manners of Ho Chi Minh. The Eisenhower administration recognized Diem's shortcomings, but Secretary of State Dulles accepted the American ambassador's conclusion "that there is no one to take his place who would serve U.S. interests better." The United States quickly realized that Diem intended to build a dictatorial regime in South Vietnam. Diem modeled his rule on Vietnamese emperors of the nineteenth century, issuing decrees and refusing to abide any criticism. "I know what is best for my people," he declared in one interview. The secret police, headed by Diem's brother-in-law, Ngo Dinh Nhu, arrested, tortured, and executed thousands of South Vietnamese accused of opposing his rule.

Most Vietminh had relocated to North Vietnam when the country split into two, but remnants of the Communist guerilla force still existed in the south. They found ample discontent with Diem among peasants, students, Buddhists, and even some South Vietnamese soldiers. Attempting to destabilize the Diem regime, the Communists unleashed a wave of assassinations targeting wealthy landlords and rural officials who worked for the repressive Diem regime. Diem fought back by trying to cut off guerilla fighters from their supply base. He moved peasants off their ancestral lands and into "strategic hamlets" protected by moats and walls and imprisoned thousands of civilians suspected of aiding the rebels. Enraged over the forced removal program, the peasants were like a "mound of straw ready to be ignited," claimed one Vietnamese Communist.

The U.S. government and press revealed none of Diem's internal difficulties to the American people. When Diem visited the United States in 1957, the American press praised him as the "tough little miracle man" who had brought stability to South Vietnam. "We can take pride in our support," *Newsweek* magazine trumpeted.

In the mid-1950s Ho Chi Minh offered southern Communists little support. He was instead preoccupied with subduing the widespread protests that greeted his forced land redistribution program in North Vietnam, a campaign that sent armed posses into the countryside to confiscate land. These "land reforms" left thousands of property owners dead, destroyed communities, and created famine. By the end of the decade, however, the North Vietnamese government began sending soldiers and supplies to southern Communists, unleashing a terror campaign meant to pave the way for a Communist takeover of South Vietnam. In 1960 the southern Communists formed the National Liberation Front (NLF) to bring the various factions in South Vietnamese society opposed to the Diem regime together into a fighting coalition. Diem derogatorily called South Vietnamese Communists **Vietcong**, slang meaning "Vietnamese Commies." The name stuck. From this point on Americans called all Communists from South Vietnam "Vietcong" and Communists from North Vietnam "Vietminh."

Why did the civil war in Vietnam reignite in the late 1950s and early 1960s?

Debates within the Kennedy Administration

John F. Kennedy assumed the presidency in 1961 having proclaimed Vietnam the "cornerstone of the free world in Southeast Asia." Kennedy also understood the negative political consequences of "losing" a nation to communism. While in the Senate Kennedy had joined the chorus hurling criticism at Truman when China succumbed to communism. In 1961 Kennedy suffered two setbacks of his own in the global war against communism with the botched Cuban Bay of Pigs invasion and his inability to stop the Soviets from constructing the Berlin Wall (see Chapter 24). His leadership during the Cuban Missile Crisis in 1962, however, eventually redeemed his reputation as a Cold War warrior. In the meantime Kennedy did not intend to let the conflict in Vietnam bring his administration down.

Faced with a worsening political and military situation in Vietnam, Kennedy received conflicting recommendations from his advisors. One group envisioned dramatically escalating the American commitment by sending in combat troops. Another wanted to seek a diplomatic resolution to the conflict. Faced with these divided opinions, Kennedy chose a middle path. Instead of infantry troops Kennedy sent more financial aid and increased the number of American military "advisors" in South Vietnam from one thousand to sixteen thousand. Officially these advisors helped train the South Vietnamese Army. In actuality many "advisors" were Green Berets, the army's special-force troops who organized South Vietnamese attacks on Vietcong supply lines, flew planes when South Vietnamese pilots were unavailable, and picked up the dead and wounded in helicopters after skirmishes. When word of these activities leaked out, Kennedy publicly denied that Americans were participating in active combat operations in Vietnam.

"Supporting the Diem regime while applying pressure for reform appears to be the only practicable alternative at this time," the joint chiefs of staff convinced Kennedy, cautioning that "any reversal of U.S. policy could have disastrous effects" throughout Southeast Asia. As South Vietnamese anger against his rule intensified, Diem privately voiced his own mounting frustration with the growing American presence in South Vietnam. "All these soldiers," he fumed, referring to the Green Berets and military advisors. "I never asked them to come here." To rid South Vietnam of Americans, Diem and his police chief brother Nhu decided to seek a negotiated settlement with North Vietnam in 1963. Upset with Diem's overture to North Vietnam, the turning point for the Kennedy administration came in June, when a Buddhist monk set himself on fire in a busy street in Saigon, the capital of South Vietnam.

The Catholic Diem had long discriminated against Buddhists. Thousands of North Vietnamese Catholics fled to the south when the Communists took over in 1954, and Diem guaranteed their loyalty by rewarding them with land and governmental positions. In May 1963 Nhu refused to let the Buddhists fly a multicolored flag honoring Buddha on his birthday. Widespread street protests ensued, which Nhu violently suppressed with soldiers who used water hoses, tear gas, and on one occasion bullets, killing a woman and eight children. On June 10, 1963, a Buddhist monk telephoned Associated Press photographer Malcolm Browne to invite him to witness "something important" the next morning. Browne arrived at the designated street crossing on June 11, 1963, and watched monks take a canister of gasoline out of the white car shown in this picture (**26.3**) and place a brown mat in the middle of the street. Moments later a Buddhist monk, Thich Quang Duc, sat down on the mat in the lotus position. After another monk poured gasoline over him, Duc struck a match. Flames instantaneously engulfed his body. "His eyes were closed, but his features were twisted in apparent pain," Browne recalled. As Browne snapped this memorable photo, a monk shouted into a microphone in Vietnamese and English: "A Buddhist priest burns himself to death. A Buddhist priest becomes a martyr." Monks (seen in the background) lined the streets to prevent any one from trying to save Duc. Immediately proclaimed a Buddhist saint, Duc's ashes were distributed to pagodas, towering Buddhist temples, throughout South Vietnam.

Duc carefully staged his suicide to gain maximum exposure for the Buddhists' political protest, using the Western press to help rally opposition to Diem within South Vietnam and the United States. The burning monk image shocked but also bewildered Americans. The American government and press had continually praised Diem as a valiant Cold War ally, but this photo suggested strong opposition to his rule at home. Students, Buddhist priests, and soldiers in South Vietnam responded to the suicide as a call to action. Street protests erupted, the military began planning a coup, and six other monks set themselves

What conflicting recommendations did Kennedy receive from his advisors about Vietnam?

26.3 Burning Monk Thich Quang Duc wanted the Western press to photograph his 1963 suicide to publicize the Buddhist protest against the corrupt Diem regime.

on fire in front of Western journalists. With a framed copy of Browne's burning monk image on his desk, Kennedy secretly agreed to support a military coup to overthrow the Diem regime.

> "I must say that during the monk episode, I had no impulse to try to go in and save him. I knew for one thing that he intended it this way."
>
> Photographer MALCOLM BROWNE, on photographing Thich Quang Duc's self-immolation in 1963

The Kennedy Assassination

The military coup supported by President Kennedy led to the murder of Diem and Nhu, but Americans had little time to reflect on these events. Three weeks later, on November 22, 1963, Lee Harvey Oswald shot and killed President Kennedy in Dallas, Texas, as Kennedy waved to onlookers from an open convertible with his wife by his side. In the midst of his presidential reelection bid, Kennedy was visiting Dallas to shore up his fading popularity among Texans angered by his support for the Civil Rights Movement (see Chapter 27). This was the first trip that Jackie Kennedy had taken with her husband since the death of their two-day-old son Patrick three months before. Kennedy decided to ride in an open-air convertible, rejecting the suggestion from his Secret Service guards that he sit within a bulletproof clear glass bubble for the ride past the gathered crowds. An amateur movie by Abraham Zapruder, a Russian immigrant and Kennedy supporter, gave the nation its most enduring images of this killing, film stills that provoked countless controversies over who killed the president. In its investigation of the assassination, the Warren Commission cited the Zapruder film as evidence that Oswald acted alone, claiming that the film footage showed bullets entering the president's body from only one direction. Counterclaims that the assassination was the result of a wider conspiracy involving other gunmen, the mafia, Cuban dictator Fidel Castro, and the CIA continue to this day.

Vice President Lyndon Baines Johnson (LBJ), who had been riding two cars behind Kennedy in the Dallas motorcade, appreciated the potent political symbolism attached to the president's grieving widow. When Kennedy died within hours of the shooting, Johnson, who was next in line to assume the presidency, insisted on taking the oath of office before Judge Sarah Hughes with Jackie Kennedy on one side and his wife on the other before the presidential airplane Air Force One left Dallas. The presence of the slain president's widow would, Johnson felt, immediately legitimatize the transfer of power in the eyes of the American people. Already on board the plane, which was carrying her husband's body back to Washington, D.C., Jackie Kennedy complied with Johnson's request, but had no chance to change her clothes. In this portrait (**26.4**) of Johnson's swearing in, photographer Cecil Stoughton carefully framed out Jackie Kennedy's skirt, which was stained with her husband's blood. Her pale and drawn expression nonetheless reflected the day's ordeal.

A wealthy Massachusetts-born Catholic, Kennedy had selected Johnson, a powerful Texan politician, as his vice presidential running mate to help broaden his appeal in the South. Johnson grew up poor and worked as a middle and high school teacher before entering national politics as an avid supporter of the New Deal in 1937. Johnson relied heavily on his superior political instincts and outgoing personality to rise to prominence. While serving in the Senate, Johnson became the most powerful majority leader in history. A larger-than-life figure, his brashness contrasted sharply with the slain president's debonair manner. His most legendary gaff came in 1965, when he lifted his shirt during a press conference to show reporters his 12-inch scar from recent gallbladder surgery. Johnson wanted to reassure the nation about his recovery, but critics lampooned the act as crude and undignified.

26.4 Jackie Kennedy
On November 22, 1963, the day President John F. Kennedy was assassinated in Dallas, Texas, the First Lady's personal tragedy became enveloped in political symbolism. Here she stands by as the new president, Lyndon B. Johnson, takes the oath of office to visibly assure the nation that she supported the smooth transition of power.

The Gulf of Tonkin

Lyndon Baines Johnson inherited a rapidly deteriorating situation in Vietnam in the wake of the Diem assassination. Like his predecessors he faced the choice of pulling back or escalating the American commitment, which at this point consisted of sixteen thousand military advisors and Green Beret troops and substantial financial aid to South Vietnam. After the Diem assassination, South Vietnam slipped into perpetual political instability as a succession of rulers failed to gain the support of the people. The shifting geopolitical situation also prompted a reappraisal of the American assumption that the Soviet Union was controlling the movements of communists throughout the world. The previous American conception of a global communist conspiracy became harder to maintain in the face of the open split between the Soviet Union and China in 1964. The Sino-Soviet alliance fell apart when the Soviets suggested that the two countries scale back their support of worldwide Communist insurgencies as a first step toward improving relations with the United States. Mao refused.

Once again elected officials and policymakers differed behind closed doors on the best course of action. National Security Advisor McGeorge Bundy told Johnson that "the right course is to continue to strengthen our struggle against the Communist terror (which is exactly what this is)." Senator

How did images both provoke and quell controversy surrounding the Kennedy assassination?

Richard Russell, a close confidant of the president, disagreed with those who claimed that "we'll lose everything in Southeast Asia if we lose Vietnam." For his part Johnson feared that withdrawal would mark him as a weak leader, emboldening conservative challenges to the civil rights laws and expanded social welfare programs for the poor that he wanted to enact. "I was determined to keep the war from shattering that dream," Johnson later admitted, by which time the war had indeed consumed the financial resources and political goodwill that the president needed to fully realize this dream (see Chapter 27).

> "No one ever won a battle sitting on his ass."
> General EARLE WHEELER, supporting the troop buildup in Vietnam

Events in the Gulf of Tonkin, the body of water off the shore of North Vietnam, soon gave Johnson an excuse to act boldly. On August 2, 1964, North Vietnamese torpedo boats attacked an American destroyer, the USS *Maddox*, in the Gulf of Tonkin. The *Maddox* easily repelled the confirmed attack. Two days later the crew of the *Maddox* and a second destroyer, the USS *Turner Joy*, both reported coming under attack from North Vietnamese torpedoes. After failing to locate any North Vietnamese boats, U.S. Navy pilot James Stockdale landed on the *Maddox* where officers met him "all with sheepish grins on their faces." Citing improperly working radar, overeager sonar operators, and no visual sightings of the torpedo boats, the ships' joint commander now doubted that a second attack had taken place. Accepting initial reports of a second attack as conclusive, Secretary of Defense Robert McNamara told Johnson that "we cannot sit still as a nation and let them attack us on the high seas and get away with it." A television reporter asked Secretary of State Dean Rusk why North Vietnam would attack an American ship. "I can't come up with a rational explanation for it," Rusk answered. Behind closed doors the president admitted to knowing better, acknowledging in a private conversation that "there have been some covert operations in that area that we have been carrying on—blowing up some bridges ... roads and so forth. So I imagine they wanted to put a stop to it."

Besides ordering reprisal bombing against North Vietnam, President Johnson used the Gulf of Tonkin incident to win congressional approval for further military action in Vietnam. In August of 1964, rallying behind the president, Congress approved the **Gulf of Tonkin Resolution** with only two dissenting votes in the Senate. The resolution gave Johnson permission "to take all necessary measures to repel any armed attack against the forces of the United States and to prevent further aggression" in Vietnam.

On March 8, 1965, the first American Marines landed at Da Nang along the northern coast of South Vietnam, where young women put leis around their necks during an official ceremony. In the years that followed, troops received a distinctly less warm welcome. As the American air force began a major bombing campaign against North Vietnam called Rolling Thunder, General Westmoreland requested a dramatic escalation in American ground forces. "You must take the fight to the enemy," General Earle Wheeler, the joint chiefs of staff chairman, agreed.

Choices and Consequences: Making Vietnam America's War (page 788) explores how Johnson reached his decision to intensify America's involvement in the war. By choosing escalation Johnson sealed his legacy as the American president who made winning the war a priority for the United States. In 1966 the political cartoonist David Levine reimagined the 1965 scene of Johnson lifting his shirt to expose his gallbladder incision. In Levine's rendition (**26.5**) the mark now assumed the shape of Vietnam, the conflict destined to scar Johnson's presidency and the nation. Johnson's willingness to expose the minute details of his health to the public contrasted sharply with the ethos of misinformation and secrecy (suggested by the Pinocchio-like nose of the caricature) he embraced as commander-in-chief.

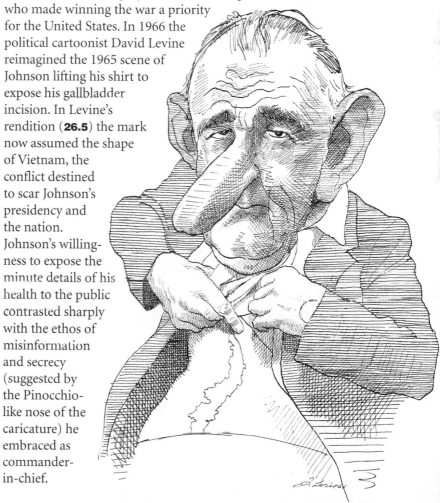

26.5 *Johnson's Scar*
In 1966 the political cartoonist David Levine transformed President Lyndon Johnson's scar into the shape of Vietnam, portraying the conflict as an ugly mark on Johnson's administration.

Choices and Consequences

MAKING VIETNAM AMERICA'S WAR

In the first part of 1965, Johnson initiated a regular bombing campaign against North Vietnam and sent 82,000 ground troops to South Vietnam. The theater commander General William Westmoreland soon requested 150,000 more. In deciding how to respond to Westmoreland's request, the president's advisors gave Johnson the following choices in the summer of 1965.

Choices

1 Avoid a war likely to become protracted with little chance for a military or political victory over the Communists and seek a negotiated settlement in Vietnam.

2 Continue at the present level of military aid to South Vietnam and push for political reforms in South Vietnam to bolster internal support for a more democratic anti-Communist government.

3 Send the requested troops, expand the bombing campaign, and work for political reforms in South Vietnam.

Decision

Johnson viewed a negotiated settlement as tantamount to losing Vietnam to communism, an outcome he viewed as a threat to both Southeast Asia and his presidency. Certain that South Vietnam would lose the war without additional U.S. aid, he publicly agreed to send fifty thousand troops immediately. He privately guaranteed Westmoreland an additional fifty thousand and promised to send more as needed. He also approved heavy bombing of Vietcong strongholds in South Vietnam and tried to institute political reforms in South Vietnam to erode support for the Vietcong.

Consequences

The United States was no longer simply aiding South Vietnam in its struggle against communism, but now took the lead in fighting the Vietcong and the North Vietnamese. By 1967 there were nearly half a million American troops in Vietnam. Over the course of the war the United States dropped more bombs there than it had in World War II.

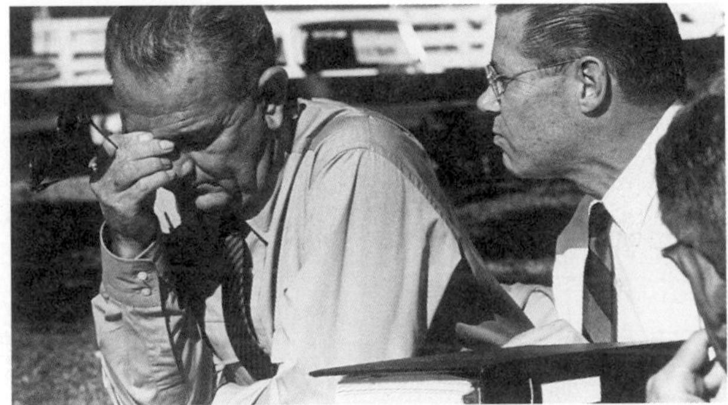

Johnson's Dilemma. He is shown here with Defense Secretary, Robert McNamara.

Continuing Controversies

Should the United States have fought a major war in Vietnam?

Detractors claim that Johnson committed the United States to an unwinnable war by trying to use the military to solve a political problem in South Vietnam. He underestimated the will of the Vietcong and exaggerated the importance of South Vietnam to containing communism in the rest of Southeast Asia. He failed to build strong domestic support for a long war, leading to eventual unrest at home over the draft and rising casualties. Johnson's supporters argue that he honored a commitment to South Vietnam made by his predecessors. This reassured American allies worldwide that they could count on the United States. Retreat would only have invited further Communist aggression in Southeast Asia and Europe. Losing Vietnam would have weakened Johnson politically, putting his controversial domestic reform and civil rights legislative agenda in jeopardy.

Why was Johnson's decision to escalate U.S. troop levels in 1965 important?

Fighting in Vietnam

David Halberstam, reporting for the *New York Times* in 1962, summed up the military dilemma in Vietnam perfectly: "It is often impossible to separate the cruel and dedicated foe you want to kill from the simple and illiterate peasant you want to woo." America and North Vietnam embraced competing strategic visions in fighting the war. While the American military preferred fighting against uniformed soldiers on a clearly defined battlefield, the Communists embraced guerilla warfare where troops blended into the civilian population or stayed hidden in underground tunnels. The American military tried to defeat Vietnamese guerilla forces by bombing enemy bases and destroying their village refuges. These tactics created another set of competing visions about the war: the soldiers' view of an unending conflict versus the image of imminent victory that the government championed at home.

The Bombing Campaign

The American military relied heavily on bombing to defeat the Vietcong and North Vietnamese. The American bombing campaign was the largest air war in world history, with American planes dropping nearly 5 million tons of bombs in eight years. The Americans hoped to pressure North Vietnam into ending the war. The North Vietnamese instead learned to live with bombs. The sighting of American planes over the North Vietnamese capital city of Hanoi sent inhabitants scurrying into bombproof underground shelters. The government built 30,000 miles of tunnels, which moved the nation's transportation and communication infrastructure underground. The sustained bombing campaign bred anti-American feelings among the civilian population that made it easier for the North Vietnamese government to mobilize the country to "foil the war of aggression of the U.S. imperialists."

Navy Captain James Stockdale led the first American air strike against North Vietnamese oil tanks in the wake of the Gulf of Tonkin incident. A year later during another air raid, he was shot down over a small coastal village in North Vietnam where angry villagers beat him and broke his knee. Stockdale spent the next seven and a half years in a prisoner of war (POW) camp. His jailers subjected Stockdale to brutal rounds of torture when he taught fellow POWs a wall-tapping code so they could communicate with one another during their long years in solitary confinement.

American planes targeted the **Ho Chi Minh Trail** as well, a 600-mile North Vietnamese supply route that ran along the western border of Vietnam through the mountainous rain forest of neighboring Laos and Cambodia. Nearly five thousand Communist soldiers and workers completed the arduous three-month journey each month, bringing additional troops, munitions, and food to the Vietcong. North Vietnamese propaganda glorified the difficult journey with images that emphasized the toughness and determination of its people. This photo (**26.6**) shows a North Vietnamese camera crew filming male and female teenage volunteers from the north as they push bicycles, which the North Vietnamese called "steel horses," through the woods to carry rice and guns to Communist troops in the south. Continued improvements turned the dirt paths into an open road by the 1970s. Surface-to-air missiles and antiaircraft guns stationed along the way helped protect trucks from bombing.

26.6 Hardships along the Ho Chi Minh Trail
North Vietnamese propaganda relentlessly publicized the arduous journey along the Ho Chi Minh Trail to highlight how Communist ingenuity had stymied the world's greatest military power. Here, a Communist movie crew films teenage volunteers transporting bags of rice and guns strapped to their bicycle handlebars in 1970.

What messages did North Vietnamese propaganda send?

Americans also extensively bombed South Vietnamese "free fire zones," the name given to villages that supposedly contained only enemy combatants. The American air campaign included spraying defoliants, usually **Agent Orange**, that stripped trees of their leaves to expose Vietcong hideouts and killed the crops that might feed enemy troops. "Only you can prevent forests," American pilots quipped, a satirical reworking of a popular environmental slogan "only you can prevent forest fires." Defoliants ultimately destroyed half of Vietnam's forests and caused lasting health problems for both American pilots and the Vietnamese that included cancers and birth defects. Responding to negative publicity at home, the military stopped using defoliants in 1971. American pilots also dropped napalm, a jellylike gasoline that ignited on impact, to destroy South Vietnamese villages hiding enemy troops. Napalm inflicted severe burns on the human body, contributing to the misery of civilians subject to bombing attacks.

> "I wanted to be a hero."
>
> Vietnam veteran RON KOVIC, explaining why he joined the Marines

Reports of mounting civilian suffering energized the U.S. **peace movement**, a loose coalition of antiwar activists that included pacifists, students, professors, clergy, hippies (young people who rejected middle-class values and adopted a bohemian lifestyle), civil rights activists, and middle-class liberals. In making his decision to go to war, Johnston had focused on placating his hawkish critics without considering the political fallout of antagonizing the left. By 1967, however, belatedly realizing the price he was paying for waging the war, the president noted, "The major threat we have [politically] is from the doves."

On the Ground

The initial wave of American troops sent to Vietnam consisted mostly of army volunteers. Raised on tales of heroism during World War II, Phil Caputo viewed joining the Marines as a way to escape suburbia and serve their country. "I saw myself charging up some distant beachhead, like John Wayne in *Sands of Iwo Jima*," noted Caputo, recalling a popular 1949 film that romanticized the battle responsible for the iconic World War II photo of six men raising the flag over Mount Suribachi (see *Images as History*, Chapter 23). The 1966 hit song "The Ballad of the Green Berets" sold nine million singles and topped the charts for five weeks, evidence of widespread popular support for the war that lasted until 1967. The song praised each member of this specially trained force as "one of America's best" who fought courageously with conviction to free the oppressed. The song's lyrics, "one hundred men, we'll test today, but only three, win the Green Beret," promoted military service as a legitimate way for young men to demonstrate their masculine prowess—a message that encouraged many working-class men to volunteer.

The realities of combat, however, quickly shattered the idealism of men like Caputo. In 1965, *Life* photojournalist Larry Burrows spent a month with helicopter crews, documenting their heroism and the harrowing combat. In this photo (**26.7**) gunner James Farley fires on enemy troops below as the pilot lands to rescue a downed American helicopter crew. Subsequent photos captured the anguish on Farley's face when he realized that the rescued pilot had died.

The drafted men sent to Vietnam in later years had fewer illusions than the initial volunteers. Conscripts were often working-class men who did

26.7 American Gunner Rescues Downed Comrades, 1965
Life photographer Larry Burrows captured the harrowing nature of combat in a photo that shows a U.S. soldier clearing the ground of enemy fire as his helicopter lands to aid a downed American helicopter crew.

What motivated American men to volunteer to fight in Vietnam?

not qualify for draft deferments, which only college-bound and married men enjoyed. Volunteers and conscripts served one-year tours in Vietnam, and as the time to return home neared, they often became more averse to taking risks in combat. Some soldiers even used their helmets as calendars, openly marking off the days left until their tour of duty ended.

In World War II American soldiers had fought against a clearly distinguishable enemy in the Pacific island jungles. Vietcong forces, however, infiltrated the civilian population. They wore civilian clothes, stored arms in the walls of huts, and sent spies to work on American military bases. Civilians gave the Vietcong crucial support, some by choice and some out of fear that the Vietcong would torture or murder them. On search-and-destroy missions, American soldiers tried to draw the enemy out of hiding to kill them and destroy their supply base with combined ground force action and air attacks. To locate the enemy American soldiers marched in darkness through the steamy jungle and tried to stay alert while sweat poured down their faces and saw-edged grass cut into their skin. They walked gingerly, on the lookout for enemy ambushes, land mines, and leaf-covered punji stake traps (holes in the ground lined with sharpened spears that would impale a soldier who fell into one).

Search-and-destroy missions reduced villages that were suspected of aiding Vietcong to mounds of rubble. American troops blew up or contaminated wells, burned straw huts, and salted the ground so no crops would grow. Even in the middle of search-and-destroy missions, however, American soldiers remained capable of compassion. It was "the paradoxical kindness-and-cruelty that made Vietnam such a peculiar war," Marine Phil Caputo remembered. On one search-and-destroy mission, for instance, men in his unit tried to treat and comfort a baby with skin ulcers. Only a few yards away, other soldiers threatened to kill an old woman for preparing metal stakes that the Vietcong placed in fields to prevent helicopters from landing.

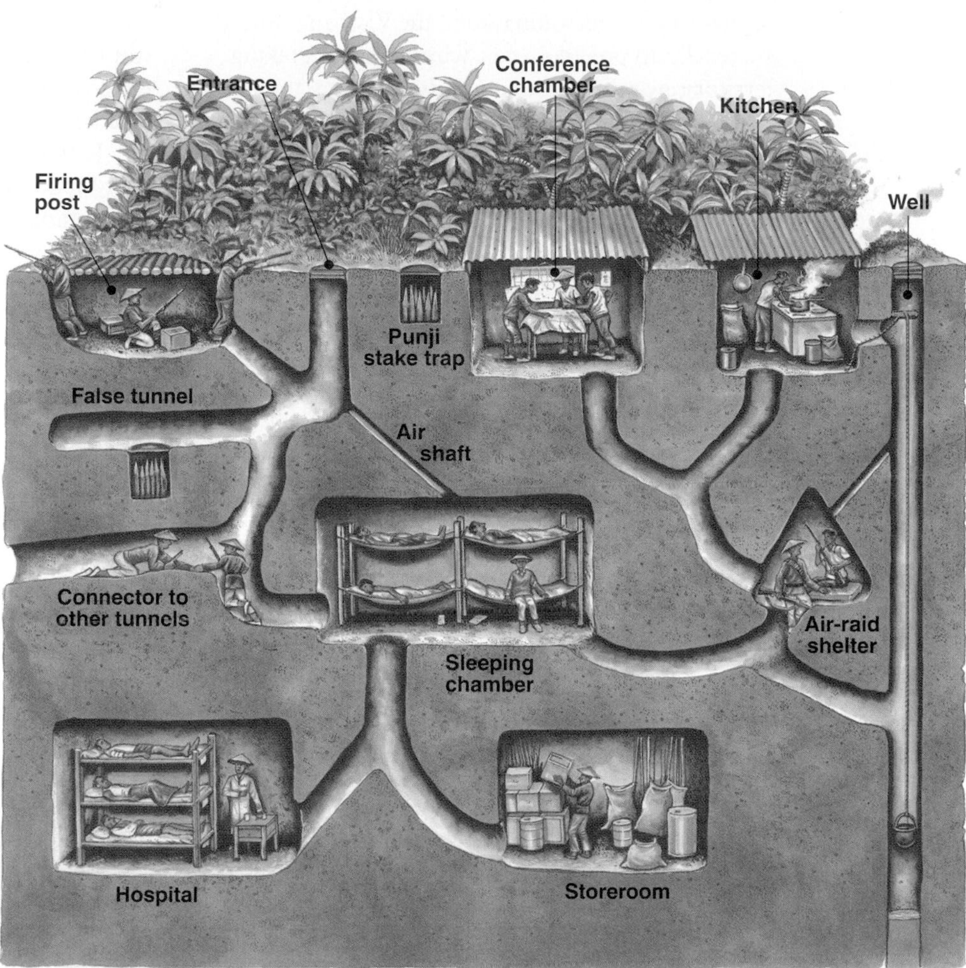

26.8 **Drawing of Vietcong Hideout** Intricate tunnel complexes concealed Vietcong guerilla forces beneath villages.

To combat American air superiority, the Vietcong moved many of their command posts, dormitories, and supply depots underground. This drawing (**26.8**) illustrates an example of an elaborate Vietcong tunnel complex. Village huts camouflaged some entrances. Punji stake traps, pictured on one side of the tunnel entrance, and hidden snipers, hiding in a hole on the other side, protected another. The Vietcong also laid traps for American "tunnel rats" who entered the complex in search of enemy troops. A wrong turn down the false tunnel meant overturning baskets of scorpions and poisonous snakes or falling into a punji stake trap. The twisted tunnel design stymied American attempts to fill the tunnels with water, while poisonous gas escaped through the airshafts. Heavy bombing ultimately demolished many tunnel complexes, but at the high cost of destroying homes and forests as well.

American soldiers fought a war of attrition, trying to kill as many Vietcong as possible while also destroying their resources and thus sapping their morale. When the enemy could no longer replace its fighters in the field, the reasoning went, the Vietcong would surrender. In previous wars, winning meant taking territory away from the enemy. In Vietnam, the United States measured victory by accumulating a high body count of enemy dead. The Communists had the same goal, hoping to create so many American casualties that the United States would abandon the war.

Compiling an accurate tally of enemy dead proved impossible, however. Soldiers encountered genuine difficulties determining how many Vietcong they had killed. The aftermath of battle often littered the jungle with assorted body parts and trails of blood rather than intact bodies to count. The military also unintentionally created incentives for soldiers to lie. "You guys want a day off, we got to be getting more kills," one commander told his men. In compiling their body counts, troops made little effort to separate friend from foe. The American soldier credo, "If it's dead and it's Vietnamese, it's VC [Vietcong]," lumped enemy soldiers with innocent civilians. Eventually the inaccuracy of body counts became common knowledge. Satirist Gary Trudeau mocked the preoccupation with body count in this Doonesbury comic strip (**26.9**). Trudeau's rendition of an American captain using the day's date as his official body count echoed an uncomfortable truth about the value of these officially circulated figures.

26.9 Doonesbury Lampoons Body Counts Cartoonist Gary B. Trudeau underscored the meaninglessness of the official body count figure. Many Americans were becoming skeptical of the government's claim that victory was imminent.

The Tet Offensive

In 1967 Americans' support for the war began to flounder. Nearly thirteen thousand American soldiers had died so far, and each month draft boards inducted another thirty thousand into the military. Johnson's call for new taxes to meet rising war expenses further dismayed Americans. Some leading policymakers changed their minds as well. Secretary of Defense Robert McNamara underwent the greatest shift in views. McNamara went from strenuously advocating war (some critics called it "McNamara's war") to conceding that "Ho Chi Minh is a tough old S.O.B. And he won't quit no matter how much bombing we do." Rather than making his breach with the president over Vietnam public, however, McNamara quietly left the administration.

In the same year General Westmoreland assured Johnson that the war of attrition had reached a crossover point, meaning that American soldiers had killed more enemy soldiers than the Communists could replace in the field. To boost morale at home, General Westmoreland publicly assured the nation that "we have reached an important point where the end begins to come into view." Johnson was also upbeat. "The enemy is not beaten," Johnson told the nation before Christmas, "but he knows that he has met his master in the field."

A major Vietnamese offensive in 1968 exposed the hollowness of these claims. On January 30, 1968, during the Vietnamese New Year holiday known as Tet, North Vietnamese and Vietcong forces launched the **Tet Offensive**, a massive, coordinated assault against more than a hundred cities and towns in South Vietnam. The map of Vietnam (**26.10**) depicts the wide-ranging attacks. "Uncle Ho was very old and we had to liberate the south before his death," one North Vietnamese officer recalled. By demonstrating their determination to fight forever, the North Vietnamese wanted to convince Johnson that the cost of any American victory was too high. The Communists also expected their attack on previously calm cities to spark a revolution within South Vietnam.

Before the Tet Offensive the Communists had successfully lured nearly fifty thousand American troops away from the cities by laying siege to a remote Marine garrison in Khe Sanh and making smaller attacks on a few isolated towns. The weakened

What problems surfaced from using enemy body counts to measure victory?

American presence in the urban centers left them vulnerable to enemy attack. A shocked American public watched on television as nineteen Vietcong commandos entered the courtyard of the American Embassy complex in Saigon and battled guards there for six hours. It took heavy fighting and more than a month before American troops regained control of South Vietnamese towns and cities. In the end the Communists paid a heavy price for forsaking the jungles and tunnels that provided such effective cover, suffering forty thousand casualties and military defeat. Nearly twelve thousand civilians died during the battle, along with thirty-five hundred American and South Vietnamese soldiers.

Yet rather than celebrating this victory over the Communists, Americans' support for the war plunged. The daily televised images of the month's fierce fighting undercut the recent rosy predictions of imminent victory issued by the White House. At a time when 60 percent of Americans got their news from television, Vietnam became the first war in which Americans viewed the fighting in the comfort of their living rooms on a nightly basis. Televised news reports suggested that no matter who won the battle the fighting would go on. These newscasts stoked the shift in public sentiment already well under way before Tet. *Images as History: The Power of the Press in Vietnam* (page 794) considers how viewers' political leanings influenced their interpretation of photographs from the battlefront. The revered CBS-TV news anchor Walter Cronkite spoke for millions when he declared the war a stalemate. "We have been too often disappointed by the optimism of the American leaders, both in Vietnam and Washington, to have faith any longer in the silver linings they find in the darkest clouds," Cronkite told his listeners on February 27, 1968. He urged the government to seek a negotiated peace.

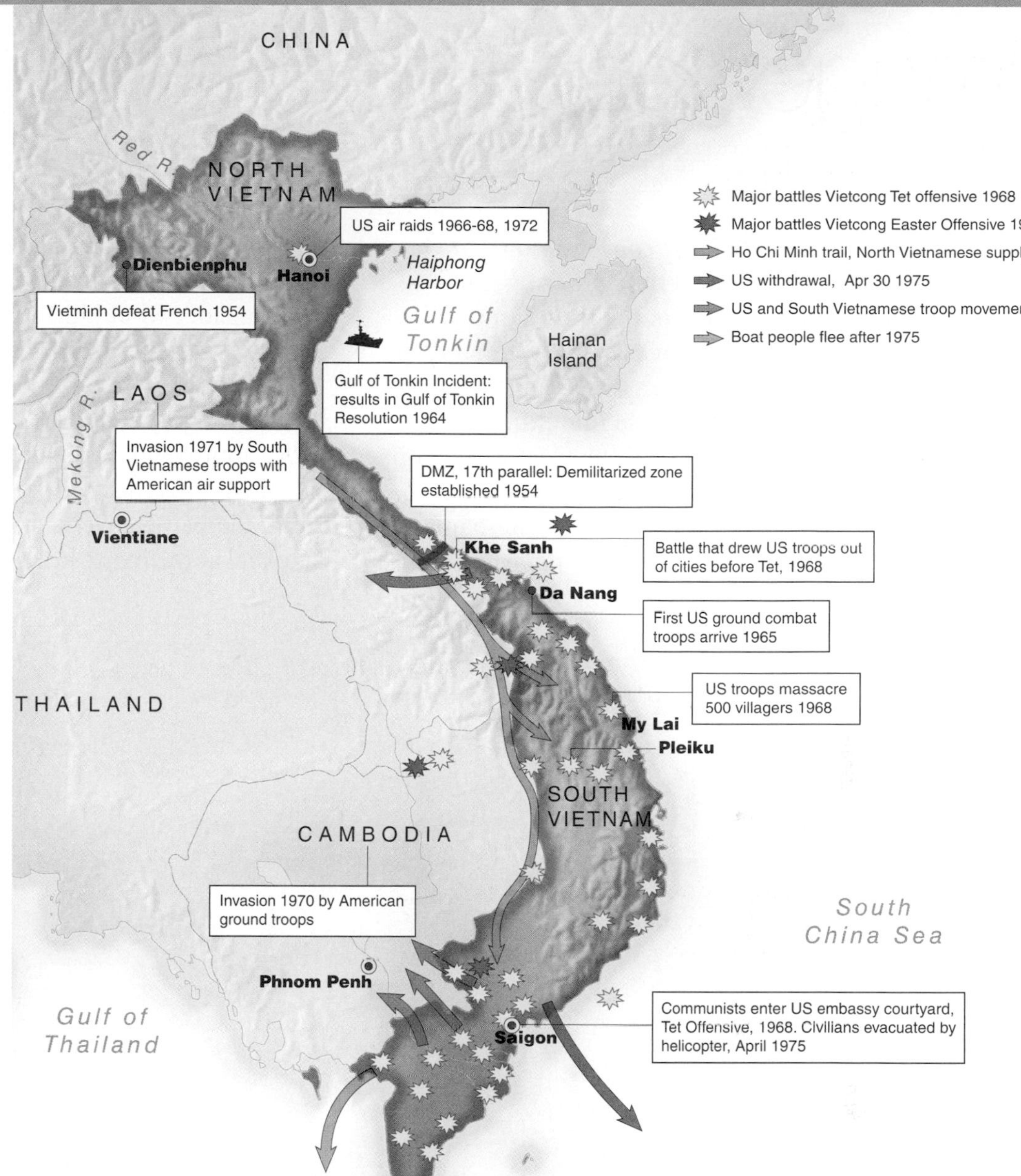

26.10 Map of Vietnam From the French defeat at Dien Bien Phu in 1954 to the final evacuation of U.S. personnel in 1975, the United States actively tried to defeat Communist forces in Vietnam.

Cronkite's assessment mirrored reports from the president's new secretary of defense Clark Clifford. As the joint chiefs pressed the president for more troops, "I couldn't get hold of a plan to win the war" [from the military], Clifford later complained. "When I asked how many more men it would take, would 206,000 more men do the job, no one could be certain." Responding to these rising doubts, Johnson made a surprise announcement in a televised address to the nation on March 31, 1968. "I want to speak to you of peace in Vietnam," Johnson told listeners. He would not seek reelection, he said. Instead of campaigning he would halt most bombing of North Vietnam and devote the rest of his time in office to peace negotiations.

Why did the 1968 Tet Offensive have such tremendous political fallout?

Images as History

THE POWER OF THE PRESS IN VIETNAM

Media photographers typically convey a point of view through their photos. However the differing interpretations surrounding some of the most famous photographs from the Vietnam War suggest that each photo took on a life of its own as Americans disregarded the photographer's original intention for taking the photo and imposed a different meaning on the image that reflected their own political views. Rather than creating new ideas or values, these images became iconic visual statements about the war because they reinforced strongly held beliefs within the population. In examining the text and photos in this box, consider what kind of power the press had to mold public opinion about the war.

In the midst of the 1968 Tet Offensive, Associated Press photographer Eddie Adams saw South Vietnamese police apprehend a Vietcong suspect in the streets of Saigon. Adams snapped his prize-winning photo just as South Vietnamese General Nguyen Ngoc Loan aimed his pistol at the man's head and pulled the trigger.

"He killed many of my men and many of your people," Loan told Adams. The *New York Times* caption echoed Loan's justification for his act. "GUERILLA DIES: Brig. Gen. Nguyen Ngoc Loan, national police chief, executes man identified as a Vietcong terrorist in Saigon. Man wore civilian dress and had a pistol."

Instead of just retribution many Americans saw an execution. Prisoners of war have the right to a trial under international law, critics argued.

This striking image of one man's death became a symbol of the failed U.S. effort to establish the rule of law in South Vietnam, prompting fears that American soldiers were killing prisoners of war as well.

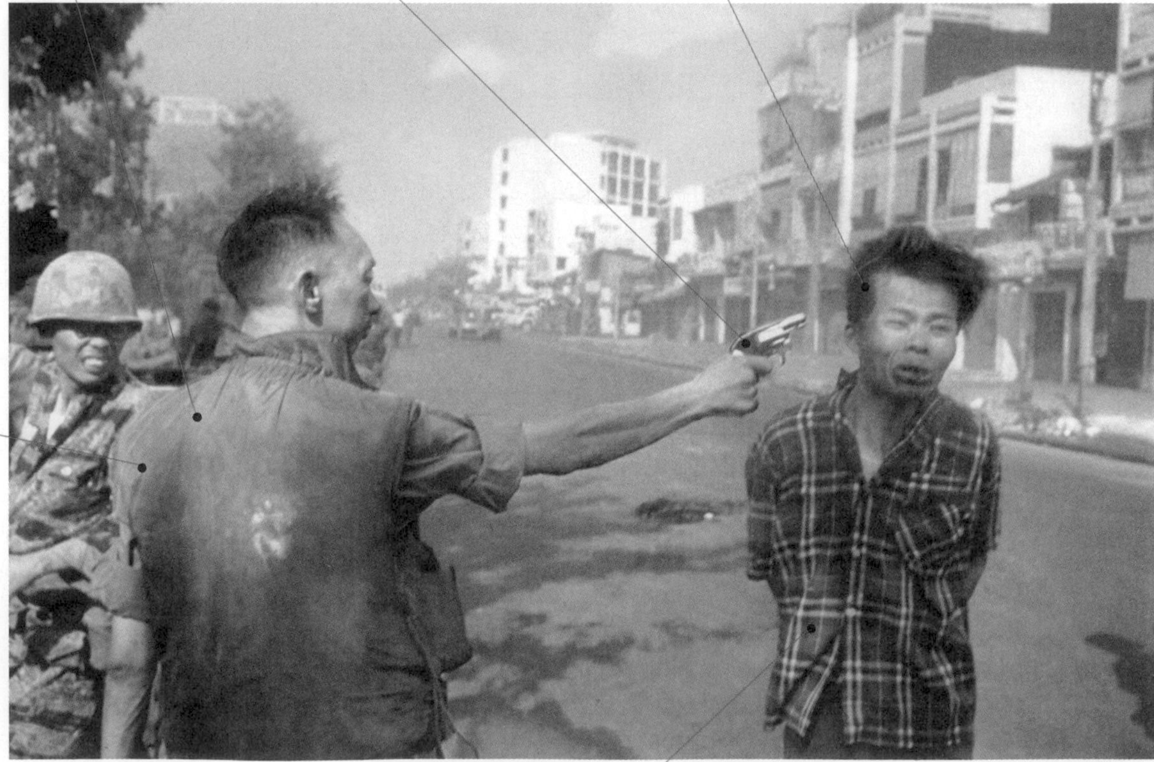

Adams regretted taking a photo that forever tarnished the reputation of Loan, whom he felt had simply acted impetuously in the heat of combat. "Pictures do not always tell the full story, and this is one case where that is true," Adams contended.

Supporters of Loan noted that the Vietcong ruthlessly executed thousands of South Vietnamese officials and police during the Tet Offensive.

Why did this image become the defining one of the Tet Offensive?

In 1966 *Life* photographer Larry Burrows went into the field with a group of marines trying to stop North Vietnamese infiltration through the demilitarized zone along the seventeenth parallel, a combat-free strip of land that separated North and South Vietnam. He snapped this image of a wounded black soldier reaching out to a white buddy sprawled on the ground. *Life* magazine published the photo twice, once right after Burrows took it and again in 1971 to eulogize Burrows when a helicopter crash in Laos took his life.

In their letters to *Life* magazine, many readers felt that Burrows's portrait illustrated how the shared burden of combat inspired men to transcend the "great racial problems" of American society. Burrows's photo gave some viewers hope that whether "purple, polka-dotted or streaked," Americans could also learn to live together as brothers at home.

In his captioning Burrows emphasized soldiers' suffering in the midst of combat, simply noting, "At a first-aid center, during Operation Prairie, a wounded GI reaches out towards a stricken comrade."

The interracial compassion captured by Burrows's photo told only one side of the story. Racial conflict permeated the armed forces in the rear and on ships, suggesting that fighting together did not magically heal the racial divide.

The wounded soldier lies in a crucifix position, establishing a symbolic link between Christ who suffered on the cross to redeem humankind and a soldier sacrificing his life to save his nation.

How does this image compare to combat photographs from World War II and the Korean War (see Chapters 23 and 24)?

Controversy on the Home Front

Advocates for peace have opposed every American war, but their dissent rarely influenced the mainstream political debate. During the Vietnam War these rebellious voices offering an alternative vision of peace moved from the fringes to the center of American political life. Building in strength as more Americans began to oppose the war, the peace movement made itself visible through mass demonstrations, propaganda posters, and press coverage of celebrities who joined. The very existence of a vocal peace movement in the midst of a war, however, also invited controversy because Americans held differing views on the legitimacy of wartime dissent. Many peace activists believed they were preserving the American tradition of freedom on speech. Public opinion polls from 1965 to 1973, however, consistently showed that the majority of Americans disliked both the war and the peace movement.

The Antiwar Movement

In announcing his 1968 decision not to run for reelection, Johnson noted that "there is division in the American house right now." In the 1960s the rise of a youth-based counterculture and a powerful civil rights movement roiled the country (see Chapter 27). The night of his announcement, however, Johnson was referring to the domestic debate over the war in Vietnam.

Although many working- and middle-class people opposed the war, overcoming existing cultural and class divisions in American society to create a unified antiwar movement proved difficult. The organized antiwar movement tended to attract mostly white, middle-class, college-educated Americans or individuals already engaged in crusades of social justice. Working-class women and African Americans, many with grade-school educations and low-paying jobs, opposed the war in large numbers, but had little interest in marching alongside middle-class college students in street demonstrations.

> "Hey, hey LBJ, how many kids did you kill today?"
>
> A popular chant during antiwar demonstrations

Uniting around one universal vision also posed difficulties for the antiwar movement. All peace activists wanted to end the war in Vietnam, but they offered different arguments for doing so. Some made a primarily moral argument. They claimed that a war involving napalm, search-and-destroy missions, and forced relocation into strategic hamlets hurt the Vietnamese more than living under Communist rule did. Others focused on the futility of fighting an unwinnable civil war. Another group accepted that the nation needed to stop Communist China from expanding its influence. They argued that working with Ho Chi Minh could accomplish this goal more effectively than fighting a war in Vietnam. These critics noted that while Ho accepted Chinese aid to fight the United States, he was leery of Chinese ambitions to control Vietnam. America had worked successfully in Europe with the independently minded communist leader Josip Broz Tito in Yugoslavia to contain Soviet ambitions in the Balkans. Why could it not do the same in Vietnam? Other activists saw a chance to open the nation's eyes to injustice at home, as well as overseas. Student leaders from the nation's top universities founded the Students for a Democratic Society (SDS) at Port Huron, Michigan, in 1962. A leader in the New Left movement, SDS combined staunch opposition to the war with a scathing critique of the inequities of capitalism (see Chapter 27).

Although peace advocates differed on their reasons for opposing the war, they agreed that the war was destroying American democracy. They noted a number of violations of American democratic values: going to war without a formal declaration of war from Congress, presidential secrets and lies, FBI surveillance of peace protesters, and unjust draft deferments for middle- and upper-class men who could afford to go to college. When civil rights leader Martin Luther King Jr. spoke out against the war in 1967, he denounced both the destruction of Vietnamese culture and the war's negative impact on African Americans. The war's

What differing visions did peace activists offer on the war?

high cost diverted funds away from antipoverty programs at home, King rightly contended. The disproportionately high numbers of African American men fighting and dying in Vietnam further illustrated ongoing racial injustice within the United States, he continued. (King's criticism was valid in 1967, but over the course of the entire war black soldiers did not incur higher casualty rates than the rest of the population.) One antiwar poster (**26.11**) captured this link between racial inequality and the war by picturing two African American soldiers as they advanced into the jungle under the headline, "The only time we're in the front is when it's time to die." The rebuke against King for these statements was swift and severe, including criticism from civil rights activists who worried that his antiwar views would discredit their cause. King died a year later from an assassin's bullet, cutting short his career as a civil rights leader and antiwar activist.

The peace movement brought the debate over the war out of the halls of government and into the streets. In 1965 University of Michigan faculty and students organized the first teach-in, a series of public lectures and debates protesting the war. Over the next eight years, scholars and students on hundreds of other college campuses held teach-ins. Some teach-ins invited counterprotests. At the conclusion of a teach-in at the University of Wisconsin, for example, six thousand students signed a petition supporting President Johnson. Like other segments of American society, college students held differing views about the war.

The draft made the war more than an abstract humanitarian or foreign policy question for millions of American men. Male college students would lose their draft deferments once they graduated, giving many personal, as well as political and moral, reasons to oppose the war. Peace activists organized ceremonies where men burned the notices from their draft boards ordering them to report for induction. When fifteen hundred peace activists gathered in New York City in 1965 to watch five men burn their draft cards, an onlooker bolted from the crowd with a fire extinguisher and doused the protesters before the cards caught fire. The shower failed to deter the activists, however, who managed to ignite their soggy draft cards while hundreds of New Yorkers stood on the other side of police barricades and chanted "Burn yourselves, not your cards!" a macabre reminder, perhaps unintentional, of the Buddhist suicides in Vietnam in 1963.

Going on the offensive Johnson tried to discredit the peace movement by claiming it was communist-run and gave solace to the enemy. Other defenders of the war openly charged the peace movement with treason. Some war supporters felt differently, however. Revulsion against the peace movement, they contended, helped bolster the resolve of Americans in the political center to stay the course.

The outcome of the 1968 presidential election suggested that the peace movement had helped the conservative cause. The presumption that Senator Robert Kennedy, brother of the slain president, would seek the Democratic Party nomination as a peace candidate had encouraged Johnson to abandon a quest for a second term. On June 4, 1968, Sirhan Sirhan, a Jordanian immigrant upset with Kennedy's pro-Israel stance, shot and killed the senator as he walked through the kitchen of a California hotel moments after finishing his victory speech for winning the state primary. At the Chicago nominating convention, the Democratic Party

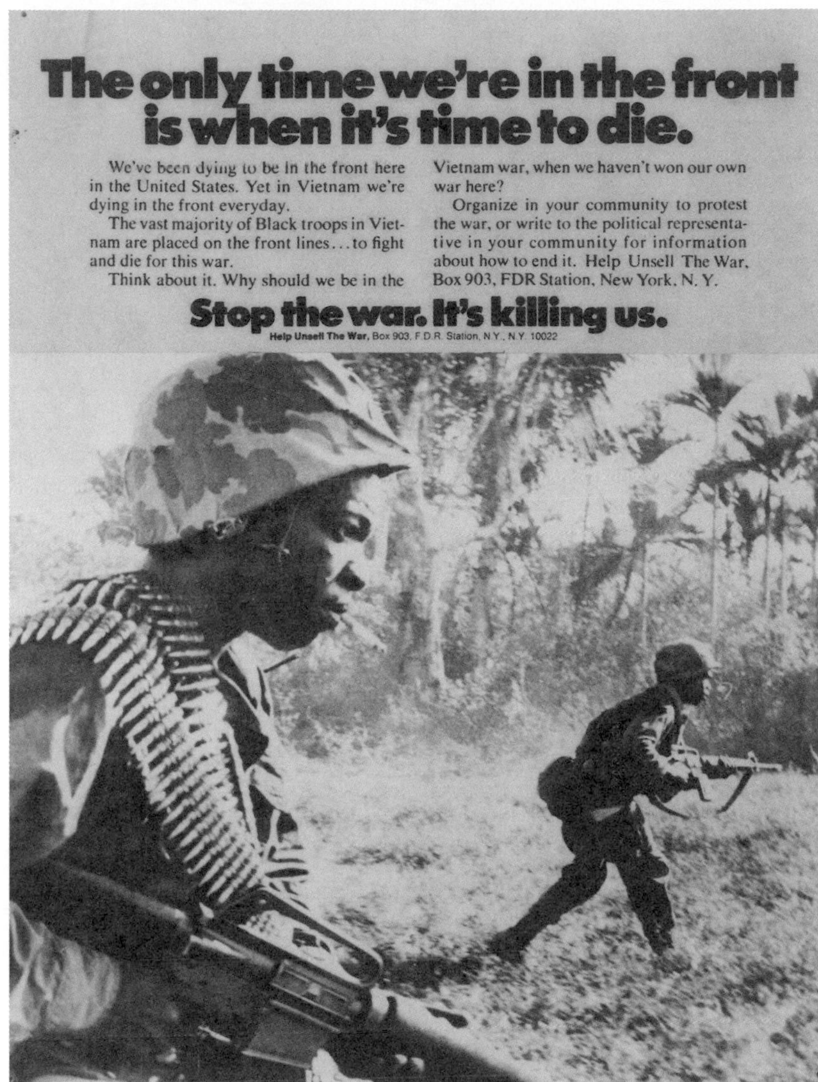

26.11 Stop the War. It's Killing Us This antiwar poster highlighted the disproportionate numbers of African Americans fighting and dying on the frontlines in the late 1960s, linking that imbalance to continued racial inequity in American society.

Dueling Bumper Stickers

"Peace Through Victory in Vietnam"

"Join the Army; travel to exotic distant lands; meet exciting, unusual people and kill them."

selected Vice President Hubert Humphrey as their presidential candidate, a man much like Johnson who supported liberal causes at home and the war in Vietnam. Instead of uniting liberal and conservative Democrats, Humphrey's candidacy badly fractured the party. Outside the convention hall radical antiwar protesters denounced his nomination and clashed violently with police. "The war is destroying our country as we are destroying Vietnam," the writer I. F. Stone lamented.

Believing that the protesters, rather than the police, had gone too far in Chicago, many working- and middle-class Americans responded positively to Republican candidate Richard Nixon's call for a return to "law and order." During the campaign Nixon suggested that he had a "secret plan" to bring about a "peace with honor" that he could not reveal to the enemy. The election became a three-man race when Alabama governor George Wallace entered as an independent candidate, attracting conservative southern whites and white northern blue-collar workers with his attacks on integration, elites in Washington, D.C., and antiwar protesters. "If any demonstrator ever lays [*sic*] down in front of my car," Wallace proclaimed, "it'll be the last car he'll ever lay [*sic*] down in front of." As election day neared Humphrey picked up some liberal support by pledging to end bombing over North Vietnam immediately. Despite losing some conservatives votes to Wallace, Nixon won the electoral college vote handily but only received 40 percent of the popular vote (**26.12**).

Rising public opposition to the war never resulted in widespread support for the peace movement. Most Americans remained staunchly anticommunist, even as their dissatisfaction with the war in Vietnam grew. Gallup Polls in 1969 revealed that by a margin of 55 percent to 31 percent, Americans labeled themselves as doves not hawks and most described the war as indefensible. Three-fifths, however, also believed that the peace movement helped the enemy and made it more difficult for the president to end the war. Americans, it seemed, wanted an end to the fighting overseas and at home.

26.12 The Presidential Election of 1968 Republican Richard Nixon won easily in the electoral college, but he received only about a half million more popular votes that his Democratic Party opponent, Hubert Humphrey.

4 Electoral vote by state	Electoral Vote (%)	Popular Vote (%)
Richard M. Nixon *(Republican)*	301 (56)	31,785,480 (44)
Hubert H. Humphrey *(Democratic)*	191 (35)	31,275,166 (42)
George C. Wallace *(American Independent)*	46 (%)	9,906,473 (14)
North Carolina *(Electors split)*	12 for Nixon 1 for Wallace	

My Lai

Johnson had calmed the American public in March 1968 by announcing he would open negotiations with the North Vietnamese. Keeping his promise, he began fruitless negotiations between Hanoi and Washington. Johnson continued trying, however, to win the war before he left office. Believing that a final push against a severely weakened enemy could finish the job, American soldiers renewed their attacks on the Vietcong. The largest search-and-destroy missions of the war occurred in March and April, involv-

Why did the peace movement have trouble winning support from mainstream America?

ing more than a hundred thousand troops. During one of these in the village of **My Lai**, American soldiers massacred five hundred civilians, an atrocity that fueled the strident domestic debate over the American mission in Vietnam.

On March 16, 1968, seventy-five American soldiers in two platoons under the command of Lieutenant William Calley entered My Lai. Leading up to the mission, these troops had spent long days wading through the rice paddies and even longer nights battling snipers and insects, looking for Vietcong forces who had killed a popular sergeant the week before. By the time the men approached My Lai, they were in an ugly mood. In making their attack during the morning hours, the company's officers anticipated that their troops would confront 250 enemy troops and very few civilians, whom the Americans expected would follow the usual daily ritual of leaving the village to visit a local market. None of these predictions came to pass. Upon entering the village the men found only unarmed women, children, and elderly in the village. The Vietcong force had retreated into the western mountains before the Americans arrived.

Rather than leaving, however, the American soldiers engaged in a systematic orgy of rape, torture, and slaughter that took four hours to complete and left more than five hundred villagers dead. Army photographer Ron Haeberle snapped this image (**26.13**) of terrified women and children huddled together moments before American soldiers killed them. "Guys were about to shoot these people, I yelled, 'Hold it' and I shot my pictures. As I walked away, I heard M-16s open up, and from the corner of my eye I saw bodies falling but I did not turn to look," Haeberle recalled. Seeing the carnage from the air, pilot Hugh Thompson landed his helicopter between the soldiers and one group of eleven survivors, whom he flew to safety. Thompson reported the atrocity to his superiors to no avail. Only the perseverance of Ron Ridenhour, a sergeant who was not even at My Lai, finally brought the massacre to light. After hearing stories from men who took part, an outraged Ridenhour wrote to President Nixon, the Pentagon, and members of Congress. When the story broke in 1969 Haeberle sold his photos to *Life* magazine. An official military investigation headed by Lieutenant General William Peers followed, resulting in the court martial of Lieutenant Calley for premeditated murder.

Calley's arrest, trial, and 1971 conviction exposed Americans' conflicting views over the meaning of My Lai. Was the atrocity a unique episode or representative of American conduct in Vietnam? *Competing Visions: Who Was Responsible for the My Lai Massacre?* (page 800) explores this question in further detail. Responding to the public outcry over Calley's conviction, the secretary of the army Howard "Bo" Callaway first reduced Calley's life sentence to ten years, and then eventually pardoned Calley after he had served only five months in prison. By this time Calley had undergone a striking transformation from villain to hero in the American imagination. People on both the left and the right of the political spectrum defended Calley. The left saw him as a scapegoat for failed American policies, while the right argued that civilians were fair targets in a guerilla war.

26.13 My Lai Villagers Moments before their Execution, 1968 Americans expressed more outrage over the publication of photographs from My Lai than over the actual killings.

Why did photos of the My Lai massacre provoke conflicting responses from Americans?

Competing Visions

WHO WAS RESPONSIBLE FOR THE MY LAI MASSACRE?

Americans disagreed over who bore responsibility for the massacre at My Lai. Some commentators focused on the individuals directly involved in the killings, others on the orders given by higher-ranking officials to destroy the village. As you read the following excerpts, try to reconstruct the domestic dispute over My Lai. Is one argument stronger than the other? Who was to blame: Calley, the two platoons, the commanding officers, or the American people?

Fellow soldier Dennis Conti told army investigators that he saw Calley and Private Paul Meadlo kill civilians in the village of My Lai.

They were bringing people out [of their huts], and then we pushed them out into the rice paddy, onto the dike there ... Lieutenant Calley came back, and said: "Take care of them." So we said: "Okay." And we sat there and watched them like we usually do. And he came back again, and he said: "I thought I told you to take care of them." I said: "We're taking care of them," and he said: "I mean kill them." So I looked at Meadlo and he looked at me, and I didn't want to do it, and he didn't want to do it ... then [Calley] said: "Come on, we'll line them up here, we'll kill them." So I told him: "I'll watch the tree line" ... Then they opened up, and started firing. Meadlo fired a while. I don't know how much he fired, a clip, I think. It might have been more. He started to cry, and he gave me his weapon.

This *New York Times* editorial suggested that higher-ranking officials than Calley bore some responsibility for ordering and observing the My Lai massacre.

Who gave the orders? Who knew what was going on? Was any attempt made to stop it? Who is responsible? ... [Paul Meadlo] was one of 18 witnesses to describe a briefing the night before the assault at which Captain [Ernest L.] Medina told the men they were going into battle with a hardened Vietcong battalion; that their mission was "search and destroy" and they were to destroy everything in the hamlet—houses, crops and people ... Helicopter pilots, radio men and artillery observers said the higher officers had flown over the scene for several hours and had seen bodies on the ground, had conference with the other officers and, as one pilot said, "knew what was going on" all through the day ... the Geneva conventions, the Nuremburg doctrines and the Army's own rules of land warfare make plain that obedience to orders is not a blanket defense, that orders that to a "prudent" or "reasonable" man seem patently illegal need not be obeyed. The question here, then, is whether the order, if that is what it was, to kill everything was one that a prudent man should obey when he found that everything included women, children, and infants.

The *National Review* rejected suggestions that the nation bore the blame and should abandon the war in Vietnam.

"That America and Americans must stand in the larger dock of guilt and human conscience for what happened at My Lai seems inescapable." So observed *Time* [magazine], adding: "Men in American uniforms slaughtered the civilians of My Lai, and in so doing humiliated the U.S. and called in question the U.S. mission in Vietnam in a way that all the antiwar protesters could never have done." One's mind staggers: Are "America and Americans" generally guilty, the same America and Americans now preparing to bring the accused to trial? And even if it turns out that atrocities were committed, how does this call in question the U.S. mission in Vietnam? Do the innumerable atrocities committed by both sides in World War II add up to the proposition that resistance to the Nazis ought to have been abandoned? ... Irrational and irresponsible comment on [My Lai] has become collective madness.

***Time* Magazine Cover, Lieutenant William Calley**

What was the ultimate historic significance of the My Lai massacre?

The Long Road to Peace

When Richard Nixon entered the White House in 1969, he told his advisors, "I'm going to stop that war. Fast." Nixon was also intent, however, on preserving America's international reputation. He had a different vision from his predecessor, he assured the public, pledging to seek "peace with honor." Nixon's promises proved empty, however. The war did not end quickly, but continued for four more years. At home Nixon benefited politically by portraying the peace movement as out of step with the values of law-abiding citizens. When Nixon extended the war into Laos and Cambodia and became embroiled in political scandal, his actions fueled the ongoing political debate over whether Americans could trust their government.

Seeking Peace with Honor

For Nixon a peace with honor meant winning the war. Nixon and his national security advisor , Henry Kissinger, pursued four different tactics to achieve this goal. First Nixon implemented **Vietnamization**, a policy that turned the bulk of the ground fighting over to the South Vietnamese Army. The gradual reduction of American forces in Vietnam took until 1971 to dramatically shrink the American presence in Vietnam. In many respects this was a return to the pre-1965 approach, when America propped up an independent South Vietnam with financial and military aid. Announcing Vietnamization in November 1969, Nixon asked for support from "the great **silent majority** of Americans," referring to the large number of Americans who supported the war quietly in the privacy of their homes. He also issued a rebuke to the peace movement. "Let us be united for peace. Let us also be united against defeat. Because let us understand: North Vietnam cannot defeat or humiliate the United States. Only Americans can do that." Polls indicated that the "silent majority" overwhelmingly supported the president's plan.

Vietnamization promised to give the country exactly what it wanted: victory with minimal loss of American lives. The United States quickly transformed the South Vietnamese Army into one of the largest and best-equipped military forces in the world. At the ongoing peace talks, a North Vietnamese negotiator wondered aloud how the United States, when it could not win with its own troops, thought it could "succeed when you let your puppet troops do the fighting." That dilemma, Kissinger admitted, "also torments me."

In implementing Vietnamization Nixon hoped to disarm the peace movement by replacing images of civilian suffering on the evening news with pictures of troops withdrawing and returning home. In March 1970 Nixon announced the incremental withdrawal of another 150,000 soldiers to "drop a bombshell on the gathering spring storm of anti-war protest." He simultaneously reformed the draft, replacing the controversial deferment system with a lottery that randomly drafted men by date of birth. Nixon hoped these policy changes would buy his administration enough time to win the war.

The controversial actions of some peace activists inadvertently helped Nixon solidify the support of Middle America. In 1972 the actress Jane Fonda accepted an invitation from the North Vietnamese government to visit Hanoi. While in the enemy capital city, she made a series of radio broadcasts urging American pilots to mutiny. A photo of Fonda joking with North Vietnamese soldiers as she sat on an antiaircraft gun used to shoot down American planes created a backlash against the peace movement that Nixon effectively exploited.

Vietnamization was more than a reaction to declining popular support for fighting in Vietnam. It was also part of Nixon's attempt to reshape the role that the United States played in global geopolitics. Nixon and Kissinger viewed the longstanding vision of a bipolar world that pitted the United States against the Soviet Union as obsolete. They embraced a competing strategic vision of multipolarity that focused on negotiating with Europe, China, Japan, and the Soviet Union to construct a new balance of power system to keep the peace. In this foreign policy reformulation, the United States would refrain from direct involvement in regional conflicts, such as Vietnam. The Nixon Doctrine, formulated in 1969 and 1970, announced that the United States expected its friends to take the lead in defending themselves.

Nixon's second tactic linked Vietnamization to the resumption of massive bombing in North Vietnam, which Johnson had halted when he

What motivated Nixon to implement Vietnamization?

Vietnam

THE WAR BY THE NUMBERS

Millions of Americans and Vietnamese fought in America's longest war to date, a conflict that exacted a high death toll and left many soldiers and civilians with lifelong wounds. The United States tried to use its air superiority to win the war, dropping more bombs in the Vietnam War than in World War II. The reliance on air power increased dramatically when the United States began pulling out troops in 1969. The numbers of draft evaders fleeing to Canada, the rising number of antiwar demonstrations, and public opinion polls illustrated the growing unpopularity of the war at home.

Total Serving in the American Military (worldwide)	8.7 million men 250,00 women
Total Serving in Vietnam	3.4 million men 6,421 women
Total Killed in Vietnam	47,415 battle deaths 10,785 other causes
Total Wounded	153,303
Total Draft Evaders	600,000 (tens of thousands fled to Canada)
Vietnamese Casualties (North and South)	2 million
Total Cost of War	$173 billion

The Human and Financial Cost of the Vietnam War, 1964–1973

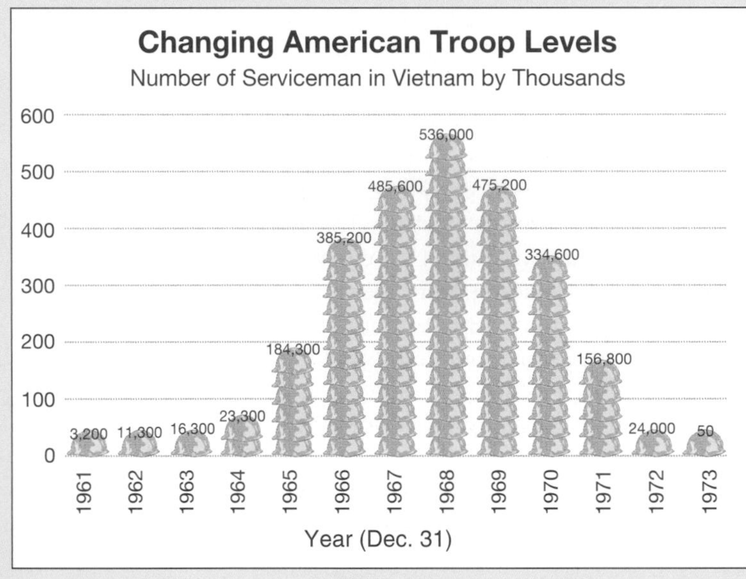

	Defoliation in South Vietnam (acres)	Crop Destruction in South Vietnam (acres)	Bombs Dropped on North Vietnam (tons)
1962	4,940	741	0
1963	24,700	247	0
1964	83,486	10,374	100
1965	155,610	65,949	63,000
1966	741,247	103,987	136,000
1967	1,486,446	221,312	226,000
1968	1,267,110	63,726	175,000
1969	1.198,444	64,961	659
1970	220,324	32,604	892
1971	0	0	1,842
1972	0	0	218,561
Total	**4,747,587**	**481,897**	**822,054**

Destruction in Vietnam, 1962–1972

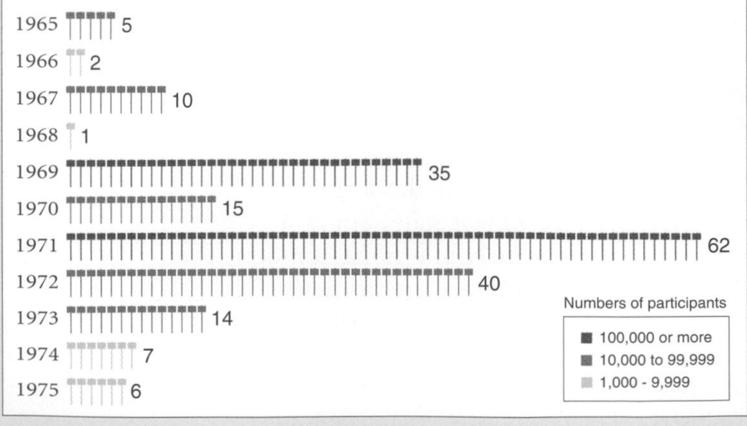

Antiwar demonstrations in Washington, D.C., 1965–1975

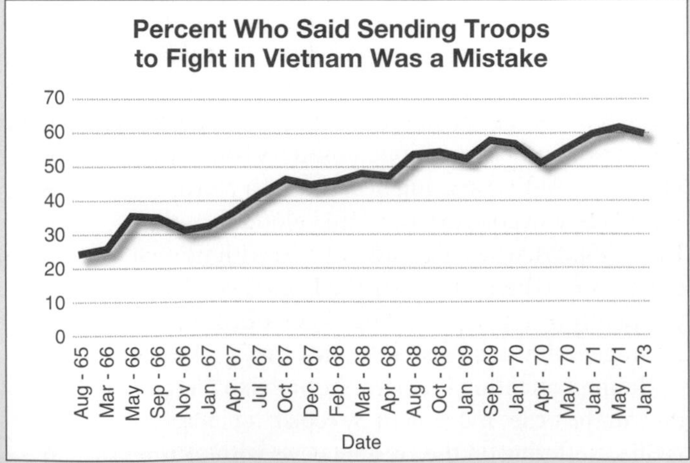

Public Opinion and the Vietnam War, 1965–1973

What does this data reveal about the various stages of America's involvement in Vietnam?

initiated peace talks in 1968. As American troops left Vietnam between 1969 and 1972, the number of bombs dropped increased spectacularly (see this shift in the "Changing American Troops Levels" and "Destruction in Vietnam, 1965–1973" charts in *Vietnam: The War by the Numbers*). America had not used enough military force to achieve victory, the president and Kissinger concluded. They intended to correct this problem. For a while the news of troop withdrawals successfully diverted attention from the intensified bombing of North Vietnam.

Alongside Vietnamization and renewed bombing of North Vietnam, Nixon and Kissinger's third tactic used diplomacy to decrease Soviet and Chinese support for North Vietnam. Recognizing the existing discord between China and the Soviet Union, Nixon pursued independent negotiations with each nation to strengthen their ties to the United States and deepen their distrust of each other. Nixon reshaped the Cold War by pursuing his vision of multipolarity through **détente**, using diplomatic, economic, and cultural contacts to improve U.S. relations with China and the Soviet Union. Fearing that the United States might form an alliance with the other, the Soviet Union and China each eagerly accepted these overtures. In return for a more congenial relationship with the United States, Nixon expected China and the Soviet Union to end their support of North Vietnam. Although both countries continued to send aid to North Vietnam, once they decided to normalize trade relations and enter into arms limitations agreement with the United States, the Soviet Union and China began pressuring Hanoi to seek a negotiated peace.

Cambodia: Invasion and Outrage

The fourth tactical component of Nixon's Vietnam policy involved the neutral country of Cambodia, which bordered Vietnam to the west. In 1969 Nixon initiated a secret bombing campaign of Cambodia. He hoped to cut off supplies filtering through the Ho Chi Minh Trail and thus pressure North Vietnam into accepting the American terms for peace that included an independent South Vietnam.

In April 1970 Nixon shattered the public consensus he had carefully created for Vietnamization by ordering an American ground force invasion of Cambodia. Before the invasion Nixon sought inspiration from repeated showings of the movie *Patton* in the White House, a film that portrayed the hard-nosed and belligerent World War II tank commander leading American forces to victory. Going public with his plans, Nixon announced in a televised speech that American troops needed to destroy Communist bases in Cambodia to help the South Vietnamese army defeat the Vietcong. The two-month-long incursion succeeded only in pushing the North Vietnamese farther into the interior of Cambodia, where they began supporting the Khmer Rouge, Communist rebels who assumed power in Cambodia in 1975 and unleashed a wave of mass murder so brutal that the country became known as "the killing fields."

Nixon's claim that he was expanding the war to end it sooner persuaded few. Protest erupted on college campuses nationwide and in Congress where the Senate symbolically terminated the Gulf of Tonkin Resolution. Many university demonstrations turned violent as protesters clashed with police and set fire to college buildings. A defiant Nixon stood his ground, assuming that the "silent majority" agreed with his assessment that the protesters were just "bums blowing up the campuses."

In Kent, Ohio, student-organized demonstrations protesting the invasion of Cambodia took a nasty turn, recalled Phil Caputo, who had left the Marines after two tours in Vietnam and was now a reporter for the *Chicago Tribune*. In a May weekend rampage, "store windows had been smashed in town, [and] radicals had burned down the ROTC building," according to Caputo. Calling the protesters "the worst sort of people we harbor in America," Ohio governor James Allen Rhodes promised to "use every weapon possible to eradicate the problem," as he sent National Guardsmen to restore order.

On Monday morning a few hundred students gathered on the campus of Kent State University for a rally, defying a campuswide ban on protests. National Guardsmen fired tear gas into the crowd to disperse the demonstrators, who responded by throwing rocks, unexploded tear gas cans, and obscenities at the troops. Suddenly, as bystanders and students on their way to class watched the mini-battle unfurl, the troops sprayed bullets into the crowd, leaving four dead and nine wounded. The National Guardsmen claimed that they had fired in self-defense when protesters began throwing concrete slabs. Two of the victims were passers-by, however, and all four were too far away from the troops to have hit them with anything more than pebbles.

Responding to Nixon's earlier characterization of the protesters, the father of one of the dead girls told reporters, "My child was not a bum." The cover of *Life* magazine (**26.14**) showed terrified students trying to save the life of one victim, underscoring that the war's killing had come home to America. This photo, along with the others inside the magazine, inspired musician Neil Young to write the song "Ohio" to protest the shootings, the war, and the Nixon administration. "A nation driven to use the weapons of war upon its youth is a nation on the edge of chaos," concluded the presidential commission that investigated the Kent State incident.

The Kent State shootings unmasked the growing "town and gown" divide over the war and latent anger at the peace movement. "They should have shot more of them," suggested one Kent resident, still angry over the weekend riot. Many radio stations refused to play Young's "anti-Nixon" song. While protests over the shooting engulfed more than half the nation's college campuses, working-class unions staged counter-protests in support of the war. In New York City hundreds of longshoremen wearing hard hats attacked students who were protesting the Cambodian invasion. During a subsequent meeting at the White House, sympathetic labor leaders presented the president a "commander-in-chief" hard hat.

The wave of protests after the Kent State shootings nonetheless bothered Nixon. At the end of a sleepless night on May 9, 1970, the president made an impulsive decision to have his valet drive him, without his Secret Service detail, to the Lincoln Memorial at five o'clock in the morning so he could talk to the antiwar demonstrators camped out there. According to the protesters Nixon talked disjointedly about college sports and surfing and assured them that he shared their wish for peace in Vietnam.

Despite his clumsy attempt to talk directly with peace activists, Nixon remained determined to see the war through to victory. Clinging to the belief that success would vindicate his methods, Nixon expanded the theater of war once again in February 1971 by ordering an invasion of Laos. This time South Vietnamese troops fought on the ground with American air support. Once again, however, the hopes of permanently disrupting enemy supply lines along the Ho Chi Minh Trail bore meager results. Administration officials claimed that the Laos invasion illustrated the success of Vietnamization. Skeptics pointed to the sight of South Vietnamese soldiers clinging in panic to the skids of departing helicopters during their chaotic retreat back into South Vietnam.

In the summer of 1971 the *New York Times* published the Pentagon Papers, a secret Department of Defense study that criticized the way Kennedy and Johnson had handled the war, further stoking the flames of antiwar sentiment in the wake of the Calley conviction, the failed Cambodian and Laos invasions,

> "Tin soldiers and Nixon coming,
> We're finally on our own.
> This summer I hear the drumming,
> Four dead in Ohio."
>
> Lyrics from Neil Young's song "Ohio," written in response to the Kent State shootings

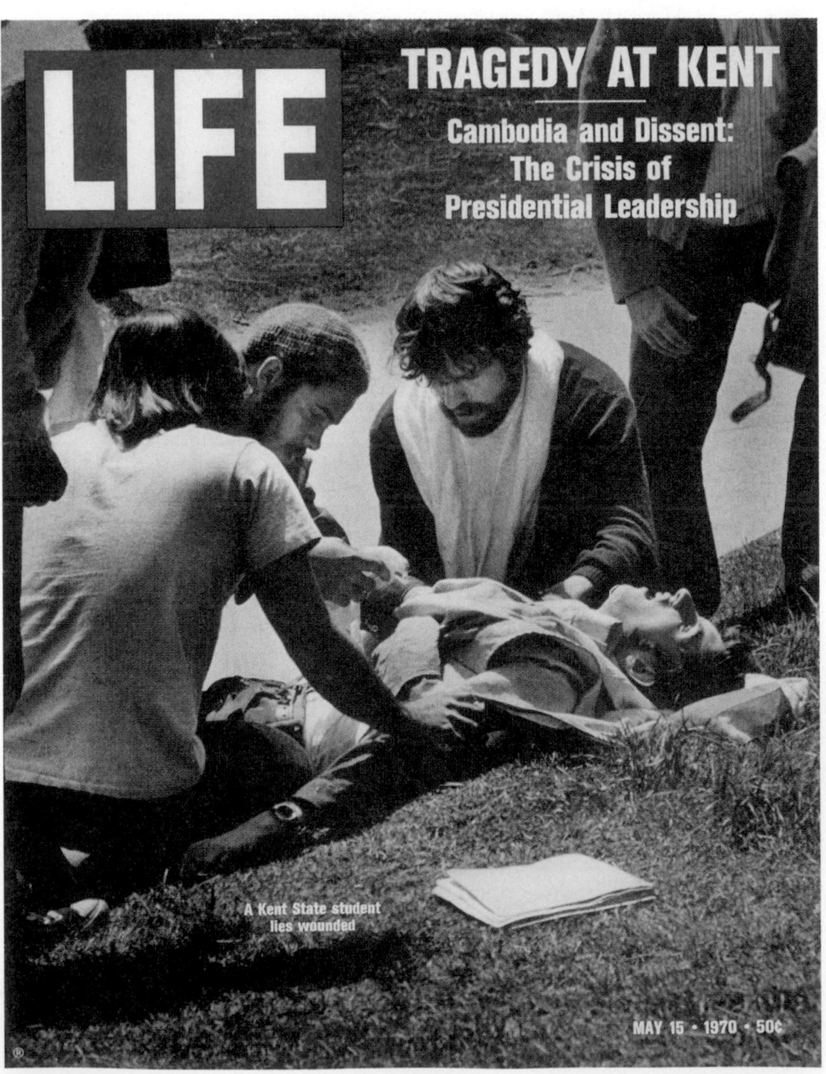

LIFE
TRAGEDY AT KENT
Cambodia and Dissent: The Crisis of Presidential Leadership
A Kent State student lies wounded
MAY 15 • 1970 • 50¢

26.14 Kent State University, 1970
The images of students wounded and killed at Kent State University by National Guardsmen prompted fears in some quarters that a war undertaken to protect American democracy was instead destroying it.

What competing visions emerged in response to the Kent State killings?

and the Kent State killings. Pentagon official Daniel Ellsberg leaked the Pentagon Papers which confirmed that presidents Kennedy and Johnson had intentionally lied to the public about the extent of previous American involvement in the war. Many Americans assumed that Nixon was misleading the country as well. By now only 34 percent of Americans approved of Nixon's handling of the war.

Controversy over the war seeped into the military as well. Morale plummeted as soldiers became increasingly unwilling to put their lives on the line for a cause that the nation seemed poised to abandon. Disobedience took a deadly turn in 1970 when the military reported nearly two hundred incidents of "fragging," deadly attacks by enlisted men on officers, named for the hand grenade fragments that did most of the damage in these fraternal attacks. Escalating use of marijuana, opium, and heroin, all readily available in Vietnam, among servicemen served as another sign of disintegrating discipline.

> "How do you ask a man to be the last man to die for a mistake?"
>
> Vietnam veteran and antiwar activist JOHN KERRY

Withdrawal

Nixon envisioned détente creating a new world order in which the United States used trade agreements and arms limitation treaties to curtail the expansionist ambitions of its enemies. The Nixon administration made great headway with this approach in 1972, beginning with a highly publicized trip to China in February and culminating with a May summit meeting in Moscow. The carefully orchestrated pictures of the staunch anticommunist Nixon toasting China's communist leader Mao during an official banquet and lauding the achievements of Chinese civilization during a trek to the Great Wall signaled an important turning point in Sino-American relations. Improved relations with China also demolished one of the main arguments used to justify the war in Vietnam. American leaders had always linked the war in Vietnam to the larger American goal of containing communism in Southeast Asia. They considered the region, rather than the country, vital to American strategic interests overseas. Nixon now demonstrated that diplomacy could perhaps achieve the goal of containing communism in Southeast Asia more effectively. Why then, many Americans wondered, was the nation still fighting in Vietnam?

North Vietnam reacted with alarm to improving relations between its communist benefactors and the United States. When the North Vietnamese grumbled about Mao shaking hands with Nixon, Mao advised them to sign a peace treaty, regroup while the Americans withdrew, and then resume the war. North Vietnam eventually followed Mao's advice. They first tried, however, to replicate the political success of the Tet Offensive by launching a major invasion of the south. The North Vietnamese timed the so-called Easter Offensive of March 1972 to coincide with the start of the American presidential campaign. In response Nixon ordered a massive retaliation against North Vietnam that included bombing, a blockade, and the mining of a key harbor.

Unlike Tet the Easter Offensive did not greatly alter the political equation in the United States or worldwide. At home Nixon's approval ratings rose for defending South Vietnam from attack. Moving from his successful meeting in China to Moscow, the U.S.-Soviet summit proceeded as planned. When Nixon returned with the first disarmament agreement ever signed by the Soviet Union, he bolstered his image as a tough negotiator who got results. The Strategic Arms Limitation Treaty (SALT I) set limits on how many intercontinental ballistic missiles and submarine-launched missiles each side could stockpile, and restricted the number of antimissile launching pads. Once again, however, Nixon's diplomatic success undercut his argument that the United States needed an anti-Communist South Vietnam to win the Cold War.

By the summer of 1972, both the United States and North Vietnam concluded that the costs of continued fighting had become too great. Recognizing that Democratic presidential candidate Senator George McGovern of South Dakota, a peace advocate who promised to withdraw U.S. troops from Vietnam, was trailing in the polls, the North Vietnamese decided to seek the best terms possible from Nixon. Although Nixon had successfully discredited McGovern by suggesting that he would abandon American POWs in Vietnam, the president was also eager to negotiate. With his reelection assured Nixon wanted to fulfill his earlier campaign promise to end the war so he could pursue his larger goal of refashioning Cold War relations among the world's superpowers.

Despite this renewed willingness on both sides to negotiate, it still took months to seal the deal.

The final 1973 peace treaty called for American withdrawal, allowed North Vietnamese troops to remain in South Vietnam, and left the existing South Vietnamese government in place. All left the Paris negotiating table knowing that the cease-fire existed only on paper. The war would go on, only now without American advisors, soldiers, or pilots.

Despite the spiral downward in Vietnam, Nixon retained a durable base of domestic support due to the success of détente with China and the Soviet Union and his effective portrayal of the antiwar movement as out of step with mainstream America. This political base, however, eroded quickly when Nixon became embroiled in a major political scandal. The **Watergate scandal (1972)**, a botched Republican-engineered break-in of the Democratic National Committee headquarters in Washington, D.C., eventually forced Nixon to resign in 1974. On June 17, 1972, members of Nixon's campaign staff had broken into the Watergate building office to fix broken wiretaps (listening devices on telephones) that they had installed during a previous burglary in May. The combined force of steady congressional challenges to his Vietnam policies and ongoing investigations into potential criminal activity by Nixon and members of his administration (see Chapter 28), severely weakened Nixon politically as he began his second term.

In the midst of the Watergate crisis, Congress passed the War Powers Resolution to curtail presidential war-making powers. The 1973 law required congressional approval for any deployment of American troops overseas that lasted for more than sixty days. Some critics pressed for even greater restrictions, arguing that the constitutional authority to declare war lay solely with Congress whether a war lasted sixty days or sixty years. Nixon countered that the law interfered with the president's constitutional role as commander in chief of the armed forces. Ignoring Congress's desire to end American involvement in Vietnam, Nixon tried to continue funneling money and arms to South Vietnam. In response Congress sharply reduced funding for South Vietnam in 1974.

When Nixon resigned the presidency on August 9, 1974 to avoid impeachment, Vice-President Gerald Ford assumed office. (Nixon had appointed Ford as his vice president in 1973 when Spiro Agnew resigned following an unrelated corruption scandal.) The political controversy at home and Americans' widespread distrust of executive power in the wake of the failed war in Vietnam and the Watergate scandal weakened President

26.15 The Final Evacuation Fleeing Vietnamese scramble for a spot aboard an American helicopter as the North Vietnamese Army approaches Saigon in 1975, a final portrait of the failed American mission in Vietnam.

How did the Vietnam War finally end for the United States and the Vietnamese?

Ford's ability to respond to the imminent collapse of South Vietnam. In March 1975 North Vietnam renewed its offensive. With no American help in the offing, South Vietnam quickly succumbed. Within eight weeks North Vietnamese troops neared Saigon. They walked along highways littered with boots and uniforms discarded by deserting South Vietnamese Army soldiers who hoped to blend into the civilian population and avoid execution.

Ho Chi Minh did not live to see the end of the war (he died in 1969), but the Communists renamed Saigon "Ho Chi Minh City" in his honor. Final victory in the thirty-year conflict did not end civilian suffering in Vietnam, however. Famine and prison camps caused thousands to flee in overcrowded boats for refuge camps in Thailand and Malaysia where they faced an uncertain future waiting for permanent asylum in the United States or Europe.

For America the war concluded with the image of South Vietnamese citizens climbing a ladder on the roof of the American Embassy to board one of the American helicopters that flew American citizens and 150,000 South Vietnamese to safety in the final days of the war (**26.15**). The frantic evacuation provided a disheartening end to America's longest war. How to remember such a divisive and controversial war continued to provoke debate within the United States. The 1982 Vietnam Veterans Memorial in Washington, D.C., listed all the names of American war dead on two black marble slabs that descended into the ground. "Hidden in a hole, as if in shame," complained one veteran. "It is exactly the right memorial for that war," countered another. Festering rumors that Vietnam was still holding American soldiers hostage deepened public bitterness against the nation's former foe. The United States finally normalized diplomatic relations with Vietnam in 1995, twenty years after the fall of Saigon. It was time, one veteran wrote, "to recognize the truth. The war is over."

Conclusion

The Vietnam War divided the country as no war had since the Civil War. The United States entered the conflict incrementally over the course of four administrations, with President Johnson taking the fateful step of sending ground troops to fight in Vietnam in 1965. His effort to win the war backfired. The political and military quagmire in Vietnam instead consumed thousands of lives and $173 billion. Antiwar activists focused unprecedented attention on the civilian casualties of war, provoking internal debate over the increasingly unpopular war and an equally disliked peace movement. On the ground American soldiers struggled against a determined guerilla force, often finding it difficult to separate friend from foe. President Nixon's attempt to parlay victory on the battlefield into success at the negotiating table also failed. When the United States withdrew in 1973, both South Vietnam and the United States suffered the consequences of the unsuccessful American war effort. North Vietnam quickly overran South Vietnam.

The war made Americans leery of embarking on other overseas military adventures and created a deeply felt cynicism that caused many to distrust any statement coming from the president. The breach of faith between Americans and the federal government temporarily weakened the presidency as Congress reasserted some control over foreign policy. The war, however, was only one part of the upheaval that Americans experienced during the 1960s. The Civil Rights Movement, the new youth counterculture, and President Johnson's effort to create a Great Society that eliminated crushing poverty combined to create a strong liberal vision that enthralled some Americans and repulsed others.

Why does the Vietnamese War continue to provoke controversy among Americans?

CHAPTER REVIEW

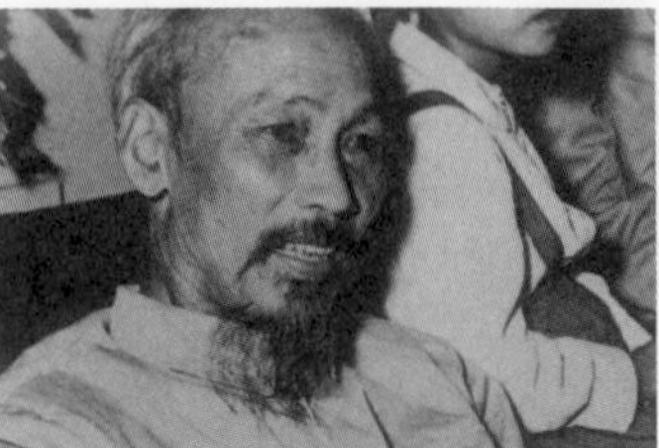

1950

Truman offers aid to French in Vietnam
United States begins financing 80 percent of France's war effort

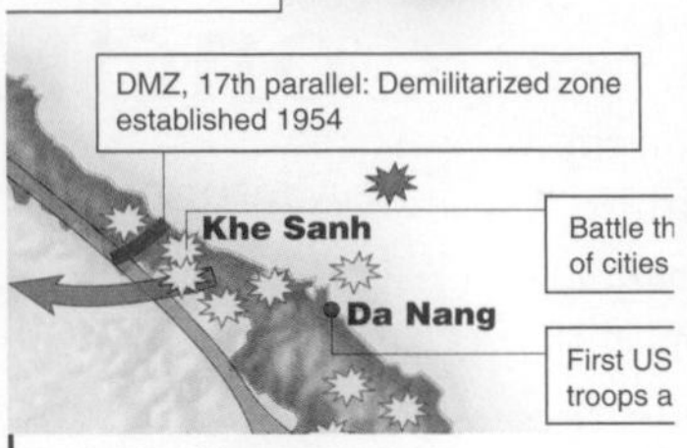

1954

Geneva Accords
Peace settlement between France and Vietminh divides Vietnam at seventeenth parallel

Eisenhower uses domino theory to explain U.S. involvement in Vietnam
Links defeating communism in Vietnam to protecting U.S. interests in Southeast Asia

1963

Buddhist monk sets himself on fire to protest corrupt Diem regime
Kennedy supports overthrow of Diem

President Kennedy assassinated
Johnson resolves to stay the course in Vietnam

Review Questions

1. Consider the nation's gradual intervention in Vietnam. How important were early decisions (1945–1954) in setting the course of U.S. involvement in the Vietnam War?
2. How did the Cold War influence presidential decision making about Vietnam from 1945 to 1975?
3. How did the political situation within Vietnam shape the war?
4. What military challenges did American troops face fighting in Vietnam?
5. How did competing images of the war create turmoil at home?
6. What do the debates surrounding the My Lai massacre and Kent State shootings reveal about Americans' competing visions about the war?

1964–1965

Gulf of Tonkin Resolution
After alleged North Vietnamese attack on U.S. destroyers, Congress gives Johnson permission for military action in Vietnam

American ground forces arrive in Vietnam
Vietnam becomes America's war

1968

Tet Offensive
Major North Vietnamese attack convinces majority of Americans that war is futile

Johnson withdraws from presidential race
Tries to win war before leaving office

My Lai Massacre
Controversy erupts over who was responsible for U.S. troops killing five hundred unarmed villagers

Nixon wins presidency
Promises peace with honor and quick withdrawal from Vietnam

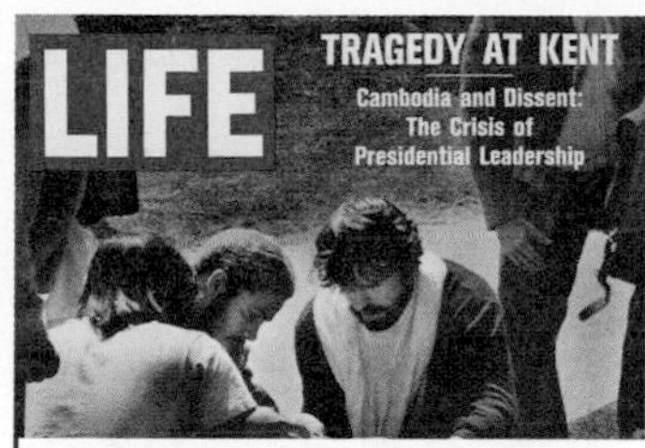

1970

U.S forces invade Cambodia
National Guardsmen fire on protesters at Kent State University, killing four

1973–1975

Paris Peace Accords
Ends direct American involvement in war

North Vietnamese troops enter Saigon
North Vietnam wins the war

Key Terms

Vietminh The term initially used to describe all Vietnamese communists, and used after 1954 solely for North Vietnamese communists. **780**

domino theory The fear that a communist Vietnam would open the door to a complete communist takeover of Southeast Asia. **781**

Geneva Accords (1954) Called for a temporary partition of Vietnam along the seventeenth parallel, with the Vietminh in the north and the French in the south, and a general election in two years to reunify the country under one government. **782**

Southeast Asian Treaty Organization (SEATO) 1954 alliance among the United States, Britain, France, Australia, New Zealand, Thailand, the Philippines, and Pakistan who pledged to "meet common danger" in Southeast Asia together. **783**

Vietcong Slang term for South Vietnamese communists. **783**

Gulf of Tonkin Resolution (1964) Gave Johnson permission "to take all necessary measures to repel any armed attack against the forces of the United States and to prevent further aggression" in Vietnam. **787**

Ho Chi Minh Trail A 600-mile North Vietnamese supply route that ran along the western border of Vietnam through neighboring Laos and Cambodia. **789**

agent orange A defoliant that stripped trees of their leaves to expose Vietcong hideouts and killed crops. **790**

peace movement A loose coalition of antiwar activists that included pacifists, students, professors, clergy, hippies, civil rights activists, and middle-class liberals. **790**

Tet Offensive (1968) A massive, coordinated Communist assault against more than a hundred cities and towns in South Vietnam. **792**

My Lai A Vietnamese village where American soldiers massacred five hundred civilians in 1968. **799**

Vietnamization A Nixon administration policy that turned the bulk of the ground fighting over to the South Vietnamese Army. **801**

silent majority Nixon's term for the large number of Americans who supported the war quietly in the privacy of their homes. **801**

détente Relaxing Cold War tensions by using diplomatic, economic, and cultural contacts to improve U.S. relations with China and the Soviet Union. **803**

Watergate scandal (1972) A botched Republican-engineered break-in of the Democratic National Committee headquarters in Washington, D.C., that eventually forced Nixon to resign in 1974. **806**

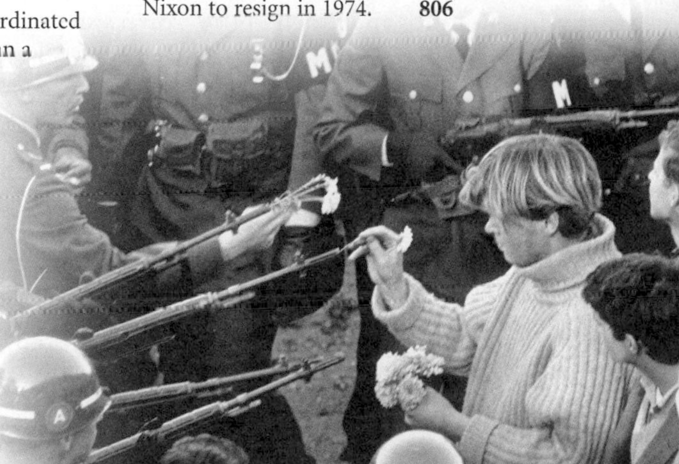

CHAPTER

27

A Decade of Discord

The Challenge of The Sixties

> "We know through painful experience that freedom is never voluntarily given by the oppressor; it must be demanded by the oppressed."
>
> MARTIN LUTHER KING JR., 1963

In April 1968 civil rights leader Martin Luther King Jr. traveled to Memphis, Tennessee, to offer his support for a black garbage men's strike. Around 6:00 pm on April 5, 1968, as King leaned over a balcony railing outside his second-story room at the Lorraine Motel to chat with two friends in the courtyard below, shots rang out. A wounded King collapsed on the floor of the balcony, and colleagues frantically tried to stem the bleeding with towels while waiting for the ambulance to arrive. Within an hour hospital doctors pronounced the thirty-eight-year-old minister dead. As news of King's assassination spread, rioting erupted in black communities throughout the nation, and images of violence saturated the television airwaves. In this photo King's thirteen-year-old daughter Yolanda sits inside a car peering at mourners, reflected in the car window, while her mother Coretta Scott King sits solemnly behind her as they leave King's funeral in Atlanta, Georgia. This somber photograph, as much as the images of rioters had, captured the crushing disappointment of dashed dreams. It was a sentiment shared by many Americans in the 1960s, white and black, who failed to fully realize their goals of either reforming America or ending the cultural turmoil.

America was rife with discord during the sixties. Much debate centered on liberalism and its willingness to use the government to protect civil rights and expand economic opportunity. Throughout the decade social reformers working within the liberal tradition advanced competing visions of social justice and shared prosperity. Some visions were bold; some, truly radical. King dreamed of using nonviolence to achieve racial equality; more militant activists advocated armed self-defense. Building on the reform legacies of the Progressive Era and the New Deal, Democratic presidents John F. Kennedy and Lyndon B. Johnson launched their own wars against poverty. Their legislative agendas were too timid for young radical activists who wanted to revolutionize American capitalism. Feminists, Chicano activists, and Native American protesters all mobilized as well to demand equal rights.

These visions of reform, especially the more radical revolutionary ones, appeared like nightmares to conservative segments of the population that abhorred liberalism. Southern segregationists organized to prevent any government-mandated dismantling of Jim Crow, and white northerners increasingly resented taxpayer-supported programs for unruly minorities. The rise of a hippie counterculture that emphasized love and pleasure convinced many working- and middle-class whites that liberalism meant the end of law and order and traditional values.

If there was one point of agreement throughout the sixties, it was that the political and cultural battles that defined the decade, for good or ill, transformed the nation. By the end of the decade, frustration over unfulfilled dreams left Americans divided over whether the nation had changed too much or not enough.

What was the larger political significance of the King family's personal tragedy?

VIETNAM
WAR
ADMINISTRATION

The Liberal Moment

The 1960s was the heyday of American liberalism, thanks in part to the reform agendas of presidents Kennedy and Johnson and pivotal Supreme Court rulings. Kennedy and Johnson viewed themselves as heirs to the New Deal legacy, and they intended to follow in Harry Truman's footsteps, who as president had desegregated the American military and secured federal funds for urban public housing, education, and public works projects. Kennedy and Johnson each believed in the power of the federal government to positively reform American society, but each faced intense resistance from conservatives who were certain that the less the government interfered in the economy or society, the better.

Kennedy and the New Frontier

Nearly 20 percent of Americans, 70 percent of them white, lived in dire poverty during the most prosperous moment in American history. Many middle- and upper-class Americans learned this startling statistic by reading Michael Harrington's *The Other America: Poverty in the United States* (1962). Harrington documented the deteriorating schools, substandard hospitals, and dead-end jobs that created a cycle of poverty that continued unabated for generations. Just like Jacob Riis's nineteenth-century exposé, *How the Other Half Lives* (see Chapter 17), Harrington made the lives of the nation's poor "visible" to the rest of the nation. Harrington claimed that a "culture of poverty" filled with extramarital sex, illegitimate children, and broken families created "a different kind of people" who did not share the values or outlook of middle-class America. Like Riis seventy years earlier, Harrington succeeded in awakening the social consciousness of affluent liberals, including John F. Kennedy.

While campaigning in West Virginia during his 1960 presidential bid against Republican Richard Nixon, Kennedy came face to face with appalling poverty as he sat and talked with coal miners, pictured here (**27.1**), about their lives. This moment of intimate conversation, one of his speechwriters noted, was "Kennedy at his best" as he gathered details about children who never drank milk and their fathers' dangerous

27.1 Presidential Candidate John F. Kennedy Speaking with Coal Miners, 1960
Kennedy's personal touch and charisma helped him create a strong connection with voters, who educated him about the entrenched poverty endemic to many rural communities.

What social problems associated with poverty became visible in the early 1960s?

work underground. "I was better off in the war than they are in the coal mines," Kennedy, a World War II veteran, told his campaign staff after this photo was taken. "It's not right."

"Let us begin anew," John F. Kennedy told the nation in his 1961 inaugural address, setting a tone of hope that inspired young people and liberals throughout the nation. After eight years with the moderate Republican Dwight Eisenhower in the White House, Kennedy wanted to reinvigorate the liberal agenda through a legislative program called the **New Frontier**. Kennedy's proposed reforms included raising the minimum wage, reducing overcrowding in schools, and providing health care for the elderly. Kennedy also advocated cutting taxes and increasing government spending to stimulate the economy, reasoning that as incomes rose more tax revenue would flow into federal coffers to pay for these programs.

> "Ask not what your country can do for you—ask what you can do for your country."
>
> Kennedy's Inaugural Address, 1961

Kennedy also needed large sums for the ongoing space race with the Soviet Union, begun when the Soviets launched Sputnik in 1957 (see Chapter 24). The Soviets sent the first astronauts into space in 1961, prompting Kennedy to announce that the United States intended to recover its reputation as the world's technological leader by putting a man on the moon.

The youngest elected president in American history, Kennedy's charisma and idealism inspired many baby boomers who were just reaching adolescence or entering college. Thousands rushed to join the **Peace Corps**, an agency established by Kennedy that sent recent college graduates to work on humanitarian projects overseas in developing nations. "I really believed that I was going to change the world," recalled one teenager. By the end of the decade, over ten thousand Peace Corps volunteers had traveled abroad to teach, build hospitals, set up water treatment plants, and establish irrigation systems.

Kennedy succeeded in raising unemployment and Social Security benefits, as well as the minimum wage, but he had trouble implementing other parts of his liberal legislative program. Unskilled in lobbying individual legislators, just over one-third of his proposals became law. Conservative congressmen balked at using deficit spending to fund the tax cuts and programs Kennedy proposed. Southerners objected to northerners' insistence that federal education funds only go to racially integrated schools, while Protestants resisted offering public monies to private Catholic parochial schools. It was one of the "great ironies of American politics," a *New York Times* reporter noted, that "JFK, the immensely popular president, could not reach his legislative goals."

A Liberal Court

Under the leadership of Chief Justice Earl Warren from 1953–1969, the Supreme Court became an aggressive champion of individual rights, fostering the liberal agenda better than Kennedy and Democrats in Congress did. Warren believed that the Constitution gave the government the power, and the responsibility, to protect the relatively powerless against oppression by the majority. By choosing to render opinions on a wide range of social justice issues, the **Warren Court** brought about a legal revolution in the United States that permanently altered American schools, politics, the criminal justice system, and cultural norms. Northern liberals cheered these court decisions, but conservatives in both parties viewed the Warren Court as an activist court that rewrote rather than upheld the Constitution.

In 1954 the *Brown v. Board of Education* decision (see Chapter 25) paved the way for school desegregation. Throughout the fifties and sixties, the court continued to dismantle Jim Crow piece by piece, striking down segregated interstate and city buses, upholding the rights of civil rights protesters to hold sit-ins, and embracing mid-1960s federal laws that desegregated public places and guaranteed the right to vote as constitutional.

Another innovative judicial premise, the right to privacy, accompanied the Supreme Court's new support for civil rights. The Court struck down a host of state laws that outlawed possession of obscene publications, prohibited the use of contraception, and prevented interracial marriages. Individual Americans, the Court ruled, had the right to decide what to read, to use birth control, and to marry whom they wanted. Other court decisions redefined how the police arrested and interrogated suspected criminals. The police now had to inform individuals of their constitutional right to have a state-funded attorney present during questioning and their right not to answer questions that might incriminate them in a crime.

Why did many young people find Kennedy inspiring?

1954	**Brown v. Board of Education** outlawed racial segregation in public schools.
1962	**Baker v. Carr** gave federal courts right to intervene if states created voting districts of unequal size.
1962	**Engle v. Vitale** outlawed official school prayer in public schools.
1963	**Gideon v. Wainwright** gave accused felons the right to free legal counsel.
1965	**Griswold v. Connecticut** established "right to privacy," overturning state laws banning use of contraception.
1966	**Miranda v. Arizona** required that police inform suspect of right to remain silent and have a lawyer present during police questioning.
1967	**Loving v. Virginia** prohibited state laws banning interracial marriages.

27.2 Major Decisions of the Warren Court The Supreme Court presided over a major "rights revolution" in the sixties.

The Court also championed freedom of speech, ruling against Red Scare–era laws that required Communist Party members to register with the government and striking down official school prayer. For many years children across America had begun their school days by reciting the "Pledge of Allegiance," to which Congress added the words "under God" in 1954 as a Cold War measure intended to contrast American religiosity with the godless communism embraced by the Soviet Union. Most schoolchildren then sang a patriotic song like "America," and some concluded this opening ritual with a short reading from the Bible. The Court's ruling against official school prayer in *Engle v. Vitale* (1962) is explored in *Choices and Consequences: Is School Prayer Constitutional?* The decision ignited a firestorm of controversy among conservative Protestants and Catholics. President Kennedy, however, endorsed the decision. Having encountered strong anti-Catholic bigotry during his 1960 presidential campaign, Kennedy welcomed the chance to make religion a strictly private matter as he geared up for his reelection campaign. The chart, *Major Decisions of the Warren Court* (**27.2**), summarizes key court decisions.

The 1964 Election

When Lyndon B. Johnson (LBJ) assumed office in the wake of Kennedy's assassination on November 22, 1963 (see Chapter 26), he took up the slain president's liberal agenda. "Let us continue," President Lyndon Johnson proclaimed, echoing Kennedy's earlier entreaty, "let us begin." Unlike Kennedy Johnson excelled at forging the deals needed to move legislation through Congress, and under his stewardship liberalism gained tremendous momentum. Over the next few months, Johnson adroitly used the nation's grief to great political advantage by cajoling Congress into enacting key pieces of Kennedy's legislative initiatives, including civil rights legislation, a tax cut, and federally funded public housing. Johnson also announced his own War on Poverty, creating an Office of Economic Opportunity that formed the Jobs Corps to teach inner-city youth vocational skills and created Volunteers in Service to America (VISTA), a domestic Peace Corps that sent privileged young adults to work on community projects in impoverished rural and urban areas.

Despite these legislative successes, Johnson knew that "for millions of Americans I was still illegitimate . . . a pretender to the throne," because he had not been elected president. Johnson saw the 1964 election as an opportunity to validate his presidency. His campaign, however, got off to a rocky start. LBJ expected to lose southern votes for having openly supported federal civil rights legislation. Alabama segregationist and former governor George Wallace's strong showing in a few northern Democratic primaries was unwelcome evidence that racism was strong in northern white working-class ethnic neighborhoods and some middle-class suburbs as well.

Racial controversy also rocked the Democratic Party's presidential nominating convention in Atlantic City when two separate delegations from Mississippi appeared. Disenfranchised blacks could not vote in Mississippi's official Democratic primary, so the Mississippi Freedom Democratic Party (MFDP) had held a shadow primary to elect their own convention delegates. This delegation traveled to Atlantic City and challenged the all-white Democratic Party's claim to represent the state.

Choices and Consequences

IS SCHOOL PRAYER CONSTITUTIONAL?

In 1962 a group of parents in New York State challenged the constitutionality of the short nondenominational prayer that the state Board of Regents had adopted in 1951 for use in the public schools. The question was whether government-directed prayer violated the First Amendment clause that "Congress shall make no law respecting an establishment of religion, or prohibiting the free exercise thereof." The Fourteenth Amendment made this clause applicable to state law.

Choices

1 The prayer was constitutional because students were not required to recite it.

2 An officially composed prayer, regardless of its content, violated the First Amendment.

3 School prayer simply recognized the importance of religion in American society without establishing an official religion.

Decision

In *Engle v. Vitale* (1962) the Supreme Court ruled 6 to 1 that state-directed school prayer was unconstitutional. Justice Hugo Black wrote the majority opinion, stating that the First Amendment prohibited "official prayers for any group of American people to recite as part of a religious program carried on by government."

Consequences

The Warren Court received more mail opposing this case than any other. In 1963 the Court also banned reciting the Lord's Prayer and Bible-reading in public school, ruling that to remain truly neutral the government could not support "the tenets of one or all religions." Shared outrage over school prayer rulings helped forge a new political coalition between southern fundamentalist Protestants and northern orthodox Catholics, whose grassroots activism against liberalism contributed greatly to the conservative right's resurgence in the late 1960s. Subsequent court decisions in the 1980s and 1990s prohibited moments of silence for private prayer, minister-led prayers at high school graduation ceremonies, and student-led prayers at high school football games.

First-graders praying

Continuing Controversies

Does school prayer violate the First Amendment?
Those who answer "yes" believe that the Founding Fathers included the establishment clause in the constitution because the union of government and religion often leads to religiously based persecution of those not adhering to mainstream religious views. Freedom of religion requires a completely secular government that neither advances nor inhibits religious beliefs. Many conservatives disagree. They argue that the Court's decisions violated their First Amendment right to exercise free speech and destroyed the spiritual heritage of the nation that stretched back to the Pilgrims.

Why did so many Americans object to the Supreme Court's ruling against school prayer?

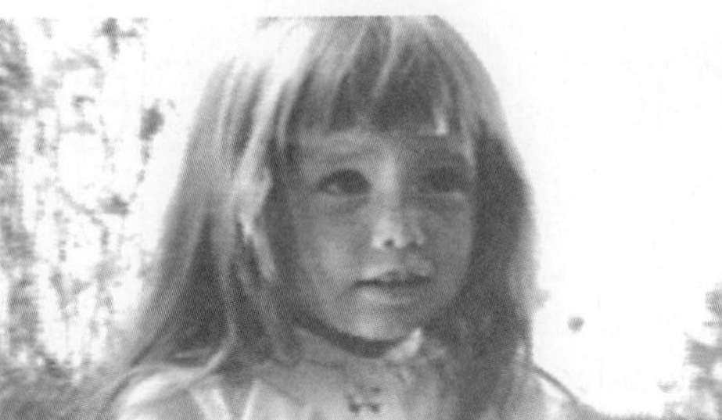
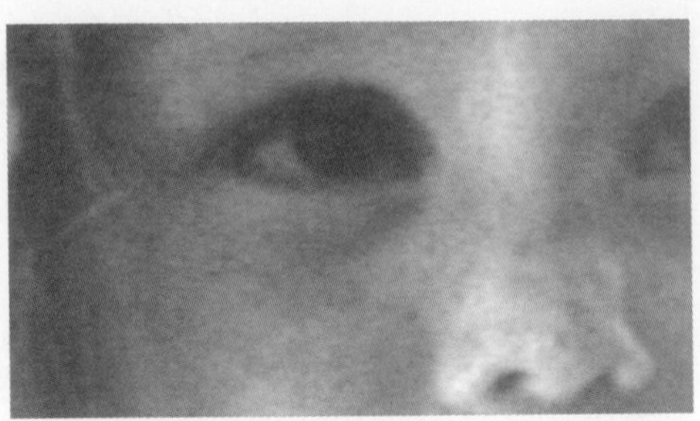

27.3 Sequence of Stills from the Daisy Girl Campaign Ad, 1964 This Democratic campaign ad implied that Republican candidate Barry Goldwater would start a nuclear war if elected. The ad script included these directions: "Ominous male voice counts down launch sequence, 10, 9, 8, 7, 6, 5, 4, 3, 2, 1. Close up of girl's face as camera progressively zooms in on her eye. Overlay an atomic explosion into the pupil of her eye."

In deciding which delegation to seat as the official delegates from Mississippi, the convention's Credentials Committee heard gripping testimony from MFDP delegate Fannie Lou Hamer. Thanks to the live television feed covering the proceedings, Americans throughout the nation heard Hamer describe being beaten, losing her job, and receiving a $9,000 water bill even though her house had no running water—all retribution for trying to register to vote. "Is this America, the land of the free and the home of the brave, where we are threatened daily because we want to live as decent human beings?" she asked before the cameras. Suddenly the networks broke away for an impromptu presidential news conference that Johnson had called to interrupt news coverage of Hamer's moving personal story. Johnson did not want the convention and his subsequent campaign to center on civil rights. To end the matter Johnson tried to broker a deal off-camera. When the MFDP rejected the offer of two delegate seats, the all-white Mississippi delegation took the floor.

In the election of 1964, the Democrat and Republican parties fielded candidates who offered starkly different visions of the role that government should play in American society. The Democrats selected Johnson, who spoke of creating a **Great Society** with social welfare reforms that would make the amenities of modern life—a decent standard of living, education, health care, clean water—available to all Americans. Like turn-of-the-century Populists and Progressives, and 1930s New Dealers, Johnson wanted to use the power of the federal government to reign in the wealthy and help economically disadvantaged Americans. Having begun his congressional career as an avid New Dealer in the 1930s, Johnson shared Franklin D. Roosevelt's desire to provide the deserving poor with a decent standard of living. Johnson, however, believed even more strongly than previous generations of liberal reformers in the ability of the government to improve the quality of life in America. Under Johnson the federal government began combating pollution, supporting the arts, and planting trees and flowers along the nation's highways—a beautification project strongly endorsed by his wife, Lady Bird Johnson. Johnson aspired to do more than put food in people's bellies; he wanted to nurture their spirits as well.

Barry Goldwater, a conservative Republican senator from Arizona, offered a radically different view of what responsibilities the government should assume. Instead of more government Goldwater proposed dismantling most of the New Deal, including Social Security, and opposed federal civil rights laws because he saw them as the first step toward creating "a police state." "My aim is not to pass laws but to repeal them," he declared. Goldwater spoke for the radical right, staunch conservatives who felt that the government's interference in the economy and society did more harm than good. Goldwater's extreme conservative views, however, alarmed some prominent moderate Republicans who openly supported Johnson.

The Democrats astutely used Goldwater's most extreme pronouncements against him in the campaign, making the liberal Johnson look almost moderate in comparison. Amplifying a remark by Goldwater that NATO commanders should have the authority to use nuclear weapons, a Democratic television campaign ad pictured a little girl counting as she picked the petals off a daisy (**27.3**). When she reached nine the camera froze on the image of her uplifted face before dissolving into the scene of a countdown to a nuclear bomb explosion. As the mushroom cloud dissipated, the screen turned dark and these words appeared: "Vote for President Johnson on November 3. The stakes are too high for you to stay home." The ad provoked its own firestorm of controversy and only aired once. It succeeded, however, in planting the image of

What competing views of government emerged during the 1964 presidential election?

VOTE FOR PRESIDENT JOHNSON
ON NOVEMBER 3.

"In Your Heart You Know He's Right."
Republican billboards

"In Your Guts You Know He's Nuts."
Democratic bumper stickers

Dueling campaign slogans in the 1964 presidential election centered on Republican candidate Barry Goldwater

Goldwater as a dangerous extremist who might lead the nation into nuclear war.

Johnson won the election with over 61 percent of the popular vote, the largest percentage of any presidential candidate in American history. The Democrats also widened their control of Congress, further strengthening Johnson's hand. Johnson knew that he had to strike immediately to enact his legislative agenda. "Hurry, boys, hurry," he told his staff. "Get that legislation up to the hill and out. Eighteen months from now Landslide Lyndon will be Lame-Duck Lyndon."

The Great Society

Admiring the trees and landscaping along a national highway, reading a food label listing nutritional content in the supermarket, buying unleaded gas at a service station, and watching a documentary on the Public Broadcasting System (PBS): these are all experiences of modern life made possible by Johnson's Great Society. Reflecting liberal faith in the power of the government to do good, the Great Society hoped to remove the causes of debilitating poverty by improving the nation's educational system, providing health care to the aged and indigent, and creating a new cabinet-level position in housing and urban affairs to oversee housing and economic relief to struggling cities. Johnson's Great Society also included a new Department of Transportation to manage the federal funds pouring into highway construction and landscaping.

Johnson worked hard to create consensus for his liberal ideals. He offered conservative industrialists tax breaks in return for supporting his social welfare programs, arguing that his programs would create highly skilled workers who consumed more. "Doing something about poverty is economical in the long run," he told them. From his long years in Congress, Johnson knew how to lobby individual legislators. To secure a needed vote, Johnson brought legislators to the White House and subjected them to "The Treatment," a mixture of cajoling, horse-trading, and intimidation. One congressman recalled the 6-foot Johnson grabbing him by the lapels of his coat, pulling him close and holding his face inches away while he "talked and talked. I figured it was either getting drowned or joining." Johnson succeeded in pushing through over 65 percent of his proposals, a level of success only surpassed by Franklin D. Roosevelt's 80 percent legislative passage rate. Unable to stop the Great Society juggernaut, Republicans complained bitterly of "the three-B Congress—bullied, badgered, and brainwashed."

What made Johnson such an effective politician?

1964 **Economic Opportunity Act** – created VISTA, a domestic version of the Peace Corps, and community-based antipoverty programs that residents designed and administered.

Wilderness Act – protected public lands from development to preserve their unspoiled state.

1965 **Social Security Act** – created Medicare, government health insurance for Americans over 65, and Medicaid, government health insurance for the poor.

Department of Housing and Urban Development – established a new Cabinet-level position to administer Great Society legislation intended to clear slums and build new public housing.

Elementary and Secondary Education Act – allocated $1 billion to improve education for impoverished children.

Higher Education Act – created federal scholarships and loans for students in need.

Immigration Act – eliminated national quotas, set new guidelines privileging family unification and desirable occupational skills.

Highway Beautification Act – provided funds for landscaping along nation's highways.

Motor Vehicle Air Pollution Control Act – set first federal standards for motor vehicle emissions.

1966 **The Department of Transportation** – established a new Cabinet-level position to administer federal funds to improve highways and urban mass transit.

Fair Packaging and Labeling Act – required manufacturers to label number of servings and nutritional information on food packages.

1967 **Public Broadcasting Act** – created public television and radio stations dedicated to educational programming.

27.4 Key Great Society Legislative Achievements
The Great Society built on liberal legislation initiated during the Progressive Era and New Deal to give the federal government an expanded role in American society.

After pushing first for federal aid to schools, Johnson turned to providing health care to senior citizens and the poor. Facing strong opposition from health insurance companies and medical professionals to government-provided health care, Johnson compromised. Medicare, government-funded health insurance for the elderly, reimbursed doctors and hospitals whatever they charged senior citizens instead of establishing government rates. Johnson also agreed to let the states, not the federal government, run Medicaid, which provided health services to the poor.

In creating the Great Society, Johnson wanted to restore America's identity as the land of opportunity for immigrants. The Immigration Act of 1965 eliminated the quota system established in the 1920s that set stringent caps on immigration from southern and eastern Europe and barred all Asian immigration (see Chapter 21). In the first great wave of immigration since the 1910s, unprecedented numbers of Koreans, Chinese, Filipinos, and Vietnamese migrated to the United States over the next thirty years. Whether immigration benefited or hurt the nation once again became a topic on which Americans offered competing visions (see Chapter 29).

By detailing the destructive impact of pesticides, Rachel Carson's best-selling book *Silent Spring* (1962) helped create a politically favorable climate for the environmental regulation that Johnson proposed. *Silent Spring* vividly detailed the destructive impact of pesticides on native bird populations, provoking general alarm over the possibility of a future silent spring when no bird songs would be heard. Johnson noted that Americans had always been proud of "America the beautiful," but the reality of polluted air, disappearing forests, and filthy rivers had already tarnished this image. The air in some major cities was so bad that motorists had to use their headlights after noon. The pronouncement that Lake Erie was "dead" and the sight of oil slicks on the Cuyahoga River in Cleveland burning for eight days after a man tossed a lit cigar into the water underscored the seriousness of environmental deterioration. These ecological catastrophes helped spawn an exploding grassroots environmental movement that included Greenpeace, a radical direct-action group, and the Sierra Club, a long-standing conservation society. Responding to environmental activism and growing middle-class concerns, Congress enacted a slew of bipartisan environmental measures that required pollution controls on cars and established national standards for acceptable air and water pollution. Johnson also created federally protected wilderness areas to safeguard endangered domestic species at risk of extinction, such as the whooping crane. *The Great Society* chart (**27.4**) contains a list of Johnson's most significant pieces of legislation.

Nonviolence Triumphant: The Civil Rights Movement, 1960–1965

Kennedy's and Johnson's strong civil rights agendas came in response to a series of carefully planned grassroots protests against segregation and disenfranchisement in Alabama and Mississippi. These highly visible demonstrations put many civil rights workers in peril, and civil rights leaders hoped to win support from white liberals and moderates nationally by showing them the face of southern segregationists' resistance. Putting increased pressure on the federal government to act, the Civil Rights Movement successfully brought an end to legalized segregation and disenfranchisement by 1965.

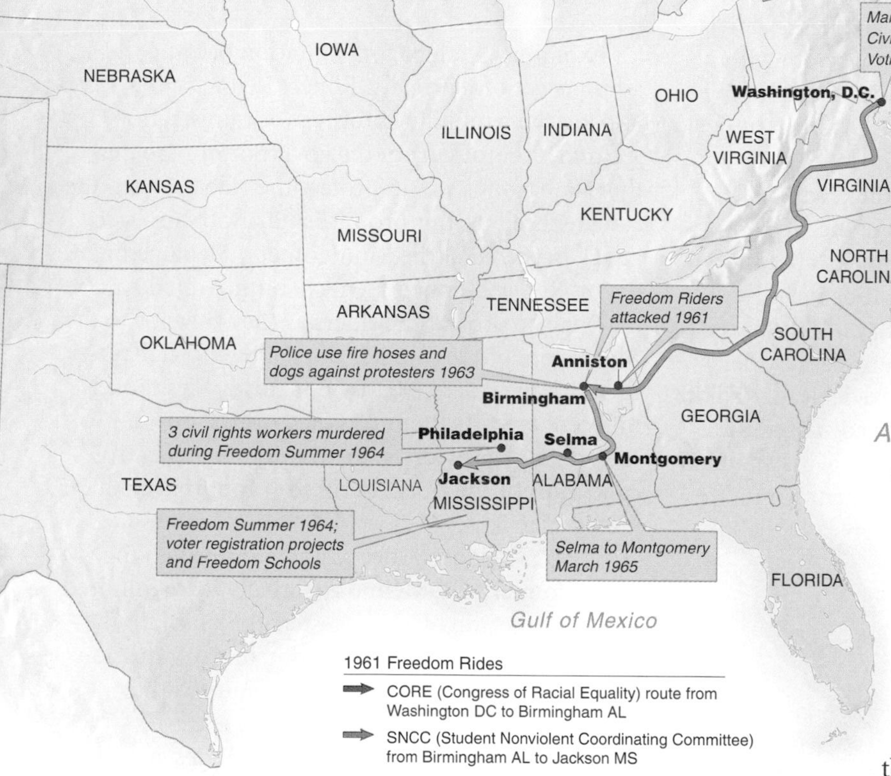

27.5 Civil Rights Milestones, 1961–1965
The Civil Rights Movement fanned out across the Deep South in the early sixties, pushing for an end to legalized segregation and disenfranchisement.

Kennedy and the Freedom Riders

Inspired by Kennedy's pronouncement during his inaugural address that "the torch has been passed to a new generation of Americans," civil rights leaders expected the new president to aggressively seek an end to Jim Crow. Kennedy, however, adopted a cautious stance, and like his predecessors, remained silent on civil rights. The movement would have to compel the new president to act.

The immediate issue centered on the enforcement of recent Supreme Court rulings that desegregated bus terminals serving interstate travelers. Faced with Kennedy's reluctance to take action, the interracial Congress of Racial Equality (CORE) organized the **Freedom Rides**, an interstate bus journey by black and white activists who entered segregated bus waiting rooms together throughout the South. "We felt we could count on the racists of the South to create a crisis so that the federal government would be compelled to enforce the law," the African American CORE leader James Farmer recalled.

The Freedom Rides began when a group of thirteen whites and blacks (including Farmer and John Lewis, a veteran of the 1960 Nashville sit-ins) boarded an interstate bus on May 4, 1961, in Washington, D.C., headed for the Deep South. Expecting the worst several riders left sealed letters for their families to open if they were killed. The map of "Civil Rights Milestones, 1961–1965" (**27.5**) traces their route. After a smooth ride through the upper South, in Atlanta the Freedom Riders decided to take two separate buses into the heart of the

What was the purpose of the Freedom Rides?

rigidly segregated Deep South. When the first bus carrying Freedom Riders entered the Anniston, Alabama, bus depot, a waiting mob pelted the bus with stones and slashed its tires. The bus driver drove away without stopping, pursued by fifty cars carrying vigilantes. When a flat tire forced the driver to stop along a deserted country road, a firebomb thrown at the bus forced the Freedom Riders into the waiting gauntlet of sticks and crowbars. State troopers arrived in time to save the lives of the traumatized Freedom Riders, two of whom sit stunned on the ground in this photo (**27.6**) of the bus burning. Meanwhile the second bus arrived in Birmingham, where a large group of Ku Klux Klansmen savagely beat white Freedom Rider James Peck, a forty-seven-year-old labor and peace activist, when he entered a white-only waiting room with a black colleague. "When you go somewhere looking for trouble, you usually find it," the governor of Alabama remarked unsympathetically.

A photo of Klan members beating Peck accompanied the front-page story in the *New York Times* that informed President Kennedy about the organized attacks on the Freedom Riders. Still dealing with the fallout from the Bay of Pigs invasion that had ended in disaster four weeks earlier and preparing for a summit with Soviet leader Nikita Khrushchev (see Chapter 25), Kennedy urged the Freedom Riders to call off the rest of their scheduled journey. Instead members of the Student Non-Violent Coordinating Committee (SNCC), the student-run civil rights group founded in 1960 during the sit-ins (see Chapter 25), rushed to Birmingham to ride alongside John Lewis, a founding member of SNCC, taking the place of riders unable or unwilling to continue.

"We can't let them stop us with violence. If we do, the movement is dead,"

SNCC leader DIANE NASH upon resuming the Freedom Rides, 1961

Avoiding a violent confrontation became the administration's priority. Robert Kennedy, the attorney general in his brother's administration, secured a promise from the governor of Alabama that state troops would protect the riders. When the state reneged on this promise and another savage attack occurred at the Montgomery, Alabama bus depot, Robert Kennedy sent six hundred federal marshals to protect the riders as they traveled to the Mississippi border. Rather than allowing vigilantes to attack the riders, Mississippi authorities took a different tack. As the riders filed off the bus in Jackson, police escorted them into waiting patrol cars. Most of the riders spent four months in jail for violating local segregation laws.

The Freedom Rides continued through the summer of 1961, and eventually three hundred white and black protesters took part. In the fall the Interstate Commerce Commission issued regulations that required the integration of all interstate travel facilities. The Freedom Rides, however, did not achieve organizers' broader goals of securing President Kennedy's enthusiastic support for the Civil Rights Movement. Despite his own integrationist views, President Kennedy remained preoccupied with protecting his white Democratic southern base and feared that open discussion of America's racial problems provided fodder for Soviet propaganda. It would take a shocking visual demonstration of racial violence in Birmingham, Alabama, to make President Kennedy a champion of civil rights.

27.6 Freedom Riders Attacked in Anniston, Alabama, 1961 Traumatized civil rights activists sit on the ground after a mob firebombed the bus the Freedom Riders were riding to protest the continued segregation of interstate bus facilities.

Who made key choices that affected the course and outcome of the Freedom Rides?

Birmingham, 1963

In 1963 the Southern Christian Leadership Conference (SCLC), Martin Luther King Jr.'s church-based civil rights organization, unfurled a carefully coordinated campaign to desegregate Birmingham, perhaps the most segregated city in the nation. SCLC's goals went beyond desegregating lunch counters or drinking fountains. "We were trying to launch a systematic, wholehearted battle against segregation that would set the pace for the nation," explained the Birmingham-based SCLC leader Fred Shuttlesworth. The city's volatile police chief Bull Connor made the city an especially dangerous place to launch such a protest. SCLC accurately predicted that they would gain the attention of the president once the world saw Connor's police force attacking nonviolent demonstrators with high-power water hoses and police dogs. Television was vital to this campaign: The images of violence pouring into living rooms would make it impossible for moderate white Americans to ignore the nation's racial problems.

In April 1963 King and the SCLC initiated their **Birmingham campaign** with economic boycotts and a limited number of sit-ins. Press coverage increased dramatically when King and Shuttlesworth led a march in defiance of a state injunction that prohibited public demonstrations. Police immediately arrested and jailed the pair. King purposefully timed his arrest to occur on Good Friday, the day that Jesus carried his cross to the site of his crucifixion, using religious symbolism to underscore the immorality of racial persecution.

As King sat in solitary confinement, the *Birmingham News* published an open letter to him from a group of white liberal southern clergymen who criticized the demonstrations as "unwise and untimely" for trying to intentionally provoke hard-core segregationists. The opinion of liberal and moderate southern whites mattered to King. The nonviolent strategy depended on swaying those who may have traditionally supported segregation but were not die-hard racists. Visitors to King smuggled out his response, written on the margins of newspapers and scraps of toilet paper during his eight-day jail stay. King's "Letter from a Birmingham Jail" did not influence the course of events in Birmingham (by the time it was published, the protests had ended), but the text was one of King's most eloquent statements on the dehumanizing aspects of racial discrimination. "For years now I have heard the word 'Wait!' It rings in the ear of every Negro with piercing familiarity. This 'Wait' has almost always meant 'Never,'" King wrote. How would whites feel about sleeping in their cars when traveling because "no motel will accept you," telling their children that they could not go to the segregated amusement parks advertised on television, and "living constantly on tiptoe stance, never quite knowing what to expect next"? These were the reasons, King explained, "why we find it difficult to wait."

Hoping to put a stop to downtown demonstrations that were keeping shoppers away and worried that the federal government might intervene, moderate white business owners initiated secret talks with SCLC leaders without Police Chief Connor's knowledge. To put increased pressure on the business owners, SCLC went ahead with a series of planned marches despite lukewarm support from Birmingham churches and adults. To fill the ranks Jim Bevel, another veteran of the Nashville sit-ins, proposed turning Birmingham into a "children's crusade" by recruiting from the city's high schools and, if necessary, middle and elementary schools. "A boy from high school has the same effect in terms of being in jail, in terms of putting pressure on the city, as his father, and yet there's no economic threat to the family, because the father is still on the job," Bevel argued convincingly.

On May 3, 1963, the second day of the protests, Carolyn McKinstry, like many others, left her high school without telling her parents that she was joining the demonstrations. When the teenagers arrived downtown, Connor was waiting with water hoses and police dogs. A shocked nation viewed television and newspaper images of firefighters directing torrents of water at McKinstry and her friends and police dogs biting protesters. (See *Images as History: Birmingham, 1963*, page 822.)

As the SCLC had hoped, northerners reacted with outrage to this blatant display of police brutality, while moderates in the South worried that Connor's heavy-handed tactics would invite more federal scrutiny of southern politics and racial customs. The Civil Rights Movement scored a major victory in Birmingham. Besides winning a commitment to desegregate lunch counters and schools as well as the promise of jobs, the protests renewed President Kennedy's interest in civil rights. Concerned about losing momentum in the Cold War, Kennedy asked the nation: "Are we to say to the world—and much more importantly to each other—that this is the land of the free, except for the Negroes . . . ?"

What various strategies made the Birmingham campaign a success?

Images as History

BIRMINGHAM, 1963

In Birmingham civil rights activists developed a strategy that included using television and news photos to their advantage. The Civil Rights Movement succeeded in getting exactly the images the activists wanted in 1963 when the Birmingham police chief Bull Connor unleashed extreme violence against protesters in the downtown area. How important was the press to the success of the Birmingham campaign? Why did the public react so strongly to these photos?

As a white child in rural Alabama, *Life* photojournalist Charles Moore had accepted segregation "as the way things were." Birmingham proved a crucial turning point in his own evolving social consciousness. "My emotional involvement in the story grew

"The water hoses hurt a lot," recalled Carolyn McKinstry, the high school sophomore girl pictured here.

Three teenage protesters clung to a doorway as water whipped their bodies, an ordeal that Moore immortalized in this iconic photograph of the Birmingham protests.

Fire Hoses, Birmingham, 1963

McKinstry remained "proud of what I had done," but afterwards she questioned "the tactics that they [SCLC] were using because I think I felt that you could actually be hurt."

Moore avoided taking photos that might send a mixed message to the public. He took no pictures of students, only partly schooled in nonviolent techniques, who threw pieces of concrete at the police—even after a slab hit him and injured some tendons.

Does knowing more about McKinstry and Moore alter this photograph's meaning?

as I saw what was happening," he noted. On the afternoon of May 3, 1963, Moore arrived in downtown Birmingham just as firefighters turned their high-pressure hoses and police dogs on teenage demonstrators. When Moore's photos appeared in *Life*, a magazine read by half of American adults in the sixties, his images, along with television coverage of the mayhem, helped transform Birmingham from a local crisis into an event that prompted national soul-searching about the state of democracy in America. Drawing inspiration from these images, civil rights activists initiated one thousand demonstrations in nearly one hundred cities throughout the South in subsequent months.

Movement leaders wanted liberal and moderate Americans to blame the police for escalating the violence in Birmingham, and Moore's pictures left little room for an alternative explanation.

The police arrested Moore when he refused to stop taking pictures. "It was scary to be a victim" of abusive police, Moore recalled, an experience that strengthened his sense of solidarity with the protesters.

"The sight of snarling dogs, and the possibility of dogs ripping flesh, was revolting to me," Moore recalled.

Moore sided with the protesters, but the story that accompanied his photos blamed extremists on both sides for the melee. "[The pictures] are frightening because of the brutal methods being used by white policemen in Birmingham, Ala. against Negro demonstrators. They are frightening because the Negro strategy of 'nonviolent direct action' invites that very brutality—and welcomes it as a way to promote the Negroes' cause, which, under the law, is right," *Life* told readers.

Police Dogs, Birmingham, 1963

How did *Life* magazine and Moore differ over the meaning of this photo?

In his address Kennedy proposed a civil rights act that would outlaw racially segregated public facilities nationwide. The white supremacist response came immediately. The next day a Klansman shot and killed Medgar Evers, the head of the National Association for the Advancement of Colored People (NAACP) in Mississippi, as Evers stood in the driveway of his Jackson home. Evers's killing was the first, but not the last, politically motivated assassination of a major political figure of the sixties.

March on Washington

Birmingham had given the civil rights cause national and international visibility, and Evers's shocking assassination reinforced Kennedy's determination to enact a sweeping civil rights bill. Southern Democratic senators were equally prepared to filibuster to prevent its passage. Intent on winning this legislative battle, King and other civil rights leaders decided to organize the **March on Washington**, a massive demonstration in the nation's capital that would demand passage of a federal civil rights act. Adopting the slogan, "Jobs and Freedom," organizers underscored the link between greater economic opportunity and civic equality. The organizing committee included African American labor leader A. Philip Randolph, founder of the Brotherhood of Sleeping Car Porters. Randolph had planned his own March on Washington in 1941, but he cancelled it when President Franklin D. Roosevelt agreed to guarantee fair protection at the workplace during World War II (see Chapter 23).

On August 28, 1963, the March on Washington for Jobs and Freedom took place as more than 200,000 marchers walked from the Washington Monument to Lincoln Memorial to listen to a three-hour program of music and speeches, forming the nation's largest political protest to date. This photo (**27.7**) of Martin Luther King Jr. talking to a reporter reveals why organizers chose to put their speakers' platform before the Lincoln Memorial. On the hundredth anniversary of Lincoln's Emancipation Proclamation, the larger-than-life statue of President Abraham Lincoln in the background offered a potent reminder of how long African Americans had waited for equal rights. "I have a dream that my four little children will one day live in a nation where they will not be judged by the color of their skin, but by the content of their character," declared King in the day's most memorable speech.

The march received the national media's full attention. It was also among the first events that television viewers throughout the world could watch live, thanks to a newly launched communications satellite. From Cairo to Amsterdam people participated in sympathy marches before American embassies and sent supportive petitions to Kennedy. By August nearly 78 percent of white Americans believed that images of racial discrimination in the United States made it harder for the nation to achieve its Cold War foreign policy goals.

Two weeks after the March on Washington, a bomb tossed into Birmingham's Sixteenth Street Baptist Church killed four little girls attending Sunday school. Carolyn McKinstry, the young woman that Charles Moore had photographed during the Birmingham protests, was in the church at the time, a friend to all four girls. The attack convinced her that she too would one day die at the hands of white supremacists. "I guess this bombing is Birmingham's answer to the march," exclaimed an enraged Anne Moody, who was working on a voter registration campaign in Mississippi. President Kennedy's assassination two months later only underscored her growing conviction that "nonviolence is through."

27.7 March on Washington, 1963 Martin Luther King Jr. speaks to a reporter while standing inside the Lincoln Memorial to underscore that one hundred years after Lincoln issued the Emancipation Proclamation blacks were still second-class citizens in the segregated South.

What symbolism and rhetoric connected the 1963 March on Washington to the past and future?

Freedom Summer

With SCLC's Birmingham campaign to desegregate public facilities successfully concluded, the spotlight turned to Mississippi. **Freedom Summer**, a multi-pronged attack on white supremacy in Mississippi during the summer of 1964, was a turning point in the Civil Rights Movement.It forced the federal government to deepen its commitment to equal rights, laid bare the rising tensions within the Civil Rights Movement, and trained a new generation of student activists who would soon spearhead new leftist and feminist movements.

In the summer of 1964, the Council of Federated Organizations (COFO) coordinated the efforts of several civil rights groups to launch Freedom Summer, including SNCC and CORE. With ambivalence SNCC recruited large numbers of northern whites to work on the voter registration projects. SNCC had reluctantly concluded that the national media, which had started to ignore blacks-only protests, would pay attention to Freedom Summer only if white students were involved. SNCC, CORE, and COFO hoped that the media spotlight would offer Freedom Summer workers some protection from racial violence, protection that the federal government was unwilling to give. This calculation proved incorrect.

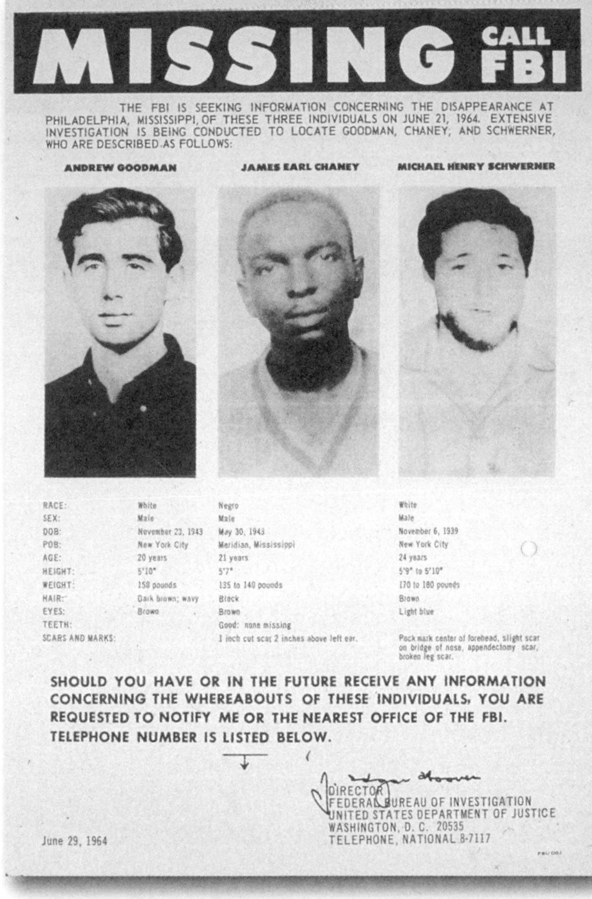

MISSING CALL FBI

THE FBI IS SEEKING INFORMATION CONCERNING THE DISAPPEARANCE AT PHILADELPHIA, MISSISSIPPI, OF THESE THREE INDIVIDUALS ON JUNE 21, 1964. EXTENSIVE INVESTIGATION IS BEING CONDUCTED TO LOCATE GOODMAN, CHANEY, AND SCHWERNER, WHO ARE DESCRIBED AS FOLLOWS:

	ANDREW GOODMAN	JAMES EARL CHANEY	MICHAEL HENRY SCHWERNER
RACE:	White	Negro	White
SEX:	Male	Male	Male
DOB:	November 23, 1943	May 30, 1943	November 6, 1939
POB:	New York City	Meridian, Mississippi	New York City
AGE:	20 years	21 years	24 years
HEIGHT:	5'10"	5'7"	5'9" to 5'10"
WEIGHT:	150 pounds	135 to 140 pounds	170 to 180 pounds
HAIR:	Dark brown; wavy	Black	Brown
EYES:	Brown	Brown	Light blue
TEETH:		Good: none missing	
SCARS AND MARKS:		1 inch cut scar 2 inches above left ear.	Pock mark center of forehead, slight scar on bridge of nose, appendectomy scar, broken leg scar.

SHOULD YOU HAVE OR IN THE FUTURE RECEIVE ANY INFORMATION CONCERNING THE WHEREABOUTS OF THESE INDIVIDUALS, YOU ARE REQUESTED TO NOTIFY ME OR THE NEAREST OFFICE OF THE FBI. TELEPHONE NUMBER IS LISTED BELOW.

DIRECTOR
FEDERAL BUREAU OF INVESTIGATION
UNITED STATES DEPARTMENT OF JUSTICE
WASHINGTON, D. C. 20535
TELEPHONE, NATIONAL 8-7117

June 29, 1964

27.8 **FBI Poster of Three Slain Freedom Summer Civil Rights Workers, 1964** The murder of these three CORE workers hardened the resolve of many Freedom Summer volunteers to continue their work registering blacks to vote, but some blacks resented that the nation seemed to care only if white activists disappeared.

> "At night, people should not sit in their rooms without drawn shades."
>
> Rule from CORE security handbook meant to protect Freedom Summer workers from sniper attacks

On the first day of Freedom Summer, three CORE workers went missing in Mississippi. Twenty-four-year-old Michael Schwerner was a white Jewish social worker from Manhattan who, one coworker recalled, "had been deeply affected by the photographs of Negroes sprawling under the dogs and fire hoses" in Birmingham. On June 21, 1964, Schwerner went with James Chaney, a twenty-one-year-old Mississippi black activist, and twenty-year-old Andrew Goodman, another white Jewish volunteer from New York, to inspect a church that the Ku Klux Klan had burned to the ground to stop CORE from opening a school there. On the return home they passed near Philadelphia, Mississippi, where local sheriff (and Klansman) Cecile Price recognized Schwerner's car and license plate from a circular the governor's office had issued concerning "outside agitators." Price arrested the trio on charges of speeding then alerted fellow Klansmen to join him for an ambush after he released the three men from jail in the middle of the night.

The trio's disappearance created national headlines, forcing the FBI to launch a massive manhunt across five states to find them. The FBI posted this circular (**27.8**) seeking information about the men's whereabouts, haunting images that conveyed more than the dangers of vigilante violence. Putting her own grief aside, Schwerner's wife Rita, herself a dedicated CORE field worker, publicly voiced her suspicion that "if Mr. Chaney, who is a native Mississippian, had been alone at the time of the disappearance, . . . this case, like so many others that have come before it, . . . would have gone completely unnoticed." As if to prove her point, sailors sent to comb through Mississippi swamps for the bodies of the three men (now assumed to be dead) discovered the corpses of three lynched black men whose previous disappearances authorities had ignored.

What interracial tensions within the Civil Rights Movement did Freedom Summer expose?

27.9 COFO Freedom School, 1964
Refusing to be intimidated when the Ku Klux Klan burned a cross in front of their Freedom School, Freedom Summer workers painted "freedom" on the blackened wood.

As the FBI investigation unfolded, Freedom Summer continued. Nearly one thousand black and white activists fanned out throughout Mississippi to register blacks in rural areas. Hoping to recruit and train a new generation of student leaders, SNCC and COFO founded summer Freedom Schools that taught high school students African American history to build pride in the long legacy of black accomplishment and gave remedial instruction in basic subjects to remedy their deficient public education. In a state with no mandatory school laws, black children often spent more time in the cotton fields than in the classroom. COFO volunteers refused to be intimidated when the Klan left a burning cross in front of a Freedom School in the Mississippi Delta (**27.9**). Writing their own counter-message of "Freedom" on the cross, Freedom Summer workers openly asserted that "COFO=Freedom Now" to underscore that it would take determined activism to meet their goals of "One Man, One Vote."

In the midst of Freedom Summer, Congress passed the **Civil Rights Act of 1964**, which banned segregation in businesses and places open to the public (such as restaurants and public schools) and prohibited discrimination in employment on the basis of race, religion, ethnicity, or sex. This landmark legislation, the most sweeping civil rights law since Reconstruction, came about because thousands of individuals risked arrest, murder, or unemployment to participate in boycotts, sit-ins, and street demonstrations in towns and cities throughout the South. Their activism went unnoticed in the national press, which focused mostly on a few dramatic moments such as the disappearance of Schwerner, Chaney, and Goodman.

A month after the Civil Rights Act's passage, after six weeks of searching, the FBI paid $30,000 to an informant who helped officers locate the three men's bodies buried in an earthen dam. All three had been shot in the head, and Chaney's shattered bones attested to the savage beating he had received. No one was ever convicted of the murders, although Price and nine others were found guilty on federal conspiracy charges in 1967 and served a few years in jail.

Like Kennedy, Johnson knew that the world was watching events unfold in Mississippi. Passage of the Civil Rights Act was front-page news overseas, and world leaders rushed to congratulate Johnson. Winning the 1964 Nobel Peace Prize, King was now an international figure who inspired social justice activists worldwide.

Passage of the 1964 Civil Rights Act was a great victory for the Civil Rights Movement, but the strain of combat-like conditions during Freedom Summer took its toll. Becoming increasingly fearful some SNCC volunteers began to arm themselves for self-defense. Many blacks resented the media attention given to white activists. Meanwhile female civil rights workers, black and white, increasingly objected to males' expectations that they would clean and cook for them. The stage was set for a fracturing within the activist community.

Selma and the Voting Rights Act of 1965

The nonviolent Civil Rights Movement registered one more significant victory before that fracturing occurred, using a stand-off in Selma, Alabama, to secure President Johnson's open support for federal

What pivotal role did college-age students play in Freedom Summer?

legislation guaranteeing blacks the right to vote. On Sunday March 7, 1965, a day soon known as "Bloody Sunday," about six hundred marchers left the small town of Selma, Alabama, and began walking across the Edmund Pettis Bridge that spanned the Alabama River. They intended to march 50 miles to Montgomery, the state capitol, to demand voting rights. At the other end of the bridge, a line of county troopers armed with clubs and tear gas waited for them. When the marchers knelt in prayer at the end of the bridge, Sheriff Jim Clark ordered the troopers to attack as white spectators cheered.

"I asked my mother and father for my birthday present to become registered voters."

Eight-year-old SHEYANN WEBB, youngest member of the first Selma to Montgomery march.

Photographers and television crews witnessed the violent attack in Selma. That evening ABC interrupted the film *Judgment at Nuremburg*, a dramatized account of the war crimes trials that convicted Nazi leaders of crimes against humanity, to show news footage of the Bloody Sunday assault. The juxtaposition between the film's portrayal of the Holocaust and events in Selma haunted many viewers. Late that evening the door opened to the chapel in Selma that served as the marchers' headquarters. "We have seen on the television screen the violence that took place today, and we're here to share it with you," announced a group of blacks and whites from New Jersey who had chartered a plane to arrive that night.

On Monday, March 15, 1965, President Johnson, who had spoken privately with King before Selma about how to win public support for voting rights legislation, announced in a televised address that he was sending a federal voting rights act to Congress. "It's not just Negroes, but really it's all of us, who must overcome the crippling legacy of bigotry and injustice," Johnson told the nation. "And we shall overcome," he concluded, quoting the anthem of the Civil Rights Movement.

A triumphant march from Selma began the following Sunday, March 21, 1965, a moment captured by James Karales's stirring photograph for *Look* magazine (**27.10**). The photograph accompanied an article on the decision of northern white ministers to join the march in Selma, reaffirming the mainstream media focus on the role of whites in the Civil Rights Movement. When the marchers arrived in Montgomery five days later, King addressed the crowd on the steps of the state capitol building, looking down at the Dexter Avenue Baptist Church where he had helped initiate the Montgomery Bus Boycott ten years earlier (see Chapter 25). "I know you are asking today, 'How long will it take?' . . . How long? Not long, because no lie can live forever," King said hopefully. Five months later Johnson signed the **Voting Rights Act of 1965**, legislation that prohibited literacy tests and poll taxes, plus authorized the use of federal registrars to register voters if states failed to respect the Fifteenth Amendment. Within a year over nine thousand blacks had registered in Dallas County, Alabama, enough to block Jim Clark's reelection as sheriff.

27.10 March from Selma to Montgomery, March 21–25, 1965
Storm clouds hovered as marchers walked along the rural highway that linked Selma to Montgomery, creating a poetic image that captured their resolve to keep moving forward, no matter what the obstacle.

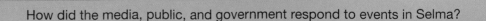

How did the media, public, and government respond to events in Selma?

The Fractured Left

Conservative Republicans and Democrats never liked the antipoverty legislative initiatives of Kennedy and Johnson, while die-hard segregationists adamantly opposed the integrationist goals of nonviolent civil rights leaders like King. The most potent attacks on these progressive visions, however, came from the left where competing visions proliferated. By the mid-sixties disaffected student activists increasingly dismissed the Great Society as too cautious and protested openly against "Johnson's War" in Vietnam, while others renounced all ties to mainstream culture. Within the Civil Rights Movement, militancy replaced nonviolence as the dominant ethos. Meanwhile many white women left the Civil Rights Movement to pursue the goal of women's liberation.

The New Left and the Counterculture

The baby boom generation came of age in the sixties. By 1968 over half of the American population was under the age of twenty-five. By then a core of white middle-class college students had created the **New Left**, a small, but highly visible, coalition of left-leaning student-based organizations that attacked racial discrimination, poverty, and the war in Vietnam.

Al Haber formed Students for a Democratic Society (SDS) in 1960 at the University of Michigan, believing "that if any really radical liberal force is going to develop in America, it is going to come from the colleges and the young." In 1962 Tom Hayden, a white activist in the Civil Rights Movement, penned the group's manifesto, "The Port Huron Statement." Hayden urged his peers to act, noting "we are people of this generation, bred in at least modest comfort, housed now in universities, looking uncomfortably to the world we inherit."

Although the majority of college-age Americans did not attend university, their ranks were increasing. By 1965 nearly 6.5 million students attended colleges or universities, compared with 2.2 million in 1950. Strict rules governed student behavior. Students lived in single-sex dormitories, had to obey curfews each evening and abide by dress codes that prohibited female students from wearing pants. The University of California, Berkeley, went one step further by forbidding all political debate or discussion on campus, a rule in place since the 1930s to prevent communist student groups from recruiting.

For years students had used a small strip just outside the campus main gate to hand out political pamphlets or give speeches. In the fall of 1964, the university administration shut this down as well, provoking the Free Speech Movement, a mass student protest that accused the University of California of denying students the right to freedom of speech. Protest leader Mario Savio, who had just returned from Freedom Summer, pointed out that "the two battlefields [in Mississippi and Berkeley] may seem quite different to some observers, but this is not the case. The same rights are at stake in both places—the right to participate as citizens in a democratic society." Aided greatly by sympathetic television coverage, the Free Speech Movement succeeded after four months of demonstrations and inspired left-leaning students on other university campuses. Most college students never joined any organized protests, but in response to those who did universities eliminated codes of conduct, introduced more elective courses into curriculums, and established black and women's studies.

After 1964 local SDS chapters took the lead in organizing antiwar demonstrations on university campuses that included teach-ins and draft-card burnings (see Chapter 26). SDS at first embraced the liberal vision of using representative government to implement incremental reforms, but in the course of its antiwar protests the group became more radical. By 1968 New Left leaders expressed open admiration for Marxist-inspired communist revolutionaries like the Vietnamese leader Ho Chi Minh and Ernesto "Che" Guevara, a colleague of Cuban dictator Fidel Castro trying to foster revolution in Bolivia and the Congo. When student-led protests roiled Europe and South America in 1968, the American New Left assumed they were part of a global youth rebellion that would ultimately reshape the world.

Once the novelty of student demonstrations wore off, getting television reporters to cover their protests

What impact did the New Left have on university life?

required more outlandish theatrics, images that increasingly radicalized student leaders eagerly provided. Press scrutiny sometimes backfired, however. Nightly news reports of demonstrators hurling bricks and expletives frightened many moderates, who increasingly viewed the New Left as unpatriotic and dangerous.

The challenge to the liberal vision went beyond the New Left. An emerging counterculture, the heir to the Beat cultural ethos of the 1950s (see Chapter 25), emphasized rejecting middle-class lifestyles more than agitating for political change. **Hippies**, youthful social rebels who renounced material acquisition and used drugs to explore their inner spiritual selves, refused to dedicate their lives to acquiring the same suburban home, car, and corporate job as their parents. The hippie utopian vision embraced peace, pleasure, sexual liberation, and sharing of material resources., an ethos captured in this 1968 photograph (**27.11**) of a hippie gathering by Robert Altman (who became a renowned filmmaker).

Drugs, especially marijuana and lysergic acid diethylamide (LSD), formed an essential part of the counterculture's challenge to the established values of middle-class society. Rock music exposed many young people to these counterculture ideals. Bob Dylan, a folk troubadour whose songs had inspired civil rights protesters, transformed himself into a rock musician with poetic lyrics steeped in drug references. The Beatles underwent a similar transformation after taking America by storm. Nearly 60 percent of the nation watched the four mop-headed British musicians sing their masterful pop concoctions during the band's first televised performance on the *Ed Sullivan Show* in 1964. In just three years the group underwent a complete makeover with the release of an album, *Sgt. Pepper's Lonely Hearts Club Band,* that broadcasted the counterculture message, "I'd love to turn you on"—a reference to taking drugs and having sex. The heyday of the marriage between rock music and the counterculture was Woodstock, a free three-day drug-infused music festival held on a farm in upstate New York, in August 1969.

New Left and young civil rights activists increasingly adopted a hippie-style of dress and experimented with drugs, but unlike hippies they remained dedicated to political activism. Most black civil rights activists, rather than rejecting white middle-class materialism, were fighting for their fair share of the nation's wealth and prosperity. New Left radicals shared the hippie belief that acquisitive capitalism bred inequality and injustice, but they were committed to engaged social action, not "tuning out."

Out of the spotlight conservatively minded college students were also active, laying the foundation

27.11 Holding Together
In their quest to define an alternative lifestyle, hippies emphasized love and harmony in their gatherings—sometimes wearing clothes, sometimes not.

How did the New Left, Civil Rights Movement, and counterculture disagree?

for the future conservative resurgence within a Republican Party dominated by moderates. A group of college students formed the Young Americans for Freedom (YAF) in 1960 under the guidance of *National Review* founder William F. Buckley. Throughout the sixties the Radical Right YAF attracted more members than the New Left SDS. Strong Goldwater supporters in 1964, these conservative students championed limited economic regulation, states' rights, respect for law and order, and staunch anticommunism. For the time being, however, the New Left had center stage.

Malcolm X: An Alternative to Nonviolence

The New Left and counterculture did not speak with one voice, and by the mid-sixties fractures within the Civil Rights Movement were also apparent. The **Nation of Islam**, an African American religious sect founded in the 1930s, rejected integration as the path to salvation for the black community and instead wanted to establish a separate black nation within the United States. As with conventional Muslims followers of Nation of Islam leader Elijah Muhammad prayed to Mecca five times a day, dressed modestly, and avoided pork and alcohol. The Nation of Islam departed from traditional Islamic thought, however, by viewing whites as "blue-eyed devils" whom Allah would condemn to eternal damnation on a forthcoming day of judgment.

> "I don't see any American dream; I see an American nightmare."
>
> MALCOLM X, ridiculing King's "I Have a Dream Speech" during the 1963 March on Washington

Nation of Islam leader Malcolm X moved ideas of armed self-defense and black separatism from the fringes to the center of the civil rights debate. A magnetic speaker Malcolm X had converted to Islam while serving a six-year stint in prison. After his release he changed his name from Malcolm Little to Malcolm X, the X signifying the lost name of his African ancestors.

Even during the heyday of nonviolence in the 1950s and early 1960s, more militant voices within the black community championed a competing vision of self-defense and racial pride that extended back to Marcus Garvey (see Chapter 21). Malcolm X openly ridiculed the nonviolent strategy of the Christian-led SCLC. "If someone puts his hand on you, send him to the cemetery," proclaimed Malcolm X in 1963. His statements received an increasingly sympathetic hearing among northern blacks who could already vote and sit alongside whites at lunch counters but encountered racial prejudice that relegated them to segregated ghettos, limited their employment opportunities, and subjected them to continued harassment by the police.

Malcolm X linked the domestic black struggle for civil rights to the global anticolonial movements underway in Africa and Asia, underscoring that the American Civil Rights Movement was just one of many liberation movements underway in the world, including a campaign to end apartheid in South Africa. Malcolm X's rhetorical links with Africa resonated well among northern blacks, who were incorporated African styles of clothing, hairstyles, and music into their daily lives. Many jettisoned the old label of "Negro" in favor of "black" to reflect their growing color consciousness and racial pride.

This photo (**27.12**) of Malcolm X smiling as he takes a photograph of boxer Muhammad Ali in a Miami restaurant after he won the heavyweight championship in 1964 conveys the charisma that each man radiated, and the strong bonds they maintained to the black urban community. Ali, who called himself "the greatest," gained fame not just for his athletic feats but, like Malcolm X, also for his defiance of authority. The day after this photo was taken he announced his conversion to the Nation of Islam, changing his name from Cassius Clay to Muhammad Ali. His mentor Malcolm X applauded Ali's announcement, knowing that the magnetic boxer would help attract other converts.

By the time Malcolm X's ideas began to gain widespread currency among disaffected blacks, however, his own philosophies were starting to shift. Viewing the increasingly powerful Malcolm X as a potential rival, Nation of Islam leader Elijah Muhammad had silenced Malcolm X a few months before this photo was taken. Malcolm X's transgression was calling the assassination of President Kennedy "a case of 'the chickens coming home to roost'" because whites were finally experiencing the vigilante violence that had terrorized blacks for years. Malcolm X left the Nation of Islam soon afterwards,

Why did some northern blacks find Malcolm X's vision appealing?

and Ali severed all ties with him. Malcolm X went on to experience a change of heart about the possibility of interracial cooperation following a 1964 pilgrimage to Mecca, Islam's holiest city, in Saudi Arabia, where he saw pilgrims "of all colors" coming together to worship. His more moderate stance did little to mollify his Nation of Islam critics. On February 21, 1965, as he stood to address a gathering in Harlem, three Nation of Islam members shot him dead.

27.12 Malcolm X Snaps a Photo of Muhammad Ali, 1964.
This meeting between two mid-sixties icons of black manhood came just after Ali won the heavyweight boxing title. Both Black Muslims, Malcolm X and Muhammad Ali enjoyed keeping whites on edge with militant rhetoric that emphasized black pride and physical prowess.

Watts and Chicago

Malcolm X did not live to help heal the fractures that ultimately unraveled the Civil Rights Movement. In the mid-sixties tensions among activists led to an overt split between those who continued to advocate nonviolence and integration and those who assumed a more militant, nationalistic approach. Stalwart civil rights veterans like John Lewis and Martin Luther King. Jr. never stopped advocating their vision of nonviolent collective action. But after 1965 the vision of armed self-defense won many new adherents.

August 6, 1965, the day that President Johnson signed the Voting Rights Act of 1965, represented the high-water mark of the nonviolent Civil Rights Movement. Five days later, with activists still basking in the afterglow of this major achievement, riots erupted in Watts, a Los Angeles black ghetto rife with high unemployment, poor schools, and rampant drug use. A routine arrest of a black man for drunk driving, which residents viewed as yet another example of the police harassment that plagued them daily, sparked the uprising. Watts burned for six days before sixteen thousand national guardsmen managed to stop the violence. The Watts riot left thirty-four dead and destroyed $35 million in property, including many businesses and homes owned by blacks.

Watts changed the image of African American protest in the white imagination from a portrait of nonviolent protesters kneeling in prayer before their attackers to one of lawless mobs shouting "burn, baby, burn." The same television cameras that helped awaken the liberal and moderate white consciousness now stoked white fears about unchecked black violence. The press ignored residents' complaints about police harassment and instead portrayed Los Angeles police as heroes who toiled tirelessly to prevent black rioters from destroying their own community. Watts was the prelude to several long, hot summers of racial rioting that rocked cities throughout the nation from 1965–1968.

The Watts riot convinced leaders like King to move aggressively to end economic inequality nationwide now that battles against legalized segregation and disenfranchisement were won. The SCLC's 1966 Chicago campaign dramatically demonstrated the limits of moderate northern whites' support for racial equality. When protesters marched through all-white neighborhoods to protest racial discrimination in renting and selling homes, white crowds pelted them with bottles and rocks, which some marchers threw back. "I have never seen—even in Mississippi and Alabama—mobs as hostile and hate-filled as I've seen in Chicago," King noted with dismay. After King's death in 1968,

"It's much easier to integrate lunch counters than it is to eradicate slums."

MARTIN LUTHER KING JR.

President Johnson successfully lobbied Congress to pass the Fair Housing Act that prohibited discrimination in selling, renting, or financing housing as a memorial to the slain leader.

Black Power and the Black Panthers

27.13 Black Panther Leader Huey Newton, 1967 This staged photo showed Newton dressed in guerrilla-style clothing surrounded by symbols of African warrior culture to convey the Black Panthers' militant, nationalistic ideology.

The "black power" slogan emerged during James Meredith's 1966 "March against Fear" in Mississippi. Meredith had faced down hostile crowds in 1962 when he became the first black student to graduate from the University of Mississippi. Four years later he decided to march 220 miles by himself from Memphis, Tennessee, to Jackson, Mississippi, hoping that his courage would inspire blacks to register to vote. On the second day of his march, a sniper waiting in the bushes shot and wounded Meredith. When activists flocked to continue Meredith's march, SNCC leader Stokely Carmichael told participants "we been saying freedom for six years, and we ain't got nothing. What we gonna start saying now is black power." **Black Power**, however, soon became a slippery term that different people employed in various ways. *Competing Visions: Defining "Black Power"* explores how black leaders with completely different ideologies embraced competing definitions of Black Power.

In 1966 Black Power militants came to the forefront of traditionally nonviolent civil rights organizations like SNCC, which expelled whites from the organization to foster black community leadership. That same year Bobby Seale and Huey Newton founded the Black Panther Party for Self-Defense in Oakland, California. The **Black Panthers** were a militant civil rights group dedicated to armed self-defense, racial pride, and inner-city renewal. The paramilitary group initiated several community projects including free breakfasts for school children and health clinics, but the press only saw their rifles. The Black Panthers organized paramilitary patrols that openly carried weapons (then legal under California law) and, Newton explained, "stopped whenever we saw the police questioning a brother or a sister" to ensure that no beatings or abuse occurred.

To project an image of strength that would appeal to inner-city youth, the Black Panthers wore commando-style attire including black leather jackets, black pants, black berets, and dark sunglasses, items already fashionable among young black men. The 1967 photo (**27.13**) that became the emblem of the Black Panther Movement depicted Newton sitting in a throne-like wicker chair surrounded by a zebra rug and warrior shields, symbols of a racial identity rooted in African culture. Wearing Western military-style clothing and holding a rifle in his right hand and a spear in his left, Newton stared into the camera with the steely resolve of a modern revolutionary.

By October, 1967 Newton was under arrest, wounded by police during a shoot-out and accused of killing a white policeman who died in the melee. FBI chief J. Edgar Hoover viewed the Panthers as "the greatest threat to the internal security of the country" and used spies to plan raids on Panther offices and create rifts within the group to weaken the Panthers internally. When the courts overturned Newton's conviction in 1970, he emerged from jail to find the Black Panthers in shambles.

The Women's Liberation Movement

Another fracture within the Civil Rights Movement, this one between men and women, energized the modern women's movement. When young white

Did the tactics used by the Black Panthers to publicize their militant vision help or hurt them?

Competing Visions

DEFINING "BLACK POWER"

The powerful image of a raised, clenched black fist became the most enduring symbol of "Black Power," but it only represented one view of the slogan's meaning. In the following excerpts civil rights leaders debate the meaning and implications of Black Power. Malcolm X never used the term directly, but his separatist message laid the groundwork for Black Power nationalism later in the decade. In contrast Martin Luther King, Jr. advocated using nonviolent methods to empower the black community. Political scientist Charles Hamilton notes the various interpretations given to the "Black Power" slogan and embraces one that emphasizes pride in being black. Are there any points of agreement among these competing definitions? How does this debate compare to the one between Marcus Garvey and W. E. B. DuBois in the 1920s (see Competing Visions, Chapter 21)?

The revolutionary, nationalist rhetoric in Malcolm X's fiery 1963 "Message to the Grassroots" greatly influenced later advocates of Black Power.

There's no such thing as a nonviolent revolution. The only kind of revolution that is nonviolent is the Negro revolution. The only revolution in which the goal is loving your enemy is the Negro revolution. It's the only revolution in which the goal is a desegregated lunch counter, a desegregated theater, a desegregated park, and a desegregated public toilet; you can sit down next to white folks—on the toilet. That's no revolution. Revolution is based on land. Land is the basis of all independence. Land is the basis of freedom, justice, and equality …

Whoever heard of a revolution where they lock arms … singing "We Shall Overcome"? You don't do that in a revolution. You don't do any singing, you're too busy swinging.

In a "Conversation with Martin Luther King," March 25, 1968, King offered a definition of Black Power that supported his strategy of nonviolence.

We have always stood up against injustices. We have done it militantly. Now, so often the word 'militant' is misunderstood because most people think of militancy in military terms. But, to be militant merely means to be demanding and to be persistent, and in this sense I think the nonviolent movement has demonstrated great militancy. It is possible to be militantly nonviolent. … I haven't advocated violence, because I do not see it as the answer to the problem. I do not see it as the answer from a moral point of view and I do not see it as the answer from a practical point of view. …

Let me briefly outline the positives [of Black Power]. First, Black Power in the positive sense is a psychological call to manhood. This is desperately needed in the black community, because for all too many years black people have been ashamed of themselves. … Secondly, Black Power is pooling black political resources in order to achieve our legitimate goals. … Thirdly, Black Power in its positive sense is a pooling of black economic resources in order to achieve legitimate power. … Withdrawing economic support from those who will not be just and fair in their dealings is a very potent weapon.

Writing to white America in the *New York Times Magazine* in 1968, Charles Hamilton outlined competing views of Black Power and stressed the importance of maintaining black racial identity.

Black Power has many definitions and connotations in the rhetoric of race relations today. To some people, it is synonymous with premeditated acts of violence to destroy the political and economic institutions of this country. Others equate Black Power with plans to rid the civil rights movements of whites who have been in it for years. The concept is understood by many to mean hatred of and separation from whites; it is associated with calling whites 'honkies' and with shouts of 'Burn, baby, burn!' Some understand it to be the use of pressure-group tactics in the accepted tradition of the American political process. And still others say that Black Power must be seen first of all as an attempt to instill a sense of identity and pride in black people. …

Black Power rejects the lessons of slavery and segregation that caused black people to look upon themselves with hatred and disdain. To be 'integrated' it was necessary to deny one's heritage, one's own culture, to be ashamed of one's black skin, thick lips and kinky hair. … The black man must change his demeaning conception of himself; he must develop a sense of pride and self-respect. Then, if integration comes, it will deal with people who are psychologically and mentally healthy, with people who have a sense of their history and of themselves as whole human beings …

Why do all three writers emphasize the importance of racial pride and manhood?

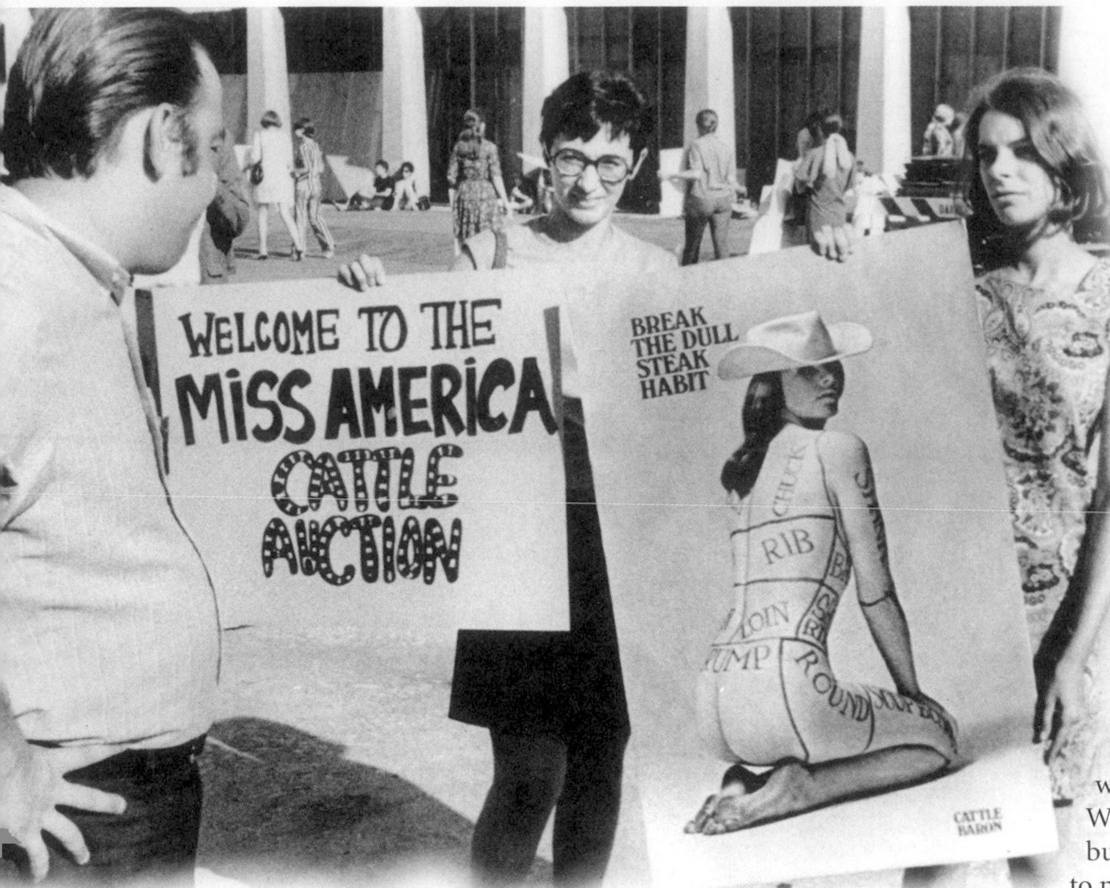

27.14 Feminists Picket the Miss America Pageant, 1968
This satirical portrait of a woman carved up like a side of beef criticizes beauty pageants for reducing a woman's value to the quality of her body parts.

female activists began leaving the Civil Rights Movement to join the women's movement, they joined a crusade already well underway. In 1963 journalist Betty Friedan reignited the feminist movement, which had faltered since the 1920s, with her treatise the *Feminine Mystique*. Calling it "the problem that has no name," Friedan challenged the widely accepted notion that women found homemaking and child-rearing fulfilling. In 1966 she founded the **National Organization for Women (NOW)**, an organization dedicated to securing equal rights for women in employment, education, and politics—areas traditionally seen as male domains. NOW also wanted to give women control over their own bodies through unfettered access to contraception and legal abortions. A relatively small organization with only five thousand members in the late sixties, NOW nonetheless convinced President Johnson to issue an executive order that required government agencies and federal contractors to create affirmative action programs to hire and promote women and minority men.

The women's movement continued to grow as younger female activists, unhappy with gender discrimination within the Civil Rights Movement and New Left, took up the cause of female liberation. The feminists who founded NOW lobbied for legislative solutions to women's problems. In contrast, more radicalized feminists, steeped in New Left ideology and nonviolent tactics, adopted a grassroots approach that used consciousness-raising—heightening awareness of social and political issues—to help women "understand the universality of our oppression." They emphasized changing attitudes rather than lobbying for legislative changes. To combat the ways that sexism pervaded normal social interactions, feminists introduced the word "Ms." into American lexicon to replace "Miss" or "Mrs.," titles that linked a woman's identity to her marital status. When activist Robin Morgan brought busloads of women to Atlantic City to protest the annual Miss America pageant in 1968, she sought maximum media coverage. Demonstrators carried the photograph (**27.14**) of an attractive, naked young woman with lines dividing her body into cuts of beef to protest how beauty pageants dehumanized women. "Welcome to the Miss America Cattle Auction," they chanted while filling a trash can with bras, high heeled shoes, mainstream fashion magazines, and copies of *Playboy*, items they believed reinforced "the Mindless Sex Object Image" of women. In deference to a local ordinance, the protesters never set the trash can on fire, but from this point onwards detractors used the dismissive term "bra-burners" to describe feminists.

Despite their different styles and messages, both moderate and radical feminists had trouble expanding their base of support beyond the white middle class. "If your husband is a factory worker or a tugboat operator, you don't want his job," noted Democratic Congresswoman Barbara Mikilski to explain why NOW's emphasis on equality in employment failed to resonate among working-class women. Similarly few black women joined the women's movement, convinced that racial oppression affected them more severely than sexual discrimination.

The End of an Era

As the Civil Rights Movement unraveled, the Great Society also floundered. Republicans widened their political appeal by promising to end the cultural strife that was tearing the nation apart. Although most liberal and radical causes lost energy after 1968, activists in the Chicano and Native American communities helped keep the protest tradition alive as the decade came to a close.

The Faltering Civil Rights Movement

Embittered by years of violent attacks in the South, young activists either left the movement altogether or migrated to more militant organizations. By 1967 King's weakening leadership reflected a movement adrift. When King spoke out against the Vietnam War, he strained his relationship with President Johnson, losing a valuable ally in the White House. King's call for a complete reconstructing of American capitalism to eliminate poverty also cost him the support of moderate blacks and whites. In the fall of 1967, after a summer of deadly race riots in Detroit and Newark, King proposed setting up a poor people's encampment in front of the White House. When the Poor People's Campaign stalled, King had time to make a quick trip to Memphis to offer his support for a garbage men's strike.

On April 4, 1968, a sniper's bullet tore through the knot in King's necktie and fatally wounded him as he leaned over the balcony of his Memphis motel. Within hours *Life* photographer Steve Schapiro entered King's motel room and snapped a haunting photograph of King's open suitcase containing a copy of his book *Strength to Love*, a wrinkled shirt, and the remnants of a meal (**27.15**). "The half-drunk cup of coffee gave me a moment of pause," Schapiro noted. "He had left his room planning to return." Completing this eerie scene King's portrait appeared on the motel television during a newscast reporting his death. The three-week urban rampage in one hundred cities across the nation that followed King's murder only further alienated the white community, who increasingly supported using troops to restore "law and order." Two months later a white man, James Earl Ray, confessed to the killing, a confession that he later retracted.

The Great Society Unravels

Diminishing sympathy for the Civil Rights Movement also meant less support for Great Society programs directed at the urban poor. Congress had written much of the legislation quickly, but the public had no appetite for waiting patiently while the Great Society worked through its growing pains. Critics from the left and right continued their attacks. The New Left advocated redistributing corporate profits more equitably throughout society. Meanwhile the Radical Right denounced the Great Society as a "hodgepodge" of

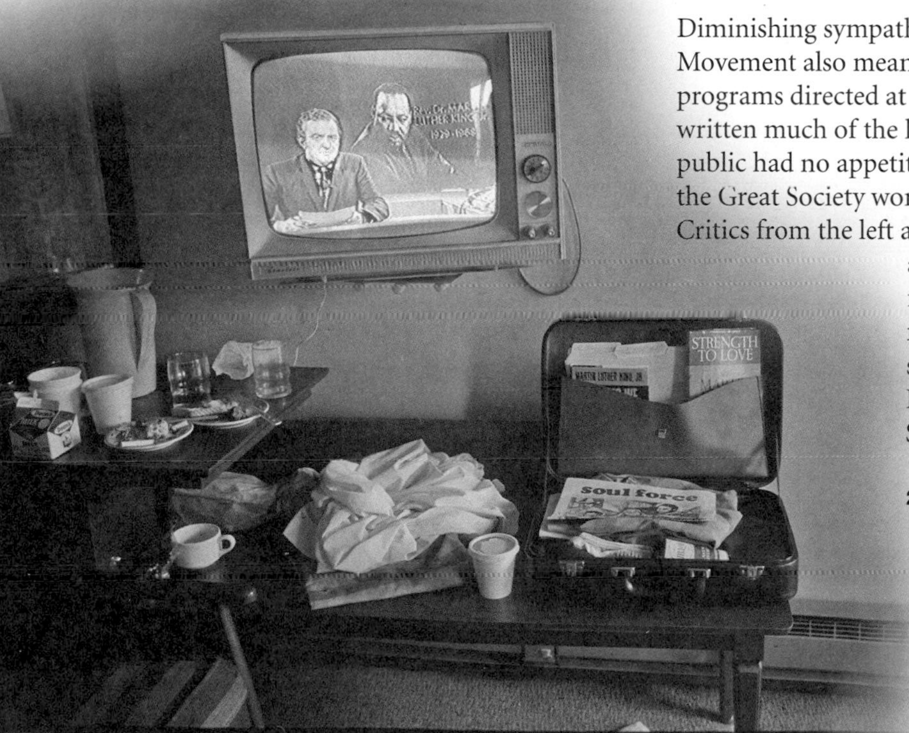

27.15 King's Room in the Lorraine Motel, April 4, 1968
King stepped out of this motel room to chat briefly with friends over the motel balcony and never returned. The television above King's suitcase announces his death to an empty room.

Why was King's death a serious blow to the Civil Rights Movement?

programs that humiliated the poor and encouraged dependency on government welfare. Ethnic working-class whites and left-leaning suburbanites, groups that had traditionally supported the Democratic liberal agenda, began to resent federal programs that they felt primarily helped black minorities. The shift in attitudes among the white working class had a significant political impact. In 1964 nearly 60 percent had voted for the Democratic ticket; four years later that percentage had dropped to 35 percent.

The Great Society's troubles reflected more than persistent racism, however. Johnson's unwillingness to raise taxes to pay for an exploding array of domestic programs and a costly war in Vietnam also contributed to its undoing. As the economy overheated interest rates doubled, the national debt exploded, and inflation caused prices to rise without any corresponding increase in wages. Americans reacted with dismay to this sudden decline in the standard of living after several decades of continued prosperity.

This 1967 Herblock political cartoon (**27.16**) illustrated Johnson's dilemma in trying to fund both the Vietnam War and the Great Society. In the drawing President Johnson prepares for an evening out with his mistress, a robust and expensively attired woman wearing a mink stole emblazoned with the words "Vietnam War." As they leave Johnson tries to assure the other woman in his life, a thin homemaker wearing a tattered apron labeled "U.S. Urban Needs," that "There's Money Enough to Support Both of You—Now, Doesn't That Make You Feel Better?" As this cartoon suggested the administration was neglecting its domestic programs and giving the war the bulk of its attention and funds. In 1968 Johnson agreed to raise taxes to finance the expanded war in Vietnam but southern conservative congressmen refused to vote for the measure until the president made substantial funding cuts to his domestic programs.

"There's Money Enough To Support Both Of You —
Now, Doesn't That Make You Feel Better?"
VIETNAM WAR
ADMINISTRATION
U.S. URBAN NEEDS
©1967 HERBLOCK

27.16 Torn between Two Mistresses, 1967 This Herblock cartoon illustrated how Johnson's escalation of the war in Vietnam deprived his Great Society programs of needed funds.

The Democratic Convention in 1968 pulled together these various strands of disenchantment with liberal politics. With Vice President Hubert Humphrey on track to secure the nomination, ten thousand antiwar activists led by New Left leader Tom Hayden organized a mass protest before the television cameras outside the Chicago Convention Center to support the antiwar candidate Eugene McCarthy. Yippies, a New Left splinter group that stood for blending "pot and politics," joined the protest. Led by Abbie Hoffman and Jerry Rubin, the Yippies issued outlandish warnings that they planned to put LSD in Chicago's water supply. As Democratic Party delegates debated the administration's Vietnam policy inside the convention hall, the police launched a premeditated attack on the demonstrators outside. Televised images of long-haired, pot-smoking protesters who waved North Vietnamese flags and threw excrement had a greater impact on public opinion than news reports of police brutality. Over 70 percent of adults supported the police crackdown.

Critics of liberalism found the public suddenly much more receptive to their competing political vision. Richard Nixon won the presidency in 1968 promising to restore "law and order," a Republican catch-phrase that fueled the political shift already underway in many traditionally Democratic blue-collar and suburban neighborhoods. With grassroots conservatism on the rise, the liberal vision appealed to fewer and fewer Americans by the end of the decade.

At the end of this divisive decade, a rare moment of national celebration occurred on July 20, 1969 when astronaut Neil Armstrong became the first man to walk on the moon. Watching the event unfurl on their television sets, Americans heard Armstrong declare "that's one small step for a man, one giant leap for mankind" as he began to stride across the moon's surface. Announcing the U.S. space race victory over the Soviet Union to the world, astronaut Buzz Aldrin planted an American flag (**27.17**) near manmade footprints that would permanently mark the moon's surface. This iconic photo of the United States conquering the moon bolstered many citizens' faith in the superiority of the American way of life, giving them another reason to reject the New Left and counterculture critique of American culture.

27.17 The First Moon Landing, 1969
National pride surged at the sight of an American flag planted on the moon. For many Americans, beating the Soviets to the moon challenged the radical left's view that American society was faltering.

The Demise of the Counterculture

As with the Civil Rights Movement and the Great Society, the hippie counterculture unraveled by the end of the decade. Heightened media coverage drew large crowds to the 1967 "Summer of Love" in San Francisco's Haight-Ashbury neighborhood, a hippie gathering dedicated to free food, drugs, sex, and music. In the fall hippie stalwarts organized a mock "Death of Hippie: Son of Media" funeral procession, blaming the over-hyped media image of the free-loving hippie for the drug-related violence and epidemic of rapes that now beset Haight-Ashbury. They then departed en masse, moving the foci of hippie culture to rural communes away from the media glare, where some succeeded in keeping the hippie utopian ideal alive.

> "Beautify America, Get a Haircut."
>
> A billboard in Rochester, New York, criticizes counterculture fashion

Ronald Reagan, the Republican governor of California, echoed the views of mainstream America in 1969 when he characterized a hippie as someone who "dresses like Tarzan, has hair like Jane, and smells like Cheetah," a reference to the counterculture's embrace of public nudity, long hair, and disdain for underarm deodorant. Worried that the counterculture had made addictive drugs such as heroin popular among the young, many states passed stringent anti-drug laws. At the federal level, in 1972 President Nixon announced a "war on drugs" aimed at disrupting the illicit drug trade.

The quick commercialization of the counterculture also hastened its demise as a potent alternative social vision. Modes of hippie dress, hippie slang, and hippie values (albeit in diluted form) swept into the mainstream. Granola appeared on supermarket shelves, and middle-aged men began growing their hair long. Affluent and educated adults increasingly smoked marijuana and listened to rock music. More sexually explicit movies and highly profitable rock record sales fueled rather than undermined acquisitive capitalism.

Keeping Protest Alive: Mexican Americans and Native Americans

The declining fortunes of the Civil Rights Movement and the counterculture did not mean the end of all campaigns for social justice in the late sixties. Mexican American and Native American activists drew inspiration from the African American struggle and launched their own highly visible, if short-lived, crusades to end ethnic discrimination. Ultimately, however, the same problems of factionalism and police harassment hurt these crusades as well.

In the 1960s the life expectancy for Mexican American migrant workers hovered around fifty years old, while infant mortality was double the national average. The short-handed hoe represented the nearly complete exploitation of California migrant workers. "The short one" forced workers to bend all day (**27.18**) as they worked in the fields, often causing crippling back pain that sidelined workers who could not afford health care. California regulators finally banned the tool in 1975.

Rallying Mexican Americans around the slogan *Si Se Puede* ("Yes, it can be done"), César Chávez, head of the United Farm Workers union, used strikes and marches to secure better working and living conditions. Chávez also appealed directly to consumers, convincing seventeen million Americans to stop buying nonunion-picked grapes, but also provoking a backlash among some. One Safeway grocery store manager reported antiunion customers loading up "their car with grapes and nothing else," while school children in the East refused to eat the grapes provided as part of their school lunches. By 1970 the economic toll of the boycott forced growers to recognize the United Farm Workers union and raise wages.

Latino urban radicals in Texas, California, and Colorado embraced a competing vision called La Raza (The Race) that emphasized racial identity over union organizing. The Brown Berets modeled themselves after the Black Panthers and proudly called themselves "Chicanos," embracing their Mexican American heritage while demanding an end to Anglo-American discrimination. In March 1968, ten thousand high school students in East Los Angeles staged a "blow-out" by walking out of their classrooms and into the streets to protest the poor education they received in their mostly Hispanic schools. By this point most white Americans had little tolerance for radical political protest and overwhelmingly supported the police for shutting the demonstrations down. Internal divisions within the Mexican American community over the wisdom of confrontational tactics like mass demonstrations and steady harassment from the police hastened the demise of the short-lived Chicano student movement.

Native American activists also drew inspiration from the integrationist vision that championed equality and the competing militant one that emphasized maintaining racial identity. After encouraging Indians to move off their reservations in the 1950s, the Bureau of Indian Affairs (BIA) began terminating the rights of some Indian tribes to federal protection. Ending their dependence on the BIA to run schools, manage their lands, and provide health care, the agency argued, would encourage Indians to assimilate into mainstream culture more quickly. Indian activists wanted the federal government to continue its financial

27.18 Hispanic Farm Workers Using Short Hoes Workers nicknamed short hoes "the devil's arm" because using them caused intense back pain. Every time César Chávez saw a head of lettuce in the supermarket, he thought of what the suffering workers had endured to grow it and was newly resolved to use strikes and boycotts to improve their working conditions.

How did the Civil Rights and labor movements influence Hispanic activists?

assistance, while at the same time allowing more self-government on Indian reservations.

On November 20, 1969, a group calling themselves "Indians of All Tribes" grabbed headlines when they occupied the abandoned federal prison on Alcatraz Island in San Francisco Bay. During their occupation of Alcatraz, Indian activists issued the sardonic **Alcatraz Proclamation** that offered to purchase the island for $24 in glass beads and red cloth, the same amount that the Dutch had paid indigenous people for Manhattan Island in 1626. The proclamation further described Alcatraz as the perfect site for an Indian reservation because it lacked running water, sanitation, schools, mineral resources, and productive soil, plus "the population has always been held as prisoner and kept dependent upon others." Eventually the cold and isolation took its toll, and the protest ended in June 1971.

In the fall of 1972 a caravan of cars and vans left the West Coast to follow "The Trail of Broken Treaties," a slogan meant to remind Americans of the "Trail of Tears," the 1838 forced removal of southeastern Indian tribes to interior lands. Stopping at individual reservations, the protesters urged tribes to fight for their legal rights. When they reached Washington, D.C., the group temporarily occupied BIA offices. Native Americans staged nearly seventy other occupations throughout the nation, including the American Indian Movement's armed takeover of the village of Wounded Knee, South Dakota, in 1973, the site of the army's massacre of three hundred Sioux in 1890. These highly visible protests prompted Nixon to increase funds for social services on Indian reservations and establish the Office of Indian Water Rights. In the early 1970s the federal government ended the policy of termination and Congress increased Indian self-rule on the reservations. Indian tribes also began suing the government for past treaty violations. At the same time, however, government harassment eviscerated radical Indian groups, part of a general crack-down on revolutionary political movements in the early seventies.

Conclusion

Whether the 1960s represented the heyday of progressive social change or a nightmare from which America needed to awake remained a point of disagreement among liberals and conservatives for decades to come. By the mid-sixties the legal edifice that had supported racial segregation and disenfranchisement through the South was gone, thanks to countless grassroots protests including the Freedom Rides, the Birmingham campaign, Freedom Summer, and the march from Selma to Montgomery. The movement effectively used mass media to create a groundswell of support for civil rights legislation, and celebrated figures like Martin Luther King Jr. along with numerous other activists lost their lives while pursuing racial justice. Nonviolent direct action lost momentum when the competing militant call for Black Power and the focus on economic inequality moved the spotlight from the South to northern ghettos. Although the movement faltered in the closing years of the sixties, it left a legacy that permanently altered the social and political fabric of the nation.

Radical and liberal politics also left a mark. Student activists transformed university life. Counterculture rejection of traditional values seeped into the mainstream, changing attitudes toward sex, drugs, and authority. Women, Hispanics, and Native Americans made the larger society aware of longstanding discrimination that limited their chances to share the American Dream. America emerged from the sixties with a new vision of itself as a multicultural society.

The Great Society laid bare a vigorous set of competing visions among radicals, liberals, and conservatives over the role of the government in American society and the value of capitalism. Dismay over Supreme Court decisions that outlawed prayer in school, Great Society programs that primarily helped minorities, and the counterculture pervaded Middle America. Unhappy with the direction of the liberal vision, many former Democrats joined a new conservative coalition whose vision appealed to more and more Americans in the 1970s.

CHAPTER REVIEW

1961

Peace Corps Established
Program sends U.S. aid volunteers worldwide

Freedom Rides
Convinces Kennedy administration to enforce Supreme Court ruling against segregated interstate travel

1962

Supreme Court rules school prayer unconstitutional
Furor lays the foundation for religiously-based conservative resurgence

Port Huron Statement
Motivates student activists to join SDS

1963

Birmingham
Outrage over fire hose and dog attacks on civil rights protesters prompts Kennedy to support a federal civil rights law

March on Washington
International press coverage turns the peaceful march into a triumphant movement for the nonviolent Civil Rights Movement

***Feminine Mystique* published**
Inspires creation of the modern feminist movement

Review Questions

1. Compare the goals and strategies of the Freedom Rides and the Birmingham civil rights campaign. Why was each an effective episode of nonviolent protest?
2. How did the Great Society compare to the New Deal? What continuities or differences existed? What lasting impact did the Great Society have on American society?
3. Why did black nationalist sentiment become more popular among African Americans after 1965?
4. What alternative visions did the counterculture and the New Left offer? What were the differences and similarities in their critiques of American society?
5. How important was leadership in the civil rights and black nationalism movements? How did grassroots activism make these movements successful? Which reform and protest movements in the 1960s were the most successful? Why?
6. Why did conservative ideals gain strength as the decade progressed?
7. How did the sixties transform American society?

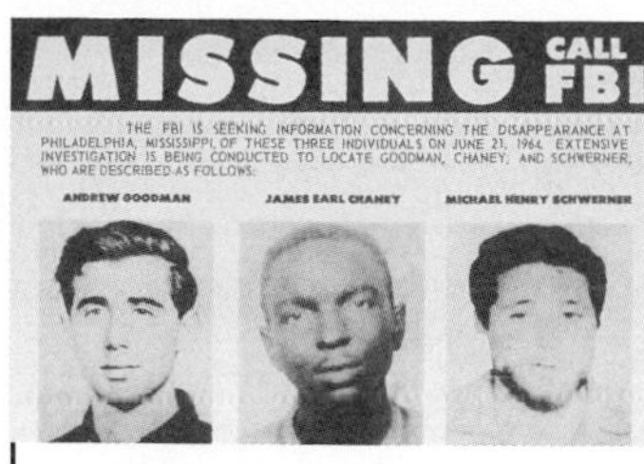

1964

Freedom Summer
Murder of three Civil Rights workers in Mississippi prompts Congress to pass the Civil Rights Act of 1964

Great Society begins
Largest legislative liberal reform effort since the New Deal

1965–1966

March from Selma to Montgomery
Congress responds to vigilante attacks on marchers by passing the Voting Rights Act of 1965

Watts Riot
Violent rampage in Los Angeles ghetto generates white backlash against Civil Rights Movement

Black Panthers founded
Black militants reject nonviolent tactics and instead advocate Black Power

1967

"Summer of Love"
Hippie gathering in Haight-Ashbury publicizes counterculture

1968

King assassinated
Nationwide rioting signals the end of the nonviolent Civil Rights Movement

Chicago Democratic presidential convention
Police crackdown on demonstrators wins general support for reinstating law and order

Feminists picket Miss America pageant
Feminists use media coverage to challenge sexist stereotypes

Key Terms

New Frontier Kennedy's legislative program that proposed raising the minimum wage, reducing overcrowding in schools, and providing health care for the elderly. **813**

Peace Corps Government agency that President Kennedy established to send recent college graduates to work on humanitarian projects overseas in developing nations. **813**

Warren Court Supreme Court that brought about a legal revolution in the United States by permanently altering American schools, politics, the criminal justice system, and cultural norms. **813**

Great Society President Johnson's wide-ranging social welfare reforms intended to make the amenities of modern life—a decent standard of living, education, health care, and clean water—available to all Americans. **816**

Freedom Rides An interstate bus journey by black and white activists who entered segregated bus facilities together throughout the South. **819**

Birmingham campaign Civil rights effort to desegregate Birmingham, Alabama, where shocking images of police brutality prompted Kennedy to push for a federal civil rights act. **821**

March on Washington, 1963 Massive demonstration in the nation's capital that demanded passage of a federal civil rights act and more economic opportunities. **824**

Freedom Summer, 1964 Multipronged attack on white supremacy in Mississippi that included a voter registration drive and the creation of Freedom Schools. **825**

Civil Rights Act of 1964 Legislation that banned segregation in businesses and places open to the public (such as restaurants and public schools) and prohibited racial and gender discrimination in employment. **826**

Voting Rights Act of 1965 Legislation that prohibited literacy tests and poll taxes, plus authorized the use of federal registrars to register voters if states failed to respect the Fifteenth Amendment. **827**

New Left A small, but highly visible, coalition of left-leaning student-based organizations that attacked racial discrimination, poverty, and the war in Vietnam. **828**

hippies Youthful social rebels who renounced material acquisition and used drugs to explore their inner spiritual selves. **829**

Nation of Islam African American sect that rejected integration as the path to salvation for the black community and instead wanted to establish a separate black nation. **830**

Black Power A call for blacks to unite politically and economically in black-only organizations to protect their racial identity as they fought for equality. **832**

Black Panthers Militant civil rights group dedicated to armed self-defense, racial pride, and inner-city renewal. **832**

National Organization for Women (NOW) An organization dedicated to securing equal rights for women in employment, education, and politics. **834**

Alcatraz Proclamation Sardonic statement issued by Indian activists who occupied the island of Alcatraz and described it as the perfect site for an Indian reservation because it lacked running water, sanitation, schools, mineral resources, and productive soil. **839**

CHAPTER 28

Righting a Nation Adrift

America in the 1970s and 1980s

> "Government is not the solution to our problem; government is the problem,"
>
> President RONALD REAGAN, 1981

The vision of the United States as a great and powerful nation suddenly seemed less assured in the 1970s. In 1973 a dispute between the United States and oil-producing Arab nations led to an oil embargo that severely restricted oil imports. Gas stations across the nation posted signs like this one as they ran out of gas, dotting the American landscape with humiliating reminders that foreign nations had the power to wreak havoc on the U.S. economy. Gas shortages also threatened the vision of America as a prosperous car culture where it was the birthright of every citizen to work, live, and shop wherever they liked thanks to the freedom of movement that automobiles provided. To many Americans images of closed gas stations (which reappeared in 1979) were just one sign of a nation adrift. Domestic political scandals, a troubled economy, and lost international prestige made the future look dim.

Americans lost confidence in the federal government in the 1970s as the Watergate scandal and cover-up brought down President Richard Nixon and the post-World War II boom times finally ended, leaving high inflation and unemployment. Ongoing economic woes and troubles abroad hampered the efforts of presidents Gerald Ford and Jimmy Carter to restore respect for the presidency. Americans did not agree over how to move the nation back onto the path of glory. Women's and gay rights groups fought to extend the social justice campaigns of the sixties, while the environmental movement focused Americans' attention on conserving its natural heritage. A new and powerful conservative coalition, however, formed around a competing vision that focused on protecting traditional values, limiting the role of the government in the economy, and flexing the nation's power overseas. In the 1980s, after two decades of grassroots activism, the conservative ascendancy was complete.

When Ronald Reagan, an ideologically committed conservative, became president in 1981, he refused to accept the notion that America had entered an age of limits. Reagan rejected the liberal vision and diagnosed government as part of the problem, not the solution to the nation's economic woes. He also moved aggressively to restore America's image as a powerful world power. An immensely popular president, Reagan restored the nation's confidence in the economy and the presidency, despite suffering some political scandals of his own.

Why did signs like this one provoke anxiety throughout the nation?

I AM
NOT
A CROOK

PRESIDENT
WHAT THE HECK ... vote Ford
JERRY FORD:
HE'S OK WITH ME ...I GUESS

ENDANGERED SPECIES

AMERICA

Downturn and Scandal

Americans enjoyed unprecedented prosperity in the 1950s and 1960s, and few expected the bubble to eventually burst. By the 1970s, however, periodic recessions returned, a shocking development for a nation that had grown accustomed to a steadily improving standard of living. The political repercussions were significant. Still reeling from the cultural and civil rights upheavals of the sixties, the nation's new economic problems exacerbated the growing feeling that the country was adrift. The economic downturn, partly caused by turmoil overseas, coincided with a decade-long crisis of presidential leadership that began when political scandal enveloped the Nixon White House.

An Ailing Economy

An ailing economy created the sense of a nation adrift by the 1970s. In the sixties Lyndon Johnson had tried to pay for both the Vietnam War (see Chapter 26) and the Great Society programs (see Chapter 27) without raising taxes. Heavy governmental spending created both a ballooning federal deficit and, by pumping so much cash into the economy, inflation. The end of the Vietnam War (see Chapter 26) added rising unemployment to the growing list of economic woes. Returning veterans entered a job market hit hard by the cancellation of government defense contracts that triggered massive layoffs in the industrial sector.

Americans also faced rising energy costs. The United States contained 6 percent of the world's population, but consumed nearly 40 percent of global energy resources. Due to increased U.S. reliance on Middle Eastern oil, the unending strife in the region affected the daily lives of Americans. The United States had offered Israel strong financial and moral support ever since the United Nations created a homeland for the Jewish people in 1947 by partitioning Palestine into Jewish and Palestinian areas. Israel claimed territory in Palestine as their ancestral land, a view supported by the United States, which also believed that the world owed the Jewish people some reparation for the horrors of the Holocaust. Arab nations viewed the creation of Israel completely differently. In their eyes the arrival of Jewish immigrants perpetuated the long history of hated Western colonization in the Middle East. A series of clashes between neighboring Arab nations and Israel ensued (detailed on **28.1**), and disputes over the fate of Palestinian refugees and Israeli land seizures continue to roil the region to this day.

Richard Nixon and subsequent presidents faced a thorny foreign policy dilemma in the Middle East. The U.S. government steadfastly supported Israel's right to exist, but given America's growing dependence on Middle Eastern oil exports, the United States could not afford to alienate oil-producing Arab nations. The Soviet push to form strong alliances in the Middle East also threatened to turn the oil-rich region into the new Cold War battlefield.

In 1973 Egypt and Syria (both armed with Soviet-provided weapons) attacked Israel on Yom Kippur (Judaism's holiest day) to regain territory lost to Israel in 1967. Nixon's decision to send military aid to Israel enraged the Arab world. In retaliation the **Organization of the Petroleum Exporting Countries (OPEC)**, an international consortium of oil-producing nations that regulates the price and quantity of oil exported to the world market, announced an oil embargo of the United States. By this point the United States depended on the Middle East for 12 percent of the oil consumed domestically. The embargo lasted five months, enough time to ravage the American economy (see image on page 843). OPEC finally lifted the embargo after Nixon persuaded Israel to withdraw from Egyptian and Syrian lands seized during the Yom Kippur War.

In 1974 the nation entered its worst recession since the Great Depression. In typical periods of recession and depression, high unemployment went hand in hand with declining prices and wages. The financial crisis of the mid-1970s was unique, however, because the economy suffered from both

How did domestic energy needs affect U.S. foreign policy?

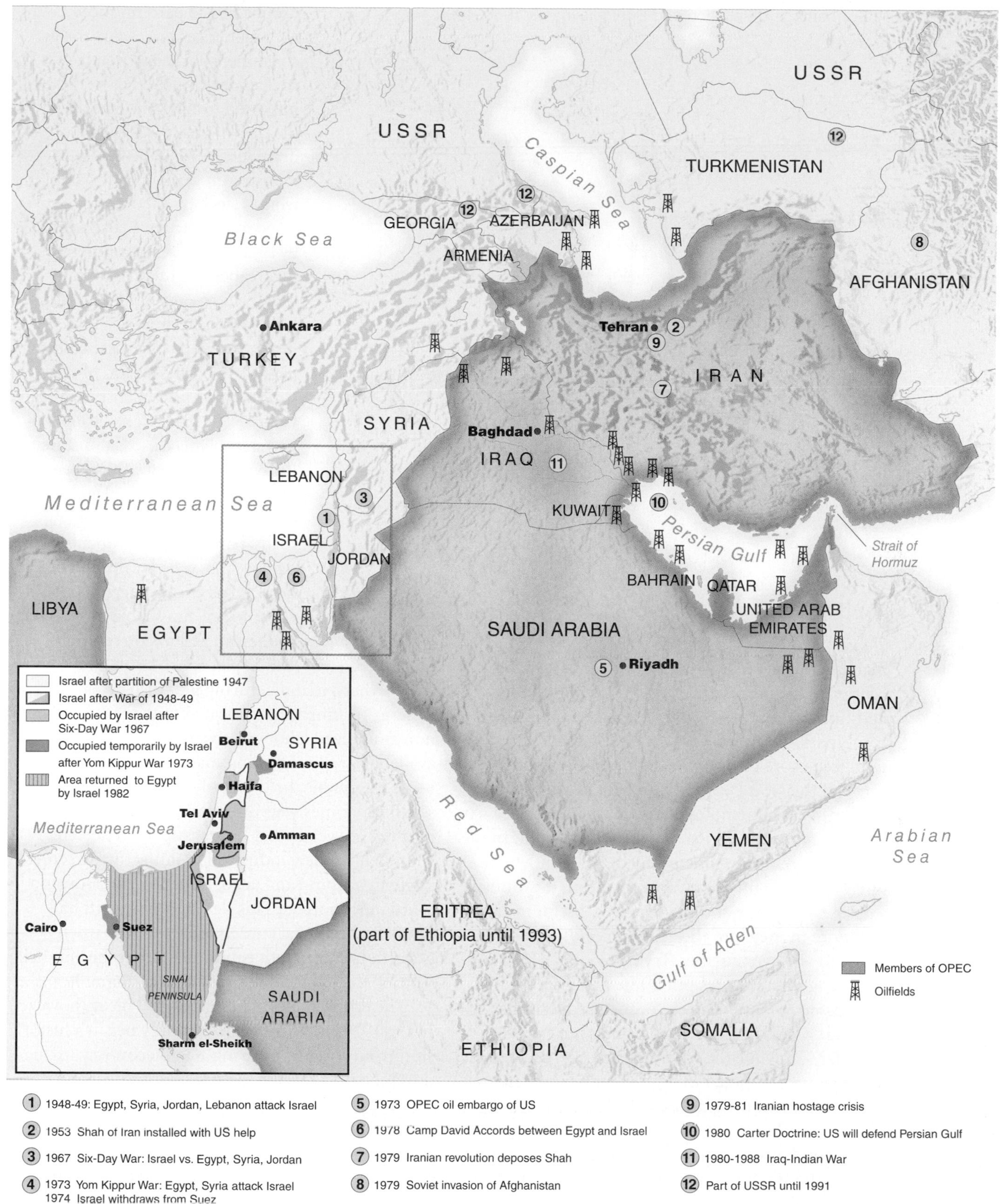

28.1 Middle East and Persian Gulf, 1947–1988
U.S. dependence on Middle-Eastern oil increased the importance of conflicts in this region for Americans.

Why did Israel's troubled relations with its neighbors concern the United States?

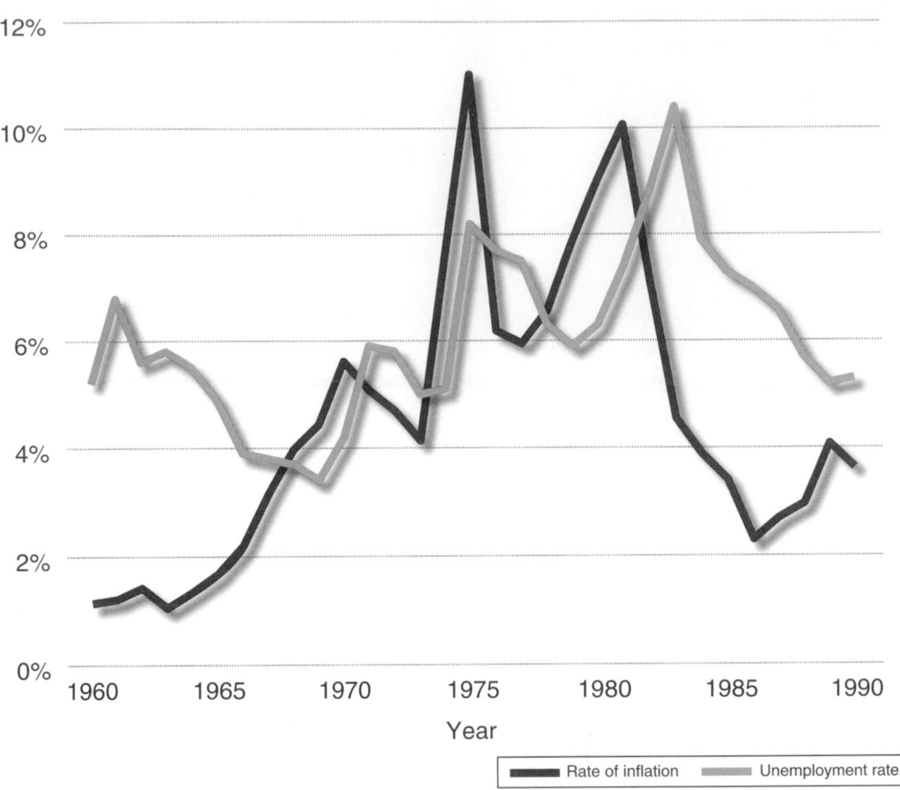

28.2 **Inflation and Unemployment, 1960–1990**
The combination of high unemployment and inflation created a phenomenon dubbed "stagflation" in the 1970s.

high unemployment and mounting inflation that kept prices rising, pictured on the graph *Inflation and Unemployment, 1960–1990* (**28.2**), an unusual combination dubbed "stagflation." In the 1930s pumping more federal money into the economy through the New Deal did not end the Depression, but it did ease unemployment and stabilize prices so farmers and businessmen could make a profit. In the 1970s trying to solve one problem, unemployment, often worsened inflation. Tax cuts meant to stimulate a business recovery and create more jobs, for instance, put more money into the economy and caused prices to rise even further. Trying to curtail inflation by raising interest rates put home mortgage and business loans out of reach for many Americans. Without access to credit the business recovery stalled. Meanwhile the federal deficit skyrocketed as tax revenue declined, but high spending on defense and entitlement programs like Social Security, welfare, and Medicaid continued.

The problem of rising unemployment had deep roots in the ailing auto and steel industries, long the backbone of the American economy. In 1970 the Big Three automakers, General Motors, Ford, and Chrysler, sold 89 percent of the cars marketed in the United States. Within ten years their market share dropped to 66 percent. Faced with higher gas prices, American consumers flocked to purchase smaller, more fuel-efficient cars imported from Japan. The decline in the steel industry was even more dramatic. In 1950 the U.S. steel industry produced nearly half of the world's steel. By 1980 that figure stood at 14 percent, a fall hastened by aggressive foreign competitors that reaped the rewards of investing heavily in research and innovation. New furnace technology, for instance, allowed Japanese competitors to produce a ton of steel for a third of the price it cost American factories. As American automobile and steel plants closed, a **Rust Belt** of decaying industrial cities appeared in the Midwest, places plagued with high unemployment, crumbling roads, bankrupt governments, and high welfare rolls. By the end of the decade, Americans increasingly chose to buy household appliances, textiles, and television sets manufactured abroad in places like Japan and Taiwan.

Northern manufacturing jobs also evaporated as American companies relocated to the South, where non-unionized labor costs were cheaper and newly available air-conditioning made the hot climate more hospitable. In 1960 only 18 percent of southern homes were air-conditioned; within the next twenty years, that figure rose to 73 percent. A "Sun Belt" of new industrial manufacturing centers stretching from San Diego, Phoenix, and Houston to Atlanta boomed. This demographic shift had important political consequences as well when grassroots conservativism took hold in the Sun Belt, shifting the electoral map in favor of Republicans.

The economic picture was not all bleak, however. In the 1970s the American economy began a historic shift from a manufacturing-based economy to one dominated by service-sector and high-tech jobs. No longer a leader in auto or steel manufacturing, America gained new preeminence in high-tech fields like aerospace, electronics, and eventually computers. In the 1890s Henry Ford had built his first car in his garage before going on to revolutionize the auto industry (see Chapter 21). In 1976 Steven Jobs and Stephen Wozniak, twenty-one and twenty-six years old respectively, followed in Ford's footsteps

What economic problems plagued the United States in the 1970s?

by constructing their first personal computer in a family garage. The pair founded Apple Computers a year later, envisioning a machine that would transform daily life. The first Apple logo showed the seventeenth-century mathematician Sir Isaac Newton sitting under the apple that supposedly fell and hit him on the head, inspiring him to develop his theory of universal gravitational pull that revolutionized modern scientific thought. The subsequent, permanent logo just retained the apple. In 1976 the claim that computers could transform the world as much as Newton's theories seemed ludicrous. Yet within a year the computer age got underway when Apple released the first home computer designed for the general public. The computer revolution received another boost when twenty-nine-year-old Bill Gates, the cofounder of an obscure start-up company called Microsoft, signed an agreement with International Business Machines (IBM) to provide operating software for its home computers. The 1980 deal made Gates a billionaire within two years.

Frustration at Home

Nixon initially embraced the same moderate course as President Dwight Eisenhower, with whom he had served as vice president from 1953 to 1961. Like Eisenhower, Nixon billed himself as a fiscal conservative who was willing to accept popular social welfare programs like Social Security and Medicare. As the economic outlook worsened, however, Nixon instituted wage and price controls in 1971 to curb inflation, the most drastic government intervention in the economy since World War II.

Conservative outrage over his fiscal policies had little effect on Nixon, who intended to stay in the political center. He hoped to bolster the moderate wing of the Republican party by turning the disgruntled southerners and northern white blue-collar and suburbanite Democrats who had voted for him in 1968 (see Chapter 27) into lifelong Republicans. Called "the silent majority" these voters rejected some, but not all, of the liberal vision. The silent majority disliked Great Society programs that primarily aided minorities, but they still subscribed to the New Deal orthodoxy that made the government responsible for ensuring permanent prosperity. Nixon's budget-cutting, therefore, targeted social-welfare programs for minorities and the poor, measures that partially appeased fiscal conservatives without touching New Deal programs like Social Security that former Democrats and many moderate Republicans viewed as sacrosanct. Nixon also tried unsuccessfully to reduce the jumble of laws and programs that made welfare assistance to the poor expensive to administer. His proposal to guarantee all Americans a minimum income drew criticisms from the poor who viewed the suggested amount of $1,600 ($8,500 in today's dollars) as too low and from conservatives who opposed redistributing income.

Nixon gained the loyalty of the silent majority by trying to tame the Supreme Court, which under the leadership of Chief Justice Earl Warren from 1953–1969 (see Chapter 27) had issued a series of controversial rulings on school prayer and desegregation. When Warren retired in 1969, Nixon appointed Warren Burger to replace him, believing that Burger would direct his colleagues to offer a more restrained interpretation of the Constitution than Warren had. Burger, however, had no intention of reducing the Court's commitment to school integration. The Court insisted that the North develop school busing programs to catch up with the South where, by 1971, 77 percent of black children attended school with white children.

The 1954 *Brown vs. Board of Education* decision outlawing segregated schools had set off waves of massive resistance throughout the South (see Chapter 26). In the 1970s opposition to court-mandated integration moved northward as members of the silent majority found their collective voice and took to the streets. Busing sent black and white children to schools outside their neighborhoods, generating tremendous opposition in northern, ethnic white enclaves where angry white parents objected to "big government" turning their children into "guinea pigs."

Boston became a hotbed of anti-busing fervor throughout the seventies. On April 5, 1976, two hundred white working-class Irish American teenagers assembled in downtown Boston to begin an adult-supervised anti-busing march. Joseph Rakes, one of the teenage protesters, who brought along his family's American flag, later recalled feeling "blind anger" at busing policies that were destroying his close-knit South Boston community. "They took half the guys and girls I grew up with and said, 'You're going to school on the other side of town.' Nobody understood it at 15," Rakes explained. When Ted Landsmark, an African American lawyer on his way to a meeting. crossed the protesters' path, the students pounced on him.

28.3 "The Soiling of Old Glory," 1976
The image of an anti-busing protester in Boston preparing to ram an African American lawyer with a flagpole underscored that deeply ingrained racial prejudices were more than just a southern problem.

Boston Herald news photographer Stanley Forman's Pulitzer-Prize winning photo "The Soiling of Old Glory" (**28.3**) showed Rakes poised to attack Landsmark with his flagstaff. In the photo Landsmark apparently struggles to free himself from the grip of another white man grabbing him from the rear. Contrary to the impression given by the photo, however, the man holding Landsmark was actually helping him to his feet after several white youths had thrown him to the ground and beaten him. Rakes never hit Landsmark with the flagstaff. Yet when Landsmark, a seasoned civil rights activist who had marched from Selma to Montgomery in 1965 (see Chapter 27), went to the hospital, he had doctors put a large bandage on his broken nose. Landsmark knew that the appearance of severe injuries would draw more press attention. The portrait of raw racial hatred captured in the photograph, and Landsmark's heavily bandaged face at a press conference the following day, shocked white Boston and encouraged the city's political leaders to initiate a sustained campaign to deescalate racial tensions. When the new school year began in September, *Time* magazine trumpeted the "Truce in Boston." By this time, however, the Supreme Court's stance had shifted, thanks to Nixon's more conservative appointments. After the court ruled that independent suburban school districts did not have to participate in inner-city busing programs, accelerated "white flight" to the suburbs created a core of all-black urban schools ringed by suburban white schools in Boston and in other cities nationwide.

The Watergate Scandal

By reshaping the political landscape, Nixon won a landslide victory against antiwar Democratic challenger George McGovern in 1972(see Chapter 27). Yet rather than ushering in an era of unchallenged Republican control, Nixon became embroiled in the **Watergate scandal**, an episode of presidential criminal

How does this photograph compare to the images of racially-inspired violence in the South seen in earlier chapters?

> "When the president does it that means that it is not illegal."
> RICHARD NIXON in 1977, defending his actions as necessary for national security

> "A government of laws was on the verge of becoming a government of one man."
> Attorney general ELLIOT RICHARDSON

wrong-doing that created a constitutional crisis, ended Nixon's political career, and helped the Democrats retake the White House in 1976.

On June 17, 1972, a night watchman caught five burglars breaking into the offices of the Democratic National Committee located in a Washington, D.C., building complex called Watergate. The plan, financed by Nixon's reelection campaign and approved by White House staffers, called for the burglars to fix a broken telephone wiretap installed during a previous break-in so the Nixon campaign could listen to Democratic phone calls. After Nixon vigorously disavowed any previous knowledge of the plot, the story slid off the front pages and Nixon easily won the 1972 election.

When the burglars went on trial in early 1973, however, one confessed to accepting a bribe to keep quiet about the White House's involvement in planning the break-in. In response the Justice Department and Senate launched two separate investigations. *Washington Post* reporters Carl Bernstein and Bob Woodward detailed the growing scandal in a series of articles based on information from a secret informant whom they identified only by the nickname, Deep Throat (recently revealed as William Mark Felt, the FBI's deputy director).

During one Senate committee hearing, Senator Howard Baker asked the key question: "What did the President know, and when did he know it?" Secret tapes that Nixon had made of all White House conversations promised to provide the answer. The showdown over gaining access to these tapes and what they eventually revealed transformed the Watergate burglary into a constitutional crisis over whether the president was above the law.

Two competing visions of presidential power emerged. Nixon refused to turn over the tapes to the Justice Department or Congress, claiming that the constitutionally protected right of executive privilege gave him the right to keep advice from counselors private. Investigators argued that the president had no constitutional right to withhold evidence of corruption or abuse of power. Nixon next tried to use his authority to control the investigation. When Archibald Cox, who headed the Justice Department investigation, secured a special court order for the tapes on Saturday, October 20, 1973, Nixon ordered his attorney general Elliot Richardson to fire Cox. Richardson refused and resigned, as did the deputy attorney general. The head of the Justice Department finally agreed to fire Cox. Public outrage greeted news of the "Saturday Night Massacre" and Nixon endured a steady cacophony of car horns sounding outside the White House day and night where protesters urged passing motorists to "Honk for Impeachment."

After much delay and controversy, Nixon finally turned over highly edited versions of his taped White House conversations, enraging his critics even further. Liberal political cartoonists lampooned Nixon as a tyrant and a crook (see *Images as History: Watergate through Political Cartoons*, page 850). In July 1974 the House Judiciary Committee issued several articles of impeachment against Nixon, charging him with obstruction of justice, abusing his presidential powers by ordering the CIA, FBI, and Internal Revenue Service (IRS) to harass his political enemies, and violating the Constitution by refusing to honor congressional subpoenas. In July the Supreme Court unanimously ruled that Nixon could not withhold information pertaining to his own potential criminal wrongdoing.

On August 6, 1974, Nixon finally released the remaining tapes, and the nation heard the president authorize a cover-up plan. On June 23, 1972, Nixon had instructed the CIA to tell the FBI to end its Watergate investigation to protect "national security." Two days later, on August 8, 1974, to avoid impeachment proceedings almost certain to remove him from office, Nixon became the first president in U.S. history to resign, and Vice President Gerald Ford became president. "Our long national nightmare is over," the new president assured the nation.

What competing views of presidential power emerged during the Watergate crisis?

Images as History

WATERGATE THROUGH POLITICAL CARTOONS

Political cartoons have been a mainstay of political debate in American society since the colonial era. "If the prime role of a free press is to serve as critic of government, cartooning is often the cutting edge of that criticism," stated Herb Block, who drew under the pseudonym Herblock. Political cartoonists like Herblock and Paul Conrad followed the long career of Richard Nixon from his early days as a Red-hunting congressman through his resignation as president. Their illustrations caricatured his face and shoulders, depicting a long beak-like nose, dark circles under his eyes, five o'clock shadow, and slumping shoulders.

Some conservative political cartoonists steadfastly defended Nixon, even as the Watergate scandal deepened. One caricature depicted the media as piranhas nipping at Nixon's heels as he tried to reach calmer waters, suggesting that he was the victim of a media witch hunt. When Nixon resigned, a Bert Whitman political cartoon in the *Phoenix Gazette* showed the president exiting center stage, leaving behind spotlights that illuminated his foreign policy successes such as ending the Vietnam War and improving relations with China and the Soviet Union. To these conservative commentators Nixon's record as a strong leader in the world mattered more than his transgressions at home.

The cartoon, Herblock later noted, "comments not only on his situation at the time, but on his veracity and honesty—without using any words other than his own."

Nixon struggles to pull the two ends of a severed tape together, a reference to the severely edited tapes of White House conversations that Nixon had released to Watergate investigators.

By depicting Nixon with the word "not" in his mouth, Herblock transformed Nixon's 1973 statement, "I'm not a crook" into "I am a crook" in this 1974 cartoon.

Herblock, *Nixon Hanging Between the Tapes, Washington Post*, 1974

Conrad satirized the president's paranoia by depicting Nixon as a despot sitting in the dark, creating pages of "enemies lists" (which eventually included thirty thousand people).

By 1973 the public knew that Nixon had instructed the FBI and IRS to harass people he considered political "enemies." The list included Paul Conrad, who drew political cartoons for the *Los Angeles Times*.

To prevent future presidents from using the FBI to spy on their domestic critics, Congress passed the Foreign Intelligence Surveillance Act (1978), which required secret judicial approval for any internal surveillance of U.S. citizens. After the terrorist attacks on September 11, 2001, Congress loosened these restrictions on monitoring Americans at home.

The cartoon title suggested that Nixon, rather than his opponents, destroyed his presidency.

His Own Worst Enemy

Paul Conrad, *His Own Worst Enemy, Los Angeles Times*, 1973

Are political cartoons an effective way to comment seriously on heady political issues of the day?

A Crisis of Presidential Leadership

The Watergate scandal and the lingering scars from the Vietnam War severely tested Americans' faith in the federal government. Congress moved to limit the powers of the president, and Americans remained divided over what direction to take in foreign policy post-Vietnam. The challenges were significant: dealing with renewed Soviet aggression, ensuring that support for Israel did not alienate oil-producing Arab nations, and fostering better relations with Central America.

A Weakened Presidency

When Gerald R. Ford became president, for the first time a man unelected as either president or vice president led the nation. Nixon had appointed Ford, then Republican House Minority leader, as his vice president in 1973, invoking the newly ratified Twenty-Fifth Amendment to fill the office after disgraced Vice President Spiro Agnew resigned for having accepted bribes while governor of Maryland. During his twenty-four years in Congress, Ford built a solid reputation as an honest, fiscally conservative Republican and won the respect of legislators in both parties. "I'm a Ford, not a Lincoln," he said when he became vice president, distancing himself from both the elite who bought luxurious Lincoln automobiles and the political genius of the nation's sixteenth president.

Ford's modesty compared favorably with Nixon's obsessive quest for power. Believing that the nation wanted to turn the page quickly on the Watergate scandal, Ford announced that he was giving Nixon a "full, free, and absolute pardon" for any illegal acts that he might have committed as president. A long trial and possibly imprisoning the former president would only prolong the nation's agony, he believed. The new president, however, had misread the public's mood. Ford's approval rating sank to 42 percent amid accusations that he was fulfilling the terms of a backroom deal made while Nixon was still president—a pardon in return for the presidency. Nixon went free but over seventy others were eventually convicted of Watergate-related crimes. Ford never fully recovered from this loss of public confidence in his leadership.

An emboldened Congress took steps to rein in presidential power. Nixon had accepted large donations from businessmen in return for favors and influence. In response Congress amended existing election laws in 1974 to create a Federal Election Commission (FEC) to monitor federal elections. Congress also set new limits on campaign contributions by individuals and official political organizations, and created a system of public funding for presidential elections. Opponents immediately challenged the constitutionality of these restrictions. In 1976 the Supreme Court struck down a provision that limited how much an individual could spend of his or her own money to win elected office, claiming that such restrictions (except for candidates who accepted matching federal funds) violated the First Amendment right to free speech. These efforts to curb influence-peddling through campaign donations had some unintended consequences. Political action committees (PACs), which represented private interest groups, such as labor, business, and retired people, were allowed to donate more money than individuals, giving them increased sway over the politicians they supported.

To repair public faith in the presidency, President Ford tried to shape a post-Vietnam foreign policy that restored America's image as an invincible superpower without reigniting fears that the nation was overextending its reach or behaving unethically. Damaging press exposés about how the United States was conducting the Cold War acquainted Americans with their government's willingness to support dictators in South America, the Middle East, and Africa who pledged friendship to the United States over the Soviet Union. In 1974 the *New York Times* exposed the CIA's covert involvement in the overthrow of Salvador Allende, the democratically elected Marxist president of Chile. With aid from CIA operatives, anti-Soviet and pro-American General Augusto Pinochet seized power and established a brutal sixteen-year dictatorship that tortured, imprisoned, and killed dissenters. Congressional investigations also exposed CIA plots to assassinate leftist leaders in the Congo, Cuba, and the Dominican Republic.

Hoping to regain public confidence in how the government was waging the Cold War, Ford issued an executive order that prohibited any government employee from engaging or conspiring in political assassination plots. Complaints over human rights violations influenced him less. Ford refused to cut off U.S. aid to Pinochet and supported the military junta that seized power in Argentina in 1976.

President Ford also tried to build on the foreign policy successes of the Nixon administration by retaining Henry Kissinger, a powerful cabinet member in the Nixon administration, as secretary of state and national security advisor. Ford initially accepted Kissinger's view that détente, the policy of using diplomatic, economic, and cultural contacts to improve U.S. relations with China and the Soviet Union, would promote global stability by lowering the risk of nuclear war. Consequently Ford abided by the terms of the 1972 **SALT I**, the first treaty between the Soviet Union and the United States that limited the deployment of intercontinental and submarine-launched ballistic missiles.

Nixon had also signed the 1972 Anti-Ballistic Missile (ABM) Treaty, in which the United States and the Soviet Union agreed to refrain from creating national missile defense systems. This treaty embraced the long-standing logic of **mutually assured destruction (MAD)**, the belief that the guarantee of a devastating nuclear counterattack would deter the United States and Soviet Union from ever employing their nuclear arsenals. By pledging to remain defenseless against a nuclear attack, each side hoped to dampen fears that it ever planned to launch a first strike against the other. Seeking further accommodation with the Soviet Union, Ford joined with the Soviet Union and thirty-one other nations to sign the 1975 Helsinki Accords, an agreement that accepted the current East-West balance of power on the continent.

Ford's moderate course invited pounding criticism from the left and the right, ultimately spelling the demise of détente. Conservative critics, led by California governor Ronald Reagan, lambasted Ford for "giving" away Eastern Europe to the Soviet Union. This objection resonated with liberal critics who shared conservatives' concerns about Soviet treatment of dissidents within the Soviet Union. Bipartisan objections also arose over letting the Soviets maintain a larger arsenal of long-range and submarine-launched nuclear missiles than that of the United States. Over time Ford began to share bipartisan concerns that the Soviet Union was untrustworthy. Certain that the Soviets were continuing to build long-range intercontinental ballistic missiles, Ford heeded the advice of his hawkish defense secretary Donald Rumsfeld and poured money into the American missile program.

The Leadership Crisis Continues: Carter in the White House

As the 1976 presidential contest approached, Ford faced a strong challenge in the Republican primaries from sixty-five-year-old Ronald Reagan, a former film actor who had just finished his second term as governor of California. Reagan's father had kept the family afloat during the Depression by working for the Works Project Administration, but some key adult experiences gradually transformed this son of the New Deal into a staunch conservative. During the Second Red Scare, Reagan became concerned about communism's influence in Hollywood, and he objected to paying nearly 70 percent of his film earnings in taxes. In 1962 he joined the Republican Party, enthusiastically supported Barry Goldwater in 1964, and became governor of California in 1966. In a breathtakingly close vote, Ford prevailed at the Republican presidential nominating convention, but Reagan vowed to "rise and fight again."

> "Don't Vote, It Only Encourages Them."
>
> A bumper sticker that reflected widespread voter apathy in the 1976 presidential election

Ford's Democratic opponent was former Georgia governor Jimmy Carter, a surprise choice who was virtually unknown to most Americans when he declared his candidacy. Carter's political ambitions even surprised his own mother. When Carter told her that he was running for president, she replied, "President of what?" Carter's strong Baptist faith and the image he cultivated of an uncorrupted Washington outsider who could restore honor to the White House attracted conservative Democrats who had voted for Nixon. "I will never lie to you," Carter assured voters.

Neither candidate generated much enthusiasm during the campaign. The made-up campaign

What competing visions arose over Nixon's efforts to reshape U.S.-Soviet relations?

slogans in this political cartoon (**28.4**)—"Gerald R. Ford: a perfectly adequate guy for the seventies" and "Oh . . . Why Not? Ford in '76"—captured the general apathy surrounding Ford's campaign. An equally lackluster campaigner, Carter benefited mostly from the nation's ongoing economic woes, residual anger over Watergate and Ford's misstep in pardoning Nixon. In winning the presidency Carter managed to temporarily reassemble the New Deal coalition of white southerners, urban blacks, and union members to carry the election by 297 to 240 electoral votes. Fewer than 55 percent of the electorate even bothered to vote, however, a historic low and disappointing follow-up to the 1960s, when countless civil rights activists had put their lives on the line to secure this right.

28.4 ***Do You Get the Feeling This Campaign Lacks a Little Something?*** Like Carter, Ford failed to generate much enthusiasm among the electorate in the 1976 presidential election.

On his inauguration day Carter chose to walk from his swearing in on the Capitol steps to the White House with his wife and family rather than ride in a limousine, the type of populist gesture that he frequently made as president. Ford had pardoned Nixon in an attempt to heal wounds quickly. Carter tried to remove another source of festering discord by immediately pardoning ten thousand Vietnam War draft resisters, many of whom had fled to Canada during the war, a move that enraged conservatives but earned him the gratitude of liberal Democrats. Seeking to solidify liberal Democratic support, Carter moved quickly to build on the liberal vision of Democrats John F. Kennedy and Lyndon B. Johnson by creating the Department of Education and successfully working with Congress to establish a "Superfund" to clean up the nation's most polluted areas. He also appointed the most women and minorities to federal office of any previous president.

Carter's outsider status and his tendency toward self-righteousness, however, soon hampered his presidency. A hard worker who rose early and went to bed late, he pored over every memorandum, even going so far as to personally handle requests to use the White House tennis court during his first six months in office. The fiscally conservative Carter had strong philosophical differences with many liberal Democrats who emphasized the advantages of deficit-spending over balancing the federal budget. Carter believed that too much government regulation was hampering the business recovery, while liberal Democrats felt certain that regulation was necessary to protect the public. The president eventually prevailed, convincing Congress to deregulate the trucking, communication, and airline industries.

Identifying rising oil costs as the linchpin of the nation's economic woes, Carter urged the nation to consume less oil in a 1977 television address that recalled Franklin D. Roosevelt's famous fireside chats. As a fire crackled behind him, Carter, dressed in a cardigan sweater, called the energy crisis "the moral equivalent of war," which was the title of a famous essay by nineteenth-century philosopher William James. To discourage consumption Carter proposed ending the price controls that kept oil and gas prices low and imposing higher federal taxes on gasoline. To prevent price-gouging he also wanted oil and gas companies to pay higher taxes on their profits. Carter tried to craft a vision that would appeal to both laissez-faire adherents who liked the idea of lifting price controls so the market determined the price of oil and liberals who believed in using government regulation to rein in corporate profits and protect the environment. The resulting energy law in 1978 offered a compromise between these conflicting visions. The law lifted price controls, raised the sales taxes on gas-guzzling cars, and offered tax incentives for using alternative energy sources such as coal and solar heating. It did not, however, include a windfall profits tax on oil and gas company profits.

The country soon felt the effects of lifting price controls without also raising taxes on oil and gas company profits. In 1979 OPEC raised prices four times in five months, and a new war between Iran and Iraq created oil shortages. Images of motorists waiting for hours in line to buy gas, last seen during the 1973 oil embargo (see the chapter opener on page 843), once again dominated the news. The crisis reached its zenith on June 13, 1979, when over half of the nation's service stations ran out of gas. Meanwhile Exxon, an American company that imported oil from overseas, announced first quarter earnings of $1.9 billion in 1980, a record profit by any American corporation.

Carter renewed his call for a windfall-profit tax on oil and gas companies, hoping to use this revenue to fund public transportation, develop alternative energy sources, and help the poor pay for heating. Trying once again to stimulate public interest in energy conservation, Carter took to the airwaves to deliver an address soon dubbed the "malaise speech." America, he lamented, was a nation enmeshed in a moral and spiritual crisis. The nation had gone from one that celebrated "hard work, strong families, close-knit communities, and our faith in God" to one that worshiped "self-indulgence and consumption." Carter's call for Americans to "seize control again of our national destiny" fell flat, arousing only resentment over his presidential sermonizing.

These two political cartoons, both drawn in 1980, encapsulated competing notions of where blame for the energy crisis lay. Bob Taylor, drawing for the *Dallas Times Herald*, focused on the nation's insatiable appetite for oil (**28.5**). He portrayed Uncle Sam as a drug addict willing to pay any price for his next fix of oil. "Hey, man . . . like I don't CARE what it's costing . . . I need it," a disheveled and stony-eyed Uncle Sam says as he prepares to inject a barrel of oil into his vein. By contrast John Milt Morris's "Profit-sharing plan!" indicted OPEC and American oil companies for price-gouging, viewing the consumer as a victim of their conspiracy to empty his pockets (**28.6**). A sign posted outside one gas station presented a third view by proclaiming "Higher prices, More Sass, Bad President, Out of Gas," putting the blame squarely on Carter's shoulders.

28.5 ***Hey, man . . . like I don't CARE what it's costing me***
This political caricature blamed Americans' oil addiction for the nation's ongoing energy problems.

28.6 ***Profit Sharing Plan***
Expressing more sympathy for the average consumer, this caricature accused oil-producing nations and oil companies of creating artificial shortages to gouge consumers.

What different opinions surfaced about the root of America's energy problems?

New Paths in Foreign Affairs

Carter had more success in foreign affairs than in domestic matters, although not without encountering serious opposition to his Wilsonian-inspired vision of America championing democracy worldwide. Constant meddling in the domestic affairs of neighboring nations, he noted, had earned the United States the reputation as an imperial exploiter throughout Latin America. Liberal Democrats rejoiced when Carter resolved to make human rights and the spreading of democracy the centerpieces of his foreign policy.

The president's first major achievement was consistent with his desire to forge a new path in American diplomatic relations. Making amends for past American wrongdoing (see Chapter 19), Carter negotiated a treaty that returned the Panama Canal to Panama in 2000. The United States had controlled the Canal Zone since 1903, but by the 1970s America's bigger submarines and ships did not fit through the canal, reducing the waterway's importance to national security and the economy. Three previous presidents had recognized these facts and opened negotiations, but Carter pushed harder than his predecessors to seal the deal and won Senate ratification for the agreement in 1978.

Giving up control of the Panama Canal failed to dramatically improve relations between the United States and Latin America. Overtures to normalize relations with the Communist Cuban dictator Fidel Castro went nowhere. Carter also faced a severe test in Nicaragua, where civil war pitted the anti-communist dictator Anastasio Somoza against the Cuban-supported Sandinista rebel force. When the Sandinistas prevailed Carter offered them economic aid in the vain hope that he could dissuade them from creating a Cuban-like authoritarian communist state. Turning to Asia, Carter continued along the path forged by Nixon and established diplomatic relations with the People's Republic of China in 1979. This decision angered conservatives who viewed Taiwan, where the nationalist government had established residence after the Communist takeover of the mainland in 1949, as the rightful government of China. "To the Communists and those others who are hostile to our country," Reagan fumed, "President Carter and his supporters in the Congress seem like Santa Claus. They have given the Panama Canal away, abandoned Taiwan to the Red Chinese, and they're negotiating a SALT II treaty (with the Soviets) that could very well make this nation NUMBER TWO."

> "An inordinate fear of communism has led us to embrace any dictator who joined in our fear."
>
> President JIMMY CARTER, making human rights a guiding principle in U.S. foreign policy

Ignoring these criticisms Carter signed the SALT II pact in June 1979, an agreement that capped missiles and bombers on each side. But as Reagan's comments revealed, American disaffection with détente ran deep. In the mid-late 1970s, Soviet-backed regimes took control of Angola, Somalia, Ethiopia, and Afghanistan, confirming skeptics' fears that détente had strengthened the enemy. Additional signs of Moscow's aggressive intentions came in 1977 when the Soviets began aiming new, highly accurate intermediate-range missiles (SS-20s) at Western Europe. Carter responded to this threat by securing the North Atlantic Treaty Organization's (NATO) authorization to install Pershing II missiles in Western Europe, missiles that could reach Moscow in ten minutes.

Strained Soviet-American relations took another hit when the Soviet Union invaded Afghanistan in December 1979 to prop up its faltering Marxist government. The Soviets were eager to keep a friendly regime in power along their border, but the United States feared their ambitions might stretch into the oil-rich Middle East. Calling the invasion "the most serious threat to peace since the Second World War," Carter announced the Carter Doctrine, a declaration that the United States would use armed forces to stop any outside power from making inroads into the Persian Gulf region. He withdrew the SALT II arms limitation treaty from the Senate, increased defense spending, cut off shipments of grain and technology to the Soviet Union, and announced that the United States would boycott the summer Olympics in Moscow. The Carter administration also sent aid to Muslim fundamentalist rebels battling the Soviets in Afghanistan, whose ranks included the Saudi-born Islamic militant Osama bin Laden. A wealthy recent college graduate dedicated to establishing an Islamic state in Afghanistan, bin Laden would later found al-Qaeda, an Islamic fundamentalist terrorist organization.

The Cold War had long held the attention of American presidents. The United States was just learning, however, to take conflicts in the Middle East as seriously. Carter hoped to remove one source

Did Carter's dealings with the Soviet Union continue or undo initiatives undertaken by Nixon and Ford?

of festering tension by negotiating an end to hostilities between Israel and Egypt. In 1978 Carter invited Egyptian leader Anwar El Sadat and Israeli leader Menachem Begin to Camp David, a presidential mountain retreat in Maryland 60 miles north of the White House. Thirteen days of tense negotiations ended with the **Camp David Accords**. Israel agreed to give the Sinai Peninsula back to Egypt in 1982 (see 28.1). In return Egypt became the first Arab state to recognize Israel's right to exist. The United States rewarded each side with pledges of substantial military aid, support that continues to this day. Befriending Egypt neutralized the only credible military threat to Israeli security and brought a previous Soviet ally into the American fold, strengthening the American position in the Middle East.

If the Middle East gave Carter his greatest diplomatic victory, it also provided the low point of his presidency. In 1953 the United States helped overthrow the left-leaning Iranian government and installed the reliably anticommunist Shah of Iran to ensure American access to Iranian oil. In 1979 radical Islamists overthrew the Shah, who fled the country. An Islamic cleric and revolutionary, the Ayatollah Ruhollah Khomeini, became the head of the world's first radical Islamist government. Khomeini's intense dark eyes, long snowy beard, and flowing robes made him appear dark and dangerous to Americans, who recoiled at his ferocious denunciations of the United States as "the Great Satan."

In October 1979 Carter made a fateful decision when he reluctantly agreed to let the ailing Shah of Iran, who was living in Mexico, into the United States for medical treatment. If the United States "turned our backs on the fallen Shah, it would be a signal to the world that the U.S. is a fair-weather friend," National Security Advisor Zbigniew Brzezinski told Carter. At 3:00 a.m. on November 4, 1979, the State Department received a telephone call from panicked officials in the American embassy in Teheran, the capital of Iran, reporting that a mob of Iranian university students had broken into the compound. The students proceeded to take embassy employees hostage. Khomeini had not ordered the hostage-taking, but he supported the students' demands that the United States return the Shah and his fortune to Iran to secure their release. Khomeini's government, worried that the United States might try to organize a counterrevolution and return the Shah to power, wanted him in hand.

The **Iranian hostage crisis** became the defining event in Carter's presidency as Iranian revolutionaries held fifty-two Americans captive for 444 days. The media coverage was unprecedented for a single event, and most reporters viewed the crisis as a humiliating blow to America's honor. ABC news created a late-night show, "Nightline," that gave constant updates on "America Held Hostage" and repeatedly showed film footage of Iranian crowds chanting "Death to America" and the blindfolded captives. Public frustration with Carter's inability to resolve the crisis caused his approval ratings to sink to 28 percent.

How to proceed was not clear, however, and Carter's key advisors offered him a competing set of recommendations. Secretary of State Cyrus Vance focused on saving the hostages' lives and argued that the United States needed to negotiate patiently, no matter how long it took. National Security Advisor Brzezinski worried more about protecting America's image as a global superpower. Brzezinski felt that the longer the crisis lasted, the weaker America appeared to the rest of the world, emboldening America's enemies to strike. The Soviet invasion of Afghanistan a month into the hostage crisis seemingly corroborated Brzezinski's vision. *Choices and Consequences: Ending the Iranian Hostage Crisis* explores Carter's options and the repercussions of his decision to try to rescue the hostages.

> "The release of the American hostages had become almost an obsession with me."
>
> President JIMMY CARTER comments on the Iran hostage crisis in his memoirs

Five months later Iraq invaded Iran, and Khomeini finally decided to negotiate in earnest. Iran could no longer afford its diplomatic isolation, needing to reestablish its global trading networks to fend off the invasion by Iraqi leader Saddam Hussein. After months of negotiations the United States agreed to give Iran $7.9 billion (the estimated value of the Shah's holdings in the United States) and pledged not to interfere in Iranian domestic affairs. Carter hoped to deliver the good news to the American people that the hostages were coming home before he left office on January 20, 1981. Instead, Khomeini waited until a few minutes after the new president Ronald Reagan was sworn into office to release the hostages, denying Carter any final moment of triumph.

Choices and Consequences

ENDING THE IRANIAN HOSTAGE CRISIS

When Iranian students stormed the U.S. Embassy and took Americans hostage in 1979, President Carter faced a choice over whether to follow the advice of Secretary of State Vance, who recommended patient negotiations, or National Security Advisor Brzezinski, who favored using military force to end the crisis. For five months Carter brokered a compromise between these two positions by freezing Iranian financial assets in the United States, engaging in secret negotiations, and beefing up the American naval presence in the Arabian Sea. Mounting public frustration as Carter began his 1980 reelection bid, along with concern that American inaction had encouraged the Soviet Union to invade Afghanistan, increased the pressure on Carter for decisive action.

Choices

1. Wait for Iran to tire of its diplomatic isolation, and then negotiate the hostages' release without alienating the rest of the Arab world.

2. Make a show of strength by bombing Iranian oil refineries and military bases and by mining harbors.

3. Use Special Forces to rescue the hostages.

Decision

When an Iranian negotiator told the administration that a possible diplomatic resolution was months away, Carter decided to act. In April, 1980, while Vance was out of town, Carter authorized a rescue mission by Special Forces.

Consequences

Swirling desert sands and a collision between American aircraft doomed the rescue mission in its first stages, further humiliating the United States. Vance immediately resigned and in July the Shah died in Egypt, ending the question of returning him to Iran. When Iraq invaded Iran in September, seeking oil-rich territory, Khomeini decided to end Iran's diplomatic isolation. Winning concessions from the United States, Iran released the hostages on January 20, 1981, the day that Ronald Reagan was inaugurated president.

"All the News That's Fit to Print"

The New York Times

LATE CITY EDITION

NEW YORK, WEDNESDAY, JANUARY 21, 1981 — 25 CENTS

REAGAN TAKES OATH AS 40TH PRESIDENT; PROMISES AN 'ERA OF NATIONAL RENEWAL'

MINUTES LATER, 52 U.S. HOSTAGES IN IRAN FLY TO FREEDOM AFTER 444-DAY ORDEAL

'ALIVE, WELL AND FREE'

Captives Taken to Algiers and Then Germany — Final Pact Complex

Teheran Captors Call Out Insults As the 52 Leave

FREEZE SET ON HIRING

Californian Stresses Need to Restrict Government and Buoy Economy

Anxious Families and Towns Erupt Into Long-Postponed Celebrations

More News And Pictures

Headline Announcing the Hostage Release, 1981

Continuing Controversies

How important was the hostage crisis for the United States in the long-term?

Some say it was very important. The hostages' prolonged captivity branded Carter as inept and contributed to his re-election loss. To gain revenge against Iran, the United States supported the Iraqi leader Saddam Hussein's regime during his ten-year war with Iran, once again using a repressive Middle Eastern dictator to advance American interests in the region. The hostage crisis also created a negative image of Islam in the United States that future Islamic terrorist attacks reinforced. The crisis was not so important, others counter, rejecting it as a major reason for Reagan's victory. In the 1980s the failed Soviet invasion of Afghanistan, the Camp David Accords, and using a secular Iraq to contain Iranian influence protected U.S. economic interests in the region, diminishing the long-term significance of the hostage crisis.

What larger significance did Carter's advisors attach to the Iranian hostage crisis?

The Rights Revolution

The nation's foreign policy problems revealed that that turbulence overseas did not end with the Vietnam War. Feminists and gay activists carried the 1960s' rights revolution into the 1970s and 1980s, demanding equal opportunities and legal protections against discrimination. These movements struck at the heart of gender identity in American society, arousing conservative fears that traditional values were disappearing. The environmental movement, seeking to reverse the toll of industrial pollution on the nation's natural habitats, had more success than the women's and gay rights movements uniting Americans around a common cause.

The Equal Rights Amendment and Abortion Controversies

Feminist political demands received unprecedented attention in the seventies. Hoping to eradicate gender discrimination and sexual inequality at the workplace, feminist organizations lobbied for equal pay for equal work, ending sexual harassment, affordable day care, and paid maternity leave. These bread-and-butter issues became even more pressing as the economic downturn of the 1970s forced more women into the workplace. The chart *Women and Work, 1950–1990* (**28.7**) shows the steady increase in the percentage of women who worked outside the home over the second half of the twentieth century. In 1950, 32.5 percent of white women and 41.5 percent of black women worked, rising to 58.8 percent and 59.1 percent by 1980. Between 1950 and 1970 the percentage of white married women holding jobs nearly doubled from 22.3 percent to 41.8 percent, compared with 33.7 percent and 53.5 percent of black married women over the same period.

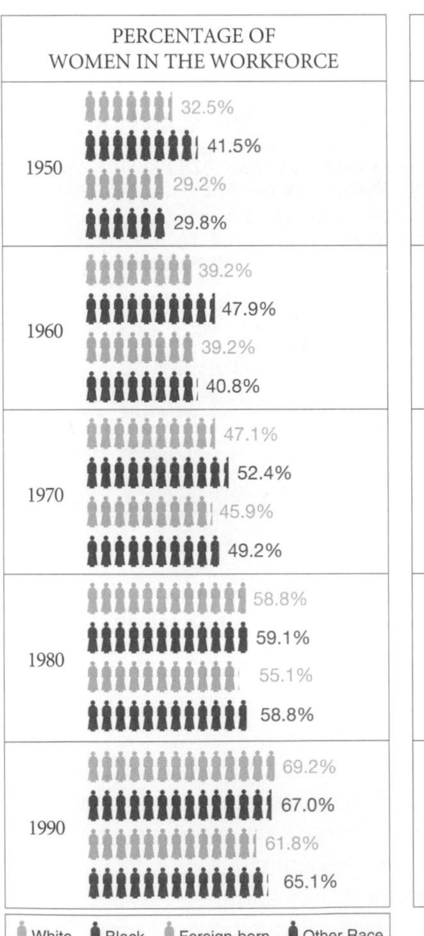

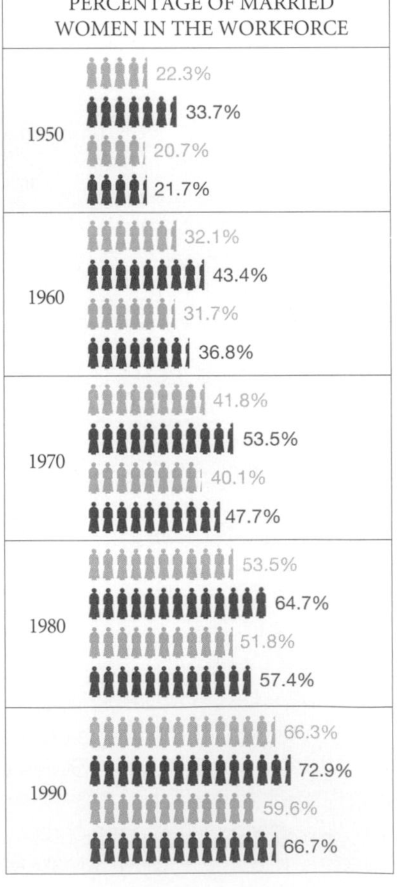

28.7 Women and Work, 1950–1990
As more women entered the workforce, combating discrimination in the workplace became a major issue for the women's movement.

The feminist movement, however, faced considerable challenges convincing these working women that feminism provided the answer to the problems they faced balancing work and home life or advancing in the workplace. The press, one activist noted, portrayed the feminist as "a total weirdo—bra-burner, man-hater, lesbian, sickie!" —exaggerated stereotypes that threatened the movement's growth. Many women proved reluctant to publicly identify themselves as feminists even if they privately supported the women's movement goals, fearing social stigmatization as unfeminine. Divisions within the women's movement created another major obstacle. Poor minority women often saw racial and ethnic prejudice as bigger obstacles to their economic advancement than gender discrimination, and regarded white, upper-middle-class feminists with suspicion. Feminism, in the words of one black woman, was "basically a family quarrel between White women and White men." Divisions between radicals and moderate feminists (see Chapter 27) also prevented women from speaking with one voice.

Despite negative media portrayals and problems attracting working-class women, the feminist

What were the social, cultural, and political consequences of shifting trends in the female workforce?

movement enjoyed a wave of success in the early seventies. Cities established shelters for battered women and rape-crisis centers. Feminist campaigning led to the passage of Title IX of the 1972 Education Act, prohibiting gender discrimination in education. This law revolutionized high school and college sports by forcing administrators to create more teams and scholarships for female students. Congress also passed the **Equal Rights Amendment** (**ERA**) in 1972, a proposal that congressional supporters had introduced regularly since 1923 that stated, "equality of rights under the law shall not be denied or abridged by the United States or by any State on account of sex." Within three years thirty-four of the thirty-eight states needed for ratification of the ERA had approved the measure, endorsing the feminist vision that the ERA guaranteed complete equality between women and men.

This avalanche of change outraged cultural conservatives who charged that the ERA would hasten the destruction of the American family. Phyllis Schlafly, a conservative Illinois lawyer with six children, led the anti-ERA crusade. Catapulting into the national spotlight, Schlafly helped forge the coalition among Catholics, southerners, antifeminists, religious fundamentalists, and fiscal conservatives that pushed the Republican Party to the right throughout the decade. Feminists branded Schlafly a hypocrite, pointing out that she was a well-educated woman who had enjoyed a satisfying career in Republican politics before spearheading the anti-ERA campaign. "She's an extremely liberated woman," asserted Karen DeCrow, the president of the feminist National Organization for Women. *Competing Visions: Defining the Ideal Woman* (page 860) further explores the spirited debate over female gender identity in the seventies. Schlafly's antifeminist message resonated in the southern and mountain states, areas without strong local feminist organizations to offer a competing view of how gender discrimination adversely affected women in the workplace. In the end the anti-ERA forces prevailed. The ERA remained three states short when the deadline for approving the measure came in 1982, the first of many conservative political victories to come in the 1980s.

The rancor surrounding the issue of legalized abortion, however, soon far surpassed the barbs exchanged over the Equal Rights Amendment. Between 700,000 and 800,000 women a year sought illegal abortions, and botched procedures by incompetent practitioners working in unsanitary conditions killed 2,000–3,000 patients annually.

28.8 *The Illegal Operation,* 1962
Edward Kienholz's sculpture of a back-alley abortionist's office evoked pain and fear to protest the inability of women to secure a safe and legal abortion in the United States.
[*Source:* Edward Kienholz, "The Illegal Operation". 1962. Sculptural installation of shopping cart, wooden stool, concrete, pots, blanket, hooked rug, medical equipment, polyester resin, pigment, etc. Dimensions: 59 x 48 x 54 in. Los Angeles County Museum of Art. Photograph © 2009 Museum Associates/LACMA]

Edward Kienholz's 1962 sculpture *The Illegal Operation* evoked the gruesomeness of visiting a back-alley abortionist (**28.8**). In the sculpture a lifeless, torn cushion (representing a woman's body) sits in a metallic chair above a white bowl filled with stained rags and crude kitchen utensils. The small stool in the foreground beckons viewers to take a seat and confront the realities of this secret butchery. The sculpture provoked little controversy when it appeared as part of a 1966 exhibition in Los Angeles. By then many Californians supported changing what the *Los Angeles Times* called "Our Archaic Abortion Law" that only allowed a woman to end a pregnancy if her life was in danger.

Bending to the popular will, then-California governor Ronald Reagan reluctantly signed a bipartisan-supported bill in 1967 that let women

What symbols does Kleinholz incorporate into his sculpture to present his view on abortion?

Competing Visions

DEFINING THE IDEAL WOMAN

What did it mean to be a woman? Cultural conservatives answered "wife and mother"; feminists disagreed. In 1972 journalist Gloria Steinem, founder of *Ms.*, a popular feminist magazine, argued that both women and men would be happier once freed from the straitjacket of culturally constructed gender roles. Conservative activist Phyllis Schlafly countered that gender identity was rooted in biology.

Gloria Steinem argued that women's liberation would benefit men as well as women.

I don't think most women want to pick up briefcases and march off to meaningless, depersonalized jobs.... We want to liberate men from those inhuman roles as well. We want to share the work and responsibility, and to have men share equal responsibility for the children. Probably the ultimate myth is that children must have fulltime mothers, and that liberated women make bad ones. The truth is that most American children seem to be suffering from too much mother and too little father.

Women now spend more time with their homes and families than in any other past or present society we know about. To get back to the sanity of the agrarian or joint family system, we need free universal day care. With that aid, as in Scandinavian countries, and with laws that permit women equal work and equal pay, man will be relieved of his role as sole breadwinner and stranger to his own children.

No more alimony. Fewer boring wives. Fewer childlike wives.... No more wives who fall apart with the first wrinkle because they've been taught that their total identity depends on their outsides. No more responsibility for another adult human being who has never been told she is responsible for her own life, and who sooner or later says some version of, "If I hadn't married you, I could have been a star." Women's Liberation really is Men's Liberation, too. ... Colleague marriages, such as young people have now, with both partners going to law-school or the Peace Corps together, ... Communes; marriages that are valid for the child-rearing years only, there are many possibilities.

The point is that Women's Liberation is not destroying the American family. It is trying to build a human compassionate alternative out of its ruins.

Gloria Steinem

Phyllis Schlafly claimed that the "Positive Woman" embraced her distinctly female role.

The first requirement for the acquisition of power by the Positive Woman is to understand the differences between men and women.... She rejoices in the creative capability within her body and the power potential of her mind and spirit. She understands that men and women are different, and that those very differences provide the key to her success as a person and fulfillment as a woman.

The women's liberationist, on the other hand, is imprisoned by her own negative view of herself and of her place in the world around her.... Women must be made equal to men in their ability *not* to become pregnant and *not* to be expected to care for babies they may bring into the world. This is why women's liberationists are compulsively involved in the drive to make abortion and childcare centers for all women, regardless of religion or income, both socially acceptable, and government-financed.... The Positive Woman looks upon her femaleness and her fertility as part of her purpose, her potential, and her power. She rejoices that she has a capability for creativity that men can never have ...

A Positive Woman cannot defeat a man in a wrestling match or boxing match, but she can motivate him, inspire him, encourage him, teach him, restrain him, reward him, and have power over him that he can never achieve over her with all his muscle.... The overriding psychological need of a woman is to love something alive. A baby fulfills this need in the lives of most women. If a baby is not available to fill that need, women search for a baby-substitute. This is the reason why women have traditionally gone into teaching and nursing careers. They are doing what comes naturally to the female psyche.

Phyllis Schlafly

Do Steinem and Schlafly offer realistic or clichéd depictions of women's lives, or a combination of both?

terminate pregnancies in cases of rape and incest and fetuses with severe physical and mental defects, a decision he later called a mistake. Texas, however, still only allowed abortions if a pregnancy jeopardized a woman's life. Feminists felt that women, not male doctors, should have the right to make medical decisions about their own bodies. In 1970 Norma McCorvey, an unmarried, poor, pregnant twenty-five-year-old, sued the state of Texas under the pseudonym Jane Roe claiming that she had the right to a legal and safe abortion based on her constitutional "right to privacy." The Supreme Court dealt the feminist movement a stunning victory when it legalized abortion in its 1973 ***Roe v. Wade*** decision. The ruling came too late for McCorvey, who gave birth to a baby girl and gave her up for adoption as the case moved through the courts.

In rendering the *Roe v. Wade* decision, the Supreme Court ruled that the "right to privacy . . . is broad enough to encompass a woman's decision whether or not to terminate her pregnancy." The Court decision prohibited states from criminalizing abortion in the first trimester, but allowed states to regulate abortion in the second trimester and prohibit it during the third trimester when a fetus became viable. The Court, however, sidestepped a key question that would provoke much future controversy. "We need not resolve the difficult question of when life begins," the Court asserted in granting women the legal right to an abortion. Critics argued that the Court had invented a right to privacy that did not exist in the Constitution. Supporters countered that court decisions over the last hundred years had firmly established this right. The debate soon seeped into national politics when the Democrats assumed the mantle of the party dedicated to maintaining a woman's right to choose an abortion and the Republicans became predominantly against the right to abortion, a position that came to be known as "pro-life."

The vocabulary embraced by each side in the abortion debate revealed competing visions of what abortion meant. Supporters of legalized abortion called themselves "pro-choice," a label encapsulating their view that abortion was a question of personal liberty. In contrast "pro-life" forces believed that human life began at conception (not when a fetus was viable outside the womb); they therefore viewed abortion as tantamount to murder. Both sides employed the language of rights, the "rights of women" (pro-choice usage) squaring off against those of "unborn children" (pro-life term). The activist women facing off in this debate had very different life experiences and conceptions of motherhood. Pro-life activists had often built their lives around children and the home, and were outraged by their suspicion that pro-choice women had abortions "as a matter of convenience." Pro-choice activists often wanted careers as well as children and refused to allow biology to dictate their life choices.

McCorvey eventually changed her mind about abortion. Twenty years after *Roe v. Wade*, she became a born-again Christian who joined the anti-abortion crusade. Her reversal illustrated the growing momentum of the pro-life movement, which used images of children, like the one affixed to the sign of this 1979 pro-life demonstrator protesting in Washington, D.C. (**28.9**), to emphasize the rights of children. In the twenty-first century, the pro-life movement took advantage of new ultrasound portraits of fetuses in the womb that showed beating hearts to underscore their argument that life began at conception. Unable to overturn the *Roe* directly, pro-life activists secured a ban on federal funding for abortions. Some states also passed laws that required parental notification when minors sought abortions.

28.9 Pro-life Protest, 1979 Pro-life demonstrators who opposed legalized abortion put the focus on the right of unborn children to have a life rather than the right of women to control their own bodies.

What different visions separated the pro-life and pro-choice camps?

Gay Rights

The rights revolution also encompassed the gay and lesbian subcultures that existed in the shadows of mainstream society until the 1960s. Unlike blacks, women, and other minority groups, gay Americans did not have a long history of organizing to defend their rights. Heterosexual Americans uniformly disparaged gays as deviant and morally reprehensible. The American Psychiatric Association categorized homosexuality as a "mental disorder," a position they did not jettison until 1973. Taking the psychological stereotyping a step further, *Time* magazine viewed homosexuality as "a pernicious sickness." "If you were gay and you accepted those societal norms, then you were at war with yourself," recalled one college student of his own private struggle to come to terms with his homosexuality. Within this social climate exposure as a homosexual or lesbian meant losing everything—job, spouse, friends, and social position.

In the sixties the black Civil Rights Movement and the hippie counterculture assault on sexual taboos inspired some gay people to "come out of the closet" and challenge the ways that American society ostracized them. The true awakening of the gay rights movement came during the **Stonewall riot** on June 28, 1969, when patrons frequenting the Stonewall Inn, a Greenwich Village male gay bar, fought back during a New York City police raid. This image of open defiance electrified the gay community, and the next morning a huge crowd gathered outside the Stonewall Inn, chanting "Gay Power," a modification of the "Black Power" slogan that black militants embraced (see Chapter 27). Energized homosexuals and lesbians founded the radical Gay Liberation Front in response to Stonewall, while hundreds of smaller gay rights groups sprouted up throughout the country. Collectively these organizations formed gay support groups on university campuses, lobbied for antidiscrimination laws, marched openly in Gay Pride parades, and followed the "sit-in" model of the Civil Rights Movement by staging "kiss-ins" in restaurants. "We should have the same right to express our affection publicly as heterosexuals have," asserted lesbian activist Barbara Gittings.

The increased visibility of the gay rights movement soon provoked a conservative response. In 1977 the deeply religious pop singer Anita Bryant, known to most Americans for her television commercials singing the praises of Florida orange juice, spearheaded a successful campaign to overturn a newly enacted gay rights law in Dade County, Florida. Her victory galvanized forces across the country on both sides of the gay rights debate.

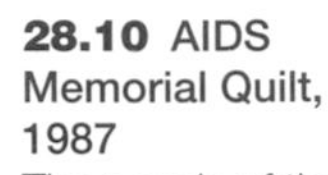

28.10 AIDS Memorial Quilt, 1987

The panels of the AIDS Memorial Quilt portrayed the disease's victims as sons, brothers, and lovers with strong ties to their families and communities to challenge stereotypes of homosexuals as diseased pariahs.

How similar were the Gay Rights and Civil Rights Movements?

Fundamentalist churches geared up to oppose any legislation granting gays legitimacy, lobbying particularly strongly for laws that prevented homosexuals from teaching in public schools. Gay rights groups ridiculed the notion that male homosexuals, because they preferred men over women as sexual partners, were pedophiles. A new, more insidious challenge loomed ahead, however.

In 1981 the mainstream press began printing stories of a mysterious ailment sweeping through the sexually charged homosexual communities in New York and San Francisco. Acquired Immune Deficiency Syndrome (AIDS), a virus transmitted through the exchange of bodily fluids, ravaged the immune system of its victims. Acquiring AIDS was a virtual death sentence in the 1980s; the disease killed over 100,000 Americans by 1990. Because in the United States AIDS disproportionately struck homosexuals, the nation viewed the epidemic as more than a public health crisis.

The raging political debate over the status of homosexuals in American society colored the competing visions about AIDS. Extreme religious conservatives viewed AIDS as God's retribution against the "morally degenerate," ignoring evidence that AIDS could strike the heterosexual population as well. Having just recently repudiated the notion that gay people were mentally ill, homosexuals now confronted widespread fears that they were all diseased. AIDS patients told heartbreaking stories of losing their jobs, being turned away from hospital emergency rooms, and facing eviction from apartment buildings by landlords who feared contamination. The gay community lobbied vigorously for increased federal funds to find a medical cure for the disease. Still, having fought so long to escape police harassment and end legal penalties for consensual homosexual acts, many gay activists were initially leery about urging homosexual men to modify their sexual behaviors. Larry Kramer chastised gay activists who "took the position that sexual promiscuity was the one freedom we had and that we had to fight to maintain it—even if it killed us. And it did kill us, a lot of us." Kramer instead worked to popularize the "safe sex" message that eventually gained currency in the gay community.

The two images shown here illustrate the competing visions within the gay community over how to best draw media attention to the mounting AIDS death toll. In 1987 the AIDS Memorial Quilt, the brainchild of San Francisco AIDS activist Cleve Jones, began touring the country after an inaugural unfurling on the National Mall in Washington, D.C. The nation's largest-ever public art endeavor, the quilt (**28.10**) made the individual stories of AIDS visible by allowing family and friends to create a square for a loved one, homosexual or heterosexual, lost to the disease. Squares were the size of a human grave and the stories they contained varied considerably, portraying a mixture of embroidered personal remembrances and treasured possessions like jewelry.

28.11 ACT-UP Protestors Stage a Funeral Demonstration in Wall Street
Militant gay activists used civil disobedience to protest high prices and slow federal approval of life-saving anti-AIDS drugs.

Radical activists adopted a less poignant and more militant tone. Embracing the slogan "silence = death," the AIDS Coalition to Unleash Power (ACT-UP) staged its first "funeral" demonstration in 1987 to demand better medical treatment. Protesters lay prone on a busy Wall Street intersection until police carried them away (**28.11**), employing the same civil disobedience tactics used successfully by the Civil Rights Movement in the 1960s. ACT UP also conducted phone "zaps" that barraged local, state, and federal officials with calls on AIDS-related issues, and barricaded the doors to the Food and Drug Administration to protest delays in approving AIDS-fighting drugs. A *New York Times* headline called ACT-UP, "rude, rash, effective." By 1996 a drug "cocktail" became available that dramatically reduced AIDS-related deaths. A relentless safe-sex campaign and screening of donated blood lowered the infection rate as well.

What competing strategies did gay activists develop to publicize the AIDs crisis?

Environmentalism

On April 22, 1970, communities throughout the nation celebrated their first Earth Day. New York City crowds walked through a block-long plastic bubble to breathe pure air; demonstrators in Boston protested noise pollution; and population control advocates in Bloomington, Indiana, handed out free birth control pills. Earth Day made environmentalism visible, but the wide variety of causes that activists championed revealed the competing visions within the environmental movement. For New Left and counterculture environmentalists, eating organically produced food grown without pesticides became a symbolic way of purging the poison of mainstream American values out of their lives. Politicians interested in securing environmentally friendly legislation framed pollution as a straightforward health issue. They focused, for example, on how lead poisoning damaged children's developing brains to win widespread support for laws mandating lead-free gas and paint. Traditional conservationist societies like the Sierra Club and Audubon Society concentrated their efforts on preserving pristine wild habitats from development. They strongly supported expanding the National Park Service to safeguard wildness areas and provide recreational sanctuaries for over-taxed citizens living in the industrial world.

28.12 Three Mile Island Nuclear Reactor Towers America rejected nuclear power after the accident at the Three Mile Island nuclear power plant. That decision, coupled with limited federal support for solar and wind-generated power, increased the nation's dependence on overseas oil.

Presidential support for environmental reforms had begun during the Kennedy and Johnson administrations (see Chapter 27), and in the 1970s Nixon and Carter also gave their blessing to increased federal environmental controls. New laws controlling toxic substances required the removal of asbestos (a cancer-causing building material) from schools. Companies had to reduce the amount of airborne toxins that their factories produced and clean up sites they had chemically contaminated. Car manufacturers installed required catalytic converters that helped reduce automobile pollution by 75 percent. Meanwhile the consumer protection movement spearheaded by activist Ralph Nader led to the creation of a federal Consumer Product Safety Commission that could ban the sale of hazardous products, from cribs to cars. While the general public applauded changes that made their lives healthier and safer, some blue-collar workers feared that new, expensive pollution controls on industry simply encouraged industrialists to move their factories overseas. "If you're hungry and out of work, eat an environmentalist," read one popular labor union bumper sticker.

Two well-publicized environmental scandals, however—one at Love Canal, a waterway near Niagara Falls, New York, and the other at Three Mile Island in Pennsylvania—convinced most Americans that their well-being depended on strict federal environmental regulation. After years of ignoring residents' complaints about rising levels of miscarriages and birth defects, New York State finally admitted in 1978 that the foul-smelling industrial waste dumped into Love Canal contained deadly toxins that had polluted the area's ground and air. Congress responded by creating a Superfund to clean up dangerously polluted areas, spending $400 million and twenty years to restore the Love Canal region.

In 1979 the partial meltdown of a nuclear reactor at the Three Mile Island nuclear power plant in Pennsylvania caused the panicked exodus of nearly 100,000 residents when radioactive steam poured into the air. No one was hurt, but the government-sponsored clean-up took fourteen years. Despite new, more stringent federal regulations for nuclear reactors, Americans equated the image of nuclear reactor towers with danger (**28.12**) and steadfastly refused to accept new nuclear power plants in their neighborhoods despite a strong industry-wide safety record.

Not all Americans applauded new environmental regulation. A "Sagebrush Rebellion" arose in the West among conservatives demanding that the federal government return federally controlled lands to the states. Viewing environmentalists as East Coast liberal elitists, Western miners, ranchers, and loggers chafed under new federal restrictions that limited their access to water, their ability to hunt predators, and their grazing rights on federal lands. Western votes helped Ronald Reagan win the presidential contest in 1980, and as president he listened sympathetically to their complaints concerning federal environmental policies. An avid outdoorsman who enjoyed riding horses at his California ranch, Reagan did not believe that the environment was in serious jeopardy. Emphasizing economic growth Reagan loosened recently enacted pollution controls on industry and reduced the size and budget of the Environmental Protection Agency (EPA), an agency founded under Nixon's watch and charged with enforcing federal environmental regulations.

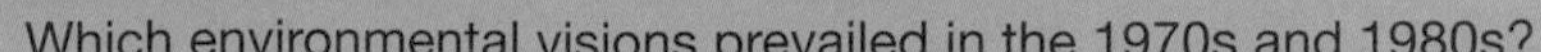
Which environmental visions prevailed in the 1970s and 1980s?

The Rise of the Right

Successful conservative attacks on environmental regulation were just one component of a resurgent conservative coalition that emerged as the dominant force in American politics in the 1980s. Through right-leaning policy institutes, magazines, lobbying groups, and direct mail campaigns, conservatives spearheaded a powerful political movement whose vision Ronald Reagan championed when he entered the White House. A charismatic leader, Reagan's unrelenting optimism changed the national mood. The vision of a nation adrift evaporated as confidence in the economy and government rebounded.

The New Conservative Coalition

The emerging conservative coalition known as the New Right created alliances among groups with very different concerns and views of what America and American government should be, reshaping the Republican Party in the process. Conservatives differed on whether a balanced budget or cutting taxes would guarantee prosperity. They disputed whether the government should play an active role in promoting conservative values or adopt a more libertarian approach that reduced governmental activity in all spheres. In the 1970s the mix of ideas grew even more complicated when neoconservatives, defectors from the liberal ranks, joined the conservative coalition. Seeking to explain his own political journey from the left to the right, Irving Kristol defined neoconservatives as "liberals who've been mugged by reality." Neoconservatives focused mostly on foreign affairs, urging the nation to cast off its Vietnam hangover and stand proud in the world once again. Their insistence that America had the right to act unilaterally in world affairs soon prevailed over lingering noninterventionist currents in conservative thinking.

Former working-class and southern Democrats also joined the emerging conservative coalition. Angry over court-ordered integration and busing, affirmative action programs that reserved jobs or school slots for minorities, and rising crime, these newcomers accepted the conservative orthodoxy of smaller government when it came to programs that primarily benefited minorities. Ethnic northern whites in the Rust Belt resented their declining economic clout as industrial jobs evaporated, and they responded well to Republican claims that "limousine liberal" elites were out of touch with the concerns of working-class America. Finally the popularity of grassroots conservative movements among burgeoning Sun Belt populations from Florida to Arizona completed the political realignment in the 1980s.

In the late 1970s simmering resentment against increasing taxes exploded into open revolt. Big business and the well-to-do had long championed lower income and corporate taxes. Now the working class and middle class joined the tax revolt by demanding lower property taxes. Voters in California spearheaded the tax rebellion in 1978 when they approved **Proposition 13**. This ballot referendum reduced property taxes by 57 percent, lost tax revenue that caused drastic cuts in funding for public schools and universities. Voters in other states soon followed suit, and increasingly found the Republican anti-tax message appealing.

The Republican Party also benefited from the rise of the **Religious Right**, a collection of conservative Christian groups that defended traditional values and supported right-wing political causes, the most sustained grassroots movement of the late twentieth century. Ronald Reagan immediately saw the benefits of reaching out to the Religious Right, hoping to create a strong conservative coalition that, in his words, would "attract those interested in the so-called 'social issues' and those interested in economic issues."

Protestant fundamentalists had mobilized their ranks for battle in the 1920s to end the teaching of evolution in southern public schools. After the Scopes Trial (see Chapter 21), the mainstream media paid little attention to religious conservatives, but Protestant fundamentalist radio stations, publishing houses, and revival meetings thrived in the South. Fundamentalists ended their self-imposed exile from mainstream politics in the 1950s when religious conservatives voiced strong support for the nation's Cold War crusade against godless communism. The

Did any significant tensions exist within the New Right?

Supreme Court's 1962 ruling against school prayer (see Chapter 27) incensed Fundamentalists, as did Carter's attempts to revoke the tax-exempt status of religious schools that failed to integrate racially.

But politics alone does not completely explain why fundamentalism became a nationwide phenomenon in the 1970s, a time when nearly a quarter of Protestant Americans (fifty million people) described themselves as born-again Christians. In an era when sprawling suburbs and rancorous cultural debates created a sense of social fragmentation, close-knit fundamentalist churches offered members cohesive communities where people with similar values spoke the same language. The fundamentalist vision of leading a morally upright life in keeping with divine will attracted white, middle-class suburbanites along with white, rural residents, creating a strong grassroots religious movement that cut across class and regional, if not racial, lines. A series of highly effective evangelical preachers, such as Pat Robertson, Jerry Falwell, Oral Roberts, Jimmy Swaggart, Robert Sculler, and Jim and Tammy Bakker, built media empires that preached the literal truth of the Bible to millions of television viewers—further popularizing the appeal of the Fundamentalist vision.

In the late 1960s Nixon claimed to speak for the "silent majority" who objected to liberal policies in the privacy of their living rooms. In the 1980s Republican politicians showered attention on the "moral majority," a well-organized network of politically active religious conservatives. In 1979 Falwell founded the Moral Majority, which he described as a "pro-life, pro-family, pro-morality, and pro-American" organization. The cover of Falwell's 1979 book, *America Can Be Saved*, showed a drawing of the preacher in front of a huge American flag, melding patriotism with religious fervor to create a vision of faith and conservative politics providing salvation to a nation adrift (**28.13**). The Moral Majority joined with other conservative religious groups to register two million new voters in time for the presidential contest of 1980. In the past Fundamentalists had distrusted Catholicism, but now, political concerns outweighed doctrinal differences. Fundamentalists formed a new political alliance with conservative Catholics who shared their concerns about religious instruction in schools, abortion, and gay rights. Along with other members of the New Right, the Religious Right voted overwhelmingly for Reagan when he ran against Carter in the 1980 presidential election.

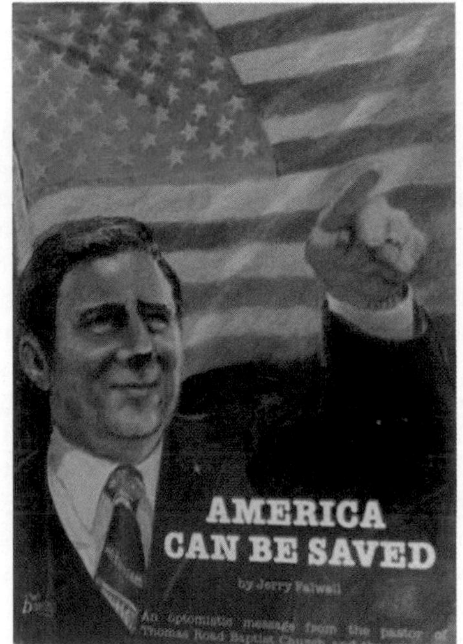

28.13 *America Can Be Saved* (1979)
The cover of Jerry Falwell's book illustrated the new connection between religious fundamentalism and political activism forged in the 1970s.

Setting a New Course: Reagan at Home

During the 1980 presidential campaign, Reagan focused voters' attention on the nation's continuing economic woes by repeatedly asking "are you better off than you were four years ago?" Reagan's cheerfulness, humor, and athleticism offered a stark contrast to Carter's more drawn and weary demeanor. Memorizing his speeches ahead of time and delivering them in a soothing baritone voice, Reagan's charisma helped him amass a devoted and almost worshipful following. Reagan's victory capped the rise of the New Right, a two-decade ascendancy that Watergate and Carter's subsequent election had temporarily interrupted. Reagan won the election by an impressive margin: 489 to 49 electoral votes. In his inaugural address Reagan entreated the nation "to believe in our capacity to perform great deeds . . . after all, why shouldn't we believe that? We are Americans." Commentators likened Ronald Reagan's victory over the unpopular Carter in the 1980 presidential election to Franklin D. Roosevelt's triumph over Herbert Hoover in 1932 (see Chapter 22). Each man created lasting political coalitions that reshaped the political landscape; each inspired the country at a moment when the nation felt besieged.

Reagan entered the presidency passionate about cutting income and corporate taxes, reducing social welfare spending, and fighting communism. He immediately sent Congress a budget that contained dramatic cuts in spending for social programs, increased allocations for defense, and lowered taxes considerably. Embracing the theory of **supply-side economics**, pro-business officials in the Reagan administration believed that letting entrepreneurs keep more of their profits would fuel economic growth, creating more and better-paying jobs that generated enough tax revenue to offset the increases in military spending that Reagan proposed.

Liberal Democrats, however, suspected that Reagan had a more sinister reason for slashing taxes. Reagan, they charged, planned to starve the budget to force Congress to undertake even more draconian cuts in New Deal and Great Society social welfare programs that conservatives longed to abolish. Liberal Democrats derided his budget proposal as trickle-down economics, an approach discredited during the Hoover administration (see Chapter 22) when aid to the wealthy failed to create more jobs for the poor.

Democrats in Congress were determined to fight Reagan's budget proposals. Then a nearly tragic turn of events gave Reagan an unexpected advantage. On March 30, 1981, a deranged twenty-five-year-old named John Hinckley (seeking to impress teenage film actress Jodie Foster) shot Reagan, his press secretary James Brady, and two others as they were leaving a Washington hotel. After hearing a firecracker-like pop, news photographer Ron Edmonds took three quick photos (**28.14**): The first shows the president grimacing as the bullet hit him; the second shows him turning to locate the source of the noise; in the third, Secret Service agent Jerry Parr pushes Reagan into the presidential limousine. In the hospital, with a bullet lodged near his heart, Reagan maintained his trademark cheerfulness, telling his distraught wife, "Honey, I forgot to duck."

Americans rallied to his side, and when Reagan returned to work a month later, he presented his 70 percent approval ratings as evidence that the nation supported his budget proposal. It passed easily with bipartisan support from conservative Democratic legislators. The top tax rate dropped from 70 percent to 50 percent, subsequently lowered to 28 percent in 1986. Reagan's image as a resolute leader got another boost when he fired eleven thousand striking air traffic controllers in August 1981, enforcing a ban on strikes by federal employees working in critical industries. Liberal critics lamented that the president's act sent a chilling message to organized labor, whose membership rolls and willingness to strike declined throughout the decade.

"Please tell me you're all Republicans."

A wounded President RONALD REAGAN to the emergency surgical team before they operated, 1981

In 1984 Reagan easily won his reelection bid against Democratic challenger Walter Mondale. Mondale energized the Democratic Party when he selected New York congresswoman Geraldine

28.14 **President Reagan Shot, 1981**
The first photo shows the president flinching as a bullet hits him, but Reagan did not realize that he had been shot until his limousine started driving away.

Ferraro as his running mate, the nation's first female vice presidential candidate, but he made a key strategic error by stating that he would raise taxes to close the deficit. Mondale expected Americans to reward him for his candor about the worrisome federal debt, but the nation was in no mood to fret. Reagan scored well with a series of television campaign ads that centered on the theme "Morning Again in America." The ads featured scenes of small-town America where content citizens celebrated marriages, schoolchildren pledged allegiance to the flag, and friends laughed together. "America is prouder, stronger, better. Why would we want to return to where we were less than four short years ago?" the voiceover asked. Many Americans agreed and Reagan won every state in the Electoral College except Mondale's home state of Minnesota and the District of Columbia, with a landslide total of 525 to 13.

Reagan remained relentlessly pro-business throughout his presidency. Driven to free private industry from government regulations that, in his view, restricted its growth, Reagan convinced Congress to deregulate the savings and loan industry. Once freed from strict government oversight, these banks subsequently lost huge amounts of depositors' money in speculative investments. In 1989 President George H. W. Bush, Reagan's successor in the White House, convinced Congress to bail them out at great cost to taxpayers rather than accept wide-scale bank failures that would certainly send the economy into a deep recession.

As the budget battles and savings and loan debacle revealed, Reagan's fiscal policies remained controversial. During his time in office, the federal debt nearly tripled (from $997 billion in 1981 to $2.6 trillion in 1988) as the hoped-for tax revenue failed to materialize and the military build-up continued unabated. After a serious recession in 1981–1983, the economy began to improve as inflation lessened and business activity picked up. The return of prosperity muted the impact of liberal criticism and helped Republicans argue that people at all class levels were doing better financially under Reagan's stewardship.

Democrats and Republicans offered competing visions on the state of the economy throughout the 1980s. Democrats lamented the increased concentration of income in the hands of the top fifth of the population. "What I want to see above all is that this remains a country where someone can always get rich," Reagan stated in 1983. Chief executive officers (CEOs) of leading corporations had no reason for complaint. Their average salaries, adjusted for inflation, rose from $3 million to $12 million a year during Reagan's eight years in office while outlays for subsidized housing dropped from $30 billion to $7 billion. In 1980 the average CEO made forty times more than the average factory worker. By 1989 CEOs earned ninety-three times more. To Democrats Reagan's economic policies helped the rich get richer while the poor got poorer. Republicans countered that consumption was a better measurement of the Americans' overall financial health than income distribution. In the 1980s Americans went on a buying spree that rivaled the postwar boom of the 1950s, purchasing nearly 88 million cars, 63 million VCRs, and 62 million microwave ovens. Items previously available only to the wealthy, such as refrigerators and telephones, were found in nearly every American household by 1990. While the poorest Americans were not living as well as the richest, their material circumstances were much improved when compared with those of previous generations.

Reagan spoke eloquently about cutting taxes and slashing welfare. He was decidedly less passionate about education, housing, health care, and the environment, often letting subordinates make key decisions in these areas. His hands-off management style differed vastly from Carter's micromanaging tendencies. Reagan rarely worked more than eight hours a day, enjoyed many vacations to his California ranch, and usually took an afternoon nap. "It's true that hard work never killed anyone, but I figure why take the chance?" he joked. Reagan's detractors viewed his detachment as senility and charged that he was just a figurehead. Supporters sometimes agreed that Reagan put his trust in the wrong hands. Over one hundred members of his administration were indicted or forced to resign amid corruption charges, stemming in part from Reagan's lax oversight of his subordinates who often acted without consulting him.

Foreign Policy Triumphs and Scandals

President Reagan did more than reject the liberal economic vision; he also overturned the foreign policy initiatives set in place by his Republican predecessors. He changed the rules of the Cold War by abandoning MAD, the doctrine embraced by American and Soviet policymakers since the 1950s, as the basis for U.S. defense against the Soviet Union. Remaining defenseless against enemy nuclear weapons was an essential component of MAD.

Why did Democrats and Republicans come to different conclusions about the state of the economy in the 1980s?

The ability to shoot down incoming missiles, the doctrine asserted, might encourage the enemy, who no longer feared its own destruction, to attack.

Reagan offered a competing view. "Let me share with you a vision of the future which offers hope," Reagan declared in 1983, announcing the **Strategic Defense Initiative (SDI)**. Challenging the view that vulnerability made America more secure, Reagan proposed building a missile shield that used lasers from space satellites to destroy incoming missiles. Publicly, Reagan argued that his plan was compatible with the 1972 ABM treaty (a point that critics disputed) since he intended to share the technology with the Soviets. Privately, he expected the Soviet Union to go bankrupt trying to match the United States in building its own missiles defenses.

Despite the billions spent on research, the SDI project failed. SDI nonetheless hurt the Soviet Union. A quick succession of elderly Soviet leaders responded to Reagan's challenge much as he expected. They increased military spending, ignoring the devastating consequences for average Soviet citizens. In the 1980s the Soviet Union spent between 15 and 20 percent of its GNP on defense, compared to 6.5 percent by the United States. Pervasive shortages meant that Soviet citizens spent hours waiting in long lines outside poorly stocked supermarkets, stoking internal discontent with Communist rule.

Closer to home, Reagan looked for ways to destabilize communist and leftist regimes in the Caribbean and Central America, activities portrayed on the map, *American Intervention in Latin America, 1980–2000* (**28.15**). In Nicaragua Reagan hoped to unseat the Sandinistas, leftist rebels who had overthrown the American-supported dictator Anastasio Somoza in 1979. Sandinista aid to Marxist rebels battling the pro-American government in nearby El Salvador confirmed Reagan's fears that communism was on the march in Central America. Reagan consequently approved covert Central Intelligence Agency (CIA) assistance to the contras, counterrevolutionary forces in Nicaragua that opposed the Sandinistas.

Congress had a different view of events in Central America. Hoping to continue the move away from direct interference in other nations' domestic affairs (a process begun by Ford and Carter), Congress prohibited the CIA and Department of Defense from funding any effort to overthrow the Sandinistas. National Security Council (NSC) Director Robert McFarlane and his assistant Marine Lt. Col. Oliver North convinced Reagan that these restrictions did not prevent the NSC from soliciting millions from the Saudi Arabian government and other private donors to aid the contras. When Congress heard about these donations in 1984, they prohibited the government from using non-American funds to unseat the Sandinistas.

Hoping to score a quick victory in thwarting the regional expansion of communism, in October 1983 Reagan ordered U.S. troops to invade the tiny

28.15 American Intervention in Latin America, 1980–2000 The United States continued to maintain Latin America as a sphere of influence in the 1980s.

Which of Reagan's foreign policy initiatives broke with policies set by Nixon and Carter?

28.16 *Speak Softly and Carry a Big Stick,* 1986
Political cartoonist Herblock suggested that the Iran-Contra scandal would mar Reagan's place in history, comparing his tepid response to the scandal with the stirring phrases associated with presidents Theodore Roosevelt, Franklin D. Roosevelt, and Harry Truman.

Caribbean island of Grenada. The president ostensibly dispatched U.S. forces to rescue American medical students trapped in Grenada when a leftist government seized control. The troops' real mission was to remove a government actively seeking Cuban and Soviet military aid. By ordering troops into battle without consulting Congress ahead of time, Reagan also used his powers as commander-in-chief (some argued unconstitutionally) to restore the strength of the presidency, badly damaged since Watergate.

Reagan supporters celebrated America's swift victory in Grenada, but critics viewed the event differently. They accused Reagan of using the Grenada invasion to distract Americans from more dismal news coming out the Middle East. Two days before the Grenada invasion, a militant Islamist suicide bomber had plowed a vehicle loaded with explosives into an unsecured barracks housing U.S. peacekeeping troops in Beirut, Lebanon, killing 241 servicemen. Over the next few months, Iranian-backed Islamist terrorist groups (angry over U.S. support for Israel and Iraq, Iran's enemy) increased their assaults against the United States by taking individual Americans hostage in Lebanon. Reagan's dual desire to end the burgeoning Middle Eastern hostage crisis and halt the spread of communism in Central America led to the biggest political scandal of his administration.

In the **Iran-Contra scandal**, Reagan administration officials sold arms to Iran to secure the hostages' release and then illegally used the proceeds to support the anti-Communist contras in Nicaragua. The problems began in 1985 when Reagan asked his new NSC director John Poindexter and North to devise a covert plan to sell arms to Iran, which needed the weapons for its ongoing war with Iraq. As part of the secret agreement, the United States demanded that Iran use its influence to secure the release of hostages held in Lebanon. After the deal went through, a few hostages were freed, but the arms-for-hostages deal soon backfired. Reagan's willingness to pay bribes to free American hostages only encouraged militant Islamist groups to seize more over the next two years. Even more troubling, Poindexter and North secretly decided to divert profits from the arms sales to the contras in Nicaragua—directly violating the congressional ban on aid to the anti-Communist rebels. When an American cargo plane carrying arms to the contras crashed in 1986, their illegal action was exposed. Convicted of breaking the law, the pair won appeals based on legal technicalities and went free.

Poindexter and North claimed that Reagan knew nothing about their illegal diversion of funds to the contras. "I made a very deliberate decision not to ask the president so I could insulate him," Poindexter testified before Congress. The public accepted this explanation, viewing Reagan as a hands-off administrator who could not always control his subordinates. This Herblock cartoon (**28.16**) reinforced that image by portraying Reagan as lacking the leadership skills of presidents Theodore Roosevelt, Franklin D. Roosevelt, and Harry Truman. With his approval rating dipping to below 50 percent, Reagan hoped to restore confidence in his leadership by improving relations with the Soviet Union.

The night before the Soviet Politburo appointed him the nation's leader in 1985, fifty-four-year-old Mikhail Gorbachev admitted to his wife, "We can't go on living like this." Gorbachev was referring to both the ironclad Soviet control over the domestic economy and the Soviet government's decades-long obsession with a possible American nuclear attack. Gorbachev embraced reform to save the Soviet Union, not destroy it. Eager to reduce Soviet outlays for defense so he could pump needed funds into the long-ignored economy, Gorbachev also moved to reduce tensions with the United States.

When Reagan and Gorbachev met in Washington, D.C., in December 1987, the pair took a historic step by signing the **Intermediate-Range Nuclear Forces Treaty** that approved the destruction of all U.S. and Soviet intermediate-range missiles in Europe. Past arms treaties had focused on curtailing the growth of nuclear stockpiles. For the first time a U.S.-Soviet pact actually reduced nuclear arms. The thaw in U.S.-Soviet relations continued when Gorbachev

Why was Reagan able to weather the Iran-Contra scandal?

withdrew Soviet forces from Afghanistan in 1988 and reduced support for Communist regimes throughout the world.

The Reagan Revolution

Reagan was an overwhelmingly popular president, but supporters' claims of a "Reagan Revolution" appear exaggerated. Reagan lowered taxes for the wealthy and he established limits that permanently curtailed the growth of the welfare state. He appointed right-leaning judges to the federal judiciary and the Supreme Court, including Sandra Day O'Connor as the first female Supreme Court justice. Cultural conservatives remained loyal to Reagan even though he offered little more than lip-service to their goals of outlawing abortion, returning prayer to public schools, or ending affirmative action.

As president Reagan always won applause when he proclaimed, "government is not the solution to our problem; government is the problem." Yet when Reagan left office, the New Deal and Great Society were as vibrant and relevant as the day he entered the White House. Americans still expected the federal government to pay pensions, guarantee unemployment benefits, curb pollution, and help educate poor children. Rather than leaving a strong institutional legacy that endured, Reagan presided over a profound shift in political vision. His pro-business policies reinvigorated faith that an unfettered free market could make Americans prosperous, and his open alliance with the Religious Right brought discussion of issues that concerned cultural conservatives into the center of American political discourse. In foreign policy neoconservatives' interventionist ideas now exerted considerable influence in Republican circles. Finally, "Reagan succeeded in reviving national confidence at a time when there was a great need for inspiration. This was his great contribution as president," reporter Lou Cannon concluded.

Conclusion

Spiritual malaise gripped the country in the 1970s as a poor economy and dissatisfying foreign policy made many Americans feel that the nation was adrift. Conflicting visions arose over women's roles and abortion, the increased visibility of homosexuals, and federal environmental regulation as Americans debated whether the country was on the right path. A crisis of presidential leadership defined American politics throughout the decade. Nixon resigned during the Watergate scandal; the first nonelected vice president, Gerald Ford, assumed the presidency; and a southern born-again Democrat, Jimmy Carter, lost support when he floundered during the Iranian hostage crisis. In the 1980s Reagan's charisma and conservative principles enthralled his supporters, but vocal critics lamented his casual style and free market economic policies. The ascendancy of the Religious Right, an important component of the new conservative coalition that elected Reagan, introduced vigorous debate over cultural issues into the political arena. Followers credited Reagan with jump-starting the economy, detractors worried about an exploding federal deficit and the inequitable distribution of wealth. Both acknowledged that Reagan presided over a rightward shift in political values in the 1980s.

The country's dependency on foreign oil and escalating tensions with the Soviet Union required a new approach to foreign affairs, a challenge that Carter met by returning the Panama Canal to Panama and injecting human rights issues into foreign policy debates. Like Carter, Reagan would enjoy his greatest successes and failures in the foreign policy arena. He rewrote the rules of the Cold War and achieved a new accommodation in U.S.-Soviet relations, but wrongdoing in the Reagan White House resulted in the Iran-Contra scandal, which brought back fears in some circles that the imperial presidency of the Nixon years had returned. In a testament to Reagan's popularity, George H. W. Bush became the first vice president since Martin Van Buren (who followed the well-liked Andrew Jackson in 1837) to win election immediately after the president under whom he served completed his term.

How does Reagan's legacy compare to the one left by Franklin D. Roosevelt?

1972–1973

Congress passes ERA
Provokes heated debate over gender roles in American society

OPEC oil embargo against the United States
Dramatizes American dependence on overseas oil exports

Watergate investigations heat up
Constitutional crisis over Nixon's abuse of power

***Roe v. Wade* legalizes abortion**
Religious conservative coalition forms in opposition

1974

Nixon resigns
Gerald Ford, the first unelected vice president, becomes president

Ford pardons Nixon
Shakes public confidence in Ford's leadership

1977–1978

First home computer marketed
Computer revolution begins

Senate ratifies treaty returning Panama Canal
Redresses past U.S. wrongdoing but provokes controversy at home

Camp David Accords
Secures lasting peace between Egypt and Israel

Review Questions

1. Why was the Watergate scandal politically significant? What different portraits of Nixon emerged in political cartoons of the 1970s? How did the Watergate scandal compare to the Iran-Contra scandal during the Reagan Administration?
2. What accounted for the nation's economic problems throughout the 1970s?
3. What changes and continuities existed in American foreign policy in the post-Vietnam 1970s and 1980s? How did concerns over human rights, communism, and the domestic economy influence the direction of foreign relations during these two decades?
4. Why did presidents Ford and Carter lose public confidence? How did Ronald Reagan's political vision differ from the ones embraced by his predecessors in the White House?
5. What different constituencies united to form the New Right?
6. What competing visions animated debates over feminism, gay rights, and environmentalism?
7. What was Ronald Reagan's lasting legacy in domestic and foreign affairs?

1979

Meltdown of nuclear reactor at Three Mile Island
Americans reject nuclear energy as an alternative to oil

Iranian Hostage Crisis begins
Carter's approval ratings plummet

Soviet Union invades Afghanistan
U.S.-Soviet relations deteriorate

1980–1981

AIDS epidemic begins
Stigmatizes gay people as diseased

President Reagan shot
Upsurge in popularity helps controversial budget plan pass

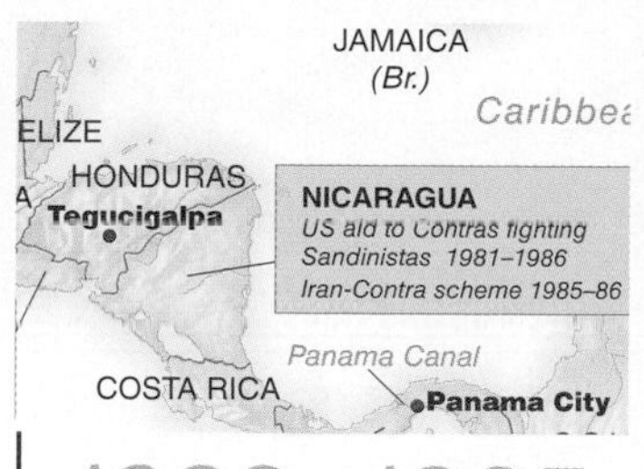

1983–1985

Reagan announces SDI
Challenges MAD doctrine

Iran-Contra scandal
Most serious presidential scandal since Watergate

1987–1988

ACT-UP stages first funeral demonstration
Puts pressure on government to fund anti-AIDS research

Intercontinental-Range Nuclear Forces Treaty signed
Spells the final phases of the Cold War

Key Terms

Organization of the Petroleum Exporting Countries (OPEC) An international consortium of oil-producing nations that regulated the price and quantity of oil exported to the world market. **844**

Rust Belt Decaying industrial cities in the Midwest, places plagued with high unemployment, crumbling roads, bankrupt governments, and high welfare rolls. **846**

Watergate scandal An episode of presidential criminal wrongdoing that created a constitutional crisis and brought an end to Nixon's political career. **848**

SALT I (1972) The first treaty between the Soviet Union and the United States that limited the deployment of intercontinental and submarine-launched ballistic missiles and the creation of missile-defense systems. **852**

mutually assured destruction The claim that the guarantee of a devastating nuclear counterattack would deter the United States and Soviet Union from ever employing their nuclear arsenals. **852**

Camp David Accords (1978) Israel agreed to give the Sinai Peninsula back to Egypt; in return Egypt became the first Arab state to recognize Israel's right to exist. **856**

Iranian hostage crisis Defining event in Carter's presidency as Iranian revolutionaries held fifty-two Americans captive for 444 days. **856**

Equal Rights Amendment (ERA) A proposed constitutional amendment, which stated that "equality of rights under the law shall not be denied or abridged by the United States or by any State on account of sex." **859**

***Roe v. Wade* (1973)** Supreme Court decision that legalized abortion. **861**

Stonewall riot A 1969 battle between patrons of a Greenwich Village male gay bar and police that became the catalyst for the gay rights movement. **862**

Proposition 13 Referendum in California that dramatically reduced property taxes, spearheading grassroots tax rebellion nationwide. **865**

Religious Right A collection of right-wing Christian groups that defended traditional values and supported conservative political causes. **865**

supply-side economics Reagan administration theory that letting entrepreneurs keep more of their profits would fuel economic growth, job creation, and more tax revenue to offset military spending. **867**

Strategic Defense Initiative (SDI) Reagan's proposal to build a missile shield that used lasers from space satellites to destroy incoming missiles. **869**

Iran-Contra scandal A law-breaking scheme that sold arms to Iran to secure the hostages' release and used the proceeds to support anti-Communists in Nicaragua. **870**

Intermediate-Range Nuclear Forces Treaty (1987) Approved the destruction of all U.S. and Soviet intermediate-range missiles in Europe. **870**

CHAPTER 29

Building a New World Order

The United States, 1989–2009

> "None of us will ever forget this day, yet we go forward to defend freedom and all that is good and just in our world."
>
> President GEORGE W. BUSH, speaking to the nation on the evening of September 11, 2001

On the morning of September 11, 2001, nineteen young Arab men boarded four planes on the East Coast. All belonged to the Islamic extremist organization known as al-Qaeda. Within a half an hour after take-off, they stormed the cockpits of their respective planes with box cutters and mace, killed the American pilots, and installed their own pilots (who had each received flight instruction in private American aviation schools) to fly the planes into predetermined targets.

At 8:46 a.m. the first plane plowed into the North Tower of the World Trade Center in New York City, an internationally recognized landmark that symbolized American dominance over the world economy. Seventeen minutes later a second plane hit the South Tower. The nation now understood that what had first looked like an unfortunate and tragic accident was actually a coordinated attack against the United States. A third plane crashed into the Pentagon, headquarters of the U.S. Department of Defense, in Virginia, the building most closely associated with U.S. military might in the eyes of the world. Meanwhile passengers in the fourth hijacked plane reached the cockpit and prevented the terrorists from flying the plane into the Capitol, a worldwide symbol of democratic government. This plane instead crashed into a Pennsylvania field.

The blazing World Trade Center towers quickly crumbled, with the office workers and firefighters still inside the buildings as onlookers ran for cover. The skeletal ruins and mountains of debris became the burial site for thousands. One onlooker echoed the nation's sense of disbelief: "This is America. How can it happen in America? How?"

The 9/11 attacks, as they came to be known, reshaped the ongoing debate about America's role in the world and the best way to protect American citizens. Only twenty years earlier Americans had savored their victory in the Cold War as communist governments in Eastern Europe and the Soviet Union collapsed. When the Cold War ended, Americans believed that their nation would take the lead in creating a new world order even as they disputed how best to spread democracy, protect the U.S. economy, and flex the nation's military muscle. Enjoying prosperous times for most of the 1990s, the country paid little attention to the new threat that loomed before the world's sole remaining superpower—terrorist strikes by anti-American Islamist extremists, such as al-Qaeda. Political debate instead centered on whether the liberal or conservative vision of government would prevail at home.

After 9/11 President George W. Bush moved with resolve to restore the image of America as a powerful and triumphant nation. He led the country into two wars: the first in Afghanistan; the second, far more controversial, in Iraq. In 2008, Americans provided a different sort of history-making moment by electing the first African American president of the United States. By then, the worst financial crisis since the Great Depression posed an additional challenge for the nation.

What meaning did Americans attach to photographs of 9/11?

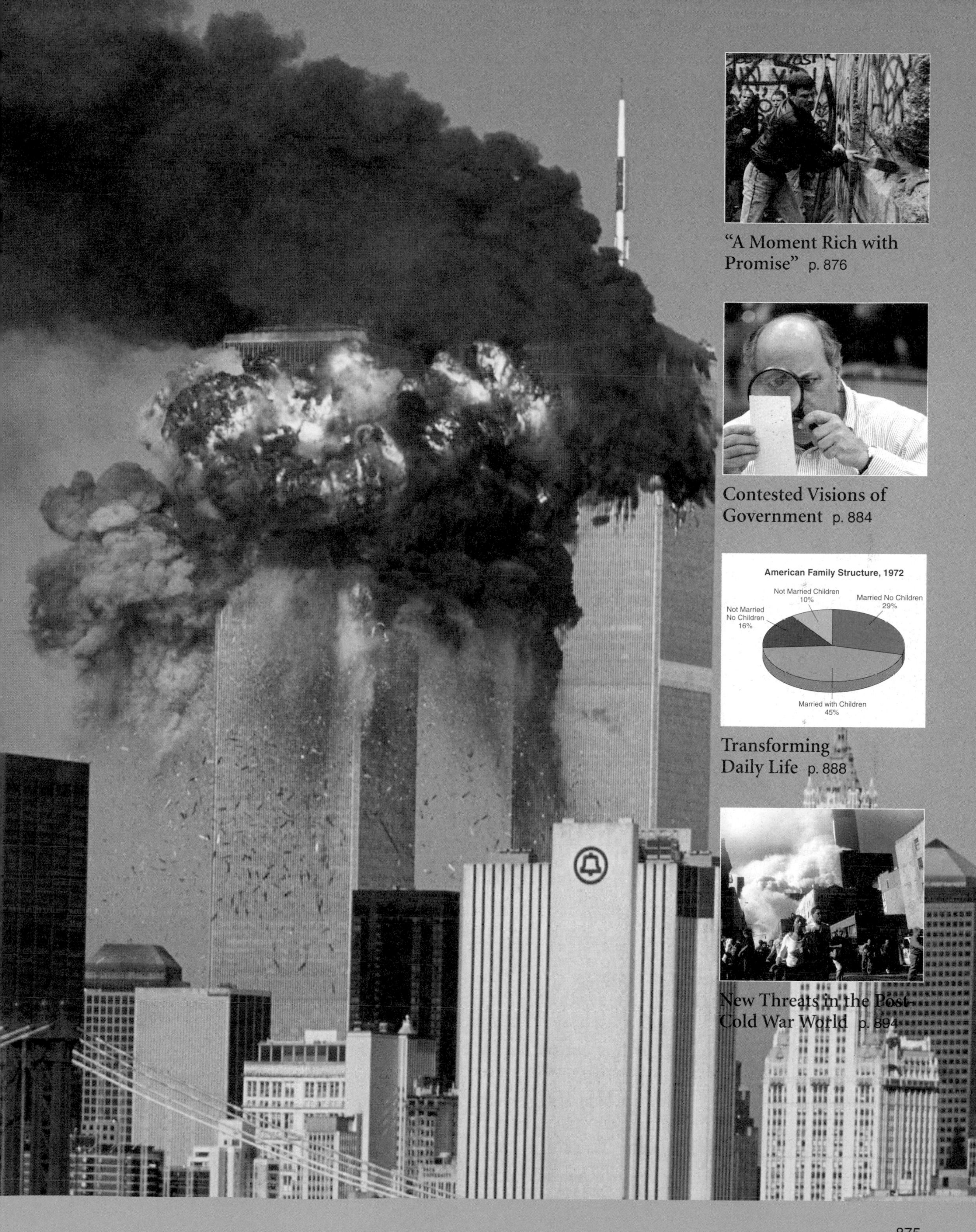
American Family Structure, 1972
Not Married Children 10%
Married No Children 29%
Not Married No Children 16%
Married with Children 45%

"A Moment Rich with Promise"

On his inauguration day in 1989, George H. W. Bush announced that he had become president "at a moment rich with promise." The fall of communism throughout Eastern Europe and the Soviet Union within the next two years seemed to confirm this judgment. However, the end of the Cold War did not mean peace; the United States immediately fought two short wars in Panama and the Persian Gulf. Conflict arose at home as well, as a huge federal deficit and simmering racial tensions that occasionally exploded into violence left some feeling that America's promise lay unfulfilled.

The Election of 1988

The son of a former Connecticut senator, George H. W. Bush served as a congressman, ambassador, Central Intelligence Agency (CIA) director, and vice president before becoming the Republican candidate for president in 1988. In this sense the decorated World War II pilot and former oilman was the ultimate insider, a man familiar with the corridors of power in Washington, D.C., and the exclusive private clubs where financial deals were negotiated. A moderate Republican with a patrician style, Bush never projected the same charisma or the passion for conservative causes that had drawn voters to Ronald Reagan, the man he hoped to follow as president. Bush's campaign had to overcome these obstacles when he faced Massachusetts Democratic governor Michael Dukakis in the 1988 presidential contest.

When Dukakis proposed increased spending on health care, education, and housing, the Bush team ridiculed the Democrat as a big-spending liberal and began calling him the governor of "Taxachusetts." In his stump speeches Bush also tapped into white peoples' fears of so-called black criminality by frequently mentioning Willie Horton, an African American prisoner who had taken advantage of a weekend furlough program in Massachusetts and gone on a crime rampage that included raping a white woman. Adding to his woes Dukakis made some critical missteps, including one ill-advised photo-op during which he donned an oversized helmet and military jumpsuit to ride a tank (**29.1**). Most

29.1 A Failed Photo-Op
Seeking to appear like a commander in chief, 1988 Democratic presidential candidate Michael Dukakis was instead ridiculed for riding around in a tank in a suit and tie.

How did George H. W. Bush prevail in the 1988 presidential election?

Americans felt that the photo made Dukakis look ridiculous, not presidential. By Election Day Bush had successfully defined Dukakis as someone who would raise taxes and let criminals out of jail, and as someone who was unprepared to be commander in chief. He defeated Dukakis 426 to 111 in the Electoral College, capturing 53 percent of the popular vote.

Popular Revolts against Communism

When Bush became the 41st president of the United States in 1989, the former director of the CIA remained suspicious about Soviet Premier Mikhail Gorbachev's true motives for instituting internal reforms and reaching out to the United States (see Chapter 28). Bush administration officials worried that Gorbachev "was attempting to kill us with kindness," according to National Security Advisor Brent Scowcroft. Gorbachev was equally distrustful of Bush and his inner circle. "These people were brought up in the years of the Cold War and still do not have any foreign policy alternative," he complained to the Politburo. Caught off guard by the quick demise of communism in Eastern Europe, within a year Bush had changed his mind about Gorbachev "by 180 degrees."

In the first sign of the upheaval to come, Hungary decided to take down the barbed wire fence between Communist Hungary and democratic Austria in May 1989. The East German government watched in dismay as thousands of its citizens drove to the Hungarian-Austrian border and then walked across to defect to the West. Turning to Moscow for help, East Germany received a surprising reply: "We can't do anything about it." A similarly uncharacteristic Soviet reaction greeted news that candidates from the democratic Polish workers' union Solidarity had won control of Poland's newly created bicameral Parliament, forming the first democratic government in postwar Eastern Europe. "This is entirely a matter to be decided by Poland," a Soviet official announced.

Soviet, Hungarian, and Polish leaders lifted restrictions on speech, voting, and economic activity to save their Communist regimes, unleashing a tide of popular revolt against Communist rule that soon overwhelmed them. Perhaps nowhere did the fall of communism come faster, and more unexpectedly, than in East Germany. On November 9, 1989, a botched news conference by a harried East German official triggered the destruction of the Berlin Wall. Instead of announcing a relaxation in rules governing travel between East and West Berlin, a confused East German official mistakenly told the press that starting immediately, East Germans could freely leave "through any of the border crossings." Electrified by the news that the wall was open, thousands of people gathered at armed crossing points, places where 1,000 East Germans had been shot trying to cross over the last twenty-eight years. When confused guards opened the gates, streams of East Germans poured across and joined with West Germans to rejoice atop the Berlin Wall.

Images as History: The Fall of the Berlin Wall (page 878) examines the media images that shaped Americans' reactions to this event. Further evidence of television's power to mold history came in the following days as thousands of East Berliners entered West Berlin and headed straight for downtown department stores. Concrete walls had not prevented East Berliners from viewing American sitcoms (dubbed in German) showing the abundance of goods available in the West. Television-stoked desires for "work-saving gadgets, [well-stocked pantries], attractive surroundings and a touch of luxury," one reporter contended, played an important role in bringing the Berlin Wall down. Gorbachev's refusal to intervene with armed force was also critical. Within a year East and West Germany had reunified into one democratic nation, an American goal since the Cold War began in the late 1940s.

By the end of 1989, the Soviet Union no longer dominated Eastern Europe, losing territory that it had controlled since the end of World War II. One by one the individual states that formed the Soviet Union demanded their independence as well, secession movements that Gorbachev tried to squash with economic embargos and, occasionally, troops. Desperate to stop the hemorrhaging, a group of hard-line Communist insiders orchestrated a coup attempt in August 1990. They put Gorbachev under house arrest in his vacation home and ringed the Soviet Parliament in Moscow with troops and tanks. Hesitating, the coup leaders lost the military's support and the overthrow attempt failed. With the populace now demanding widespread economic reforms and Communist Party officials blaming Gorbachev for losing control, the freed premier resigned on August 24, 1990. Five days later the Soviet Communist Party dissolved. By December 25, 1991, the Soviet Union ceased to exist as all its member states, including Russia, became independent nations. After decades

What role did ordinary citizens play in ending communism in East Germany and the Soviet Union?

Images as History

THE FALL OF THE BERLIN WALL

Photographs of Berlin had already punctuated key moments in the Cold War for Americans, beginning with images of the 1948–1949 Berlin airlift to the wall's construction in 1961 to prevent East Berliners from defecting to West Berlin (see Chapter 24). Presidents John F. Kennedy and Ronald Reagan had made well-documented pilgrimages to the site where they publicly denounced the Berlin Wall as a towering symbol of Communist oppression. Now, from the comfort of their living rooms, TV-viewing Americans watched as East and West Berliners climbed atop the wall throughout the night on November 9, 1989 to demand the reunification of their divided city.

The fall of communism in Europe reinforced American faith in the superiority of capitalism over communism, but some commentators urged the United States to undertake economic reforms at home to ensure that capitalism operated more fairly. What competing views do this photograph and political cartoon offer Americans about the importance of the Berlin Wall falling? What counter-arguments could critics offer?

After the evening celebrations East German guards reclaimed the top of the wall and impassively watched German civilians attack the graffiti-laden western side of the wall with chisels and hammers.

President Bush told the press that he had no desire "to dance on the wall," worried that any gloating might goad Gorbachev into sealing up the wall or prompt Soviet hardliners to overthrow Gorbachev.

Both reporters and ordinary people brought cameras to document this historic moment.

The image of one man destroying the wall piece-by-piece with his hammer resonated with Americans—it symbolized the ability of common people to make history and their desire to collect pieces of the wall as souvenirs.

Attacking the Berlin Wall with a Hammer

Would the fall of Communism usher in a better world? Many Americans believed so, but cartoonist Pat Oliphant offered a competing view by implying that free market capitalism did not always benefit everyone equally.

Pat Oliphant Questions the Triumph of Capitalism over Communism

The befuddlement of the hungry, homeless man dressed in rags suggests that there is no "we" in the United States—rich and poor view events like the fall of the Berlin Wall differently.

In the 1980s, the number of homeless people living and begging on the streets grew to a level not seen in urban America since the Progressive era.

Many Americans celebrated the fall of the Berlin Wall as a triumph of the nation's democratic, capitalist vision over a competing autocratic, anti-capitalist Communist one.

What symbolic importance did the Berlin Wall have during the Cold War?

of devising strategies to contain, weaken, and defeat the Soviet Union, the United States declared victory in the Cold War. "The Soviet Union did not simply lose the Cold War; the Western democracies won," Bush announced.

The U.S. battle against communism was not over, however. On the other side of the world, the Chinese Communist regime made different choices when faced with a popular revolt. In April 1989 university student demonstrators occupied Tiananmen Square in central Beijing to protest the removal of a high-ranking Communist official who had called for economic and political reforms. A vigorous debate took place behind closed doors among Chinese Communist officials over whether to end the demonstrations with troops or adopt a Gorbachev-like approach and accommodate some of the students' demands. On the morning of June 4, tanks appeared in Tiananmen Square, signaling that discussion within the inner circle had ended. Troops shot hundreds as they cleared the area of protesters. Two days later a lone man walking down the deserted Avenue of Eternal Peace made a solitary gesture of defiance by standing steadfast in the middle of the street as a column of seventeen patrolling tanks approached. When the lead tank swerved right to avoid hitting him, the man stepped right. When it swerved left, he stepped left. Finally the tanks stopped and the man jumped onto the first one, shouting to its driver, "Why are you here? My city is in chaos because of you." Associated Press photographer Jeff Widener captured this encounter in an award-winning photo seen on newspaper front-pages around the globe (**29.2**). Americans hailed "Tank Man," as he became known, for his inspirational defense of peace and human rights. No one in China, however, except for the bystanders who whisked him away and the Chinese authorities who probably executed him, ever knew of this encounter.

As the economic relationship between the United States and China changed, China's violent suppression of democracy movements provoked competing visions over how to proceed. In 1900 America wanted to sell China goods; by 1990 American companies increasingly outsourced work on manufactured products to China, using cheap Chinese labor to satiate American consumers' demands for affordable goods. Some critics argued that by aiding the Chinese government in its quest to improve the standard of living for ordinary citizens, Americans were helping autocratic Communist leaders stay in power. Others countered that recent events in Eastern Europe demonstrated that exposing Chinese citizens to Western values and goods would sow the seeds for an eventual democratic and capitalist revolution. A third faction saw the issue differently; they worried that a prosperous and industrially strong China might eventually replace the United States as the world's strongest power.

29.2 Standing Up for Democracy in China, 1989 Two days after the Chinese military brutally suppressed a popular rebellion in Tiananmen Square, a lone man stopped army tanks in their tracks; the world cheered his courageous stand.

Why did popular uprisings against communism in Europe and China have different outcomes?

Domestic Policy in the Bush Administration

The growing trade deficit with China (the United States bought more than it sold) was only one economic issue troubling Americans during the Bush years. "Read my lips: No new taxes," Bush had proclaimed during the 1988 campaign. Once in office, however, Bush reneged on his pledge by raising income taxes. Faced with the largest deficit in American history, the result of increased defense spending during the Reagan years without any corresponding tax increases and Bush's own decision to bail out the failing savings and loan industry in 1989 (see Chapter 28), he saw no other option. Bush's decision angered many conservative Republicans, and some never forgave him. "Read My Lips: I Lied," ran one condemning *New York Post* headline.

The combination of a huge deficit and an unfriendly Democratic majority in Congress discouraged Bush from proposing any dramatic new domestic initiatives. A revolution of sorts nonetheless occurred when Bush signed the **Americans with Disabilities Act**, a 1990 civil rights law that prohibited discrimination against the disabled in employment, public accommodations, and telecommunications. The disabled gained unprecedented freedom of movement as legally required elevators, ramps, and sloped curbs became commonplace.

During the campaign Bush had courted the conservative wing of the Republican Party by promising to appoint like-minded judges. He fulfilled this pledge by nominating a conservative African American lawyer, Clarence Thomas, to the Supreme Court when Thurgood Marshall, the Court's first African American judge, retired. Controversy erupted when Anita Hill, a former colleague, accused Thomas of sexual harassment and Thomas responded by calling the televised confirmation hearings a "high-tech lynching." The Senate ultimately confirmed Thomas by a narrow majority in 1991. With workplace sexual harassment front-page news, an unprecedented number of women won congressional seats in the 1992 elections, including the first female African American senator, Carol Mosley Braun, a Democrat from Illinois.

While the Thomas hearings exposed gender discord, the 1991 Los Angeles riots brought simmering racial and ethnic tensions to the surface. In March a 78-mile car chase along Los Angeles freeways ended with white police brutally beating Rodney King, an African American, when he resisted arrest for speeding. A nearby resident captured the incident on film, but Americans differed on what the video revealed (**29.3**). Most blacks and some sympathetic whites saw a poorly trained and racist police force that unfairly harassed blacks, echoing complaints that had set off the Watts riots in 1965 (see Chapter 27).

29.3 Los Angeles Police Beat Motorist Rodney King, 1991
Many whites saw the police trying to control an unruly black man who had resisted arrest for speeding, but many blacks saw racist police brutality.

Which gender and racial issues dominated the headlines in the early 1990s?

Others, including the jury (consisting of ten whites, one Latino, and one Asian American) that eventually acquitted the officers, offered a competing vision. They saw overworked police doing their job to protect law and order in a dangerous neighborhood. The "not guilty" verdict set off four days of rioting in Los Angeles during which Latinos also took to the streets to air their frustration with failing schools and entrenched poverty. Television networks continuously aired footage of black youths assaulting a white truck driver, but paid little attention to the Asian American–owned stores that blacks and Latinos ransacked as payback for allegedly having previously refused to serve or hire young men of color.

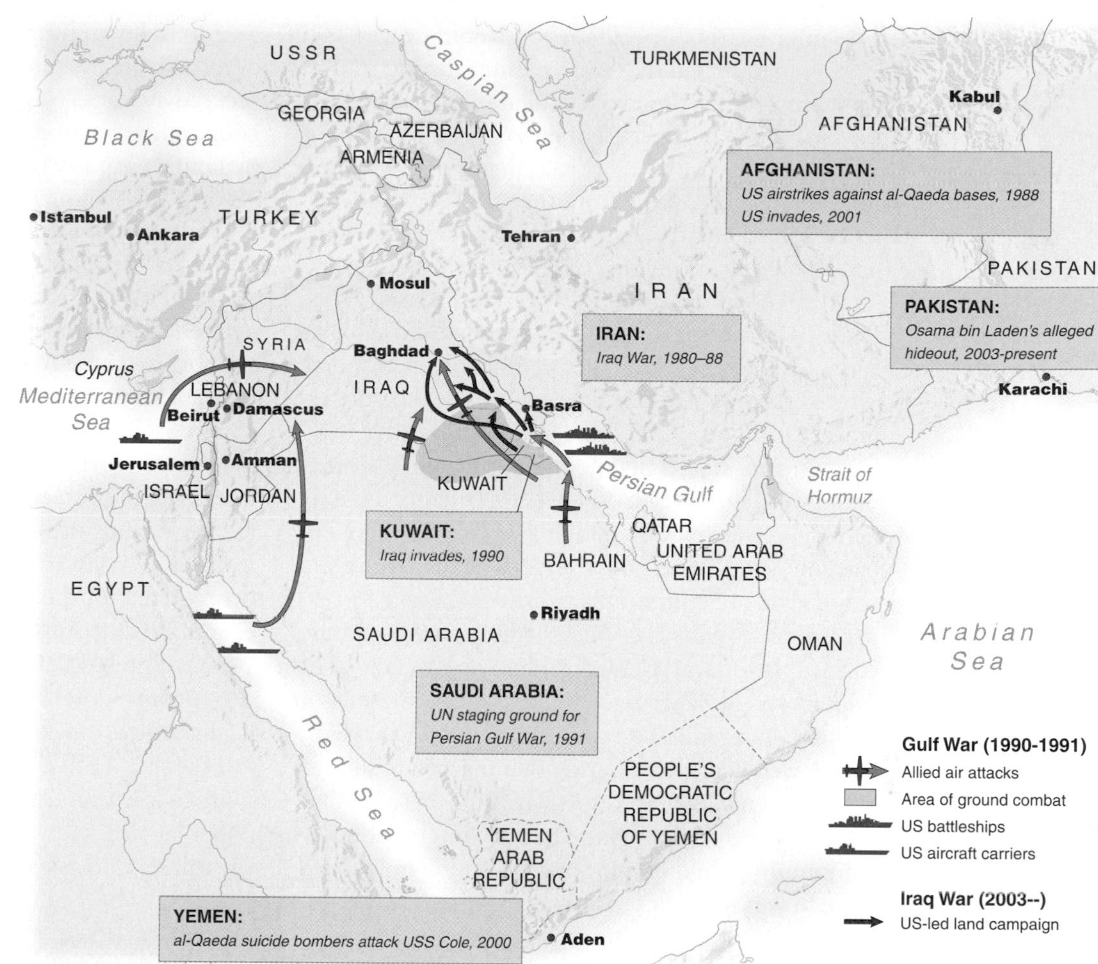

29.4 America and the Middle East, 1980–2003
The United States fought two major wars against Iraq, one in 1991 and the other beginning in 2003.

Panama and the Persian Gulf War

Bush did not propose any new initiatives to address gender, racial, or ethnic inequities; his real interest lay in foreign affairs. As he contemplated the new role that the United States should assume in a post–Cold War world, Bush moved to address a festering problem close to home. The Bush administration felt particularly uneasy about returning the Panama Canal in 1999 (see Chapter 28) to a Panamanian dictator who ruthlessly suppressed political opponents and oversaw lucrative drug-trafficking schemes. In December 1989 Bush launched Operation Just Cause, the largest American military campaign since the Vietnam War, to remove Manuel Noriega from power. The Panamanian invasion continued the nation's long tradition of maintaining Central America as a U.S. sphere of influence.

A crisis in the Middle East, however, offered Bush the opportunity to propose a new focus for U.S. foreign policy now that the Cold War was over. Bush faced the severest test of his administration when Iraqi dictator Saddam Hussein, whose nation's oil fields supplied 11 percent of global oil exports, invaded the neighboring nation of Kuwait, a small country that provided 9 percent of the world's oil, on August 2, 1990 (**29.4**). The 1979 Carter Doctrine (see Chapter 28) had already established the oil-rich Persian Gulf as a region vital to national economic and strategic interests. Throughout the 1980s Iranian-financed terrorist attacks and hostage crises in Lebanon (see Chapter 28) convinced the U.S. government that the fundamentalist Islamic government in Iran, not Iraq, posed the major threat in the Persian Gulf. During the eight-year Iran-Iraq War over a disputed waterway that separated the two nations, the United States supplied Iraq with weapons and intelligence. Oil-rich Arab nations, including Saudi Arabia and Kuwait, had also lent Iraq billions of dollars to prevent Iranian revolutionary religious fervor from spreading to their kingdoms. When the war ended inconclusively in

What problems did the United States face in the Middle East from 1980–2003?

1988 after nearly one million combatant deaths, Hussein demanded that Arab nations forgive Iraq's debt. Hussein harbored particular animosity against Kuwait, which he accused of exporting too much oil and depressing world oil prices, thereby hurting the Iraqi financial recovery from the war. When Kuwait refused his demands, Hussein declared that Kuwait had historically been part of Iraq, and invaded.

After the Iraqi army easily overran Kuwait, President Bush rushed American troops and ships to Saudi Arabia. Operation Desert Shield, the president assured the public, was solely a defensive measure to prevent Iraq from attacking Saudi Arabia. After Hussein announced that he was permanently annexing Kuwait, Bush began to question whether a purely defensive strategy was enough. Now in control of 20 percent of the world's oil, overnight Iraq became a major rival of Saudi Arabia, which contained 26 percent of global oil supplies. With the president now contemplating war, General Colin Powell, chair of the Joint Chiefs of Staff, urged Bush to follow the rules of military engagement established in the Reagan years. The **Powell Doctrine** asserted that the nation should go to war only as a last resort when the president had full support from the nation and the international community, could employ overwhelming military force to win without serious loss of American life, and had a clear exit strategy.

To amass overwhelming military strength, Bush sent Secretary of State James Baker on a diplomatic tour to build an international coalition that eventually included thirty-four nations. Bush secured a United Nations (UN) resolution authorizing military action if Hussein did not withdraw by January 15, 1991. With Saudi Arabia agreeing to serve as the staging ground for the invasion, 460,000 U.S. troops and sixty-five warships made their way to the Persian Gulf.

The Powell Doctrine called for more than overwhelming force; it also required enthusiastic support from the American people for an overseas military campaign. Bush faced stiff opposition from congressional Democrats, who argued that the president, a former Texas oilman, was primarily interested in protecting the lucrative profits of his former oil-business associates who imported oil from the Persian Gulf. Instead of war, Democrats promoted a competing vision that relied on economic sanctions to force Hussein to withdraw. Bush countered that Hussein's atrocities against his own people, notably his 1988 poison gas attacks against Kurdish villagers in northern Iraq, made him "worse than Hitler." Echoing Bush's claim, this political cartoon (**29.5**) showed Hussein holding a paper labeled "Kuwait takeover" as he looked into the mirror and asked Adolf Hitler's smiling reflection, "how'm I doing?" Bush, a decorated World War II veteran, reminded Americans that the world's failure to act when Hitler began his wars of conquest in 1939 had led to World War II. If an emboldened Hussein next attacked Saudi Arabia, he would control nearly half of the world's oil reserves. Bush also claimed that Hussein was actively trying to acquire nuclear weapons, and if he succeeded, he would be unstoppable. These arguments did not sway Democrats. With a vote split mostly along partisan lines, Congress voted to authorize war according to the terms spelled out in the UN resolution. When the UN deadline for withdrawal passed, the American-led UN coalition attacked Iraq the next day. Once the fighting started public debate ceased and Americans rallied around the flag.

29.5 "Mirror, Mirror on the Wall–How'm I doing?"
This 1990 political cartoon supported President George H. W. Bush's claim that Iraqi dictator Saddam Hussein was a modern-day Hitler.

How did the Powell Doctrine influence Bush's preparations for war against Iraq in 1991?

The Persian Gulf War unfolded in two phases. In the first phase U.S. forces bombed Iraqi installations in Kuwait and major cities in Iraq for thirty-nine days. In Kuwait the massive bombing terrified many poorly trained occupying Iraqi soldiers, and nearly one-quarter of the 400,000-man force deserted. A news team from the cable television news network CNN stayed in Baghdad, the capital of Iraq, throughout the bombing, and each night Americans watched their own nation's missiles streak across the sky and explode. The bombing inside Iraq destroyed the nation's power grid, water treatment plants, radio and television stations, and roads—hampering its military activities but also leaving civilians without power or clean water.

With Iraqi defenses in shambles from the air attacks, the war's second phase began when ground troops attacked the Iraqi forces occupying Kuwait on February 23, 1991. General Norman Schwarzkopf led coalition forces during **Operation Desert Storm**, a massive assault that soundly defeated the Iraqi army within four days, pushing it out of Kuwait. When American soldiers crossed into Iraq, Bush ordered an abrupt halt to the fighting. The total war had lasted forty-two days.

American forces, Bush declared, had met their goal of ending Hussein's occupation of Kuwait and had no intention of conquering Iraq. The United States would henceforth rely on sanctions to curb Hussein, returning to the strategy of containment that the United States had employed successfully against the Soviet Union to win the Cold War. Neoconservatives embraced a competing vision. They viewed the war as an opportunity to remove Hussein from power. Bush advisors, including Secretary of Defense Dick Cheney, however, saw no advantage to staying in Iraq. They argued that it would be difficult, if not impossible, to bring together the nation's three different ethnic groups (Sunnis, Shiites, and Kurds), each of which inhabited distinct regions, to form a democratic government. Abiding by the Powell Doctrine's emphasis on a clear exit strategy, Bush wanted to avoid a long, protracted war that could become a Vietnam-like quagmire. Having suffered relatively few casualties (148 battlefield deaths) and successfully avoided widening the war beyond its original goal, Bush's approval ratings soared to 89 percent.

The UN peace agreement prohibited Hussein from rearming or acquiring nuclear weapons, restrictions enforced by UN inspectors who stayed in Iraq until 1998. The establishment of no-fly zones over Shiite and Kurdish areas prevented Hussein and his Sunni-dominated government from launching aerial attacks against these minorities within his own nation. The UN also instituted an oil embargo to prevent Hussein from acquiring funds to reconstitute his nuclear weapons program. Critics charged that the embargo led to widespread food and medicine shortages among the civilian population, and failed to prevent Iraq from rearming. Instead of caring for his people, Hussein used the nation's meager cash flow to continue his lavish lifestyle and secured funds to amass a large arsenal of conventional weapons by illegally smuggling oil through Jordan, Turkey, Syria, and Egypt. When the UN initiated a "food-for-oil" program in 1996 that allowed Hussein to export some oil legally if he used the profits for humanitarian purposes, civilian conditions improved slightly.

"By God, we've kicked the Vietnam Syndrome once and for all."

An exultant President GEORGE H. W. BUSH at the end of the Persian Gulf War, 1991

Victory in the Persian Gulf War, along with the end of the Cold War, led to a revaluation of American foreign policy goals. After defeating Iraq Bush took to the airwaves to announce that the United States would build a "new world order," which he defined as playing an active global peacekeeping role dedicated to spreading democracy and prosperity. Some of Bush's defense advisors encouraged the president to go even further to protect American dominance. In 1992 Cheney and his neoconservative aide Paul Wolfowitz asserted that the United States needed to respond immediately, and preemptively, to any foreign nation that challenged American military superiority or attempted to "overturn the established political and economic order." Bush never publicly embraced these neoconservative principles, but his son George W. Bush, the 43rd president of the United States, proved more receptive to these ideas.

What vision of American world leadership did neoconservatives promote?

Contested Visions of Government

The Reagan years had redefined the American political landscape, shifting the political center away from New Deal and Great Society liberal assumptions that government could be a positive force in citizens' lives. To succeed in this changed political climate, a new breed of Democratic politician was needed—socially liberal but fiscally conservative. The most successful and most controversial "New Democrat" was William "Bill" Jefferson Clinton, who defeated George H. W. Bush in the 1992 presidential election and won reelection in 1996 against Kansas Senator Bob Dole. When Republican George W. Bush won the presidency in the heavily disputed 2000 election, he moved swiftly to restore the conservative vision of low taxes and limited regulation that the political right had long championed.

Clinton's New Democrats

Clinton was relatively unknown when the 1992 presidential campaign began. While governor of Arkansas, at just forty-four years of age, Clinton had chaired the Democratic Leadership Council, a group committed to shifting the Democratic Party to the political center by accepting market-based solutions to social problems and ending deficit spending. Exuding boundless energy and a vast knowledge of government policy, Clinton's magnetic personality and compassionate nature soon won him a dedicated following. "I feel your pain," became Clinton's mantra as he bear-hugged voters on the campaign trail. Clinton, one commentator noted, cultivated the image of "the president as the guy next door," who "struggles like the rest of us with his weight, his marriage, and his golf game."

Worried about the nation's finances, third-party candidate Ross Perot, a self-made Texas billionaire, entered the race and focused his campaign almost exclusively on how the federal deficit had ballooned under Bush's watch. Winning 19 percent of the popular vote, Perot registered the best third-party showing since Theodore Roosevelt's run as the Progressive Party candidate in 1912. Clinton defeated Bush in the Electoral College, 370 to 168, but only 43 percent of the electorate voted for him.

Widely praised for his superior political skills, Clinton nonetheless stumbled badly during his first few weeks in office when he tried and failed to fulfill a campaign pledge to lift the ban against gays in the military. Proponents viewed the issue as a straightforward question of protecting civil rights; opponents countered that ignoring heterosexual soldiers' objections to serving alongside gay soldiers would undermine military discipline and hurt recruitment. Clinton pleased no one with his compromise approach. Rather than lift the ban, Clinton instituted a policy of **"Don't Ask, Don't Tell,"** which allowed closeted homosexuals and lesbians—gays who kept their sexual preferences hidden—to serve in the military.

Clinton's domestic agenda contained a number of other ambitious proposals, including a comprehensive plan to provide all Americans with health care. Clinton delegated this major policy initiative to Hillary Rodham Clinton, his wife, an attorney with extensive experience in public service. Republicans successfully attacked the plan as "socialized medicine" that would deprive Americans of the freedom to choose their healthcare providers. The plan failed to win congressional approval. Clinton achieved a more modest victory with his tax proposals. Overcoming Republican opposition, he passed an economic stimulus package that offered tax incentives for job creation and increased taxes for large corporations and wealthy Americans—reversing Reagan's decision to lower taxes on the richest citizens.

Clinton also addressed economic problems caused by the recent globalization of the American economy. As late as 1970 most U.S. businesses manufactured strictly for the American market, and few stores stocked items made overseas. By the early 1980s the United States exported and imported more goods than ever before. Exports rose from $43 billion in 1970 to $178 billion in 2000, while imports surged from $40 billion to $519 billion in 2000 (all figures adjusted for inflation). Importing more than it exported, the nation questioned whether this trade deficit hurt or helped the overall economy. American companies selling products at home now faced stiff competition from

How did Clinton's centrist vision affect his policy decisions?

foreign manufacturers, while U.S. companies shifted production to places like China and Mexico where workers earned less. Globalization, however, also lowered costs for consumers and gave them a greater selection of products.

Clinton helped accelerate the trend toward globalization when he broke with organized labor to back the 1992 **North American Free Trade Agreement** (NAFTA), a treaty that lifted trade barriers between the United States, Mexico, and Canada. Labor unions opposed NAFTA because they feared that it would encourage U.S. factories to relocate to Mexico, resulting in fewer jobs for American workers. American businesspeople liked NAFTA because it prohibited Mexican companies from manufacturing knock-offs of American films, drugs, clothing, and accessories—essentially protecting their overseas and domestic markets by stopping the flow of counterfeit goods.

Clinton's emphasis on free trade reflected his desire to move the Democratic Party to the political center, but his Republican opponents cited his failed healthcare initiative as evidence that Clinton subscribed to the same 1960s liberal vision that had spurred the creation of the Great Society (see Chapter 27). In the 1994 midterm elections, Georgia congressman Newt Gingrich successfully mobilized the New Right (see Chapter 28) with his call to end the "corrupt liberal welfare state." The Republicans captured both the House and the Senate for the first time since 1952. Gingrich's manifesto, **"The Contract with America,"** envisioned smaller government, less regulation, term limits for members of Congress, welfare reform, and adding a balanced budget amendment to the Constitution. Little of Gingrich's ambitious agenda was enacted, partly because Clinton stole some of his thunder by undertaking his own program of welfare reform. Modifying legislation passed during the New Deal, Clinton joined with Republicans and conservative Democrats in Congress to reduce the time that families (mostly single mothers) with dependent children could receive financial assistance. Clinton also tried to appeal to fiscal conservatives by balancing the federal budget for the first time in thirty years.

Clinton used his superior political skills not only to weaken the Republican resurgence but also to survive the scandals that plagued his presidency. In 1994 a special federal prosecutor, Kenneth Starr, began investigating charges that the president had participated in a fraudulent land deal during his tenure as Arkansas attorney general. In the course of his investigation, Starr learned that President Clinton had engaged in a sexual relationship with a White House intern named Monica Lewinsky. Clinton was not the first or only president to have extramarital dalliances, but when giving testimony under oath on an unrelated matter he denied the affair. Seven months later the president publicly acknowledged that he had lied as seen in this *New York Daily News* headline reporting his televised address to the nation (**29.6**). Republicans argued that Clinton's failure to tell the truth warranted impeachment. In 1998 the Republican-controlled House of Representatives completed the first stage of impeachment by voting that the president had lied under oath and obstructed justice. The Senate now had to decide whether these infractions met the constitutional test of "high crimes and misdemeanors" needed to remove a president from office. Ten Republican senators joined with Democrats in defeating the first charge of perjury by a vote of 55 to 45. The second charge of obstructing justice resulted in a 50 to 50 tie. Neither charge obtained the requisite two-thirds vote required to remove Clinton from the White House.

Clinton survived impeachment by cultivating the same "everyman" appeal that won him the presidency. "The essence of Clinton's success has been to persuade America that this scandal is about human weakness, not crime, and that at its core is not a string of felonies but a sin familiar to all—adultery," lamented conservative commentator Patrick Buchanan. The strong economy also helped keep Clinton's approval ratings near 60 percent throughout the ordeal.

29.6 Clinton's Sex Scandal
When Clinton finally admitted to an "inappropriate relationship" with White House intern Monica Lewinsky, the lies he had previously told to cover it up led to his impeachment.

How does Clinton's sex scandal compare to the Reagan-era Iran-Contra scandal (see Chapter 28)?

The Disputed Election of 2000

The election of 2000 once again offered voters two competing notions of the role that the government should play in American society. Democrat Al Gore, then serving as vice president under Bill Clinton, ran against Republican George W. Bush, the son of former president George H. W. Bush. More liberal than Clinton, Gore was a well-known environmentalist whose pedantic manner often made him appear wooden. Bush was a born-again evangelical Christian who had cultivated a folksy persona while governor of Texas.

Reflecting the generally prosperous times, the two candidates put forward competing visions on how to spend the projected federal surplus. Calling it "the people's money," Bush proposed enormous tax cuts that he argued would fuel investment and economic growth. Rejecting the Democrat emphasis on federal government activism, Bush vowed to create an "ownership society" where people had more control over their wealth, Social Security retirement accounts, health care, and property. Gore adhered to the traditional competing Democratic vision of using government regulation and federally funded programs to promote equity, environmental responsibility, and prosperity. He charged that Bush's tax cuts would disproportionately help the wealthy and starve federal programs for the poor. Gore proposed saving the surplus to prepare for the coming explosion in Social Security payments once the baby boom generation began retiring. Green Party candidate Ralph Nader, a consumer advocate who railed against corporate greed, and the Conservative Patrick Buchanan, who ran on the Reform Party ticket, also entered the race.

In an age of machine-counted votes and instantaneous communication, Americans expected complete results on election night. However, with several states too close to call that evening, it took a few days before Gore emerged with 267 electoral votes, three short of the 270 required to win the presidency, to Bush's 246. All eyes now turned to Florida where a riveting thirty-six-day drama unfurled over recounting ballots that vote-counting machines had rejected because voters had not completely punched the perforated box next to the candidate's name. Gore's team went to state court and won a hand recount in four primarily Democratic counties. Election inspectors, like the one pictured here (**29.7**), spent hours examining "hanging chads," the name given to partially punched boxes, to determine voters' intent. Arguing that time for a recount had run out, Republican Florida officials certified that Bush had won the state.

The battle now moved to the Supreme Court, where conservative justices accepted the Republican argument that the different standards used by inspectors to include or reject ballots violated the "equal protection" clause of the Fourteenth Amendment. As the map (**29.8**) shows, although Gore won the national popular vote, by winning Florida, Bush had the 271 electoral votes that he needed to win the election. Echoing the outraged Democratic response to the Supreme Court's decision to halt the recount, Justice John Paul Stevens wrote, "Although we may never know with complete certainty the identity of the winner of this year's Presidential election, the identity of the loser is perfectly clear. It is the Nation's confidence in the judge as an impartial guardian of the rule of law." Subsequent privately funded recounts undertaken by several major news organizations all concluded that Bush had indeed won Florida.

The election results continued to rankle Democrats. Besides questioning poor ballot design and Supreme Court partisanship, Democrats charged that Florida Republicans had used a variety of shady tactics to disenfranchise some African Americans, such as incorrectly claiming they were felons who could

29.7 Hanging Chads
A Florida election worker uses a magnifying glass to try to determine which candidate this voter had selected, reflecting the closeness of the 2000 presidential election.

Why was the 2000 presidential election so controversial?

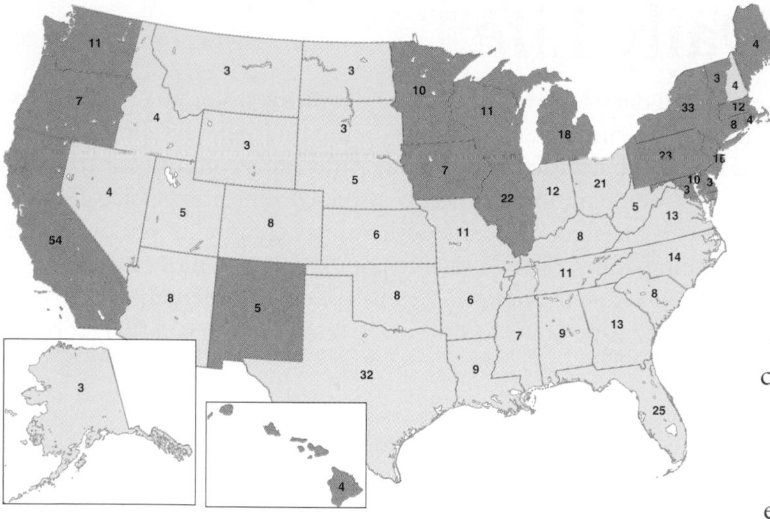

Electoral vote by state	Electoral Vote (%)	Popular Vote
George W. Bush (Republican)	271 (50)	50,456,062 (48)
Albert Gore, Jr. (Democrat)	266 (50)	50,996,582 (48)
Ralph Nader (Green Party)	0 (0)	2,882,955 (3)

29.8 Presidential Election, 2000
A mere 537 votes in Florida decided the outcome of the 2000 presidential contest.

not vote. The post-election recriminations also targeted liberals who had rejected the centrist direction of the Democratic Party and voted for Nader. The Green Party candidate received 97,488 votes in Florida—a state that Bush won by a mere 537 votes.

Compassionate Conservatism

Bush entered office proclaiming that his administration would move away from the laissez-faire, antigovernment message championed by past Congressional Republican leaders like Gingrich. He instead embraced a new vision termed "**compassionate conservatism**," a philosophical approach to governing that emphasized using private industry, charities, and religious institutions, rather than the government, to provide community services. Adherents to compassionate conservatism argued that the poor quickly became dependent on government-run social welfare programs, losing the motivation and drive to improve their circumstances themselves. As one Bush administration official put it, compassionate conservatives believed that "the government should encourage the effective provision of social services without providing the service itself." In keeping with this philosophy, the president championed faith-based initiatives that funded church-run community programs, arguing that local clergy understood their neighborhood problems better than government bureaucrats. Federal money flowed to churches offering after-school tutoring to students, transportation for the elderly, counseling for drug addicts, and soup kitchens for the homeless.

Critics saw little compassion for the poor in some of Bush's other economic initiatives. Ignoring the election's evidence that strong competing visions of governing continued to divide the nation, President Bush relied on the Republican-controlled Congress to win swift congressional approval for the tax cuts and deregulation of financial markets that he had proposed during the campaign. Faced with the beginnings of a recession as overinflated stock prices collapsed, Bush and other conservative Republicans offered a new rationale for slashing taxes by an average of 15 percent. Over 40 percent of the tax cuts went to the wealthy, the very people whose companies and investments would provide the jobs and capital needed to jump-start the economy, the president argued. When the short recession ended, Bush and his congressional supporters credited their tax cutting. Some economists suggested that the overinflated housing market was the real reason for the economic rebound. Home prices increased nearly 45 percent between 1997 and 2005 as speculators bought and sold homes quickly to take advantage of rising prices. Low-interest loans encouraged homeowners to use their houses as collateral to borrow money, which they used to purchase consumer goods. For the moment the credit-fueled rise in housing prices infused cash into the economy, but the day of reckoning was ahead.

Despite his antigovernment philosophy Bush sometimes proved willing to strengthen the federal government's power. The bipartisan 2001 "No Child Left Behind" law tried to improve public schools by linking federal funding to student performance on annual standardized exams. Bush also dramatically increased the investigative powers of the Justice Department in the wake of the terrorist attack against the United States on September 11, 2001.

Transforming Daily Life

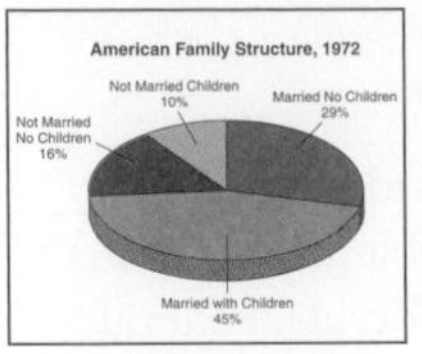

In the 1990s computers altered daily life in countless ways, quickly becoming essential to work and leisure. The Monica Lewinsky scandal broke on the Internet, revealing how the emergence of the World Wide Web transformed the way Americans communicated with one another in the 1990s. Key demographic shifts also reshaped American society. Fewer heterosexual American couples married, while the desire of gay couples to wed provoked heated debate over the meaning of marriage. A sizable population of senior citizens emerged, and new immigrant communities formed across the nation. Meanwhile environmentalists worried about human-induced climate changes and entreated Americans to stop using fossil fuels to run their cars and factories.

The Computer Age

At key moments in American history, transportation or communication breakthroughs transformed the contours of daily life. Past accomplishments such as building the intercontinental railroad and federal highway system quickened the movement of goods and people throughout the nation. Telegraphs, telephones, and televisions broke down the barrier of distance among people living in different regions. Thanks to these inventions Americans could speak directly to loved ones living elsewhere, learn instantaneously about events far from home, and laugh at the same jokes told on weekly television shows. In the 1990s computer technology, especially personal computers and the Internet, once again changed how Americans communicated, shopped, and received information.

First introduced in the 1980s (see Chapter 28), by the late 1990s millions of Americans spent hours a day at work or home typing on personal computers. The lucrative computer industry, fueled by the constant invention of ever-improving components and programs, supplanted the car and steel industry as the engine that drove prosperity. As manufacturing plants continued to close in the Midwest, areas where high-tech enterprises clustered, like Silicon Valley in northern California, boomed. Computer giants Microsoft (which produced the computer operating system Windows) and Apple became powerful corporations that employed highly educated workers and developed global markets for their products.

> "When I took office [in 1993], only high energy physicists had ever heard of what is called the Worldwide Web… Now even my cat has its own page.
>
> President BILL CLINTON, 1996

Going the way of the horse and buggy when cars were invented, typewriters became obsolete when people ranging from office workers to students began using computers to write letters and essays. At first computer-users printed copies of these documents and delivered them in traditional ways—such as mailing letters or handing a teacher a completed assignment. By the end of the decade, however, more and more Americans relied on the Internet to deliver business and social correspondence electronically.

The Internet evolved from a primitive computer system designed in the sixties to facilitate the exchange of computer information among geographically disparate military installations. The creation in the late 1980s of a computer network linking universities and five national supercomputer centers paved the way to providing instantaneous computer communication among civilians. At the same time engineers in Switzerland developed the **World Wide Web**, a system for organizing electronic information transmitted through the Internet. With these tools in place, Internet use exploded. In 1994 six million Americans were connected to the Internet. By 2001 the 130 million Americans who surfed the web daily in offices, libraries, schools, or at home accounted for a quarter of all global Internet traffic.

Computers and the Internet quickly reshaped how Americans worked and played at the dawn of the twenty-first century. Virtual business meetings now took place among geographically dispersed colleagues who looked into small cameras attached to their computers to converse with the people they saw on their screens. Office workers working in the same building sent a steady stream of e-mails to each other throughout the day, rather than telephoning or delivering a message in person. Many companies jettisoned paper records in favor of computer databases that stored personal and commercial data.

Americans differed on the benefits that children derived from this new technology. A generation of youth hooked on computer games alarmed commentators who worried that their sedentary lifestyle was fueling an epidemic of childhood obesity. Others fretted that children who played violent computer games became desensitized to real-world violence. Schools, however, quickly brought the Internet into the classroom. By simply typing a phrase into an Internet search engine, researchers of all ages gained instant access to information from libraries throughout the world. The Internet facilitated the spread of misinformation as well. Anyone could create a Web site, allowing virtual communities to form around almost any issue. A great resource for researching a medical condition, the Internet also helped terrorists publicize their causes and killings around the world.

The Internet reshaped commerce as well, becoming a virtual shopping mall and entertainment center as entrepreneurs rushed to market their wares. Shopping on the Internet, however, differed from taking a stroll down Main Street. The Internet-based company Amazon.com not only sold books more cheaply but built virtual communities in which readers posted their own reviews of books and sold used copies. The privacy and accessibility that the Internet afforded gave the pornography and gambling industries a boost, drawing millions of customers on a daily basis. To pay the credit card bills that they accumulated while shopping online, many Americans stopped sending checks through the mail and began using the Internet to pay their bills electronically. Droves of Americans stopped watching their favorite shows on TV, preferring instead to watch them on the Internet when it was convenient.

The Changing Face of Families

In 1992 George H. W. Bush's vice president Dan Quayle attacked a popular television series *Murphy Brown* for positively portraying the unmarried title character's decision to have a child. Quayle voiced the New Right's lament that marriage had lost ground to other nontraditional family arrangements. The charts "American Family Structure, 1972" and "American Family Structure, 1998" (**29.9**) show that the composition of the American family had indeed changed radically in less than a generation. By 1998, 47 percent of American families lived in non-married households, both with and without children, compared to 26 percent in 1972. Longstanding gender roles within families also changed. In the traditional model of marriage, the husband worked and the wife stayed at home. By the end of the 1990s, most married couples worked outside the home.

Changing family structure prompted sometimes acrimonious debate between the New Right who wanted to reverse these trends and liberal Democrats who championed the right of non-married partners to cohabitate and single women to have children. Many people who considered themselves liberal on a myriad of economic and social issues, however, joined with the New Right in condemning same-sex or gay marriage. The gay rights movement had made overt discrimination against homosexuals and lesbians less socially acceptable (see Chapter 28).

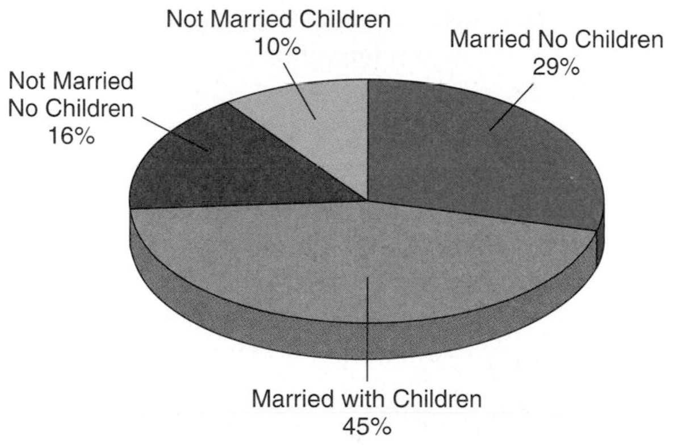

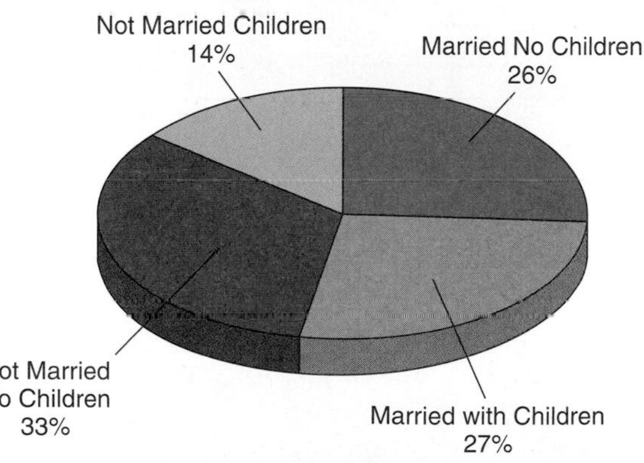

29.9 **Changes in American Family Structure, 1972–1998** These graphs reveal that the percentage of married households with children dropped significantly by the end of the twentieth century.

What changes in family structure do these graphs illustrate?

> "Regardless of how you feel about marriage, it's wrong to treat people differently under the law."
>
> An ad equating bans against gay marriage with past laws prohibiting interracial marriages

> "I can marry a princess."
>
> In a competing ad a young girl suggests that schools will promote legalized gay marriage

While many Americans were willing to tolerate same-sex couples living together, people on both ends of the political spectrum drew the line at same-sex marriages. In 1996 Congress overwhelmingly passed the Defense of Marriage Act, a law that defined marriage as a legal union between a man and a woman. Under this statute states that banned same-sex marriages did not have to accept legal marriages performed in other states if a gay couple moved to their jurisdiction. Gay-rights advocates argued, with limited success, that every American had the right to marry a partner of their choosing. In 2009 only Massachusetts, Connecticut, Vermont, Maine, and Iowa allowed same-sex marriages. Seven other states authorized "civil unions" between same-sex partners that granted them either all or some of the rights accorded married couples. The remaining states, either through referendum or stature, prohibited same-sex marriage.

The debate over gay marriage received a tremendous amount of press exposure, but few reporters paid much attention to how the graying of America was altering family life. Life expectancy had increased thanks to improved medical care and decreasing poverty. Many middle-aged parents finished raising their children only to discover that their aging parents needed full-time caretaking.

29.10 Competing Views on Immigration Americans continue to debate whether immigrants are a burden or an asset.

As the population aged, Social Security and Medicare payments went up, but a declining birthrate meant that there were fewer native-born workers available to pay the taxes that kept this social welfare system afloat. Over the last twenty-five years, the birth rate had declined from 18.4 births for every 1,000 people in 1970 to 14.8 in 1996. Faced with a labor shortage of able-bodied workers, the nation turned, as it had in the past, to immigrants to fill available jobs.

A Wave of Immigration

The massive wave of immigration that began after Congress eliminated national quotas in 1965 initiated another important social transformation. Between 1931 and 1965 around 5 million immigrants came to the United States. These numbers skyrocketed to 4.5 million in the 1970s; 7.3 million in the 1980s; and 9.1 million in the 1990s. Hundreds of thousands more entered the country illegally. Most of these immigrants came from Asia, Africa, and Latin America—only two million Europeans settled in the United States between 1980 and 2000. Some Americans satirically referred to the exploding Hispanic immigrant population in the Southwest as the *reconquista*, or re-conquering of territory that Mexico had lost to the United States in the nineteenth century after the Mexican-American War of 1848 (see Chapter 11). Overall the United States attracted twice as many immigrants as all of the other nations in the world combined.

Competing claims about the economic benefits of immigration emerged, a debate explored more fully in *Competing Visions: The Economic Costs of Immigration.* The different meanings attached to the word "benefits" in this political cartoon by Brian Fairrington (**29.10**) encapsulated the debate over whether immigrants drained the economy by seeking a wide array of taxpayer-funded social services or contributed to overall prosperity by working for very little. The New Right also feared dire cultural

Competing Visions

THE ECONOMIC COSTS OF IMMIGRATION

To this day Americans continue to disagree about the economic costs associated with immigration. In the following passage Harvard economist George J. Borjas paints a pessimistic economic portrait. Tamar Jacoby disputes Borjas's claim that three decades of high immigration have hurt the U.S. economy. What different factors does each emphasize to make his case?

George J. Borjas suggested that immigration affected socioeconomic groups differently in his 1996 article "The New Economics of Immigration: Affluent Americans Gain: Poor Americans Lose."

New research has established a number of points. The relative skills of successive immigrant waves have declined over much of the postwar period. In 1970, for example, the latest immigrant arrivals on average had 0.4 fewer years of schooling and earned 17 percent less than natives. By 1990 the most recently arrived immigrants had 1.3 fewer years of schooling and earned 32 percent less than natives ...

The large-scale migration of less-skilled workers has done harm to the economic opportunities of less-skilled natives. Immigration may account for perhaps a third of the recent decline in the relative wages of less-educated native workers ...

The increasing welfare dependency in the immigrant population suggests that immigration may create a substantial fiscal burden on the most-affected localities and states ...

There exists a strong correlation between the skills of immigrants and the skills of their American-born children, so that the huge skill differentials observed among today's foreign-born groups will almost certainly become tomorrow's differences among American-born ethnic groups. In effect, immigration has set the stage for sizable ethnic differences in skills and socioeconomic outcomes, which are sure to be the focus of intense attention in the next century ...

Current immigration redistributes wealth from unskilled workers, whose wages are lowered by immigrants, to skilled workers and owners of companies that buy immigrants' services, and from taxpayers who bear the burden of paying for the social services used by immigrants to consumers who use the goods and services produced by immigrants. ... Immigration changes how the economic pie is sliced up. ... The harmful effects of immigration will not go away simply because some people do not wish to see them.

In his 2002 article "Too Many Immigrants," Tamar Jacoby argued that large-scale immigration benefited the United States economically.

The most commonly heard complaint about foreign workers is that they take jobs from Americans. Not only is this assertion untrue—nobody has found real evidence to support it—but cities and states with the largest immigrant populations (New York, Los Angeles, and others) boast far faster economic growth and lower unemployment than cities and states that do not attract immigrants. In many places, the presence of immigrants seems to reduce unemployment even among native-born blacks—probably because of the way immigrants stimulate economic growth. ... Even if Borjas is right that a native-born black worker may take home $300 less a year as a result of immigration, this is a fairly small amount of money in the overall scheme of things. More to the point, globalization would have much the same effect on wages, immigrants or no immigrants ...

What about the costs imposed by immigrants, especially by their use of government services? It is true that many immigrants—though far from all—are poorer than native-born Americans, and thus pay less in taxes. It is also true that one small segment of the immigrant population—refugees—tends to be heavily dependent on welfare. As a result, states with large immigrant populations often face chronic fiscal problems. ... [But] If we shift the lens to the federal level, and include the taxes that immigrants remit to the IRS, the calculation comes out very differently: immigrants pay in more than they take out. ... 28 million immigrants form but a small part of the $12-trillion U.S. economy, and most of the fiscal costs and benefits associated with them are relatively modest. Besides, fiscal calculations are only a small part of the larger economic picture. How do we measure the energy immigrants bring—the pluck and grit and willingness to improvise and innovate?

Not only are immigrants by and large harder-working than the native-born, they generally fill economic niches that would otherwise go wanting.

Are contemporary concerns about immigration similar or different from objections made earlier in the twentieth century?

consequences as the nation fragmented into permanent ethnic enclaves. "If America is to survive as 'one nation, one people' we need to call a 'time-out' on immigration, to assimilate the tens of millions who have lately arrived," exhorted conservative columnist Patrick Buchanan, who unsuccessfully ran for president in 2000. To protect the nation's cultural cohesion, these right-leaning critics organized campaigns to make English the nation's official language.

Both Democrats and Republicans worried that immigrants, who were willing to work for less, took jobs away from native-born workers. Critics especially denounced illegal immigration, arguing that people who sneaked across the border often violated other laws as well. Illegal immigrants sent their children to school and received health care in hospitals, all at taxpayer expense, they charged. Unions and their supporters complained that undocumented workers could not join labor unions, making it more difficult to organize labor to improve working conditions and wages.

Champions of immigration, mostly from the political left, pointed to the nation's past success in assimilating large numbers of immigrants and argued that immigrants took the low-paying jobs such as busboys, gardeners, and nannies that few Americans wanted. Countering claims that new immigrants failed to assimilate, advocates of immigration noted the high rate of interethnic marriages among second-generation immigrants. They also viewed complaints about multiculturalism as a racist attempt to protect the United States as a primarily white society.

Climate Change

The computer revolution and shifting demographics were not the only factors changing American daily life. Scientists worried that accelerated climate change threatened to reshape the physical space that Americans inhabited and urged the nation to take steps to reverse human-induced environmental damage. They entreated Americans to alter their consumption habits by switching from gas-guzzling cars like sport-utility vehicles (SUVs) to automobiles that burned little or no fossil fuels. Americans, 4.5 percent of the global population, drove 24 percent of the 590 million cars in the world. Ingrained driving habits, however, were hard to change.

Environmental scientists claimed that average temperatures had risen 1.8 degrees Fahrenheit over the last one hundred years, a phenomenon called **global warming**. They attributed this climate shift to the widespread burning of fossil fuels (coal and oil) that pumped carbon dioxide into the air. Carbon dioxide was one of several greenhouse gases that trapped the sun's heat in the Earth's atmosphere. While the sun's rays were essential to human life, environmentalists blamed the rapidly rising levels of greenhouse gases for global warming.

This 2007 world map (**29.11**) shows which nations emitted the greatest amount of carbon dioxide from burning fossil fuels. The United States, China, Russia, India, and Japan head the list. Developing nations in Africa with few cars or heavy industry emitted relatively little carbon dioxide. Besides emitting more total greenhouse gases than most other nations, the United States ranked tenth in the amount of greenhouse emissions per person.

Why did global warming matter? The quicker-than-normal melting of the Arctic ice cap, environmentalists warned, was causing sea levels to rise. If unchecked, rising waters would soon wash over sea-level lands throughout the world including the Mississippi Delta in the United States. Scientists also speculated that global warming affected rainfall patterns and storms, leading to an increase in devastating droughts, wildfires, and hurricanes. Not everyone in the United States accepted these dire predictions. Some Americans questioned the scientific evidence linking climate change to human activity. Fluctuations in the earth's average temperature had occurred before, they argued, disputing the claim that any permanent or catastrophic change in the atmosphere was underway.

In 1997 the United States signed the Kyoto Protocol, an international agreement that set targets for reducing greenhouse emissions in industrial nations. In 2001, however, President George W. Bush argued that the agreement was flawed because it exempted China and relied on governmental controls, not market incentives, to develop "green" technology. The United States subsequently became the only nation besides Australia to sign, but not ratify, the treaty.

For Americans to reduce the amount of fossil fuels burned in cars and factories, a significant shift in lifestyle needed to occur. Enjoying low gas prices few Americans felt compelled to invest time or money into developing "green" technology. National security concerns proved more effective in motivating the nation to re-examine its energy

What core arguments support and refute the theory of global warming?

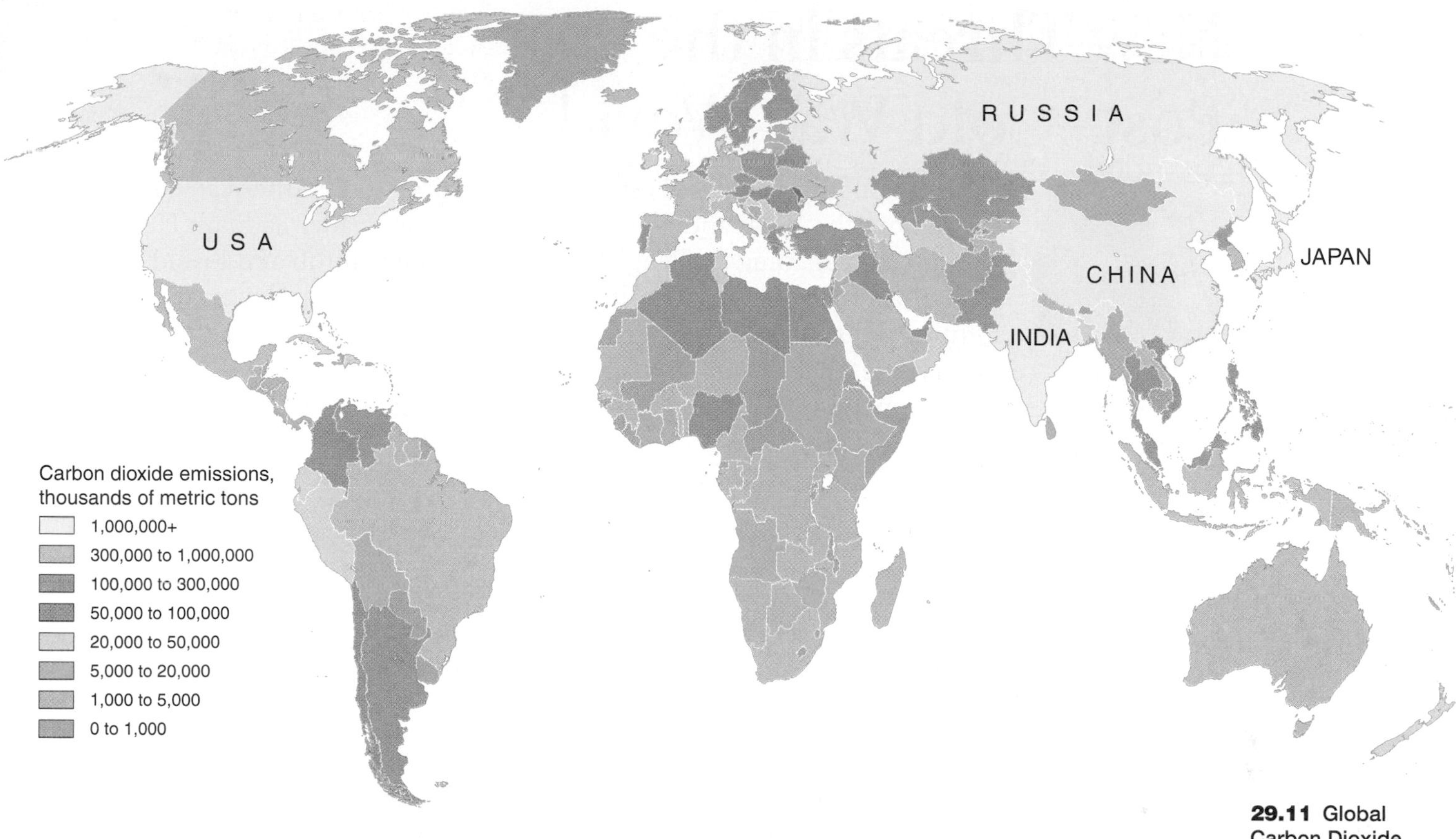

29.11 **Global Carbon Dioxide Emissions**
This 2007 map depicts the proportion of carbon dioxide gases emitted from burning fossil fuels (mostly in factories and cars) by each nation. The United States and China were the worst polluters, along with Japan, Russia, and India.

policy. The United States imported 65% of its oil, with Canada providing the largest share. After 9/11 a consensus emerged that the ongoing American presence in the Middle East (which provided 11% of the oil Americans consumed) bred resentment among Arab populations that helped Islamist fundamentalist terrorist groups. Republicans and Democrats, however, disagreed over how to wean the nation off its dependence on foreign oil. The Bush administration championed bolstering oil production at home by lifting restrictions on drilling in the Arctic National Wildlife Refuge, a nationally protected wilderness area in Alaska. This proposal enraged a wide swath of environmentalists and Democrats who worried that drilling accidents could potentially contaminate this pristine wilderness. They also feared losing valuable time in the battle against global warming by continuing, rather than ending, fossil fuel consumption.

"We are entering a period of consequences."

AL GORE, who won the 2007 Nobel Peace Prize for publicizing the global warming crisis

"Global warming—at least the modern nightmare version—is a myth."

British botanist DAVID BELLAMY

What accounts for the disparity in carbon dioxide emissions on this map?

New Threats in the Post–Cold War World

Access to oil in the Middle East remained critical to the American economy throughout the 1990s and 2000s. Containing Iraqi leader Saddam Hussein presented an ongoing challenge for President Bill Clinton and President George W. Bush. Ethnic cleansing in Eastern Europe and Africa raised additional questions of much responsibility American should assume to prevent massacres worldwide. When Islamic fundamentalist terrorists attacked U.S. targets overseas and at home, competing visions also arose over how to best defend the nation from this new threat.

Ethnic Cleansing and Terrorism

In the 1990s the nation faced a new foreign policy dilemma: when to intercede on humanitarian grounds to stop massacres in parts of the world strategically unimportant to the United States. In 1992 images of a civil-war induced famine in Somalia, a country in East Africa, flooded American airwaves and newspapers. This image of a Somali woman and her starving child (**29.12**) echoed the Madonna and child compositions used by Jacob Riis during the Gilded Age (see Chapter 17) and Dorothea Lange during the Depression (see Chapter 22) to rally popular support for aiding the poor. President George H. W. Bush responded to the public outcry by sending U.S. troops to help UN peacekeepers restore order, aid that incoming president Bill Clinton continued. Public opinion shifted dramatically in 1993 when news cameras captured the image of cheering Somalis dragging the corpse of an American soldier through the streets of Mogadishu, the capital city of Somalia, after rebel Somali warlords downed a U.S. Black Hawk helicopter (**29.13**). The public now demanded

29.12 and 29.13 Competing Views of Civil Turmoil in Somalia, 1992 and 1993 Photographs like this one of a starving Somali woman and child prompted Americans to demand that the United States send troops to end the civil war responsible for the famine. A year later, angered by a photograph of Somali rebels dragging the corpse of an American soldier through the streets, Americans called for the return of U.S. troops. Both images encouraged Americans to view African nations as dysfunctional places where famine and fighting were endemic.

How did media coverage influence American views of Africa?

an immediate withdrawal, and Clinton complied. The UN withdrew its troops as well, and years of anarchy in Somalia followed. Reluctant to put American soldiers' lives in jeopardy again, Clinton proceeded cautiously in April 1994 when Hutus, the majority ethnic group in Rwanda, another East African nation, unleashed a one-hundred-day genocidal rampage that killed 800,000 Tutsis, a minority ethic group. This time Clinton came under attack for failing to intervene decisively with force.

The photo of Somalis desecrating the corpse of an American soldier had other repercussions as well. Osama bin Laden, the Saudi exile who headed **al-Qaeda**, a fundamentalist Islamic terrorist organization, concluded that terrorist attacks against the United States would work because Americans had no stomach for casualties. "One American pilot was dragged in the streets of Mogadishu [and] you left. . . . the extent of your impotence and weaknesses became very clear," he jeered in 1996. Such pronouncements caused Paul Watson, the photojournalist who took the Pulitzer-prize winning image, to conclude that the "storm of outrage" over his photo taught terrorists that they could rely on publicity in the Western media to amplify the impact of their terrorist attacks.

During his first few years in office, Clinton also had to formulate a response to "**ethnic cleansing**," the intentional mass killing of one ethnic group by another, in the Balkans, a mountainous region of southeastern Europe. When Communist Yugoslavia dissolved in 1991, ethnic and religious differences provoked a civil war among Croatia, Bosnia, and Serbia, all former parts of Yugoslavia. Clinton resisted intervening until July 1995 when Serbian forces forced 25,000 Bosnian Muslim women and children to leave the town of Srebrenica, and murdered the 7,500 Muslim men and boys who remained behind. The United States participated in North American Treaty Organization (NATO) air strikes of Serbian military positions and helped broker the 1995 Dayton Peace Accords, which settled disputed territorial boundaries and placed NATO troops (including Americans) on the ground as peacekeepers.

Preoccupied with humanitarian tragedies overseas, Americans paid less attention in the early 1990s to signs that the terrorist threat was moving closer to home. Many residents in Arab nations saw the United States and Israel as one, blaming both for taking away land that rightfully belonged to the Palestinians. A spate of overseas hostage-takings and plane hijackings in the 1970s and 1980s kept the Arab-Israeli conflict in the news. In 1993 Kuwaiti and Iraqi-born terrorists exploded a massive car bomb in the parking garage of the World Trade Center, two towering skyscrapers located in the heart of New York City's financial district that housed governmental agencies and companies involved in foreign trade. The explosion killed six people and created a six-story hole in the ground. The FBI captured the culprits easily when one tried to recover his deposit from a car rental agency for the van used in the attack. Reassured that law enforcement agencies had done their job and that the terrorists were inept, the public and government quickly forgot the incident.

But al-Qaeda, which maintained training bases in Afghanistan, resolved to try again. Determined to launch a *jihad*, or holy war against Western nonbelievers, bin Laden relied on his family's fortune and large donations from individuals in Saudi Arabia to construct a clandestine terrorist network that recruited disciples from the Middle East, Asia, and Africa.

Not all terrorist threats during this period originated overseas. On April 19, 1995, Timothy McVeigh parked a rental truck filled with explosives in front of a federal building in Oklahoma City. The blast killed 168 people, including many children in the building's day care center, and wounded 800. McVeigh and his accomplice Terry Nichols viewed the attack as payback for the federal government's recent assaults against private paramilitary groups and their rural compounds filled with large caches of weapons. Militia supporters like McVeigh rejected any legal restriction on their Second Amendment right to bear arms, citing gun laws as just one example of government tyranny. The attack stunned the country and remained the deadliest terrorist attack against American civilians until 9/11.

Meanwhile al-Qaeda made plans to attack U.S. targets overseas. Issuing a *fatwa*, or death sentence, against all Americans, bin Laden demanded that the United States remove its troops from Saudi Arabia (stationed there since the 1991 Persian Gulf War) and end its support of Israel. "It is more important for Muslims to kill Americans than other infidels," bin Laden declared. This pronouncement was more than rhetoric. In August 1998 al-Qaeda terrorists bombed the U.S. embassies in Nairobi, the capital of Kenya, and Dar es Salaam, a city in Tanzania. Clinton ordered an immediate retaliatory attack, and tomahawk cruise missiles rained down on eight al-Qaeda training camps in Afghanistan and on a pharmaceutical plant in Sudan accused of supplying bin Laden with chemical weapons.

What motivated foreign and domestic terrorists to attack Americans?

The president's advisors presented Clinton with a set of competing views over the next step to take. Clinton's antiterrorist advisor recommended continuing the bombing until the Taliban, Afghanistan's fundamentalist Islamic government, turned bin Laden over to the United States. Pentagon officials opposed sustained bombing, worried that mounting civilian casualties would inflame anti-American sentiments throughout the Middle East. Assassinating bin Laden, others argued, would turn him into a martyr whose death fundamentalists would certainly avenge. Faced with these conflicting views, Clinton chose instead to rely on the CIA to thwart terrorist attacks against U.S. targets overseas. These covert agents uncovered several planned attacks but failed to prevent al-Qaeda from sending a small explosive-laden boat into the side of an American navel vessel, the *USS Cole*, which was anchored near the Middle Eastern country of Yemen. The October 12, 2000, assault killed seventeen sailors and injured forty more. Clinton left office still waiting for verification that al-Qaeda was behind this attack. Incoming President George W. Bush received that confirmation, but had not yet settled on a clear policy response when al-Qaeda struck again on September 11, 2001.

29.14 The World Trade Center Collapses
This photograph conveyed the panic that spread through lower Manhattan as rubble and smoke from the collapsing World Trade Center towers rained down on the streets.

How did the nation and government respond to the 9/11 attacks?

9/11

On the morning of September 11, 2001, in an attack that became known as **9/11**, nineteen terrorists operating from al-Qaeda cells located inside the United States hijacked four planes. The terrorists, from Saudi Arabia, Egypt, Lebanon, and the United Arab Emirates, flew two planes into the World Trade Center towers, and a third into the Pentagon. The fourth plane crashed in Shanksville, Pennsylvania, after the passengers seized control of the cockpit, thwarting the terrorist plan to fly the plane into the Capitol. On this "day of terror," Americans watched in horror as the World Trade Center towers crumbled, causing rescue workers, victims, and onlookers to run for safety as the massive structures collapsed in a heap (**29.14**). A total of 2,973 people died in the attacks.

President Bush immediately announced that "we will make no distinction between the terrorists who committed these acts and those who harbor them." He issued an ultimatum to Afghanistan's Taliban government: turn over al-Qaeda members living there, including bin Laden, or face invasion. The Taliban refused. Receiving overwhelming support from Congress, the American people, and most foreign nations, the United States attacked Afghanistan on October 7, 2001. U.S. forces first bombed al-Qaeda training camps and arms depots, and then joined with the Northern Alliance, an Afghan rebel group, to drive the Taliban from power. The two-month conflict failed, however, to capture bin Laden, who had likely escaped into the mountains of neighboring Pakistan with help from Pakistani sympathizers.

29.15 **Security versus Privacy, 2002**
This cartoon suggests that invading the privacy of Americans under the guise of increasing security reduced, rather than improved, their standard of living.

Most Americans had supported the invasion, but a growing number grew uneasy about how the Bush administration was conducting the war. These critics accused Bush of condoning torture by allowing CIA agents to use water-boarding, an interrogation tactic that simulated drowning, in an effort to extract information from captured al-Qaeda suspects held prisoner at the U.S. naval base in Guantánamo Bay in Cuba. The decision to incarcerate captured prisoners indefinitely at Guantánamo Bay, denying them the right to a fair trial, also aroused controversy.

Responding to criticism that the nation's security agencies had failed to prevent the 9/11 attack, the president created the Department of Homeland Security, a new umbrella organization that housed the nation's intelligence-gathering and law enforcement agencies. He also secured congressional approval for the 2001 **Patriot Act**, a law that greatly expanded the government's investigative and police powers. Critics soon attacked the law as an unconstitutional assault on civil liberties. This 2002 Pulitzer Prize–winning political cartoon (**29.15**) by Clay Bennett exposed a familiar wartime dilemma—how to protect the nation against enemy agents operating on American soil while simultaneously safeguarding the privacy rights of Americans. In the cartoon determined federal workers remove planks from a couple's home to build a security fence, exposing their personal lives to public scrutiny. In the weeks after the 9/11 attacks, the FBI arrested hundreds of Arabs and Muslims in an effort to destroy any remaining al-Qaeda cells in the United States. Acting hastily, and often on flimsy evidence, resulting in innocent people getting caught up in the FBI dragnet and some spent substantial periods in jail before being released. Scores of Arab Americans, like Japanese Americans in World War II, hung American flags outside their businesses to counter lingering suspicions that all Muslims were terrorists. In 2007 a federal court overturned parts of the Patriot Act that made it easier for the government to secure search warrants and Internet and phone records.

Were governmental efforts to prevent internal enemy attacks after 9/11 similar to the steps during World War I and II?

The Iraq War

America's "war on terror" soon spread to Iraq. Containing Hussein's ambition to acquire weapons of mass destruction (nuclear, chemical, and biological weapons) had been an ongoing issue since the end of the 1991 Persian Gulf War. In 1998 the UN halted its weapons inspection program after Hussein refused to continue cooperating. President Clinton subsequently authorized Operation Desert Fox, a four-day bombing campaign in December 1998 against one hundred Iraqi military targets to punish Hussein and destroy any weapons he was hiding. Neoconservatives publicly urged Clinton to make removing Hussein a key goal of American foreign policy. They had the chance to advance their views more forcefully once Bush appointed key neoconservatives to defense-related positions, including Secretary of Defense Donald Rumsfeld and Deputy Secretary of Defense Paul Wolfowitz.

This core of key neoconservative defense policy advisors included Vice President Dick Cheney. Reversing his previous stand when he had urged the first President Bush to stop the Persian Gulf War without attacking Bagdad, Cheney, along with others, urged the president to attack Iraq while public concern about national security remained high. "Do we wait and hope he doesn't do what we know he is capable of, which is distributing weapons of mass destruction to anonymous terrorists, or do we take preemptive action?" asked neoconservative Richard Perle, chairman of the Defense Policy Board. These advisors championed the doctrine of **preemptive war**, the notion that the United States should remove hostile regimes with force before they could pose a serious threat.

> "Our security will require all Americans to be forward-looking and resolute, to be ready for preemptive action when necessary to defend our liberty and to defend our lives."
>
> President GEORGE W. BUSH, announcing a shift in foreign policy from containment to preemption, 2002

State Department officials, especially Secretary of State Colin Powell, disagreed. They offered a competing vision that relied on the same Cold War–era containment policies that had eventually toppled the Soviet Union. Those urging restraint worried that a hostile fundamentalist Islamic government might replace Hussein's secular regime, fueling rather than dampening the terrorist threat against the United States. "Better the devil we know than the one we don't," one high-ranking intelligence official reasoned. *Choices and Consequences: Launching a Preemptive War* examines the options before Bush as he made his decision to attack Iraq.

Having privately resolved to topple Hussein, Bush began laying the groundwork for sending American troops into Iraq. In September 2002 his administration announced a new national security strategy. The **Bush Doctrine** established the unilateral right to attack nations that harbored terrorists, to launch preemptive military strikes to prevent future attack on the United States, and to replace autocratic governments with democratically elected ones. The inclusion of preemptive war was new, but other parts of the Bush Doctrine reiterated key principles announced by Bush's father when he defined a new post–Cold War direction for American foreign policy in 1992. Neoconservative Paul Wolfowitz played a key role in both administrations, devising a foreign policy that aggressively protected America's singular status as the world's strongest military power.

In building his case for war, the president repeatedly claimed that Hussein possessed weapons of mass destruction and had links to terrorist organizations, including al-Qaeda. By the summer of 2002, this rhetoric had convinced 72 percent of the American public of the falsehood that Hussein was responsible for the 9/11 attacks. Working to win support in the international community and at home, Bush sought both a UN resolution demanding that Iraq readmit weapons inspectors and a congressional joint resolution authorizing the use of force to enforce UN mandates and remove the "continuing threat" that Hussein posed. In arguing for war the administration pointed to secret correspondence between Iraq and Niger provided by Italian intelligence agents indicating that between 1999 and 2001 Hussein had tried to buy uranium oxide, material used to build a nuclear bomb, from Niger. Some CIA agents, including the envoy sent to Niger to investigate, privately doubted that Hussein had made any direct overture to buy uranium from Niger. This charge, however, convinced wavering Democrats to support the war. When the International Atomic Energy Agency later anounced that these letters were indeed forgeries, antiwar advocates charged that Bush had deliberately misled the country while building his case for war.

What debates occurred within the Bush administration over going to war against Iraq in 2003?

Choices and Consequences

LAUNCHING A PREEMPTIVE WAR

In 2002 the Bush administration feared that Iraqi dictator Saddam Hussein had acquired, or was on the verge of acquiring, nuclear weapons and was actively developing chemical and biological weapons. President Bush worried that once Hussein acquired a sizeable arsenal, he would use it against his neighbors, including Israel, and help terrorists attack the United States. Facing a critical decision about how to proceed, his advisors gave Bush several options.

Choices

1 Launch a preemptive war to remove Hussein from power.

2 Work through the UN to impose economic sanctions and send weapons inspectors to Iraq.

3 Support Iraqi exiles' plan to organize a coup d'état that might trigger a mass uprising.

Decision

In February 2002 Bush decided to fight. He announced that Hussein harbored weapons of mass destruction and had aided al-Qaeda. He made a half-hearted effort to work with the UN to reconstitute the weapons inspection program halted in 1998, and secured support from a handful of potential allies it the United States declared war. Announcing that Hussein had refused to cooperate with UN weapons inspectors adequately, the United States attacked Iraq on March 20, 2003.

Consequences

Active combat operations lasted three weeks and successfully removed Hussein from power. No weapons of mass destruction were found. Iraq elected a democratic government that struggled to contain ethnic and religious strife. U.S. forces came under daily attack until a surge of troops in 2008 weakened rebel insurgencies.

***Looking for a coherent Iraq policy*, Jack Ohman, *The Oregonian*, 2002**

Continuing Controversies

Was the Iraq War justified?

Supporters of Bush's policies argued that removing Hussein benefited the Iraqi people and the world. Building a stable, democratic and militarily weakened Iraq was necessary to protect American interests in the strategically and economically important Persian Gulf. The 9/11 attacks demonstrated that the United States must act aggressively and preemptively overseas to prevent future strikes on its own soil.

Critics argued that Bush misled the American people by making false claims that Hussein possessed weapons of mass destruction and had ties to al-Qaeda. The war made America less secure by fanning anti-American sentiments in the Middle East that helped al-Qaeda recruit and diverted needed resources from the war in Afghanistan, where al-Qaeda was regrouping. Preemptive war set a dangerous precedent that lowered the threshold for declaring war to simply feeling threatened by another nation.

What justifications and criticisms did the doctrine of preventative war arouse?

The Iraq War followed the same pattern as the 1991 Persian Gulf War—intense bombing followed by a ground troop invasion. The bombing campaign began on March 19, 2003, and within three weeks American troops were in Baghdad. On April 10, 2003, *USA Today* was one of many newspapers and television newscasts (**29.16**) showing an Iraqi crowd enlisting the aid of U.S. Marines to pull down a huge statue of Hussein. "The toppling of Saddam Hussein's statue in Baghdad will be recorded alongside the fall of the Berlin Wall as one of the great moments of liberty," Bush subsequently proclaimed. Although the event was initially seen as emblematic of Iraqi happiness over the fall of Hussein, subsequent reports suggested that American army personnel had staged it in a square across from the hotel housing international journalists to create a positive iconic image of the war similar to the World War II image of U.S. Marines raising the flag on Iwo Jima (see Chapter 23). The controversy over the picture mirrored Americans' ongoing debate over whether the war was based on lies or was, as Bush and his supporters maintained, spreading democracy to the Middle East.

After active combat operations ceased, American troops faced a host of problems that kept them in Iraq. Widespread looting greeted the fall of Saddam Hussein, who eluded capture until December 13, 2003. He was held in prison, then put on trial and executed on December 30, 2006. Restoring law and order and creating a new democratic government proved difficult as Sunnis, Shiites, and Kurds divided along ethnic and religious lines. American soldiers caught up in the emerging civil war provided inviting targets for suicide bombers, while Iran and al-Qaeda penetrated Iraq to expand their influence in the region.

Controversy over the war continued at home, especially when scandalous photographs taken by soldiers at the American-run Abu Ghraib prison circulated in the mainstream media and on the Internet in 2004. While interrogating prisoners U.S. guards had taken photos of the prisoners forced into humiliating sexual positions and being threatened with dogs. Some photos showed smiling American soldiers standing beside beaten and bloody corpses. As with the 1968 My Lai massacre in Vietnam (see Chapter 26), Americans held strong competing visions on what they felt the photos represented. Some saw rogue soldiers acting on their own; others blamed the president for authorizing brutal

www.usatoday.com THE NATION'S NEWSPAPER 50 CENTS

LATE SPORTS

Masters goes on today

Tiger eyes third title; protests planned ■ Preview, 1, 10-11C

By Timothy A. Clary, Agence France-Presse

Thursday, April 10, 2003

USA TODAY

NO. 1 IN THE USA

Battles still rage in the north

Kurdish fighters, above, join U.S. troops in the field, 5A

Baghdad falls

Why capital fell so quickly, 2A

Jubilant crowds swarm U.S. troops as 3-week war topples regime; 'Game is over,' Iraqi diplomat says

29.16 "Baghdad Falls," April 10, 2003
Initial news reports spoke of jubilant crowds cheering as U.S. Marines helped them pull down a statue of Saddam Hussein, but later reports suggested that the army had staged the incident.

What accomplishments and setbacks did the United States experience in the Iraq War?

interrogating techniques on suspected terrorists. Another group sidestepped the moral question and instead debated whether torture produced valuable information or simply encouraged suspects to say what interrogators wanted to hear.

When an influx of U.S. troops in 2008 reduced insurgent attacks, the public's views of the war improved. Debate nonetheless continued over how long American troops would stay in Iraq and whether the war had made the nation safer. How the new president who entered the White House in 2009 would handle these questions remained to be seen.

The Election of 2008

In 2004 Bush successfully won reelection against Democratic challenger Massachusetts senator John Kerry, a Vietnam War veteran whose record both as a decorated officer and peace activist came under Republican attack during the campaign. Despite the growing unpopularity of the war in Iraq, the fresh memories of 9/11 bolstered Bush's argument that only he could adequately protect the nation against terrorism. In a close election Bush won the popular vote by 3 percent and captured the Electoral College 286 to 252.

By 2008, however, the president's approval rates had sunk to historic lows. These lows reflected the nation's unease with its seemingly permanent presence in Iraq and recoil at the White House's initial failure to react when Hurricane Katrina devastated predominantly black New Orleans neighborhoods in 2005. In the 2008 presidential contest, Democrat and Republican candidates all repudiated the Bush administration and ran campaigns that promised change.

The election soon assumed historic dimensions when Hillary Rodham Clinton, the former First Lady and now a senator from New York, announced her candidacy. Clinton had a long record of public service dedicated to healthcare issues, but her initial support for the war in Iraq angered staunch antiwar Democrats. First-term Illinois senator Barack Obama, the forty-seven-year-old son of a white woman from Kansas and an African father, astutely campaigned on his own consistent opposition to the war. When the crowded Democratic field narrowed to Clinton and Obama, the 2008 election was guaranteed to make history. For the first time either a woman or an African American would head the national Democratic Party ticket. At the end of a bruising primary battle, Obama prevailed and became the Democratic nominee. Fervent Clinton supporters, holding fast to their dream of electing the first female president, for the moment appeared reluctant to switch allegiances to Obama.

In the general election Obama faced Republican John McCain, a former military pilot whom the Communist Vietnamese had held captive for six years during the Vietnam War. The seventy-two-year-old senator from Arizona had developed a reputation as a maverick for occasionally breaking ranks with fellow Republicans. Hoping to make some history of his own, and perhaps woo some Clinton supporters, McCain selected Alaska governor Sarah Palin as his running mate—only the second time that a woman had received this honor.

Obama pledged to end the war in Iraq quickly and roll back the Bush-era tax cuts for the wealthy, while McCain supported both. Debate over the Iraq War faded when a cascade of bank and insurance company failures sent the stock market into a tailspin. In the midst of the crisis, economists offered the following explanation for the downturn that future investigations may or may not confirm. During the last five years, as housing prices rose dramatically and Congress deregulated the banking and financial industries, banks had made numerous risky loans that let some people purchase homes they could not afford, and Wall Street brokers had invested heavily in mortgage-backed securities. When housing prices started declining in the summer of 2007, the dominos began to fall. Bank foreclosures on people who could not pay their mortgages increased, and even more ominously, the declining value of mortgage-backed securities threatened to bankrupt leading Wall Street firms, wiping out many Americans' retirement investments. Trying to stabilize the mortgage market, the government took over two leading lenders, Freddie Mac and Fannie Mae. Treasury Secretary Henry Paulson refused to intervene when Lehman Brothers, a major investment firm, went bankrupt in September 2008. This bankruptcy sent shock waves through the financial sector. Credit markets froze as banks stopped lending and investors began moving money from stocks and bonds to government-backed Treasury notes.

By mid-September the Bush administration decided that an infusion of $700 billion was needed to unfreeze the credit markets and stop the stock market's freefall. Enraged House Republicans revolted. In their view the government "bail-out" used taxpayer money to reward bad behavior. Many Democrats accepted the competing view that the government would recoup this money when the

What factors led to the economic downturn in 2008?

29.17 "Out of Many, We are One" Almost overnight Barack Obama became an American icon, and his soaring rhetoric inspired this flag-shaped montage of his supporters.

economy and value of these investments improved. Congress eventually authorized the funds, which Paulson used to infuse capital directly into banks rather than buying low-valued assets. What happened to this money emerged as a major political question in the months to come.

Obama was a captivating orator who drew thousands to his rallies. His supporters came to hear him speak of "that American spirit, that American promise, that pushes us forward even when the path is uncertain; that binds us together in spite of our differences; that makes us fix our eye not on what is seen, but what is unseen, that better place around the bend." Inspired by his trademark phrase "out of many, we are one," photographer Anne Savage superimposed Obama's image on snapshots of people who attended his campaign events, and arranged them to look like an American flag (**29.17**). As the mosaic reveals, Obama succeeded in drawing enthusiastic support from whites and blacks; young and old; Hispanic and Asian. Eventually even Hillary Clinton campaigned for him. Exuding confidence, calm, and charm, Obama amassed an inspired following who put his likeness on posters, vans, t-shirts, bridges, and boats. Some supporters even sported Obama tattoos.

With the nation facing its most severe economic crisis since the Great Depression, the focus of the 2008 presidential race changed. An intensely disciplined candidate, Obama stuck to a clear message of economic reform. The McCain campaign was more erratic, one day highlighting economics; the next portraying Obama as the heir to sixties-era radical politics. Thanks to support from swing voters (those without strong ideological convictions), momentum for Obama built steadily throughout the fall. As this *New York Times* headline announced (**29.18**), on November 4, 2008, Barack Obama became the first African American elected president of the United States by winning a decisive victory: 365 to 173 electoral votes, and 53 percent of the popular vote.

How did past civil rights activism help make Obama's election possible?

> "If there is anyone out there who still doubts that America is a place where all things are possible, who still wonders if the dream of our founders is alive in our time, who still questions the power of our democracy, tonight is your answer."
>
> BARACK OBAMA after becoming the first African American elected president, 2008

Conclusion

Americans had good reason to feel hopeful when the forty-year Cold War came to an end as Communist governments collapsed in Europe and the Soviet Union disintegrated. Rather than entering into a period of sustained peace, however, the United States almost immediately faced new challenges from an aggressive dictator in the Middle East and Islamic fundamentalist terrorist attacks that culminated in 9/11. Taking stock of these new threats, three consecutive presidents tried to set a new direction in post–Cold War foreign policy. George H. W. Bush spoke of using U.S. leadership to create a new world order where democracy and prosperity prevailed, a vision that his son expanded to include the use of preventative war to ensure that America remained the world's sole superpower. Clinton accepted that the nation had a global responsibility to prevent massacres and used missile strikes to punish rogue states. These new foreign policy forays, which included several wars, all sparked controversy at home over the role that the United States should play in the world.

Competing visions also emerged over how to manage domestic affairs. Americans disagreed over whether to place faith in an activist, regulatory government or the free market to protect prosperity and individual rights. With the political center shifting toward the right, Democratic president Bill Clinton embraced issues popular with moderates in both parties such as welfare reform and free trade agreements. Adept at surviving political scandal, Clinton's attempt to reinvigorate the liberal vision by melding fiscal conservatism with social liberalism halted when George W. Bush won a hotly contested presidential race in 2000. Bush and the Republican-controlled Congress moved quickly to cut taxes and deregulate the financial and banking sector, but his administration failed to foresee the economic meltdown that began in the summer of 2008.

"All the News That's Fit to Print"

The New York Times

Late Edition

NEW YORK, WEDNESDAY, NOVEMBER 5, 2008

$1.50

OBAMA

RACIAL BARRIER FALLS IN DECISIVE VICTORY

Democrats in Congress Strengthen Grip

PRESIDENT-ELECT

SENATE

29.18 Obama Makes History The United States turned a page on its troubled racial past when it elected Barack Obama as the nation's first African American president in 2008.

Bush was widely unpopular when he left office in 2009, and high expectations to end the war in Iraq and solve the nation's growing financial crisis awaited the incoming president Barack Obama. In difficult economic times the liberal vision of government gained new currency amid demands for increased government spending and regulation. How Obama planned to shape the liberal vision to meet these new circumstances, and the competing conservative response, lay in the future.

CHAPTER REVIEW

1989

Fall of the Berlin Wall
Symbolizes demise of communism in Eastern Europe

Chinese students occupy Tiananmen Square
Communist government violently suppresses pro-democracy movement

1991

Persian Gulf War
United States announces intention to build "a new world order"

Soviet Union ceases to exist
United States declares victory in the Cold War

Los Angeles police acquitted of wrongfully beating Rodney King
A four-day riot erupts in Los Angeles minority neighborhoods

1998

UN withdraws weapon inspectors from an uncooperative Iraq
Growing U.S. alarm over Hussein's drive to acquire nuclear weapons

Home prices begin to surge
Encourages banks and Wall Street to invest in risky mortgages

President Bill Clinton impeached
Cleared of charges, but scandal mars Clinton's second term

Review Questions

1. What factors contributed to the ending of the Cold War?
2. What competing ideas emerged over the role that America should play in the world from 1989 to 2009? How did these ideas shape key American foreign policy decisions in this period?
3. How did technological and demographic changes affect American society? What controversies emerged over immigration, gay marriage, and computers?
4. How did liberals and conservatives modify their long-standing visions of the role government should play? How successful were they in realizing their new, modified visions?
5. Compare the differences and similarities in the U.S path to war in the 1991 Persian Gulf War and the 2003 Iraq War. Why was the 2003 war more controversial at home than the 1991 one?
6. What role did the media play in shaping American attitudes about world events?
7. How did the United States reconcile its domestic values with its new imperialistic ventures in the world from 1989-2009?

2000

al-Qaeda attacks *USS Cole* near Yemen
Precursor to 9/11 attacks inside the United States

George W. Bush elected president
Controversy over disputed recount in Florida divides the nation

2001

al-Qaeda terrorists attack U.S. targets
United States begins "war on terror" overseas and at home

United States rejects Kyoto Protocol
Stalls domestic campaign to reduce greenhouse gas emissions

Congress passes the Patriot Act
Americans debate whether law protects nation or violates civil liberties

2003

Iraq War begins
Preemptive war puts U.S. troops in Iraq indefinitely

2008

Economic downturn begins
Economists predict worst financial crisis since the Great Depression

Barack Obama elected president
First African American elected president

California rejects gay marriage
Joins majority of states in banning same-sex marriages

Key Terms

American with Disabilities Act A 1990 civil rights law that prohibited discrimination against the disabled in employment, public accommodations, and telecommunications. **880**

Powell Doctrine General Colin Powell's assertion that the nation should go to war only as a last resort when the president had full support from the nation and the international community, could employ overwhelming military force to win without serious loss of American life, and had a clear exit strategy. **882**

Operation Desert Storm A massive U.S. ground assault during the Persian Gulf War that soundly defeated the Iraqi army within four days. **883**

"Don't Ask, Don't Tell" The policy instituted during the Clinton era that allowed closeted homosexuals and lesbians, gays who kept their sexual preferences hidden, to serve in the military. **884**

North American Free Trade Agreement (NAFTA) A 1992 treaty that lifted trade barriers between the United States, Mexico, and Canada. **885**

"The Contract with Americas" A 1994 Republican manifesto that envisioned reducing the size of government, less regulation, term limits for members of congress, welfare reform, and adding a balanced budget amendment to the Constitution. **885**

"compassionate conservatism" A philosophical approach to governing that emphasized using private industry, charities, and religious institutions, rather than the government, to provide community services. **887**

World Wide Web A system for organizing electronic information transmitted through the Internet. **888**

global warming The scientific theory that widespread burning of fossil fuels emitted greenhouse gases into the atmosphere that caused average global temperatures to rise. **892**

al-Qaeda A fundamentalist Islamic terrorist organization led by Saudi exile Osama bin Laden. **895**

"ethnic cleansing" The intentional mass killing of one ethnic group by another. **895**

9/11 September 11, 2001, was the day of al-Qaeda attacks on the United States; terrorists hijacked four planes and flew two into the World Trade Center towers and one into the Pentagon; one crashed on a field in Shanksville, Pennsylvania. **896**

Patriot Act A controversial 2001 law that greatly expanded the government's investigative and police powers. **897**

preemptive war The notion that the United States should remove hostile regimes with force before they could pose a serious threat. **898**

Bush Doctrine Established the unilateral right to attack nations that harbored terrorists, to launch preemptive military strikes to prevent future attack on the United States, and to replace autocratic governments with democratically elected ones. **898**

Appendix

- **The Declaration of Independence**
- **The Articles of Confederation**
- **The Constitution of the United States of America**
- **Amendments to the Constitution**
- **Presidential Elections**
- **Presidents and Vice Presidents**

For additional reference material, go to
www.pearsonamericanhistory.com
For the on-line appendix, click on Pearson American History Study Site.
The on-line appendix includes the following:

- The Declaration of Independence
- The Articles of Confederation
- The Constitution of the United States of America
- Amendments to the Constitution
- Presidential Elections
- Vice Presidents and Cabinet Members by Administration
- Supreme Court Justices
- Presidents, Congresses, and Chief Justices, 1789–2001
- Territorial Expansion of the United States (map)
- Admission of States of the Union
- U.S. Population, 1790–2000
- Ten Largest Cities by Population, 1700–1900
- Birthrate, 1820–2000 (chart)
- Death Rate, 1900–2000 (chart)
- Life Expectancy, 1900–2000 (chart)
- Urban/Rural Population, 1750–1900 (chart)
- Women in the Labor Force, 1890–1990
- United States Physical Features (map)
- United States Native Vegetation (map)
- Ancient Native American Communities (map)
- Native American Peoples, c. 1500 (map)
- Present-Day United States (map)

The Declaration of Independence

In Congress, July 4, 1776

The Unanimous Declaration of the Thirteen United States of America

When, in the course of human events, it becomes necessary for one people to dissolve the political bonds which have connected them with another, and to assume, among the powers of the earth, the separate and equal station to which the laws of nature and of nature's God entitle them, a decent respect to the opinions of mankind requires that they should declare the causes which impel them to the separation.

We hold these truths to be self-evident: That all men are created equal; that they are endowed by their Creator with certain unalienable rights; that among these are life, liberty, and the pursuit of happiness; that, to secure these rights, governments are instituted among men, deriving their just powers from the consent of the governed; that whenever any form of government becomes destructive of these ends, it is the right of the people to alter or to abolish it, and to institute new government, laying its foundation on such principles, and organizing its powers in such form, as to them shall seem most likely to effect their safety and happiness. Prudence, indeed, will dictate that governments long established should not be changed for light and transient causes; and accordingly all experience hath shown that mankind are more disposed to suffer, while evils are sufferable, than to right themselves by abolishing the forms to which they are accustomed. But when a long train of abuses and usurpations, pursuing invariably the same object, evinces a design to reduce them under absolute despotism, it is their right, it is their duty, to throw off such government, and to provide new guards for their future security. Such has been the patient sufferance of these colonies; and such is now the necessity which constrains them to alter their former systems of government. The history of the present King of Great Britain is a history of repeated injuries and usurpations, all having in direct object the establishment of an absolute tyranny over these states. To prove this, let facts be submitted to a candid world.

He has refused his assent to laws, the most wholesome and necessary for the public good.

He has forbidden his governors to pass laws of immediate and pressing importance, unless suspended in their operation till his assent should be obtained; and, when so suspended, he has utterly neglected to attend to them.

He has refused to pass other laws for the accommodation of large districts of people, unless those people would relinquish the right of representation in the legislature, a right inestimable to them, and formidable to tyrants only.

He has called together legislative bodies at places unusual, uncomfortable, and distant from the depository of their public records, for the sole purpose of fatiguing them into compliance with his measures.

He has dissolved representative houses repeatedly, for opposing, with manly firmness, his invasions on the rights of the people.

He has refused for a long time, after such dissolutions, to cause others to be elected; whereby the legislative powers, incapable of annihilation, have returned to the people at large for their exercise; the state remaining, in the mean time, exposed to all the dangers of invasions from without and convulsions within.

He has endeavored to prevent the population of these states; for that purpose obstructing the laws for naturalization of foreigners; refusing to pass others to encourage their migration hither, and raising the conditions of new appropriations of lands.

He has obstructed the administration of justice, by refusing his assent to laws for establishing judiciary powers.

He has made judges dependent on his will alone, for the tenure of their offices, and the amount and payment of their salaries.

He has erected a multitude of new offices, and sent hither swarms of officers to harass our people and eat out their substance.

He has kept among us, in times of peace, standing armies, without the consent of our legislatures.

He has affected to render the military independent of, and superior to, the civil power.

He has combined with others to subject us to a jurisdiction foreign to our constitution, and unacknowledged by our laws, giving his assent to their acts of pretended legislation:

For quartering large bodies of armed troops among us;

For protecting them, by a mock trial, from punishment for any murder which they should commit on the inhabitants of these states;

For cutting off our trade with all parts of the world;

For imposing taxes on us without our consent;

For depriving us, in many cases, of the benefits of trial by jury;

For transporting us beyond seas, to be tried for pretended offenses;

For abolishing the free system of English laws in a neighboring province, establishing therein an arbitrary government, and enlarging its boundaries, so as to render it at once an example and fit instrument for introducing the same absolute rule into these colonies.

For taking away our charters, abolishing our most valuable laws, and altering fundamentally the forms of our governments;

For suspending our own legislatures, and declaring themselves invested with power to legislate for us in all cases whatsoever.

He has abdicated government here, by declaring us out of his protection and waging war against us.

He has plundered our seas, ravaged our coasts, burned our towns, and destroyed the lives of our people.

He is at this time transporting large armies of foreign mercenaries to complete the works of death, desolation, and tyranny already begun with circumstances of cruelty and perfidy scarcely paralleled in the most barbarous ages, and totally unworthy the head of a civilized nation.

He has constrained our fellow-citizens, taken captive on the high seas, to bear arms against their country, to become the executioners of their friends and brethren, or to fall themselves by their hands.

He has excited domestic insurrection among us, and has endeavored to bring on the inhabitants of our frontiers the merciless Indian savages, whose known rule of warfare is an undistinguished destruction of all ages, sexes, and conditions.

In every stage of these oppressions we have petitioned for redress in the most humble terms; our repeated petitions have been answered only by repeated injury. A prince, whose character is thus marked by every act which may define a tyrant, is unfit to be the ruler of a free people.

Nor have we been wanting in our attentions to our British brethren. We have warned them, from time to time, of attempts by their legislature to extend an unwarrantable jurisdiction over us. We have reminded them of the circumstances of our emigration and settlement here. We have appealed to their native justice and magnanimity; and we have conjured them, by the ties of our common kindred, to disavow these usurpations, which would inevitably interrupt our connections and correspondence. They, too, have been deaf to the voice of justice and of consanguinity. We must, therefore, acquiesce in the necessity which denounces our separation, and hold them, as we hold the rest of mankind, enemies in war, in peace friends.

We, therefore, the representatives of the United States of America, in General Congress assembled, appealing to the Supreme Judge of the world for the rectitude of our intentions, do, in the name and by the authority of the good people of these colonies, solemnly publish and declare, that these United Colonies are, and of right ought to be, FREE AND INDEPENDENT STATES; that they are absolved from all allegiance to the British crown, and that all political connection between them and the state of Great Britain is, and ought to be, totally dissolved; and that, as free and independent states, they have full power to levy war, conclude peace, contract alliances, establish commerce, and do all other acts and things which independent states may of right do. And for the support of this declaration, with a firm reliance on the protection of Divine Providence, we mutually pledge to each other our lives, our fortunes, and our sacred honor.

John Hancock

Button Gwinnett
Lyman Hall
Geo. Walton
Wm. Hooper
Joseph Hewes
John Penn
Edward Rutledge
Thos. Heyward, Junr.
Thomas Lynch, Junr.
Arthur Middleton
Samuel Chase
Wm. Paca
Thos. Stone
Charles Carroll of Carrollton
George Wythe
Richard Henry Lee
Th. Jefferson
Benj. Harrison
Thos. Nelson, Jr.
Francis Lightfoot Lee
Carter Braxton
Robt. Morris
Benjamin Rush
Benja. Franklin
John Morton
Geo. Clymer
Jas. Smith
Geo. Taylor
James Wilson
Geo. Ross
Caesar Rodney
Geo. Read
Tho. M'kean
Wm. Floyd
Phil. Livingston
Frans. Lewis
Lewis Morris
Richd. Stockton
Jno. Witherspoon
Fras. Hopkinson
John Hart
Abra. Clark
Josiah Bartlett
Wm. Whipple
Saml. Adams
John Adams
Robt. Treat Paine
Elbridge Gerry
Step. Hopkins
William Ellery
Roger Sherman
Sam'el Huntington
Wm. Williams
Oliver Wolcott
Matthew Thornton

The Articles of Confederation

Between the States of New Hampshire, Massachusetts Bay, Rhode Island and Providence Plantations, Connecticut, New York, New Jersey, Pennsylvania, Delaware, Maryland, Virginia, North Carolina, South Carolina, Georgia

ARTICLE 1

The stile of this confederacy shall be "The United States of America."

ARTICLE 2

Each State retains its sovereignty, freedom and independence, and every power, jurisdiction, and right, which is not by this confederation expressly delegated to the United States, in Congress assembled.

ARTICLE 3

The said states hereby severally enter into a firm league of friendship with each other for their common defence, the security of their liberties and their mutual and general welfare; binding themselves to assist each other against all force offered to, or attacks made upon them, or any of them, on account of religion, sovereignty, trade, or any other pretence whatever.

ARTICLE 4

The better to secure and perpetuate mutual friendship and intercourse among the people of the different states in this union, the free inhabitants of each of these states, paupers, vagabonds, and fugitives from justice excepted, shall be entitled to all privileges and immunities of free citizens in the several states; and the people of each State shall have free ingress and regress to and from any other State, and shall enjoy therein all the privileges of trade and commerce, subject to the same duties, impositions, and restrictions, as the inhabitants thereof respectively; provided, that such restrictions shall not extend so far as to prevent the removal of property, imported into any State, to any other State of which the owner is an inhabitant, provided also, that no imposition, duties, or restriction, shall be laid by any State on the property of the United States, or either of them.

If any person guilty of, or charged with treason, felony, or other high misdemeanor in any State, shall flee from justice and be found in any of the United States, he shall, upon demand of the governor or executive power of the State from which he fled, be delivered up and removed to the State having jurisdiction of his offence.

Full faith and credit shall be given in each of these states to the records, acts, and judicial proceedings of the courts and magistrates of every other State.

ARTICLE 5

For the more convenient management of the general interests of the United States, delegates shall be annually appointed, in such manner as the legislature of each State shall direct, to meet in Congress, on the 1st Monday in November in every year, with a power reserved to each State to recall its delegates, or any of them, at any time within the year, and to send others in their stead for the remainder of the year.

No State shall be represented in Congress by less than two, nor by more than seven members; and no person shall be capable of being a delegate for more than three years in any term of six years; nor shall any person, being a delegate, be capable of holding any office under the United States, for which he, or any other for his benefit, receives any salary, fees, or emolument of any kind.

Each State shall maintain its own delegates in a meeting of the states, and while they act as members of the committee of the states.

In determining questions in the United States, in Congress assembled, each State shall have one vote.

Freedom of speech and debate in Congress shall not be impeached or questioned in any court or place out of Congress: and the members of Congress shall be protected in their persons from arrests and imprisonments, during the time of their going to and from, and attendance on Congress, except for treason, felony, or breach of the peace.

ARTICLE 6

No State, without the consent of the United States, in Congress assembled, shall send any embassy to, or receive any embassy from, or enter into any conference, agreement, alliance, or treaty with any king, prince, or state; nor shall any person, holding any office of profit or trust under the United States, or any of them, accept of any present, emolument, office or title, of any kind whatever, from any king, prince, or foreign state; nor shall the United States, in Congress assembled, or any of them, grant any title of nobility.

No two or more states shall enter into any treaty, confederation, or alliance, whatever, between them, without the consent of the United States, in Congress assembled, specifying accurately the purposes for which the same is to be entered into, and how long it shall continue.

No State shall lay any imposts or duties which may interfere with any stipulations in treaties entered into by the United States, in Congress assembled, with any king, prince, or state, in pursuance of any treaties already proposed by Congress to the courts of France and Spain.

No vessels of war shall be kept up in time of peace by any State, except such number only as shall be deemed necessary by the United States, in Congress assembled, for the defence of such State or its trade; nor shall any body of forces be kept up by any State, in time of peace, except such number only as, in the judgment of the United States, in Congress assembled, shall be deemed requisite to garrison the forts necessary for the defence of such State; but every State shall always keep up a well regulated and disciplined militia, sufficiently armed and accoutred, and shall provide, and constantly have ready for use, in public stores, a due number, of field pieces and tents, and a proper quantity of arms, ammunition and camp equipage.

No State shall engage in any war without the consent of the United States, in Congress assembled, unless such State be actually invaded by enemies, or shall have received certain advice of a resolution being formed by some nation of Indians to invade such State, and the danger is so imminent as not to admit of a delay till the United States, in Congress assembled, can be consulted; nor shall any State grant commissions to any ships or vessels of war, nor letters of marque or reprisal, except it be after a declaration of war by the United States, in Congress assembled, and then only against the kingdom or state, and the subjects thereof, against which war has been so declared, and under such regulations as shall be established by the United States, in Congress assembled, unless such States be infested by pirates, in which case vessels of war may be fitted out for that occasion, and kept so long as the danger shall continue, or until the United States, in Congress assembled, shall determine otherwise.

ARTICLE 7

When land forces are raised by any State for the common defence, all officers of or under the rank of colonel, shall be appointed by the legislature of each State respectively, by whom such forces shall be raised, or in such manner as such State shall direct; and all vacancies shall be filled up by the State which first made the appointment.

ARTICLE 8

All charges of war and all other expences, that shall be incurred for the common defence or general welfare, and allowed by the United States, in Congress assembled, shall be defrayed out of a common treasury, which shall be supplied by the several states, in proportion to the value of all land within each State, granted to or surveyed for any person, as such land and the buildings and improvements thereon shall be estimated according to such mode as the United States, in Congress assembled, shall, from time to time, direct and appoint.

The taxes for paying that proportion shall be laid and levied by the authority and direction of the legislatures of the several states, within the time agreed upon by the United States, in Congress assembled.

ARTICLE 9

The United States, in Congress assembled, shall have the sole and exclusive right and power of determining on peace and war, except in the cases mentioned in the 6th article; of sending and receiving ambassadors; entering into treaties and alliances, provided that no treaty of commerce shall be made, whereby the legislative power of the respective states shall be restrained from imposing such imposts and duties on foreigners as their own people are subjected to, or from prohibiting the exportation or importation of any species of goods or commodities whatsoever; of establishing rules for deciding, in all cases, what captures on land or water shall be legal, and in what manner prizes, taken by land or naval forces in the service of the United States, shall be divided or appropriated; of granting letters of marque and reprisal in times of peace; appointing courts for the trial of piracies and felonies committed on the high seas, and establishing courts for receiving and determining, finally, appeals in all cases of captures; provided, that no member of Congress shall be appointed a judge of any of the said courts.

The United States, in Congress assembled, shall also be the last resort on appeal in all disputes and differences now subsisting, or that hereafter may arise between two or more states concerning boundary, jurisdiction or any other cause whatever; which authority shall always be exercised in the manner following: whenever the legislative or executive authority, or lawful agent of any State, in controversy with another, shall present a petition to Congress, stating the matter in question, and praying for a hearing, notice thereof shall be given, by order of Congress, to the legislative or executive authority of the other State in controversy, and a day assigned for the appearance of the parties by their lawful agents, who shall then be directed to appoint, by joint consent, commissioners or judges to constitute a court for hearing and determining the matter in question; but, if they cannot agree, Congress shall name three persons out of each of the United States, and from the list of such persons each party shall alternately strike out one, in the petitioners beginning, until the number shall be reduced to thirteen; and from that number not less than seven, nor more than nine names, as Congress shall direct, shall, in the presence of Congress, be drawn out by lot; and the persons whose names shall be drawn, or any five of them, shall be commissioners or judges to hear and finally determine the controversy, so always as a major part of the judges who shall hear the cause shall agree in the determination; and if either party shall neglect to attend at the day appointed, without shewing reasons which Congress shall judge sufficient, or, being present, shall refuse to strike, the Congress shall proceed to nominate three persons out of each State, and the secretary of Congress shall strike in behalf of such party absent or refusing; and the judgment and sentence of the court to be appointed, in the manner before prescribed, shall be final and conclusive; and if any of the parties shall refuse to submit to the authority of such court, or to appear or defend their claim or cause, the court shall nevertheless proceed to pronounce sentence or judgment, which shall, in like manner, be final and decisive, the judgment or sentence and other proceedings being, in either case, transmitted to Congress, and lodged among the acts of Congress for the security of the parties concerned: provided, that every commissioner, before he sits in judgment, shall take an oath, to be administered by one of the judges of the supreme or superior court of the State where the cause shall be tried, "well and truly to hear and determine the matter in question, according to the best of his judgment, without favor, affection, or hope of reward": provided, also, that no State shall be deprived of territory for the benefit of the United States.

All controversies concerning the private right of soil, claimed under different grants of two or more states, whose jurisdictions, as they may respect such lands and the states which passed such grants, are adjusted, the said grants, or either of them, being at the same time claimed to have originated antecedent to such settlement of jurisdiction, shall, on the petition of either party to the Congress of the United States, be finally determined, as near as may be, in the same manner as is before prescribed for deciding disputes respecting territorial jurisdiction between different states.

The United States, in Congress assembled, shall also have the sole and exclusive right and power of regulating the alloy and value of coin struck by their own authority, or by that of the respective states; fixing the standard of weights and measures throughout the United States; regulating the trade and managing all affairs with the Indians not members of any of the states; provided that the legislative right of any State within its own limits be not infringed or violated; establishing and regulating post offices from one State to another throughout all the United States, and exacting such postage on the papers passing through the same as may be requisite to defray the expences of the said office; appointing all officers of the land forces in the service of the United States, excepting regimental officers; appointing all the officers of the naval forces, and commissioning all officers whatever in the service of the United States; making rules for the government and regulation of the said land and naval forces, and directing their operations.

The United States, in Congress assembled, shall have authority to appoint a committee to sit in the recess of Congress, to be denominated "a Committee of the States," and to consist of one delegate from each State, and to appoint such other committees and civil officers as may be necessary for managing the general affairs of the United States, under their direction; to appoint one of their number to preside; provided that no person be allowed to serve in the office of president more than one year in any term of three years; to ascertain the necessary sums of money to be raised for the service of the United States, and to appropriate and apply the same for defraying the public expences; to borrow money or emit bills on the credit of the United States, transmitting, every half year, to the respective states, an account of the sums of money so borrowed or emitted; to build and equip a navy; to agree upon the number of land forces, and to make requisitions from each State for its quota, in proportion to the number of white inhabitants in such State; which requisitions shall be binding; and, thereupon, the legislature of each State shall appoint the regimental officers, raise the men, and cloathe, arm, and equip them in a soldier-like manner, at the expence of the United States; and the officers and men so cloathed, armed, and equipped, shall march to the place appointed and within the time agreed on by the United States, in Congress assembled; but if the United States, in Congress assembled, shall, on consideration of circumstances, judge proper that any State should not raise men, or should raise a smaller number than its quota, and that any other State should raise a greater number of men than the quota thereof, such extra number shall be raised, officered, cloathed, armed, and equipped in the same manner as the quota of such State, unless the legislature of such State shall judge that such extra number cannot be safely spared out of the same, in which case they shall raise, officer, cloathe, arm, and equip as many of such extra number as they judge can be safely spared. And the officers and men so cloathed, armed, and equipped, shall march to the place appointed and within the time agreed on by the United States, in Congress assembled.

The United States, in Congress assembled, shall never engage in a war, nor grant letters of marque and reprisal in time of peace, nor enter into any treaties or alliances, nor coin money, nor regulate the value thereof, nor ascertain the sums and expences necessary for the defence and welfare of the United States, or any of them: nor emit bills, nor borrow money on the credit of the United States, nor appropriate money, nor agree upon the number of vessels of war to be built or purchased, or the number of land or sea forces to be raised, nor appoint a commander in chief of the army or navy, unless nine states assent to the same; nor shall a question on any other point, except for adjourning from day to day, be determined, unless by the votes of a majority of the United States, in Congress assembled.

The Congress of the United States shall have power to adjourn to any time within the year, and to any place within the United States, so that no period of adjournment be for a longer duration than the space of six months, and shall publish the journal of their proceedings monthly, except such parts thereof, relating to treaties, alliances or military operations, as, in their judgment, require secrecy; and the yeas and nays of the delegates of each State on any question shall be entered on the journal, when it is desired by any delegate; and the delegates of a State, or any of them, at his, or their request, shall be furnished with a transcript of the said journal, except such parts as are above excepted, to lay before the legislatures of the several states.

ARTICLE 10

The committee of the states, or any nine of them, shall be authorized to execute, in the recess of Congress, such of the powers of Congress as the United States, in Congress assembled, by the consent of nine states, shall, from time to time, think expedient to vest them with; provided, that no power be delegated to the said committee for the exercise of which by the articles of confederation, the voice of nine states, in the Congress of the United States assembled, is requisite.

ARTICLE 11

Canada acceding to this confederation, and joining in the measures of the United States, shall be admitted into and entitled to all the advantages of this union; but no other colony shall be admitted into the same, unless such admission be agreed to by nine states.

ARTICLE 12

All bills of credit emitted, monies borrowed and debts contracted by, or under the authority of Congress before the assembling of the United States, in pursuance of the present confederation, shall be deemed and considered as a charge against the United States, for payment and satisfaction whereof the said United States and the public faith are hereby solemnly pledged.

ARTICLE 13

Every State shall abide by the determinations of the United States, in Congress assembled, on all questions which, by this confederation, are submitted to them. And the articles of this confederation shall be inviolably observed by every State, and the union shall be perpetual; nor shall any alteration at any time hereafter be made in any of them, unless such alteration be agreed to in a Congress of the United States, and be afterwards confirmed by the legislatures of every State.

These articles shall be proposed to the legislatures of all the United States, to be considered, and if approved of by them, they are advised to authorize their delegates to ratify the same in the Congress of the United States; which being done, the same shall become conclusive.

The Constitution of the United States of America

PREAMBLE

We the People of the United States, in Order to form a more perfect Union, establish Justice, insure domestic Tranquility, provide for the common defence, promote the general Welfare, and secure the Blessings of Liberty to ourselves and our Posterity, do ordain and establish this Constitution for the United States of America.

ARTICLE 1

Section 1

All legislative Powers herein granted shall be vested in a Congress of the United States, which shall consist of a Senate and House of Representatives.

Section 2

The House of Representatives shall be composed of Members chosen every second Year by the People of the several States, and the Electors in each State shall have the Qualifications requisite for Electors of the most numerous Branch of the State Legislature.

No Person shall be a Representative who shall not have attained to the Age of twenty five Years, and been seven Years a Citizen of the United States, and who shall not, when elected, be an inhabitant of that State in which he shall be chosen.

Representatives and direct Taxes shall be apportioned among the several States which may be included within this Union, according to their respective Numbers, *which shall be determined by adding to the whole Number of free Persons, including those bound to Service for a Term of Years, and excluding Indians not taxed, three fifths of all other Persons.** The actual Enumeration shall be made within three Years after the first Meeting of the Congress of the United States, and within every subsequent Term of ten Years, in such Manner as they shall by Law direct. The Number of Representatives shall not exceed one for every thirty Thousand, but each State shall have at Least one Representative; *and until such enumeration shall be made, the State of New Hampshire shall be entitled to chuse three, Massachusetts eight, Rhode-Island and Providence Plantations one, Connecticut five, New York six, New Jersey four, Pennsylvania eight, Delaware one, Maryland six, Virginia ten, North Carolina five, South Carolina five, and Georgia three.*

When vacancies happen in the Representation from any State, the Executive Authority thereof shall issue Writs of Election to fill such Vacancies.

The House of Representatives shall chuse their Speaker and other Officers; and shall have the sole Power of Impeachment.

Section 3

The Senate of the United States shall be composed of two Senators from each State, chosen by the Legislature thereof, for six Years; and each Senator shall have one Vote.

Immediately after they shall be assembled in Consequence of the first Election, they shall be divided as equally as may be into three Classes. The Seats of the Senators of the first Class shall be vacated at the Expiration of the second Year, of the second Class at the Expiration of the fourth Year, and of the third Class at the Expiration of the sixth Year so that one third may be chosen every second Year; and if Vacancies happen by Resignation, or otherwise, during the Recess of the Legislature of any state, the Executive thereof may make temporary Appointments until the next Meeting of the Legislature, which shall then fill such Vacancies.

No Person shall be a Senator who shall not have attained to the Age of thirty Years, and been nine Years a Citizen of the United States, and who shall not, when elected, be an Inhabitant of that State for which he shall be chosen.

The Vice President of the United States shall be President of the Senate, but shall have no Vote, unless they be equally divided.

The Senate shall chuse their other Officers, and also a President *pro tempore*, in the Absence of the Vice President, or when he shall exercise the Office of President of the United States.

The Senate shall have the sole Power to try all Impeachments. When sitting for that Purpose, they shall be on Oath or Affirmation. When the President of the United States is tried the Chief Justice shall preside: And no Person shall be convicted without the Concurrence of two thirds of the Members present.

Judgment in Cases of Impeachment shall not extend further than to removal from Office, and disqualification to hold and enjoy any Office of honor, Trust or Profit under the United States: but the Party convicted shall nevertheless be liable and subject to Indictment, Trial, Judgment and Punishment, according to Law.

Section 4

The Times, Places and Manner of holding Elections for Senators and Representatives, shall be prescribed in each State by the Legislature thereof; but the Congress may at any time by Law

*Passages no longer in effect are printed in italic type.

make or alter such Regulations, except as to the Places of chusing Senators.

The Congress shall assemble at least once in every Year, *and such Meeting shall be on the first Monday in December, unless they shall by Law appoint a different Day.*

Section 5

Each House shall be the Judge of the Elections, Returns and Qualifications of its own Members, and a Majority of each shall constitute a Quorum to do Business; but a smaller Number may adjourn from day to day, and may be authorized to compel the Attendance of absent Members, in such Manner, and under such Penalties as each House may provide.

Each House may determine the Rules of its Proceedings, punish its Members for disorderly Behaviour, and, with the Concurrence of two thirds, expel a Member.

Each House shall keep a Journal of its Proceedings, and from time to time publish the same, excepting such Parts as may in their Judgment require Secrecy; and the Yeas and Nays of the Members of either House on any question shall, at the Desire of one fifth of those Present, be entered on the Journal.

Neither House, during the Session of Congress, shall, without the Consent of the other, adjourn for more than three days, nor to any other Place than that in which the two Houses shall be sitting.

Section 6

The Senators and Representatives shall receive a Compensation for their Services, to be ascertained by Law, and paid out of the Treasury of the United States. They shall in all Cases, except Treason, Felony and Breach of the Peace, be privileged from Arrest during their Attendance at the Session of their respective Houses, and in going to and returning from the same; and for any Speech or Debate in either House, they shall not be questioned in any other Place.

No Senator or Representative shall, during the Time for which he was elected, be appointed to any civil Office under the Authority of the United States, which shall have been created, or the Emoluments whereof shall have been encreased during such time, and no Person holding any Office under the United States, shall be a Member of either House during his Continuance in Office.

Section 7

All Bills for raising Revenue shall orginate in the House of Representatives; but the Senate may propose or concur with Amendments as on other Bills.

Every Bill which shall have passed the House of Representatives and the Senate, shall, before it become a Law, be presented to the President of the United States; If he approve he shall sign it, but if not he shall return it, with his Objections to the House in which it shall have originated, who shall enter the Objections at large on their Journal, and proceed to reconsider it. If after such Reconsideration two thirds of that House shall agree to pass the Bill, it shall be sent, together with the Objections, to the other House, by which it shall likewise be reconsidered, and if approved by two thirds of that House, it shall become a Law. But in all such Cases the Votes of both Houses shall be determined by yeas and Nays, and the Names of the Persons voting for and against the Bill shall be entered on the Journal of each House respectively. If any Bill shall not be returned by the President within ten Days (Sundays excepted) after it shall have been presented to him, the Same shall be a Law, in like Manner as if he had signed it, unless the Congress by their Adjournment prevent its Return, in which Case it shall not be a Law.

Every Order, Resolution, or Vote to which the Concurrence of the Senate and House of Representatives may be necessary (except on a question of Adjournment) shall be presented to the President of the United States; and before the Same shall take Effect, shall be approved by him, or being disapproved by him, shall be repassed by two thirds of the Senate and House of Representatives, according to the Rules and Limitations prescribed in the Case of a Bill.

Section 8

The Congress shall have Power To lay and collect Taxes, Duties, Imposts and Excises, to pay the Debts and provide for the common Defence and general Welfare of the United States; but all Duties, Imposts and Excises shall be uniform throughout the United States;

To borrow Money on the credit of the United States;

To regulate Commerce with foreign Nations, and among the several States, and with the Indian Tribes;

To establish an uniform Rule of Naturalization, and uniform Laws on the subject of Bankruptcies throughout the United States;

To coin Money, regulate the Value thereof, and of foreign Coin, and fix the Standard of Weights and Measures;

To provide for the Punishment of counterfeiting the Securities and current Coin of the United States;

To establish Post Offices and post Roads;

To promote the Progress of Science and useful Arts, by securing for limited Times to Authors and Inventors the exclusive Right to their respective Writings and Discoveries;

To constitute Tribunals inferior to the supreme Court;

To define and punish Piracies and Felonies committed on the high Seas, and Offences against the Law of Nations;

To declare War, grant Letters of Marque and Reprisal, and make Rules concerning Captures on Land and Water;

To raise and support Armies, but no Appropriation of Money to that Use shall be for a longer Term than two Years;

To provide and maintain a Navy;

To make Rules for the Government and Regulation of the land and naval Forces;

To provide for calling forth the Militia to execute the Laws of the Union, suppress Insurrections and repel Invasions;

To provide for organizing, arming, and disciplining, the Militia, and for governing such Part of them as may be employed in the Service of the United States, reserving to the States respectively, the Appointment of the Officers, and the Authority of training the Militia according to the discipline prescribed by Congress;

To exercise exclusive Legislation in all Cases whatsoever, over such District (not exceeding ten Miles square) as may, by Cession of particular States, and the Acceptance of Congress, become the Seat of the Government of the United States, and to exercise like Authority over all Places purchased by the Consent of the Legislature of the State in which the Same shall be, for the Erection of Forts, Magazines, Arsenals, dock-Yards, and other needful Buildings;—And

To make all Laws which shall be necessary and proper for carrying into Execution the foregoing Powers, and all other Powers vested by this Constitution in the Government of the United States, or in any Department of Officer thereof.

Section 9

The Migration or Importation of such Persons as any of the States now existing shall think proper to admit, shall not be prohibited by the Congress prior to the Year one thousand eight hundred and eight, but a Tax or duty may be imposed on such Importation, not exceeding ten dollars for each Person.

The Privilege of the Writ of Habeas Corpus shall not be suspended, unless when in Cases of Rebellion or Invasion the public Safety may require it.

No Bill of Attainder or ex post facto Law shall be passed.

No Capitation, or other direct, Tax shall be laid, unless in Proportion to the Census or Enumeration herein before directed to be taken.

No Tax or Duty shall be laid on Articles exported from any State.

No Preference shall be given by any Regulation of Commerce or Revenue to the Ports of one State over those of another: nor shall Vessels bound to, or from, one State, be obliged to enter, clear, or pay Duties in another.

No Money shall be drawn from the Treasury, but in Consequence of Appropriations made by Law; and a regular Statement and Account of the Receipts and Expenditures of all public Money shall be published from time to time.

No Title of Nobility shall be granted by the United States: And no Person holding any Office of Profit or Trust under them, shall, without the Consent of the Congress, accept of any present, Emolument, Office, or Title, of any kind whatever, from any King, Prince, or foreign State.

Section 10

No State shall enter into any Treaty, Alliance, or Confederation; grant Letters of Marque and Reprisal; coin Money; emit Bills of Credit; make any Thing but gold and silver Coin a Tender in Payment of Debts; pass any Bill of Attainder, ex post facto Law, or Law impairing the obligation of Contracts, or grant any Title of Nobility.

No State shall, without the Consent of the Congress, lay any Imposts or Duties on Imports or Exports, except what may be absolutely necessary for executing its inspection Laws: and the net Produce of all Duties and Imposts, laid by any State on Imports or Exports, shall be for the Use of the Treasury of the United States; and all such Laws shall be subject to the Revision and Controul of the Congress.

No State shall, without the Consent of Congress, lay any Duty of Tonnage, keep Troops, or Ships of War in time of Peace, enter into any Agreement or Compact with another State, or with a foreign Power, or engage in War, unless actually invaded, or in such imminent Danger as will not admit of delay.

ARTICLE II

Section 1

The executive Power shall be vested in a President of the United States of America. He shall hold his Office during the Term of four Years, and, together with the Vice President, chosen for the same Term, be elected, as follows:

Each State shall appoint, in such Manner as the Legislature thereof may direct, a Number of Electors, equal to the whole Number of Senators and Representatives to which the State may be entitled in the Congress: but no Senator or Representative, or Person holding an Office of Trust or Profit under the United States, shall be appointed an Elector.

The Electors shall meet in their respective States, and vote by Ballot for two Persons, of whom one at least shall not be an Inhabitant of the same State with themselves. And they shall make a List of all the Persons voted for, and of the Number of Votes for each; which List they shall sign and certify, and transmit sealed to the Seat of the Government of the United States, directed to the President of the Senate. The President of the Senate shall, in the Presence of the Senate and House of Representatives, open all the Certificates, and the Votes shall then be counted. The Person having the greatest Number of Votes shall be the President, if such Number be a Majority of the whole number of Electors appointed; and if there be more than one who have such Majority, and have an equal Number of Votes, then the House of Representatives shall immediately chuse by Ballot one of them for President; and if no Person have a Majority, then from the five highest on the List the said House shall in like Manner chuse the President. But in chusing the President, the Votes shall be taken by States, the Representation from each State having one Vote; A quorum for this Purpose shall consist of a Member or Members from two thirds of the States, and a Majority of all the States shall be necessary to a Choice. In every Case, after the Choice of the President, the Person having the greatest Number of Votes of the Electors shall be the Vice President. But if there should remain two or more who have equal Votes, the Senate shall chuse from them by Ballot the Vice President.

The Congress may determine the time of chusing the Electors, and the Day on which they shall give their Votes; which Day shall be the same throughout the United States.

No person except a natural born Citizen, *or a Citizen of the United States, at the time of the Adoption of this Constitution,* shall be eligible to the Office of President; neither shall any Person be eligible to that Office who shall not have attained to the Age of thirty five Years, and been fourteen Years a Resident within the United States.

In Case of the Removal of the President from Office, or of his Death, Resignation, or Inability to discharge the Powers and Duties of the said Office, the Same shall devolve on the Vice President, and the Congress may by Law provide for the Case of Removal, Death, Resignation or Inability, both of the President and Vice President, declaring what Officer shall then act as President, and such Officer shall act accordingly, until the Disability be removed, or a President shall be elected.

The President shall, at stated Times, receive for his Services, a Compensation, which shall neither be encreased nor diminished during the Period for which he shall have been elected, and he shall not receive within that period any other Emolument from the United States, or any of them.

Before he enter on the Execution of his Office, he shall take the following Oath or Affirmation:—"I do solemnly swear (or affirm) that I will faithfully execute the Office of President of the United States, and will to the best of my Ability, preserve, protect and defend the Constitution of the United States."

Section 2

The President shall be Commander in Chief of the Army and Navy of the United States, and of the Militia of the several States, when called into the actual Service of the United States; he may require the Opinion, in writing, of the principal Officer in each of the executive Departments, upon any Subject relating to the Duties of their respective Offices, and he shall have Power to grant Reprieves and Pardons for Offences against the United States, except in Cases of Impeachment.

He shall have Power, by and with the Advice and Consent of the Senate, to make Treaties, provided two thirds of the Senators present concur; and he shall nominate, and by and with the Advice and Consent of the Senate, shall appoint Ambassadors, other public Ministers and Consuls, Judges of the supreme Court, and all other Officers of the United States, whose Appointments are not herein otherwise provided for, and which shall be established by Law: but the Congress may by Law vest the Appointment of such inferior Officers, as they think proper in the President alone, in the Courts of Law, or in the Heads of Departments.

The President shall have Power to fill up all Vacancies that may happen during the Recess of the Senate, by granting Commissions which shall expire at the End of their next Session.

Section 3

He shall from time to time give to the Congress Information of the State of the Union, and recommend to their Consideration such Measures as he shall judge necessary and expedient; he may, on extraordinary Occasions, convene both Houses, or either of them, and in Case of disagreement between them, with Respect to the Time of Adjournment, he may adjourn them to such Time as he shall think proper; he shall receive Ambassadors and other public Ministers; he shall take Care that the Laws be faithfully executed, and shall Commission all the officers of the United States.

Section 4

The President, Vice President and all civil Officers of the United States, shall be removed from Office on Impeachment for, and Conviction of, Treason, Bribery or other high Crimes and Misdemeanors.

ARTICLE III

Section 1

The judicial Power of the United States, shall be vested in one supreme Court, and in such inferior Courts as the Congress may from time to time ordain and establish. The Judges, both of the supreme and inferior Courts, shall hold their offices during good Behaviour, and shall, at stated Times, receive for their Services, a Compensation, which shall not be diminished during their Continuance in Office.

Section 2

The judicial Power shall extend to all Cases, in Law and Equity, arising under this Constitution, the Laws of the United States, and Treaties made, or which shall be made, under their Authority;—to all Cases affecting Ambassadors, other public Ministers and Consuls;—to all Cases of admiralty and maritime Jurisdiction;—to Controversies to which the United States shall be a Party;—to Controversies between two or more States;—between a State and Citizens of another State;—between Citizens of different States;—between Citizens of the same State claiming Lands under Grants of different States, and between a State, or the Citizens thereof, and foreign States, Citizens or Subjects.

In all Cases affecting Ambassadors, other public Ministers and Consuls, and those in which a State shall be Party, the supreme Court shall have original Jurisdiction. In all the other Cases before mentioned, the supreme Court shall have appellate Jurisdiction, both as to Law and Fact, with such Exceptions, and under such Regulations as the Congress shall make.

The Trial of all Crimes, except in Cases of Impeachment, shall be by Jury; and such Trial shall be held in the State where the said Crimes shall have been committed, but when not committed within any State, the Trial shall be at such Place or Places as the Congress may by Law have directed.

Section 3

Treason against the United States, shall consist only in levying War against them, or in adhering to their Enemies, giving them Aid and Comfort. No person shall be convicted of Treason unless on the Testimony of two Witnesses to the same overt Act, or on Confession in open Court.

The Congress shall have Power to declare the Punishment of Treason, but no Attainder of Treason shall work Corruption of Blood, or Forfeiture except during the Life of the Person attainted.

ARTICLE IV

Section 1

Full Faith and Credit shall be given in each State to the public Acts, Records, and judicial Proceedings of every other State. And the Congress may by general Laws prescribe the Manner in which such Acts, Records and Proceedings shall be proved, and the Effect thereof.

Section 2

The Citizens of each State shall be entitled to all Privileges and Immunities of Citizens in the several States.

A Person charged in any State with Treason, Felony, or other Crime, who shall flee from Justice, and be found in another State, shall on Demand of the executive Authority of the State from which he fled, be delivered up, to be removed to the State having Jurisdiction of the Crime.

No Person held to Service or Labour in one State, under the Laws thereof, escaping into another, shall, in Consequence of any Law or Regulation therein, be discharged from such Service or Labour, but shall be delivered up on Claim of the Party to whom such Service or Labour may be due.

Section 3

New States may be admitted by the Congress into this Union; but no new State shall be formed or erected within the Jurisdiction of any other State; nor any State be formed by the Junction of two or more States, or Parts of States, without the Consent of the Legislatures of the States concerned as well as of the Congress.

The Congress shall have Power to dispose of and make all needful Rules and Regulations respecting the Territory or other Property belonging to the United States; and nothing in this Constitution shall be so construed as to Prejudice any Claims of the United States, or of any particular States.

Section 4

The United States shall guarantee to every State in this Union a Republican Form of Government, and shall protect each of them against Invasion; and on Application of the Legislature, or of the Executive (when the Legislature cannot be convened) against domestic violence.

ARTICLE V

The Congress, whenever two thirds of both Houses shall deem it necessary, shall propose Amendments to this Constitution, or, on the Application of the Legislatures of two thirds of the several States, shall call a Convention for proposing Amendments, which, in either Case, shall be valid to all Intents and Purposes, as Part of this Constitution, when ratified by the Legislatures of three fourths of the several States, or by Conventions in three fourths thereof, as the one or the other Mode of Ratification may be proposed by the Congress; Provided that *no Amendment which may be made prior to the Year One thousand eight hundred and eight shall in any Manner affect the first and fourth Clauses in the Ninth Section of the first Article;* and that no State, without its Consent, shall be deprived of its equal Suffrage in the Senate.

ARTICLE VI

All Debts contracted and Engagements entered into, before the Adoption of this Constitution, shall be as valid against the United States under this Constitution, as under the Confederation.

This Constitution, and Laws of the United States which shall be made in Pursuance thereof; and all Treaties made, or which shall be made, under the Authority of the United States, shall be the supreme Law of the Land; and the Judges in every State shall be bound thereby, any Thing in the Constitution or Laws of any State to the Contrary notwithstanding.

The Senators and Representatives before mentioned, and the Members of the several State Legislatures, and all executive and Judicial Officers, both of the United States and of the several States, shall be bound by Oath or Affirmation, to support this Constitution; but no religious Test shall ever be required as a Qualification to any Office of public Trust under the United States.

ARTICLE VII

The Ratification of the Conventions of nine States, shall be sufficient for the Establishment of this Constitution between the States so ratifying the Same.

Done in Convention by the Unanimous Consent of the States present the Seventeenth Day of September in the Year of our Lord one thousand seven hundred and Eighty seven and of the Independence of the United States of America the Twelfth* IN WITNESS whereof We have hereunto subscribed our Names,

*The Constitution was submitted on September 17, 1787, by the Constitutional Convention, was ratified by the Convention of several states at various dates up to May 29, 1790, and became effective on March 4, 1789.

George Washington
President and Deputy from Virginia

Delaware
George Read
Gunning Bedford, Jr.
John Dickinson
Richard Bassett
Jacob Broom

Maryland
James McHenry
Daniel of St. Thomas Jenifer
Daniel Carroll

Virginia
John Blair
James Madison, Jr

North Carolina
William Blount
Richard Dobbs Spraight
Hugh Williamson

South Carolina
John Rutledge
Charles Cotesworth Pinckney
Charles Pinckney
Pierce Butler

Georgia
William Few
Abraham Baldwin

New Hampshire
John Langdon
Nicholas Gilman

Massachusetts
Nathaniel Gorham
Rufus King

Connecticut
William Samuel Johnson
Roger Sherman

New York
Alexander Hamilton

New Jersey
William Livingston
David Brearley
William Paterson
Jonathan Dayton

Pennsylvania
Benjamin Franklin
Thomas Mifflin
Robert Morris
George Clymer
Thomas FitzSimons
Jared Ingersoll
James Wilson
Gouverneur Morris

Amendments to the Constitution

AMENDMENT I

Congress shall make no law respecting an establishment of religion, or prohibiting the free exercise thereof; or abridging the freedom of speech, or of the press; or the right of the people peaceably to assemble, and to petition the Government for a redress of grievances.

AMENDMENT II

A well regulated Militia being necessary to the security of a free State, the right of the people to keep and bear Arms, shall not be infringed.

AMENDMENT III

No Soldier shall, in time of peace be quartered in any house, without the consent of the Owner, nor in time of war, but in a manner to be prescribed by law.

AMENDMENT IV

The right of the people to be secure in their persons, houses, papers, and effects, against unreasonable searches and seizures, shall not be violated, and no Warrants shall issue, but upon probable cause, supported by Oath or affirmation, and particularly describing the place to be searched, and the persons or things to be seized.

AMENDMENT V

No person shall be held to answer for a capital, or otherwise infamous crime, unless on a presentment or indictment of a Grand Jury, except in cases arising in the land or naval forces, or in the Militia, when in actual service in time of War or public danger; nor shall any person be subject for the same offense to be twice put in jeopardy of life or limb; nor shall be compelled in any criminal case to be a witness against himself, nor be deprived of life, liberty, or property, without due process of law; nor shall private property be taken for public use, without just compensation.

AMENDMENT VI

In all criminal prosecutions, the accused shall enjoy the right to a speedy and public trial, by an impartial jury of the State and district wherein the crime shall have been committed, which district shall have been previously ascertained by law, and to be informed of the nature and cause of the accusation; to be confronted with the witnesses against him; to have compulsory process for obtaining witnesses in his favor, and to have the Assistance of Counsel for his defence.

AMENDMENT VII

In Suits at common law, where the value in controversy shall exceed twenty dollars, the right of trial by jury shall be preserved, and no fact tried by a jury, shall be otherwise reexamined in any Court of the United States, than according to the rules of the common law.

AMENDMENT VIII

Excessive bail shall not be required, nor excessive fines imposed, nor cruel and unusual punishments inflicted.

AMENDMENT IX

The enumeration in the Constitution, of certain rights, shall not be construed to deny or disparage others retained by the people.

AMENDMENT X *

The powers not delegated to the United States by the Constitution, nor prohibited by it to the States, are reserved to the States respectively, or to the people.

AMENDMENT XI

[ADOPTED 1798]

The Judicial power of the United States shall not be construed to extend to any suit in law or equity, commenced or prosecuted against one of the United States by Citizens of another State, or by Citizens or Subjects of any Foreign State.

AMENDMENT XII

[ADOPTED 1804]

The Electors shall meet in their respective states, and vote by ballot for President and Vice President, one of whom, at least, shall not be an inhabitant of the same state with themselves; they shall name in their ballots the person voted for as President, and in distinct ballots the person voted for as Vice President, and they shall make distinct lists of all persons voted for as President, and of all persons voted for as Vice President, and of the number of votes for each, which lists they shall sign and certify, and transmit sealed to the seat of the government of the United States, directed to the President of the Senate;—The President of the Senate shall, in the presence of the Senate and House of Representatives, open all the certificates and the votes shall then be counted;—The person having the greatest number of votes for President, shall be the President, if such number be a majority of the whole number of Electors appointed; and if no person have such majority, then from the persons having the highest numbers not exceeding three

*The first ten amendments (the Bill of Rights) were ratified and their adoption was certified on December 15, 1791.

on the list of those voted for as President, the House of Representatives shall choose immediately, by ballot, the President. But in choosing the President, the votes shall be taken by states, the representation from each state having one vote; a quorum for this purpose shall consist of a member or members from two-thirds of the states, and a majority of all the states shall be necessary to a choice. And if the House of Representatives shall not choose a President whenever the right of choice shall devolve upon them, before the fourth day of March next following, then the Vice President shall act as President, as in the case of the death or other constitutional disability of the President.—The person having the greatest number of votes as Vice President, shall be the Vice President, if such number be a majority of the whole number of Electors appointed, and if no person have a majority, then from the two highest numbers on the list, the Senate shall choose the Vice President; a quorum for the purpose shall consist of two-thirds of the whole number of Senators, and a majority of the whole number shall be necessary to a choice. But no person constitutionally ineligible to the office of President shall be eligible to that of Vice President of the United States.

AMENDMENT XIII

[ADOPTED 1865]

Section 1

Neither slavery nor involuntary servitude, except as a punishment for crime whereof the party shall have been duly convicted, shall exist within the United States, or any place subject to their jurisdiction.

Section 2

Congress shall have power to enforce this article by appropriate legislation.

AMENDMENT XIV

[ADOPTED 1868]

Section 1

All persons born or naturalized in the United States, and subject to the jurisdiction thereof, are citizens of the United States and of the State wherein they reside. No State shall make or enforce any law which shall abridge the privileges or immunities of citizens of the United States; nor shall any State deprive any person of life, liberty, or property, without due process of law; nor deny to any person within its jurisdiction the equal protection of the laws.

Section 2

Representatives shall be apportioned among the several States according to their respective numbers, counting the whole number of persons in each State, excluding Indians not taxed. But when the right to vote at any election for the choice of electors for President and Vice President of the United States, Representatives in Congress, the Executive and Judicial officers of a State, or the members of the Legislature thereof, is denied to any of the male inhabitants of such State, being twenty-one years of age, and citizens of the United States, or in any way abridged, except for participation in rebellion, or other crime, the basis of representation therein shall be reduced in the proportion which the number of such male citizens shall bear to the whole number of male citizens twenty-one years of age in such State.

Section 3

No person shall be a Senator or Representative in Congress, or elector of President and Vice President, or hold any office, civil or military, under the United States, or under any State, who, having previously taken an oath, as a member of Congress, or as an officer of the United States, or as a member of any State legislature, or as an executive or judicial officer of any State, to support the Constitution of the United States, shall have engaged in insurrection or rebellion against the same, or given aid or comfort to the enemies thereof. But Congress may by a vote of two-thirds of each House, remove such disability.

Section 4

The validity of the public debt of the United States, authorized by law, including debts incurred for payment of pensions and bounties for services in suppressing insurrection or rebellion, shall not be questioned. But neither the United States nor any State shall assume or pay any debt or obligation incurred in aid of insurrection or rebellion against the United States, or any claim for the loss or emancipation of any slave; but all such debts, obligations and claims shall be held illegal and void.

Section 5

The Congress shall have power to enforce, by appropriate legislation, the provisions of this article.

AMENDMENT XV

[ADOPTED 1870]

Section 1

The right of citizens of the United States to vote shall not be denied or abridged by the United States or by any State on account of race, color, or previous condition of servitude.

Section 2

The Congress shall have power to enforce this article by appropriate legislation.

AMENDMENT XVI

[ADOPTED 1913]

The Congress shall have power to lay and collect taxes on incomes, from whatever source derived, without apportionment among the several States, and without regard to any census or enumeration.

AMENDMENT XVII

[ADOPTED 1913]

The Senate of the United States shall be composed of two Senators from each State, elected by the people thereof, for six years; and each Senator shall have one vote. The electors in each State shall have the qualifications requisite for electors of the most numerous branch of the State legislatures.

When vacancies happen in the representation of any State in the Senate, the executive authority of such State shall issue writs of election to fill such vacancies: *Provided*, That the legislature of any State may empower the executive thereof to make temporary appointments until the people fill the vacancies by election as the legislature may direct.

This amendment shall not be so construed as to affect the election or term of any Senator chosen before it becomes valid as part of the Constitution.

AMENDMENT XVIII

[ADOPTED 1919, REPEALED 1933]

Section 1

After one year from the ratification of this article the manufacture, sale, or transportation of intoxicating liquors within, the importation thereof into, or the exportation thereof from the United States and all territory subject to the jurisdiction thereof for beverage purposes is hereby prohibited.

Section 2

The Congress and the several States shall have concurrent power to enforce this article by appropriate legislation.

Section 3

This article shall be inoperative unless it shall have been ratified as an amendment to the Constitution by the legislatures of the several States, as provided in the Constitution, within seven years from the date of the submission hereof to the States by the Congress.

AMENDMENT XIX

[ADOPTED 1920]

The right of citizens of the United States to vote shall not be denied or abridged by the United States or by any State on account of sex.

Congress shall have power to enforce this article by appropriate legislation.

AMENDMENT XX

[ADOPTED 1933]

Section 1

The terms of the President and Vice President shall end at noon on the 20th day of January, and the terms of Senators and Representatives at noon on the 3d day of January, of the years in which such terms would have ended if this article had not been ratified and the terms of their successors shall then begin.

Section 2

The Congress shall assemble at least once in every year, and such meeting shall begin at noon on the 3d day of January, unless they shall by law appoint a different day.

Section 3

If, at the time fixed for the beginning of the term of the President, the President elect shall have died, the Vice President elect shall become President. If a President shall not have been chosen before the time fixed for the beginning of his term, or if the President elect shall have failed to qualify, then the Vice President elect shall act as President until a President shall have qualified; and the Congress may by law provide for the case wherein neither a President elect nor a Vice President elect shall have qualified, declaring who shall then act as President, or the manner in which one who is to act shall be selected, and such person shall act accordingly until a President or Vice President shall have qualified.

Section 4

The Congress may by law provide for the case of the death of any of the persons from whom the House of Representatives may choose a President whenever the right of choice shall have devolved upon them, and for the case of the death of any of the persons from whom the Senate may choose a Vice President whenever the right of choice shall have devolved upon them.

Section 5

Sections 1 and 2 shall take effect on the 15th day of October following the ratification of this article.

Section 6

This article shall be inoperative unless it shall have been ratified as an amendment to the Constitution by the legislatures of three fourths of the several States within seven years from the date of its submission.

AMENDMENT XXI

[ADOPTED 1933]

Section 1

The eighteenth article of amendment to the Constitution of the United States is hereby repealed.

Section 2

The transportation or importation into any State, Territory, or possession of the United States for delivery or use therein of intoxicating liquors in violation of the laws thereof, is hereby prohibited.

Section 3

This article shall be inoperative unless it shall have been ratified as an amendment to the Constitution by conventions in the several

States, as provided in the Constitution, within seven years from the date of the submission hereof to the States by the Congress.

AMENDMENT XXII

[ADOPTED 1951]

Section 1

No person shall be elected to the office of the President more than twice, and no person who has held the office of President, or acted as President, for more than two years of a term to which some other person was elected President shall be elected to the office of the President more than once. But this Article shall not apply to any person holding the office of President when this Article was proposed by the Congress, and shall not prevent any person who may be holding the office of President, or acting as President, during the term within which this Article becomes operative from holding the office of President or acting as President during the remainder of such term.

Section 2

This article shall be inoperative unless it shall have been ratified as an amendment to the Constitution by the legislatures of three-fourths of the several States within seven years from the date of its submission to the States by the Congress.

AMENDMENT XXIII

[ADOPTED 1961]

Section 1

The District constituting the seat of Government of the United States shall appoint in such manner as the Congress shall direct:

A number of electors of President and Vice President equal to the whole number of Senators and Representatives in Congress to which the District would be entitled if it were a State, but in no event more than the least populous State; they shall be in addition to those appointed by the States, but they shall be considered, for the purposes of the election of President and Vice President, to be electors appointed by a State; and they shall meet in the District and perform such duties as provided by the twelfth article of amendment.

Section 2

The Congress shall have power to enforce this article by appropriate legislation.

AMENDMENT XXIV

[ADOPTED 1964]

Section 1

The right of citizens of the United States to vote in any primary or other election for President or Vice President, for electors for President or Vice President, or for Senator or Representative in Congress, shall not be denied or abridged by the United States or any state by reason of failure to pay any poll tax or other tax.

Section 2

The Congress shall have the power to enforce this article by appropriate legislation.

AMENDMENT XXV

[ADOPTED 1967]

Section 1

In case of the removal of the President from office or his death or resignation, the Vice President shall become President.

Section 2

Whenever there is a vacancy in the office of the Vice President, the President shall nominate a Vice President who shall take the office upon confirmation by a majority vote of both houses of Congress.

Section 3

Whenever the President transmits to the President pro tempore of the Senate and the Speaker of the House of Representatives his written declaration that he is unable to discharge the powers and duties of his office, and until he transmits to them a written declaration to the contrary, such powers and duties shall be discharged by the Vice President as Acting President.

Section 4

Whenever the Vice President and a majority of either the principal officers of the executive departments or of such other body as Congress may by law provide, transmit to the President pro tempore of the Senate and the Speaker of the House of Representatives their written declaration that the President is unable to discharge the powers and duties of his office, the Vice President shall immediately assume the powers and duties of the office as Acting President.

Thereafter, when the President transmits to the President pro tempore of the Senate and the Speaker of the House of Representatives his written declaration that no inability exists, he shall resume the powers and duties of his office unless the Vice President and a majority of either the principal officers of the executive department or of such other body as Congress may by law provide, transmit within four days to the President pro tempore of the Senate and the Speaker of the House of Representatives their written declaration that the President is unable to discharge the powers and duties of his office. Thereupon Congress shall decide the issue, assembling within 48 hours for that purpose if not in session. If the Congress, within 21 days after receipt of the latter written declaration, or, if Congress is not in session, within 21 days after Congress is required to assemble, determines by two-thirds vote of both houses that the President is unable to discharge the powers and duties of his office, the Vice President shall continue to discharge the same as Acting President; otherwise, the President shall resume the powers and duties of his office.

AMENDMENT XXVI

[ADOPTED 1971]

Section 1

The right of citizens of the United States, who are 18 years of age or older, to vote shall not be denied or abridged by the United States or any state on account of age.

Section 2

The Congress shall have the power to enforce this article by appropriate legislation.

AMENDMENT XXVII

[ADOPTED 1992]

No law, varying the compensation for the services of the Senators and Representatives shall take effect, until an election of Representatives shall have intervened.

Presidential Elections

Year	Candidates	Parties	Popular Vote	Electoral Vote	Voter Participation
1789	**George Washington**		*	**69**	
	John Adams			34	
	Others			35	
1792	**George Washington**		*	**132**	
	John Adams			77	
	George Clinton			50	
	Others			5	
1796	**John Adams**	**Federalist**	*	**71**	
	Thomas Jefferson	Democratic-Republican		68	
	Thomas Pinckney	Federalist		59	
	Aaron Burr	Dem.-Rep.		30	
	Others			48	
1800	**Thomas Jefferson**	**Dem.-Rep.**	*	**73**	
	Aaron Burr	Dem.-Rep.		73	
	John Adams	Federalist		65	
	C. C. Pinckney	Federalist		64	
	John Jay	Federalist		1	
1804	**Thomas Jefferson**	**Dem.-Rep.**	*	**162**	
	C. C. Pinckney	Federalist		14	
1808	**James Madison**	**Dem.-Rep.**	*	**122**	
	C. C. Pinckney	Federalist		47	
	George Clinton	Dem.-Rep.		6	
1812	**James Madison**	**Dem.-Rep.**	*	**128**	
	De Witt Clinton	Federalist		89	
1816	**James Monroe**	**Dem.-Rep.**	*	**183**	
	Rufus King	Federalist		34	
1820	**James Monroe**	**Dem.-Rep.**	*	**231**	
	John Quincy Adams	Dem.-Rep.		1	
1824	**John Quincy Adams**	**Dem.-Rep.**	**108,740 (31%)**	**84**	**26.9%**
	Andrew Jackson	Dem.-Rep.	153,544 (44%)	99	
	William H. Crawford	Dem.-Rep.	40,856 (12%)	41	
	Henry Clay	Dem.-Rep.	47,531 (14%)	37	
1828	**Andrew Jackson**	**Democratic**	**647,286 (56.0%)**	**178**	**57.6%**
	John Quincy Adams	National Republican	508,064 (44.0%)	83	
1832	**Andrew Jackson**	**Democratic**	**688,242 (54.2%)**	**219**	**55.4%**
	Henry Clay	National Republican	473,462 (37.4%)	49	
	John Floyd	Independent		11	
	William Wirt	Anti-Mason	101,051 (7.8%)	7	

Year	Candidates	Parties	Popular Vote	Electoral Vote	Voter Participation
1836	**Martin Van Buren**	**Democratic**	**762,198 (50.8%)**	**170**	**57.8%**
	William Henry Harrison	Whig	549,508 (36.6%)	73	
	Hugh L. White	Whig	145,342 (9.7%)	26	
	Daniel Webster	Whig	41,287 (2.7%)	14	
	W. P. Magnum	Independent		11	
1840	**William Henry Harrison**	**Whig**	**1,274,624 (53.1%)**	**234**	**80.2%**
	Martin Van Buren	Democratic	1,127,781 (46.9%)	60	
	J. G. Birney	Liberty	7069	—	
1844	**James K. Polk**	**Democratic**	**1,338,464 (49.6%)**	**170**	**78.9%**
	Henry Clay	Whig	1,300,097 (48.1%)	105	
	J. G. Birney	Liberty	62,300 (2.3%)	—	
1848	**Zachary Taylor**	**Whig**	**1,360,967 (47.4%)**	**163**	**72.7%**
	Lewis Cass	Democratic	1,222,342 (42.5%)	127	
	Martin Van Buren	Free-Soil	291,263 (10.1%)	—	
1852	**Franklin Pierce**	**Democratic**	**1,601,274 (50.8%)**	**254**	**69.6%**
	Winfield Scott	Whig	1,386,580 (43.9%)	42	
	John P. Hale	Free-Soil	155,825 (5.0%)	—	
1856	**James Buchanan**	**Democratic**	**1,832,955 (45.3%)**	**174**	**78.9%**
	John C. Frémont	Republican	1,339,932 (33.1%)	114	
	Millard Fillmore	American	871,731 (21.6%)	8	
1860	**Abraham Lincoln**	**Republican**	**1,865,593 (39.8%)**	**180**	**81.2%**
	Stephen A. Douglas	Democratic	1,382,713 (29.5%)	12	
	John C. Breckinridge	Democratic	848,356 (18.1%)	72	
	John Bell	Union	592,906 (12.6%)	39	
1864	**Abraham Lincoln**	**Republican**	**2,213,655 (55.0%)**	**212†**	**73.8%**
	George B. McClellan	Democratic	1,805,237 (45.0%)	21	
1868	**Ulysses S. Grant**	**Republican**	**3,013,421 (53%)**	**214**	**78.1%**
	Horatio Seymour	Democratic	2,706,829 (47%)	80	
1872	**Ulysses S. Grant**	**Republican**	**3,597,132 (55.6%)**	**286**	**71.3%**
	Horace Greeley	Dem.; Liberal Republican	2,834,761 (43.8%)	66‡	
1876	**Rutherford B. Hayes§**	**Republican**	**4,036,572 (48.0%)**	**185**	**81.8%**
	Samuel J. Tilden	Democratic	4,284,020 (51.0%)	184	
1880	**James A. Garfield**	**Republican**	**4,454,416 (48.5%)**	**214**	**79.4%**
	Winfield S. Hancock	Democratic	4,444,952 (48.1%)	155	
1884	**Grover Cleveland**	**Democratic**	**4,874,986 (48.5%)**	**219**	**77.5%**
	James G. Blaine	Republican	4,851,981 (48.2%)	182	
1888	**Benjamin Harrison**	**Republican**	**5,439,853 (47.9%)**	**233**	**79.3%**
	Grover Cleveland	Democratic	5,540,309 (48.6%)	168	
1892	**Grover Cleveland**	**Democratic**	**5,556,918 (46.1%)**	**277**	**74.7%**
	Benjamin Harrison	Republican	5,176,108 (43.0%)	145	
	James B. Weaver	People's	1,041,028 (9%)	22	

Year	Candidates	Parties	Popular Vote	Electoral Vote	Voter Participation
1896	**William McKinley**	**Republican**	**7,104,779 (51.1%)**	**271**	**79.3%**
	William Jennings Bryan	Democratic People's	6,502,925 (47.7%)	176	
1900	**William McKinley**	**Republican**	**7,207,923 (51.7%)**	**292**	**73.2%**
	William Jennings Bryan	Dem.-Populist	6,358,133 (45.5%)	155	
1904	**Theodore Roosevelt**	**Republican**	**7,623,486 (57.9%)**	**336**	**65.2%**
	Alton B. Parker	Democratic	5,077,911 (37.6%)	140	
	Eugene V. Debs	Socialist	402,400 (3.0%)	—	
1908	**William H. Taft**	**Republican**	**7,678,908 (51.6%)**	**321**	**65.4%**
	William Jennings Bryan	Democratic	6,409,104 (43.1%)	162	
	Eugene V. Debs	Socialist	402,820 (2.8%)	—	
1912	**Woodrow Wilson**	**Democratic**	**6,296,547 (41.9%)**	**435**	**58.8%**
	Theodore Roosevelt	Progressive	4,118,571 (27.4%)	88	
	William H. Taft	Republican	3,486,720 (23.2%)	8	
	Eugene V. Debs	Socialist	900,672 (6.0%)	—	
1916	**Woodrow Wilson**	**Democratic**	**9,129,606 (49.4%)**	**277**	**61.6%**
	Charles E. Hughes	Republican	8,538,221 (46.2%)	254	
	A. L. Benson	Socialist	585,113 (3.2%)	—	
1920	**Warren G. Harding**	**Republican**	**16,152,200 (60.4%)**	**404**	**49.2%**
	James M. Cox	Democratic	9,147,353 (34.2%)	127	
	Eugene V. Debs	Socialist	917,799 (3.4%)	—	
1924	**Calvin Coolidge**	**Republican**	**15,725,016 (54.0%)**	**382**	**48.9%**
	John W. Davis	Democratic	8,386,503 (28.8%)	136	
	Robert M. La Follette	Progressive	4,822,856 (16.6%)	13	
1928	**Herbert Hoover**	**Republican**	**21,391,381 (58.2%)**	**444**	**56.9%**
	Alfred E. Smith	Democratic	15,016,443 (40.9%)	87	
	Norman Thomas	Socialist	267,835 (0.7%)	—	
1932	**Franklin D. Roosevelt**	**Democratic**	**22,821,857 (57.4%)**	**472**	**56.9%**
	Herbert Hoover	Republican	15,761,841 (39.7%)	59	
	Norman Thomas	Socialist	884,781 (2.2%)	—	
1936	**Franklin D. Roosevelt**	**Democratic**	**27,751,597 (60.8%)**	**523**	**61.0%**
	Alfred M. Landon	Republican	16,679,583 (36.5%)	8	
	William Lemke	Union	882,479 (1.9%)	—	
1940	**Franklin D. Roosevelt**	**Democratic**	**27,244,160 (54.8%)**	**449**	**62.5%**
	Wendell L. Willkie	Republican	22,305,198 (44.8%)	82	
1944	**Franklin D. Roosevelt**	**Democratic**	**25,602,504 (53.5%)**	**432**	**55.9%**
	Thomas E. Dewey	Republican	22,006,285 (46.0%)	99	
1948	**Harry S Truman**	**Democratic**	**24,105,695 (49.5%)**	**304**	**53.0%**
	Thomas E. Dewey	Republican	21,969,170 (45.1%)	189	
	J. Strom Thurmond	State-Rights Democratic	1,169,021 (2.4%)	38	
	Henry A. Wallace	Progressive	1,157,326 (2.4%)	—	

Year	Candidates	Parties	Popular Vote	Electoral Vote	Voter Participation
1952	**Dwight D. Eisenhower**	**Republican**	**33,778,963 (55.1%)**	**442**	**63.3%**
	Adlai E. Stevenson	Democratic	27,314,992 (44.4%)	89	
1956	**Dwight D. Eisenhower**	**Republican**	**35,575,420 (57.6%)**	**457**	**60.6%**
	Adlai E. Stevenson	Democratic	26,033,066 (42.1%)	73	
	Other	—	—	1	
1960	**John F. Kennedy**	**Democratic**	**34,227,096 (49.9%)**	**303**	**64%**
	Richard M. Nixon	Republican	34,108,546 (49.6%)	219	
	Other	—	—	15	
1964	**Lyndon B. Johnson**	**Democratic**	**43,126,506 (61.1%)**	**486**	**61.7%**
	Barry M. Goldwater	Republican	27,176,799 (38.5%)	52	
1968	**Richard M. Nixon**	**Republican**	**31,785,480 (44%)**	**301**	**60.6%**
	Hubert H. Humphrey	Democratic	31,275,166 (42%)	191	
	George Wallace	American Indep.	9,906,473 (14%)	46	
1972	**Richard M. Nixon**	**Republican**	**46,740,323 (60.7%)**	**520**	**55.2%**
	George S. McGovern	Democratic	28,901,598 (37.5%)	17	
	Other	—	—	1	
1976	**Jimmy Carter**	**Democratic**	**40,828,587 (50.0%)**	**297**	**53.5%**
	Gerald R. Ford	Republican	39,147,613 (47.9%)	241	
	Other	—	1,575,459 (2.1%)	—	
1980	**Ronald Reagan**	**Republican**	**43,901,812 (50.7%)**	**489**	**52.6%**
	Jimmy Carter	Democratic	35,483,820 (41.0%)	49	
	John B. Anderson	Independent	5,719,437 (6.6%)	—	
	Ed Clark	Libertarian	921,188 (1.1%)	—	
1984	**Ronald Reagan**	**Republican**	**54,455,075 (59.0%)**	**525**	**53.3%**
	Walter Mondale	Democratic	37,577,185 (41.0%)	13	
1988	**George H. W. Bush**	**Republican**	**48,886,097 (53.4%)**	**426**	**50.3%**
	Michael S. Dukakis	Democratic	41,809,074 (45.6%)	111	
1992	**William J. Clinton**	**Democratic**	**44,908,254 (43%)**	**370**	**55.1%**
	George H. W. Bush	Republican	39,102,343 (37.5%)	168	
	H. Ross Perot	Independent	19,741,065 (18.9%)	—	
1996	**William J. Clinton**	**Democratic**	**45,590,703 (50%)**	**379**	**49%**
	Robert Dole	Republican	37,816,307 (41%)	159	
	Ross Perot	Reform	7,866,284	—	
2000	**George W. Bush**	**Republican**	**50,456,062 (47.88%)**	**271**	**49.3%**
	Al Gore	Democratic	50,996,582 (48.39%)	266[‖]	
	Ralph Nader	Green	82,955 (2.72%)	—	
	Other		834,774 (less than 1%)	—	
2004	**George W. Bush**	**Republican**	**60,934,251 (51.0%)**	**286**	**55.6%**
	John F. Kerry	Democratic	57,765,291 (48.0%)	252	
	Ralph Nader	Independent	405,933 (less than 1%)	—	
2008	**Barack H. Obama**	**Democratic**	**69,456,897**	**365**	**56.8%**
	John McCain	Republican	59,934,814	173	
	Ralph Nader	Independent	738,475	0	

*Electors selected by state legislatures.

†Eleven secessionist states did not participate.

‡Greeley died before the electoral college met. His electoral votes were divided among the four minor candidates.

§Contested result settled by special election.

‖One District of Columbia Gore elector abstained.

Presidents and Vice Presidents

	President	Vice President	Term
1.	**George Washington**	John Adams	1789–1793
	George Washington	John Adams	1793–1797
2.	**John Adams**	Thomas Jefferson	1797–1801
3.	**Thomas Jefferson**	Aaron Burr	1801–1805
	Thomas Jefferson	George Clinton	1805–1809
4.	**James Madison**	George Clinton (d. 1812)	1809–1813
	James Madison	Elbridge Gerry (d. 1814)	1813–1817
5.	**James Monroe**	Daniel Tompkins	1817–1821
	James Monroe	Daniel Tompkins	1821–1825
6.	**John Quincy Adams**	John C. Calhoun	1825–1829
7.	**Andrew Jackson**	John C. Calhoun	1829–1833
	Andrew Jackson	Martin Van Buren	1833–1837
8.	**Martin Van Buren**	Richard M. Johnson	1837–1841
9.	**William H. Harrison (d. 1841)**	John Tyler	1841
10.	**John Tyler**	—	1841–1845
11.	**James K. Polk**	George M. Dallas	1845–1849
12.	**Zachary Taylor (d. 1850)**	Millard Fillmore	1849–1850
13.	**Millard Fillmore**	—	1850–1853
14.	**Franklin Pierce**	William R. King (d. 1853)	1853–1857
15.	**James Buchanan**	John C. Breckinridge	1857–1861
16.	**Abraham Lincoln**	Hannibal Hamlin	1861–1865
	Abraham Lincoln (d. 1865)	Andrew Johnson	1865
17.	**Andrew Johnson**	—	1865–1869
18.	**Ulysses S. Grant**	Schuyler Colfax	1869–1873
	Ulysses S. Grant	Henry Wilson (d. 1875)	1873–1877
19.	**Rutherford B. Hayes**	William A. Wheeler	1877–1881
20.	**James A. Garfield (d. 1881)**	Chester A. Arthur	1881
21.	**Chester A. Arthur**	—	1881–1885
22.	**Grover Cleveland**	Thomas A. Hendricks (d. 1885)	1885–1889
23.	**Benjamin Harrison**	Levi P. Morton	1889–1893
24.	**Grover Cleveland**	Adlai E. Stevenson	1893–1897
25.	**William McKinley**	Garret A. Hobart (d. 1899)	1897–1901
	William McKinley (d. 1901)	Theodore Roosevelt	1901
26.	**Theodore Roosevelt**	—	1901–1905
	Theodore Roosevelt	Charles Fairbanks	1905–1909
27.	**William H. Taft**	James S. Sherman (d. 1912)	1909–1913

	President	Vice President	Term
28.	**Woodrow Wilson**	Thomas R. Marshall	1913–1917
	Woodrow Wilson	Thomas R. Marshall	1917–1921
29.	**Warren G. Harding (d. 1923)**	Calvin Coolidge	1921–1923
30.	**Calvin Coolidge**	—	1923–1925
	Calvin Coolidge	Charles G. Dawes	1925–1929
31.	**Herbert Hoover**	Charles Curtis	1929–1933
32.	**Franklin D. Roosevelt**	John N. Garner	1933–1937
	Franklin D. Roosevelt	John N. Garner	1937–1941
	Franklin D. Roosevelt	Henry A. Wallace	1941–1945
	Franklin D. Roosevelt (d. 1945)	Harry S Truman	1945
33.	**Harry S Truman**	—	1945–1949
	Harry S Truman	Alben W. Barkley	1949–1953
34.	**Dwight D. Eisenhower**	Richard M. Nixon	1953–1957
	Dwight D. Eisenhower	Richard M. Nixon	1957–1961
35.	**John F. Kennedy (d. 1963)**	Lyndon B. Johnson	1961–1963
36.	**Lyndon B. Johnson**	—	1963–1965
	Lyndon B. Johnson	Hubert H. Humphrey	1965–1969
37.	**Richard M. Nixon**	Spiro T. Agnew	1969–1973
	Richard M. Nixon (resigned 1974)	Gerald R. Ford	1973–1974
38.	**Gerald R. Ford**	Nelson A. Rockefeller	1974–1977
39.	**Jimmy Carter**	Walter F. Mondale	1977–1981
40.	**Ronald Reagan**	George H. W. Bush	1981–1985
	Ronald Reagan	George H. W. Bush	1985–1989
41.	**George H. W. Bush**	J. Danforth Quayle	1989–1993
42.	**William J. Clinton**	Albert Gore, Jr.	1993–1997
	William J. Clinton	Albert Gore, Jr.	1997–2001
43.	**George W. Bush**	Richard Cheney	2001–2005
	George W. Bush	Richard Cheney	2005–2009
44.	**Barack H. Obama**	Joseph R. Biden, Jr.	2009–

Glossary

agent orange (p. 790) A defoliant that stripped trees of their leaves to expose Vietcong hideouts and killed crops.

Alcatraz Proclamation (p. 839) Sardonic statement issued by Indian activists who occupied the island of Alcatraz and described it as the perfect site for an Indian reservation because it lacked running water, sanitation, schools, mineral resources, and productive soil.

Alien and Sedition Acts (p. 183) Four laws designed to protect America from the danger of foreign and domestic subversion. The first three, the Alien laws, dealt with immigration and naturalization. The Sedition Act criminalized criticism of the federal government.

Allies (World War I) (p. 594) Initially composed of Britain, France, Belgium, and Russia, and would eventually total eighteen nations, including Italy and the United States.

Allies (World War II) (p. 688) Name for powers fighting Germany, eventually including the United States, Britain, France, and the Soviet Union.

American Expeditionary Forces (p. 612) Two million American soldiers who fought overseas under the command of General John J. Pershing.

American Federation of Labor (AFL) (p. 678) A craft-based organization that accepted only skilled workers, like carpenters or cigar makers, who practiced a trade.

American System (p. 226) Henry Clay's comprehensive national plan for economic growth that included protective tariffs for American industry and government investment in roads and other internal improvements.

Angel Island (p. 581) Immigration processing station in the San Francisco Bay for Asian immigrants.

Anglicization (p. 67) The colonial American desire to emulate English society, including English taste in foods, customs, and architecture.

Anti-Federalists (p. 149) The name reluctantly adopted by opponents of the Constitution who insisted that they, not their opponents, were the true supporters of the ideal of federalism. Anti-Federalists opposed weakening the power of the states and feared that the Constitution yielded too much power to the new central government.

Archaic Era (p. 5) Period beginning approximately nine thousand years ago lasting an estimated six thousand years. This period was marked by more intensive efforts on the part of ancient societies to shape the environment to enhance food production.

Articles of Confederation (p. 138) America's first constitutional government in effect from 1781–1788. The articles created a weak decentralized form of government that lacked the power to tax and compel state obedience to treaties it negotiated.

artisan production (p. 260) A system of manufacturing goods, built around apprenticeship, that defined the pre-industrial economy. The apprentice learned a trade under the guidance of an artisan who often housed, clothed, and fed the apprentice.

assumption of the state debts (p. 164) Hamilton's scheme for the federal government to take over any outstanding state debts.

Axis (p. 688) Name for nations fighting the Allies, including Germany, Italy and Japan.

Aztec (p. 6) Led by the Mexica tribe, the Aztec created a powerful empire whose capital, the great city of Tenochtitlán, was created on an island in Lake Texcoco in 1325 CE.

baby boom generation (p. 758) The 76.4 million Americans born between 1946 and 1964.

Bacon's Rebellion (p. 54) A popular uprising in Virginia in 1676 named after its leader, Nathaniel Bacon.

Bank of the United States (p. 166) A bank chartered by the federal government. The Bank served as a depository for government funds, helped bolster confidence in government securities, made loans, and provided the nation with a stable national currency.

Bank Veto Speech (p. 241) Jackson's veto of a bill to re-charter of the Bank of the United States, in which he explained why he opposed the bank and laid out his own vision of American democracy and constitutional government.

Battle of Little Bighorn (p. 456) Lt. Col. George A. Custer and the Seventh Cavalry are wiped out by a force of Cheyenne, Sioux, and Arapaho warriors on June 25, 1876; hardens white attitudes toward Native Americans.

Bay of Pigs operation (1961) (p. 745) Failed attempt to use an amphibious invasion by Cuban exiles to overthrow the Cuban dictator Fidel Castro.

Beats (p. 763) Members of the bohemian communities of poets, novelists, and artists that flourished in New York's Greenwich Village and San Francisco's North Beach and who rejected middle-class suburban values.

Berlin airlift (1948–1949) (p. 726) Americans and British used planes to resupply West Berlin to stymie the Soviet blockade of the city.

Bill of Rights (p. 161) The first ten of the original twelve amendments to the Constitution, which included protections for basic individual liberties and protections for the states.

Birmingham campaign (p. 821) Civil rights effort to desegregate Birmingham, Alabama, where shocking images of police brutality prompted Kennedy to push for a federal civil rights act.

Black Belt (p. 273) A swath of dark rich soil well suited to cotton agriculture that stretched from Alabama westward, and eventually reached the easternmost part of Texas.

Black Codes (p. 413) Laws designed by the ex-Confederate states to sharply limit the civil and economic rights of freedmen and create an exploitable workforce.

blacklist (p. 485) A list of workers that employers in a particular town or industry refused to hire because they were considered troublemakers.

Black Panthers (p. 832) Militant civil rights group dedicated to armed self-defense, racial pride, and inner-city renewal.

Black Power (p. 833) A call for blacks to unite politically and economically in black only organizations to protect their racial identity as they fought for equality.

Black Republican (p. 359) A racist pejorative that Democrats used to suggest that Republicans were dangerous radicals who favored abolition and racial equality.

Bleeding Kansas (p. 358) A phrase used to describe the wave of vigilante reprisals and counterreprisals by proslavery and antislavery forces in Kansas in 1856.

Bonus March (p. 660) A two-month-long demonstration by forty thousand impoverished World War I veterans in Washington, D.C., that ended violently when the army expelled the protesters.

Border States (p. 379) The four slave states,Missouri, Kentucky,Maryland, and Delaware, that bordered the Confederacy. The Lincoln administration succeeded in keeping them in the Union.

Boston Massacre (p. 101) A confrontation between a group of Bostonians and British troops on March 5, 1770, during which the troops opened fire on the citizens, killing five of them.

***Brown v. Board of Education* (1954) (p. 766)** Supreme Court decision that segregated schools violated the equal protection clause of the Fourteenth Amendment.

"Buffalo Bill's Wild West" (p. 462) A circuslike production begun in 1883 that helped create a romantic and mythological view of the West in the American imagination.

Camp David Accords (1978) (p. 856) Israel agreed to give the Sinai Peninsula back to Egypt; in return Egypt became the first Arab state to recognize Israel's right to exist.

capitalism (p. 11) An economic system in which the market economy determined the prices of goods and services.

carpetbagger (p. 418) White Southerners' derogatory term for Northerners who came south after the war to settle, work, or aid the ex-slaves. It falsely suggested they were penniless adventurers who came south merely to get rich.

"cash and carry" (p. 687) A policy that required belligerent nations to pay cash for goods and transport them on their own ships.

central business districts (p. 512) Sections of cities devoted exclusively to commercial enterprises such as banks, department stores, and the offices of corporations, accountants, lawyers, and other professions.

Central Powers (p. 594) Initially Germany and Austria-Hungary, expanded by 1915 to include the Ottoman Empire and Bulgaria.

Cherokee Cases (p. 236) *Cherokee Nation v. Georgia* (1830) and *Worcester v. Georgia*, the two cases in which the Supreme Court of the United States determined that Indian nations retained certain rights of sovereign nations, but did not enjoy the full powers of a sovereign nation.

Chesapeake Affair (p. 202) An incident in 1807 when the British ship the *Leopard* fired at an American navy ship, the *Chesapeake*. The British abducted four American sailors, whom they charged were deserters from the Royal Navy.

Chinese Exclusion Act (p. 486) An 1882 law barring Chinese immigration to the United States for ten years. Renewed several times. It remained in effect until 1943.

City Beautiful Movement (p. 510) A movement begun in the 1880s that advocated comprehensive planning and grand redesign of urban space to eliminate pollution and overcrowding.

civil disobedience (p. 772) A strategy of nonviolence used by demonstrators to protest a law or a policy considered unjust.

Civil Rights Act of 1875 (p. 426) Passed by Congress in 1875, it required state governments to provide equal access in public facilities such as schools and to allow African Americans to serve on juries. In 1883 the U.S. Supreme Court ruled it unconstitutional.

Civil Rights Act of 1964 (p. 826) Legislation that banned segregation in businesses and places open to the public (such as restaurants and public schools) and prohibited racial and gender discrimination in employment.

Clayton Anti-Trust Act (1914) (p. 539) The act prohibited interlocking company directories—the practice of setting up shadow companies that appeared to compete but were actually run by the same board of directors—and exempted trade unions from prosecution under the 1890 Sherman Anti-Trust Act.

Cold War (p. 721) A full-scale ideological and military conflict between the United States and the Soviet Union and their allies that led to several hot wars around the globe, although the Americans and Soviets, fearful of a nuclear showdown, never fought each other directly.

Columbian Exchange (p. 16) The term used by modern scholars to describe the biological encounter between the two sides of the Atlantic, including the movement of plants, animals, and diseases.

Committee on Public Information (p. 606) Government agency that controlled the flow of information and shaped public opinion about the war with posters, Four-Minute Men, pamphlets, and films.

***Common Sense* (p. 107)** Thomas Paine's influential pamphlet that forcefully argued for American independence, attacked the institution of monarchy, and defended a democratic theory of representative government.

companionate marriage (p. 124) A term used by scholars to describe a more egalitarian relationship between husband and wife in which the two act as companions to each other.

company town (p. 524) A town built and owned by a corporation and rented to its employees, reflecting both the corporation's desire to help their workers and to control them.

complex marriage (p. 299) A system developed by John Humphrey Noyes's followers at Oneida, where any man or women who had experienced saving grace was free to engage in sexual relations with any other person.

Compromise of 1850 (p. 348) An attempt by Congress to resolve the slavery question by making concessions to both the North and South, including admission of California and a new Fugitive Slave Act.

Compromise of 1877 (p. 427) Resolution of the disputed presidential election of 1876 that handed victory to Republican Rutherford B. Hayes over Democrat Samuel J. Tilden. Democrats agreed to the deal in exchange for patronage and the continued removal of federal troops from the South.

Congress of Industrial Organizations (CIO) (p. 679) A brand-new type of labor organization that organized workers within an entire industry rather than by their trade orientation.

Conscription Act (p. 390) A law passed by Congress in March 1863 to offset declining volunteers to the Union Army. It declared all male citizens (and immigrants who had applied for citizenship) aged twenty to forty-five eligible to be drafted into the Union Army. The rich could pay a $300 fee to avoid the draft.

conscientious objectors (p. 609) Those who opposed participating in military service because of religious, philosophical, or political belief.

conservationist (p. 540) An environmentalist who wanted to meet present economic needs and conserve natural resources for future generations.

conspicuous consumption (p. 517) A term used to describe lavish displays of wealth by the rich, including construction of opulent mansions and hosting lavish balls.

containment (p. 722) The label affixed to multiple American foreign policy initiatives meant to prevent the Soviet Union from expanding its influence around the globe.

contraband of war (p. 384) The term introduced by General Benjamin Butler to justify his refusal to return fugitive slaves to their owners because they were seized property.

Copperheads (p. 390) Northern Democrats (sometimes called "Peace Democrats") who opposed the war and the Lincoln administration and favored a negotiated settlement with the Confederacy.

corporation (p. 472) Businesses owned by people who buy shares of stock in the company.

"corrupt bargain" (p. 227) Term presidential candidate Jackson's supporters used to attack the alliance between John Quincy Adams and Henry Clay that deprived Clay of the presidency.

cotton embargo (p. 380) A ban imposed by Confederates in 1861 on the export of cotton, the South's most valuable commodity, to prompt cotton-importing nations like England and France to intervene to secure Confederate independence.

cotton gin (p. 212) Eli Whitney's invention for removing seeds from cotton.

Coxey's Army (p. 523) A protest march from Ohio to Washington, D.C., in 1894 organized by Jacob Coxey to publicize demands for the federal government to alleviate the suffering brought on by the Panic of 1893.

Crittenden Compromise (p. 369) An unsuccessful proposal by Kentucky senator John J. Crittenden to resolve the secession crisis in the spring of 1861 with constitutional amendments to protect slavery.

Cuban Missile Crisis (1962) (p. 745) A showdown between the United States and the Soviet Union over Khrushchev's decision to place Soviet missiles in Communist Cuba aimed at America.

"cult of true womanhood" (p. 295) A set of beliefs in which women's values were defined in opposition to the aggressive and competitive values of the marketplace.

Dawes Plan (1924) (p. 650) International agreement that loaned Germany $200 million in gold to pay a reduced reparation bill and gave Germany more time to meet its debt.

Dawes Severalty Act (p. 458) 1887 law that started the breakup of reservations by offering Native Americans allotments of 160 acres of reservationland to encourage them to become independent farmers.

Declaration of Independence (p. 110) On July 4, 1776, Congress approved the final text of the Declaration of Independence, a public defense of America's decision to declare independence from Britain that was to be printed and sent to the individual states.

Democratic-Republican Societies (p. 169) A new type of political organization informally allied with the Republicans whose function was to help collect, channel, and influence public opinion.

Denmark Vesey Uprising (p. 216) An alleged plot led by a free black man, Denmark Vesey, to free slaves in Charleston and kill their masters.

depression (p. 483) A contraction of economic growth, widespread business failure, and high rates of unemployment lasting several years.

deserving poor (p. 676) Needy Americans who were legitimately entitled to public support, a category open to differing interpretations.

détente (p. 803) Relaxing Cold War tensions by using diplomatic, economic, and cultural contacts to improve U.S. relations with China and the Soviet Union.

domino theory (p. 781) The fear that a communist Vietnam would open the door to a complete communist takeover of Southeast Asia.

double-victory campaign (p. 699) Civil rights call for victory against both fascism overseas and racial prejudice at home.

Draft Riots (p. 392) Four days of rioting in New York City in July 1863 by mostly poor, immigrant, and working-class men who opposed the draft.

***Dred Scott v. Sandford* (p. 360)** The highly controversial 1857 Supreme Court decision that rejected the claim of the slave Dred Scott, who argued that time spent with his owner in regions that barred slavery had made him a free man. It also declared that Congress lacked the right to regulate slavery in the territories.

Dust Bowl (p. 670) Drought and soil erosion caused massive dust storms across southern and plains states throughout the thirties.

Eighteenth Amendment (1919) (p. 633) Constitutional amendment that banned the sale, manufacture, and transportation of intoxicating liquors.

electoral college (p. 160) A group of electors appointed by each state who had the responsibility of picking the president.

Emancipation Proclamation (p. 385) The decree announced by Lincoln in September 1862 and taking effect on January 1, 1863, declaring slaves in the seceded states not under Union army control "forever free."

Embargo Act of 1807 (p. 202) The cornerstone of Jefferson's plan of peaceable coercion that attempted to block U.S. trade with England and France to force them to respect American neutrality.

Enlightenment (p. 72) An international philosophical movement that extolled the virtues of reason and science and applied these new insights to politics and social reform.

Equal Rights Amendment (ERA) (p. 858) A proposed constitutional amendment, which stated that "equality of rights under the law shall not be denied or abridged by the United States or by any State on account of sex."

Era of Good Feelings (p. 209) A term that the press coined to describe the absence of bitter partisan conflict during the presidency of James Monroe.

Espionage Act (1917) (p. 606) Legislation that made it a crime to obstruct military recruitment, to encourage mutiny, or to aid the enemy by spreading lies.

ethnic enclaves (p. 501) Urban neighborhoods dominated by one particular immigrant group, often leading to names such as Little Germany and Little Italy.

Eugenicists (p. 646) Those who wanted to improve the human race by controlling its hereditary qualities.

Exodusters (p. 444) More than twenty thousand exslaves who in 1879 left violence and poverty in the South to take up farming in Kansas.

Fair Deal (p. 754) Truman's proposals for national health care, public housing, education, and public works projects.

farmers' alliances (p. 520) Organizations in the 1870s and 1880s dedicated to helping farmers struggling with rising costs and falling crop prices by advocating farmer cooperatives and laws to regulate banks and railroads.

fascist state (p. 686) A type of dictatorial regime that arose in Germany, Italy, and Spain that glorified the state over the individual.

Federal Reserve Act (1913) (p. 539) The act creating a federally run Federal Reserve to serve as a "banker's bank" that held a portion of bank funds in reserve to help member banks in time of crisis, set rates for business loans, and issued a new national paper currency.

Federal Trade Commission (1914) (p. 539) A federal agency with the power to order companies to cease unfair trading practices whose decisions were subject to court review.

Federalists (p. 149) The name adopted by the supporters of the Constitution who favored a stronger centralized government.

Fifteenth Amendment (p. 421) Constitutional amendment passed by Congress in 1869 providing an explicit constitutional guarantee for black suffrage.

First Red Scare (1919–1920) (p. 634) Period when the Justice Department arrested and deported alien anarchists and Communists suspected of trying to destroy American democracy and capitalism.

Force Bill (p. 232) A bill enacted by Congress that gave President Jackson the power to use military force to collect revenue, including tariffs.

Fourteenth Amendment (p. 416) Drafted by Congress in June 1866, it defined citizenship to include African Americans, guaranteed equal protection before the law, and established the federal government as the guarantor of individual civil rights.

Freedmen's Bureau (p. 408) Relief agency for the war ravaged South created by Congress in March 1865. It provided emergency services, built schools, and managed confiscated lands.

Freedom Rides (p. 819) An interstate bus journey by black and white activists who entered segregated bus facilities together throughout the South.

Freedom Summer, 1964 (p. 825) Multipronged attack on white supremacy in Mississippi that included a voter registration drive and the creation of Freedom Schools.

free labor (p. 364) A procapitalist Northern philosophy that presented an idealized vision of the industrial North, celebrating the virtues of individualism, independence, entrepreneurship, and upward mobility.

Frontier Thesis (p. 464) Historian Frederick Jackson Turner's 1893 theory that extolled the positive role the frontier had played in shaping the American character and consequently American institutions.

Fugitive Slave Act (p. 348) A component of the Compromise of 1850 that increased the federal government's obligation to capture and return escaped slaves to their owners.

fundamentalism (p. 636) An evangelical Christian theology that viewed the Bible as an authentic recounting of historical events and the absolute moral word of God.

Gabriel's Rebellion (p. 186) A slave insurrection in Richmond, Virginia, that drew together free blacks and slaves in a plot to seize the Richmond arsenal and foment a slave rebellion.

gag rule (p. 293) A procedural motion that required that the House of Representatives automatically table antislavery petitions and not consider them.

Geneva Accords (1954) (p. 782) Called for a temporary partition of Vietnam along the seventeenth parallel, with the Vietminh in the north and the French in the south, and a general election in two years to reunify the country under one government.

Gentleman's Agreement (1907–1908) (p. 581) Japanese agreement to deny passports to Japanese workers intending to immigrate to the United States.

Gilded Age (p. 498) The name for the period 1877–1900 that suggested the amazing achievements of the period were like a thin gold layer that covered many unresolved social problems.

Glorious Revolution (p. 56) The relatively bloodless revolution that led to the ascension of William and Mary, which was widely seen as a vindication for English liberty.

Grange (p. 449) Originally founded in the fall of 1867 by Oliver H. Kelley as a social and educational society for farmers, it became a major political force in the Midwest in the mid-1870s.

Great Awakening (p. 72) A religious revival movement that emphasized a more emotional style of religious practice.

Great Compromise (p. 146) Compromise plan proposed by Roger Sherman and Oliver Ellsworth of Connecticut that called for equal representation of each state in the upper house and a lower house based on population.

Great Depression (p. 659) The most devastating and longest economic crisis in American history that lasted from 1929 to 1939.

Great Plains (p. 443) Vast open territory stretching east to west from present-day Missouri to the Rocky Mountains, and north to south from North Dakota to Texas.

Great Society (p. 816) President Johnson's wideranging social welfare reforms intended to make the amenities of modern life—a decent standard of living, education, health care, and clean water—available to all Americans.

Gulf of Tonkin Resolution (1964) (p. 787) Gave Johnson permission "to take all necessary measures to repel any armed attack against the forces of the United States and to prevent further aggression" in Vietnam.

Harlem Renaissance (p. 638) An outpouring of African American artistic expression in the 1920s and 1930s.

Hartford Convention (p. 207) A meeting of Federalists in Hartford, Connecticut, to protest the War of 1812. The convention proposed several constitutional amendments intended to weaken the powers of the slave states and protect New England interests.

Haymarket Incident (p. 493) A violent incident touched off when a bomb exploded amid a group of policemen as they broke up a peaceful labor rally in Chicago's Haymarket Square on May 4, 1886.

headright (p. 39) An incentive system to encourage additional immigrants by giving 50 acres to any man who would pay their own fare to Virginia and 50 additional acres for each person brought with him.

hippies (p. 829) Youthful social rebels who renounced material acquisition and used drugs to explore their inner spiritual selves.

Ho Chi Minh Trail (p. 789) A 600-mile North Vietnamese supply route that ran along the western border of Vietnam through neighboring Laos and Cambodia.

holding company (p. 477) A huge corporation that bought and ran other corporations by purchasing their stock.

Hollywood blacklist (p. 739) A list of individuals with suspected past or present communist ties whom film studios refused to hire.

Holocaust (p. 708) German-engineered wartime extermination of Jews and other peoples that Germans considered inferior.

Homestead Act (p. 440) Passed in 1862, it provided 160 acres of free land to any settler willing to live on it and improve it for five years; promoted massive westward migration.

horizontal integration (p. 475) Business organization where one company buys many other companies producing the same product to eliminate competition and achieve greater efficiency.

humanists (p. 13) Individuals who advocated a revival of ancient learning, particularly ancient Greek thought, and encouraged greater attention to secular topics including a new emphasis on the study of humanity.

immediatism (p. 291) Abolitionist doctrine that rejected gradualism and advocated an immediate end to slavery.

Immigration Act of 1924 (p. 63) Law that allowed unrestricted immigration from the Western Hemisphere, curtailed all Asian immigration, and used quotas to control how many immigrants emigrated from individual European nations.

imperialism (p. 562) The late nineteenth-century term for colonizing foreign nations and lands, relying primarily on business, political, and military structures rather than settlers to rule colonized peoples and exploit their resources.

impressment (p. 202) The practice of forcing merchant seamen to serve in the British navy.

indentured servants (p. 83) A form of bound labor in which servants had their passage to America paid in return for a specified number of years of service.

Indian Removal Act of 1830 (p. 236) Legislation that gave President Jackson the authority to remove Indians tribes to lands west of the Mississippi.

Industrial Workers of the World (IWW) (p. 543) This group envisioned "one big union" that welcomed all workers regardless of sex, race, ethnicity, or skill, which would one day take over all means of production in the United States.

initiative (p. 552) Provided a way, usually by gathering signatures on petitions, for the electorate to introduce legislation before state legislatures.

internment camps (p. 694) Camps in the United States that held people of Japanese descent under armed guard in isolated areas.

interventionists (p. 686) Those advocating direct engagement in overseas conflicts.

Intermediate-Range Nuclear Forces Treaty (1987) (p. 870) Approved the destruction of all U.S. and Soviet intermediate-range missiles in Europe.

Intolerable Acts (p. 102) Legislation passed by Parliament to punish Bostonians for the Boston Tea Party. It closed the Port of Boston; annulled the Massachusetts colonial charter and dissolved or severely restricted that colony's political institutions; and allowed British officials charged with capital crimes to be tried outside the colonies.

Iran-Contra scandal (p. 870) A law-breaking scheme that sold arms to Iran to secure the hostages' release and used the proceeds to support anti-Communists in Nicaragua.

Iranian hostage crisis (p. 856) Defining event in Carter's presidency as Iranian revolutionaries held fifty two Americans captive for 444 days.

iron curtain (p. 722) Churchill's characterization of the military and ideological barrier erected by the Soviet Union that separated Western and Eastern Europe into free and unfree halves.

Islam (p. 10) Monotheistic faith whose teachings followed the word of the prophet Muhammad, and whose followers controlled most of the overland trade routes to the Far East.

Jay's Treaty (p. 172) Diplomatic treaty negotiated by Federalist John Jay in 1794. According to the terms of the treaty, Britain agreed to compensate America for cargoes seized in 1793–1794 and promised to vacate forts in the Northwest Territory. However, America failed to win acceptance of the right of neutral nations to trade with belligerents without harassment.

The Jazz Age (p. 642) Nickname for the twenties that reflected the popularity of jazz music.

John Brown's raid (p. 366) A failed assault led by the radical abolitionist on the federal arsenal at Harpers Ferry,Virginia, on October 16, 1859, intending to seize the guns and ammunition and then touch off a wave of slave rebellions.

Kansas-Nebraska Act (p. 354) An 1854 act designed to resolve the controversy over whether slavery would be permitted in the Western territories. It repealed the ban on slavery north of 36° 30' (the Missouri Compromise) and created two separate territories, Kansas west of Missouri and Nebraska west of Iowa.

Kellogg-Briand Pact (1928) (p. 648) Treaty that renounced aggressive war as an instrument of national policy.

Kennedy and Nixon debate (p. 761) First televised presidential election debate in 1960 watched by nearly 77 million Americans, or 60 percent of the adult population.

Knights of Labor (p. 492) A labor organization founded in 1869 that in the 1880s accepted workers of all trades and backgrounds and became the world's largest industrial union.

Know-Nothings (p. 356) The nickname for the constituents of the nativist, or anti-immigrant, American Party who called for legislation restricting office holding to native-born citizens and raising the period of naturalization for citizenship from five to twenty-one years.

Korean War (1950–1953) (p. 729) The United States fought Communist North Koreans and Chinese to a stalemate, frustrating Americans who had to learn to accept only a partial victory.

Ku Klux Klan (p. 422) The best-known of the many secret white terrorist organizations that first arose in the South in 1866; they targeted freedmen and symbols of black self improvement and independence and played a key role in reestablishing white supremacy by the late 1870s.

laissez-faire (p. 471) (French for "let do" or leave alone) A philosophy that argued that the government should impose no restraints on business.

League of Nations (p. 615) An international collective security organization composed of member nations where member nations agreed to mediate future international disputes to prevent wars and work together to improve global human conditions.

Lend-Lease (p. 689) A 1941 policy that circumvented "cash and carry" by loaning rather than selling arms to the Allies.

Levittowns (p. 758) Planned suburban communities where developers standardized every part of the construction process.

Liberty Party (p. 329) The staunchly antislavery, antiannexation, party was short lived, but captured 62,000 votes, a small number, but enough to effectively rob Henry Clay of electoral victories in New York and Michigan thereby handing Polk the presidency in 1844.

Little Rock Nine (p. 771) Nine black teenagers who integrated Central High School in Little Rock, Arkansas, in 1957 and became the focus of a national crisis that required the intervention of federal troops to resolve.

Lincoln-Douglas debates (p. 366) A series of highprofile debates in Illinois in 1858 between Senate candidates Stephen A. Douglas and Abraham Lincoln that focused primarily on the slavery controversy.

***Lochner v. New York* (1905) (p. 544)** A Supreme Court ruling that unless long work hours directly jeopardized workers' health, the government could not abridge an employee's freedom to negotiate his own work schedule with his employer.

Long Drive (p. 449) The annual cattle drives of more than 1,000 miles from Texas to the Great Plains that started in 1866 and established the ranching industry in the West.

"long telegram" (p. 722) An influential five-thousand-word missive by diplomat George F. Kennan that outlined why America needed to develop an aggressive foreign policy aimed at containing Soviet expansionist impulses.

Lord Dunmore's Proclamation (p. 105) Official announcement issued by Lord Dunmore, royal governor of Virginia. It offered freedom to any slave who joined the British forces in putting down the American rebellion.

Louisiana Purchase (p. 198) The acquisition by the United States of the Louisiana Territory from France in 1803, thereby securing control of the Mississippi River and nearly doubling the size of the nation.

Loyalists (p. 110) Colonists who remained loyal to the king and Britain.

Ludlow Massacre (1914) (p. 544) Colorado state troops set a striking miners' camp ablaze, killing thirteen women and children, an act that outraged laborers throughout the nation.

***Lusitania* (p. 598)** British passenger ship sunk by a German U-boat on May 7, 1915, an attack that killed 1,198 passengers, including 128 Americans.

Manhattan Project (p. 711) Secret U.S. wartime project to develop an atomic bomb.

Manifest Destiny (p. 320) A term coined by editor and columnist John O'Sullivan to describe his belief in America's divine right to expand westward.

March on Washington, 1963 (p. 824) Massive demonstration in the nation's capital that demanded passage of a federal civil rights act and more economic opportunities.

market revolution (p. 254) A set of interrelated developments in agriculture, technology, and industry that led to the creation of a more integrated national economy. Impersonal market forces impelled the maximization of production of agricultural products and manufactured goods.

Marshall Plan (1948–1952) (p. 724) Aimed to restore Europeans' faith in capitalism by sending $13 billion ($119 billion in today's dollars) overseas to rebuild Europe's ruined roads, bridges, factories, and farms.

McCarthyism (p. 739) The government's anticommunist crusade named for Senator Joseph McCarthy from Wisconsin, who, along with the House Committee on Un-American Activities (HUAC), spearheaded numerous governmental investigations into communist activities, many of them spurious.

Meat Inspection Act (1906) (p. 552) Law gave federal inspectors the authority to condemn meat unfit for consumption and established federal sanitary standards for meatpacking plants.

mercantilism (p. 60) Theory of empire that advocated strict regulation of trade between colonies and the mother country to benefit the latter.

middle ground (p. 87) A cultural and geographical region of the Great Lakes in which Indians and the French negotiated with each other for goods and neither side could impose its will on the other.

middle passage (p. 79) The harrowing voyage across the Atlantic from Africa to the Americas during which slaves endured meager rations and horrendously unsanitary conditions.

"Migrant Mother" (p. 673) Dorothea Lange's 1936 photograph of a destitute woman, which became an iconic portrait of Depression-era suffering.

militia (p. 104) An organization of citizen soldiers regulated by the laws of the individual colonies that provided the primary means of public defense in the colonial period.

military-industrial complex (p. 755) Eisenhower's term for the close ties between the defense industry and the Pentagon that might influence government policy.

mission system (p. 326) The colonial system devised by the Spanish to control the Indian population, forcing them to convert to Catholicism and work the land.

Mississippi Plan (p. 426) Campaign of violence and intimidation waged by armed groups of whites closely allied with the Democratic Party that drove Republicans from power in the Mississippi state elections of 1874. Copied by other Southern states.

modern warfare (p. 383) Military conflict involving enormous armies that utilize the technologies of the Industrial Revolution in the areas of communications, transportation, and firearms. Victory is secured by destroying the enemy's army and inflicting suffering on civilian populations.

modernism (p. 636) A liberal Christian theology embraced in many urban areas that emphasized the ongoing revelation of divine truth.

monopoly (p. 474) The control of an industry or market by one corporation.

Monroe Doctrine (p. 212) A foreign policy statement by President Monroe declaring that the Americas were no longer open to colonization and that the United States would view any effort to reassert colonial control over independent nations in the Western Hemisphere as a threat to America.

Montgomery Bus Boycott (1955–1956) (p. 768) A year-long bus boycott that brought a new leader,Martin Luther King Jr., and a new strategy of nonviolent protest to the forefront of the Civil Rights Movement.

Mormons (p. 445) A religious sect founded in upstate New York in 1830. Driven by persecution they headed west in 1846 and settled in a valley in Utah near the Great Salt Lake.

muckrakers (p. 533) Progressive Era term for investigative journalists who wrote exposés on government and business corruption.

mutually assured destruction (p. 852) The claim that the guarantee of a devastating nuclear counterattack would deter the United States and Soviet Union from ever employing their nuclear arsenals.

***Muller v. Oregon* (1908) (p. 546)** The Supreme Court upheld maximum hour laws for female workers because protecting women's reproductive health served the public good.

Munich Conference (1938) (p. 687) Hoping to avoid war, Britain and France agreed to let Germany occupy the Sudetenland, a German-speaking part of Czechoslovakia.

My Lai (p. 799) A Vietnamese village where American soldiers massacred five hundred civilians in 1968.

National Organization for Women (NOW) (p. 834) An organization dedicated to securing equal rights for women in employment, education, and politics.

Nation of Islam (p. 830) African American sect that rejected integration as the path to salvation for the black community and instead wanted to establish a separate black nation.

Nat Turner's Rebellion (p. 277) The 1831 Virginia slave uprising led by Nat Turner shocked many in the South and led to a host of new repressive measures against slaves.

Neutrality Acts (p. 687) A series of laws from 1935 to 1939 that restricted arms sales, loans, and transport of goods with nations at war.

New Deal (p. 662) An avalanche of legislation from 1933 to 1938 intended to promote economic recovery, reform American capitalism, and offer security to ordinary Americans.

New Deal coalition (p. 680) A political partnership formed in the midthirties among liberals, trade unionists, Catholics, and Northern blacks that redrew the nation's political map.

New Frontier (p. 813) Kennedy's legislative program that proposed raising the minimum wage, reducing overcrowding in schools, and providing health care for the elderly.

New Jersey Plan (p. 146) Proposal made by William Patterson of New Jersey as an alternative to the more nationalistic Virginia Plan that would have retained the principle of state equality in the legislature embodied in the Articles of Confederation.

New Left (p. 828) A small, but highly visible, coalition of left-leaning student-based organizations that attacked racial discrimination, poverty, and the war in Vietnam.

New Lights (p. 76) Supporters of the Great Awakening and its more emotional style of worship.

New Negro (p. 642) Spirit of black racial pride and militancy that set a younger generation of African American artists and civil rights leaders apart from their predecessors.

New South (p. 428) Optimistic phrase white Southerners used to describe the post-Reconstruction South, reflecting the South's development of a new system of race relations based on segregation and white supremacy and pointing to a profound economic transformation that swept across the region.

New Woman (p. 514) A phrase used to describe young women in the 1890s and early 1900s that reflected their rising levels of education, economic independence, and political and social activism.

Nineteenth Amendment (p. 605) Constitutional amendment that granted women the right to vote; it was ratified August 26, 1920.

nonimportation movement (p. 100) A boycott against the purchase of any imported British goods.

non-interventionists (p. 686) Those urging the nation to stay out of overseas conflicts.

North Atlantic Treaty Organization (NATO) (p. 722) A post-World War II military alliance between the United States and Western European powers.

Northwest Ordinance of 1787 (p. 141) One of several laws adopted by the Confederation Congress designed to provide a plan for the orderly settlement of the Northwest Territory (the area north of the Ohio River and west of Pennsylvania). In addition to providing for a plan for self-governance, the Ordinance also prohibited slavery from the Northwest Territory.

nuclear fallout (p. 734) The deadly pollution that descends through the air after a nuclear bomb explosion.

nullification (p. 231) A constitutional doctrine advanced by supporters of states' rights that held that individual states could nullify unconstitutional acts of Congress.

"Old Hickory" (p. 228) The nickname that General Andrew Jackson earned for seeming as stout as an "Old Hickory tree" in fighting against the British in the War of 1812.

Old Northwest (p. 139) The region of the new nation bordering on the Great Lakes.

Old Lights (p. 76) Opponents of the Great Awakening who favored traditional forms of religious worship.

Organization of the Petroleum Exporting Countries (OPEC) (p. 844) An international consortium of oil-producing nations that regulated the price and quantity of oil exported to the world market.

Overland Trail (p. 320) The 2,000-mile route taken by American settlers traveling to new settlements in Oregon, California, and Utah.

Paleo-Indians (p. 4) The name given by scientists to the first inhabitants of the Americas, an Ice Age people who survived largely by hunting big game, and to a lesser extent by collecting edible plants and fishing.

Panama Canal (p. 584) A manmade waterway through Panama completed in 1914 to link the Pacific and Atlantic oceans.

Panic of 1819 (p. 214) A downturn in the American economy in 1819 that plunged the nation into depression and economic hardship.

Panic of 1873 (p. 424) A financial panic on Wall Street that touched off a national economic recession causing financial houses, banks, and businesses to fail. Hundreds of thousands of workers lost their jobs.

pan-Indian resistance movement (p. 200) Shawnee leaders Tenskwatawa and Tecumseh's plan to unite Indian tribes to repel white encroachments in Ohio and Indiana, thus defending indigenous lands and reasserting the traditional values of Indian culture.

Patriots (p. 110) Colonists who supported American independence.

Peace Corps (p. 813) Government agency that President Kennedy established to send recent college graduates to work on humanitarian projects overseas in developing nations.

peace movement (p. 790) A loose coalition of antiwar activists that included pacifists, students, professors, clergy, hippies, civil rights activists, and middle-class liberals.

Pearl Harbor (p. 690) A U.S. naval base in Hawaii that the Japanese attacked on December 7, 1941.

"peculiar institution" (p. 294) A term that John C. Calhoun coined to describe Southern slavery. In Calhoun's view slavery was not "an evil" or a cause of shame but rather "a good—a positive good" to be championed.

Peninsular Campaign (p. 382) The complex plan developed by General George B.McClellan to capture the Confederate capital, whereby four hundred ships deposited 120,000 soldiers just east of Richmond at Fortress Monroe between the James and York Rivers.

penitentiary (p. 289) A new reform-based model of incarceration that isolated individuals from one another and gave them a chance to repent and reform. This method was a radical departure from earlier approaches to crime, which cast behavior in terms of sinfulness, innate depravity, and punishment.

People's Party (p. 518) A third party effort launched in 1890 by a coalition of farmer organizations, reformers, and labor unions and dedicated to curbing corporate power and increasing the voice of the masses in politics.

plantation (p. 29) An English settlement or fortified outpost in a foreign land dedicated to producing agricultural products for export. (Later the term would become synonymous with a distinctive slave-based labor system used in much of the Atlantic world.)

Platt Amendment (p. 572) Law linking U.S. withdrawal from Cuba to Cuban government granting the United States the right to maintain a naval base at Guantánamo Bay, to intervene militarily in Cuban domestic affairs, and to establish a privileged trading relationship with Cuba. The Cuban government also needed permission from the United States before entering into treaties with other nations.

political machines (p. 503) Powerful urban political organizations that mobilized large blocs of working-class and immigrant voters and often engaged in corrupt and illegal activity.

popular sovereignty (p. 335) An approach to the question of slavery in a newly acquired territory that would have allowed the people in each territory to decide for themselves whether to permit slavery.

preservationist (p. 539) An environmentalist who championed preserving nature in its unspoiled state.

privateer (p. 30) A form of state-sponsored piracy, usually directed against Spanish treasure fleets returning from the Americas.

Proposition 13 (p. 865) Referendum in California that dramatically reduced property taxes, spearheading grassroots tax rebellion nationwide.

proprietor (p. 40) This English legal title carried with it enormous political power, giving its possessor almost king-like authority over his domains. Colonial proprietors carried similar powers.

Pullman strike (p. 524) A bitter strike that began on May 11, 1894, at the Pullman Palace Car Company and soon spread nationwide, paralyzing the railroad system. President Cleveland sent in federal troops and broke the strike.

Pure Food and Drug Act (1906) (p. 552) Law levied federal fines for mislabeling food or medicine.

Quakers (p. 47) The Society of Friends, who believed each individual possessed a divine spark of grace, an inner light that could lead them to salvation.

recall (p. 553) Used special elections to remove unpopular officials from office before their term expired.

reconcentration (p. 565) Spanish policy that herded Cuban peasants off their farms into heavily fortified cities followed by systematic destruction of the crops that fed the rebel armies.

Redeemers (p. 426) Name for white Southern political leaders who successfully returned their states to white Democratic rule in the mid-1870s. The name was intended to depict these leaders as saviors of Southern society from rule by freedmen, scalawags, and carpetbaggers.

referendum (p. 553) Put legislative proposals on the ballot, letting the voting public decide whether a measure became law.

Reformation (p. 13) The movement for religious reform started by Martin Luther.

Religious Right (p. 865) A collection of right-wing Christian groups that defended traditional values and supported conservative political causes.

Republicans (p. 162) An opposition movement led by Jefferson and Madison that opposed Federalists' efforts to create a more powerful centralized government.

rendezvous (p. 318) A festive annual gathering held in the Rocky Mountains in which Indians, mountain men, and traders would gather together to exchange pelts for a variety of goods.

Restoration (p. 50) In 1660 Charles II became king of England, restoring the monarchy to power after the Civil War and Cromwellian rule.

robber barons (p. 476) A pejorative name for big business leaders that suggested they grew rich by devious business practices, exploitation of workers, and political manipulation.

***Roe v. Wade* (1973) (p. 861)** Supreme Court decision that legalized abortion.

Roosevelt Corollary (p. 587) (1904) Corollary to the 1823 Monroe Doctrine that announced the U.S. intention to act as an "international police power" in Latin America.

Rough Riders (p. 570) A volunteer unit of cowboys, Ivy League athletes, city police officers, and Pawnee scouts led by Theodore Roosevelt that gained fame by charging up the San Juan Heights during the Spanish-American War.

Rust Belt (p. 865) Decaying industrial cities in the Midwest, places plagued with high unemployment, crumbling roads, bankrupt governments, and high welfare rolls.

SALT I (1972) (p. 852) The first treaty between the Soviet Union and the United States that limited the deployment of intercontinental and submarine-launched ballistic missiles and the creation of missile-defense systems.

Sand Creek Massacre (p. 454) A massacre of some two hundred Cheyenne Indians on November 29, 1864, in Colorado by a military outfit known as the Colorado Volunteers under Colonel John M. Chivington.

scalawag (p. 418) White Southerners' derogatory term for fellow whites considered traitors to their region and race for joining the Republican Party and cooperating with Reconstruction policy.

The Schlieffen Plan (p. 596) A military plan that called for Germany to attack and quickly defeat France while the cumbersome Russian army mobilized.

scientific management (p. 543) The effort to use scientific knowledge to secure maximum output and profit.

Second Red Scare (p. 737) Widespread effort to root out Communist spies after World War II that lasted for nearly a decade.

Sedition Act (1918) (p. 606) Legislation that went even further than the Espionage Act by prohibiting anyone from uttering, writing, or publishing "any abusive or disloyal language" concerning the flag, constitution, government, or armed forces.

self-determination (p. 601) Giving people a voice in selecting their own government.

Seneca Falls Convention (p. 297) A convention of women's rights supporters, held in Seneca Falls, New York, whose resolves emphatically declared that "all men and women are created equal."

settlement houses (p. 510) Institutions established in cities beginning in the 1880s and dedicated to helping the poor by providing a wide range of social and educational services.

Seventeenth Amendment (1913) (p. 553) A constitutional amendment that allowed voters, rather than state legislatures, to elect federal senators.

share our wealth (p. 674) Louisiana Senator Huey Long's plan to redistribute money from the rich to the poor.

Shays's Rebellion (p. 142) Uprising in western Massachusetts in which farmers organized themselves as local militia units and closed down courts to prevent their farms from being seized by creditors.

Sherman's March to the Sea (p. 399) The 285-mile "scorched earth" campaign of General William T. Sherman across Georgia in late 1864 and early 1865. Sherman's soldiers seized or destroyed $100 million in goods, hurting Southern morale and depriving the Confederate army of supplies.

Sherman Anti-Trust Act (p. 477) Authorized the Justice Department to prosecute any illegal contract, combination, or conspiracy among corporations that eliminated competition or restrained free trade.

silent majority (p. 801) Nixon's term for the large number of Americans who supported the war quietly in the privacy of their homes.

sit-down strike (p. 679) Workers occupy a factory to paralyze production lines and prevent strikebreakers or management from entering the building.

sit-ins (p. 772) Nonviolent demonstrations where civil rights protesters employed the tactic of civil disobedience to occupy seats at whites-only lunch counters.

Sixteenth Amendment (1913) (p. 538) The constitutional amendment authorizing federal income taxes.

social Darwinism (p. 490) The belief that the principles of evolution, which Darwin had observed in nature, also applied to society. Advocates argued that individuals or groups achieve advantage over others as the result of biological superiority, an idea expressed as "survival of the fittest."

Social Gospel (p. 534) The religious belief that Christians had a responsibility to create an ethically sound and morally upright society.

socialism (p. 486) A theory that rejected capitalism and advocated common ownership of property and social and economic equality.

Southeast Asian Treaty Organization (SEATO) (p. 783) 1954 alliance among the United States, Britain, France, Australia, New Zealand, Thailand, the Philippines, and Pakistan who pledged to "meet common danger" in Southeast Asia together.

Southern Christian Leadership Conference (SCLC) (p. 770) Civil rights organization founded by Martin Luther King Jr. that used black churches to devise a new nonviolent strategy of direct action.

Spanish Influenza (p. 614) A lethal flu virus that killed millions worldwide.

Spanish Inquisition (p. 15) A Spanish tribunal devoted to finding and punishing heresy and rooting out Spain's Jews and Muslims.

Special Field Order No. 15 (p. 400) The directive announced by General Sherman in January 1865 during his March to the Sea that set aside more than 400,000 acres of seized Confederate land for distribution to former slaves in 40-acre plots.

sphere of influence (p. 579) The term used to describe the exclusive political and trading rights that a foreign nation enjoyed within another nation's territory.

***Spirit of St. Louis* (p. 630)** The plane that Charles Lindbergh piloted on the first-ever nonstop solo flight from New York to Paris on May 21, 1927.

spirituals (p. 276) Religious songs created by slaves. Spirituals' symbolism drew heavily on biblical themes.

spoils system (p. 230) The name applied to Jackson's system of replacing government officeholders with those loyal to him.

Stamp Act (p. 99) Legislation that required colonists to purchase special stamps and place them on all legal documents. Newspapers and playing cards had to be printed on special stamped paper.

states' rights (p. 185) The theory that the Constitution was a compact among the states and that the individual states retained the right to judge when the federal government's actions were unconstitutional.

***Steve v. Mann* (p. 276)** The 1829 North Carolina Supreme Court case that involved a white man's assault on a slave. The case asserted that the domination of the master over the slave was complete.

stock market crash of 1929 (p. 657) A ten-day period beginning on October 20, 1929, when the value of stocks plummeted as panicked investors sold off their stock in droves. This moment is usually considered the official start of the Depression.

Strategic Defense Initiative (SDI) (p. 869) Reagan's proposal to build a missile shield that used lasers from space satellites to destroy incoming missiles.

Student Nonviolent Coordinating Committee (SNCC) (p. 775) Student-run civil rights organization founded in 1960.

Stonewall riot (p. 862) A 1969 battle between patrons of a Greenwich Village male gay bar and police that became the catalyst for the gay rights movement.

suburbs (p. 512) Middle- and upper-class residential communities established just beyond a city's boundary but connected to the urban center by mass transit.

Sugar Act (p. 98) British tax aimed at imported sugar, molasses, and other goods imported into the colonies; it also created a new mechanism for enforcing compliance with custom's duties.

supply-side economics (p. 867) Reagan administration theory that letting entrepreneurs keep more of their profits would fuel economic growth, job creation, and more tax revenue to offset military spending.

Taft-Hartley Act (1947) (p. 753) Law that abolished the closed shop, banned so-called sympathy boycotts, and required that all union officers sign affidavits certifying that they were not members of the Communist Party.

telegraph (p. 258) Invention patented by Samuel Morse in 1837 that used electricity to send coded messages over wires, making communication nearly instantaneous.

Teller Amendment (p. 568) Congressional promise "to leave the government and control of the [Cuban] Island to its people" at the end of the Spanish-American War.

temperance (p. 285) A reform movement that developed in response to concern over the rising levels of alcohol consumption in America society.

Ten Percent Plan (p. 408) Pardoned all Southerners (except high-ranking military officers and Confederate officials) who took an oath pledging loyalty to the Union and support for emancipation. As soon as ten percent of a state's voters took this oath, they could call a convention, establish a new state government, and apply for congressional recognition.

tenements (p. 502) Multiple family dwellings of four to six stories housing dozens of families that became the most common form of housing for poor city dwellers by the 1860s.

Tet Offensive (1968) (p. 792) A massive, coordinated Communist assault against more than a hundred cities and towns in South Vietnam.

"the white man's burden" (p. 575) The Anglo-Saxon quest to better the lives of so-called racially inferior peoples by spreading Western economic, cultural, and spiritual values and institutions.

Transcendentalism (p. 303) A loose set of philosophical and literary ideas focused on the spiritual power of the individual. Transcendentalists looked to nature for inspiration and philosophical insights.

transcontinental railroad (p. 441) A line spanning the continental United States. Congress helped the Union Pacific and Central Pacific railroads build it by providing land grants, cash incentives, and loans..

trans-Mississippi West (p. 440) The region of the United States west of the Mississippi River.

The Treaty of Guadalupe Hidalgo (p. 332) This treaty formally ended the war between the United States and Mexico (1848). In addition to settling the border dispute between Texas and Mexico, the United States gained a significant swath of new territory in the Southwest.

Treaty of Paris (1783) (p. 116) Treaty between the newly created United States of America and Britain that officially ended the war between the two and formally recognized American independence.

Treaty of Paris (1898) (p. 571) Agreement that ended the Spanish-American War with Spain relinquishing its claim to Cuba and the United States receiving Puerto Rico, some smaller Caribbean islands, and the Pacific island group of Guam. In return for $20 million, Spain turned the Philippines over to the United States.

Trent Affair (p. 380) A diplomatic incident in November 1861 when a U.S. Navy vessel stopped the British ship *Trent* and removed two Confederates heading for Europe to press for British and French intervention.

Truman Doctrine (p. 724) A foreign policy initiative that gave the United States an active role in stopping the global spread of communism by supporting "free peoples who are resisting attempted subjugation by armed minorities or by outside pressures."

trust (p. 476) A legally binding deal bringing many companies in the same industry under the direction of a board of "trustees."

trust-busting (p. 536) Governmental action to dissolve monopolies.

Twenty-First Amendment (1933) (p. 633) Constitutional amendment that repealed the Eighteenth Amendment.

U-boat (p. 598) German submarine, a new weapon that launched surprise torpedo attacks against Allied merchant and naval ships.

Underground Railroad (p. 349) A network of safe houses and secret hiding places along routes leading to the North and into Canada (where slavery was prohibited) that helped several thousand slaves gain their freedom between 1830 and 1860.

unicameralism (p. 118) A form of representative government with only one legislature. Pennsylvania's 1776 constitution created a unicameral system.

Universal Negro Improvement Association (UNIA) (p. 640) Organization founded by Marcus Garvey to spread his message of racial pride, economic self-sufficiency, and returning to Africa.

Versailles Peace Treaty (p. 615) The controversial treaty that required Germany to pay reparations and disarm.

vertical integration (p. 475) Business organization where one company controls the main phases of production of a good, from acquiring raw materials to retailing the finished product.

Vietcong (p. 783) Slang term for South Vietnamese communists.

Vietminh (p. 780) The term initially used to describe all Vietnamese communists, and used after 1954 solely for North Vietnamese communists.

Vietnamization (p. 801) A Nixon administration policy that turned the bulk of the ground fighting over to the South Vietnamese Army.

Virginia Plan (p. 145) A plan framed by James Madison and introduced in the Constitution Convention by Edmund Randolph that called on delegations to abandon the government of the Articles and create a new, strong national government.

virtual representation (p. 71) A theory of representation in which legislators do not serve their localities but rather the whole nation.

Volstead Act (1919) (p. 633) Law that established criminal penalties for manufacturing, transporting, or possessing alcohol.

Voting Rights Act of 1965 (p. 826) Legislation that prohibited literacy tests and poll taxes, plus authorized the use of federal registrars to register voters if states failed to respect the Fifteenth Amendment.

Wade-Davis Bill (p. 408) A Reconstruction program designed to punish Confederate leaders and permanently destroy the South's slave society.

Waltham System (p. 261) Also known as the mill town model, a system that relied on factories housing all the distinctive steps of cloth production under a single roof. The Waltham System depended on a large labor force housed in company-owned dormitories.

war bonds (p. 606) Short-term loans that individual citizens made to the government that financed two-thirds of the war's costs.

War Hawks (p. 204) Young Republican congressmen from the South and Western regions of the country who favored Western expansion and war with Britain.

War of 1812 (p. 204) The war fought between Britain and America over restrictions on American trade. British trade with American Indians, particularly trade in weapons, was also an issue.

Warren Court (p. 813) Supreme Court that brought about a legal revolution in the United States by permanently altering American schools, politics, the criminal justice system, and cultural norms.

Washington Conference (1921–1922) (p. 647) Meeting of world powers that resulted in agreements that limited naval arms, reaffirmed America's Open Door policy that kept Chinese trade open to all, and secured pledges of cooperation among the world's leading military powers.

Watergate scandal (1972) (p. 806) A botched Republican-engineered break-in of the Democratic National Committee headquarters in Washington, D.C. that eventually forced Nixon to resign in 1974.

welfare capitalism (p. 541) The notion of using benefits to gain workers' loyalty, improve worker morale, and weaken interest in unions.

Western Front (p. 596) Complex system of trenches and earthworks that ran for 550 miles from the North Sea to Switzerland that pitted Germany against Belgium, France, Britain, and the United States.

Whigs (English, 17th Century) (p. 59) The group that supported parliamentary power after the Glorious Revolution.

Whigs (American, 19th Century) (p. 239) Anti-Jackson political party; the name evoked the seventeenth-century English opponents of absolute monarchy and the Patriot leaders who had opposed the tyranny of George III during the American Revolution. Whigs supported Clay's American System and a stronger central government.

Whiskey Rebellion (p. 173) The armed uprising of western Pennsylvania farmers protesting the Whiskey excise in 1794 was the most serious test of the new federal government's authority since ratification of the Constitution.

Wilmot Proviso (p. 335) Bill introduced by Congressman David Wilmot would have banned slavery from the territories acquired from Mexico.

women's suffrage (p. 513) The effort to obtain voting rights for women that eventually gained passage of the Nineteenth Amendment (1920).

Wounded Knee Massacre (p. 461) U.S. soldiers open fire on a group of Sioux Indians on December 29, 1890, killing between two hundred and three hundred.

XYZ Affair (p. 182) The furor created when Americans learned that three French officials, identified in diplomatic correspondence as "X," "Y," and "Z," demanded a bribe from America's diplomats as the price of beginning negotiations.

yellow press (p. 565) Tabloid journalists and newspapers that reported sensationalist stories with a strong emotional component.

Young America (p. 352) The movement within the Democratic Party that embraced Manifest Destiny and promoted territorial expansion, increased international trade, and the spread of American ideals of democracy and free enterprise abroad.

Zimmermann Telegram (p. 600) German foreign minister Arthur Zimmermann offered to help Mexico recover Texas, New Mexico, and Arizona if Mexico would start a borderland war with the United States and ask Japan to join them.

zoot-suiters (p. 700) Name given to Mexican American youths who wore oversize suits.

Credits

Page abbreviations are as follows. **T** *top,* **C** *center,* **B** *bottom,* **L** *left,* **R** *right.*

CHAPTER 1

2 The Granger Collection, New York **1.2** Pete Bostrum/Lithic Casting Lab **1.4** The Granger Collection, New York **1.5** Hans Collaert, "Sculptura in Aes". The workshop of an engraver (Sculptura in Aes), plate 19 from "Nova Reperta", Netherlandish. c. 1600. Engraving. After Stradanus (Jan van der Straet), 10⅝" × 7⅞". The Metropolitan Museum of Art, New York, NY, U.S.A. Image copyright © The Metropolitan Museum of Art **12L** The Courtauld Institute of Art Gallery, London **12R** The Bridgeman Art Library International **1.6** Snark/Art Resource, N.Y. **1.7** The Granger Collection, New York **1.9** Private Collection/The Stapleton Collection/Bridgeman Art Library **1.10** Museo Provincial de Bellas Artes Salamanca/Dagli Orgi/Picture Desk, Inc./Kobal Collection **20L** The Granger Collection, New York **20R** Image courtesy of Rare Books and Special Collections, Thomas Cooper Library, University of South Carolina **1.12** Kunsthistorisches Museum, Vienna, Austria **24** © CORBIS All Rights Reserved **1.14** Edgar Fahs Smith Collection/University of Pennsylvania, Van Pelt Library **1.15** Cristobal de Villalpando (1639–1714), "Central Square of Mexico City". 1695 (oil on canvas). Corsham Court, Wiltshire. The Bridgeman Art Library, NY **1.16** Musees des Ursulines de Quebec, Collection du Monastere des Ursulines **1.17** George Gower (1540–96), "Elizabeth I, Armada Portrait", c. 1588 (oil on panel), Gower, George (1540–96) (attr. to)/Woburn Abbey, Bedfordshire, UK/The Bridgeman Art Library **1.18** Private Collection/The Bridgeman Art Library **1.19** The Granger Collection, New York

CHAPTER 2

35 Virginia Historical Society **2.1** Art Resource/The New York Public Library, Rare Book Division **38** © Bettmann/CORBIS **2.2** Erich Lessing/Art Resource, N.Y. **2.3** Virginia Historical Society **2.4 & 52L** Courtesy of Enoch Pratt Free Library, Central Library/State Library Resource Center, Baltimore, MD **43** Erich Lessing/Art Resource, N.Y. **2.6** The Vindication of Christmas or, His Twelve Yeares Observations upon the Times, concerning the lamentable game called Sweepstake, 1653 (woodcut), English School, (17th century)/British Library, London, UK/© British Library Board. All Rights Reserved/The Bridgeman Art Library **2.8** University of Virginia Library, Special Collections Department **2.10** Art Resource, N.Y. **52R** The Granger Collection, New York **2.11** Historic Map Works **2.12** © National Maritime Museum Picture Library, London, England **2.13** The Image Works **2.15** © The Trustees of the British Museum

CHAPTER 3

65 The Warner House **3.1** Room from the Hart House, Ipswich, Massachusetts, American, 17th Century. Oak beams, pine panels and white plaster walls. The Metropolitan Museum of Art, Munsey Fund, 1936 (36.127). Photograph © 1995 The Metropolitan Museum of Art. **3.3L** Woodwork of a Room from the Colden House, Coldenham, New York, American, ca. 1767, Pine, 252" × 213" × 113" (640.1 × 541 × 287 cm). The Metropolitan Museum of Art, Purchase, The Sylmaris Collection, Gift of George Coe Graves, by exchange, 1940 (40.127). Photograph ©1995 The Metropolitan Museum of Art **3.3R** Detail, Desk and Bookcase, English, 1700–1720; Oak, pine, 81⅛ × 43⅞ × 23½ in. The Metropolitan Museum of Art, Gift of James DeLancey Verplanck and John Bayard Rodgers Verplanck, 1929 [39.184.1a,b] Image copyright © The Metropolitan Museum of Art **3.4** The Smithsonian Institution. Neg. #2003-34020 **3.5** William Owens/Alamy Images **3.6** Courtesy, The Winterthur Library: Printed Book and Periodical Collection **69** The Maryland Historical Society **3.7** Getty Images Inc.—Hulton Archive Photos **3.8** National Portrait Gallery, London **3.9** Courtesy of the Georgia Historical Society **74** The Granger Collection **3.10** Mason Chamberlain (1727–1787), "Portrait of Benjamin Franklin". 1762. Oil on canvas, 50⅜ × 40¾ inches (128 × 103.5 cm). Gift of Mr. and Mrs. Wharton Sinkler, 1956. Location: Philadelphia Museum of Art, Philadelphia, Pennsylvania, U.S.A./Art Resource, NY **3.11** From the Collection of the Moravian Historical Society, Nazareth, PA **3.13** The Art Archive/Picture Desk, Inc./Kobal Collection **3.14** Carolina Art Association/Gibbes Museum of Art **3.15** Abby Aldrich Rockefeller Folk Art Museum, The Colonial Williamsburg Foundation, Williamsburg, VA **3.18** Collection of The New-York Historical Society **3.21** Benjamin West (1738–1820), "The Death of General Wolfe," 1770. Oil on canvas, 152.6 × 214.5 cm. Transfer from the Canadian War Memorials, 1921 (Gift of the 2nd Duke of Westminster, England, 1918). Photo © National Gallery of Canada, Ottawa, Ontario **92** The Historical Society of Pennsylvania

CHAPTER 4

97 Lilly Library **4.1** Courtesy of the Library of Congress **4.3** A Society of Patriotic ladies at Edenton in North Carolina's Metropolitan Museum of Art Bequest of Charles Allen Munn **4.4** Corbis/Bettmann **4.5** The Granger Collection **4.6** Courtesy of the Library of Congress **4.8** Courtesy of the Library of Congress **108–109** Art Resource/Yale University Art Gallery **4.9** Susan Van Etten/PhotoEdit Inc. **4.10** Courtesy of the Library of Congress **112** The Granger Collection, New York **4.11** Reproduced with permission of the Minor White Archive, Princeton University Art Museum. Copyright © The Trustees of Princeton University **4.14** Courtesy of the Library of Congress **4.15** Charles Willson Peale's, "Timothy Matlack," c. 1790, oil on canvas. Access. # 1998.218/ Photograph © 2010 Museum of Fine Arts, Boston **4.16** John Vanderlyn, "The Murder of Jane McCrea". 1804. Oil on canvas, 32½ × 26½ in. Wadsworth Atheneum Museum of Art, Hartford, CT. Purchased by Subscription. Acc# 1855.4 **123L** The Granger Collection **123R** "White House Historical Association (White House Collection)" (25) **4.17** Charles Willson Peale, "Portrait of John and Elizabeth Lloyd Cadwalader and Their Daughter Anne". 1772. Oil on canvas, 50½" × 41¼" (128.3 × 104.8 cm). Photo: Graydon Wood. Philadelphia Museum of Art: Purchased for the Cadwalader collection with funds contributed by the Mabel Pew Myrin Trust and the gift of an anonymous donor, 1983. Acc: 1983-90-3 **4.18** Harvard Law School Library

CHAPTER 5

129 The Library of Virginia **5.1** Getty Images **5.2** Courtesy, Winterthur Museum **5.3** Samuel McIntire, "Chest-on-chest (detail)"; Mahogany, mahogany veneer, ebony and satinwood inlay, pine; Eighteenth-century American Arts No. 4; the M. and M. Karolik Collection of Eighteenth-Century American Arts, 41.580. Museum of Fine Arts, Boston (41.58). Photograph © 2010 Museum of Fine Arts, Boston. **5.4** American Antiquarian Society **5.5** U of North Carolina/Wilson Library **134L** Courtesy, Winterthur Museum. **134R** © 2007 Museum of Art, RISD. All Rights Reserved. **5.6** Charles Wilson Peale (American 1741–1827), "William Smith and his Grandson". 1788. Oil on Canvas, 51¼" × 40⅜" (130.2 × 102.5 cm). Signed and dated lower right C W Peale painted 1788. Virginia Museum of Fine Arts, Richmond. Museum Purchase with Funds provided by The Robert G. Cabell III and Maude Morgan Cabell Foundation, and The Arthur and Margaret Glasgow Fund. Photo: Katherine Wetzel © Virginia Museum of Fine Arts **5.10** William Clements Library, University of Michigan **143L** The Granger Collection, New York **143R** The Granger Collection, New York **5.12** Independence National Historical Park **5.15** Courtesy of the Library of Congress **516L** Corbis/Bettmann **516R** The Granger Collection, New York **153** Courtesy of the Library of Congress **5.17** Collection of The New-York Historical Society, [1903.12]

CHAPTER 6

159 Collection of The New York Historical Society, PR010, #1795-1; Neg. #2737 **6.1** Courtesy of the Library of Congress **6.2** Corporate Art Directions, Inc. Collection Credit Suisse **6.3** Courtesy of the Library of Congress **6.4L** Trumbull John (1756–1843). Portrait of Alexander Hamilton (1755-57-1804). Statesman, 1806. Oil on canvas, 76.2 × 61 cm(30 × 24 in.) Gift of Henry Cabot Lodge. National Portrait Gallery, Smithsonian Institution, Washington, DC, USA/Art Resource **6.4R** The Granger Collection, New York **6.5** The Granger Collection, New York **6.6** This item is reproduced by permission of The Huntington Library, San Marino, California. **6.8** The Ohio Historical Society **6.9** Courtesy of the Atwater Kent Museum of

Philadelphia **175** The Granger Collection, New York **6.10** Photograph Courtesy Peabody Essex Museum **6.11** The Granger Collection, New York **179** The Library Company of Philadelphia. **6.12** Gilbert Stuart. Portrait of George Washington. Landsdown Portrait. Anonymous Loan. National Portrait Gallery. Washington, D. C., USA. Art Resource, NY **6.14** Dagli Orti/Picture Desk, Inc./Kobal Collection **6.15** This item is reproduced by permission of The Huntington Library, San Marino, California. **184** The Granger Collection **6.16** The Granger Collection, New York

CHAPTER 7

191 The Granger Collection, New York **7.1** Will Pryce/Thames & Hudson/Arcaid/ Alamy Images **7.2** Courtesy of The Maryland Historical Society **7.4** American Antiquarian Society **197** The Granger Collection, New York **7.6** Monticello/Thomas Jefferson Foundation, Inc. **7.7** Collection of The New-York Historical Society, Acc. #1931.58 **7.8** The Granger Collection, New York **7.9** Courtesy of the Library of Congress **205** Courtesy of the Library of Congress **7.11** Courtesy of the Library of Congress **7.12** Courtesy of the Library of Congress **7.13** Getty Images Inc.—Hulton Archive Photos **7.14** Corbis/Bettmann **211** Samuel F. B. Morse, "The Old House of Representatives". 1822. Oil on Canvas. 86½ × 130¾. Museum Purchase, Gallery Fund. Corcoran Gallery of Art **7.15** Rhode Island Historical Society Library and Museum **7.17** Colonial Williamsburg Foundation, Williamsburg, VA

CHAPTER 8

221 George Caleb Bingham, American, (1811–1879). Stump Speaking, 1854, oil on canvas. The Boatmen's National Bank, St. Louis. **8.2** The Granger Collection, New York **224** The Historical Society of Pennsylvania (SHP), John Lewis Krimmel **8.3** Courtesy of the Library of Congress **8.5** Collection of The New-York Historical Society, New York City **8.6** CORBIS All Rights Reserved **8.7** The Granger Collection, New York **8.8** Courtesy of the Boston Art Commission 2009 **8.9** © Bettmann/CORBIS All Rights Reserved **8.10** The Library Company of Philadelphia **8.11** Library of Congress **237L** Getty Images Inc.—Hulton Archive Photos **237R** Courtesy of Oklahoma Historical Society; Dr. Joseph Thoburn Collection **8.13** Courtesy of the Library of Congress **8.14** The Granger Collection, New York **8.15** Collection of The New-York Historical Society, New York City **244** The Library Company of Philadelphia **245** North Wind Picture Archives **8.16** Courtesy of the Library of Congress

CHAPTER 9

253 Courtesy of the Library of Congress **9.1** Alan Fisher, "Corn Husking Frolic". 1828. Oil on Panel, 70.8 × 62.23 cm Museum of Fine Arts, Boston Assc. #62.27 Photograph © 2010 Museum of Fine Arts, Boston. **9.2** Fenimore Art Museum, Cooperstown, New York. Photo by Richard Walker. New York State Historical Association **257** George Inness, "The Lackawanna Valley". 1856. Oil on Canvas, 33⅞" × 50³⁄₁₆". Image © 2010 Board of Trustees, National Gallery of Art, Washington, D.C. **9.4** Corbis/Bettmann **9.5** Courtesy of the Library of Congress **263** American Textile History Museum **9.7** The Granger Collection **9.8** The Library Company of Philadelphia **9.10** Courtesy Library Company of Philadelphia. **9.11** Collection of The New-York Historical Society, Neg. #40696 **9.13** Manuscripts, Archives and Rare Books Division, Schomburg Center for Research in Black Culture, The New York Public Library, Astor, Lenox and Tilden Foundations **9.14** The Granger Collection, New York **9.15** The Granger Collection, New York **9.16** Corbis/Bettmann **9.17** Jan White Brantley/The Historic New Orleans Collection **9.18** Courtesy of the Library of Congress **278** Manuscripts, Archives and Rare Books Division, Schomburg Center for Research in Black Culture, The New York Public Library, Astor, Lenox and Tilden Foundations

CHAPTER 10

283 Courtesy of the Library of Congress **10.1** From the Collection of the New Bedford Whaling Museum. **10.2** James G. Clonney, "Clonney: Militia Training". 1841. Oil on Canvas. Pennsylvania Academy of the Fine Arts, PA **287** Courtesy of the Library of Congress **10.3** The Library Company of Philadelphia **10.4** Division of Rare and Manuscript Collections, Cornell University Library **10.5** Library of Congress 292L Hiram Powers (1805–1873), The Greek Slave, 1851, after an original of 1844. Marble, 65¼ × 21 × 18¼ in. (165.7 × 53.3 × 46.4 cm). Olive Louise Dann Fund. 1962.43. Location: Yale University Art Gallery, New Haven, Connecticut, U.S.A. Photo Credit: Yale University Art Gallery/Art Resource, NY **292R** Courtesy of the Library of Congress **10.6** Courtesy of the Library of Congress **10.7** The Granger Collection, New York **10.8** Lilly Martin Spencer, "Domestic Happiness". 1849. Oil on canvas, Spencer, Lilly Martin (1827–1902)/The Detroit Institute of Arts, USA/Gift of Dr and Mrs James Cleland Jr./The Bridgeman Art Library **10.9** Courtesy of the Library of Congress **10.10** Courtesy of the Library of Congress **300** From the Collection of the Oneida Community Mansion House, Oneida, NY. **10.12** Courtesy of the Library of Congress **10.13** Used with Permission of Documenting the American South, The University of North Carolina at Chapel Hill Libraries **10.14** Asa Ames (1824–1851), "Phrenological Head". Evans, New York. c. 1850, paint on wood. American Folk Art Museum **10.15** The Warner Collection of Gulf States Paper Corporation, Tuscaloosa, Alabama **10.16** Central Park Conservatory **10.17** Thomas Chambers, "Mount Auburn Cemetery". Mid-19th C. Oil on Canvas, 14" × 18⅛". Image © 2010 Board of Trustees, National Gallery of Art, Washington, D.C. Gift of Edgar William and Bernice Chrysler Garbisch **10.18** Courtesy, Winterthur Museum. **10.19** The Henry Francis du Pont Winterthur Museum, Inc. **10.20** Lyndhurst, A National Trust Historic Site **10.21** Watertown Historical Society

CHAPTER 11

317 Corbis/Bettmann **11.1** Alfred Jacob Miller (American, 1810–1874), The Trapper's Bride, oil on canvas, Museum purchase. Joslyn Art Museum, Omaha, Nebraska **11.3** Emigrants Crossing the Plains, 1867, Albert Bierstadt, oil on canvas, 60 × 96 in., A.011.1T, National Cowboy Hall of Fame, Oklahoma City **11.4** Charles Ferdinand Wimar, "Attack on Immigrant Train". 1856. Oil on Canvas. 139.9 × 200.8 cm. Bequesst of Henry C. Lewis. University of Michigan Museum of Art. Acc #1895.80 **323L** George Catlin (1796–1872), "Mah-to-toh-pa, Four Bears, second chief, in full dress (Mandan)". 1832. Oil on fabric; canvas mounted on aluminum, 29 × 24 in. Smithsonian American Art Museum, Washington, DC/Art Resource, NY. 323R Getty Images **11.5** Minnesota Historical Society **11.6** Courtesy of The Bancroft Library. University of California, Berkeley. **11.7** The Granger Collection, New York **11.8** Courtesy of the Library of Congress **11.10** Amon Carter Museum **11.11** Courtesy of the Library of Congress **334** Beinecke Rare Book and Manuscript Library, Yale University **11.12** Courtesy of the Library of Congress **11.13** Courtesy of the Library of Congress **338** Courtesy of the Library of Congress

CHAPTER 12

343 The Granger Collection, New York **12.1** The Granger Collection, New York **12.2** California State Archives **12.3** Eon Images; www.eonimages.com. All Rights Reserved **12.5** The Granger Collection, New York **12.6** Indiana State Library **351** Courtesy of the Library of Congress **12.8** Emanuel Gottlieb Leutz (1816–1868), "Westward the Course of Empire Takes Its Way (Mural Study, U.S. Capitol)", 1861. Oil on canvas, 33¼" × 43⅜" (84.5 × 110.1 cm). Smithsonian American Art Museum, Washington, DC/Art Resource, NY. **12.10L** Courtesy of the Library of Congress **12.10R** Architect of the Capitol **357T** The Granger Collection, New York **357B** Courtesy of the Library of Congress **12.11** Courtesy of the Library of Congress **12.12** The Granger Collection, New York **12.14** MPI/Stringer/Hulton Archive/Getty Images **12.15 (inset)** Courtesy of the Library of Congress **12.15** © Museum of the City of New York/CORBIS All Rights Reserved **12.16T&B** Courtesy of the Trustees of the Boston Public Library/Rare Books **12.17** Augustus Washington/National Portrait Gallery, Smithsonian Inst./Art Resource, N.Y. **12.19** © Bettmann/CORBIS All Rights Reserved **12.20** National Archives and Records Administration

CHAPTER 13

375 The Granger Collection, New York **13.2** Connecticut Historical Society **13.3** Duke University **13.4** Anne S. K. Brown Military Collection, John Hay Library, Brown University **13.6** The Granger Collection, New York **13.9R&L** National Civil War Museum **13.10** Theodor Kaufmann (1814–1896), "On to Liberty," 1867, Oil on canvas, 36 × 56 in (91.4 × 142.2 cm). The Metropolitan Museum of Art. Gift of Erving and Joyce Wolf, 1982 (1982.443.3) Photograph © The Metropolitan Museum of Art./Art Resource, NY **386** Courtesy of the Library of Congress **387** Courtesy of the Library of Congress **13.11** The Boston Athenaeum **391** The Granger Collection, New York **13.12** The Granger Collection, New York **13.13** Courtesy of frankleslie.com **13.14** Courtesy of frankleslie.com **396** Courtesy of the Massachusetts Historical Society, Boston. **13.15** Courtesy of the Library of Congress **13.18** The Granger Collection, New York **13.19** National Archives and Records Administration/Presidential Library **13.20** The Boston Athenaeum

CHAPTER 14

405 National Museum of American Art, Smithsonian Institution/Art Resource, N.Y. **14.1** Collection of The New-York Historical Society, [37628] **14.2** The Granger Collection, New York **14.3T&B** Chicago History Museum **14.4** The Granger Collection, New York **14.5** Courtesy of the Library of Congress **14.6** The Granger Collection, New York **14.7** Picture History **414** The Granger Collection, New York **14.8** The Granger Collection, New York **14.9** The Granger Collection, New York **14.10** Used with Permission of Documenting the American South, The University of North Carolina at Chapel Hill Libraries **14.11** Corbis/Bettmann **14.12** David J. and Janice L. Frent **14.14** Frank Leslie's Illustrated Newspaper, October 7, 1871/The Granger Collection, New York **425T** Harper's, Aug. 5, 1865/Courtesy of the Library of Congress **425BL** Harper's Sept. 5, 1868/Courtesy of the Library of Congress **425BR** The Granger Collection, New York **4.16** The Granger Collection, New York **14.19L** Keene **14.19R** Lee Monument Unveiling Ribbon Accession #TBMR 277-1 (2). The Museum of the Confederacy **14.20** Lauren Rogers Museum of Art **14.21** Brown Brothers **14.23** Courtesy of the Library of Congress **434** The Granger Collection, New York **14.24** Charles Blankenship, descendant of H. R. Nicks

CHAPTER 15

439 © Christie's Images Inc. 2004 **15.1L** Courtesy of the Library of Congress **15.1R** U.S. National Archives and Records Administration **15.2** The Granger Collection, New York **15.4** George Catlin (1796–1872) "Buffalo Chase Over Prairie Bluffs". 1832–33. Smithsonian American Art Museum, Washington, DC/Art Resource, NY **15.5** The Granger Collection, New York **15.6** The Burndy Library, Dibner Institute for the History of Science and Technology, Cambridge, Massachusetts **15.8** © Nebraska State Historical Society Photograph Collections **15.9** The Granger Collection, New York. **15.10** George Ranch Historical Park **15.11** Minnesota Historical Society **452** Albert Bierstadt (1830–1902), "Among the Sierra Nevada Mountains, California", 1868. Oil on Canvas, 71 × 120" (183 × 305 cm). Smithsonian American Art Museum, Washington DC. Copyright © Smithsonian American Art Museum, Washington DC/Art Resource, NY. **15.12** Courtesy of the Library of Congress **15.13** Getty Images Inc.—Hulton Archive Photos **15.14** "Courtesy of the Burton Historical Collection, Detroit Public Library" **15.15** Collection of Sandy Bernard, Wake Forest, NC/AST Press **15.16** The Granger Collection, New York **459T&B** Bureau of Indian Affairs/U.S. Department of the Interior **15.17** Getty Images **15.19** © Nebraska State Historical Society Photograph Collections **463** Getty Images Inc.—Hulton Archive Photos **15.20** Montana Historical Society, Helena **15.21** Colleen Cutschall, "Spirit Warriors". bronze sculpture, 34 ft. × 14 ft. in an arc. Little Bighorn Battlefield Natioal Monument, Montana. Brandon University, Canada

CHAPTER 16

469 Robert Koehler (1850–1917), "The Strike" 1886. Oil on canvas. Deutsches Historisches Museum, Berlin, Germany/The Bridgeman Art Library, NY. **16.2L** AP Wide World Photos **16.2R** Lynn Historical Society **16.3** Provided courtesy HarpWeek., LLC **16.4** Manning's Books, Prints Old & Rare **16.5** Courtesy of The Bancroft Library. University of California, Berkeley. **16.7** The Granger Collection, New York **16.8** Getty Images Inc.—Hulton Archive Photos **480** Reproduced from "The Century Magazine", November, 1887 in The History and Development of Advertising by Frank Presbrey, Doubleday, Dowan & Company, Inc. 1929 **481** Courtesy of David Briggs; briggsdavi@gmail.com **16.9** National Museum of American History/Smithsonian Institution **16.10** Courtesy of George Eastman House **16.11** Special Collections & Archives **16.12** The Granger Collection, New York **16.13** Courtesy of The Bancroft Library. University of California, Berkeley. **487** Special Collections & Archives **16.15** Courtesy of the Clara Barton National Historic Site, CLBA #659 **16.16T&B** Reproduced from the original held by the Department of Special Collections of the University Libraries of Notre Dame, Photo by Cornell Engraving Company, Lincoln, Neb., Fisher & Lawrie, Architects, Omaha, Neb. **16.17** Courtesy of Center for Southwest Research, University Libraries, University of New Mexico, Seder Dime Novel Collection, MSS 312 BC, Box 3, Folder 63 **16.18** John Hay Library, Brown University **16.19** The Granger Collection, New York **16.20** Courtesy of the Library of Congress **494** Bryan Mawr College Library

CHAPTER 17

499 Collection of the New York Historical Society **17.2** Edward T. O'Donnell **17.3** Chicago Historical Museum **17.4** Culver Pictures, Inc. **17.5** The Granger Collection, New York **505** The Granger Collection, New York **17.6** Ohio State University Cartoon Research Library **17.7** Courtesy of the Library of Congress **509T** Filippo Lippi, "Madonna and Child," 1440/1445. Tempera on panel, .797 × .511 (31⅜ × 20⅛); framed: 1.172 × .854 × .095 (46⅛ × 33⅝ × 3¾). Samuel H. Kress Collection, Photograph © 2001 Board of Trustees, National Gallery of Art, Washington. 1939.1.290(401)/PA **590B** Jacob A. Riis "Italian Mother and Her Baby in Jersey Street", in the home of an Italian rag-picker, Jersey Street, circa 1890. Museum of the City of New York, The Jacob A. Riis Collection (#157) **17.8** © Bettmann/CORBIS **17.9** The Granger Collection, New York **17.10** National Archives and Records Administration **17.11** The Granger Collection, New York **17.12** Courtesy of the Library of Congress **17.13** Collection of the New-York Historical Society, Box 1.f 10. Negative no. 80433d **17.15** The Granger Collection, New York **17.16** The Granger Collection, New York **17.17** From "The River Ran Red, Homestead 1892" by David P. Demarest Jr. Editor, University of Pittsburg Press, with image credited to Marge Rybar. **17.18** The Ohio Historical Society **17.19** Chicago Historical Museum **525** Library of Congress **17.20** The Granger Collection

CHAPTER 18

531 Victor Joseph Gatto (1893–1965), "Triangle Fire: March 25, 1911". c. 1944 [depicting 1911], oil on canvas, 19 × 28", Gift of Mrs. Henry L. Moses, 54.75. The Museum of the City of New York **18.2** Brown Brothers **18.3** Courtesy of the Library of Congress **18.5** Corbis/Bettmann **18.6** Courtesy of the Library of Congress **18.7** From the Collection of the Henry Ford, THF23871 **18.8** Courtesy of the Library of Congress **545** Joseph Lochner/National Geographic Image Collection **18.9L** Kansas State Historical Society **18.9R** Corbis/Bettmann **18.11** Widener Library **550** Lewis Wickes Hines/Courtesy of the Library of Congress **551T** Lewis Wickes Hines/Courtesy of the Library of Congress **551B** Courtesy of the Library of Congress **18.12L** Baker Library Historical Collections, Harvard Business School **18.12R** Baker Library Historical Collections, Harvard Business School **556** © Bettmann/CORBIS All Rights Reserved **18.13** Francis Johnson/Courtesy of the Library of Congress

CHAPTER 19

566 ICHIi-08428; Destruction of the battleship Maine in Havana harbor; in the Spanish-American War; Havana (Cuba) 1898 Feb. 15; Creator-Kurtz & Allison/Chicago Historical Society **566T** Frederic Remington Museum **566B** Courtesy of the Library of Congress **19.3** The Granger Collection, New York **19.4** Courtesy of Andy Moursund **19.5** © CORBIS All Rights Reserved **19.6** Provided courtesy HarpWeek., LLC **19.7** Widener Library, Harvard College Library, Harvard Depository **19.8** CORBIS-NY **19.9** Do You Graphics for "The National Archives" **19.11** © Bettmann/CORBIS **583** Science Museum/SSPL/The Image Works **19.12** Map of the Panama Canal from the Atlantic to the Pacific Ocean, 1913 (litho), American School, (20th century)/Private Collection/Peter Newark American Pictures/The Bridgeman Art Library International **19.13** Corbis/Bettmann **19.14** The Granger Collection, New York.

CHAPTER 20

593 Courtesy of the Library of Congress **20.4** Keene **20.5** Brown Brothers **20.6L** © CORBIS All Rights Reserved **20.6R** Cornell University, Carl A. Kroch Library, Division of Rare and Manuscript Collections **20.7** Courtesy of the Library of Congress **20.8** Jacob Lawrence born in Atlantic City, New Jersey, 1917, "The Migration of the Negro" 1940–41. Panel no. 1 "During the World War there was a great migration North by Southern Negroes." Tempera on masonite 12 × 18" (30.5 × 45.7 cm). Acquired through Downtown Gallery, 1942. In series of 60. [Odd numbers at Phillips]. E © 2010 The Jacob and Gwendolyn Lawrence Foundation, Seattle /Artists Rights Society (ARS), New York. **20.9** © Bettmann/CORBIS All Rights Reserved **607L** Poster Collection, Hoover Institution Archives **607R** Courtesy of the Library of Congress **20.10** From "World War I: A History in Documents" by Frans Coetzee and Marilyn Shevin-Coetzee, Oxford University Press. 2002 **610** © Bettmann/CORBIS All Rights Reserved **20.11L&R** Courtesy of the Library of Congress **20.14** © Bettmann/CORBIS All Rights Reserved **20.15** © CORBIS All Rights Reserved **619** © Bettmann/CORBIS All Rights Reserved **20.16** Property of the Westervelt Company and displayed in The Westervelt-Warner Museum of American Art in Tuscaloosa, AL.

CHAPTER 21

625 © Underwood & Underwood/CORBIS All Rights Reserved **21.1** The Center for American History, The University of Texas, No. 3_bb_4311 **21.2** © Terry Donnelly **21.4** Paramount/The Kobal Collection/The Picture-Desk **21.5** © Underwood & Underwood/CORBIS All Rights Reserved **21.6** Courtesy of the Library of Congress **21.8** © Bettmann/CORBIS All Rights Reserved **21.9** © Bettmann/CORBIS All Rights Reserved **21.10** © Bettmann/CORBIS All Rights Reserved **21.11** © Bettmann/CORBIS All Rights Reserved **641** © David J. & Janice L. Frent Collection/CORBIS All Rights Reserved **642T** Corbis/Bettmann **642B** Corbis/Bettmann **643** Janet Sommer/Getty Images Inc.—Hulton Archive Photos **21.12** Used with Permission of Documenting the American South, The University of North Carolina at Chapel Hill Libraries. **645** Courtesy of the Library of Congress **21.13** © Bettmann/CORBIS All Rights Reserved **21.14** Courtesy of the Library of Congress **649** Courtesy of the Library of Congress

CHAPTER 22

655 Courtesy of the Library of Congress **22.1L** James N. Rosenberg, American, (b. 1874). Oct 29 Dies Irae, 1929, Lithograph. Philadelphia Museum of Art, Lola Downin Peck Fund. **22.1R** © Bettmann/CORBIS All Rights Reserved **661** Picture History **22.4** Franklin D. Roosevelt Library **22.5** Franklin D. Roosevelt Library **22.6** © Bettmann/CORBIS All Rights Reserved **22.7** Reproduced with permission of The Kansas City Star © Copyright 2007 The Kansas City Star. All rights reserved. Format differs from original publication. Not an endorsement. **22.8** NARA/Getty Images **22.10** Marci Penner/Kansas Sampler Foundation **22.11** Hulton Images/Getty Images **22.12** Courtesy of the Library of Congress (LC-USF34-018191-E). Dorothea Lange **673T&B** Courtesy of the Library of Congress **675** Prentice Hall School **22.13** Courtesy of the Library of Congress **22.14** Courtesy of the Library of Congress **22.15** © UPI/CORBIS All Rights Reserved **22.16** Time & Life Pictures/Getty Images

CHAPTER 23

685 National Archives and Records Administration **23.3** National Archives and Records Administration **23.4** Mandeville Special Collections Library **23.5** U.S. Naval Historical Center, Collection of Fleet Admiral Chester W. Nimitz **23.6** Courtesy of the Library of Congress **23.7** TIME Life Magazine/Courtesy of the Library of Congress **23.8T** Courtesy of CSUN Oviatt Library, Special Collections & Archives **23.8B** Courtesy of the Library of Congress **23.9** Franklin D. Roosevelt Library **23.10** National Archives and Records Administration **696** Courtesy of the Library of Congress **23.11** Adel Precision Instruments **23.12L** Franklin D. Roosevelt Library **23.12R** The National Archives, Records of the Office of War Information. Do You Graphics **23.13** Horace Pippin (1888–1946), "Mr. Prejudice," 1943. Oil on canvas, 18 × 14 inches. Philadelphia Museum of Art, Gift of Dr. and Mrs. Matthew T. Moore. Photo by Graydon Wood. 1984-108-1 **23.16** National Archives and Records Administration **23.17** Ralph Crane/Time & Life Pictures /Getty Images/Time Life Pictures **706T** George Strock/Time & Life Pictures/Getty Images/Time Life Pictures **706B** National Archives and Records Administration **23.18** Robert Capa/Cornell Capa Photos/Magnum Photos, Inc. **23.19** National Archives and Records Administration **713** National Archives and Records Administration **23.21** Alfred Eisenstaedt/Stringer/Getty Images, Inc.

CHAPTER 24

719 © Bettmann/CORBIS All Rights Reserved **24.1** © Yevgeny Khaldel/CORBIS All Rights Reserved **24.3** The Granger Collection, New York **24.4** University College London **24.6** © Bettmann/CORBIS All Rights Reserved **24.7** W. Eugene Smith/Getty Images **24.9** © Sfc. Al Change/CORBIS All Rights Reserved **24.10** © Bettmann/CORBIS All Rights Reserved **24.11** Photofest **735T** © CORBIS All Rights Reserved **735Ba-b, d-e** © CORBIS All Rights Reserved **735Bc** Getty Images **24.12** MPI/Stringer/Hulton Archives/Getty Images **24.13** Elliot Erwitt/Magnum Photos, Inc. **740** © Bettmann/CORBIS All Rights Reserved **24.14** © Dorling Kindersley **24.16** John Waterman/Stringer/Hulton Archive/Getty Images **24.17** Keystone/Stringer/Hulton Archives/Getty Images **746** © CORBIS All Rights Reserved

CHAPTER 25

751 © Bettmann/CORBIS All Rights Reserved **25.1** © Bettmann/CORBIS All Rights Reserved **25.2** Courtesy of the Library of Congress **25.3&25.4** Dean Loomis/Time Life Magazine/Getty Images **759** © Bettmann/CORBIS All Rights Reserved **25.5** © Bettmann/CORBIS All Rights Reserved **25.6** Cecil Stoughton, White House/John Fitzgerald Kennedy Library, Boston **25.7** Hulton Archives/Getty Images **25.8** Mark Rothco(1903–1970), "Number 10". 1950. Oil on canvas. 7' 6⅜" × 57⅛". Gift of Philip Johnson. (38.1952) Location:The Museum of Modern Art, New York, NY, U.S.A. Digital Image © The Museum of Modern Art/Licensed by SCALA/Art Resource, NY. Estate of Mark Rothco © 2010 Artists Rights Society (ARS), NY **25.9** Bruce Davidson/Magnum Photos, Inc **25.10** Courtesy of the Library of Congress **767T** The Chicago Defender **767B** © Bettmann/CORBIS All Rights Reserved **769** AP Wide World Photos **25.11** Ernest C. Withers/Panopticon Gallery **25.12** © Jack Moebes/CORBIS All Rights Reserved **25.13** Fred Blackwell Photography/Wisconsin Historical Society

CHAPTER 26

779 Washington Post Writers Group **26.1** © Bettmann/CORBIS All Rights Reserved **26.2** Courtesy of the Library of Congress **26.3** Malcolm Browne/AP Wide World Photos **26.4** Lyndon Baines Johnson Library Collection **26.5** Kathy Hayes Associates **788** © Yoichi Okamoto/CORBIS All Rights Reserved **26.6** Trong Thanh/Doug Niven **26.7** Larry Burrows/ Time Life Pictures/Getty Images **26.9** Universal Press Syndicate **794** Eddie Adams/AP Wide World Photos **795** Larry Burrows/Getty Images **26.11** Courtesy of the Library of Congress **26.13** Ronald S. Haeberle/Time & Life Pictures/Getty Images **800** Time & Life Pictures/Getty Images **26.14** Howard Ruffner/Time & Life Pictures/Getty Images **26.15** © Hubert Van Es/CORBIS All Rights Reserved

CHAPTER 27

811 Santi Visalli, Inc/Contributor/Hulton Archives/Getty Images **27.1** Hank Walker/Getty Images **815** © Bettmann/CORBIS All Rights Reserved **27.3** Democratic National Committee **27.6** UPI/Corbis/Bettmann **822** Charles Moore/Black Star **823** Charles Moore/Black Star **27.7** © Bettmann/CORBIS All Rights Reserved **27.8** MPI/Hulton Archive/Getty Images **27.9** Tamio Wakayama **27.10** Courtesy of James Karales **27.11** Robert Altman Photography **27.12** Bob Gomel/Getty Images **27.13** Courtesy of the Library of Congress **833** © David J. & Janice L. Frent Collection/CORBIS **27.14** AP Wide World Photos **27.15** Steve Schapiro/Steve Schapiro **27.16** A 1967 Herblock Cartoon, copyright by "The Herb Block Foundation **27.17** NASA/Phototake NYC **27.18** Walter P. Reuther Library/ Wayne State University

CHAPTER 28

843 © H. Armstrong Roberts/ClassicStock/CORBIS All Rights Reserved **28.3** Stanley J. Forman/Stanley Forman **850T** A 1974 Herblock Cartoon, copyright by "The Herb Block Foundation" **850B** Paul Conrad/© Tribune Media Services, Inc. **28.4** Tribune Media Services, Inc. All Rights Reserved. Reprinted with permission. **28.5** Keene **28.6** Keene **857** From The New York Times 1981 © 2010 The New York Times. All Rights Reserved **28.8** Edward Kienholz, "The Illegal Operation". 1962. Sculptural installation of shopping cart, wooden stool, concrete, pots, blanket, hooked rug, medical equipment, polyester resin, pigment, etc. Dimensions: 59 × 48 × 54 in. Los Angeles County Museum of Art. Photograph © 2009 Museum associates/LACMA **860L** Corbis/Bettmann **860R** AP Wide World Photos **29.9** © Bettmann/CORBIS All Rights Reserved **28.10** Value RF/© Hirsham Ibrahim/Corbis Royalty Free **28.11** John Sotomayor/Redux/The New York Times **28.12** © W. Cody/CORBIS All Rights Reserved **28.13** Cindy Elgrably/Cindy Elgrably **28.14** AP Wide World Photos **28.16** The Herb Block Foundation/Courtesy of the Library of Congress

CHAPTER 29

875 Robert Clark/Aurora Photos, Inc. **29.1** Michael Samojeden/AP Wide World Photos **878T** © Reuters/CORBIS **878B** OLIPHANT © Universal Press Syndicate **29.2** Jeff Widener/AP Wide World Photos **29.3** CNN via Getty Images **29.5** Used by permission of Pelican Publishing Company, Inc. **29.6** © Najlah Feanny/CORBIS All Rights Reserved **29.7** Robert King/Getty Images, Inc. **29.10** © 2003 Brian Fairrington and PoliticalCartoons.com **29.12** © Andrew Holbrooke/CORBIS All Rights Reserved **29.13** Paul Watson/Toronto Star **29.14** Susan Meiselas/Magnum Photos, Inc. **29.15** Clay Bennett/© 2001 The Christian Scienc Monitor (www. CSMonitor. com) **899** The Permissions Group, Inc./ Ohman/TMS Reprints **29.16** USA Today **29.17** Courtesy of Anne Savage **29.18** From The New York Times Nov. 5, 2008 © 2010 The New York Times. All Rights Reserved. The New York Times/PARS International

Index

C

E

F

G

I

J

K

L

M

O

P

Q

R